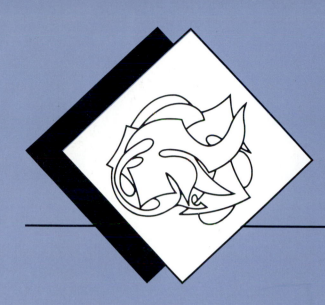

Understanding
Human Behavior

James V. McConnell
The University of Michigan

Understanding Human Behavior

FIFTH EDITION

Holt, Rinehart and Winston
New York Chicago San Francisco
Philadelphia Montreal Toronto London
Sydney Tokyo Mexico City Rio de Janeiro
Madrid

Dedication

For Ted Newcomb who helped get it all started, and for Mary, too
For Roz, Johnna, and Louise,
For Nick and Jim
For Dan and Tracy and Mike and my many friends
And most of all, with great thanks to all the students. . . .

Publisher **Bob Woodbury**
Acquisitions Editor **Susan Meyers**
Senior Developmental Editor **Rosalind Sackoff**
Senior Project Manager **Arlene Katz**
Production Manager **Pat Sarcuni**
Art Director **Lou Scardino**
Interior Design **Caliber Design Planning**
Cover Design **Albert DiAgostino**
Photo Researcher **June Lundborg Whitworth**

(Photo credits appear after Appendix.)

Library of Congress Cataloging in Publication Data

McConnell, James V.
    Understanding human behavior.

    Includes bibliographies and indexes.
    1. Psychology. 2. Human behavior. I. Title.
[DNLM: 1. Behavior. 2. Psychology. BF 121 M478u]
BF121.M42 1986   150   85-8599

ISBN 0-03-071096-0

CBS COLLEGE PUBLISHING
Holt, Rinehart and Winston
The Dryden Press
Saunders College Publishing

Preface

Shortly after I had finished preparing the third edition of this text in 1978, a friend suggested that the book was "now so good that it wouldn't need much in the way of changing in the future." I laughed. "No," I said, "I don't think the book will reach its peak until at least the fifth edition."

And, as it turned out, I was right. The fourth edition was a significant improvement over the previous versions. However, it was not until a couple of years ago, when I began work on the fifth edition, that I felt experienced enough at producing an introductory text to make it into what I really had wanted the book to be all along.

The fifth edition, then, represents a complete and thorough rewriting of *Understanding Human Behavior*—the most complete revision yet, by far. Some of the changes are immediately noticeable: The number of chapters has decreased by two, and there is much more material than ever before on cognitive psychology and on developmental issues. The introductory chapter is almost entirely new. There are five new chapter-opening vignettes in Chapters 1, 12, 18, 19, and 25. And the art work is almost entirely redone. However, the most significant alterations are probably invisible to the casual reader. For these changes involve the *integration of the material in UHB*. Not only is the range of topics covered much broader, but the depth at which each topic is surveyed is greater as well. Also, the interrelatedness of the various topic areas in psychology is much more obvious in this edition. I think most readers will be pleased by all these revisions.

However, not everything about the book has changed. In discussing UHB-5, then, I would like to describe three things: (1) What's new; (2) what's similar to the previous editions (but greatly improved); and (3) what things appeared to satisfy readers the most about previous editions and hence are relatively unaltered in this edition.

What's New

1. The "stories" that begin and end each major chapter in the book help set UHB apart from most other introductory textbooks. These vignettes serve many functions: They introduce the student to the topics to be covered within the chapter, they are rewarding experiences for many readers, and they "humanize" psychology in ways that tables of data and descriptions of experiments never can hope to. Indeed, most students list the stories as *one of the main reasons they like UHB so much.* I have written several new stories for this edition, mostly to replace ones that either seemed out of date or that pleased only a limited sample of readers.

2. One of the most exciting and rapidly-developing areas of psychology is that of cognitive psychology. The emphasis in previous editions was more on social learning theory than on cognitive activities themselves. However, Chapter 9 is now devoted almost entirely to cognition. You'll find data on information processing, attention, the orienting reflex, psychophysics, thinking, reasoning, problem solving, and artificial intelligence in Chapter 9, all of it new to UHB. Likewise, Chapter 18 now includes material on the *development* of cognitive processes in children. As you will see, too, there is expanded coverage of cognitive activities in several other chapters.

3. A "chapter-by-chapter" analysis of the changes reveals the following:

   Chapter 1 Almost entirely new, including a "story" about a little girl who supposedly reads minds. The emphasis is more on cognitive activities (and the issue of "science versus magic") than in previous editions.

   Chapter 2 An update of the material on hemispheric functions, including more detail on laterality effects in normal individuals. Also raised is the issue of whether the right hemisphere has a type of "consciousness" all its own.

   Chapter 3 Much new information on sleep and dreams, including an entire new section on sleep disorders. Also added is material on synaptic transmission and inhibition, biological clocks, and the opioid peptides.

   Chapter 4 A more balanced presentation of Gall's theories, and an update of the studies on violence and aggression, including recent data on the effects of TV on aggressive behavior in children and adults. Also added are some new thoughts on psychosurgery.

   Chapter 5 Addition of Jerry Fodor's theory of "commonsense mentalism" and a discussion of the problem of consciousness. Much new material on history and systems, including greater coverage of structuralism and functionalism.

   Chapter 6 New data on the skin receptors from research by Herbert Hensel, on smell and its qualities from work by John Amoore, and on emotion and olfaction by Trygg Engen.

   Chapter 7 New material on hearing aids that involve implantation of electrodes directly in the cochlea, and recent information on color deficiencies and theories to account for same.

   Chapter 8 A complete reworking of the material on visual perception, plus the addition of material on speech perception. The chapter begins with a survey of the four main theories of visual perception, and continues by showing how each of the four theories would explain various visual phenomena (including developmental patterns). Many new illusions and illustrations have been added.

   Chapter 9 Combines material from Chapters 8 and 10 in UHB-4, but adds much new material on cognitive processes.

Chapter 10 Expanded coverage of homeostasis and arousal theory, the biology of hunger (particularly the effects of the endorphins on eating), set-point theory, and social influences on obesity. Most important, there's a whole new section on eating disorders, including anorexia and bulimia.

Chapter 11 Another major revision. New material includes information on sexual dimorphism, the effects of hormones on sexual orientation, intersexuality, gender identity, sex-role stereotypes, and sociobiology.

Chapter 12 Begins with a new story, then covers the five major elements of emotionality. There's an update on Selye's research, and new information on Type A personalities. Next comes a discussion of several theories of emotion: Plutchik's evolutionary theory, Arnold's theory, Tomkin's theory of facial expression, Seligman's theory of learned helplessness, Lazarus's cognitive theory, and Carol Tavris's theory of emotion as a social response.

Chapter 13 New data on the polygraph, and additional information on desensitization and the controversy between Wolpe and the psychoanalysts.

Chapter 14 A new comparison of operant and respondent conditioning, and new material on biofeedback. However, the major change is the addition of material on the "controlled drinking controversy," an attempt by Marlatt and others to utilize the laws of learning to help problem drinkers acquire better self-control.

Chapter 15 A whole new section has been added on Sensory Information Storage and on Short-term Memory. Also included are recent data on the aphasias, on Alzheimer's disease, and additional material on mnemonics.

Chapter 16 Includes new material on the effects of placebos and hypnotism. However, the major addition is a section on cognitive strategies for controlling pain, and coverage of new data suggesting the body has two separate "pain control systems."

Chapter 17 The three chapters on developmental psychology in UHB-4 have been combined into two much larger chapters in UHB-5. Chapter 17 is organized around four major developmental issues, and includes new material on the developmental disorders, on prenatal and neonatal learning, emotion in neonates, the effects of hormones on parenting behavior, and a major section on Down's syndrome.

Chapter 18 Begins with a new story, then launches into coverage of recently published material on cognitive development. Includes a discussion of language development and language acquisition, the Chomsky-Skinner debates, data on concept formation and the development of thought processes, new information on Piaget's theory of the equilibration process, more complete descriptions of Piaget's four stages, and additional comments and criticisms of Piaget's approach.

Chapter 19 Starts with a new story, then compares traditional and personological personality theories. There's additional material on the conflict between Freud and his fellow analysts (chiefly Jung and Adler), much more information on Erikson, a new section on Henry Murray, a comparison of social learning theory with the more traditional theories, a section on "Recent Trends in Personality Theory," and much new material on aging and old age.

Chapter 20 The material on personality measurement is reorganized, and includes an evaluation of trait theory by Anne Anastasi, new data on the effects of the social environment on IQ, and new material on the MMPI.

Chapter 21 Begins with a discussion of the controversy about "what's normal," including past attempts to define normality. Gives a more balanced presentation of DSM-III, and presents recent attempts to measure the reliability and validity of DSM-III. Included in the description of the diagnostic categories are recent (1984) data on the incidence of mental illness in the

United States. Concludes with an attempt to relate psychodiagnostics to research on concept formation by Nancy Cantor and her associates.

Chapter 22 Includes new data and evaluations of biological, intra-psychic, and social/behavioral therapies. New material on psychodrama, TA, and Gestalt therapy. Covers attempts to use meta-analysis to validate the effectiveness of psychotherapy, and ties these attempts to Marlatt's thoughts on therapy as a learning process (from Chapter 14).

Chapter 23 Begins with a new section on Darley and Fazio's description of the "Social Interaction Sequence." Includes new material on self-fulfilling prophecies, first impressions, non-verbal behavior, stereotyped responses to body language, territoriality in married and non-married couples, a fuller explanation of the attribution process, and a more complete description of social exchange theory.

Chapter 24 Adds new material on Milgram's research on obedience, on bystander apathy and social intervention, European research on inter-group conflict, and Tajfel's Social Identity Theory.

Chapter 25 Begins (and ends) with new but related stories. Includes new data on student activists, the sleeper effect, fear-arousing communications, and adds sections on mass hysteria and psychological traps.

Chapter 26 Concludes the book with new thoughts on genetic engineering, hemispheric laterality, behavioral medicine, biological computers, applied developmental and cognitive psychology (including the effects of computers on everyday life), community mental health, industrial psychology, organizational development, and applied social psychology. Includes a whole new section on recent research on cortical blindness.

What's Revised or Improved

There are many physical improvements in UHB-5. The most important thing to note is that, while we've *decreased* the number of chapters (by two), we've actually *increased* the amount of coverage of the more important topics in psychology.

Cutting the number of chapters also gave us the space to add more research reports. You'll find almost twice as many reference citations in the text itself as in previous editions. However, our continuing studies of student responses to UHB (and other texts) shows us that it is better to give enough information *in the text itself* for students and instructors to find the cited articles or books in the library. The complete list of references appears in the *Instructor's Manual.* At the end of Chapter 1 of UHB-5, I urge the student who wishes additional references to seek help from the instructor (who presumably will have the *Instructor's Manual* available).

Also available to the instructor are a series of computerized "literature searches" on various topics included in UHB. We've published three of these volumes so far, each containing selected abstracts on 25 or more important content areas in psychology. Any instructor who adopts UHB can obtain these volumes of abstracts from Holt, Rinehart and Winston.

More than a million students have read one of the first four editions of this text, and we have kept their needs in mind while preparing UHB-5. Al Siebert and Tim Walter have greatly revised their outstanding *Student Manual,* while Tom Carskadon and Mike Thorne have completely rewritten the *Unit Mastery/ PSI Workbook.* Terry Sissons has prepared a bank of test questions that is far better than any we've had before. The test bank is also available in a computerized format to operate on the APPLE IIe, II+, IIc and the IBM PC. The Instructor's Manual was again ably prepared by Bob Johnson. In this edition, he has added sections on the cross-cultural aspects of psychology and on using the methodology. There is also a slide package and a set of transparency masters available upon adoption of the text. Our newest ancillary with this edition is the computer assisted instruction prepared by David Glanzer and Galen Lehman. Your Holt, Rinehart and Winston representative can help you with further information about any piece of this package. I hope that all instructors will make effective use of these first-rate ancillary materials.

What's Much the Same

So much has been changed or revised in this new edition that I feel compelled to assure both teachers and students of one important thing: We have managed to retain all those good things that have made UHB so popular in the past. As I mentioned earlier, the "stories" that begin and end each major chapter are still there, as are the glossary items that appear *in the book* (where students find them most useful) rather than in the back of the book (where most students never manage to find them at all). The stories, the "running glossary," the cartoons by Sidney Harris, the simple language, and the integrated approach to psychology are the five features of the previous editions that students found particularly useful to them in their attempts to master the field of psychology.

There is no doubt that UHB-5 is as different from other introductory psychology textbooks as were the first four editions. If you read *Teaching of Psychology*—the journal put out by Division Two of the American Psychological Association—you know that research performed both in the United States and in Canada shows that students rate UHB *higher than any other text*. I take great pride in this fact, for I have attempted to write the book so that it will both *please and teach* the introductory student. To me, these are two of the most important goals of any psychology text—that readers enjoy what they read, and understand and remember the material *for a long time thereafter*. As best we can tell, UHB both "pleases and teaches" better than any other book that we have been able to test.

I have tried, as well, to present psychology in such a way that most students will give at least passing consideration to making it their undergraduate major. As I have noted elsewhere, it doesn't help any of us if our classes (and texts) are so boring that most of our students can't wait to finish the introductory class so that they can take something more interesting.

The question remains, "What should a student get out of the introductory psychology course? Facts? An understanding of what psychology is all about?" Many of the so-called encyclopaedic texts contain a lot of facts, true. But how many students appreciate or recall those facts a month after the final exam? It seems to me that these texts miss the real point of what a college course should be about—that of encouraging *long-term changes* in human thoughts, feelings, and actions. According to a survey published in *Teaching of Psychology*, UHB cites at least as many facts and research studies as does the average psychology text, but explains the data and theories in such a way that the facts "come to life" and thus are important and real enough to be memorable and useful to the reader.

Finally, UHB-5 is as personal a book as the previous editions were. Our research shows that most students are put off by a very formal, academic approach to their first psychology course. The students are interested in *people*—themselves and others—and not in esoteric data, statistical equations, and the fine points of experimental design. Many of us who teach the first course forget that 95 percent of our students are *not* psychology majors. And probably 90 percent of them will *never* perform a real psychological experiment. Why then should we rub their noses in scientific esoterica when that's the last thing that will "turn them on" to psychology? UHB-5 is a practical, people-oriented textbook that deals in real-life issues and gives students material that they can put to practical use immediately. Is there any better way to make science understandable to students than by exciting their interest and giving them practical rewards for learning?

Let's hope that you find UHB-5 as great an improvement over previous editions as I do.

Acknowledgments

According to the title page, this is "my" book. Nothing could be farther from the truth. It takes the combined efforts of hundreds of people to produce a decent introductory psychology text. The author gets most of the credit, but the others do much of the real work. Yet without their contributions, no book would ever see final publication. In this brief note, let me acknowledge my great indebtedness to many individuals.

To begin with, my continuing thanks to Louise Waller and Johnna Barto, who helped the first three editions through their various birth pangs.

Next, let me thank Nick Suino, who helped me "put it all together," and who prepared the references.

Perhaps most important, there's Rosalind Sackoff. She was the developmental editor for UHB-4, and stayed on to help guide both the planning and production of the current edition. Much of the credit for making this version "the best ever" goes to her. She was a joy to work with, a very talented colleague and contributor, and someone I am happy to call "friend."

My special blessings too to Bob Woodbury, Susan Meyers, David deCampo, and Carol Einhorn for their considerable efforts to make UHB so successful.

I would also like to thank Harry McQuillen, Robert Rainier, Susan Katz, John Wood, Barbara Kimball, and Ann Heath for their many kindnesses.

Louis Scardino and Howard Leiderman designed the book and supervised the illustration program. Albert DiAgostino designed the marvelous cover. June Lundborg Whitworth researched all the new photographs. Pat Sarcuni guided matters wisely and well through the production process. My special thanks to Vic Calderon for his continued assistance in matters large and small. Arlene

Katz efficiently shepherded the book through the editorial process, coordinating all of the day-to-day activities that take the manuscript to bound book.

In final analysis, a good share of the success of previous editions was due to the enthusiastic reception given UHB by many HRW marketing and salespeople. I cannot begin to name them all, but would like to extend thanks particularly to Patti Arneson, Diana Badger, Russ Boersma, George Bergquist, Laura Coaty, Wendy Conner, Ken Crabb, Keith Collins, Dave Cummins, Sheila Dinges, Sally Fabian, Donna Fletcher, David Hall, Jerry Holcomb, Cecile Higgins, Eve Howard, Lori Hatcher, John Howard, Candace Hetherington, Bobby Knight, John Lannefeld, Jim Lizotte, Roger MacQuarrie, Carol Mikenas, Lisa McGlynchey, Lisa Miller, Liz Miller, Paul Murphy, Marilyn Moran, Terry Nelson, Gerry Novakoske, Ginny Pease, Joan Rainer, Jerry Riley, Chuck Pensinger, Andy Paprocki, Don O'Guin, Dan Slegal, Nadine Tracy, Jane Vaicunas, Linda Winer, Don Welch and DeVilla Williams.

Many of my professional colleagues gave generously of their time in reading all or parts of the manuscript and offering their thoughtful comments. In particular, there are the "Senior Consultants" who gave so willingly of their collective wisdom: William Uttal, University of Michigan; Robert Bolles, University of Washington; David Edwards, Iowa State University; Margaret Matlin, State University of New York at Geneseo; Neil Salkind, University of Kansas; Nancy Cantor, University of Michigan; Brian Bate, Cuyahoga Community College; Leona Tyler; Christopher Monte, Manhattanville College; Theodore Newcomb, University of Michigan; Jeffrey Rubin, Tufts University; Kay Deaux, Purdue University; Daniel Kimble, University of Oregon.

I would also like to thank the following people for their letters, reviews, criticisms, and most useful comments: David Berg, Community College of Philadelphia; William Schellenberger, AIMS College; Donald Gates, Northwestern State University; David Mayne, Rio Saladao College; Douglas Beneway, Marist College; John Lakey, University of Evansville; William Calhoun, University of Tennessee; George Mount, Mountain View College; Pat Murphy, Spokane Community College; Harold Hartstein, Hillsborough Community College; Joan Erber, Florida International University; Thomas Eckle, Modesto Junior College; Peter Gram, Pensacola Junior College; Betty Henry, Old Dominion University; Don Fischer, Southwest Missouri State University; Jean Alvers, Johnson County Community Junior College; Kenneth Coffield, University of Alabama; Larry Plant, Niagra Community College; Ralph Hansen, Augustana College; Joseph Palladino, Indiana State University; Ted Barnes, Coastline Community College.

Then there are my many friends in Ann Arbor and elsewhere, comrades all, who gave me most of my ideas and whose names I have taken in vain in some of the short stories. To my poker-playing cronies—Brian Healy, Bill Meyer, Nick Suino, Jim Samons, W. Robert Dixon, John Holland, Peter Steiner, Chuck Phillips, Art Rich, Dean Patrides, R.M. Dougherty and Ralph Heine—my thanks for keeping me amused (and broke) during the book's gestation period.

Last, but most assuredly not least, it is my students—past and present—who deserve my thanks. They taught me how to write; they shaped me into learning more about psychology and about people than I had any intention of learning. Whatever is best in this book is their doing, not mine.

Bless 'em all.

—J.V.McC.

Senior Editorial Consultants

Part I   Biological Bases
William Uttal, *University of Michigan*
Daniel Kimble, *University of Oregon*

Part II   Sensation and Perception
William Uttal, *University of Michigan*
Margaret Matlin, *State University of New York, Geneseo*

Part III   Motivation
Robert Bolles, *University of Washington*
David Edwards, *Iowa State University*

Part IV   Learning and Memory
Robert Bolles, *University of Washington*
Margaret Matlin, *State University of New York, Geneseo*

Part V   Maturation and Development
Neil Salkind, *University of Kansas*

Part VI   Personality
Nancy Cantor, *University of Michigan*
Christopher Monte, *Manhattanville College*
Brian Bate, *Cuyahoga Community College*
Leona Tyler

Part VII   Social Psychology
Theodore Newcomb, *University of Michigan*
Jeffrey Rubin, *Tufts University*
Kay Deaux, *Purdue University*

Contents

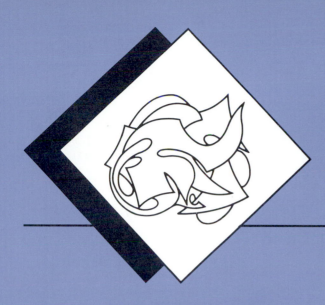

Understanding
Human Behavior

1

Introduction

"Talk of Mysteries"

"Talk of mysteries! Think of our life in nature—daily to be shown matter, to come in contact with it—rocks, trees, wind on our cheeks! the *solid* earth! the *actual* world! the *common sense! Contact! Contact! Who* are we? *where* are we?"

Henry David Thoreau, *The Maine Woods, Ktaadn*

I was sitting at my kitchen table, reading the newspaper, when the phone rang. "Hello," I said.

"Hello, Jim? This is Marcello Truzzi. How would you like to drive down to Toledo to look at a little girl who can read minds?"

Marcello Truzzi is a long-time friend of mine. He is also professor of sociology at Eastern Michigan University, a very good school that is some five miles from the kitchen table I was sitting at.

"Why me, Marcello?" I asked. "You're the expert on mind-readers, not me." And indeed he is an expert on such things. For many years, Professor Truzzi has made a study of the *paranormal*, which we can define as "events that seem to be beyond normal explanations." The news media often contain sensational reports of

people who (so it is claimed) can read other people's thoughts, or bend spoons through "mental effort," or predict the future. As you might have guessed, most of these reports turn out to be hoaxes or delusions. But since there is always the chance that a mind-reader or spoon-bender may actually have genuine paranormal powers, scientists like Dr. Truzzi try to investigate as many of these reports as possible.

"I called you because the little girl is also supposed to be autistic," Marcello replied.

"Oh," I said, suddenly realizing why Marcello had called me. For the past several years, my colleagues and I at Michigan have been working with autistic children. *Juvenile autism* is a psychological disorder that affects about one child in 2,000. Most autistic children are quite normal in appearance, and few of them have any measurable brain damage. It is their *behavior* that is unusual or abnormal. These youngsters seldom talk, even though they are physically capable of doing so. For the most part, they are unable (or unwilling) to relate to the people around them, including members of their own families. For some time now, my colleagues and I at the University of Michigan have been trying to find ways to help autistic children communicate more effectively.

"Okay, Marcello, tell me about this little girl who can read minds," I said to my friend.

"It's a very interesting story," he said with considerable enthusiasm. "The girl's name is Mary Smith. She's nine years old. She apparently suffers from some kind of brain damage, and limps a bit when she walks. She seldom if ever speaks, which is why she was diagnosed as autistic, I gather."

"Who did the diagnosis?" I asked.

"The school psychologist, I presume," Dr. Truzzi replied. "Mrs. Smith said Mary's teachers believe she's retarded as well as autistic. And Mrs. Smith thinks the teachers are wrong. She says Mary is potentially quite bright, even though the girl doesn't talk. That's why she taught Mary to communicate with her by using a computer."

"A computer?" I said, puzzled. "I thought Mary could read minds."

"Oh, she *supposedly* does," Marcello said. "At least, that's what Mrs. Smith claims. Whether she *really* can read minds remains to be proven scientifically, of course. However, since Mary can't talk, she needs some way of expressing her thoughts. It was only when Mrs. Smith taught Mary how to type on a computer keyboard that the mother learned that her daughter could read minds. Because, up until then, Mary had no way of letting people know what her mental skills were."

"I see," I said, scratching my head. "How long did it take Mary to learn to use the computer?"

"I don't know," Dr. Truzzi said. "But I gather she learned fairly quickly."

"How does she use this computer?"

Marcello paused for just a fraction of a second, as if searching his memory banks. "I think the mother stands behind the girl and asks her questions. Mary then types on the keyboard, and the answers appear on the computer screen."

"Oh?" I said. "Marcello, are you sure this thing is 'for real?'"

Dr. Truzzi laughed. "Of course not. You're never sure about these things until you investigate. But a psychiatrist who studied the girl says she really can read minds. And one of the Toledo TV stations broadcast a story about her that apparently impressed a lot of people. So there may be something to it after all. That's why it's important that someone checks this thing out. I don't have time right now, but I thought perhaps you'd be interested in looking into the situation because the girl presumably is autistic."

I stalled for time. "Well, I don't know . . ."

"Oh, come on, Jim. It's a fascinating mystery story, and I know how much you love mysteries."

"Well, all right . . ."

The Mystery of Human Behavior

Marcello had me dead to rights. I *do* love mysteries. That's one of the reasons I find human beings so intriguing. Like many psychologists, I consider human behavior a fascinating puzzle, begging to be solved. If you enjoy guessing what other people are really like, you probably feel much the same way. So, just for the moment, let's assume that you and I are detectives, trying to figure out whether nine-year-old Mary Smith can really read minds.

Like most sleuths, we'll gather evidence and follow our hunches. But, as you will soon learn,

Your author, James V. McConnell.

modern psychologists have several tools available to them that not even the great Sherlock Holmes possessed. The first tool is that collection of data and theories called *scientific psychology*. Because psychologists have been studying human behavior in the laboratory and in real-life settings for more than a century, we simply know more *facts* about people than most detectives do. And we also have many *theories* about human behavior that have stood the test of time. We frequently draw on these theoretical viewpoints to help us understand human behavior. Our second tool is just as important. It's called the *scientific method*, and it gives us an extremely powerful way of collecting and evaluating the information we need to help us solve human mysteries.

Reading this book can be a useful first step as you try to master the facts and theories that make up modern psychology. And following my train of thought as I puzzle over the matter of Mary Smith may demonstrate rather dramatically why psychologists depend so heavily on the scientific method.

There is another point I should make immediately. I have immense respect for people's privacy. So, I've changed some of the names and descriptions of the people involved in this case history, particularly those involving the "Smith" family. But I also respect accuracy, so I've done my best to report what I actually saw and experienced.

Please keep these points in mind as we return to the mystery of "Mary Smith."

Clues and Data

As I listened to Dr. Truzzi describe Mary Smith, I paid much more attention to some things he said than to others. Several events that Marcello described bothered me. (When you read Chapter 8, you'll learn that the way you perceive the world is strongly influenced by certain *perceptual principles*. One such principle is that you tend to "see what you expect to see." When you perceive something that violates your expectancies, you often tend to focus on it. Small wonder, then, that I focused more on what was unusual in Marcello's description than in what was—to me—rather predictable.)

Let's call the things that bothered me "discrepancies," or *clues*. If we can resolve enough of these discrepancies, perhaps we can decide whether Mary Smith could really read minds, or whether we should explain what she was doing in other ways.

Clue #1. Some children diagnosed as *autistic* do suffer from obvious brain damage. But, as I've already said, most of them appear to have fairly normal nervous systems. So the first thing I asked myself was, "Is Mary Smith really autistic, or is there something else wrong?"

Clue #2 is related to #1. Most autistic children are *mute*. It's very difficult to teach them to speak, or to write, or even to communicate using sign language. While some autistic children do learn to talk eventually, they usually express themselves rather poorly and imprecisely. Thus, it seemed highly unlikely to me that Mary Smith could (a) be autistic, and (b) quickly learn to communicate using the precise language demanded by a computer.

The third discrepancy was more a vague hunch than a clue. For, as Marcello described how Mary "typed out the answers to her mother's questions," I got the uncomfortable feeling that I had heard this story before. I couldn't recall quite where or when I had encountered something similar in the past. But I was pretty sure that if I could just remember, I might come up with a solution to the mystery of Mary Smith. So I asked Dr. Truzzi a few more questions in an attempt to jog my memory.

Mr. van Osten and his star pupil, a horse named "Clever Hans."

More about Mary

"Marcello, tell me something. You said she's brain-damaged and limps a bit. So she probably has poor control of her hands as well as of her legs. If that's the case, how does she use the computer?"

"The mother had a special keyboard made with very large letters on it. All Mary has to do, really, is to poke a finger at the letters and she can type out whatever words she supposedly reads in her mother's mind."

I thought for a moment. "Can Mary read anybody else's mind other than her mother's?"

"I haven't seen Mary perform," Marcello said, "so I don't know whether she can read *my* mind or not. But I'm told she can answer almost any question you care to ask her."

"*Any* question?" I asked, my memory stirring a little.

Dr. Truzzi responded almost immediately. "Remember I said a psychiatrist went to see her? Well, she apparently knew things about him that she couldn't have learned in any ordinary way. Or, at least, that's what Mrs. Smith claims."

My memory nudged me again. "Where does the mother stand when Mary's answering all these questions?"

"Behind the girl. But I think the mother usually touches Mary on the head, supposedly to establish telepathic contact."

Telepathy is usually defined as "the ability to read thoughts over a distance." But to qualify as telepathy, there must be no *physical contact* between the telepath and the mind he or she is "reading." Thus, if Mary Smith was actually a telepath, why would her mother need to touch her on the head in order to establish telepathic contact? Surely this was Clue #4, so I asked another question.

"Couldn't Mrs. Smith be giving her daughter cues as to what to type?"

"That's always possible," Marcello responded in a bemused tone of voice. I sensed that he was almost leading me along, hoping I'd raise the same sort of questions that had already occurred to him. "But the girl apparently types out her answers very quickly. Wouldn't she have to be awfully clever to respond that fast to just a light touch on the head?"

And then the clues all fell into place, and I was sure I had part of the solution to the mystery of Mary Smith. "Clever Hans," I said.

"Clever Hans indeed," Dr. Truzzi replied. "I presumed you'd see the possible similarities."

A Horse Named "Clever Hans"

Some 80 years ago, the newspapers of Berlin, Germany, were filled with exciting stories about a horse named Clever Hans. According to these reports, Hans could not only "read minds," but could also solve difficult mathematical problems. People by the thousands flocked to see Hans perform his amazing feats.

Hans was owned by a Mr. van Osten, who was so impressed by the horse's abilities that he built a large "answer board" for Hans to use (see photo). If you gave Mr. van Osten a question for Hans, the man would look directly at the horse and repeat the question in what seemed a normal tone of voice. Hans would then lift his hoof and tap out the answer. If you asked, "What is $2 + 2$?", Hans would tap the ground four times. But if your question was "Who is president of the United States?", Hans would point at the letters on the answer board that spelled out the correct response. Frequently, after Hans had done well, Mr. van Osten would pat the animal on its neck or give it a bit of food as a reward.

There were a number of intriguing aspects to Hans's performance. First, if you tried to trick him, he'd almost always catch you at it. For instance, if you said, "$2 + 2$ is 5, isn't it?", Hans would usually signal "NO," using the answer board. Many people believed this response proved Hans was an "independent thinker," and wasn't just responding to subtle cues given him by Mr. van Osten. Second, if the answer to your question was a long one, Hans would tap much more rapidly than if the answer were short. Many newspaper reporters took this as evidence that Hans was so bright, he knew the length of the answer *before he started responding*. (If the horse merely started and stopped responding when given some cue by Mr. van Osten, the animal obviously wouldn't know in advance which answers were going to be long, and which would be short.) Third, Hans would respond to questions given to him even by strangers. Thus, the horse obviously wasn't just picking up on unintentional cues from his owner.

Given these facts, it's not surprising most people concluded Hans was a genuine telepath. But a few skeptics remained convinced that the animal was merely reacting to cues of some kind from the people who asked Hans questions. The controversy became so heated that, in 1904, several of the best-known scientists in Germany formed a "commission" to study the animal. The commission included a zoologist, a physiologist, a veterinarian, a psychologist, the director of the Berlin Zoo, and even the manager of a circus that featured animal acts. After months of study, the commission issued its report. These distinguished scientists stated boldly that they could find no evidence Hans was responding to external cues from his questioners. Hence, the commission said, Hans was a "special case," and perhaps really could read minds.

However, like most scientific commissions, this distinguished group recommended that "further research be done." So Professor Carl Stumpf, the psychologist on the commission, told one of his graduate students to look into the matter. This student, a young man named Oskar Pfungst, did just that.

Pfungst to the Rescue

Unlike Professor Stumpf, Oskar Pfungst simply didn't believe that Hans could "read minds." So, for many months, he observed Mr. van Osten very carefully as the owner talked to his horse. Then, in a controlled and systematic way, Pfungst began to change the conditions under which Hans worked. For example, Pfungst put blinders on Hans so the animal couldn't watch the people who were asking him questions. The horse's ability to respond correctly decreased significantly. This result suggested strongly that Hans was responding to some unintentional visual cue given him by the person asking the questions. And when Pfungst found ways to keep Hans from hearing the tiny noises that people made when asking him questions, Hans did even worse. Indeed, when Pfungst cut out *both* visual and auditory cues after someone asked the horse a question, Hans either refused to respond or gave the wrong answer entirely.

To test the animal's ability to "think independently," Pfungst did something a little different. First, he asked Hans to add two numbers, such as $23 + 49$. Hans immediately responded by tapping out 72. Then Pfungst asked a friend of his to select a number at random and whisper it in the horse's ear. Pfungst then did the same, and asked Hans to add the two numbers. If *either* Pfungst or his friend knew *both* numbers, Hans invariably got the correct answer. But if neither man was aware of what number the other had chosen, the horse usually failed the test.

These results indicated Clever Hans was indeed a "genius of a horse," but surely wasn't a mind-reader. Rather, the animal was superb at reading "body-language" cues that questioners almost always gave to the animal. But these cues were so slight and so subtle that most people were completely unaware they were giving Hans signals.

For example, the moment most people finished asking Hans a question, they inclined their heads forward a fraction of an inch. This was a signal to Hans to start tapping. When Hans had tapped out the correct response, the people leaned back just slightly. This cue told Hans to stop tapping. (Other people inhaled sharply when they asked a question, and then exhaled when Hans had reached the right number of taps.) Similar cues helped the animal point his hoof to letters on the "answer board" that Mr. van Osten had constructed.

Pfungst also noticed that people tended to lean farther forward when they asked questions requiring long answers than when they asked questions with short answers. This response gave Hans his cue as to how fast to tap. Indeed, the horse was so sensitive to slight head movements that if anyone present raised an eyebrow or twitched a nostril while Hans was responding, he would stop instantly.

A final point: Once Pfungst became aware that Clever Hans was reacting to the body-language cues he was giving the horse, he deliberately tried to stop making these tell-tale twitches and snorts when he asked Hans questions. But no matter how hard Pfungst struggled to control his bodily movements, Hans could almost always detect some sort of signal that told the animal when and how to respond.

After months of study, Pfungst concluded Hans was a very bright horse indeed, even if the animal couldn't "read minds."

From Horses to People

Once Pfungst had identified the cues that Hans was responding to, Pfungst moved his research from Mr. van Osten's barn to a psychological laboratory at the University of Berlin. And he began studying the effects of "social cues" on human rather than animal behavior.

In one study, Pfungst tried to play the role of Clever Hans himself. That is, he invited 25 people to ask him questions that only they could answer. Pfungst then tapped out the answers much as Hans did, trying to stop responding when the people gave him the same sort of body-language cue they might give the horse. With 23 of the 25 people, Pfungst's answers were right on target!

One Reason People Are a Puzzle

The Clever Hans story is important for several reasons. First, it taught psychologists that most of us continuously give cues in our body language that suggest how we feel and what we're thinking about. Usually, we're unaware we're giving off these signals, but they're visible (or audible) to anyone who cares to notice. (For example, research studies show that most of us usually lean toward people we like when talking to them, but lean back when conversing with individuals we dislike or don't trust.) The reverse is also true—we often respond to body-language cues from other people, even though we typically are unconscious of what signals we're reacting to. It's hardly surprising, therefore, that many of us find human beings such insoluble puzzles. For most of us never become aware of the wide range of external cues that strongly influence our emotions and actions.

Second, the Pfungst research demonstrates just how critical a knowledge of the scientific method is to understanding human behavior. The commission of distinguished scientists that studied Clever Hans knew a great deal about human and animal psychology. They observed the horse carefully, they asked questions, and they gave the matter a lot of thought. Then they concluded that Hans could "read minds." But they didn't do *adequately extensive scientific experiments* to test out their conclusions. Pfungst observed the animal too, because the scientific method always begins with careful observations. But he alone took the crucial next step. He guessed at the environmental stimuli (or cues) that could be affecting the horse's behavior, and then he altered these stimulus cues in a very systematic way. This creative use of the scientific method led Pfungst to quite a different set of conclusions about Clever Hans than the commission had reached.

Third, when the name "Clever Hans" popped into my memory, I thought I had come up with an answer to the mystery of Mary Smith—even if it was one that Marcello Truzzi had already considered. But, like Pfungst, I couldn't be sure of my conclusions until I too had put the scientific method to good use.

We'll get back to the Mary Smith story in just a moment. First, however, we need to take time out for what we might call an "academic commercial"—that is, a plug for the scientific method.

Science as a "Detective Story"

One of the main purposes of any science is that of solving mysteries. Nature gives us a puzzle, human or otherwise. For some reason, perhaps due to our own peculiar nature as human beings, we are motivated to solve the puzzle. We could just use our "hunches," of course, and make wild guesses about the answer. But scientists prefer to adopt a logical process of some kind when trying to find the solution to the puzzle.

The approach most scientists use is called the *scientific method*, and it is based on the belief that most mysteries have *measurable causes*. To use the scientific method properly, you must follow several steps:

1. First, you have to recognize that a mystery of some kind exists that needs solving, and that the mystery probably has a natural cause. We might call this step *perceiving the problem*.

2. Then you make as many *initial observations* about the mysterious circumstances as you can. And you try to make your observations as exact and complete as possible.

3. You use the results of your initial observations to come up with a *tentative solution* or "first guess" as to what the answer is. Scientists often call this step "making a hypothesis." The solution you pick, however, will be determined by how you view the problem—and the world. If you think events that take place in the world around you are affected primarily by *supernatural powers*, then the scientific method won't help you much. But if you believe that the mysterious event might have a *natural cause*, then perhaps you can state your "tentative solution" or hypothesis in a way that will help you determine what that cause is.

4. Next, you draw up a plan for *testing objectively* whether or not your first hunch about the solution was correct. This test may merely involve making further observations about the puzzling affair. Or it may involve performing an experiment in which you "do something" to the puzzle in order to get a reaction of some kind.

5. Whether you merely observe things, or whether you undertake an experiment of some kind, you then look over the data and try to decide as unemotionally as possible whether your tentative solution to the problem was right or wrong. If your initial hypothesis was wrong, you will revise it and make some more observations. But if your first hunch was correct, you probably will refine your solution to the mystery by *testing it again and again*. And to do so, you will need to make further predictions about future events.

6. If these further predictions turn out to be accurate, then most likely your solution to the puzzle was correct. But if your predictions were incorrect, you should realize that you "goofed" somewhere along the way. And you will have to start the problem-solving process all over again.

The Importance of Objectivity

The key concept in any definition of the scientific method is *objectivity*. And "being objective" means standing back and looking at the puzzle as unemotionally and impersonally as you can.

True, your subjective, personal feelings are very useful in *motivating* you to want to solve problems, but your emotions can cloud your judgment if you don't know how to control them when necessary.

For example, Pfungst was *objective* in his study of Clever Hans. His initial hypothesis was that the horse was responding to unconscious cues from Mr. van Osten and other questioners. As Harvard psychologist Robert Rosenthal states in the book, *Clever Hans: The Horse of Mr. van Osten*, Pfungst liked Hans and respected Mr. van Osten. Pfungst notes, for example, that van Osten never charged anyone for talking to Hans, and made not a penny out of the animal's fame. But Pfungst didn't allow his affection for either the man or the horse to get in the way of his pursuit of objective truth. Mr. van Osten, on the other hand, let his emotions blind him to what was really going on. He loved Hans and was convinced the horse could "read minds." Shortly after Pfungst proved otherwise, van Osten went into a deep depression. A few months later, he died, a bitter and surely very disappointed man.

Given these facts, perhaps you can understand why I worried a bit how Mrs. Smith might react if someone proved scientifically that Mary was merely responding to subtle cues from her mother. As you will see, however, those fears were groundless.

A Trip to Toledo

As I suggested, Marcello was pleased when I said the words "Clever Hans." For, like most behavioral scientists, Dr. Truzzi knew all about Mr. van Osten's horse. Indeed, as I discovered later on, Marcello had published an article on the subject in 1981.

"Oh, yes," he said. "The girl could just be responding to subtle cues from her mother. But what are the cues, and how does the whole thing work? That's what I hope you can find out."

And so we agreed that I would pay a visit to the Smiths. Thus, a week or so later, I drove down to Toledo with a man I'll call Charles Barnwell. Charlie was trained as a social worker, had a long-standing interest in autistic children, and had been to the Smith house previously. He also was convinced that Mary Smith could actually "read minds." After all, he had asked the girl questions himself, and she had gotten the right answers! How could she possibly fake something like that?

I had two answers to that question. First, I told him briefly about Clever Hans. Second, I reminded him that, as far as I knew, no instance of "mind reading" had ever held up under the scrutiny of scientific investigation. When Charlie doubted my statement, I referred him to two journals that deal with such matters. The first is called *The Skeptical Inquirer*, which is the official journal of the Committee for the Scientific Investigation of Claims of the Paranormal. The second is *The Zetetic Scholar*, journal of the Center for Scientific Anomalies Research, which is edited by Dr. Truzzi. (*Anomalies* is a technical term meaning "events that are inconsistent with what would be normally expected." I'll list addresses for both journals at the end of this chapter.)

I also told Charlie that no one—not even the most convinced of the skeptics—had ever proved that mind reading and other paranormal events *couldn't occur*. So we must surely keep an open mind about such things. However, as a careful reading of either of these two journals suggests, the evidence supporting most types of paranormal occurrences is dubious at best.

At any rate, after an hour's drive, Charlie and I arrived at the Smith house. It was a small but well-kept home on the outskirts of Toledo. Mrs. Smith smiled at us warmly as she opened the door, took our coats, and then invited us back to the kitchen.

My first impression was that I had wandered by mistake into a computer showroom, for the tiny kitchen and dining room were filled with electronic equipment of various kinds. I spotted an Apple computer, a slide projector and a movie screen, a voice synthesizer, and a large keyboard connected to the computer by wires. A sort of highchair, covered with comfortable cushions, sat in front of the computer screen. "This is what Mary uses to communicate with me," Mrs. Smith explained. "The equipment was given to us by one of the service clubs when they learned about Mary's special talents."

I asked about the slide projector. "Mary doesn't see very well," Mrs. Smith said. "She can't always read the tiny letters on the computer screen. I hooked the slide projector up so it can magnify what she types and project it on the movie screen."

Next I asked about Mary herself. "She's adopted, you know," the woman said. "Our first child was born handicapped. Most people are a little put off by handicapped children. Very few people will adopt a handicapped child. But my husband and I think they're the most loving children there are. We think we can help them, maybe more than most people can. So we've adopted three of them."

"How old was Mary when you adopted her?" I asked.

"About five," Mrs. Smith replied. "She was like a frightened little animal when we first got her. She hid in the bathroom and wouldn't come out. So I just stayed in the bathroom with her for the first six weeks or so, until she calmed down. Now she's quite comfortable with me. Of course, she still has a few problems, but she's a very special child, as you'll see."

"What kind of problems does she have?"

"Well, her brain didn't develop properly. She's hydrocephalic, you know. The doctors have operated on her brain, to relieve the pressure. And it does seem to have helped a little. But she's very bright, despite all her difficulties."

Hydrocephalic is a medical term, which comes from the words "hydro" (meaning water) and "cephalo" (meaning brain). Special cells in the brain continuously secrete a watery fluid that surrounds and cushions the brain. In a normal child, this fluid drains off through a sort of tube and becomes the spinal fluid. In the hydrocephalic child, however, the tube is blocked so the fluid can't escape. The pressure inside the skull becomes so great that the child's brain cells can't grow properly. The child is left with a skull full of fluid—and with an underdeveloped brain.

(Put more technically, Mary Smith had little in the way of cortex, cerebrum, or midbrain. Thus, she had to make do with little more than the stem of the brain. For a more complete description of the parts of the brain and what they do, see Chapter 4.)

Since Mary Smith had much less brain tissue than a normal child has, it was understandable that she "had a lot of problems." It also seemed likely she was profoundly handicapped rather than autistic. But, as I soon learned, Mrs. Smith didn't like to think of her daughter as being "retarded." She preferred to call Mary "autistic" instead.

"Mary's teachers have always underestimated her abilities," Mrs. Smith said. "They don't think she'll ever learn to talk. But a lot of the things she did early on suggested she wanted to express herself. Since she wasn't speaking out loud, I thought maybe she could learn to use a computer to tell me what she's thinking about."

"And she learned quickly?"

Mrs. Smith smiled. "No, it wasn't that easy. Mary can't control her hands very well, so she can't use the keyboard that came with the computer. So I had that big alphabet board built. Even so, it seemed to take her a long time to learn how to use it. And then one day she just started typing out words and complete sentences."

"Just like that?" I asked.

"Well, more or less. You see, I made the mistake of trying to move her hands for her at first. I'd ask her a question, like, 'How do you spell cat?' And then I'd guide her fingers over the board, and show her how to type out the answer. But she just didn't seem to understand what I was trying to get her to do. And then one day I got frustrated and stopped pushing her fingers around."

"How did she respond?"

"I was teaching her how to spell a word—'dog,' I think it was. Well, she got angry with me when I tried to help her type the answer. So I just let go of her hands. She began poking at the keys, slowly. I was screaming DOG, DOG, DOG in my mind, I was so angry. Then I looked over at the screen. She had typed out DOG, DOG, DOG on the keys. 'My Lord,' I said to myself. 'Mary can read my mind.'"

A Mother's Touch

For several seconds, the three of us were completely silent. I glanced at Charlie, who was wide-eyed, as if in amazement. I looked back at Mrs. Smith. Her face wore a quiet smile.

Finally I said, "And ever since that day, Mary has been able to read your thoughts and type them out on the computer?"

Mrs. Smith nodded. "Of course, she got better at it, as time went on."

I cleared my throat. "That first day, when Mary typed out the word 'dog' for you, were you touching her?"

"Oh, yes. I was standing behind her, resting my hands on her head, like I always do when she types. She can't read my mind unless I'm touching her, you know."

"Do you always touch her on the head?"

"No. Her teachers came and saw her perform. They said I must be giving her cues of some kind—turning her head, or something. So now I touch her on the arm instead."

Charlie interrupted. "But it still works, doesn't it?"

Mrs. Smith nodded again.

"Could we see Mary?" Charlie continued. "Could you show us how it works?"

"Of course," the woman said. "I'll get her right away. She's just downstairs, playing."

As soon as Mrs. Smith had left the room, Charlie turned to me. "Amazing, isn't it?"

I sighed. "Yes, it is. Mrs. Smith knows, doesn't she?"

"Knows what?"

"Knows that Mary can't really read minds, Charlie. Knows that she's cueing the girl's responses in some fashion."

Charlie frowned. "Well, I suppose you could be right. But it certainly does seem like the girl can read minds. I mean, I've seen it with my own eyes!"

An Eye-Opening Demonstration

Before I could respond, Mrs. Smith returned with her daughter. Charlie and I shook hands with the girl. Then Mrs. Smith put her up on the well-cushioned highchair in front of the computer screen.

"Dr. McConnell, if you'd care to write out some questions on a piece of paper, I'll try to have Mary answer them for you." Mrs. Smith said this as she turned on the equipment.

"What kinds of questions?" I asked.

"Oh, anything at all. Write out some words, for example. Show them to me, but don't say them out loud."

"Okay," I said, and began jotting some words down on a piece of paper. While I was writing, Mrs. Smith got out the alphabet board and put it in Mary's lap. It was a long, thin, flat piece of equipment. The front of the board contained letters and numbers, divided into a sort of grid.

A	B	C	D	E	F	1	2	3
G	H	I	J	K	L	4	5	6
M	N	O	P	Q	R	7	8	9
S	T	U	V	W	X	Y	Z	0

Mrs. Smith showed us that just touching any of the squares on the grid would make the computer display the appropriate letter or number.

I wrote the words, "Rat," "Banana," and "Weather" on the paper and gave it to Mrs. Smith. She read the words, nodded, and then stood behind Mary's chair, draping her arms around the girl's shoulders. Almost at once, the girl lifted her right hand and pointed her right index finger at the letter "A." Without touching any of the squares, her finger swept across the top row of the board. When she reached the end of the first row, her hand jerked back and rapidly swept across the second row. As she neared the "R" in the third row, her hand slowed slightly. Her index finger hovered over the "R" for a fraction of a second. Then she touched it, and the letter "R" appeared on the computer screen.

Instantly, Mary's hand returned to the "A" on the top row. She hesitated momentarily, touched the letter, and then began to sweep out the rest of the top row. This time, her hand didn't slow until she reached the bottom row. She touched the "T." The word "RAT" now appeared on the computer screen. It had taken Mary less than five seconds to produce the first word I had shown to Mrs. Smith.

"Incredible!" Charlie said, staring at the screen in astonishment.

"Yes, it is," I said, staring at Mrs. Smith's hands as they gently caressed her daughter's arms. "Try the second word, would you please?"

Mrs. Smith nodded. Mary touched the "B" and "A" so quickly that I couldn't follow her movements. But as her finger neared the "N," I was looking intently at the tendons on Mrs. Smith's right hand. The closer the little girl's finger came to the "N," the more visible the tendons on the mother's hand became. And when Mary's finger was right over the letter "N," the mother's tendons popped into full view for a fraction of a second. Mary touched the "N." The tendons in the mother's hand relaxed, and Mary's fingers moved to the top row of the alphabet board once more. Each time the mother's hand tensed, Mary poked the keyboard. Within a few seconds, the word "BANANA" showed on the computer screen. A few moments later, so did the word "WEATHER."

"Fantastic," Charlie said. "I wouldn't have believed it if I hadn't seen it with my own eyes."

"It is fantastic," I said. I thought for a moment. "Mrs. Smith, I noticed that you were looking at Mary's fingers as she typed. Can she read your mind if you have your eyes closed?"

"No, she can't," the woman replied. "I've tried

shutting my eyes, and looking away. Mary just gets confused when I do. That's one of the things that puzzles me."

"What else puzzles you?" I asked.

The woman frowned. "Well, at first I thought she was a mathematical genius. That made me happy, because it would prove to her teachers that she's brighter than they think she is. Anyhow, I'd write out two numbers, add them myself, and then give her the numbers to do on her own. She always got the right answer very quickly. Except one day I added the numbers wrong myself, and Mary typed out the same wrong answer I had, not the correct answer."

"What did you conclude from that?"

"That's when I realized she was reading my mind, not doing the math on her own."

I nodded. "And what did you conclude from the fact that she can't read your mind when you shut your eyes?"

Mrs. Smith gave a deep sigh. She patted Mary lovingly on the head, and then sat down wearily in a kitchen chair. She glanced at the floor for a moment, then looked up at me. "Maybe I am giving her a cue of some kind, maybe not. If I am, I don't know what it is. But that isn't what bothers me."

Mary slid down from her highchair and limped over to her mother. She climbed up in the woman's lap and began pulling at her mother's earring. "Don't do that, dear," Mrs. Smith said gently. She gathered the girl into her arms to keep her quiet.

"What does bother you?" I asked.

The woman sighed again. "The fact that I can't seem to reach *her*. I can hold her in my arms, like this, but I can't reach deep down inside her. Even if she's reading my mind, she's just telling me what *I* think, not what *she* thinks and feels. She may have a damaged brain, but there's a little girl in there somewhere. How do I get to her, Dr. McConnell? How do I find out who my little girl really is?"

Three Explanatory Views of Human Behavior

How would you have answered Mrs. Smith had you been in my place? There are thousands of responses I might have given, all of them accurate in a limited sort of way. For example, I could have replied, "She's a nine-year-old, hydrocephalic human female." Or, "She's your *daughter*, someone you have a warm, loving relationship with." Or even, "She's *herself*, that's who she is."

If you asked a thousand psychologists to define Mary Smith, the answers you'd get would probably include one or more of the descriptive terms listed above. For these responses represent the three major theoretical viewpoints within the behavioral sciences today. Let's look briefly at these three main ways of explaining human behavior.

The Biological Viewpoint

Some psychologists emphasize the importance of biological factors in determining who you are and what you do. These scientists believe that everything you think and feel is controlled by electrical and chemical activity in your brain and the rest of your body. Thus, to these theorists, the body controls the mind, and not the other way around (see Chapter 5).

From the *biological viewpoint*, Mary Smith would be defined primarily in terms of her damaged nervous system. Her inability to speak, her lack of muscle coordination, her limited comprehension—all these *psychological* or *behavioral* difficulties would be viewed as "natural consequences" of her poorly developed brain. And given this perspective, biological psychologists might well recommend that the best way to help Mary Smith would be through surgery, or the use of drugs.

"DELUSIONS OF GRANDEUR?
I AM GRAND!"

Mary Smith did have physical handicaps, and there's no way of "defining" her without taking these problems into account. But just as we cannot explain who you are merely by describing the flow of electricity through your nervous system, so we cannot take just a narrow biological view of who Mary Smith really is.

The Intra-Psychic Viewpoint

The majority of behavioral scientists would probably take an *intra-psychic viewpoint* toward Mary Smith. (The term *intra-psychic* means "inside the mind.") Most psychologists believe that everything that goes wrong (or right) about someone's psyche or mind or behavior cannot be explained in simple, biological terms. These scientists try to look (as best they can) at what goes on *inside the individual's mind*, rather than just looking at how a person's brain functions.

But what does the word "mind" really mean? In fact, it comes from an Old English term meaning "memory." *Webster's New Collegiate Dictionary* defines mind as "that element or complex of elements in an individual that feels, perceives, thinks, wills, and especially reasons." The same book also calls mind, "The conscious mental events and capabilities in an organism." Mind, then, has to do with your *inner* experiences.

Scientists define "mind" in many different ways. But if there is one fact that almost all psychologists are agreed upon, it's this one: What goes on inside your mind is a *private set of events* we can never inspect directly. (Had Mary Smith actually been able to read minds, she might have helped advance the science of psychology more than anyone else in history!)

Put it this way: I could see Mary Smith's body, and I could measure her physical behavior objectively. Her *mind* was hidden from my direct view, however. All I could do was study her behavior as objectively as possible, and then draw conclusions from what I observed.

Intra-psychic psychologists are primarily interested in *mental processes*. Scientists study these inner processes in many ways. First, they observe what people actually do and say in a variety of settings. Second, they give people standardized tests of various kinds, and then compare their responses with those that other individuals make (see Chapter 20). Third, they listen very closely to statements that people make about their inner thoughts and feelings. The intra-psychic psychologists then try to explain the behaviors they've measured *objec-*

tively in terms of *subjective* mental processes—such as perceptions, motives, values, attitudes, memories, and personality traits.

From the biological viewpoint, the body exercises almost complete control over the mind. From the intra-psychic standpoint, however, the mind dominates most bodily activities.

Both viewpoints can be very useful in helping you understand yourself (and others). But both viewpoints are—in and of themselves—incomplete.

The Social/Behavioral Viewpoint

Mary Smith had both a mind and a body. But she was also a *social being*. Mary's thoughts and behaviors were strongly influenced by the people and things around her, and her thoughts and behaviors strongly influenced the people she was around. Even her "mental disabilities" were affected as much by her environment as by her hydrocephalic condition. Children with very similar brain damage often show quite different behavior patterns, depending on what type of home they have grown up in.

Mary had a mother and father, two adopted sisters, and a brother. She had many friends living in her neighborhood, and at school she worked and played with teachers and schoolmates. In the past she had been in a hospital and an adoption agency home. At the moment, she was in contact not only with her mother, but also with a psychologist and with someone trained in social work. In her brief life, therefore, Mary Smith had met and interacted with hundreds of other individuals, all of whom had played their parts in helping make her what she was today. Indeed, from the *social/behavioral viewpoint*, there was little about Mary's actions and emotions that couldn't be explained in terms of what she had learned from her social environment.

Most people ignore the importance of the environment in shaping human thoughts and actions. For example, Mrs. Smith apparently defined her daughter primarily in intra-psychic terms, since she explained the girl's behaviors in terms of "mental telepathy." In fact, mother and daughter had become a smoothly functioning *social team*. Each gave subtle cues to the other, and each responded to subtle cues received from the other. Do we have to know anything at all about brain damage or mental processes in order to explain how both members of this social team responded? Indeed, wouldn't appealing to such concepts as "hydrocephalism" and "mind reading" tend to blind us to the social factors that were actually determining Mary Smith's responses?

The Holistic Approach

Which of the three viewpoints—the biological, the intra-psychic, or the social/behavioral—gives you the greatest understanding of Mary and her problems?

The answer is, *all three of them taken together*. Like Mary, you are an incredibly complex living system. There is a biological side to your nature, a mental side, and a social side. You cannot hope to understand yourself—or Mary, or anyone else—unless you are willing to view human beings from these three different perspectives.

And if you are to learn to understand yourself better—or to understand Mary, your parents, your friends, and your loved ones—you too must learn to see people as being complex *systems* made up of interacting parts.

Let's keep this *holistic* viewpoint in mind as we look more closely at Mary Smith.

Mary and the Three Viewpoints

What had I learned about Mary so far?

From a biological viewpoint, I knew that she had much less brain tissue than a normal child her age would have. The surgeons had surely helped with the operation to relieve the pressure within her skull, but they couldn't help her recover the brain cells she had lost. Those cells were gone forever. However, this fact didn't necessarily mean she couldn't recover *psychologically* and *socially* if given the proper training. As you will learn in Chapter 26, psychologists have recently become fairly adept at helping people with severely damaged nervous systems.

From an intra-psychic viewpoint, I knew that Mary suffered from behavioral and mental problems related to her physical difficulties. She couldn't speak, she couldn't control her movements in a normal fashion, and her teachers considered her "mentally retarded." She had also been through several frightening experiences in the past that surely had left psychological scars on her personality. However, she had strengths and abilities as well as weaknesses and disabilities. Like Hans the horse, Mary was particularly clever at picking up subtle cues from the people around her—cues that most "normal" children probably would have missed.

She could communicate her needs and feelings in at least a rudimentary way. And most of all, she could *learn*. (As you will discover when you read Chapters 17–19, the ability to adapt to the environment is perhaps the most important survival skill a developing child can have.)

From a social/behavioral viewpoint, it was clear that the girl and her mother made up an incredible team. The woman's love for Mary was obvious. Few of us would have had the stamina, motivation, or guts to stay in a bathroom for weeks just to calm a frightened child's fears. And few of us probably would have worked as hard, or spent as much money, trying to devise ways to help a brain-damaged child learn to communicate with the world around her. Thus, to find out more about who Mary was—and what sort of person she could become—I obviously would need to discover more about how she and her mother interacted.

Now, at last, we can begin to answer our original question, "Who is Mary Smith?" The answer is that she is a biological, intra-psychic, and social *organism*—just as we all are. Viewing her from all three perspectives *simultaneously* is what I mean by "taking the holistic approach in psychology." As it happened, I chose to look at her social behavior more closely at first. But I was equally interested in all aspects of this young girl called Mary Smith.

And I needed to use the scientific method to help me accomplish my task.

The Scientific Method

Once Mrs. Smith admitted that she was cueing most of Mary's responses at the computer keyboard, I was reasonably confident the girl wasn't a telepath. Oddly enough, however, Charlie remained unconvinced.

"I still think she can read minds," he said. "I mean, I was watching pretty carefully, and I didn't see you give her any cues."

"But if she can read my mind, why can't she type out answers if I'm not looking at her?" Mrs. Smith replied. "That still puzzles me."

"Maybe your mind goes blank when you shut your eyes," Charlie said quietly. "Maybe looking at her helps establish the telepathic contact."

"What do you think, Dr. McConnell?"

I paused for a moment, trying to put my thoughts in order. Before I could say anything, however, Mary demanded that her mother take her to the bathroom. While the two were gone, I talked at length with Charlie.

"Look," I said. "You have one explanation for Mary's behavior—you call it 'mind reading.' I have another explanation. Probably we could come up with several more theories if we really tried. The important thing is to find some way to put our notions to a scientific test of some kind. That's the best way to determine which of us has the right answer, isn't it?"

Charlie nodded in agreement.

"Okay, when Mrs. Smith and Mary come back, suppose we ask Mrs. Smith to help us run an experiment. Okay?"

When Charlie nodded again, I told him what I had in mind.

Independent, Dependent, and Intervening Variables

When psychologists perform experiments to test their hunches, they typically "do something new or unusual" to some organism or group. Then they sit back to see what *changes* occur.

When you "do something new or unusual" to an individual, you decide on the ways you are going to *vary* that person's environment. Since *you* make the choice, this *variable* in the experiment is "independent" of the subject's wishes. Psychologists call "what you do to a subject" the *independent variable* because it is under the experimenter's control.

When you act, people react. The subject's reaction is called the *dependent variable* because the response the person makes obviously depends on what you've done to the individual.

To summarize, the "independent variable" is what the experimenter does to the subject, while the "dependent variable" is the reaction the subject gives. But *why* do subjects react as they do? Psychologists aren't always sure. When we find that a certain act of ours almost always evokes the same response in someone else, however, we can often "make guesses." These guesses or hypotheses are our ways of explaining what goes on inside the person that *connects* the act with the reaction. Put another way, we guess at what processes inside the person "intervene" between the independent and dependent variable. And we call these inner processes *intervening variables*. We can't observe or measure these intervening variables directly, for they are just our guesses about why the person acts as he or she does.

Suppose you show Mary Smith a kitten because you want to see how she will react to it. She smiles and pets the animal. "Aha!" you say.

"She petted the beast because she loves cats." Showing Mary the kitten is the *independent variable*, because you could have shown her a snake. Smiling and petting are *dependent variables*, because her response depended on what you showed her. If you'd shown her a snake, she might have run away. "Love" is an *intervening variable*, because it's your explanation of why she responded as she did.

You can *see* kittens and petting behaviors. So independent and dependent variables are things that you can measure objectively. But you *can't see* "love" or "fear" or "mental telepathy." Therefore, intervening variables are usually *internal processes* that you can't measure directly. Indeed, you can't even be sure they actually exist. You merely presume that they do, because intervening variables give you a way of *explaining* the relationship you have observed between the independent and the dependent variables.

Charlie had watched Mary Smith perform at the computer keyboard, and had come up with an explanation for what he saw. The words I had shown to Mrs. Smith were the independent variable in this case, because I could have written three other words. Mary's responses at the keyboard were the dependent variable, because what she wrote obviously depended on the words I had chosen. Charlie then *invented* an intervening variable called "mind reading" to explain the relationship between my independent variable and Mary's dependent response.

I had watched the same performance, but offered a different intervening variable—one called "social cueing." Either hypothesis could be correct. How shall we judge between the two?

How do you decide which of two financial experts is the better? You ask both of them to predict what the stock market will do in the next months or so, and then you check to see which expert gave the more accurate prediction. Scientists do the same sort of thing when they test two competing hypotheses. They design an experiment and then let each hypothesis predict what will happen. Then they actually run the experiment and compare the results with the predictions. The theory that *predicts and explains* things better usually wins.

With this thought in mind, I said, "Charlie, weren't you surprised when Mrs. Smith said Mary couldn't read her mind when she looked away or closed her eyes?"

"Well, yes. But there are explanations . . ."

In science, explaining things *after the fact* is not nearly as convincing as predicting what will happen *before the fact*. So, I wanted to compare

Charlie's theory with mine, using predictions rather than explanations.

"But let's assume that Mrs. Smith is giving Mary cues, and that she needs to watch the girl in order to give her the proper signals. Then we'd be surprised only if Mary could respond correctly when her mother *wasn't* looking at her. Right?"

Charlie frowned. "I suppose so. But what cues does Mrs. Smith give?"

"The hands, Charlie. Watch her hands." And then I told Charlie what I had observed and what I wanted to do next.

Using Control Groups in Experiments

Suppose we wanted to run some additional tests to see if my hunch about Mary Smith was correct. What could we do next? As you might guess, we'd perform additional tests, sometimes letting her mother cue her, sometimes removing the cues. If the *only* time Mary responded appropriately was when she got the cues, then we could place some faith in the "cueing" hypothesis.

Whenever psychologists run experiments, they typically expose one group of subjects to what the psychologists believe is the important variable. Then, to make sure they can depend on the results they've gotten, the psychologists expose one or more additional groups of subjects to unimportant or trivial variables. By *comparing the responses* of these various groups, the scientists can usually decide whether the independent variable they're studying is really important in determining the subjects' responses.

For instance, let's assume you discovered a drug you thought would cure headaches. How would you prove it really worked? You could just give the drug to 100 people with headaches and count how many of your subjects got better. Suppose 65 percent of them got immediate relief. Wouldn't that prove that your drug was effective? Not really. For, suppose someone with a different theoretical viewpoint pointed out the following facts: Many scientific studies show that a large number of people get better immediately even if you just give them a sugar pill. And many subjects recover even if you give them nothing at all. So, maybe your new drug is just another sugar pill.

To compare these two competing theoretical explanations, you'd need to test some additional groups. You might give a sugar pill to one such group, and nothing at all to a second bunch of subjects. You could then *compare* the recovery rates shown by these two groups with the recovery rate shown by your original subjects.

In this study, the subjects you gave the "real" pill to would be called the *experimental group*. The two "comparison groups" are referred to as *control groups*. Each comparison group you run actually "controls" for another possible explanation of the results shown by the experimental group. In this case, your theory would predict that significantly more subjects in the experimental group would get better, because you believe your drug actually "works." The sugar-pill theory would predict that just as many subjects in the comparison groups would recover. You "control" for this competing explanation by comparing the experimental group with the control groups.

Now, suppose the experimental-group subjects showed a significantly higher recovery rate than did the subjects in the two control groups. The fact that you compared their responses with those of the two control groups *strongly suggests* that your drug was effective in curing headaches.

In this case, your theory wins, because you predicted the group given the drug would do better than the groups given sugar pills or nothing at all. The "control" hypothesis loses, because it predicted there would be no differences among the three groups.

Many things can affect the outcome of a scientific study. In the experiment we've just described, for instance, you'd want to assign the subjects to the various groups in a *random fashion*. And you'd have to make sure that neither the person giving out the pills nor the subjects themselves knew which was the "real" drug and which was the sugar pill. We'll talk more about such matters both in Chapter 16 and in the Statistical Appendix at the end of this book. Generally speaking, however, the more astute you are at picking the proper control groups, the more dependable the results of your experiments are likely to be. For each comparison group you use rules out an alternative explanation for the results your experimental group showed.

"Between-Subjects" and "Within-Subjects" Designs

Scientists use many different types of experimental designs to test their theories. In the "headache" study, you actually used a technique called the *between-subjects design*, because you ended up comparing the results *between* two or more groups. The "between-subjects" design almost always calls for using several groups of subjects—and testing each subject in each group just once.

However, you could have accomplished much the same thing using quite a different experimental procedure. You could have tested each subject *several times, under different conditions*. That is, you could find people who get frequent headaches and use them as subjects. The first time they complain of a headache, you give them the sugar pill. This is called "Independent Variable A." (It's an *independent* variable, because you decide what you're going to give the subjects.) The second time, you give them the drug instead. This is "Independent Variable B." To be absolutely sure you could trust your results, you'd probably switch back and forth between A and B several times.

You'd also want to randomize your order of presentations—give some people A-B-A-B, others B-A-B-A, still others A-B-B-A, and so forth. And, of course, you should make sure the subjects didn't know which pill they were taking.

Once you test all the subjects several times, you then look at each subject's response to *both variables*, A and B. By comparing these two sets of reactions for *each subject*, you can dis-

"IT WAS MORE OF A 'TRIPLE-BLIND' TEST. THE PATIENTS DIDN'T KNOW WHICH ONES WERE GETTING THE REAL DRUG, THE DOCTORS DIDN'T KNOW, AND, I'M AFRAID, NOBODY KNEW."

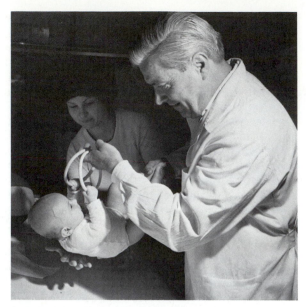

Developmental psychologists study problems of human development, from infancy to old age.

Clinical psychologists help people solve their problems.

cover whether your drug is significantly more effective than a sugar pill is. We call this experimental approach the *within-subjects design*, because your comparisons are "within" subjects rather than "between" subjects.

When you employ the "between-subjects" design, you use different subjects in your experimental and control groups. However, when you employ the "within-subjects" design, you actually use each subject *as his or her own control*.

Psychologists tend to use the "between-subjects" design when they have a lot of subjects available. The more subjects they test, of course, the more likely it becomes that the results will apply to all people everywhere.

We typically use the "within-subjects" design when we have just a few subjects available—or when we're primarily interested in discovering some of the factors influencing the responses of just one person.

Since I had but one Mary Smith available, I decided to use the "within-subjects" design in trying to discover what variables actually controlled her "mind-reading" responses.

Using Mary as Her Own Control

Once Mrs. Smith and her daughter returned to the kitchen, I asked Charlie to write out some words and show them to Mrs. Smith. Mary typed them out on the computer just as quickly as she had the words I selected. But this time, of course, Charlie was watching the tendons on Mrs. Smith's hands rather than looking at what Mary was doing. I could tell by the look on his face that he saw what I had seen.

Next, we asked Mrs. Smith to close her eyes and try to communicate with Mary. The girl typed out a couple of random letters and then quit responding.

We were, of course, using Mary as her own control. In this case, Condition A was letting her mother cue the girl. In Condition B, we removed the cues. And just to make sure, we switched back and forth between the two conditions several times.

"Amazing," Charlie said. "Simply amazing."

"Yes, she is an amazing little girl, isn't she?" I replied. "We can learn a lot from her."

What You Can Learn from Mary Smith—and from This Book

Learning about psychology doesn't consist of finding a set of magic keys that will unlock the "great secrets of your mind." Rather, understanding human behavior is chiefly a matter of discovering thousands of things that you've been thinking and feeling and responding to— but were never really aware of.

Many fields of knowledge can offer you a *subjective* understanding of human behavior. Art, literature, and religion are good examples of subjective approaches that can give you important information about people. But psychology offers you two things that no other field can: (1) a set of *objective* facts about how you think, feel, and behave; and (2) theories and insights that attempt to explain in *objective* terms why you think, feel, and act as you do.

But taking an unbiased, objective view of yourself (and others) is a skill that you have to "learn by doing." And not everyone appreciates—or even agrees with—the facts that psychologists have discovered about human nature. Whether it's worth your time and effort to learn how to be objective about people, only you can decide. Perhaps it will help if we discuss what types of psychologists there are, and what these psychologists actually do.

What Psychologists Do

There are many types of psychologists. Some psychologists *generate* facts and theories; others *apply* this information in real-life settings. Many psychologists do both.

Experimental and Academic Psychology

Experimental psychologists mostly work in scientific laboratories. These scientists typically perform experiments to help develop a basic understanding of human nature. Some of these individuals study such processes as perception, learning, or motivation in human and animal subjects. Others, called biological psychologists, investigate such things as the effects of drugs and surgery on performance. We will describe biological psychology in Chapters 2–5, and other types of experimental psychology in Chapters 6–15. Reading these chapters will give you some idea of what experimental psychologists are like, and the sorts of things they do and are interested in.

Developmental psychologists look at how people grow and mature from conception to old age. They study human behavior in a variety of settings, from hospitals and nurseries to homes for the elderly. We will discuss the sorts of experiments that developmental psychologists perform in several chapters, but primarily in 17 and 18.

Social psychologists study the behavior of people in groups and organizations. Some social psychologists work primarily in laboratories, where they can maintain tight controls over the variables that affect the behaviors of the subjects they study. Other social psychologists work "in the field," which is to say that they perform their research in real-world environments. We will describe both types of studies in Chapters 23–25.

Educational psychologists are primarily interested in how humans learn in schools and other educational settings. The creation of standardized tests and other measures of academic and intellectual performance is one of the chief tasks performed by educational psychologists. We will discuss these sorts of tests in Chapter 21.

In addition to the research they perform, most *experimental psychologists* teach in academic settings such as colleges and universities. Others work in government and industrial laboratories, or at private institutes.

Clinical and Applied Psychology

More than half of the psychologists in the US work in what are called "applied settings." While many of these professionals perform occasional research studies or teach classes, their main focus is generally that of helping people solve real-life problems.

Clinical psychologists, for example, usually deal with individuals who have personal difficulties, or who suffer from mental or behavioral disorders of some kind. Most clinical psychologists work in clinics or hospitals, or treat patients in their own offices. We will have more to say about clinical psychology in Chapters 22–23.

Counseling psychologists usually offer expert advice on personal, educational, or career problems. Some counseling psychologists are in private practice; others work in schools or clinics. Generally speaking, counseling psychologists deal with less severe problems than do clinical psychologists. For example, a person wanting help deciding on a career might well go to a counseling psychologist. However, someone with a major emotional difficulty might well seek the aid of a clinical psychologist. We will describe some of the work done by counseling psychologists in Chapters 13 and 21.

Industrial psychologists tend to be employed by business or government organizations. For the most part, they deal with personnel problems and management decision making. You will find a description of industrial psychology in Chapter 26.

Experimental psychologists may observe behavior either in the laboratory or in real-life settings. They also create tests and take surveys. Generally speaking, experimental psychologists try to be as objective as possible in their descriptions of people.

Applied psychologists may also develop knowledge in a variety of ways. But chiefly they conduct interviews, give tests, and apply information gathered from experiments and surveys. Clinical and counseling psychologists usually deal with one person at a time, although occasionally they work with groups. Industrial psychologists tend to focus on work groups and organizations.

The Author's Biases

Some psychologists are primarily teachers. Although they may do some research, their main goal is passing information along to the students who take their classes or read their textbooks. As you will see in Chapter 15, I spent many years studying the biochemistry of memory in a scientific laboratory. In recent years, though, I've spent most of my research time studying autistic children. However, I've also done a fair amount of industrial consulting and, during the late 1970's, I helped run a private psychological clinic. So, like most psychologists, I'm something of a hybrid.

And like all other psychologists, I have my own set of biases or subjective viewpoints about people and psychology. I've mentioned some of these prejudices already. But there are others you should be aware of too, if you are to be able to read this book both with subjective enjoyment, and with objective understanding.

1. To begin with, I believe the study of human behavior is the most fascinating, awe-inspiring, and important occupation imaginable. I hope that some of my enthusiasm for psychology rubs off on you by the time you finish the book, for it is the greatest gift I can give you.
2. I believe that learning should be both challenging *and* fun. My way of making the study of psychology enjoyable to you in this book is to focus on the experiences of people such as Mary Smith. For example, I begin and end each chapter with a story or a case history built around the lives of real or imagined human beings. You may find that you can *understand* the people in the stories

better after you have read the scientific material in the chapter itself.
3. At various points, I have included "thought questions" that often are not answered directly in the text. The purpose of these questions is to push your mind beyond the facts on the printed page. However, if you find these questions a bore, or if the answers don't come easily, pass the questions by or ask your instructor to help you.
4. I place a great deal more faith in facts than I do in theories and opinions. Most arguments in science revolve around speculations and interpretations of data—not around the data themselves. In science, you usually gather data first, then attempt to discover what the data mean. If you try to understand people before you have enough facts, you run the danger of seeing what you want to see—instead of seeing *objectively* what the people are like. (See Chapter 8.)
5. I am an incurable optimist. I believe that, through the wise and humane application of the *holistic approach*, we can all come closer to achieving our personal goals in life (see Chapter 5). This moral viewpoint, like most others, rests on faith as well as on science; but it is a faith that is shared by most psychologists or they wouldn't *be* psychologists.
6. You have theories about human behavior, just as I do. But unless you have studied psychology before, chances are your present theories are based more on your subjective impressions than on objective data. Thus, you may find that many of your feelings or theories about yourself and others are challenged by the facts presented in this textbook. I do not ask that you give up your present views, merely that you try to examine them afresh in the light of what new information this book gives you.

All of which brings us back again to Mary Smith. For, as it turned out, the results of our little experiment caused both Charlie and Mrs. Smith to re-examine the way in which they perceived the girl.

Psychology's Limits

As you know, we used the "within-subjects" design in testing Mary. And after we were done, Charlie, Mrs. Smith, Mary, and I sat around the kitchen talking.

"What cues am I giving her?" Mrs. Smith asked.

I told her how she tensed her grip on Mary's arm when the girl's finger got close to the correct key.

Mrs. Smith nodded in understanding. "I didn't *feel* myself doing that. But I guess you're right." She thought for a moment, then asked, "How bright do you think Mary is?"

"Bright enough to pick up very subtle cues from you," I replied. "Bright enough to learn how to use a computer keyboard."

"Yes, but is she bright enough to *communicate* with me?"

"She does that all the time. She tells you that she loves you when she seeks you out, and when she cuddles in your arms. By her actions, she tells you when she's happy, when she's angry, when she's excited, and when she's bored. You read her social cues as precisely as she reads yours."

"All mothers do that," the woman said. "That's part of what being a parent is all about— learning to respond to your child's needs, even when the child can't tell you in words. But that's the problem, you see. Do you think Mary is bright enough so that she can learn to talk in words?"

I gave the matter serious consideration. What Mrs. Smith was really asking me was this— what are my child's limits? And whatever these limits are, has my child reached them yet, or can she go farther?

From a biological point of view, Mary's limits were obvious—hydrocephalic children are often profoundly retarded. From an intra-psychic viewpoint, Mary was nine and still wasn't talking. And her teachers apparently considered her incapable of learning more than the simplest of words (if that). From a social/behavioral point of view, Mary had lived for several years in a warm and encouraging family environment, but she hadn't produced speech yet. All these facts suggested the girl probably never would be able to converse with the fluency her mother desired.

From a holistic point of view, however, Mary was more than the sum of her parts, more than just a brain-damaged child living in a warm family setting. She was a unique human *system*, with a unique set of capabilities. Many of her disabilities were obvious. Her potential was much harder to guess at. I could predict that she'd never become an Einstein, or a concert pianist, or a brain surgeon. But would she ever learn to talk? I simply didn't know the answer to that question.

However, like Mrs. Smith, I did suspect that "deep down inside" there was more to Mary than met the eye. Given the amount of time and effort Mrs. Smith would surely devote to the task, it seemed barely possible that some day Mary might learn to speak. I didn't want to delude Mrs. Smith, but I didn't want to discourage her either.

"Look, I haven't worked with children like Mary before, so I don't know what's possible— or impossible. But I do know that she has two things going for her that might help."

"What two things?" Mrs. Smith asked.

"First, your loving desire to help her. That's a big plus. Second, she's bright enough to pick up on very subtle cues. You taught her how to use a complicated computer keyboard. Perhaps you can use her sensitivity to your cues to teach her to express herself either in speech, or through the computer. Give it a try. But don't expect miracles."

Mrs. Smith frowned, but after a few seconds, she nodded rather reluctantly. She asked what I had in mind, so we talked about the specifics of what she might do. And then, finally, Charlie and I left and drove back to Ann Arbor. The next day, I called Marcello Truzzi and told him he had been right to remind me of the "Clever Hans" story. And I thought the matter would end there.

But a few months later, Mrs. Smith called on the phone. She wanted me to write a letter encouraging her to continue her work with Mary. The girl's teachers remained skeptical that Mary would ever show any progress. Mrs. Smith hoped that a letter from a psychologist might get them to change their minds. I told her I'd be happy to oblige. Then I asked how Mary was doing.

"She's coming along. Slowly, of course, but I do see some change. And working on this brings us closer together. So it's a benefit, no matter how things turn out."

"How far do you think you can go with Mary?"

"I don't know. I'm still convinced she'll learn to express herself some day. But that's my faith talking. The fact is that she still doesn't talk."

"Does that fact bother you still?"

"No, not really. How can you understand people, or hope to help them, if you don't know the objective facts about them?" Mrs. Smith laughed gently. "I remember you told me not to expect miracles. But I'll tell you something. Now that I understand her better, I know I'll love her just as much whether she talks or not. Maybe that's the real miracle."

"Maybe it is," I said.

Recommended Readings

At the end of each chapter, I will list several books and articles that you might read if you want to go into the content of that chapter more deeply. Should you wish a more detailed list of readings (chapter by chapter), ask your instructor for help.

There are two good books on the Clever Hans story. One, *Clever Hans*, edited by Robert Rosenthal, was published by Holt, Rinehart and Winston in 1965. The other, *The Hans Legacy*, is by Dodge Fernald, and was published by Lawrence Erlbaum Associates in 1984. Marcello Truzzi's article, "Reflections on Paranormal Communication: A Zetetic's Perspective," was published in 1981 in Volume 364 of the *Annals of the New York Academy of Sciences*. This volume, entitled *The Clever Hans Phenomenon: Communication with Horses, Whales, Apes, and People*, was edited by Thomas A. Sebeok and Robert Rosenthal.

For information about *The Skeptical Inquirer*, write to Box 229, Central Park Station, Buffalo, New York 14215. The address for the *Zetetic Scholar* is Box 1052, Ann Arbor, Michigan 48106.

Psychology Today is far and away the best popular magazine dealing with behavioral topics, but articles on the behavioral sciences also appear in *Discover*, *OMNI*, and *Science 85* (which becomes *Science 86* in 1986, *Science 87* in 1987, and so forth). There are also dozens of scientific journals, most of which focus on one particular aspect of human or animal behavior. Any psychology teacher or librarian will surely be happy to help you find the journal most interesting to you.

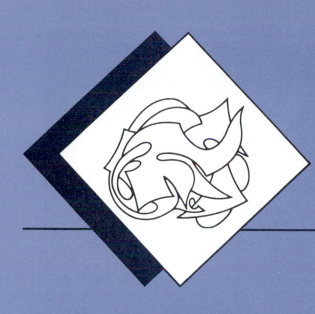

PART I

Biological Bases of Behavior

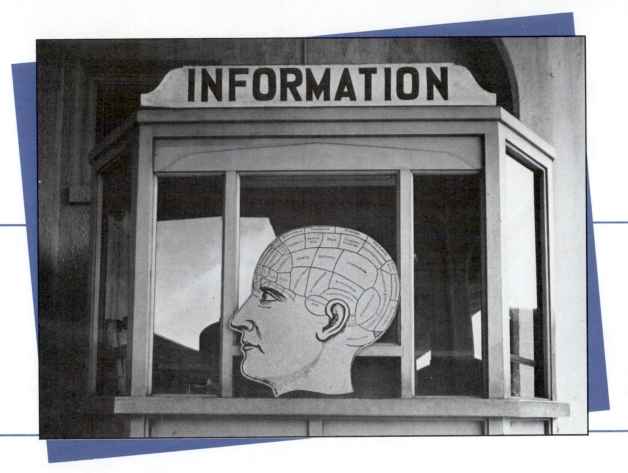

Did You Know That...

- Your brain looks something like a wrinkled mushroom?
- Your nervous system may contain almost a trillion nerve cells (neurons)?
- The cortex, or outer layer of your brain, contains most of the "decision-making centers" that influence what you do, feel, and think?
- The major function of your brain is to process information?
- Some four million people in the United States suffer from epilepsy?
- Brain waves are the result of the electrical excitation occurring in thousands or even millions of your brain cells?
- The left half of your brain looks like a mirror image of the right half?
- If you are right-handed, the left hemisphere of your brain is dominant and controls the right half of your body?
- If you are right-handed, your left hemisphere contains your "speech center," and seems responsible for most language?
- Left-handed people are more likely to suffer from migraine headaches and language disorders than are right-handers?
- If a surgeon separated the two hemispheres of your brain, you might end up with two quite separate and distinct "minds" inside your skull?

2

The Brain

"On the Other Hand"

"Young man, you are an epileptic?"

Patrick looked the woman over carefully. Her closely-cropped white hair was peppered with black, rather like ashes sprinkled on fresh snow. She was wearing a colonel's uniform with a lot of gold braid on it. The other soldiers seemed to be afraid of this woman, so Pat guessed she was a pretty important person. But Pat's friend, Dr. Tavela, had told him not to fear people just because they wore fancy uniforms. So Pat looked straight at the woman and said, "I used to be."

Colonel Garcia picked up a yellow pencil and began tapping it slowly on her desk. She looked squarely at the youth sitting in front of her for a moment, then said, "Before Dr. Tavela operated on you, then, you were subject to epileptic attacks?"

"Yes."

"These attacks occurred frequently?"

Pat shivered a bit, then ran his fingers nervously over the plaster cast on his left hand. It had been six weeks now since he had last felt the "aura," that strange feeling that hit him each time just before he had an epileptic seizure. He had gone six weeks now without the headaches—without once losing consciousness, falling to the floor, and embarrassing himself by "having a fit." Despite the bandages on his head and all the terrible things that had happened since his operation, Pat felt so different now that he tried not to think of what the seizures had been like. But since she asked, Pat answered truthfully. "The attacks came several times a day, sometimes."

Colonel Garcia turned to the officer sitting beside Patrick in front of her desk. "Captain Hartman, this has been confirmed?"

The blond-haired man nodded quickly. "Yes, Colonel. When Patrick was three, a severe fever caused considerable damage to his cortex.

We have tested him on the EEG machine. Abnormal, spike-shaped brain waves show up in the motor areas of his right hemisphere. Epileptic seizures are almost always associated with 'spikes' in the motor cortex."

"Yes, of course," the woman responded, gazing back at Patrick. "And after the operation, you have been free of these attacks?"

Pat tried to smile politely. "Yes, ma'am."

"Then how did you hurt your left hand?"

Pat rubbed his right hand over the plaster cast covering his entire left hand and forearm. Only the tips of his fingers were free of the plaster. "After the operation, I couldn't walk very well at first. I fell and broke my hand."

Colonel Garcia looked back at Captain Hartman. "This too is confirmed?"

"Yes, Colonel. The X-rays show a compound fracture of the metacarpal bone. The wound is about three weeks old. Patrick will not be able to use his left hand freely for another month or so—except to scratch his nose."

Patrick gently rubbed a finger along the side of his nose.

"Was Dr. Tavela angry with you for breaking your hand?" the woman asked.

Patrick frowned. "He was angry because he said I might have hurt my head. But then, just before he left, he smiled and said it was a good sign."

"A sign of your recovery?"

Pat thought about it a moment. "He didn't say."

"I wish he had," Colonel Garcia said, then breathed a deep sigh. "Patrick, although Dr. Tavela lived in a foreign country, he was our friend."

Pat interrupted. "You

mean he was your spy. Anyhow, that's what the secret police said when they questioned me."

Colonel Garcia glanced uneasily at Captain Hartman, then back at the boy. "You know Dr. Tavela was a good man, and he would want you to cooperate with us. I know you have told your story many times, Patrick. But I would like to hear it again. Tell me everything that happened, if you don't mind."

The young man shrugged his shoulders. "I don't mind."

"First, why were you sent to see a surgeon in a foreign country? Are there no good physicians here?"

"Because they said that Dr. Tavela was the only doctor in the world who did the sort of operation I needed."

"Dr. Tavela was a brilliant neurosurgeon," Colonel Garcia said quietly. "We will miss him. But tell me what happened to you at his clinic."

"He gave me a lot of tests for a week or so, and then my seizures got real bad. He said it was the stress that made them worse. Then they shaved my head and put me to sleep and he cut out the part of my brain that was making me sick."

"How soon afterwards could you get up out of bed?"

"After a few days. Just to go to the bathroom. I guess it was a week or so before I could really walk much."

Colonel Garcia nodded sympathetically. "You said Dr. Tavela gave you some tests before the operation. Did he test you afterwards?"

"Yeah. He had this sort of mask that I looked into. It blocked off part of what I could see. Then he showed me things and asked what they were."

The woman smiled with growing excitement. "What sort of things did he show you?"

"Oh, pictures of cows and horses. Circles and squares. Sometimes he showed me printed words and asked me to read them. Sometimes he made me wear earphones and then he asked me to do things or say things."

"What kind of things?"

"Oh, point at a circle, or say words like 'cat' and 'dog.'"

Colonel Garcia leaned forward eagerly. "And perhaps he talked about a chemical formula, or even showed you a drawing of a particular molecule?"

Pat laughed. "That's what the secret police asked, too. Did I know anything about chemistry? And did Dr. Tavela read me the name of a formula, or show me a picture, or anything like that?"

"And you said . . ."

"I said that he never read anything to me except the Bible. Mostly Proverbs."

"Why Proverbs?"

Patrick had never thought to question the actions of the adults around him. "I don't know. He seemed to like them. He said they contained all the wisdom of Solomon."

A startled look appeared on Captain Hartman's face. "Colonel . . ."

The woman interrupted. "Yes, Captain, I know. Tavela's first name was Solomon. You will please get a copy of the Bible from the library."

Captain Hartman rose and left the room.

Putting the pencil carefully down on her desk, Colonel Garcia continued. "Patrick, just before Dr. Tavela was killed by the secret police, a man brought him a very important secret—the outline of the molecular structure of a new chemical compound."

"That would be the funny little man in the dark overcoat, I suppose," Patrick said, trying to be helpful.

"Perhaps so, Patrick. Tell me about him."

Pat picked at one of the bandages on his head with his right hand. "It was that last day, you know, the day the secret police came and . . . and . . ."

"I know. Go on, please."

"Well, I had the earphones on and was looking into the mask. Dr. Tavela was showing me some pictures and asking me questions over the earphones. Sometimes it hurt a little."

"Hurt?"

"Yeah. My ears. Sometimes he would whisper in one ear while he was making a very loud noise in the other. The noise hurt sometimes."

"What did he whisper to you, Patrick?"

Pat sighed. "I couldn't hear most of the time because of the noise. I guess he asked me to point to something, sometimes with my left hand, sometimes with my right."

"But your left hand is in a cast."

"I can point with my fingers," Pat said, poking his left index finger at the pencil on the woman's desk to demonstrate his abilities. "That wasn't the problem."

"What was the problem, Patrick?"

"You're going to think this is pretty funny. I could do what he told me to do over the earphones. I pointed my left fingers at the thing he wanted me to touch. But I never was sure what it was he had asked me to do, even

when I did it just like he said to do it." The young man stopped, a puzzled look on his face. "I mean, how can you do something when you don't know what it is you're supposed to be doing?"

Colonel Garcia frowned. Then she said, "Tell me about the man in the overcoat, please."

"Well, Dr. Tavela was testing me when this man came into the lab. He looked nervous and excited, I guess. He pulled on Dr. Tavela's arm, and they went out of the room for a while. Then when Dr. Tavela came back, he was awful excited too. He said that something good had happened, something he had been waiting for for a long time." Patrick's left hand reached out and touched the pencil again, almost unconsciously.

"And then . . ."

"And then he said we had work to do. So he whispered at me for a long time, maybe half an hour or so, and had me trace things with my left hand again and again."

Colonel Garcia leaned forward. "What sort of things, Patrick? Numbers and letters?"

"That's what the secret police asked, but I don't know. I really don't!" Patrick's voice cracked with emotion. "I couldn't see the things, I just pointed at them with my left hand. The usual cat and dog pictures, I guess. That's what we usually worked on."

"You told the secret police about this?"

"Of course, but they didn't believe me at first. So they hooked me up to a polly . . . a polly . . ."

"A polygraph, Patrick. That's what you would call a 'lie detector.'"

"Yeah, well, they stuck this wet, metal thing on the palm of my right hand. It was connected with wires to a machine that made squiggles on a sheet of paper. And they asked me questions and looked at the squiggles." Patrick sighed deeply. "They did it for hours and hours and hours. One man kept insisting that I was lying and said they ought to give me a whipping for lying so much."

"Did they punish you?"

Patrick shook his head. "No, the other man kept saying that the squiggles showed I was telling the truth. And I was!"

Colonel Garcia nodded sympathetically. "I believe you, Patrick. You see, the secret police thought that Dr. Tavela had given you the formula or the drawing of the shape of the molecule. We put a lot of pressure on them, but they wouldn't release you until they made sure that you didn't know what it was."

The woman picked up the pencil again and tapped it nervously. "He must have known they would arrest him shortly, and I'll bet a million dollars he told you something. He must have hidden some clue deep within your brain, where the secret police couldn't find it, but we could."

"He didn't tell me anything, ma'am." Patrick started to cry a little. "Except, when the police came to the door to get him, he told me to be brave, and tell the truth. He said he was glad I had broken my hand, and that whenever I was troubled, I should read the Bible and seek out a pattern of understanding."

Captain Hartman entered the Colonel's office bearing a tattered book. "You'd be surprised how difficult it was to find a copy of the Bible around this place," he said, handing the book to the woman.

Colonel Garcia gave the man a bemused look, then turned to Patrick. "What part of Proverbs did Dr. Tavela read to you the most?"

"The third chapter, I think it was."

The woman leafed through the book, found a place, then began to read. "'Happy is the man that findeth wisdom, and the man that getteth understanding.'" The woman looked at the boy. "Is that the part?"

"Further on, I think."

"'Understanding is more precious than rubies: and all the things thou canst desire are not to be compared unto her. Length of days is in her right hand; and in her left hand riches and honor.'"

Patrick became excited. "Yes, that's it. He read that verse to me several times."

Colonel Garcia put the Bible face down on the desk, and picked up the pencil in her right hand. She tapped it gently on the desk, again and again. After a moment she stared at Patrick's left hand, encased as it was in the plaster cast. She gazed intently at the bandages on his shaven head. Next she looked at the innocent smile on the young man's face.

Then she laughed warmly, jubilantly. "Of course!" she said loudly.

Captain Hartman was startled. "Have you found the secret, Colonel?"

"Of course I have, Captain. Where the secret police failed, I have succeeded. Thanks to Dr. Tavela's clue from the Bible, and my knowledge of Patrick's problems, I know the truth." She got up and walked around the desk, pulling up a chair to sit by Patrick. She hugged him in her arms momentarily, then gently touched his head.

"What an appropriate place to hide a secret," she said.

(Continued on page 50.)

Your Brain

Your brain is the master organ of your body. During open heart surgery, a machine can take over for your heart, just as a machine can take over some of the functions of your kidneys. But even with mechanical methods of cleaning and pumping your blood, you remain YOU. Which is to say that your thoughts, dreams, hopes, and general behavior patterns aren't much affected by mechanical substitutes for most of your bodily functions.

However, even a small amount of damage to certain *critical parts of your brain* may—under certain circumstances—cause you to lose consciousness for the rest of your life. More extensive damage might even cause rather dramatic changes in your personality. Why? Because your brain is the seat of your self-awareness, the locus of your intelligence, your compassion, and your creativity. All of your mental activities—your thoughts, emotions, and feelings—and all of your bodily processes are affected by the functioning of your brain.

On the other hand, sometimes people can sustain massive damage to major portions of their brains, and still recover all the mental and physical abilities they had before the damage occurred. So, while your brain is very much the master organ of your body, YOU are a great deal more than the mere sum of all the complex physical activities that occur inside your skull.

Still and all, from a psychological point of view, your brain is the single most important part of your body. Thus, if you are to understand why you think and feel and act as you do, you *must* first have some notion of how this master organ operates. Therefore, we will begin our survey of the field of psychology by looking closely at your brain and nervous system.

Inputs, Internal Processes, Outputs

First, let us see what your brain actually looks like. If you enjoy analogies, consider this one for a moment. In a very limited sense, your brain is like a wrinkled mushroom packed tightly inside a bony shell we call the skull (see Fig. 2.1A & B). Not counting the skull, your brain weighs about 1.3 kilograms (3 pounds). In their 1980 book *Behavioral Neuroscience*, Carl Cotman and James McGaugh state that the human nervous system contains almost a trillion nerve cells (1,000,000,000,000). Most of these **neurons**, or nerve cells, are in the brain. The biological activities of these nerve cells help determine what you think and feel and learn

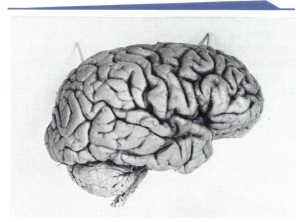

Fig. 2.1A The human brain, viewed from the right. The *cerebellum* (a Latin word meaning "little brain") at the bottom of the photograph is not a part of the cerebrum but is one of the "lower centers." The cerebellum is involved in coordinating such complex movements as walking, playing the piano, driving a car, and so on.

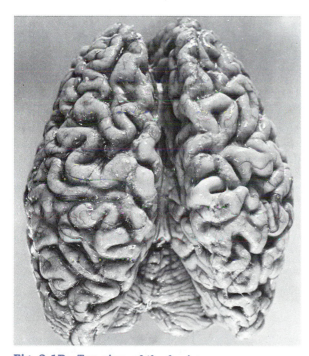

Fig. 2.1B Top view of the brain.

A NOTE ON THE GLOSSARY ITEMS

Most texts have word lists or glossaries at the end of the book that give definitions of technical terms. These glossaries are often difficult to find and to use, and few of them tell you how to say the word aloud. In this book, we have reserved the top of the right-hand column of each odd-numbered page for definitions and explanations of the sometimes complicated words or phrases you may encounter in each chapter. We call this the "running glossary." Every time you see a **boldfaced** word on a page, you will know that the word is defined (and often a pronunciation given) in the "running glossary" at the top of the right-hand column of the odd-numbered page.

If you already understand the boldfaced word, don't bother checking it out immediately. However, if you have any doubts about the meaning of the word—or if you are interested in the Latin or Greek derivation of the term—you may wish to check the item at once, without having to lose your place by turning to the back of the book (where the glossary is located in most other texts).

Also, when you study for an examination, you may find it helpful to check all the terms in the "running glossary" since most of the key words or thoughts will appear there. Many of these same important terms will also be **boldfaced** in the summary that appears at the end of most chapters.

If you run across a word you don't understand that does *not* appear in the "running glossary," please check the index at the end of the book to see if the word is defined elsewhere in the text. You will find both an index of people's names and an index of subjects at the end of the book.

The pronunciations given in the definitions are in the "Midwestern dialect" that is used by many radio and TV announcers and newscasters. Pronunciations of many words vary from one part of the country to another. If you have doubts about how to say a word, please ask your teacher about it.

And finally, one very important point: Any dictionary contains thousands of words that you know, as well as thousands that you don't know. I hope you will use the "running glossary" in this text as you would a dictionary. Don't be upset if I define terms you think every student ought to be familiar with. I selected the terms in the glossary by asking several hundred students to circle every word they didn't understand. The items that appear are those that *at least 10 percent* of these students weren't sure of—including some words that have no direct connection with the science of psychology.

This book is for *everybody*—for people with large vocabularies, and for people with limited knowledge but a large desire to learn. If you know most of the words defined in the "running glossary," congratulations! However, you should remember that other students may need all the help any of us can give.

and do. But these neurons do not all have the same tasks to perform. Sometimes groups of your neurons function rather independently. More often, they cooperate to achieve some common goal.

As we will see in Chapter 5, psychologists often consider business organizations to be "complex social systems," much as your body is a "complex living system." To make this point clearer, let's compare your body to a corporation. This analogy is pertinent, since the word "corporation" actually comes from the Latin word meaning *body*.

All living systems have three main types of functions—**inputs**, **internal activities**, and **outputs**. A large manufacturing company such as Ford takes in orders from customers and purchases raw materials. These are its *inputs*. The cars that Ford produces are its *outputs*. But producing cars also involves such tasks as "information processing" and "decision making," which are *internal processes*. The management at Ford serves as the "brain" of that corporation and thus processes the information and makes the decisions that keep the company functioning smoothly.

You too take in information from the world around you and make decisions based on these informational inputs. For example, you must decide what food to eat, what material to study for your next exam, and how you should act in most situations. Food and information are *inputs* to your body. Decision making and digestion are *internal activities* in your own "corporation." And what you say and do are your *outputs*. Your brain is your own "top management" that helps run your body in an efficient manner.

Corporate Organization

Ford could not survive unless its management team was organized into various levels of decision making. At the top are the executive officers, who send orders *down* the organizational ladder to "middle-level management." The men and women in middle-level management supervise the various internal functions that keep the organization alive and carry out the orders they receive from top management. Middle-level managers also send messages *up* to the executive officers, letting them know how things in the offices and factories are going.

At the bottom of the organizational chart are the front-line supervisors and workers. Some of these lower-level employees receive messages from the outside world, process them, and send them up the chain of command. Other employees produce most of the actual "outputs" of the car company. But what these people do, for the most part, is to follow instructions they receive from higher management.

Organization of Your Brain

Your brain is organized in "levels" much as is Ford. For instance, a large collection of neurons (nerve cells) gathered together at the very top of your brain serves as your own "top management." These neurons make up what is called the **cortex** of your brain.

Cortex is a Latin word meaning the "bark" of a tree or the "skin" of a mushroom. The thin outer skin of a mushroom is often darker and tougher than the tissue inside, and the cortex or thin outer layer of your brain is likewise different from the neurons inside. Your cortex contains millions of very special neurons that seem to be intimately related to your "stream of consciousness," or your moment-to-moment thoughts. It is mostly in your cortex that conscious decisions are made about what your own "corporation" or body is going to do. But your cortex must have informational inputs to process if it is to function properly. And your cortex must have ways of sending messages to the muscles and glands in your body if you are to produce the proper outputs.

Sensory and Motor Pathways

Information about the outside world flows into your cortex along a number of routes called **sensory pathways**. Your eyes, ears, nose, tongue, and skin all send messages to your brain about what is happening around you—and inside you. These inputs go first to the lower parts of your brain, and then to your cortex. Your cortex pays attention to this incoming sensory information, checks its memory files, and then "decides" what you should do or think or feel in a given situation. Paying attention, checking memory files, and "deciding how to respond" are some of the ways in which your cortex *processes* sensory inputs (see Chapter 9).

Once your cortical "top management" has processed an input and decided on a response, it sends command messages along **motor pathways** to your body's muscles and glands telling them how to react. But before these messages reach your muscles, they must first pass through the lower parts of your brain.

Lying beneath your cortex are a large number of **neural sub-centers** which are the "middle management" of your brain. These "neural sub-centers" have many functions. They screen out trivial inputs from your body and from the outside world. But they send important inputs on up to your cortex. The lower centers in your brain also execute commands they receive from "upper management" (such as your cortex). However, they make certain types of response outputs on their own.

The sub-centers of your brain are most important to your very existence, for they control such *automatic* responses as breathing and digestion. They also execute the complex muscle movements involved in walking and running. For example, when you decide to walk to class, the *decision* to do so is made in your cortex. But are you conscious of each tiny movement the muscles in your legs and feet must make to get you there? Surely not, for you would be hard-pressed to keep up with the millions of different neural commands that the lower centers in your brain must issue to your muscles each time you take a simple stroll. Your neural sub-centers handle these movements automatically, without conscious effort on your part. However, in emergency situations, your cortex may assume direct and voluntary control over almost any of your automatic responses.

For the most part, though, your cortical "top management" is free to dream and scheme as it wishes, leaving most of your physical behavior to be directly controlled by the lower parts of your brain.

Question: If you had to *consciously* think about keeping your heart pumping and your lungs breathing, what would happen when you went to sleep at night?

The Cerebrum

If you would like to get a better feel for the physical structure of your brain, you might try this little *exercise*. Pause for a moment and go look at yourself in a mirror. If by some magic the flesh and bone of your head could be made invisible, you would see the front part of your brain as you stared into the mirror. Viewed this way, your brain would look much like the mountain ranges along the California coast as seen from an airplane. That is, your brain

INSPIRATION POINT

FOR THOSE WHO THINK VISUALLY: PAINTERS, SCULPTORS, ARCHITECTS

FOR THOSE WHO THINK VERBALLY: WRITERS, PSYCHOLOGISTS, PHILOSOPHERS, TRY NEXT INSPIRATION POINT. ¼ MILE ➞

Neuron (rhymes with "YOUR on"). A single nerve cell.

Inputs, internal activities, and outputs. The three functions of all living systems. Food is a type of input that your stomach digests (internal activity) and converts into energy so that you can think and behave (outputs). The remains of the food are also released as waste products (outputs).

Cortex (CORE-tex). The thin outer layer of the brain, about 0.6 centimeters (1/4 inch) thick. The millions of nerve cells (neurons) in your cortex influence most of what you think, feel, and do.

Sensory pathways. Bundles of nerves rather like telephone cables that feed information about the outside world (inputs) into your brain for processing.

Motor pathways. In biological terms, the word "motor" means "muscular," or "having to do with movement." The motor pathways are bundles of nerves rather like telephone cables that run from your brain out to your muscles (also called "output pathways").

Neural sub-centers. The word "neural" means "having to do with neurons or nerve cells." Certain groups or "centers" of neurons in your brain have highly specific functions, unlike those of any other part of your brain. For instance, one neural sub-center called the thalamus (THALL-ah-muss) acts as a sort of switchboard through which most input messages pass before reaching your cortex. The thalamus is called a *sub*-center because it is "lower" than your cortex, which is the "highest" part of your brain.

Cerebrum (sair-REE-brum). The big, thick "cap" on the top of your brain. Humans have bigger cerebrums than any other animal. The word "cerebral" (meaning "mental") comes from "cerebrum." Most of your important mental functions take place in your cerebrum.

would appear to be a series of rounded hills with deep valleys in between.

The outer crust of this brainy landscape is, as we said, the *cortex*. It is about 0.65 centimeters (1/4 inch) thick. This cortical "peel" covers the biggest part of your brain, which is called the **cerebrum** (from the Latin word for "brain").

Your cerebrum sits on top of the rest of your brain much as the huge cap of a mushroom sits on top of its skinny stem. If you could look at your brain from the top, all you would see would be the cortical covering, or the cap of the cerebral mushroom. The lower centers, or subunits, are all buried deep in your cerebrum or in the stem itself.

Evolution of the Cerebrum

In evolutionary terms, the cerebrum has been one of the last parts of the brain to develop. If you inspected the brains of lower animals, you would find that a human has a better-developed cerebrum than a monkey, that a monkey has more cerebral tissue than a dog, a dog more than a rat, a rat more than a pigeon, and a pigeon more than a goldfish. Most psychologists believe that, in general terms, the better developed an animal's cerebrum is, the more complex its behavior patterns are likely to be.

Complex intellectual functions—such as writing song lyrics and performing scientific experiments—are controlled by your cerebrum and its cortex. Perhaps this fact explains why biology students are able to study the earthworm, but no one has ever noticed a worm taking notes on human behavior. It takes a very large corporate structure indeed to produce such complex outputs as songs or automobiles.

The Brain and Behavior

Most companies manufacture a specific product or a series of products that keeps them in business. From a biological point of view, your brain *manufactures thoughts and behaviors.*

The primary purpose of your brain is to create neural, muscular, and glandular reactions, just as Ford's primary purpose is to produce cars and profits. The "employees" that make up your corporate brain and produce your thoughts, feelings, and behaviors are your individual nerve cells, or neurons. When your neurons are functioning well, they take in messages properly and make the right "corporate decisions." In consequence, your reactions flow off this neural assembly line in satisfactory fashion. When your neurons become sick or disturbed, various parts of this input-output process are badly upset.

If your *input* neurons were damaged or drugged, you might suffer from various kinds of *hallucinations.* That is, you could (1) see objects that weren't there, (2) hear voices when no one is speaking, (3) smell or taste or feel things not physically present, or (4) fail to detect important changes in your sensory environment. We will discuss these problems in the next chapter, when we investigate the effects that various drugs can have on your brain.

If your *processing* neurons are disturbed, several things may happen to you: (1) You could suffer a memory loss, (2) you might under-react or over-react to emotional situations, (3) your judgment might become clouded, (4) you could faint or fall into a type of unconsciousness called a **coma**, or (5) your cortex might become confused and issue "output orders" that were abnormal in one way or another. In the latter case, your behavior (including speech) probably would be *coordinated,* in that it wouldn't be clumsy. But *what you did or said* simply wouldn't be appropriate to the circumstances.

We will have a great deal more to say about some of these situations in later chapters.

If for any reason your *output* neurons started functioning abnormally, their behavioral product might become very clumsily put together. The "processing centers" in your brain might still issue appropriate "output orders." But the output centers in your brain simply wouldn't be able to coordinate your actions in the usual manner. Damage to the output systems of your brain can lead to any of the following: (1) A loss of muscular coordination; (2) paralysis of the muscles in your arms, legs, or any other part of your body; or (3) to a condition known as **motor epilepsy** or a **grand mal seizure.** We will have more to say about that abnormal condition called epilepsy later in the chapter. For the moment, let's see how your neurons function under normal conditions.

Question: Suppose a young man was hit over the head in a fight, and his doctor suspected brain damage even though the man's skull wasn't broken. How might the young man's *behavior* give the doctor a rough idea of whether the injury was to the input, processing, or output areas of the brain?

The Neuron

One major purpose of the individual nerve cells in your brain is to *pass information from one part of the body to another.* Although neurons vary considerably among themselves in size and shape, they all have three main parts—the **dendrites**, the **soma** (cell body), and the **axon**. As you will see, all three parts of the neuron are involved in transmitting "neural messages" through your body—and hence help produce thoughts and behaviors.

The Dendrites

The front end, or *input* side, of a cortical neuron is a network of tiny fibers called *dendrites.* The dendrites project out from the cell body like the branches of a tree to make contact with surrounding nerve cells. The major activity of the dendrites is to *receive information* from other nerve cells. We will see how the dendrites accomplish this miracle in a moment. Dendrites also generate electrical activity that causes the *brain waves* we will discuss later on.

The Soma

The main part, or body, of the cell is called the *soma.* The soma seems to have two major functions. First, like the dendrites, it can receive inputs from other neurons. But second and just as important, the soma is the neuron's "housekeeper." Most of the complex chemical reactions involved in cellular **metabolism**—which keep the cell functioning in a healthy fashion—take place inside the soma.

The Axon

The action end, or *output* area, of the neuron is called the *axon*. The axon stretches back from the soma like a branching telephone cable. At the end of each axonic branch or cable are tiny fibers which make contact with the dendrites and cell bodies of nearby neurons, or with the muscles and glands in the rest of the body. The axon is the *output area* of the neuron because the axonic fibers actually pass messages along to other nerve cells, and to the muscles and glands.

Many axons are covered with an *insulating sheath* that serves to speed up neural transmission (see Chapter 16) and prevent "message mixing." This sheath is actually a special type of "support cell," separate from the neuron. The support cell wraps itself around the axon early in life, when the brain is first developing.

As we will see in a moment, the axonic fibers come close to, but *do not touch*, the dendrites and cell bodies of the neurons and muscles they make contact with.

Action Potentials

One of the major functions of the neuron is to send information from one part of your body

Coma (KO-mah). An unusual form of deep sleep from which the person usually cannot be easily awakened. Often caused by drugs, fever, or brain injury.

Motor epilepsy (EP-ee-LEP-see). A type of muscular seizure or attack usually caused by damage to the brain.

Grand mal seizure (grahn mahl). Perhaps the most dramatic, terrifying type of motor epilepsy. The French words *grand mal* mean "big sickness" (the final "d" in "grand" is not pronounced).

Dendrite (DEN-dright). Tiny fibers at the front or "input" end of a neuron that are chemically excited by neurotransmitters released into the synapse.

Soma (SO-mah). The cell body of a neuron. Contains the cell nucleus (NEW-klee-us). The center or main part of a neuron that "processes" some types of inputs to the cell.

Axon (AX-on). The "tail" or "output" end of a neuron. Axonic end-fibers release into the synapse neural transmitters that stimulate the next neuron in line.

Metabolism (mett-TAB-boh-lism). From a Greek word meaning "change." The sum total of biological processes inside the cell that (a) build up energy to be released, and (b) repair the cell and keep it functioning in a normal fashion.

to another. Each nerve cell contains a certain amount of stored-up electrical energy—the *resting potential*—that it can discharge in short bursts. The battery in your car releases a similar burst of stored-up electrical energy when you turn the ignition key. These bursts of energy are called *action potentials*.

The action potential is one of the key parts of the complex electro-chemical process by which your neurons pass messages from one part of your body to another. For example, consider three nerve cells in your brain that are connected together in sequence, in *A-B-C* fashion. As Fig. 2.2 shows, one axonic branch of *A*

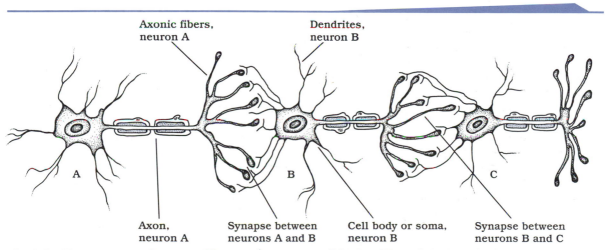

Axonic fibers, neuron A

Dendrites, neuron B

A   B   C

Axon, neuron A

Synapse between neurons A and B

Cell body or soma, neuron B

Synapse between neurons B and C

Fig. 2.2 Three neurons in a row. The axonic fibers of A make synapse with the dendrites and cell body of B, and the axonic fibers of B make synapse with the dendrites and cell body of C.

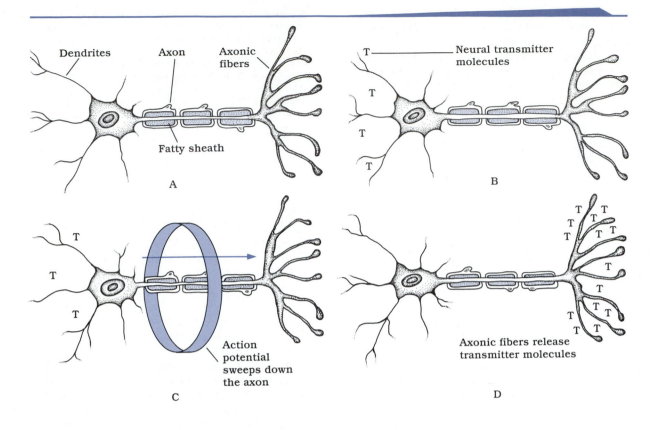

A

B

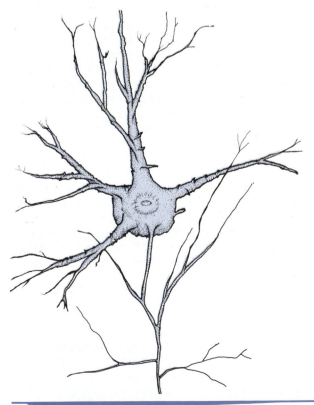

C

Action
potential
sweeps down
the axon

D

Axonic fibers release
transmitter molecules

Fig. 2.3 Transmitter molecules (T's) excite the dendrites of a neuron, causing the neuron to fire. During "firing," a wave of electrochemical activity sweeps down the axon causing the axonic fibers to release more T's (transmitters) which stimulate the next neuron in line.

Fig. 2.4 A motor output neuron in the brain. The treelike structures at the top are the dendrites, the pyramid-shaped structure in the middle is the soma, and the thin "wires" at the bottom are part of the axon.

makes contact with the dendrites and soma of B, and one axonic branch of B makes contact with the dendrites and soma of C.

A, B, and C all have a certain (and very similar) resting potential to call upon when necessary. When a message is to be passed from A to C, a chemical change occurs in the axon of A that affects both the dendrites and the cell body of B. Neuron B responds by releasing its stored-up electrical energy. That is, when A stimulates B, an *action potential* sweeps down the length of B's axonic branches in much the same fashion as fire sweeps down a fuse. When the action potential reaches the tips of B's axonic fibers, it causes a chemical change to occur that sets off a similar burst of electrical energy in neuron C (see Fig. 2.3 and Fig. 2.4).

Thus, the message passes from A to B to C as each cell produces an action potential that stimulates the next neuron in line.

Neural Firing

Whenever an action potential passes along a neuron's axon, we say that the nerve cell has *fired*, because the action involved is much like the firing of a gun. For example, consider how a gun actually "fires." There is a great deal of potential energy stored in the chemical gunpowder in a bullet. When you pull the trigger on a gun, you translate this *potential* chemical energy into the *active* energy of an explosion, and the bullet is propelled down the barrel of the gun. And when a neuron fires, it translates its resting potential into an action potential.

Let's carry the bullet analogy a step further. The neuron behaves in some ways as if it were a machine gun loaded with electro-chemical bullets. To begin with, a machine gun either fires, or it doesn't. The bullets travel at the same speed whether you fire one or a hundred in a row. In similar fashion, a neuron either fires, or doesn't fire. All its action potentials are of the same strength whether the neuron produces one action potential a second, or a hundred.

Second, if you press and release the trigger on a machine gun very quickly, you can fire the shells slowly, one by one. But if you hold the trigger down, you can fire off whole bursts of bullets in a second or two. In like manner, if you tap lightly on your arm, the receptor (input) nerve cells in your skin will fire at a very slow rate—a few times a second. If you press very hard on your arm, these same input neurons can fire hundreds or even thousands of times per second.

Every time you move a muscle—or think a thought, or experience an emotion—you do so

in part because groups of nerve cells in your brain *fire off messages* to your muscles, glands, or to other groups of neurons.

The Synapse

Now, let's go back to neurons A, B, and C. As we noted, the axonic end-fibers of A come close to, *but do not actually touch*, the dendrites of cell B. The general area where two neurons come in contact with each other is called the **synapse**. This synapse (or "area of contact") is so tiny you would have trouble seeing it even using a powerful microscope.

As we said, neurons A and B don't actually touch at their synapse. Instead, there is a tiny space between them called the **synaptic cleft**. This cleft is filled with fluid that contains many different types of chemical substances. These chemicals all have a definite effect on your behavior.

When a neuron fires, the action potential causes the axonic fibers to release tiny drops of chemicals into the synaptic cleft. These chemicals move across the cleft and stimulate the dendrites and soma of the next cell. These stimulating chemicals are called "neural transmitters" or **neurotransmitters**. The function of the neurotransmitters is to *transmit* information from one cell to another. The more neurotransmitters that A's axonic end-fibers release into the synaptic cleft between A and B, the more often cell B will be triggered into firing.

Nerve Cell Functions

Nerve cells have many functions. There are special neurons in your eyes and ears and other parts of your body called *receptor cells*. These

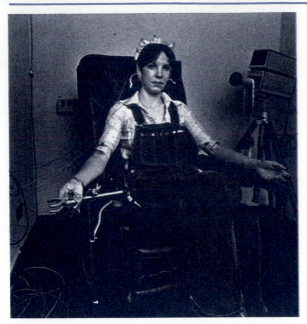

A subject hooked up to an EEG machine.

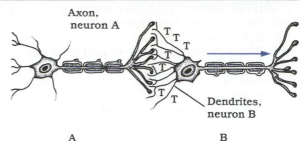

Fig. 2.5 When neuron A fires, its axonic fibers release transmitter (T) molecules into the synapse with neuron B. These molecules bind to receptor sites on the dendrites and cell body of B, causing B to fire.

receptor cells are actually "input neurons" that detect changes in the world around you and relay information about those changes to your brain. Specialized *processing cells* react to this incoming sensory information by checking your memories to determine the input's importance and emotional value, and then decide how your body should react.

Motor neurons relay the output decision to your muscles and glands, thus causing your body to go into action. When a motor neuron fires, it releases *neural transmitters* into the synaptic cleft between its own axon and the muscle it connects to (see Fig. 2.5). These transmitter chemicals cross the synaptic cleft and cause the muscle to twitch or contract. Even the most complex muscular reactions—a rock musician playing a crashing chord on a guitar, or a secretary typing 100 words a minute on a typewriter—are made up of *orderly patterns of individual muscle contractions*. And all these reactions are brought about by the *orderly firing of motor neurons* and the release of transmitter chemicals at the *neuro-muscular synapse* (nerve-muscle connection).

If all your neurons were connected in simple *A-B-C* fashion, your behaviors would be no more complex than those of an earthworm. In fact, in the decision-making centers of your brain, the dendrites of any nerve cell *B* are likely to receive messages from axonic fibers from a thousand or more different *A*s. And *B*'s own axonic end-fibers are likely to pass messages along to the dendrites of a thousand or more *C*s. Thus, any given neuron in your brain is likely to make contact with *thousands* of its neighboring neurons.

The EEG

Under normal conditions, the nerve cells in your brain act together in small units. But each unit (and each individual neuron) works toward the common goal of keeping you alive and functioning well. If a scientist wanted to get an idea of how your brain was performing, she or he might place one or more small pieces of metal—called **electrodes**—on the outside of your head. These electrodes would be connected by wires to an **electro-encephalo-graph**, or EEG machine.

This EEG machine translates electrical energy from your brain into *visual patterns on a screen*—much as a television set translates electrical energy into patterns you can see on the picture tube. The dendrites in your brain produce "waves of electrical activity" that are related to (but different from) the "action potentials" already described. An electrode placed on your head can detect these "brain waves," just as a TV antenna can detect the electrical waves in the atmosphere that make up the television signal. The electrode then sends the "brain waves" over a wire to the EEG machine, just as the TV antenna sends the TV signal to the TV set. And the EEG machine displays the brain waves on a tube just as the TV set displays the TV signal. (Some EEG machines print the waves out on a piece of paper rather than showing them on a screen.)

The EEG doesn't "read" the activity of one or two *specific* neurons, however. Rather, the EEG gives you the same sort of fuzzy, imprecise picture of what is going on inside the skull that you would get outside a huge football stadium if you tried to guess what was happening inside by listening to the roar of the crowd. Standing outside the stadium, you could tell whether the football game was exciting, and when an important play had been made. But you couldn't always tell which team had the ball, or what the score was—much less what individual members of the crowd were doing or experiencing.

The EEG electrode "listens" outside the skull to the electrical noise made inside by the dendrites of thousands of individual neurons. But all the EEG record can tell you is how active the *bulk* of the nerve cells are, not the precise behavior patterns of each *single* neuron.

Brain Waves

When you are actively engaged in thought—trying to work through a difficult problem, for example—your EEG record would show a rapid but rather irregular pattern of electrical activity. We call this sort of electrical output **beta waves**, or the **activity pattern** (see Fig. 2.6). The appearance of this irregular brain wave pattern on the EEG usually means your mind is engaged in some kind of "deliberate mental processing."

The visual areas of your cortex are located primarily on the rear surface of your brain. When you relax and close your eyes, these visual parts of your brain will show regular but rather fast waves called **alpha waves**.

When you go to sleep, your brain wave activity generally slows down. The large, slow *sleep waves* that occur when you are deeply asleep are called **delta waves**. (We will have more to say about sleep and delta waves in the next chapter.)

The Cerebral Hemispheres

Now that you've learned a few simple facts about how your neurons work, let's go back to your brain's basic structure. As we noted earlier, your cerebrum has "mountains" and "valleys." The biggest "valley of the brain" is a deep groove that runs down the center from front to

Electrode (ee-LEK-trode). A device used to detect electrical activity in the brain. Disk electrodes are coin-shaped pieces of metal that can be placed against the head to read brain waves. Needle electrodes are thin wires inserted through holes in the skull directly into the brain.

Electro-encephalo-graph (ee-LEK-tro-en-SEF-uh-low-graf). An electronic machine that makes a graphic record of brain waves. *Cephalo* is from the Greek word for "head."

Beta waves (BAIT-tah). Low voltage, rapid brain waves with rather a random pattern that signal alertness or awake attention.

Activity pattern. Another name for beta waves.

Alpha waves (AL-fa). When you are resting peacefully with your eyes closed, the visual regions of your brain at the back of your head will show a brain wave that repeats itself about 9–12 times per second. These are alpha waves. If you are listening to music with your eyes closed, the visual regions of your brain will show alpha waves, but the hearing regions will typically show the activity pattern. When you are reading a good book, the situation is often reversed—the visual brain will show the activity pattern and the hearing regions of your brain will show alpha waves.

Delta waves (DELL-tah). Much of the time when you are deeply asleep, your brain will produce big waves that repeat themselves less than 4 times per second.

Cerebral hemispheres (ser-REE-bral HEM-ee-spheres). The two halves of the globe-shaped or spherical cerebrum.

Aphasia (a-FAZE-ya, or uh-FAZE-ya). The inability to recognize the meaning of words, or to speak or write in meaningful terms. Some experts limit aphasia to an inability to process spoken language, and use the term agraphia (a-GRAF-ya) to refer to the inability to process written language. Either disorder is usually a symptom of some kind of brain damage.

back, dividing your brain in two parts called the **cerebral hemispheres**. For the most part, the two hemispheres are physical *mirror images* of each other—just as the left half of your face is (more or less) a mirror image of your right half, and your left hand is a mirror image of your right hand.

Despite the fact that your two cerebral hemispheres are reversed images of each other, however, there are important physical and psychological differences between them. The major *physical* difference between the two halves of the brain is that the left hemisphere is usually slightly larger in the area just above the left ear (see Fig. 2.7 and Fig. 2.8). The major *psychological* difference is the fact that, in most people, the left hemisphere "dominates" in producing language and other coordinated muscular reactions. As you might guess, these physical and psychological differences are closely related. Damage to the part of the left hemisphere that is "larger" usually produces a disorder known as **aphasia**, or the inability to recognize

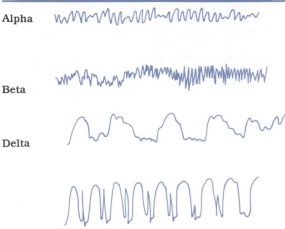

Alpha

Beta

Delta

Petit mal epilepsy

Grand mal epilepsy

|← 1 sec. →|

Fig. 2.6 Alpha waves in the brain made up of electrical waves that have a frequency of 9 to 12 or so cycles per second. The delta waves register on an EEG machine as large, slow waves with a frequency of about 0.1 to 4 cycles per second. The brain waves that occur during epileptic seizures are larger and more synchronous than normal.

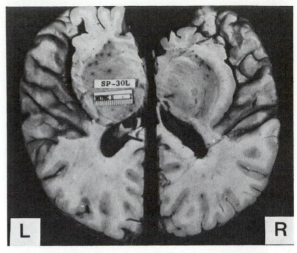

Fig. 2.7 A "slice" through the middle of the human brain at the level of the "speech center" in the temporal lobe. Notice that there is more brain tissue in the area below and to the left of the marker (Sp-30L) in the left hemisphere than in the right hemisphere.

and produce spoken language. Damage to the same part of the right hemisphere usually has a less severe effect on language production—and often no effect at all.

Question: If you are right-handed, you probably can't write very well with your left hand. Why is this the case? Do you think the problem lies in your hands (which are almost identical) or in your brain? And why is it that some people seem to be able to write better with their left hands?

Handedness and Hemispheric Dominance

As confusing as it may seem to you at first, your *right* cerebral hemisphere controls the *left* side of your body, and your *left* cerebral hemisphere controls the *right* side of your body. Thus, the left half of your brain controls your right hand (and foot), and the right half of your brain controls your left hand (and foot).

If you are strongly right-handed, your *left* hemisphere is your *dominant hemisphere*. A better name for the left half of your brain, however, might be "motor control hemisphere," since this is the side of your brain that coordinates most of your body movements. When you write, your left hemisphere issues the orders that your right hand and fingers follow. And when you speak, it is this same "dominant" left

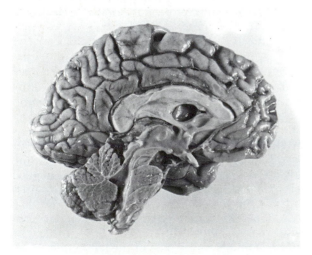

Fig. 2.8 If you cut the human brain in half from front to rear, then looked at the "inside view" of the left hemisphere, this is what you'd see. The *Corpus callosum* that connects the two hemispheres is the white tissue in the center of the photograph.

side of your brain that makes your tongue, lips, and vocal cords move. Even when you think or scheme about something by "talking to yourself," you probably do so with this same left hemisphere.

Your *right* hemisphere is called by many names—*minor hemisphere*, "perceptual" hemisphere, "emotional" hemisphere, or "monitoring" hemisphere. It understands language, but neither talks nor writes except under rather unusual circumstances.

If you are left-handed, it may be that the right half of your cerebrum is the "talking hemisphere" and produces most of your spoken and written language. Or it may be that your left hemisphere is dominant despite the fact that you are left-handed. However, in some left-handers, both hemispheres share the ability to speak and write, and neither of them is really "dominant." We don't really know why the pattern of hemispheric dominance is so confused in left-handed people.

Left-Handedness

According to most experts, about 90 percent of the world's population is right-handed. Of the remaining 10 percent, about half are "strongly" left-handed. Which is to say, in about 5 percent of the people, the *right* hemisphere is dominant and controls language. These left-handers tend to write with the pen or pencil *above* the fingers (see Fig. 2.9), just as most right-handers do. Some left-handers, however, "crook their fingers around" when they write. These individuals are more likely to have dominant *left* hemispheres, even though they perform most tasks with their left hands.

Left-handedness is associated with many traits—some good, some not so good. Almost twice as many males as females are left-handed. And according to British psychologist Marian Annett, more than twice as many artists, musicians, mathematicians, and engineers are left-handed as would be expected by chance. Annett notes that both Michelangelo and Leonardo da Vinci were left-handed. However, Annett says, about 10 percent of left-handers suffer from language disorders and reading disabilities, while only 1 percent of right-handers do. And recent studies suggest that left-handers are three times more likely to suffer severe **migraine headaches** and certain types of **autoimmune** diseases than are right-handed people.

According to Harvard **neurologist** Norman Geschwind, the cause for left-handedness may lie in **testosterone**, the male hormone. Geschwind believes testosterone slows the growth of

Migraine headaches (MY-grain). From the Greek word "hemicrania", meaning "half-head." A migraine headache usually involves intense pain in just half of the brain, often accompanied by nausea and vomiting.

Autoimmune (AW-toe-im-MUNE). The immune system in your body attacks and destroys intruders such as germs. To function effectively, therefore, it must have some way of "recognizing" your own body parts so it doesn't attack them too. Autoimmune diseases are characterized by a breakdown in the immune system's recognition system, which leads your body to attack itself.

Neurologist (new-RAWL-oh-gist). A scientist who studies nerves or treats nervous disorders.

Testosterone (tess-TOSS-ter-own). A hormone (HORR-moan) or chemical produced chiefly by the male sex organs. See Chapter 11.

AIDS. Short for "Acquired Immune Deficiency Syndrome," a recently described disease characterized by a loss of effectiveness of the body's immune system. The person suffering from this disorder loses the ability to fight such diseases as influenza and some types of cancer. AIDS is often transmitted by sexual contact. In the US, most AIDS victims are male homosexuals, more than 4,000 of whom had died of the illness by 1985.

the left hemisphere, thus favoring greater development of the right. "Consequently, males end up right-handed less often than females," Geschwind says.

Since the *left* hemisphere is specialized for language, males in general might be expected to experience more reading and speech disorders than do females. According to Geschwind, several studies suggest this is the case. But the problems are most severe in left-handed males. However, because the *right* hemisphere is specialized for spatial perception and pattern recognition, left-handers "tend to be more talented in these areas," Geschwind believes.

Geschwind's latest research suggests that, during the time a child is in the womb, testosterone attacks not only the left hemisphere, but parts of the body's *immune system* as well. Thus, as males grow up, they are much more likely to suffer from such diseases as the Acquired Immune Deficiency Syndrome, or **AIDS**. However, Geschwind says, being left-handed is neither a curse nor a blessing. "My own belief is that the same population at high risk for the diseases I am talking about is probably going to be found to be at lower risk for other diseases

Fig. 2.9 Left-handed people who write in a "normal" fashion tend to have dominant right hemispheres. Left-handers who write in "inverted" fashion either have dominant left hemispheres or have no dominant hemisphere at all.

[such as cancer and certain types of infections]. I doubt that the left-hand population is declining."

Question: Why does it seem logical that right-handers should be better at language, while left-handers are better at painting and mathematics?

The Corpus Callosum

We will continue our discussion of "handedness" and "hemispheric dominance" in just a moment. First, let's look at how the two halves of your brain manage to cooperate.

The two cerebral hemispheres of your brain are joined together by a bridge of very special tissue—much as the north American hemisphere is joined to the southern by a narrow bridge of land we call Central America. The tissue connecting the two hemispheres of your brain is called the **corpus callosum**, two Latin words meaning "thick or hardened body." The corpus callosum contains a large number of axonic fibers that act like telephone cables running from one side of your brain to the other. Your "talking" hemisphere and your "perceiving" hemisphere keep in touch with each other *primarily* through your corpus callosum.

Sensory inputs that reach one of your hemispheres are almost automatically flashed to the other. Thus, if one of your hemispheres learns something, it usually shares the information with the other hemisphere almost immediately.

The situation is similar with your behavioral *outputs*. Suppose, for instance, your left hemisphere sends a message to the muscles in your right hand telling them to write the word "dog" with a pencil. Your dominant hemisphere would immediately let your right hemisphere know what it had commanded your hand to do.

Your left hemisphere is dominant in executing most muscle movements. But *emotional reactions* are controlled to a great extent by your right hemisphere. If you experienced something that upset or aroused you, your right hemisphere would send out the neural commands that caused you to blush, smile, laugh, or even "feel sick to your stomach." But your "emotional" hemisphere would also send a message across the corpus callosum to let your left "executive" hemisphere know what was happening—in case you might need to respond to the situation with more than a blush or a smile.

Your left hemisphere, then, *directly controls* the right half of your body. Your right hemisphere *directly controls* the left half of your body. However, most *coordinated body movements* originate in the left hemisphere (in right-handed individuals).

Your right hemisphere seems to take the lead when it comes to such simple emotional reactions as laughing or crying. The right hemisphere also strongly influences how you *perceive* the world, but not necessarily how you *respond* to the world with integrated movements.

Question: Because our society is built primarily for "right-handed" people, some parents attempt to impose right-handedness on children who are naturally left-handed. What might happen to speech development in a left-handed child who was forced to learn to write and speak with the "wrong" hemisphere of her or his brain? (Hint: A large number of stutterers are left-handed.)

Why a Dominant Hemisphere?

At birth (or shortly thereafter), one hemisphere starts to gain the lead over the other and eventually takes over major control of the whole body. Why the left hemisphere usually "wins out" is a matter for **conjecture**. But psychiatrist George F. Michel reported in the May 8, 1981 issue of *Science* that 65 percent of the newborn infants he studied preferred to lie with their heads turned to the right. Only 15 percent of the infants showed a distinct preference for lying with their heads turned to the left. At 5 months of age, almost all of the children who had shown a "head right" orientation at birth reached for things with their right hands, while almost all of the infants with a "head left" orientation reached for objects with their left hands.

"I CLAIMED MY LEFT BRAIN DIDN'T KNOW WHAT MY RIGHT BRAIN WAS DOING, BUT THEY DIDN'T BUY IT."

Corpus callosum (KOR-pus kah-LOW-sum). The bridge of nerve tissue that connects the major and the minor hemispheres.

Conjecture (kon-JEKT-sure). From a Latin word meaning "to throw together." A conjecture is a guess or hypothesis (high-POTH-ee-sis).

Optic nerve (OP-tick). The visual input pathway that runs from each eye to the brain. Half of the optic nerve from each eye runs to the left brain, half to the right brain. In order to make sure that input from the cat's left eye went only to its left hemisphere, and that input from the right eye went only to the right hemisphere, Sperry and Myers had to cut half of the optic nerve from each eye.

Michel believes that almost all infants are born with a tendency to orient their heads one way or another. This inborn "head orientation" then *determines* which hand—and which half of the brain—becomes dominant in later life.

Once the left hemisphere has become dominant (for such tasks as talking and motor movements), how does it exercise control over the right hemisphere? R.W. Doty and his colleagues reported in 1979 that the left half of the brain actively *inhibits* the right half when issuing motor output commands. Thus, if you are right-handed, your left hemisphere *suppresses* any attempts the right might make to speak or "take control" of your body movements. These "suppression orders," of course, are sent from the left hemisphere to the right across the corpus callosum.

Now, with all these facts in mind, can you guess what would happen to you if your corpus callosum were cut, and the two hemispheres of your brain were suddenly split apart?

This is precisely the question that psychologists R.W. Sperry and R.E. Myers were trying to answer when, in 1953, they performed their first split-brain operations on cats. They ended up making one of the most exciting discoveries in modern psychology. Sperry has continued in this field of research for the past 30 years. In 1981 he was awarded the Nobel Prize in medicine and physiology in large part because of his split-brain studies.

Two Minds in the Same Body

The surgical technique used by Sperry and Myers involved opening up the cat's skull, then slicing the animal's corpus callosum. They also split part of the optic nerve that runs from the cat's eyes to its brain.

Normally, sensory input from *each* eye goes to *both* cerebral hemispheres along the **optic**

Roger Sperry

nerve. When Sperry and Myers cut the corpus callosum—and also split part of the optic nerve—they left the cat's *eyes* as isolated from each other as were the *two halves of its cerebrum*. Now, whatever the animal's left eye saw was recorded only in the left hemisphere. And whatever the animal's right eye saw was recorded only in the cat's right hemisphere.

Immediately after the operation the cats had difficulty coordinating their movements. But after a while their behavior became fairly normal again. Either the two hemispheres had learned to cooperate with each other, or both sides of the brain took turns in controlling the entire body.

Once a cat seemed recovered from the surgery, Sperry and Myers gave the animal a variety of behavioral tests. First, they blindfolded its left eye and taught the cat to solve a visual problem using *just* its right eye (and, of course, just the right hemisphere of its brain). The cat learned this lesson very well.

Next, they covered the trained right eye with the blindfold and tested the cat on the same problem with its untrained left eye (and left hemisphere). The question was, would any information about the problem have "leaked" from the right half of the cat's brain to the left?

The answer was a resounding *no*. Using just its untrained left eye/left brain, the cat appeared to be entirely ignorant of what it had learned with its right eye/right brain. When Sperry and Myers trained the left eye in similar fashion, the right eye (and hemisphere) seemed unaware of what the left part of the brain had learned.

Sperry and Myers concluded that the cat now had two "minds," either of which was capable of learning *on its own*—and of responding intelligently to changes in the world around it *on its own*.

Subsequent experiments with rats and monkeys gave similar results. However, the animals recovered so nicely that, if you hadn't known about their operation, you might not have guessed there were two more-or-less independent "entities" inside each animal's body.

The split-brain surgery was seemingly safe and relatively easy to perform in animals. But what would the operation do to a human, and why would anyone want to find out? To answer that question, we must look once more at that odd and unfortunate condition known as epilepsy.

Epilepsy

Although 4,000,000 people in the US suffer from epilepsy, most of us have little understanding of what causes the condition, nor do most of us appreciate the problems that epileptic individuals must face. Just for a moment, then, try to imagine what it might be like if you were unfortunate enough to sustain brain damage and have an epileptic attack.

If the site of the damaged nerve cells were in the *input* or *processing* areas of your brain, you might never recognize that you suffered from epilepsy. In fact, it was not until very recently that we realized epilepsy could affect these parts of your nervous system, for seizures in the input and processing areas of the brain typically lead to little more than momentary lapses in consciousness. This type of epileptic attack is called a **petit mal seizure**.

If the injured neurons were in your *output* system, however, you might suffer from *motor epilepsy*—a condition that is very hard to overlook. During a full-blown motor seizure, most of the muscles in your body would suddenly contract. As your lungs squeezed shut, the air forced out might cause you to moan or scream. You would lose consciousness and fall to the ground, stiff as a board. For a moment or two, you would stop breathing. Then your arms and legs would begin twitching or jerking rhythmically, and you might lose control of your bladder and bowels.

Your motor seizure would be over and done with in five minutes or less, but you would be confused and sleepy—or have a headache—for some time thereafter. Typically, you would have little or no memory either of what led up to the seizure itself, or for the period of confusion that followed. Within an hour or so, you might be completely back to normal—until the next attack hit.

If your epilepsy resulted from mild brain

damage—or if the attack was caused by an overdose of some drug—your seizures would occur infrequently. But if your brain damage were severe, your attacks might happen several times a day—so frequently that you did not regain consciousness between seizures. This rare condition must be treated promptly, for it can lead to death.

Hypersynchrony

As we noted earlier, the neurons in your brain tend to function in small but relatively independent units. In brain-damaged people, however, *all* the nerve cells in a given part of the brain occasionally begin to fire in unison. We call this type of neural activity **hypersynchrony**, and it typically shows up on an EEG record as **spikes** (see Fig. 2.6).

When hypersynchrony occurs, huge and jagged waves of electrical activity sweep across the surface of the brain like a thunderstorm sweeping across the Atlantic Ocean. And just as you can tell something about the intensity of an Atlantic storm by measuring the size and shape of the ocean waves it stirs up, so you can tell something about that "stormy condition" called epilepsy by reading EEG records taken when a seizure occurs.

Epilepsy and the Corpus Callosum

The brain damage that causes most epileptic seizures usually has a specific *focus* or location on *one side of the brain*. If you took an EEG record from this damaged area, you would see continuous "spike" responses.

But remember that the two hemispheres are more-or-less "mirror images." What would happen if you took an EEG record at the same point in the undamaged hemisphere? In fact, the EEG record from the unscarred hemisphere would usually look pretty normal. However, at the onset of an epileptic attack, you would detect spikes on *both sides of the brain*.

How could there be spike responses coming from apparently healthy tissue?

Almost every neuron in your *left* hemisphere has a nerve cell in your *right* hemisphere that is its "identical twin," or mirror image. Many of these nerve cells are tied together by axonic fibers that pass through the corpus callosum. Whenever a neuron in your dominant hemisphere fires, it may send a "command message" telling its mirror-image cell in the minor hemisphere to fire too. And whenever the mirror-image neuron fires, it sends a message back to the dominant hemisphere saying that it *has* fired.

These command messages are the primary way in which your dominant hemisphere coordinates muscular activities on both sides of your body.

Whenever an epileptic seizure begins at a focal point in one hemisphere, the mirror-image neurons in the other hemisphere receive a "seizure message" via the corpus callosum. This "seizure message" causes the mirror-image neurons to fire very, very rapidly themselves. The cells may even start showing spike activity on their own as they "catch fire" from all the stimulation they are receiving from the other hemisphere. So the spike activity begins to build up simultaneously at the *same spot in both hemispheres*.

In addition, the mirror-image neurons may send seizure messages back to the original site of the trouble. This return message from the undamaged hemisphere sets off even more spiking in the damaged area, which then sends even wilder messages back to the mirror-image cells, which causes them to fire even more rapidly.

Each time the seizure message flashes back and forth across the corpus callosum, a few more cells in each hemisphere get caught up in the spiking. Within a few seconds, the whole brain can become involved, and a *grand mal* attack occurs.

An epileptic seizure, therefore, is a good example of what is called a *positive feedback loop*.

"Cutting the Feedback Loop"

When medical doctors learned of the Sperry-Myers split-brain operation, they reasoned that if they cut the corpus callosum and separated the two hemispheres of the brain, they could *cut the positive feedback loop* that typically causes an epileptic attack. And by "cutting the loop," they might prevent full-blown seizures

 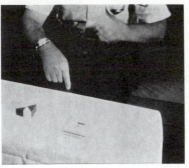 

Fig. 2.10 A film sequence of a split-brain patient in Gazzaniga's laboratory, asked to use blocks to copy a design with his right hand. The patient's poor performance using right hand/left brain apparently upsets the patient's right hemisphere which is much better at perceptual tasks. The experimenter must restrain the patient's left hand from "correcting" the right.

from occurring in patients whose seizures couldn't be controlled by drugs or other medical treatment.

And the doctors were right. They tried the operation on a middle-aged man whom we shall call John Doe. During the Korean War, John Doe had served in the armed forces. After parachuting behind the enemy lines, he had been captured and put in a concentration camp. While in the prison camp, he had been struck on the head several times with a rifle butt.

Shortly thereafter, John Doe's epileptic seizures began. By the time he was released from the concentration camp, his brain was in such bad physical shape that drugs couldn't help very much. His seizures increased in frequency and intensity until they were occurring a dozen or more times a day. Without the split-brain operation, John Doe would probably have died—or committed suicide, as had many other epileptic patients with similar problems.

After the surgeons cut John Doe's corpus callosum, his seizures stopped almost completely—just as the surgeons had expected. Obviously, "cutting the positive feedback loop" had prevented the *grand mal* attacks from occurring. But when the doctors split John Doe's brain, they apparently cut his "mind" into two separate but similar personalities as well. Each of these "minds" seemed to exist more-or-less independently of the other, and each of them had its own unique claim on his body.

As far as his mental activities were concerned, John Doe had suddenly become Siamese twins!

John-Doe-Left and John-Doe-Right

Immediately after the operation, John Doe was able to communicate in almost normal fashion. Some of his speech was slurred, as if he didn't have complete control over the muscles in his tongue. But his thinking seemed clear and logical, and he suffered no noticeable loss in intelligence.

But John Doe did have moments of confusion, and he was often unable to coordinate his body movements and his emotional reactions. Every now and then, he reported, the left half of his body "did odd things," *as if it had a will of its own.*

John Doe was right-handed, so his "talking hemisphere" controlled his right hand and leg. Occasionally, when John was dressing, his right hand would zip up his pants (as it normally did) and John would start to go about his business. Moments later, however, his left hand (controlled by the right hemisphere), would casually reach down and unzip his pants. His left hand did other odd things too, mostly in fairly emotional situations. These behaviors almost always embarrassed John Doe's dominant hemisphere, because he could offer no logical (verbal) explanation for why his left hand was behaving so peculiarly.

The doctors soon began to suspect that when John Doe answered their questions and reported his thoughts, it was *only* his left hemisphere that was doing the talking. Indeed, the left side of his brain seemed blissfully unaware of the perceptions and emotions that were occurring in his right hemisphere. And since his left hemisphere controlled speech output, the right hemisphere couldn't communicate by talking. So, it offered its comments behaviorally—by occasionally doing odd things that would *disrupt* the ongoing flow of behavior controlled by John Doe's left hemisphere.

The psychologists working with John Doe soon devised ways of communicating with either side of his brain without the other side's knowing what was going on. John-Doe-Left responded *verbally* to most questions the psychologists asked him, since this hemisphere possessed full language control. John-Doe-Right could not talk, but he could *point to things* (with the left hand) in response to questions that John-Doe-Left couldn't hear.

Question: As soon as John-Doe-Left responded out loud to a question that only it could hear, why would John-Doe-Right usually know what the question had been?

Similar Personalities

According to Roger Sperry, psychological tests showed that both John Does had remarkably similar personalities. Except for language ability, they were about as much alike as identical twins. Their attitudes and opinions seemed to be the same; their perceptions of the world were the same; and they woke up and went to sleep at almost the same times.

There were differences, however. John-Doe-Left could express himself in language and was somewhat more logical and better at orderly planning than was John-Doe-Right. John-Doe-Right tended to be somewhat more aggressive, impulsive, emotional—and frequently expressed frustration with what was going on. Sperry believes this frustration was caused by the fact that John-Doe-Right often knew what he wanted to say or do, but was unable to express himself verbally.

The split-brain operation was so successful in reducing epileptic attacks that it was tried with more than a dozen patients who might otherwise have died from uncontrollable seizures. In some of these patients, one hemisphere (usually the dominant one) was able to gain control of both sides of the body. In most cases, however, the two halves learned to cooperate and share control, but the dominant hemisphere was in the driver's seat most of the time. In one or two patients, though, neither

half of the brain ever gained the ability to coordinate all bodily movements.

How the Hemispheres Differ

The split-brain studies have given us fascinating insights into the ways that the two hemispheres may function in individuals (like yourself) with intact brains. The research to date suggests that if you are right handed, your left hemisphere is much better at handling written and spoken language, and at executing sequences of coordinated movements. However, the right half of your brain seems superior at perceiving and remembering visual patterns, at processing emotional responses, and at "monitoring" your actions than is your left hemisphere.

Let us now examine in some detail the experiments that led to these conclusions.

Visual Perception, "Monitoring," and the Right Hemisphere

Research performed by Roger Sperry (and many others) suggests that the right hemisphere is much better at *perceiving visual patterns* than is the left. In one experiment, Sperry showed a male patient a complex design and then asked the man to reproduce the pattern by putting colored blocks together. When the patient used his left hand (right hemisphere), he completed the task rapidly. But when the man tried to match the design using his right hand (left hemisphere), he proceeded slowly, clumsily, and made many mistakes. And much to the annoyance of both Sperry and the patient, the man's left hand often tried to "correct" the mistakes the right hand made.

The right hemisphere not only seems to *perceive* complex visual patterns better than the left, it also seems to *remember* them more readily. In research reported in 1978 by Michael Gazzaniga and Joseph LeDoux (see Fig. 2.10), a split-brain patient was asked to reproduce patterns with either the left or right hand. The superiority of the left hand was much greater when the patient had to create the pattern from memory than when the pattern was physically present.

Oddly enough, there are no reports of cases in which the left hemisphere tries to correct any responses made by the right half of the brain. Indeed, as we will soon see, the left hemisphere

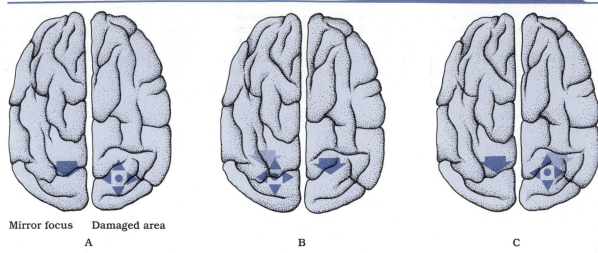

Mirror focus   Damaged area

A   B   C

Fig. 2.11A Damaged cells in the left hemisphere cause abnormal electrical activity in nearby cells and send an "excited" message to their "mirror image" cells in the right hemisphere.

Fig. 2.11B The "mirror image" cells are stimulated to fire by this abnormal input and feed an "excited" message back to the right hemisphere.

Fig. 2.11C Soon the whole brain is "on fire" with neural excitation, and an epileptic seizure results. Cutting the corpus callosum "cuts the feedback loop" and reduces the likelihood of a seizure.

usually tends to *deny responsibility* for any of the right hemisphere's actions. It would appear, then, that the right hemisphere is better at "monitoring" the activities of the left than the left hemisphere is at observing and recording the activities of the right.

Emotions and the Right Hemisphere

There is a fair amount of data connecting the right hemisphere with emotionality. For instance, several studies suggest that most smiles, grins, and frowns begin on the *left* side of the face in right-handed individuals—as surely would be the case if the *right* hemisphere took the lead in expressing joy or sorrow. Research on brain-damaged patients (see Fig. 2.11) tends to confirm the role of the right hemisphere in emotional reactions. For example, in 1979 Elliott Ross and Marek-Marsel Mesulam reported the case histories of two people who suffered from **strokes** that affected the right half of the brain.

One of these patients—a 39-year-old woman—had to give up teaching school for a time after her stroke because she no longer could "put emotion into her speech and actions." All her words came out in a flat tone of voice, and neither her pupils at school nor her own children could tell when she "meant business" when she talked. To compensate, she learned to say things like "I am angry and mean it" when she wanted to express dissatisfaction. She found it impossible to laugh, and was unable to cry even at her father's funeral. Some six months after the stroke, she started to regain the ability to express her feelings. Two months later she was again able to express emotions normally. Apparently, various undamaged parts of her brain had been able to "take over" the right-brain functions lost when the stroke occurred.

Similar evidence about the importance of the right hemisphere in processing emotional responses comes from a female split-brain patient studied by Roger Sperry and his associates. They showed pictures of various people and things to the woman's right hemisphere and asked her to evaluate the visual stimuli by giving a "thumbs up" or "thumbs down" response with her left hand. Her left hemisphere then tried to guess (and describe verbally) what the right was looking at.

Throughout the testing, the left hemisphere seemed to be playing a game like "20 questions" with the right. The right hemisphere would view a photo—of Adoph Hitler, for instance—and would give a vigorous "thumbs down" response. The left hemisphere would then attempt to figure out what the right had seen. When the left hemisphere guessed wrong, the right would respond with a "thumbs down." When the left was "on target," it got a "thumbs up" response and other positive emotional clues from the right. Indeed, as Sperry reports, he often had to restrain the woman's left hand from "tracing the initials" of the name of the object to help the left hemisphere with its guesses.

At one point in the testing, Sperry and his colleagues showed the woman's right hemisphere a photograph of herself. She responded, "Oh, no! Where'd you g— . . . what *are* they?" Then she laughed loudly and said, "Oh, God!" After a moment—in quite a different tone of voice—the woman asked hesitantly if there were people in the photograph. Sperry believes that the first (and rather emotional) reaction came from the right hemisphere before the left had time to exercise its usual dominance. Once the left hemisphere had gained control, though, it hesitantly asked about the picture in very unemotional tones.

Language and the Left Hemisphere

The split-brain research—and many other studies with both normal and brain-damaged individuals—suggests strongly that language is *primarily* processed on the left side of the brain. For instance, in 1978 Ruben Gur and his colleagues at the University of Pennsylvania gave 13 right-handed males various tasks to solve. Half of these tasks involved the use of complex language. The other half of the problems involved the visual perception of incomplete patterns. When the subjects were working on the verbal problems, the blood flow through their *left* hemispheres increased markedly, but the blood flow through their *right* hemispheres did not increase at all. And those subjects who did best at solving the visual problems showed an increased blood flow through their *right* hemispheres, but not through the *left* half of their brains.

In a similar set of experiments, David Galin and his associates at the Langley Porter Institute in San Francisco found that normal sub-

Strokes. Brain damage usually caused by ruptured blood vessels. When deprived of blood, the neurons in a given area of the brain die. The stroke victim then loses the psychological and biological functions controlled by that part of the brain.

Gestalt (guess-TALT). A mental or perceptual pattern. From the German word meaning "figure," "pattern," or "good form." The ability to see something "as a whole"—rather than just see its parts—is the ability to "form a Gestalt."

jects show increased electrical activity in their left hemispheres when attempting to solve verbal tasks, but increased activity in their right hemispheres when solving tasks requiring spatial ability.

Galin believes that "each hemisphere is specialized for a different cognitive style—the left for an analytical, logical mode for which words are an excellent tool, and the right for a holistic **Gestalt** mode, which happens to be particulary suitable for spatial relations."

Cooperation across the Corpus Callosum

If it seems highly unlikely to you that you have two minds locked away inside your skull, the reason is not hard to find. Although the split-brain research suggests that each of your hemispheres *specializes* in certain types of tasks, for the most part the two halves of your brain *cooperate* so quickly and efficiently that they operate as a "functional unit" rather than as two separate entities. It is only when the two hemispheres are isolated that their differing abilities can readily be measured. And even these "differences" are not always obvious to the split-brain patient.

Roger Sperry reports that, following the operation, none of his split-brain patients was aware that "anything was missing." Although their left (verbal) hemispheres had lost *depth perception*, and could no longer hear music in "full stereophonic sound," the patients did not become aware of this loss until it was demonstrated to them in the laboratory.

More than this, the patients often verbally rejected those few responses that clearly came from their right hemispheres. When Sperry would show a picture of some kind to the right hemisphere, the left hand would identify the picture correctly—but the patient would frequently deny having seen anything at all. And just as often, when the patient's left hand would "correct" the right hand as it tried to reproduce a pattern, the patient would say something like, "Now, I know it wasn't *me* who did that!"

Case of J.W.

Studies in which only *part* of the corpus callosum is cut tell us even more about how the hemispheres communicate with each other. In 1981 Michael Gazzaniga and his colleagues reported the case history of J.W., a bright young man whose epileptic seizures became so severe that he underwent split-brain surgery when he was 26. The operation took place in two stages, however. During the first stage, the surgeon cut *just the rear half* of the callosum. Then, 10 weeks later, the surgeon cut the *front half* as well. Gazzaniga and his co-workers gave J.W. psychological tests several times—before any surgery at all, after the first stage of the operation, and again after the entire corpus callosum had been cut.

Prior to the operation, when the word "knight" was shown just to J.W.'s right hemisphere, he immediately said the word aloud. After the rear half of the callosum was cut, however, J.W. gave the following response when his right hemisphere was again shown the word "knight": "I have a picture in my mind but can't say it . . . Two fighters in a ring . . . Ancient . . . wearing uniforms and helmets . . . on horses . . . trying to knock each other off . . . Knights?"

We will describe J.W.'s responses after the *entire* corpus callosum was cut in just a moment. But two important points emerge from his reactions when just the *rear half* of the callosum was severed:

1. When the front half of his callosum was still intact, J.W.'s left hemisphere did not deny having experienced stimuli presented to the right half of his brain. Instead, he claimed he could "see" the stimulus in his mind, but just couldn't name or describe it very well.
2. When the rear half of his callosum was cut, J.W.'s right hemisphere could no longer send *specific stimuli* (such as words) to the left hemisphere. But it could transmit a *general impression* of the stimulus across the callosal tissue that still remained. His left hemisphere could then make educated guesses about what his right hemisphere was viewing.

After his entire corpus callosum was cut, though, J.W. was unable to report *anything at all* about the stimuli presented to his right hemisphere. Indeed, he now denied having "seen" anything, and his guesses at what the right hemisphere had been shown were no better than chance.

Gazzaniga believes that words and other types of *specific* sensory information pass back and forth between the two hemispheres in the rear half of the corpus callosum. However, the front half of the callosum apparently is the highway across which the two hemispheres exchange perceptual and emotional information (thoughts, feelings, "pictures," and "meanings").

Question: When J.W.'s right hemisphere was shown the word "knight" after the first operation, his left hemisphere responded by talking about "two fighters in a ring wearing ancient armor." But the printed word "knight" sounds just the same as "night" when the two words are spoken aloud. What does the fact that J.W.'s left hemisphere didn't confuse "knight" with "night" tell you about what kind of sensory information the right hemisphere was sending to the left?

The Whole Brain Versus the Split Brain

The chances are very good that no surgeon will ever cut your corpus callosum, and that you will not suffer the type of stroke that destroys your ability to express emotions. What then can all this study of brain-damaged individuals tell you about the normal functioning of the whole, intact brain? Although the split-brain research does give a partial answer to this question, you should realize five things:

1. Almost all of the theories we have today are "subject to being recalled," which is to say they may be drastically changed as new data come from the laboratory.
2. Because we place a high premium on language production and coordinated activities, we tend to call the left hemisphere the *dominant* half of the brain. The term "dominant" may be a poor choice of words, however, for the right hemisphere surely "dominates" the production of emotional and perceptual responses. And, in normal individuals, both hemispheres are involved in almost all activities. For example, when you talk, your left hemisphere may select (and produce) the words you say. But according to Elliott Ross, your right hemisphere controls the intonation, rhythm, and pitch of your speech. And it may actually take the lead when you sing.
3. Until recently, many experimental psycholo-

gists assumed that the "mind" was a highly complex biological machine that "processed information" much as a giant computer might "process data." Other psychologists preferred to view the mind as a mental (or even spiritual) thing. But almost everybody thought of the mind as being a *single* system. The incredible conclusion some scientists draw from the split-brain research, however, is that you have *at least two different types of brains*, and thus two different types of "mind."

One half of your brain apparently takes in information from the outside world and processes it in a *linear* or logical fashion, rather as most modern computers do. The other half of your brain deals with "patterns," "meanings," and "emotions" rather than with "bits of information." It perceives the world in what seems to be a *holistic* fashion. It apparently monitors the actions of the other hemisphere, and gives emotional feedback to the left side of your brain to keep its thoughts and behaviors "on target" (see Chapter 5).

4. The split-brain research has taught us a great deal about human *individuality*, par-

ticularly as regards our "mental processes." Roger Sperry puts it this way: "The more we learn, the more we recognize the unique complexity of any one individual intellect and the stronger the conclusion becomes that the individuality inherent in our brain networks makes that of fingerprints or facial features gross and simple by comparison."

5. As Sigmund Freud put it years ago, studying the abnormal often tells us what the normal is like. Trying to figure out what the right hemisphere's "stream of consciousness" is like has taught us much about what "ordinary consciousness" consists of. But so has research on "altered states of consciousness," such as sleep, dreaming, and drug-induced "highs." Some of the experiences people have when asleep or "on drugs" may well be caused by a disruption of the orderly flow of thoughts and emotions back and forth across the corpus callosum.

To understand better how your *whole brain* works when it is functioning normally, then, we must turn once more to the abnormal—to such "altered states of consciousness" as sleep and drug intoxication.

Summary

1 The **brain** is the master organ of your body that coordinates or controls many of the functions of the other organs.

2 The largest parts of your brain are the two **cerebral hemispheres** that sit atop the stem of your brain like the cap on a mushroom.

3 The thin outer covering of the cerebral hemispheres is called the **cortex**. Many of the functions of the brain that relate to conscious decision-making are located in the cortex.

4 There are nearly one trillion nerve cells or **neurons** in the human nervous system, most of them in the brain.

5 Most cortical neurons have three main parts—the **dendrites**, the cell body or **soma**, and the **axon**.

6 The main purpose of most neurons is to pass messages from one part of the body to another. These messages are really waves of electro-chemical energy called **action potentials**.

7 When the dendrites are stimulated by **neurotransmitters**, the action potential sweeps down the axon like a bullet speeding down the barrel of a gun.

8 When the action potential reaches the end of the axon, it causes the axon to release **neurotransmitters** into the **synapse**—the fluid-filled space between the axon of one neuron and the dendrites and cell body of a second neuron.

9 Neurotransmitters released into the synapse excite the dendrites of the second neuron. It responds by **firing**, or generating an action potential of its own.

10 **Sensory input neurons** receive information from the outside world and transmit this information to **neural sub-centers**, which then pass the information along to your cortex, which decides how to respond.

11 **Command messages** telling your muscles to respond go out from the brain via **motor neurons**.

12 Electrical activity in the dendrites creates **brain waves** that show up on an **EEG** machine. When you are actively thinking, your brain produces **beta waves**. When you are resting peacefully with closed eyes, the visual areas in your

brain generate **alpha waves**. When you are deeply asleep, your EEG record will show **delta waves**.

13 Left-handers are more likely to suffer **developmental disorders** and **language difficulties**, and are three times more likely to experience **migraine headaches** and **autoimmune disorders** than are right-handers. However, a higher percentage of left-handers are artists, musicians, mathematicians, and engineers.

14 The two hemispheres of your brain are connected by a bridge of tissue called the **corpus callosum**.

15 Damage to various parts of the brain can cause a condition known as **epilepsy**. Epileptic seizures show up on an EEG machine as **spike-shaped brain waves**.

16 If epileptic seizures become too frequent or severe, a surgeon may cut the corpus callosum. This **split-brain operation** may leave the patient with "two minds in the same body."

17 In right-handed people, the left hemisphere is **dominant**, has the power of speech, and controls coordinated movements of the body.

18 The minor or **perceptual/emotional hemisphere** can understand most language, but does not usually speak. It seems more specialized to handle perceptual patterns and emotional expression than is the dominant hemisphere.

(Continued from page 28.)

"What an appropriate place to hide a secret," Colonel Garcia said, caressing Patrick's head again.

"I don't understand," said Captain Hartman. "How can the boy have a secret in his brain that the police over *there* could not discover?"

Colonel Garcia beamed. "Because Tavela knew more than they did, for one thing. Because they are atheists and God-haters, for another."

"Are you trying to tell me that Tavela hid the secret in Patrick's *soul*?" Captain Hartman said, a touch of sarcasm in his voice.

"Not quite, Captain, but perhaps you are closer than you know." The woman turned to the young man sitting beside her. "Tell me, Patrick, did you mention the Bible to the secret police when they questioned you?"

"Yes."

"And I'll bet they laughed, didn't they? And spoke of fairy stories and capitalist fancies, didn't they?"

Patrick nodded his agreement.

"But 'understanding is more precious than rubies,' Patrick. Don't ever forget that. Tavela knew we would understand. And we do."

"I don't understand at all," said Captain Hartman.

Colonel Garcia grew serious. "It is simple, when you know how the brain actually works. Patrick, when Dr. Tavela operated on you, he cut your corpus callosum, didn't he?"

"Yes, I think that was it. He said it would stop the seizures."

Nodding, Colonel Garcia continued. "And then he tested the two hemispheres of your brain to determine what each could see and hear and respond to."

"What has that got to do with the pattern of the secret molecule?" asked the Captain.

"*Everything*, if you understand the third chapter of Proverbs. You see, the 'mask' that Patrick looked into was a device that presented stimuli to just one half of his brain. If Dr. Tavela showed something to the left hemisphere, Patrick would be conscious of it and could answer questions about it verbally." She looked at the young man. "Is that not so? Didn't he ask you what you could see?"

"All the time," replied Patrick. "Sometimes I could tell him, and sometimes I couldn't."

"But even if you couldn't tell him what you saw, you could point to it with your left hand, couldn't you? You could trace patterns with your left hand, couldn't you? Not with your right hand, of course, but with your left hand?"

Patrick considered the matter. "Yeah, you're right."

"Ah," said Captain Hartman. "I think I see what you mean. 'And in her left hand is riches and honor.' When Tavela knew the police were coming for him, he had half an hour to hide the pattern for the new molecule where we could find it later. Not in the cast or in the bandages, because the police would check them."

Patrick nodded excitedly. "Yes, they took off my cast and and changed my bandages. And they took lots of X-rays."

"And they didn't find anything, because they rejected the clue to the Bible," continued the Colonel.

Hartman smiled. "Because Dr. Tavela had hidden the pattern in the right half of Patrick's brain. But how did he do that?" he asked.

"He must have shown it to Patrick's right hemisphere, and had Patrick trace it again and again with his left hand," replied Colonel Garcia.

Hartman seemed confused. "But his left hemisphere doesn't *know* what the formula is at all! The lie detector tests showed that."

"They tested Patrick's *right* hand during the lie detector test, Captain. And the right hand is controlled by the left hemisphere, which was ignorant of what the right hemisphere had learned. They couldn't test Patrick's *left* hand during the polygraph tests because he's wearing a cast on his left hand. That's why Dr. Tavela said the broken left hand was a 'good thing.' So his right brain knows, but Patrick doesn't know, eh?" She smiled at the young man. "You really aren't conscious of knowing the pattern for the secret molecule, are you?"

"No," he said, a puzzled look on his face.

"We'll see about that." The woman picked up the pencil from her desk and wrote "Yes" and "No" on a sheet of paper. Then she put the paper close to Patrick's left hand. "Now, Patrick, I'm going to ask you some questions, but I don't want you to answer out loud. Instead, I want you to point to 'Yes' or 'No' on the paper with your *left* hand. All right?"

"All right," he responded, his left hand moving toward the paper.

"Patrick," the Colonel continued, "I want to talk to your right hemisphere. If you hear what I am saying, please point to 'Yes.'"

Patrick's fingers touched "Yes."

"Patrick, did Dr. Tavela show you the drawing of the secret molecule?"

"No," said Patrick out loud. But his left hand pointed to "Yes."

"Weird," muttered Captain Hartman.

Patrick stared at his left hand in amazement. "I don't understand what I'm doing."

Colonel Garcia gave the young man a hug. "In the world of espionage we tell our agents, 'Never let your right hand know what your left is doing.' You are the only person I know of who can actually follow that advice. Because of your special brain, you have helped us, and Dr. Tavela, and even yourself. Be proud of that." Then she sighed and stood up. "Come, Patrick. It is time that your left hand had a long talk with one of our chemists."

Patrick's left hand pointed to "Yes."

Recommended Readings

Brown, T.S. & Wallace, P.M. (1980). *Physiological psychology.* New York: Academic Press.

Cotman, Carl W. & McGaugh, J.L. (1980). *Behavioral neuroscience: An introduction.* New York: Academic Press.

Galin, D. (1974). Implications for psychiatry of left and right cerebral specialization. *Archives of General Psychiatry, 31,* 572–583.

Gazzaniga, M.S. & LeDoux, J.E. (1978). *The integrated mind.* New York: Plenum Press.

Kimble, D.P. (in press). *Biological psychology.* New York: Holt, Rinehart and Winston.

Sperry, R.W. (1982). Some effects of disconnecting the cerebral hemispheres. *Science, 217,* 1223–1226.

Springer, S.P. & Deutsch, G. (1981). *Left brain, right brain.* San Francisco: Freeman.

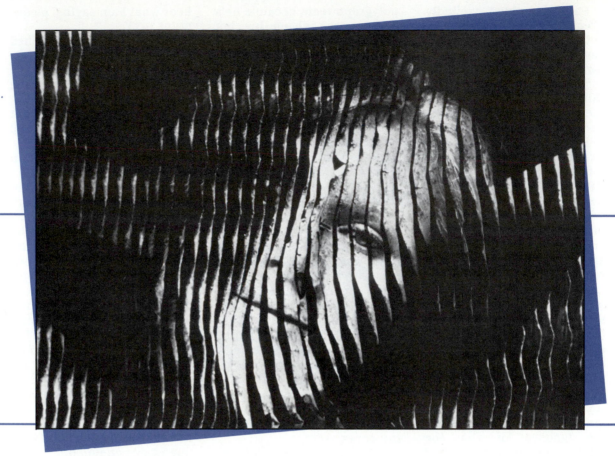

Did You Know That...

- "Consciousness" is a "primitive term" that is almost impossible to define?
- Your body has "biological clocks" that control your sleep-wake cycle and other bodily processes?
- No one really understands why people sleep and dream?
- You go through several 90-minute sleep cycles nightly?
- When you dream, your muscles are paralyzed so you won't act out your dreams?
- Some people are able to control what they dream about?
- Nightmares frequently occur after you've stopped taking sleeping pills?
- Your brain produces natural pain-killers called endorphins that are similar to morphine?
- "Runner's high" may be due to endorphins?
- Under controlled conditions, alcoholics cannot tell the difference between tonic water and vodka?

3

Sleep, Drugs, and Altered States of Consciousness

"Perchance to Dream"

The Washington Bureaucrat leaned back in his over-stuffed chair, puffed on his pipe, and meditated quietly as he looked at the man and woman sitting in front of his desk. They were nice people, really—bright, eager academics—and he did want to help them. They needed research funds to study some savages living in a jungle in South America, and were obviously good at their jobs. But it was a pity they knew so little about the savages who lived in that "jungle by the Potomac" called Washington, D.C.

"Look," the Bureaucrat said, putting down his pipe.

"It's a simple trade-off, really. You, Dr. Ogdon, and your husband are both psychologists. You want to go study language development in some very primitive people who live near the Amazon. Right?"

Susan Ogdon looked at her husband and then nodded assent.

"Well," continued the Bureaucrat, "our department wants someone to study marijuana use, and in just the same sort of back-woods people. We don't care what language these people speak or how they learn to speak it. But we do want to find out how pot-smoking affects

their lives, their health, and their ability to get along in the world. You make our study for us, and we'll pay for the research." The Bureaucrat picked up his pipe again and leaned back in his chair. "What you choose to do on your spare time is your own affair, naturally. If you want to study language development on the side, we couldn't care less."

The woman cleared her throat. "What do you wish us to prove for you?"

The Bureaucrat sat bolt upright. "Nothing! Nothing at all! We have no preconceived notions of what your findings will be." The man paused, remembering how upset the Deputy Assistant Secretary got at the mere mention of marijuana. "Well, no *official* preconceived notions, you understand. But truthfully, we'll accept and let you publish whatever results you get."

"Why us?" asked Roger Ogdon.

"Because you've been there, and you know the people. Otherwise you wouldn't want to do your own research there." The Bureaucrat's voice softened and he put on his warmest smile. "Speaking personally, I do happen to be quite interested in language development. But the department simply is not able to fund such projects these days. So, when I read the proposal you sent us on language development in primitives, I thought . . ." He let his words drift slowly toward the ceiling like verbal pipe smoke.

The woman's face brightened. "Roger," she said, turning to her husband, "I do believe we ought to consider it. But we'd surely have to think about how to measure the effects of long-term marijuana smoking on *anybody*, much less on the natives."

"You're right, Sue," Roger Ogdon said. He turned in his chair and looked straight at the Bureaucrat. "Why do you want us to study Amazon primitives? If you want to know the effects of pot-smoking on American citizens—and I suspect you do—why not do your research right here in Washington? Surely there are enough people in government who . . ."

"You're thinking of the Previous Administration," said the Bureaucrat quickly. "But really, you two, you know we can't get a really random sample of long-term pot smokers here, because the people who would volunteer wouldn't be representative. Besides, I suspect those natives have been smoking pot for many generations. You can look for long-term genetic effects as well as measuring the problems it gives them today."

Sue Ogdon frowned. "I thought you said you had no preconceived notions of what we'd find. What if there aren't any long-term genetic effects, or any real problems today?"

Now it was the Bureaucrat's turn to frown. These people were giving him a mild headache. Surely they saw that he was trying to help them. Why didn't they just take the money, and do what they were told? He reached in a desk drawer and took out an aspirin. Taking a sip of water, he swallowed the tablet quickly.

"Look, Dr. Ogdon," he said. "I will be frank with you. It would greatly please certain people upstairs if you found that marijuana had bad effects on the natives. Maybe that's what you'll find, and maybe not. But let's get things straight. I don't care what you find. Just plan the best study possible, use as many controls as you can, and get the facts. We'll pay the bills no matter what."

"Haven't you supported similar studies before?" asked the woman.

The Bureaucrat's face went slightly white. "Er, yes, I believe so. A couple, perhaps. But the more research is repeated, the more firmly we can believe in the data. As my senior professor said in graduate school, 'Replication is good for the soul.'"

Susan Ogdon persisted. "What did the other investi-gators find?"

"Now, now," said the Bureaucrat in a soothing tone of voice. "I'd rather you approached this problem with fresh minds. Just make sure that you measure the biological, psychological, and social effects of marijuana use, and do so as objectively as you can. That's the important thing."

Roger Ogdon was puzzled. "I don't think I've read the results of those 'couple of studies' you've already funded."

"Well," said the Bureaucrat, reaching for another aspirin. "I don't believe we've published the results yet. Later this year, perhaps . . ." He let his words drift off again.

Susan Ogdon frowned in surprise. "You mean, you didn't publish the results because the data didn't come out the way you expected them to? Then why do you want to pay for still another study whose results you may have to suppress?"

The Bureaucrat put down his pipe in an angry gesture. "Listen to me. You both are psychologists, and you're supposed to be able to understand why people and organizations act like they do. You know perfectly well that it takes a long time for an organization to change its mind on a subject. It takes a lot of data to accomplish that miracle, and a lot of gentle pushing from inside. You go do the study, and report *anything* you find. Do your own work on the side, if you wish. And leave it up to me to see that your data have the maximum impact. Okay?"

The man and woman exchanged glances. Then the man said, "Well, I think we understand each other. We'll go plan a study, and submit a proposal to you. If we agree on the details, you'll get us the funding. And, as you said, any other research we do 'on the side' is our business."

The Bureaucrat beamed. "Marvelous! I hoped you'd see it that way. Now, let's go find a drink somewhere and celebrate!"

(Continued on page 83.)

Consciousness

This chapter is about altered states of *consciousness*. Some altered states of consciousness occur naturally. For instance, that blissful state called sleep, and those sometimes unblissful experiences we call nightmares, are examples of "natural" altered states of awareness. But there are "unnatural" states, as well—unnatural in the sense that they are *artificially* brought about. The **intoxication** that you get from drugs such as alcohol is a good example of an artificially induced altered state of consciousness.

However, if you wish to find out some new things about drugs, sleep, and dreams, you will have to pay a small price for that pleasure. That is, you will have to learn a bit more about the *systematic interactions* among your brain, your mind, and your social environment. For, unless you know something about what goes on inside your brain, and how the *synapse* really works, the new information about your states of mind may not make much sense to you.

So let us begin with what may seem a dumb question. What do we mean by the term *consciousness*? After all, if the main theme of this chapter is *altered* states of consciousness, perhaps we had better first make sure we know what it is we're altering.

Primitive Terms

Every science has what are called *primitive terms*. That is, every science has ideas or concepts which are so elemental that they are exceptionally difficult to define.

For example, "energy" and "matter" are two primitive terms in the field of physics. You must have a rough notion of what these words mean, but you should also realize that great philosophical battles have been fought over their exact definitions.

Psychology has its primitive terms too. One of these is *consciousness*. (Another, in case you're wondering, is *mind*.) The dictionary gives many definitions of "consciousness," most of which have to do with awareness, awakeness, understanding, being alert, or even being alive. Some of the dictionary meanings have to do with *self*-awareness, or the experience of knowing that you are having the experience of knowing. But no two psychologists will agree completely on the precise meaning of "consciousness" (nor of "mind," for that matter).

Three Important Points About Consciousness

We will have more to say about primitive terms (and consciousness and mind) in Chapter 5. For the moment, there are three important points we should make about consciousness.

First, it is a *process*, not a thing. Processes are much harder to measure—and to describe scientifically—than are things. You can describe a track shoe rather easily. Describing the *process of running*, however, is a more difficult task.

Second, consciousness is usually marked by a subjective awareness of the passage of time. When you are awake, you are aware that "the meter is running." When you are asleep, or when you are intoxicated, your sense of temporal duration is usually badly distorted, if not entirely absent. Thus, one important characteristic of an altered state of consciousness is a *change in your perception of the passage of time*.

The third point has to do with what we might call the "reality" of consciousness. Writing in the May 1984 *Contemporary Psychology*, Stevan Harnad notes that "self-awareness" is marked by a kind of *immediate certainty* that "settles all my doubts about whether *I* really have experiences." When you are in a state of "ordinary consciousness," Harnad believes, you are generally immediately certain that you are awake and aware of what is going on. You don't have to ask people around you if you're dreaming; you *know* you're not. But when you've drunk too much booze, or gotten "high" on some drug, you may not always be so sure.

Thus, a *change in the subjective experience of reality* is another hallmark of an "altered state of consciousness."

Consciousness is a *subjective state* or "internal process." But it is controlled in large part by physical activities in our brains and bodies. Before we can discuss consciousness further, therefore, we must take a closer look at the biological rhythms that influence our states of awareness.

Biological Rhythms

Your body goes through rather regular *biological cycles* every day. Many of these cycles reach a peak at some regular point during the day or night. These cycles are often called **circadian rhythms**, a technical term that means "a repeating pattern of activity that runs about 24 hours in length."

Your temperature, for instance, is usually lowest in the middle of the night. It begins to rise a few hours before you get up in the morning, and reaches the "normal" 98.6° F. around 6 p.m. Then your temperature begins to drop, moving down toward its nighttime low.

According to a 1973 book by G.G. Luce, your blood-sugar level, pulse rate, and blood pressure also reach peaks around 5 or 6 p.m. Luce says that your sensory abilities—hearing, vision, taste, and smell—also are at their best in the late afternoon. Unlike blood pressure and temperature, however, your sensory acuity reaches a second peak around 3 a.m.

Other biological cycles reach their high points at different times of day. For example, the amount of male hormone present in the bodies of most men is greatest at about 9 a.m. And the amount of calcium in the blood in both males and females usually peaks at midnight.

The most obvious circadian rhythm is probably the sleep/waking cycle. Most of us are active for some 16 hours each day, but are inactively asleep for the other 8 hours. Before we discuss the sleep/waking cycle, though, there are several general points we should make about biological rhythms.

First, most **biological clocks** run on a circadian rhythm (under normal conditions). But some cycles are shorter or longer than 24 hours. Second, there is tremendous individual variability among people as far as their biological rhythms are concerned. And third, human activity cycles are strongly influenced by the external environment. Let's look at all three points in detail.

Short and Long Cycles

Sleep is a good example of a biological rhythm that runs less than a day in length. As you will soon see, sleep is actually made up of a repeating sequence of events. Each individual sleep cycle runs about 90 minutes.

The female menstrual cycle, which runs about 28 days, is an example of a much longer biological rhythm.

Individual Variability

Your biological rhythms may peak at quite different times than do those of the people around you. And, as you surely know, your own cycles may be disrupted under many different circumstances.

As an example of differences among people, a 1976 study by T. Akerstedt and J.E. Froberg suggests there may be "morning persons" and "evening persons." Akerstedt and Froberg asked Swedish soldiers a series of questions designed to find out whether the men were more active during the day or at night. Some of the men preferred daytime activities and were early risers (the "morning persons" group). Others said they typically did better at night and hence were late risers (the "evening persons" group). The rest of the soldiers (the "intermediate group") had no clear-cut preference.

Next, Akerstedt and Froberg measured the soldiers over a period of several months. The scientists found that, overall, **adrenalin** levels for "morning persons" tended to be higher than for "evening persons." Thus, "morning persons" probably are a bit more active physically than "evening persons" are. However, as you might suspect, adrenalin levels were higher *early in the day* for "morning persons," but higher *at night* for "evening persons." The circadian rhythm for temperature differed significantly for the two groups as well. The results for the "intermediate group" were, as expected, in between these two extremes.

Resetting Your Biological Clocks

Most biological clocks are like alarm clocks. That is, they run on a 12- or 24-hour cycle. You can speed up or slow down the *rate* at which the clock "ticks" to some small extent. But you *can't ordinarily change the length of the cycle itself* in any significant fashion.

But your biological clocks are typically *set* by external events. If you live on the east coast of the US, your clocks will normally operate on Eastern Time. If you fly to Los Angeles, you will often experience several days of confusion as your body tries to reset all its clocks so they operate on Pacific Time. When you fly back to the east coast, you will undergo a similar sort of *jet lag*. In either case, however, once your biological clocks have stabilized, they still will run on a 24-hour cycle.

Scientists have, on occasion, studied the effects of putting people in highly controlled environments that ran on "22-hour days" or "28-hour days." In these laboratory situations, for example, the lights might be on for 11 hours, then off for 11 hours. Generally speaking, the subjects adapted fairly readily to a change in length-of-day that wasn't more than an hour or two different from the normal 24-hour cycle. They did not adjust well to extremes, however, such as 18-hour or 30-hour days.

Oddly enough, if we remove all environmental cues, you won't set your own "24-hour cycle" and follow it without fail. Rather, if you have *no sensory inputs* to tell you what time of day it really is, your sleep-waking rhythm will soon settle down on a day-length of about 25.8 hours. There is little agreement among scientists as to why your sleep-waking rhythm runs on a 25.8-hour cycle rather than a 24-hour cycle in the absence of all external cues.

Question: When President Reagan flew to China a couple of years ago, he stopped en route for several days in Hawaii. What have you learned about jet lag that would suggest this was a good idea?

"IF YOU TAKE OUR TWO-DAY ROUND TRIP, YOU NOT ONLY SAVE $35, BUT YOUR BIOLOGICAL CLOCK IS QUICKLY READJUSTED."

Intoxication (in-tocks-ee-KAY-shun). From the Latin word *toxicum*, meaning "poison." To intoxicate yourself is to "poison" your body with alcohol or some other drug.

Circadian rhythms (seer-KAY-dee-an). From the Latin words *circa*, meaning "about," and *dies*, meaning "day." A biological rhythm that is "about a day (24 hours) in length."

Biological clocks. Internal "time givers" or bodily processes that seem to function like built-in clocks. Although the starting point of each rhythmic cycle can be set by external stimuli, and the clocks sped up or slowed down slightly, the basic rhythm seems determined primarily by the genes.

Adrenalin (add-DREN-ah-linn). One of two "arousal" hormones secreted by the adrenal glands. See Chapter 12.

Relationships among Various "Biological Clocks"

We are not entirely sure what physical activities in your body control your various biological clocks. As we noted, many of your cycles seem to "peak" at about the same time each day. But there is evidence that each important biological rhythm is controlled by a different physical mechanism.

Under normal conditions, you tend to go to sleep when your body temperature is falling and wake up as your temperature starts to rise. Thus, it might seem as though these activities are controlled by the same clock—or that one circadian rhythm strongly affects the other. However, under certain conditions, the sleep cycle and the temperature cycle can be separated. Writing in the August 17, 1983 *Nature*, Timothy Monk and his colleagues at Cornell and Harvard report a study in which they forced a subject to live on a rigid 25.8-hour-day schedule. The young man's sleep cycle soon adjusted, but his temperature cycle remained on a 24.8-hour schedule and soon departed noticeably from the sleep cycle. Monk notes that peaks in the man's *physical* performance seemed tied to the temperature cycle. However, peaks in the man's *mental* performance were closely related to his sleep cycle. Under normal conditions, of course, both peaks would come at about the same time, because the temperature and sleep cycle would be "set" by the same environment stimuli.

We will have more to say about these experiments in a moment. But first we have to ask a most important question: Why do you bother to go to sleep at all?

Wilse Webb

Question: Timothy Monk believes his findings have important implications as far as assigning people to "shift work" in the military and in industry is concerned. Can you see why?

The Function of Sleep

Sleep is obviously an interruption in your normal stream of consciousness—that much is clear. But scientists are still uncertain as to what sleep actually is or what functions it serves. In his book *Sleep: The Gentle Tyrant*, University of Florida psychologist Wilse Webb notes there are two major theoretical explanations for sleep. The first is that sleep is an **adaptive response** that increases an organism's chances of surviving. The second theory is that sleep is a "restorative process" that allows the body (and perhaps the mind) to repair the day's damages. Let's look briefly at both these theories.

Sleep as an Adaptive Response

Imagine yourself as a primitive human living on earth thousands of years ago. What sorts of behaviors would increase your chances of surviving? During the day, you'd have to be actively engaged in finding things to eat—and in protecting yourself from those animals that would like to dine on *you*.

During the day you could see rather well, since your vision is "tuned" for the daylight hours. But what would you do at night? For, without artificial light, you wouldn't be able to *see* either food or danger. So you might well end up wasting a lot of energy and getting in trouble. If you went to sleep at night instead of remaining active, however, you could conserve your energy and avoid the terrors of the night.

As Wilse Webb puts it, "Sleep, then, can be thought of as an instinctive response which is useful in 'keeping us out of harm's way.'"

Early humans probably retired to the safety of caves and slept through the night. Little did we know, thousands of years ago, that one day Edison would develop the electric light, turn night into day, and badly disrupt our "instinctual sleep patterns." We'll return to this point shortly.

Sleep as a Restorative Process

If you ask people why they sleep, Wilse Webb says, most of them will respond, "To rest." According to the "restorative theory of sleep," you burn up energy during the day. Thus, you need to remain quiet for long hours each night to "recharge your batteries." Sleep, then, *restores* your body.

It certainly is true that you often go to bed feeling tired and out of sorts, and wake up the next day feeling much better. It's also the case that, when you're weary, you *feel the need* for sleep—just as you feel the need for food when you're hungry. But does *unconscious sleep* help your body recover more than would "deep rest" in which you stayed peacefully awake? The answer seems to be "no." For scientists have yet to discover any type of restorative process that functions *only* when you are unconscious.

Comparing the Two Theories

Wilse Webb points out there is no way to know which of the two approaches to explaining sleep is correct. Indeed, Webb says, both theories have some validity to them. By making you relatively immobile, sleep does tend to keep you out of harm's way. But it is also more likely you will get your daily "restorative rest" if you feel a need for sleep—and if you are unconscious while resting.

Question: People spend about one-third of their lives in sleep. But less than two percent of all psychological research is on sleep and dreaming. How many reasons can you think of to explain why scientists have studied "awakeness" so much more than "sleep"?

Sleep Cycles

Sleep is part of your daily activity cycle. But how much you sleep—and when and how deeply you sleep—are determined as much by psychological and social factors as by biological "needs."

Amount of Sleep

Generally speaking, the younger you are, the more you sleep and the deeper your sleep is likely to be. Newborn infants sleep about 16 hours out of 24. This sleep is scattered in six or more short bursts of a few hours each. Newborns sleep as much during the day as at night. During the first year of life, the amount of sleep decreases by two hours or more. By six months of age, 80 percent of the infants in one recent study were "sleeping through the night" and taking short naps during the day. By age two, the child sleeps about 12 hours a day, including about 90 minutes of daytime naps. According to Wilse Webb, the major change during the infant's first two years is a decrease in the *amount of daytime sleep*. This change occurs in almost all infants. Therefore, this developmental sequence probably is controlled primarily by genetic factors.

By adolescence and early adulthood, the amount of daily sleep has dropped to about 8 hours. Wilse Webb found that University of Florida students averaged about 7 hours and 40 minutes of sleep at *night*. In addition, they napped about 25 minutes per day. During the two-week period the students were studied, 84 percent of them took at least one nap and about 42 percent napped daily or almost every day. There was considerable variation, however. Some students averaged but 6 hours per day; others got as much as 10 hours of sleep per 24-hour period. And almost all the students slept more on weekends than during the week.

Older people tend to sleep less deeply than do infants or young adults. By 40 or 50 years of age, people wake up more frequently during the night. And by age 60, almost everyone naps on a regular basis. A recent study of 77-year-old men and women suggests these older individuals nap (on the average) twice a day and get about 10 percent of the daily sleep during the day.

These data, however, are for people in the US living in more-or-less normal circumstances. In other countries, a nap or "siesta" is part of the daily routine for people of all ages. And in the US, people in institutions, individuals who work at night, and persons who are sick or experiencing other unusual situations will often show quite different sleep patterns, no matter what their age.

Sleep Stages

As Wilse Webb puts it, "Sleep is not simply a 'turning off' or 'going flat' or a 'nothingness' in

which we lie awash. It is a very busy and active state of affairs." In fact, there are five different stages of sleep (see Fig. 3.1), each marked by its own pattern of brain waves that can be measured with an EEG machine. If you are an average sleeper, your cycle will go something like this:

Stage 0 Sleep

When you first try to fall asleep, your muscles will relax, and your breathing will slow and become quite regular. Your brain waves slow down a bit too, with alpha waves predominating (see Fig. 3.2). This period is called *Stage 0 sleep*, or "pre-sleep." Stage 0 sleep is little more than a transition from being awake to being asleep. According to Wilse Webb, you spend from 0 to 3 percent of a night's sleep in Stage 0.

Stage 1 Sleep

For the next few minutes, as you relax more deeply, you will be in *Stage 1* of the sleep cycle. Alpha waves disappear and your brain waves show irregular patterns. The disappearance of the alpha rhythm marks the real start of sleep. You spend from 1 to 10 percent of a night's sleep in Stage 1 sleep.

Stage 2 Sleep

It is during this stage that your brain shows **sleep spindles** (see Fig. 3.2), which are bursts of waves that occur about 13–16 times per second. According to Webb, you spend from 40 to 60 percent of a night's sleep in Stage 2.

Stage 3 Sleep

Stage 3 sleep is a brief transition period, during which your brain waves slow down even more and sleep spindles tend to disappear. The slow waves that characterize deep sleep also begin to appear. From 3 to 12 percent of sleep generally occurs at the Stage 3 level.

Stage 4 Sleep

Then, about 40–60 minutes after you lose consciousness, you will have reached the deep-

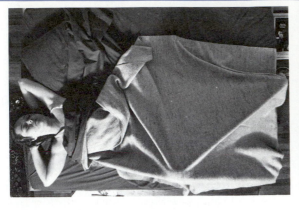

Fig. 3.1A In first of normal sleep's four stages, small, fast brain waves appear on EEG record (below sleeper).

Spindle

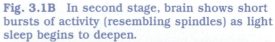

Fig. 3.1B In second stage, brain shows short bursts of activity (resembling spindles) as light sleep begins to deepen.

Fig. 3.1C In the third stage, larger, slower brain waves appear as the half-hour descent to deep sleep continues.

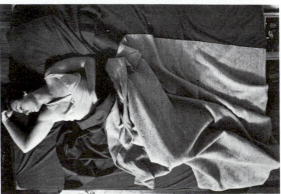

Fig. 3.1D Fourth stage, with large delta waves, is followed by ascent to lighter sleep, then to dreaming (REM sleep).

EEG
Awake-like activation

EOG
Rapid eye movements

EMG
Muscle tone absent

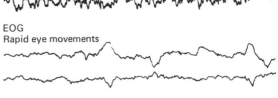

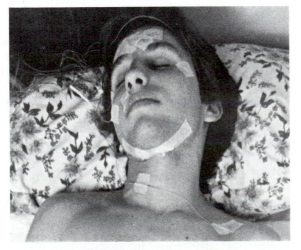

Fig. 3.1E In Stage 1-REM sleep, when dreams take place, a volunteer's polygraph shows brain waves similar to waking state (top row), intense rapid eye movement (middle), and virtually no activity of chin muscles (bottom).

est sleep of all. Your brain will show *delta waves*, and it will be very difficult for anyone to awaken you. This is *Stage 4* sleep, and it is during this stage that sleeptalking, sleepwalking, nightmares, and (in young children) bedwetting occur. Webb states that from 5 to 25 percent of your night's sleep is at Stage 4.

Stage 1-REM Sleep

You may think that you stay at this deep fourth stage all the rest of the night, but that turns out not to be the case. Instead, about 80 minutes after you fall into slumber, your activity cycle will increase slightly. The delta waves will disappear, to be replaced by the *beta waves* that signal an active or "awake" brain. Your eyes will begin to dart around under your closed eyelids as if you were looking at something occurring in front of you. This period of *Rapid Eye Movements* is called **REM** sleep. During the first sleep cycle, REM sleep usually lasts from 8 to 15 minutes. In subsequent cycles, REM sleep may last for 40 minutes or more. Overall, you spend from 15 to 35 percent of the night in REM sleep.

The description we've just given is for the first sleep cycle, which usually lasts about 90

Stages of Sleep

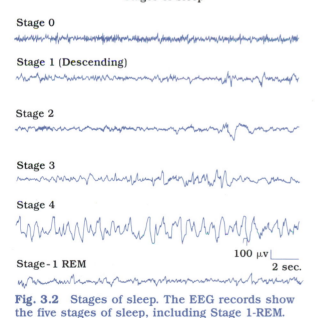

Stage 0

Stage 1 (Descending)

Stage 2

Stage 3

Stage 4

100 μv
2 sec.

Stage-1 REM

Fig. 3.2 Stages of sleep. The EEG records show the five stages of sleep, including Stage 1-REM. The brain-wave activity during Stage 0 is similar to the "activity rhythm" (beta waves) present when you are awake and conscious.

REM. Rapid eye movement sleep that occurs toward the end of each 90-minute sleep cycle. It is during this period that most dreaming seems to occur.

minutes. Occasionally (particularly if you are older) you may wake up briefly during the transition between Stage 4 and Stage 1-REM sleep. But if you don't awaken, your brain waves will slow again. If this is your first cycle of the night, you probably will slip down all the way to Stage 4 sleep once more. Later in the evening, you may go only as deep as Stage 2 or 3. Whatever the case, in the later stages of each subsequent cycle, your brain waves will speed up and you will go through another REM period.

If you are like most people, you will experience four to five complete sleep cycles per night. But both the quality and the intensity of the experiences change, the longer you stay asleep (see Fig. 3.3). Your first cycle usually yields the longest period of Stage 4 deep sleep, while your first Stage 1-REM period is typically the shortest.

According to Wilse Webb, "It is rare, once sleep has begun and is not interrupted, that a stage is 'skipped,' for instance, from 1 to 4 or 4 to 2. REM typically emerges from Stage 2."

REM Sleep

Your eyes do not move constantly during REM sleep. Rather, as Webb notes, eye movements "tend to occur in 'bursts' of different 'densities' (eye movements per minute), with as much as five minutes between such bursts." However, there is much individual variation in such matters. Generally speaking, people who don't recall their dreams very well tend to have fewer eye movements per unit of time than do those who recall their dreams readily.

At the onset of Stage 1-REM sleep, most males experience an erection of the penis, and most females experience vaginal swelling and sometimes a hardening of their nipples. This sexual arousal typically occurs at the onset of each Stage 1-REM sleep period.

Dreams, in one form or another, tend to occur throughout the sleep period. The way we know this is by waking people up at different points in the sleep cycle and asking them if they were dreaming. Generally speaking, most *organized* and *detailed* dreams occur during REM sleep. However, the connection between dreaming and REM sleep depends on how you define *dreaming*. After looking over several experi-

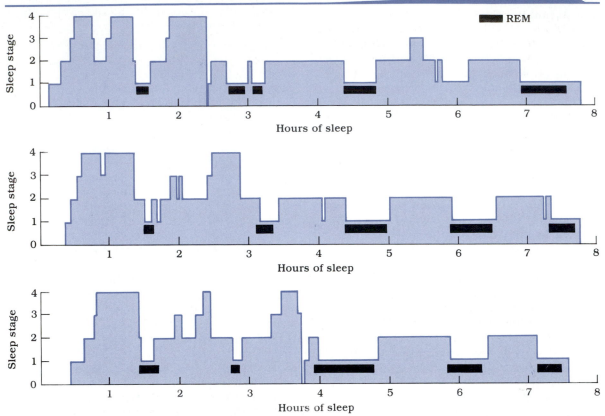

Fig. 3.3 The sleep record of one subject tested for three nights by Wilse Webb at the University of Florida. The first night, the subject had some difficulty adjusting to sleeping in the laboratory. Note that the REM periods increase significantly in length in the later sleep cycles of each night. In a good night's sleep, wakefulness gives way to deep sleep, then to the REM stage where most dreams occur. As the night wears on, dreams tend to lengthen.

ments in which subjects were awakened at various times, Webb concludes that "if one required the dream to be a clearly present, visual, storylike event, then almost all such 'dreams' occurred with REM awakenings." However, Webb says, "If one accepted the presence of any mental content—'thinking about something' or a brief or vague recall of 'something' . . ." then *dreaming* occurs during all stages of sleep. Webb states that REM dreams produce more of what we tend to think of as dreams—visual, hallucinatory-type events. Non-REM awakenings produce more "thoughtlike" and realistic material.

Dreaming seems to be primarily a function of the right hemisphere. Scientists from several laboratories have found that the right half of the brain is much more active electrically during dreaming than is the left. And Roger Sperry notes that while many of his split-brain pa-

tients reported having vivid dreams prior to the surgery, they reported no dreams at all after the operation. However, patients in other laboratories have given different reports, so the question is still in some doubt. It does seem possible, though, that the right hemisphere takes the lead during dreaming.

Question: Why might you have trouble consciously remembering your dreams unless you say the dream out loud as soon as you awaken? And when you first awaken in the morning, why might you have difficulty "talking sensibly and getting your act together" for a short period of time?

Dream "Paralysis"

During REM sleep and dreaming, you are almost incapable of moving. The muscles in

your body are relaxed but capable of movement during both light and deep sleep. However, as you slip into REM sleep, most of the **voluntary muscles** in your body become *paralyzed*. Although your brain often sends orders to your muscles telling them to move, they simply don't respond. In more technical terms—as we will see later in this chapter—we can say that REM sleep is accompanied by extensive *muscular inhibition*.

No one knows why this muscular inhibition takes place during REM sleep, but many scientists speculate that it serves to keep you from acting out your dreams. At least that is what Adrian Morrison at the University of Pennsylvania reported to be true of cats in an article in *Scientific American* in April 1983. Morrison destroyed a very small amount of tissue in one of the lower brain centers of his animals. While awake, the cats behaved normally. When a REM period occurred during their sleep, though, the animals raised their heads, moved about, and struck out at imaginary objects. Morrison believes that the lower brain center he destroyed *actively inhibits* the acting out of dream behavior in normal animals.

Effects of Sleep Deprivation

You can go for many days without sleep—if circumstances force you to stay awake. But eventually your body will force you to drift off into slumber. Missing one night's sleep causes little change in your behavior. However, if you stay awake for more than 48 hours, you will probably begin to show an increased irritability and impulsiveness. Your decision-making processes will be affected, and you will react more slowly and make poorer intellectual judgments than you would when rested.

If you are deprived of sleep for 100 hours or more, you will very likely show considerable stress. You may experience "moments of confusion," lose your train of thought, become momentarily irritated, feel "spacy," or become quite **apathetic**. You may "misperceive" what is going on around you, become inattentive, and show bursts of anger. A few people—perhaps 5 to 10 percent of those tested in several studies—show panic behaviors or symptoms of some type of mental disorder. The surprising thing is, however, that most individuals can tolerate long periods of total sleep deprivation with so little change in performance.

Whenever you are allowed to sleep after being severely deprived, your cycles may change to include much *more* Stage 4 (deep) sleep than

usual—and a good deal *less* REM sleep than than usual. However, several studies suggest that you are unlikely to sleep for more than 11–16 hours, even after you've been kept awake for 10 days straight.

The record for sleep deprivation seems to be held by a 17-year-old San Diego man. In 1966, he stayed awake for 11 days and nights (264 hours) in an attempt to set a record. When he finally went to bed, he slept but 14 hours, and needed no more than 8 hours a night thereafter.

REM-Sleep Deprivation

Several researchers have attempted to deprive human subjects of REM sleep by waking the subjects up each time REM sleep occurred. These subjects were allowed all the Stage 2, 3, and 4 sleep they needed. But whenever the subjects cycled up to Stage 1-REM, they were awakened. A few experimenters reported their subjects soon became cross, anxious, and showed some signs of mental disturbance. However, most recent studies show little or no evidence of these kinds of symptoms. What *is* true, though, is that when REM-deprived subjects are allowed to sleep normally, they show what is called a **rebound effect**. That is, they show a great increase in Stage 1-REM sleep, and a marked decrease in Stage 4 deep sleep, for a night or two thereafter.

Wilse Webb calls sleep a "gentle tyrant," and this tyrant struggles to assert its rights. We can go for long periods of sleeplessness without experiencing any real physical or mental damage. But sleep is not just a "bad habit" that we can break if we wish to. As Webb puts it, "Sleep cannot be ignored or lost without worry or care. Sleep is a fundamental, built-in way of behavior. It is not something we can choose to do or choose not to do," except for short periods of time. We simply aren't at our best when we're sleep-deprived to any great extent.

Sleep Disorders

There are a number of different types of *sleep disorders*. These include such things as involuntary falling asleep, the inability to get to sleep in the first place, the inability to stay asleep for very long, and walking and talking while asleep. Let's look at these problems in some detail.

Narcolepsy

Suppose you were sitting in a chair after lunch, listening to a friend tell a very funny joke. At the "punch line," of course, you laughed loudly. And just as you did so, you fell asleep involuntarily and stayed asleep for several minutes. How would you explain this odd behavior?

The best explanation would be that you had just experienced an attack of **narcolepsy**, or a "sleep attack." This rare condition seems to be inherited and affects 2–5 people per 1,000.

Narcolepsy can strike at any time. Usually, the person with this problem can "ward off" the attacks in dangerous situations—but not always. The attacks typically occur one or more times per day, and are often set off by strong emotions such as anger or laughter. Fatigue or a heavy meal can also increase the chances that an attack will occur.

During a "sleep attack," the person will often experience the sort of paralysis that shows up during REM sleep. And about half the time, the individual will have vivid visual or auditory hallucinations at the onset of the attack. These facts become understandable if you realize that narcoleptic attacks almost always involve Stage 1-REM sleep rather than Stage 4 deep sleep.

Narcolepsy is *not* a form of epilepsy, since the EEG record shows the normal Stage 1-REM sleep pattern during an attack. Nor are there any known personality traits that are associated with narcolepsy. Drugs that suppress REM sleep are sometimes of considerable help to narcoleptic patients.

In his 1983 article, Adrian Morrison states that narcolepsy may be related to the "muscle paralysis" that accompanies REM sleep. Morrison notes that sudden excitation often is followed almost immediately by certain types of muscular inhibition. For example, when you are walking across a street and see a car bearing down on you, you may experience indecision or even "freeze" for a fraction of a second before jumping out of the way. Morrison believes people who suffer from narcolepsy have a very low "paralysis threshold." Thus, they are much more likely to slip into Stage 1-REM sleep (or some other type of paralysis) any time they are aroused.

Insomnia

People who suffer from narcolepsy have trouble staying awake. Individuals who experience **insomnia** have the opposite problem. According to Wilse Webb, *insomnia* is "a summary term for all real and imagined failures of the sleep process." The word "imagined" is important for, as Webb notes, some people who claim to be insomniacs in fact show normal sleep when tested in the laboratory.

There are four main types of *real* insomnia:

1. Sleep-onset insomnia, in which the person cannot get to sleep in the first place.
2. Sleep-awakening insomnia, in which the person goes to sleep normally, then wakes up five or more times per night and spends at least 30 minutes awake during the night (while trying to go back to sleep).
3. Early-termination insomnia, in which the person wakes up after less than 6 hours of sleep and can't return to sleep at all.
4. Light-sleep insomnia, which is characterized by excessive amounts of Stage 1-REM sleep and/or greatly reduced amounts of Stage 4 "deep sleep."

About one person in seven suffers from insomnia fairly often. But at least half the population have "troubled sleep" on occasion. Generally speaking, older women tend to complain about the problem more than any other group. There are now numerous sleep clinics around the country that deal with insomnia and related sleep disorders with varying degrees of success. What we can say with some confidence is that—except in fairly rare cases—sleeping pills are not a long-term solution to "the insomnia problem."

Question: Since sleep is a "gentle tyrant," you eventually get what sleep you really need. Why does this fact suggest that the *psychological discomfort* of insomnia is more important than the *physical effects*?

Sleepwalking

Until the 1960's, sleepwalking was considered either a personality disorder of some kind or an "acting out of dreams." Recent research suggests there is little connection between personality problems and sleepwalking, however. It does seem to "run in families," however, and is associated with other deep-sleep disturbances, such as night terrors, sleeptalking, and (to some extent) bedwetting.

Sleepwalking almost always occurs during Stage 4 deep sleep, and almost never during Stage 1-REM sleep. Since almost all well-formed dreams occur during REM periods, we can be reasonably sure that the sleepwalker is not merely acting out a dream. And since the voluntary muscles are paralyzed during REM sleep—but not during deep sleep—we can be sure that most sleepwalking occurs during Stage 4 and not during Stage 1.

Movements during sleepwalking tend to be of the "automatic" or "ritualistic" type. The person may get up, go to the door, get partially dressed, go to the kitchen and get out some pots and pans, or even get in the car and finish out the night's sleep there. The sleepwalker is usually quite insensitive to the outside world and is hard to awaken. The person usually can't remember the episode the next day.

Children—particularly those between 9 and 12 years of age—tend to sleepwalk more than do adults. And the problem seems to be more common than originally was thought to be the case. In one recent survey, almost 20 percent of the people questioned could recall one or more sleepwalking episodes.

Sleeptalking

Although there are many old beliefs that people who talk in their sleep tend to "tell secrets," the truth is quite different. Some 90 percent of sleeptalk occurs during dream-free sleep and is marked by rather unemotional and "situation-bound" discussions. The 10 percent or so of sleeptalk that occurs during dream sleep is more emotional and usually relates to the "dream in progress."

Generally speaking, most sleeptalk occurs during Stage 0 or dreamless Stage 1 sleep. Thus the "talker" is really more awake than asleep—which explains why the person can respond to questions. There is no indication that sleeptalking is related to any personality traits or disorders.

Bedwetting

Bedwetting is one of the most common types of sleep disorders. In a large sample of children aged 4 to 14, some 29 percent reported recent episodes of bedwetting. The problem is more common in younger children than in older ones. But a recent survey suggests 1 percent of the 14-year-olds still wet the bed with some frequency. Boys are significantly more likely to experience the problem than are girls.

Narcolepsy (NARK-oh-LEP-see). From the Greek words *narke*, meaning "sleep" or "unconscious," and *lepsis*, meaning "seizure." The word "narcotic" comes from the same Greek source.

Insomnia (in-SOM-knee-ah). From Latin and Greek words meaning "sleeplessness." The most common type of sleep disorder.

Bedwetting tends to occur during non-REM sleep, and often happens during Stage 4 deep sleep. It may occur for many reasons, including stress, physical problems, and poor training. The behavior therapies (see Chapter 14) are often of some help in solving the problem.

Question: Why can we be reasonably sure that neither sleeptalking nor bedwetting would generally occur during REM sleep?

Dreams

People have studied dreams and dreaming since the dawn of time, but it has been only in the last century that we have had the tools to investigate the subject scientifically. The most important tool of all in studying sleep and dreams has turned out to be the EEG machine.

The presence of "brain waves" in animals was discovered by Richard Caton in 1875. But it wasn't until 1930 that a German scientist named Hans Berger developed the first practical EEG machine. Thus, it was Berger who first noted the changes in brain waves that occur during waking and sleep periods. (Alpha waves are still sometimes called the *Berger rhythm* in his honor.) Before Berger's pioneering studies, all we could do was to ask people to give us their *subjective* impressions about their sleep experiences. Thanks to the *objective* data we have gotten from EEG records, we have learned more about sleep in the past 50 years than we did in the previous 50,000.

The Dream Cycle

We've always known that sleeping people dream, but we didn't know much about the frequency of dreaming until the early 1950's. Prior to that time, scientists could do little more than record what people remembered about their dreams. Some people insisted they never dreamt at all; other individuals were confident that they dreamed the whole night long. We now know, however, that everyone dreams *several times a night*, during each sleep cycle. For in

An artist's reconstruction of a night terror.

1953 Nathaniel Kleitman and Eugene Aserinsky discovered the connection between REM sleep and dreaming by waking up their subjects at various times during the sleep cycle.

If Kleitman and Aserinsky woke up their subjects during deep sleep (Stages 3 and 4), the subjects seldom reported they were dreaming. However, if the subjects were awakened during Stage 1, or particularly during REM sleep, the subjects frequently stated they had been dreaming and could almost always describe what they had just dreamed.

Dream Frequency

According to Kleitman (and most other authorities), you usually have several dreams within each REM period. Each dream probably runs from a few seconds to several minutes in length. And since REM periods at the beginning of your sleep tend to be the shortest, you probably dream less in the early evening than later on.

Dream Content

If you are like most people, your first dreams of the night will tend to be rather dull and trivial—mostly having to do with things you have done during the day. In later REM periods, however, your dreams will probably become more unusual, vivid, colorful, easier to remember, and sometimes more anxiety-provoking. During any one REM period, you are likely to experience a *sequence of related dreams*, or to run through the *same dream two or three times*. Mostly, though, you will dream about things that are of some interest or importance to you.

Lucid Dreaming

Most people state they have little conscious control over what happens in their dreams. In recent years, however, psychologists have reported a number of techniques by which some individuals seem to be able to influence both the content and the outcome of their dreams. And other scientists have developed ways of helping people maintain "conscious awareness" that they are dreaming, even while the dream is taking place.

As an example of how you can "control the destiny of your dreams," consider a recent report by Rosalind Cartwright. She claims that, by holding discussions with people before they went to sleep, she was able to train people to influence the outcome of their dreams. Apparently, when some individuals "want" their dreams to have happy endings, their brain (probably the right hemisphere) often obliges.

The act of maintaining some low level of consciousness during REM periods is often called *lucid dreaming*. According to Stanford psychologist Stephen P. La Berge, lucid dreaming is most likely to occur during the last dream cycles of the night. La Berge states that, during a lucid dream, you are aware that your "experiences" are dreams rather than reality, and you can remember the dream quite well after you have wakened. Sometimes you can even evaluate what is happening during the dream, and take an active role in resolving the conflict that occurs in a lucid dream.

If you could control the content of your dreams, you'd probably make them pleasant experiences. However, the most vivid (and disturbing) type of dream you are likely to have is one that you seldom have much influence over—the *night terror*. Let us now examine these terrifying dreams in some detail.

Question: How might the differing abilities of the two hemispheres help explain lucid dreaming—that is, the fact that one part of your mind can be dreaming while another is aware that a dream is taking place?

Night Terrors

Imagine yourself comfortably sleeping in your bed, unaware of everything around you. Then you begin to sense—deep down inside you—that something has gone very wrong. Slowly, almost dimly, you regain enough consciousness to realize that you are suffocating, that some heavy weight is lying on your chest and crushing your lungs. Suddenly you realize your breathing has almost stopped, and you are dying for air. Terrified, you scream! At once, you seem to awaken. There is this *thing* hovering over you, crushing the very life out of your lungs. You shout at the *thing*, but it won't leave you alone.

Despite a strange feeling of paralysis, you start to resist. Your pulse begins to race, your breathing becomes rapid, and you push futilely at the *thing* that is choking you to death. Your legs tremble, then begin to thrash about under the covers. You sweep the bedclothes aside, stumble to your feet, and flee into the darkness. You run clumsily through the house, trying to get away from the *thing*.

And then, all at once, you find yourself in your living room. The lights come on, the *thing* instantly retreats to the shadows of your mind, and you are awake. You are safe now, but you are intensely wrought up and disturbed. You shake your head, wondering what has happened to you. You can remember that you were fleeing from the *thing* that was crushing you. But you have forgotten your scream and talking in your sleep.

Stage 4 Night Terror

The *thing* dream is a classic example of a *night terror*. According to Anthony Kales, a scientist at the Penn State Medical School, night terrors occur to but one person in several hundred. However, if someone else in your family has a history of night terrors, you are 10 times more likely to experience night terrors than would ordinarily be the case.

Unlike most other dreams, the night terror begins during Stage 4 (deep) sleep and *not* during a REM period. According to a 1982 report by Vanderbilt psychologists Charles Carlson and David White, night terrors are a "nighttime disorder of arousal" that are often stress-related. Night terrors can also be triggered off by highly emotional environmental events, and by antidepressant drugs.

Night terrors are more frequent in children than in adults. They are almost always associated with sleepwalking, sleeptalking, and other types of sleep disorders. In a recent study by Charles Fisher and his colleagues at Mount Sinai Medical Center in New York, some 58 percent of the subjects who suffered from night terrors could remember part of what they experienced during the attack. The dream episodes included such things as being crushed, being enclosed, being abandoned, choking, dying, falling, and aggressive acts by others. Their sleeptalk typically matched the content of the dream. However, the subjects seldom remembered the extensive sleeptalking and screaming that characteristically appeared at the start of the attack.

Night terrors can be dangerous. In the August 1983 *Journal of Nervous and Mental Disease*, Ernest Hartmann reports the case history of a man who experienced a night terror while sleeping in his car by the side of a major highway. The man "sleep-drove" his car onto the highway and crashed into another automobile, killing three people. Hartmann admits this is an extreme case, but believes that night terrors are always a *potentially* dangerous experience for those few people who experience them (and for others who are around when the attack occurs).

There are several reports in the literature suggesting that psychotherapy, behavior therapy, and use of tranquilizing drugs can be effective in reducing both the number and the severity of *night terror* attacks.

Anxiety REM Nightmare

Much more common than the night terror is the *anxiety nightmare*, which typically occurs

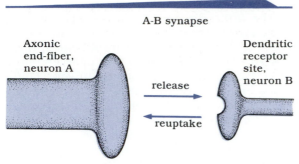

Fig. 3.4 Chemical transmitters released by axonic end-fibers of neuron *A* find a receptor site on the dendrites (or cell body) of neuron *B*, causing *B* to fire. The transmitters then break up, and the pieces are taken up by *A* and put together again.

late in the sleep cycle at the end of a very long REM period. If you have an anxiety nightmare, your body will seldom be aroused to a panic state. In fact, there will really be little change in your body's *biological responses* during the nightmare. It is, therefore, the *psychological content* of the dream itself (being chased, falling, witnessing frightening events) that leads to the anxiety attack.

Anxiety nightmares are most frequent when your psychological need for *REM sleep* is greatest. In his book *The Sleeping Pill*, Ernest Hartmann notes that various illnesses and high fevers often reduce the amount of REM sleep you experience. So do sleeping pills. Thus, anxiety nightmares often occur when you are recovering from sickness, or just after you have stopped taking sleeping pills. Hartmann warns that taking drugs to help you sleep can be dangerous. For once you stop using the drug, your REM sleep "rebounds" and you may have almost constant anxiety nightmares for several nights in a row. You may then return to the pills—not to put yourself to sleep, but to reduce your REM periods and hence get rid of all those disturbing anxiety nightmares.

Sleep and dreams are altered states of consciousness that most of us experience every evening. Now that we have talked about them at some length, suppose we look at some other types of altered awareness and then try to determine what *causes* your conscious awareness to shift from one state to another.

Question: A common anxiety nightmare is that of "running through molasses"—trying to escape something terrible, but not being able to move. What happens to your muscles during REM sleep that might help explain the commonness of this type of anxiety nightmare?

Altered States of Consciousness

Psychologists generally assume that everything you feel or experience is reflected by the functioning of your body—particularly by the way in which your nervous system reacts. When your brain is alert (beta waves), you are consciously alert. When your brain sleeps (delta waves), you become almost totally unconscious. And when your brain waves speed up during sleep, you quite frequently dream. If your nerve cells fire at a faster-than-normal rate, you may experience great anxiety, fear, or pain—or great pleasure. If your neurons fire more slowly than usual, you may feel relaxed, peaceful, dreamy—or even mildly "down" and a bit depressed.

In short, when some change occurs in the *speed* at which your brain takes in and processes information, there is usually some corresponding change (1) in the way that you think and feel about yourself, and (2) in how pleasant or unpleasant you perceive the world around you to be.

Direct and Indirect Methods of Altering Consciousness

Drugs are a *direct* method of speeding up or slowing down neural firing—a quick if sometimes deadly way that people have chosen for a great many centuries. When we look at the effects of drugs on human behavior in just a moment, we will find there is a chemical compound that can affect your brain almost any way you wish—*but usually at a cost of some kind*. However, before we can discuss the rather abnormal brain states that drugs can bring about, we first must delve a little more deeply into the manner in which your brain functions under more normal conditions.

The Molecules of the Mind

From a biochemical standpoint, your whole body is little more than a bag of complex molecules kept in place by your skin and skeleton. You take in such molecules as oxygen and food. Then you digest or "process" them, and return the molecules in altered form back to the environment as waste products. If you don't get enough of the right kinds of chemical inputs, or get too much of the wrong kinds, you die.

The cells in your body are bags of chemicals too, kept together by a cellular "skin" or membrane. Your cells take in oxygen and food from your blood and excrete wastes back into the blood. The neurons in your brain are highly specialized in the way that they function, but primarily they are *cells* that keep alive by maintaining a delicate balance between the chemicals inside the membrane and the chemicals that must remain outside if the neuron is to survive. But neurons do more than excrete waste products—they **secrete** very complex substances that affect everything that happens in your brain.

As you know from reading Chapter 2, when a neuron fires, a wave of electrical energy sweeps down the axon. This *action potential* generally does little in and of itself, except to cause the neuron to *secrete more molecules.*

Nerve cell *A* usually cannot stimulate nerve cell *B* by shocking it *electrically*. Rather *A* must stimulate *B* *chemically*—by releasing neural transmitters into the synaptic cleft between *A* and *B*. The more frequently that neuron *A* fires, the more neurotransmitter molecules it launches into the synaptic cleft. And the more neurotransmitter molecules there are in the *A-B* synaptic cleft, the more likely it is that *B* will fire.

Receptor Sites

The dendrites and cell bodies of neurons have tiny **receptor sites** that are particularly sensitive to neural transmitters. These "receptor sites" are really *complex molecules* that are embedded in the membrane covering the dendrite or cell body (see Fig. 3.4). As we will see shortly, these molecules form "pockets" into which neurotransmitters fit. If a neurotransmitter from *A* lands on one of the receptor "pockets" on *B*, the neurotransmitter triggers off a chemical reaction that causes *B* to fire. An action potential then pulses down *B*'s axon, causing *B*'s axonic end-fibers to release neurotransmitters at the synapse between *B* and *C*.

If a neurotransmitter molecule from neuron *A* doesn't land on a receptor site—*or if the "pockets" are already filled by other molecules*—the transmitter will rapidly break down chemically and lose its effectiveness. And even if the transmitter molecule *does* find a receptor site on *B*, it still will break down quickly—so another transmitter molecule can take its place and cause *B* to fire once more. The broken pieces of the transmitter will, *in either case*, mostly be taken up by *A*'s axon, put together, and used again (see Fig. 3.4).

Secrete (see-KREET). The cells in your body manufacture many types of chemicals that are released or secreted into the blood or onto your skin. Cells in glands at the corners of your eyes secrete tears onto the surface of your eyes.

Receptor sites (re-SEPT-er sights). Only certain small spots or sites on the dendrites or soma seem to be sensitive to the transmitter chemicals. If nerve cell *B* is to be stimulated into firing by nerve cell *A*, the transmitter molecules must cross the synaptic space and reach one of these receptor sites.

Of course, you are not directly aware of all the chemical activity that goes on inside your brain. Yet it is exactly true that you cannot lift a finger, see a sunset, solve a problem, or even remember your own name unless these transmitter substances in your brain function properly.

"Lock and Key Hypothesis"

Twenty years ago, brain researchers knew of only one or two neurotransmitters. Now, however, we realize there are hundreds of different molecules that can act as neurotransmitters. And even 10 years ago, most scientists believed that a given neuron could secrete just one neurotransmitter. However, recent research suggests strongly that almost all nerve cells produce two or more neurotransmitters. Writing in the July 1982 *Proceedings of the National Academy of Science*, Harvard scientist Victoria Chan-Palay and her colleagues discuss their work on synaptic transmission. They find that most neurons have several different types of transmitter molecules in them at any given point in time.

Just as there are many different neurotransmitters, there also are many different kinds of receptor sites. We presently believe that only one general class of transmitter molecule will "fit into" a given receptor site. When a molecule of the right size and shape from *A* lands on the proper receptor site on neuron *B*, the transmitter "unlocks" *B* and causes *B* to fire. A molecule of the wrong shape can't "unlock" *B*—just as a key of the wrong shape can't unlock your front door (see Fig. 3.5).

The belief that *specific transmitters* will fit only into *specific receptor sites* is called the *lock and key hypothesis* of synaptic transmission. As we will see, this hypothesis helps explain why various drugs can affect *highly specific parts of the brain.*

Finally, this brief discussion of the "lock and key hypothesis" should illustrate one important fact: We are gathering new information about the nervous system at an explosive rate of

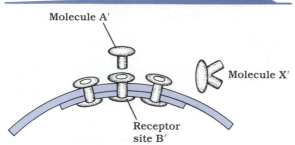

Fig. 3.5 The "lock-key" hypothesis states that a transmitter molecule (the "key") must be the right size and shape to fit into a given receptor site (the "lock") on neuron B. In this drawing, molecule A fits receptor site B and thus can "unlock" neuron B and cause it to fire. Molecule X, however, has the wrong shape and thus cannot "unlock" neuron B.

speed. Thus, we may well take a substantially different view of neural functioning in the 1990's than is presented in these pages. As you read this book, therefore, please remember that *everything you learn* is "subject to revision" as further data come from the laboratory.

Function of the Synapse

The neurons in your cortex are so incredibly tiny that 20,000 of them could fit on the head of a pin. The synaptic cleft *between* neurons is much smaller yet. Indeed, several transmitter molecules placed one atop the other are enough to bridge the gap between most neurons.

The major purpose of the synapse seems to be this—it helps control the flow of information through your nervous system. With certain minor exceptions, neurons "fire" in just one direction—from the dendrite to the axon. Thus, in the illustration we have been using, A can cause B to fire, and B can cause C to react. But C can't fire B, and B can't fire A.

Information about the world around you enters your body through such sensory receptors as your eyes and ears. Your receptors respond by sending messages to your brain along *input pathways* in your nervous system up to your brain. But to get from your eye to your brain, a visual input must pass along several neurons in A-B-C fashion, crossing many synapses in the process. When you respond to these inputs, messages from your brain flow down *output pathways* in A-B-C fashion, again crossing several synapses before they reach your muscles.

Input and output pathways are one-way streets that carry neural messages in just one direction. The synapses act as "traffic cops" that prevent the messages from going the wrong way.

The *amount* of traffic passing along a neural pathway is determined by the number of transmitter molecules each neuron secretes. Anything that causes your neurons to fire faster—and hence release more neurotransmitters—will increase the number of messages the pathways carry.

Drugs such as marijuana, alcohol, heroin, cocaine, and LSD can influence your brain in a variety of ways. Chiefly, they act by speeding up or slowing down the frequency with which *specific neurons fire*. And as surprising as it may seem, a drug-induced change in the *speed* at which your nerve cells release transmitter molecules may cause a profound change in the subjective *quality* of your conscious experience.

To appreciate why a *quantitative* change in neural firing can bring about a *qualitative* change in your conscious experience, you need to know something about neural *excitation* and *inhibition*.

Excitation and Inhibition

Suppose that, later on today, you are sitting quietly in your chair, reading. Suddenly you get an urge to eat an apple lying on the table beside you. So you decide to reach out and take the apple in your hand. Both the "urge" and the "decision" are communicated from one part of your brain to another by electrochemical means.

The motor centers in your cortex transmit the order "reach for the apple" by sending an output message to the muscles in your arm telling them to get to work. The motor nerves that make synapse with your arm muscles respond by dumping transmitter chemicals into those "neuro-muscular" synapses. These neurotransmitters cause *chemical reactions* in your muscles so they extend and contract in just the right way for your arm to be guided toward the apple.

Now, let's add some complications. Suppose that, just as your hand nears that big red fruit, you notice something that greatly disturbs you. Crouched just behind the apple is a huge, hairy, black spider that you recognize as a tarantula! Suddenly a great many nerve cells in your brain that were sitting back resting will shift into emergency gear. These neurons will begin dumping a great many transmitter chemicals into a great many synapses all over your nervous system!

Your first impulse may be to jerk back your hand as quickly as you can. But any quick movement on your part might disturb the spider and make it jump at you. So what you really should do is to *freeze* for a moment before you slowly retract your hand. (And then maybe you should exit from the scene as gracefully but as rapidly as possible.)

Excitatory and Inhibitory Synapses

At the instant you spotted the spider, your hand was in the process of *reaching out* for the apple. How do you go about explaining to your hand that you've changed your mind, and that it should *freeze*? The problem is, your motor nerves have already dumped a rather large supply of neurotransmitters into their synapses. So how does your brain *recall* those molecules once they've been launched into the synaptic cleft?

Actually, your brain will do three things at once. For each muscle that (when chemically stimulated) will cause your hand to reach out, there is another muscle that will make your hand pull back. So first, your brain will order the "pull-back" muscles to get *excited* and rescue you. Your neurons will obey this first order by releasing neurotransmitters into the synapses that control the "pull-back" muscles.

Second, the motor centers in your cortex will *stop* sending output messages to the "stretch-out" muscles, so that no further neurotransmitters are released into those synaptic canals.

But third, your brain goes one step farther. There are many neurons in your brain that can *inhibit* other nerve cells from firing. Whenever your brain needs to "shut down" neural transmission, it simply orders the inhibitory neurons to do their job.

Pre- and Post-Synaptic Inhibition

How can the *firing* of one neuron *inhibit the firing* of another? We're not entirely sure, but there seem to be two rather distinct types of inhibition. One is called **pre-synaptic** inhibition, because it prevents the axon from *releasing* neurotransmitters into the synapse. The other is called **post-synaptic** inhibition, because it prevents the dendrites and cell bodies from *responding* to neurotransmitters.

Pre-synaptic inhibition is shown in Fig. 3.6. Here, neuron *A* makes synapse with *B*, as usual. As you can see, neurotransmitters released by *A*'s axonic end-fibers cross the *A-B* synapse, find receptor sites on *B*, and cause *B* to fire. However, as Fig. 3.6 shows, if neuron *I* happens to fire, it releases molecules that prevent *A*'s

axon from *releasing* its transmitters. If *A* doesn't release any transmitters, obviously *B* won't become excited and fire. In this figure, *I-A* is an *inhibitory synapse*, while *A-B* is an *excitatory synapse*.

Post-synaptic inhibition is shown in Fig. 3.7. Here, again, *A* releases its excitatory neurotransmitters into the *A-B* synapse. But now neuron *I* releases its inhibitory molecules *directly* into the *A-B* synapse, just as *A* does. The synapse has now become an *A-I-B* synapse. Whether *B* fires at any moment in time depends on whether *A* or *I* happens to release the most neurotransmitters.

In truth, most synapses in the central nervous system are of the *A-I-B* type. That is, any given neuron (*B*) in your brain is likely to receive simultaneous inputs from dozens of *A*s and dozens of *I*s. Whether *B* fires at any given moment depends on the *balance* of excitatory and inhibitory neurotransmitters it receives at that point in time. If there are more excitatory molecules than inhibitory molecules present in the synaptic cleft, *B* will fire. If there are more inhibitory than excitatory molecules present, *B* will be inhibited and won't fire.

Excitation and inhibition are not just chemical events, however. They also exist at the intrapsychic and the social/behavioral level. To show you how changes in your body chemistry can affect both your mind and your behavior, let us explore the subject of *drugs*.

Drugs

A *drug* is usually defined as any substance that can affect the structure or functioning of your body. Actually, that definition doesn't mean very much. Because almost any chemical will have some kind of effect on you—if you take a large enough dose, or take it the wrong way. For instance, water is not usually considered a drug, but if you get too much of it in your lungs, you may drown.

A more useful definition is the one we will use in this book: A drug is any chemical that, when taken in relatively small amounts, *signifi-*

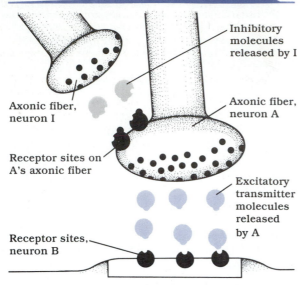

Fig. 3.6 Pre-synaptic inhibition. *A's* released neurotransmitters find receptor sites on *B* and cause *B* to fire. If, however, I happens to fire, it releases molecules that prevent *A's* axon from releasing its transmitters, and thus *B* will not fire.

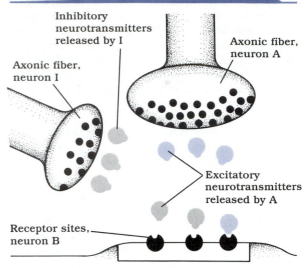

Fig. 3.7 Post-synaptic inhibition. Neurotransmitters released by *A's* axonic fibers find receptor sites on neuron *B* and thus "excite" *B* into firing. But inhibitory neurotransmitters released by neuron I compete for receptor sites on *B* with those released by *A*. I's transmitter molecules inhibit *B* from firing. Whether *B* fires or not depends on the relative number of excitatory or inhibitory molecules that land on *B's* receptor sites.

cantly increases or decreases cellular activities somewhere in your body.

Most of the drugs we will discuss in this chapter have their main effects on neural firing, usually by altering the rate or *speed* at which your nerve cells release synaptic transmitters. There are other ways that drugs can affect neural responses, but changing the rapidity of neural firing is perhaps the most common. Some drugs—such as caffeine—tend to increase the rate at which your neurons fire. Other drugs—such as sleeping pills—have an inhibitory effect on neural firing.

However, the actual effects a particular drug will have on a particular person are often complex and hard to predict. Thus, a drug that affects you one way might affect another person in quite a different manner. And a drug that has a mild effect on you at one time of day may be much more potent at some other point in your daily activity cycle. For example, according to G.G. Luce, *stimulants* are much more dangerous if taken at the height of your daily activity cycle than at the low point. We might assume, therefore, that "morning persons" should particularly avoid stimulants early in the day, while "evening persons" should particularly avoid stimulants at night. (And, since

stimulants are dangerous drugs, the safest course is not to take them at all.)

Thus, in categorizing drugs, we will find it useful to ask three questions:

1. Does the drug have a *specific* or a *general* effect on neural transmission?
2. If the effect is general, does the chemical tend to *increase* or to *inhibit* neural firing?
3. If the effect is specific, does the drug mostly affect inputs, cortical processes, or outputs? That is, *where* in the brain does the drug produce its effects?

Let us begin by looking at drugs that influence almost every one of your nerve cells.

Drugs Affecting General Activity Levels

One of the most common effects a drug can have is to change your activity level. The more active you are physically, the more rapidly *most* of your neurons must fire. Anything that increases your activity level also causes more transmitters to be dumped into the excitatory synapses in your brain and also into the synapses between your motor nerves and your muscles.

"Uppers"

"Uppers," or *psychic energizers*, are drugs that typically facilitate or increase synaptic transmission. "Uppers" therefore usually make you physically and mentally more active. They do this by affecting nerve cells in your **autonomic nervous system**, which controls such involuntary activities as breathing, heart rate, and so forth. We will have more to say about your autonomic nervous system in Chapter 12. For the moment, all you need to know is that psychic energizers *speed up* many of your bodily processes that are controlled by synaptic transmission.

"Uppers" are also called *stimulants*, because they chemically stimulate your neurons into firing more often. As your nerve cells release more transmitters into the synaptic canals, your whole body speeds up its tempo. As a result, any or all of the following responses may occur:

1. Your heart beats more quickly.
2. Your mouth becomes dry.
3. Blood rushes to the surface of your skin.
4. The pupils in your eyes open or *dilate*.

"I'LL HAVE TO GET DR. CURTIS TO REDUCE HIS DOSAGE OF THE MOOD-ELEVATOR."

5. You breathe more rapidly.
6. Your hair stands on end.
7. Your digestion is shut down.
8. Your appetite vanishes.
9. Your urine flow and bowel movements are inhibited.
10. You may become sexually excited if the environment or your own thought processes encourage you to do so.
11. Your muscles become tense, and your reaction times are speeded up.
12. You typically wake up and become alert, but often find it difficult to concentrate.

Caffeine is perhaps the most common "upper" in our society. Less common—and considerably more dangerous—is a class of drugs called by such names as **amphetamines**, or pep pills. Amphetamine itself is often referred to as Benzedrine. Two other similar but more powerful drugs are Dexedrine and Methedrine. Since they all increase neural activity, any or all of these "uppers" can be referred to as *speed*.

Like any other drugs, "uppers" can be dangerous. For example, continued use of amphetamine (or any other type of "speed") can produce symptoms that are much the same as a severe mental disorder called **paranoid schizophrenia**.

"Downers"

Drugs that slow down or inhibit neural activity go by the general name of "downers." The strongest "downers" in general use are the **barbiturates**, which are sometimes called "sleeping pills" because they depress neural activity so much they often put a person to sleep.

The *tranquilizers* are both more specific in their effects and usually less powerful than the

Solomon H. Snyder

barbiturates. Tranquilizers affect the nervous system in several different ways. However, many of them act by exciting those neurons (such as *I* in Fig. 3.6) which *inhibit* other nerve cells from firing.

The general effects of "downers" are the opposite of those produced by "uppers." That is, "downers" slow the beating of your heart, take blood away from the surface of your body, and retard the rate at which you breathe. They also cause your pupils to close or constrict, and generally slow down mental and physical reactions.

"Downers" have physical and psychological side effects that range from mildly unpleasant to downright deadly. Wisely used, these drugs can be of considerable medical help. When abused, these chemicals can lead to depression and other severe types of mental disorders. According to many reports, "downers" are particularly likely to be abused by women.

Drugs Affecting Sensory Input

Information about the world around you comes to you through your sensory receptors. As we will see in Chapter 9, if you were totally cut off from the outside world, you would rapidly stop being a normal human being. But not all of the sensory messages that reach your brain bring pleasant news. Some messages involve the experience of *pain*, a highly complex psychological experience we will discuss more fully in Chapter 16.

In part, pain is a *sensory input* that tells you something has gone wrong with the functioning of your body. Pain commands your attention because "it hurts." And because "it hurts," humans have long made use of various chemicals in order to rid themselves of pain. Some of these drugs—such as aspirin—have their **anal-** **gesic** or pain-killing effects at the site of a wound. Thus, they reduce the number of pain messages that are sent to your brain. Other drugs—particularly those derived from the opium poppy—are analgesic because they inhibit the *processing* of the painful inputs in various neural centers in your brain.

Aspirin is perhaps the most common pain-killing drug known to humans. It is one of the few drugs that almost everyone reading this book will have tried at least once. Aspirin occurs naturally in the bark of the willow tree and was first *synthesized* in 1860. Some 12 million kilograms (27 million pounds) of aspirin are consumed annually in the United States—enough to treat 17 *billion* headaches. As potent a pain-killer as aspirin is, though, it is also a deadly poison that must be treated with respect. Perhaps 20 percent of the deaths by poisoning that occur in the United States each year are due to an overdose of aspirin. And when taken in large doses by a pregnant woman, aspirin may either kill the unborn child or cause the child to be badly deformed.

The Opiates

Aspirin is a mild pain-killer. In case of severe pain, a more potent medicine—such as an **opiate**—is needed. *Opiates* are derived from opium, a drug used for centuries as an analgesic in the Near and Far East. When the seed pods of the opium poppy are slashed, a sticky resin oozes out. This resin is collected by hand, heated and rolled into balls, and then smoked in tiny pipes as opium.

In 1806, **morphine** was first synthesized from opium. Since morphine can be injected directly into the body in controlled amounts, and since it lacks some of the side effects of opium, morphine rapidly gained wide use in medical circles.

No one really knows why the opiates reduce or kill the experience of pain. It seems likely, however, that these drugs stimulate inhibitory neurons, which then "turn off" the synapses in your brain that are involved in processing the painful inputs (see Fig. 3.6 and Fig. 3.7).

The Opioid Peptides

Morphine has one terrible side effect: it is very *addictive*. The exact biological mechanism underlying addiction is still not fully understood. However, there is considerable evidence suggesting that *natural pain-killers* produced by the the body itself may be involved. These naturally-occurring analgesics have many names, including **enkephalin**, **endorphin**, and

opioid peptides. And when you learn how these natural analgesics work, you will understand a bit more about how they may be involved in morphine addiction.

During the 1970's, scientists both in Great Britain and in the United States isolated the first of these natural pain-killers. The name they gave to this opioid peptide was *enkephalin*. We now know there are two slightly different types of enkephalin, and that both are included in the general category of natural pain-killers called "the endorphins." When enkephalin—or any other endorphin—is injected into the body, it appears to reduce pain at least as much as does morphine. However, the effects of the endorphins on both physical and mental processes are complex and—as we will see at the end of this chapter—perhaps a little surprising.

Solomon Snyder and his associates at Johns Hopkins University were among the first to identify enkephalin. Snyder believes the natural pain-killers your body normally produces are sufficient to protect you from many of the ordinary aches and pains of life. When you experience severe pain, however, you are likely to turn to stronger medicine, and morphine is one of the strongest yet available.

Opiate Addiction

If, for medical reasons, you were to take morphine, it would act much as the enkephalins and other endorphins do. That is, morphine (1) would block neural transmission in your pain centers, and (2) would stimulate certain nerve centers involved in experiencing pleasure. But according to Snyder, morphine also *inhibits the production of the endorphins*. So, when you take morphine for any length of time, your body *stops* manufacturing its natural pain-killers almost entirely.

If you use morphine daily for a month or so, you are likely to become **addicted** to the drug. Then, if you don't get your "daily fix," you feel miserable, you ache all over, you are depressed, and you may even experience convulsions. Why? Because, when you stop taking morphine, your body needs several weeks before it can replenish its supply of natural pain-killers. During this period of time, your body has no defense against pain. Thus, even the slightest cut or bruise will be extremely unpleasant. Little wonder, then, that so few morphine addicts voluntarily withdraw from using the drug.

When enkephalin was first discovered, Snyder hoped that it might be useful in treating morphine addiction. After all, if we could find

Analgesic (an-al-GEE-sick). From the Greek words meaning "no pain." Technically speaking, any drug that reduces pain without causing a loss of consciousness.

Opiate (OH-pee-ate or OH-pee-at). Any of the narcotic drugs that come from the opium poppy. Almost all opiates are habit-forming.

Morphine (MORE-feen). A product of opium. Morphine is a dream- or sleep-inducing drug and, like all opiates, is a powerful pain-killer.

Enkephalin (enn-KEFF-uh-linn). A natural pain-killer discovered in the brain by scientists in the United States and Great Britain. There are two known types of enkephalins.

Endorphin (en-DORF-in). The general class of pain-killers produced in the brain. The two enkephalins are both endorphins.

Opioid peptides (OH-pee-oid PEP-tides). Peptides are a specific type of small molecules. The endorphins are all peptides that resemble opiates such as morphine. Thus the endorphins are a class of molecules called opioid peptides.

Addicted. There are at least two types of addiction, biological and psychological. In biological addiction, some "outside" drug (such as morphine) replaces an internal product, such as the endorphins. Thus, the body develops a physical "need" for the replacement chemical. Psychological addiction is a very strong habit not usually marked by a physical need. Most drug addictions have both physical and psychological components.

Withdrawal symptoms. Those physical and psychological changes that accompany giving up a drug after you have become addicted to it. Vomiting, fever, loss of appetite, compulsive shivering, and hallucinations often accompany withdrawal from narcotics such as heroin.

some way to get the body to manufacture large amounts of opioid peptides, we could probably reduce the **withdrawal symptoms** that occur when an addict is cut off from morphine. However, research reported in 1976 by Eddie Wei and Horace Loh suggests that the enkephalins are as addictive as morphine. If this is indeed the case, history will have repeated itself.

Late in the 1800's, scientists hunting for a non-addictive opiate (to replace morphine) stumbled upon *heroin*, which is also made from opium. Heroin is several times more powerful than morphine as a pain-killer. It gets its name from *hero*, because this drug was supposed to be a "heroic" solution to the "morphine problem." So, in the early 1900's, morphine addicts were given heroin instead. Unfortunately, heroin soon proved to be even more addictive and dangerous than morphine. Because of its addictive qualities, heroin is seldom used as an analgesic in the United States today—except by the million or so drug addicts who take it as regularly as their funds allow them to.

Cocaine has become a highly abused drug.

Oakley Ray

Local Anesthetics

Laughing gas, or nitrous oxide, is another example of a pain-killer that once enjoyed great medical popularity but which is not used as much today as it once was. First discovered in 1799, nitrous oxide was employed by dentists and surgeons as an analgesic because it made their patients so "happy" that tooth pulling and minor surgery didn't seem to hurt very much.

The effects of laughing gas were often unpredictable, however, and dentists soon began using **procaine** or Novocain instead. Both procaine and Novocain are synthetic forms of *cocaine* that kill pain by *inhibiting neural transmission* wherever they are injected into the body.

Cocaine is a moderately strong drug made from the leaves of the coca plant. Cocaine, or "coke," is notorious for the rush of pleasure or **euphoria** it gives almost immediately after a person takes it (usually by sniffing). Frequent use of cocaine can lead to a variety of problems, however, including severe damage to the nose and throat.

Cocaine was first used as a local anesthetic in the late 1800's by a Viennese doctor named Carl Koller. Sigmund Freud, who also lived in Vienna, learned of Koller's work and began ex-perimenting with the drug. Freud found it such a pleasurable medication he recommended it to his patients as a substitute for aspirin. When he saw the bad effects cocaine occasionally had, though, he changed his mind.

Americans were much slower to use cocaine "recreationally" than were Europeans. According to a 1979 government report, some 10 million people in the US now use cocaine fairly regularly, and another 5 million people have tried it at least once. In the March 1982 issue of *Scientific American*, Craig Van Dyke and Robert Byck estimate that cocaine sales run more than 30 billion dollars a year in the US alone. These scientists suggest that cocaine is not *physically* addictive, but is severely habit forming. Surprisingly enough, Van Dyke and Byck also report that even experienced users could not tell the difference between sniffing cocaine and sniffing a **placebo**. Van Dyke and Byck believe that the effects of cocaine depend as much on the user's past experiences, expectations, and present environment as on the drug's effects on body chemistry and neural transmission.

Vanderbilt psychologist Oakley Ray takes a different view. In his 1983 book *Drugs, Society, and Human Behavior*, he writes, "It has been known for many years that prolonged high doses of either cocaine or amphetamine produce the same toxic syndrome: enhanced sense of physical and mental capacity, loss of appetite, grinding of teeth . . . repetitious behavior, and paranoia." Ray notes as well that by mid-1981, the National Institute on Drug Abuse put cocaine 12th in drug-related deaths (up from 18th in 1978).

Oakley Ray also points out that alcohol affects the way in which the body reacts both to uppers and downers. Thus, taking these drugs in combination with alcohol is particularly dangerous.

Drugs Affecting Central Processing

Analgesics reduce pain in one of two ways: They either prevent painful inputs from occurring, or they keep the inputs from stimulating the "pain centers" in your brain by inhibiting neural transmission. Which is to say that analgesics "work" because they prevent you from experiencing the world (and your body) as it really exists.

Hallucinogens

The *hallucinogens* are a class of drug that work in quite a different way. Rather than affecting inputs, hallucinogenic drugs act on the central processing areas of the brain that try to "make sense" out of these sensory messages (see Chapter 9). And by speeding up some brain centers and inhibiting others, hallucinogens make you experience or perceive the world as it actually *isn't*. **LSD**, **mescaline**, **psilocybin**, and **PCP** are perhaps the best-known hallucinogens in our society, although a wide variety of other drugs also fall into this category.

LSD

According to Oakley Ray, LSD is an artificial or synthetic chemical not found in nature. It was first made in a Swiss laboratory in 1938. However, its rather profound effects on human behavior were not appreciated until five years later. In 1943 Albert Hofmann—the Swiss scientist who had first synthesized LSD—accidentally licked some of the drug off his fingers. About half an hour later, knowing that something unusual was happening to him, Hofmann decided to stop work and bicycle home from the lab. Wobbling and weaving all the way, he finally made it. But by the time he reached his house, everything he saw looked so terrifying, Hofmann was sure he had gone mad.

Because LSD caused people who took it to experience some of the symptoms associated with schizophrenia, Hofmann believed the drug might be useful in brain research. Therefore, he suggested it be given to people with mental disorders. LSD was first tried with patients in a Swiss mental hospital. And, as is often the case, a few of these patients did seem to get better. Whether this improvement was due to the drug or to the special attention the patients got was never proven, however. Oakley Ray notes that, "The potential value of the hallucinogens in the treatment of many disorders is still very much discussed and studied, and, as with most issues, a final resolution has not yet been reached." However, a 1975 report from the National Institute of Mental Health states that, "Research on the therapeutic use of LSD has shown that it is not a generally useful therapeutic drug."

Procaine (PRO-cane). Like Novocain (NO-voh-cane), a synthetic form of cocaine.

Euphoria (you-FOR-ee-ah). From the Greek word meaning "good feeling," hence a rush of pleasure.

Placebo (pla-SEE-boh). From the Latin words meaning, "I please." A harmless substance, such as a sugar pill. In drug experiments, any neutral or inactive substance given to subjects to make them think they are taking "the real thing."

LSD. Common name for d-lysergic acid di-ethyl-amide (dee-lie-SIR-jick A-sid die-ETH-ill-A-midd). Also called "acid." Synthetic hallucinogen first synthesized in Switzerland.

Mescaline (MESS-ka-lin). An hallucinogen found in the peyote (pay-YO-tee) cactus.

Psilocybin (SILL-oh-SIGH-bin). An hallucinogenic drug that comes from a wild mushroom.

PCP. Common name for phencyclidine (fenn-SIGH-kli-deen). Also called "Angel dust."

Dissociative anesthetic (diss-SOH-see-ah-tive ann-ness-THET-tick). To dissociate means "to pull apart." A dissociative anesthetic is a drug that kills pain by separating the mind from the body.

Mescaline and Psilocybin

Mescaline is a chemical found in buttons on the peyote cactus. It can also be produced in synthetic form in a laboratory. The hallucinogenic effects of mescaline have been known for centuries to American Indians, who at times have eaten peyote buttons as part of their religious ceremonies.

Less well known is a drug called *psilocybin*, found in a mushroom that grows wild in certain parts of the world. Psilocybin also produces hallucinations and also has been used in religious ceremonies.

PCP

PCP, or "Angel Dust," has replaced LSD and mescaline as the most abused hallucinogen in the United States. Discovered in 1956 by Victor Maddox and Graham Chen in Detroit, PCP was used for a time as an anesthetic for both humans and animals. However, it was banned for human use after tests showed that in large doses it produced convulsions, uncontrollable rage, *coma*, and death.

In his 1981 book on PCP, Edward Domino notes that PCP acts as a **dissociative anesthetic**. That is, the drug doesn't make patients unconscious. Rather, it "disconnects" them from their bodies—and from their environments. One male subject who took PCP in an experiment reported his legs were "ten miles long." A female subject said, "I feel like the head of a pin in a completely black atmosphere." Domino believes that PCP inhibits neural activity in the *processing areas* of the brain. And by doing so, it induces psychological symptoms similar to those reported by people suffering from a variety of mental disorders.

One of the greatest dangers of PCP seems to be the *unpredictability* of its effects. Sometimes it causes euphoria, sometimes fear, sometimes rage, sometimes severe depression, and sometimes a complete loss of reality. In 1980, almost 50 percent of the patients admitted to mental hospitals for drug-related problems suffered from PCP **psychosis**. However, as Domino said recently, by 1984 abuse of PCP seemed to be falling off markedly.

Effects of Hallucinogens

No one really knows why the hallucinogens affect people as they do. But according to Edward Domino, hallucinogenic drugs seem to influence neural processing in two important ways. First, they decrease the brain's ability to *screen out* many types of sensory inputs. And second, the drugs seem to disrupt the brain's attempts to *integrate complex stimuli*. Let us look at both effects in more detail.

First, there are parts of your nervous system that allow you to *gate out* unimportant sensory inputs and pay attention only to those sensory messages you wish to focus on. Hallucinogens, however, seem to open up the sensory gates and let almost all inputs come through with equal intensity. People who take LSD or PCP often appear to become confused and frightened by this onslaught of uncontrollable inputs. Terrified by this loss of sensory control, the drug-taker may withdraw from the world in order to try to "make sense out of sensory experience."

Second, people who are "high" on hallucinogens often cannot put complex inputs together to make a *unified experience*. For example, if you have taken LSD, you may not be able to match the sight of a friend's face with the sound of the friend's voice because the hi-fi distracts you. So you end up perceiving your friend as singing instead of talking—or see your friend's face whirling around inside the loudspeaker. This type of experience may be amusing—or terrifying.

Hallucinogens cause little physical damage to the body. Their danger comes from their effects on mental processes and behavior. One of the most frequent problems associated with use of these drugs is that the user "loses control" of his or her flow of thoughts and emotions. This sort of experience is often called a "bad trip." In a recent interview, Albert Hofmann notes that almost everyone who takes LSD has a bad trip now and again. And Edward Domino believes that almost anyone who takes a sufficiently large dose of PCP—or who takes small doses regularly—is likely to need medical or psychological help.

Marijuana

Marijuana is a product of the hemp or **cannabis** plant, a weed found in abundance in many parts of the world. The "active ingredient" in marijuana is a chemical that goes by the complex name of delta-9-trans-tetrahydrocannabinol—which we can gladly abbreviate as **THC**.

As Solomon Snyder points out in his book *Uses of Marijuana*, cannabis has a long and interesting history. A century ago cannabis was almost as commonly used for medicinal purposes as aspirin is today and could be purchased without a prescription in any drug store. Cannabis became illegal in the US in 1937, but scientific evidence suggests that it still might be useful as a medicine. It seems particularly effective against diseases caused by tension and high blood pressure, menstrual bleeding, and glaucoma (a build-up of pressure within the eyeball). But its most important use may be that of helping relieve the nausea that cancer patients often experience when given **chemotherapy**.

Very little is known about how cannabis affects the central nervous sytem, for it is chemically very different from the opiates, from all other known hallucinogens, and from cocaine. In small doses cannabis can produce a pleasant change of mood. In larger amounts it can produce mild hallucinations similar to those brought about by a small dose of LSD or mescaline. In very large doses it can induce vomiting, chills, and fever—as well as the bad-trip "loss of control" caused by hallucinogens.

Is Marijuana Dangerous?

In the spring of 1982, the National Academy of Sciences released a study on the dangers of marijuana. According to this report, there is no evidence that cannabis produces permanent, long-term health effects in humans. But a number of short-term reactions to the drug "justifies serious national concern." The scientists con-

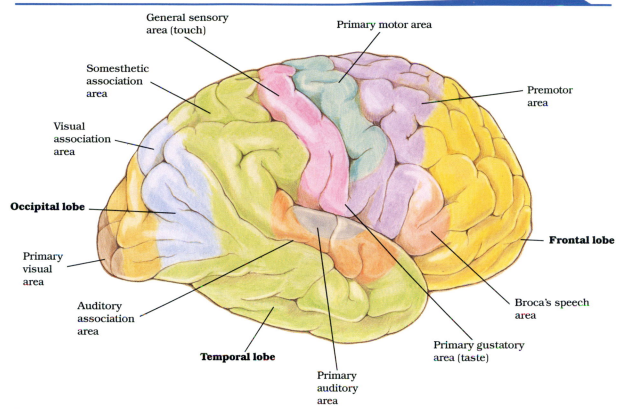

General sensory
area (touch)

Primary motor area

Somesthetic
association
area

Premotor
area

Visual
association
area

Occipital lobe

Frontal lobe

Primary
visual
area

Broca's speech
area

Auditory
association
area

Primary gustatory
area (taste)

Temporal lobe

Primary
auditory
area

Plate 1 Map of the cerebral cortex showing the lobes and some
of the functional areas.

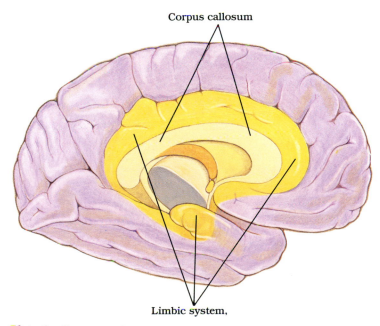

Corpus callosum

Limbic system,

Plate 2 Cross section of the left cerebral hemisphere showing
the limbic system.

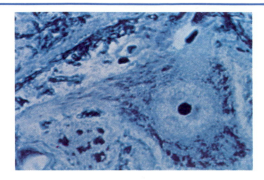

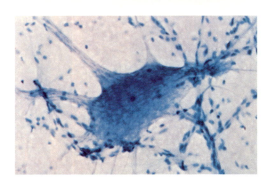

Plate 3 Neurons take many forms in different portions of the nervous system. Above left: the large cell body is a motor neuron (multipolar) from the grey matter in the spinal cord. Above right: A pyramidal neuron in the cerebral cortex. Right: One large multipolar neuron from the myenteric (intestinal) plexus. (from Leeson and Leeson, *Descriptions and Explanations: Practical Histology, A Self-Instructional Laboratory Manual in Filmstrip*, Philadelphia, W.B. Saunders Company, 1973 [right], from Curtis, Jacobson and Marcus: *An Introduction to the Neurosciences* [filmstrip], Philadelphia, W.B. Saunders Company, 1972.)

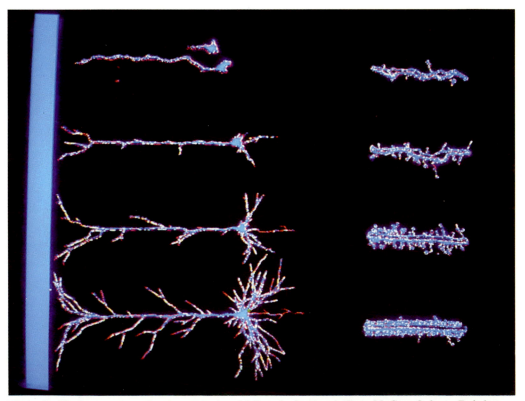

Plate 4 Brain neurons from young to old (top to bottom) (Dan McCoy © from Rainbow. Credit also Scheibel.)

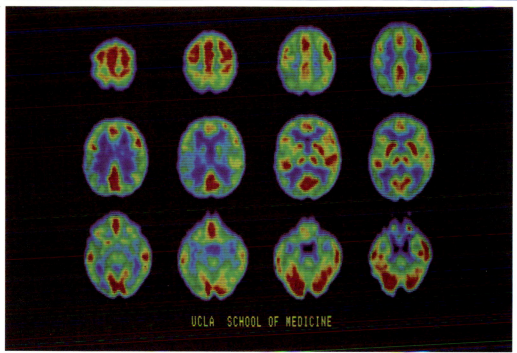

Plate 5 CAT (computer assisted tomography) scan of a normal brain. The red and yellow areas show those parts of the brain that are most active, while the green and blue areas are those that are least active. Had the scan been of a schizophrenic brain, the left half would show much more red and yellow than would the right half. (Courtesy of M.E. Phelps, J.C. Mazziotta, E.J. Hoffman, et al., UCLA School of Medicine, Los Angeles, California.)

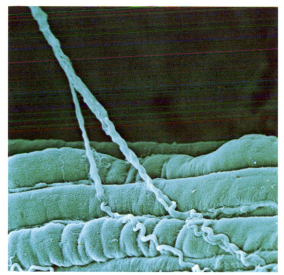

Plate 6 Photograph of the nerve-muscle synapse. Axonic fibers (upper left) reach down to make a synapse with thick muscle fibers. (Photograph by Lennart Nilsson from Behold Man. © 1973 by Albert Bonniers Förlag, Stockholm, published by Little Brown and Company, Boston, 1974.)

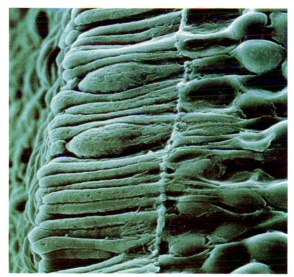

Plate 7 The rods are the slim, pencil-shaped cells on the left of the photograph; the cones are the two fat cells squeezed in between the rods. Light enters the retina from the right; the back of the eye (choroid coat) is to the left in this photograph. (Photograph by Lennart Nilsson from Behold Man. © 1973 by Albert Bonniers Förlag, Stockholm, published by Little Brown and Company, Boston, 1974.)

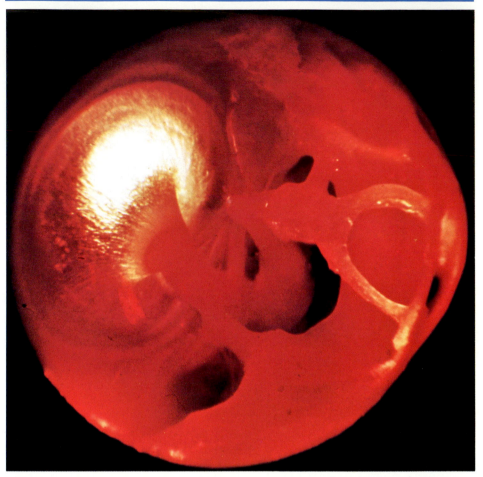

Plate 8 A cross section of the middle ear. The hammer is connected to the eardrum which is the bright spot in the middle of the photograph. The stirrup, seen on the right, is connected to the oval window. The anvil connects the hammer to the stirrup. (Photograph by Lennart Nilsson from Behold Man. © 1973 by Albert Bonniers Förlag, Stockholm, published by Little Brown and Company, Boston, 1974.)

ducting the NAS study state there is no conclusive evidence the drug is addictive, that it leads to use of "harder" drugs, affects the structure of the brain, or causes birth defects. But it does affect motor coordination, short-term memory, oral communication, and may disrupt sperm production in males and ovulation in females—at least on a temporary basis.

All drugs have their dangers. But most of the other "recreational" drugs seem considerably more damaging than is cannabis. Indeed, in 1973 a Presidential Commission on Marijuana and Drug Abuse came to the following conclusions on the subject:

1. Alcoholism is our worst drug problem.
2. Heroin dependence is our second-worst problem.
3. *Legal* use of "downers," particularly by housewives, is our worst "hidden" drug problem.
4. Cannabis use is a minor problem compared with the abuse of alcohol and other drugs.

Drugs Affecting Motor Output

Almost all of the "uppers" and "downers" affect motor outputs as well as sensory inputs and central processing. However, many drugs have their major influence on muscular reactions.

Perhaps the best known of these drugs is **meprobamate**, also called Miltown or Equanil. When meprobamate was first introduced, it was called a "psychic" tranquilizer. Later research indicated it does not affect central processing all that much, but rather increases the output of inhibitory molecules at the neuro-muscular synapses, thus lowering the level of muscular activity.

Alcohol

The April 1983 issue of *American Psychologist* has a number of articles on alcoholism. Alcohol is partially or wholly responsible for more than 100,000 deaths each year, and it is involved in some half of the automobile accidents on American highways. More than half the people in the US who commit murders each year have measurable amounts of alcohol in their blood at the time of the crime. Alcohol abuse costs the US some 50 billion dollars each year in medical care and in time lost from work. At least 25 percent of the admissions to US mental hospitals involve alcohol abuse.

An estimated 5 to 10 percent of the work force suffers from alcoholism. Employees with

Psychosis (sigh-KO-sis). A very severe form of "mental illness" which often requires hospitalization. Schizophrenia is a type of psychosis.

Cannabis (KAN-ah-biss). The common hemp plant, from which come such drugs as marijuana (also spelled marihuana) and hashish. In the Western world, the most widespread species is *cannabis sativa* (SAT-ee-vah), which grows wild in most of the continental US.

THC. An abbreviation for tetra-hydro-cannabinol (TET-trah-HIGH-dro kan-NAB-uh-nol). Marijuana contains many chemicals, of which THC seems the main one that induces a "high." The "street drugs" sold as THC are usually some other substance, since THC loses its powers when exposed to air.

Chemotherapy (KEY-moh-THER-a-pee). Treatment that involves giving a person drugs or other chemicals to help the person get better.

Meprobamate (mepp-pro-BAMM-ate). A drug that acts to relax the muscles.

drinking problems are absent 16 times more often than are non-drinkers. They have an accident rate four times greater, use a third more sickness benefits, and have five times more compensation claims than do other employees. Some 40 percent of industrial fatalities and 47 percent of industrial injuries can be traced to alcohol abuse.

Alcohol affects the brain in many ways, but two effects seem most important. First, alcohol kills nerve cells—but in a highly selective fashion. In the January 30, 1981 issue of *Science*, Charles Golden and his associates report that alcohol tends to destroy brain tissue *primarily in the dominant hemisphere*. The behavioral changes associated with chronic drunkenness tend to support Golden's findings. For example, the slurred speech, the inability to think logically and to plan effectively, and the emotional outbursts shown by many alcoholics all suggest that alcohol disrupts the dominance normally shown by the left hemisphere. Indeed, Golden and his colleagues believe these symptoms result from the right hemisphere's attempts to take over the functions lost through destruction of tissue in the left hemisphere.

Second, alcohol appears to affect the same inhibitory synapses in the brain that are blocked by cocaine and morphine. Consumed in larger amounts, however, alcohol disrupts motor coordination—presumably by making it difficult for the person to inhibit many types of muscle movements.

We will have much more to say about alcoholism (and its treatment) in Chapter 14. At the moment, we will merely note the problems asso-

The Behavioral Alcohol Research Laboratory (BARLAB) is a simulated tavern facility at the University of Washington that is equipped with audio-videotaping and one-way-mirror observation facilities, stereo music system, dim lighting, and full wet bar. G.A. Marlatt and his colleagues use this unique laboratory to study drinking behavior unobtrusively in a naturalistic setting.

"Runner's high" is apparently caused by a massive stress-related release of endorphins.

ciated with alcohol consumption. For a study released early in 1984 by the Institute for Social Research at The University of Michigan shows that consumption of marijuana, PCP, LSD, and heroin is *decreasing* in high-school students. However, consumption of alcohol is still quite high. Almost 6 percent of the teenagers questioned used alcohol daily, almost 70 percent used alcohol at least once a month, and 41 percent said they had consumed five or more drinks at a time during the two weeks before the survey.

Drugs and Mental Processes

For the most part, we take drugs because certain chemical compounds make us feel better than we do without the drugs—or because we *believe* the drugs will make us feel better. And beliefs often can have just as strong an influence on the "drug experience" as does the biochemistry of the drug itself.

For example, in the 1980 book *Advances in Substance Abuse*, G.A. Marlatt and D.J. Rohsenow report that most of the "social effects" of alcohol may be due to people's *expectations* about the drug. Subjects who drank tonic water

but thought it was alcohol showed most of the "classic" symptoms of intoxication, while subjects who drank alcohol but thought it was tonic water failed to get "high." More specifically, men who thought they had consumed alcohol became less anxious in social situations. They also became more aggressive and sexually aroused. Women who consumed tonic water thinking it was alcohol became more anxious in social situations and less aggressive. The women *reported* they became sexually aroused, but physically they actually became less so.

The social setting has a strong influence on how you react to all drugs, including alcohol. According to Marlatt and Rohsenow, solitary drinkers describe the effects of drinking primarily in terms of physical symptoms—they feel dizzy or numb. Drinkers in social situations (who have consumed the same amount of alcohol) tend to say they feel more "outgoing" or "friendly."

Marlatt and Rohsenow also tested alcoholics by giving them tonic water but telling them it was vodka. The alcoholics experienced the same "craving" for more alcohol after drinking the tonic water as they typically did when consuming alcohol. They did *not* report this craving after drinking vodka they thought was just tonic water.

Marlatt and Rohsenow conclude that the setting in which alcohol is consumed and the drinker's expectations are even *more* influential in determining the drinker's reactions than are the physical effects of the alcohol itself. Put another way, the effects your thought patterns have on your body are at least as important as the effects your body has on your mental processes. Indeed, there is now evidence that what you think and feel and do may *change your body chemistry* as much as your body chemistry changes what you think and feel and do.

Question: Some people believe alcoholism is a "disease," and that even one drink will set off a strong *physical* reaction in an alcoholic. Why does the research by Marlatt and Rohsenow cast some doubt on this belief?

Shock, "Getting High," and the Endorphins

Almost all descriptions of "getting high" have two important aspects to them: (1) The person feels no pain; and (2) the person feels detached from his or her body and from ordinary reality. Oddly enough, these experiences may well be like those brought about by great shock—and with the release of massive amounts of the endorphins (and other opioid peptides) inside the brain.

Writing in the December 20, 1980 issue of *The Lancet*, William McDermott of the Harvard Medical School speculates that the onset of intense shock may lead the brain to create an abnormal amount of one or more of the endorphins. The sudden release of all these "natural pain-killers" apparently puts the organism in a **trance state** similar to that occasionally achieved by Eastern mystics. This altered state of consciousness is also akin to the euphoria caused by some drugs, and to the insensitivity to pain associated with hypnosis.

What led McDermott to this conclusion was a passage from the journals of David Livingstone, a noted surgeon who spent many years exploring the wilds of Africa. In the journal, Dr. Livingstone describes what he experienced when he was attacked by a large male lion:

I heard a shout. Starting and looking half round, I saw the lion just in the act of springing upon me. I was on a little height; he caught my shoulder as he sprang and we both came to the ground below together. Growling horribly close to my ear, he shook me as a terrier does a rat.

Trance state. A state of partly suspended animation or the inability to function normally. A sleep-like state in which the body moves slowly if at all, while the mind is usually focused narrowly or on a single thought. See Chapter 17.

The shock produced a stupor similar to that which seems to be felt by a mouse after the first shake of a cat. It caused a sort of dreaminess in which there was no sense of pain nor feeling of terror, though [I was] quite conscious of all that was happening. It was like what patients partially under the influence of chloroform describe, who see all the operation but feel not the knife.

McDermott notes there is currently no scientific proof the opioid peptides are associated with the sort of trance state Livingstone experienced when the lion attacked. However, in the March 6, 1981 issue of *Science*, Barbara Herman and Jaak Panksepp state that *decreasing* the amount of enkephalin in an animal's brain seems to *increase* its sensitivity to pain and to social isolation.

There is additional evidence relating the release of endorphins to stress and pain. University of Michigan researchers Huda Akil and Cheryl Cahill report in the 1984 *Annual Review of Neuroscience* that pregnancy causes women's bodies to make more of one type of endorphin. In a study of 10 women from early pregnancy to labor, Akil and Cahill state, the amount of endorphin in the blood "doubled or tripled in every subject from the first trimester until birth."

In 1981, several scientists reported that the endorphins seem responsible for the "high" that runners often experience. And as we will see in Chapter 16, when you are hypnotized—or when you are given a placebo you *think* is a pain-killer—your brain may secrete more endorphins than usual.

Given these data, it is tempting to speculate that *almost all altered states of consciousness* are associated with the release of natural pain-killing chemicals within the brain. Sometimes you secrete endorphins because of the drugs you have taken. But just as often, you secrete them because of your *expectations* about how the drugs will affect you. Thus, *some* of the effects of alcohol, the opiates, marijuana, and cocaine are due to biochemical changes these drugs cause at various synapses. But *other* effects of these drugs are caused by the types of neural transmitters and inhibitors your brain secretes in response to what you *think* the drugs ought to be doing to you.

To restate a point we have already made, your mental processes have as much influence on the behavior of your neurons as the behavior of your neurons has on what you think and feel.

We have already described the electro-chemical functions of the *individual neuron*. In the next chapter we will look at how *groups of neurons* cooperate in order to help you cope with the pleasures and pains of life.

Summary

1 **Consciousness** is a **primitive term** that is defined as your ordinary state of mental functioning.

2 Certain experiences—such as falling asleep, dreaming, and taking various drugs—can lead to unusual or **altered states of consciousness**.

3 Your body has certain **biological rhythms**, such as daily fluctuations in temperature, that follow predictable patterns. These **circadian rhythms** suggest there are **biological clocks** in the body that control many physical processes, including sleep and waking.

4 Sleep is both an **adaptive response** that helped early humans survive, and an innate **restorative process** that allows the body and mind to rejuvenate themselves.

5 **Infants** sleep about 16 hours per 24. **Young adults** sleep about 8 hours, but **older people** sleep slightly less. Both infants and elderly individuals nap more than do young adults.

6 The stages of sleep run from **Stage 0** (pre-sleep) to **Stage 4** (deep sleep).

7 Each **sleep cycle** is about 90 minutes long, including a REM period that runs from 8 to 15 minutes (first cycle of the night) to more than 40 minutes (final sleep cycle of the night). Stage 4 (deep) sleep predominates during the first and second sleep cycles of the night. Stage 2 sleep, Stage 1-REM periods, and **dreaming** increase during later cycles.

8 Stage 1-REM sleep usually develops out of Stage 2 sleep. During REM, most of the **voluntary muscles** in your body are paralyzed—except for those that control eye movements.

9 Dreaming seems to be primarily a function of the right hemisphere.

10 People deprived of REM or Stage 4 sleep usually show a **rebound effect** when allowed to sleep normally.

11 Sleep disorders include **narcolepsy** (involuntary "attacks" of sleep), **insomnia**, **sleepwalking**, **sleeptalking**, and **bedwetting**.

12 You **dream** several dreams during each REM period. REM dreams are noted for their completeness and their fantastic quality. Dreams that occur during Stage 2, 3, or 4 sleep are at best **brief and fragmentary**, and are "reality-oriented."

13 Some people have **lucid dreams** in which they can control the content and outcome of their dreaming.

14 There are two main types of nightmares: **anxiety nightmares** and **night terrors**. Anxiety nightmares develop out of Stage 1-REM sleep, while night terrors develop out of Stage 4 sleep and occasionally are followed by sleepwalking.

15 Neurons have **receptor sites** on their dendrites and cell bodies that are particularly sensitive to **neurotransmitters**.

16 The **lock and key hypothesis** states that if a specific transmitter molecule "fits" a specific receptor site, it "unlocks" the neuron and makes it fire.

17 Your brain contains both **excitatory** and **inhibitory synapses**.

18 **Pre-synaptic inhibition** prevents the axon from releasing neurotransmitters. **Post-synaptic inhibition** prevents the dendrites and cell bodies from responding to neurotransmitters.

19 **Drugs** can affect many neural processes, but typically cause either an increase or decrease in **neural firing** at specific synapses.

20 The **opiates** inhibit sensory inputs and thus reduce the intensity of painful stimulation.

21 Your brain produces a variety of natural pain-killers called the **endorphins** or **opioid peptides**.

22 **Morphine** inhibits the production of the natural pain-killers. **Withdrawal** from morphine addiction is painful because your body has no **opioid peptides** and other natural pain-killers to protect itself.

23 **PCP** is a **dissociative anesthetic** that disconnects people's minds from their bodies.

24 **Alcohol** is the most widely abused drug in the US and is a major health and social problem.

25 The effects of all drugs are strongly influenced by **psycho-social factors**, including expectations. Experienced drinkers cannot tell the difference between alcohol and tonic water.

26 The brain reacts to shock and stress by secreting endorphins. In large amounts, the endorphins can bring about a **trance state** or **euphoria**.

27 Your mental processes have as much influence on the behavior of your neurons as the behavior of your neurons has on what you think and feel.

(Continued from page 55.)

"Well," said the Bureaucrat, puffing nervously on his pipe. "Back from the Amazon so soon?"

"It's been 18 months," said Dr. Susan Ogdon.

"Ah, yes. Well, time certainly flies, doesn't it?" The Bureaucrat carefully inspected the faces of the two psychologists sitting in his office. They seemed tanned and relaxed. He wished that he could go buzzing off to tropical climes any time he wished. "And how were the pot-smoking natives? Still lost in the 'Stoned Age,' I suppose?" He chuckled over his little joke.

Roger Ogdon smiled wanly. "The natives are decent human beings, just like you and me. Some of them do smoke marijuana, of course, but I doubt theirs is any more of a 'Stoned Age' than ours."

"Um, yes," said the Bureaucrat, quickly swallowing his chuckle. "And what were the results of your study?" In fact, he had a copy of the Ogdons' report lying on his desk in front of him. But he had found time to skim only the first page or so. Besides, he preferred to hear such things first-hand. "I trust you didn't come up with anything too radical?"

Susan Ogdon sighed. "No, our results were about the same as those that Vera Rubin and Lambros Comitas found in their study of marijuana use in Jamaica, and that Paul Doughty and his colleagues at the University of Florida found in their work in Costa Rica."

The Bureaucrat frowned. "Oh, you read those studies, did you?" He wondered why scientists were always checking out the literature when it seemed that tackling a problem with a fresh mind might be so rewarding. He stirred his cup of coffee and took a small sip to perk him up a bit.

"Well," said the woman, "we began by looking at the various ways in which our natives used marijuana. They chew it, smoke it, brew it as tea, and use it in their cooking."

"Oh, my," said the Bureaucrat. "That much, eh?"

"Yes," Roger Odgon responded. "And they give it to their children as a medicine, so they start using cannabis at a very early age. But, of course, not all of the natives use it."

"Good," the Bureaucrat said. "That means that you could find a control group of non-users, I presume?"

"Yes," said Susan Ogdon. "We found 30 men who were long-time, heavy pot smokers, and 30 who had never used it at all. The users smoked an average of 8 'joints' a day, except that they call them 'spliffs' instead of joints. And, as we note in our report, they refer to pot as 'ganja,' just as the Jamaicans do. It has much more THC in it than does the pot that usually finds its way to the US."

"Excellent!" said the Bureaucrat, reaching for his pipe. "And the non-users were similar to the users in all respects other than the use of this 'ganja?'"

Roger Ogdon nodded. "They were of about the same height, age, occupation, and educational background. And the men in both the experimental and control groups were heavy smokers of tobacco."

The Bureaucrat refilled his pipe and lit it. "Well, if the groups were that similar, then any differences in their mental or physical health most probably was due to the fact that one group smoked marijuana, and the other didn't, right?"

"That's what we presume," said the woman.

"And what was the major difference?" asked the Bureaucrat. "Something startling, I presume?"

Susan Ogdon laughed softly. "Very startling. The ganja smokers weighed, on the average, seven pounds less than did the non-smokers."

The Bureaucrat frowned. "Seven pounds?" he asked. He rubbed his stomach and wondered if he shouldn't lose a little weight. Perhaps those diet pills his wife was taking would help. Then a stray thought popped into his mind. "Wait a minute," he said. "I thought pot-smoking gave you 'the blind munchies.' How come the ganja smokers weighed less, not more, than the natives in your control group?"

Roger Ogdon answered. "It's a cultural thing, I suppose. Here the myth is that pot makes you hungry. In the Amazon, they believe it calms your stomach. As I'm sure you know, our feelings and behaviors often reflect our cultural backgrounds and social biases."

"Everyone knows that," responded the Bureaucrat. "But stop teasing me. What else did you find? Surely the ganja smokers had poorer health . . ."

"No," said Susan Ogdon. "Not at all. We took X-rays of their lungs. Both groups showed fairly normal tissue, except that the men who *didn't* smoke ganja had a bit more scarring of the lungs. But then, as we said, both groups were heavy tobacco smokers as well."

The Bureaucrat put down his pipe. "Well, imagine that. But what about genetic damage?"

Susan Ogdon responded. "The ganja smokers all had parents and grandparents who had been heavy smokers. You'd expect some genetic problems from that, wouldn't you? Yet the ganja smokers actually showed slightly fewer genetic abnormalities than did the men in our control group."

"Oh, my," replied the Bureaucrat as he poked a nasal inhaler up one of his nostrils and inhaled deeply. "I don't think the Deputy Assistant Secretary is going to like your data at all. But that's his problem, now isn't it?" He put the inhaler back in his desk before continuing. "Well, what about personality differences between your experimental and control group subjects?"

"None," said the woman. "We found no significant differences in personality, intelligence, tendency toward mental illness, or brain-wave recordings between the two groups."

The Bureaucrat reached in a desk drawer and extracted a small, white capsule. He had spent the morning in a conference with the Deputy Assistant Secretary, and the meeting had not been particularly pleasant. A mild "downer" might help soothe his nerves, he told himself. He swallowed the pill and then picked up the thread of the conversation. "But what effect did the ganja have on the men's intelligence?"

"No effects that we could detect," the woman said. "Which is just what we might expect, given the July 24, 1981 *Science* article by two psychiatrists at UCLA."

"They studied savages in the Amazon too?"

"No," Susan Ogdon replied, "they studied 10 Americans living in a Southern state who had been smoking ganja daily for an average of 7.4 years as part of their religious ceremonies. The UCLA psychiatrists found no impairment of cognitive function among their subjects."

"Um," said the Bureaucrat. "But what of the social consequences? What of motivation? Some scientists insist that pot-smoking decreases the desire to work and to get along in society. Did you find that was true in the Amazon?"

"Of course not," Roger Ogdon replied. "The smokers had no more trouble getting or holding a job than did the non-smokers."

"But how long had the pot smokers been puffing on this 'ganja?'" asked the Bureaucrat.

"On the average, about 18 years," said Susan Ogdon.

"And all that ganja didn't even affect their sex lives?" the Bureaucrat said with a gasp.

Roger Ogdon laughed. "Not that we could tell. Or at least not that their wives or girl friends noticed. More objectively, the men in both groups had normal amounts of male hormone."

"But wasn't there an article in *Science* back in 1979 suggesting that marijuana may affect the sex hormones?"

"There are several such studies in the literature," Roger replied. "But an article in the March 25, 1983 *Science* may give us a clue as to what's really happening. Several investigators gave high doses of THC to female monkeys and found their menstrual cycles were badly disrupted for several months. After this period, though, the animals adapted and returned to normal. Any new drug you introduce into a subject's system is likely to cause a temporary disruption of many bodily processes. Eventually, people simply adjust and go about their lives. And you must remember that the men we studied in the Amazon had been smoking pot for an average of 18 years."

"Oh, my," said the Bureaucrat. He couldn't imagine how he'd explain this to the Deputy Assistant Secretary. His stomach rumbled. He patted it gently, then helped himself to an antacid tablet he had tucked away in his desk for just such emergencies.

"You aren't going to object to our publishing the results of our study, are you?" Susan Ogdon asked.

The Bureaucrat smiled. "No, surely not. As you obviously know, your findings really aren't all that surprising, given the results of the Jamaica and Costa Rica studies."

"But what about your Deputy Assistant Secretary?" she questioned.

"Well," responded the Bureaucrat, "I take my cue from Winston Churchill. He once said, 'The truth is incontrovertible. Panic may resent it; ignorance may deride it; malice may distort it; but there it is.'" The man chuckled for a moment. "Leave the Deputy Assistant Secretary to me. Besides, rumor has it that he will be leaving for another position shortly. So let the truth prevail."

"'And the truth will set you free,'" replied Roger Ogdon, smiling.

"Let's hope so," said the Bureaucrat. "But the truth is, I still don't understand why some of the natives smoke ganja, and others don't."

"Individual choice, we presume," Roger Ogdon replied.

The woman nodded. "Yes, and perhaps some difference in their sensitivity to pain."

"Pain?"

"Look," Roger Ogdon continued. "Those men work 10 hours a day or more in the fields, doing very difficult manual labor. They use cannabis as a pain-killer. They probably produce less per hour when they're stoned, but they seem to be able to work longer."

"Then what do they do at night, when they want to relax?" asked the Bureaucrat?

Donald Ogdon laughed. "They drink alcohol."

"No kidding?" responded the Bureaucrat. "Perhaps they're not so different from us after all. But that's what we wanted to find out about, and that's why we supported your research. Please do publish it, wherever you wish. And in conclusion, let me say that it's been a real pleasure to work with you two."

The Bureaucrat shook their hands and walked the two psychologists to the door. Then he returned to his desk, gathered up his papers, and put them in his briefcase. He tossed in a box of aspirin, and then glanced briefly at his watch. It had been a long, hard day, and he hoped his wife would have a martini waiting for him at home.

Then a sad thought crossed his mind. "Pity about those natives having to work so long and hard in the fields," he said aloud. "I suppose they need a little something too, just to get them through the day." He picked up his pipe and tucked it into his briefcase. "Ah, well, different smokes for different folks."

Recommended Readings

Domino, E.F. (Ed.). (1981). *PCP (phencyclidine): Historical and current perspectives*. Ann Arbor, Mich.: NPP Books.

Garfield, P. (1974). *Creative dreaming*. New York: Simon & Schuster.

Krieger, D.T. (1982). Brain peptides: What, where, and why? *Science, 222,* 975–985.

Luce, G.G. (1973). *Body time: Physiological rhythms and social stress*. Toronto: Bantam.

Snyder, S.H. (1984). Neurosciences: An integrative discipline. *Science, 225,* 1255–1257.

Webb, W.B. (1975). *Sleep: The gentle tyrant*. Englewood Cliffs, N.J.: Prentice-Hall.

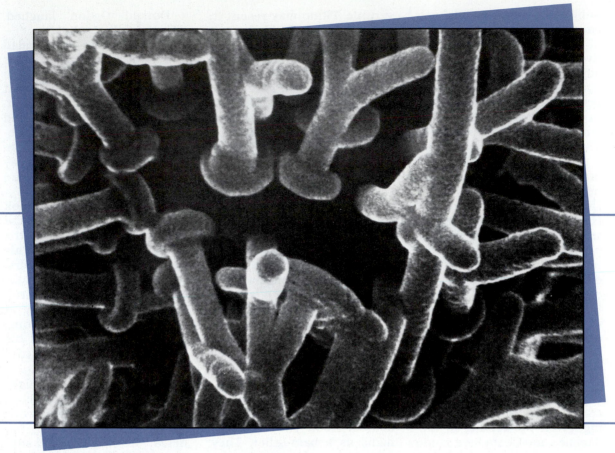

Did You Know That...

- Many early Greeks believed the mind was located in the heart?

- Many people once believed you could read someone's personality by studying the bumps on the person's head?

- If you electrically stimulate certain parts of your brain, your arms and legs will twitch and move about whether you want them to or not?

- About 80 percent of the murders committed each year involve people related to or friendly with each other?

- Most murderers and their victims are under 30 years of age?

- British studies suggest that young boys who commit violent acts are very likely to be "heavy" TV watchers?

- Males who watch sexually violent films often become desensitized about rape and aggression toward women?

- A rat shocked in a confined space will almost always attack anything handy?

- Some scientists believe that much human violence is due to hidden brain damage?

- There apparently is no simple cure for the violence we find in the world?

4

Structure and Function of the Brain

"The Riddle of Rage"

"Peace," the young woman said as she got into the car. "Nice of you to give me a ride."

"No trouble at all," the older woman said as she put her car in gear and drove off down the dusty road. "My name's Jane Hughes. What's yours?"

"Jennifer Ahearn," the younger woman responded. "But my friends call me Jeff."

Mrs. Hughes nodded cordially. "Pleased to meet you, Jennifer. Don't get many hitchhikers up here in the back woods of Manitoba. Where are you headed?"

"To the Hutterite colony, about 15 miles away," Jenni-fer responded. "Are you going that way?"

Mrs. Hughes nodded. "Drive right past there." Then, taking her eyes from the road for a second or two, the woman looked Jennifer over. Noticing the young woman's slacks, the beads around her neck, and her loose-flowing hair, Mrs. Hughes chuckled. "Well, you sure don't *look* like a Hutter-ite."

"I'm not," Jennifer replied. "I'm just visiting."

"What you plan on doing with them folk?"

"I'm going to study their peaceful ways," Jennifer re-plied earnestly. "It's my Action Project for the sum-mer. I'm majoring in psychol-ogy, and we're supposed to spend our summers either working in a laboratory or out in the field somewhere. Last summer I worked at a clinic, you see, and that's why this year I decided to come live with the Hut-terites."

Mrs. Hughes pursed her lips. "No, I reckon I don't see."

Jennifer Ahearn frowned. "At the clinic we mostly worked with battered women and abused children. I got sick to my stomach seeing wives with black eyes and broken bones, and kids whose bodies were covered with bruises and whip marks. The 'aggressive instinct' at work, you know."

Jane Hughes shook her head in dismay. "Were you able to help the women and children very much?"

Nodding positively, Jennifer said, "Oh, yes. We helped as much as we could. But we were just cleaning up after the damage had been done, if you know what I mean. We couldn't *prevent* violence, just fix things up afterwards."

"So?" Mrs. Hughes said, steering her car deftly around a large pothole in the road.

"So, I studied up on violence and aggression. And then I read an article by Gertrude Huntington in *Natural History* on the Hutterites. They fled to America from central Europe because they refused to join the army and fight in wars. They may be the most peaceful people in the world."

"They are peaceful, I'll give them that," Jane Hughes said.

"And my professor, Dr. Sackoff, says there simply is no child abuse among the Hutterites, and practically no violence of any kind. That's why I decided to come study them for the summer."

"To see if maybe you can learn how to prevent wife beating and child abuse back where you live, eh?"

Jennifer laughed. "You got it! I figure the Hutterites must have a secret of some kind. I want to learn what it is and then teach other people how to live in peace the way the Hutterites do."

Mrs. Hughes was silent for a few moments. Finally she said, "What does your teacher back at the univer-

sity—Dr. Sackoff, you said?— what does she say about this project of yours?"

The young woman shrugged. "Well, when I told her I was sure I could find a way to end war and violence on earth, her enthusiasm wasn't exactly overwhelming. But finally she agreed to my coming up here. She said, if nothing else, it ought to be a 'learning experience.'"

Jane Hughes roared with laughter. "Yes, dear," she said, "it really ought to be that." Then she stopped the car at the side of the road. "See that big white building over there between the trees? That's the Hutterite 'long house,' as they call it. Just walk straight down that path, and you can't miss it."

Jennifer Ahearn gathered her gear together and got out of the car, then turned to smile at Mrs. Hughes. "Thanks so much for the ride," she said.

"Oh, you're welcome, dear," the older woman replied. "And I just hope that you like what you learn from the Hutterites." Then, with a laugh, she put the car in gear and roared off down the dusty road.

"Children are born with stubborn natures, Miss Ahearn," the Hutterite woman said as she shook a birch switch at her son to warn him he was misbehaving. "Like my Donny, here, all children are willful and selfish. They're born aggressive, and inclined to misbehave." Then the woman smiled warmly at the boy. "Of course, Donny's only three yet, and that's very young. But I don't doubt he'll need many a switching before his will is broken."

Jennifer frowned. "That's

what you send them to kindergarten for, then? To break their wills?"

"Certainly," the woman said. "What else should a child learn at Donny's age other than to obey the will of God, and of the group? But kids naturally want to fight, and do things on their own. That's their evil tendencies showing through. So we break their wills in kindergarten to teach them to be obedient, loving, God-fearing, and peaceful."

"You mean," Jennifer said, "you teach them to understand right from wrong, and to be ethical. That way they will grow up wanting to be peace-loving citizens."

The woman shook her head. "No, Miss Ahearn. Doesn't matter what they *want* to be, or whether they *understand.* They're too young to do anything but memorize, and act like we tell them to act. So we teach them to obey the rules."

"But if they don't think the right thoughts . . ."

The Hutterite woman laughed heartily. "That's the trouble with you 'outsiders.' You keep talking about what goes on inside the mind. Oh, wrong thinking is bad, I agree. But if you keep your thoughts to yourself, what does it matter? *Thinking* bad is not a sin. But bad *behavior* is a sin, because everybody can see that you're transgressing the law. And that goes against God's will."

Jennifer Ahearn was puzzled. "But don't you ever have aggressive impulses? I mean, when Donny here misbehaves, don't you ever get angry and feel like hitting him until he acts the way he ought to?"

"Hit a child in anger? You

must be joshing," the woman said. "Why, that's against our rules. A couple of licks with a birch switch is enough, anyhow. We punish a child to teach him a lesson, not to make ourselves feel better."

"But doesn't your anger ever get out of control . . .?"

The woman grinned. "I'm not saying I don't *feel* anger down inside me. But it doesn't matter. If I tried to harm Donny in any way, the rest of the group would keep me from doing so." She sighed deeply. "That's one of the great joys of living among the Brethren. They keep you walking the straight and narrow path, even when you might be inclined to stray from the true way."

"And the true way is . . ."

"The way of the God of love," the woman said immediately. "The way of truth. We follow the example set by our martyrs, who were burned at the stake or died of starvation rather than fight in wicked wars. We forsake all worldly things, and all the sinful and corrupt ways of you outsiders. Because, as we learn in our schools, 'It is better to die the bitterest death, yea ten deaths, than to forsake the truth.'"

Jennifer's face flushed in anger. "I may be an 'outsider,' but I'm not sinful and corrupt. I love God and peace as much as you do."

The Hutterite woman snorted in amusement. "Not likely, Miss Ahearn. Look at your clothes! You wear pants, like a man. Sinful! And you should cover your head with a scarf and a cap, instead of letting your hair flow free like a harlot's!"

"But it's too hot to wear a scarf and a cap today," Jennifer replied angrily.

"Humph," the woman said. "You can't expect to be comfortable in *this* world and in the hereafter both."

"And as for the slacks I'm wearing, they're *sensible*! Back at school, *all* the girls wear slacks, so you'll just have to forgive me . . ."

The woman frowned. "Can't forgive wicked behavior, no matter where it occurs. Of course, I *understand* you didn't grow up here in the colony. And so your will wasn't broken when you were young, and you don't know the godly way to dress. 'By their fruits ye shall know them,' God says in the Good Book. God judges you by what you wear, and what you do, because those are the fruits you bear to others. Your trouble is, you just weren't taught obedience when the time was right. But now you've been here a while, and you ought to be learning."

"I came here to learn how to stop child abuse, and how to teach people to love each other," Jennifer said. A tear rolled down one cheek. "I don't see what wearing a scarf and cap has to do with stopping war and aggression. Besides, I don't look good in floppy old clothes like the ones you're wearing."

"Pride goeth before a fall, Miss Ahearn," the woman replied, clucking her tongue as she did so. "You must learn to submit yourself to the will of the group, to God's way, if you want to be pure of heart and give up your evil, aggressive behaviors."

"I am *not* evil and aggressive!" Jennifer shouted.

"Stubborn, stubborn, stubborn," the woman said. "You're worse than Donny, here. And he's only three."

The woman pulled her son to her and hugged him. After a moment she sighed again. "But then, maybe our way is just too difficult for you to learn, you being a woman and all that."

"I can learn anything I want to learn!" Jennifer said loudly.

The woman shook her head in disagreement. "No, still full of sinful pride, because your will wasn't broken at the right time. But there's hope for you, I think."

"Hope?"

The Hutterite reached out and patted Jennifer tenderly on the arm. "Yes, hope. Come live with us, and learn the true path to peace. It will be hard, I know. But we'll help all we can, Miss Ahearn. We'll tell you when you're right and wrong, we'll guide your behaviors as we would a child's. And you'll get your reward in the hereafter."

"You'll *guide* me along the path to peace?"

"Oh, yes," the woman said. "It won't be easy because, like a child, you place your own needs above those of the group. But submit yourself to the will of the colony, and we'll wring the disobedience and aggression from your heart. And then we'll help you discover what love and peace are all about."

"You'll *tell* me what I have to do . . .?"

The woman patted Jennifer's arm again. "Of course we'll tell you! That's why we live together, to tell each other when we stray from the path of God. Learning to live in peace isn't something you can do on your own. You need someone observing you each minute of the day, to correct your misdeeds and show the proper way to dress and act."

And then a saintly smile lit up the Hutterite woman's face. "Come live with us, Miss Ahearn, and you'll be the most fortunate of women. For here there are always a hundred helpful eyes watching you."

(Continued on p. 111.)

The Mind-Body Problem

What makes you tick?

A simple-sounding question, perhaps, but one humans have debated (sometimes violently) for a great many centuries. Most of the time when people raise this question, they are asking, "Who are you?" That is, they want to know what biological, psychological, and social events have made you into the person you are today. (To anticipate a bit, we will spend the rest of this book trying to answer *that* particular question.)

But there is an even more basic problem hiding behind the innocent-appearing phrase, "What makes you tick?" Namely, what do we really mean when we use the pronoun YOU? At this deeper level of analysis, the question becomes not "WHO are YOU?" but "WHAT are YOU?"

Are you merely a biological machine, a body full of complex clockwork run by a motor called the brain? Or are you a unique psychological or spiritual identity that happens to inhabit a certain body the way that you also happen to inhabit a certain house, apartment, or dorm room? Put this way, the original question becomes, "Does your mind (whatever that is) run your body, or does your body run your mind?" (Or, to raise a more disturbing thought, are they both perhaps controlled by outside forces neither your mind nor your body is entirely aware of?)

This kind of questioning may seem odd to you, or even downright stupid, if you've never encountered it before. For, if you are like most people, you *know* what your mind is. And you probably *assume* your mind controls your body. After all, YOU make up your mind to go to the store, so your legs carry you there. YOU decide to have dinner, so your hands get the food and your mouth eats it. From this viewpoint, your "psychological" mind gives the commands that your "biological" body executes.

But consider the following troublesome facts: First, you spend about one-third of your life asleep, yet your body continues to function beautifully even when your mind is unconscious. Who runs your body when your cortex takes a nap?

Second, if you take a couple of drinks, or smoke some pot, YOU become intoxicated. It is easy to understand how the chemicals in alcohol and cannabis can affect the ticking of your nerve cells. But how can *physical* reactions in your brain cause the *psychological* or *spiritual* YOU to get high?

And third, if your mind controls your body, *how does it do so*? When you drive a car, you sit in the driver's seat, you push on the pedals with your feet, and you turn the wheel with your hands. If you consider your body to be a biological machine "driven" by your mind, where does the driver "sit"? And how does your purely spiritual or psychological "mind" pull the biological strings that make your neurons fire and your muscles move?

What and Where Is Your Mind?

The question, "What and where is the mind?" has puzzled people at least since the time of the early Greek philosopher Plato. Yet we still do not have one simple, agreed-upon answer as to what the mind is, and how it manages to interact with the body. For buried away within the question "What is the mind?" is a psychological nettle that stings almost everyone who attempts to grasp it. Philosophers call this nettle the *mind-body problem*. This age-old problem has to do with the complex relationship between your mental and your physical processes—and where inside your body those "mental" processes take place.

As you will see, we still don't know as much as we'd like about what the mind is and what its relationship to the body is. But we do assume that mental activities take place (for the most part) inside the head. Ancient humans, however, were not quite so **sophisticated**.

Aristotle's "Radiator Theory"
Aristotle—a Greek scholar who lived long before the birth of Christ—believed that our minds (or souls) reside in our hearts. Aristotle had observed humans wounded in battle and

animals being slaughtered. Thus, he knew the heart was in constant motion—beating, beating, beating. If you pierced a man's heart with a sword or arrow, the man almost always died. The brain, on the other hand, was quiet. No matter how much you poked or prodded it, the brain *simply did not respond.* Many early Greeks considered the brain to be little more than a radiator where blood was pumped to be cooled off when a woman or man flew into a "hot rage."

The Homunculus Theory

Another view, supposedly held by the early Egyptians, was that a "little man" lived inside each person's skull. This **homunculus** (to use the Latin word for "little man") supposedly peered out through your eyes and listened through your ears. Once the "little man" decided how to *process* or react to incoming sensory information, he pulled the strings that operated your muscles, much as a puppeteer pulls the strings that make marionettes behave.

Nor was this *homunculus theory* as ridiculous as it may seem at first. Ancient people knew that if you looked directly into a friend's eyes, you would see a "little man" or "little woman" looking out at you (try it—it works!).

Furthermore, the theory established our superiority over lower animals. If you stare into a dog's eyes, you will see a human face looking out at you, not a dog's. So "little men" obviously pulled the strings for animals as well as for humans. (What the dog sees when it looks into *your* eyes is a question the early theorists apparently forgot to ask.)

Even today, the homunculus theory has its believers. How many TV commercials have you seen in which "little men" or "little women" chase about the human body causing headaches or stomach upsets?

Question: If a "little man" pulls the strings that move your muscles, who pulls the little man's strings?

Descartes' Theory of Separate Substances

Three centuries ago, the French philosopher **René Descartes** offered one of the first modern solutions to the mind-body problem. Descartes believed mind and body were made of *separate substances.*

According to Descartes, your body is composed of *physically measurable* substances such as blood and guts. Thus, your body's actions are purely mechanical. Your mind is sup-

Sophisticated (so-FISS-tic-kay-ted). A group of philosophers called Sophists lived in Greece several hundred years before Christ was born. The Sophists were very good at winning arguments, more through their ability to "shoot the bull" effectively than through logical thinking. Our English words "sophomore" and "sophisticated" come from "Sophist."

Homunculus (ho-MUN-cue-lus). The Latin word *homo* means "man." A homunculus is a "small man," such as a dwarf or midget.

René Descartes (ren-nay day-cart). Usually considered the greatest of French philosophers. He was born in 1596 and lived until 1650. A world-famous scholar who made many great contributions to physics, mathematics, psychology, and philosophy.

posedly a ghostly something that exists *spiritually* or *psychologically*, but has no physical existence.

Descartes thought that mind and body were *coupled*, like man and wife. The mind did not control the body directly, nor did the body control the mind. But, like a married couple, mind and body were very closely related and they did *interact* with each other. The brain (which was physical) was the most important part of the body because it was the "marriage bed"—that is, *the point of maximum interaction between mind and body.*

René Descartes knew precious little about the functioning of the brain, for modern biology didn't exist at the time Descartes lived. But he was one of the first scientists to insist that the seat of consciousness (YOU) lies within the skull. Thus, he turned the mind-body problem into the mind-brain problem.

Question: Suppose we could transplant your brain into another body. How would your personality be affected by the operation? Would "you" go with your brain, or stay with your body? And if "you" went with your brain, how would your feelings and behaviors be affected if your new body were of the opposite sex?

Phrenology

By the year 1800, medical doctors were convinced of the psychological importance of the brain. But they could not begin to unlock the brain's secrets because they knew so little about chemistry and electricity. So the medical profession studied this magnificent organ as best it could—by cutting and poking at it as if it were a lump of muscle tissue. Some scientists decided the brain was a *unitary organ* that functioned "as a whole." Others believed the

René Descartes   M.J.P. Flourens

The phrenologist, an 1839 cartoon by Honoré Daumier.

brain was made up of *many separate organs*, each of which controlled a basic "mental function" of some kind.

Around the year 1800, a European medical doctor named Franz Joseph Gall stated that there were as many "organs of the brain" as there were "psychological faculties." Most behaviors, Gall said, were the result of *cooperation* among the various "organs of the brain." However, if you studied people carefully enough, you could determine what the "underlying faculties" and "brain organs" really were. And how did Gall study people? By investigating the "bumps on their heads." Let's see what led Gall to do so.

Most of us are right-handed (and left-brained). Because we do most of our heavy labor with our right hands, the muscles in our right arms are slightly larger and better developed than are the muscles in our left arms. Now, if your "brain organs" reacted like muscle tissue, then the more you used one of these "organs," the larger that part of the brain should grow. Right?

Well, that was what Gall believed. After studying inmates in jails and insane asylums, Gall found (or so he thought) that most pickpockets and thieves had a "bump" on their skulls just above their ears. Thieves spend a lot of time "acquiring" other people's property. So the "organ of their brains" associated with the trait of "acquisitiveness" should be *swollen from exercise*. And since the bump above the thieves' ears was the only swelling Gall could find, he stated that the "acquisitive organ" must be located just under this bump!

Now, suppose you adopted Gall's rather odd viewpoint. How would you go about determining anybody's personality? Obviously, all you would have to do would be to "read the bumps" on a person's skull!

Gall gave the practice of bump-reading a very fancy name, **phrenology**, which he made up from the Greek words meaning "to study the mind." He went around Europe hunting for people with special talents or *psychological traits*, and then tried to find a bump that matched each trait. For instance, Gall placed the trait of "destructiveness" just behind the ear because he found bumps there (1) in a medical student who was "so fond of torturing animals that he later became a surgeon," and (2) in a man who worked as an executioner and who apparently enjoyed his work immensely.

Phrenology became very popular in the United States during the early 1800's, since it seemed to offer practical-minded Americans an easy way to improve themselves. But the phrenology fad didn't last very long for at least two reasons: First, Gall never could give his clients a workable set of "mental exercises" to reshape their personalities. And second, the bumps *didn't change*, no matter what the client did.

As silly as Gall's "bump-ology" may seem, however, he did make many significant contributions to neuro-anatomy, to the study of fetal development, and to clinical psychology. Most of all, Gall was one of the first to insist that the *organization of behavior* must be related in some way to the *organization of the brain*. As Georgetown University psychologist Daniel Robinson says in the August 1982 *American Psychologist*, "None of the silliness of [Gall's] 'bumpology' can cancel these contributions."

Question: What sort of experiment could you perform to test the correctness of Gall's hunches about the brain?

Science Versus Phrenology

In the long run, however, it was the scientific method that effectively bashed phrenology over the head. **Pierre Flourens**, the great French physiologist, demolished most of Gall's claims in the 1820's. Flourens did so by performing actual *experiments* on brains instead of merely reading bumps on people's skulls and then trying to **correlate** the bumps with psychological traits.

Gall had located the "bump of amativeness" (or sexuality) on the back part of the head, in areas we now know are associated with visual sensory inputs. What would happen, Flourens asked, if this part of the brain were destroyed? Presumably, the person's sex life would be greatly changed. As a surgeon, Flourens was occasionally called upon to remove this part of a patient's brain in order to save the person's life. But on recovery from the operation, these patients seldom showed decreased sexual activity. They might be partially blinded, but they could still make love (and did!). In fact, Flourens found he could remove large areas of the cortex from badly wounded patients without destroying the psychological traits Gall said were lodged in those areas of the brain.

Because Flourens knew little or nothing about electricity and chemistry, he studied the brain by cutting out parts of it to see how surgery would affect people's behaviors. Since patients with brain damage had trouble taking care of themselves, Flourens decided the cerebral hemispheres were the seat of perception, intelligence, and all *voluntary activity*. Which is to say that Flourens believed that the hemispheres were "the seat of the mind." And perhaps in reaction against Gall's wildly incorrect ideas, Flourens decided the brain "functioned as a whole." That is, Flourens believed psychological traits or abilities had no *specific locus* or homesite within the brain.

It took a lunatic to prove Flourens wrong.

Phrenology (free-NOLL-oh-gee). Reading the bumps or depressions on a person's skull in order to make guesses about the person's psychological abilities. Phrenology, which was invented by Franz Joseph Gall, doesn't work very well.

Pierre Flourens (pee-air flu-rans). A noted French medical scientist who, in the 1800's, made many brilliant discoveries about how the brain works.

Correlate (CORE-e-late). Two things are said to be "correlates" if they are so closely related or complementary to each other that one implies the other. However, to *imply* something doesn't mean *causing* that thing, nor are all correlations perfect. Blondness and blue eyes are highly correlated traits. But blondness doesn't cause you to have blue eyes, because some blonds don't have blue eyes. And having blue eyes doesn't cause you to be blond, because some people with blue eyes have dark hair.

Autopsy (AW-top-see). A careful inspection of a dead body to determine why the person died.

The Speech Center

In 1831 there came to an insane asylum near Paris a young Frenchman whose only mark of madness was that he wouldn't talk. He could communicate by making signs, but he refused to write or speak. Although he appeared to be normal in all other respects, he was put into the insane asylum because the French authorities decided no sane man would refuse to talk to his fellow beings. The doctors could find no cure for his silence, so the man remained in the hospital for 30 years.

In April of 1861 the man caught an infection and was put under the care of Paul Broca, a noted French surgeon. Broca examined the man carefully, determined that the man's vocal cords were perfectly sound and that the patient was intelligent enough to be able to speak. Five days later—unfortunately for the man, but perhaps fortunately for millions of other patients—the man died of the infection.

Broca put the man's body to **autopsy** at once and discovered a mass of scar tissue in the *left hemisphere* just about where the man's temple would have been. Broca assumed, rightly, that this site in the brain must contain the neural tissue that controls speech.

Gall assumed the brain had "many organs," and *each organ of the brain* had a highly specific function. Gall was proven wrong by Flourens. Flourens assumed there was *no specific locus within the brain* for specific psychological functions or traits. But Flourens was proven wrong by Broca, who correctly located the speech center in the left half of his patient's brain.

And for the next century, the battle seesawed between these two viewpoints. Many scientists

Paul Broca

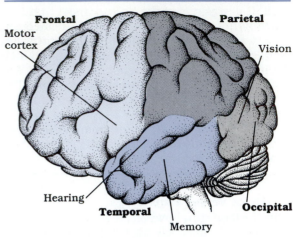

Fig. 4.1   The four lobes of the brain.

believed there must be a *specific center* or site in your brain for each type of behavior you are capable of. However, many other scientists were convinced that almost *every part of your brain* participates in producing each thought or action that you experience.

As is usually the case in such scientific free-for-alls, the truth actually lies somewhere between these two extreme viewpoints.

The Lobes of the Brain

Let us return once more to that magic mirror that allows you to inspect your own brain. If you could look into that mirror, you would probably first notice the huge, deep valley between the left and right hemispheres of your brain. But if you inspected your brain a little more closely, you would see that each hemisphere is actually divided into *sections* (see Fig. 4.1).

Viewed from the top, as we mentioned earlier, your hemispheres look much like a mountainous landscape—there are dozens of smoothly rolling hills which are separated by steep-sided valleys. Some of the valleys are so large they seem to separate the cerebrum into definite areas or sections. We call these sections the **lobes** of the brain.

There are four main sections or lobes in *each* cerebral hemisphere:

1. The **frontal lobe**, which lies just under the skull in the region of the forehead.
2. The **temporal lobe**, which lies under the skull just above each ear, in the general region of your temple.
3. The **parietal lobe**, which lies under the top center of your skull.
4. The **occipital lobe**, which lies at the back of your head, just above your neck.

It was tempting to Broca to assign highly specific psychological functions to each of these lobes. And Broca was *partially* correct in doing so. But as much as he learned about the brain from his surgery and his autopsies, he didn't know enough to help hundreds of his patients who were sick or dying from brain disease. For, like all of his colleagues at that time, Broca did not understand that the nerve cells work electro-chemically.

What the scientists of the 1860's obviously needed was an *electrical* method of investigating brain reactions. And in 1870 they got just that—but it took the violence of a major war to give it to them.

The Electrical Probe

The Franco-Prussian War between Germany and France reached its climax late in the summer of 1870 near the small French town of Sedan. The immediate political consequences of that war have long since been forgotten—even by most German and French citizens. But a discovery two German doctors made on the battlefields outside the sleepy little village of Sedan changed the course of modern medicine.

G. Fritsch and E. Hitzig were trained as medical doctors. When the Franco-Prussian War broke out, they both entered the armed forces of Germany. During the battle of Sedan, Fritsch and Hitzig wandered among the wounded men, helping those whom they could. Some of these soldiers had skulls blown open by cannon fire. Nothing could be done to save these men, all of whom were unconscious and dying. But perhaps, thought Fritsch and Hitzig, these soldiers could contribute priceless medical information to the world in their final moments of life.

In 1870, biologists were already speculating that electrical currents might flow through the brain. What would happen, Fritsch and Hitzig asked themselves, if they provided *electrical stimulation* to the brains of the dying soldiers? So they did just that. And as inhumane as these actions might seem after the fact, they led to important insights on brain functions. Indeed, this research by Fritsch and Hitzig has probably helped millions of brain-damaged patients.

Fritsch and Hitzig applied electrical stimulation to an area at the top-rear of the *frontal lobe*, just where it joins with the parietal lobe. When they did so, the arms and legs of their human subjects would show repeated, jerky movements. Once the war was over, Fritsch and Hitzig performed similar studies with animals and reported they had discovered what seemed to be a "motor output center" in the cortex of both frontal lobes.

Fritsch and Hitzig had also pioneered a new tool for investigating the functioning of the brain and for curing some of its ills—the *electrical probe*.

Mapping the Cortex Electrically

If someone stuck a pin in your arm, you would experience pain. Surprisingly enough, though, if someone stuck a pin directly into your exposed cortex, you probably wouldn't *consciously* experience any discomfort at all.

With certain minor exceptions, there simply are no "pain receptors" in the brain. (There *are* pain receptors in the membrane covering the brain, however.) Because brain tissue is insensitive to pain, patients undergoing brain surgery are often conscious, so they can help the doctor locate whatever damaged section might need to be removed or treated. During such surgery, the doctor may stimulate various parts of the patient's cortex electrically and ask what the patient feels the moment the current is turned on.

What would you experience if you were willing to let a scientist "map" your *entire cortex* with an electrical stimulator? Well, the most dramatic results of all would surely come if the scientist touched the probe to your *motor output area* (motor cortex), which lies at the rear of each frontal lobe (see Fig. 4.1). Stimulation of the nerve cells in the motor cortex in your left hemisphere would cause the muscles on the right side of your body to twitch or jerk—even though you didn't *consciously will* these mus-

Lobes. Rounded bumps that typically project out from the organs of the body. Each half of your cerebrum has four main lobes or projections.

Frontal lobe. The part of your cerebrum that lies just above your eyes. Experiments suggest this part of your brain may be involved in decision making, among many other things. The motor cortex is part of the frontal lobe.

Temporal lobe (TEM-por-al). Part of your cerebrum that lies just above your ears. It seems to be involved in hearing, in speech production, and in emotional behavior, among many other things.

Parietal lobe (pair-EYE-eh-tal, or puh-RYE-eh-tal). Part of your cerebrum at the very top of your brain. Sensory input from your skin receptors and muscles comes to this part of your cerebrum.

Occipital lobe (ox-SIP-it-tull). The lower, rear part of your cerebrum just above the back of your neck. The visual input area of your brain, among other things.

cles to move. Stimulation of the motor cortex in your right hemisphere would, of course, make the muscles on the left side of your body move involuntarily.

When the probe was applied to the *occipital* lobe at the back of your head, you would see brief flashes of light or "shooting stars."

If the scientist stimulated parts of your *temporal* lobe, you would hear brief bursts of sounds.

And if the probe were touched to parts of the *parietal* lobe at the top of your head, you might feel odd "prickly" sensations in your skin.

Strangely enough, however, the scientist could apply the probe to large areas of all four lobes without your experiencing *anything at all!*

Sensory, Motor, and "Silent" Areas

The researchers who first mapped the brain electrically concluded that your cerebral cortex has three general types of areas:

1. *Sensory input areas*, where nerve axons carrying messages from your sense organs make synapse with dendrites of cortical neurons. We will discuss these areas in detail beginning with Chapter 6.
2. *Motor output areas*, which contain nerve cells whose axons reach out to make contact with the muscles and glands of your body.
3. *"Silent" areas*, which have no function that can be determined directly from electrical stimulation.

The early brain researchers were surprised to find that *most of the surface area of the cortex* is "silent" to an electrical probe. At first, these early scientists assumed the silent areas were where memories—or *associations* between sensory inputs and motor outputs—were located. So these silent parts of the cortex were nicknamed the *association areas*. But many lines of evidence now suggest that these are the cortical *processing areas*, for it is in these regions that incoming sensory information is processed and evaluated, and where "command decisions" seem to be made.

The Birth of Psychology

When electrical probing of the brain first began, many early *biologists* were convinced they were about to resolve the mind-body problem in favor of the body. These scientists presumed they would be able to find a specific locus in your brain that matched each unique hope, fear, dream, thought, hatred, and desire you might ever experience. (Had they been able to find such specific brain sites, biology would have swallowed up psychology, and you would be reading quite a different book than this one.)

Imagine the frustration of these scientists, then, when electrical stimulation of much of the brain failed to call forth any "mental" responses at all! The biologists were convinced "the mind" was lurking somewhere in that 3-pound mass of neural tissue inside the skull. But somehow the most important parts of human experience kept eluding (and still elude) their needle-like probes.

In a sense, intra-psychic and social/behavioral psychology grew out of the successes and failures of the early biologists. For while these biological scientists failed to solve the mind-body problem to everyone's satisfaction, they did demonstrate that the *scientific method* could be successfully applied to the study of human behavior.

In the late 1800's, then, a group of scholars who called themselves *psychologists* started applying the scientific approach to the study of what humans thought and did. Some psychologists began to develop "mental probes" to map out the mind as the biologists had mapped out the brain. Other psychologists tried to measure and record the visible behavior of the human organism as precisely as the biologists had measured and recorded the electro-chemical behavior of cortical neurons. Still other psychologists started studying the effects of the social environment on human thoughts and actions.

Out of this sudden burst of scientific activity, there emerged three quite different ways of answering the question, "What makes you tick?"

These three are the *biological*, the *intra-psychic*, and the *social/behavioral* approaches to psychology. Each of the three has its own strengths and weaknesses, and its own contributions to make in answering the mind-body riddle.

To help us put all three approaches in perspective, let us first look at them briefly, then discover how each attempts to explain a pressing human problem—the occurrence of such *violent behaviors* as war, rape, and murder.

The Mind-Body Problem: Three Theoretical Viewpoints

The Biological Viewpoint

As we have noted, psychology partially grew out of the sciences of medicine and biology. That area of psychology concerned with studying how bodily functions affect behavior is called **physiological psychology**. This old and highly respected field is now sometimes referred to by such newer names as *biological psychology*, *psychobiology*, or *biopsychology*. Some biopsychologists work primarily with animals, while others usually work with human subjects.

For the most part, biopsychologists are interested in the *interactions* between body processes and behavior. That is, they study how changes in your biology are *related to* changes in your behavior.

At times, a biopsychologist may induce a change in an organism's behavior and then look for changes in the organism's body. For instance, the scientist might teach a dog to perform a trick and then study what happens in the dog's brain as a result of the change in its performance. Mostly, though, the biopsychologist is likely to alter the functioning of the brain in some way to see how the organism's behavior changes *as a consequence*. For example, if you stimulate parts of a cat's motor cortex, the animal's legs will move. If you stimulate other parts of the cat's brain electrically, the animal will fly into a rage.

Perhaps because biopsychologists tend to "do something physical" to an animal and then note its behavioral changes, these scientists occasionally talk as if biology *causes* psychology. Not all biopsychologists prefer this biological answer to the mind-body problem, of course. But many of their theories do suggest that the interaction between brain and mind is a one-way street. That is, their theories imply that physical events in your nervous system are the *major cause* for all the subjective experiences in your mind. This is a viewpoint that the intra-psychic psychologists object to strongly.

The Intra-Psychic Viewpoint

At the beginning of this chapter, when we asked where the "essential, psychological YOU" resides, we were speaking in intra-psychic terms. That is, we were asking about the location of your own subjective world, of your own stream of consciousness, or of your *mind*. Traditionally, the intra-psychic or mental viewpoint has dominated the psychological sciences, just as it dominates most of the material in this book.

From an intra-psychic standpoint, YOU are a conscious entity separate from but somehow related to your body. That is, your mind has *voluntary control* over your body (brain), and not the other way around. Our legal system takes this intra-psychic point of view, for the laws of the land don't view you as a machine. Rather, they hold YOU responsible for your actions.

Scientists who study the "inner woman" or "inner man" will usually admit that your genes help determine what your mind is like. And they realize that a brain-damaged person cannot be expected to act and think exactly as normal people do. But from a strictly "mentalistic"

Physiological psychology (fizz-ee-oh-LODGE-uh-cal). That part of psychology which looks upon humans primarily as biological organisms. Physiology is that division of biology dealing with the activities and processes of living systems. *Physio* means "of the body." *Psycho* means "of the mind."

viewpoint, the condition of your body merely *sets limits* to what your mind can accomplish. Within these biological limitations, YOU are presumed to become whatever YOU decide you should be.

The social and behavioral psychologists, however, offer many important reasons why the intra-psychic viewpoint simply cannot explain everything that we know about human beings.

The Social/Behavioral Viewpoint

As the poet John Donne said, you are not an island unto yourself. Rather, you grew up around other people who helped determine your ideas, your values, your joys, your disappointments, your speech, and your behaviors. However, because the biological and the intra-psychic viewpoints have dominated our thinking for so many centuries, it has taken us a very long time to realize the importance of the social and physical environments we live in.

Those psychologists who emphasize the strong influence the outside world has on what we think and do typically have adopted the social/behavioral viewpoint as their solution to the mind-body problem. For the most part, these scientists are referred to as *social psychologists*.

As we will see in Chapters 24–26, social psychologists are interested in many aspects of human behavior. They spend much of their time, however, studying how your attitudes and behaviors are affected by the actions of the *groups* and *organizations* you belong to. In social psychology, your family is considered a "group," while the school you attend is an organization.

From the strict *social viewpoint*, your body creates your mind at birth and has a minor influence on it thereafter. But the outside world creates all your important attitudes and behavioral reactions while you are growing up. From this social viewpoint, therefore, if you want to change your mind, you must first change your environment (or the way that it treats you).

Behavioral psychology goes a step farther. To a behaviorist, your thoughts, feelings, and emotions are *subjective* events. Because these

"Having someone get hit 73 times is unnecessary violence. Have him get hit, say, 49 times."

Donald Lunde

mental experiences take place inside the privacy of your own mind, they cannot be seen or measured directly by a scientist. However, your *behavior* most certainly can be seen and recorded by a scientific observer. *What* you do—the movements you make and the things you say—are non-mental events. Your behavior therefore can be treated as an object and hence can be measured *objectively*—just as one can measure the "behavior" of such other objects as a falling stone, an ocean wave, or a neuron firing. And because behavioral psychologists prefer to study human behavior objectively, they tend to ignore your subjective (mental) experiences and focus instead on what you do and say.

Behaviorists admit your actions are determined partly by your biological inheritance. But they note that one of the main ways your genes influence your behavior is by making you sensitive to your environment. For example, you seem to be "biologically programmed" to seek pleasurable inputs and avoid painful inputs. However, since these pleasures and pains come to you primarily from your *social and physical environment*, behaviorists believe all your mental and physical reactions are the *consequences* of external inputs.

Social learning theory is a fairly recent approach that combines some of the best aspects of social and behavioral psychology. Social learning theorists believe that, when you were young, your environment determined most of your thoughts and actions. You *acquired* these behaviors both because you were rewarded for learning them, and because you tended to *imitate other people* who displayed these behaviors. As you matured, however, you discovered ways of deliberately *changing your outputs* so that your environment would give you *different inputs*. Eventually, social learning theorists believe, you and your environment became an *interacting system*, each influencing the other in predictable and measurable ways.

We will discuss social learning theory more fully in Chapter 19. For now, we might note that behavioral and social psychology have one main point in common: Both approaches focus on the role of the external environment in "shaping" behavioral outputs.

Which View Is Correct?

Despite occasional arguments psychologists may have on the subject, very few of them hold rigidly to just one of the three viewpoints we have described. Instead, psychologists use whatever view seems most appropriate or useful in solving whatever human problem they happen to face at the moment. Different psychologists may *emphasize* the value of one viewpoint or another, but almost all psychological theories make reference to biological, intra-psychic, and environmental influences.

We need to learn as much as we can about all three points of view, for no one of them *all by itself* can explain the rich complexity of human experience. To demonstrate this point as vividly as possible, let us now study one aspect of human behavior—*violence*—as seen from the social/behavioral, the intra-psychic, and the biological points of view.

Violence: Three Theoretical Viewpoints

To many people, the most terrifying form of violence probably is murder. If you have ever walked the empty streets of a big city late at night, surely you have feared that some madman might leap out of the shadows to attack you. And if you have seen the results of some particularly bloody massacre on TV, surely you have wondered why the police don't do a better job of protecting innocent people from such criminals. But as Donald T. Lunde points out in his fascinating book *Murder and Madness*, the facts about violent death are probably quite different from your fantasies and fears.

To begin with, you are quite right to worry about violent death. For according to Reynolds Farley, of the University of Michigan Population Studies Center, there were 21,000 murders in the US in 1978. And by 1985, the number of murders was even higher. Indeed, more of us in the US were killed by *other Americans* in the last 4 years than were killed in Vietnam during the entire war there. Farley notes as well that there are at least 30,000 rapes and more than 300,000 cases of violent assault per year in this country.

However, in some ways you may be much safer on the streets than in your own home, and better off with strangers than with people you know and love. For almost 80 percent of the murders committed each year involve people related to or friendly with each other, and about 40 percent of the killings occur in homes or apartments.

Daytime is safer than night, for few murders take place during business hours. In most big cities, Lunde reports, two-thirds of the killings occur on weekends, most of them on Saturday night between 8 p.m. and 2 a.m. And perhaps because we're around friends and family more during summer holidays and at Christmas, the murder rate peaks in July and in December. For a variety of reasons, the South is more dangerous than the North. Some 44 percent of all recent murders occurred in the southern states, while the lowest murder rate **per capita** is found in New England.

Some Violent Statistics

As far as violence is concerned, young people are much more dangerous than are older people. For instance, less than 10 percent of all murders are committed by people over the age of 50. The average killer is, in fact, about *20 years of age*. It is also true that older people get killed a lot less frequently than do younger ones, for most murder *victims* are under 30 years of age.

As you might suspect, men are three times as likely to kill someone as are women. But women are frequent victims. One-fifth of all the people killed in the US are women murdered in their own bedrooms (usually shot to death by husbands or lovers). When a woman is the murderer, she is most likely to kill a husband or lover by stabbing him to death or shooting him in the kitchen.

According to Lunde, race plays an important part in murder. In some 90 percent of all killings, the victim and the murderer are of the *same race*. However, black men are 10 times as likely to be victims as are white women. Indeed, as Reynolds Farley notes, murder is now the fourth most common cause of death for black males in the United States.

When cross-racial murders do occur, whites are much more likely to kill blacks than vice

Per capita (purr KAPP-it-tuh). A Latin phrase that means, roughly, "to take an average" or "to count heads." If a city of 1,000 people has one murder per year, and a city of 10,000 people has 10 murders per year, the per capita murder rate is the same in both cities.

versa. Blacks are more likely to use knives as murder weapons than whites, while whites are more likely to use guns.

In at least one-third of the cases, the victim seems to have *precipitated the killing*—either by taunting or goading the murderer, or by pulling out a weapon first.

And despite common views on the subject, there is only the slimmest connection between murder and mental illness. A patient released from a mental hospital is no more likely to commit a murder than is the average person— *unless* the patient was hospitalized for being violent. And then the patient is only slightly more likely to commit a crime than is anyone else.

If we cannot blame most acts of violence on mental illness, what is it that causes people to kill each other? Probably each of us has her or his own answer to this question. But most of our explanations will fall within the social/behavioral, intra-psychic, or biological viewpoints. Let's see what each point of view has to say about violence.

Question: Knowing these statistics, what things could you do to decrease the likelihood that you would either commit a murder or be a murder victim?

Social Determinants of Violence

Does the society you grow up in affect the probability that you will harm another individual? Do some cultures repress violent behaviors, while other cultures reward or encourage rape, assault, and murder? Perhaps so. For many research studies suggest that the attitudes held by the majority of people within a given society have a marked effect on the level and type of violence found within that society.

In the United States, as we just mentioned, there are more than 20,000 murders a year. The majority of these deaths are the result of gunshot wounds. About 51 percent of the murders are committed with pistols or hand guns, while rifles and shotguns account for another 15 percent or so of the recorded *homicides*.

Research suggests that some (but not all) children may be affected by violence on television.

Leonard D. Eron

The city of Detroit has a population of about two million people who, according to police estimates, own an average of one gun per person. In 1984, there were some 700 murders in Detroit, the majority of these being deaths from firearms. By contrast, during the same year, there were fewer than 150 murders in *all* of Great Britain—a land of 50 million people. Americans, in general, take a fairly positive attitude toward the private ownership of hand guns, and almost all of our police are armed. In Great Britain, hand guns are illegal. Not even the police wear pistols, except on rare and very special occasions.

Does the fact that British society takes quite a different attitude toward guns and violent behavior help explain why there are 100 times as many murders (per capita) in the United States each year as in Great Britain? Or should we point the finger of shame at television and other cultural influences instead?

Effects of TV on Violence

In 1969 the US Senate, worried about the impact of television violence on the personality development of young children, asked the Surgeon General to undertake an extensive study on this subject. In 1972, after an expenditure of one million dollars in research funds, Dr. Jesse Steinfeld (the Surgeon General) reported some interesting findings.

Is there violence on television? Yes, indeed. In 1967, according to the National Commission on the Causes and Prevention of Violence, a staggering 94.3 percent of cartoon shows contained violent episodes. That same year, 81.6 percent of all prime-time entertainment shows on TV contained violence. The Commission estimated that a normal child, growing up during the 1960's and 1970's, would have watched at least 20,000 incidents of violence on television by the time she or he was 19.

In 1983, the National Institute of Mental Health released a "10-year follow-up" on the 1972 Surgeon General's report. The authors of the 1983 study conclude as follows:

> After 10 more years of research, the consensus among most of the research community is that violence on television does lead to aggressive behavior by children and teenagers who watch the programs. . . . Not all children become aggressive, of course, but the correlations between violence and aggression are positive. In magnitude, television violence is as strongly correlated with aggressive behavior as any other behavioral variable that has been measured.

Belson's London Study

What sorts of studies led the NIMH scientists to draw the conclusions they did? One important example came from England. In 1978 William Belson reported that young British men who are "heavy" watchers of TV violence are much more likely to commit aggressive acts than are boys who view such violence only occasionally.

The several hundred subjects in Belson's study were selected by **random sample** from all parts of London. Belson interviewed and observed the young men for some 10 hours to determine how many violent TV programs they had viewed in recent years. He then divided the boys into two groups—the "heavy watchers" and the "occasionals"—and studied them further.

Surprisingly enough, there were no obvious social, physical, or educational differences between the boys in the two groups. But when Belson asked the boys to report secretly how many acts of violence they had *actually engaged in* during the six months, he found rather shocking results. The "heavy watchers" admitted to a much larger number of violent acts than did the "occasionals." (Some of the acts reported were dropping lighted matches into a shopper's bag, busting open pay telephones, kicking other boys in the crotch, and beating on automobiles with hammers.)

One important point about Belson's work: Some 50 percent of the boys in the study did not report *any violent acts at all*. A mere 12 percent of the boys were "active" aggressors— and most of them were "heavy" watchers of violence on television. But each of these "actively" violent young men reported having performed *at least 10 acts of serious violence* in the six months before being interviewed.

Eron's Chicago Circle Studies

In the February 1982 issue of the *American Psychologist*, Leonard D. Eron answers some of the questions raised by Belson's research. Eron and his colleagues at the University of Illinois at Chicago Circle have studied violence in children for more than two decades. In their most recent work, they have found that TV has an effect on aggressive behaviors not only in boys, but in girls as well. But *which* boys and girls does TV affect most, and why?

Eron states that aggressive children have certain common characteristics. First, they tend to be disliked by other children. Second, they indulge in active aggressive fantasies. Third, both aggressive boys and girls prefer masculine activities. Fourth, they are low achievers in school. And fifth, they enjoy watching violence on TV and often identify strongly with the violence they see on the television screen.

The *parents* of these aggressive children have certain things in common, too. First and foremost, Eron says, "Those parents who punish their children physically and express dissatisfaction with their children's accomplishments and [social behaviors] have the most aggressive children." Both the mothers and fathers of aggressive boys also tend to be aggressive themselves. The younger and the less educated the father, the higher his son's aggression. And the

lower-paying the father's job, the more aggressive his daughter is likely to be.

Eron believes one of the main reasons some children are aggressive is that they have poor models, both in their parents and in the programs they watch on television. Furthermore, these young people apparently cannot differentiate between the fantasy violence they watch on the tube and aggressive behaviors in real-world situations. In his 1982 article, Eron reports that he and his colleagues gave "reality training" to a group of aggressive children in order to help them learn the difference between televised fantasy and reality. The technique involved teaching children the "tricks" TV producers use in filming their programs. The children were also exposed to the sorts of attitude-change procedures we will describe in Chapter 25. Eron states that the "aggression therapy" apparently was successful. He concludes, "There are simple instructional procedures that can be used by parents and teachers to counteract the negative effects television is having on our children."

Question: If parents of aggressive children tend to be punitive, rejecting, and of low educational status, how likely are they to use the sorts of instructional procedures that Eron has developed? What sorts of things could be done to encourage the parents to learn and use these techniques?

Violence and Pornographic Films

On American television—and in American movies—violence and sexual aggression are often combined. Almost always, it is the male who takes out his aggressive feelings on a female. Does this combination of sex and violence in the media somehow encourage men to be violent toward women in "real life settings"? Recent research suggests this may be the case. However, the research also shows that the *explanations* the male gives for his aggression typically do not include the fact that he's seen so much violence on TV and in the movies.

Massachusetts psychologist Michele Bograd recently interviewed 15 abusive men and 15 battered women. In a 1983 report, Bograd states that the men tended to believe their violence was caused by *temporary factors*—they were drunk or experiencing job-related problems. Thus, the men seldom felt "responsible" for their acts. Indeed, most of them blamed the wives—because the women "failed to live up to their expectations." The men also viewed their violence as a "positive act, intended to facilitate communications or end an argument." The women, however, perceived the violence as stemming from their husbands' "chronic emotional problems." Thus, they blamed their husbands' personalities, not themselves (or the media). And they saw the violence as "coercive, hostile, and intended to cause injury." (We will have more to say about the way married couples *attribute* motives to each other in Chapter 23.)

According to Murray State University psychologists Rosemarie Bogal-Albritten and Bill Albritten, "wife battering" may get its start long before the marriage ceremony. In a 1983 report, the Albrittens state that 20 percent of the college students they questioned had had a personal experience with *premarital violence*. The reasons the students gave for their acts were, for the most part, similar to those reported by Michele Bograd.

Why do American men "batter" their women? Obviously, the couples involved tend to put the blame on stress or personality factors. However, University of Wisconsin psychologist Edward Donnerstein and his colleagues offer quite a different reason. In an article in the January 1984 issue of *Psychology Today*, Donnerstein and Daniel Linz suggest that TV and the movies *desensitize* men to the negative effects of violence.

Donnerstein and his colleagues showed several groups of men four movies featuring violence and explicit sexuality. The films included such "classics" as *Tool Box Murders*, *Vice Squad*, *Texas Chainsaw Massacre*, and *I Spit on Your Grave*. The subjects watched one film a day for four days straight. They filled out a "mood questionnaire" after watching each movie. One group of subjects viewed the films in the order listed above. A second group saw the movies in reverse order. Donnerstein and Linz report that, after watching the first film, the men were "significantly above the norm for depression, anxiety, and annoyance." However, by the time they had watched the fourth film, their moods had "returned to normal." The subjects rated the last film they watched (no matter which one it was) as significantly "less offen-

sive" and "less violent" than the first one they viewed. All these films contain scenes depicting graphic violence against women. After watching the fourth film, the male subjects considered this violence as "significantly less debasing and degrading to women, more humorous and more enjoyable, and they claimed a greater willingness to see this type of film again."

Next, Donnerstein and his associates showed a filmed re-enactment of a rape trial to two groups of male subjects. According to Donnerstein and Linz, "The victim of rape was rated as significantly more worthless and her injury as significantly less severe by those men who had been exposed to filmed violence than by a control group who saw only the rape trial and did not view any of our films."

Donnerstein and Linz believe the widespread availability of films linking sex and violence "desensitizes" men to actual effects of aggression against women. The movies may also "perpetuate the myth that women enjoy rape" and thus encourage males to practice violent behaviors. However, Donnerstein and Linz note that when they "debriefed" their subjects, they were able to "resensitize" the men. The debriefing sessions "produce a marked decrease in the acceptance of rape myths and violence against women," according to the Wisconsin psychologists.

It is the *combination* of violence and sexuality that "desensitizes" people to aggression, however. Erotic movies that are *non*-violent apparently do not lead to any increase in aggression. Indeed, under the right circumstances, they may even have a positive effect on behavior. As California psychologist Edward Nelson points out in the 1982 book *The Influence of Pornography on Behavior*, "Sexually explicit materials have a definite place as an adjunct to a wide variety of procedures in sex education and therapy."

The "Body Language" of Victims

Some people get mugged frequently; others never do. Is there any connection at all between the actions of the *victim* and the aggression the *criminal* shows toward that victim? Psychologists Betty Grayson and Morris Stein believe there is. In the August 1980 issue of *Psychology Today* they report that the way that you walk may (in part) determine whether a mugger will select you as a victim—or leave you alone.

Grayson and Stein began by secretly filming 60 people as they walked along the streets of

New York City. Then the psychologists showed these films to 65 prisoners who had been convicted of assault and asked the prisoners to rate the "walkers" in terms of their "muggability." Grayson and Stein state there was an exceptionally high level of agreement among the prisoners as to which of the "walkers" would make easy targets, and which would not.

Grayson and Stein then inspected the films carefully to analyze the way in which the pedestrians walked. Those individuals with high "muggability" scores tended to walk in a dreamy, exaggerated way. Their strides were either very long or very short, and they acted as if they were in conflict with themselves. Grayson and Stein believe that the *body language* of the victims was a loud and clear signal to the **assailant**, "Here is an easy target."

It takes two to tango, and it takes both a victim and an assailant for a violent crime to take place. The Grayson and Stein research suggests that the victim picks the aggressor as much as the other way round.

Question: *What kinds of behaviors by the children* would you imagine are most likely to trigger off child abuse by parents? Would the child have been abused if he or she didn't display these "trigger behaviors"? Then who is to blame for the abuse, the child or the parents?

Violence: A Multi-determined Behavior

If we put together the various studies on violence, it seems likely that the most likely "candidate" for aggressive behaviors would be a young person who grew up in a family that approved of violence, whose parents watched violent TV shows and discouraged the young person from expressing any sympathy for the victim of aggression. And judging from the little research so far reported, the most likely victim would probably be someone confused about life, whose parents had not taught the person much about self-control and getting along with others.

But are social factors the only—or even the major—determinants of violent actions? Is all aggression learned by "imitation," or is the situation much more complex than that?

Bowling Green University psychologist J.P. Scott has studied aggression in people and animals for a great many years. Scott believes violence is usually *multi-determined*. That is, aggressive attacks almost always have biological, intra-psychic, and social/behavioral causes.

Scott says that, at the human level, societal factors are usually the most important of all. He points out that males in our culture are encouraged to leave home when they reach sexual maturity, but typically do not form new family ties until several years afterwards. Perhaps this is why, in the US, violent crimes are most likely to be committed by single or divorced males between the ages of 16 and 25.

Scott believes we will not do away with violence and aggression until we create societies that promote peace, stability, and positive interpersonal relationships—particularly among disadvantaged young people in all cultures.

But do we need to teach "peaceful thoughts and behaviors" to *all* people, or are there some individuals whose "inborn personalities" are such that they are likely to become violent—or victims—no matter what social environment they grow up in?

Intra-Psychic Determinants of Violence

In the later chapters of this book, when we discuss a topic called *personality theory*, we will find that some psychologists view violence

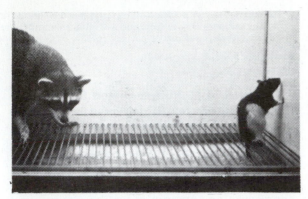

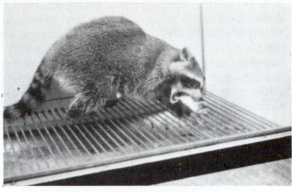

Fig. 4.2 A raccoon and a hooded rat remain far apart in cage before shock.

Fig. 4.3 Two seconds after receiving shock, the animals move toward each other.

Konrad Lorenz   Nathan Azrin

as a mental trait that is determined by a person's subjective outlook on life. From this intrapsychic position, personality traits are produced both by one's biological inheritance and by what happens during certain critical stages in a person's early development.

Many social/behavioral psychologists theorize that we are born without any strong tendency either to be violent or non-violent—we thus become what our environment *teaches* us to become. But according to many intra-psychic theorists, we are born with an aggressive **instinct** we must somehow *learn to control.* Thus, one of the major functions of civilization is to train us to **repress** our aggressive instincts.

Konrad Lorenz

As evidence to support their view, intra-psychic theorists often point to the research of **Konrad Lorenz**, a German scientist who got his ideas about human aggression from spending many years studying the behavior patterns of wild animals. Lorenz found that instinctual

behavior patterns in lower animals are primarily controlled by two factors: (1) such internal biological factors as hormone levels, and (2) environmental inputs that seem to "release" the instinctual response. During mating season, for example, most male animals will immediately attack another male that wanders into their territory. However, this aggressive behavior occurs only when (1) the level of male hormone in the animal's body is very high, and (2) the first male sees, hears, or smells another male. Furthermore, this aggression is almost never directed toward females or infants.

Lorenz believes that while aggressive instincts first evolved in lower animals, the tendency toward senseless violence has reached its peak in human beings. Human males, for instance, often attack others (including women and children), whether or not the attacking males have high levels of male hormone. Humans also kill each other out of hatred, prejudice, politics, or "just for fun"—not just because the victim has intruded into the killer's home territory.

Not all scientists agree with the conclusions Lorenz draws from his research. Thus, it is still an open question whether or not human beings are *born* with an aggressive "instinct" we must learn to control. But in seeking further data on this matter, it might help if we asked the following question: Do animals ever show the kind of "vindictive nastiness" we see too often in humans—both on television and in real life?

Pain and Aggression

Psychologist Nathan Azrin and his colleagues, working at the Anna State Hospital in Illinois, fell into the study of violence quite by accident. Azrin is a behavioral psychologist who believes in the importance of rewards and punishments in determining behavior, and he wanted to see if he could train two rats to become "more social." In this research, Azrin defined *social behavior* as "moving toward each other." Azrin presumed the more he could reward the rats for "seeking each other's company," the more social behavior they would show.

Azrin and his group began by putting the two rats in a "shock box" (see Figs. 4.2 and 4.3). The psychologists planned to shock the animals and then reward them for moving toward each other by turning the electricity *off*. To the great surprise of Azrin and his group, however, they never got the chance to reward the rats for "social movements." For the moment the shock went on, the two animals turned on each other and attacked each other violently.

Wisely enough, Azrin ***et al.*** abandoned their original objective and began to study aggression.

First, the psychologists had to make sure they knew what they were studying. Think about it for a moment. How would you go about defining *aggression* in a rat? Azrin et al. found the animal had a characteristic "aggressive posture": As soon as the rat was shocked, it would stand up on its hind legs, face another rat, open its mouth, bare its front teeth, and then strike out at the other animal with its forepaws. Oddly enough, if another rat (or some similar object) was not present, the shocked animal would show none of this behavior, but would keep its mouth closed and would cling with all four paws to the metal grid on which it stood.

Second, Azrin and his group had to determine whether the aggression was caused by the *shock*, not by incidental factors they had failed to control for. The psychologists tested the relationship between shock and violent behavior by varying the *intensity* of the electrical current. They found that (1) the stronger the shock, the longer the aggression lasted; and (2) the more frequently the shock was given, the more vigorous and vicious the animal's attack was. Furthermore, the rats did not ever seem to get used to or *habituate* to the shock. The animals would display the attack behavior several thousand times a day if the experimenters shocked them that often.

Azrin et al. also showed that this aggressive response was instinctual and not learned, for animals raised from birth in complete isolation from other rats still demonstrated the violent attack pattern when they were first shocked. Rats that lived together from birth attacked one another just as often as they attacked animals

Instincts. Inherited desires or behavior patterns. An innate reflex is a highly specific stimulus-response pattern that is inherited. For instance, if a mother touches her infant's cheek, the infant will reflexively turn its head as if to suckle. An instinct is a less specific behavioral pattern. For example, the "maternal instinct" is the set of behavior patterns women are supposed to inherit that makes them *want* to take care of their infants. The maternal instinct is not a reflex, since the mother presumably will respond to *any* need that the infant expresses. Many psychologists doubt that humans inherit such ill-defined desires or instincts.

Repress. To block out or to forget something deliberately.

Konrad Lorenz (CONE-raht LOR-rents). A noted German biologist who became famous for his studies of animal instincts. Lorenz believes that humans have stronger killer instincts than do other animals, but not all psychologists agree with Lorenz. Technically speaking, Lorenz should be called an *ethologist* (ee-THOL-oh-gist)—that is, a scientist who is interested in the biological basis of behavior. Lorenz received the Nobel Prize in 1973 for his ethological research.

Et al. (ett-all). From the Latin term *et alia*, meaning "and others." Scientists like to give each other credit. If an experiment was performed by Smith and Jones, it is usually referred to as "the study by Smith and Jones." But some experiments are performed jointly by a dozen or more scientists. Rather than writing Smith, Jones, Johnson, Ginsburg, Washington, Lee, Brodsky, Blanc, and Gonzalez each time we speak of the study, we usually say "Smith et al." Usually—but not always—the first name listed is that of the "senior scientist" who had the greatest responsibility for the research.

that were complete strangers. And since both males and females aggressed against members of either sex, Azrin concluded that neither sexual competition nor attraction was responsible for this reaction.

Azrin believes it was the *pain* of the shock that brought the instinctual behavior pattern into *readiness*. But it was the *sight* of another animal that "released" the innate response.

Question: Why does the research of Azrin et al. support the notion that violence is almost always triggered off by the presence of a "victim"?

Violence Induced by Frustration

Is there something special about the *physical* pain caused by electrical shock that triggers off aggressive behavior? Or would a *psychologically* painful stimulus do just as well?

In their next series of experiments, Azrin and his group found that almost any situation that caused the animal psychological discomfort or *frustration* would set off an attack. If a hungry pigeon is rewarded with a piece of grain each time it pecks at a button, it will soon learn to peck the button vigorously. If, after it has been pecking away for some time and earning its

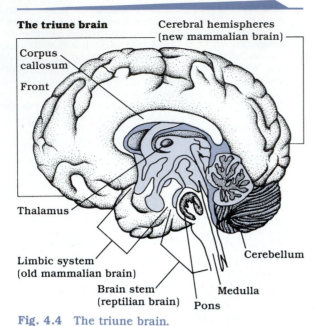

The triune brain

Cerebral hemispheres
(new mammalian brain)

Corpus
callosum

Front

Thalamus

Limbic system
(old mammalian brain)

Brain stem
(reptilian brain)

Pons

Cerebellum

Medulla

Fig. 4.4 The triune brain.

corn, you suddenly stop giving it the reward, the pigeon will typically first attack the button. Then it will peck viciously at any other object (such as another pigeon) that happens to be handy. If we *assume* the pigeon is "frustrated" by failing to receive its expected reward, we might conclude that "psychological discomfort" can lead to violence as readily as can electric shock. (Whether the pigeon experiences "frustration" and "discomfort" similar to that reported by humans is a question still hotly debated by many psychologists.)

Fortunately, as Azrin et al. found, there is a way to prevent violence from being the natural consequence of frustration and pain. The aggressive **syndrome** usually does not occur if the frustrated animal is given a chance to *escape* rather than *attack*. A rat cooped up in a small box with another animal will aggress because it apparently has no alternative. The same rat, if shocked in an open field, will escape rather than take out its frustration on nearby objects. The attack behavior will also not occur if the animal is given the opportunity to *avoid* the pain or frustration in the first place, or if the animal can *terminate* the pain by a peaceful gesture.

Question: From an intra-psychic viewpoint, why might violence be expected to occur more frequently in crowded, big-city slums than in surburban areas? And why would riots be more

likely to take place during times of high unemployment than when jobs are easy to get?

Frustration-Aggression Hypothesis

Perhaps the greatest modern contributor to the intra-psychic viewpoint was Sigmund Freud, the Viennese psychiatrist who developed an intra-psychic theory of personality called psychoanalysis. As we will see in later chapters, Freud believed there is a childish part of our personalities which demands immediate gratification of all its wishes. Whenever this "child" in our minds is frustrated, it may either throw a temper tantrum or display other immature forms of emotion.

Using Freud's basic idea, several psychologists jointly derived what they called the *frustration-aggression hypothesis*. According to this theory, frustration occurs whenever you are (1) highly motivated, and (2) encounter a barrier of some kind that prevents you from reaching a much-desired goal. The barrier may be physical, psychological, or symbolic. If you cannot get around the barrier, you experience frustration, and your behavior typically becomes less logical and more strongly emotional than would usually be the case. Thus, you are very likely to aggress whenever you're frustrated. However, you may *express* your aggression in a variety of ways. You may hit the person—which is physical violence. You may cruelly deny the person something the individual needs, which is psychological aggression. Or, you may poke fun at the person, which Freud considered a symbolic form of aggression.

As intriguing as the frustration-aggression hypothesis is, the theory takes far too limited a view of the problem of violence and aggression. As Scott points out, aggression is *multi-determined*. Thus, frustration doesn't always lead to violence, nor is aggressive behavior always the result of frustration. We have already mentioned some of the social and intra-psychic determinants of violent behavior. Now, let's see what we can learn about the biological factors that might be associated with aggressive acts.

Biological Determinants of Violence

We are not entirely sure what takes place inside the brain of an animal (or human) who flies into a rage and attacks someone else. However, certain parts of the brain do seem to be heavily involved in aggressive behavior. And certain chemicals do appear to *inhibit* violent reactions while other chemicals *excite* them. Before you can understand the neuro-chemistry of aggression, though, you will need to know a bit more about the parts of your brain.

The Triune Brain

Paul MacLean is a noted neuro-physiologist who serves as chief of brain evolutionary research at the National Institute of Mental Health. MacLean believes the human brain evolved over millions of years from the brains of lower animals. But this evolution took place in three main stages, says MacLean, and thus the human brain has three main parts. MacLean calls this belief the *theory of the triune brain*.

According to MacLean, the first animals to develop a true brain were the ancient reptiles. This *reptilian brain* still exists inside your head, says MacLean, in the form of your **brain stem** (see Fig. 4.4). The stem of your brain sits atop your spinal cord, and reaches up to your cerebrum, much as the stem of a mushroom reaches from the roots of the plant up to the big, fleshy cap.

Your brain stem includes such neural structures as the **pons** and the **medulla**. The pons and the medulla are nerve centers that help control such vital activities as walking, breathing, swallowing, and adjusting your heart rate. The brain stem also is the main pathway for conducting messages between your brain and your spinal cord.

Over millions of years, the ancient mammals evolved from the reptiles. And in the evolutionary process, MacLean says, many additional neural structures got tacked onto the reptilian brain. MacLean calls these "tacked on" nerve centers the *old mammalian brain*. The most important parts of this old mammalian brain are the **thalamus**, the **hypothalamus**, and the **limbic system**. Your *thalamus* acts as a giant switchboard that routes sensory inputs to the proper areas of your cortex, and transmits output commands from your cortex to the muscles you want to move. As we will see in Chapter 10, your *hypothalamus* is intimately involved in the process of motivation. And the *limbic system* we will discuss in detail in just a moment.

According to MacLean's theory, as the mammals themselves evolved (from rat to cat to elephant to monkey), they acquired the huge cerebral hemispheres that make up the major part of the human brain. MacLean calls this the *new mammalian brain*, which is composed of the

Syndrome (SIN-drome; rhymes with "BEEN home"). A group of symptoms or signs typical of a particular disease or reaction pattern. The aggressive syndrome varies from one animal to another. In cats, for instance, it usually includes spitting, scratching, biting, arching of the back, flattening of the ears, baring of the teeth, twitching of the tail, and so forth.

Brain stem. The lower area of the brain that connects the spinal cord with the middle parts of the brain.

Pons, medulla (me-DULL-ah). Neural centers in the brain stem that control vital activities such as walking and breathing.

Thalamus, hypothalamus (THALL-ah-mus, HIGH-poh-THALL-ah-mus). Neural centers in the middle part of the brain. Your thalamus is a giant switchboard which routes input messages to various areas of the cortex. Your hypothalamus influences emotions and motivated behaviors (see Chapters 10–12).

Limbic system (LIM-bick). A related set of nerve centers in your brain that influences your emotional behavior.

Cerebellum (ser-ee-BELL-um). From the Latin word meaning "little brain." A large center of neural tissue at the rear of the brain, just below the occipital lobe, that coordinates muscle movements (among other things).

the cerebrum (and the cortex), the corpus callosum, and the **cerebellum**.

Functions of the "Three Brains"

MacLean notes that your "reptilian brain" is incredibly more complex than the brain of any snake or lizard. And your "old mammalian" brain is likewise much more developed than (say) the brain of a rat or cat. Small wonder, then, that your thoughts and feelings and actions are so much more complicated than either a snake's or a rat's.

MacLean tends to assign certain psychological functions to the three types of brain. For instance, he believes that the brain stem controls certain *inherited* types of behaviors, such as walking and breathing. According to MacLean, these "automatic" behavior patterns are primarily determined by your genes and function almost entirely at an unconscious level.

The old mammalian brain, too, operates at an unconscious, instinctual level. Thus, this part of the brain is responsible for emotional responses, including such "instinctual" behaviors as aggression and physical violence. The old mammalian brain also controls those activities involved in satisfying bodily needs. The old mammalian brain is, however, capable of *learning* new response patterns and thus is not restricted entirely to expressing inherited behaviors.

It is your "new brain," though, that gives you the capacity for learning to speak, to think cre-

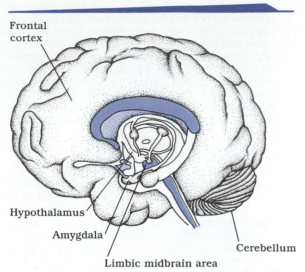

Frontal cortex

Hypothalamus

Amygdala

Limbic midbrain area

Cerebellum

Fig. 4.5   The limbic system, including the amygdala. The "new mammalian brain" is the outer covering of the brain. The "limbic lobe" and the midbrain area make up the "old mammalian brain."

atively, and to deal with the rich array of informational inputs that come to you from the complex world you live in. It is also true, MacLean says, that your cortex and your cerebral hemispheres are capable of coordinating the activities of the two more "primitive" areas of your brain. Thus, given the proper training, you can learn to control such instinctual behaviors as aggression. However, anything that *disrupts* neural activity in the old mammalian brain might well disrupt cortical control of emotional responses as well.

Not all scientists agree with MacLean's notions of how the three main parts of the brain evolved. But to show you how they operate—and how your cortex exercises control over the lower centers in your brain—let us now look more closely at what goes on in your limbic system.

The Limbic System

The Latin word *limbus* means "border." The limbic system is so named because it makes up the "border" or inner surface of both your cerebral hemispheres. There are identical limbic systems in both your hemispheres. But since they are usually in close touch with each other (via the corpus callosal bridge), we can consider the two systems as one unit.

Your limbic system has several parts or structures to it (see Fig. 4.5). One of these structures

is the **amygdala**, which is buried deep within the temporal lobe on each side of your head. The amygdala is a nut-shaped group of neurons that gets its name from the Latin word for "almond." Since the amygdala in each of your temporal lobes has a decided influence on how violent you are, and on your sex life, it is well worth studying.

Cortex vs. Limbic System

Under normal circumstances, your cortex maintains control over the primitive, emotional reactions that are set off by activity in your limbic system. But what happens when you take a drug that reduces the ability of your "new brain" to dominate the two more primitive brains? According to the Triune Brain theory, you would regress to a more "animalistic" way of behaving. The theory assumes, for instance, that intoxicated people act in a childish, aggressive manner because alcohol knocks out cortical control of the limbic system.

Support for this assumption comes from experiments on cats. It isn't easy to get a cat drunk because most animals tend to refuse alcohol. But we can remove the animal's cortex surgically while leaving the limbic system intact. How do you think a cat would react if we used a surgical knife rather than a drug to free the limbic system from cortical inhibition?

To begin with, this "de-cortex-ed," or **decorticate**, animal gets along surprisingly well, considering that it has been deprived of more than 10 percent of its brain. There seems to be no basic change in the animal's personality—friendly cats remain friendly, and aggressive felines remain aggressive. However, even *very slight pain or frustration* is enough to set these animals into an explosive, violent rage.

Question: How does MacLean's belief that alcohol makes you "regress" to a more primitive brain agree with the data on the social and psychological influences on alcoholic behavior discussed in Chapter 3?

Sex and Aggression

Next, what do you think would happen if we "reversed" the kind of operation just described? That is, what would happen if we removed parts of the limbic system in animals but left most of the cortex intact? Heinrich Klüever and Paul Bucy were probably the first scientists to perform this operation. Their experimental animals were rhesus monkeys, a species of *primate* noted for its vile temper and its readiness to aggress. Kluever and Bucy removed the temporal lobes from both hemispheres in their animals—thus taking out the amygdalas and other parts of the limbic system.

After the monkeys had recovered, their personalities appeared to have changed rather profoundly. They were gentle and placid in almost all circumstances, even when attacked by another animal. They also became markedly *oversexed*. For example, the males would attempt to mount anything handy, including inanimate objects.

Later studies by other scientists confirmed the Kluever and Bucy experiment by showing that removal of the amygdala in wild animals makes them relatively tame.

Stimulating the Amygdala

Given the results of the Kluever-Bucy study, what do you think would happen if you could somehow *stimulate* the amygdala in a normal cat electrically? The answer is not particularly surprising. If you insert a long, thin needle electrode into a cat's amygdala and turn on the current, the animal flies into a rage. Its hair stands on end, its back arches, it spits and screams, and it will usually attack anything nearby (including the experimenter).

There are at least two explanations for this rage response. First, the electrical stimulation may cause the animal *intense pain* and the cat merely responds as did Azrin's rats. Second, the current may actually trigger off an unconscious *aggressive reflex*, which may or may not cause the animal to feel pain. The first explanation seems more likely, however, since recent studies show that pain-killing drugs such as morphine and enkephalin have an *inhibitory effect* on neural activity in various parts of the limbic system. It is also true that the *precise rage response* the animal makes is dependent on what objects are present in its environment when you stimulate its brain, and how it has learned to respond to ordinary rage in the past.

Now, knowing how cats respond to electrical stimulation of their limbic systems, what do you think would happen if someone stuck a needle electrode in *your* amygdala and turned on the current? More to the point, perhaps, why would anyone wish to do such a thing?

Brain Damage and Violence

Most humans can tolerate a fair amount of stress without becoming violent. Others of us, however, seem to fly off the handle at the slightest provocation. Could it be that individuals who are particularly bad-tempered might suffer

Amygdala (a-MIG-dah-lah). An almond-shaped nerve center in your temporal lobe that is part of your limbic system. Removal of the amygdala makes a monkey rather unemotional and easygoing, but has other effects as well.

Decorticate (de-CORT-uh-cate). An animal or human whose cortex has been removed, usually through surgery.

from some subtle damage to their amygdalas?

Vernon Mark and Frank Ervin—two brain scientists who worked together in Boston for many years—believe that senseless human violence is almost always associated with some form of brain damage. Mark and Ervin studied many patients who were hospitalized because they had killed or maimed others in "fits of rage." Some of these patients also had epileptic-type seizures, and EEG recordings often suggested the presence of scar tissue in their amygdalas.

When drugs and psychotherapy failed to reduce the number of violent attacks these patients had, Mark and Ervin decided to remove the damaged amygdalas surgically. Some of the patients showed a dramatic improvement following the operation. Unfortunately, many of the patients either were unchanged in their behaviors, or even became worse.

"Psychosurgery"

Physicians call operations such as the removal of the amygdala *psychosurgery*, because the purpose of the surgery is to "cure" patients of inappropriate *thoughts or behaviors* that seemingly cannot be removed by pills or psychotherapy.

But before we routinely chop up people's brains in order to "make them behave," there are several dangers we should take note of. First, Mark and Ervin have been able to demonstrate clear-cut brain damage in but a *small fraction* of the patients they have studied. Second, as we noted, not all the patients were improved after the surgery. And third, not all scientists have been successful in their attempts to repeat the Mark and Ervin research.

Karl Pribram, a noted neurosurgeon at Stanford, points out there is no doubt at all that a damaged amygdala *can* lead to episodes of violent rage in human beings. But, according to Pribram, we would be very wrong to assume that the reverse is true—*that episodes of violence are a universal sign of scar tissue in the amygdala*. In fact, *most* assaults and aggressive behaviors seem to be caused by psychological and social factors, not by brain damage.

E. Valenstein

Psychosurgery, then, not only doesn't work very well in most cases, but seems to be aimed at the wrong goal—that of changing the *brain*, rather than changing the violent person's *mental processing* or *social environment*.

Furthermore, the moral questions raised by such operations are complex and often frightening. Pribram reminds us, too, of another factor we must always consider in evaluating research such as that performed by Mark and Ervin. Even if a patient does cease being violent after psychosurgery, we cannot be certain that it is the *surgery* that was responsible for the behavioral change. It may be that the changed *attitudes* of the patient's family, friends, and the medical staff after the operation caused the decrease in aggression. If we *expect* psychosurgery patients to behave more maturely after parts of their brains are removed, the patients may *respond* to our expectations even if the surgery itself was not particularly successful.

Despite the evidence showing that psychosurgery is not a particularly effective way to change behavior, the technique continues to be used on some patients. The people in favor of psychosurgery are primarily medical doctors who believe the brain controls the mind, and not the other way around. In his 1980 book *The Psychosurgery Debate*, Michigan psychologist Elliot Valenstein explains why the issue can't be settled merely on the basis of experimental results:

> I have concluded that only part of the conflict can be attributed to arguments about the data. Perhaps more significant are the divergent views of human nature and of the proper relationship between the individual and society. Such contrasting views often generate strong passions.

Your brain is an organ of marvelous complexity. And everything you think, feel, or do is influenced by neural activity in your brain. Thus, you must learn something about how your brain functions if you want to figure out "what makes you tick." However, you cannot understand the richness of human experience merely by studying electro-chemical discharges in your neurons, any more than you could comprehend the beauty of a Beethoven symphony merely by studying the physics of sound waves.

Your thoughts and actions are always affected by your biological inheritance, your past experience, and what is going on in your present environment. To give up any of the three main viewpoints in psychology would be to short-circuit your understanding of why you think and act as you do.

As the debate over psychosurgery suggests, though, the major conflict among the three viewpoints comes not so much in explaining "what makes you tick," as it does in suggesting how to repair the human clockwork when it gets violently out of adjustment. Or to put the matter another way, your *theoretical viewpoint* toward people almost always determines the type of *treatment* you think they should have in order to "tick better."

We will begin our discussion of theories and therapies in the next chapter.

Question: What kind of experiment might you perform to determine if it were the *removal of the amygdala* that decreased the patient's violent episodes, or merely the fact that the patient had *had an operation* of some kind?

Summary

1 The complex set of interactions among brain, mind, and environment is often referred to as the **mind-body** problem.

2 **Descartes** stated that mind and body were made of **separate substances** that interacted like husband and wife.

3 Gall theorized that there was a separate "organ of the brain" for each **psychological trait**. As the trait was "exercised," the "organ" associated with that trait should swell, cause a "bump" in the skull. Gall developed a technique for "reading the bumps on the head," which he called **phrenology**.

4 Phrenology failed when Pierre Flourens showed he could remove large parts of

the brain without removing the "psycho-logical traits" Gall said were located in those parts. Flourens believed the brain **functioned as a whole**.

5 Paul Broca disputed Flourens. Broca first located the **speech center** in the left hemisphere in 1861. We now know that some behaviors are mediated by specific sites in the brain, but others are not.

6 Each cerebral hemisphere is divided into four parts—the **frontal lobe**, the **temporal lobe**, the **occipital lobe**, and the **parietal lobe**.

7 Large areas of the cortex are silent to electrical probing. These so-called **association areas** are presumably the parts of the cortex where information processing and decision making occur.

8 That area of psychology concerned with studying how body functions affect behavior is called **physiological psychology**, **biopsychology**, or **psychobiology**.

9 Violence is caused by many factors, including social, intra-psychic, and biological influences.

10 The violence on TV may serve as a **model** for some but not all young people.

11 Males who have watched films featuring sexual aggression toward women become **desensitized** to violence and tend to believe the myth that most women "enjoy" rape.

12 The **body language** of mugging victims may signal their weakness to their assailants.

13 According to the **frustration-aggression hypothesis**, violent attacks are an instinctual (unlearned) response to frustration. Research suggests, however, that organisms aggress only if they cannot escape from the frustrating (or painful) situation.

14 According to the **theory of the triune brain**, the **brain stem** evolved from the reptilian brain, the **old mammalian brain** evolved into the lower centers of the cerebrum such as the **limbic system**, while the **new mammalian brain** evolved into the **cerebrum** and **cortex**.

15 Emotional behavior is correlated with electrical activity in the limbic system, a set of neural centers that includes the **amygdala** in the temporal lobe. Stimulation of the amygdala is often followed by aggressive attacks. Removal of the amygdala leads to a marked reduction in aggressive behavior in animals, but not necessarily in humans.

16 **Psychosurgery** is an attempt to change thoughts and behaviors by removing parts of the brain. It seldom is effective.

17 Behavior is **multi-determined**. There is no one unique solution to the problem of violence in today's world because almost all violence involves biological, psychological, and environmental factors.

(Continued from p. 90.)

"Peace," Jennifer Ahearn said as she slipped demurely into the chair in front of Professor Rosalind Sackoff's desk.

"Looks more like 'pieces' to me, Jeff," Dr. Sackoff said. "Pieces of this and that, which you dragged out of a trunk of old clothes you found in the attic. Where did you get that Mother Hubbard dress, not to mention that black polka-dot scarf tied around your head?"

"Oh, this is the typical dress of a Hutterite woman," Jennifer said quietly. "I thought you might like to see how they dress."

Rosalind Sackoff laughed. "Whatever happened to blue jeans and T-shirts?"

Jennifer shrugged. "They made me change."

"*Made* you change?"

The young woman nodded. "That was the price I had to pay in order to learn the secret of their peaceful ways."

"Well, don't keep me in suspense," Dr. Sackoff said. "You know how I adore secrets."

Jennifer stared at her hands for a moment or two.

"The Hutterites *are* peaceful, you know. They are totally opposed to violence of any kind. No wars, no wife beatings, no child abuse. They live together in almost total harmony."

"Okay, I'll give you that," Rosalind Sackoff said. "But what's their secret? Do they put Miltown in the water, or Pheno-barb in the potato salad?"

"No, they don't believe in drugs of any kind," Jennifer replied. "Not even pain-killers. They believe that discomfort is a part of life, and you've just got to get used to it."

Dr. Sackoff shrugged. "So it must be yoga. They sit in the lotus position all day long to achieve oneness with the Universal Spirit."

Jennifer shook her head. "No, they work all day long. Every day. Sometimes they work 16 hours a day, or more. Happily. Contentedly. Peacefully."

A grin creased Rosalind Sackoff's face. "Well, if working 16 hours a day is their secret, it's one I'd like all my students to learn."

"No, their 'secret,' as you put it, is something else."

"Okay, Jeff, I give up. What do the Hutterites do that makes them so non-violent?"

Jennifer Ahearn sighed. "They brainwash their children."

"They *what*?"

"They call it 'breaking the will.' It isn't really 'brainwashing,' of course, because they don't isolate the kids. But it is a pretty severe type of mental indoctrination, as far as I can tell. They train the child for years and years to do exactly what the group wants the child to do. They make the child give up all its own desires, and force it to obey the Hutterite rules and regulations. And since they have very strict rules against any behavior that would harm another person, they all turn out to be peace-loving."

Dr. Sackoff stared intently at the young woman. "And how do the Hutterites accomplish this miracle? I mean, if it's all that easy, I've known a couple of kids I wouldn't mind trying the technique on."

"Oh, no," Jennifer said. "You couldn't. You see, everyone in the group has to agree

on what's right and what's wrong. Everybody has to think the same thoughts and feel the same feelings. And each of them has to give up his or her individuality in order for the system to work."

"Sounds like what we have to go through in order to get tenure," Professor Sackoff said with a laugh. "But seriously, Jeff, how do they manage to achieve such uniform value systems? Do they beat self-discipline into the kids, or something?"

"No," Jennifer replied. "And that's maybe the most terrifying thing about their child-rearing techniques. As far as the Hutterites I lived with are concerned, there *is* no self. There is only the group. They don't teach their kids self-discipline, because no one is allowed to decide what is right or wrong. Only the group can do that. All the individual is allowed to do is to obey the will of the group."

Rosalind Sackoff frowned. "No self-discipline at all? Don't they have any feelings of guilt or shame when they break the rules?"

"They don't teach self-guilt," Jennifer said, "because they believe it's only natural for people to want to misbehave."

"But who punishes you when nobody else is around and you misbehave?

Jennifer Ahearn smiled wanly. "You're *expected* to sin when nobody is watching you. In her article in *Natural History*, Gertrude Huntington describes how her teen-aged daughter reacted to the Hutterite children's lack of self-guilt. The girl got very angry because the Huntingtons expected her to be 'good' even when no adults were

around. But the other children didn't have to behave when they weren't being observed by adults. And, of course, the kids *did* misbehave occasionally when they were off by themselves."

"Because that was what the group expected them to do."

"Of course," Jennifer said.

"And so the *real* purpose of the group is to watch you continuously so that your evil nature doesn't assert itself," Dr. Sackoff said.

Jennifer nodded in agreement. "Makes a weird sort of sense, doesn't it?"

"Eternal vigilance is the price of peace, eh?"

"Yes, but vigilance by the 'hundred friendly eyes always watching you,'" the younger woman said.

The older woman sighed deeply. "That's a pretty expensive price to pay, at least from my biased point of view."

"But it *works*!" Jennifer said loudly. "They have no child abuse, no women battered to bits by their husbands, no murders, and no violence at all."

"And, if I remember correctly, they also don't have any real art, music, science, or literature to call their own. Would you give up Shakespeare and Beethoven and all the miracles of modern medicine in exchange for cutting the murder rate to zero?"

Jennifer Ahearn stared quietly at her hands for a few seconds. "I don't really know."

"Would you give up self-awareness, free will, and the ability to choose things for yourself? Would you surrender all individuality as the price for everlasting peace?"

After a moment, Jennifer

said, "I haven't figured that one out yet. You see, their system does work, for them, at least. And it does turn out the most peace-loving kids in the world. And you know something?"

"What?"

"After a while, when I got used to the rigid sex-roles, and the loss of privacy, I sort of got to like it. A little bit, anyhow. I mean, I felt very safe, and very secure, and very much a part of the group. But . . ."

"But you aren't about to go back, are you?"

Jennifer shook her head.

"No, it was a nice place to visit . . ."

"But you wouldn't want to live there?" Dr. Sackoff said, laughing.

"Not just yet. But I did get to know myself—and other people—a little better while I was there."

"It was a real learning experience, eh?" the professor said.

"It was that," Jennifer said, smiling. "And it gave me a lot of things to think about."

Rosalind Sackoff grinned. "Good. And generous me, I'll give you the whole semester

to figure out how to achieve the Hutterite goals without paying the penalty they do. In 20 pages or less, typewritten, double-spaced, and with lots of references, of course."

Jennifer laughed. "Of course," she responded, getting up from her chair and heading for the door.

"Peace," Dr. Sackoff said.

Jennifer turned and looked thoughtfully at the woman. "Yes, peace," she said finally. And then she opened the door and went out.

Recommended Readings

Belson, W. (1978). *Television violence and the adolescent boy*. London: Teakfield.

Lunde, D.T. (1975). *Murder and madness*. New York: Charles Scribner's Sons; San Francisco: Freeman.

MacLean, P. (1978). A mind of three minds: Educating the triune brain. In *Education and the brain*, 77th Yearbook of the National Society for the Study of Education, Part II. Chicago: University of Chicago Press.

Mark, V.H. & Ervin, F.R. (1970). *Violence and the brain*. New York: Harper & Row.

Valenstein, E.S. (Ed.). (1980). *The psychosurgery debate: Scientific, legal, and ethical perspectives*. San Francisco: Freeman.

Did You Know That...

- The better the predictions that a scientific theory makes about future events, the more accurate it probably is?

- The most important reason for accepting or rejecting a scientific theory is usually its usefulness?

- The most widespread theory of human behavior is called "commonsense mentalism"?

- According to General Systems Theory, you are a "living system"?

- The first psychological laboratory was founded about 100 years ago?

- All living systems are capable of learning how to alter their behaviors in order to get the inputs they want?

- When you "decide" to do something, you typically make use of "feed-forward" and "feedback"?

- Early in this century, the behaviorists denied that "mind" existed?

- Learning to help others often means learning to change yourself first?

5

General Systems Theory

"The System Is the Solution"

"Well, Tom," Dr. Donald Severeid asked, "how are you doing with Patti?"

Tom Watson smiled broadly. He was a graduate student in educational psychology, and he had a strong love for young children. Thus when Dr. Severeid had offered him the chance to work with a severely retarded child named Patti, Tom had jumped at the opportunity. "Things are going beautifully."

"But when you first saw her, you thought there would be real problems. Remember?"

A serious expression wiped the smile off Tom's face. "Yeah, I know. When I met Patti, all I could see were the things she did wrong. I thought she was little more than an animal."

"A pig, as I recall," Severeid said.

"Well, she *was* a pig then," Tom replied defensively. "She was four years old, but she acted like a spoiled two-year-old. She was fat from over-eating, she couldn't talk very well, and she had a mean streak in her that was a mile wide."

Professor Severeid frowned. "A *mean streak*?"

Tom nodded. "Every time she got angry at you, she'd pinch you as hard as she could. And that young lady has *strong* fingers."

"I thought we had agreed to be objective about Patti's problems, Tom. Wouldn't it be better to say that her response to stress and frustration was to display aggressive behavior?"

"What's the difference?" Tom asked.

Dr. Severeid sighed. "To say that she has a 'mean streak in her' implies that you can actually see inside her mind. And having looked, you have *perceived* an innate personality characteristic you call 'meanness.' In truth, all you can say *objectively* is that she responds to stressful inputs by pinching you. This 'mean streak' business is simply your theoretical way of trying to explain why she acts as she does."

Tom Watson nodded. "I see what you're getting at. But if I really love the kid—and you know I do—does it really matter how we describe her?"

"Of course it does," the professor said. "If you say she has a mean streak, therapy consists of trying to 'change her personality.' But if you say that pinching is a 'learned response to frustration,' then you try to teach her better ways of handling stress. Which technique do you think would work best with Patti?"

Tom sighed. "I *know* which way works best. I tried lecturing her, and appealing to her pride, and she just pinched harder. Then I did what you suggested, and taught her how to get what she wants without pinching."

"And?"

"And she doesn't pinch much anymore. Particularly when I remember to reward her when she behaves well."

Dr. Severeid smiled. "Yes, of course. Good for you, Tom. And what else have you done? What about her overeating? Did you work on her 'piggishness,' or did you try to find out what was causing her to ingest all that food?"

Tom laughed in response. "You're right again. Her parents had scolded her for eating too much, and her reaction was to eat more. So I didn't really work on 'piggishness' as such."

"What did you do?"

Tom leaned back in his chair. "Well, I looked at her behavior in terms of inputs, outputs, and consequences. I decided that she just hadn't learned how to get what she wanted, so she grabbed everything in sight and stuffed it in her mouth. And when her parents fussed at her, they were merely rewarding her inappropriate behaviors."

"So?"

"So I taught her the names for food, and to say 'please' when she wanted something and 'thank you' when she got it." Tom Watson frowned thoughtfully. "I must say that she learned a lot faster than I thought she would, given the fact that she was born with such a damaged brain. I guess nobody had tried the right sort of treatment with her before. Maybe we just blamed her for being brain-damaged instead of blaming ourselves for not finding a way to help her effectively."

Dr. Severeid's face brightened into a smile. "Nice insight, Tom. But what about self-control?"

"Well, after I taught her to ask for things politely, I started to delay giving her the food for a few seconds. She learned to handle the delay because she could always see the reward she was waiting for, and she knew she'd get it if she just waited a moment or two longer."

"And what about her screaming? Didn't that bother you a lot at the start of treatment?"

Tom grinned. "Yeah, it bothered everybody. I remember once I took her to the supermarket, to help her learn the names of some new foods. And we had this slight disagreement about what to do next. I wanted to go home; Patti wanted to stay. I started pulling, and she started screaming. Three women came over and bawled me out for hurting the little darling." Tom smiled wistfully. "Patti pinched all three of them. I think they got the message."

"I'm sure they did," Dr. Severeid replied in an amused tone of voice. "But how did you handle the screaming response, Tom?"

The young man laughed. "One day when we were heading home from a walk, we took a shortcut across the football field. Not a soul in sight. Patti decided she didn't want to go home, so she started yelling. I just sat down, covered my ears, and let her scream. Every once in a while, when she was catching her breath, I'd tell her quietly that we'd go home when she stopped the noise. It took 20 minutes or so before she calmed down, but finally she gave in. Funny thing, she hasn't screamed at me much at all lately."

Professor Severeid nodded. "Extinction of a learned response. If you don't reward her for screaming, she eventually stops it. A bit wearing on the ears, but it works." After a moment, the man went on. "Have you tried extinguishing any of her other inappropriate behaviors?"

"A couple of them," Tom said. "Mostly having to do with soiling her pants. You know, her doctor said she might be too retarded to learn to control her bowels, but that's not her problem at all. She's got too much control! When she gets tired of working on food names, she begins to whine. If I don't stop right away, she cries, 'Oh, oh! B.M.!' And then she dumps. Takes about 10 minutes to clean her up, and by then I don't feel like doing much of anything except go home."

"How are you handling the soiling response?" the professor asked gently.

"I asked her doctor if I could put her back in training pants. He agreed. Now when she cries, 'Oh, oh! B.M.!' I just let her sit in her own mess for a while and continue the lesson. She hasn't tried that little trick on me now for a couple of weeks."

Dr. Severeid nodded soberly. "Well, Tom, it sounds like you're making real progress. I wonder if you wouldn't like to bring Patti over to show to my class. You might talk with her parents and, if they approve, you can give her a lesson in that demonstration room with the one-way mirror. The class can watch what you're doing without Patti's seeing them. And afterwards, they can ask you questions about your work."

A week or so later, Tom escorted four-year-old Patti into the demonstration room. As the door clicked shut solidly behind them, Tom led her over to the table and dumped a bag of goodies on the table.

"Food," Patti said, pointing at the bag.

"Yes, food," Tom responded, pulling two chairs up to the table. He looked at the mirror-like window set in one wall. The students in Dr. Severeid's class presumably were behind the glass, watching. They could hear Tom's voice—and Patti's—through a loudspeaker. He nodded briefly at the students and then turned his attention to the little girl.

Holding up a piece of sweet cereal so that Patti could see it, Tom asked, "Patti, would you like this?"

"Oh, yes," Patti squealed delightedly.

"Ask for it politely, by name, and you can have it."

Patti frowned. "Froot Loop," she said, and reached for the sweet.

"No, ask for it politely, and I'll be happy to give it to you."

"Please Tom can I have the Froot Loop?" she said, struggling to get the words right.

"Patti, you can have anything at all if you ask for it nicely," Tom said in an encouraging tone of voice, giving her the piece of cereal.

Patti devoured the sweet greedily. "More!" she cried.

Tom ignored her and pulled a fresh green grape from the bag of goodies. "What is this, Patti?"

"I want it," was the girl's eager reply.

"Tell me what it is, and ask for it politely, and you can have it. Now, what is it, Patti?"

"Groop," said Patti.

"That's good, very good. You said it almost right. Grape, Patti, grape. Now you say it."

"Grape," she squealed, and grabbed for the piece of fruit.

"Say 'please,' Patti."

"Please give me the groop."

Tom could hear some muffled giggles from the other side of the one-way mirror. He tried a little harder. "Please give me the grape."

"I want it!" Patti wailed.

"I'll give it to you when you ask politely," Tom said, fearing that the students wouldn't appreciate what a great improvement even this behavior was over the way she had acted before he had started working with her.

"Please give me the grape, Tom," Patti said, all sweetness and smiles.

Tom handed her the grape. "You're doing beautifully, Patti. Just keep it up so that everyone will know know smart you really are." He reached in the bag again and pulled out a small cookie, knowing it was one of her favorites.

"Cookie!" Patti squealed with delight. "Gimme."

"Yes, you're right. It's a cookie. But you have to ask for it, and then when I give it to you, you have to wait 30 seconds before you eat it. Okay? If you can wait for 30 seconds, you can eat that cookie, and another one too!" He pulled another cookie out of the bag. "Now ask for it politely . . ."

"Please, please, can I have the cookie?" She held out her hand.

"Okay," Tom said, placing the bit of cookie on her open palm. "Now just hold it there safely until I say 'Go.'" He started counting off the seconds. "One, two, three . . . that's marvelous, Patti. You're really doing beautifully . . . twelve, thirteen, fourteen . . . You're a good girl, Patti. You're really learning self-control. Now just a little longer . . . twenty-eight, twenty-nine, thirty, EAT!"

Patti gobbled the cookie down at once. Tom smiled and gave her the second cookie, which she pushed into her mouth even before she had finished the first.

"Good girl, Patti," Tom said. "You did just beautifully. I bet you could wait 40 seconds next time, couldn't you?"

Patti nodded, still munching on the cookies.

"Okay, now it's time to learn a new word." Again Tom reached into the bag and pulled something out. It was a tiny sweet pickle. "Do you want this, Patti?"

Patti turned up her nose. "Don't like. Wanna go home."

Tom panicked. "No you don't. You want to learn some new names today, don't you?

This is a pickle, Patti. A sweet pickle. Say 'sweet pickle' and I'll give you a bite."

Patti turned away from him. "Don't like."

"You'll get us both in a pickle if you don't behave, Patti. Tell you what, if you try to say 'sweet pickle,' I'll give you another cookie. Okay?"

"Wanna go home!" Patti shrilled.

"Not yet, darn it. We've got a lot of work to do, and . . ."

"Oh, oh! B.M.!" Patti screamed.

There was a strange noise, and a contented look spread over the little girl's face.

Tom ignored the whole episode. "Okay, Patti, just a little longer, and then we'll go home, okay? Now, please try to say 'sweet pickle.' Please?"

Patti squirmed uncomfortably in her chair. A peculiar and rather upsetting smell arose from her vicinity.

"Don't like. Wanna go home," she said, rather softly.

"I know. I'll take you home just as soon as you try to say 'sweet pickle.' So please, Patti, try to say it. I'm really proud of what you've done, and I want you to look good. So try, Patti, try."

The smell got worse.

"Sweat puckle."

"That's close. Very close." He patted her on the back. She squirmed again, and the odor became more intense. "Sweet pickle. Just say it right once, and we can go home."

"Sweet buckle."

The stench was now so bad that Tom was feeling a bit sick. But then he remembered the students watching him. Since they couldn't smell anything through the mirror, they didn't know what he was putting up with. So he tried again.

"One more time, Patti. You're doing really good. Just say 'sweet pickle,' and we'll go home right now. And I do mean now."

"Sweet pickle," Patti said, smiling brightly.

"Beautiful, Patti. I knew you could do it. Here's the cookie." He gave her the reward, and gathered up what was on the table and stuffed it into his bag. "And now let's get out of here," he said, gagging a bit as he spoke.

Grabbing the little girl by the hand, he led her to the door. He reached for the knob and pulled hard. The door

wouldn't budge. Tom tried again. And again. The door didn't move even a fraction of an inch. It was obviously locked from the outside.

Tom turned toward the mirror. "Hey, you guys. The door is locked. Somebody come open it before I die of asphyxiation."

There were noises from the other room, and soon other noises outside the door. Patti began to cry softly, and the stink became unbearable.

Moments later, Tom heard a muffled voice outside the room. "The door is locked, and we haven't got a key. You'll just have to stay there until we can find the janitor."

"Well, hurry up!" Tom yelled.

"I wanna go home," Patti wailed, and pinched Tom's arm.

"Listen," Tom said angrily. "You do that once more and I'll pinch you back right where it will hurt the most." He reached down, his fingers threatening painful revenge.

Patti screamed in terror. "Oh, oh! B.M.!"

"Oh, oh," Tom moaned. "Sweet pickle!"

(Continued on page 135.)

How to "Tick Better"

In the last chapter we asked, "What makes you tick?" And we found that "ticking" is *multi-determined*. Your attitudes, your feelings, and the things you say and do are influenced by biological, mental, and environmental factors. In this chapter, we ask, "What do you have to know or do in order to tick *better*?"

The answer to that question turns out to be surprisingly complex. For in order to help yourself, you often must learn how to understand,

deal with, and help other people. And in order to work successfully with others, you typically must have some understanding of—and control over—your own thoughts and actions.

It is at this very practical level of trying to help ourselves (and others) that most of us run into difficulty. For most of us have never been trained to look at human behavior *systematically*. That is, most of us have not learned how to identify—and deal with—the biological, intra-psychic, and social influences on our thoughts, emotions, and behaviors. Put more precisely, most of us have never acquired a **holistic** or *unified* theory of human nature.

The major purpose of this chapter, then, is to give you a *theoretical perspective* that may enable you to see yourself and others in a more unified way. And once you learn to *perceive* the world differently, you may find new ways to *reshape* that world to bring it closer to your heart's desire.

Scientific Theories

All sciences, including psychology, are built on **theories**. Scientific theories are summaries of what we *know* about a given topic. And since they gather past knowledge together in a structured form, they help us predict future events. Thus, theories are extremely handy things to have around, for they give you a framework for understanding yourself and the world around you. But these theoretical explanations may mislead you if you don't remember one fact— theories are merely *approximations to the truth.*

Even our best scientific explanations are *limited in their usefulness.* For theories are merely verbal or mathematical descriptions of the world. And the world is far too complicated for the simple words and mathematical symbols we presently have available to us. Therefore, all theoretical frameworks are somewhat *incomplete* and somewhat *inaccurate* descriptions of real-world systems.

But we cannot live without theories, because they help us organize what we know about ourselves and the rest of the world. And theories not only give meaning to the facts we already have available to us, they also tell us what we should do in the future to learn more about a variety of subjects. The question then becomes, How should we pick and choose among the many psychological explanations of human behavior available to us?

Judging a Scientific Theory

Scientists have many different **criteria** by which they judge theories. Some scientific scholars want a theory that leads them to further research and to exciting new ways of perceiving the world. Other scientists prefer *hypotheses* that tell them which facts have practical importance, and which don't seem very valuable at present. Some scholars believe

Holistic (ho-LISS-tick). From an old English word *hool*, meaning "whole." A holistic theory is one that assumes that "the whole is greater than the sum of its parts." Put another way, you are more than a collection of organs and cells, for you have properties (such as consciousness) that cannot be explained in terms of the actions of your parts.

Theories (THEE-or-rees). From the Greek word meaning "to behold, or view." A "theorem" (THEE-or-em) is a scientific or mathematical statement whose truth has been proven, or at least assumed. A theory is a set of related theorems, thus a collection of statements about some aspect of science. Generally speaking, a theory is a set of assumptions about the way the world (or a part of it) works. A theory is also a collection of facts, or data. It is thus a *viewpoint* that is capable of being disproved by additional factual evidence. A theory that is incapable of being *disproved* is, scientifically speaking, not worth the paper it's written on. The word "theater" comes from the same Greek word as does "theory," and a theory presents the same condensed view of things that a play or movie does.

Criteria (cry-TEER-ee-ah). Plural of *criterion* (cry-TEER-ee-on). From a Greek word meaning "to judge, or decide." The criteria for success in school usually include good grades, the ability to read and write effectively, to think logically, and so forth.

the theories that come from physics and chemistry—which emphasize exact measurement—should be "models" for psychological theories. Others prefer a more "commonsense" approach to psychology that emphasizes the uniqueness of human beings and their ability to control their own actions. Still other scholars—mostly those who are politically active—desire theories that reinforce their notions about how people ought to behave in a variety of situations.

There is, therefore, *no one set of guidelines* that all scientists agree upon when it comes to judging the "goodness" of a theory. However, most scientists do admit that the following four criteria are quite important:

1. How accurate is the theory?
2. How complete is the theory?
3. How elegant or impressive is the theory?
4. How useful is the theory?

Let us look at these four criteria one by one.

Accuracy
In order to test the accuracy of a theory, we usually follow the *scientific method.* That is, we use the theory to *make a prediction* about something, and then we run experiments or make observations to see how accurate the prediction was. If the theory does a good job of predicting, we tend to accept or believe in the theory. If it does a poor job of predicting, we should either revise the theory or switch to another one.

Completeness

Some theories give us detailed descriptions of one limited part of the world, while other theories give us broad descriptions of "the whole big ball of wax." Psychology has both types of theories.

For example, *perceptual theories* and *cognitive theories* are an attempt to describe one small part of your life—how you take in information about your world and process it so that it makes sense (see Chapters 6–9).

Motivational theories are a way of describing another limited aspect of your life—your goals, and how you attempt to reach them (see Chapters 10–12).

Learning theories treat yet another small segment of your psychological world—how you acquire habits, and how you store and recall memories (see Chapters 13–16).

Behavior theories are a subset of "learning theories." Behavioral theories describe how outputs change over time as a function of changing inputs (see particularly Chapters 13 and 14).

Developmental theories are a bit more complex. These theories attempt to describe where all your perceptions, motives, habits, and memories come from—and how they develop over the span of your life (see Chapters 17–18).

Personality theories are even more complicated. For they try to lay out in systematic terms not only how you became the person you are, but also how you might go about changing yourself (see Chapters 19–22).

Social theories are ultimately the broadest of all, for they attempt to tell us two important things: first, how individuals react to each other; and second, how social systems (such as groups and organizations) grow and develop (see Chapters 23–25).

In psychology, then, our theories run from the simple to the complex. But what we need in addition is a sort of "master viewpoint" that would let us put all these individual theories together into one comprehensive whole. By far the most holistic or unified of the "master viewpoints" is *General Systems Theory*. We will talk more about this approach in just a moment.

Elegance

The noted French physicist Paul Dirac once said, "It is more important to have beauty in one's [theoretical] equations than to have them fit the data." Some scientific theories may delight you because they are particularly simple or *elegant*. Other theories may impress you be-cause they match the world as you see it. For example, if you stand on the beach and look out at the ocean, the world surely *looks* flat. We now know that "looks are deceiving." But up until 1520—when Ferdinand Magellan and Juan del Cano sailed around the world—most people refused to question the "flat earth" theory because it fit what they saw.

Other viewpoints are impressive because they tell us what we want to hear. For instance, consider the very strange theory of intelligence dreamed up 100 years ago by Paul Broca. Broca was the noted French scientist who discovered the "speech center" in the brain. He began with an incorrect assumption, namely, "the bigger the brain, the brighter the person." He then performed rather a sloppy study of the *size* of human brains. Broca concluded—incorrectly—that males had larger brains than females, and that whites had larger brains than blacks. Broca then announced he had *proven* that men were more intelligent than women, and whites were innately smarter than blacks.

Actually, there is no known relationship between "brain size" and "intelligence" in humans. But because what Broca said confirmed what many French citizens believed anyhow, his work was accepted as "fact" rather than "theory."

If you are like most people, you will tend to prefer beautiful, elegant, simple theories that reinforce your own observations and prior beliefs. And once you have accepted a theory because it impresses you favorably, you may find yourself reluctant to give it up, even when newly discovered facts show it is less accurate or complete than another theory.

Usefulness

Although not all scientists agree, one of the most important criteria by which a theory is typically judged in real-life situations is this one: How useful is it to you?

The *usefulness* of a theory can be measured in many ways. At a personal level, a theory can give you emotional pleasure because it offers new insights into the world and the people you live with. If you are a practicing scientist, and a theory suggests new and exciting experiments to perform, then it may be useful to you professionally. Personal theories tend to be loosely stated, such as "fat people are jolly," or "spare the rod and spoil the child." Scientific theories tend to be more formal and mathematical, such as Einstein's famous equation, $E = mc^2$.

However, the ultimate joy for most of us is

that of reaching our own personal goals. In the long run, therefore, you will most likely adopt the personal or scientific theories that give you the best predictions about yourself and others—and thus give you sufficient control over yourself and your environment so you can get what you want from everyday life.

You already have a great many *personal* theories about human behavior you probably believe in rather strongly—but that you aren't conscious of believing in. One of the major purposes of this book, then, is to make you aware of the personal theories you already hold. But a second major purpose is to impress you with the usefulness of various *scientific* viewpoints you might wish to consider adopting.

The theoretical approach most people take in explaining human behavior is what MIT psychologist Jerry Fodor calls *commonsense mentalism*. According to this viewpoint, your mind controls your body. And you act as you do because of your "belief systems" and your "emotions." As we will see in a moment, commonsense mentalism does a fairly good job of explaining human behavior—but only in very general terms. Thus, commonsense mentalism is often useful, but isn't very accurate, elegant, or complete.

Quite the opposite is a broad-scale scientific viewpoint called *General Systems Theory*. Unlike commonsense mentalism, General Systems Theory is very comprehensive and elegant. And

because the "systems approach" gives us a better technology for changing ourselves than does commonsense mentalism, General Systems Theory is ultimately more useful.

Let's first look briefly at the commonsense approach. Then we will spend a few pages describing General Systems Theory. Finally, we will compare the two.

Commonsense Mentalism

In the July 1981 issue of *Contemporary Psychology*, Jerry Fodor says, "By *commonsense mentalism*, I mean the doctrine that the behavior of higher organisms is typically caused by their mental states." What are "mental states?" Fodor says they are such things as "beliefs and desires." The commonsense approach states that these beliefs and desires control behaviors.

For example, suppose we see a young man named John eat a hamburger, and we ask ourselves *why* he did so. The commonsense answer would be that John *desired* the hamburger because he felt hungry. In the past, John has learned that eating a hamburger reduces his hunger pangs. Therefore, John ate the hamburger not merely because he desired it, but because he *believes* that eating the sandwich will satisfy his desires.

The commonsense approach is a simple and fairly accurate way of explaining why people act as they do. However, as Fodor notes, because commonsense mentalism lacks *explicit accuracy*, we are slowly shifting to a more scientific approach. However, elements of commonsense mentalism can still be found in most psychological theories.

General Systems Theory

Commonsense mentalism *appears* to offer a relatively complete understanding of human behavior. In fact, it does not. For the commonsense viewpoint tends to overemphasize the importance of intra-psychic variables such as "beliefs" and "desires." And it tends to ignore the importance of biological and social/behavioral variables.

General Systems Theory, to the contrary, strives to give equal weight to all three classes of variables. We can give you a better "feel" for what the systems approach is like—and show how it differs from the commonsense viewpoint—by asking you to think for a moment about your first child.

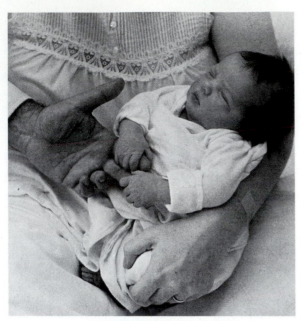
Family groups are fairly simple social systems.

Your First Child

If you are like most people, you will marry and raise a family sometime in your future life. Perhaps you are already doing so. In either case, at some point after the birth of your first child you probably will give considerable thought to what your child's future might be.

So, imagine that you are sitting beside a crib, and in that crib is your own first child. The infant is now a healthy six weeks old. Chances are good that, as you look at this marvelous youngster, you will perceive the child (theorize about it) in several ways. First, you will see the youngster as being *your* child. That is, you will *assume* the infant is an extension of your own mind and body. Second, you will see the child as being a normal *human being* which, according to most theoretical (and moral) viewpoints, you ought to love and help as best you can.

But just for a moment, stand back and—like a physician judging your infant's state of health—look upon this child of yours as being a **living system**. This child has biological needs that must be met if the youngster is to survive. No matter how much you may love the child, if you do not give the youngster food, air, and water—and if you do not protect the child from germs and other physical dangers—the child will die before reaching maturity.

From a systems viewpoint, then, your infant is a *biological system* that requires certain inputs from the environment in order to maintain that miraculous internal process we call "life."

But infants are more than mere biological machines. For each human being is a unique *psychological system* as well, and each of us is a part of such larger *social systems* as groups, organizations, and societies.

Thus, in order for you to best meet *all* the needs of your infant—biological, social, and psychological—you may have to *perceive* this tiny child as being much, much more complicated than you had ever dreamed a child could be. And to help your youngster survive, you must come to *understand* how the child interacts with you and the rest of the environment. But to achieve these goals, you may need more than just a "commonsense" theory to guide you.

Question: In some present-day cultures with very high rates of infant mortality, parents understand very little about germs and disease. The parents thus see no reason for boiling their drinking water or keeping their children clean. Why would it be difficult for you to reduce the number of infant deaths in these cultures without first changing the parents' "theoretical viewpoint" toward dirt and germs?

What Is Life?

What does it mean—in practical terms—to view your infant as a *living system*? Before we can answer that question, we must first define a few terms.

A Pattern of Interactions

As we noted earlier, *primitive terms* such as "life" are terribly slippery things to define. Life is a *process*, not a lump of coal or a piece of concrete reality. An instant after you die, much of your body will still be *physically* what it was the moment before. But because most of your organs would no longer be actively interacting with each other, you would be dead rather than living. From a systems point of view, then, life is determined by a *pattern of interactions* among the various parts of your body.

This pattern of interactions *among* your body parts is so complex that we understand very little about how the miracle of life occurs. Indeed, we don't really know all that much about how any *one* part of your body takes care of itself, much less how it communicates with other parts. But at least we have learned some of the *biological characteristics* that all living things seem to possess. We know, for example, that biological systems function as if their *major purpose* in life was that of *survival*.

Goal-Oriented Behaviors

Oddly enough, as soon as we use the word "purpose," we have switched from a biological to a psychological viewpoint. For "purposes" imply actions and behaviors, and it is difficult to discuss *behavior* in purely biological terms.

So we might note that, *psychologically speaking*, all living systems possess certain specific characteristics too. For instance, from the tiniest cell to the largest animal, all living things behave as if they were *goal oriented*. Which is to say that all living systems have ways of achieving the inputs (or goals) that they require in order to survive.

Motivation and Emotion

If you observe your child carefully, you will soon note an interesting fact. The infant cries when hungry, but stops crying when full. Why? Children cry because they experience hunger and are motivated to reduce their hunger pangs. They stop crying when the food they eat reduces their hunger and thus their motivation.

As we will see in Chapters 10–12, the term *motivation* almost always refers to goal-oriented behavior. Hunger is a type of motivation the infant experiences as a painful event (input). The crying is the child's way of expressing (outputting) *emotional feelings* about a need for food.

When deprived of something needed for life—or when kept from achieving a goal—almost all living systems show *agitated movements* that we typically call "emotional behavior." *Emotion*, therefore, is another psychological characteristic of all living systems.

Question: In what ways is this description of "hunger" different from, and similar to, the commonsense explanation mentioned above?

Learning

The first time newborn infants cry for food, they usually don't stop their agitated actions until long after they have begun to eat. After a few days or weeks, however, the infants often cease their crying as soon as the mother or father appears. For they have *learned* that the arrival of a parent (or whoever feeds the child regularly) means food is at hand. Eventually the infants learn to cry in one way when hungry, but cry another way when wet or cold or they want to be played with.

Of all the psychological characteristics of life, *learning* is probably the most important. For

Living system. The cell, organ, organism, group, organization, and society are all examples of living systems. All systems are made up of related parts (sub-systems), are open to the environment (have inputs and outputs), act as if they were motivated to achieve goals, are controlled by feed-forward, expectancies about consequences, and feedback, and are capable of a certain amount of self-control.

without the ability to change, to adjust, and to grow, we surely wouldn't survive.

Life is a process, then, with many different biological and behavioral aspects to it. But this process of life occurs only in *systems*, so before we can appreciate fully what life is, we must define the second word in the term "living systems."

Question: How does the infant's ability to learn to cry in "different tones of voice" aid its survival? What would happen if the parents responded the same way no matter how the infant cried?

What Is a System?

What do you think of when a person says, "I have a system"? Probably you will imagine some technique or series of steps the person has in mind for achieving a particular goal. But what do you think of when a friend of yours says, "I want to beat the system!"? Now you will probably see "the system" as being a social organization of some sort.

An Organization of Related Parts

The key word in defining the term "system" is *organization*. Technically speaking, a system is *an organization of related parts*. These parts are often called "sub-systems." And for the parts of a living system to be "related," these sub-systems must be in some kind of *communication* with each other. As an example, the organs in your body communicate with each other in many different ways. Your heart pumps food and oxygen to your brain, while your brain sends neural messages to your heart telling your heart when it should become excited and pump blood faster, and when it should relax and pump slower. Your heart thus communicates *energy* to your brain, while your brain communicates *information* to your heart.

Inputs, Processes, Outputs

In order to survive, each living system must take in such things as food and water from its environment. The system then uses (or *pro-*

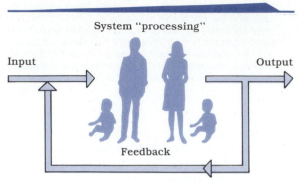

Fig. 5.1 The interconnection of input, output, and feedback.

The boy inputs information from the machine, processes it, and responds. The machine gives the boy feedback as to whether his response was appropriate or not. The boy uses this feedback to change his outputs, and thus comes closer to his goals.

cesses) what it gets, and releases its wastes back to the environment. One of the major characteristics of living systems, therefore, is that they have *inputs, internal processes, and outputs* (see Fig. 5.1).

Look back at the beginning of this chapter, to the point where we were telling you how to judge a scientific theory. Under the criterion of "completeness," we described a number of psychological approaches, including "perceptual theories," "motivational theories," and "behavioral theories." Some of these approaches emphasize *inputs*, some *outputs*, but most of them focus on *internal processes* (as does commonsense psychology). General Systems Theory is one of the few to give as much importance to inputs and outputs as it does to internal processes.

Information vs. Energy

Generally speaking, there are two major types of inputs, internal processes, and outputs: those having to do with *energy*, and those having to do with *information*.

When you eat supper, your body takes in food, which it then digests or processes internally. Later, your body will release energy (and matter) back to your environment—in part through waste products, in part through behavior.

As you read this book, you are "inputting" information of one kind or another. You process this information as you evaluate it, try to understand it, and as you file the material away in your memory. And you output that information by talking or responding in new ways.

Most inputs, internal processes, and outputs involve *both* energy and information. You learn what to eat, and what not to eat. And you need

food in order to learn new habits that will help you survive.

In general, when we talk about "information," we're talking at the level of "mind." And when we talk about "energy," we're analyzing the system from a physical or "body" point of view. Thus, the General Systems Theory solution to the mind-body problem is this: What we call "mind" and "body" are simply two different ways of looking at the functions of living systems. But the term "mind" doesn't exist when we're describing how energy and matter flow through a system. And the term "body" doesn't have its usual meaning when we're describing how a system processes information.

Question: What solution does commonsense mentalism offer to the mind-body problem?

Controlling Your Inputs

Think back again to your infant lying in the crib. We have already said that your child is strongly goal oriented, and that the infant's major goal is that of survival.

But how does an infant survive? By now, perhaps you can see that no living system (including both you and your infant) can survive unless that system can somehow *control its environmental inputs*.

Now think a little bit further. In order to control your *inputs*, you usually must control your *outputs*. That infant of yours needs food in order to survive. The child soon learns that he or she is more likely to get food (rather than a fresh diaper) by crying in one tone of voice when hungry, but in another tone of voice when wet. Crying is thus *information* about the infant's internal energy needs that the infant *outputs* to the environment. By controlling the "crying output," your newborn child influences what sorts of inputs she or he gets from you and other people.

Question: How do infants reward their parents when the parents help satisfy the child's needs?

Controlling a Living System

Generally speaking, systems are controlled by their inputs. Some of these inputs concern energy; others concern information. But how do you (as a living system) achieve the inputs you "desire"?

As we noted earlier, you get the inputs you want by learning how to control your outputs. But to achieve this miracle, you must make use of three processes you may not have given much thought to. First, you must be able to plan a series of actions (outputs) that presumably will yield the inputs you want. You then execute the plan by telling your body the *sequence of behaviors* it must perform. In systems terms, this "sequence" is called **feed-forward**. And *feed-forward* is the first process you employ in learning how to control your outputs.

But how do you know this sequence will yield the reward you want? Because you are able to *guess the consequences* of most of the things you do. *If* you eat, *then* your hunger will be satisfied. *If* you pick up a crying baby, *then* the child mostly likely will quit crying. *Predicting consequences* is the second process in learning how to control your outputs.

And how did you learn that food satisfies hunger? Because your body and your environment give you **feedback** about the results of your actions. And if the consequences of your behavioral outputs aren't those you predicted (or desired), then you do something else until you get the inputs you wanted in the first place. *Using feedback* is the third process you must employ in learning how to control your outputs.

"Feed-forward," "predicting consequences," and "feedback" may seem rather strange con-

Feed-forward. A series of commands or orders that you issue (usually all at once) that are to be executed in sequence at some time in the future. The "rules and regulations" issued by any group or organization are feed-forward in that the rules tell the members of the group or organization what behaviors are allowed, what behaviors are forbidden, and what the *consequences* of obeying or disobeying the rules will be. Your own personal "code of ethics" (conscience) is also a type of feed-forward in that this code tells you what sequences of actions to perform in certain situations in the future.

Feedback. Information about a system's present or past performance which is fed back into the system to control the system's present or future actions.

cepts to you at first. But they are really just new terms for ideas you probably are already familiar with. So let us look at these concepts in detail, because you will need to understand them if you are to make much sense out of General Systems Theory.

Feed-forward

How do you get a computer to solve an equation for you? The first thing you do is to feed the machine information about the *sequence* of steps it should follow in order to generate a solution to the equation. The computer then carries out your commands "one step at a time" until it completes the task you have given it. The "programming" inputs you initially give the machine are called "feed-forward" because you tell the computer *now* what you want it to accomplish during some *future* (forward) time period.

Living systems too make use of "feed-forward" in order to plan and execute a series of responses that will lead them toward some goal. Suppose you are reading a book when you suddenly "feel hungry." So you decide to get an apple from the refrigerator. But your "mind" can't accomplish this goal on its own—your body must do the actual moving (and eating). Thus, when you "make up your mind" to get the apple, parts of your cortex decide on a *sequence of movements* that will get your body up from the chair and walking toward the refrigerator in the kitchen. Your cortex next "feeds forward" the sequence of commands to the lower centers of your brain. These lower centers then execute the movements without any conscious effort on your part.

Whenever you read the term "feed-forward" in this book, you will know we are referring to *future behaviors designed to achieve some goal.*

A graphic display of some of the long-distance lines operated by AT&T. The phone system is, indeed, a system—that is, an organization of related parts or subsystems.

Karl H. Pribram

Predicting Consequences

Telling your body what movements it must make to get you an apple from the refrigerator is but a small part of the process of satisfying your hunger needs, however. All along the way, your brain must generate predictions about what the actual *consequences* of your actions will be. For example, why do you want an apple when you feel hungry? Because you have learned that eating an apple reduces your hunger pangs. Drinking a glass of water or standing on your head are behavioral sequences that just don't have the consequences devouring an apple will have.

Many psychologists believe that one of the main purposes of your "mind" is that of predicting what the results of your actions will be. Indeed, these scientists view your mind as an incredibly complex computer that does little more than the following three things:

1. It measures your internal needs and the demands placed on you by your environment.
2. Then it plans behaviors (sequences of outputs) that will meet these needs in a predictable manner.
3. Finally, it compares the actual consequences of your actions with what it expected and adjusts your outputs accordingly.

Feedback

How did you learn that standing on your head doesn't usually reduce your hunger pangs? Well, perhaps once when you were starving, your mind told your body to stand on its head because your mind predicted this output might help. But your stomach growled just as loudly as before. This painful *feedback* from your gut informed your mind that the first plan it fed forward to your muscles didn't get the job done. So your mind generated another plan which, when fed-forward and executed, got you an apple and reduced your hunger.

Feed-forward is defined as a planned sequence of outputs that your mind predicts will move you toward some goal. Feedback is information about whether those outputs actually did or did not get the job done. From a General Systems viewpoint, *all* your motivated activities involve planning (feed-forward), predicting (guessing consequences), and adjusting (using real-world feedback to stay on target).

Question: Does your mind predict the *actual consequences* of your actions, or does it generate predictions about *what kind of feedback* your behaviors will yield?

Self-Control

At first glance, it may seem that General Systems Theory views you (or at least your mind) as little more than a giant computer. Not so, because your mind is but a small part of YOU. There's also your brain, *and* the rest of your body, *and* your environment. Indeed, some systems theorists believe that *consciousness* is not just a property of the "mind." Rather, it may be a process that is *generated* by a complex set of interactions among mind, body, and environment.

In a 1976 book entitled *Consciousness and the Brain*, Stanford psychologist Karl Pribram states, "Consciousness describes a property by which organisms achieve a special relationship with their environment." Thus, Pribram says, you can't locate consciousness as being "in the mind," or "in the brain," because consciousness always implies the existence of an environment "to be conscious of." Pribram believes that consciousness *emerges* from our attempts to predict and control both our inputs and our outputs. Therefore, we will not be able to construct a computer that "approximates consciousness" until we discover ways to teach the computer **self-control**. That is, we won't have conscious machines until we can program them to predict the environmental consequences of their own actions. And, to date, no one has come close to achieving that computing miracle.

Thus, "consciousness" and "self-awareness" may well result from the need most living systems have to *gain voluntary control* over their own outputs and inner processes so they can get the inputs they need from their environments.

Question: Pribram says if we ever developed a "conscious" computer, someone would immediately found a Society for the Prevention of Cruelty to Computers. What does this amusing possibility tell you about the commonsense approach to explaining human behavior?

Systems Within Systems

Now that we have gotten the definitions out of the way, let us view YOU through the eyes of General Systems Theory—both to add to your understanding of yourself, and to demonstrate why you must learn as much about relationships *among* systems as you do about individual systems themselves (see Fig. 5.2).

Biological Systems

The Cell

Every cell in your body is a living system. Cells are made up of complex molecules, but these molecules do not exhibit the property of *life*. Only when these molecules interact with each other in very complicated ways does the property of life *emerge* in the living cell.

Self-control. Living systems have the ability to make use of feed-forward and feedback in order to grow, mature, change, learn, and hence achieve their goals more effectively. Self-control is the ability voluntarily to change your outputs so that you can gain the present or future inputs you desire. Children learn self-control when they discover that reducing their temper tantrums and impulsive actions will yield them rewards they can't otherwise get.

Organ. From the Greek word meaning "tool, instrument, or parts that work together." An organ is thus a means of accomplishing something. Your heart is an instrument for pumping blood. Your brain is a tool for processing informational inputs.

Emergent properties (ee-MER-jent). From a Latin word meaning "to rise, or come out of concealment." When you put the pieces of a jigsaw puzzle together, the "picture" emerges. But you cannot usually predict what the *whole* picture will look like just by looking at a single piece or two. Thus, the visual properties of the picture emerge from concealment only when the pieces are put together in a *systematic* way.

Like other biological systems, the cell is affected by its genetic inheritance and by any damage it may have sustained in its past history. In a sense, then, each cell in your body is as much a unique, individual living system as you are yourself.

The Organ

One cell isn't enough to keep a heart going—any more than one person is enough to keep a group going. The various types of cells in your heart play quite different *biological roles*. Yet, working together, they manage to keep the blood pumping through your body.

Your heart itself is an **organ**—an *organ*ized group of individual cells. But it is also a system in and of itself. You can learn a great deal about hearts by studying the behavior of individual cells. However, if you want to view the heart as an *organ*, you must study the *relationships among cells*. For if the cells did not relate to each other in some way, they would not be organized enough to form a system as complex as your heart.

The major **emergent properties** at the organ level seem to be those of *cooperation* and what we might call *role specialization*. Heart cells *specialize*. Some of them are built for working, others for support and protection, still others for circulating food and oxygen. A few nerve cells inside the heart act as "organ regulators" by controlling the rate at which the organ beats. And because each of these many types of cell is specialized for a single task, they cannot sur-

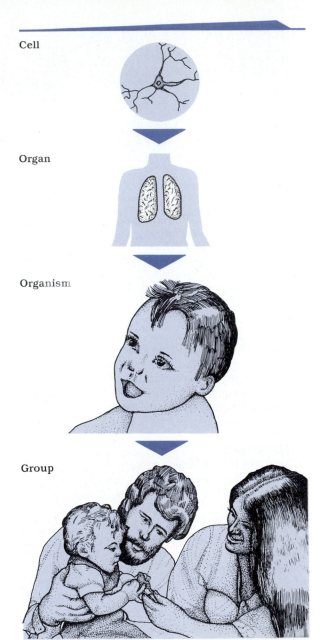

Cell

Organ

Organism

Group

Fig. 5.2 Various types of systems: a cell, an organ, an organism, and a group. All systems have certain characteristics in common.

vive on their own. The heart cells must *cooperate* with each other—or die.

It is this *cooperation* (born of *specialization*) that allows the heart cells to create a more complex system—the organ.

Question: How long would a "General Hospital" survive if its staff were made up just of kidney

specialists? What other "medical roles" are needed in order to keep the hospital functioning smoothly?

Psychological and Social Systems

The Organism

Each organ in your body is a complex living system with its own types of inputs, internal processes, and outputs. But your body itself is an *organism*, a much more complex living system than any one of its component organs.

For instance, YOU, as a living organism, are surely something more than a heart, a liver, a brain, and a few other organs loosely thrown together inside your skin. For YOU have properties (such as perceptions, thoughts, memories, and attitudes) that your individual organs simply do not possess. Your heart is not "conscious"—and never will be—because *consciousness* is a characteristic that emerges only at the level of the organism.

Question: As we noted, consciousness actually emerges from a complex set of interactions between the organism and its environment. If you didn't have other people around, would you be likely to develop "self-consciousness"?

The Group

You do not live your life in social isolation. Rather, you share your existence with and are dependent upon other human beings. To put the matter in more technical terms, organisms form *groups* in much the same way that your individual organs unite to form organisms such as yourself.

From the standpoint of General Systems Theory, the group is a kind of *super-organism* with emergent properties that are unique to it. Sexual reproduction is one such property. Spoken language is another property that emerges at the level of the group. Cells and organs communicate with each other chemically and electrically. Members of family groups communicate with each other using verbal and non-verbal signals. *Speech*, then, is a system of informational inputs and outputs that emerges at the level of the group.

Question: Family therapy is a relatively new type of treatment based in part on systems theory. We will discuss family therapy later. But, given what you already have learned about systems theory, can you guess how family therapy might differ from individual therapy?

The Social Organization

Social organizations are much like your body. They typically start small and develop slowly into highly complex systems. And since social organizations don't have "genes" to guide them, they must have *formal* rules and regulations to control their functioning. Being able to write these "rules and regulations" down in formal language can aid an organization in many ways. Thus *written language* is a property that probably emerged when people first began to form large organizations.

It is also at the level of the organization that **social roles** first appear, including those of "teacher," "student," "parent," "worker," "manager," and "police officer" (see Chapter 23). As perhaps you can guess from the titles we usually assign these roles, they are actually a set of *expected outputs*. Individual organisms who play the role of "teacher" are expected to act and think in one way, while organisms who play the role of "student" are expected to produce quite a different set of behavioral outputs.

From an *organizational* point of view, however, it often doesn't matter which organism fills what role—any more than it matters to you which of your cells becomes a part of your liver and which becomes brain tissue. All you care about—and all the system cares about—is that all the roles are filled, and all the goals are met, so that you (and the organization) can survive.

Question: Does an organization have the ability to control its outputs *voluntarily*?

Societies and Cultures

A society or culture is an extremely complex social system that is composed of organizations, each of which plays its role in supporting the society. (See Fig. 5.2.)

Organizations sometimes act as if they were free to work toward any goals their members wish. But, in truth, no complex social organization can long endure without the strong support of the rest of society. Thus, the better an organization fulfills its cultural expectations, the better off will be the society, the organization, and each individual member thereof.

Question: A scientific experiment usually consists of changing the inputs to a system and then

Social roles. A role is a stereotyped or systematic way of behaving or thinking about something. When you say, "The good guys always wear white hats," you are describing a social role both in terms of the actor's behaviors and style of dress. A social role is thus a set of feed-forward instructions telling you how to act if you wish to play a certain part or role in society.

Structuralism. An early "school" of psychology started by the German scientist Wilhelm Wundt (VILL-helm Voondt). The structuralists attempted to model psychology after chemistry, thus hunted for the "atoms" or "elements" that composed the mind.

noting what changes occur in the system's outputs. What would be the easiest system to study scientifically—a cell, an organ, an organism, a group, an organization, or a society? Which science seems most advanced these days—biology, psychology, or sociology? Why is this so? Biology actually got its start as a science more than a century before psychology did. Why was this so?

Psychology: From Structuralism to Systems Theory

Psychology, as a science, is a little more than 100 years old. The first psychological laboratory was opened in Germany in 1879 by Wilhelm Wundt, who is usually considered to be the "father of experimental psychology." Many of the early American psychologists—such as James Angell and William James—studied in Germany with Wundt.

To Wilhelm Wundt, psychology was the "study of the contents of consciousness." And the way to discover what these contents were, Wundt said, was to study the *structure* of conscious experience. Wundt's approach is now called **structuralism**.

Structuralism

Wundt and his structuralist colleagues were probably the first "mentalists" in modern psychology. Taking their cue from physics, the structuralists assumed the mind was constructed of "mental atoms" just as a lump of coal is made up of carbon atoms.

But how do you study consciousness? You can poke and prod a lump of coal in various ways to determine its inner structure. As we noted, however, most psychologists consider consciousness to be a "process," not a material substance. To get around this problem, Wundt

Wilhelm Wundt   William James   John Dewey   John B. Watson

used a technique called **introspection**. That is, he trained observers to "look inside their minds" and "analyze their own mental experiences." He assumed that, by "introspecting" their own inner experiences, his observers would be able to identify what the "atom" of the mind actually was.

In a typical experiment, Wundt would present some stimulus input to his observers and ask them to report what they were conscious of. For example, he might sound a musical note and ask the observers to analyze their mental experiences. Wundt (and the other structuralists) hoped all observers would break the tone down into the same mental components. Alas, each observer tended to analyze the tone in quite different ways. Thus, the search for "mental atoms" was unsuccessful.

Wundt's structuralism had its day. But it passed from the scene early in this century because it offered too limited and too "mentalistic" a view of human nature.

Question: Did structuralism focus on inputs, outputs, or internal processes? Did it emphasize biological, intra-psychic, or social/behavioral variables?

Functionalism

Two of Wundt's best-known students were James Angell and William James. By the 1890's, they became dissatisfied with the search for "mental structures." They viewed Wundt's approach as too static, too theoretical, and (to be truthful) too European. America was bursting with vitality, and Americans seemed to demand "practical solutions to life's problems." To meet this demand, James and Angell developed a school of psychology called **functionalism**. They were helped enormously in their venture by a noted philosopher and educator, John Dewey.

In the *Encyclopedia of Human Behavior*, Robert M. Goldenson states that functionalism is a "general psychological approach that views behavior in terms of active adaptation to the environment." According to Goldenson, functionalism got its "official start" in 1896 when John Dewey published an important paper on **reflexes**. Dewey insisted that the distinction between "mind" and "body" was an artificial one. Every act, Dewey said, has both mental and physical aspects. Nor can we view our mental activities "in isolation," as Wundt did. Instead, we must try to understand our mental processes in terms of the conditions from which they arise and the consequences they produce.

The functionalist approach has had a strong influence on American psychology. To begin with, by emphasizing the importance of environmental inputs on mental activities, the functionalists encouraged the development of both sensory psychology and biological psychology. Second, by looking at the "consequences of mental acts," the functionalists got psychologists interested in behavioral outputs and what we now call "feedback." Third, because the functionalists said the purpose of behavior was to help organisms "meet the demands of daily living," they spurred the development of applied and clinical psychology.

Goldenson concludes that "functionalism was never a systematized, well-defined theory of psychology. It can best be viewed as a trend rather than a school." Indeed, functionalism no longer exists as a distinct approach "because it has been so fully incorporated into the psychology of this country."

Question: What similarities do you see between functionalism and General Systems Theory? What are the differences between the two?

The Behaviorist Revolution

One problem the functionalists had was this—they never got around to telling psychologists how to measure inputs and outputs very precisely. Another problem came from the fact that, like Wundt, the functionalists believed in using introspection as a psychological tool. A third difficulty was that, while they talked a lot about "helping people improve their lot," the functionalists never came up with a very good *technology of personal change*. It took the behaviorists to accomplish that practical goal.

In 1913, John B. Watson began the behaviorist revolution by throwing out the concept of "mind" entirely. Why did Watson take such a radical step? For several reasons. First, Watson was never very happy with such **nebulous** concepts as "consciousness" and "free will." Watson believed psychology should deal with concepts that were both *substantial* and *measurable*. "Mind" and "consciousness" didn't meet that criterion, but *behavior* surely did.

According to Watson, the "theoretical goal" of behaviorism "is the prediction and control of behavior." But to take this stance, Watson had to deny the commonsense view that people control their own actions. Rather than being "self-controllers," Watson said, people are like simple adding machines. A stimulus input comes along, presses a button in people's brains, and out pops a response of some kind. And the response occurs *because of the input*, not because of any "mental state" inside the individual.

Second, Watson saw that it was often easier to change behavioral outputs than it was to change inner mental processes. Why bother with the mind, then, when behavior is so much easier to deal with?

While Watson's brand of behaviorism did appeal to those individuals who desired "practical ways of changing (or controlling) human behavior," it had several fatal flaws. To begin with, Watson focused almost entirely on inputs. He saw humans as *passive organisms* that merely responded to environmental stimuli in ways their genes programmed them to respond. Since he never could gain complete control over the environment (past and present), he never produced the practical solutions to everyday problems he promised. Second, Watson failed to appreciate the importance of *feedback* in shaping human thoughts and behaviors. It thus fell to Harvard psychologist B.F. Skinner to take the next step—that of adding "feedback" and "consequences" to the behavioral equation.

> **Introspection** (inn-tro-SPECT-shun). The act of "inspecting" what's going on within your own mind. To introspect is to attempt to perceive and analyze your own mental processes.
>
> **Functionalism.** Early American psychologists—particularly John Dewey (1859–1952) and James R. Angell (1869–1949) were more interested in the functions of the mind than in its structures. Dewey proposed that psychology should study "what mind and behavior *do*." The "school" of psychology Dewey founded is called *functionalism*.
>
> **Reflexes** (REE-flex-es). Automatic responses, such as the knee-jerk, that are made (usually without conscious effort) whenever the appropriate stimulus input appears.
>
> **Nebulous** (NEBB-you-lus). From the Greek word meaning "cloud." Anything that is "misty" or "cloudy" or whose details are hard to determine is said to be nebulous.

Skinner's Contributions

B.F. Skinner took Watson's half-formed ideas on behaviorism and made them work in real-world situations. Skinner did so by demonstrating that organisms are particularly sensitive to the *consequences* of their actions. If a hungry pigeon gets a piece of corn when it pecks a button in a training box, this "positive feedback" encourages the pigeon to repeat the response that yielded the corn. But if the feedback is negative instead of positive—or if there is no feedback at all—the pigeon will try some other response instead of continuing to peck at the button. In Skinner's view, organisms use external feedback to guide their actions through long sequences of goal-oriented behaviors.

"Behavior is determined by its consequences," is one of Skinner's best-known sayings. And with this slogan as his motto, Skinner developed one of the most impressive *technologies* of behavioral change the world has ever known (see Chapter 14).

Evaluating Behaviorism

What are we to make of Watson and Skinner? To begin with—as we will see in many later chapters—the behaviorist tradition has given us highly effective ways of changing ourselves and of helping others do likewise. Thus, we would be foolish to reject behaviorism out of hand. However, the fact remains that "things go on inside our heads" that influence our behaviors—even if we cannot prove the existence of our mental processes to the behaviorist's satisfaction.

B.F. Skinner

Furthermore, as we will note in Chapter 14, even Skinner's brand of behaviorism has its practical limits. For, in the 1960's, many of Skinner's students developed even more effective ways of helping people change themselves by *putting the mind back in the human equation*. The first of these approaches is called **cognitive behavior modification**, and involves teaching people to use behavioral techniques to control their thoughts as well as their actions. The second is referred to as **social learning theory**, which teaches people to change their environments in order to achieve their personal goals.

In a sense, modern-day psychology has turned full circle and returned to the functionalist position. Wundt got psychology started in commonsense fashion, by overemphasizing the importance of the mind. Dewey and the functionalists rectified matters by placing equal importance on inputs, internal processes, and outputs. But because their concepts lacked precision, the functionalists offered little in the way of a full-fledged theory or practical solutions to human problems. The behaviorists threw mentalism out the window, but the cognitive behaviorists and social learning theorists brought the mind right back in.

As you might have guessed by now, General Systems Theory is an outgrowth of functionalism. But it is functionalism some 90 years after Dewey published his 1896 paper. Because we have learned so much more about human behavior now than Dewey knew of, General Systems Theory is much more precise than functionalism ever could be. And because the systems approach is compatible with behaviorism and social learning theory, General Systems Theory offers a type of practicality that the early functionalists could only dream of.

Now that we have described Systems Theory and given its historical background, it is time to evaluate it briefly, using the criteria we mentioned earlier in this chapter. As you will see, there are many things to be said in its favor. But there also are several problems associated with adopting the "holistic" approach to psychology.

Evaluating General Systems Theory

Accuracy

Most psychological theories are *qualitative* rather than *quantitative*. That is, psychologists tend to describe things in words rather than in the sorts of mathematical symbols used by physicists, chemists, and biologists. It was perhaps for this reason that functionalist William James described physics as a "hard-headed" science, but called psychology a "soft" science. Thus, James said, it is not very easy to judge the accuracy of most psychological theories because they are based more on hunches than on **empirical** data.

Briefly put, General Systems Theory is probably as accurate as any other broad-scale theory in that "soft" science we call psychology. However, it is not as precise as many "mini-theories" that attempt to explain just a small part of human thought, emotion, or behavior.

Completeness

The General Systems approach seems by far the most complete psychological theory presently available. However, General Systems Theory does not *disprove* or *displace* any of the other theories in psychology—it merely helps pull many of them together into a more coherent whole.

Impressiveness

Writing in the June 1979 issue of *Contemporary Psychology*, Harvard psychologist Brendan Maher states that, "Those who seek universal, coherent, elegant formulations in the grand manner" will find the systems approach to their liking. However, if you prefer a simpler view of human nature—or a more complex one—you may not find the General Systems Theory very impressive at all. Whatever the case, it is not important that you *believe* the theory—just that you understand it well enough to translate the material in this book into terms that make sense to you.

Usefulness

General Systems Theory may be useful to you in at least three ways:

1. It offers you a more "functional" understanding of yourself than do most other theories.
2. It can give you a better technology for personal change than do most other approaches.
3. It is a very optimistic theory indeed.

A Functional Approach

Because it grew out of functionalism, General Systems Theory offers a more holistic approach to understanding human behavior than do many other theories. For this reason, perhaps, it gained greatest acceptance in such function-oriented disciplines as family medicine, family therapy, and marriage counseling. For in these fields, the emphasis is on treating the *system*, not the individual.

Better Technology

From a technological point of view, you don't always have to understand *why* a system changes in order to *get* it to change. Indeed, in many cases, you can help systems acquire new responses without ever knowing for sure which "internal processes" **mediated** this learning.

General Systems Theory yields a stronger "technology of change" because it helps you find the inputs you need in order to alter your own outputs (and those of other systems).

An Optimistic Approach

All cultures have certain "commonsense" prejudices about human conduct built into them. As an example, our society has dozens of "folk sayings" that seem to tell us that people cannot change very much, no matter how hard they try. One such saying is, "You can't change human nature." Others are "You can't teach an old dog new tricks," "Leopards never change their spots," and "You can lead a horse to water, but you can't make him drink." All of these sayings seem designed to convince you that human change is difficult if not impossible.

From a General Systems Theory standpoint, however, *change is always possible* (at least theoretically). A system will *always* change its internal processes and its outputs *if* you are bright enough to find the input that will cause the change you desire. If you desire change, then—in yourself, in someone else, or in a group, organization, or society—it is up to you to discover the inputs that will do the job. And if change doesn't occur, you can't fault "human

Cognitive behavior modification. The use of behavioral techniques to change thoughts instead of merely changing observable behaviors. See Chapters 13 and 14.

Social learning theory. According to Skinner, all behavior is determined by external inputs. The social learning theorists believe that this statement is true only of infants. As children grow and mature, they learn not only because they are reinforced for some behaviors (and not reinforced for others), but also because humans are capable of acquiring new thoughts and actions by *observing* how other people behave and what the consequences of the behaviors of others are. Eventually, people acquire the ability to initiate behaviors on their own, and to alter their own environments voluntarily. See Chapters 14 and 19.

Empirical (em-PEER-ih-cal). From a Greek word meaning "experience." To be empirical is to rely on experience rather than on theory, to deal with facts and not with assumptions or guesses.

Mediated (ME-dee-ated). From a Latin word meaning "to take the middle position." If you mediate a dispute, you help the people arguing with each other come to some resolution of their conflict—usually by taking a position that is between the positions held by the parties having the dispute.

Dilemma (dye-LEMM-ah). From a Greek word meaning "involving two assumptions." When you are "caught between the devil and the deep blue sea," you face a dilemma. That is, you must choose between two equally unpleasant alternatives.

nature." Instead, you must blame yourself for not finding the way to achieve your goals.

Question: What inputs do you think you could give an "old dog" to help it acquire a new set of "tricky" outputs?

Problems With General Systems Theory

We have already mentioned some of the benefits involved in taking the systems approach to psychology. Now, let us discuss some of the problems you may encounter in trying to look at yourself and others from this new viewpoint.

Some New Insights Are Painful

Suppose your child doesn't learn as fast as you wish it to. If you adopt a "human nature" explanation of the child's slowness, you might blame "fate" or "bad genes." But if you adopt the General Systems viewpoint, you may experience a serious **dilemma**. For you will have to face the fact that many of the unpleasant things that happen to you (and the people around you) are at least partially your own fault.

To put the matter in different terms, when

you look at yourself in objective terms, you may grow painfully dissatisfied with your past actions. Under these circumstances, you must either make some fundamental changes in the ways you think and behave, or you must find some excuse for rejecting your new insights.

Attitude Change Is Not Always Enough

All of us occasionally must own up to a very thorny problem—the fact that our attitudes don't always agree with our actual behaviors. As we will note in Chapter 24, psychologists have frequently studied what happens when a person's attitudes come in conflict with that person's actual behavioral outputs. For the most part, people tend to reduce this type of conflict by producing complicated **rationalizations** for their actions—and then go on behaving just as they always had. The problem with General Systems Theory is this—it continually reminds you that changing your internal processes (such as attitudes) isn't enough. You must keep working until you change your behavioral outputs as well.

Helping Others Means Changing Yourself First

According to the systems view, your own personal growth will occur most readily when the feedback you get from others is rewarding or encouraging. However, if you do not first "reflect back" to others' information about the good things they are doing, can you really expect them to give you the sort of encouragement you need from them?

The Biblical "Golden Rule" has been around for many thousands of years, and it is an excellent theoretical statement of how people *ought* to behave. General Systems Theory—like many over viewpoints—accepts the Golden Rule as a goal well worth achieving. But unlike most other approaches, the systems approach offers a step-by-step *technology* for putting the rule into practice. The first step, though, involves making changes in your own actions and attitudes.

Learning Is Time Consuming

Before you can begin to make use of *any* psychological theory, you must first learn as much as you can about the "nuts and bolts" that hold the theory together. Put another way, in dealing with any science you must learn facts first and practical applications later.

By now you probably understand that, from a General Systems Theory point of view, all psychological processes *begin with inputs*. If you want to "make sense" out of what goes on inside your head, therefore, you may find the most sensible approach is to start by learning what your senses actually do for you.

Now that we have described and evaluated General Systems Theory, therefore, let us next turn our attention to *sensory psychology*—the scientific study of inputs to the mind-brain. Once we know something about how organisms handle inputs, we will look at such internal processes as cognition, motivation, emotion, and learning. Then we will discuss behavioral outputs. Only when we've mastered these "nuts and bolts" topics can we go on to such fascinating topics as child and developmental psychology, abnormal patterns of thoughts and behaviors, and psychotherapy.

Summary

1 Science is a mixture of facts and theories. The facts describe the world in very concrete or **empirical** terms. A **theory** organizes these facts systemically in order to describe the world in words or mathematical **symbols**.

2 Scientists judge theories by at least four **criteria**: Accuracy, completeness, impressiveness, and usefulness.

3 The psychological theory most people hold is **commonsense mentalism**—the belief that behavior is determined by **beliefs** and **desires**. The commonsense approach has many virtues, but is inaccurate and imprecise.

4 **General Systems Theory** is an attempt to analyze the world in terms of the **living systems** that inhabit the world.

5 Living Systems:
   a Are goal oriented, their major goal being that of survival.
   b Show emotional reactions associated with achieving or not achieving their goals.
   c Are capable of learning and adapting.
   d Are made up of organized parts or **sub-systems** that are in some kind of communication with each other.
   e Have **inputs, internal processes**, and **outputs**.
   f Are capable of **self-control**—which is to say they can alter their outputs in order to achieve the inputs they desire.

6   In order to achieve self-control, systems make use of **feed-forward**, **predicting consequences** of their actions, and **feedback**.

7   Feed-forward is a **sequence of responses** the system can make at some future time. Feedback is information about the system's past or present performance.

8   **Consciousness** emerges as individual organisms establish a "special relationship with their environments," and as they attempt to gain **self-control** and explain their own actions.

9   The **cell** is the smallest living system.

10 When cells cooperate with each other—and take on different **role specializations**—they can combine to form **organs**.

11 The **organism** is a collection of specialized organs that cooperate to produce the emergent property of **consciousness**.

12 Organisms form **groups** by learning how to communicate and cooperate with each other.

13 Groups form **social organizations** in which **formal rules** and written language typically emerge.

14 Social organizations can combine to form such complex **social systems** as societies and cultures.

15 The structuralists attempted to study the **contents of consciousness** using a tool called **introspection**.

16 The functionalists viewed behavior as an **active adaptation to the environment**.

Rationalizations (rah-shun-nall-ee-ZAY-shuns). From the Latin word meaning "to reason, or compute." To explain something in rational terms is to make it seem reasonable. To rationalize, however, is to offer "logical excuses" for what you wanted to do anyhow—to explain your emotional impulses in reasonable terms. Freud considered *rationalization* to be a mechanism by which the ego defended some of its more neurotic actions (see Chapter 21).

They held the major goal of mental activities was that of helping people solve life's problems.

17 John B. Watson was the father of **behaviorial psychology**. He threw out the notion of "mind" and focused on measuring behaviors instead.

18 B.F. Skinner added the concept of **feedback** to Watson's behaviorist and developed an impressive **technology** of personal change.

19 General Systems Theory seems to be a reasonably accurate and complete theory. It can be useful in three ways—it offers a **functional** viewpoint of the world, it yields a **strong technology of personal change**, and it is **optimistic** about the possibility of change.

20 The problems associated with adopting General Systems Theory include the facts that some new insights are painful, that the theory requires you to change both your behaviors and your attitudes, that helping others often means changing yourself first, and that you must learn many facts before you can use the theory.

(Continued from page 118.)

The party was marvelously noisy. There were a great many people on hand, all to help Patti's parents celebrate their "lucky seventh" wedding anniversary. Dr. Donald Severeid and his graduate student, Tom Watson, sat quietly in a corner, ignoring the turmoil. They knew very few of the other guests.

"I still don't believe you took Patti back to the table and continued her lesson after you found out the door was locked," Dr. Severeid said, taking a sip from his glass. "Surely that was above and beyond the call of duty."

Tom Watson gave a bemused groan. "It was either that, or sit down on the floor and cry. Especially since it took them 45 minutes to find the janitor."

"Has she stopped the voluntary 'soiling' behavior now?"

"It was a case of 'one-trial learning' on both our parts," Tom responded. "I never threatened to pinch Patti again, and she never soiled her pants to try to control me."

Dr. Severeid nodded "hello" to Patti's mother as the woman walked through the room, headed for the kitchen. "What about her self-control with food? Can she really hold a cookie in her hand for several minutes without eating it?"

"You won't believe this, Dr. Severeid, but we've timed her at 30 minutes by the clock. Of course, she did grind the cookie up a bit with her fingers, but she didn't eat a bite of it before I told her to. That's why I asked Patti's parents to invite us to the party tonight. I figure we've been giving Patti and her parents a private class in systems technology. You know—teaching them about inputs, outputs, feedback, and consequences. And I wanted you to help grade their final examination."

"Final examination? What do you mean?"

Tom leaned back in his chair. "Well, it used to be that her parents could either have a party, or Patti, but not both. Once the food was put out, she'd run screaming from plate to plate, grabbing everything in sight and stuffing it into her rosebud mouth. She'd even snatch food from the guests. But she's learned so much self-control that tonight she's going to be allowed to show off."

"How so?" Professor Severeid asked.

Tom grinned. "She's going to pass a tray of goodies among the guests. If she doesn't snitch any food, she gets to eat whatever she wants. Her parents and I have been practicing with her for several days now. They've learned a great deal about how to handle Patti, and I'm sure she'll make it."

At that moment, Patti's mother came into the room. "Listen, everybody," she said loudly. "Patti is going to serve you some food. Please help yourself to anything you want." The little girl came into view holding a large platter heaped high with delicacies. "But please don't encourage Patti to eat anything, because she has promised to wait until you've all been served before she eats."

Patti smiled and, at her mother's direction, walked up to an elderly woman and offered the plate to her. The woman beamed, took a little sandwich, and patted the girl on her cheek. Patti walked to the next guests, a young couple, and presented the plate to them. Both the man and the woman took something to eat from the platter and thanked Patti warmly.

Then she was in front of Tom. "Can you have a cookie, please?" she said, giggling just the smallest amount.

"Thank you very much, Patti. You're doing beautifully."

Patti offered Dr. Severeid the plate and, after he thanked her, moved to the next bunch of guests. Watching her actions carefully, the professor sighed softly. "Amazing progress for a little girl we all thought was too badly retarded to learn very much."

Tom smiled paternally. "She's an amazing person. I suspect we were the ones who retarded her progress,

really. As long as we viewed her as being 'incurably brain-damaged,' or 'piggish,' or 'mean,' there wasn't much we could do to help. But when we took a broader view . . ."

"When you saw her as a living organism, imbedded in a social system . . ."

"Then we realized we first had to change the way we treated her, in order to get her to grow and develop as she always could have. Patti can probably learn anything we're smart and patient enough to teach her."

Professor Severeid nodded in agreement. "It's like the telephone company used to say, Tom. Sometimes 'the system is the solution.'" The man thought for a moment, then continued. "Her parents are the most important part of the system, of course, and they've obviously changed considerably."

"Oh, they have. I think they understand that, for the most part, Patti just responds to their inputs. So they helped Patti rehearse for tonight, and they give her lots of love and encouragement. And they're making a big sacrifice for me tonight."

The professor looked puzzled. "What do you mean?"

"Although it's one of Patti's mother's favorites, there's one item of food she promised me wouldn't be on the menu tonight."

"What's that?" the older man asked.

Tom grinned. "Sweet pickles."

Recommended Readings

Miller, J.G. (1978). *Living systems.* New York: McGraw-Hill.

Morton, A. (1980). *Frames of mind: Constraints on the common-sense conception of the mental.* Oxford, Eng.: Clarendon.

Pribram, K.H. (1976) Problems concerning the structure of consciousness. In G.G. Globus, G. Maxwell, & I. Savodnik (Eds.), *Consciousness and the brain.* New York: Plenum.

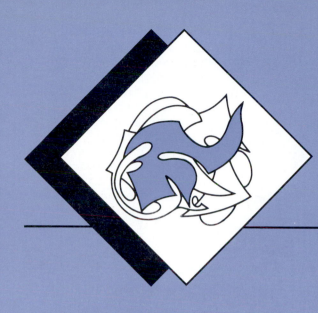

PART II

Sensation and Perception

Did You Know That...

- Your skin is primarily sensitive to warmth, cold, pressure, and, in a complex way, to pain?
- Some 95 percent of your skin is hairy?
- Muscle receptors tell your brain where your arms and legs are, and what they are doing?
- Special receptor cells in your inner ear help you detect "up" from "down"?
- Your sense receptors primarily detect *changes* in your environment?
- Even the best steak doesn't *taste* much different from old shoe leather?
- There are only four basic taste qualities: sweet, sour, salty, and bitter?
- Smell is an "ancient sense" related more to emotion than to cognition?
- A woman's sensitivity to tastes and odors varies with her menstrual cycle?
- Sex-related odors can change the way many women *perceive* other people?

6

Introduction to Sensory Psychology: "Touch," Taste, and Smell

"How to Build a Better Robot"

The mile-long chunk of rock hung suspended in the dark of outer space like a frayed cigar floating on the surface of a huge black lagoon. The little NASA space ship circled the asteroid-rock twice, and then dropped toward it slowly for a landing. The ship's directional jets hissed nervously as it twisted this way and that, now slowing its speed a bit, now correcting its slippery course through space with just the briefest puff of gas from one of the many jet nozzles protruding from its sides.

The space ship was millions of kilometers from earth, probing the ring of asteroids that girdled the dis-

tant sun like the belt around a fat man's belly. But this belt was a circle of rocks flung far out in space, sandwiched somewhere between the orbits of the planets Mars and Jupiter. A few of the asteroids were large enough to be seen by telescope from earth. Most of them, though, were so small you had to be right on top of them to detect them.

No one knew where the asteroid belt had come from— probably from some planet that had blown up a billion years ago. And only a few scientists really cared one way or another. But everybody knew and cared that some of these hunks of celestial gar-

bage were loaded with valuable metals. And that's what the little NASA space ship was out here for—to search for such earth-rare metals as radium, uranium, and plutonium. The National Aeronautics and Space Administration had a long-time need for these radioactive substances.

Major Jack Amundsen watched the dials and displays on the ship's control panel cautiously. The asteroid toward which he was guiding his craft was not all that large. But if the space ship's radioactive detector was right, the asteroid contained a chunk of uranium big enough to make the NASA brass back in Houston very happy indeed—and to earn him a very accelerated promotion. And Amundsen was the sort of man who found promotions very accelerating indeed.

As the ship inched in for a landing on the cigar-shaped rock, Amundsen switched on the landing lights. For the most part, the asteroid's surface seemed pitted with cracks and craters. But almost in the center, running around the rock like an equator, was a shallow groove that appeared to have a reasonably flat bottom. Amundsen dropped the little ship down into the depression carefully. When the ship made contact, Amundsen pressed a button on his control panel. Immediately, high-speed drills in the ship's legs chewed into the hard rock underneath and effectively bolted the ship to the asteroid. Only then did Major Amundsen lean back in his command chair and relax.

"Pretty good piloting, don't you think, Mark? Bet you couldn't do half that good."

Robot XSR 5 Mark III/21, sitting next to the Major, turned its head from the control panel. Its metallic eyes sparkled as if in amusement.

"You know, Major, that I am not programmed for landings except in emergency conditions. I am an exploratory space robot, not a pilot robot." The machine's voice was so musical that it almost sounded human.

"Then go explore. And don't let any meteorites puncture your space suit." The Major smiled at his little joke, for the robot wore no space suit at all.

Raw space was dangerous to man, as the deaths of sev-

eral U.S. and Russian astronauts had proved only too dramatically. The NASA brass had split down the middle on how to overcome the dangers. Several top administrators wanted all exploration done by machines. But the astronauts insisted machines were not flexible enough to meet the challenge of unknown conditions.

So an odd sort of compromise occurred. Humans would go into space, but would be mostly confined to the ship. As their companions, the astronauts would have highly complex robots to perform all the dangerous work outside the ship.

At first, Amundsen had resented the robot, wishing it were flesh and blood rather than metal and plastic. But during the long trip out, the Major had grown to accept Mark as being "almost human."

Mark lumbered clumsily into the space lock, pumped the precious air back into the ship, then moved slowly down a ladder onto the surface of the asteroid. Being a robot, Mark did not need much protection from the vacuum and cold of space. But Mark did need a searchlight and a radiation detector to help discover the substances that NASA was after.

As the robot moved away from the ship, the needle on its radiation detector hinted that the lode of uranium should be a few hundred meters ahead and very close to the surface. Mark moved cautiously, testing each step, the balance sensors in its head working overtime as it attempted to remain upright while walking weightlessly up the side of the small depression into which the ship had settled.

"How are you doing?" came Amundsen's gruff voice over the radio.

"Major, all is well. The stick-tite shoes grip the surface of the asteroid tightly, my walking reflexes function well; I have not stumbled once." The robot rounded a boulder and stopped, directing the light fastened to its head toward the mouth of a cavern near where it was standing.

"Major, the uranium appears to be buried inside a cave. May I descend?"

All hazardous procedures had to be approved by the human pilot.

"You may descend," came the Major's quick response.

Mark III/21 moved slowly into the mouth of the cave, stopping each few feet to daub a spot of fluorescent paint on the rocks. The paint marks would help guide the robot back to the surface should it lose its way inside the cave. Then Mark moved onward. The deeper underground the robot went, the more wildly the needle on the radiation detector danced. When the robot had pushed its way more than three hundred meters into the ground, it came to the top of a large, hollow chamber in the cave.

As the robot crawled to the bottom of the chamber, the detector needle jumped off the dial. Mark stopped and swung around, the light on its head flooding the chamber with brightness. Then the robot knelt, put its tools down beside it, and picked up a handful of black, soft, somewhat sticky material. Under the light, the soft stuff looked like pitchblende, one of the most common ores containing uranium.

"Major, we have apparently struck paydirt, if I may use

that phrase."

Back at the space ship, Amundsen was sitting at the control console waiting for news. When he heard what Mark said, he grinned.

"That's great, Mark, super great. Just gather up a sample in your bag and then . . ."

And then their world nearly ended.

Coming up from their blind side at a high speed, one of the asteroid's smaller brothers smacked into the rock's mid-section, just a few hundred meters from the ship. The asteroid shuddered like a punching bag hit by a world heavyweight. The smaller rock then bounced off into space again, leaving its devastation behind for the Major and the robot to handle as best they could.

Amundsen had been knocked from his seat when the crash occurred, and he thrashed about in midair momentarily. Because there was no gravity on the ship, objects knocked loose by the collision floated about the cabin lazily. The Major grabbed at a seatbelt and pulled himself to the control console. A quick glance at the dials and lights assured him that the ship was intact and safe. But the robot?

"Mark!" he called into the microphone. "What happened? Are you all right?"

The answer was slow in coming, and the robot's voice seemed distorted, fluttery, and very unmusical.

"Major, I survive, but barely. A rock hit my head. My light is gone. My vision circuits are inoperative. I am blind. I have lost contact with the bottom surface of the large chamber I was in. I float. Rocks and other objects float by me. What am I to do?"

The Major thought a while, picturing the robot tumbling about in the hollow underground bubble like a piece of meat in a bowl of stew.

"Reach out your arms and legs and wait until you make contact with one of the chamber walls."

"I obey, Major," the robot said. A minute or so later, it reported success, but in a doleful tone of voice. "I have touched the wall, Major. But what do I do now? My light is gone, and I cannot see. I cannot find the trail markers. I cannot find the tiny entrance to this large chamber. I have but three hours' power left in my batteries. How do I find my way back to the ship, Major?"

The problem was serious. Amundsen was under strict orders not to leave the ship even if the robot became endangered. He could return to earth safely without Mark, but when the robot's batteries were exhausted, its heater would no longer function. Then its delicate "brain" circuits would freeze and warp. For all practical purposes, the robot would be "dead." NASA would be furious at the loss of a multi-million dollar piece of equipment, and Amundsen would have lost a . . . friend?

Amundsen retraced the robot's path in his mind's eye. Always Mark had reported going down, down, deeper into the ground. Suddenly the solution seemed obvious.

"Mark, just keep moving upward. If you move upward, you'll get to the surface eventually and I can pick you up then with the ship. No sweat at all, really, Mark. Just keep moving upward."

"Major," said the robot after a while. "There is no gravity here and I do not know in which direction I am pointed. Major, which way is up?"

(Continued on page 160.)

The Senses

According to popular opinion, there are but five senses—vision, hearing, taste, smell, and touch. But there is also "common sense," which is unfortunately rare; "non-sense," which is unfortunately common; and the "sixth sense," which some people claim warns them of impending disaster (and which may be just ordinary "horse sense").

In truth, there are *more* than five senses, no matter how you wish to define the word "senses." For example, in this chapter, you will discover that what most people call "touch" is not one sense but several: (1) pressure, (2) temperature, (3) feedback from your muscles that lets you know where your arms and legs are, and (4) detection of changes in motion. To make matters even more complex, you will also find out that taste is both simpler and more complicated than you might have imagined, and that smell has a decided effect on your sex life. And in case you have any doubts, some of these facts are guaranteed to be sensational!

In order to help you "make sense" of your senses, let's begin by seeing what sorts of sensory information a *robot* would need in order to survive in outer space. For if you can understand what inputs a complex machine would need to survive "out there," perhaps you'll understand better what sorts of sensory experiences *you* require in order to survive on the planet Earth.

"Project Robot"

A few years from now, our first real interplanetary space ships will blast off from earth and take *people* out to one or more of the planets. As you may know, the U.S. space program is directed by the National Aeronautics and Space Administration. Let us suppose that, some time in the future, NASA decides that the environments on the eight other planets are so hostile that *robots* should be sent out first to investigate—to make sure human beings can survive in space suits if and when we do arrive.

For many reasons, NASA further concludes that the robot ought to be man-sized. It should be mobile, and it must carry its own protection against the elements. The robot should also have a means of sensing and measuring its environment, and a way of sending messages back to its home base to report the data it gathers.

Let's assume further that you are hired by NASA to help with "Project Robot." Your first assignment is to worry about what kind of *sensory inputs* the robot should have. You begin by asking yourself, "What kinds of sensory stimulation are humans sensitive to, and what use do we make of the information we get from our bodies and the world around us?"

Sensory Coherence

The robot you will design will have a purpose of some kind. That is, it must execute certain commands, maintain itself in reasonable order, and be able to move about in one fashion or another. All of these actions require that the robot be in touch both with the external world and with its own body functions. And in this respect, the robot is little different from you. For if *you* are to survive, you too must be able to interact with your environment and know what's going on inside your own body.

The *major purpose* of sensory inputs, then, is to give you a **coherent** picture of both your internal and your external environments, so that you can achieve your goals in life (includ-

ing that of surviving). You might be the brightest person ever born, but if you don't get the proper inputs (or don't use them correctly), you won't be around for very long.

Getting the proper inputs is not too difficult for most of us—we have but to open our eyes and ears and "take in the world." But how do you *make sense* out of these inputs? Well, that's one of the chief functions your brain serves—to tie together sight and sound and touch and smell and taste into one *coherent whole*.

To "make sense" of an input may seem easy—after all, your brain performs this task routinely millions of times a day. But think about the *sensory process* for a moment. Suppose you look at a bright red sports car passing by. You "see" the car because of light rays that are reflected to your *eyes* from the automobile. But your *brain* itself is not sensitive to light. So somehow your eyes must *translate* or **transduce** those light rays into a pattern of neural messages. Then your eyes send those input messages to your brain. Your brain momentarily "stores" these neural signals while it checks its memory banks, and "recognizes" the pattern as one it has experienced before. Your brain then combines the *sight* of the car with the deep rumbling *sounds* its engine is making (and perhaps the *smell* of the exhaust) and somehow produces a coherent mental image—that of a noisy, smelly, bright red sports car.

Sensory psychology deals with each of the various types of inputs you can detect—sight, sound, smell, taste, and "touch." *Perception* is the means by which your brain puts these inputs together to make a coherent experience. *Cognition* is the set of "inner mental processes" describing how you acquire, store, retrieve, and use knowledge about yourself and the world. Thus, cognition includes both perception and sensory inputs.

We'll have more to say about perception and cognition in later chapters. For the moment, let's first try to figure out what your sensory inputs *really are*, and how your brain *detects* what's going on inside your body and in the outer world.

The Skin

What is your most important sensory organ? Your eyes? Your ears, perhaps? Before you answer, think of the many blind people you know who get along quite well in this complex world. And think of how many deaf people manage to survive without being able to hear. But have you ever known anyone *without a skin to cover their flesh and bones*?

As you can perhaps now realize, your skin is the one of the *most important sensory organs* your body has. For your skin not only gives you sensory information, it gives you physical protection from the elements as well. Thus, when your boss at NASA assigns you the task of deciding what kind of "skin" the robot should have, you are rather pleased. Because you have been asked to design one of the most critical parts of the robot's body.

To start matters off, you ask yourself a very important question: What purpose does the skin serve? A little thought convinces you that your skin answers many needs. It keeps your vital organs "inside" where they belong, and keeps the outside world "outside" where it belongs. Your skin stretches as you gain weight and shrinks when you shed a few pounds. It also helps regulate your internal temperature, for it has several layers to it that help insulate you against the cold. And when you get too hot, your skin has sweat glands that release water, which cools you by evaporation.

Most important, however, your skin is filled with *receptors* that let you know what the world

around you is like. If you had no skin receptors, you wouldn't know when you had hurt yourself. You also wouldn't know when you were touching something, and whether what you touched was hard or soft, cold or hot. How long could you survive without this kind of sensory knowledge?

But would *your* skin serve a robot's specialized needs? After due consideration, you conclude you can't tell what type of covering the robot ought to have until you know more about what this robot is going to have to do. So you begin to think about what types of *sense organs* the robot is going to need in whatever skin it gets.

The Skin Receptors

If you like to experiment on yourself, please go find several small objects—things like a pencil, a glass, a rubber band, a ring, a key, a piece of cloth—and put them on a table near you. Now, close your eyes and *feel* each object. Begin by just pressing the palm of your hand down on the objects.

What can you tell about these small objects without fingering them? That they are hard or soft, large or small, that they have points or sharp edges or rounded **contours**—and that is about all you can tell. A pencil or key is hard, a rubber band or an eraser yields when you press on it and hence feels soft.

But to ask what may at first seem a stupid question, *how do you know what is hard and soft?*

The Pressure Receptors

When you touch an object gently, you depress or deform your skin. Very sensitive nerve cells detect this *deformation of your skin* and fire off a message to your cortex. This input message

"WHAT I LIKE ABOUT THIS OFFICE IS I CAN SEE THE CITY, BUT I CAN'T HEAR IT OR SMELL IT."

People who are sightless "see" art through their fingertips in a special museum for the blind in North Carolina.

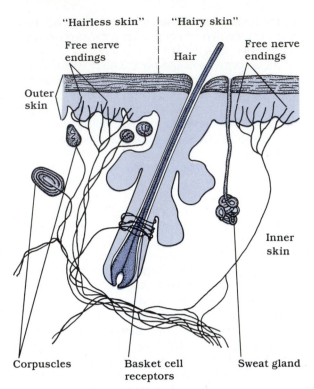

Fig. 6.1 A schematic diagram of the skin. Basket cell receptors are found only in hairy skin. Corpuscles are found primarily in hairless skin. Free nerve endings are found in both hairy and hairless regions.

moves down the axons of the receptor cells until it reaches your spinal cord, then moves up the cord to the stem of your brain. From your brain stem, the message flows through several "lower centers" and finally works its way up to your cortex. Your body may respond automatically and unconsciously to these inputs *before* they reach your cortex. But only when the sensory message arrives at your cortex do you realize *consciously* that your skin has encountered a foreign object of some sort.

Now, with the fingers of one hand, gently pinch the palm of your other hand. You will notice that the skin on your palm feels fairly thick. Next, gently pinch the skin on your forearm. The skin is much thinner there. But the major *biological* difference is that the skin on your forearm has hairs on it, while the skin on your palm does not. Some 95 percent of the skin on your body (whether you are male or female) is *hairy* skin. Only the palms of your hands, the soles of your feet, your lips and mouth, your eyeballs, some parts of your sex organs, and a few other scattered areas are made up of *hairless* skin.

Hairless Skin

Hairless skin contains tiny receptor cells that are called **encapsulated nerve endings**. Some of these encapsulated nerve endings look much like small onions and are known as **corpuscles**. The corpuscles are more or less round in shape, much like small onions. And if you were to cut one open, you'd find that these "onion-shaped" corpuscles have many layers to them (see Fig. 6.1).

Hairy Skin

Hairy skin has a few encapsulated nerve endings in it. But it also has a unique type of touch-receptor neuron buried at the base of each hair. The fibers of these nerve cells are woven around the bottom of each stalk of hair. Whenever the hair-stalk is pushed or pulled in any direction, the nerve fibers are squeezed so that they fire off a "pressure" message to your brain. These hairy-skin receptors are called *basket cells* because they look like a wicker basket wrapped around the bottom of the hair stalk. (It is the basket cell, not the hair itself, that is the "receptor," of course.)

Free Nerve Endings

Both hairy and hairless skin also contain receptor neurons called *free nerve endings.* "Free" in this case means the "input ends" of the receptor are not attached to any particular place (see Fig. 6.1). The free nerve endings are very simple nerve cells whose fibers spread out freely like the branches of a vine just under the outer layers of your skin. Since the free nerve endings are found everywhere on the surface of your body, they are by far the *most common sort* of skin receptor that you have.

All three types of receptors—the encapsulated nerve endings (including the corpuscles), the basket cells, and the free nerve endings—yield a simple "pressure sensation" when they are stimulated. (As we will see, however, some of the free nerve endings and basket cells are also sensitive to temperature.)

Primary Sensory Qualities

Now, go back to the objects you were feeling on the table near you. Close your eyes and have someone place first a *wooden* object and then a *metal* object in your hands. You can tell wood from metal in two ways: (1) The wood is softer than the metal; and (2) the wood will feel warm, while the metal feels cold.

Your skin receptors give rise to two qualitatively different sensory experiences—*pressure* and *temperature*. The encapsulated nerve endings in the hairless regions are primarily *pressure receptors*. The free nerve endings and the basket cells around each hair detect both *pressure* and *temperature*.

It may come as a surprise to you that these two sensations (plus pain, which we will discuss later) are the *only primary sensory qualities* your skin can tell you about. However, most psychologists believe that all the information you get from your skin about the world around you is merely a *combination* of pressure sensations and temperature sensations—plus, occasionally, the experience of pain (see Chapter 16).

Complex Pressure Sensations

Next, rub the palm of your hand over your clothes, the surface of the table, the cover of this book, the upholstery of a chair, or the top of a rug. Some objects feel smooth to your touch, others feel rough. How does your skin tell you which is which if it can experience *just* pressure and temperature?

The answer comes from this fact—when you move your hand across a surface, you stimulate many receptors at once. If the surface of an object is rough, parts of your skin "stick" as you rub your palm across the object. This "sticking" causes your skin to wrinkle as it rubs across the object. Where your skin wrinkles the most, the receptors fire vigorously. But where your skin is unwrinkled and smooth, the receptors fire hardly at all. Your brain perceives this *pattern*

Encapsulated nerve endings (en-CAP-sue-lated). Encapsulate means to enclose or to envelop. When you put on a cap, you encapsulate your head.

Corpuscles (KOR-pus-sulls). The Latin word *corpus* means "body." We get our English words "corpse" (a dead body), "corps" (the Marine Corps), and "corporation" (a body of people) from this same Latin term. A corpuscle is a "little body" or "little cell," particularly one that is isolated from others like it. The red blood cells, for instance, are called the "red corpuscles."

of incoming sensory information as "roughness" or "smoothness."

If the robot you are helping build for NASA is going to stroll about the surface of some distant planet, you will want it to be able to bend over, pick something interesting off the ground, and examine it. If you put pressure receptors of some kind in the robot's fingers, you will be able to tell if the object is hard or soft, or rough or smooth, simply by decoding the *pattern of signals* from the robot's pressure receptors.

You could also put temperature detectors in the robot's fingers and learn whether the object was hot or cold.

But hot or cold in relation to what?

The Temperature Receptors

When you first crawl into a tub of hot water, it may seem that you are going to be boiled alive before the bath is over. The water feels intensely hot, and your skin turns lobster red as your brain orders an increase in the flow of blood through your skin to help cool you off. If you manage to stay in the tub for a while, the water feels cooler and cooler, even if you keep the temperature of the water constant. When you get out, the air in the bathroom may seem surprisingly cool to your naked skin.

"Hot" and "cold" are *relative* terms that, in your body's case, are always related to *whatever your skin temperature is*. Anything you touch that is *colder* than your skin will seem *cool* to you. Anything you touch that is *hotter* than your skin will seem *warm*. The warmer or colder the object is in relation to your skin temperature, the more rapidly your temperature receptors will fire.

Many years ago, it was thought there were separate receptors for "warm" and for "cold." In his 1982 book on temperature receptors, however, German psychologist Herbert Hensel notes that this simply isn't the case. Areas of hairy skin with no receptors other than the basket cells can detect both warmth and cold. So can

In zero gravity conditions, your balance detectors can't tell "up" from "down."

areas of the white of the eye, which contains only free nerve endings. Most scientists now believe that the basket cells and the free nerve endings can signal *either* warm or cold. And they do so primarily by detecting *changes* in the temperature of the skin. Thus, the receptors actually are sensitive to temperature *changes* rather than to "warm" and "cold" in any absolute sense.

Question: After you have been soaking in a warm tub for some time, the hot water typically will seem cooler to you than when you first got in the tub. How does this fact support Hensel's view that the skin is sensitive to temperature changes rather than "hot" or "cold" in any absolute sense?

The Somatic Cortex

The messages that your skin receptors send to your brain tell you four things:

1. The *location* of the experience—that is, what part of your body is detecting the sensations.
2. The *quality* of the experience—that is, pressure or temperature.
3. The *quantity* or strength of the experience—

intense pressure or weak, slightly warm or very cold.
4. The *duration* of the stimulation—whether it is brief or continuing.

Let's see why all four of these things are important. Suppose you are walking along barefooted and you step on a tack. As you probably well know, you realize almost instantly *what part* of which foot has been punctured, *how intense* the wound is, and whether the tack is *still* in your foot or has fallen out. How do you become conscious of all this information so quickly?

Well, think for a moment about the NASA robot you are helping design. If you want the robot to *localize* its skin sensations, how would you hook the robot's skin receptors up to its brain? Probably you would want to put in a direct "telephone line" between each receptor and a *specific* part of the "brain." Each receptor would, in effect, have its own "telephone number." The robot could tell where the stimulation was coming from simply by checking to see which telephone line the message was coming over.

Your nervous system is "constructed" in much the same way. Each receptor cell in your skin is connected to a specific region in the *sensory input areas* in your **parietal lobes**. Thus, your brain can tell the location of any stimulation on your body by noting *where* the input message arrives in the parietal lobe.

You may recall from Chapter 4 that the parietal lobe in each of your cerebral hemispheres is located at the very top center of your brain. The front edge of the parietal lobe is immediately adjacent to the *motor output area* at the rear of the frontal lobe. The cortex at this front edge of the parietal lobe is often called the *somatic cortex*. "Soma" is the Greek word for "body," and it is to this part of your cortex that all of your body or *somatic receptors* send their sensory messages. Receptors in the left side of your body send their inputs primarily to the somatic cortex in the right half of your brain. The receptors in the right side of your body send their messages to your left somatic cortex.

The Deep Receptors

If you made the NASA robot much like yourself, it could tell the hardness, smoothness, and temperature of an object it had picked up just by noting what its "skin" receptors were signaling. But what about the object's size, shape, and weight?

Pick up a pencil, close your eyes, and roll the pencil around in your hand. You can tell at once what size, shape, and weight the pencil has. But it is *not* your surface or skin receptors that give you this information. For we could anesthetize all the nerves in the skin of your hand, and you would still be able to tell the size, shape, and weight of the pencil.

The muscles, joints, tendons, and bones in your hand (and in much of the rest of your body) all have sensory receptors in them. These are called *deep receptors*, to distinguish them from the *surface receptors* in your skin. Whenever you contract a muscle in your hand, a tiny nerve cell buried in that muscle sends a feedback signal to your somatic cortex saying the muscle is in operation. The heavier an object is, the harder your muscle must work to lift the object and hold it steady. And the harder the muscle pulls or contracts, the more vigorously the tiny receptor neuron buried in the muscle fires—and the more intense feedback you get.

Distribution of Receptors

If you were building a robot, you would surely want its *fingers* to be more sensitive to pressure and temperature than, say, the middle of its

Parietal lobes (pair-EYE-uh-tull, or puh-RYE-uh-tull). That part of each cerebral hemisphere located at the very top of the brain. Sensory input from the skin receptors and the muscles comes to this part of your cerebrum. See Chapter 4.

back. For robots (like people) would seldom be called upon to make fine discriminations about objects with the "skin" on their backs. So you would probably put *more* sensory receptors in the robot's fingers than on its back.

There are more pressure receptors in your fingertips, your lips, your eyeball, and on the tip of your tongue than elsewhere on your body. Thus, the skin on your back and buttocks contains far fewer receptors per square inch of tissue than the skin on your lips contains.

Generally speaking, the distribution of the sense receptors in your body is just about the same as you would logically decide should be the case for your robot. Those parts of your body that you use most to make sensory discriminations have the most pressure receptors, while those parts that you use least have fewer receptor neurons.

Motion-Change Detectors

By using electronic circuits that would operate much the way the neural circuits in your body operate, you could design a robot able to pick things up, measure them with its fingers, and keep track of where its arms and legs were in the process. But what if your robot fell over and ruined its vision tubes? How would you get it upright and walking again? How would it know which way was up?

Contact receptors in the soles of your robot's feet might be helpful, but they would not tell the robot whether its head was bent over or upright. You could add position detectors in the robot's "muscular" system that could monitor the location of all its limbs and its head. But even these receptors would not be enough. For the robot still could not tell "up" from "down" just by getting feedback about where its arms and legs were.

Two Types of Motion

Whether you are considering robots or people, there are two basic types of motion that a "body" must be sensitive to: (1) straight-line or linear movements, and (2) rotary or circular movements. Buried away inside each of your

Children use their balance detectors in order to learn how to maintain an upright posture.

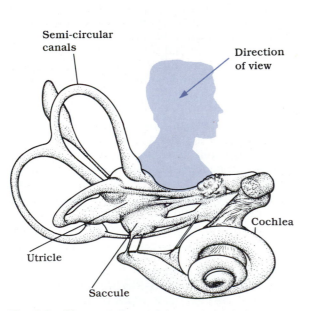

Fig. 6.2 The saccule, utricle, and semi-circular canals are motion detectors in the inner ear.

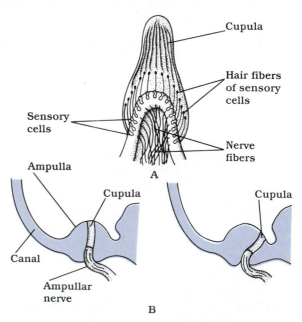

Fig. 6.3 Receptor cells in the cupula of the semi-circular canals detect rotary motion.

ears are two types of receptor organs that detect *changes* in the motion of your body. One type of receptor responds to changes in "straight-line motion." The other type responds to changes in "circular" motion. Both types of receptor organs function by obeying Newton's **law of inertia**.

Linear Motion-Change Detectors

The "flip-flop" movements that your body makes when an automobile speeds up or slows down are usually straight-line or linear movements. The detectors in your ear that sense *changes in linear motion* are two small organs called the **saccule** and the **utricle**.

Both the saccule and the utricle are made up of Jello-like or gelatinous tissue filled with tiny stone-like particles—rather as if someone had made a bowl of cherry Jello and put in just the pits instead of the cherries. When your head begins to move in a straight line, the saccule and utricle flip-flop in your inner ear the same way that your body flip-flops in an automobile. The "rocks in your head"—that is, the bits of stone in the saccule and utricle—increase the quivering of Jello-like material.

Hair cells buried in this gelatinous tissue are pushed or pulled this way and that by the "quivering" in the saccule and utricle. These *hair cells* are stimulated by the flip-flopping and signal your somatic cortex that your body is starting or stopping a straight-line (linear) movement (see Fig. 6.2).

Rotary Motion-Change Detectors

Any *change* in rotary motion your body makes is detected by the *semi-circular canals* in your ear. These three canals are positioned at right angles to each other inside your ear so they can detect changes in circular motion in any of the three dimensions of space (see Fig. 6.3).

When you turn your head, the fluid in the semi-circular canals accelerates more slowly than does the rest of your head. This fluid presses against a small mound of gelatinous tissue at the base of each canal. When this Jello-like tissue is pushed one way or the other, hair cells in the gelatin are twisted or pulled. These *hair cells* then signal your somatic cortex that your head has either stopped or started some kind of rotary motion.

Law of inertia (in-ER-sha). After studying apples falling from trees (and other things), Sir Isaac Newton "discovered" the law of inertia: An object at rest tends to remain at rest, while an object in motion tends to maintain that motion. *Inertia* thus means "resistance to change."

Saccule (SACK-you'll). One of the two small organs in your inner ear that detects straight-line movements of your head (and hence of your body). The Greek word *sakkos* means "bag" or "sack." The saccule is thus a "little bag."

Utricle (YOU-trick-ull). From the Latin word meaning (you guessed it!) "little bag." The second of the small organs in your inner ear that detect linear motion.

Centrifugal Force

If you have ever been to a carnival or amusement park, you may have ridden on a "loop-the-loop" roller coaster. If you have taken one of these frightening yet thrilling rides, you may have asked yourself why you didn't fall out of the car when it turned you upside down at the top of the "loop."

The answer is, *centrifugal force*. Centrifugal force tends to throw any object in the roller coaster car *away* from the center of the rotation. As the car makes the loop, therefore, centrifugal force plasters you firmly against your seat cushion despite the fact that you are upside down.

Centrifugal force is actually an example of Newton's law of inertia, and your motion-change detectors respond to centrifugal force just as they do to any other form of movement. If you could stand up in the roller coaster car just as you reached the top of the "loop," your head would be pointed straight at the earth. Yet the bottom of the car would seem "down" to you, while the earth itself would seem to be "up."

The people at NASA have designed wheel-like space ships we might use to visit the planets. During the journey, the wheel would turn just rapidly enough to create an artificial gravity so the men and women on board could walk comfortably around the inside of the outer wall of the wheel—with their heads pointed to the center of the wheel. Since the motion-change detectors in the travelers' ears couldn't tell the difference, centrifugal force presumably could make a pleasant substitute for gravity.

Question: The earth is turning at a speed of some 1,000 miles per hour. Why don't your motion receptors detect this rotary movement?

People who live close to an airport soon habituate to the sound of passing airplanes. This is an example of "central habituation."

Adaptation and Habituation

Your brain is your main organ of survival. And if you are to survive, you must usually pay more attention to *changes* in your environment than to stimuli that *remain constant* for a period of time.

There are at least two ways in which your nervous system adjusts to constant inputs: first, by what we will call *receptor adaptation*; second, by what we will refer to as *central habituation* to a stimulus input. Receptor adaptation occurs in the receptor neurons themselves, while central habituation occurs in your brain.

Receptor Adaptation

As an example of *receptor adaptation*, consider what happens when you first sink into a tub of water that is 20° warmer than your skin. As you know, your temperature receptors will begin to fire vigorously. But as you remain lying in the tub, your skin itself warms up. After a short period of time, your free nerve endings will fire less vigorously because the temperature of your skin is now much closer to that of the water. Because your skin and your free nerve endings have *adapted* to the heat, the water will now seem much less hot to you.

Central Habituation

As an example of *central habituation*, think of what happens when you move into a house beside a busy highway. At first, you notice the sounds of the traffic almost continuously. But after a few days, your brain will stop paying much attention to the continual drone of the passing cars and trucks. Indeed, you may be surprised when a visiting friend asks how you can stand the noise. But in this case, it is your *brain* that has changed its way of responding to a constant input, not the receptors in your *ears*.

In general, we use the term *adaptation* whenever your receptor cells themselves slow down or reduce their firing rates in response to a contant stimulus. We use the term *habituation*, however, to refer to your brain's tendency to ignore sensory inputs that seem of little interest or importance.

Adaptation and habituation are complex subjects we will discuss often in this book. For the moment, you should remember that the human body has a great ability to adjust to the world around it. But this adjustment hinges on your body's being able to notice and react to what is *changing* in the environment.

Question: When you have been soaking in a hot tub for a while, can you make the water "feel" warmer just by paying attention to it? When you have lived by a noisy highway for a while, can you hear the traffic just by paying attention to it? What do your answers to these two questions tell you about the differences between receptor adaptation and central habituation?

A Window of Skin

Your skin senses are surely as critical to your survival as are vision and hearing. And yet, since you seldom use them for communication or artistic expression, you may have overlooked their complexity, their beauty, and their incredible usefulness.

As an example of your skin's importance, consider the story of Helen Keller. She was born a normal child, but an illness when she was 19 months old left her deaf and blind. Although she had learned to say a few words before the illness, she soon stopped speaking. For the next several years, Helen Keller was little more than an animal, trapped in a black and silent cage, completely unable to communicate with those around her.

When Helen Keller was 6, however, her parents appealed to Alexander Graham Bell for help. Bell, the inventor of the telephone, recommended as a teacher a young woman named Anne Sullivan. Within a month Anne Sullivan had taught Helen to make sense of the myriad sensations her skin receptors poured into her brain. Helen learned how to "talk" using her fingers, and how to "listen" when someone "wrote" on the palm of her hand. Later she learned to "read speech" by placing her fingers on the lips of the person who was speaking.

Helen Keller's skin was her only window to the world, but she "saw" through this window with exceptional clarity.

Every scrap of knowledge you have about the world around you, including the images you have of people you love and hate, first came to you as a pattern of neural inputs that your sense organs sent to your brain for processing. If you understand where your inputs come from—that is, how your receptor neurons react and why they function as they do—you will certainly be able to build a better robot if you ever have to. But, more important, you will also come closer to understanding your own internal psychological processes—and your behavioral outputs—than if you choose to ignore the "input side" of your own body's functioning.

Taste

Your skin is an important "input organ," in part because it protects you from things in the outside world that shouldn't get inside your body. But there are times when you *must* "input" certain items—such as food and water—if you are to survive. And much as it may surprise you, your skin helps you determine what to eat and drink—and what not to. For, as we will soon see, receptor cells in the skin that lines your tongue, mouth, and nose are responsible for mediating those sensory qualities we call "taste" and "smell."

Let's look first at what taste is all about. Pick your favorite food and imagine it in your mind's eye. Let's say you picked a steak—3 inches thick, wrapped in bacon, and cooked just the way you like it. Now, ask yourself what may seem a very stupid question: Why does the steak *taste* good to you?

Whatever reasons you come up with, chances are they're partly wrong. For even the best of steaks has almost no *taste* at all—at least if we restrict "taste" to the sensory qualities that come from the skin receptors in your tongue. Steak *smells* good; it *looks* good; it has a fine *texture* to it as you chew it. And if it comes to your table sizzling hot, steak both *sounds* good and has just the right *temperature*.

But none of these sensory qualities has anything to do with the *taste* of steak. In fact, if we could block out all the other sensory qualities except those that come from your taste receptors, you'd find you could hardly tell the difference between the taste of steak and that of old shoe leather.

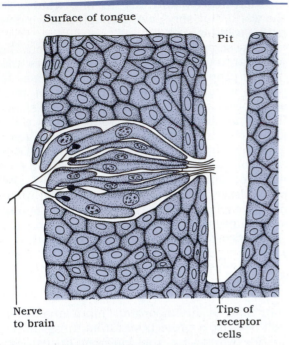

Fig. 6.4 A single taste bud.

Surface of tongue

Pit

Nerve to brain

Tips of receptor cells

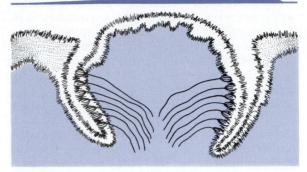

Fig. 6.5 A papilla in the tongue.

The sense of smell affects not only what you eat and drink, but also influences sexual attractiveness.

All tastes are made up of mixtures of just four basic qualities: sweet, sour, bitter, and salty.

The Taste Receptors

Your *taste buds* contain the hair cells that are your taste receptors. The taste buds are your body's "poor relations" (see Fig. 6.4). Impoverished in almost every sense of the word, your taste buds are scattered in nooks and crannies all across the surface and sides of your tongue. Mostly, however, they are found clumped together in bumps on your tongue called **papillae** (from the Latin word meaning "nipples"). If you stick out your tongue and look at it, you will see the papillae very clearly.

Most of the papillae have grooves around their sides, like the moats or canals that circled old European castles. The taste buds line the sides of the papillae, like windows in the outer wall of a castle (see Fig. 6.5).

There are about 10,000 taste buds in your mouth, each made up of several receptor cells. Most of the buds are on your tongue, but there are also a few scattered elsewhere in your mouth. Each of the receptor cells in the taste bud has a hair at one end which pokes out into the "moat" around the papillae much as the hairs on the skin of your arm stick out into the air. When you eat or drink something, the liquids in your mouth fill up the moats around the papillae. Various molecules in the food stimulate the hair cells *chemically*. The cells then fire off sensory input messages to your brain, and you experience the sensation of taste.

The chemical processes that lead to the experience of taste are not entirely known. But it appears that the food molecules fill in specific *receptor sites* on the hairs and receptor cells, much as the transmitter molecules in the synaptic clefts find receptor sites on the dendrites and cell bodies of the neurons in your brain. Certain types of food molecules apparently fit

into one receptor site but won't fit into others—much as a key will fit some locks but not others. When a molecule fits into a taste receptor site, it causes the receptor cell to fire. Your brain then figures out what kinds of chemicals are present in your mouth by noting which receptors have been "unlocked," or stimulated.

Not all scientists agree that this is how you detect the various taste qualities. However, much of the research data does support this position.

Taste Qualities

There are only four basic taste qualities: *sweet, sour, bitter,* and *salty*—a paltry few *primary* qualities compared to the richness of the sensory experiences you get from vision, hearing, and smell. The noted psychologist E.B. Titchener once estimated that you can discriminate about 3,000 different tastes. However, all of them appear to be *mixtures* of the four basic taste qualities.

Research by G. von Bekesy suggests there are four different taste receptors—one for each of the four primary taste qualities. However, more recent work by Carl Pfaffman indicates that your nervous system *processes* information from the taste receptors in a complex manner we still don't fully understand. Thus, as simple a sense as taste is, so far it has defied our attempts to understand it completely.

One point about taste is clear, however. It plays a very important role in your life. For, along with your nose, your tongue acts as *guardian of your stomach*. That is, things that innately "taste good" typically are good for you, while foods and liquids that innately "taste bad" often are harmful. You can, however, *acquire* a taste for many things that aren't pleasing to your **palate** the first time you sample them. As an illustration of all these points, consider the following facts: Newborn infants will usually drink milk shortly after birth, but will spit out sour or bitter substances. The liking for sweet or slightly salty substances thus seems "built into your genes." But a fondness for beer or for "gin and tonic" would seem to be

"MY COMPLIMENTS TO THE FOOD TASTER."

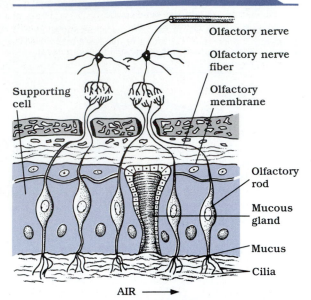

Fig. 6.6 Schematic representation of olfactory membrane, showing the olfactory rods and the cilia in the layer of mucus. (Adapted from Gardner, E. *Fundamentals of Neurology,* 6th ed. Philadelphia: Saunders, 1975).

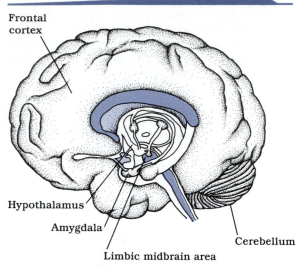

Fig. 6.7 The olfactory receptors send messages directly to the limbic system and other emotional centers in the brain.

John Amoore

Question: When you catch a cold, and your *nose* is clogged but your *tongue* is not affected, why does food suddenly lose its "taste?"

a learned response, since infants don't care much for such tastes, but adults often do.

Some people are very insensitive to the taste of certain foods—you must really saturate their tongues with these foods for these people to detect the substance at all. This *taste blindness* is far from rare, and seems to be caused by some inherited deficiency in the chemical composition of the person's saliva. However, the taste-blind individual can usually detect the substance rather easily if you first dissolve the food in the saliva of a person with normal taste sensitivity.

The taste receptors in your tongue apparently are "worn down" by the act of chewing and swallowing food—and thus must be continuously repaired or replaced. Older individuals often cannot regrow lost tissue as readily as younger individuals and therefore may have reduced numbers of receptors in their later years. Perhaps this fact explains why some older people add more seasoning to their food than most younger individuals prefer.

Taste is a necessary but not a particularly rich "sense." For the truth is, most of the food qualities that you ascribe to your tongue really should be credited to your nose.

Smell

Your nose has two cavities or open spaces inside it. The roof of each of these nasal cavities is lined with a thick covering called the **olfactory membrane**, which is really a type of skin. Covering the olfactory membrane is a thin layer of **mucus**. Embedded in the membrane itself are millions of receptor cells called *olfactory rods* (see Fig. 6.6).

At the base end of each of the olfactory rods is an axon that runs directly to your brain. At the front end is a branched set of **cilia**, which act in much the same fashion as dendrites do. These cilia stick out of the olfactory membrane into the layer of mucus.

The stimuli that excite your olfactory rods are complex chemicals in *gaseous form* that are suspended in the air you breathe. As air passes over the olfactory membrane, some of the complex chemicals in the air are absorbed into the mucus. These gaseous molecules appear to lock onto specific receptor sites on the cilia. This "locking on" causes the olfactory rods to fire off an input message to your brain.

Smell Qualities

There have been several attempts to break the experience of smell down into its "primary qualities," such as the "salt, sweet, sour, and bitter" qualities of taste. Perhaps the most successful scheme is that proposed by John Amoore, at the University of California Medical Center in San Francisco. Amoore believes that there are seven primary smell qualities:

1. camphor (moth balls)
2. musky
3. floral (roses)
4. peppermint
5. ethereal (dry-cleaning fluid)
6. pungent (vinegar)
7. putrid (rotten eggs)

Amoore believes that there are several different kinds of *receptor sites* on the olfactory cilia. Stimulus molecules that fit within a *single* receptor site trigger off a *single*, "primary" smell experience. However, most molecules will fit within two or more receptor sites. Thus, you perceive most smells as being complex mixtures of the seven primary smell qualities.

Smell—an Ancient Sense

Smell is a unique sense in at least two important ways. First, it is perhaps the most ancient sense of all. Single-celled organisms could detect molecules in the water around them long before they became sensitive to sights or sounds. The fact that the olfactory nerve bypasses the thalamus and runs directly to the amygdala and other parts of the "old mammalian brain" (see Chapter 4) is good evidence of the ancientness of smell. All other sensory inputs pass through the thalamus before going on to the cortex.

Second, smell seems more directly related to emotion and motivation than are the other

senses (see Fig. 6.7). In his 1982 book *The Perception of Odors*, Brown University psychologist Trygg Engen puts it this way: "Functionally, *smell may be to emotion* what sight or hearing is to cognition. . . . When odor is involved it may well cause a feeling before it elicits a concern with the meaning of odor." Engen notes, for instance, that many attacks of **mass hysteria** are set off by a new or unusual odor. And many epileptic patients report they experienced an "odd odor" (real or imagined) just prior to a grand mal seizure.

Question: How might the fact that the olfactory nerve runs directly to the amygdala support Engen's view that smell is closely related to emotion?

Hormones and Sensory Acuity

According to John Amoore, many of us lack the ability to smell specific substances. Amoore found that 47 percent of the people he tested could not smell the urinous odor, 16 percent were "blind" to malty smells, 12 percent couldn't detect musky odors, and 3 percent could not smell sweat. These "smell blindnesses" apparently are present from birth.

Judging from Amoore's research, your genes influence your ability to detect various odors. But recent experiments suggest that your olfactory thresholds are also influenced by the amount of sex hormones present in your body. *Hormones* are chemicals secreted by various glands in your body that have a profound influ-

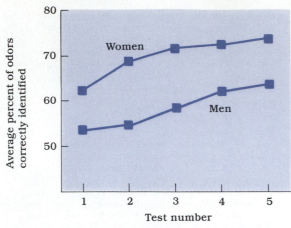

Fig. 6.8 Outcome of an experiment by William Cain, who tested men and women on their ability to learn 80 odors. The ability of both women and men to come up with the correct names improved over time. But, on the average, women correctly identified more items on the initial test and maintained this superiority in four later trials.

ority is a matter of experience, however, for *all* the subjects showed improvement over time. And by the fifth test, the men were performing as well as the women had at the start of the experiment. In present-day American society, Cain says, women are more likely to deal with foods, perfumes, and other "smelly" objects than men are.

Research by University of Pennsylvania psychologist Richard Doty, reported in the March issue of *Science 83*, tends to support Cain's work. Doty had 33 male and female college students breathe into glass tubes passing through a screen. Judges on the other side tried to guess the sex of the "breather" by smelling the breath. Doty states the majority of judges were accurate most of the time. But several female judges were correct on 95 percent of the tests, and were particularly good at picking out men's breath. Doty concludes, "Though humans don't use their sense of smell in many situations, in some cases people can be as discriminating as animals."

Question: William Cain notes that learning to give a "verbal label" to an odor helps considerably in identifying it at a later time. Why might attaching a name to a smell help you remember it?

Smells and the Menstrual Cycle

The relationship between smells and sexual behavior is a complex but very interesting one. To begin with, the menstrual cycle itself seems to be controlled in part by olfactory inputs. There are many "old wives' tales" suggesting that women who live together tend to have menstrual periods that are "in synch" with each other. In 1971, Martha McClintock tested this folk belief by studying the menstrual cycles of 135 women living in a dormitory at Wellesley College. McClintock found that, as the college year progressed, the menstrual cycles of good friends and roommates did in fact become more similar.

An explanation for this "menstrual synchrony" may come from research reported in 1977 by California psychologist Michael Russell and his colleagues. Russell believes that when we sweat, the **apocrine glands** under our arms release sexual substances. To test this notion, Russell and his group asked a woman with a very regular menstrual cycle to wear cotton pads under her arms daily. The experimenters then rubbed portions of these pads on the

ence on your growth and behavior. As we will see in Chapter 11, the sex hormones are created primarily in the sex organs and serve to regulate sexual development and behavior.

Berkeley psychologist Frank Beach reports that before and during menstrual bleeding, a woman's body is almost totally deprived of sex hormones. As a consequence, during menstruation most women become less sensitive to inputs in *all* their sensory **modalities**. In fact, only in the middle of their menstrual cycle are women at the peak of their sensitivity to most types of sensory inputs. However, women who are "on the pill" maintain a continuously high hormone level. Hence their sensory **acuity** also remains high.

Beach and many other psychologists have noted as well that men are more sensitive to some odors just after receiving injections of the male sex hormone **testosterone**.

In the February 2, 1979 issue of *Science*, William Cain reports that women appear to be superior to men at such tasks as *identifying* and *remembering* smells. Cain asked 102 men and 103 women subjects to name and identify 80 different odors. Cain exposed the subjects to the smells a total of five times. As Fig. 6.8 shows, the women were superior to the men on each of the tests. Cain believes that this superi-

upper lips of female volunteers who agreed not to wash their faces for several hours afterwards. A "control" group of volunteers was treated with pads not containing human sweat. The women in the control group maintained their normal menstrual cycle. However, the menstrual cycles of the women who smelled the sweat pads daily became strikingly similar to that of the woman who had donated the sweat.

The Sweet Smell of Sex

It has long been known that both male and female animals secrete chemicals that attract the opposite sex. These chemicals are called **pheromones**. But what about humans? Do we secrete sex pheromones as do other mammals?

Naomi Morris and Richard Udry have studied the relationship between smells and sexual intercourse for more than a decade in various groups of married women. In 1968, Udry and Morris reported that many of the subjects in their first study were more likely to engage in intercourse—and to achieve orgasm—during the middle of their menstrual cycles than at any other time. The woman's hormone production (and hence her sensitivity to smells) is, of course, greatest in mid-cycle. But how could an increase in olfactory acuity account for an increase in sexual behavior?

Copulins

In 1974, Richard Michael and his colleagues at Emory University reported that female monkeys secrete pheromones called **copulins** which are sexually attractive to males. More recently, Michael has discovered that these same copulins are produced by human females. Michael believes that the peak production of copulins occurs in the middle of the menstrual cycle.

Although some scientists have criticized Michael's work, a study reported in 1978 by Morris and Udry does seem to support the belief that women release chemicals that can *sometimes* act as **aphrodisiacs**. Morris and Udry asked 62 married women to rub one of four different perfumes on their chests before going to bed at night. Only one of the four perfumes contained copulins, and the women were not told which perfume was which. The women used a different perfume each night, and kept records of their sexual activities and of their menstrual cycles.

Morris and Udry report that the sexual behavior of only 12 of the 62 couples apparently

Modalities (moh-DALL-it-tees). From the Latin word meaning "measures" or "manners." A modality is a way of doing or arranging something, or a type of sensory experience. Vision is one sensory modality; taste is another.

Acuity (ack-CUE-it-tee). The ability to detect very weak stimulus inputs, or to make fine sensory discriminations—that is, to judge very small differences between quite similar stimuli.

Testosterone (tess-TOSS-tur-own). One of the male sex hormones, secreted primarily by the testes (TESS-tees) or testicles (TESS-tickles) of the male. Masculine behavior patterns are strongly influenced by the presence of testosterone in the body.

Apocrine glands (AHP-oh-krin or APP-oh-krin). Glands in your armpits that, when stimulated by sex hormones, release a "smelly" type of sweat.

Pheromones (FAIR-oh-moans). Chemicals released by one organism that serve to induce one or more behavioral responses in other organisms of the same species.

Copulins (KOPP-you-lins). Chemicals released by female animals (including women) that act as sexual attractants for many males. Thus, chemicals that stimulate organisms to copulate, or engage in sexual activity.

Aphrodisiacs (AFF-roh-DEE-see-acks). Sexual stimulants. The Greek goddess of sexual love and beauty was Aphrodite (AFF-roh-DEE-tee). The Romans called her Venus. According to the famous Greek poet Homer, Aphrodite "overcomes all mortal men and immortal gods with desire." Thus, anything to eat, drink, or be merry with that raises the passions—among other things.

Exaltolide (ex-ALL-toe-lide). A chemical compound that smells much like androstenol.

Androstenol (an-DROSS-tee-noll). From the Greek word *andro*, meaning "male." A substance that may be a sex pheromone released in urine. Men secrete twice as much androstenol, on the average, as do women. Supposedly an aphrodisiac for women, but not for men (who apparently cannot detect its smell).

was affected by the copulin-containing perfume. It would seem, then, that while human females do secrete copulins, these sexual attractants do not affect all men in the same way.

Question: How might differences in *olfactory sensitivity* help explain the Morris and Udry data?

Androstenol and Exaltolide

Do men secrete sex pheromones too? The answer seems to be a qualified "yes." In 1952, a French scientist named J. LeMagnen reported that women seem to be particularly sensitive to the odor of a synthetic chemical named **exaltolide**. This musky fragrance—which is found in many well-known perfumes—is chemically similar to a chemical called **androstenol**. Androstenol and exaltolide have almost identical smells.

Androstenol is excreted in human urine, but men produce about twice as much of it as do women. Androstenol is also secreted in the sweat of adult men—but not in adult women or in children of either sex.

Sexually mature women can detect the smell of exaltolide (and androstenol) readily, particularly in the middle of their menstrual cycle when their hormone levels are highest. Men are relatively insensitive to the odor. Women who have had their ovaries removed—and hence are no longer producing female sex hormones—are as insensitive as are males. But even a woman without ovaries becomes highly sensitive to the smell shortly after receiving an injection of female sex hormone.

Although LeMagnen believes the smell of exaltolide is sexually attractive to women, the matter has not as yet been proved scientifically.

Effects of Smell on Perception

In the late 1970's, J.J. Cowley and his colleagues at Hatfield Polytechnic in England reported they had been able to use smells to influence the judgments women students made about political candidates. Cowley and his group presented a large class of psychology students with printed information about six people who were competing for a student government position. Three of the candidates were men, three were women. The psychology students were asked to judge each candidate in terms of her/his personality and fitness for office.

While the members of the class were making their judgments, they were asked to wear paper masks—supposedly to keep their classmates from noticing their facial expressions. In truth, some of the masks had been coated with small amounts of sexual attractants. One third of the masks contained exaltolide, and one third contained copulin-like chemicals. The final third contained no attractants at all, so the students who wore these masks made up the "control group" in this experiment.

Crowley reports the male psychology students were seemingly not affected at all by the "smelly" masks. The sex-related odors did alter the judgments of the women students, however. Those women exposed to exaltolide tended to favor the more assertive and aggressive of the six candidates for office. Those women exposed to copulins, however, preferred the shy and unaggressive candidates. The odor inputs thus apparently affected the manner in which the women students actually *felt about* the office-seekers.

However, in a 1982 article in *Behavioral and Neural Biology*, two Canadian scientists dispute Crowley's findings. Stephen Black and Colette Biron, psychologists at Bishop's University, used both male and female subjects in their study. Each subject was asked to sit for about 15 minutes in close proximity to another person who was actually a *confederate* of the experimenters. Male subjects were paired with a female confederate, and female subjects were paired with a male confederate. After sitting close to the confederate, each subject was asked to tell how attractive he or she thought the person was. One-third of the time, the confederate had been liberally doused with exaltolide. Another third of the time, the confederate smelled heavily of androstenol. The remaining times, the confederate had a "neutral smell." Black and Biron report that neither exaltolide nor androstenol seemed to affect the subjects' judgments of the physical attractiveness of the confederate. These experimenters conclude "it is premature to classify androstenol as a human pheromone."

Question: Crowley asked his subjects to pick which candidate they *liked*, while Black and Biron asked their subjects to judge how *attractive* the confederate was. How might this *procedural* difference explain the difference in the *results* of the two studies?

"Local" versus "Distance" Senses

Smell and taste are often called **chemical senses** because the stimulus that excites the receptors in your tongue and nose are *complex chemical molecules*.

But there is a very important difference between taste and smell—whatever your tongue tastes must ordinarily be brought to your mouth, while your nose can detect stimuli that are some distance away.

The skin senses, including taste, are *local* receptors—that is, they give your brain information about the exact point on your body that is being stimulated. Olfaction, hearing, and vision are *distance* receptors—that is, they typically tell your brain what is going on some distance away from the surface of your body.

However, to borrow a phrase from the world of high-fidelity music, taste and smell are essentially **monaural** or "mono" senses. It may take you some time to locate the body of a mouse that had the misfortune to die in some out-of-the-way corner of your home, or to find in July an egg that was hidden too well at Easter. Why? Because your nose doesn't give you good *directional cues* as to the location of the "smelly" stimulus in three-dimensional space. Your eyes and ears, on the other hand, are strictly "stereo." Standing quite still in the middle of a strange room with your eyes closed, you can point out rather precisely the location of some noisy object like a ticking clock. And if you cover your ears but open your eyes, you can see the exact position of a clock even if it's on a tower miles away.

Chemical senses. Taste and smell are called the chemical senses because the stimulus input that sets them off is a chemical molecule of some kind.

Monaural (mon-AWR-al). Sound produced by a single source, as through just one loudspeaker.

If you wish to find out why your eyes and ears are so much better than your tongue and nose at helping you judge the *location* and *distance* of of a stimulus object, "lend an ear" and "see" what you find out about yourself in the next chapter.

Summary

1 Your skin is your window to a great part of the outside world. **Receptor cells** in your skin provide sensory inputs to your **somatic cortex (parietal lobe)** telling your cortex what your body is doing, what your skin is touching, and whether the outside world is warm or cold.

2 The **corpuscles** in the hairless regions of your skin detect pressure. The **basket cells** in the hairy regions, and the **free nerve endings** found in all skin, detect both pressure and temperature.

3 The **deep receptors** in your muscles, joints, tendons, and bones tell your cortex the position and condition of various parts of your body.

4 Buried away in your inner ear are your motion-change detectors—the **saccule**, the **utricle**, and the **semi-circular canals**. The saccule and utricle sense changes in straight-line or **linear motion**. The semi-circular canals respond to changes in circular or **rotary motion**.

5 Receptor **adaptation** is a slowing down of the firing rate of your sensory receptors, which occurs when the receptors are stimulated at a constant rate. Central **habituation** is a process that occurs in your brain when you no longer pay attention to a **constant stimulus input**.

6 Taste and smell are called "chemical senses" because the receptors in the nose and tongue are stimulated primarily by complex chemical molecules.

7 The primary receptors for taste are the receptor cells in the **taste buds**, which are located in mushroom-shaped bumps called **papillae**.

8 The four basic taste qualities are **sweet**, **sour**, **bitter**, and **salty**.

9 Most of the "taste" of food is really the smell of the food rather than its taste.

10 The smell receptors are the **olfactory rods**, which lie on the **olfactory membrane** inside each of the two nostrils. Chemical molecules in the air are absorbed into the **mucus** covering the olfactory membrane and excite the **cilia** of the olfactory rods.

11 The primary smell qualities seem to be **camphor**, **musky**, **floral**, **peppermint**, **ethereal**, **pungent**, and **putrid**.

12 Smell is an **ancient sense** more associated with **emotion** and **motivation** than with cognition.

13 Women are more sensitive to all types of sensory inputs in the middle of their **menstrual cycles**—when their **hormone level** is high—than at any other point in the cycle.

14 Women who are housed together tend to experience similar menstrual cycles. This **menstrual synchrony** seems to be caused by chemicals that the women release in their sweat.

15 Women (and many female animals) release chemicals called **copulins** that can be sexually attractive to some males. Both men and women release a chemical called **androstenol** in their urine, but

men produce twice as much of it as do women.

16 **Exaltolide** is a synthetic chemical similar to androstenol. Some research suggests the odor of exaltolide can affect the

way women perceive or feel about other humans.

17 Smell and taste are both **mono** (one dimensional) senses in that they seldom help us locate objects in space very well.

(Continued from page 141.)

Major Jack Amundsen turned down the volume on the radio link between him and the robot. Mark III/21 was trapped somewhere in the very heart of the asteroid, clinging to the walls of a cave that had no top or bottom as far as the robot could sense. Amundsen could rescue Mark easily, quickly, if he could only find some way to let the robot know in which direction it should move to get out of the cave. But how to tell Mark which way was "up" on an asteroid that had no gravity?

But what is gravity, after all, but a force that keeps the human race glued to the earth? Were it not for gravity, the Major reminded himself, the centrifugal force created by the earth's rotation would have flung us all into outer space long ago. Could he perhaps substitute one force for the other?

"Listen, Mark," the Major said on the radio. "I'm going to try something. Our spaceship is bolted to this cruddy piece of rock. If I aim the positioning jets just right, I can probably set the whole asteroid spinning slowly like a top. If it does, your direction detectors will start operating again."

The robot was silent as Amundsen calculated what to do. The ship was parked almost dead center on the asteroid. If the positioning

jets could generate enough sideways power—that is, create enough thrust at right angles to the surface of the asteroid—the asteroid would start to rotate. Amundsen turned on the jets and watched the dials on his control console. Slowly, ever so slowly, the huge piece of cosmic debris started to rotate like a wheel.

"Major, I feel it moving. The loose rocks that were floating around in the cave are falling to the floor of the chamber. Your idea worked." Mark's voice was as unemotional as ever, but Amundsen could swear the robot was smiling electronically.

"Major, my sensors are now functioning. I now know which way is up. I shall return to the ship shortly."

Amundsen suddenly panicked. "Wait a minute, Mark! Which way are you moving?"

"Up, Major, ever upward," came the calm reply.

"Stop, Mark! You're going the wrong way! Your sensors are giving you the right information, but you're interpreting it incorrectly. What seems to be 'up' to you is actually the center of the centrifugal rotation, the center of the asteroid. To get up to the space ship, you've got to move in the opposite direction of what seems up to you right now. It may seem screwy to you, Mark, but you've got to walk *down* in

order to get *up*."

"But Major, my reflexes are all wrong. I see the logic of what you say, yet my motion detectors indicate that I would be going in an inappropriate direction if I move downward. Help me, Major. I cannot decide which way to go."

Major Amundsen grinned. Wait till he told the boys back in Houston about this! There were some things that a robot couldn't handle after all!

Amundsen pressed the button on his microphone and issued a command:

"Robot XSR 5 Mark III/21, this is your superior officer, Major Jack Amundsen, speaking. I hereby order you to continue moving in what seems a downward direction until you reach the surface of this asteroid and can then return to the space ship."

"Yes, Major. I hear and will obey."

Major Jack Amundsen breathed a sigh of relief, and then said gruffly, "Listen, Mark, be careful. The asteroid is whirling around fairly rapidly. So when you get to the surface, use your stick-tite shoes to keep from flying off into outer space."

Amundsen paused to think of what had happened to him and his robot companion, then laughed out loud. "And Mark, may the centrifugal force be with you!"

Recommended Readings

Black, S.L. & Biron, C. (1982). Androstenol as a human pheromone: No effect on perceived physical attractiveness. *Behavioral and Neural Biology*, 34(3), 326–330.

Boring, E.G. (1942). *Sensation and perception in the history of experimental psychology*. New York: Appleton-Century-Crofts.

Engen, T. (1982). *The perception of odors*. New York: Academic Press.

Hensel, H. (1982). *Thermal sensations and thermoreceptors in man*. Springfield, Ill.: Charles C. Thomas.

Hopson, J. (1979). *Scent signals: The silent language of sex*. New York: William Morrow.

Uttal. W.R. (1978). *The psychobiology of mind*. Hillsdale, N.J.: Erlbaum.

Did You Know That...

- You can locate sounds in the left-right dimension better than in the up-down dimension?
- Three little bones in your middle ear act like stereo amplifiers?
- The two most important attributes of a sound wave are its frequency and its amplitude?
- Your hearing is most sensitive to the range of frequencies produced by the human voice?
- Animals can often hear higher frequency sounds than can humans?
- Loss of hearing can produce behavioral symptoms similar to those of paranoia?
- Visual acuity is best in a tiny spot in your eye called the "fovea"?
- Each of your eyes has a blind spot almost in the middle of your visual field?
- The retina of the eye is sometimes considered to be an extension of the brain?
- You can have better than 20/20 vision?
- About 1 person in 20 is markedly color-deficient?

7

Hearing and Seeing

"The Eyes and Ears of the World"

"Okay, dear, which kid do you want?"

Judy Jones looked around the room. There were children of all ages, all sizes, all colors. Some were playing together, some were fighting, some were sitting quietly in corners minding their own business. Judy glanced quickly at Mrs. Dobson, the woman who had asked the question, and then gazed back at the dozens of children packed into the room.

"How about that little girl over there, in the pink dress?" Judy asked, pointing her finger at a dark-skinned but handsome girl who was playing with several other youngsters. "She looks adorable."

Mrs. Dobson turned to see which child Judy was pointing to. "Oh, Arabella. Sorry, dear, but somebody's already working with her. The pretty ones are always picked first, you know. Pick an ugly one instead, if you want my opinion. They're starved for love, and they need your help just as much as the cute ones do."

Judy was shocked at Mrs. Dobson's bluntness, but guessed the woman might be right. Judy inspected the room carefully, then spotted a little boy with red hair sitting by the window, looking at a magazine. He was by far the most unattractive child in the room. His eyes were watery, his hair uncombed, his skin covered with brown blotches and blemishes. His face was lopsided, and his head seemed too large for his body. Not only that, but he was white. Judy, a black student at a college near the Children's Home, had hoped to work with someone of her own race.

"What about him?" Judy said, pointing again.

"Oh, that's Woodrow Wilson Thomas. Ten years old.

Nice little fella, but ugly as home-made sin."

"Home-made sin?" Judy asked.

"Sorry, dear. It's a saying I got from my mother," Mrs. Dobson replied. "Appropriate enough in his case. Woodrow is a bastard, you see."

Judy was shocked. "You mean, he's nasty?"

"No, dear," came the calm response. "I mean bastard in a technical sense. A love child, a natural-born child, the offspring of an unwed mother. I read his record a couple of years back. His mother was 16 when she got pregnant, and she didn't quite remember who the father was. Maybe somebody in the family, for all we know. Anyhow, the mother got rubella—that's the German measles—while she was carrying poor little Woodrow, and he just didn't turn out right. They thought of putting him up for adoption when he was born. But he was so ugly, they figured nobody would take him. So they kept him for a while."

"For a while?" Judy asked, beginning to sympathize with the little boy more and more.

"Yes, 'for a while.' Woodrow not only got off to a bad start in life, he didn't grow up very well either. The record says he crawled and walked at a normal age, but his speech was very retarded. Made animal noises and grunts instead of talking words. Still does, poor little fella. Doesn't understand much when you talk to him, and he won't usually do what you tell him to do. When you try to get through to him, he just stares at you with those watery eyes, and then he looks out the window while you're trying to say something. No wonder his folks put him in the Home here, so the state could take care of him. Retarded, that's what Woodrow Wilson Thomas is."

Judy turned the matter over in her mind. "Do you think there's anything I can do for him? I mean, it's part of an assignment for my psych class. We're supposed to show that we can help a retarded or emotionally disturbed child. Can I help Woodrow?"

Mrs. Dobson sighed. "I don't see why not. There must be something you can do. We're so overcrowded here, and we've got such a small staff, I reckon nobody's worked with that child for 2 or 3 years. He's no trouble, you see. Doesn't have temper tantrums or act up. Never plays with the other kids, or gets into difficulties. He just sits by the window and looks at his books and magazines all day long."

"Well, if he can read magazines at his age, he can't be all that retarded."

Mrs. Dobson laughed. "Read? Don't be foolish, dear. He just looks at the pretty pictures, and smiles. One day, a year or so ago, I saw him puzzling over a picture like he was trying to figure out what it was. So I asked him what he saw. He just ignored me. Maybe you can get through to him, but I don't promise. But you should learn a lot, and he won't give you any trouble."

Judy accepted the challenge. She went over to the window and tried to talk to Woodrow, but he didn't seem to want to listen. Finally, in desperation, she tugged on his shirt and pulled him over to a nearby table. Woodrow seemed happy to come along with her.

"Now, Woodrow, we're going to draw some pictures. You like pictures, don't you?"

The boy's watery blue eyes drifted toward the window.

Judy pulled on his shirt again until he looked back at her, then she picked up a crayon. She drew a crude picture of a cow while Woodrow watched, seemingly interested. She gave him the crayon and motioned to him that she wanted him to draw. Woodrow took the crayon carefully in his right hand, then looked up at Judy, a puzzled stare on his face.

"Draw a cow, please, Woodrow," Judy said, making scribbling motions with her hand and pointing to the drawing she had just made.

Woodrow smiled serenely as he touched the crayon to the paper. Within three minutes, he handed back to her a crude but recognizable picture of a cow. Judy was so pleased that she wrote the letters C-O-W beneath the drawing. Woodrow took the scratch paper back and copied his own version of the letters underneath those Judy had written.

Judy was thrilled by his response. She got out some of the textbooks she had brought along and hunted through them until she found other pictures for Woodrow to draw. He made a horse, and an auto, and a house. When Judy wrote their names on the scratch paper, Woodrow copied the letters as carefully as he could.

When her time with Woodrow was up, and she had to catch the bus back to the college, Judy kissed Woodrow on the forehead.

"I don't care if you are retarded, young man. You're going to learn to read. I just know you are!"

Then she gathered up her textbooks and rushed off.

In her excitement at wanting to tell the other students how well things had gone, Judy failed to notice that she had left her algebra textbook behind. Woodrow picked it up and began to look through it. Although it didn't have any real pictures in it, he found the book utterly fascinating.

The next week, when Judy came back to the State Home for the Retarded to be with Woodrow again, he solemnly presented her with a sheet of scratch paper. On one side were childish drawings of a cow, a tree, a car, and a house, each correctly labeled several times over. On the other side, in very poor but legible script, were written out the first two review problems at the end of the introductory chapter of the algebra textbook.

"My God," said Judy when she saw them, "You've done the algebra correctly!"

(Continued on page 188.)

The "Cognitive" Senses

In the last chapter, we discussed "touch," taste, and smell. And we pointed out that these senses are important for several reasons—they help you locate your body in space, they protect you from harm, and they assist you in finding the "energy inputs" you need in order to survive. But neither man nor woman survives by bread alone, for you need "informational inputs" as much as you need food and water.

As we mentioned in Chapter 5, the sub-units of any system must be in *communication with one another*, or the system will soon collapse. And that's one of the things your senses help you do—communicate with others. But some sensory inputs are better suited for communications than are others. Perhaps we could use our skins and our chemical senses to "talk" with each other, as some animals do. But for many reasons, humans communicate primarily through the written and spoken word, through music, and through pictures and visual symbols. Vision and hearing, then, are the two main "communication senses," because these sensory modalities allow us to pass complex symbols and other types of information rather easily from one person to another. And since we tend to think in words and pictures too, vision and hearing dominate most of our *cognitive processes*.

Hearing and vision are much more than mere "channels of communication," of course. They are also rich sensory experiences in their own right. But as we look at these two modalities, we should keep in mind that our social systems would disintegrate if we could not see and hear each other. And our own personalities would be greatly impoverished if we could not think and reason as we presently do—in language and visual symbols. So if you want to learn about your own cognitive processes, and how you share information with others, you first must discover something about the *sensory channels* that carry human communications.

Hearing

From a physical point of view, what do your eyes and ears have that your skin, nose, and tongue lack? One answer is—*separation*.

Let's first compare hearing with olfaction. If you block one of your ears with cotton, your ability to localize the *position* of sounds diminishes considerably. But if just one of your nostrils is stopped up when you have a cold, you could locate a rotten egg just about as rapidly as if both your nasal chambers were operating unimpaired.

One important difference between hearing and smell, then, is this: Your ears are some 6 inches apart; your nasal chambers are separated by less than half an inch.

If you would like to demonstrate to yourself the importance of the "space between your ears," you might try a musical experiment. Find a **stereo** hi-fi set with two *movable* speakers. Put the speakers as far apart in the room as you can. Now put on your favorite stereo record and sit between the two speakers with your eyes closed. You will hear music coming at you from all directions. But some sounds will seem to be on your left, while others seem to be on your right.

Now, put the two speakers right next to each other and repeat the experiment. Chances are, the music will seem compressed, pushed together, cut down in size to a *point source*. In short, the stereo music will now sound monaural or "mono."

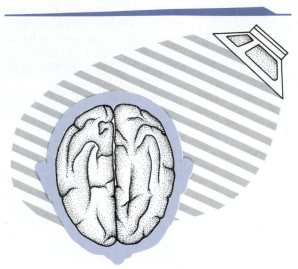

Sounds from objects to the right of you arrive at your left ear later (and weaker) than they do at your right ear. Your brain interprets these differences as meaning that the object is to your right.

Your ears are like the two speakers spread far apart. Your nose and tongue are like the two speakers put close together.

Localizing Sounds

In a sense, your ears are similar to the microphones used to record music. To get a stereo effect, the record company must use at least two mikes that are some distance apart. When a band performs, each mike "hears" a slightly different version of the music.

Suppose the lead guitarist in the band is on the left. The mike on the left would then "hear" the guitarist much more loudly than would the mike on the right. If the drummer is on the right, then the right microphone would pick up the sounds of the drum more loudly than would the mike on the left.

Record companies typically make a *completely separate* recording of what the left mike "hears" and what the right mike "hears." These two different records make up the two channels of stereophonic music that are pressed on stereo disks or dubbed on tapes.

By keeping the two channels separate during both recording and playback, you can maintain left-right relationships. That is, when you hear the record, the sounds made by the lead guitarist come primarily from the left speaker. The drummer's beat, however, will come to you mostly from the right speaker.

Your ears are just far enough apart so that you can readily detect left-right differences in sound sources. Sound waves travel at a speed of some 750 miles per hour at sea level. If a cricket six feet to the left of your head chirps loudly, the noise will reach your left ear a fraction of a second before it reaches your right ear. And since the insect is closer to your left ear than to your right, the noise will be louder when it reaches your left ear than when it finally gets around your head and reaches your right ear.

Your brain *interprets* the difference in the auditory inputs from your left and right ears to *mean* that the cricket is to your left. But, as we will soon see, your brain can be fooled in such matters if you know how to go about it.

The farther apart your ears are, the more precisely you can detect the location of a sound—because there is a greater difference in what your two ears would hear. When a recording company sets its microphones 10 feet apart, they are effectively increasing the *apparent* distance between your ears to 10 feet—particularly if you listen to the music with stereo headphones.

Now go back to your stereo set and put one speaker on the floor and the other as high up in the air as you can, directly above the first. Sit with your head upright between the two speakers. When you play music now, it will seem strangely "mono," for each of your ears is the *same distance from both speakers*. In fact, you may find that you tilt your head to one side without realizing it, as your brain attempts to turn monaural music into a stereo message that carries much more interest and information.

Your ears can detect the location of sounds spread out in the *left-right* dimension rather well. But your ears do very poorly in locating sounds in the *up-down* dimension.

Question: Why might it help to "cock your head to one side" when trying to locate the source of a sound over your head?

The Auditory Stimulus

Hearing is a *vibratory sense*. That is, the **auditory** receptors in your ears are sensitive to *vibrations* of the molecules in the air around you. These vibrations usually come in waves, which we call "sound waves." Thus, the stimulus for hearing (or "audition") is usually a vibratory wave of some kind. (Words such as "audition," "audio," and "auditorium" all come from the Latin word *audire*, meaning "to hear.")

Imagine yourself seated a couple of feet above a very quiet pool in a forest. You take a stone and toss it in the center of the pond, and what happens? Wave after wave of ripples circle out from the center until they strike the edges of the pool. If you looked closely, you would see that when one of the waves reached the shore, it "bounced back" in a kind of watery echo.

The sound waves that stimulate the *auditory receptors* in your ear are not very different from the ripples that you create by dropping the rock in the pond. Whenever any fairly rigid object is struck forcibly, it tends to *vibrate*. As this object vibrates back and forth, it "makes ripples" in the molecules of air around it. These "ripples" are really *sound waves*. That is, they are waves of molecules that pass through the air just as the ripples pass across the surface of the water when you throw a stone in the pond. When these *sound waves* reach your ear, they set part of your eardrum to moving back and forth in rhythm with the vibrating object. Other parts of your ear then translate the vibrations of the eardrum into *patterns of neural energy* that are sent to your brain so that you can "hear."

Parts of the Ear

Your ear has three main divisions: (1) the outer ear, (2) the middle ear, and (3) the inner ear (see Fig. 7.1).

"I HEARD WHAT YOU SAID. I'M PROCESSING IT."

1. The **outer ear** is that fleshy flap of skin and other tissue sticking out from either side of your head. Your outer ear tends to "catch" sound waves and direct them into a narrow tunnel called the **auditory canal**. At the inner end of this auditory canal is your *eardrum*, a thin membrane stretched tautly across the auditory canal like the skin on a drum. The eardrum separates your outer ear from your middle ear.

2. The **middle ear** is a hollow cavity in your skull that contains three little bones called the **hammer**, the **anvil**, and the **stirrup** (see Color Plate 8). If you inspected these three little bones under a microscope, they would look much like the real-world objects they are named after. One end of the hammer is connected to the eardrum. When your eardrum moves, it pulls the hammer back and forth rhythmically.

The hammer transmits this "wave" of sound energy to the anvil, making the anvil move back and forth. The anvil pulls the stirrup back and forth in similar fashion.

The stirrup is connected to another membrane stretched across an opening called the **oval window**. As the stirrup moves, it forces part of the membrane on your oval window to wiggle back and forth in rhythm, too.

The three little bones and the two membranes act as the *amplifiers* in your own biological stereo system. By the time the sound stimulus has reached your oval window, it is many times louder or stronger than it was when it first struck your eardrum.

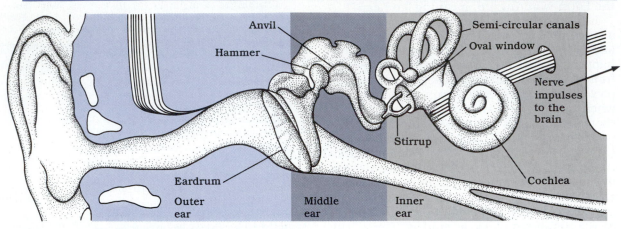

Fig. 7.1 Structure of the human ear.

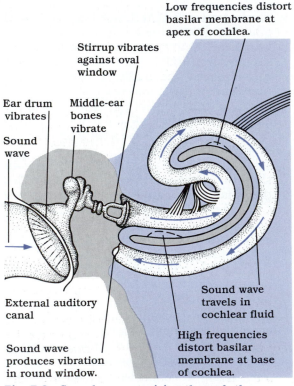

Fig. 7.2 Sound waves arriving through the auditory canal make the ear drum (tympanic membrane) vibrate. The three small bones in the inner ear amplify the sound and cause the oval window to vibrate. Sound waves travel through the cochlear fluid and cause the basilar membrane to distort or vibrate. The hair cells lying on the basilar membrane respond by sending an input message along the auditory nerve (not shown).

Your middle ear is like a bubble of air trapped inside your skull bone. When you go up in an airplane, the air pressure around you decreases, but the pressure inside your middle ear remains the same. This pressure difference would rupture your eardrum, were it not for the **eustachian tube**, which connects your middle ear to your throat. When you swallow, the tube opens momentarily, allowing air to escape from your middle ear. Each time your ears "pop" on a plane ride, your eustachian tube has opened briefly to reduce the pressure difference between air in your middle ear and the air outside.

3. The oval window separates the middle ear from the **inner ear**. Your inner ear is a fluid-filled cavity that runs through your skull bone like a tunnel coiling through a mountain. This inner ear of yours has two main parts: (1) The **cochlea**, and (2) the motion detectors we discussed in Chapter 6 (the saccule, the utricle, and the semi-circular canals).

The cochlea gets its name from the Latin word for "snail shell," which is just what your cochlea looks like. Your auditory receptors are the 24,000 hair cells that are part of the **organ of Corti** inside your cochlea. The organ of Corti lies on the **basilar membrane**, which runs the length of the cochlea (see Fig. 7.2). Input messages from the hair cells pass along the auditory nerve to the lower centers of the brain, which relay them up to the temporal lobe of your cortex. Generally speaking, you are not *consciously aware* of hearing anything until the auditory message reaches your cortex.

Frequency and Amplitude

Sound waves have two important *physical* aspects: **frequency** and **amplitude**.

The frequency of a musical tone is related to how *high or low* the tone sounds to your ear. Put more precisely, the psychological *pitch* of a tone is primarily determined by the physical *frequency* of the sound wave.

The amplitude of a musical tone is related to how *loud or soft* the tone sounds to you. Put more precisely, the subjective *loudness* of a tone is primarily determined by the objective *amplitude* of the sound.

"Pitch" and "loudness" are terms that describe *psychological* attributes of the subjective experience of hearing. "Frequency" and "amplitude" are terms that describe the *physical* characteristics of the auditory stimulus.

Pitch and Frequency

If you drop a stone in a deep pond, you set up just one big wave that moves out from the point at which the stone hits the water. But if you drop several pebbles in, one after the other, you set up a *series of waves.* If you dropped in 10 pebbles each second, you would set up 10 waves a second (under perfect conditions). The *frequency* of the waves would then be 10 per second.

When you pluck a string on a guitar, you are doing much the same thing as dropping a rock in a pond. For the string creates sound waves that have *exactly the same frequency* as the number of vibrations that the string makes per second. Your ear detects these sound waves, and your brain turns them into musical tones. The *faster* a particular string vibrates, the *more* "waves per second" it creates—and the *higher* the pitch of the tone will seem to be when you hear it.

If you plucked the "A" string on a guitar, it would vibrate 440 times per second. This number is called the *frequency* of the musical tone "A." In technical terms, we would say this tone has a frequency of 440 "cycles per second," or 440 **Hertz** (440 Hz). In general, the thinner and shorter a string is, the higher the frequency at which it vibrates—and the higher the pitch of the tone that it makes.

Amplitude and Loudness

The loudness of a tone is determined primarily by the tone's *amplitude*, not by its fre-

Eustachian tube (you-STAY-shun). A narrow canal connecting the middle ear to the throat. Opens briefly when you swallow to allow the air pressure in the middle ear to equalize with the pressure of outside air.

Inner ear. A fluid-filled "worm hole" in your skull that contains both the motion detectors (the saccule, utricle, and semi-circular canals) and your receptor neurons for hearing.

Cochlea (COCK-lee-ah). The snail-shaped portion of your inner ear that contains the basilar membrane.

Organ of Corti (KOR-tie). A highly complex structure lying on the basilar membrane that contains the sensory receptor cells for hearing.

Basilar membrane (BASS-ill-ar). A ribbon of tissue that supports the organ of Corti. One end of the basilar membrane connects to the oval window, the other to the round window.

Frequency. In auditory terms, the number of times a sound source vibrates each second. The frequency of a musical tone is measured in Hertz.

Amplitude (AM-plee-tood). From the Latin word meaning "muchness." We get our word "ample" from the same Latin source. Amplitude is the amount of sound present, or the strength of a musical tone. Literally, the "height" of a sound wave.

Hertz (hurts). The frequency of any wave, such as a sound wave. Used to be called "cycles per second," or cps. Named for the German scientist Heinrich Hertz who made the first definitive studies of energy waves.

quency. If you happen to pluck the "A" string of the guitar *very gently*, it vibrates 440 times per second. But if you plucked the string *as hard as you could*, it would still vibrate at about 440 Hz. If it didn't, you wouldn't hear the note as being an "A."

But surely something different happens, for the more energetically you pluck a string, the louder the note sounds. The answer is that the string moves *farther up and down* during each vibration—but it still vibrates at about 440 times per second (see Fig. 7.3A and Fig. 7.3B). In similar fashion, if you gently drop 10 pebbles per second into a pond, you create 10 very small waves. But if you throw 10 pebbles per second into a pond as hard as you can, you create 10 very tall waves. In either case, however, there are still just *10 waves per second.*

In technical terms, the "taller the wave," the greater its *amplitude*. And the greater the amplitude that a sound wave has, the louder it will sound to you.

The Range of Hearing

What kinds of musical tones can your ear hear?

Your range of hearing is, roughly speaking, from *20 Hz to about 20,000 Hz.* But you are not

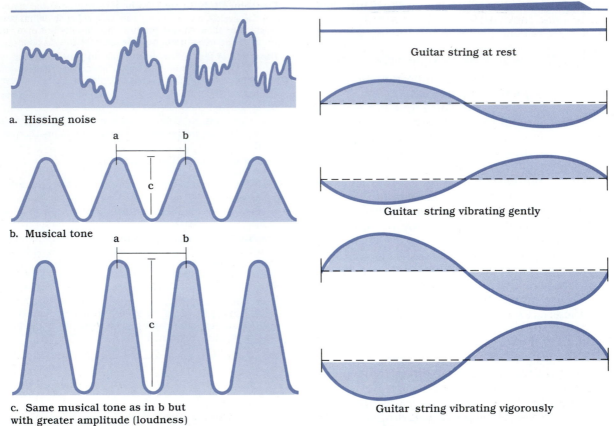

a. Hissing noise

b. Musical tone

c. Same musical tone as in b but
with greater amplitude (loudness)

Fig. 7.3A A sound wave "cycle" or "Hertz" is measured from peak to peak.

Guitar string at rest

Guitar string vibrating gently

Guitar string vibrating vigorously

Fig. 7.3B A vibrating guitar string.

Deaf children have trouble learning to speak because they cannot hear the sounds their vocal cords produce.

Older people with hearing losses sometimes show symptoms of paranoia if they cannot understand what is being said to them.

equally sensitive to all frequencies within this range. Your hearing is best from about 400 to 4,000 Hz. Human conversation ranges between 200 and 800 Hz. The lowest tone a bass singer can produce is about 100 Hz, while the highest tone most sopranos can produce is about 1,000 Hz. Thus, your ear is "tuned" to listen to other people speak (and sing).

There seems to be a general rule that holds *across animal species*: The smaller the cochlea, the higher the animal's range of hearing is likely to be. The dog can hear notes at least as high as 25,000 Hz, while the bat is sensitive to tones as high as 100,000 Hz. Elephants, on the other hand, probably have a hearing range that cuts off at about 7,000 Hz.

Question: If you wanted to design a whistle that could be used for calling dogs but couldn't be heard by human beings, what frequency range would you want to investigate?

Deafness

What difference would it make to your life if you became deaf?

Hearing is the major channel for *informal* social communication. Our customs, social graces, and moral beliefs are still passed down from one generation to another primarily by

Loud noises can cause nerve deafness by damaging the hair cells in the inner ear.

Spectrum (SPECK-trum). From the Latin word meaning "to look," from which we also get the words "specter" (ghost) and "spectacle." The word "spectrum" means a set or array of related objects or events, usually a set of sights or sounds.

word of mouth rather than in writing. And most of us (textbook writers included!) prefer the informal transmission of knowledge that comes from talking to the formalness of the written word.

Bone Deafness and Nerve Deafness

When people grow older, the three small bones in the middle ear often become brittle and thus do not work properly. Since the hammer, anvil, and stirrup serve to *amplify* the sound waves as they come into the ear, you could become deaf (or partially so) when these bones malfunction. This type of *bone deafness* can usually be corrected if you are fitted for a hearing aid, a device that acts like a miniature hi-fi set and "turns up the volume" electronically. The more severe types of bone deafness sometimes require surgery.

Many types of infection can attack the hair cells on the organ of Corti. If your receptor cells were permanently damaged for any reason, you would suffer from *nerve deafness*. If only a small section of your basilar membrane were affected, you would lose the ability to hear just high notes, or low notes, or even notes in the middle of the auditory **spectrum**. If the damage to your nerve cells were widespread, however, you might become totally deaf for *all frequencies*.

In the past, nerve deafness could seldom be corrected either by surgery or by a hearing aid. In the past few years, however, scientists at the University of Utah and at the University of Melbourne (Australia) have begun implanting tiny electrodes *directly into the ear*. These electrodes deliver short bursts of electricity to the auditory nerve. Normal speech is picked up by a small microphone and "translated" into pulses of electrical current by a pocket-sized computer. These devices by-pass the damaged receptor cells on the basilar membrane by stimulating the auditory nerve itself. Writing in the February 25, 1983 issue of *Science*, Y.C. Tong and his colleagues at Melbourne report that the deaf patients they have worked with can now hear "some sort of unnatural type of speech—like a robot's." Tong believes the implantation technique has great promise for helping many people who suffer from nerve deafness.

There are two major causes of nerve deafness—disease, and exposure to extremely loud sounds. The jet engines on modern airplanes create ear-splitting sounds, which is why people who work around jets wear protective earphones. The sound levels in many factories can also cause damage, if the workers are exposed to the noise for too long a time.

Question: The sound levels produced in rock concerts often equal those of jet engines. What conclusions can you draw from this fact concerning the risk factor that rock musicians face in terms of possible hearing loss?

Deafness and Paranoia

According to Philip Zimbardo, older individuals who slowly lose their hearing may be reluctant to admit their growing deafness. To do so, Zimbardo says, would be to admit that they are "growing old." Thus, many older people with hearing losses tend to blame their hearing problems on the behavior of others rather than on their own faulty ears. This "blaming behavior" often takes the form of a mild **paranoia**, in which the older person grows highly suspicious that other people are whispering about the person behind her or his back.

In the June 26, 1981 issue of *Science*, Zimbardo and two of his associates report the results of a study they performed on "experimental deafness" at Stanford. The psychologists began by hypnotizing some of their subjects and telling them that they would have severe difficulties hearing other people talk. This sort of temporary hearing loss under hypnosis is completely reversible (see Chapter 16).

Zimbardo and his colleagues then asked the temporarily hard-of-hearing subjects to work together in discussion groups with normal subjects. The tasks the discussion groups had to accomplish were, for the most part, the sort of "problem-solving exercises" that psychologists often ask subjects to engage in. The experimental subjects were given personality tests both before and after the problem-solving sessions.

Zimbardo and his colleagues report that most of the temporarily deaf students showed marked signs of mild paranoia. That is, the subjects became convinced other members of their discussion groups were "talking ill of them," or were trying to do the subjects harm. They also became more hostile, confused, agitated, irritable, and less creative. Zimbardo believes that the tendency to blame other people for one's own faults may explain many personality disorders, including some types of paranoia.

Question: If you don't "speak up" around a person with hearing problems, how might your own behaviors increase the deaf person's feelings of paranoia?

Language Learning, Deafness, and Feedback

Learning to sing, dance, play the guitar, or drive a car—all these complex motor tasks require *feedback*. A girl who is born deaf—or partially deaf—has trouble learning to *talk* because she cannot *hear* what noises her voice is making. Without the auditory feedback from her vocal cords, the girl can never learn to shape her spoken words properly, because she simply does not know *what her own voice sounds like*.

Until scientists discovered how necessary some kind of feedback is in learning to talk, we often thought that partially deaf children were dumb or stupid. Occasionally we mistakenly confined these children to homes for the mentally retarded—although many of them were very intelligent. Fortunately, now that hearing tests for young children are much more common than they used to be, we are less likely to confuse partial deafness with mental retardation.

Question: Suppose that a very bright but partially deaf child is mistakenly put in a home for the mentally retarded. Would anyone be likely to try to train the child to read? Under some circumstances, could the child perhaps learn to read on his or her own?

Vision

Psychologically speaking, hearing is a far more complex sense than is "touch," taste, or smell. But when it comes to "richness" of sensory experience, vision is perhaps more complicated than all the other sensory modalities put together. And because vision dominates so much of our lives, psychologists have studied it in greater detail than the other senses. As a result, we know more about how and why you *see* than we do about how you experience the rest of your sensory world.

Vision has often been called "the sense of wonder." To appreciate how your ability to see influences your thoughts and behaviors, how-ever, you need to understand at least three things:

1. What the visual stimulus (light) is like.
2. How your eye converts light into a sensory input to send to your brain.
3. How your brain interprets this incoming sensory information.

The Visual Stimulus

The stimulus for vision is *light*, which is a very small part of the **electro-magnetic spectrum**. The electro-magnetic spectrum also includes X-rays and radio waves.

The smallest, most elementary unit of light is called the **photon**, which gets its name from the Greek word meaning "light." The flame from one match produces millions of photons. A flashlight produces a great many more photons than does a match. Thus, in general, the *stronger* the light source, the *more* photons it produces in a given unit of time (such as a second).

When you turn on a flashlight, photons stream out from the bulb at an incredible speed or **velocity**. To give you a better "feel" for this speed, consider the fact that the velocity of sound waves is about 750 miles per *hour*. The speed of light, on the other hand, is about 186,000 miles per *second*.

If you could travel as fast as a photon, you could zoom all the way around the world *seven times* in just a second. And you could go to the moon and back in less than three seconds.

Wave-Lengths of Visual Inputs

The bulb of a flashlight produces photons in *waves*—much as the string on a guitar produces sound waves when the string vibrates, or the wind produces waves on the surface of the ocean. If you want to understand how scientists study light waves, learning something about ocean waves first might be of help.

If you wanted to, you could take a boat out on the sea and actually measure the distance *between* one ocean wave and another. And if you did so, you would find the distance between the crests of the waves was remarkably consistent. On a calm, peaceful day, as the waves moved slowly and majestically, the distance *between* waves would be rather large. But on windy, choppy days, this wave-length would be rather small. Thus, if you knew the strength of the

Paranoia (pair-ah-NOI-ya). A severe type of mental disorder characterized by delusions of grandeur and suspicions that people are whispering or trying to control your behavior.

Electro-magnetic spectrum. The entire range of frequencies or wave-lengths of electro-magnetic radiation ranging from gamma rays to the longest radio waves. Includes the visible spectrum.

Photon (FO-tohn). A tiny packet of energy which is the small-est unit of light. Under ideal circumstances, your eye is so incredibly sensitive that it can detect a single photon.

Velocity (vee-LOSS-sit-tee). The speed at which an object or wave moves. From the Latin word meaning "to be quick."

Visible spectrum (SPECK-trum). When you look at a rainbow in the sky, you see the array (spectrum) of visible colors that make up sunlight. For most purposes, "rainbow" and "visible spectrum" can be considered the same things.

Nanometers (NAN-oh-meters). A nanometer is one-billionth of a meter, or about 1/40,000,000,000th of an inch.

wind, even without going out on the water you would have some notion of what the *length* be-tween the crests of the ocean waves would be.

Much the same sort of consistency holds for the wave-length of light and what color it ap-pears to be. In the **visible spectrum** blue colors have very short wave-lengths. The reds, at the other end of the spectrum, have much longer wave-lengths. The colors between red and blue have wave-lengths that fall between these two extremes.

Thus, if you know what *wave-length* a visual input has, you will know what *color* it ordinarily will appear to be.

However, the distance between the crests of light waves is much, much smaller than the dis-tance between any two ocean waves. The wave-length for red is so short that it takes about 38,000 "red waves" to make an inch. The wave-length for blue is much shorter—it takes about 70,000 "blue waves" to make an inch.

Scientists seldom measure the wave-length of light in fractions of an inch, because the fig-ures are just too clumsy to use. Instead, scien-tists measure wave-lengths in **nanometers**. The Greek word for "dwarf" is *nanos*. From this fact, you can perhaps guess that the nanometer is a "dwarf" or fraction of a meter (39.37 inches). In fact, there are one billion nanome-ters in each meter.

Amplitude of Visual Inputs

The physical wave-length of a light stimulus usually determines the color that it will appear to you, such as blue or red. But some blue lights are bright, while others are dim. The physical

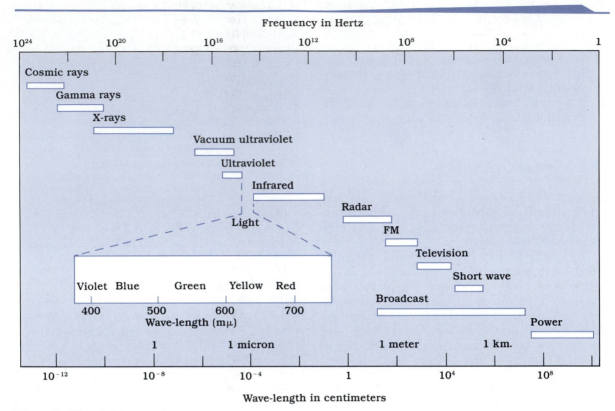

Frequency in Hertz

10^{24} 10^{20} 10^{16} 10^{12} 10^8 10^4 1

Cosmic rays

Gamma rays

X-rays

Vacuum ultraviolet

Ultraviolet

Infrared

Radar

Light

FM

Television

Short wave

Broadcast

Violet Blue   Green   Yellow Red

Power

400   500   600   700
Wave-length (mµ)

1   1 micron   1 meter   1 km.

10^{-12} 10^{-8} 10^{-4} 1 10^4 10^8

Wave-length in centimeters

Fig. 7.4 The visible spectrum.

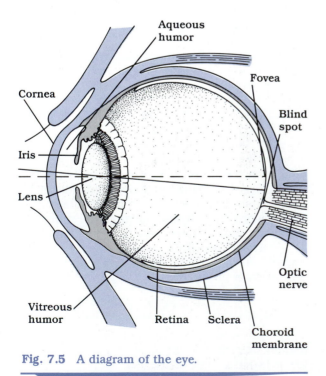

Aqueous humor

Fovea

Cornea

Blind spot

Iris

Lens

Optic nerve

Vitreous humor

Retina Sclera

Choroid membrane

Fig. 7.5 A diagram of the eye.

intensity of a light determines how bright it will seem, and *intensity* can be specified in terms of the height or *amplitude* of the wave.

If you measured the *length* between crests of ocean waves on a calm day, you might find that the wave-length was about 20 feet. The *height* of each wave, however, might be no more than 3 feet. During a storm, the wave-length might still be 20 feet, but the height of each ocean wave might now be 10 to 13 feet.

In similar fashion, a dim blue light might have a wave-length of 423 nanometers. If you "turned up the intensity" of this blue light until it was so bright it almost blinded you, it would still have a *wave-length* of 423 nanometers—but the *amplitude* (height) of each wave would be many times greater.

When you make a light brighter, you *amplify* the height of each light wave—just as when you turn up the volume on your stereo set you *amplify* the height of each sound wave the machine puts out.

The *psychological color* of a visual input, therefore, is determined primarily by its *physical wave-length*. And the *psychological bright-*

ness of a visual stimulus is determined primarily by the *physical amplitude* of the light wave.

The Visible Spectrum

In a manner of speaking, light waves are much like X-rays and radio waves—except that X-rays have such short wave-lengths that they are invisible to your eye, and radio waves have such a long wave-length that you can't see them. As Fig. 7.4 suggests, the only waves you can *see* lie between 400 and 760 nanometers. We call this range of waves the *visible spectrum*.

Why does a psychologist interested in human behavior bother with such technical measures as wave-length and amplitude? For two reasons, really.

First, visual inputs *stimulate* people to act and respond. And the more precisely we can specify the *stimulus* that evokes a certain reaction, the better we can understand the *behavior* itself.

Second, we are often interested in individual differences. If we show *exactly the same* visual stimulus to two people, and they report *different* psychological experiences, we know these reports are due to differences in the people and not to some variability in the physical stimulus itself. We will have more to say about this point when we discuss color vision disorders (or "color blindness") later in this chapter.

The Eye

What biological processes occur when you see? These processes are so complex we still don't understand them completely.

If we stretch the facts a bit, we can say that your eye is like a color TV camera. Both are essentially "containers" that have a small hole at one end that admits light. The light then passes through a lens that focuses an image on a **photo-sensitive surface**. In both your eye and in the color TV camera, the "hole" can be opened to let in more light, or closed to keep light out. And in both, the lens can be adjusted to bring near or far objects into focus.

In the case of the color television camera, the light coming through the lens falls on an electronic tube that contains several complex chemicals. These chemicals are photo-sensitive—that is, they react chemically when struck by photons. The camera then produces several different images which, when properly combined on a TV set, reproduce the scene in vivid color.

Photo-sensitive surface. Light waves can set off rather dramatic reactions in some chemicals. These light-sensitive chemicals are said to be "photo-sensitive." The film in a camera reacts to light—hence, film is photo-sensitive. The inner surface of your eye contains pigments (colored chemicals) that are also photo-sensitive.

Cornea (CORN-ee-ah). From the Latin word meaning "horn-like." We get our words "horn" and "corn" (the kind of blister you get on your foot) from this same Latin source. The cornea is the tough, transparent tissue in front of the aqueous humor.

Aqueous humor (A-kwi-us). The watery substance between the iris and the cornea that keeps the front of your eyeball "inflated" to its proper size and provides nutrients to the cornea.

Pupil (PEW-pill). The opening in the iris through which light passes into the eye.

Iris (EYE-riss). The colored or pigmented area of the eye. When you say that someone has brown eyes, you really mean the person has brown irises. The Greek word for "rainbow" is *iris*.

Vitreous humor (VITT-tree-us). From the Latin word meaning "glass." The vitreous humor is a clear, glass-like substance in the center of the eyeball that keeps your eye in its proper rounded shape. Light must pass through the vitreous humor before it strikes your retina.

In the case of your eye, light first passes through the **cornea** and the **aqueous humor** (see Fig. 7.5). The cornea helps focus light rays as they enter your eye. The aqueous humor is a watery substance that helps nourish your cornea and keeps your eyeball filled out in its proper shape.

Once past the aqueous humor, light enters your inner eye through an opening called the **pupil**. The **iris** is the colored part of your eye which, by expanding and contracting around the pupil, controls the amount of light admitted inside your eye.

Just beyond the pupil is the lens. The purpose of the lens in your eye—like the lens in a camera—is to allow you to *focus clearly* whether you are looking at something close or far away. As you change your point of focus from a near object to something several feet away, muscles inside your eye pull on the lens to change its shape and thus refocus the light.

The lens *focuses* the image of what you are looking at. The lens also *projects* this image through the **vitreous humor** onto the inner surface of your eyeball—just as the lens in a camera focuses an image and projects it on the film in the back of the camera.

The vitreous humor is a transparent, Jello-like substance that, like the aqueous humor, acts to keep your eyeball "inflated" in its proper, rounded shape.

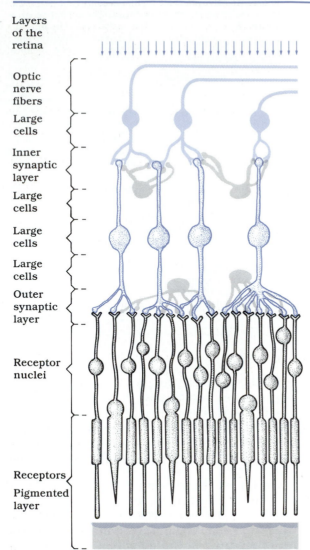

Layers of the retina

Optic nerve fibers

Large cells

Inner synaptic layer

Large cells

Large cells

Large cells

Outer synaptic layer

Receptor nuclei

Receptors

Pigmented layer

Fig. 7.6 The layers of the retina, including the rods and cones. The rods are the slim, pencil-shaped receptors at the bottom of the drawing. The cones are the fatter cells at the bottom. Three cones are shown.

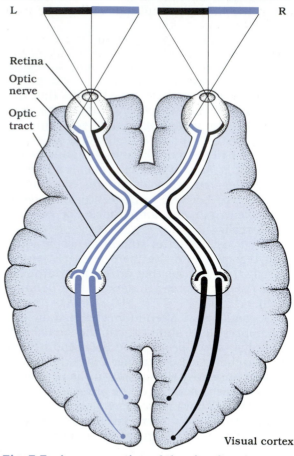

L R

Retina

Optic nerve

Optic tract

Visual cortex

Fig. 7.7 A cross section of the visual system. Any object (such as the black part of the line) in the left half of your visual field will be focused on the right half of the retinas in both your left and right eye. Inputs from the right half of both retinas are sent to the visual cortex in your right hemisphere. Inputs from the left half of both retinas go to the left visual cortex. In this drawing, your left brain perceives the colored half of the line, while your right brain perceives the black half of the line.

The inner surface of your eyeball is called the **retina**, from the Latin word meaning "net" or "network." Your retina is a network of millions of cells that—like the picture tube in the TV camera—contains several photo-sensitive chemicals.

The Retina

In a sense, your eyeball is a hollow sphere whose shell has three layers.

The outer layer—which contains the cornea—is called the **sclera**. The sclera is really the "skin" of your eyeball. Like most other skin tissue, the sclera contains *free nerve endings* that are sensitive to pressure, temperature—and pain.

The middle layer of the "shell" of your eye is a dark lining that is called the **choroid membrane**, or coat. The choroid coat contains blood vessels and dark pigment cells. The blood vessels supply the visual receptors with food and oxygen. The dark pigment cells absorb stray rays of light that might otherwise interfere with your vision.

The third layer is the *retina*, which is really the inner surface of your hollow eyeball.

The Fovea

Your retina contains the *receptor cells* that translate the physical energy of a light wave into the patterns of neural energy that your brain interprets as "seeing." There are two special parts of your retina that you should know about. The first is called the **fovea**. The second is your **blind spot**.

Fovea is the Latin word for "small pit." The fovea in your eye is a tiny pit in the center of your retina where your vision is at its sharpest. Although the fovea is only about the size of a head of a pin, the fovea is crucial for such specialized tasks as reading or inspecting the fine detail of any object.

The *blind spot* is a small area of your retina near the fovea, which is, for all practical purposes, totally "sightless." We will discuss the blind spot in greater detail later in this chapter. The reason that this part of your eye is sightless, however, is that it has *no receptor neurons* in it.

While your eye is like a TV camera in some ways, there are many differences between the two. The camera is large, bulky, clumsy to operate, and requires an external power source of some kind. Your eye is small and, in a sense, self-powered. The photo-sensitive plate or picture tube in a camera is flat, while the retina in your eye is *curved* to cover almost the entire inner surface of the eyeball.

But perhaps the major difference between your eye and a TV camera is the way that each mechanism *translates* light waves into patterns of electrical energy. The picture tube in a black-and-white TV camera contains just one kind of photo-sensitive chemical, while the tube in a color camera has several such chemicals. Your eye is something like a combination of the two, for it has *both* black-and-white detectors and a separate set of color detectors.

The Rods and Cones

The receptor neurons for vision are the *rods* and *cones*. Their names are fairly descriptive of their shapes. In the human eye, the rods are slim, pencil-shaped nerve cells. The cones are thicker and have a cone-shaped tip at their "business" end. (See Fig. 7.6 and color Plate 7 in color insert).

Both the rods and cones contain chemicals

Retina (RETT-tin-ah). The photo-sensitive inner surface of your eye. Contains the visual receptor organs.

Sclera (SKLAIR-ah). The tough outer layer of the eyeball.

Choroid membrane (KOR-oid). The dark, middle layer of the eyeball that contains blood vessels and pigment cells.

Fovea (FOE-vee-ah). The tiny "pit" or depression right at the center of your retina that contains only cones, and where your vision is at its clearest and sharpest.

Blind spot. That small part of the retina near the fovea where blood vessels and nerve pathways enter and exit from inside the eyeball. The blind spot contains no visual receptors.

Rhodopsin (ro-DOP-sin). From the Greek word meaning "reddish-purple." We get our words "rose" and "rhododendron" from this same Greek source. Rhodopsin is a purple-colored, photo-sensitive pigment found in the rods.

Periphery (pair-IF-er-ee). From the Greek word meaning "to move around the outside." The periphery is the outer edge of any closed surface, such as a circle.

that are very sensitive to light. When a beam of light strikes a *rod*, it causes the *bleaching* or breakdown of a chemical called **rhodopsin**, or visual purple (the Greek word *rhod* means "rose-colored"). In ways that we still don't entirely understand, this bleaching action causes the rod to respond electrically. This visual input message passes up through the lower centers of your brain and eventually reaches the occipital lobe (see Fig. 7.7). At this point, you become "consciously aware" that you have actually seen something.

The Rods

Your rods are *color-blind*. They "see" the world in blacks and whites, no matter how colorful the world actually is. Your rods respond much like a "fast but grainy" black-and-white camera film. That is, the rods need less light to operate than the cones do, but they give a less detailed picture of the world than the colorful view provided by your cones.

For the most part, the rods are concentrated in the outer reaches or **periphery** of the retina. There are almost no rods in the central regions of the retina, and none at all in the fovea. All told, there are about 120 million rods in each of your eyes.

The Cones

Your cones contain photo-sensitive chemicals that break down when struck by light waves. This chemical reaction triggers off an electrical response in your cones, which passes along the optic nerve until it reaches the visual input area in your occipital lobes.

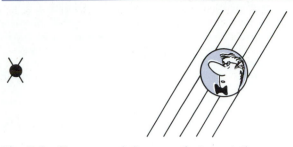

Fig. 7.8 Close your left eye and stare at the crossed dot with the book held about 6 inches away. The face should disappear.

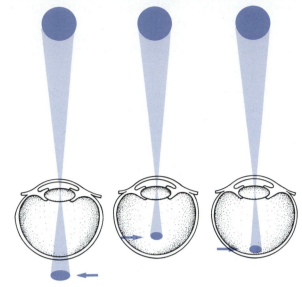

Fig. 7.9 A far-sighted, a near-sighted, and a normal eye. Notice where the image focuses in each case.

Current research suggests there are three different types of cones. One type of cone is sensitive primarily to *red* light, a second is sensitive to *blue* light, and a third is sensitive to *green*. Each type of cone has its own unique photo-sensitive chemical.

The cones are your *color receptors*. There are a few cones in the periphery of the retina, but most of the cones are bunched together in the center of your retina near the fovea. The fovea contains *only cones*. There are between six and seven million cones in each of your eyes.

Since your cones are located *primarily* in the center of your retina, this is the part of your eye that is *most sensitive to color*.

When you look at something straight on, the light waves coming from that object strike your fovea and stimulate the cones, giving you clear color vision. When the same object is at the outer edges (periphery) of your vision, the light waves from the object strike primarily the rods in the periphery of the retina. Since the rods are color-blind, you will see anything that appears at the edges of your visual world as lacking in color. However, you can see some color (very weakly) even in the periphery of your vision, because there are a few cones scattered about in the periphery.

Structure of the Retina

If you were called upon to design the eyes for a NASA robot, the odds are that you would never think of making the robot's retina like yours.

To begin with, your retina has *ten distinct layers*, with the rods and cones making up the *back layer*. The tips of your rods and cones—which contain the photosensitive chemicals that react to light—are actually pointed *away* from the outside world. For light to strike your rods and cones, it must first pass through *all nine other layers of your retina* (see Fig. 7.6).

The receptor cells in your *skin* are a part of your **peripheral nervous system**. That is, they are nerve cells that lie outside your brain and spinal cord. The retina evolved directly from the brain, however, and is considered by most authorities to be a part of the central nervous system.

The top layers of your retina contain a great many "large neurons" that are very similar in structure to those found in your cortex. These "large neurons" begin processing visual information right in the retina, before sending messages along to your visual cortex (in the occipital lobes at the back of your brain). Your retina is the *only receptor organ* in your body that processes inputs so extensively before sending them along to the cortex.

The top layers of your retina also contain a few of the tiny blood vessels that serve the retina. Surprisingly enough, light must pass through these "large neurons" and the blood vessels before it can stimulate the rods and cones. Fortunately, these neurons and blood vessels are pushed aside at the point of the fovea. This fact helps explain why the fovea looks like a "pit," and why vision is clearest at this point.

The Blind Spot

It is probably hard for you to imagine that each of your eyes has a spot that is, for all practical purposes, *totally blind*. Thus, there actually is a "hole" in your visual field where you see nothing at all.

Why this hole in your visual field? Well, your eyeball is hollow like a balloon, and your retina is *inside* the eyeball. The axons from the "large neurons" must somehow get through the walls of the eyeball if they are to reach their destinations in your brain. These axons meet at a point near the fovea to form the *optic nerve*, which exits from your eye at the *blind spot*. There are no receptors at this point in your retina—only axonic fibers and blood vessels. So, the part of your visual world that falls on the blind spot is not recorded in your brain.

You are usually unaware of this "hole in your vision," because what one eye misses, the other

usually picks up (see Fig. 7.7). However, it is also true that your brain "cheats" just a bit. That is, your brain fills in the hole by making the empty spot in your visual world look like whatever surrounds it. You can prove this to yourself by following the instructions given in Fig. 7.8. If you look at the picture from just the right position, the man's face disappears. But notice too that the spot where the man's face should be is filled in by your brain with the lines that surround the man's picture.

Optical Defects

Many distortions of your visual world are caused by misinterpretations made by your brain. But quite a few distortions stem from physical problems with the eye itself.

For example, the chances are one in four you either wear glasses or should wear them to help you overcome correctable visual difficulties. Many of these problems come from slight abnormalities in the *shape* of your eyeball.

Near-sightedness and Far-sightedness

If your eyeball is *too long*, the lens tends to focus the visual image a little *in front* of your retina rather than clearly on it. You then see *near* objects rather clearly, but distant objects appear fuzzy and blurred to you. We call this condition *near-sightedness* (see Fig. 7.9).

If your eyeball is *too short*, the lens tends to focus the visual image *behind* the retina rather than directly on it. Close objects are therefore indistinct to you, but *far* or distant objects are usually in clear focus. We call this condition *far-sightedness*.

If you watch carefully in the next movie you attend, you may notice something like the following: A woman standing close to the camera is talking with a man some distance away. When the woman is speaking, the camera focuses on her face, which you see clearly—but the image of the distant man is blurred and

"K, C, Ǝ..."

A view of a scene as a nearsighted person sees it.

The same scene as viewed by a farsighted person.

fuzzy. *This is approximately the way the nearsighted person sees the world* (see *left* photo this page).

Now, as the dialogue in the movie continues and the man begins to speak, the camera changes focus (but not position). Suddenly the woman's face, which is close to the camera, becomes blurred—but the distant image of the man sharpens and becomes distinct. *This is approximately the way the far-sighted person sees things in the world* (see *right* photo this page).

The lens in your eye operates much the same as does a camera lens, changing the focus from far to near as the occasion demands. As you grow older, however, your lenses become brittle, and you cannot focus back and forth between near and far objects as well as when you were young. This condition is called **old-sightedness**, or *presbyopia*. The typical solution to this problem is *bifocal glasses*. The upper part of the lens gives a clear picture of distant objects, while the lower half of the lens allows the person to see near objects clearly.

If your cornea is irregularly-shaped, you could suffer from a common visual defect called **astigmatism**. Fortunately, you can usually overcome this problem by wearing the proper prescription glasses.

Visual Acuity

When you go to an eye doctor to be tested for glasses, or when you apply for a driver's license, you will be given one of several tests to determine how accurately your eyes *discriminate* small objects. Your ability to discriminate such things as the small print in a phone book is called your *visual acuity*.

One very common visual test is the **Snellen chart**, which presents letters of different sizes for you to read (see Fig. 7.10). A person with normal vision can barely read the largest letter on this chart at a distance of 200 feet (60 meters), and can just make out the next largest letters standing 100 feet away.

If you took this test yourself, you probably would be asked to stand 20 feet away from the Snellen chart. If you could read the "normal" line of letters at this distance, we would say that you can "see at 20 feet what the normal person can see at 20 feet." Hence, you would have 20/20 vision.

If you stood 20 feet away from the chart and could read only what the normal person can easily see at 100 feet, your vision would be 20/100, which is fairly poor. But if you could make out the very small letters on the bottom line when you were standing 20 feet away, you would be able to read letters that normal people can discriminate only when they are *10* feet away from the chart. In this case, you would have 20/10 or superior visual acuity.

Visual Sensitivity

In order to discriminate objects in your visual world, you typically depend on your cone vision. Under normal circumstances—in daylight, for

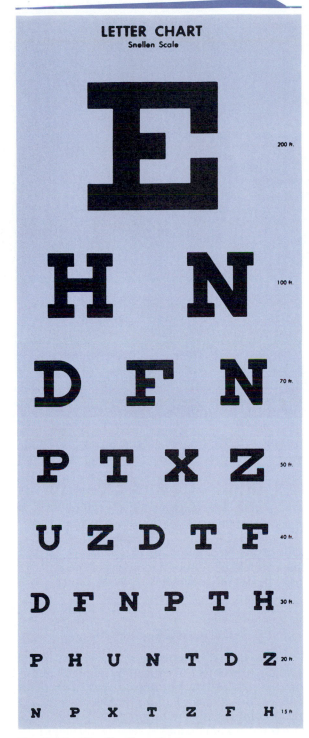

LETTER CHART
Snellen Scale

E — 200 ft.

H N — 100 ft.

D F N — 70 ft.

P T X Z — 50 ft.

U Z D T F — 40 ft.

D F N P T H — 30 ft.

P H U N T D Z — 20 ft.

N P X T Z F H — 15 ft.

Fig. 7.10   The Snellen chart.

instance—your *visual acuity* depends primarily on your cones.

The involuntary *reflexes* of your eye are so arranged that the visual image of anything you want to inspect closely will fall on your fovea, where there are millions of tiny cones packed together in a tiny area. During daylight hours, when there is plenty of illumination, your color vision dominates and you can easily make out the details of objects using foveal vision.

But at night or in any dim illumination—when you are often more interested in *detecting* faint sources of light than in *discriminating* fine details—your rods come into play. Your rods are much more sensitive to light than are your cones. Which is to say that the rods are better light detectors than the cones are. Your cones, however, are better than your rods at "seeing things in fine detail."

Visual Adaptation

When light strikes one of your rods or cones, the light causes the photo-sensitive chemicals in your receptors to *bleach*. Bleaching is a chemical reaction in which molecules *break apart* because they have been struck by a beam of light. It is this "breaking up" of the photo-sensitive molecules that causes your rods and cones to become electrically excited and to send input messages to your brain.

Your eye replaces the "broken down" photo-sensitive molecules fairly rapidly. If it didn't, you'd "see" only until all the light-sensitive chemicals in your eye were exhausted.

As you might guess, your eye can replace these "visual chemicals" more rapidly in the dark than in bright illumination. Thus, after you have "adapted" to the darkness for a while, your ability to detect faint light sources is much better than when you've been sitting in bright sunlight.

Dark adaptation is caused by at least two things. First, you must have a surplus of rho-

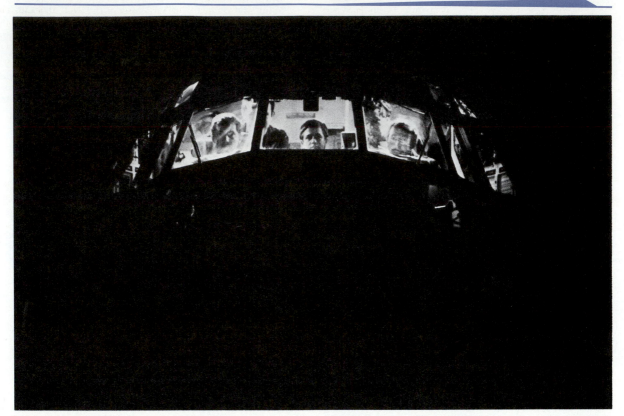

Pilots should dark adapt for around 30 minutes before flying at night.

dopsin (visual purple) in your rods and a surplus of the red, green, and blue photo-sensitive chemicals in your cones. And second, according to Michigan psychologist William Uttal, darkness causes certain neural changes in the rods and cones themselves that help you to see better under conditions of dim illumination. These neural changes in the rods and cones appear to be similar to those that occur in your skin receptors when you sit in a tub of warm water for a period of time. There are changes that take place in your brain, too, during dark adaptation. But these are more a matter of central *habituation* than of receptor *adaptation*. (See Chapter 6.)

Your *cones* adapt more quickly in darkness than do your *rods*. Your cones become almost as sensitive as they are ever going to get in a matter of 10 minutes or so. Your rods continue to adapt for 30 minutes or more. Because they build up a larger "surplus" of photo-sensitive chemicals, your rods are a thousand times bet-ter at *detecting* weak visual inputs when fully dark-adapted than are your cones.

Question: How long do you think an airplane pilot should be required to adapt to the dark before she or he is allowed to fly at night?

Night-blindness

Some people do not see at all well at night. Usually this defect is caused by some disability of the rods. Night-blindness may have many causes, but a lack of Vitamin A is perhaps the most common one. Vitamin A is necessary for the build-up of rhodopsin (visual purple) in the rods.

In daylight, your eyes automatically focus the image of an object on your fovea—where your visual acuity is best in good illumination. But your fovea contains only cones, hence it is "blind" at night. So when you stare directly at an object in dim light, the object may "disappear" because you're trying to see it with your cones. And the harder you try to focus the image of the object on your fovea, the less you will be able to see it!

If you want to see something at night, don't try to look directly at it. Instead, remember that your rods are most numerous in the *periphery* of your retina. So you should try to stare at the object "out of the corner of your eye," so that the object's visual image will fall on the periphery of your retina. That way, you can look at the object with your rods, not your cones. And that way, you can actually see better in dim illumination.

Question: Why do most objects look less colorful at twilight than at bright noon? (Hint: Remember the distribution of cones in the retina.)

Color Vision

One of the main problems in studying your senses is this: Scientists tend to use two quite different languages in describing sensory processes. Theoretically speaking, we should use the language of physics to describe the *physical properties* of sensory inputs, but we should employ psychological terms to describe the *behavioral effects* these inputs have on living systems such as yourself. The difficulty comes from the fact that we sometimes confuse the two languages, and thus end up confusing ourselves as well.

For example, perhaps you've heard the old riddle, "If a tree fell in a forest and no living thing were around to hear it fall, would the tree make any sound?" To a physicist, the answer is clearly *yes*. For in physics, "sound" is a physical event described in terms of the frequency and amplitude of the sound source. But to a psychologist, the answer is clearly *no*. For in the behavioral sciences, "sound" is a stimulus that has reality only when it is *experienced* by a living system of some kind. To a psychologist, then, "sound" is a behavioral process measured in terms of subjective pitch and loudness.

We run into the same two types of descriptive languages in the field of color vision. To a physicist, "red" is a light-wave that has a certain wave-length—about 700 nanometers. But to a psychologist, "red" is an internal process that may or may not be associated with a physical event. For instance, close your eyes momentar-

Hue (rhymes with "few"). The colors of the rainbow, or of the visible spectrum. Technically speaking, "color" includes not only the hues of the rainbow, but all the mixtures of hues plus blacks, whites, and grays. Black and white are not considered hues, although technically they are "colors." Pink (red + white) is a color; its hue, however, is red.

ily and picture a luscious, ripe tomato "in your mind's eye." Did it look red to you? Probably so. But the "input" that caused you to "see" the tomato surely wasn't a light-wave with a wave-length of 700 nanometers!

More to the point, perhaps, suppose you happened to glance at a ripe tomato out of the corner of your eye in very dim twilight. What "color" would it be? Unless you have a very vivid imagination, it probably would look gray to you, not red—despite the fact that the light rays coming from the tomato would still have a wave-length of about 700 nanometers. Why? Because in dim illumination, you tend to focus objects on the periphery of your retina. Thus, you would "see" the object with your rods, not with your cones. (To a physicist, of course, the tomato would still be "red," no matter what color you saw the tomato as being.)

As you learn more about your own ability to "see color," you might keep this fact in mind— to a physicist, *color resides in objects* (or, more precisely, in the light-waves the objects generate or reflect). But to a behavioral scientist, *color is an internal psychological process*. For the most part, there is a very close connection between the physical attributes of a stimulus and the psychological experiences the stimulus creates inside your head. That's why it is very important that you learn something about the physical aspects of various stimuli. As we will see, however, there are times when your eyes (and brain) respond to inputs in ways that cannot be explained in purely "physical" terms.

Question: Why would it be almost impossible to describe the color "red" to someone who was totally color-blind, despite the fact that you could specify precisely what the physical stimulus was?

Hue

In *physical* terms, when you speak of the color of something, you really are talking about that object's **hue**, or the wave-length of light the object produces or reflects. Each wave-length of light in the rainbow (visible spectrum) produces a unique *hue*. The psychological experience of *color* is closely associated with the physical *hue* or wave-length of the stimulus object.

Most of the familiar colors appear on what psychologists call the *color circle*, which is made by joining the ends of the rainbow (see Color Plate 10). Arranged around the outer edge of this circle are all of the spectral colors that you can see, and each point on the circle has a unique hue and wavelength.

Saturation

Hue alone is not enough to explain all the colorful visual experiences you have. For example, what is pink? It isn't a mixture of any two colors, but rather is a pale or *diluted* red. The vividness or richness of a color is what we call **saturation**.

Saturated colors are rich-looking and strong. Desaturated colors are weak and diluted. For example, suppose you poured red coloring into a bowl filled with tap water. The water would become deep red—a highly saturated color. Now suppose you pour in a lot more tap water. What happens? The ruby red soon becomes a pale, *desaturated* pink.

The hues around the outer edge of the color circle were carefully picked to be the most saturated possible (see Color Plate 10). As you move inward toward the center of the circle, the colors become less and less saturated until you reach gray, which has *no hue at all*. The color solid shown in Color Plate 9 is an "expansion" of the color circle into three-dimensional space. Notice, though, that the color solid is not a perfect globe. The light blue colors simply do not seem as *saturated* to most observers as do the dark blue colors. And the dark yellow colors do not seem as saturated as do the light yellows. There is no general agreement among scientists as to why light blue and dark yellows aren't as fully saturated as are dark blues and light yellows.

Question: What does the shape of the color sphere tell you about the psychological relationship between yellow and blue?

Complementary Colors

Any two colors that are *opposite* one another on the color circle are *complementary*. If you **(additively)** mix two complementary colored lights in more or less equal amounts, you get a completely desaturated gray. Thus, if you *add* green to a red, the red becomes less and less saturated until it becomes gray. However, the red light *never turns green* until it has passed through gray.

If you (additively) mix two colors that are *close to each other* on the circle, you get a "mixture color," not a gray. Thus, if you add yellow to red, the red turns first orange and then finally becomes a slightly reddish yellow—without first passing through gray.

Lightness

Look again at the color solid shown in Color Plate 9. As we mentioned, this globe is really a three-dimensional "color circle." The hue changes as you go around the figure, while saturation decreases as you move from the outer edge toward the the center of the globe. But there is a third dimension to this figure aside from hue and saturation. This third dimension is called *lightness*. The "north pole" of the solid is pure white. The "south pole" is pure black. Gray lies in the very center of the solid. The "lightness" of a visual stimulus, then, ranges from white to gray to black.

By definition, black and white are completely desaturated colors. And like gray, black and white are "colors," but not "hues."

By making careful use of color, saturation, and lightness—or their physical attributes—we can describe almost any color experience you have in very precise terms.

Question: What is the difference between "lightness" and "brightness"? (Hint: Does the saturation of a colored light change when you make it brighter? What about when you make it lighter?)

Color Deficiencies

Suppose you wanted to determine whether other people "saw the world" in the same colorful way that you do. How would you go about finding out?

Well, you might just show a variety of objects—a rose, a lime, a blueberry, and a lemon—to a random sample of subjects and *ask* them what colors the objects were. But even if everyone in your sample announced that "the rose is red-colored," how would you know the subjects actually *saw* the rose as being the same color you did? Red, after all, is a *subjective experience*, not a physical dimension. One way to bring some objectivity to your experiment might be to show your subjects a rose and then ask them to *mix three colored lights* until they just matched the redness of the rose (an additive mixture). You could pick almost any three colored lights from the spectrum for your "mix colors," of course. But let's say you picked red, blue, and a yellowish-green because you know you have a specific cone-receptor for each of these colors. You could then use these same three "mix colors" when you asked your subjects to match the greenness of a lime, the yellow of a lemon, and the blue of a berry.

Color Weakness

If you tested enough people, using an additive color mixture technique, you would soon find that a few of your subjects needed an abnormally large amount of red in order to reproduce the redness of a rose. These people would be *red-weak*. That is, they *see* the color red, but it appears much weaker to them than do green, blue, and yellow. If you asked a red-weak individual to mix red and blue to match the purpleness of a plum, this person would mix in much more red than would a subject with normal "red vision."

A few other subjects might need an unusually large amount of yellowish green to match a lime-colored light. These people would be *green-weak*. If you asked a person with normal color vision to mix green and blue to match a turquoise-colored light, the person might mix the two colors in equal proportions. A green-weak individual, however, might well need 80 percent green and 20 percent blue to get a "subjective match" for the turquoise-colored light.

Most *color-weak* individuals have difficulties seeing either red or green—or have problems with both these hues.

Color Deficiencies

About 5 percent of the people in the world are almost totally insensitive to one or more hues on the color circle, although they can see most of the other hues perfectly well. The majority of these **color-deficient** people are *men*, for color deficiency is a sex-linked, inherited problem that seldom affects women.

The color-deficient person can reproduce all of the colors she or he can see by mixing just *two* basic hues. The main types of color deficiency involve a red deficiency or a green defi-

Saturation (sat-your-RAY-shun). The intensity or richness of a color. Pink is a weak (desaturated) red. The colors of the rainbow are about as saturated as any colors can be.

Additively. There are two types of color mixtures, additive and subtractive. If you shine a blue light and a yellow light on the same spot on the movie screen, the screen reflects back almost all of the light and thus "adds" the blue to the yellow light. This is an additive mixture. The pigments in most paints, however, give a subtractive mixture. If you shine a white light on an object painted blue, the pigments in the blue paint will "subtract" or block out all the spectrum other than the hues in the blue area (that is, all the hues except blue and a little green). Thus, the object appears blue because the pigments subtract all but the blue hues. Yellow paint blocks out ("subtracts") all the hues in white light except those at the yellow end of the spectrum (that is, all but yellow and a little green and a little orange). If you mix blue and yellow paints, the blue pigments subtract out the yellows and the yellow pigments subtract out the blues. But both pigments will leave some of the greens unblocked. Thus, a subtractive mixture of blue and yellow paints often yields a green color.

Color-deficient. A person who is "red-weak" sees red, but not very well. A "red-deficient" individual usually sees yellows and blues quite well, but cannot see red at all.

ciency. Blue or yellow color deficiency is very rare.

A person suffering from either red or green deficiency sees the world almost entirely in terms of blues and yellows (plus black and white). Colors at the blue-green end of the spectrum appear blue, while colors at the red-yellow end of the spectrum appear yellow. Thus, to someone with *either* red or green deficiency, a bright red fire engine will look a dull yellow, and grass would appear to be a desaturated blue.

The rare individual who is blue/yellow-deficient sees the world entirely in reds and greens (plus black and white).

According to recent research by W.A.H. Rushton, red-deficient individuals simply don't have any red photo-sensitive pigment in their cones. Similarly, green-deficient individuals lack the green photo-sensitive pigment.

There are many different theories of color vision that attempt to explain why some people see colors normally, while other people don't see colors as they should. Since these theories are highly complex, we won't discuss them here. We might note, however, that so far none of the theories has proved itself fully acceptable to all psychologists.

Total Color-Blindness

Only about one person in 40,000 is totally color-blind. A few of these totally color-blind individuals were born with normal vision, but as a result of disease lost the ability to see hues. Others became totally color-blind because their cones were poisoned by such pollutants as lead or carbon disulfide. Many of these people can recover at least some of their color vision if given proper therapy—including large doses of Vitamin A.

Most totally color-blind people, however, suffer from **albinism**—an inherited condition involving a lack of pigment throughout their bodies. Like albino rabbits and rats, these people have colorless hair, pink-white skin, and pinkish irises. Since the photo-sensitive chemicals in the cones are, in fact, *pigments*, albino people lack functional cones and *cannot see color at all.*

All albino humans have foveas that are *totally blind*, so the albino must learn to defeat the usual visual reflexes that tend to focus images in the area of the fovea. Most albinos develop rather jerky eye movements that prevent their visual images from focusing in on the fovea. But even so, their visual acuity is well below average. For if they look straight at something, it disappears from their sight.

Since albino individuals have only rod (or night) vision, they find normal day illumination blinding-bright. They usually compensate by learning to keep their eyelids half-closed, or by wearing dark glasses. Put more accurately, they use their *brains* to help them perceive the world in situations where their visual inputs are somewhat imperfect.

Tests for Color Deficiencies

Odd as it may seem, many color-deficient individuals reach maturity without knowing they have a visual defect. For instance, Karl Dallenbach, a psychologist who spent his professional life studying sensory processes, learned of his red deficiency in an introductory psychology class.

Students in this particular class were seated alphabetically to make checking attendance easier for the teacher. Dallenbach was in the front row. During a lecture on vision, the professor wished to demonstrate an old color-deficiency test called the **Holmgren wools**. The test consists of a large number of strands of colored wool that the subject is asked to sort into various piles according to their hues. Dallenbach was tapped for the honor of being a subject sim-

Karl M. Dallenbach

ply because he was right under the teacher's nose.

When asked to sort the reds into one pile, Dallenbach included all the wools with a greenish hue as well as those that were clearly red. When asked to sort all the greens, he included the reds.

At first the teacher thought that Dallenbach was playing a joke, but subsequent tests proved he was red-deficient. Like most color-deficient people, Dallenbach had learned to compensate for his handicap while growing up. Since everyone said that grass was green, he saw it as being somehow different from red roses—although, under controlled conditions, Dallenbach could not tell the color of grass from that of most red roses.

Despite this visual problem, however, Dallenbach went on to become a noted psychologist. But perhaps because of his red deficiency, Dallenbach specialized in the study of taste and smell—not of color vision.

The Holmgren wools are but one (and perhaps the least accurate) of many different tests for color deficiences. Most of the other tests contain hundreds of tiny dots of colors. These dots are so arranged that a person with normal vision sees letters, numbers, or geometric figures in the dots. A person with color deficiency, however, sees only a random jumble of dots or a different number than would the normal person. An example of this sort of color deficiency test is shown in Color Plate 15.

Question: Red and green were picked as the colors for our traffic signal lights before we realized that millions of drivers are "deficient" or "weak" to these two hues. How might we slightly alter the traffic-light colors to make it easier for drivers with red-green deficiencies to tell the difference between a "stop" light and a "go" light? (Remember, these drivers can see blue and yellow quite well.)

Sensation and Perception

Sensory inputs are but the first stage of that marvelous process called *perception*. Now that we know how your nervous system handles sensory inputs, suppose we look at how your brain "gives meaning" to sensory stimuli.

Albinism (AL-been-ism). From the Latin word *albus*, meaning "white." Albinism is an inherited condition that involves a failure to produce colored pigments in the hair, skin, and elsewhere in the body.

Holmgren wools (HOLM-gren). A color vision test devised by a Swedish scientist named Alarick F. Holmgren. The test consists of strands of colored wool yarns that the subject must sort according to their hues. The test is seldom used these days.

Summary

1 Hearing is a **stereo** sense. Because your two ears are several centimeters apart, sounds reach your left ear at slightly different times and loudnesses than they reach your right ear. Your brain converts these differences into an understanding of whether the source of the sound is to the left or right.

2 When sound from any source arrives at your ear, the sound passes through the outer and middle ear until it reaches the hair cells in your inner ear. The middle ear contains three bones—the **hammer**, **anvil**, and **stirrup** that amplify sound waves. The **eardrum** separating the outer from the middle ear is connected to the hammer. The stirrup is connected to the **oval window**, which separates the middle from the inner ear.

3 The inner ear is a snail-shaped space called the **cochlea**. The hair cells that are the true **auditory receptors** are part of the **organ of Corti**. The organ of Corti lies on the **basilar membrane** which runs the length of the cochlea.

4 Sound waves have both **frequency** and **amplitude**. Frequency is measured in **Hertz**, or Hz. The greater the frequency of a musical tone, the higher it generally sounds. The larger the amplitude of a sound, the louder it will usually seem to be.

5 **Bone deafness** is a hearing loss caused by improper functioning of the bones in your middle ear.

6 Nerve deafness results from damage to the hair cell receptors.

7 The stimulus input for vision is light, which is made up of waves of very tiny energy particles called **photons**.

8 The **frequency** of a light wave helps determine the color the light will appear to be. The **amplitude** (intensity) of the light wave generally determines how bright it will seem.

9 The **visible spectrum** (or rainbow of colors) runs from blue through green, yellow, and orange to red.

10 The **wave-lengths** for the visible spectrum run from 400 **nanometers** (blue) through 760 nanometers (red).

11 The eye is something like a color TV camera. Light enters your eye through the **cornea** and **aqueous humor**, then passes through the **pupil**, the **lens**, and the **vitreous humor**. The light then strikes your **retina**, which is the **photosensitive** inner surface of the hollow eyeball.

12 Muscles attached to your lens help focus the visual input so that it falls squarely on your retina.

13 The retina contains your **visual receptors**—the **rods** and **cones**. There are three types of **photo-sensitive pigments** in the cones, one sensitive to red, one to blue, and one to yellowish-green. The rods contain **rhodopsin**, and are sensitive only to blacks, whites, and shades of gray.

14 In the center of your retina is a small pit called the **fovea** that contains only cones. Your vision is at its sharpest when the visual image falls on the fovea.

15 Near the fovea is the **blind spot**, which contains no visual receptors. The optic nerve, which runs from your retina to your brain, exits from the eyeball at the blind spot.

16 **Near-sighted** people typically see close objects more clearly than they do far objects. **Far-sighted** people typically see distant objects more clearly than they do objects that are close to their eyes.

17 **Old-sightedness** is a condition caused by hardening of the lens.

18 A person with normal **visual acuity** (keenness of vision) is said to have **20/20 vision**.

19 When you sit in the dark, your rods and cones adapt to this decrease in light intensity. **Dark adaptation** is mostly complete in about 30 minutes or so. Your rods are more sensitive at night (or in dim illumination) than are your cones. If your rods malfunction, you may suffer from **night-blindness**.

20 Colors have **hue** (red, green, blue, yellow) and **saturation** or richness.

21 Black, white, and gray are completely **desaturated colors**.

22 If a person can see a color, but only when it is very intense, the person is said to be **color-weak**.

23 If a person cannot see a particular color no matter how intense it is, that person is said to be **color-deficient**.

24 The most common form of color deficiency is the failure to see reds and/or greens as people with normal color vision do.

25 **Albino** humans and animals lack the pigments necessary for normal color vision. They therefore see only with their rods and are **totally color-blind**.

(Continued from page 165.)

Dear Judy Jones:

I was going through some of my stuff today, packing it all up, when I found this old sheet of scratch paper. It had a cow on it, and a horse and an automobile. On the back were a couple of algebra problems, written out in long hand. My ticket to the world, I always used to call it. Reminded me that I hadn't written you a letter in some time, so maybe I ought to catch you up with the news.

I'm going to college! Can you believe it! That's what I was packing for, when I found the scratch paper. Bet you never thought, the first time you saw this ugly boy, Woodrow Wilson Thomas, that he'd be going off to college someday. I don't remember that first day you came to the Home too well, maybe because I didn't know the words to remember things with, back then. But the alge-bra book, that is something I sure won't ever forget. I guess I learned how to read with that book. And your help too, and then Mrs. Dobson's. She told me later you had a real argument with her. She thought I was retarded, but you insisted I must just be deaf. Then there was a doctor checking me out, and the hearing aid that the state bought me. Did I ever tell you, the first day I had the hearing aid, I just sat and listened to the birds all day long? Can you imagine not knowing what a bird sounds like until you're 10 years old?

Anyhow, as you know, it took me a couple of years to learn how to talk like normal people do. Still not too good at it, I guess. But I went to school, and I caught up, and now I'm going to college. I still can't believe it. I guess I did pretty good in high school, except maybe in English. But real good in math. Good enough to get a scholarship. How 'bout that? I'm going to study math in college. Hope to be a teacher some day. My complexion has cleared up a lot since you saw me last, and maybe I'm not so ugly any more. Anyhow, I've got me a girl friend. Sort of.

It's been so long, maybe you're married now and have kids of your own. If you do, I bet you'll have their ears checked out early, won't you?

Anyhow, I just wanted to let you know how things are going, and about the college bit. I guess if it hadn't been for you, I'd still be at the Home, sitting in the window, looking at the pretty pictures in the magazines. I guess I really owe the world to you, Judy Jones. So I thought I'd write and say thank you.

Best,
Woody

Recommended Readings

Braginsky, D.D. & Braginsky, B.J. (1971). *Hansels and Gretels: Study of children in institutions for the mentally retarded*. New York: Holt, Rinehart and Winston.

Moore, B.C.J. (1982). *An introduction to the psychology of hearing (2nd ed.)*. London: Academic Press.

Rushton, W.A.H. (1975). Visual pigments and color blindness. *Scientific American, 232*(3), pp. 64–74.

Uttal, W.R. (1981). *A taxonomy of visual processes*. New York: LEA.

Did You Know That...

- A person born blind who recovers sight as an adult has great difficulty in recognizing people's faces?
- You probably learn to judge distances by moving about?
- You tend to see all objects as appearing on a background of some kind?
- You typically group objects together according to such principles as proximity, closure, and continuity?
- Infants usually prefer to look at human faces rather than at random visual patterns?
- Infants only 10 days old will mimic the facial expressions of adults around them?
- Blind children are slow to build up an adequate concept of themselves?
- The pupils of your eyes often open wider when you are staring at something of interest to you?
- Your brain may suppress inputs that disturb or annoy it?
- You see what you expect to see?

8

Visual Perception and Speech Perception

"Great Expectations"

The Professor was sitting on a large box, cursing like a trooper and sweating like a stallion. Several other boxes, covered with address labels, were stacked nearby. On the smallest label of all there was just room for

Dr. M.E. Mann
Dept. of Psych.
Univ. of the Mid-West, USA

Moments before, a group of porters had unloaded the boxes from an ancient pickup truck and trundled the cartons inside the airport, dumping them near the Customs office. Professor Mann sat on the cartons, sweating and cursing.

Outside the airport the African sun shone fiercely, roasting any man or beast foolish enough to venture forth unprotected. Even inside the airport building the temperature was nearly 100°, reason enough for the Professor's clothing to be soaked with sweat. The cursing was no doubt due to the fact that Dr. Mann was going home royally frustrated.

A small, dark man walked briskly out of the Customs office and headed toward Mann. Despite the heat, he looked as crisp and elegant as a fashion model in his silk suit.

"Ah, my dear Professor, all is in order, all is in readiness," the man said in an elegant tone of voice. "I assure you we will tuck your boxes of scientific equipment on the plane as gently as a mother tucks a child into bed. Let no one say that the Republic of Lafora treats visiting scientists shabbily." The elegantly dressed man smiled radiantly. "And now, perhaps we might repair to what passes for a cocktail lounge in this ancient airport. I am certain that the limited budget of the Ministry of Science and Technology can be stretched to provide us with a glass or two of cheer while we await the arrival of your jet."

Mann's response was sharp and unprintable.

"Ah," the small man replied. "You are still angry because we cannot approve your venturing into our back country to complete your research. But surely, my dear Professor, you understand my country's position. We are responsible for your safety, and the tribes you wish to study are still little more than savages."

The Professor made a savage remark.

"No, no," the small man continued hastily. "We could not in good conscience let you go among those tribes unprotected, for they would surely murder you. Your research grant is not of sufficient magnitude to allow you to hire a private troop of soldiers to protect you. And, as you know, all of our military personnel are required at our borders at this dangerous time in our nation's existence. Now, come and have a drink and soothe yourself while we wait . . ."

Mann interrupted. "Oh, come off it, Freddie. All this formality and politeness is just a cover up for the truth. It's prejudice. Pure and simple prejudice. You're a city-born, Oxford-educated, wealthy, sophisticated man. You hold two cabinet posts in the Laforan government. You've been wined and dined in half the capitals of the world, but I'll bet a year's pay that you've never broken bread with one of your backland natives. If they occasionally do wipe out one of your tax collectors or military types, I don't doubt they've been provoked into doing so. But *murderers*? No, that's pure, superstitious prejudice on your part. I've talked to those natives, and many of my anthropologist friends have been out there. You

don't understand the backlanders, so you're afraid of them. You shouldn't be. The truth is that they're frightened to death of you city people."

The sharply dressed Minister of Science and Technology began to sweat a little. "My dear Professor, I took your case to the highest authorities in my government, and the answer was no. Absolutely not. What more could I do?"

"You could have pleaded my case with the President himself, that's what," the irate American continued.

"Our great leader is too busy to concern himself with such trivial matters. As you no doubt are aware, we are threatened by enemies on all sides. Even though you are a noted scientist from a country that has long supported our freedom and independence, I would not dare bother the President with such minor problems at this time."

Mann laughed sharply. "That's hogwash! You still see the world in terms of absolutes, in blacks and whites. You wouldn't dare turn down my request if your native prejudice wasn't so great that . . ."

The scream of a shrill siren interrupted them. A large black automobile screeched to a halt in front of the airport, and out popped a huge man dressed in the uniform of a Laforan general. The big man came striding into the building at top speed. Then, catching sight of the Minister and Mann, the General rushed up to them.

"Ah, Freddie," said the General, "Thank God I found you. We have a terrible emergency on our hands. Perhaps you can help."

Freddie said, "Of course," and then quickly introduced General Chambro, head of security for the Republic of Lafora, to Professor Mann.

"Charmed, I'm sure," the General said, bowing slightly to acknowledge the American's presence. Then he continued in an excited tone of voice, "Freddie, the Snake is coming!"

Freddie looked puzzled. "The Snake?"

"Yes, on the next airplane. We just got the message from our agents in Paris. They're sure he's coming to kill the President! You must help us figure out what to do!"

"Well, why don't you just arrest this 'Snake' as soon as he gets off the airplane?" asked the American in a matter-of-fact tone of voice.

"I'm afraid you don't understand," the General said, giving Dr. Mann a withering look. "The Snake is the most dangerous terrorist in the world, responsible for some of the foulest political assassinations you could imagine. The problem is, we simply don't know what the Snake looks like! Not a jot or tittle of information about this assassin do we have. Is he young, old, tall, short, fat, skinny? All we know is that he usually kills his victims by injecting snake venom into them with a fang-shaped needle. The victim dies in horrible convulsions. And to arrange to arrive on this plane! No wonder they call him the Snake!"

Freddie paled visibly during the General's speech. Turning to the American, he said quietly, "There is something you don't understand, Dr. Mann. This particular flight brings to Lafora almost a hundred of the biggest munitions dealers in the world. They are wormy characters, all of them. But we need them because, as you know, we refuse to accept military supplies from any of the major powers. So we spread the word that we wished to buy guns, and chartered a special plane to bring in from Europe anyone interested in selling us weapons. That is one of the reasons I am at the airport now, to greet these men and make them welcome. If we treat them badly . . ."

The General interrupted. "And we cannot check out their passports because most of them travel with forged papers."

"What about giving them a lie-detector test?" Freddie asked.

"They wouldn't submit to such a test, of course," said the General contemptuously.

"The lie detector measures emotionality, not truthfulness," the American added. "And I'd guess that your 'Snake' isn't exactly the sort who would lose his cool very readily."

"Too true," said the General, and mopped his face again. "But we must find some way of separating the Snake from—er, the worms, or we are in grave danger."

Freddie cleared his throat and ventured a question. "Professor Mann, you are an expert in the field of perceptual responses. You told me you wished to give certain tests to our backland natives that would tell you about their minds even if they did not understand the purpose of the tests, and even though you could not speak their language. I don't suppose that now . . ."

Professor Mann was suddenly all business. "Yes, Freddie, it might work. We could set up my equipment right here in the airport and test everyone as they get off the plane. I would have to draw up some new stimulus cards, but that shouldn't take long. Of course, I don't guarantee anything. The error rate is really very high, you know, and I could easily make a dreadful mistake. But if you're really desperate, perhaps it's better than nothing."

The General looked confused. "I don't understand . . ."

Freddie turned to the military man and said, "You aren't expected to understand—this is a matter for scientists such as Dr. Mann and me. We will screen the men on the plane with the Professor's equipment. You have your soldiers standing by, looking as innocent as possible. When we detect the Snake, we will give you a signal and you must move in for the arrest at once. More than that, you need not know."

"But what will we tell the arms dealers?" the General wailed. "They will want an explanation . . ."

"We will say that Paris has reported an outbreak of a highly infectious eye disease, and we must check each person on the flight to make sure they are not carrying the illness," Dr. Mann said brusquely. "I will put on a white uniform and be very efficient about it all."

At this final comment, Freddie smiled broadly. "You are a positive genius, my dear Professor. We will do just what you say!" And then he turned to some porters standing idly by. "Here, you men! Help us open these crates and set up this equipment!"

(Continued on page 221.)

Perception

Psychology is, in many ways, the scientific study of the obvious. For example, look at Fig. 8.1. Obviously, it's a photograph of a coin. But what *shape* is it, and how do you know it's a "coin"? Well, you say, it's round, and you know it's a coin because you recognize it from past experience. However, let's push matters a bit. How do you *know* the shape of the coin is "round"? And how do you *use* "past experience" to recognize that the object is a coin?

These are the sorts of "obvious questions" that seldom concern people other than philosophers and behavioral scientists. And, as you have already learned, different theorists are likely to answer such questions in radically different ways. For example, one answer to the first question might be, "You know the shape of the object is round because you have *innate knowledge* about such shapes as roundness." Put more precisely, we might assume that your genes "hard-wired" the circuits in your brain so you perceive certain visual patterns in a con-

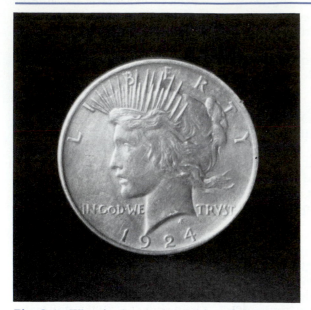

Fig. 8.1 What is the shape of this coin?

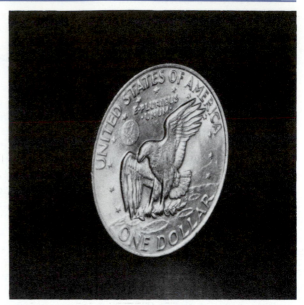

Fig. 8.2 What is the shape of this coin?

sistent manner. You obviously *learned* to call the object a "coin." But did you have to learn how to "see" the shape as *round*? Or was your brain *created* to perceive such shapes correctly in the first place?

Nature Versus Nurture

One of the great battles in psychology is this: How much of what you experience is learned, and how much is innately determined by your genes? We call this the *nature-nurture problem*, and we will discuss it frequently in future chapters (as well as in this one). In the field of perception, the "nature" position is represented primarily by two theoretical schools—the **Gestalt** psychologists, and the **Gibsonians**. The "nurture" position is best represented by the **empirical** approach, and by what is now called the *information-processing* viewpoint. Let's look briefly at all four positions.

The Gestalt Approach

The Gestalt movement began in Germany around 1912. It was started by several psychologists who believed the perception of *shape* was inborn. To the Gestalt theorists, the circle was a "perfect form." Thus, to the Gestalt psychologists, you perceive the coin as "round" (or circular) because your brain has a built-in concept of "roundness" or circularity. When you look at

the coin, the "perfect form" of roundness is called into your mind automatically. So you *impose* the innate concept of "circularity" on your sensory inputs. True, you *learn* to call this particular example a "coin" through experience. But, according to Gestalt theory, your *perception of roundness* (or circularity) is a psychological experience that is a *gift of nature*.

The Gibsonian Approach

The Gestalt view is that your mind *imposes* a kind of psychological order on the inputs you get from the outside world. Cornell psychologist James J. Gibson took the opposite point of view. He held that perception is *direct* and *immediate*. Gibson believed sensory inputs *impose order on your mind*.

In his 1950 book *The Perception of the Visual World*, Gibson stated that your brain is "hard-wired" to *see the world as it really is*. The coin *is* round, and the light rays coming from the coin are rich in sensory cues describing its roundness. The pattern of excitation the light rays make on your retina is round. Thus, how could you perceive the coin as anything other than circular in shape?

Put more precisely, James Gibson said we can explain almost all perceptual experiences in terms of information to be found in the stimulus itself. Therefore, we should study *stimuli*, not "internal processes." Gibson believed there is a one-to-one correspondence between sensory inputs and perceptual experiences, and that this correspondence is determined by the genes. As one of Gibson's followers put it in a 1977 paper, "James J. Gibson's strategy for perceiving: Ask not what's inside your head, but what your head's inside of."

Look at Fig. 8.2. Here's the same coin again, but now it's turned away from you in space. Do you still see it as round? Probably so, even though the "image" the coin casts on your retina is actually an **ellipse**. The Gestalt view would be that, since the circle is a "more perfect form" than the ellipse, your brain *forces* you to perceive the coin as round. Gibson, however, would say that sensory cues determine what you perceive, not some "innate tendency to see good form." Notice that the "detail" on the face of the coin is bold and clear on the left side of the coin. But the features on right side are "compressed" and less distinct. These *sensory inputs*, Gibson said, would force you to perceive the coin as round but turned away from you in space.

The Empirical Approach

Both Gibson and the Gestalt psychologists took the genetic (or "naturist") viewpoint. And, as we will see, both approaches contributed greatly to our understanding of perceptual processes. However, the more traditional view-

point puts greater emphasis on learning ("nurture") than on nature. According to the *empirical* position, perception is determined by two independent factors—*present sensations* and *mental images of past experiences*. Put another way, the empirical view is that "perception = sensory inputs + memories."

The empirical position holds that you were not born with the innate knowledge that the coin is round, nor with the ability to make use of the sensory stimuli coming from the coin. Rather, you *learned* through empirical observations that these types of inputs are typically associated with a class of "round objects called coins." From the *empirical viewpoint*, you acquired the ability to see the world the way you see it—including the "roundness" of coins.

The Information-Processing Approach

According to the empirical viewpoint, *sensations* are "pure experiences not influenced by learning." Thus, sensory inputs presumably arrive at your cortex "unprocessed" in any significant way by the lower centers in your brain. Once these inputs **register** on your consciousness, your mind checks through its memory files and *interprets* the inputs according to past experience. To the empiricists, perception is the process by which your mind "adds meaning to sensations."

Much of perception does seem to consist of "adding meaning to sensory inputs." But the *manner* in which your mind accomplishes this miracle is far more complex than most early empiricists dreamed. For instance, many neurons in your visual system seem sensitive to certain *critical features* of visual inputs. Dozens of studies suggest that some cells in your *retina* probably are more responsive to movement

TAE CAT

Fig. 8.3 After you read the words, look at the middle letter in each word.

Fig. 8.4 The "contour" of this circle is the outer edge.

Fig. 8.5 Do you see a solid white triangle that partially covers up a triangle with black edges? Look again, and see if the solid white triangle is really there.

than to stationary objects. Other studies show that some neurons in your brain respond to vertical lines, but not to horizontal lines. Yet other nerve cells react to corners and sharp angles, but not to straight or curved lines. Thus, by the time a "circle" has *registered* on your consciousness, this input surely has been "analyzed" or "processed" in a variety of ways. (We will have more to say about all this in Chapter 9.)

According to the information-processing approach, information flows up to your brain in a series of steps or *stages*. For example, your rods and cones translate light rays coming from the coin into patterns of neural energy. The rods and cones then pass this information along to complex cells in your retina. These complex cells respond to *critical features* of the visual input, and send this "processed information" to the thalamus (and other lower brain centers). Neurons in the thalamus detect certain *patterns of information* coming from the retinal cells, and pass the information "upstream" to your visual cortex.

The cells in your cortex search for their own type of specific features. Does this input have corners? (No.) Does this input have rounded lines? (Yes.) The cortical neurons then check through your memory banks to see if you have

experienced this type of input before. (You've seen a lot of circles.) Your cortex then tries to *match* the present input with an image stored in memory. Since the input matches the image of a coin, you "perceive" a coin!

There are several different types of information-processing theories. However, they all assume that, at each "processing stage," your neurons *extract* some types of information from the input and pass it on. But your neurons also *simplify* the input by failing to pass on "unimportant" information. Thus, you don't really see "what's there." Rather, these theories say, you typically perceive only certain *critical features* of the stimulus input.

The Four Viewpoints Compared

The Gestalt and Gibsonian positions emphasize the *innate properties* of perception. The empirical and information-processing theories focus on those aspects of perception that are *learned*.

Gibson made the stimulus the most important part of perception. The other views emphasize "internal processing."

Gibson, the Gestalt psychologists, and the empirical theorists believe that "sensations" arrive at the brain relatively unprocessed and thus free of cortical influence. The information-processing viewpoint is that the input is highly processed by "lower centers" in your brain, and that your cortex can influence what goes on in the "lower centers" in a variety of ways. For example, look at Figure 8.3. Did you read the words as "The cat"? Look again. The "h" and the "a" are identical, thus they must have identical "critical features." But you *perceived* them in different ways because your brain *forced* these letters to fit within the images of well-known words. The other viewpoints have problems explaining this type of perceptual "error."

Gibson saw sensation and perception as being pretty much the same thing. The Gestalt and empirical theorists believe that sensation and memory are totally independent processes, but that both influence perception. However, the information-processing theorists hold that sensation, perception, memory, and **cognition** are all part of the same "global process." We cannot separate them because each affects the other. We will have more to say about this point later.

Each of the four views has made its own contributions to our understanding of how you perceive the world. As we discuss perception, we will try to show what the strengths (and problems) of each of the theories seem to be.

Visual Perception

Your eyes are more than "the windows to your soul." Unless you are visually handicapped, your eyes are also the main sensory route by which you acquire information about the outside world. Thus, the bulk of perceptual research deals with vision—as does much of the material in this chapter. So let us begin by asking, "How do you perceive the world around you visually?"

Contours

The simplest form of visual information is the difference between light and darkness. A visual **contour** is a place where there is a sharp or sudden change in brightness—from light to dark, or vice versa. Fig. 8.4 has two contours—one at the inner edge of the circle, and one at the outer edge. It is these two contours, actually, that give *shape* to the circle.

The two contours shown in Fig. 8.4 are *objective*. That is, there is a *real* change in brightness between the black of the circle and the white paper it is printed on. But now look at Fig. 8.5. Do you see two triangles? Most people

Cognition (cog-NISH-shun). From the Latin word meaning "to know." The dictionary definition of cognition is "The act or process of knowing including both awareness and judgment." Roughly speaking, cognitive activities are those "internal processes" that involve information processing, thinking, reasoning, remembering, perceiving, and so forth, but that (usually) do *not* include emotions or feelings.

Contour. The edge or outer shape of any object. Your eye and brain have innate elements that allow you to detect contours of objects at birth.

see a large white triangle (pointing up) superimposed on a triangle pointing down. If this is what you see, look at the center of the white triangle. Doesn't it somehow look *whiter* than the background outside the figure does? And don't you see a sharp contrast between the *imaginary lines* setting off the top triangle and the space outside the triangle? These are *subjective* contours, since they are generated by your brain, not by objective changes in brightness.

What causes subjective contours? One interesting answer was given by Canadian psychologist Stanley Coren in 1971. Coren believes we have an innate tendency to perceive the world in meaningful but simple terms. You could perceive Fig. 8.5 as a collection of (1) three black circles with pie-shaped wedges cut out of them and (2) three V-shaped black lines. However, Coren says, it is both simpler and more meaningful to see the drawing as a white triangle lying on top of three black circles and thereby partially covering a second triangle as well.

Question: Fig. 8.5 contains an important clue about depth perception. We will discuss it later, but can you guess what it is?

Shape

Look at Fig. 8.6. What do you see? Most people see a solid black circle and a rather formless blob of black ink. Notice that the *contours* give shape to both figures.

Now, close your eyes and try to imagine both black figures. Chances are, you have no problem with the circle. But what about the blob? Why is it so difficult to remember *in detail*?

There are many answers to this question. For one thing, the blob is a much more complex figure than is the circle. For another, you are quite familiar with circles, but you probably never have seen a blob just like this one before. (These facts should tell you something about the im-

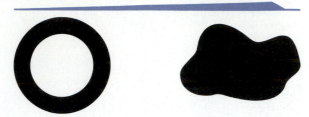

Fig. 8.6 Both the circle and the "blob" have contours.

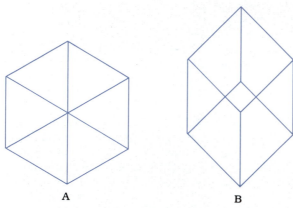

A   B

Fig. 8.7 Most people see the figure on the left as two-dimensional, but see the figure on the right in three dimensions. Why?

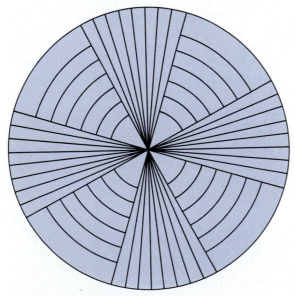

Fig. 8.8 What is figure and what is ground in this drawing? Why?

portance of memory in shaping your perceptions.)

When the Gestalt psychologists tried to answer this same question, they came up with the **Law of Praegnanz**. According to this law, you have an innate tendency to perceive shapes or figures as "good," "simple," and "regular." The circle is the "best" of all possible figures. Therefore, it is the simplest to perceive.

Generally speaking, you will attempt to force any object you see to take its simplest or "best" form. For example, look at Fig. 8.7. Most people see the drawing on the left as a six-sided figure with three lines in the middle. But what about the drawing on the right? Do you see it as a two-dimensional figure, or does it somehow project itself into three dimensions? Since the two drawings are really quite similar, why do you perceive Fig. 8.7A as two-dimensional, but Fig. 8.7B in three dimensions?

According to Gestalt theorist Julian Hochberg, Fig. 8.7A is a simple figure when viewed in two dimensions. Therefore, you see it in two dimensions, although you could project it into three dimensions as well. However, Fig. 8.7B is a very complex figure when viewed in two dimensions—*but a simple figure in three dimensions.* Thus, following the Gestalt Law of Praegnanz, you "make it simple" by projecting it into three dimensions.

Question: Why was the "subjective triangle" in Fig. 8.5 easier to see in "depth" (three dimensions) than the "box" in Fig. 8.7B?

Figure-Ground Relationships

According to the Gestalt position, you never perceive an object such as a circle "all by itself." Rather, you always see a circle as a shape *on a background.* The contours that define the circle as a "shape" also differentiate the circle from its surroundings. Part of "good form," therefore, is the fact that any form always appears against a background of some kind.

In studying the Law of Praegnanz, the Gestalt theorists made many discoveries about *figure-ground relationships.* One such fact is that the figure almost always seems *brighter* and *closer* to you than does the background. Look again at Fig. 8.5. Doesn't the (subjective) white triangle seem brighter than its surround? And doesn't it seem closer to you than the rest of the figure?

Another aspect of figure-ground relationships is this—the background seems to *con-*

tinue behind the figure. Look at Fig. 8.8. Which is figure and which is background? Probably you see a cross on a background of concentric circles. Does the cross seem nearer to you than the circles? Why? If you stare at this figure long enough, you may get a "reversal" and see a cross with radial lines as the "figure." Why is it so hard to see the "radial cross" as *figure*? (Hint: Remember that the background always "continues behind the figure.")

Ambiguous Figure-Ground Relationships

Now look at Fig. 8.9. What do you see? A white vase on a black background? Or two black profiles facing each other? Or do these two perspectives alternate?

Fig. 8.9 is a very famous example of what the Gestalt psychologists called **ambiguous** figure-ground relationships. Almost all these ambiguous figures involve *reversible perspectives*. Notice that when the vase is figure, it seems closer. But when the faces become figure, the vase retreats into the background and becomes *less important* psychologically. Generally speaking, you will also perceive the figure as having more *reality* or "thing-ness" than does the background.

Now, try to see *both* the vase and the faces as "figure" *at the same time*. Chances are, you'll find it impossible to do. Why? According to Gestalt theory, you *always* must perceive a figure on a background. Therefore, you can't see both as figure at the same time.

Law of Praegnanz (PREG-nants). A Gestalt law that states that perceptions tend to take the most stable possible form or configuration in any given set of circumstances.
Ambiguous (am-BIG-you-us). Anything that is vague or indefinite. If you ask someone to go on a date, and the person says "maybe yes, maybe no," the person has given you an ambiguous answer.

Reversible Perspectives

Look at the "impossible figure" in Fig. 8.10. Do the stairs go up or down, or both ways? Is the platform on the right higher or lower than the platform on the left? What is there about the perspective of this figure that "fools" your eyes?

Now look at Fig. 8.11, the famous Necker Cube. Does it project upward or downward? Actually, it projects *either way*. And, if you stare at it long enough, it will "reverse its perspective" from time to time. The *frequency* with which the Cube changes perspective may depend in part on what sort of person you see yourself as being, however. Judith and Bruce Bergum at Texas A. & M. showed the Cube to 128 students and asked them how frequently the Cube "changed directions." The Bergums reported in 1981 that students who had the *highest* reversal rates tended to perceive themselves as being more (1) creative and original, (2) enthusiastic and optimistic, and (3) excitable and appreciative than did students with the *lowest* reversal rates.

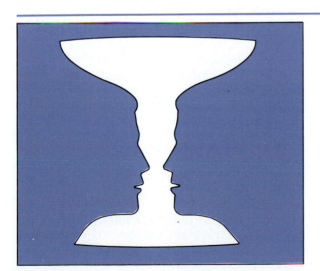

Fig. 8.9 Do you see two profile faces? Or a wine glass?

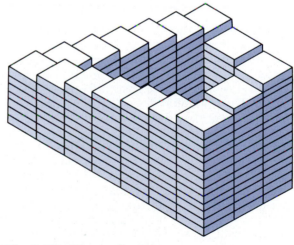

Fig. 8.10 The magic stairs.

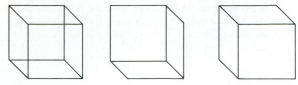

Fig. 8.11 The Necker Cube. It can be seen as projecting up or down in three dimensions in the first cube. In the other two cubes the perspective is stabilized.

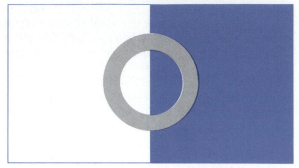

Fig. 8.12 The gray circle appears darker when viewed against a light background than when viewed against a dark background.

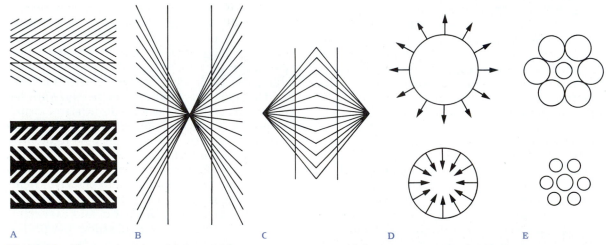

A   B   C   D   E

Fig. 8.13 The context in which an object appears affects the way you perceive it. The two parallel straight lines in Figs. 8.13A, 8.13B, and 8.13C seem "bent" because of the backgrounds on which they appear. In 8.13D the arrows make the top circle appear larger than the identical bottom circle. In 8.13E the two center circles are the same size.

Can you learn to make the Cube reverse its perspective at a faster rate? Perhaps so. The Bergums note that architecture students at Texas A. & M. tended to have much *higher* reversal rates on the Cube than did business students. The Bergums believe the architecture students were probably rewarded by their teachers for being able to "change perspectives" rapidly. Students in business administration, the Bergums say, were probably expected to take a much more stable view of the world. The Bergums' results suggest that, with training, you can learn to make the Cube "reverse perspective" almost as frequently or infrequently as you wish.

Question: How else might the Bergums' findings be explained? (Hint: Are students with a "creative, unstable view of the world" more likely to study architecture or business?)

Effects of Surround

One of the major beliefs of the Gestalt position can be found in a phrase they made famous in psychology: "The whole is greater than the sum of its parts." In truth, the phrase really means that the whole is *different* from the sum of its parts. As we noted in Chapter 5, when the sub-units of a system interact, they often produce *emergent properties*. The visual "whole," then, has perceptual properties that can't be deduced just by looking at the individual parts. For the background (or *surround*) has a strong influence on how you perceive the figure itself.

Look at Fig. 8.12. Here is a gray circle displayed on a surround that is half white, half blue. As you look at the circle, the gray seems uniform. But if you cover the border between the blue and white sections with a pen, the gray semi-circle on the white background will look much darker than the semi-circle on the blue surround. Why?

Figure 8.13 gives five examples of how the background changes the perception of the figure itself. One of the most striking examples of this effect, however, appears in Fig. 8.14. Do you see a spiral moving in toward the center of the drawing? If you do, use your finger to trace out where the spiral actually goes.

Question: How would you attempt to explain these illusions from the "information-processing" viewpoint of perception? From the "empirical" approach? How do these explanations differ from that offered by the Gestalt psychologists?

Visual Grouping

As you look out at the world, your mind makes use of several Gestalt principles in trying to bring some kind of order to its perceptions.

Proximity and Closure

One Gestalt principle is that you tend to *group things together* according to how close they are to each other. In part 1 of Fig. 8.15, you probably see three "pairs" of lines. You will group *a* and *b* together because they are close to each other.

In part 2, however, things have changed. Now *b* and *c* seem to go together—to form a rectangle of some kind. Indeed, if you stare closely at the *b-c* rectangle, you will see rather faint but *imaginary* lines as your brain attempts to fill in or close up the open figure.

Part 1 illustrates the Gestalt principle of *proximity*, or physical closeness. Part 2 illustrates the principle of *closure*—your brain's tendency to join broken lines together to make a closed figure of some kind.

Question: How might you derive the principles of proximity and closure from the Gestalt Law of Praegnanz?

Continuity

A third perceptual principle is that of *continuity* and is illustrated in part 1 of Fig. 8.16. In this illustration you will probably see a wavy

Fig. 8.14 If you perceive one line that "spirals" in to the center, trace the line with your finger. The "spiral" is actually a set of circles. What in this illusion actually fools your eye?

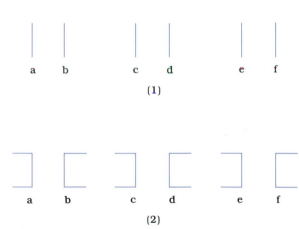

Fig. 8.15 Which lines seem to relate in part 1? in part 2?

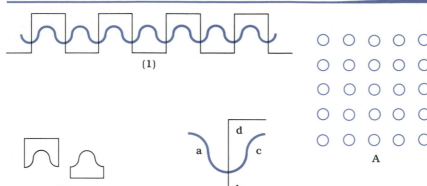

(1)

(2)

(3)

Fig. 8.16   The Gestalt principle of continuity.

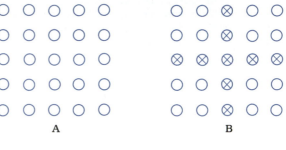

A

B

Fig. 8.17   How do you "group" these circles? Why do you group the circles in A in Fig. 8.17 differently than you do those in B?

Fig. 8.18   Bisection illusion.

line superimposed on a square-cornered line. If we now break up the pattern somewhat differently, as in part 2, you see not two lines but two closed figures joined together. Why do you think this is so? And if you wish, you may even break the figure up into a different set of components, shown in part 3.

Once you have learned what the parts of the figure can be, you can perceive it many different ways. But, at the beginning, your eye tends to follow the wavy line because it is *continuous*.

Similarity

A fourth principle of perceptual grouping is that of *similarity*. Fig. 8.17A shows a series of 25 circles arranged in a square. If you fixate on this figure, you will notice that sometimes you "group" the circles together in bunches of 4, or

9, or 16. And sometimes you see 5 horizontal rows of circles, sometimes 5 vertical columns. In such ambiguous situations, your brain apparently tests out various possibilities, attempting to see which fits the stimulus pattern best.

Visual Depth and Distance

So far, we have mostly discussed the viewing of two-dimensional objects. However, when you look at the world (beyond the printed page), it doesn't seem to be flat and two-dimensional. Rather, the world is *three-dimensional*. It has *depth* to it. This fact poses a problem to perceptual theorists. For the retinas in your eyes are, for all practical purposes, little more than flat "screens" on which the lenses in your eyes project two-dimensional images. How does your mind take these "flat" retinal images and *create* a third dimension—that of *depth*?

We are not entirely sure of the answer to this question. We do know, though, that true depth perception occurs only in people who have two eyes. And these two eyes must have slightly different views of the world for the third dimension to appear. It may also be the case (as we will see later in this chapter) that the *concept* of depth is innate. However, we are quite sure that some aspects of depth perception are *learned through experience*.

So, let's ask another of those supposedly obvious questions: What would your world be like if you had been born blind and only now opened your eyes? The answer to that question, as it happens, is anything but "obvious."

The Case of S.B.

Some years ago, British psychologist Richard L. Gregory reported the case of a man who had been blind from infancy, but whose vision was restored at age 52. This patient—whom Gregory calls S.B.—was an intelligent person whose vision had been normal at birth. At age 10 months, S.B. developed a severe infection of the eyes that left his corneas so badly scarred he couldn't see objects at all.

Enough light leaked through his damaged corneas so that S.B. could just tell day from night. But he saw the world much as you would if someone cut a ping pong ball in two and placed the halves over your eyes. S.B.'s corneal scars were so bad, in fact, that for most of his life no doctor would operate on him. Nonetheless, S.B. led an enjoyable and very active life. He went places by himself, waving his white cane in front of him to let people know he was blind. He often went for rides on a bicycle, with a friend holding his shoulder and guiding him.

S.B. spent considerable time making wooden objects with rather simple tools. He had an open-faced watch that let him tell time by feeling the positions of the hands. He took care of animals and knew them all by touch, sound, and smell. And he always tried to imagine what things looked like. When he washed his brother's car, he would vividly try to picture what color and shape it really was. When S.B. visited the zoo, he would get his friends to describe the animals there in terms of how different they were from the dogs and cats in his home.

S.B.'s Operation

When S.B. was well past his 50th year, he prevailed upon a surgeon to attempt an operation in which his damaged corneas were removed and new ones were **grafted** on in their place. The operation was a great success but, as Gregory reports, S.B. was anything but happy with the results. When the doctor first removed the bandages, S.B. looked straight into the doctor's face—and saw nothing but a blur. He knew what he saw had to be the doctor's face, because he recognized the man's voice. But it was several days before he could begin to tell one person from another merely by *looking* at them. And he never became very good at identifying people visually.

Nonetheless, he progressed rapidly in some areas. Within a few days, S.B. could successfully navigate the halls of the hospital without running into things. He could tell time by looking at the face of a very large clock. And he dearly loved to get up early in the morning and

Grafted. Joining parts of one organism to another is called "grafting." In corneal grafts, part of the donor's cornea is surgically removed and transplanted to the eye of the recipient. If the corneal graft "takes," the grafted tissue will connect up to the recipient's bloodstream and function more or less normally.

sit at his window watching the traffic rumble by on the street far below his hospital room.

But there were problems. S.B. rapidly learned the names of the colors red, black, and white. However, he had trouble identifying most other colors. He could judge *horizontal* distances fairly well when looking at objects whose size he was familiar with. But *heights* of any kind always confused him. One day the nurses found him crawling out the window of his fourth-floor hospital room, presumably because he wanted to inspect more closely the automobile traffic in the street below. He looked at the ground 40 feet beneath him and thought it to be no more than 6 feet away.

Prior to the operation, S.B. had crossed even the busiest intersection alone without the faintest fear. He would plunge into traffic waving his white stick in front of him. And somehow the river of cars and trucks would part for him, much as the waters of the Red Sea parted for Moses in Old Testament times. But after S.B. got his vision back, he was absolutely terrified of crossing a street. Gregory states it usually took two people holding his arms to force him across an intersection.

Often when S.B. saw a familiar object for the first time, he would be unable to identify it until he closed his eyes and felt it. Then he knew it by touch. And once he "had the picture in his mind," he could recognize it visually after he had looked at it a few times.

But objects he hadn't (or couldn't) run his hands over before regaining his sight always gave him problems. The moon, for instance, puzzled him greatly. The full moon he could make out, but the quarter moon he had expected to be wedge-shaped, rather like a large slice of pumpkin pie. And when S.B. looked at Fig. 8.18, he saw the horizontal and the vertical lines as being the same length. How do they look to you?

S.B.'s Depression

Immediately after his operation, S.B. was very enthusiastic and happy. He loved bright colors (although he couldn't always give their right names), and he enjoyed being able to see

Fig. 8.19 According to the principle of linear perspective, parallel lines appear to meet at the horizon.

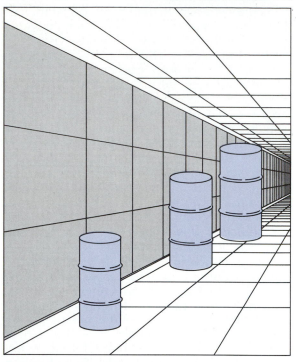

Fig. 8.20 Although the three cylinders are actually the same size, they appear to be different. Why? (From James J. Gibson, *The Senses Considered as Perceptual Systems*. Copyright © 1966 by James J. Gibson. Reprinted by permission of Houghton Mifflin Company.)

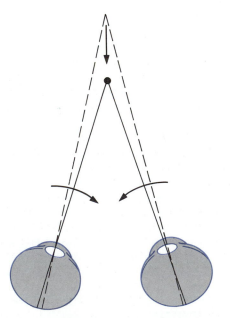

Fig. 8.21 An example of convergence. When you focus on a near object, your eyes "converge" (turn toward each other).

the faces of people he knew. But then he began to get depressed. He complained bitterly about the ugliness in the world around him—houses with the paint coming off, buildings with dirty walls, people with blemishes on their faces. He would spend hours sitting in his local tavern watching people *in the mirror*. Somehow their reflections seemed more interesting to him than their real-life images.

Often S.B. would withdraw from human contact and spend most of the day sitting in darkness, claiming he could "see" better when there was no light.

There have been no more than half a dozen confirmed cases of people who have gained sight as adults. According to Gregory, depression and unhappiness are common consequences of their getting back their vision. We should note, however, that not all patients who recover sight late in life have the same problems—or the depression—that S.B. experienced. One woman who recovered her sight in

1980 had no problem at all seeing and naming colors the moment her bandages were removed. Nor did she become unhappy with her new-found sight. These facts suggest that S.B.'s early illness may have *damaged* his rods and cones. Thus, many of the difficulties S.B. had in perceiving the world were probably due to retinal damage rather than to an inability to learn to see the world correctly so late in life.

Clues to Visual Distance

S.B. gained the ability to perceive *horizontal distance*. That is, he could tell how far away you were if he saw you walking down a hallway toward him. But he never could perceive *depth* very well. As we noted, depth is a three-dimensional property. People with **monocular** vision—that is, people who have just one functional eye—can also usually judge distance fairly well. However, like S.B., they typically don't perceive depth.

These facts suggest that *distance* cues are different from cues to *depth*. As James Gibson noted many years ago, distance cues are typically embedded in the visual stimuli themselves. However, your mind judges distance using more inputs than just those that come from the retina. It also takes into account the way your eyes move in their sockets, the sounds your ears report, the smells around you, your body posture, and all the memories it can dredge up.

For example, an automobile passes you on the street. You know it is about 30 feet away because you remember what size cars ought to be, how long it takes you to walk 30 feet, and how the visual image of the car will change as you walk toward it.

The *apparent size* of an object gives you a good notion of how far away the object is. You tend to perceive small objects as being far away, and large objects as being closer. But you do this only if you know what the "real size" of the object is, and after taking into account the *background* the object appears on. There are other clues your brain uses, too, even though you are often unaware of what these clues are.

Linear Perspective

Look at Fig. 8.19. Notice that all the lines seem to meet at a point right in the center of the drawing. Figure 8.20 shows part of the same sort of illusion, but something new has been added. The three cylinders are actually the same size. But the cylinder on the far right appears more than twice as large as the cylinder

on the far left. Can you use the lines on the drawing to explain why?

The apparent *convergence* of parallel lines as they approach the horizon is called **linear perspective**—one of the cues your brain uses to judge distance.

Question: If an artist paints a scene that lacks linear perspective, does this mean the artist actually does not *see* perspective in his or her own visual world? How could you *prove* experimentally that your answer is correct?

Convergence

Humans are essentially two-dimensional animals, bound to those parts of the surface of the earth our two feet can walk on. We judge distances rather well—if they are no greater than those we can walk or run or ride. But we judge heights rather poorly, at least in comparison with animals such as birds and fish that move readily through all three dimensions of space.

When you look at something in the distance, both your eyes point straight ahead. When you look at something up close, however, both of your eyes turn inward, toward your nose (see Fig. 8.21). The amount of strain this **convergence** creates in your eye muscles is an index of how far away the object is.

To judge how *distant* an object is, you have merely to let your eyes converge and notice the strain on your eye muscles. But to judge *height*, you usually have to move your head up and down or crane your neck. For most of us, the neck muscles are poorer judges of distance than are the eye muscles.

Fig. 8.22 *Les Promenades d'Euclide*, a 1955 painting by the Belgian artist René Magritte. See text.

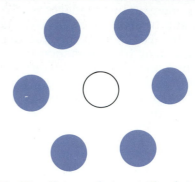

Fig. 8.23 The distance between the dots is actually the same as the size of each dot.

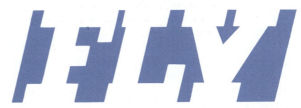

Fig. 8.25 Do you see a word or five odd-shaped blue objects?

SHADOW SHADOW

Fig. 8.24 The word *shadow* on the right is actually made up of "shadows" of the word on the left.

Question: Why are airplane pilots usually better at judging heights than are non-pilots?

Aerial Perspective and Texture

Anyone who has grown up in a smog-ridden city knows there often are days when you can't see more than a block or two away. But there are parts of the world still blessedly free from this aerial pollution. In some of our deserts, for instance, the air is often so clear that the visibility is practically unlimited. The city dweller who first visits these regions is sometimes shocked at how badly she or he actually judges distances in clean, fresh air. A mountain peak that appears to be no more than 5 or 10 miles away may actually be more than 50 miles down the road.

The more hazy and indistinct a remote object seems to you, the farther away it appears to be. Psychologists refer to this "distance cue" as the **aerial perspective** of an object (see Fig. 8.22).

Texture is a distance cue very similar to aerial perspective. In real life, the texture of objects near to you is more detailed than the texture of distant objects. Over time, you learn to use texture as a cue. Notice in Fig. 8.22 that you can see the bricks or stones in near buildings, but not in distant ones.

Light and Shadow

Often we use the *lightness* of an object to give us some notion of its size or distance from us.

Plate 9 The purple-blue to yellow color solid on the left is viewed from the green side. The yellow to purple-blue range on the right side is viewed from the red side. (Munsell Color, Macbeth Division of Kollmorgen Corporation.)

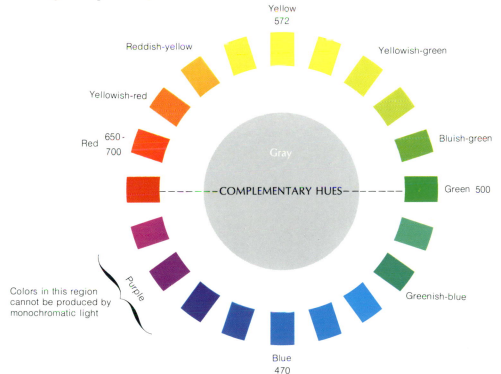

Plate 10 The color circle illustrates the facts of color and color light mixture. The color names and their corresponding wavelengths (in nanometers) are given along the outside of the circle. Complementary colors are those colors opposite each other in the circle (such as reddish-yellow and greenish-blue); they will result in gray when mixed. The mixing of any two other wavelengths gives us an intermediate color. By proper mixing of three wavelengths equidistant in the circle (such as blue, green and reddish-yellow), we can produce all color sensations. (From Bourne and Ekstrand, 1985.)

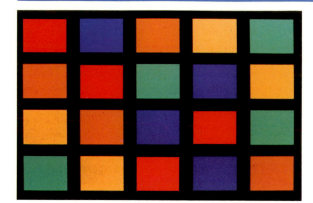

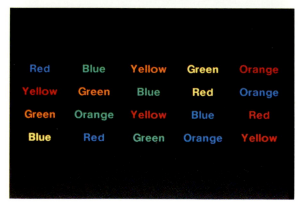

Plate 11 These three illustrations reproduce the Stroop effect. The first illustration is a series of colored squares. Starting at the upper left corner, quickly call out the *names* of the colors in sequence. For the second illustration, simply read the names of the colors *as printed*. For the third illustration, quickly *name the color in which the word is printed.* You will probably find that the meaning of the stimuli interferes with direct perception of their physical characteristics.

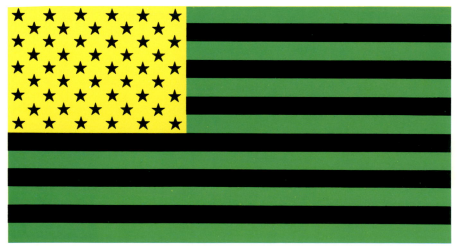

Plate 12 Stare at the center of this flag for about 30 seconds. Then look at a white wall or sheet of paper. You will see a negative after-image in the colors complementary to those shown here.

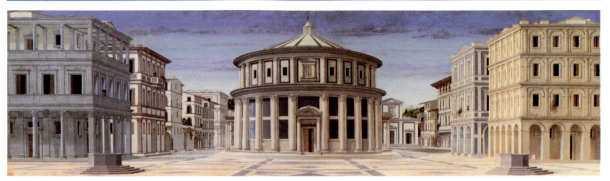

Plate 13 Ignoto sec. XV; Veduta di citta ideale. Urbino
Gallery Nazionale. (Art Resource.) This fifteenth century
painting of an ideal city illustrates the property of linear
perspective.

Plate 14 Vincent Van Gogh's "The Starry Night" (1889)
illustrates the painter's imperfect sensory perception. Look
at the concentric rings of color around the "starry lights."
(Oil on canvas, 29 × 36¼″ Collection, The Museum of
Modern Art, New York. Acquired through the Lillie P. Bliss
Bequest.)

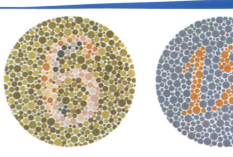

Plate 15 These two illustrations are from a series of color-blindness tests. In the left plate, people with normal vision see a number 6, while those with red-green color-blindness do not. Those with normal vision see a number 12 in the right plate; red-green blind people may see one number or none. These reproductions of color recognition texts cannot be used for actual testing. The examples are only representative of the total of 15 charts necessary for a complete color recognition examination. (American Optical Corporation from their AO Pseudo-Isochromatic Color Tests.)

Horse	Horse
Table	Table
Wheel	**Wheel**
Water	Water
Tiger	**Tiger**
Whale	Whale
Chair	Chair
Train	**Train**
Field	Field
Shark	Shark

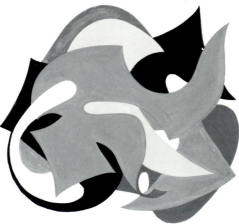

Plate 16 Look at the design on the cover of this book. A person with normal color vision would see all the colors. At the top of this panel, the cover design is reproduced as it might look to someone with red-green color-blindness; and in the middle as a person with yellow-blue color-blindness might see it. At the bottom is a black-and-white reproduction of the cover design as a totally color-blind person might see it.

Plate 17 The "serial position effect" described in chapter 15 predicts that, if you had to memorize the list of ten words at the left, you'd be more likely to remember those items at the beginning of the list (horse, table) and at the end of the list (field, shark) than items in the middle. However, if some of the middle items are printed in color (wheel, tiger, train), the serial position effect is counteracted by a "novelty effect," and you will remember the items printed in color more than those at the start and end of the list.

For reasons we still don't understand, dark objects often appear to be smaller than light-colored objects. For example, look at the 7 dots in Fig. 8.23. Although it doesn't look like it at first glance, the distance *between* the dots is exactly the same as the size of the dots themselves.

Sometimes we make judgments about the visual world from what we *don't* see, instead of from what we do see. Look at Fig. 8.24, a simple representation of the word "shadow." Notice that each of the six letters in this word is printed in full. Now look at the next word. Here there are no letters, just the shadows themselves. But look carefully. Doesn't your eye actually *see* the forms of the letters as if they were really there? And what about the five black figures in Fig. 8.25? Can you see the word "fly" spaced between the figures? And after you recognize the word "fly," can you perceive the drawing as just a collection of odd-shaped black figures? Why not?

You also make use of shadows in judging whether you are looking at a mountain or at the hole left when somebody dug up the mountain and carted it away. When you look at a photograph of a crater (see Fig. 8.26), you automatically make an assumption about how the sunlight is falling on the landscape. If you make the *wrong assumption*, then your brain will show you a hill instead of a crater.

Aerial perspective (AIR-ee-ull). Literally, the "way you see an object through the air." Fuzzy objects seem distant; clear (distinct) objects seem close.

Question: S.B. often mistook shadows for real objects. Why do you think this was the case?

Interposition

If one object seems to block another, you will usually perceive the "blocking" object as being closer to you than the object it masks. Look back at Fig. 8.22, a famous painting by the noted Belgian artist René Magritte. Notice how the conical tower in the foreground blocks your view of some of the buildings. And notice too how the buildings and trees in the lower part of the painting mask the buildings "behind them." Your mind uses these *interposition* cues to perceive distance rather readily.

This painting actually illustrates several of the distance cues we have already discussed. See if you can find examples of linear and aerial perspective, texture, and light and shadows (as well as interposition). How do these cues give "apparent depth" (that is, distance) to the painting?

Fig. 8.26 Light and shade as a cue for depth. Turn the book upside down and the crater turns into a hill.

Fig. 8.27 If the lights go on and off in rapid sequence—with a slight pause between lights 4 and 5—you will perceive the gray rectangle as being in front of the row of lights.

Fig. 8.28 Do you see an old woman or a young girl?

Fig. 8.29 A coin viewed on edge.

Question: Notice that the conical tower and the street in this painting are actually very similar triangles. How does the *context* of the other objects in the painting affect your perception of these two triangles?

Real and Apparent Motion

Motion can also be a cue to distance. Imagine you are riding in a car, looking out the window. You will see telephone poles flash by rapidly, but a cow in a distant meadow will move across your field of vision slowly. Objects (such as the cow) that seem to move *slowly* as you are moving rapidly will seem *distant*. However, the telephone poles will seem *near* because they move *rapidly*. They also momentarily block out objects "behind them," such as the cow.

Apparent motion can also be a cue to distance. Look at Fig. 8.27. Here you have eight light bulbs and a black rectangle. If you turned the bulbs on and off quickly in the order they

are numbered, you might perceive just one bulb moving from left to right. (This sort of "apparent movement" is best illustrated by the flashing lights on theater marquees.) Now imagine that you turned on the first four light bulbs in Fig. 8.26 in 1-2-3-4 order, then waited a second or two. Now you turn on 5-6-7-8 in sequence. The apparent movement of the lights might convince you that the row of bulbs continued *behind* the black rectangle. Thus, you would perceive the rectangle as being closer to you than the lights.

Now, imagine you are standing in a dark hallway. Some distance from you is a large, white globe suspended in air. As you first look, the globe is dimly illuminated from within. But as you continue watching, the globe grows brighter and brighter. If you have no other cues as to distance, you will perceive two different effects. First, the globe will seem to get *larger*. And second, the globe will seem to *move closer*— even though it hasn't really moved at all. The change in brightness gives rise to apparent movement, for you tend to see bright objects as being nearer than dim objects.

Expectancy

One of the principle laws of perception is this: *You see what you expect to see.* As you experience the world, you learn that objects typically grow brighter as they move closer to you. Thus, when you see an object growing brighter, you expect it to be moving closer to you. So you *perceive* it that way. Any clues you get from your environment that change your expectancies will also have a strong influence on your perceptual processes.

Keep that thought in mind as you look at Fig. 8.28. As you can see, it is a drawing of an *ugly old woman* with her chin buried in a fur coat. Look at it carefully and try to figure out what this old woman is thinking of.

The artist who drew the picture claims she is dreaming of her daughter. And if you inspect the drawing again, you will see the face of the old woman change into that of the daughter.

Several experimenters have shown this picture to groups of college students. If the students are told to expect a picture of an *old woman*, most of them discover the mother's face before finding the daughter's. But if the students are told they will see a drawing of a *young woman*, they tend to see the daughter's face easily, but often have trouble "finding" the picture of the mother.

Question: Were you "fooled" by the ending to the story that begins this chapter? If so, can you discover the "false clues" that gave you the wrong expectancy?

Constancies and Illusions

Expectancy is closely related to another perceptual principle, that of *constancy*. A knowledge of both principles may help you understand some of the visual *illusions* that you experience daily.

Imagine yourself in the same situation S.B. faced, when he gained sight at the age of 52. Before your operation, you crossed streets safely. You knew people would stop for you—but you could also judge the flow of traffic reasonably well by *listening* to it. You knew what a truck sounded like when it was 200 feet away, and what it sounded like when it was but 20 feet away and still moving rapidly. Now, sud-

Size constancy (KON-stan-see). Your brain gets a rough idea of the physical size of an object by noting how large a visual image the object casts on your retina. Generally speaking, the larger the visual image, the larger the object will be. However, an object very close to you will cast a much larger image on your retina than will the same object if it is far away from you. If the object is very familiar, your brain will interpret any change in the size of the retinal image as a change in the distance the object is from you. This is the principle of size constancy. If the object is unfamiliar, you may overestimate its size if it is up close, and underestimate its size if it is far away from you.

denly, you can *see*. When you *look* at that truck 200 feet away, it seems incredibly tiny, almost insignificant. Why? Because the truck's visual image on your retina is also incredibly small. As the truck moves rapidly toward you, the *size* of the image it casts on your retina grows by leaps and bounds. But would you see the truck as changing *position*? Why couldn't you perceive a stationary truck that was suddenly swelling up in *size* like a balloon?

Size Constancy

Like most sighted people, you learned long ago that trucks don't change size. So you *interpret* changes in the *apparent size* of objects like trucks as evidence that they (or you) are moving. Put another way, there is a relationship between the perceived size of an object and its perceived distance. As long as you have some clue as to how far an object is from you, the object will appear to be the same "real size," whether it casts a large or small image on your retina. We call this relationship between size and distance the principle of **size constancy**.

Size constancy does break down under certain conditions. First, if you don't have any cues as to the object's distance, you will often make mistakes about its real size. Unless, that is, the object is something familiar, such as a football or a pack of cigarettes. Then, *expectancy* (from past experience) will give you a clue as to the object's real size. Second, size constancy often fails when you look at objects from a great distance. If you view the objects below you from an airplane or the top of a tall building, they often look like "toys" rather than the real thing.

Shape Constancy

Look at Fig. 8.29, which is the same as one we showed you earlier in this chapter. Here's your old friend, the coin. And chances are, you

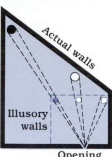

● Actual place and size of "smallest" man

● Illusory place and size of "smallest" man

○ Actual place and size of "medium" man

○ Illusory place and size of "medium" man

□ "Largest" man

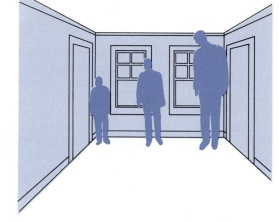

Fig. 8.30 The Ames "distorted room" as seen from the top (diagram) and from the front.

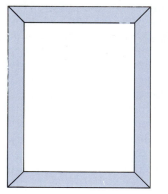

Fig. 8.31 The same picture frame head-on and at an angle of 45 degrees is no longer visually the same.

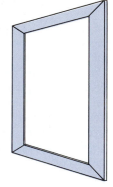

Fig. 8.32 The Mueller-Lyer illusion.

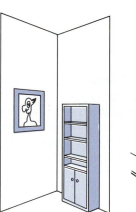

Fig. 8.33 The vertical line in the corner of the room is the same length as the vertical line that makes up the corner of the building. These two drawings make up a sort of "real-life Mueller-Lyer illusion."

still see it as a round coin turned away from you in space.

As objects rotate in space, or as you move around the objects, the actual image they cast on your retina changes dramatically. The tendency to perceive objects as *maintaining their known shape*, despite the image they project on the retina, is known as **shape constancy**.

Generally speaking, shape constancy is good when you have cues as to whether you're viewing the object straight on, or whether it is tilted or slanted in space. As Gibson pointed out, there are many such cues, including light and shadow, texture, and linear and aerial perspective. Shape constancy breaks down in extreme conditions, however, or when you lack sufficient cues to guess the object's orientation in space.

The Ames Distorted Room

Adelbert Ames, a U.S. psychologist who began his professional life as a painter, took advantage of *shape constancy* to produce a number of very amusing illusions that illustrate the Gestalt principles of perception. The best-known of these illusions is Ames's "distorted room," shown in Fig. 8.30.

When looked at head-on, the "distorted room" appears quite normal—until you see three people standing in the room. And then you know that something is very definitely wrong.

The windows in the room *look* square. In fact, the windows are really **trapezoids**, like the window frame on the right in Fig. 8.31. But your mind *assumes* windows ought to be rectangular, hence you "see" them as being rectangles.

In order to keep the windows looking like rectangles, your brain must produce *distance distortions* that make one of the men in the room look much larger than his smaller companions. Given the choice between preserving "good form" (the shape of the windows) or "size constancy" (the size of the men), your cortex typically votes in favor of good form.

Question: How does the Ames distorted-room illusion tend to confirm the Gestalt Law of Praegnanz?

Mueller-Lyer Illusion

Look at Fig. 8.32. This is the famous Mueller-Lyer illusion. Don't the two lines with the outward-pointing "V's" seem much longer than the

Shape constancy. The tendency to perceive the shape of an object as invariant (in-VER-rhee-ant) or unchanging, even when the shape of the image the object casts on your retina changes considerably.

Trapezoids (TRAP-ee-zoids). Four-sided figures with two sides that are parallel. In the drawing of the picture frame "tilted away from you" on this page, notice that the left and right sides of the frame are parallel, but the top and bottom sides are not. The picture frame—as viewed from this angle—is a trapezoid.

Diagonal (die-AG-oh-null). If you were standing straight up, then leaned over at an angle, your body would be diagonal to the floor. The "slant mark" (/) on the typewriter is a diagonal line.

two lines with the inward-pointing "V's"? Yet if you measure the lines in both these figures, you'll see they are exactly the same length.

Why does one line look longer than the other? Richard Gregory believes this illusion is based on your perception of corners (see Fig. 8.33). If you are reading this book indoors, look at one of the corners of the room you're in. Notice that the angles the wall makes with the floor or the ceiling form lines much like those in the figures with the outward-pointing "V's." If you are sitting outdoors, look at the corner of a building. You will see that the angles made by the roof and the ground are similar to the same lines in the figures with the inward-pointing "V's."

Question: It is rather simple to train a pigeon in a laboratory to peck at the shorter of two lines in order to get a bite of food. How might you use this procedure to test whether pigeons are as fooled by the Mueller-Lyer illusion as humans are?

Other Illusions

You seldom see an object *all by itself*. Instead, you almost always see an object in relationship to the other objects around it. In the Mueller-Lyer illusion, for example, the "V's" at the ends of the horizontal lines affect your perception of how long the lines are.

Now look at Fig. 8.34. Is the hat taller than it is wide? If you think so, take out a ruler and measure the distances.

The apparent straightness of a line can easily be affected by whatever objects the line seems to penetrate. In Fig. 8.35, the **diagonal** line crossing the two bars seems to be three disconnected lines. In fact, as you can determine by using a

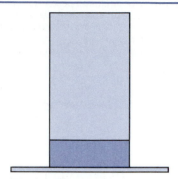

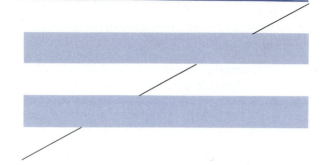

Fig. 8.34 Top hat illusion.

Fig. 8.35 Is the diagonal line straight?

Fig. 8.36 The "round culture" of the Zulus.

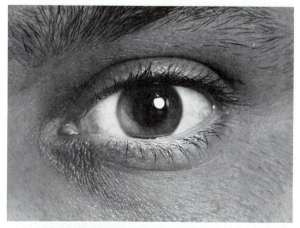

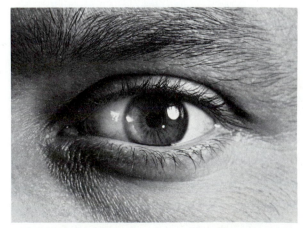

Fig. 8.37 Your pupil usually dilates (opens), as in the photo at the left, when you are looking at something of interest, and closes a bit, as at the right, when you are not.

ruler, the line is absolutely straight. Oddly enough, the illusion disappears for most people if they turn the drawing around so that the line is straight up and down.

Cultural Influences on Illusions

You grew up in a world of straight lines, corners, and sharp angles. But suppose you had lived as a child in an environment where straight lines were **taboo**? How would you perceive these illusions?

The answer is—you probably wouldn't see some of them at all. The Zulus—a tribe of primitive people in South Africa—live in what Richard Gregory calls a "circular culture." Their huts are round mounds with circular doors (see Fig. 8.36). They plow their fields in curved lines, and even their toys and tools lack straight edges. When shown the Mueller-Lyer illusion, the typical Zulu native sees one line as being only very slightly longer than the other. Some illusions, such as the "top hat" drawing, affect the Zulu hardly at all.

Pupil Responses

As the illusions we've just described suggest, perception is an exceptionally complex process. From the "information-processing" point of view, visual inputs are processed at various stages as they work their way up to your brain from your eyes. However, once you have perceived something, your mind can send commands back to the lower centers (and your eyes). These "downward commands" affect what you perceive *next*. Now that we have discussed simple eye-to-brain illusions, let's look at some complex perceptions that are created *after* your mind has made its initial response to a visual input.

One of the major purposes of your visual system is to gird you for *action*. When you walk out of a darkened movie theater, your pupils decrease in size rapidly to keep you from being blinded by the sudden increase in light. Your brain didn't have to *learn* how to make your pupils close under these conditions—the response is *innate*. And at dusk, when the sunlight dims, your pupils automatically open up or *dilate*. The wider your pupils open, the more light comes through and the better you can see and react to objects in your visual environment. Again, this response is determined by your genes, not by previous learning.

Your pupils also dilate when you look closely at some object, even though there is no change

Taboo (tab-BOO). Sometimes spelled "tabu." Any object or behavior that is prohibited because it is illegal or immoral. The most common form, found in almost all cultures, is the incest taboo—the strong belief that you are not supposed to have sexual experiences with close relatives.

in illumination. The harder you stare at the object, the wider your pupils will open (see Fig. 8.37). *What* you choose to inspect closely, of course, is determined primarily by your past experience. So *this* type of pupil dilation is influenced by what you have learned about the world.

Psychologist Eckhard Hess made use of this information to test a hunch of his. Hess reasoned that people would stare *more* at something they were really interested in than at something they disliked. So he showed pictures of many different objects to the college students he used as subjects in his experiments.

Hess found that women typically had much larger pupil openings when he showed them pictures of babies or nude males than when he showed these women pictures of landscapes or nude females. Men, on the other hand, usually had wider pupils when shown pictures of nude females than when they were shown photographs of babies, landscapes, or nude males.

Hess's research suggests you can often discover a person's *real* interests simply by noting when the person becomes "wide-eyed."

Question: Is the tendency for women to become "wide-eyed" when looking at babies or nude males learned, innate, or both? How might you prove your answer is correct?

Visual Suppression

Under certain very special conditions, your mind can be forced to *choose* between two entirely different visual inputs.

Imagine a large black box with two eyeholes in one side. There is a wooden partition inside the box that divides it in half. Thus, when you look through the holes, your left eye sees a different scene than does your right eye. How would your mind handle this odd situation?

Generally speaking, you will make one of two responses when faced with conflicting visual inputs. Most of the time your nervous system simply *suppresses* or rejects one of the pictures and *concentrates* on the other. But on rare occasions, your cortex may *combine* the two inputs into one.

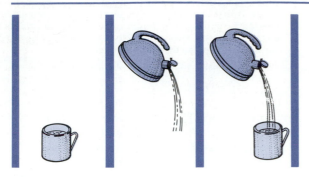

Fig. 8.38 The teapot pouring liquid and the teacup can be fused visually so that the tea seems to flow into the cup.

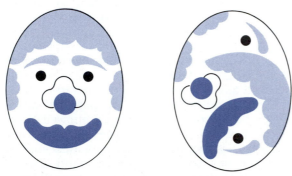

Fig. 8.39 Infants tested in Fantz's apparatus looked at the simple face longer than they did at the design with randomly placed facial features.

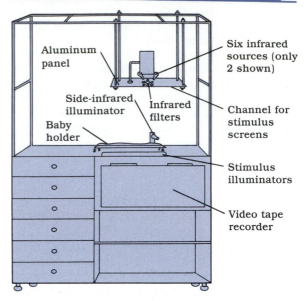

Fig. 8.40 Drawing of Haith's apparatus. Infrared lights provide illumination for recording of image of the eye via infrared TV camera onto videotape. Stimulus illuminators light stimulus screen above baby holder so that a baby, lying in the holder, sees only the screen and stimulus spray painted on it. TV camera records through screen.

If we show a different scene to your left eye than to your right, which scene will you suppress? If your vision is clearer in one eye than in the other, you will almost always pick the scene that you see best. But if both your eyes are in good shape, you face a **dilemma**.

If your left eye is looking at a cup, while your right eye is looking at a teapot that is pouring liquid from its spout, your mind may actually *fuse* the two scenes together so that you see a pot pouring tea into a cup (see Fig. 8.38). If one of your eyes sees a baby hanging in mid-air, while the other sees a woman holding out empty arms, your brain may superimpose one scene on the other so that you see the woman holding the child.

But suppose the two pictures are so different they can't be fused? Then you typically concentrate on whichever scene you find *more interesting*, and suppress the other scene almost completely. In many cases this suppression takes place so rapidly, you are not aware you are being shown two different objects or photographs.

Research suggests you are more likely to suppress unpleasant or frightening scenes than you are to block out pleasant or stimulating scenes.

Question: Suppose you need to determine whether a group of workers has unconscious prejudices about female supervisors. How might you use photographs of male and female supervisors—presented in the "black box" apparatus—to help determine the workers' underlying attitudes?

The Development of Perception

You are *born* with the tendency to suppress some types of threatening visual inputs. But *what* you find threatening is, of course, determined by your past experience. These facts bring us back to *nature-nurture problem* mentioned earlier in this chapter. There are some aspects of perception that appear so early after birth that they can be considered *primarily* innate. And there are other parts of the perceptual process that emerge only when the infant has had a fair amount of "worldly experience." As we discuss this issue in detail, however, you should keep the following two points in mind: First, infants begin to learn about the world around them *even before the infants are born.* And second, all learning is based on innate responses the infants have available at birth. Perception, then—like all other parts of human experience—is truly multi-determined.

Innate Aspects of Perception

Al Yonas of the University of Minnesota's Institute of Child Development believes that many aspects of visual perception are controlled by the child's genetic blueprint. Yonas has shown that 3-week-old infants will blink and recoil slightly from a black triangle moving toward them—even when no physical contact occurs. However, these same babies will be unresponsive when the triangle moves away from them. Yonas also notes that early visual development tends to be better in female infants, those who are above average in size, and those born after their due dates. These facts are better explained in terms of genetic inheritance than in terms of early visual experience.

Face Perception in Infants

Recent research suggests that, just an hour or so after birth, infants will mimic the facial expressions of adults (see Chapter 18 for details). This work indicates there is something rather special about the human face—at least from an infant's point of view.

Look at Fig. 8.39. One drawing is that of a face with the nose, eyes, and other features in their proper places. The other drawing has the same elements, but they are oddly scrambled. Now imagine a very young infant lying comfortably on her or his back looking up at these figures. What do you think the baby would spend more time looking at—the normal face, or the scrambled one?

Psychologist Robert L. Fantz photographed the eye movements of young babies. The infants he measured spent much more time looking at the normal than at the scrambled face. This finding suggests children have innate response patterns that allow them to recognize what the human face looks like.

Fantz also found that babies prefer looking at simple round objects rather than at two-dimensional drawings of the same objects. Fantz believes infants may have an *innate appreciation of depth.* He points out, however, that his experimental results may also mean that babies learn about faces and depths very early in their lives.

Visual Processing in Infants

Marshall M. Haith and his colleagues at the University of Denver have made extensive studies of the ways in which infants learn to process visual inputs during the first weeks of life (see Fig. 8.40). According to Haith, a four-week-old child is not mature enough to *process* such "complex visual stimulus patterns" as the human face. Therefore, very young infants gaze *away* from their mother's face about 80 percent of the time, and *fixate* on her face only about 20 percent of the time. Even when the four-week-old child does gaze directly at the mother, the infant tends to fixate mostly at the *edge* of her face. Haith and his colleagues report that four-week-old infants fixated on the *center* of the mother's face (her eyes, nose, mouth) but 22 percent of the time.

By seven weeks of age, however, the normal infant has learned how to "process" faces. So the child gazes directly *at* the mother's face almost 90 percent of the time the child can see her. And when looking at her face, the infant fixates on the *center* of the face rather than the edges. Haith also reports seven-week-old infants looked at the mother's *eyes* almost twice as much as at her nose or mouth.

Haith believes newborn infants are innately attracted to *edges* or contours of objects in their visual world. By seven weeks of age, however, the baby is sufficiently experienced to begin to perceive the human face as a unified "whole" rather than as a "collection of parts." We call this "unified whole" a perceptual **schema**.

Dilemma (die-LEM-mah). A problem that has two or more equally good solutions. To be "caught on the horns of a dilemma" is the same thing as being "caught between the devil and the deep blue sea," in that any solution you pick is equally good—and equally bad.

Schema (SKEEM-mah). You recognize an apple as being an *apple* whether you see the fruit from above, from the side, or cut in half. You also recognize it as an *apple* whether it is green, yellow, or red—or even just a black-and-white drawing in a book. "Appleness" is the "schema" or set of related percepts that allows you to recognize the apple under these various conditions, but may also include strategies for relating to or responding to apples.

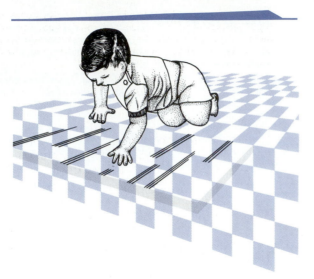

Fig. 8.41 The "visual cliff."

Haith notes that a nine-week-old infant is more likely to gaze at the mother's face when she is *talking* to the child than when she isn't. But Haith also points out the baby is more likely to gaze at the mother's *eyes* when she is talking than at the mother's *mouth*. Although Haith doesn't say so, it seems likely that the sound of the mother's voice speeds up the infant's visual development—perhaps by soothing the child's fears. The infant responds to the soothing sounds by gazing at the mother's eyes more often. The mother usually interprets increased "eye gazing" as a sign the child is "paying attention." Thus, she talks to the child—and cradles the infant—more frequently. Whatever the case, Haith's research suggests that visual perception in the human infant is as strongly influenced by auditory and skin-receptor inputs as it is by visual stimuli.

Question: Haith's research seems to contradict Fantz's belief that infants are born with the ability to recognize the human face. How might you resolve this contradiction? (Hint: How old might Fantz's infants have been when he tested them?)

The Visual Cliff

Another intriguing bit of evidence concerning the innate properties of perception comes from a series of experiments pioneered by Eleanor Gibson. Although she frequently collabo-

rated on research with her husband, James J. Gibson, she is one of America's best-known perceptual psychologists in her own right.

One day several years ago, Eleanor Gibson found herself eating a picnic meal on the rim of the Grand Canyon. Looking straight down into that deep and awesome river bed, she began to worry about the safety of the children around her. Would a very young child be able to perceive the enormous drop-off at the edge of the cliff? Or would the child go toddling right over the edge if no adult were around to restrain the child?

Gibson was really asking two very important questions about perception. First, are babies born with an *innate ability to perceive depth*? And second, do infants have a *built-in fear mechanism* that would make them retreat from sharp drop-offs even without having been trained to do so?

Once Gibson had returned to her laboratory at Cornell University, she attempted to answer both these questions. And to do so, she designed an artificial *visual cliff* on which she could test infants safely (see Fig. 8.41).

Running down the middle of the apparatus was a raised plank of wood painted in a checkerboard pattern. To one side of the plank was a sharp drop-off. On the other side was a normal "floor" an inch or so below the center plank. The entire apparatus was covered with sturdy glass so the infant could see the cliff but could not fall off it.

When an infant was tested, the child was put on the center board and allowed to explore freely. Very few of the infants crawled off onto the "cliff" side, although most of them freely moved onto the "floor" side. Even when the child's mother stood at the side of the apparatus and attempted to coax the child to crawl out over the "cliff," most infants refused to do so. Instead, they began to cry loudly. If the mother stood on the "floor" side of the box, however, the infant would crawl toward her willingly.

A variety of newborn animals—lambs, kittens, puppies, and rats—have been tested on the visual cliff too. For the most part, these animals showed an immediate perceptual awareness of the "dangers" of the cliff. Gibson concludes that many higher species have behavioral mechanisms built into their brains at birth that tend to protect them from the dangers of falling from high places.

However, not all infants, nor all species, react to the visual cliff as did the babies in Gibson's studies. Nancy Rader of U.C.L.A. points out there are great individual differences between infants in their response to the visual cliff. Some babies seem to be *visually oriented*. These infants recoil with fear from the sight of the cliff. Others tend to be *touch oriented*. These children apparently trust their skin senses more than their eyes, and crawl right out on the glass covering the cliff as long as it offers firm support. Thus, the issue of whether infants are born with an innate fear of heights is far from settled.

Developmental Handicaps of the Blind

Some innate visual tendencies are so subtle we tend to overlook them—except when we observe the development of the child who is born blind. In her book *Insights from the Blind*, Selma Fraiberg says the blind youngster has two severe problems to overcome: (1) learning to recognize his or her parents from sounds alone, and (2) acquiring a healthy *self-concept* or perceptual "self-schema."

Fraiberg notes that normal eight-month-olds will reach out their arms the moment they hear their mother's voice—*anticipating* the sight of the parent even before she appears in the child's view. The blind baby does not show this reaching response until much, much later. The blind infant *hears* and *feels*, but cannot "integrate" these sensory experiences very well to form a unified schema of *mother*. Vision, then, is particularly important to a youngster because sight allows the child to pull the other sensory modalities together in her or his mind.

Blind children are frequently retarded in their speech development. They talk later and more poorly than do sighted children. Much of this speech retardation seems due to their slowness in recognizing the *permanence* of objects in the world around them (see Chapter 18). Blind children also have problems "imagining" things while young and do not identify readily with a doll or with a character in a story their mother reads to them. And they often do not learn the correct use of "I" and "you" until they are five or six.

Fraiberg concludes blind youngsters cannot *picture* themselves as objects that exist separate from their environments. And since they cannot *visualize* themselves as independent entities, they are slow to develop any real notion of "self."

In brief, *seeing* yourself may be the easiest and most natural way of building up a perceptual schema of your own *self*.

Congenitally (kon-JEN-it-tally). From the Latin words meaning "to bring forth." A "congenital" defect is one present at birth. The defect may be innate (caused by genetic damage) or may be caused by trauma the infant experiences in the womb or during the birth process.

Innate or Learned?

The question of which aspects of vision are learned and which are innately determined may never be entirely solved. For instance, while children blind from birth are sometimes slow to develop social and verbal skills, they usually are able to move around in the world fairly readily. Indeed, according to Barbara Landau and her associates at the University of Pennsylvania, **congenitally** blind children perceive *physical space* (as distinct from "visual space") about as well as sighted children do.

Landau and her group tested Kelli, a 2 1/2-year-old girl who was blind from birth, on a variety of tasks. When Kelli was allowed to explore a room on her own, she could thereafter take the shortest path from any spot to any spot in the room. Landau and her colleagues believe Kelli could "perceive" the physical layout of the room even if she couldn't "see" the room visually.

Apparently, then, infants are born with an innate ability to *create three dimensional space in their minds*. But even with this inborn tendency, they still need "worldly experience" if they are to learn to perceive "objects in space."

Question: How might *auditory* perception help a child like Kelli develop a perception of physical space?

Auditory Communication

More than 80 percent of all research in the field of perception deals with vision. In consequence, the other sensory modalities have been somewhat neglected. Much of the non-visual research is on auditory perception. The remainder deals with the so-called "minor senses." We have already described some of the recent studies on the perception of taste and smell in Chapter 6. Experiments on the perception of "touch" deal mostly with pain, which we will save for a later chapter. There *is* good work going on in these other fields. But studies on the "minor senses" tend to be focused either on *sensory processes* (as opposed to complex perceptions) or on solving practical problems. How to make

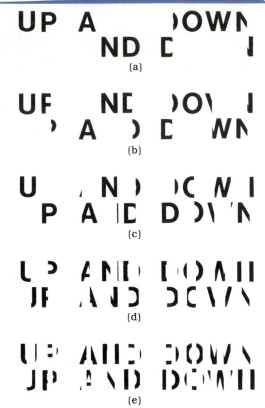

Fig. 8.42 "Chopped speech." The top line in each figure shows the sounds presented to the left ear. The bottom line shows the sounds presented to the right ear. The sounds alternate between ears, giving a "chopped" effect. From Neisser, U. *Cognitive Psychology* (Englewood Cliffs, N.J.: Prentice-Hall). Copyright © 1966 Prentice-Hall, Inc. Reprinted by permission.

food taste better or perfumes more attractive are examples of this kind of research.

Much of the research on *auditory perception* has a practical orientation, as well. The corporations that make music-reproduction systems obviously benefit from learning how people hear musical sounds. Many of these companies either have their own laboratories, or they support auditory research performed at universities and private laboratories. The telephone companies too have a long-standing interest in audition, as does the military. Indeed, several of the studies we will discuss in this section either were performed at Bell Labs (owned by AT&T) or were supported by grants from some military organization.

Because one of the main functions of our ears is to let us hear what other people are saying to us, much of the research on auditory perception has traditionally involved *communication*. As such, this work has often been classified under such titles as "language learning" or "cognitive processes." We will discuss cognition in the next chapter, and language learning in Chapter 18. To set the stage for our coverage of cognitive processes, however, let's look at **speech perception** in some detail.

Speech Perception

In discussing visual perception, we tended to ignore a very important variable—*time*. Generally speaking, you see a circle "all at once." And unless you or the circle is moving, your perception of the circle doesn't change much from one second to another. But think of speech. When a friend *says* something to you, you receive the verbal inputs (words) one at a time, in *temporal sequence*. Often, you won't know the *meaning* of what your friend is trying to say until he or she has completed at least a sentence or two. Thus, you not only have to *recognize* the words as they hit your ear, you must also have some means of *storing* the first words until you hear the ones at the end of the sentence.

Speech perception differs from other types of auditory perception in another way too. When you listen to a baby crying, or the wail of a police siren, you typically are trying to discover two things: *what* (or *who*) is making the sounds, and *where* the sounds are coming from. Thus, when you hear these types of sounds, your nervous system attempts to detect any "special features" the sounds have that might identify the source and its location. When you listen to speech, though, you usually know who's talking and where the person is. What you're trying to perceive is the *meaning* of the message the speaker is trying to pass along to you. And to accomplish this chore, you must somehow identify the *basic units of speech* and put these units together into words and concepts.

The Syllable
Several types of research suggest the basic unit of speech perception is the **syllable**. For example, consider a study reported by A.W.F. Huggins in 1964. Huggins used a technique called "chopped speech." First, he *recorded* someone saying a sentence aloud. Suppose the person said, "Up and down the avenue, the hungry lion roamed." Then Huggins had his subjects listen to the recording over special ear-

phones. These special earphones allowed Huggins to present sounds to *either* the left or right ear, but *not to both ears simultaneously.*

While his subjects listened to the recording of the sentence, Huggins switched the sounds back and forth between earphones at regular intervals. This switching technique effectively "chopped" the speech into small "units of sound." The frequency with which Huggins switched the sounds determined the *size* of the "unit." In order to understand the sentence, the subjects had to *combine the units in their minds to make words.*

Figure 8.42 shows *visually* what Huggins actually did with *sounds.* Please look at this figure carefully before you read further.

When the "chopped units of sound" contained at least one syllable of speech (Fig. 8.42a), the subjects had no trouble understanding. When the units contained less than a full syllable (Fig. 8.42c), the subjects had difficulty comprehending what was being said. Apparently, when you listen to people talk, you search for syllables and put these basic units together to make words.

Question: Huggins reports the recording became understandable again at very rapid rates of alternation (Fig. 8.42e). Why do you think this was so? (Hint: Could you get the entire message by reading *just the top line* of Fig. 8.42a or 8.42c? What about Fig. 8.42e?)

Context Effects

The syllable may be the basic unit of speech perception, but the *context* in which a sound occurs affects how you "hear" the sound. Proof for this statement comes from a 1970 *Scientific American* article by R.M. and R.P. Warren.

Suppose you heard the following sound: Someone coughs and immediately says "eel." We can represent the "coughing" sound as *. Therefore, what the subjects actually heard was "*eel." Chances are, if *eel was *all* you heard, you would describe the sound accurately as "cough-eel." But now, suppose you listened to a recording of one of the following four sentences:

1. It was found that the *eel was on the axle.
2. It was found that the *eel was on the shoe.
3. It was found that the *eel was on the orange.
4. It was found that the *eel was on the table.

Warren and Warren played tape-recorded versions of these four sentences to their subjects. The Warrens report that, almost uniformly, the

listeners *heard* the word "wheel" in the first sentence rather than "cough-eel." And, as you might guess, they heard the word "heel" in the second sentence, "peel" in the third, and "meal" in the fourth. What they *never* heard was "cough-eel."

The Warrens then played a recording of another sentence to their subjects: "The state governors met with their respective le/gis/latures convening in the capital city." This time, the Warrens cut out the syllable /gis/ from "legislatures" and substituted a cough. When the subjects heard the sentence, however, they were unaware of the missing syllable. Indeed, they reported the word "legislatures" was pronounced as clearly as any other word in the sentence. The Warrens then informed the subjects that a sound was missing from the sentence and asked the subjects to find it. The subjects did report (for the first time) hearing the cough. But they insisted the cough *co-existed* with the syllable "gis," not that the cough *replaced* the syllable!

Question: Suppose a friend said to you, "Howja liketah go tahshow thuh seevnin?" What *features* about this "stream of speech" would help you analyze what your friend actually meant? And how would *context* help you decide?

Theories of Speech Perception

There are many theories that attempt to explain *how* you make sense out of spoken words. Some of these theories emphasize the "special features" certain speech sounds have. For example, the "s" always has a hissing sound in English. Other theories focus on "hypothesis making." That is, these theories assume you "input" certain sounds and then try to *guess* what they mean. But most of the newer viewpoints tend to take the "information-processing" approach we described at the beginning of this chapter.

In truth, the information-processing theory deals more with *cognition* than with *percep-*

tion. According to this viewpoint, we should not speak of visual "perception" or speech "perception." Rather, we should talk about visual "cognition" and speech "cognition."

The older theories viewed sensation, perception, and memory as *separate psychological processes*. The information-processing approach insists these are all part of a unitary *cognitive process*. The importance of this shift from "perceptual theories" to a "cognitive theory" will become evident when you read the next chapter.

Summary

1 There are four major theories of visual perception: the **Gestalt** approach, the **Gibsonian** viewpoint, the **empirical** position, and the **information-processing** approach.

2 Gestalt psychologists believe your brain was "hard-wired" to perceive the world in certain ways. Thus, your brain **imposes** innate perceptual concepts (such as roundness) on the world.

3 James Gibson believed perception is **innate** and **direct**. You **see the world as it actually is**, because visual stimuli are rich in sensory cues that tell your brain what the objects actually look like.

4 The empirical approach states that you **learn** to perceive through experience. Thus, empirically speaking, **perception = sensory inputs + memories**.

5 The **information-processing approach** holds that inputs are highly processed before they reach your cortex. Special nerve cells **detect critical features** of visual inputs and pass this patterned information along to your cortex. Perception, therefore, is an indivisible part of **cognition**.

6 The simplest type of visual information is **contours**, or a sudden change in lightness/darkness. Contours give **shape** to objects perceived visually.

7 The Gestalt **Law of Praegnanz** states that you tend to perceive shapes or figures as the simplest or **best possible form** they could take. The circle is the best possible visual form.

8 **Figure-ground** relationships have a strong influence on perception. You tend to see **salient** objects as "figure" rather than as "background."

9 **Ambiguous figures** show **perspective reversal**.

10 You tend to group things together perceptually according to the Gestalt principles of **proximity**, **closure**, **continuity**, and **similarity**.

11 Humans who lose their sight in childhood but regain it as adults often have severe problems adjusting.

12 **Linear perspective**, **convergence**, **aerial perspective**, **texture**, **light and shadow**, **interposition**, and **real and apparent motion** give you clues that allow your brain to perceive visual distance.

13 **Expectancy** has a strong influence on perception. For the most part, **you see what you expect to see**.

14 **Size constancy** and **shape constancy** are the tendencies to see objects as maintaining proper size and shape despite changes in the image they cast on the retina.

15 Your pupils open wider when you look at something interesting than when you look at something boring.

16 When your two eyes are shown different scenes, your mind may **suppress** one of the scenes, or it may **fuse** the two together to make a "Gestalt."

17 Some aspects of visual perception occur so soon after birth they seem *primarily* determined by your genes.

18 Three-week-old infants tend to look away from their mothers' faces because they are not mature enough to have developed a **perceptual schema** of the mother. Nine-week-old babies are experienced enough to gaze directly at the mother's eyes and mouth.

19 Some (but not all) infants will avoid a **visual cliff**.

20 **Blind children** are slow to develop language and a **self-concept**, but do seem to have an innate appreciation of **physical space**.

21 **Speech perception** is the study of how humans comprehend spoken language. Unlike most visual perception, speech perception always involves **temporal sequencing** of inputs and **memory**.

22 The **syllable** is the basic unit of speech perception. However, the **context** in which syllables are heard strongly influences your perception of them.

(Continued from page 193.)

The last of the male passengers came out of the little airport waiting room sweating profusely and shaking his head. "Bunch of bloody nonsense," the man muttered to himself as he passed by the elegant figure of the Laforan Minister of Science and Technology.

Freddie glumly watched the man depart. They had held the passengers of the special Paris jet in a quarantine waiting room, letting them pass one by one through the office where Professor Mann had inspected their eyes. Mann had agreed to signal Freddie if the tests detected the Snake, but no signal had come.

And now the waiting room was empty, save for a number of attractive but overdressed young women and one rather forlorn-looking matron cradling a baby in her arms. Freddie was confident the pretty women were girl friends of the munitions dealers. The matron was probably a wife of one of the dealers—although why a man would bring a wife and child to Lafora on a business trip, Freddie wasn't sure.

Freddie sighed. It seemed certain that Dr. Mann's tests had failed him—and failed the Republic of Lafora as well. The former fault he could tolerate. The latter came close to treason, and he mentioned this point to the U.S. Professor.

"What have you done, and why didn't it work?" Freddie demanded.

Mann looked annoyed at the Minister's bluntness. "First I showed a series of drawings to each man and measured the size of his pupils while he was watching. One of the drawings was of a snake. I had thought that our friend the assassin would show a larger pupil size to this drawing than to any other. Three of the men did so, but they failed the second test."

"Which was . . . ?"

"A suppression test. I have a variety of drawings—a pile of money, guns, airplanes, a picture of your President, a number of animals, and a snake striking at something with dripping fangs. I had the men look into my little black box that shows one drawing to the person's left eye, another to the right eye. And then I simply asked them to report what they saw. I figured most of the men would suppress the image of the snake, since most people are afraid of snakes."

Freddie snorted inelegantly. "But wouldn't the Snake see through your little tricks?"

"Perhaps, although I figured that, at the very least, he'd hesitate or be a little confused. But every man on the plane suppressed the picture of the snake without a moment's hesitation."

"And so your oh-so-scientific tests have failed," Freddie said glumly.

"No, Freddie, we're not through yet. There are still people in the waiting room."

Freddie looked around. "Just women and children, my dear Professor. We might as well let them go."

"You'll do nothing of the kind. Send them along for the eye checks, or their boy friends are going to be rather suspicious, don't you think?"

Freddie paused to consider the matter. As he did so, the matron approached them hesitantly and spoke to Freddie. "Excuse me, sir, my little boy is not feeling well. I'd like to get some warm milk for him and change his diaper. I wonder if you would allow us to go on through to the ladies' room?"

Before Freddie could respond, Professor Mann said loudly, "Right after you have your eyes checked, Madam. Part of the health inspection, you know. Now if you'll just look into this black box and tell me what you see . . ."

"Of course," the matron said, "if you'll promise to hurry."

The woman turned to Freddie and handed him the infant, which immediately set up a lusty bawling. Freddie's nose crinkled at the moist little bundle he had been handed, and he held the child clumsily and with obvious distaste. "Hurry it up, will you?" he said loudly to the Professor.

"Here's the first picture. What do you see?"

The matron leaned back a bit. "It's a gun of some kind," she said. "I don't approve of guns, you know."

"And how about this second picture?"

The matron glanced into

the eyeholes in the black box, then leaned forward a bit. "Why, it's a snake—a big, black, ugly snake."

Freddie glanced up immediately. The Professor smiled at him with wide-open eyes.

"And now we'll try another test entirely. When I say 'Now,' I want you to look into the apparatus and tell me as quickly as you can what you see. All right?"

"Certainly," said the matron demurely, as Professor Mann adjusted the slides inside the box.

"Now."

The woman leaned forward to look. She paused for several seconds, then responded. "That's odd, very odd indeed. I seem to see two things at once. First I see that snake again, and then I see a picture of the Laforan President, and then . . . then I see the snake biting the President. Now why would I see something like that?"

Freddie knew perfectly well why. He moved the infant to one arm and signaled vigorously with the other. Two large guards swooped down on them at once.

"Arrest this woman and search her baggage carefully," he told the guards.

General Chambro hurried up to them, a worried look on his big, round face. "Freddie, you've gone mad! This woman can't be the Snake!"

"How can you be sure, if you don't know what the Snake looks like?" the Professor asked, as the guards removed the matron from the scene.

"Yes, my dear General," Freddie said, a smile on his face. "I'll bet you a month's pay that Professor Mann has snared the Snake for us. The perceptual tests are posi-

tive."

"Perceptual tests be damned," said the General loudly. "Killing is a man's business, and everybody knows that the Snake is a man . . ."

"And that's why nobody ever caught her," replied Professor Mann. "She gave you a beautiful illusion to fool yourselves with. Down through history, the snake has always been a symbol of masculine sexual power and ruthlessness. Take the primitive tribe that I had hoped to visit, for instance. The chief warrior has a snake carved on the staff he carries. And if you look closely at those gold buttons that cover your uniform, General, you'll find the snake symbol on them all."

The General inspected his buttons, then frowned.

Professor Mann continued. "But of course the Snake did give you one clue to her identity—isn't poison a woman's weapon? Or was it just your minds she was attempting to poison?"

Freddie grinned, the General sputtered in protest, and Professor added a footnote. "I'll offer one more suggestion. Look through those baby things very closely. What more unlikely place to carry snake venom than in a child's rattle?"

A few moments later the guards reported that they had found a tiny hypodermic needle and a small bottle of white liquid inside the bottle of milk that the woman carried.

General Chambro was beside himself with happiness. He embraced Professor Mann in a huge bear hug, then hurried off to tend to his nation's security.

"He smells a promotion, I'm sure," said Freddie caus-

tically.

"Helping catch the Snake won't hurt your image any either, now will it, Freddie?"

"My dear Professor Mann, you speak with a forked tongue. But you are right, of course. The President will be very pleased . . ."

"And as for me?"

Freddie frowned. "Whatever do you mean?"

"What about those 'murderous savages' that I want to visit? If I can catch a snake for you, can't I manage to handle a few frightened primitives?"

"Well, my dear friend . . ."

The Professor interrupted. "You're still showing your prejudices, Freddie. You get very, very angry at all the whites in this world who judge a man by his skin color rather than by his true capabilities. Yet your view of women is just as biased and as distorted as their view of skin color. Isn't it about time you saw through some of your own illusions?"

Freddie smiled. "You psychologists! Ah well, I suppose that I might just mention to the President what your part in this afternoon's activities was. And our President is a very generous man indeed."

Freddie looked around and saw a couple of porters lounging near one of the doors.

"Here, you men! Get this equipment packed up again, then take it outside and put it back on the truck. Professor Mann will need it in the back country."

The American smiled softly. "Thanks, Freddie. I do appreciate your changing your mind. And now, how about that drink you promised me two hours ago?"

They walked off, arm in arm, headed for the cocktail lounge. The porters began to load up the heavy crates with the perceptual apparatus.

The boxes were covered with address labels. On the largest label of all, written in scrawling print, was:

Dr. Mary Ellen Mann
Department of Psychology
University of the Mid-West
USA

Recommended Readings

Coren, S., Porač, C., & Ward, L.M. (1984). *Sensation and perception*, 2d ed. New York: Academic Press.

Fraiberg, S. (1977). *Insights from the blind: Comparative studies of blind and sighted infants.* New York: Basic Books.

Gregory, R.L. (1977). *Eye and brain: The psychology of seeing*, 3rd ed. New York: World University Library.

Haith, M.M. (1980). *Rules that babies look by: The organization of newborn visual activity.* Hillsdale, N.J.: Erlbaum.

Maitlin, M.W. (1982). *Perception.* Boston: Allyn and Bacon.

Did You Know That...

- Thinking is a complex process that begins by "paying attention"?
- People tend to pay attention primarily to new inputs that have some significance to them?
- Although you can consciously attend to just one thing at a time, lower centers in your nervous system may attend to many inputs simultaneously?
- These lower centers sometimes respond to stimuli so weak you simply aren't conscious of them?
- When your conscious mind puts your body on "automatic pilot," these lower centers may execute overlearned habits (like driving) without your being aware of what they are doing?
- Your mind tends to create a "prototype" of concepts such as "dog" and "cat"?
- Sometimes you do poorly at problem solving because you can't break your "mental set" to perceive situations in the "same old way"?
- You tend to solve many problems faster than computers do because you use "rules of thumb" rather than exact formulas?
- If you were totally cut off from all inputs, you might not be able to "think" at all?

9

Cognition

"Cogito, Ergo Sum"

Philip Cassone laughed when they shut the door. This was going to be a cinch, no doubt about it. Imagine those crazy psychologists wanting to pay him $20 a day for just doing nothing!

Plus room and board!

He just might stay here for weeks, maybe for months. Let them go bankrupt, as far as he was concerned.

The bed Phil was lying on was narrow but comfortable. The long cardboard tubes into which his arms were stuck were annoying, but Phil was sure he could adjust to them with little difficulty.

The goggles covering his eyes let in some light. But he couldn't make out any details of the room he was in, except that the walls were painted black. He knew the room was small, though—maybe 6 feet wide by 10 feet long. Big enough to live in if you didn't move around very much, and the crazy psychologists were paying him for not moving.

All Phil could hear was the quiet, gentle, soothing whirr of an air-conditioning unit. Black as a tomb, that's what the room was.

Phil yawned, stretched a little on the narrow bed, and relaxed. A lead-pipe cinch, that's what it was going to be. He drifted gently off into sleep.

Some time later, Phil awoke. He had a moment of panic when he couldn't remember just where he was. But then he smiled and relaxed.

"Inside the little black box," he said to himself. That's where he was. He must have slept for, oh, maybe 3 hours. Or was it more like 4 or 5? Phil couldn't tell exactly, and that bothered him a bit.

How long had he been in the room so far? Maybe 6 hours? How much had he earned? Maybe $5? Not bad for just sleeping.

A few minutes later, Phil decided that he needed to go to the bathroom, so he yelled out, "I want to go to the john." There was a microphone in his cubicle that carried his voice to the crazy psychologists in the next room—if they were still there, like they said they would be. They could talk to him too, over a loudspeaker hanging on the wall. But so far they hadn't said anything at all.

The door opened and someone came in and touched him on the shoulder. Phil hopped out of bed and almost fell flat on his face. Funny he should be so clumsy. Maybe he was still half asleep. He spoke several times to the person leading him, but got no answer. After he had urinated, he was led back to the little black room by his silent escort. Strange the man wouldn't talk to him . . . if it was a man.

Phil lay down on the bed again and started to contemplate the world. He thought about his school work; he thought about his family; he gave serious attention to several girls he had encountered in recent weeks. And then, when he ran out of things to think about, he started over again.

It was all getting pretty boring. Maybe he'd only stay in the room for a few weeks after all, until he had earned enough money to make a down payment on that car he had seen in the showroom. What did that car look like anyway? He could barely remember . . .

"Phil, are you awake?"

The voice sounded remote and at first he couldn't be sure that he wasn't imagining it.

"Hello, Phil, are you awake?"

He told the crazy psychologist he was, but his own voice sounded odd and hol-

low to him.

"Okay, Phil, I want to give you some tests now. Are you ready?"

Phil said he was.

The psychologist's voice came out of the black haze again. "All right, let's start with the letter H. How many words can you think of that begin with the letter H? Don't use verbs and don't use proper names. Go ahead and start now."

H? What begins with H? Hell, for one thing. And Horse and House and Heart and Hurt and Help. And Hungry. Am I hungry? Maybe that was what was wrong. What will they give me for dinner? Maybe a hamburger. Oh, yes. Hamburger begins with H. And Horse. No, I said that. Horsemeat in the Hamburger . . .

What else? Celery? No that doesn't begin with an H. Helpless? Honda. No, that's a proper name. Hello out there. Happy? No, that isn't a word, is it? More a state of mind, really. Head! Yes, Head would do.

Then Phil thought and thought, but nothing else popped into his head. Finally he asked, "Is that enough?"

"If that's all you can think of, that's fine, Phil."

He smiled and relaxed. That ought to show them.

My God, it's quiet, he said to himself a few moments later. The silence seemed to stab at his eardrums like an ice pick. How could silence be so loud, so overwhelmingly bright?

And the colors, the sparks of colors. Banners of different colors waving back and forth. The wallpaper was wiggling, writhing, pulsating, just the way it did that time he had foolishly taken that

drug his friend Van had given him.

Oh, what in the world was that sound? A dark green clunking noise. Could it be the air conditioner? Sounded more like an elephant stomping around. Clunk, clunk, clunk. My God, it was a herd of elephants!

The elephants changed color. Now they were sort of black, with pink and blue and purple . . . elephants moving . . .

No, the elephants are standing still, aren't they? It's the picture that's moving, and the elephants are like cutouts in a moving picture. There they go, over the hill . . .

"Hey. You people listening in. Do you know there's a herd of elephants marching around in here?"

Why didn't the crazy psychologists answer?

And the quiet again. How long has it . . .

"Now, Phil, we have some recordings you can listen to if you wish. Would you like to hear them?"

Recordings? Why not? Maybe some good rock . . .

But no, it's a voice talking about ghosts. Who the hell cares about ghosts? Dullsville. But at least it's a voice, talking . . .

Yes, play it over one more time. This is getting interesting. Yes, play it again, Sam . . . It sure sounds more sensible this time round. Yes, ghosts are for real. Why hadn't he realized that before? Yes, play it just one more time . . .

"Hey, you people. What time is it? Why don't you answer? Don't you know I can't stay in here too long? Why don't you say something? It's been at least 24 hours, hasn't it? I've earned my 20 bucks, now tell me what time it is . . ."

Floating . . . looking down . . . Who was that strange person lying on that little bed down there with the cardboard tubes on his arms? Maybe he was dead and nobody knew it . . .

. . . There's that dark green clunking sound again. They must be letting something else into the room. Last time it was elephants. Wonder what it is . . .

My God, it's a spaceship! It's only six inches long, but it's a real spaceship. How did

they manage that? It's buzzing around the room like Darth Vader chasing Luke Skywalker . . .

"Hey, you crazy psychologists, what are you trying to pull? Get that spaceship out of here! Shooting at me, that's what it's doing. It's shooting laser beams at me!"

"Ouch! Oh, my God, I'm hit! Hey, you stupid people, stop that! If you don't stop that, I'll have to come out right away. You know that. What are you trying to do, make me quit? I can't take this much longer. Darth Vader is going to kill me with his laser beams . ..."

"Why won't you help me?

If you don't do something right now, I'm coming out. Don't you understand, it's your fault!"

Philip Cassone angrily stripped the tubes from his arms and jumped off the bed. He jerked the door open and stumbled into the room next door where two startled psychologists sat working at a table containing recording equipment.

"You bastards ruined the experiment. You made me come out. Now aren't you sorry you let Darth Vader get at me?"

And then Phil started to cry.

(Continued on page 255.)

Cognition

Had you taken a course in psychology 75 years ago, you probably would have been told that *consciousness* could be divided into three major functions or processes: **conation, affect,** and *cognition.* Let's look briefly at each of these three terms.

Conation

Conation is the act of "willing." As such, it is intimately tied up with such concepts as "mind," "soul," and "ego." These rather slippery concepts were all developed by people trying to explain their own actions, and those of others.

Why do you do the things you do? The functionalists (see Chapter 5) decided there were two basic types of responses. First, many of your actions are reflexive. As you will see in Chapter 13, reflexes are *involuntary* response patterns. Some reflexes are unlearned or "instinctual." Other reflexes are acquired, but are still *automatic* reactions. Your mouth "waters" instinctively when someone puts food into it. But you have to *learn* that the smell of bacon may lead to a pleasant breakfast. Once you learn this response, however, your mouth may "water" automatically whenever you're hungry and smell bacon cooking. You don't have to "will" such reflexive reactions.

However, from a conative viewpoint, many of your reactions are *voluntary.* You act as you do because you *want* to, because you *will* yourself to think and behave in a certain fashion. The decision to eat bacon—or to avoid it—usually is a voluntary choice rather than a reflexive response.

As we mentioned in Chapter 5, the behaviorists threw "voluntary acts" out the window some 50 years ago. Thereafter, the term *conation* disappeared from most psychology textbooks. However, the concept remains buried in the definitions of such terms as "ego strength," "motivation," and "decision making."

Affect

Affect is a technical term for "feelings" or "emotions." We will discuss "affect" in several other chapters, particularly in Chapter 11. The important thing to realize at this point is that many psychologists still separate the process of "thinking" from that of "feeling."

Cognition

Cognition has many different definitions. However, almost all of these definitions refer to "mental activities" of one sort or another. For example, *Webster's New Collegiate Dictionary* defines cognition as "the act or process of knowing, including both awareness and judg-

"information processing," "decision-making strategies," and even **artificial intelligence**.

By 1980, cognition had become a respectable part of the behavioral sciences again. Psychologists had discovered they could not explain all of the human experience in terms of an organism's responding *passively* to environmental stimulation. Instead, psychologists began viewing people as *actively involved* in person-environment interactions. This new approach is one you are familiar with by now: namely, the belief that you receive inputs from the outside world, "process" them in a variety of ways, and then respond. Much of this internal processing, of course, involves such cognitive acts as *knowledge* and *judgment*.

The study of cognitive processes is now one of the most exciting areas in psychology. But the behavioral revolution has left its mark, for psychologists now take a much more systematic (or "information-processing") view of cognition than they did half a century ago. Indeed, the terms "cognitive processes" and "information processing" now have almost the same meanings for many psychologists.

Cognition: A Complex Process

For our present purposes, cognition can be defined as the scientific study of how organisms make use of informational inputs. As such, cognition is a complex set of operations:

1. Cognition begins with **attention**, the process by which you *detect* and *orient* toward sensory inputs. (Input Detection)
2. Then you must *receive* these inputs at the level of your sensory receptors. (Input Reception)
3. Your receptor organs "process" the inputs by *converting* physical energy (such as light rays and sound waves) into patterns of neural energy. (**Input Transduction**)
4. Lower centers in your nervous system detect *critical features* and send information about these features up to higher centers. (Critical Feature Selection)
5. The lower centers also *screen out* certain types of information. (Input Screening)
6. Your cortex attempts to match the input with items stored in memory. (Pattern Recognition)
7. At this point, the input *registers* on your consciousness. (**Registration**)
8. You *perceive* the input, or become aware of it. (Perception)
9. Your nervous system *stores* the input for a brief period. (Temporary Memory Storage)

Fig. 9.1 Your brain is like a TV control room, in that you have inputs coming in over many different sensory channels. When you choose to "pay attention" to one channel, your brain typically suppresses temporarily the inputs on all other channels.

ment." The hallmark of "cognition," then, is that it refers to activities that go on inside your mind.

The behaviorists banished conation from "scientific psychology" because the concept of "willing" didn't fit their view that *all* responses were reflexive or automatic. The behaviorists threw out cognition, too, because "mental activities" are private events, and thus can't be measured objectively.

Because of the behavioral revolution, the study of cognitive processes *as such* went into a temporary decline from about 1940 to the mid-1960's. However, many psychologists remained interested in the topic even during these "cognitive Dark Ages." And during the 1960's, the tide turned. Some of Skinner's followers developed *cognitive behavior modification*, a technique that employs behavioral methods to control thought processes. At about this same time, scientists interested in learning and memory began using such cognitive terms as

10. You *think about* the input for a period of time. (Reasoning, Problem Solving, Mental Imagery)
11. Eventually, you must *decide* what to do about the input. (Decision Making)
12. You may decide to *ignore* the input. (Forgetting)
13. Or, you may *store* the input in your Long-Term Memory. (Permanent Memory Storage)
14. You may also *respond* to the input. The "response-output sequence" involves such activities as issuing motor commands (feed-forward), generating predictions about consequences, and monitoring feedback. (Response Output)
15. The *environment* then *responds* to your output, and the sequence begins all over again.

We have already talked about sensory inputs and perception (Chapters 6–8), and about the response-output process (Chapter 5). We will cover learning and the memory storage processes in Chapters 13–15. However, we have not as yet touched on *attention*, so we will begin this chapter by discussing that topic. Next, we will look at how your cortex influences what goes on in the "lower centers," and vice versa. Then we will "turn our attention" to *reasoning* and *problem solving*. Finally, we will investigate what happens when you experience either too many or too few inputs.

Let's start this lengthy journey by returning to our old friend, the NASA robot.

Question: Can computers "think"? (Hint: What do you mean by "thinking"?)

Attention

In Chapter 6, we asked you to "make some decisions" about what *sensory receptors* a robot would need in outer space. As you can now see, however, input detection is but one of the first steps in the cognitive process. If the robot is to be of any real use to you, it must process these inputs and then make the same sorts of decisions about them that you would. Thus, we must find some way of programming the robot's computer-brain so that it perceives and thinks about the world much as you do.

Before the robot can *perceive* the world—much less *think* about it—the machine must first *attend* to sensory inputs. More than this, the robot must somehow be programmed to pay

Conation (co-NAY-shun). From the Latin word meaning "to attempt." Conation is the act of willing, desiring, or acting purposefully.

Affect (AFF-ect). A feeling, or an emotion. More properly, the psychological aspect of an emotion. The "affective disorders" are mania and depression, so called because they are disorders of the emotions.

Artificial intelligence. The attempt by psychologists, philosophers, and computer experts to describe human intelligence in sufficiently mechanical terms so that they can build computers (or other "expert systems") that can reason and solve problems "in the human style."

Attention. From the Latin word meaning "to stretch to." To attend class is to be physically present when the class is in session. To *attend* to the teacher is to "pay attention" to what the instructor is saying and doing. According to *Webster's New Collegiate Dictionary*, attention involves "a selective narrowing or focusing of consciousness and receptivity."

Input transduction (trans-DUCT-shun). To transduce is to convert energy or information from one form to another. An electric heater transduces electricity into heat. The rods and cones in your retinas transduce light waves into patterns of neural energy, or informational inputs.

Registration. An input "registers" in your mind when you become conscious of it. See Chapter 8.

attention to some inputs, while ignoring others.

Question: Suppose the robot is sitting quietly in a room, reading a textbook on psychology. Presumably, it is focusing all its attention on visual inputs. Now, you walk into the room and call to the robot. How will it know to stop "looking" and start "listening"?

Sensory Channels

In a sense, your brain is rather like the control room of a television station. The director of a TV show usually sits in front of a bank of video monitors, each of which shows a different scene (see Fig. 9.1). The director must select—from instant to instant—which of the channels to send out on the air.

In similar fashion, inputs arrive at your brain over a *number of sensory channels*. But at any one moment in time, you typically "pay conscious attention" only to the inputs coming in on one channel. These inputs continue to arrive at the lower centers of your brain, however, even when your mind is not "watching that channel." For example, when you are concentrating on studying for a test, you may not hear the hi-fi playing softly in the background. However, if you closed your eyes momentarily, you probably would become aware of the music almost immediately.

Part of the problem of explaining attention, therefore, is trying to figure out *which sensory channel* is likely to become prominent at any given instant in time. As you might suspect, which channel you pay attention to is determined by several factors—the physical qualities of the stimulus, intra-psychic factors such as "novelty" and "importance," and social factors including learned cultural values. We will have more to say about these matters in a moment.

However, before your robot can "pay attention" to a new input—no matter how important or novel that input is—the machine first has to realize the new input is *there*. Then it must *arouse* itself sufficiently to "change channels." Finally, it must *orient* its receptor organs so that they are facing the new stimulus.

Question: Imagine that your dog is lying on the floor with its eyes closed. What is the *first* visible response the dog is likely to make if you whistle softly to the animal? (Hint: Think of the dog's ears.)

Orienting Reflex

The process of "paying attention" to a new input is often called the **orienting reflex**. Another name for the *orienting reflex* is the "Where is it?" response. The orienting reaction is automatic and involuntary. A simple version of the reflex appears in newborn infants, so some aspects of the response are unlearned. However, as we will see, the reflex can also be modified by experience.

Arousal

The orienting reflex always includes a general state of physical *arousal*. For example, imagine you are gazing out the window at a beautiful sunset. Then, without your realizing it, someone sneaks up behind you and explodes a big balloon just a few inches away from your left ear. How would you react?

Chances are, you would show a classic reaction called the **startle reflex**, which is an extreme form of the orienting reflex. You might blink or close your eyes momentarily. When you opened them again, though, your pupils would be slightly **dilated**. You might gasp, and stop breathing for a second or two. Your pulse would quicken, and there would be a change in the pattern of your brain waves. Your mouth would open slightly, as it might if you were grinning.

Irving Maltzman

Your neck and head would thrust forward slightly. A second or two later, you would involuntarily turn to your left, toward the source of the sound.

Before you can either be startled or orient toward a new sensory input, though, some part of your nervous system must *detect a sudden change in your environment*. This new input *disrupts* your ongoing cognitive processes and *arouses* you in a reflexive way. The amount of your arousal—and the intensity of your reaction—both depend in large part on the *strength* of the new stimulus. You react with a simple "orienting reflex" toward most novel inputs. But you respond with a full-blown startle reflex if the input is particularly intense.

The Galvanic Skin Response (GSR)

Any time you are emotionally aroused, sweat glands in your skin release tiny amounts of water. This sweating reaction changes the *resistance* of your skin to electrical current. We call this the **galvanic skin response**, or GSR. The GSR is frequently used as a rough measure of arousal and emotionality.

As you will see in Chapter 13, the **polygraph** or "lie detector" actually measures emotional arousal, not "lies." If you took a "lie-detector" test, the person giving the test would put electrodes on your palms or finger tips. These electrodes measure your GSR. A significant change in the GSR usually suggests you are having an emotional reaction of some kind.

A change in skin resistance also typically *precedes* physical movement during the orienting reflex. That is, first you are aroused, then you turn toward the source of the new input to determine *consciously* what the stimulus is. However, as we will see, the "lower centers" in your nervous system may *already* have detected some of the "critical features" of the input.

Novelty or Significance?

Some psychologists believe the orienting reflex is primarily a response to *novelty*. They believe you make the orientation response to any stimulus input that *differs* from (1) what you are presently experiencing, or (2) what you expect will happen next.

Other theorists, such as U.C.L.A. psychologist Irving Maltzman, believe you "orient" primarily to stimuli that are *significant* to you in some fashion. For example, in a 1980 study with Joseph Wingard, Maltzman asked undergraduate males what sorts of recreational activities they were interested in. Wingard and Maltzman selected 16 subjects who were *exclusively* interested in chess, or in fishing, or in surfing. The experimenters showed slides of a number of recreational activities to these 16 students. The subjects gave a much larger GSR (galvanic skin response) to slides of their *chosen type of recreation* than to slides of other activities. According to Maltzman and Wingard, the larger GSR suggests the subjects were more likely to orient to "significant" stimuli than to non-significant inputs.

What makes a stimulus *significant*? Motivation, for one thing. Subjects tend to give a stronger orienting reflex to food-related inputs when hungry than when they have just eaten. But social factors and "expectancy" can also make an input significant. In a recent study, Maltzman and his colleagues showed that subjects are more likely to "orient" toward weak stimuli they have been *warned to expect* than to weak stimuli that are unexpected. If the orienting reflex were set off merely by novelty, Maltzman says, the subjects would have responded to the unexpected stimuli at least as strongly as to those they anticipated. But telling the subjects to expect certain inputs made those stimuli "significant," according to Maltzman.

The difficulty in deciding between the "novelty" and "significance" approaches lies in the definition of these terms, for the importance of many stimuli is the very fact they *are* new or different in some way. Generally speaking, however, those psychologists who emphasize "novelty" tend to believe that the orienting reflex is a weaker form of the startle reflex, and therefore is primarily an innate response. Those theorists who emphasize "significance" admit that

Orienting reflex. To "orient" is to turn toward some goal or chosen direction.

Startle reflex. An inborn response that involves the disruption of all on-going activities due to a sudden change in the environment. If you are holding an infant and cautiously "drop" the child an inch or so, the infant will usually show a full-blown startle reflex.

Dilated (DYE-lay-ted). Your pupils dilate (open wider) whenever you are startled, or whenever you need to take in more visual information from your environment.

Galvanic skin response (gal-VAN-ick). Abbreviated GSR. "Galvanic" means an electric current, particularly a direct current (DC) produced by chemical action. Named after a famous Italian scientist, Luigi Galvani, who studied the effects of direct current on muscles in the late 1700's.

Polygraph (POL-ee-graff). A machine that makes many different records or graphs simultaneously. Usually, a device that records body responses such as pulse rate, GSR, blood pressure, and so forth. Often referred to, incorrectly, as a "lie detector." See Chapter 13 for an explanation of why lie detectors are misnamed.

the reflex occurs innately to *biologically important inputs*. But they point out that the reflex often fails to occur to unimportant inputs despite their novelty. The orienting response also occurs to many psychologically significant stimuli despite their *lack* of newness.

Habituation

In Chapter 6, we pointed out that your receptors tend to stop responding to constant stimulus inputs. We used the term "receptor adaptation" to refer to this decrease in responsiveness. We noted as well that your brain *learns to ignore* certain unimportant changes in your environment. We referred to this higher-level process as *central habituation*.

One of the characteristics of the "orienting reflex" is that it *habituates* over a period of time. When you first move into a new house, you are aware of all sorts of new and unusual noises. You turn your head toward the source of these sounds and try to figure out where they come from and what they mean. Eventually, though, you habituate to most of the sounds. Put another way, instead of "orienting" to overly familiar inputs, eventually you just ignore them.

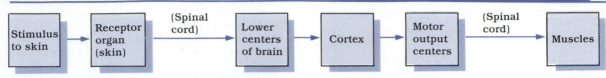

Fig. 9.2 Until recently, scientists believed a stimulus input passed up your spinal cord to your cortex, which processed the input and sent command messages to your muscles. This is the "straight-line sensory system."

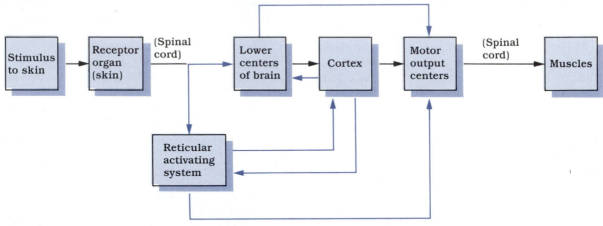

Fig. 9.3 Now we know that sensory input messages "split" at the top of the spinal cord. Unless activated by the reticular system, the cortex does not respond to the message coming through on the "straight-line" system. But activity in the cortex can inhibit or enhance activity in the reticular system as well.

H. W. Magoun

Input Screening

Obviously, you would want to program your robot so that it paid attention to you whenever you said something to it. Just as obviously, you'd want the machine to habituate to unimportant stimuli so it wouldn't be continually distracted from whatever task you gave it to perform.

But how is the robot to become aroused just by *important* stimuli unless it has some mechanism for "screening out" *trivial* inputs? And how can it decide which inputs are trivial unless it first attends to them and identifies them in some fashion?

The answer to these questions comes from research performed by H.W. Magoun and his colleagues at U.C.L.A. In fact, Magoun (pronounced mah-GOON) was interested in the problem of *arousal*—that is, the biological and psychological mechanisms that wake us up and keep us functioning at a peak level of performance. By the time he had finished his work, though, Magoun and his associates not only had discovered what most of these mechanisms were, they also identified many of the factors that influence the orienting reflex.

Input Control

Prior to Magoun's work, psychologists generally assumed that sensory information reached your brain in only one fashion (see Fig. 9.2). Inputs from your receptor cells would pass up your spinal cord to your thalamus. Cells in your thalamus would relay the message on to your cortex. Your brain then processed this message. And, if you needed to respond, the motor centers in your frontal lobes caused your muscles to move.

This approach to sensory functioning was correct as far as it went. But scientists holding this viewpoint assumed that information flowed in *one direction only*—from receptors up to the brain and then out from the brain to the muscles. As Magoun and his group showed, this view was far too narrow.

Magoun made three remarkable discoveries. First, incoming information actually reaches your cortex through *two* quite different pathways. Second, the sensory routes to your brain are "superhighways" where messages flow in *both* directions. And third, your cortex exercises considerable *control* over what information gets through to it, and over what messages are blocked out in lower centers and thus never reach conscious awareness.

The road map for this maze of interconnected pathways is far from being completely drawn, but we can at least sketch in some of the landmarks.

Two Important Sensory Pathways

As far as "input control" is concerned, almost all of your sensory modalities operate in similar fashion. So let us see what happens when a free nerve ending in your skin responds to an external stimulus such as the warmth of a fire. The process begins when the receptor cell "fires." As you know by now, "firing" actually involves *converting* physical inputs into a patterned burst of neural energy. This patterned burst is an "input message," which travels up your spinal cord to your brain stem (the "stem" of the cerebral mushroom). Up to this point, only one input route is involved.

In your brain stem, however, the road to your cortex "splits" into two pathways. One road leads directly to the somatic sensory cortex in your parietal lobe. This route is called the **straight-line sensory system**, which lets your brain know what part of your body has been stimulated and how strong the stimulation is (see Fig. 9.3).

A second road leads into the *reticular activating system*, which gets its name (like the retina) from the Latin word for net or network. The reticular system is a network of cells that begins at the top of your spinal cord and runs up through the brain stem to the lower parts of your cerebrum. The reticular system acts as an

alerting system for the rest of your brain—rather like the bell on your telephone. When the reticular system is activated, it rings up your cortex to let it know an important message is coming through on the straight-line sensory "telephone."

The message from the free nerve endings in your skin will usually reach your somatic sensory cortex *whether or not* your reticular system is aroused. However, unless the reticular system "rings the bell" and activates your cortex, your brain appears to *ignore* any information coming through on the straight-line system. And your brain acts in this fashion whether the message comes from your skin, your eyes, your ears, or from any other sensory receptors.

The Reticular Activating System (RAS)

Magoun's experiments demonstrating the function of the **RAS** (reticular activating system) were performed on animals rather than humans. So let us talk about cats first, and people second.

Suppose we implant a "stimulating electrode" in the RAS of a cat. Then we let the animal continue its daily life. But, occasionally, we deliver a small amount of electrical current to the cat's RAS. What happens?

If we stimulate the cat's RAS when it is awake and moving about, it shows the classic *orienting reflex*. That is, the animal suddenly becomes alert, as if its environment had suddenly *changed* dramatically and the cat realized it ought to pay attention to what was going on around it.

If we wait until the cat goes to sleep, a short burst of electrical energy delivered to the RAS causes the cat to open its eyes and jump up, rather as if someone had stepped on its tail.

If we remove the cat's RAS surgically, the animal lapses into deep sleep from which it seldom

At times your cortex can focus on one task, while the lower centers in your brain go on "automatic pilot" and execute overlearned tasks such as walking or driving.

if ever recovers. If we shook the cat violently, it would wake up momentarily and move around for a minute or two. But even if it were starving to death, the animal would soon lie down and drift off to sleep.

Next, suppose we put a "recording electrode" in the somatic sensory cortex (parietal lobe) of the cat whose RAS we had removed. Then we pinch the animal's tail. The signal coming from the recording electrode would show that the neural message from the the cat's tail does in fact reach the animal's parietal lobe. So the animal's straight-line sensory system is still functioning properly. But since there is nothing to *arouse* the animal's brain—to *alert* it that information is coming through that needs to be acted on—the cat remains asleep.

Stimulus Screening

Since your RAS sits atop your spinal cord—and extends up into your lower brain centers—the RAS is in a perfect position to act as a toll booth or *gate* through which incoming sensory information must pass if it is to have an effect on your cortex. If the incoming message is trivial or routine, the RAS will allow your cortex to ignore the stimulus by "screening it out" before the input reaches consciousness. But if the message seems important, the RAS *alerts* the higher centers of your brain and they pay attention to what is coming through on your straight-line sensory system.

What do we mean by *important* messages? Any dramatic change in your environment will reflexively trigger off the RAS. But experiments with animals suggest your RAS also *learns* which stimuli need your instant attention—and which stimuli are unlikely to require a conscious response.

The important point to remember is that the RAS tells the cortex that a message is important—but *not what the message actually is*. The "content" of the message is handled by the straight-line sensory system.

Question: Suppose you are reading something interesting when a friend speaks to you. Why do you often have to ask your friend to repeat what was said, even though you know that your friend said something important?

Cortical Influence on the RAS

The road between the cortex and the RAS is, as we suggested earlier, a two-way street. Early studies on the RAS showed it had a marked influence on activity in the cortex. But later experiments proved the cortex has ways of affecting the RAS as well.

Whenever you choose to concentrate or focus your attention on something, your cortex tells your RAS not to bother it for a while. Your cortex exerts this control directly by *inhibiting* neural activity in the RAS. On the other hand, if you decide to cram for an exam by studying all night, your cortex is usually able to keep itself awake by continuing to *stimulate* the RAS—which feeds this stimulation back to the cortex itself.

Question: Presumably, you will want to program your robot to become aroused when something in its environment changes significantly. But *how much* must the environment change before the change is actually "significant"?

Thresholds

When does a difference *make* a difference? More than 150 years ago, a German scientist named Ernst Weber (pronounced VAY-bear) gave what is still a reasonably good answer to this question: If you can *notice* the difference, it probably is significant. Weber's definition gave rise to one of the first basic measuring units in psychology, the *Just Noticeable Difference*, or **JND**.

The JND

Imagine you are looking at two tiny white lights in a dark room. One is the "reference" light that *never changes* in intensity. The other is called the "variable" light, which *can* change in brightness. At first, the two lights are absolutely identical. Then, the variable light slowly begins to *increase* in intensity.

Since the first step in this "change process" is incredibly tiny, you don't notice the difference. But as the variable light keeps on getting brighter, bit by bit, there will come a time when you suddenly *perceive* the variable light is *different* from the reference. At this point, some aspect of the stimulus input has just crossed the **difference threshold**. That is to say, you have moved from a cognitive state where you *couldn't* perceive a difference, to a new state where you *can* perceive a difference between two stimuli. The size of the "difference threshold" is, by definition, one JND.

Weber's Law

Now, the question is, how different are the two lights *physically* when you've just noticed a *perceptual* difference between them? Weber found that, when dealing with the *brightness of lights*, he had to increase the intensity of the variable light by about 1/60th to make it noticeably different. For example, if the reference light was as bright as 60 candles, Weber had to make the variable as bright as 61 candles for his subjects to see any difference. If the reference light was as bright as 120 candles, he had to make the variable as bright as 122 candles before he got a JND.

Weber's research led him to propose the following relationship: The JND is always a *constant fraction of the reference stimulus*. This relationship is now known as "Weber's Law."

Weber's Law holds for most sensory modalities—but only in the middle ranges of intensities. That is, the law breaks down when you deal with very weak or very strong stimuli. And, as you might guess, the actual fraction varies from one sense modality to another. The Weber fraction for the brightness of lights, as we noted, is 1/60. For the loudness of sounds, however, the fraction is 1/10. That means you must increase the loudness of a variable sound by about 10 percent before you cross the difference threshold.

You must realize, too, that *your* thresholds (or Weber fractions) for detecting various stimuli would be slightly different from anyone else's. And your thresholds would *vary* from moment to moment, and from day to day. In-

JND. Just noticeable difference. The amount of *change* in a stimulus input that is just great enough so that you notice it half the time, but fail to notice it half the time.

Difference threshold. Another name for the JND.

Signal-detection theory. Your nervous system is "noisy," which is to say there is a lot going on at any given time inside your brain that can affect what you perceive and how you respond. If you are told a very weak stimulus input may occur during the next minute, you may "detect" it even if it doesn't occur. In fact, you are really responding to the "noise" in your nervous system because of your *expectancy* that a signal would occur, and thus what you reported was a "false alarm" and not a real "input." Signal detection theory is a mathematical way of predicting the likelihood that a given response is a "false alarm" or a true stimulus input.

deed, thresholds vary so much that some psychologists prefer to use what is called **signal-detection theory** instead. However, if we measured you hundreds of times—across many months—your *average* threshold for detecting differences in visual brightness would probably be fairly close to 1/60.

Question: If the reference light had the brightness of 300 candles, how bright would the variable have to be before you probably would notice a difference?

Measuring the Threshold

What does the word "threshold" mean? If you stand on the threshold of a room, you are obviously in the doorway—neither entirely *in* the room nor all the way *out* of it.

The threshold, then, is a *halfway point* between two places or states of being. Indeed, the technical definition of a JND is "that amount of change in a stimulus which is perceived as 'different' half the time—but which is *not* perceived as 'different' the other half of the time." Let's see what this statement really means.

Suppose on Monday at 4 p.m. we test your threshold for visual brightness. The reference light is as bright as 60 candles and, at the start, so is the variable light. We then increase the brightness of the variable by very tiny amounts. On the first trial, you notice a difference when the variable is as bright as 61.1 candles. So we reset the lights and try again. The second trial, you don't notice a difference until the variable is as bright as 61.2 candles. On the third trial, though, you perceive the two as different when the variable reaches the intensity of 60.8 candles. And on the fourth trial, you perceive the difference when the variable reaches the intensity of 60.9 candles (see Fig. 9.4).

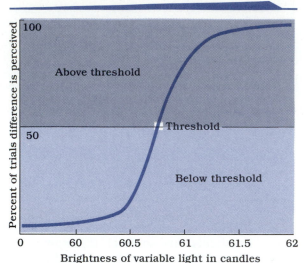

Fig. 9.4 The difference threshold when reference light is as bright as 60 candles.

Elliott McGinnies

These figures tell you two important things. First, if you add up the numbers and take an average, your Weber fraction (JND) is 1/60. Second, you actually *perceived* 1/60 as being "different" on half of the trials, but *failed to perceive it as different* the other half of the trials.

To restate the case, the threshold is that intensity of stimulus (or stimulus change) you perceive 50 percent of the time, but *don't* perceive 50 percent of the time.

Question: Could you ever *respond* to a stimulus input that you weren't consciously aware of at the time you responded?

The Limen

The Latin word for "threshold" is **limen**. A stimulus input that is "above threshold" is **supraliminal**. An input that is "below threshold" is called a **subliminal** stimulus.

There are many types of thresholds, or limens. The JND is a *perceptual* limen, because you must be *conscious* of the difference between the reference and the variable stimulus. So the JND is a measure of *supraliminal* stimulus inputs. A stimulus that was too weak to break through to consciousness would be called a *subliminal* stimulus.

Most of the time when you respond, you are aware of what stimulus input prompted your response. On some occasions, though, you may not be conscious of what stimuli you're reacting to. The orienting reflex is one such example.

But there are three other well-known situations in which "responding without awareness" occurs. The first is called *overlearned responding*. The second is known as *perceptual defense*. The third goes by the name of *subliminal perception*. Oddly enough, all three seem to involve the reticular activating system (RAS).

Overlearned Responding

Just because a stimulus is supraliminal (above the conscious threshold) doesn't mean you will be aware of it at any given moment in time. For example, have you ever been driving a car along a highway while you were thinking about something important? And then you suddenly "woke up" to the fact that you had been paying no attention at all to the traffic? Yet somehow you managed to stay on the road, slow down at the right moments, and speed up when necessary. How is it that you didn't have an accident?

After you have been driving for a while, most of the motor skills necessary to keep the car on the road become *automatic*. That is, the responses your hands make on the steering wheel and your feet make on the pedals are so *overlearned* that they become *reflexive*. We call this ability *overlearned responding*, and it is a very common experience for most of us.

Overlearned responses are processed by lower centers in the nervous system. As long as the responding goes smoothly, your RAS screens knowledge of these automatic reactions from your cortex. When the situation changes dramatically, however, your RAS arouses your cortex and orients your receptors toward the change. And because the stimulus controlling the overlearned response is *supraliminal*, you become conscious of it the instant your attention focuses on the stimulus.

Put another way, your RAS can sometimes act like an "automatic pilot." But it not only *executes* well-learned responses automatically, it also *screens* the inputs controlling these reactions from consciousness, so that your train of thought won't be interrupted.

Perceptual Defense

In addition to screening out "trivial" inputs, your RAS (and other lower centers) probably can block out *threatening* stimuli that might disturb you emotionally if you had to pay attention to them. Evidence for this statement comes from the "dirty word" experiments performed in the 1950's and 1960's by Elliott McGinnies and several other psychologists.

McGinnies began by determining the *perceptual threshold* for ordinary words. He did this by showing students words such as "table" and "chair" at faster and faster speeds. With each subject (and for each word), McGinnies was able to calculate an exposure time so rapid that the subject would perceive the word *exactly 50 percent of the time* (and not perceive it 50 percent of the time).

For a word such as "whale," this perceptual threshold might be about 100 **milliseconds**. For an emotionally laden word such as "whore," however, the threshold was typically much *higher*—200 milliseconds or more.

McGinnies believed his subjects were *unconsciously defending* against perceiving such "disturbing" words as "whore." He called this effect **perceptual defense**.

Many psychologists objected to McGinnies's studies, claiming he had not *controlled* for all the outside influences he ought to have taken into account. For instance, we know the more common a word is, the *lower* its perceptual threshold will be. You can recognize the word "put" in a much shorter time than you can recognize the old English word "tup," although both are made up of the same letters. In the 1950's, words such as "whore" seldom appeared in print, so the students might well have been relatively unfamiliar with the printed form of the word.

We also know that, in some circles, speaking such "dirty" words out loud is unacceptable—particularly if both sexes are present. McGinnies's critics speculated that if a male student were presented with the word "bitch," he might indeed recognize it. But he might be afraid to say·it in public. Instead, he might say "botch" or "batch" or "butch." And he might keep on doing so until he clearly saw it was "bitch." These critics guessed that male stu-

dents would be more likely to report "dirty" words if the psychologist testing them were male than if the experimenter were female. And, as further experiments showed, the critics were quite right.

Perceptual Vigilance

The critics also noted that a few students actually had *lower* thresholds for "dirty" words than for "clean" words. How might this finding be explained?

The answer given by McGinnies is that, while most people *defend* against sexual stimuli, a few of us are vigilantly searching the world around us for anything that might be slightly smutty. McGinnies called this *lower* threshold **perceptual vigilance**. Whether a person tends to seek out, or to defend against, sexual stimuli seems to be a matter of each individual's own past experience and moral upbringing.

Question: How can you *defend* against perceiving a "dirty" word before you *perceive* the word and recognize that it's "dirty"?

GSR and the Orienting Reflex

The major objection to the "dirty word" experiments came from psychologists who perceived the nervous system in pre-Magoun terms. That is, these scientists believed that *all* important processing of inputs took place consciously, at the level of the cortex. As we now know, that isn't the case. Your RAS and other lower centers can recognize and respond to stimuli without your being aware of what they are doing.

K. D. Broota   Graham Wagstaff

The interesting question then becomes, *How do the lower centers manage to defend against conscious recognition of emotion-laden words?* The answer may come from a series of studies performed by Robert McCleary. In one experiment, McCleary measured his subjects' GSRs while also testing their visual thresholds. When he showed his subjects "dirty words" at speeds *far below* their perceptual thresholds, the subjects *denied* seeing the stimuli. But the subjects often showed significant changes in GSR even when they insisted they hadn't the foggiest notion what the word was. And, just as McCleary had predicted, the GSR changes occurred just to "dirty words," not to words such as "table" or "chair."

Question: How does McCleary's research support the belief that you only orient to "significant" stimuli?

Perceptual Thresholds

McCleary's research suggests that emotionally laden stimuli can *raise perceptual thresholds.* Evidence supporting this view can be found in a study published by Indian psychologist K.D. Broota in 1978. Broota *paired* three-letter **nonsense syllables**, such as DAX, either with "dirty" words or with neutral words. Once the subjects had *learned* such associations as "ZOK-table" and "DAX-bitch," Broota measured their visual recognition thresholds. The subjects had much higher recognition thresholds for nonsense syllables paired with "dirty" words than those paired with neutral words.

Apparently, then, neutral inputs can become "significant" if you come to associate them with emotional stimuli. And when the previously neutral inputs do become significant, your recognition threshold for them is raised.

McCleary's research also suggests that the RAS may occasionally respond to *subliminal* inputs—if they are emotionally "significant." Support for this belief comes from a 1974 paper by Graham Wagstaff, published in the *British Journal of Psychology.* Wagstaff showed 23 male and 23 female students pairs of identical lights. **Superimposed** over *each* light, Wagstaff projected the subliminal image of a word. The words were projected at such a weak intensity the students never were conscious the images were there. Some of the subliminal words were "dirty," some were neutral.

While the subliminal words were being superimposed over the lights, Wagstaff asked the students to tell him which of the two lights was brighter. The two lights were, as mentioned, identical in intensity. However, Wagstaff's subjects tended to perceive one light as significantly *dimmer* than the other. Most of the time, the "dim light" was the one the "dirty" word was being superimposed on. The "dirty" word, therefore, *raised the perceptual threshold for brightness* of the light it was associated with—even though the "dirty" word was far too subliminal to break through to conscious awareness.

These studies suggest that **subliminal perception** does exist. But it is a very weak effect, and probably can be detected only under highly controlled conditions in a laboratory. Given these facts, you wouldn't think subliminal perception would pose much of a threat to civilization. But that's just what many Americans feared was the case some 30 years ago. Let's look at what caused their fears.

Question: What is the purpose of running "control groups" in psychological experiments?

Subliminal Advertising

In 1956, a public-relations executive named James Vicary held a press conference that set New York City on its ear. At that conference, Vicary announced to the press he had discovered a new advertising technique that (so he claimed) would revolutionize America's buying habits. According to Vicary, the technique was so powerful that almost no one would be able to resist it. And it was so subtle that most Americans would never realize that their behaviors had been affected.

What Vicary did was to project "subliminal ads" on the screen of a movie house in Fort Dix,

New Jersey. The ads said, "Drink Coke," and "Eat Popcorn." These hidden advertisements were flashed on the movie screen (by means of a slide projector) while the audience was watching a feature film. The subliminal ads were projected at such rapid speeds, the audience wasn't *consciously aware* of the "hidden messages."

According to Vicary, sales of both Coca Cola and popcorn rose dramatically. Vicary explained his results by claiming the "secret ads" stimulated the *unconscious* portions of the mind. Thus, he said, people in the audience purchased Coca-Cola and popcorn because their conscious minds couldn't resist the demands their unconscious minds made.

Vicary called his technique *subliminal advertising*. Within a few days after the 1956 press conference, the newspapers and magazines were full of anguished articles denouncing Vicary for having thrust a new and terrible method of "mind control" upon an unwilling world.

Question: James Vicary did not use "control groups" in his study of subliminal advertising, nor did he test the effects of using different feature films. What kinds of control groups do you think he should have used in order to be sure that it was the "hidden messages" that caused the increase in sales? (Hint: Would the audience have bought more Coke *even without the hidden ads* had the feature movie been "Lost in the Desert" than if it had been "Lost in the Arctic"?)

Vicary's Claims versus the Awful Truth

In point of fact, *subliminal advertising* was neither new nor is it an effective way of pushing people around without their knowledge. As Richard Cutler, Elton McNeil, and I pointed out in 1958, the technique had been tried many times earlier. All previous researchers had abandoned it because, as an *advertising technique*, it simply didn't work very well. Indeed, after the press conference, many scientists repeated Vicary's study in other movie houses. Not one of these attempts yielded the same results Vicary reported!

To tell the awful truth, there has never been a well-controlled, *scientific* study demonstrating that "hidden advertisements" can affect people's buying behaviors in real-life settings. However, "negative results" seldom get splashed about on the front page of newspapers, nor highlighted on prime time television. So sub-

Nonsense syllables. "Manufactured" syllables, usually consisting of two consonants and a vowel, such as DAJ. The fact that the syllables are "nonsense" means most subjects will be unfamiliar with them, a useful thing when you wish to study how people learn and remember verbal material.

Superimposed. In most studies of subliminal perception, the experimenter shows the subject a supraliminal stimulus and then projects a very weak (subliminal) stimulus on top of the strong stimulus, using a slide projector. In one study, subjects saw a drawing of an emotionless human face and were asked if the face was "happy" or "sad." If the experimenter superimposed the word "happy" (flashed for just a few milliseconds), the subjects tended to perceive the face as "happy" but didn't consciously perceive the word "happy."

Subliminal perception. Responding unconsciously to stimuli too weak to break through to consciousness. Occurs primarily in the laboratory, or in real-world situations where the person is *forced* to guess about something but has inadequate supraliminal information to make a good guess. Given the ease with which most people actively suppress loud TV commercials and other supraliminal forms of advertising, it seems unlikely most individuals would be affected by ads too weak to break through to consciousness.

Preconscious processing system. Abbreviated PPS. Term used by Norman Dixon to refer to all those "lower centers of the brain" that do the initial processing and screening of informational inputs.

liminal advertising still crops up in horror movies (such as "Agency"). And the technique is presently marketed by several individuals who boldly claim it can reduce shop-lifting and increase productivity—but who cannot offer *scientific proof* to back up their claims.

Need we worry about men and women of evil intent who might practice "mind control" using subliminal advertising? The laboratory studies we've mentioned suggest we have little to fear in this regard. However, subliminal perception *does* occur under some conditions, as does perceptual defense. In his 1981 book *Preconscious Processing*, British psychologist Norman Dixon states that the evidence in this regard is "irrefutable." The question then becomes, What *purpose* do these effects serve in everyday life?

"Preconscious Processing"

Norman Dixon notes that the "lower centers" of the nervous system evolved long before the cortex did (see "Theory of the Triune Brain" in Chapter 4). Dixon calls these primitive centers the **preconscious processing system**, or PPS. Originally, these primitive centers mostly mediated orienting reflexes, arousal, and emotional responses. When the cortex evolved, however, the PPS took on a new function—that of prelim-

Norman Dixon

inary screening of *informational* inputs before they reach the "conscious processing system" in the cortex.

According to Dixon, the PPS can *attend simultaneously* to inputs from *all* the sensory modalities (sight, hearing, and so forth). The PPS also has much lower thresholds than does the conscious system. Thus, the preconscious system can process a large amount of information in a small amount of time. The PPS responds in a reflexive (automatic) fashion to many of these inputs. But the PPS is better at *detecting* the emotional significance of stimuli than at *making logical decisions* about these inputs. So, when the PPS detects important inputs, it sends these stimuli along to the cortex for "conscious processing."

In contrast to the PPS, Dixon says, the conscious system is relatively insensitive to weak stimuli. And the conscious system has a limited capacity for processing data. Therefore, it can attend to only one input at a time. However, according to Dixon, the cortex only *needs* to pay attention to one thing at a time because the PPS has already screened the inputs for emotional significance. And *because* the cortex can focus on a limited number of alternatives, the conscious system can make decisions *quickly* in emergency situations.

Not all psychologists would agree with Dixon's position. However, the data do suggest that one purpose of lower centers in your brain is to screen out trivial stimuli. Thus, they keep your cortex from being overloaded by inputs. And almost everyone agrees that the major psychological purpose of your cortex is *logical decision making*.

Question: What psychological abilities should a robot have if it is to make *good* decisions?

Concepts and Categories

One manner in which the lower centers "process inputs" is to search for *critical features* (such as contours) that will allow you to perceive real-world objects correctly. Your cortex makes conscious use of these critical features as it tries to sort the perceived objects into various **cognitive categories**.

Research suggests that there are two major types of cognitive categories: *natural* and *artificial*. Natural categories are those that occur in real-world situations, and that are immediately understandable to most people. Examples of natural categories would be such things as "big or small," "hard or soft," "red or green," "male or female," and even "normal or abnormal." Artificial categories are contrived or synthetic groupings. Usually they are "made up" by humans (particularly by academics!). Dividing college departments into the physical sciences, natural sciences, social sciences, and the humanities is an example of one artificial classification scheme. Classifying students by such titles as freshman, sophomore, junior, senior, and graduate is another artificial set of categories.

Question: Suppose, some time in the future, you buy a "household robot." One night as you are reading, you tell the robot to go to your bedroom and fetch your slippers. What perceptual and cognitive abilities would the robot have to possess in order to execute this apparently simple command?

Attributes and Rules

The *purpose* of categories is to allow you to put objects, events, or concepts into convenient groupings. And you do so by looking for *attributes* that each member of the category shares with other members. For example, a birthday cake, a bowl of soup, and an apple all share at least one common attribute—they are edible. Therefore, these objects fall within the natural category, "food." A tennis shoe and a tuxedo wouldn't fit within this category. Shoes and suits would fit within the "clothing" category, though, while soup and apples wouldn't.

Attributes allow you to group objects together (into a category) by *including* some objects while *excluding* others. However, most categories are complex. That is to say, an object must often possess several attributes to fit within a certain category—and perhaps *not* possess certain other attributes.

Rules tell you how to *combine attributes* to form a certain category. For example, suppose you told your robot to go to the store and bring back some "fresh fruit." To respond appropriately, the robot would have to create a category with at least two attributes, "fruit-ness" and "fresh-ness." The *rule* in this case is the "and" rule, since the object selected must be both fresh *and* fruit. Frozen fruit and canned fruit would be excluded.

Another common rule is the "or" rule. You could have said to the robot, "Get me some fresh *or* frozen fruit." In this case, canned fruit would be excluded even though it had the single attribute "fruit-ness."

There are many other types of *rules* for combining attributes to form categories. Of these, the "if-then" rule is perhaps the most important. You might have said to the robot, "*If* the fresh peaches are really ripe, *then* get me some. But canned peaches are fine too." Using the "if-then" and the "and" rules, the robot would include ripe fresh peaches and canned peaches in the category, but exclude frozen peaches and peaches that were fresh but still green.

Question: If you sent your robot to get your slippers, and it brought you a pair of boots instead, what would this tell you about the robot's cognitive categories?

Superordinate, Basic, and Subordinate Categories

How are a dog and a cat alike? They are both *animals*. But how are a collie and a cocker spaniel alike? They are both *dogs*.

Natural categories generally fall into *three levels of generality*. **Superordinate** categories—such as "animal"—tend to be extremely broad. For example, you are an animal, and so is an earthworm. What attributes do you share with an earthworm?

Basic categories—such as "dog"—tend to be of moderate generality. They are neither too specific nor too general.

Subordinate categories—such as "collie"—are highly specific (see Fig. 9.5).

Generally speaking, *basic* categories are easy to create and easy to think about. As you will discover in Chapter 18, young children learn to use basic categories long before they master either subordinate or superordinate categories. At age two or three, a child may call the family cat a "doggie." The child usually must be four or five before she or he can perceive the relation-

Cognitive categories. Mental schemes that allow you to group certain objects together because the objects share certain attributes.

Superordinate (SOO-per-OR-din-ate). Anything is "superordinate" if it is "above the ordinary," that is, superior to the basic or usual category.

Basic categories. The most common of the cognitive categories. "Dog" is a basic category. "Animal" is a superordinate category that includes dogs, cats, and other beasts.

Subordinate categories (Sub-OR-din-ate). If you are a boss, the people who work for you are your subordinates. Collies and poodles are types of dogs, thus they are subordinate to the basic category "dog."

Concepts. Cognitive schemas, or ways of perceiving a situation. A "mental abstraction" that usually is generalized from specific examples.

Defining features. The most important aspects of an informational input, or a cognitive category. The defining features of a square are four straight lines that make 90° angles (or "square corners").

ship between such words as "collie," "cat," and "animal."

Question: When you think of the basic category "bird," what example first comes to mind?

Prototypes

What we call **concepts** are usually artificial categories. Over the years, there has been a fair amount of psychological research on "concept formation." An example of the sorts of concepts usually studied in these experiments can be found in Fig. 9.6.

Berkeley psychologist Eleanor Rosch has criticized most of the work on concept formation because it involves *artificial* rather than *natural* categories. If you tried to figure out what the critical attribute in Fig. 9.6 was, for instance, you probably came to the conclusion that it was "eyebrows." Any face with rounded eyebrows fitted within the concept/category. Any face with peaked eyebrows didn't fit. But how often in real life do you see faces like these, or "peaked" eyebrows?

Now, think of the basic category "bird." How did you form this category? And how do you know what animals to include in it, and which to exclude? You could make up a list of **defining features**, such as "it flies," "lays eggs," and "has feathers." Then, when you were faced with putting an animal into this category or in some other category, you could check to see how many of the defining attributes the animal possessed. When you tried to solve the puzzle in Fig. 9.6, you had to use the *defining-features*

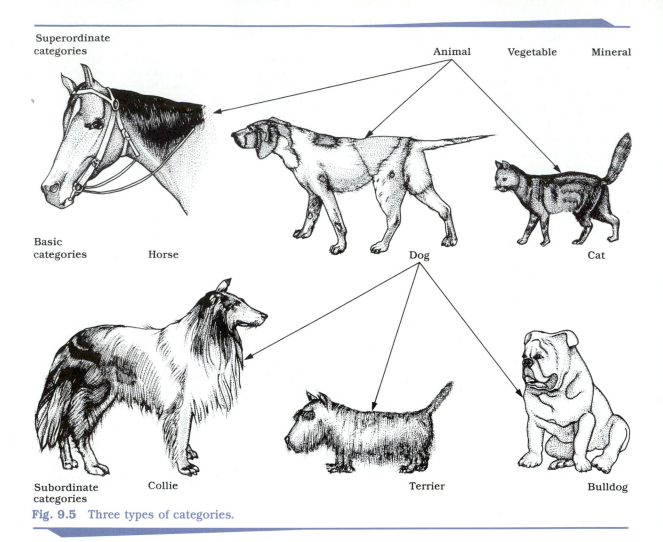

Superordinate categories

Animal   Vegetable   Mineral

Basic categories   Horse   Dog   Cat

Subordinate categories   Collie   Terrier   Bulldog

Fig. 9.5 Three types of categories.

approach because that's the way the puzzle was structured.

According to Eleanor Rosch, that's not the way the human mind usually functions. Instead, she says, you tend to create a **prototype** for each basic category and compare any new possibility to the prototype. Most people in the United States tend to use either the robin or the sparrow as a prototype of a "bird." Now, suppose you have never seen a canary. If someone showed you a canary, you wouldn't ask, "Does it fly?" or "Does it lay eggs?" Rather, you'd immediately say it *was* a bird because it is very much like your prototype, a robin or a sparrow.

Rosch has shown that concept formation is quick and easy if you have a ready-made prototype available. You can readily sort colored objects into categories such as "blue," "green,"

"red," and "yellow" because these are natural categories for which you already have clear-cut prototypes. It is much more difficult to sort colored objects if the categories you must use are "aquamarine," "magenta," "turquoise," and "chartreuse."

"Fuzzy" Boundaries

Is a penguin a bird? You know the answer to that question, of course. But compare a penguin with that prototype of a bird, a robin. The two animals are quite dissimilar, yet both are birds.

Natural categories (such as "bird") often have fuzzy or indistinct boundaries. For instance, both "wolf" and "dog" are basic categories. But if you mated the two, which basic category would the offspring fall into? However, artificial categories often have fairly clear-cut boundaries. After all, they were artificially structured so that the boundaries would be as clear as possible.

The "fuzzy boundary" problem becomes worse if you tend to categorize according to prototypes rather than using "distinctive features." For example, "chair" is a basic category. What does your prototype of a chair look like? Does it have arms and legs? A seat and a back? Now think of a large canvas bag filled with beans. Does it *look* like your prototype of a chair? Probably not. And yet, if we call this object a "bean-bag chair," you can fit the object into the category "chair."

Prototype (PRO-toe-type). From the Greek word meaning "giving rise to," or "the first in line." In psychology, a prototype is a mental representation (or concept) of such cognitive categories as "bird," "airplane," and "human being."

Analogies (an-AL-oh-jees). An analogy is a way of pointing out that since two things are like each other in some respects, they probably are similar in other regards as well. If you compare the human brain to a computer, you are drawing an analogy between the two by pointing out their similarities.

Similes (SIM-ih-lees). From the word "similar." A simile is a figure of speech that compares two things, often by using the terms "like" or "as." For example, "My love is *like* a red, red rose."

Metaphors (MET-ah-fors). From the Greek words meaning "to transfer." A metaphor is a figure of speech in which you transfer the meaning of one word to another, such as "My love *is* a red, red rose." Metaphors and similes are subordinate examples of the basic category "analogy."

Answers

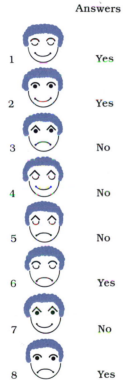

1		Yes
2		Yes
3		No
4		No
5		No
6		Yes
7		No
8		Yes

Fig. 9.6 An attribute discovery task. Before you begin, place a piece of paper so that it hides the correct answers in the right-hand column. Looking only at the figures on the left-hand side, say "yes" if you believe that the figure is an example of the concept, and "no" if you believe that it is not. Only one attribute is relevant in this task. After judging each pair, move the paper down to see the answer. Continue until you think you know what the concept is, and then check the text to see whether you are correct. (From Matlin, *Cognition.* New York: Holt, Rinehart and Winston, 1983, p. 180.)

Fuzzy Boundaries and Analogies

Some of what we call "creative thinking" turns out to be a blurring of the boundaries between common categories. For example, consider **analogies**, **similes**, and **metaphors**:

"Your brain functions much as a computer does." (Analogy)

"My love is like a red, red rose." (Simile)

"Tree trunks are straws for thirsty leaves and branches." (Metaphor)

In all these cases, you have blurred the boundaries between two categories. Put more precisely, if you view an object in a new light, you may discover it has attributes that allow you to fit it into new and unusual categories.

Question: Suppose you asked your robot, "What's 2 + 2?" When your robot answers, you then ask, "What is the purpose of life?" What is the *difference* between these two questions?

Problem Solving

Imagine that you volunteered to be a subject in a psychology experiment. The researcher asks you to put on a bathing suit, then escorts you into an almost empty room. Two cord-like ropes are hanging from the ceiling. In one corner of the room there is a pair of pliers. Otherwise, the room is bare. Your job is to tie the two ropes together. Now, how would you go about solving this problem?

The Goal

To begin with, the experimenter has made things easy for you by *specifying the goal*. The first two steps in most types of problem solving are (1) realizing that a problem exists, and (2) defining what goal you are trying to achieve. If you don't *know* there's a problem, of course, you won't do much of anything. And if you don't know *what goal* you're trying to reach, you won't know when the problem is solved. Generally speaking, the more specific you can be in describing the goal, the more likely it is you will reach it (see Chapter 14).

Your goal in the experiment, of course, is to tie the two ropes together. Since that's a fairly specific goal, you should *know* when you've achieved it.

The Original State

The next step in problem solving is to find out where you're starting from. Some psychologists call this "determining the original state." Other researchers—as you will see in Chapter 14—call it "taking a **baseline**.

What is your "original state" in the rope experiment? Well, you start with two ropes hanging from the ceiling, a pair of pliers, and your own body. That's it.

Rules

In most problem situations, there are rules that determine what you can do and can't do. In the rope experiment, you're told right away what the rules are. First, you can't pull the ropes from the ceiling or change them in any way. Second, you can't use anything not presently in the room. Third, you can't take off your bathing suit and use it. (A fourth rule is usually unstated, but almost always exists: namely, you can't behave in an abnormal way, such as assaulting the experimenter, setting the place on fire, and so forth.)

Trial Solutions

Once you know the goal and the rules, you can try out some possible solutions. You go over to one of the ropes, take hold of it, and walk toward the second rope (see Fig. 9.7). You pull on the first rope as hard as you can (to stretch it a bit, perhaps). Then you extend your free arm as far as it will go. Unfortunately, you can't quite reach the second rope. So you drop the first rope, take hold of the second rope, stretch it out, and try to grab the first rope with your free hand. But that, of course, won't work either. Now, what do you do?

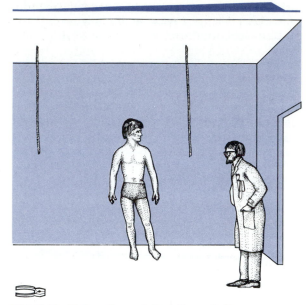

Fig. 9.7 Maier showed that the solutions subjects offered for "the rope test" depended on how they perceived the problem.

Question: Suppose you gave your robot a picture, a nail, and a pair of pliers. Then you told the robot to pound the nail into the wall and hang the picture on the nail. What would you do if the robot demanded a hammer?

Conceptualizing the Problem

In truth, you didn't really know what the *problem* was until you tried to tie the ropes together and found they wouldn't reach. At this point, you have to stop and think. Which is to say, you have to *conceptualize* the problem. "Conceptualizing" means to "construct an internal representation" of the problem. This "internal representation" really is a set of **mental images** of the elements or categories involved in the problem. A "prototype," for instance, is a *mental image* of a basic category.

Once you conceptualize the problem using mental images, you can manipulate the various elements of the problem *cognitively* rather than *physically*.

Maier's Research

The "rope problem" was developed many years ago by Norman R.F. Maier. When he tested University of Michigan students on the problem, Maier found they tended (at first) to conceptualize the problem in fairly standard ways. Some students decided "their arms were too short." Their first trial solution was to "extend their arms" using the pair of pliers. They would pull one rope over as far as they could, then reach out for the other rope holding the pliers in their free hand. Unfortunately, using the pliers to "extend their arms" didn't work.

Other students conceptualized the difficulty as being, "The rope is too short." These students would "extend the rope" by grasping it with the pliers. Then they'd try to reach the other rope with their free hand. Again, no luck. (Before Maier learned to dress the students in bathing suits and tell them, "Don't take off your clothes," some of the students used their belts or shirts to "extend the rope.")

Still other subjects decided the problem was that "the rope won't come to me." They would stretch out one rope as far as it would go, then beckon to the other rope as if they could "will" it to swing toward them. These students sometimes solved the problem. Can you guess how they did so?

Functional Fixedness

Once you have conceptualized a problem in a certain way, you may find it difficult to see the problem in a different light. Psychologists call this **functional fixedness**, or "mental set."

Abraham Luchins made an extensive study of functional fixedness. Find Fig. 9.8 and work through the problems before you read any farther.

As you probably found, the best solution to problem 1 is first to fill up jar B. That gives you 130 gallons. Then you dip jar A into B and remove 24 gallons. That leaves 106 gallons. Now you dip jar C into B twice and remove 6 more gallons. That operation leaves you with 100 gal-

lons in B, which is your goal. The best way to solve problems 2 through 5 is in much the same fashion. Check your answers and see if that's the way you solved the first five problems.

If you did solve 1–5, how about 6? In fact, you can solve 6 and 7 exactly the same way. However, that's a very round-about way. Look at the last two problems again and see if you can't find an easier method.

When Luchins asked students to solve 1–5 *first*, they did so. But then they almost always used the round-about solution to solve problems 6 and 7 as well. However, when he gave students *just problems 6 and 7* (without exposing them to 1–5 first), the subjects almost always came up with the "easy" solution first. The success the first group of students had solving problems 1–5 tended to "fix" a certain procedure in their minds. Because of this "mental set," the students continued to use the round-about solution even when better solutions existed.

Question: How does "functional fixedness" relate to the perceptual principle that "you see what you expect to see"?

Imagine that you have three jars, A, B, and C. In each of seven problems the capacity of the three jars is listed. You must use the three jars in order to obtain the amount of liquid specified in the "Goal" column. You may obtain the goal amount by adding or subtracting the quantities listed in A, B, and C. (The answers can be found in the discussion of the experiment.)

Problem	A	B	C	Goal
1	24	130	3	100
2	9	44	7	21
3	21	58	4	29
4	12	160	25	98
5	19	75	5	46
6	23	49	3	20
7	18	48	4	22

Fig. 9.8 Luchins' water-jar problem.

Reconceptualizing the Problem

One good way to break a "mental set" is to *re*conceptualize the problem. That is to say, you often need to look at a problem from a fresh perspective, or create new mental images (or prototypes) to describe the problem situation.

Maier's Rope Problem

As you may have guessed by now, the solution to Norman Maier's rope problem is to break your "mental set" about pliers. That is, you must see that pliers are not only tools—they can also be placed in a basic cognitive category called "pendulum weights." If you tie the pliers to the end of one rope, you can set it swinging back and forth. Then you can pull the other rope out far enough to catch the swinging rope when it comes close to you.

Many of Norman Maier's students failed to solve the problem because they couldn't "categorize" the pair of pliers as a pendulum weight. So Maier gave them some clues. First, he brought a type of pendulum into the room and set it in motion. This clue helped a few of the subjects. But most still conceptualized the problem in terms of "my arm is too short" or "the rope is too short." Then Maier gave them a more important clue. He started talking to the subject, to get the person's attention. Then Maier slowly walked toward the student. As he walked, he deliberately brushed into one of the ropes, so it caught against his body. When Maier walked past the rope, it slid over his shoulder and swung back and forth a couple of times. Shortly thereafter, almost all of the students solved the problem!

Maier then asked the subjects what gave them the clue to solving the problem. Oddly enough, almost all the students said, "The pendulum." Very few of them were conscious of having seen the rope swing back and forth. However, if Maier just showed them the pendulum but *didn't* brush into the rope, few of the students found the solution.

Question: How does Maier's experiment demonstrate the importance of "input processing" by the lower centers of the brain?

Artificial Intelligence

Let's return to a question we asked earlier: What perceptual and cognitive processes would your robot need in order to bring you a pair of slippers from your bedroom? As you probably realize by now, this is an extremely difficult task for any robot to accomplish. But it happens to be the sort of problem that researchers working in the field of *artificial intelligence* love to tackle.

More than 30 years ago, scientists interested in cognitive processes asked themselves a very sticky question: Can we program a computer so that it *thinks* like a human being? With perhaps more enthusiasm than good sense, the scientists plunged into the problem headfirst. And hit bottom rather quickly. They had assumed that, since the human brain "processes" information in much the same way that computers do, it should be simple to get computers to handle such tasks as translating a book from one language to another. In the mid-1960's, the AI people (as scientists working in *artificial intelligence* are called) promised a breakthrough on machine translation "in a year or two." As of the mid-1980's, computers still can't translate language more complex than, say, a six-year-old child would use. In other areas, however, the AI people have made real progress.

Computer Recognition of Speech

Spoken language is even more difficult for computers to comprehend than is the written word. So you may have to wait a few years before your robot can respond to your command to fetch your slippers.

According to M.I.T researcher Robert Berwick, computers can now recognize perhaps 1,000 spoken words. In comparison, you can probably recognize 50,000 to 100,000 words. Furthermore, you can understand someone speaking in "British" English, or a man with a Texas drawl, or a woman with a "cold in her nose." Berwick notes that computers have difficulty comprehending single words, even when you speak to them in clear, distinct tones.

Recognizing single words is one thing. Putting several words together into a comprehensible *sentence* is much harder. And a sustained interchange of speech between computer and human is presently almost impossible. Robert Berwick states that "we can analyze a single sentence, but we still don't understand what happens in a conversation."

One major problem is that words can mean quite different things, depending on the *context* in which they appear. Take "hotdog," for example. It could mean a sandwich, or a family pet that got too close to the fire. It could also refer to a skier who was a show-off, or it might just be an exclamation of pleasure. Your brain automatically takes the context of the word into account when you hear it. Teaching a computer your "context recognition" skills has proved to be a particularly difficult task.

One important thing that AI research on speech perception has already taught us, however, is the fact that humans often do *misperceive* what others say to them. Studying how to communicate with computers, therefore, may well teach us how to communicate with each other more effectively.

Search Strategies

Presuming your robot could comprehend your spoken command to "fetch my slippers from the bedroom," it would then have to navigate to the bedroom. It would have to maintain its balance, avoid obstacles, and probably open and close doors. (For a discussion of the difficulties involved in planning and executing these motor behaviors, see Chapters 5 and 6.)

Algorithms and Heuristics

Once in the bedroom, the robot would have to use a *search strategy* to find the slippers. It

Algorithm (AL-go-rhythm). A step-by-step procedure for solving some problem.
Heuristics (hyour-IS-ticks). From the Greek words meaning "to discover." A problem-solving technique that involves making use of what you find to change the direction of your search. If you make use of feedback as you try to learn how to drive, you are using a heuristic learning technique.

might search the room in a completely random fashion. Or it might use some formula or **algorithm**, such as "always start at the far left wall and search diligently to the far right wall."

More likely, it would use **heuristics**, which is a fancy name for a set of "rules of thumb." Using heuristics, the robot would rely on all it knew about slippers to shorten the search. For instance, its memory banks might tell it that slippers are often left under beds or on closet floors, but seldom are found under sheets or in suitcases. Therefore, it would first look under the bed and on the floor of the closet. It would look in the bed and suitcases only after it failed to find the slippers in the most likely places.

Computers can be programmed to use algorithms rather easily. For instance, a chess-playing computer will search through millions of possible chess moves, following a simple formula that tells it how to evaluate each possibility.

Human chess players tend to employ heuristics. That is, humans learn from experience which moves are most likely to be effective in any given situation. However, no one has yet developed high-level, general heuristic techniques for computers.

Pattern Recognition

Look at Fig. 9.9. What are all those objects? It won't take you more than a moment or two to recognize them all as *slippers* and other footwear. But pity your poor robot. If the machine has but one "image" of a pair of slippers stored in its memory (such as Fig. 9.9A), how will it identify a slipper that's upside down, or twisted into an odd shape, or even viewed "on end?" And how will it differentiate slippers from boots, shoes, galoshes, socks, or even *photographs* of slippers? Worse yet, how will the robot know which are *your* slippers if more than one person keeps slippers in the same bedroom?

Templates versus Prototypes

Computers have been programmed to recognize simple objects using inputs from TV cam-

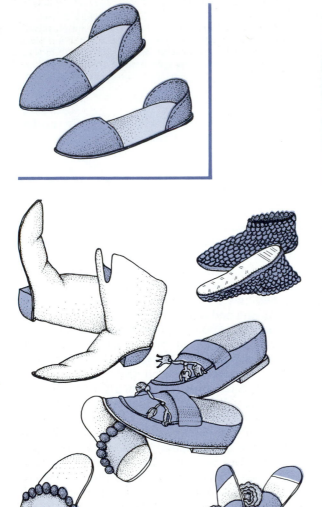

Computers use algorithms when playing chess; humans use hueristics, or rules of the thumb, thus usually can beat computers.

Robert Glaser

Fig. 9.9 Computers have problems recognizing simple objects such as a pair of slippers because they must "know" what the object looks like from any perspective.

eras. They usually do so by comparing each object they "see" with a **template**, or *exact* visual reproduction of the object, which is stored in the computer's memory. Using an algorithm, the computer can rotate its image of the template through three dimensions, so it can recognize the object no matter what its orientation in space.

The problem with using templates is that they are *exact copies* of a particular object. Given the template of a "robin," the computer could recognize most robins. But what would it

do if it encountered a crow, much less a penguin or an ostrich?

Computers can also be programmed to identify *critical features* or *attributes* of various objects. And it can use algorithms or "rules" that will allow it to combine these features or attributes in standard ways. However, *you* do much better at identification tasks, because you use prototypes rather than templates. Prototypes are much fuzzier "mental images" of concepts or categories than are templates. And that is why prototypes are so useful in real-life situations, for what prototypes lack in the way of precision, they make up in terms of generality.

AI researchers have learned, rather painfully, that the human mind is a very "noisy" or "sloppy" processing system. It can tolerate a lot of error and imprecision, and still come up with the right answer. To date, no one has been able to program this type of "creative and practical sloppiness" into a robot's information-processing system.

Question: Years ago, "playboys" in movies used to drink champagne out of their lovers' satin slippers. How might your robot react if you told it to "fetch a satin champagne glass"?

Parallel Processing

The chess-playing computer is a good example of a *serial processor*. The machine evaluates one move at a time. And while it takes but a tiny fraction of a second to make each decision, the machine must look over millions of possibilities in *serial* fashion.

Your brain is both slower and faster than a computer. It takes each of your neurons longer to "process" a single input than it does the individual "chips" in a computer's brain. However, each neural circuit in your brain is really a "little computer." When you look at a picture, therefore, millions of individual "neural computers" work on parts of this input *at the same time*. That is, your brain automatically "breaks the picture up" into millions of tiny parts. Then separate circuits process each part *simultaneously*. AI researchers call this approach **parallel processing**. As you might guess, "shared" or "parallel" processing is extremely efficient—and extremely fast.

We probably won't have computers *physically capable* of parallel processing until the 1990's. And it may take us longer to figure out how the computer should *divide up the task* into a million parts than it takes us to build the computer itself.

Question: To repeat a question asked earlier, how will your robot *know* when it's completed the task of "fetching the slippers"?

Knowledge = Facts plus Rules

Twenty years ago, AI specialists tried to program a computer to diagnose various types of illnesses by asking patients for their symptoms. In its simplest form, this sort of "medical diag-

Template (TEM-plate). A pattern or mold used to guide the formation of an object. A cookie cutter is a simple type of template.

Parallel processing. Most computers use algorithms. That is, they solve problems one step at a time. Parallel processing involves breaking a problem up into many different parts, and then working on the parts *simultaneously*—rather as if you had hundreds of computers linked together, each solving part of the same problem. Your brain uses parallel processing. Presumably, so will the "fifth generation of computers" (due in the 1990's)—if anyone can figure out how to program them to accomplish this miracle.

nostics" is really an exercise in *categorization*. So, the AI researchers told themselves, diagnostics should involve little more than (1) identification of "defining attributes," and (2) rules for combining these attributes. Therefore, the AI experts created various highly logical algorithms that would make the computer ask the patient various types of questions. The computer would then try to combine the answers into a precise description of the patient's illness. This algorithmic approach has succeeded fairly well with a few well-defined illnesses. However, computers do rather poorly with complex medical problems. And they fail miserably when trying to diagnose "mental disorders."

By 1980, the AI specialists started looking at medical diagnostics in rather a different light. That is, rather than building logical algorithms, they tried to *mimic* the decision-making skills of human experts. For example, University of Pittsburgh psychologist Robert Glaser and his associates studied how highly experienced physicians made medical diagnoses just from inspecting X-rays of patients. They tried to discover what kinds of "critical features" the skilled physicians looked for in the X-rays, and how they put these features together to make a diagnosis. Glaser and his group then compared the approach used by *experienced physicians* with that employed by *young doctors* who were just learning how to "read an X-ray."

In an article in the February 1984 *American Psychologist*, Glaser suggests that skilled and beginning doctors use quite different decision-making strategies. An expert looks at an X-ray and immediately perceives features that a beginner either overlooks or finds only after a lengthy search. The young doctor may have all the *facts* he or she needs to arrive at a correct diagnosis, but the beginner uses an *algorithm*—a "logical search." The expert has learned to use *heuristics*. That is, the expert uses "rules-of-thumb" plus facts. The rules—or heuristics—tell the experienced doctor which features (or facts) are important, and which aren't. And these heuristics are *acquired through experience*.

According to Robert Glaser, knowledge equals facts plus rules. "As individuals acquire knowledge, they also should be empowered to think and reason," Glaser says. If and when we gain enough knowledge about the ways in which humans *acquire and use knowledge*, then perhaps we will know enough to teach a robot to "think and reason" too.

Question: Suppose a robot has three human masters, and they all start shouting orders at the machine at the same time. How would you expect the robot to react?

Channel Capacity

Thinking, reasoning, and decision making are learned skills. But when you think and reason, you typically are "processing" inputs from the outside world. Therefore, anything that disrupts the flow of information from your receptors to your cortex will also affect your ability to make good decisions.

Informational inputs move up to your brain through various *sensory channels*. Each of your sense modalities—vision, hearing, taste, smell, and "touch"—is a "channel" that information flows through. These various modalities (or channels) have a certain *physical capacity* for handling inputs. AI experts call this *channel capacity*, or the amount of information you can input in a given amount of time through one sensory modality.

Let's see what "channel capacity" is all about. Imagine a large city (such as Los Angeles) that depends on distant lakes and rivers for much of its water supply. Water is brought into Los Angeles through large pipes. These pipes, of course, have a certain capacity for handling water. If you try to push too much water through the pipes in a given amount of time, the pipes burst from the pressure and you get a disruption called a flood. If you drastically restrict the amount of water, you get a disruption called a drought. In either case, the people of Los Angeles suffer.

Now, think of your own brain. If you try to force too much information into your head in a short period of time—say, by "cramming" for an exam—you get a disruption called **information**

overload. You experience stress, and you may not do very well on the exam. Oddly enough, you may suffer stress as well if you *restrict* your inputs too drastically—for then you will experience a situation called **information underload**.

We will discuss information *overload* in Chapter 12, when we look at stress (and how to manage it). To end this chapter on cognition, therefore, let's take a look at its mirror-image, information *underload*. You may be surprised at how people react when they are *deprived of inputs*.

Sensory Isolation

The information-processing approach to cognition tends to emphasis *inputs*. The reason for this emphasis should be clear by now. You can't survive unless you can gain some *measure of control* over what your environment gives to you. Thus, you spend a fair amount of your "mental processing time" trying to figure out how to predict and control your inputs.

If you doubt the importance of inputs, ask yourself this question: What would happen to you if, as you were reading these lines, you suddenly lost *all* your sensory inputs?

That is, what would you *experience mentally* if something unexpectedly blocked off all incoming information both from your body and from the outside world? What if you couldn't hear, see, smell, taste, or feel anything at all? How would you know where your arms or legs were? How would you discover whether you were wearing clothes or not, or whether it was hot or cold where you were? How would you react if you couldn't determine whether any parts of your body were moving, or whether you were standing up or lying down?

Question: If your robot lost all its inputs, would it react any differently than you would? Why (or why not)?

Consequences of Input Underload

Whenever you are deprived of the inputs you want or need in life, you respond in a variety of ways. To begin with, your motivational systems are *aroused*. If you get no food, you become hungry. If you are deprived of informational inputs, you hunger for intellectual stimulation. If you are cut off from other people, you will surely yearn for the sight of a familiar face.

The second important consequence of input underload has to do with your *values*. The hungrier you are, the more important food becomes to you. The more significant food is to you, the more your orienting reflex is directed toward food-related inputs. And the more you orient toward food, the more rewarding it will be when you finally get it. Furthermore, the greater your deprivation, the more likely it is that you will work for food, and the more probable it becomes that you will eat new or unusual items. In short, the *greater your need*, the *more flexible and changeable you are likely to become* in your attempts to satisfy that need.

The third consequence of input deprivation has to do with the voluntary control you have over your thoughts and actions. Although you may not realize it, your mind and body are so constructed that they *cannot operate normally if you are cut off from your environment.*

You can't make hamburger if you don't have meat to grind, and you can't digest food until you've swallowed it. Nor can you *think* about things for very long if you don't have sensory inputs to process. Thus, under conditions of severe sensory deprivation (input underload), you could lose voluntary control of your thought processes. And if someone then gave you inputs aimed at changing your values and behaviors, you might well accept these inputs as uncritically as a starving person sometimes accepts rotten food.

"Brainwashing"

During the 1930's and 1940's, strange rumors began circulating in the scientific world that the Russian and Chinese governments were using some form of sensory isolation on prisoners. The term **brainwashing** apparently was first applied to these techniques by journalist Edward Hunter in his 1951 book *Brainwashing in Red China.* Hunter took the term from the Chinese words *hsi nao*, which literally mean "to wash the brain."

According to Hunter, "brainwashing" typically involved isolating a prisoner from almost all normal sensory inputs for a period of time. This isolation seemed to "soften the person up," allowing the authorities to "wash out all the old thoughts" from the prisoner's mind. The authorities could then replace the old values with new ones more acceptable to the Communist way. The "brainwashing" technique also involved *rewarding* prisoners for becoming more Communistic in their thoughts and actions,

Information overload. Input overload. Having to process too many inputs in too short a period of time.

Information underload. Input underload. Having so few inputs to process that your brain cannot function normally.

Brainwashing. Technically speaking, brainwashing is a "mind-change" technique that *always* involves sensory (or social) isolation as well as rewards and punishment.

Isolation chamber. Any small room or large container in which a person can be deprived of most sensory inputs for a period of time.

Translucent (trans-LOO-sent). Any material that transmits light but not patterns. Milk is translucent because you can see light through it, but not objects. Water is transparent because you can see both light and patterns through it.

Poltergeists (POLE-ter-guy-sts). From the German words meaning "noisy spirits." Perhaps you have read about old houses where the dishes suddenly fall off the shelves or where strange noises come from the attic or basement. Supposedly, poltergeists are responsible for such frightening experiences.

and *punishing* them when they resisted change.

The reports on "brainwashing" in China and Russia had one immediate effect—Western governments became worried that the Communists had discovered some kind of psychological magic. The Canadians were perhaps the first to react. As early as 1951, the Canadian government commissioned a group of psychologists at Donald Hebb's laboratory at McGill University to investigate the effects of sensory isolation on *attitude change*. While the experiments were supervised by Hebb, the actual work and planning were done by four of Hebb's students and associates—W. Heron, W.H. Bexton, T.H. Scott, and B.K. Doane.

The McGill Experiments

Heron and his colleagues at McGill began by building a small **isolation chamber** (see Fig. 9.10). They then paid students $20 a day to lie on a small bed, their arms inside cardboard mailing tubes. The students' eyes were covered by **translucent** goggles, and their hearing was masked by a noisy air conditioner.

The students were fed and watered when necessary, but were asked to remain as motionless as possible during the entire experiment.

Prior to undergoing the sensory deprivation, the students were given a battery of tests and questionnaires. The subjects received similar tests while in the isolation chamber, and after the deprivation experience had ended.

While the students were in the chamber, they were exposed to a series of propaganda mes-

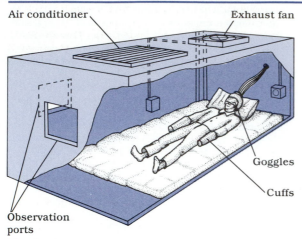

Air conditioner   Exhaust fan

Goggles

Cuffs

Observation ports

Fig. 9.10 A sensory-deprivation chamber.

Fig. 9.11 An iron lung used to force air into the lungs of polio victims who cannot breathe for themselves. (Birth Defects Foundation, March of Dimes)

sages read in a rather boring monotone. These messages concerned such supernatural events as mental telepathy, ghosts, and those noisy spirits called **poltergeists**.

In order to make sure any changes in the subjects' attitudes or behaviors were due to the isolation and not merely to exposure to the propaganda, Heron and his colleagues hired a separate group of students to serve as a *control group*. These students simply sat in a quiet room and listened to the same propaganda speeches through earphones without undergoing any real sensory isolation.

Intellectual Impairment and "Blank Minds"

The results of the McGill experiments were somewhat surprising. First, there was the matter of "length of stay." Heron and his colleagues had expected most of the subjects to withstand the isolation for several days. In fact, almost half of the students quit during the first 48 hours.

Second, those subjects who did stay showed considerable intellectual impairment during the sensory deprivation itself and for some hours afterward. Simple problem-solving exercises often seemed beyond the students' mental capacities. Furthermore, they had difficulties with motor coordination, and they did not adapt well to new situations.

Not all of the isolated subjects lasted long enough to be exposed to the dull and repetitious propaganda messages. But those who did usually asked to hear the speeches again and again

and again. These subjects were also much more profoundly affected by what they heard than were the students in the control group.

Of equal interest were the subjective reports the subjects gave of their experiences while in the "black box." At first, they thought a great deal about their various personal problems. But as time went on, they found such organized thinking more and more difficult. They could no longer concentrate on much of anything, so they just relaxed and let their minds drift.

Eventually most of these subjects experienced "blank periods" during which they simply could not *think* at all. They were conscious—which is to say that they were not asleep. But their minds simply were not functioning in a logical fashion. During these periods, their emotions often ran wild.

All of the students found the sensory deprivation very stressful and even very frightening.

Hallucinations

Some 80 percent of the McGill subjects reported *visual hallucinations*. For reasons no one yet understands, the *content* of these hallucinations seemed beyond the mental control of the subjects. One student, for example, could see nothing but eyeglasses, no matter how hard he tried to think of something else.

Many subjects reported disturbances in their *body images*. For instance, one student had the impression his body had turned into *twins*. That is, he was convinced there was another body lying on the bed with him, and that his own body partially overlapped this "twin." A second student stated that his mind seemed to leave his body and roam around the cubicle. Occasionally this "free mind" would look back at the "body" lying quietly on the bed to see what it was doing.

Still other students had "floating" feelings, as if their bodies had somehow overcome gravity and were hanging suspended in midair.

Other Deprivation Studies

Once the results of the McGill experiments were made public, psychologists in many laboratories in the United States began paying students to stay inside "black rooms" too. The results of these studies soon showed a common trend—the reactions a subject showed to sensory deprivation were mostly a function of what the subject's personality was like prior to entering the isolation chamber.

For example, students judged as being "normal and healthy" tended to *underestimate* the length of time they had been isolated. However, subjects who were judged as being "somewhat psychologically disturbed" before isolation often *overestimated* the length of time they had been in the cubicle. These subjects also broke off the experiment more readily than did subjects with apparently stronger or more mature personalities.

In general, the greater the state of deprivation, the less the subjects were able to tolerate the isolation. If the subjects were allowed to move around freely (in a totally dark room), they could often stand the experience for several days. But if they were forced to remain lying motionless on a bed, the subjects quit much sooner.

The shortest stays of all were reported by a group of scientists who asked their subjects to lie inside an iron lung—that is, a small tank-type **respirator** used by some victims of polio (see Fig. 9.11). Most of these subjects were terrified at being trapped inside such a narrow space and demanded to be released after spending but a few hours in the iron lung.

Respirator (RESS-pirr-ray-torr). A mechanical device that helps people breathe, often by pressing rhythmically on their chests.

Restricted Environmental Stimulation Therapy. Also called REST. Use of sensory isolation in order to reduce stress and motivate people to change their attitudes and behaviors.

The "REST" Cure

Although sensory isolation was first used as a way of "brainwashing" people, recent research suggests it may have therapeutic value in certain situations. For example, Canadian psychologist Peter Suedfeld has performed a series of experiments in which he has put clients in very restricted environments. Some of these people were overweight and simply could not keep to a diet. Others were heavy smokers who found it almost impossible to give up cigarettes, no matter what kind of therapy they tried. Suedfeld calls this technique **Restricted Environmental Stimulation Therapy**, or the "REST Cure."

Suedfeld's clients typically remained in a sensory isolation chamber for 24 hours or so. During this period of time, Suedfeld played recorded messages aimed at convincing them either to lose weight or to stop smoking. The clients were also given "booster sessions" two months later in which they again spent some time in the chamber. In his recent book *Restricted Environmental Stimulation*, Suedfeld reports considerable success. For example, all of the smokers on whom he tried the technique reported a significant reduction in their "craving" for cigarettes. And a majority of them were able to give up smoking for at least a period of several months.

In another set of studies, psychologists G. David Cooper and Henry Adams worked with a group of 60 people who were heavy social drinkers. Half of the group were men, half were women. The drinkers voluntarily spent some three hours in a sensory isolation chamber similar to the one used in the McGill studies described earlier in this chapter. After the subjects had been in the cubicle for 90 minutes, they heard anti-alcohol messages.

Cooper and Adams also tested several *control groups* of people who had similar drinking problems. One control group heard the messages, but not while in sensory deprivation. A second control group spent time in the isolation chamber, but heard no messages. A third control group was given no treatment at all.

A subject of Peter Suedfield in a sensory-deprivation chamber.

Peter Suedfield

According to a 1981 report by Cooper and Adams, the experimental subjects showed a significant reduction in their consumption of alcohol. Even though given no additional treatment, the subjects maintained their reduced rate of drinking for at least six months. The subjects in the three control groups, however, continued to drink about as much as they did prior to the study.

Therapeutic Isolation: An Evaluation

The REST technique combines sensory isolation with "suggestions for improving your behavior." Several studies indicate the REST technique may reduce stress temporarily and may also decrease the frequency of some types of bad habits. We need a great deal more research on this topic, however, before we will know "for sure" just how effective therapeutic isolation is—or isn't.

The success of sensory isolation as a therapeutic tool seems to be due to three factors. First, it increases the *attention* a subject pays to inputs received while in isolation. Second, it increases the *acceptability* or social value of those inputs. And third, isolation apparently *motivates* people to make changes in their thoughts and behaviors.

Cognition is the study of *how* you process and respond to inputs from your body and from the outside world. Motivation is the study of *why* you bother to do so in the first place. Now that we have "paid attention to" cognition, it's time to "think about" the subject of human motivation.

Question: At the beginning of the chapter, we noted that the behaviorists threw out conation and cognition because they believed that "mental activities" (if they existed) were completely controlled by environmental inputs. What have you learned from this chapter that supports the behaviorist view? What seems to contradict it?

Summary

1 Years ago, psychologists divided **consciousness** into three processes: Conation, affect, and cognition.
2 **Conation** is the act of "willing."
3 **Affect** is a technical term for "feelings" and "emotions."
4 Cognition is a complex process. Initial stages include **attention**, **input reception**, **input transduction**, **critical feature selection** and **input screening**. These processes occur primarily in the lower centers of the brain.
5 Later stages of cognition include **pattern recognition**, **registration**, **perception**, **temporary memory storage**, **thinking**, **decision making**, **forgetting** and

memory, and **responding**. These processes occur primarily in the cortex.

6 Attention often begins with the **orienting reflex**, which includes a general state of **arousal**. Arousal is often measured with a **polygraph** that records the **galvanic skin response**.

7 Some psychologists believe the orienting reflex is a response to **novelty**. Others hold that the reflex occurs primarily to **significant** inputs.

8 Inputs reach your cortex by two routes, the **straight-line sensory system** and the **reticular activating system**, or RAS. The straight-line sensory system handles information. The RAS screens inputs for significance and **arouses** the cortex when an important message is coming through on the straight-line system.

9 Two stimuli that are **just noticeably different** 50 percent of the time are one **JND** apart.

10 **Weber's Law** states that the difference threshold, or JND, is always a **constant fraction** of the reference stimulus.

11 **Overlearned responding** occurs when the lower centers automatically execute reactions that the cortex is unconscious of.

12 Research suggests that the lower centers block weak **emotionally-laden inputs** from reaching the cortex by increasing their conscious thresholds, an effect known as **perceptual defense**.

13 Studies on **subliminal perception** indicate that the lower centers may respond reflexively to inputs too weak ever to reach conscious awareness.

14 According to one theory, the RAS and other lower centers make up the **preconscious processing system**.

15 The PPS may **attend simultaneously** to inputs from all modalities and screens inputs for **significance**.

16 Only significant inputs reach the conscious system, which can attend to just **one input at a time**.

17 There are two types of cognitive categories, **natural** and **artificial**.

18 There are three levels of categories, **superordinate**, **basic**, and **subordinate**. Basic categories are the easiest to deal with cognitively.

19 Humans often create **prototypes** of basic categories to speed concept formation.

20 **Problem solving** typically begins with **goal setting** and a description of the **original state** or **baseline**. It continues with **conceptualizing the problem**, which involves creation of **mental images**.

21 Problem solving continues with **trial solutions** that are governed by **rules**.

22 Finding solutions to problems is often inhibited by **functional fixedness**, or mental set.

23 The study of **artificial intelligence** is a search for ways to program computers to **reason** (process inputs) as humans do.

24 Computers typically must use **algorithms** or exact formulas to solve problems. Humans tend to use **heuristics**, or "rules of thumb."

25 Humans identify objects using **prototypes**, while computers must use **templates** or exact copies.

26 Computers process inputs **sequentially**, while humans use **parallel processing**.

27 All information-processing systems have a limited **channel capacity**. Both **input overload** and **input underload** lead to stress.

28 Humans undergoing **sensory isolation** could not think straight, suffered from hallucinations, and uncritically accepted any inputs.

29 **Restricted Environmental Stimulation Therapy** has been used successfully to help people stop smoking, lose weight, and reduce their drinking.

(Continued from page 227.)

A few hours after he got out of the "black room," Philip Cassone returned to the laboratory to take some more tests. The psychologists explained that they were giving him the tests to find out how soon he had recovered from the effects of the sensory deprivation.

When he took the tests again, Phil did much better than when he had taken them in isolation. Although, to be truthful, he still didn't seem to be as sharp as he usually was. Obviously some of the effects were still lingering on.

But the psychologists assured him that within a few days he would be as good as ever.

"How did I do as a subject?" Phil asked the man in charge when the tests were done.

"Let's see," the man said, putting down his pipe and checking the records. "You stayed in for about 26 hours. That's about average. Not bad at all."

Phil was annoyed. He had hoped to do much better than average. He turned to leave in disgust, when he spotted a tape recorder sitting on one of the tables.

"Did you record my voice?" Phil asked.

The psychologist put his pipe in his mouth and nodded gravely.

"Could I listen to some of it?"

The man picked a tape up off the table, put it on the machine, and started the tape in motion.

Phil was shocked to hear the way his voice came out. "Do I really sound like that?"

When the psychologist again nodded soberly, Phil paid even closer attention to the tape. He heard himself demand to know what time it was, heard himself insist that the psychologists talk to him, listened to his scream that if they didn't say something right away he was com-

ing out.

And then he heard a door open and his voice come faintly from a distance . . . "You bastards ruined the experiment. You made me come out."

Phil blushed. "Did I really call you guys bastards?"

Again the psychologist nodded his head slowly in agreement.

Phil groaned. It was the first time he had ever called a professor such a name—at least to his face. "I must have lost my mind to have said something like that," Phil said.

The psychologist just puffed on his pipe and smiled.

Recommended Readings

Dixon, N.F. (1981). *Preconscious processing.* Chichester, Eng.: Wiley.

Matlin, M. (1983). *Cognition.* New York: Holt, Rinehart and Win-ston.

Suedfeld, P. (1980). *Restricted environmental stimulation: Research and clinical applications.* New York: Wiley.

Wingard, J.A., Maltzman, I. (1980). Interest as a predeterminer of the GSR index of the orienting reflex. *Acta Psychologica, 46*(2), 153–160.

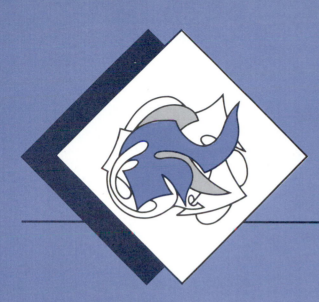

PART III

Motivation

Did You Know That...

- Motivation can be viewed as a series of questions about *why* you do what you do?
- Some psychologists consider the need for "self-actualization" the most mature need of all?
- Stimulation of a rat's "feeding center" will cause the animal to eat huge amounts of food?
- Stimulation of a rat's "satiation center" will cause the animal to refuse almost all food?
- Colleges often discriminate against overweight students?
- More lower-class than upper-class persons in the United States are overweight?
- Some husbands seem to push food on their wives to keep the women fat and faithful?
- Some upper-class young women go on "food binges" during which they consume up to 15,000 calories, then try to purge themselves of the food?
- Almost anyone can gain or lose weight by using a technique called Cognitive Behavior Modification?

10

Introduction to Motivation

"By Bread Alone"

Thelma Green shook her plump face in dismay. "It's a dirty shame the way they treat people who are a trifle overweight," she said. "They don't consider our problems at all, and we've got lots."

Annette Holmes smiled and nodded encouragingly. Thelma Green certainly did have "lots"—about 280 pounds of "lots." But Annette liked the woman and, because Annette was a therapist at the Weight Control Clinic, she wanted to help Thelma shed some of those pounds if she could. So Annette just nodded and smiled and waited to see what Thelma had in mind.

"Take, for instance, clothes." Thelma Green picked at the blouse she was wearing. "Who makes good-looking clothes for somebody as fat as me? Potato sacks is what they sell us, and we have to buy them because there's nothing else available."

Annette looked carefully at Thelma's clothes. They didn't look all that bad. The woman was neat in her appearance despite her size. But Annette continued to nod her head.

"And anyhow, what kind of wardrobe can you have when you shoot up or down 30 pounds every six months?"

Thelma continued. "I'm like a yo-yo. I gain a little, so I don't fit most of the things I have. And then I go on a crash diet, and I lose 40 pounds, and I *still* don't fit my clothes because now they're too big for me. I tell you, I've been on so many diets I think I'll puke if I ever see another bowl of cottage cheese!"

"Diets don't do all that much good, it's true," Annette said. "It's not losing pounds that is the difficult part, as you know. It's learning how to eat sensibly so that you reach and maintain a reasonable weight. That's what is so terribly hard for most overweight people."

"Why is that?" Thelma asked plaintively.

Annette warmed to her subject. "Starving yourself is a just a short-term change in behavior. And you pretend that when you've lost a few pounds, you've solved your basic problem. But you haven't really made any fundamental changes in your eating habits, your exercise habits, or in your self-image. If you want to keep your weight down permanently, you have to learn to eat sensibly, and keep on eating that way. Most overweight people just aren't motivated to make that drastic a change in the way they live and think and feel."

"But I don't eat all that much," Thelma replied, an edgy tone in her voice. "I just can't understand why I stay so heavy."

Annette smiled. "Look, Thelma. Fatness is caused by just one thing—you take in more calories than you burn up. Some people eat too much. Other people eat fairly sensibly but exercise too little. But the real problem is that most people don't *measure* what they're doing. So they never face the fact that they're inputting too much and outputting too little."

"That can't be my problem," Thelma said a bit testily. "Because I know what I eat, and it's very little, I assure you. No breakfast at all, and I have a very light lunch. I eat a sensible dinner, and that's it. Maybe 1,500 calories per day. But I gain weight on that, so maybe there's something wrong with the way my body utilizes food, or something."

Annette sensed the woman's impending anger and backtracked a little. "Well, there is a recent medical study indicating some people can eat less to maintain their weight than others have to eat. So I suppose that could be the difficulty. Have you seen a doctor yet?"

"I've seen a dozen," Thelma said unhappily. "They've put me on a dozen different diets, they've given me pills, and they've given me hundreds of lectures. Hasn't helped a bit. I saw one guy last week. He told me I had a possible heart problem, that something might be wrong with my kidneys, and that I was going to die if I didn't lose 100 pounds right away. I asked him how I was going to shed those pounds, and he said that any dummy knew how to lose weight. Then he gave me another diet and said it would be my fault if I got sick and died because I was too stubborn to lose weight."

"So how did you react to this news?" Annette asked.

Thelma pulled out a handkerchief and dabbed it at her eyes. "I got so discouraged and depressed I went home and cooked a huge meal to make me feel better."

Annette had heard that one before. She just wished medical doctors would look at the actual consequences of the "little lectures" they gave their patients. Perhaps they'd lecture less and give their patients emotional support more often. "Well, I can understand your reaction to what your doctor said," Annette said, smiling warmly. "But it does seem as if you ought to try to learn how to eat better so that you can get back into shape medically as well as socially. Suppose we start off by taking a baseline of what you really eat . . ."

"It isn't much, I told you that."

Annette smiled again. "I know, but we want exact figures. Here's a form I'd like you to fill out. Please record everything you eat and drink. Put down the time, the place, the amount, who else is present, what you're doing, and how you feel. That will give us a good baseline or starting point. Once we have those data, we can talk seriously about how to help you learn some new eating and exercise habits."

"Fifteen hundred calories a day, it's no more than that. And I still gain weight!"

Annette nodded. "Perhaps, but you may be surprised. What I want you to do next is to decide how much you'd like to weigh a year or so from now. Then make a list of all the benefits and gains you'd receive if you got down to that weight."

"Well, my clothes would fit better," Thelma responded. "And I could go bowling again, and there's my friend Shirley in Miami I want to impress . . ." Her voice trailed off pensively.

"Very good thoughts!" said Annette. "Please put all those things down on your list, and any others you can think of. And come see me again on Friday at this same time. We'll have our dietician see you then."

Thelma Green gathered herself together and stood up. "Do you really think there's any hope for me?" she asked softly. "Can I really get things under control?"

Annette looked the woman squarely in the eye. "Certainly there's hope. You can do it—if you really want to."

"I really want to," Thelma said. "I really do."

Three days later Annette got an urgent telephone call. "I don't believe it!" Thelma wailed. "I wrote down everything I ate and drank, just like you said I was supposed to do . . . "

"The baseline, yes . . . " said Annette. "That's good."

"No, it's terrible! Absolutely terrible! I added it up, and I'm taking in 5,000 calories a day. Can you believe that?"

"I can believe it," Annette said, thinking of the woman's size.

"Listen," said Thelma, "I want to go on a 1,000-calorie-a-day diet right away. Do you hear, right now!"

For just a second, Annette panicked. Cutting down from 5,000 to 1,000 a day would surely be too big a change. So Annette stalled a bit. "Listen, Thelma, you said you didn't eat much breakfast or lunch and had just a light dinner. When are you taking in all those calories?"

"At night, after dinner, sitting in front of the boob tube," the woman replied. "I snack and snack and snack. About 3,000 calories worth an evening, to tell you the truth."

Annette nodded to herself, then spoke again into the phone. "And how do you feel when you're snacking?"

"Bored," came the reply. "I had a bad day at work yesterday. I got depressed, and I came home and started dinner and just kept on eating all night long."

"Well," said Annette, "what happened at work that got you so depressed?"

Thelma paused a moment before replying. "To tell you the truth, one of the women I supervise screwed up a report, and when I told her to get her ass in gear and do it over again, she threw the report in my face. I'm just trying to be helpful, and she throws a temper tantrum like a 3-year-old."

Annette frowned. Weight control therapy seemed so simple when you first went into it. Just help people learn to eat correctly, right? But very often you had to help people clean up their emotional problems before you could teach them to control their overeating. Annette suspected she'd have to teach Thelma some new job skills so she wouldn't get depressed at work and then overeat when she came home.

"Listen," continued Thelma, "I've gone through the kitchen and thrown out all the junk food I could find. But now there's practically nothing left to eat. I'd go to the grocery store right now, but I don't know what to buy or how to cook low-cal stuff. Can you help me?"

"Of course I can help," Annette responded. "That's what I'm here for. Tell you what. I'll come over and we can make up a shopping list. Then we can have a light dinner somewhere and go to the grocery store."

Thelma snorted loudly. "Go to the store *after* you eat?"

"Certainly," Annette replied. "That way you cut down on the impulse buying. I'll bring over a really good diet plan our dietician has prepared. We can look it over and then go shopping. I'll bring over a nice exercise plan too."

"Exercise?" Thelma said in a shocked tone of voice. "I don't go for that stuff very much. Except for bowling, which I've given up for the duration."

"Why?"

Thelma sighed. "Well, I used to belong to this bowling league, and I really did like it. But I got so big I didn't fit my bowling clothes any more. And then we usually had three or four drinks, and you know how many calories there are in alcohol. And, well, to tell the truth, sometimes when I got a little snockered I had these arguments with my buddies . . . "

Annette could see it all quite clearly. Thelma simply didn't know how to get along very well with people. So she avoided company and stayed home by herself and got depressed and watched the tube and snacked. "Listen," Annette said, "You should go back to bowling even if your clothes don't fit. You can tip the bartender to give you a glass of icewater with lots of cherries and orange slices in it, and everyone will think you're drinking gin. And we can do some role playing so that you'll learn how to handle any social situations that might bother you. Okay?"

"Okay," came the reluctant response.

"But we're going to have to get you on a regular exercise program too."

"None of that crazy jumping around stuff, do you hear?"

Annette grinned. "Of course not. We'll start with walking. Just walking. For instance, you tend to eat when you first come home from work, right?"

"Right."

"Well, we can interrupt that habitual behavior by having you walk for 10 minutes when you get home. That way . . . "

Thelma suddenly sounded excited again. "That way I don't associate eating with getting home from work, right? Hey, that's great. And you know I live in an apartment house, so even if it's raining I could just walk up and down the stairs for a while. Probably meet a lot of my neighbors for the first time, too. Might even be fun . . .''

"Of course it will be," Annette said enthusiastically. "Tell you what. Why don't you go for a walk and meet me at the parking lot in a quarter of an hour. Then we can look at the diet, have supper, and go grocery shopping."

"Okay, it's a deal. But listen, no grapefruit and no cottage cheese, or I'll upchuck right there in the supermarket."

Annette laughed. "Okay, but no cookies and no potato chips either."

Thelma moaned softly and hung up the phone.

A month later, Annette sat quietly in her office, a worried look on her face. For the first time ever, Thelma had missed an appointment. She had asked to see Annette at 9 p.m., because she was going bowling right after work. Annette had agreed, because Thelma was doing beautifully. She had lost 22 pounds in four weeks, which was amazing. She was walking at least 30 minutes each day, and she had made several new friends while marching up and down the apartment stairs. Now it was nearly 11 p.m., but where was Thelma?

Annette reviewed the situation mentally. Thelma had gotten many insights into her own personality in the process of trying to lose weight. As Annette had guessed, Thelma tended to be rather bossy and punishing to her friends. But during their role-playing exercises, Thelma had learned how to express affection and gratitude openly instead of converting it into criticism.

She also was doing much better on the job. Before treatment, Thelma had ignored the people she supervised unless they goofed up. Now she spent most of her time helping them set goals for themselves and letting them know when they were showing progress. So she seldom came home depressed, and she had so many invitations to visit her friends that she almost never spent the evening alone watching TV.

Annette dialed Thelma's number again, but there still was no answer.

Of course, the woman still had a long way to go—both physically and psychologically. She had a terrible self-image, and she wouldn't use cosmetics at all. "I don't deserve to look good," Thelma had said. "No one as fat as me deserves to look anything but ugly."

Annette had solved the problem by teaching Thelma how to use lipstick and rouge, and by getting her to write down daily at least one good thing that she thought about herself. But Thelma frequently got depressed when she felt she "wasn't getting anywhere," so the two women had talked at length about Thelma's real goals in life.

The one thing that Thelma wanted was the respect and affection of others. Her feelings about Shirley, the friend who lived in Miami, were an example. "Shirley's a doll," Thelma had said. "She's stuck by me through thick and thin. Mostly thick, of course, given my size. Anyhow, what I want to do most is to lose 100 pounds, and fly to Miami without telling her I'm coming. I've seen that scene a thousand times in my mind's eye. Shirley opens the door, and she is thunderstruck. 'Hi, Shirl,' I say to her. 'It's the new me.'"

What better motivation? Annette had asked herself. So, at her suggestion, Thelma had started putting away $2.00 in her piggy bank every day that she stuck to her diet. Half the money went for cosmetics, but the other half she put in the bank to pay for the projected trip to Miami. But Thelma still had a few dozen pounds to lose before she flew south.

Annette gave Thelma's number one last try. After three rings a discouraged and somewhat intoxicated voice answered.

"Thelma? This is Annette. What's happened?"

After a moment's silence, Thelma sobbed, "Oh, Annette. I'm so sorry. I'm just no damned good. I just don't deserve to get better."

The crisis, Annette thought. It almost always happens when the person is right on the brink of success.

"Look, Thelma, I want to come over to see you. Right now."

"You better hurry, honey," came the tearful reply. "There may not be much left to see if you don't."

(Continued on page 288.)

David Edwards

Motivation (mote-tee-VAY-shun). From the Latin word *motivare*, meaning "to move." Motivation is defined in many different ways, the most common being that it is a series of questions that you ask about *why* people think, feel, and behave as they do.

Motivation: Fact and Theory

What do psychologists mean when they use the term **motivation**? Many things. For, as David Edwards of Iowa State University notes, motivation isn't really an "area in psychology." Rather, it is a *series of questions* we ask as we try to explain *why* people act as they do. Different psychologists tend to ask quite different sorts of questions. Therefore, there are about as many definitions of *motivation* as there are behavioral scientists.

Almost all scientists agree, however, that humans have *needs*, and that the study of needs makes up a large part of what we call "motivation." So, suppose we begin this chapter by asking four important questions about needs:

1. First, what *kinds* of needs do you have? Obviously, you have a biological requirement for things such as food and water. But can we explain everything you do in terms of your attempt to satisfy these basic *physical* needs? Or do you have intra-psychic and social needs that are (in their way) as strong as your need for food and water? If so, what are these psychological and social needs? Do they vary much from person to person, or do all people develop about the same sort of social and psychological motives at the same stage in life?

    In a sense, this is the "mind-body problem revisited." Those psychologists who take a biological viewpoint tend to emphasize bodily needs. Those theorists who emphasize "mental" and "social" activities often hold that psychological needs are as "basic" as are physical needs.

2. Second, *where* do your motivations come from? Your basic needs are surely determined by your genetic blueprint. But pre-

suming we allow for social and intra-psychic motives, what causes them? Are they also determined (even in part) by your genetic blueprint? Or are they entirely imposed on you by your culture and your past experiences?

In brief, how much of your motivation is *innate*, and how much is *learned*? This is, of course, the "nature-nurture" debate extended to the field of motivation.

3. Third, what are the various *mechanisms* by which you satisfy your needs? Are all your behaviors aimed at reducing stress and pain? Or are you motivated primarily by the promise of pleasure? That is, do you eat to reduce your hunger pangs, or because food tastes so good? Or are your eating behaviors (and their associated feelings) primarily controlled by such environmental inputs as cultural values and social expectations?

    Put briefly, are motivated behaviors determined by such single factors as stress and arousal? Or are motivated acts multi-determined?

4. Last but not least, what is the relationship between motivation and conation? As we pointed out at the start of Chapter 9, *conation* is the act of "willing." Does your mind do anything more than yield to your body's itches and urges (the behavioral viewpoint)? Or can you voluntarily *choose* among a variety of behaviors in any given situation (the conative viewpoint)?

    Put more simply, can we explain your motives entirely in terms of blind biological drives, or is motivation a matter of your consciously selecting among various behaviors available to you at a given time?

These are some of the thorny questions you must try to answer when you try to explain *why* people do what they do. Little wonder, then, that the study of human motivation is one of the most fascinating but also one of the most frustrating areas in all of psychology.

Suppose we begin by looking at some early definitions of this slippery concept called motivation.

5. Self-actualization needs
4. Esteem needs (Social learning theory operates on this rung)
3. Belongingness or love needs (Perceptual theory operates on this rung)
2. Safety needs (Arousal theory operates on this rung)
1. Physiological needs (Drive theory operates on this rung)

Fig. 10.1 Maslow's hierarchy of needs.

According to Maslow, biological needs such as food are the most basic of all.

Abraham Maslow

Motivation and Self-Movement

The word *motivation* comes from the Latin term meaning "to move." Ancient scholars were fascinated by the fact that some objects in the world seem to be *self-movers*, while other objects remain stationary unless *acted upon* by some outside force. The ancients assumed that self-initiated motion was caused by a *spirit* inside the object—a "little man" of some kind—that pushed or impelled the object into action. Whenever the "spirit was moved," so was the object or body that the spirit inhabited.

It was not until about the 16th century that Western scientists gained enough knowledge of physics to explain the "behaviors" of such *inan-*

imate objects as rocks and rivers in purely *mechanical* terms. Thus, it was not until a few hundred years ago that we managed to get the **animus** out of inanimate objects. And once scientists had made this giant intellectual step, they began to wonder if the actions of *living* organisms couldn't also be understood in physical or non-spiritual terms. Therefore, many of our theories of motivation are based on the belief that human activities are just as mechanical as are the movements of bedbugs and bacteria. The best-known of these mechanistic approaches are *drive theory* and *arousal theory*.

Opposed to these biological viewpoints are a variety of psychological and social theories that stress the importance of intra-psychic and environmental influences on behavior. But these approaches are limited too, in that most of them neglect the importance of biological needs.

Fortunately, there is one holistic theory that more or less encompasses the biological, the social, and the intra-psychic approaches to motivation. Although it too is far from being complete, let's talk about that approach first, and then explain drive theory and arousal theory. Finally, we will attempt to show the real complexities of motivation by discussing one very human problem in some detail—why some people overeat, while others deliberately undereat.

Maslow's Theory of "Self-Actualization"

According to Abraham Maslow, human needs can be placed on a **hierarchy**, or ladder. This hierarchy runs from the simplest biological motives up to the most complex of intra-psychic and social desires. As you develop in life, you move up the ladder until you reach the top rung, which Maslow calls *self-actualization* (see Fig. 10.1).

Maslow assumes that you start life at the lowest level of the motivational hierarchy. He believes you are born with innate reflexes that help you satisfy your basic biological needs. Once you are blessed with biological life, however, you must secure some control over your physical environment. Thus, almost immediately after birth, you begin to move up to the second level of the motivational hierarchy, that of safety needs.

The next two rungs of the ladder involve the social environment. You need people to love,

Animus (ANN-ee-muss). The Latin word meaning "spirit."
Hierarchy (HIGH-er-ark-key). To make a hierarchy is to list things (or people) in order of their importance.

and you need people to love you. Part of these needs are satisfied by your family, but there are also work groups and various social organizations you can join. These groups not only offer you rewards for performing well, they can also help you learn what self-respect is all about.

If you are fortunate, you will finally reach the top rung of Maslow's hierarchy and achieve *self-actualization*. This term is difficult to define. Put simply, it means reaching your own greatest potential, doing the things you do best in your own unique way, and then helping those around you achieve these goals too. But you can get to this final stage of human development only by first solving the problems associated with the four lower levels.

Now that we have given Maslow's theory in broad outline, let's look at what he says in more detail.

Maslow's Hierarchy of Needs

Maslow says there are five primary levels on the ladder of human motivation:

1. *Biological needs.* Bodily needs come first. You must always satisfy your physical needs or you won't live long enough to take care of any psychological or social needs you may have. You cannot take the next step up the motivational ladder unless, and until, your primary biological needs are met. (As we will soon see, *drive theory* operates at this rung of the ladder.)
2. *Safety needs.* Neither man nor woman lives by bread alone. Once an infant's basic needs are satisfied, the child is ready to explore the physical environment. But as we will show in later chapters, young children typically don't explore unless they feel secure. A predictable world is, generally speaking, a much safer environment than one that is unpredictable. Thus, one reason you "move about" in your environment is to reduce your uncertainty about what the world has to offer. With this knowledge, you can choose sensibly among the various physical inputs you need to sustain life. And once you know what to expect from the world, you can move on to the next rung of the motivational ladder. (Arousal theory operates in part at this stage of development.)

According to Maslow all people have "belongingness" needs that are innately determined.

As children gain emotional security they begin to explore their physical world.

Maslow states that "self-actualization" or desire to reach the limits of your own potential is at the top of the needs hierarchy. The photograph shows a father and daughter graduating from college at the same time.

These three people are blind. Do you think their ability to ski adds to their "self-esteem"?

3. *Belongingness* and *love needs*. Once you have gained control over your physical environment, you can then turn your attention to social inputs. As the poet John Donne once said, "No man is an island, entire of itself." Donne knew quite well that, to be a *human* being, you must have other people around you. Therefore, according to Maslow, you have an innate need for affection and love that can be satisfied only by other people. You must *affiliate* with others, and identify yourself with one or more like-minded individuals. When you identify with someone else, you learn to perceive part of the world as that person presumably does. (As we will learn in Chapters 11 and 12, perceptual and emotional theories of motivation apply primarily to the first three rungs of the ladder.)

4. *Esteem needs*. One reason you need other people is to help you set your life's goals. Under the right conditions, the groups you affiliate with can offer you *models* or *feed-forward* on what your future behavior might (or should) be. Groups also offer you external *feedback* on how close you are coming to achieving your targets in life. And the better you get at reaching your goals, the more esteem you will likely have for yourself (and the more esteem you will probably get from others). According to Maslow, "esteem needs" are just as important for *human* life as are food and water. (Social learning theory and the various theories of social motivation we will discuss later in this book operate at levels 2, 3, and 4 of the hierarchy.)

5. *Need for self-actualization*. Until you have achieved self-esteem, you probably will not feel secure enough to become a "fully-actualized person." Unless you have confidence in yourself, Maslow says, you will not dare to express yourself in your own unique way, make your own special contribution to society, and thus achieve your true inborn potential.

And once you have achieved self-actualization for yourself, Maslow says, you will find you have a strong urge to help others get where you have gotten. And to do *that*, you will need to teach others the lessons you learned as you worked your way up the four lower levels of the motivational hierarchy. (The many theories of personality and human development discussed later apply to all the rungs of Maslow's ladder, but primarily to the fifth rung.)

Question: How far up the ladder would a frequently abused child be likely to climb? Or a student whose teachers gave the student nothing but criticism?

Criticisms of Maslow's Theory

Like all theories in psychology, Maslow's *hierarchical* approach to human motivation has been subjected to many criticisms. As we will see in Chapter 19, Maslow based his theory on the study of highly successful people in the Western world. Thus, his viewpoint is most applicable to middle- and upper-class individuals in our present society. But this theory may not apply to other cultures, nor even to all segments of our own society.

More than this, Maslow's is one of many "stage" theories. That is, Maslow presumed that *all* humans move up through five clearly definable steps as they mature. Whether there are actually *five* rungs to the motivational ladder, or 15, or 150, is something that Maslow never really proved. Furthermore, he assumed you must somehow "conquer" the problems associated with each lower rung before you could move on to a higher one. This assumption is, at best, highly debatable.

Nor does Maslow tell us what biological and psychological *mechanisms* underlie the types of human needs he describes. For example, he admits you need food, but he doesn't describe how your body senses and responds to this need. And he states you strive for self-esteem and self-knowledge, but doesn't say how you manage to learn what these concepts are all about.

Last but not least, other than the case histories Maslow offers, there simply is no *experimental* evidence proving Maslow's approach is correct. Indeed, it is rather difficult to imagine how one might put many of Maslow's notions to a critical test.

Strengths of Maslow's Theory

Despite these criticisms, Maslow's approach has many strengths to it. To begin with, it is one of the few theories that emphasizes the importance of *individual choice* in determining behavior. That is, Maslow views the human organism as being capable of choosing between alternative courses of action. True, many of the things you do are influenced by your biological state and your social environment. But given these limitations, you still are able (in Maslow's view) to exercise voluntary choice in most situations.

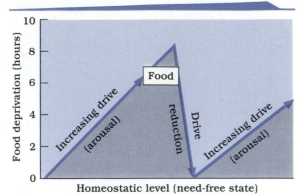

Fig. 10.2 A simple diagram of drive theory, using food deprivation as an example.

Figure labels: Food deprivation (hours); Homeostatic level (need-free state); Food reduction; Increasing drive (arousal); Drive; Increasing drive (arousal)

Second, Maslow's hierarchy is by far the best-known of the *holistic* approaches to the study of motivation. Indeed, Maslow's theory is one of the few that give relatively equal value to biological, intra-psychic, and social/behavioral influences on behavior. Drive theory—which we will discuss momentarily—does a good job of explaining how organisms react in situations of extreme deprivation. Arousal theory incorporates the best aspects of drive theory and adds a number of its own strengths. However, none of these narrow theoretical viewpoints can begin to explain the enormous complexities of even the simplest of human activities, such as eating.

Suppose we first take a quick look at drive and arousal theory. Then we will discuss a highly specific problem—that of **obesity**—and show how drive and arousal theory simply cannot explain why we eat as we do. Next, we will talk about a very strange type of self-induced starvation. Finally, to make the matter both more interesting and more practical, we will use what psychologists know about human motivation to develop a highly workable recipe for *losing weight* (or *gaining weight*).

Now that we have set the stage, let's see what drive theory is all about.

Drive Theory

For the past century, many psychologists have attempted to imitate the "hard" sciences by reducing the complexities of human motivation to fairly uncomplicated *biological* equations. Rather than assuming people (or animals) are capable of self-determined actions, these psychologists theorized that organisms are *driven* or pushed into motion much the way an automobile engine is cranked into activity when you turn the ignition key or step on the starter.

At its simplest, the biological approach to motivation is often called *drive theory*. As David Edwards notes, psychologist Clark Hull was one of the first great drive theorists. Hull assumed that *biological* needs are the ones that rule your life. Biological pain arouses or *drives* you to movement. *Reducing* your drives gives you biological pleasure and "rewards" those movements that led to the drive reduction. Hull made the concepts of drive and drive reduction the cornerstones of his theory of learning (see Chapter 14).

You do have motives other than biological pain and pleasure, of course. But drive theorists such as Hull assume that you *learned* these needs by associating them with your attempts to reduce the physical arousals that propel you along life's highway.

Homeostasis

The key concept in understanding drive theory is that of **homeostasis**. The term itself comes from a Greek word meaning "home state" or "normal condition." To a drive theorist, your body is like an automobile engine. To keep a car's engine in a state of fine tune—its "normal condition"—you need to take constant care of it. For example, you must give the engine oil, water, fuel, and lubrication. And you must protect it from damage. To keep your body in "fine tune"—or *homeostasis*—you must also give it the things it needs to function properly. These needs include food, water, air, a given range of temperatures, and protection from germs and accidents.

Whenever the engine in your car departs from its normal condition, red lights blink on the dashboard telling you what is wrong. Perhaps you need to add oil, or buy some fuel. Whatever the case, those lights will continue to flash until you satisfy the engine's needs. In similar fashion, whenever your body runs low on food or water, warning signals go off inside you telling you something is wrong. That is, you experience hunger or thirst. And you go on being hungry or thirsty until you satisfy your body's need—and return your body to its usual *homeostatic* condition.

"Homeostasis," then, simply means the innate biological urge you have to keep your bodily processes in a balanced or need-free state.

Primary Needs and Drives

Most drive theorists refer to those things you absolutely must have to survive as *primary needs*. These basic needs include such things as air, food, water, and a proper temperature. Whenever you run short of one of these things, built-in mechanisms in your body detect that need. As the need increases, the firing rates in various neural centers in your brain start to increase. This increased neural activity creates a *primary drive* inside you that *arouses* you to action. When your arousal is great enough, you are *driven* to seek out whatever you need.

Generally speaking, the longer you are deprived of something you need, the faster your nerve cells will fire. And the more *aroused* your nervous system becomes, the *greater* the primary drive you will experience. And the stronger the drive becomes, the more "motivated" you are to reduce that drive.

For example, you have a "primary need" for food. The longer you are deprived of food, the greater your primary drive (hunger) becomes, and the more aroused or driven you are to find something to eat. If you go hungry long enough, your aroused movements will probably bring you into a position to satisfy your need. Once you do so, the "hunger centers" in your brain stop firing. At this point, your drive level decreases, your arousal (motivation) disappears, and your normal homeostatic *balance* is reinstated. (See Fig. 10.2 for a diagram of drive theory, using food deprivation as an example.)

Intra-psychic and Social Needs

You need to take in food in order to maintain your normal homeostatic "good biological health." But *what* you eat depends in large part on what drive theorists call learned or *secondary needs*. Other psychologists refer to these as "intra-psychic needs" and "social needs."

Primary (biological) needs are innately determined. But secondary needs presumably are learned through some association with the satisfaction of a primary need. For example, suppose you "get hungry for a steak." According to drive theory, this *specific hunger* is an acquired, secondary drive. At some time in the past when you were hungry, you ate a steak. This behavior reduced your hunger drive, and you were thus rewarded for consuming a steak. As a consequence, when you get hungry in the future, you are more likely to "want" a steak than some food you've never eaten before.

Obesity (oh-BEE-sit-tee). From a Latin word meaning "to eat up." To be obese (oh-BEES) is to be excessively fat.

Homeostasis (home-ee-oh-STAY-sis). The tendency to move toward a need-free or drive-free condition. Any action by an organism to reduce drives is called a "homeostatic behavior."

Drive Theory: A Summary

The drive approach to motivation is what we might call a biologically oriented, *one-level* theory. It is biological in orientation because physical needs are presumed to be primary. All other motives are said to be acquired or learned. And the theory operates on only one level because it claims that the feelings, perceptions, cognitive activities, and social behaviors of the organism are learned *because* they are associated with the reduction of primary (biological) drives.

Question: What position do drive theorists appear to be taking with regard to solving the mind-body problem?

Criticisms of Drive Theory

Many objections have been raised to the simple form of drive theory we have just outlined. Three of the major objections are as follows:

1. Not all psychologists agree with drive theorists that intra-psychic needs are *learned*. For instance, most young animals (including children) seem to have an innate desire to explore their environment. This "exploratory drive" apparently is specified by the genetic blueprint, but it is difficult to think of "exploration" as being a *biological* need. Indeed, although we have some notion of the physical mechanisms that underlie the hunger drive, we simply don't know what parts of the brain control "exploration." Thus, to many psychologists, it seems more appropriate to consider exploration an innately determined *intra-psychic* drive.

2. In similar fashion, not all psychologists believe social needs are merely acquired by association with the reduction of some biological drive. For example, most newborn animals seem to have an innate urge to identify with a "mother figure." And as we will see in later chapters, most female animals readily develop an intense "social bond" with their infants immediately after birth. Therefore, many mother-infant behaviors seem to

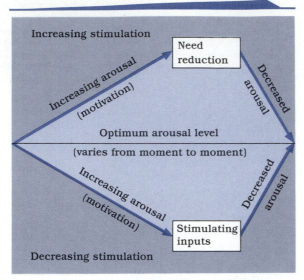

Fig. 10.3 A simple diagram of arousal theory.

be specified by the genetic blueprint. However, we don't know what biological mechanisms underlie these instinctual needs. And it is difficult to think of these highly motivated social behaviors in terms of "homeostasis."

3. Drive theory equates an *increase* in neural excitation with an *increase* in motivation. Yet, as we learned from the sensory-deprivation experiments, sometimes a *decrease* in excitation can cause an *increase* in psychological arousal.

As we will see, the scientists who raised these objections often were "driven" to create competing motivational theories of their own.

Question: Under what conditions do you become bored, and how do you typically react? Why might a drive theorist have difficulties explaining your highly motivated response to boredom?

Arousal Theory

In the late 1950's, Elizabeth Duffy (and others) made a telling criticism of classical drive theory. Duffy had spent many years studying the exploratory drive in animals. Her work convinced her that arousal is not always caused by a lack of such things as food, air, or water. For you have *informational needs* that are as innate

and as highly motivating as are your life-sustaining or *energy needs* (see Chapter 5). However, classical drive theory almost totally ignores informational inputs.

This objection led Duffy and other scientists to create a new approach to motivation called **arousal theory**. The basic **postulates** of this position can be summarized as follows:

1. Homeostasis isn't really a point of *zero* neural excitation, but rather is a point of **optimum** stimulation. The *optimum* point is the level at which you function best *at any given moment in time.*
2. This optimum point—often called the **set point**—may *change* from time to time, depending on your biological condition.
3. There are *opposing processes* associated with each "set point." Some of these processes are excitatory, and come into play when you move *below* your optimum set point. The other processes are inhibitory, and start to function when you move *above* your optimum set point. Working together, these *opponent processes* help you maintain your homeostatic set point.
4. You have *set points* for informational needs as well as for physical needs.

Boredom and Homeostasis

The concept of *boredom* was always a difficult one for the drive theorists to handle. For example, consider the hunger drive. Technically speaking, any balanced diet should satisfy all of your biological needs for food. Therefore, from a drive-theory point of view, you might well be expected to eat the same menu at every meal. But eating *exactly the same foods* at every meal gets boring, so you tend to vary what you consume. Yet, according to classical drive theory, you should eat primarily those foods you've eaten most often in the past. And it's difficult for a drive theorist to explain why you should ever eat something entirely new to you, when old (and satisfying) foods are available.

In similar fashion, lying quietly in a sensory isolation chamber theoretically should be a very pleasant thing—if all of your biological needs are being met. However, as you know, most subjects deprived of their usual level of informational inputs were highly motivated to seek *increased* sensory arousal. Yet according to classical drive theory, a *decrease* in excitation is always rewarding, while an *increase* in neural firing presumably is always painful or punishing.

The conclusion Duffy drew from these points is as follows: You do not have a single "homeostatic level" that is set at birth and never varies thereafter. Rather, you have a different "set point" for each type of need, whether that need is related to energy inputs or informational inputs. Furthermore, each "set point" changes according to your past experience and present conditions. You are motivated to maintain this optimum level, Duffy says, whenever your inputs *increase* too much or *decrease* too much. For a movement in either direction will take you away from your optimum level of performance.

Question: Some people occasionally "pig out" on rich foods, then starve themselves for days afterward. Why would it be easier for Duffy to explain this type of behavior than it would for a drive theorist to do so?

Optimum Arousal

According to Duffy, the optimum level of stimulation that you need *varies from moment to moment.* There is good reason why this is so. If your sensory inputs become too constant, your receptors "turn off" and leave you with little or no stimulation at all. And if your inputs vary too much, your environment becomes too unpredictable.

Thus, you need a certain amount of *stability* in the world around you—just as the homeostatic model would predict. However, you also need a certain amount of *variability* in stimulation. According to Duffy, your "set point of optimum arousal" will fluctuate from moment to moment in response to the level of inputs that you receive from your environment. But this optimum point will always lie somewhere between complete stability and complete predictability. Figure 10.3 illustrates how we might diagram arousal theory.

Question: In Chapter 3, we noted that certain drugs such as LSD lead to a stressful experience called "loss of personal control." In Chapter 9, we noted that sensory deprivation can cause a panic-inducing experience in which subjects can no longer control their thought patterns. How might both these unpleasant situations be related to a need to predict and control your inputs?

> **Arousal theory**. A one-level, biologically oriented theory in which motivation comes from some departure from a norm or optimum point of neural excitation. Any increase or decrease in neural firing moves the organism away from this optimum point and hence is arousing.
>
> **Postulates** (POSS-tew-lates). To postulate is to make a guess about something, or to insist that something exists or is very important. Postulates may or may not be facts.
>
> **Optimum** (OPP-tee-mum or OPP-tuh-mum). From the Latin word meaning "best." Literally, the most favorable point or condition. In arousal theory, optimum means "the point at which we operate most efficiently in our work, personal lives, and so forth."
>
> **Set point**. Your body has a "set point" for internal temperature—98.6°F. If your temperature rises above this point, you sweat. If your temperature falls below this point, you shiver or seek warmth. Your body tends to have a set point for weight, too. That is, your body tends to "defend" or maintain a given weight in a homeostatic manner.

Problems with Arousal Theory

Arousal theory was a noticeable improvement over drive theory in that Duffy could explain a number of motivational situations that early drive theorists had difficulties with. But the arousal position still is a "homeostatic" theory that tends to reduce motivation to what seem to be purely physical processes.

There is an appealing simplicity to homeostatic models such as those proposed by Duffy and by the drive theorists. For these models attempt to explain *all* human behavior in terms of an innate urge to "return to a pre-set level of normal functioning." Unfortunately, as R.C. Bolles points out in his 1980 book *Analysis of Motivational Processes*, the experimental data just don't give much support to homeostatic theories. According to Bolles, "the arousal of a motivational state in the individual has no necessary bearing on the homeostasis of the body; it is quite irrelevant to the solution of most regulatory problems." Bolles goes on to say, "What appears to be homeostasis is often only a constancy of environmental conditions. . . . All of the factors in a feeding control system are interrelated and interconnected; if the system is loaded with new environmental conditions, all of the components of the system will adjust to some degree."

To show why psychologists such as Bolles prefer a broader, more *systematic* view of motivation, suppose we look in considerable detail at an important American problem, that of people who overeat.

Robert C. Bolles   Marshall R. Jones

Obesity: A Holistic Approach

Dietitians estimate that 10 to 25 percent of the American public are **overweight**. The average family doctor treats more than 10 patients a month who want to lose weight. Perhaps 1 in 20 of these patients has a *physical* problem that is responsible for the fatness. And with these patients, the medical profession can often be of considerable help. The other 19 out of 20 people are fat simply because they take in more **calories** than they use up, and their bodies store the surplus energy as fat tissue. And with these patients, medical science has not done particularly well.

A decade ago, at a meeting on the topic of fatness, Alvan Feinstein of the Yale Medical School reported that the success rate of most *medical* weight-loss programs is "terrible, much worse than in cancer." In 1984, Feinstein noted that the situation hasn't changed much in the last 10 years. According to Feinstein, only some 12 out of 100 patients who seek a *physician's* help actually lose weight, and 10 of these 12 gain back their excess pounds within a year or two.

Presuming that your own weight is normal, why should you worry about such things? First, because fatness could happen to you someday, and probably has already happened to several of your friends or relatives. Second, because fat people are a very discriminated-against minority.

Problems Overweight People Face

If you are overweight, you have difficulty buying attractive clothes. You may also find it hard to get out of many chairs and to squeeze into some small cars. Finding a job can also be a problem, since many employers are hesitant to hire overweight individuals.

Fatness can even affect your academic career. Several years ago, H. Canning and J. Mayer studied the effects of obesity on high-school students. These scientists report that school counselors are less likely to write letters of recommendation for fat students than for normals. Canning and Mayer also found that college admissions committees discriminate against fat students during interviews. Faced with two students with equally good grades and equally high test scores, college committees tend to accept the non-obese student and to shut out the one who weighs too much.

Unfair? Of course it is. So is our society's discrimination against people with dark skins or slanted eyes. Of course, most of us realize you had little to say about your skin color—but fatness is primarily a *voluntary choice*, isn't it?

No, in a very strange way, you are not entirely responsible for how much you weigh. First, there is strong genetic component in fatness, and you are no more to blame for inheriting "fat genes" than for inheriting a certain skin color. Second, the psychological and social influences on fatness or thinness are just as important as the genetic factors. So if you happen to be snacking on something delicious, perhaps you'll want to put the food aside while we look at various biological, intra-psychic, and social/behavioral influences on **gluttony**.

The Biology of Hunger

Marshall Jones, who has spent most of his career studying problems of motivation, points out an interesting fact: Motivated behaviors are often *related sequences of responses*. And to understand behavioral sequences, you must answer the following questions:

1. Why does a given behavioral sequence begin? That is, what inputs prompt the thought or get the action going?
2. Why does the behavior go in a particular direction once it begins?
3. Why does the thought or behavior eventually come to an end? That is, once a behavioral sequence has begun, what brings it to a stop?

Eating is a motivated behavior—but so are overeating and undereating. Therefore, to understand why you eat as you do, we must answer three critical questions: Why do you start eating, why do you prefer steak and ice cream to fried worms and boiled monkey brains, and why do you eventually stop eating?

As we will see, drive theory and arousal theory offer partial answers to these questions. But they have little to say about why you select the foods you choose to consume, much less why you eat when you're not really hungry.

Question: From a motivational point of view, fat people might be overweight for at least four reasons: (1) They eat too frequently; (2) once started, they don't know when to quit; (3) they prefer rich, fat-laden foods; and (4) they don't burn up enough energy through exercise and physical labor. Would you think that different forms of therapy would be needed depending on what combination of these four behaviors the person engaged in?

Blood-Sugar Level

When you eat a dish of ice cream for dessert, how does your body make use of this fuel? To begin with, your digestive system breaks the food into tiny molecules, most of which contain sugar. These molecules enter your bloodstream, flow through your body, and pass sugar on to any cell that might be "hungry." A few hours after you have eaten a large meal, your blood contains a great many sugar molecules. However, if you starved yourself for 24 hours or so, your blood would contain relatively few of these energy particles.

Here is our first clue as to what the *hunger drive* is all about. To maintain its homeostatic balance, your body needs a certain level of sugar in its blood. And when this level drops below a certain point, you experience hunger "pangs" and you are aroused to seek out food. Therefore, if we could somehow control the molecules floating around in your bloodstream, might we not be able to control your sensation of hunger directly?

From a purely biological point of view, the answer is a probable yes. Under normal conditions, your body secretes a chemical called **insulin,** which stimulates your body to digest sugar. If we let a hungry rat eat all that it wants, then take a blood sample from the animal a little later, we would find a lot of sugar molecules in the rat's blood. If we now inject the animal with insulin, its blood-sugar level drops—and to our surprise the rat will soon begin to eat again (even though it had just consumed a very large meal).

Somewhere in your body, then, there must be a "sugar detector" that lets your cortex know how many sugar molecules are floating around

Overweight. Scientists have worked out an "ideal weight" for people, depending (mostly) on their age and height. Anyone who tips the scales at 10 percent more than this "ideal" is usually considered to be "slightly overweight," and anyone more than 25 percent above this "ideal" is usually considered to be "noticeably overweight." The definition of "overweight," however, varies considerably from one expert to another.

Calories (KAL-or-rees). The Latin word *calor* means "heat." The caloric (kal-LOR-ick) content of anything is the amount of heat it will generate when burned. Your body "burns" food when it converts what you eat into energy to keep you alive. Rich, sweet, fatty foods have lots of calories (that is, a high caloric content). Water has no calories at all. Fat burns; water doesn't.

Gluttony (GLUT-tone-ee). From the Latin word meaning "to gulp or swallow." A glutton (GLUT-tun) is someone who enjoys overeating. A "glutton for punishment" is someone who "eats up punishment with pleasure."

Insulin (IN-sull-in). A hormone secreted by the pancreas (PAN-kree-as), which is a small organ near the stomach. Insulin makes it easier for the cells in your body to take in sugar molecules. People whose bodies do not secrete enough insulin may suffer from a disease called diabetes (die-uh-BEET-ease). Diabetics (die-uh-BETT-ticks) have to control the amount of sugar they eat, and may have to take daily injections of insulin.

Hypothalamus (HIGH-po-THALL-ah-muss). A very important neural center lying just under the thalamus. The hypothalamus influences many types of motivated or emotional behavior, including eating and drinking.

Thalamus (THALL-uh-muss). Sensory messages from your eyes, ears, and skin all pass through the thalamus before being passed on to your cortex (and other higher centers of your brain). The thalamus is thus a sort of "giant switchboard" in your brain.

in your bloodstream. Recent research suggests that this "detector" is located in a central part of your brain called the **hypothalamus**.

The Hypothalamic "Feeding Center"

Sitting right at the top of your *brain stem* is a neural center called the **thalamus**. The thalamus is a sort of "central switchboard" through which sensory inputs pass before being relayed to your cortex. The word "hypo" means "below" or "beneath." The hypothalamus is a bundle of nerve cells lying just under the thalamus. The hypothalamus exercises rather strong control over many of your biological motivations and emotions (see Fig. 10.4).

One small part of your hypothalamus contains neurons that are particularly sensitive to the amount of sugar in your blood. When the blood-sugar level drops too low, the cells in this region of your hypothalamus begin to fire more rapidly—and you typically begin to feel hungry.

If we put a metal electrode into this part of a rat's brain and stimulate the cells electrically,

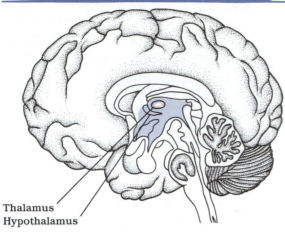

Thalamus
Hypothalamus

Fig. 10.4   The hypothalamus and thalamus.

Fig. 10.5   Surgical removal of the "satiation center" in the hypothalamus causes a rat to overeat.

the rat will begin to eat at once (even if it has just had a big meal). If we stimulate this hypothalamic *feeding center* continuously, the rat will eat and eat and eat—until it becomes so obese that it can barely move around (see Fig. 10.5). If we continue the electrical stimulation even when food is not present in the rat's cage, the animal will often gnaw on anything handy—including air.

If we destroy this "feeding center" in the rat's hypothalamus, the animal often refuses to eat at all. Some of the animals will die of starvation unless we force-feed them.

Does this one "feeding center" in the hypothalamus control all aspects of eating behavior? Certainly not. To begin with, even the "dumb rat" knows better than to overeat continuously, no matter what we do to it. If we give rats continual hypothalamic stimulation, the animals will become very, very fat. But eventually they will reach a cut-off point beyond which they will not go. Their weights will stabilize at this "set point" and we cannot induce them to become much fatter.

(You will probably be pleased to know that, when we stop prodding the rat's brain with electrical stimulation, the animal will typically go on a "crash diet" and return to its normal body weight.)

Stress and Overeating

As we noted in Chapter 3, your body produces a number of natural pain-killers called *endorphins*. According to R.L. Atkinson of the University of Virginia, the endorphins may be related to fatness.

A number of experiments show that when you are stressed, endorphin secretion increases dramatically. In the May 1981 issue of *Science 81*, Atkinson reports that the endorphins not only kill pain, they also increase the production of insulin. The insulin then reduces the blood-sugar level, causing you to feel hungry. So you eat—in response to the stress, not because you really need more food. But the food you consume causes your body to release even more insulin, which again lowers your blood-sugar level. And soon you are caught in a stress-related cycle in which the act of eating causes you to eat some more.

R.L. Atkinson believes many people are overweight because their bodies produce too much endorphin. As of 1982, Atkinson had shown that a chemical that reduces the endorphin level in rats caused the animals to lose weight. Whether or not this chemical will be of help to humans, however, is something Atkinson is still testing. (We will have more to say about the odd relationship between the endorphins and eating later in this chapter.)

Problems with the "Hunger Drive"

Drive theory can explain rather readily why you start to eat. As the sugar content in the blood reaching your brain *decreases*, electrical activity in your hypothalamic "feeding center" *increases*. Your cortex translates this *increased neural activity* into the psychological experience of "hunger pangs." And you go looking for a decent meal, just as drive theory would predict. But why do you stop eating once you've begun? Why don't you munch away for hours and hours?

Because, you say, as soon as you start eating, the sugar content in your blood goes up dramatically and your "feeding center" turns off. That explanation would surely fit drive theory, but it happens not to be so. For eating behavior doesn't have a simple explanation, even at a biological level.

If you ate a big steak right now, it would take several hours for the meat to be digested and assimilated into your bloodstream. It takes only 10 to 20 minutes for you to eat the steak, though. Therefore, you actually *stop eating* long before that steak can greatly affect your blood-sugar level. In fact, if you're a quick eater, your "feeding center" may still be signaling "eat—eat—eat!" at the top of its neural voice at the very moment when you push yourself away from the table, so stuffed with food that you can't imagine ever being hungry again.

So a lowered blood-sugar level can turn *on* your hunger. But what biological mechanism turns it *off*?

The Hypothalamic "Satiation Center"

As arousal theory points out, homeostasis is more a *balance* between opposing processes, rather than being a point of zero excitation. Thus, for every biological function that pushes you in one direction, there presumably is another function that tends to pull you back toward an optimum level of existence.

So if there is a "feeding center" in your hypothalamus that causes you to *start* eating, wouldn't you guess there might also be a center that, when stimulated, causes you to *stop* eating? It is called the **satiation center**, and it is also located in your hypothalamus, close to your "feeding center."

Suppose we implant an electrode in a rat's hypothalamic "satiation center." Then, just as the hungry animal starts to eat, we pass a weak electrical current through this "satiation center." The animal will suddenly refuse its meal. And if we continue the simulation for a long enough time, the animal will come close to starving itself to death.

On the other hand, if we surgically remove the rat's "satiation center," the animal will go on an eating jag. Soon it will become as obese as the rats whose "feeding centers" were electri-

Satiation center (say-she-A-shun). Our word "satisfied" comes from the Latin words *satis*, meaning "enough," and *facere*, meaning "to do" or "to make." Satiation is the condition of being completely satisfied. The "satiation center" is that part of the hypothalamus which, when stimulated electrically, causes a hungry animal to stop eating—that is, to behave as if it were already satisfied.

cally stimulated. But as you might already have surmised, eventually the animal will reach its "obesity set point" and will taper off its wild consumption of food.

Under normal conditions, your "satiation center" functions *symmetrically* with the "feeding center." When your blood-sugar level goes up, the neurons in your "feeding center" *decrease* their response rate and the nerve cells in your "satiation center" *increase* their firing rate. When your blood-sugar level falls, your "feeding center" turns on and your "satiation center" turns off.

Furthermore, your "satiation center" seems sensitive to inputs from your digestive system as well as to your blood-sugar level. In the August 12, 1980 issue of *Science*, R.D. Myers and M.L. McCaleb report that receptor cells in the stomach are connected directly to the "satiation center." When Myers and McCaleb injected food into the stomach of rats, these receptors sent messages to the hypothalamus that caused neurons in the "satiation center" to increase their firing rate. The Myers and McCaleb research is important because it may tell us why you stop eating *before* your blood-sugar level falls—the mere presence of food in your stomach may cause your "satiation center" to start responding (and thus decrease your hunger pangs).

Additionally, the stomach apparently secretes chemicals that circulate to the brain and affect the satiation center. James Gibbs and his colleagues at the New York Hospital in White Plains reported in the May 14, 1983 *Science News* that these chemicals are released from the gut whenever an animal ingests most types of food. When Gibbs and his associates injected rats with these chemicals prior to giving them *bland* food, the animals ate little or nothing at all. (Oddly enough, the chemicals had no effect on the consumption of *sweet* foods. We will return to this point in a moment.)

So now we know why you start eating and stop eating, don't we? No, we've learned only part of the answer. For what do you think would happen if we surgically removed *both* the "feed-

Eliot Stellar

Walter B. Cannon

ing center" and the "satiation center" from a rat's hypothalamus? Would the animal starve, or would it become obese?

The answer is, some animals will starve, but many will continue to eat pretty much as they did before the operation. So there must be systems in the brain other than the "feeding" and "satiation" centers that strongly influence eating behaviors.

The "Swallow Counter"

One mechanism for turning off eating behavior is what we might call the *swallow counter*.

A young rat eats almost continuously. As it grows up, however, it soon learns to associate the intensity of its hunger pangs with the amount of food that it ought to eat. When the rat has been deprived of food for a couple of hours, it eats a small amount. But when it has gone without eating for 12 hours, it will consume a great deal more food. The question is, how does the rat *know* how much food it actually needs?

Research indicates that some part of the animal's brain actually *counts* the number of swallows the animal makes as it eats. When the rat has had enough to satisfy its *present* state of hunger, it stops eating. And it stops *before* there is much of a change in its blood-sugar level, or in the firing rates in its "feeding" and "satiation" centers. So *learning* plays as much of a role in turning the hunger drive on and off as do the centers in the hypothalamus.

Stellar's Experiments

But even the "swallow counter" doesn't give us the whole answer to the puzzling question, Why do you stop eating? For example, experiments by Eliot Stellar and his associates at the University of Pennsylvania suggest that people are able to control their food inputs even if they can't "count" what they're swallowing.

Stellar and his colleagues asked students to swallow a tiny plastic tube that pumped liquid food directly into their stomachs when the students pressed a lever. The students could not see, smell, taste, chew, or swallow the food. But they somehow learned to control the amount they consumed just as readily as if they were drinking it from a glass. Perhaps the most interesting result of these experiments was the fact that the students were completely unable to explain to Professor Stellar how they managed this feat!

Stellar's experiments suggest that your stomach "knows" things about your eating habits that your "feeding" and "satiation" centers are only dimly aware of. For example, when you've packed your stomach with a huge meal (or with liquid), the muscles in your stomach are stretched out or distended. The feedback nerve cells in your stomach would surely let your brain know how inflated your stomach was. Then your cortex could inhibit or block out the input messages from your "feeding center" even before your blood-sugar level changed.

It is possible that Stellar's results could be explained by appealing to the research just cited by Myers and McCaleb, and by James Gibbs and his colleagues. That is, perhaps the liquid food merely stimulated the stomach receptors that are connected to the "satiation center." Or perhaps the liquid food caused chemicals to be released in the gut that "turned on" the satiation center. However, research by Walter Cannon suggests that yet another mechanism may be involved.

Cannon's Experiments

Long before the "feeding center" had been discovered, physiologist Walter Cannon performed a very important experiment on hunger. He got a student volunteer to swallow a balloon attached to a long hose. Once the balloon was inside the man's stomach, Cannon pumped air through the hose and inflated the balloon until it pushed firmly against the walls of the subject's stomach. (Fortunately, the man suffered little or no pain from this procedure.) Now, whenever the man's stomach contracted, the balloon was pinched and air was forced up the tube. By measuring the air pressure in the tube, Cannon got a rough reading of when the man's stomach muscles churned about.

Cannon found that "stomach contractions" began an hour or so before the man would normally have eaten a meal. As lunch time approached, for instance, the man's stomach began to contract more and more vigorously—and the man reported an increased interest in food. An hour or so after the man's usual lunch time, the stomach contractions almost stopped—*despite the fact that the man hadn't eaten a thing.* The man's subjective experience of hunger also decreased.

If you eat lunch every day at 12 noon, your "feeding center" and other parts of your brain begin to *anticipate* when they will have to go to work. An hour or so before noon, your brain starts sending neural signals to the muscles in your stomach telling them to "wake up" and get ready to start performing. The muscles contract in response to these signals, and your stomach "growls."

Other parts of your brain notice the growling (and the input signals coming from your "feeding center") and decide you're probably hungry. The closer the clock gets to noon, the more vigorously your stomach muscles respond.

Oddly enough, if you once get past the lunch hour without eating, your stomach will often calm down just as it does after you have eaten. Then your hunger pangs will decrease, only to rise again as supper time approaches.

Question: Why do both your hunger "pangs" and your stomach contractions tend to decrease after lunch even though you didn't eat anything?

The Hunger Habit

The hunger pangs that come from stomach contractions are **conditioned**. But almost any conditioned habit can be unlearned if you go about it the right way. If you stop eating *entirely*, your subjective experience of hunger will rise to a maximum in three to five days, as the centers in your brain and the muscles in your stomach continue to anticipate meal after missed meal. By the end of five days of *complete* starvation, however, your body will have learned that food simply isn't going to be coming along as it once did. Your stomach contractions will *habituate*, and your subjective experience of hunger will drop to a low ebb. However, if you go on a diet and "eat just a little" at each regular meal time, your "habitual" stomach contractions will take a very long time to change, and you may experience biting, gnawing hunger for weeks on end.

The fact that people on a complete fast soon lose the subjective experience of hunger suggests that hunger is to some extent a "habit."

Conditioned (konn-DISH-shunned). When an organism is trained to give a particular response to a specific stimulus, we say that it has been conditioned to respond to that stimulus. As we will see in Chapter 14, there are several types of conditioning. Psychologists often use the words "learning" and "conditioning" as if they were the same.

Metabolic rates (met-ah-BOLL-ick). Metabolism (met-TAB-oh-lism) is the sum of internal processes that provide the energy to keep your body going. People with high metabolic rates are usually more active and thinner than people with low metabolic rates.

Thus, if you want to lose weight, it might help if you eat on a highly irregular schedule prior to going on a diet. Once the "hunger habit" is broken, dieting might well be less painful (psychologically speaking).

Obesity and Metabolic Processes

In their 1982 book *The Dieter's Dilemma,* William Bennett and Joel Gurin make several controversial claims. To begin with, they believe "fat people" are born that way. That is, Bennett and Gurin theorize that people who tend to be overweight have a higher "weight set point" than do thin people, and that this "high set point" is inherited and thus can't be readily changed. As evidence to support their claim, Bennett and Gurin note that "no reputable study of calorie consumption has demonstrated that fat people eat more than others do."

Then why do fat people remain overweight? Because of their **metabolic rates**, Bennett and Gurin claim. Overweight individuals have much *lower* metabolic rates than do thin people. So fat people "burn up" food at a much slower pace than do thin people. That's why fat people can eat the same amount as thinner individuals, yet the fat people remain fat while the thin individuals remain thin. The fat person's body simply uses food *more efficiently* than does the thin person's body.

Then, what about dieting? It's a waste of time, Bennett and Gurin believe. Unless you're diabetic or have high blood pressure, Bennett and Gurin say, there's no scientific evidence that being overweight harms you in any significant manner. Not all doctors would agree with this statement, of course, but the "weight of evidence" does seem to be on Bennett and Gurin's side on this point.

Suppose you decide to lose weight anyhow. Why not diet? Because, Bennett and Gurin say,

Hilde Bruch   **Stanley Schachter**   **Albert J. Stunkard**

your body will simply "adjust" by lowering its metabolic rate. Therefore, you may *consume* less, but you also *use* less food to maintain your normal "set point." If you cut your caloric intake sharply, of course, you *will* lose weight. But when you go off your diet, your body's metabolic rate *remains low.* So, now you gain weight on the same amount of food that previously was just enough to maintain your weight. And your metabolic rate will "lag behind" until your weight again reaches your innately determined "weight set point."

How do you lose weight, then? According to Bennett and Gurin, the only way is to change your metabolic rate. And the most effective way to do that, they claim, is by exercising more. However, as we will see, Bennett and Gurin are probably wrong on this point. There is considerable evidence that your "weight set point" is strongly influenced by past experience and present environmental inputs. And despite Bennett and Gurin's claims, several studies suggest you can lower your "metabolic set point" if you voluntarily control your food intake *for a long enough period of time.* Keep these points in mind as we look at intra-psychic influences on eating and obesity.

Question: Bennett is a medical doctor, and Gurin is a professional writer. Why might they be more likely to take a *biological* view of obesity than would a psychologist?

Intra-Psychic Influences on Obesity

Consciously or unconsciously, many parents train their children to be overeaters. Sometimes the parents are overweight themselves and, without realizing it, *overfeed* their children in order to make the children like themselves. Other parents may believe that "fatness" and good health are pretty much the same thing. If the usual reward the parents offer the child for good behavior is an extra helping of pie or cake, the child will soon come to associate rich foods with the act of winning parental approval. Food then takes on the *symbolic meaning* of love and acceptance. Later, as an adolescent or young adult, the person may feel a yearning to "raid the refrigerator" whenever she or he feels rejected or disappointed by life.

Data to support this view come from a series of studies by psychoanalyst Hilde Bruch, who found that many overweight people felt unwanted, inadequate, and insecure as children. According to Bruch, these subjects began overeating not only to gain attention from their parents, but also because eating too much made them feel big and important to themselves.

Schachter's Studies of Obesity

If fat people eat to satisfy symbolic needs, then one would expect eating behavior to be primarily under the control of internal or intra-psychic drives.

A decade or so ago, Columbia psychologist Stanley Schachter disputed this view—at least as far as fat people are concerned. In the late 1960's and early 1970's, Schachter came to the following conclusion: Normal people eat when their bodies tell them to—that is, when their stomachs contract and their "feeding centers" are active. However, Schachter said, obese people *don't listen to their bodies.* Rather than being driven to eat by internal cravings and desires, overweight individuals are simply abnormally sensitive to the world around them. In one set of studies, Schachter and his group showed that fat subjects tended to "eat by the clock" rather than eating when their stomachs were contracting. In another study, Schachter showed that fat people tend to be "plate cleaners" who eat everything set before them whether they need it or not. People of normal weight, however, paid attention to their stomachs and ate only what they needed, even if this meant "leaving a little something on the plate."

Fat people are also more affected by the *taste* of food than normals, according to Schachter's early findings. When offered food of average or above-average taste, fat individuals ate a great deal more than did normals. When offered food of below-average or miserable taste, however, fat people ate a great deal less than normals did. Obese individuals were also less likely to perform physical labor for food, or to suffer mild amounts of pain to get to eat, than were people of normal weight.

Recently, however, Schachter has changed his position slightly. He now sees obesity as a *multi-determined problem*. As one of his former students, Judith Rodin of Yale, put it recently, being fat is "determined by a combination of genetic, metabolic, psychological, and environmental events." In a recent interview, Schachter remarked that Rodin's views are "really closer to the way God sees things."

When we see someone who is grossly overweight, we often assume their problem is that they are greedy, psychologically immature, or that they must have a medical difficulty of some kind. That is, we *attribute* their obesity to some sort of "character defect." But if Rodin and Schachter are right, we do the overweight individual an injustice by presuming the problem is always internal. For to make this assumption, we have neglected the strong effects that our culture has on our eating habits.

Let us look briefly at how the social environment influences what and how people eat.

Question: As we noted, James Gibbs and his colleagues found that chemicals released by the gut inhibit the ingestion of bland food, but not of sweet foods. What possible relationship do you see between this fact and Schachter's finding that fat people will work hard to get rich foods but not bland or bad-tasting foods?

Social/Behavioral Influences on Obesity

The culture you live in plays a great part in controlling what you eat—and when you eat it. In some places where food is or has been scarce,

Social classes. A way of grouping or classifying people according to their occupations, incomes, family histories, where they live, and their social relationships. There are three general classes. About 5 percent of the US population is said to be "upper class." These people are mostly very rich. About 40 percent of the US population is considered to be "middle class." These people are white-collar workers, middle-level executives, or professional people. About 55 percent of the population is said to be "lower class." These people are blue-collar workers, who perform unskilled or semi-skilled jobs and who have less education and (usually) smaller incomes than do members of the other two classes.

being fat is a sign of wealth. In other societies, "eating regularly and frequently" is not only a habit, but a status symbol of sorts.

For example, European farm workers often have five or six "regular" mealtimes per day. When they are working in the fields 12 to 14 hours daily, they need all this fuel to stay healthy. But many of them continue to eat just as frequently when they move to the city and take jobs in offices. They may even continue their five meals a day when they move to a new country.

A study by A.J. Stunkard shows that farm women from central Europe who immigrate to the United States are four to five times more likely to be overweight as are women from the same background whose families have lived in the United States for several generations.

People from different **social classes** in the United States have quite different types of eating habits. Men and women who belong to the wealthiest or "upper class" tend to be thinner, healthier, and to live longer than do men and women of the so-called "lower class."

Many upper-class women jokingly remark that "you can't be too thin or too rich." A recent study of 1,660 adults living in New York City tends to confirm this view. Some 32 percent of the men and 30 percent of the women in the lower classes were found to be obese. However, only 16 percent of the men and 5 percent of the women in the upper class were overweight. Four times more upper-class women were "thin" than were women in the lower class. And the chances that an upper-class individual will go on a diet are two to three times as great as are the chances that a person from any other social class will start to lose weight voluntarily.

Question: Can you be "too thin?"

Individuals suffering from anorexia perceive themselves as being "fat" even though they may be little more than skin and bones. A painting by an anorectic made during the severest stage of illness.

Fat Wives and Insecure Husbands

Many of our social needs are pressed upon us by the people around us. Thus, we may overdrink or overeat because individuals we love may be *rewarded* in various ways when we are drunk or fat.

Richard B. Stuart worked for many months with married women who were complete failures at losing weight. Stuart eventually began to suspect that the women's husbands were partially responsible for keeping their wives **corpulent**. To test his hypothesis, Stuart asked these couples to make tape recordings of their dinner-table conversations.

Stuart found that, although all the women were on diets and their husbands knew it, the husbands were 12 times more likely to *criticize* their wives' eating behaviors than to praise them. The men were also four times more likely to offer food to their wives than the wives were to offer food to the husbands. These "food-pushing" husbands fell roughly into four groups:

1. Some husbands enjoyed demonstrating their masculine power by coaxing or forcing their wives to become fat. If the wife was overweight, the husband sometimes found this a useful fact to bring up in family arguments. The man could win almost any battle by calling the woman "a fat slob." Stuart believes the husbands realized (perhaps unconsciously) that if the wife lost weight, the husband would lose more arguments.
2. Other husbands viewed dinner time as being the main social event of the day. When the wives refused to eat very much, the husbands saw this as a rejection of themselves and the rest of the family group.

3. Some men had lost any sexual interest in their wives. They seemed to want to keep their wives fat as an excuse for their "playing around" with other women. Stuart's data also indicate that the husband lost sexual interest first, and then began rewarding the woman for overeating, rather than losing interest after the wife was already fat.
4. Other husbands apparently feared their wives might be unfaithful to them if the women were too attractive. These men encouraged their wives to overeat in order to keep their wives ugly—and therefore faithful.

Question: Do you think even a superb therapist could help these women change their eating behaviors unless the husbands were somehow motivated to solve their own psychological problems?

Corpulent (KOR-pew-lent). From the Latin word *corpus*, or "body." We get our words "corpse" and "corporation" from the same Latin source. To be "corpulent" is to have too much body—that is, to be somewhat obese.
Anorexia (an-or-REX-ee-ah). From the Greek words meaning "no appetite." A psychological disorder that involves self-starvation in order to achieve certain unusual or "disordered" personal goals.
Bulimia (byou-LEE-me-ah). From the Greek words meaning "great hunger." A psychological disorder that involves massive overeating, usually followed by an attempt to purge the body of the food.
Pathological (path-oh-LODGE-ee-cal). Pathology is the study of the "essential nature of diseases." A pathological behavior pattern, therefore, is one that is "diseased" or "a deviation from the normal."

Eating Disorders

So far, we've talked entirely about the problems associated with being overweight. However, there are also a number of eating disorders that are related to being too thin—or to attempts to maintain a very low weight through rather unusual eating behaviors.

The two major types of eating disorders associated with abnormal thinness are **anorexia** and **bulimia**. *Anorexia* involves self-induced starvation, even to the point of death. *Bulimia* is also known as the "binge-purge" syndrome. Both disorders are about ten times as likely to affect women as men. And both disorders are found primarily among young upper-middle-class and upper-class women who firmly believe that "you can't be too rich or too thin."

Anorexia

Hilde Bruch was one of the first psychiatrists to take an interest in anorexia. She states there are two types, *primary* (or true) anorexia, and *atypical* anorexia.

Primary anorexia is a **pathological** fear of "being fat." The disorder is found primarily in young women in their teens. A woman suffering from this condition usually has a skeleton-like appearance. She also denies that she is abnormal in any way, but strives actively to maintain all her abnormal behavior patterns.

Atypical anorexia, Bruch says, differs from primary anorexia in just one important way:

The woman *knows* her behaviors are abnormal, but *feels helpless* about changing them.

Three Symptoms of Anorexia

According to Bruch, there are three main symptoms that define primary anorexia. First, the anorexic woman has a false perception of her own body image. Thus, even though the woman weighs but 80 pounds, she may *perceive* herself as being "grossly fat." So the woman starves herself and frequently engages in abnormal amounts of exercise. If she doesn't receive help, the woman may well starve herself to death in a desperate attempt to "avoid obesity."

The second symptom is a disturbance in the manner in which the woman "processes" bodily sensations. Bruch believes many overweight individuals confuse arousal with hunger. Therefore, she says, they eat when they are frightened or stressed in any way. The anorexic woman, on the other hand, does just the opposite: She confuses hunger with stress. When her body gives her "hunger signals," she *interprets* them as signs of stress or fear. Therefore, she denies she feels hungry, insisting she is merely "anxious" or even "depressed" instead.

The third symptom is that of abnormally low self-esteem. Bruch says the anorexic woman typically perceives herself as "enslaved by others, exploited by family and friends, and thus incapable of living a life of her own." Therefore, she isolates herself from "the exploiting others" whenever she can. And her refusal to eat, Bruch believes, is really a "struggle to attain self-respect." By not eating, she attempts to show others (and herself) that she can maintain some control over her life.

Research suggests that some compulsive male runners may have psychological motives similar to those of female anorexics.

anorexic patients are males. Squire reports that these men share some of the same concerns as do female patients. For example, the men have a pathological fear of obesity and feel a need to "control their bodies" in some rigorous fashion. They also tend to come from the upper classes and to be intelligent and well educated.

However, male anorexics differ from female anorexics in many ways. For one thing, the males frequently are homosexuals, while the females are chiefly heterosexual. The women tend to be overachievers; the males, under-achievers. The women often develop "work rituals" and are almost obsessive about being "orderly." The men usually are hard workers, but their attempts at getting things done are often ineffectual and haphazard. And the families of male anorexics typically are more "emotionally disturbed" than are the families of female patients, Squire says.

Susan Squire believes that male anorexics are much more difficult to treat than are women patients. However, Squire says, the "success rate" for therapy with either male or female anorexics is fairly low.

Question: How can you "eat your cake" and *not* have it too?

The Anorexic's Family

According to Hilde Bruch, the family plays an important role in bringing about the anorexic disorder. Almost all anorexic women are from the upper class, or from the top levels of the middle class. The mothers of anorexic women are typically "high achievers, but are frustrated in reaching their desired goals in life." They also tend to be subservient to their husbands. The fathers of anorexic women tend to be successful, athletic, and good-looking. But they frequently perceive themselves as being "second best," Bruch says. The fathers are also "enormously preoccupied with outer appearances," particularly with maintaining physical fitness and beauty.

Bruch states that few parents of anorexic women are sensitive to the problems their daughters experience. The parents tend to carry an "idealized image" of the young woman in their minds, which is quite different from reality. Bruch claims that treatment of anorexia is seldom successful unless the parents participate actively, and unless they are willing to change the way in which they perceive (and relate to) the daughter.

The Male Anorexic

In her 1983 book *The Slender Balance*, Susan Squire states that about 10 percent of

Bulimia

Bulimia is an eating disorder characterized by "binges" of caloric intake followed by desperate attempts to get rid of the food consumed. The three most common ways of ridding the body of the food are by self-induced vomiting, by "purging" (using laxatives), and by post-binge starvation.

Anorexia and bulimia are similar in some ways, different in others. Like the anorexic patient, the bulimic individual tends to fear "fatness" and to prize "thinness." And both types of disorders are primarily found in upper-middle-class and upper-class individuals. Both anorexics and bulimics usually have a lengthy history of failure in trying to control body weight. And both types of person tend to rely almost exclusively on eating as a means of coping with stress. However, the bulimic individual seldom denies reality to the extent that anorexics do. Indeed, the "binge-purge" person often feels guilty about his or her behaviors and hides them from family and friends as much as possible. In addition, most bulimic individuals engage in "binge-purge" activities only on occasion, but most anorexics starve themselves continuously.

Some anorexic individuals are also bulimic. And some bulimic individuals are extremely thin. However, most people who suffer from bulimia are of normal weight. A few are even overweight.

Writing in the February 1983 *Behavior Therapist*, Billy Barrios and James Pennebaker state that caloric intake during a "food binge" may range from 1,500 to 15,000 calories. In comparison, the average "balanced meal" contains from 1,000 to perhaps 2,000 calories. And the average caloric intake for most adults in the United States is between 2,000 and 3,500 calories per day.

Bulimia is much more common than is anorexia. Studies reported in 1983 on Chicago high-school students and on college students in New York City suggest that as many as 20 percent of women students and some 5 percent of men students engage in bulimia occasionally. Some 8 percent of the women stated they go on uncontrollable "food binges" fairly regularly, and then use vomiting or purging to control their weight. According to Barrios and Pennebaker, "episodes of gorging and vomiting vary in frequency from once every two months to six times per day."

Barrios and Pennebaker believe that bulimia can be successfully treated if the disorder is detected in its early stages. The problem is, Barrios and Pennebaker say, most people who suffer from bulimia are extremely secretive and hence are unlikely to seek help.

Question: Bulimics almost always "binge" on rich, sweet foods. How might this fact be related to James Gibbs's finding that chemicals released by the gut inhibit the consumption of bland foods, but not the consumption of sweet-tasting foods?

◇?

Compulsive Eating and Compulsive Running

Alayne Yates, Kevin Leehey, and Catherine Shisslak are behavioral scientists at the University of Arizona. In the February 3, 1983 *New England Journal of Medicine*, these scientists compare "compulsive runners" to "compulsive eaters" (bulimics) and "compulsive non-eaters" (anorexics).

Yates, Leehey, and Shisslak define *compulsive runners* as "those who are consumed by running, who run in spite of illness, and who

Asceticism (as-SET-tih-cism). From the Greek word meaning "laborious." An ascetic (as-SET-tick) is someone who practices strict self-denial as a means of achieving personal and spiritual goals.

suffer depression when they cannot run." The typical compulsive runner is an upper-middle-class or upper-class male. Like anorexic women, these men tend to be "introverted, compliant, self-effacing and unable to express anger." Most compulsive runners are high achievers, just as anorexic women tend to be. And, like anorexic women, most of these men have "an unstable self-concept," according to Yates, Leehey, and Shisslak. The men perceive themselves as being "out of shape" even when they are "dangerously overtrained," just as anorexic women perceive themselves as being "grossly fat" even when they are mere skeletons. There are differences, however. The men tend to focus on controlling "physical strength," while the women tend to focus on slimness. And the disorder hits women during adolescence, while it primarily appears in men during middle age.

The Arizona scientists believe the same "psychological disorder" underlies both compulsive running and anorexia. They see the major problem as being a pathological reaction to stress. *Society shapes the symptoms*, however. Controlling "strength" is an acceptable activity for men, but not for women. But society places a higher value on "thinness" in women than in men.

Yates, Leehey, and Shisslak believe that the self-destructive behaviors associated with anorexia and compulsive running become *self-rewarding* because they lead to the release of endorphins, the body's "natural pain-killers." According to Yates *et al.*, anorexic women often have elevated *endorphin* levels. These women also often report that starvation gives them a euphoric feeling similar to "runner's high." And, as we reported in Chapter 3, "runner's high" is related to abnormal amounts of endorphin in the brain. Thus, both anorexia and compulsive running may be learned reactions to social or personal stress that are maintained by the release of endorphins.

According to the Arizona scientists, however, the most striking characteristic shared by both compulsive runners and compulsive eaters (or non-eaters) is this: Both groups share "a grim **asceticism** and an assiduous avoidance of passive, receptive pleasures."

Not all scientists agree with the position taken by Yates, Leehey, and Shisslak. Nor do all compulsive runners seem to fit the pattern the Arizona scientists describe. However, their research surely does give us "food for thought."

Question: What personality characteristics does our culture often attribute to fat people? (Hint: Think of Santa Claus.) What about thin people? (Hint: Think of paintings of saints and religious martyrs.)

Symptom Choice in Eating Disorders

There is almost no life-sustaining behavior that isn't considered abnormal if you engage it in too frequently—or too infrequently. Sleep, sex, and eating all offer evidence supporting this statement. The question then becomes, If you depart from the norm, why do you deviate in one direction and not the other?

Generally speaking, disordered behaviors are as multi-determined as are "ordered" activities. Some people overeat in response to stress, while others undereat when faced with the same problems. The *choice* between undereating and overeating, however, is affected by biological, intra-psychic, and social factors. And it is a problem we can only speculate about, since scientists have gathered little valid data in the area of "symptom choice."

Consider the difference between anorexia and bulimia. Both anorexics and bulimics come from the same social backgrounds, experience similar social stresses, and share the same distorted perceptions of body image. The fact that both problems are found chiefly among upper-class women shows that cultural factors help bring about both disorders. But anorexics get a "high" from starving themselves, while bulimics get "high" from food binges. Could it be that bulimics are simply more sensitive to sweet tastes than anorexics are? Or that bulimics inherited higher "weight set points" or more efficient metabolic rates than anorexics did? We do not know. However, it would be surprising if symptoms people display in *all* psychological disorders weren't the result of an *interaction* of many different types of influences.

We will return to this point frequently in future chapters. For the moment, though, let's assume that your weight is relatively normal and your eating behaviors are not particularly disordered. Still, the time might come when

you *choose* to gain or lose a few pounds. Let's close this chapter by looking at one relatively effective system for gaining or losing weight. But as you will see, you have to know something about *why* you choose to gain or lose weight before you can do so efficiently.

How to Gain or Lose Weight

You eat not just because you've been without food for a while, but also because (a) your blood-sugar level has fallen, (b) your stomach is contracting, (c) your "feeding center" has increased its neural activity, (d) your "satiation center" has decreased its neural activity, (e) your "swallow counter" has been silent for a while, (f) your regular dinner time is approaching, (g) you smell food in the air and hear other people talking about "what's for lunch," and (h) because food and eating have a variety of symbolic values for you.

Obviously, then, if you want to gain or lose weight, your dietary program must take into account not just the calories you consume and how you burn them up, but your *motives* and *mannerisms*, and your *perceptions* and *emotions*, as well as the behavior of the people around you.

If you wish to embark on a well-rounded weight-loss or weight-gain program, the first thing you should do is to have a medical check-up. That way you can make sure you are not that 1 American in 20 who is under- or overweight because you have a physical problem of some kind. If you want to gain or lose more than 10 to 20 pounds, you probably should do so under medical guidance. Your physician may wish to prescribe drugs to help increase or decrease your appetite, and may also send you to see a registered dietician.

However, diets and pills are only the first step in a long journey. The real problem usually lies in learning enough about yourself to recognize what internal and external *stimulus inputs* affect your eating behavior. You must somehow *measure* these inputs—and their consequences—and then change the way you react to these inputs.

Using Cognitive Behavior Modification to Gain or Lose Weight

If you wish to gain or lose weight, you might consider using *cognitive behavior modification* to help you do so. For a variety of studies show this approach yields the best long-term results as far as controlling your weight is concerned. Many behavioral therapists recommend a program that has ten steps to it:

1. Begin by recording *everything* you eat and drink for a period of at least a week. Psychologists call this "taking a baseline." Your own baseline should include a record of where you eat, the events that occurred just before you started eating, what you thought about just before you ate (and afterward), how you perceive food and the act of eating, and how you felt about eating as you did. And, *most important,* you should note who is around when you eat and what their response is to your food intake. Is anyone in your life (other than yourself) rewarded by your being too fat or too thin? In brief, your baseline should be a measure of: (1) *what you eat*; (2) the *thoughts and feelings* associated with eating; and (3) the personal and social *consequences* of your eating behaviors.

2. Write down all the rewards and pleasures that will come to you if you gain better control over your eating behavior.

3. If you are trying to lose weight, you might try "breaking the hunger habit" by changing your meal times to a very irregular schedule several weeks before you begin your diet. If you are underweight and eat irregularly, you may wish to force yourself to eat on schedule

"I JUST LOVE THESE FAD DIETS. I'M ON FOUR OF THEM RIGHT NOW."

in order to help build up the hunger habit so that your stomach muscles will begin urging you to eat more.

4. If you wish to lose weight, increasing your physical activities will help you burn off excess fat. If you are out of shape, begin by walking a few minutes each day and work up from there. *Don't* push yourself to do too much at any one time. If you are underweight and exercise frequently, you may wish to reduce your activities.

5. Once you have your baseline material available, you may want to talk things over with a psychologist. You may be using your fatness or thinness as a psychological defense, or as a substitute for healthier behaviors. Unless you solve your own psychological problems first, you are not likely to be particularly successful at gaining or losing weight. Put another way, it will help you change your eating behaviors if you simultaneously change your cognitive processes and your emotional responses. You may even have to learn some new social skills—and better ways to control your thoughts and actions—as a part of your weight-change program.

6. Habits are difficult to change, and you will probably need all the help you can get. So you may find it wise to involve as many people as possible in your program. If someone close to you unconsciously wants you to remain fat (or thin), you may well have to find some substitute reward for this person. Otherwise, the person may try to sabotage your weight-loss or weight-gain program.

7. When you start your program, make a large chart or graph on which you record each aspect of your daily routine (including exercise). Post the graph in a prominent place so everyone can see your progress and comment on it. Have someone give you regular rewards (money, special privileges, a gold star on your chart, or praise) each time you meet your daily goal. Give yourself a bonus for meeting that goal every day for a whole week. This graph is perhaps the *most important part* of any weight-control program, for it gives you immediate feedback on your progress. Learning to eat correctly is a matter of establishing voluntary self-control over your actions. And without feedback, you will find it almost impossible to acquire the self-discipline you will need both to change your weight and to maintain this change.

8. Don't expect too much too fast. Unless you alter your diet drastically, your average weight loss or gain will be about two pounds

a week. Because your weight fluctuates from day to day, it is a better idea to keep track of what you eat and the exercise you engage in than merely to record how much you weigh daily. However, do weigh yourself at least weekly and put this information on your chart.

9. Prepare yourself *in advance* for the occasional failure. Most people "bust their diets" now and again. And most of these individuals feel depressed and unworthy afterward. Many weight-control therapists urge their clients to use these temporary setbacks as a way of learning how to perceive themselves (and their actions) in a different light. Once you find you can readily recover from your mistakes, you probably won't make as many (or be as bothered by them) in the future.

10. Don't think of your program as being a "weight-loss" or "weight-gain" program. Rather, think of it as your way of increasing self-control by finally learning how to eat properly.

The Concept of Choice

There is a great deal more to the field of motivation than just those behaviors (and thoughts and emotions) involved in eating. We will discuss sexual motivation in Chapter 11, stress and emotionality in Chapter 12, and the influence of motivation on learning in Chapters 13–15. However, now that we've looked at eating in some detail, perhaps you can understand several things about motivation better than when you started the chapter.

To begin with, probably you can now see why a simple question such as, "Why do some people overeat?" is so difficult to answer. For even when we attempt to study the simplest of human behaviors, there are biological, intra-psychic, and social influences that we always must take into account. So, even though we certainly don't know all the answers about human motives, at least we can guess at some of the questions we ought to be asking.

Many of these questions concern the *biology* of hunger. And, at first glance, it might well seem that we know more about this topic than about the intra-psychic and social/behavioral factors that influence food consumption. In a sense, that's true, for there have been many more experiments on the biological variables that affect eating than on the psychological and social aspects of the problem. But few of these biological studies do us much good when we try

to help you *change* your eating patterns. There are at least three reasons why this is the case.

First, most of the laboratory studies have used animal subjects rather than humans. We know little or nothing about the intra-psychic processes of the white rat, and next to nothing about the social influences of one rat's actions on the amount of food that another rat eats. And even if we did know more than we do, we couldn't be sure our knowledge about rats would *generalize* to the level of human beings.

Second, most research on the biology of hunger has focused on subjects who were severely deprived of food. Indeed, much of this work has dealt with animals who were near starvation. Little wonder, then, that the animals seemed preoccupied with obtaining food. As University of Washington psychologist R.C. Bolles has pointed out, biological mechanisms tend to dominate behavior in cases of extreme deprivation—but not at any other time in an organism's life.

Given a crisis of some kind, your body may well "take over" your behavior. Most of the time, though, you "pick and choose" what you want to do, because your biological needs are almost always being met on a regular basis. Bolles believes most eating and drinking—in humans as well as rats—is "secondary." That is, these behaviors are not really related to any *immediate biological need*. Thus, most human activities simply cannot be explained by drive theory, arousal theory, or any other "narrow" viewpoint.

Third, *medical intervention* has a very low "cure rate" when it comes to helping people gain or lose weight. The behavioral program outlined above is much more effective, because it pays attention to a wide range of intra-psychic and social factors that influence eating behavior. And if these factors are most influential in helping people gain or lose weight, they are also likely to be involved in *causing* people to undereat or overeat in the first place.

You Help Choose What "Moves You"

R.C. Bolles believes motivation is best described as a "response selector mechanism." He notes that you are always active, always doing something—even if that "something" is just daydreaming or watching television. Thus, you are always *aroused* (behaviorally speaking) both to your external world and to your internal thoughts and needs.

According to Bolles, you "behave" when you (1) respond to external stimulation, or (2) commit yourself to some course of action. In extreme situations, your responses will probably be governed primarily by your physical needs. But in most circumstances, you will *select* the one thing you want to do "right now" from a long list of possible actions. And the factors that most influence (but do not totally determine) what you select are your past experiences and your present social environment.

What "moves" you? According to Bolles, you move yourself. True, many of your actions are fairly predictable—but only if we know a great deal about who you are, what you have experienced in the past, and what your present environment is like. The study of motivation, then, boils down to knowing as much as we can about you and your own set of personal choices.

To repeat our opening quote from David Edwards, motivation is a set of questions you ask in order to determine *why* you do what you do. As you must realize by now, those questions are so numerous and so complex that you may never answer them to your complete satisfaction. However, the study of human behavior remains a delightful and rewarding journey for most people. And a journey of a thousand miles begins with the motivation to take the first step.

Summary

1   **Motivation** is not so much an area in psychology as a series of questions about *why* people do what they do.

2   Many "why" questions involve human **needs**—what kinds of needs do you have, are these needs **learned** or **innate**, what are the **mechanisms** by which you satisfy your needs, and do you exercise any voluntary **choice** over your behavior patterns?

3   Motivation implies **movement**. Ancient scholars differentiated between objects that were **animate** or "self-movers" and those that were not.

4   According to Maslow, human needs can be placed on a **hierarchy** with five levels: **biological**, **safety**, **belongingness**, **esteem**, and **self-actualization**.

5   **Drive theory** focuses primarily on biological needs. Clark Hull assumed that associated with each physical need was a **primary drive**. Whenever your body lacks something needed for life, the appropriate drive increases, causing you pain and thus motivating you to satisfy that need and return your body to **homeostasis**.

6   Hull assumed that **secondary needs** or social needs were learned by being associated with the pleasures that accompany primary **drive reduction**.

7   Criticisms of drive theory include the fact that you have **information** needs as well as **energy needs**, and the fact that some social behaviors seem innately determined rather than being learned.

8   **Arousal theory** was developed by Elizabeth Duffy to counter the criticisms of Hull's drive theory. Duffy assumed that homeostasis is a point of **optimum arousal**, and that a decrease in sensory inputs can be as arousing as an increase in biological drives. The optimum homeostatic **set point** changes from moment to moment.

9   At a biological level, the **hunger drive** is affected by **blood-sugar level**. When you go without food, your **hypothalamic feeding center** detects a decrease in blood sugar molecules and motivates you to eat. Stress increases the production of the **endorphins**, which stimulate your body to produce **insulin**, which also decreases your blood-sugar level. Thus, you may overeat because of stress.

10   Your **hypothalamus** also contains your **satiation center** which, when stimulated, causes you to stop eating. Hunger pangs are also affected by your **swallow counter**, by your knowledge of how much you have already eaten, by **conditioned stomach contractions**, and by your **metabolic rate**. Chemicals released by the gut decrease consumption of bland foods but not **sweet-tasting foods**.

11   Intra-psychic influences on obesity include the fact that some parents train their children to be fat, thus giving overeating a **symbolic** value.

12   Social/behavioral influences on obesity include the fact that in some cultures fatness suggests wealth, and that some **social classes** place more of a premium on thinness than do others.

13   Stuart has shown that **insecure husbands** often reward their wives for remaining fat.

14   The most common **eating disorders** are

anorexia (self-starvation) and **bulimia** (the "binge-purge" syndrome). Both disorders affect primarily upper-class women who have a **distorted self-image** and low **self-esteem**.

15 Men with similar social backgrounds and psychological problems as female anorexics often engage in **compulsive running**.

16 **Cognitive behavior modification** offers an excellent method for losing or gaining weight. The technique involves taking a **baseline** of present food input, **establishing goals**, **exercise**, keeping precise **records** of food-related activities, and establishing personal and social **rewards** for progress.

17 According to Robert Bolles, **drives** affect behavior primarily in times of severe deprivation. For the most part, humans appear to be able to **choose** which behavior patterns are most satisfying to them.

(Continued from page 262.)

The crisis, Annette thought as she rushed up the stairs to Thelma's apartment. People like Thelma often did well for a while, and then failed momentarily. It was almost as if they were testing themselves, because they didn't understand why they should succeed. So they failed, and that was so devastating to them, they were tempted to give up. Giving up, at least, confirmed their negative self-image. When the crisis hit, you had to catch them right away and talk out their problems, or else . . .

A bedraggled-looking Thelma answered the door and quietly invited Annette in. Her eyes were moist and puffy from crying. "Listen, Annette," she said when they were seated. "I'm terribly sorry about tonight. I just sort of lost control, you know?"

"I know," Annette replied.

"I mean, it was a rotten day at the office. I jumped all over people, and they were nasty to me in return. I knew what I was doing wrong, but I just couldn't stop myself. Anyhow, I went bowling after work, and I was feeling so damned rotten, I decided to have just one little drink.

Just one, you know . . ."

Annette nodded. "I know."

"And then before I knew it I was on my fourth Tom Collins, and I bowled really lousy, and I told one of my friends to go to hell." Thelma started weeping. "I mean, I *knew* I was hurting people, and I just couldn't seem to stop."

"Yes, we all do that sometimes," said Annette quietly.

"Then I got so mad at myself I just ran out to the car and started driving. I couldn't bear to face you right then. Does that make sense to you?"

"Of course."

"I must have driven for three hours anyway. I kept hoping the car would run out of gas way out in the country somewhere, and I'd just die or something before anybody found me." Thelma sighed. "But finally I just gave up and drove back here. And then you called."

"I'm glad I did."

Thelma nodded, trying to smile a bit. "So am I, Annette. I think I finally figured it out, what went wrong. But I want your advice on it."

"Of course," said Annette, brightening considerably.

"It sounds screwy, I know,

but I think I got depressed because I was doing so well. You know what I mean?"

Annette nodded. "I know exactly."

"I mean, I've lost 22 pounds in a month, I've done better at the office—except for today—and you've helped me like nobody else ever has. But *I* was the one who did it, you understand? I mean, *you* didn't resist all those hunger pangs in the middle of the night, *I* did. And *you* didn't have to do all that exercise, *I* did."

"I know," Annette said reassuringly. "And you really did beautifully."

"That's the trouble!" Thelma cried. "I lost weight, I did better on the job, I've got my friends back, I look better, I feel better, I'm happier than I've been in years."

Annette smiled. "And that's the problem, isn't it?"

"Of course," Thelma said in a weary tone of voice. "I kept asking myself, why did I have to wait so long to make all these changes? Why did I need you to help me do what should have been obvious? And I kept thinking about all of the wasted times in my life, the people I'd hurt because I didn't know any better."

"You've got a lifetime left to make up for it," said Annette.

"Oh, I know. And I suppose I will. But even that isn't the real problem, is it?"

Annette grinned broadly. "No, Thelma, it isn't."

"I mean, the problem is, I *know* I can change myself. I've already done it. So I guess I could do some more, right?"

"Right," said Annette. "You've got both the motivation and the technique."

Thelma nodded. "That's the scary part. Now that I can do just about anything I want to do, what the hell do I really want to do?" Thelma giggled a bit. "I mean, as long as I was failing, I could blame it all on God, or my parents, or just about anybody. Now I've got nobody to blame except myself. I finally have all the freedom anybody could ask for. That's frightening."

"Of course," said Annette. "Because there's no freedom without responsibility. Freedom's pretty expensive, when you stop to think about it."

Thelma laughed. "Well, I guess I can afford it now." She shook her head, as if in wonderment. "You know, I guess I must be the happiest person in town. No, that's wrong. I must be the happiest person in the whole wide world."

Now it was Annette's turn to cry a bit. "Can I be number two?"

Thelma reached over and squeezed Annette's hand tightly. "Sure. And thanks for everything, you know?"

"I know," said Annette, wiping her eyes with a tissue.

Thelma released Annette's hand and leaned back in her chair. "Listen, we've got some things to plan. I've been thinking about getting a new job in a year or so, after I've lost another hundred pounds or so. But you know what I want to be?"

"No, tell me."

Thelma grinned. "An airline stewardess."

"You're kidding!"

Thelma nodded. "They're so slim and trim, you know. I've wanted to be just like that, all my life. And now maybe I can be." She paused for a second. "And there's another thing about being a stewardess, you know."

"What?"

Thelma roared with laughter until she almost cried again. "Well, it sure would beat buying my own ticket to Miami!"

Recommended Readings

Bennett, W. & Gurin, J. (1982). *The dieter's dilemma.* New York: Basic Books.

Herbert, W. (1983). Modeling bulimia. *Science News, 123* (May 14), p. 316.

Maslow, A. (1971). *The farthest reach of human nature.* New York: Viking.

Pfaff, D.W. (Ed.). (1982). *The physiological mechanisms of motivation.* New York: Springer-Verlag.

Did You Know That...

- Sexual motivation is more complex than hunger because sex involves at least two behavior patterns (male and female) as well as child-care activities?

- John B. Watson lost his professorship for undertaking pioneering studies of the human sexual response in 1917?

- The sex life of animals is controlled primarily by hormones?

- No matter what your sex, you have both male and female sex hormones in your body?

- Giving injections of male hormones to gay males causes them to become more active sexually, but doesn't make them heterosexual?

- The vast majority of children reared by homosexual parents turn out to have a heterosexual orientation?

- Most parents begin to teach their children "appropriate sex roles" the day the infants are born?

- You have "pleasure centers" in your brain which, when stimulated electrically, make you "feel good"?

11

Sexual Motivation

"The Mating Game"

Clare Wilson put down her library book and smiled warmly at her fiancé, Bill Meyer. "I think we should have a girl first. And don't you think that Christine would be a nice name for her?"

Bill's eyes opened slightly, but his gaze never strayed from the TV set. He was watching the U.S. Open Golf Tournament, and didn't really want to be disturbed. One of his favorite golfers, Greg Norman, was two strokes ahead of the other players, and Bill was trying to give Norman some moral support. Norman sank a difficult 30-foot putt on the 14th hole, and the crowd cheered. "You

drive for show, but you putt for dough," Bill said approvingly.

"You won't mind if our first child is a girl, will you, dear?"

Bill glanced quickly at Clare, then looked back at the television. "I don't think I have much choice in the matter," he said.

"Oh, I know that. But if it *is* a girl, you won't mind, will you?"

Bill sighed. It was difficult to concentrate on the golf tournament when Clare wanted to talk about things. "I don't really care, Clare. But how will you feel if she turns out to be a boy?"

Clare shrugged her shoul-

ders. "We'll name him Christopher, and try again."

With a sly grin on his face, Bill replied, "I don't mind that 'trying again' business at all."

Clare laughed. "Sex. That's all you men ever think about, isn't it?"

"Way to go!" Bill said loudly, as Greg Norman hit a ball that flew 250 yards through the air before landing in the middle of the fairway on the 15th hole.

"Well, isn't it?" Clare demanded.

"Isn't it what?" Bill asked.

"Sex," Clare said, a touch of laughter in her voice. "Isn't that all that guys ever think about?"

Bill shook his head in dismay. "You brought the topic up, not me. I was just sitting here, minding my own business, watching a golf tournament on the tube."

"I did *not* bring the topic up," Clare said, teasing Bill a bit. "I was talking about what we were going to name our first child. And you had to go and drag sex into the discussion."

"Well, how in the world are you going to have kids if you don't have sex first?" Bill asked.

Clare raised an eyebrow. She knew Bill was trying to concentrate on the golf tournament, but she enjoyed twitting him a bit when he got too involved in sports. Besides, this was a very important issue between the two of them—at least as far as she was concerned. So she said, "Having children is primarily a matter of love and commitment, not sex. It means getting married, building a stable relationship, and taking a responsible role in life."

A TV announcer extolling the virtues of a new automobile interrupted the tournament. Bill stood up, pretended he had a golf club in his hands, and began taking practice strokes. "*Right* down the middle," he said as he hit a phantom golf ball down an imaginary fairway.

"Bill, I know that you're really into golf. But I do wish you'd listen a bit more attentively when I'm trying to have a serious discussion with you," Clare said.

"Sorry about that," Bill replied, a touch of guilt in his voice. He stopped pretending he was playing golf, sat back down in his chair, and smiled at Clare. "Now, let's see. You were talking about sex . . ."

"I was *not* talking about sex, Bill Meyer! I was talking about our *relationship*. You're the one who dragged the conversation into the gutter."

"The gutter!" Bill said in dismay.

"That's right," Clare replied, delighted that Bill was giving her his full attention now. "I asked if you would object to calling our first child Christine, and you said . . ."

"I said that having children involves having sex first. Which it does. But, okay, I apologize for not paying attention. Now, tell me, why do you think we ought to have a daughter before we have a son."

Clare smiled happily. "Because, the way my career is going, I'll have more time to spend with our first child than with the second. So, Christine ought to be the first, because I want to make sure that she grows up to be a completely liberated young woman. And that will take a lot of work on my part."

Bill gazed back at the television set. Pleased to see that Greg Norman was still ahead of the other golfers, he looked back at Clare. "I'm not supposed to play much of a role in bringing up our daughter, I gather."

"Oh, of course you'll pay a part," Clare said. "An important part, too. But you're such a *traditionalist* when it comes to women, Bill. Sometimes I suspect that you think our only purpose in life is cooking and having babies . . ."

"Keep 'em barefoot and pregnant, huh?"

"There you go, talking about sex again," Clare replied in mock seriousness. "Anyway, that's why I want to make sure that Christine

picks up her social values from me instead of from you. You can train Christopher, when he comes along. But Christine is going to be my responsibility, since I want her to break free of the usual social constraints that you men impose on women."

"Constraints?" Bill muttered. "I never met a woman yet I could constrain in any way imaginable."

"Don't be silly," Clare replied. "You are perfectly aware that women are not allowed to do most of the things that you men do."

"Like what?" Bill said, his gaze wandering back to the golf tournament again.

"Like, be president of the United States, or be chairperson of General Motors, or win the Heisman trophy in college football . . ."

"Well, we've got a woman on the Supreme Court now, and we had a woman vice-presidential candidate, as you'll surely recall since you campaigned for her."

Clare gave him an annoyed look. "But Ferraro lost, as you'll surely recall. And as for Sandra Day O'Connor, she's one out of nine. A token appointment to keep the natives from getting restless."

"Way to go!" Bill cried, as one of the golfers sank a very long putt. In his excitement, he stood up and started swinging his imaginary golf club again.

"See what I mean?" Clare responded. "You don't take the women's equality movement as seriously as you take that golf tournament you're watching. Which reminds me. Why don't you pay as much attention to women's golf as you do to the men's tours?"

"Because they won't let me play in the women's tournaments. Although the way my game is going lately, I'm not sure I could win, even playing against the ladies."

"You see!" Clare said teasingly. "You think women are inferior to men, even on the golf course. Typical, chauvinistic male attitude. And that's why I want to make sure I'm the one who trains our daughter, Christine. If I didn't, you'd dress her up in frilly clothes and hair ribbons, and make her think her only purpose in life was to attract young men."

A commercial featuring Joe Namath flashed on the television screen. Bill smiled, remembering the time that "Broadway Joe" had stirred up so much controversy by starring in a pantyhose commercial. Then he turned his attention back to Clare. "Well, our daughter Christine would look a lot better in frilly dresses and hair ribbons than our son Christopher would."

"So, you would *constrain* our daughter from dressing any way that suits her, eh? See what I mean about the typical male attitude?"

Bill thought a moment. "No, I don't care how Christine dresses. That's up to her."

"And me," Clare said.

"And you," Bill agreed. "But what about Christopher? How are you going to rear him?"

Clare gave the matter some thought. "Well, I want him to be healthy and happy, of course. And I do want him to realize that his sister is his equal. But aside from that, he's chiefly your responsibility."

"You don't want to make sure he learns how to cook and sew and change diapers?"

Clare paused. "Well, those would be useful skills, I suppose. And I do think that a man and woman should share responsibility for household chores. But I'm sure you'll want him to learn how to play golf, and football, and those sorts of things. I'd go along with that, just so Christine is free to participate in sports too."

"Wouldn't you prefer for Christopher to grow up wanting to stay home and cook and run the vacuum and take care of our grandkids? While his wife earned the money by being chairperson of G.M.?"

Clare frowned. "If he *wanted* to do that sort of thing, I suppose I wouldn't object. Not too much, anyhow." Then her face brightened. "Besides, if our daughter-in-law is chairperson of G.M., they could afford to hire a maid, and Christopher could do whatever he liked."

"But suppose he really *wanted* to be a househusband."

"Well, I don't really know," Clare said, realizing that the conversation had reached a delicate turn. "I just can't imagine that any son of mine would want to stay home and do the household chores."

Joe Namath appeared on the television set again, talking sincerely about another product. Bill thought about Namath for a moment, then said, "Well, what if Christopher was so liberated that he wanted to wear dresses and pantyhose?"

"Don't be silly!" Clare said in a shocked tone of voice.

"Aren't you the one who's being conventional now? I mean, you think it's okay if our daughter Christine wears slacks and sneakers and T shirts . . ."

"Of course it's okay, because she'll be liberated from the traditional feminine role . . ."

"But our son Christopher can't be liberated enough to wear pantyhose . . ."

"That's not 'being liberated,' that's being *abnormal.*"

Bill grinned. "And you're the one who said that men can do anything they want, while women are constrained by the wicked, chauvinistic males in our society."

"That's absolutely true, Bill, and you know it. Men are free, and women aren't."

"But Christopher can't wear pantyhose, right?"

"No son of mine would *want* to wear pantyhose!"

"Why not, Clare? Why not?"

(Continued on page 310.)

Sexual Motivation

Sex has always posed something of a problem for the psychologist. Part of the difficulty lies in finding a theoretical explanation for sexual motivation. But sometimes the problem has existed at a personal or social level, as well.

As far as theory goes, it would seem that sexual needs should be explainable in the same terms as are hunger, thirst, and the other biological needs. However, there is a crucial difference: Food, air, and water are necessary for the survival of the *individual*, but sex is necessary for the survival of the *species*. In order for reproduction to occur, two individuals of opposite sex must find each other and adjust to each other's needs—at least momentarily. Unlike hunger, then, sex involves at least two different sets of behavior patterns, male and female. Men and women breathe the same way, drink the same way, eat the same way. But their sexual behaviors are typically quite different, and so presumably their sexual motivations are different too.

If we look at sex from a *species* perspective, reproduction involves more than just a one-time act. For, in higher animals, species survival depends on keeping one or both parents around to care for the young until they are large enough to face the world on their own. An adequate theory of *species* sexuality, then, must explain not only the differing sexual desires and responses of male and female, but maternal and paternal activities as well.

Given these complexities, it shouldn't surprise you to learn that motivational theories that account fairly well for hunger and thirst often do a poor job of explaining sexual behaviors.

Sexual Motivation: Theoretical Issues

In Chapter 10 we said that the study of human motivation is really an attempt to answer questions about *why* people do what they do. And we quoted Marshall Jones's belief that the answers to these questions must tell you why people *begin* a certain activity, why the behavior goes in the *direction* it does, why it *continues* for a period of time, and why it eventually *stops*.

Most people assume that sexual behavior *begins* because of some innately determined "sex drive." And there are some data suggesting a connection between *hormone* levels and sexual activities. However, as we will see, hormones don't directly determine the *directions* in which our sexual desires take us. Nor can we appeal to hormones for an explanation of why some people are *inhibited* in their sexual activities, nor why a particular sex act may be *prohibited* in some societies but allowed in others.

We face similar problems when we try to explain why human sexual behaviors "continue" once started, and why they cease when they do.

One reason for our ignorance is the difficulty many people have in being objective about human sexuality. But suppose we try to put our preconceptions aside, and look at two things: what we know about sexual motivation and behaviors, and why our knowledge of these subjects has been so difficult to gain.

Early Research on Sexuality

In the first half of this century, a few scientists tried to bring human sexual behavior into the laboratory, to study it as objectively as other scientists had studied the digestion of food. Almost without exception, however, these pioneers were rejected by their scientific colleagues for daring to perform experiments on what most people believed was an intensely private aspect of human life.

Back in the early 1900's, psychologists at Cornell asked their graduate students to record their **introspections** during sexual activities (as well as at other times). And Clelia Duel Mosher, a physician who taught at Stanford from 1910 until 1929, made an extensive study of sexuality in college women. However, the Cornell data never appeared in print, and Mosher's results were first published in 1974, almost 35 years after her death.

Watson's Studies

The most famous of these early investigators was John B. Watson, who started the behaviorist tradition in psychology. In 1929 Watson wrote that sex "is admittedly the most important subject in life. . . . And yet our scientific information is so meager. Even the few facts that we have must be looked upon as more or less bootlegged stuff." Since the medical sciences had studiously ignored the subject of human sexuality, Watson set out in 1917 to investigate the matter himself.

Watson tackled the issue directly—by constructing a set of instruments to measure the physical responses of a woman during sexual arousal. Watson's wife refused to participate in such a project. However, Watson apparently talked his laboratory assistant, Rosalie Rayner, into serving as a subject.

With Rayner's help, Watson gathered what were probably the first reliable data on the female sexual response. And since this was a topic he could obviously study with pleasure, he acquired several boxes of scientific data. Unfortunately for all concerned, Watson's wife eventually discovered why her husband was spending so much time in the laboratory. Watson's wife not only sued him for divorce, she also confiscated the scientific records!

Although Watson was one of the brightest and most creative men of his time, his academic career was ruined by this episode. He had to resign his professorship at Johns Hopkins University, and most of his friends and colleagues deserted him. The Baltimore newspapers reported the divorce in lurid detail, and the judge presiding at the trial gave Watson a severe tongue-lashing—calling him, among other things, an expert in *mis*behavior.

After the divorce, Watson and Rosalie Rayner were married. But Watson still could not find a job at any other college or university. In desperation, he took a position with a large advertising agency and stayed there the rest of his professional life. Although he continued to write books and scientific papers, he considered himself a ruined man and soon slipped into the solace of alcohol. He died at the age of 80 in 1958.

Sex Research in Columbia, Missouri

In 1929 Watson wrote, "The study of sex is still fraught with danger. It can be openly studied only by individuals who are not connected with universities." As H.W. Magoun points out in the November 1981 issue of the *Journal of Sex Research*, Watson's warning was not an idle one. In 1929 a young man named O. Hobart

Introspections (in-troh-SPECK-shuns). To introspect means "to look inward." Your own personal inner thoughts and feelings. See Chapter 5.

Biased (BUY-est). From a Latin term meaning "to cut or go against the grain." In psychological terms, to be biased is to have preconceived notions about a situation, or to perceive things as you want to see them, not as they actually are. A "biased sample" is one not selected randomly, but rather selected according to some (often unconscious) scheme.

Mowrer was an undergraduate at the University of Missouri in Columbia. As part of a project in a sociology class, Mowrer gave out a questionnaire on "The Economic Aspects of Women" to some 600 Missouri students. Three of the questions Mowrer included in his survey concerned attitudes toward extramarital sexual relations.

When the newspapers discovered what Mowrer was doing, they raised a furor. The townspeople in Columbia circulated a petition demanding that the "people responsible" for this outrage be fired. The state legislature agreed, and the president of the university responded by firing the professor who had taught the course. Mowrer fortunately survived the incident and went on to a distinguished career in psychology. In 1954 he became President of the American Psychological Association.

Kinsey's Interviews

Watson's influence on the scientific study of human sexuality was profound, but largely indirect. One of Watson's students, Karl Lashley, did undertake some work in the area. But Lashley's major contribution came when he got a noted biologist interested in studying sexual responses—a man named Alfred Kinsey.

The first survey of sexual behavior based on an adequately large segment of the public did not come until 1948, when Kinsey and his associates published their monumental volume, *Sexual Behavior in the Human Male*. Using a standardized set of questions, the Kinsey group got many thousands of men to describe their sexual feelings and behaviors. A surprisingly large number responded to the questions without apparent shame or evasion.

However, as many critics noted, there were methodological problems with Kinsey's survey. Since Kinsey depended on volunteers, it may be that his sample was **biased**. That is, it may be that the sexuality of those people who wouldn't talk to Kinsey was quite different from the sexuality of those who did. Nonetheless, Kinsey did

"HEY, GUYS — WAKE UP!"

Alfred C. Kinsey

Virginia Johnson and William Masters

show that a large group of normal-appearing males regularly engaged in a wide variety of sexual practices that "nice people" were not even supposed to know about.

In 1953 Kinsey and his group published a similar book about female sexual behavior. And in 1981, scientists at the Kinsey Institute reported a study of **homosexual** activities.

The public response to Kinsey's efforts was decidedly a mixed bag. Shortly after the study on women was published, New York Congressman Louis B. Heller had this to say about Kinsey: "He is hurling the insult of the century against our mothers, wives, daughters and sisters, under the pretext of making a great contribution to scientific research." In 1954 a special House committee accused the Rockefeller Foundation of "directly supporting subversion" and of promoting communism because the Foundation gave money to the Kinsey Institute. In a 1982 article, Harvard biologist Stephen Jay Gould notes, "Kinsey never did find an alternate source of support [after the Congressional attack]; he died two years later, overworked, angry, and distressed that so many years of further data might never see publication . . ."

Masters and Johnson's Research

The writings of Kinsey and many others all sprang from conversations and case histories rather than direct observations. Subjects were asked to *talk* about their sex lives while the scientists recorded what the subjects *said*. It was not until the 1950's that William Masters and Virginia Johnson began to study what people actually *did*.

Masters was trained as a **gynecologist**—that is, a physician who has specialized knowledge of the female reproductive system. Johnson re-

ceived her training in social work and psychology. They started their work in St. Louis, using female prostitutes as paid subjects. Following Watson's lead, Masters and Johnson made recordings of their subjects' bodily reactions while the women experienced various types of sexual arousal (chiefly masturbation). Later, they studied the biological changes that accompany sexual excitement in males, as well.

When Masters tried to present his early data to a gathering of U.S. gynecologists, the majority of these physicians urged him to give up his research. Many of the best-known medical journals would not publish his findings, and political pressure prevented his getting governmental support for his work. Thus, the first public discussion of Masters and Johnson's work was delayed until 1962, when they presented their findings at a meeting of the American Psychological Association.

The Early Studies: A Summary

Almost all the early research on human sexuality focused on intra-psychic or social variables. Those few scientists who attempted to look at the biology of *human* sexuality paid the price for so doing. Thus, much of what we know of the biological factors affecting sexual motivation comes from studies conducted on animal subjects. How much this animal research can be generalized to humans is still a matter of debate. However, let's look at what the facts seem to be, and then turn our attention to the intra-psychic and social/behavioral factors that influence sexual motives and acts.

The Biology of Sex

Most of the cells in your body contain 23 *pairs* of **chromosomes**, or 46 chromosomes in all. The only exceptions to this rule are the sperm cells and unfertilized egg cells. The sperm cell, like the egg cell, contains only 23 chromosomes. But the sperm cell is somewhat different from the egg. Its 23rd chromosome can be either the large X type or the smaller Y type (see Fig. 11.1 and Fig. 11.2). The 23rd chromosome of the egg cell is *always* a large X type.

If an X-type sperm is the first to enter the egg cell, the fertilized egg will have an XX 23rd chromosome *pair*—and the child will be a *genetic* female. If a Y-type sperm fertilizes the egg, the 23rd chromosome pair will be of the XY variety and the child will be a *genetic* male.

Hormones

The X and Y chromosomes determine whether the cells in your body will carry the XX or XY pattern. However, *becoming* a male or a female is a much more complicated process. The actual *shape* of your body—and of your sex organs—is affected by many factors. The most important of these factors are the hormones produced by various *glands* in your body.

Glands are small chemical factories that release their products into the bloodstream, or onto the tissues surrounding the gland, or even into the outside world. Some of these chemicals primarily have a local effect. For instance, the tear glands in your eyes secrete that clear but romantic liquid which lubricates the movement of your eyes in their sockets. Other types of glands secrete their products directly into your bloodstream, and thus have their primary effects *some distance away* from the glands. These "action-at-a-distance" chemicals are the *hormones*.

The Sex Hormones

You have two **adrenal glands**—one atop each of your kidneys (see Fig. 11.3). Your adrenals secrete more than 20 different hormones. The majority of the adrenal hormones regulate such bodily functions as digestion, urine excretion, and blood pressure. As we will see in the next chapter, many of these hormones play a role in your response to stress. However, some of these chemicals also have a direct effect on your sex life. These are called the *sex hormones*.

Sex hormones are also produced by your **gonads**, or sex glands—the testes in the male, and the ovaries in the female. From shortly after conception onward, your adrenals and your gonads worked together to provide your body with the chemicals it needed to develop into— and to remain—a sexually mature adult.

Homosexual (HO-mo-SEX-you-all). Sexual activities between two (or more) males, or between two (or more) females. As opposed to *heterosexual* (HETT-er-oh-SEX-you-all) activities, which occur between a male and a female. Homosexual behaviors are frequently found in lower animals and, according to Kinsey, take place more often among humans than "prudish people" are willing to admit. Freud—and most other scientists who have studied human sexuality—believe that homosexual activities are as "normal" and as "genetically determined" as are heterosexual behaviors.

Gynecologist (guy-nuh-COLL-oh-jist, or jin-nuh-COLL-oh-jist). The Greek word *gyne* means "woman." A medical doctor whose speciality is treating the reproductive problems of women is called a gynecologist.

Chromosomes (KROH-moh-sohms). From the Greek words *chromo*, meaning "colored," and *soma*, meaning "body." The genes of a cell are strung together like strands of colored beads. These "strands" are the chromosomes.

Adrenal gland (add-DREE-nul). A small gland at the top of the kidney that secretes many different hormones, including those that affect sexual growth and behavior. You have two adrenal glands—one for each of your kidneys.

Gonads (GO-nads). The primary sex glands—the ovaries in the female and the testes in the male. The ovaries produce the egg cells that are fertilized by the sperm secreted by the testes.

Androgens (ANN-dro-jens). From the Greek words meaning "producer of males." There are several male hormones; collectively these are known as androgens.

Testosterone (tess-TOSS-ter-own). The most important of the androgens, or male hormones. Found in small quantities in females, as well as males. Many psychologists believe testosterone is the "major hormonal motivator" for many types of behaviors in both men and women.

Estrogens (ESS-tro-jens). The Latin word *estrus* (ESS-truss) refers to the period in a female's reproductive cycle when she is fertile and hence capable of becoming pregnant. Estrogens are the hormones that generate or bring about estrus.

Progesterone (pro-JEST-ter-own). One of the several female sex hormones.

Male hormones are called **androgens**. The best-known of these is **testosterone**. The two main types of female hormones are known as the **estrogens** and **progesterone**. Whether you are a woman or a man, however, your adrenals and your gonads produce *both* male and female hormones. As we will see, though, it is the *relative amount* of these two types of hormones that is important for sexual differentiation.

Primary and Secondary Sex Characteristics

When scientists speak of *primary sex characteristics*, they mean the actual sex organs themselves—the ovaries, vagina, uterus, and clitoris in the female, and the penis and testes in the male. Additionally, those parts of the reproductive organs that can be seen by the naked eye are called the *external genitalia*, or

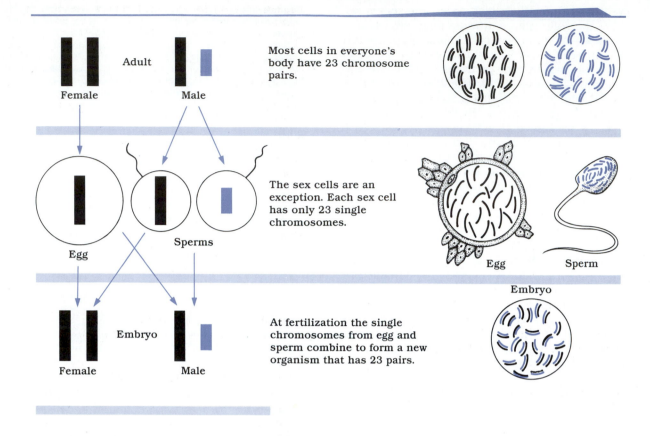

Most cells in everyone's body have 23 chromosome pairs.

The sex cells are an exception. Each sex cell has only 23 single chromosomes.

At fertilization the single chromosomes from egg and sperm combine to form a new organism that has 23 pairs.

Adult

Female

Male

Egg

Sperms

Embryo

Female

Male

Egg

Sperm

Embryo

X chromosome

Y chromosome

Fig. 11.1 Sex is determined by the sperm cell. An egg and sperm unite to form a new being.

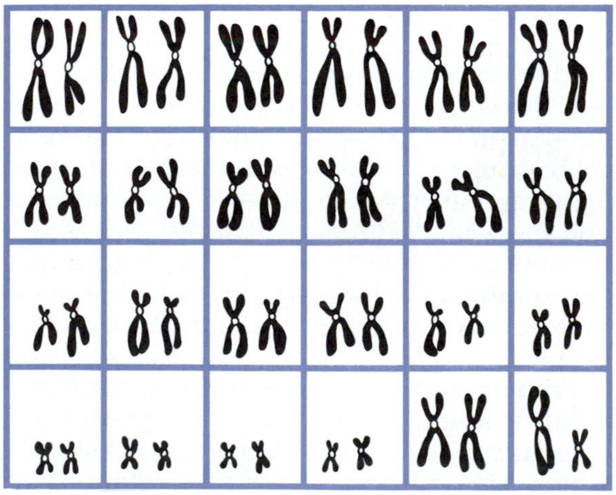

Female or male

Fig. 11.2 Human chromosome cells. Only the 23rd pair differ—XX for female, XY for male.

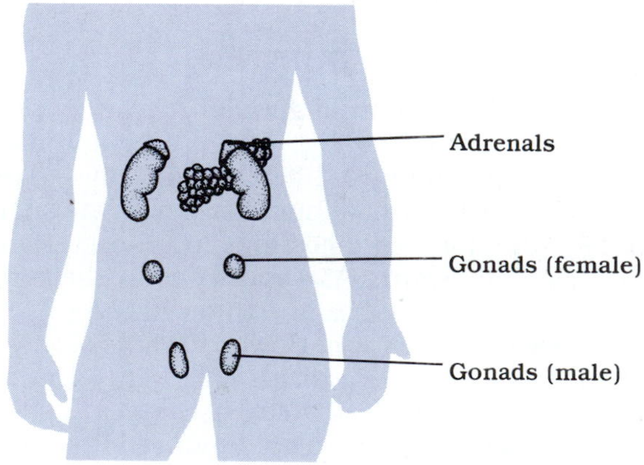

Adrenals

Gonads (female)

Gonads (male)

Fig. 11.3 The location of some major endocrine glands.

genitals. Male-female differences in *primary* sex characteristics are usually present at birth.

The *secondary sex characteristics* are those that appear at **puberty**—the growth of facial hair and deepening voice in the young man, the development of the breasts and broadening of the hips in the young woman. The appearance of both primary and secondary sexual characteristics is controlled almost entirely by *hormones*.

If a young boy's adrenals and testes *overproduce* androgens—or *underproduce* estrogens—he will experience early puberty. That is, his voice will change and his beard will begin to grow sooner than expected. But if the boy's glands *underproduce* androgens or *overproduce* estrogens for some reason, his puberty will be delayed and his body may take on feminine characteristics—a high voice, overdeveloped breasts, and a lack of facial hair.

If a young girl's adrenals and ovaries *overproduce* estrogens—or *underproduce* androgens—the girl will come to sexual maturity earlier than expected. If the reverse is true, her puberty will be delayed, and she may even develop such masculine secondary characteristics as flat breasts, excess facial hair, and a low voice.

Androgens and Sexual Behavior

Estrogens and progesterone seem to be correlated with child bearing and child rearing. It is testosterone—in both men and women—that tends to promote *sexual behavior itself*. Thus, either a man or woman with a low testosterone level is likely to experience a low *biological* sex drive. However, cultural inhibitions can suppress sexual behavior even in someone with a high testosterone level. And stimulation from the environment may be so strong at times that even someone with a low testosterone level may engage in a variety of sexual behaviors.

Thus, both the strength of the sex drive—and the types of behaviors that the organism produces—are *always* affected both by genes and by social factors.

Question: How many sexes are there?

Sexual Dimorphism

The division of the animal kingdom into male and female is called **sexual dimorphism**. However, nature often blurs the line between female and male body types. For even in higher animals, where sexual dimorphism is most pronounced, some offspring are born who possess part or all of both male and female sex organs.

Genitals (JEN-it-tulls). From the Latin word meaning "to beget, to reproduce, to generate children." The external sex organs, or *genitalia* (jen-it-TAIL-ee-uh).

Puberty (PEW-burr-tee). The onset of sexual maturity, when the person becomes physically capable of sexual reproduction. Usually between the 11th and the 14th year, the female's ovaries begin producing eggs and menstrual (MEN-strew-ull, or MEN-strull) bleeding begins. At about the same age, the male's testes begin producing semen and ejaculation becomes possible.

Sexual dimorphism (dye-MORE-fism). *Morph* (MORF) comes from a Greek word meaning "form" or "type." There are, generally speaking, two sexual "forms," male and female.

Intersex. Many lower organisms are hermaphrodites (her-MAFF-rho-dights). That is, each organism contains both male and female reproductive organs. Although sexual dimorphism is fairly strong in higher animals, some individuals (including humans) are *intersexed*, in that they contain parts or all of both the male and female organs.

These **intersex** individuals range from "mostly female" to "mostly both" to "mostly male."

Critical Periods in Sexual Development

The March 20, 1981 issue of *Science* includes a number of articles on the effects of hormones on sexual dimorphism in humans and animals. According to these papers, both male and female hormones can be found in most fetuses while they are in the womb. It is the *balance* of the hormones during certain *critical periods* that biases the fetus toward male or female behavior patterns.

Generally speaking, the critical period for most species is just when the central nervous system is beginning to develop. If androgens predominate during this critical time, the fetus will develop male *genitalia*. In addition, various *parts of the brain* involved in masculine behavior patterns will be activated, and the brain centers that mediate feminine behavior patterns will be suppressed. If the androgens do not predominate during the critical period, the fetus typically will develop female genitalia and behaviors, while the brain centers that control masculinity will be suppressed.

To summarize, the sex hormones affect sexual behavior during fetal development in two ways: first, by determining whether the organism will have male or female primary sex characteristics; second, by determining which sex-related centers in the brain will develop, and which won't. However, as we will see, it is the *combination* of hormonal bias, past experience, and present environmental stimulation that determines most adult sexual behaviors.

The male ring dove bows and coos before the female as part of a mating ritual.

The "bow-coo" dance performed by the male triggers the production of hormones in the female, which leads to egg laying and nesting.

Mating and Nesting in Doves

The complex interplay between hormones and environmental stimulation is nicely illustrated in a classic series of studies by Daniel Lehrman and his colleagues at Rutgers.

Lehrman and his group studied mating and nesting behaviors in the ring dove. During the mating season, the male ring dove approaches the female and dances around her. At one point in his ritual, he bows low in front of her and utters a characteristic "coo" sound. Under normal circumstances, the female accepts the male's advances, and the two subsequently mate. Both birds then build a nest. When the female lays her eggs, both birds sit on them and care for the young after they hatch.

If the male ring dove is castrated, he shows no interest at all in the female and simply won't mate. If he is subsequently injected with testosterone, he will perform the "bow-coo" dance and will mate with the female. But he won't help with nest building, nor will he sit on the eggs. If the male is now injected with estrogen, he will help the female construct the nest, but he won't hatch the young. If he is also given progesterone, the male will complete the sequence and care for the young doves as well.

As far as the female dove is concerned, it is the *sight* of the male's dance and the *sound* of his voice that trigger the production of estrogen. The increase in estrogen causes her to mate, gather materials for the nest, and then lay her eggs. The *act* of nest building causes her ovaries to secrete progesterone, which encour-ages her to hatch the eggs and care for the young.

As Lehrman notes, in the case of the ring dove, sexual behavior affects hormone production as much as hormone production affects sexual behavior.

Question: Some biologically oriented scientists believe that sexual behavior is determined almost entirely by the hormones. What does Lehrman's research suggest is the case?

Intra-Psychic Aspects of Sexual Motivation

Sexual behavior is strongly—but not completely—influenced by hormones and other biological factors in the lower animals. But what about humans? Surely we *choose* the sexual activities we engage in. Were that not the case, our laws against certain types of sex acts—with certain types of partners—would be scientifically indefensible.

Not all sexual behaviors are the product of voluntary choice, of course. A woman does not "choose" to engage in rape; she is forced into that behavior. Children who are molested by adults are often powerless to prevent the acts that are thrust upon them. And strong social pressures may make almost anyone engage in sexual behaviors that seem "personally unnatural" to the individual concerned. Many of these "personally unnatural" acts involve sexual **orientation**.

Sexual Orientation

Psychologists don't entirely agree as to which factors affecting voluntary sexual behavior are the most potent. However, one obvious influence is *sexual orientation*. Women tend to be primarily attracted to men as sexual partners, and vice versa. Perhaps because heterosexuality is so "natural" to most people, it has been infrequently researched.

Those acts—such as homosexuality—that "go against the grain" of natural heterosexuality have received some scientific attention, however. Sigmund Freud once said we learn about the normal by studying the abnormal. Perhaps, then, we can learn something about heterosexual orientation by investigating the factors that influence supposedly "abnormal" thoughts, feelings, and behaviors.

Homosexuality

There are few topics in the entire field of psychology so emotionally charged as that of homosexuality. There are many reasons why this topic raises such intense feelings. First, homosexual acts are viewed as a "crime against nature" by many people. Second, effeminate males and masculine females appear to be rejecting their "normal sex roles." Third, homosexuals are often perceived as poor role models for children. Last, but surely not least, people with a strong heterosexual orientation frequently have difficulty imagining any other point of view. Thus, they may view a homosexual orientation as evidence of a "mental disorder."

Suppose we look briefly at these points, then discuss the factors that apparently influence sexual orientation.

Is Homosexuality Unnatural?

In his 1980 book *Homosexual Behavior: A Modern Reappraisal*, psychiatrist Judd Marmor states that homosexuality is far from being "unnatural" in the *statistical* sense. It occurs in all higher species, even when members of the opposite sex are present and presumably available for mating. Therefore, we can presume that the *possibility* of homosexuality is as "coded for in the genes" as is the *possibility* of heterosexuality.

Homosexual acts among humans are fairly common in western societies. Some 40 percent of Kinsey's male subjects admitted to having had "at least one homosexual experience" at some time in their lives. However, only 10 percent of the men stated they had a homosexual orientation. Another 10 percent or so were bisexual, or weren't strongly attracted either to males or females. Judging from these figures, having a same-sex orientation in the United States today is about as "unnatural" *in the statistical sense of that word* as is being Jewish, black, or being a blue-eyed blond.

Do Homosexuals Violate Standard Sex Roles?

In a 1981 study from the Kinsey Institute, Alan Bell and his colleagues report that the major *developmental* difference between "straights" and "gays" is that both male and female homosexuals experienced *gender nonconformity* while young. That is, the boys tended not to like sports and other "masculine" activities all that much, while the girls tended to prefer "non-feminine" activities. In terms of adult masculine and feminine sex-role behaviors, however, there is little difference between "gays" and "straights." Some gay males are effeminate; most are not. Some lesbians show strongly masculine behaviors; most do not. And some straight males and females show "nontraditional" sex-role behaviors.

If we look at adult *sexual* behaviors and fantasies, the difference between heterosexuals and homosexuals becomes more pronounced. According to University of Kansas psychologist Michael Storms, female and male homosexuals have "values" and "self-images" that are identical to those of heterosexual women and men. However, the homosexuals tend to fantasize about (and engage in) same-sex relations, while the heterosexuals tend to fantasize about (and engage in) cross-sex relations.

Homosexuality and Children

One standard objection to homosexuality is that it does not lead to childbearing. In fact, as Alan Bell and his colleagues have shown, this is not always the case. In a 1981 survey of more than 1,000 homosexuals in San Francisco, Bell

Sexual orientation is determined early in life and is affected by a combination of biological, psychological, and social factors.

sexual experiences. If children are seduced by homosexuals, won't that affect the children's sexual orientation? Again, the data suggest this isn't the case. In their 1981 study, Alan Bell and his colleagues compared 1,000 homosexuals with a carefully matched group of 500 heterosexual men and women. These scientists report that the majority of both groups "knew" their sexual orientation at a very early age, several years before they actually engaged in any overt sexual acts. A great many of the heterosexuals had homosexual encounters at an early age, but became "straight" anyhow. And most of the homosexuals had a number of heterosexual encounters early in life. They didn't find these experiences "traumatic," just less rewarding than same-sex relationships.

Is Homosexuality a Mental Disorder?

Until fairly recently, most psychologists and psychiatrists considered homosexuality a "mental disorder." However, in the early 1970's, both the American Psychological Association and the American Psychiatric Association removed homosexuality from the list of "standard mental disorders." To be entirely truthful, however, a significant minority of both professional groups still believe that gayness is a type of personality disorder. However, the prevailing opinion is that homosexuality is an "alternate life style."

Heterosexual Orientation

This rather lengthy discussion of homosexuality is important for two reasons. First, it tells us something about what may be the largest "hidden" minority in our society. Second, it gives us some of the data we need to discuss *heterosexual attraction.* For, as we mentioned earlier, most of the research on sexual orientation has focused on homosexuality rather than on heterosexuality.

We must also differentiate sexual *orientation* from sexual *identity* and sex *roles.* Orientation has to do with whether you are attracted to the opposite sex, the same sex, or both. Sexual identity involves whether you "feel" yourself to be male or female without regard to your sexual orientation. Sex roles have to do with displaying socially accepted patterns of "masculine" and "feminine" thoughts, attitudes, and behaviors.

Sexual Identity

Most scientific research on sexual identity has focused people who, because of hormonal

and his associates found that 20 percent of the gay males had been married. About a third of the white lesbians and half the black lesbians had been or still were married. And many of these individuals had gotten (and remained) married precisely because they wished to have children.

A second objection raised against homosexuality has to do with sexual identity. Many people assume that children reared by gay parents will have a greater-than-normal chance of becoming gay themselves. However, the data suggest otherwise. U.C.L.A. psychiatrist Martha Kirkpatrick studied the children of single lesbian and single heterosexual mothers. She could find no difference between the two groups of children, either in terms of emotional disturbances or sexual identity. Similar results come from a recent study by Richard Green, a psychiatrist at the State University of New York at Stony Brook. Green evaluated 37 children being reared either by female homosexuals or by parents who had undergone a sex-change operation. Of these 37, 36 showed no signs of confused sexual identity. And all of the teenagers in this group were decidedly "straight" in their sexual orientation.

A third objection has to do with a child's early

problems, are born with both male and female sex organs. Perhaps the best-known studies are those that Julianne Imperato-McGinley and her colleagues at the Cornell Medical Center performed in the late 1970's. The subjects of this research were 38 individuals who grew up in rural villages in the Dominican Republic. The subjects were all XY males who had normal levels of testosterone, but whose bodies could not produce a related male hormone called *dihydro-testosterone*. As a consequence, these *intersex* individuals were born with such ambiguous genitalia that more than half of them were reared as girls. However, at puberty, the subjects developed most of the male primary and secondary sex characteristics. Their voices deepened, they showed the male pattern of musculature, and their breasts did not enlarge. Their penises grew and became capable of erections and ejaculation.

The question that interested Imperator-McGinley was this: How would these men react when they developed male primary and secondary sex characteristics after being reared all their lives as girls?

Of the 25 living subjects, Imperator-McGinley and her colleagues were able to gather detailed information on 18. The Cornell scientists report that 17 of the 18 switched to wearing male clothing at puberty and thereafter considered themselves to be "men."

According to Imperator-McGinley, these 17 subjects began to question their sexual identity sometime between the ages of 7 and 12. Over this period, the men passed "through stages of no longer feeling like girls, to feeling like men, and finally to conscious awareness that they were indeed men." Imperator-McGinley concludes that hormones, rather than social factors, are the major determiners of sexual identity.

However, in an article published in the March 20, 1981 issue of *Science*, Robert Rubin and his colleagues dispute this conclusion. They point out that one subject whom Imperator-McGinley claims "developed a male sex identity" continued to wear dresses. Rubin and his associates believe that only 13 of the 18 actually had clearly defined male identities. These scientists also report on 8 intersex individuals in the United States who had similar hormonal problems and who were reared as girls. All 8 "maintained their female gender identity of rearing" despite the development of male genitalia at puberty.

According to Rubin and his colleagues, "Most investigators now regard the factors contributing to the development of gender identity to be neither 'nature' nor 'nurture' alone, but rather an interaction of hormonal and psychosocial influences."

Question: Why might intersex individuals living in a highly traditional culture such as the Dominican Republic be more likely to adopt a male identity than similar individuals living in the United States?

Why Are You "Straight" (Or Otherwise)?

Until fairly recently, most scientists assumed that hormonal bias determined whether a person turned out to be heterosexual, homosexual, or bisexual. However, as Robert Rubin and his colleagues suggest, this doesn't seem to be the case. With certain minor exceptions, the hormonal patterns of gay males is the same as that of heterosexual males. And no one has yet reported reliable hormonal differences between lesbians and "straight" females. Furthermore, injecting gay males with testosterone *increases their homosexual activities* rather than "turning them 'straight.'" Writing in the March 20, 1981 issue of *Science*, psychologists Anke Ehrhardt and Heino Meyer-Bahlburg conclude, "The data available . . . indicate that prenatal hormones do not rigidly determine sexual orientation."

Like all other human behaviors, sexual orientation and sexual identity are multi-determined. And both aspects of your sexuality seem to be more a matter of "discovery" than of "choice." During your early years, you slowly became aware of what sex you were, and what sex you were attracted to. You did not sit down, think things over, and then logically "decide" to be what you are. Rather, you simply became aware of what motives nature and your environment had given you.

Question: Men in Scotland and Greece have traditionally worn skirts. How would "wearing dresses" affect their sexual identity *within those cultures*?

Social/Behavioral Influences on Sexual Motivation

Society cannot control which hormones are present in your body. Nor can society entirely determine whether you are attracted to same-sex or opposite-sex partners (or both). But your culture does strongly influence your *feelings* about sex and about yourself—and how you *express* those feelings. Society does so by specifying which sexual *roles*, *behaviors*, and *values* are "acceptable" within that culture.

Society not only sets sexual standards, it enforces them as well—in at least two ways: first, by surrounding you with *models*—that is, with people (such as your parents and peers) who have adopted society's standards; and second, by rewarding you when you imitate these models, and by punishing you when you don't.

We will describe the "socialization process" by which you incorporate society's values in several later chapters. However, much of that socialization process involves learning **sex-role stereotypes**.

Question: Suppose you are a heterosexual male, hence strongly attracted to females. If men and women dressed and acted alike, how would you know whom to pursue sexually?

Sex-Role Stereotypes

In her chapter in the 1982 *Handbook of Developmental Psychology*, Dee Shepherd-Look defines sex-role stereotypes as "widely shared and pervasive concepts that prescribe how each sex ought to perform." According to Shepherd-Look, "there is considerable agreement both within and between cultures as to the appropriate sex-role behaviors for males and females." In most societies, a man is expected to be "competent, independent, assertive, aggressive, dominant, and competitive in social and sexual relations." A woman, on the other hand, is supposed to be "passive, affiliative, affectionate, nurturant, intuitive, and supportive, particularly in her familiar role as wife and mother."

Why are these sex-role stereotypes so similar from one culture to another? The answer scientists give to this question depends on the viewpoint they take toward human motivation. Most *biologists* presume that sex roles reflect genetic traits. *Intra-psychic psychologists*, such as Sigmund Freud, see sex roles as individual responses that develop out of a conflict between biological tendencies and social influences. However, *social/behavioral theorists* believe sex roles are primarily *learned*. We will discuss the Freudian and developmental viewpoints in Chapters 17–19. For the moment, let's look more closely at the biological and the social/behavioral explanations of what sex roles are, and where they come from.

Question: In most societies, men frequently seek casual affairs, while women seem to prefer long-lasting relationships. Why?

Sociobiology

In 1975, Harvard biologist Edward O. Wilson published a book entitled *Sociobiology: The New Synthesis*. In this work, Wilson tries to solve a very sticky problem. As we noted, sex is necessary for the survival of the species, but not for the survival of the individual. Why, then, do people (and animals) engage in sex and rear offspring, when these acts can be very costly to the individual organism?

Wilson argues that the major motive all organisms have is not that of *individual* survival, but rather that of *helping their genes survive*. You do not eat, drink, and breathe to ensure your own good health. Rather, Wilson says, you try to survive because you have an overwhelming urge to reproduce your own genes.

Male and Female "Roles"
According to Wilson, stereotyped sex roles developed because men and women must have different reproductive strategies. These strategies stem from "genetic reality," Wilson says. And since men and women in all societies have similar genes, their sex roles in all cultures should also be similar.

Wilson believes the best strategy men can adopt to make sure their genes get passed on is to have sex with as many women as possible. Therefore, Wilson says, the "masculine role" is that of being aggressive, dominant, and **promiscuous**. Women, however, must bear and care for children. Their best chance to help their genes survive is to make sure their offspring thrive. So, Wilson says, the "feminine role" is that of being submissive, because this is women's instinctual way of getting men to protect the women's children (i.e., genes).

Sociobiology: An Evaluation
Wilson's theory does have its strengths. It fits neatly within the framework of Darwinian evolution, and it allows biologists to explain many behaviors without delving too far into the organism's "mind."

However, according to social psychologists such as Dee Shepherd-Look, Wilson's point of view is not supported by the data. For example, Shepherd-Look notes that the traditional sex roles are reversed in many primitive cultures, and in some segments of industrial society.

Therefore, she says, sex-role stereotypes cannot be part of the "genetic code," as Wilson claims they are. So, where do they come from? According to Shepherd-Look, most sex-role stereotypes are *learned*. Originally, these roles may have developed because only women can bear and nurse children. However, once these roles were established, they were passed on to subsequent generations through learning, not through the genes. Thus, Shepherd-Look says, as society changes, so do sex-role stereotypes.

Before evaluating Wilson's position further, let's look at the social/behavioral viewpoint on sex roles.

How Sex-role Stereotypes Are Formed

Dee Shepherd-Look cites several studies suggesting that sex-role differentiation is controlled by the environment and starts at birth. For example, in 1974, Jeffrey Rubin and his associates interviewed parents within 24 hours after their infants were born. The parents were asked to rate their new child on a number of scales. Both mothers and fathers of daughters described their infants as being "softer, finer featured, weaker, smaller, prettier, more inattentive, more awkward, and more delicate" than did parents whose infant was a male. Sons were described as "firmer, larger featured, more coordinated, alert, stronger, and hardier" than were daughters. Fathers saw their daughters as

"cuddly," but not their sons. Mothers, on the other hand, perceived their sons as "cuddly," but not their daughters. Despite these parental *perceptions*, however, Rubin and his colleagues note that there were no *measurable* physical or behavioral differences between the male and female infants.

In a similar sort of study, J.A. Will, P.A. Self, and N. Datan asked a number of women to play with a six-month-old child while the investigators watched. The women were all mothers who had small children (of both sexes) of their own. Half the time, the infant was dressed in blue pants, and the mothers were told the child's name was "Adam." The other half of the time, the child was called "Beth," and was clothed in a pink dress. The mothers who played with "Adam" almost uniformly offered him a masculine toy (such as a train). The mothers who played with "Beth" typically offered the child a doll. The women also smiled at "Beth" more than at "Adam." J.A. Will and his associates note that the mothers seemed entirely unaware they were engaging in sex-role stereotyping.

Question: What benefits do you gain from having ready-made social responses to make to the males and females you meet?

Childhood Stereotyping

According to Dee Shepherd-Look, children learn by age two that there are some toys that "boys" play with, and others that "girls" play with. By that age, they *self-select* games that are stereotypically "correct" for their gender.

During childhood, boys are more likely to avoid sex-inappropriate activities and toys than are girls. Apparently the boys' choices are strongly influenced by their parents. Several investigators have found that parents were not concerned when their daughters engaged in a sex-inappropriate activities. However, both parents tended to react negatively (and punitively) when their sons made sex-inappropriate choices.

"POP, IS IT TRUE MEN CAN BE SEXUALLY ACTIVE EVEN WHEN THEY'RE OVER 21?"

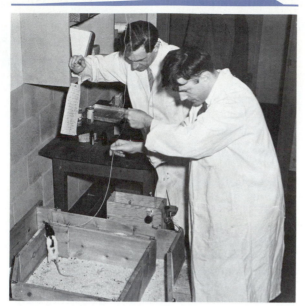

Fig. 11.4 James Olds (right) and Peter Milner discovered that stimulating certain parts of a rat's brain seems "rewarding" to the animal.

Dee Shepherd-Look believes that, by the time children reach puberty, society has "shaped" them into *perceiving their own sexuality* in a socially-approved manner.

Question: As we noted, homosexuals tend to show "gender-inappropriate" behaviors as children *despite* strong societal pressures to conform. What does this fact tell you about the relative importance of genetic and social/behavioral factors in determining sex roles?

"Choice" Versus Genes and Society

There is ample evidence that sexual motivation is influenced by your genes *and* by what society has taught you is "appropriate" to your gender. However, both the biological and the social/behavioral viewpoints are incomplete in one important respect: Neither approach pays much attention to *personal feelings and motives*. Despite Wilson's theorizing on the matter, most humans apparently do not marry, mate, and rear children *primarily* because they consciously wish to reproduce their own genes. And many people engage in a variety of sexual activities *despite* society's standards rather than *because* of them.

Most intra-psychic psychologists would argue that *pleasure* is a critical element in shaping all aspects of sexuality. From an intra-psychic point of view, you *choose* your sexual acts for many reasons, but primarily because they "feel good"—that is, because they are rewarding or satisfying in some way.

With that thought in mind, let's look at what pleasure is, and where it may come from.

The Pleasure Centers

When scientists first began sticking electrodes into the brains of rats and other animals, they found that stimulation of a few parts of the **limbic system** caused the animals to react as if they had experienced sharp, biting pain. This discovery was, at first, surprising because, as we saw earlier, there are *no pain receptors* in the brain itself.

These scientists suspected they had tapped into what are now called the "avoidance centers" of the brain. So they began to map out as many different regions of the brain as they could, trying to find out how extensive these "avoidance areas" really were. As it turned out, these centers are not very extensive at all. You can stimulate more than 99 percent of the brain electrically without getting an avoidance reaction from the animal. However, this search paid unexpected dividends when, in the early 1950's, two psychologists working in Canada discovered that electrical stimulation to certain parts of the brain can have *pleasurable* consequences.

Olds and Milner's Discovery

James Olds took his doctorate in psychology at Harvard in 1952. Then, because Olds was interested in the biological processes underlying motivation, he went to McGill University in Montreal to work with the noted psycho-biologist, Peter Milner.

Olds and Milner implanted electrodes in the "avoidance areas" in the brains of white rats, then let the animals run about on the top of a table. When the rat would move toward one particular corner of the table, Olds and Milner would turn on the current. The rat would stop, then turn around and move in the opposite direction. The animal subsequently *avoided* that particular corner of the table even if not given any more electrical stimulation.

However, one day Olds and Milner made a glorious mistake—they stuck an electrode in the wrong place in one rat's brain. When this animal started moving toward one of the corners of the table, Olds and Milner turned on the electrical current as usual. But this rat stopped, sniffed, and then moved a step or two *forward!*

Olds and Milner assumed the current wasn't strong enough to have any effect, so they turned up the juice and stimulated the animal again. And once again, the rat twitched its nose rather vigorously, and then moved several steps forward. The more Olds and Milner stimulated the rat's brain, the more eager it became to get to the corner. Finally, the animal reached the corner, sat down, and refused to move! It is to Olds and Milner's credit that, instead of thinking the rat was "sick" or "abnormal," they realized at once they had discovered a part of the rat brain where electrical stimulation was obviously very *rewarding* (see Fig. 11.4).

We now know there are dozens of **pleasure centers** in the brains of most mammals (including humans) which, when stimulated electrically or chemically, will give the animal the subjective experience of *pleasure*. Most of these "pleasure centers" are located either in the hypothalamus or in the limbic system (see Fig. 11.5).

Pleasure or Compulsion?

In animals such as the white rat, neural excitation in these "pleasure centers" causes a strange and oddly *compulsive* set of behaviors to occur. Suppose we rig up a small, rat-sized box with a lever in it (see Fig. 11.6). The lever is connected to an electrical stimulator so that every time the rat presses on the lever, the animal stimulates one of the "reward centers" in its own brain. Will the rat press the bar very often?

The answer is yes—very often indeed. Under these conditions, a rat will "self-stimulate" (by pressing the lever) as often as a hundred times a *minute*. It will continue to do so hour after hour after hour—until it collapses in exhaustion. Then the rat will sleep a while until it regains its strength. But as soon as it wakes up, it typically starts pressing the lever again. And if we offer this rat the chance to bar-press as a reward for problem-solving behavior, it will learn highly complicated mazes just to get a few whacks at the lever.

Obviously, something about the electrical stimulation of the "pleasure centers" is highly *motivating* to a rat. But is the motivation that of pleasure, or that of yielding to a "compulsion"?

Limbic system (LIM-bic). Part of the "old mammalian brain" that mediates emotional responses. See Chapter 4.

Pleasure centers. Various areas of the brain that, when stimulated electrically, seem to be rewarding to the organism or give it "mental experiences" akin to pleasurable sensory inputs. Stimulation of the pleasure centers in rats causes them to engage in compulsive behaviors. Stimulation of similar areas in the human brain gives mildly pleasurable experiences, but does not cause compulsive behaviors.

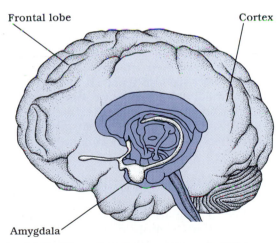

Frontal lobe | Cortex

Amygdala

Fig. 11.5 The colored areas are part of the limbic system.

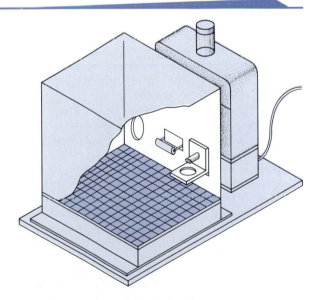

Fig. 11.6 A single-lever rat box.

In humans, sexual behavior is predominantly under the control of the *brain* rather than just hormones.

Two Types of Pleasure

Until the discovery of the "pleasure centers" by Olds and Milner, sexual behavior had always posed something of a problem to motivational theorists. Knowing nothing about the "pleasure centers" in the brain, early drive theorists assumed that *pain reduction* was the chief motivational force underlying all behavior.

But sexual excitement is almost entirely a matter of pleasurable *arousal*—the more stimulated an organism is, the more pleasure it feels. How then could an *increased* drive level be associated with pleasure rather than with pain?

We now know there are two distinctly *different* types of pleasure: (1) the generalized feeling of relief when pain ceases, and (2) the sensory thrill associated with what we might call "pleasurable inputs." For example, food not only reduces hunger, it tastes good as well. Therefore, there must be a direct connection of some kind between the taste receptors in your tongue and the "pleasure centers" in your brain. Once Olds and Milner had shown the way, psychologists began looking for just those connections.

Specific and Generalized Pleasures

Current animal research indicates that some parts of the rat brain are associated with sexual pleasure, while other parts are associated with eating or drinking pleasures. Stimulation to still other brain areas seems to give the rat a "general glow of satisfaction" that isn't tied to any specific biological drive yet known.

If we implant an electrode in those "pleasure centers" related to eating behavior, the rat will bar-press compulsively *only* if it is hungry. If we feed the rat first, it will ignore the lever for sev-eral hours until its hunger drive mounts a bit. If we implant the electrode in those parts of the brain connected with drinking behavior, the rat will bar-press only if it is thirsty.

In similar fashion, if we put an electrode in one of the "sex reward centers" of a male rat's brain, the animal will bar-press much more vigorously if it has been sexually deprived than if it has copulated recently. However, if we castrate the rat, we find that it presses the lever less and less frequently on the days following the operation. Apparently, as it uses up all the male hormone left in its body after castration, it finds the electrical stimulation less and less pleasurable. We can restore the castrated rat to its original level of sexual performance, however, by giving it an injection of testosterone. Within a short period after the injection, it begins to press the lever vigorously.

Oddly enough, once the rat begins bar-pressing, it typically prefers electrical stimulation to "natural pleasures" such as food, water, or sex. Perhaps direct brain stimulation yields stronger rewards than do "natural pleasures." Or perhaps the electrical current triggers off *both* pleasurable feelings and compulsive behaviors. The answer to this problem awaits further study.

Human Pleasures

When Olds and Milner first reported their results, many people feared governments might seize upon electrical stimulation of the brain as a new way to control people against their wills. However, these fears proved to be groundless. For the "compulsiveness" one can create in a rat with brain stimulation seems to be lacking in humans. Those women and men who have volunteered to have their "reward centers" tickled with electricity have all reported the experience as being mildly pleasant—but something they could take or leave. It may well be that this "lack of compulsiveness" is why humans are so much better at "self-control" than animals are.

Sex Is Multi-Determined

Sexuality in humans is obviously a complex experience that is multi-determined. The androgens, estrogens, and progesterone shape our bodies, bias our brains, and energize our behaviors. But *overriding* these biological motivations are the neural commands that come from the higher centers of our brains. And these neural commands are primarily learned or the product of voluntary choice.

For example, many types of sexual behaviors cause an increase in neural firing in the pleasure centers in your brain. The resulting "subjective experience of pleasure" surely motivates you to participate in sexual activities. But *what* you find pleasurable depends on your sexual orientation, your gender identity, the sex role you adopt, and your own personal values.

Society influences your choice in such matters by providing you with models of "appropriate" behaviors. However, society's standards may occasionally be in conflict both with your genetic urges and with your personal desires and pleasures. Put another way, "choosing" often involves a certain amount of *stress*. So, it is to this topic that we must next turn our attention.

Summary

1 Sexual needs have a **biological basis**, but differ from hunger and thirst in that they are necessary for the survival of the species, but not the individual.

2 John B. Watson studied the female sexual response, but lost his professorship because of his research.

3 Alfred Kinsey published the first **scientific survey** of sexual behavior in 1948. The first studies of actual **human sexual behavior** were made by Masters and Johnson.

4 You began life as a single **egg cell** that contained 23 **chromosomes**. At the moment of **fertilization**, one of your father's sperms penetrated the egg and added 23 chromosomes of its own.

5 If an **X sperm** unites with the egg, the 23rd chromosome will be **XX**, and the child will be a genetic female. If a **Y sperm** unites with the egg, the 23rd chromosome will be **XY**, and the child will be a genetic male.

6 The **sex hormones** are secreted by the **adrenal glands** that sit atop the kidneys and by the **gonads**, the **testes** in males and the **ovaries** in females.

7 The male hormones are called **androgens**, the best-known of which is **testosterone**. The female hormones are the **estrogens** and **progesterone**.

8 Testosterone promotes sexual behavior in **both sexes**. The female hormones primarily influence **childbearing** and **child rearing**.

9 Both male and female hormones are found in both sexes. It is the relative amount of these hormones during **critical developmental periods** that determines **primary** and **secondary sex characteristics**.

10 The sexual behavior of the **ring dove** is controlled by a complex interaction between hormone levels and the **mating behaviors** of the male and female dove.

11 **Intra-psychic** aspects of sexual motivation include **sexual orientation**, **sexual identity**, and **sex roles**.

12 The three main types of sexual orientation are **heterosexual**, **bisexual**, and **homosexual**. Orientation is influenced by biological, intra-psychic, and cultural factors.

13 Although heterosexuality is the dominant orientation, some 10 percent of the population is primarily homosexual in orientation. Another 10 percent is probably bisexual.

14 **Children** reared by homosexual parents show little **gender confusion** and mostly have a **heterosexual orientation**. Children with **hormonal problems** who are reared as the "wrong sex" tend to respond to **cultural pressures** concerning gender identity rather than to biological urges.

15 Children **become aware** of their sexual orientation and gender identity long before **puberty**.

16 **Sex role stereotypes** are widely shared concepts that prescribe how each sex ought to behave.

17 **Sociobiology** is a theory by Edward O. Wilson, who assumes your **major motive** in life is to increase the odds your **genes** will survive. Wilson believes **sex roles** stem from the differing strategies males and females adopt to gain **reproductive advantage**.

18 **Stereotyping** begins at birth and affects the way people **perceive** males and females—and the way they perceive themselves.

19 Sexual behavior is strongly influenced in lower animals by **pleasure centers** in the animals' brains. Electrical stimulation of these centers leads to **compulsive behaviors** in the rat, but not in the human.

(Continued from page 293.)

"Why not, Clare?" Bill Meyer asked his fiancée. "You assume that our daughter Christine would *want* to wear men's clothes. So why wouldn't our son Christopher *want* to wear dresses and pantyhose?"

Clare Wilson frowned as she considered the matter. "Well," she said finally. "I guess I see what you're getting at. I know only too well the sort of stupid male prejudices against women my daughter will face. Maybe I'd never given much thought to what sorts of social constraints my son will have to put up with."

"Right on," Bill said. "You women are convinced that men have locked you into a rigid social role of some kind. Well, men are at least as locked into a male 'role model' as women are—and maybe more. It always ticked me off that women demanded the right to wear men's clothes, and heaven help the man who got upset. Yet if a man appears on television dressed in pantyhose, you think he's a disgrace of some kind."

Clare grinned. "Yes, and so do you."

"Not if he's making as much money as Joe Namath did," Bill said, laughing. "But the point is, why do you approve of women who take on male characteristics, but get upset when a man acts in a feminine way?"

Clare paused for a moment. "It is odd, isn't it? I guess I see men as being socially superior in some strange way. When women dress like men—or act in a traditionally masculine way—they're just trying to improve their status in society. But when a man acts like a woman . . ."

"Then he's giving up status," Bill said. "And that does seem unnatural to all of us. But if men and women are *really* equal, then . . ."

". . . Then both men and women should be free to act as they wish," Clare said thoughtfully. "Yes, I can understand the logic behind that point. And maybe it's the same thing with blacks or any minority group. We can understand when they dress and behave like the dominant group in society. We even encourage them to take on the values of white, middle-class Americans, and think it's great when they do."

Bill nodded. "But saints preserve any white, middle-class person who tries to act or talk 'black.' Unless they're doing it as an obvious joke, we see 'black talk' by whites as being abnormal because it involves a voluntary loss of social status."

Clare sighed. "I guess we won't really be an unprejudiced society until we allow all people to act and feel any way their genetic makeup dictates, eh?" After a moment's hesitation, she continued. "But how can we be sure it's our genes, and not our social prejudices, that make us feel that a particular behavior is either normal or abnormal? There *must* be some way to tell the difference."

Bill glanced at the television screen. Greg Norman was still ahead in the golf tournament, but Calvin Peete was only one stroke behind going into the 17th hole. "You mean, like, men are more interested in sports, while women are more interested in library books and opera and stuff like that."

"Now, Bill," Clare said teasingly. "You know that women are just as sports-minded as men are."

"No, they're not," Bill replied, refusing to be baited by Clare's comment. "There's never been a culture in the history of the world where that was true. My psych prof was talking about that just a few days ago. Young male monkeys roughhouse three times as much as female monkeys do. Same thing with all the primates. The males are almost always bigger, stronger, and more physically active. Now, don't get me wrong. Women are *good* at lots of sports—better than men at olympic swimming, for instance. And maybe at long-distance running, too. And they're better at skills that require fine motor coordination. But, on the average, men are just more interested in physical challenges than women are."

Clare smiled. "And you think that's a genetic difference between men and women?"

Bill nodded. "Sure, just like their sexual interests are different."

"There you go again, Bill."

"Oh, come off it, Clare," Bill replied, having temporarily forgotten the golf tournament. "Women are just as interested in sex as men are. It took me a long time to realize that, but it's true. It's just that men and women are concerned about different aspects of the sexual experience."

"I should hope so."

"I should hope so too. If we weren't, we wouldn't have families and children," Bill replied.

"What do you mean?"

Bill thought a minute. "Well, somebody's got to make sure that sex occurs, so there will be children. And maybe that's the man's job. And maybe that's part of what sports and social aggression are all about. But historically speaking, at least, it's been the woman's job to see that the children were fed and taken care of properly. And you've got a biological advantage over men in that department, you must admit."

Clare straightened her shoulders. "Now, Bill . . . ," she said demurely.

"It's true, and I'm glad of it," Bill said in a playful tone of voice.

"But that still doesn't give you the right to talk about sex all the time," Clare said, trying to regain control of the conversation.

"You talk about it all the time, too, Clare. Only you call it 'commitment,' or 'our relationship,' or 'feelings.' But it amounts to the same thing."

"It does *not* amount to the same thing," Clare replied.

"Yes, it does. To a man, sex is an act that leads to child bearing. So the man thinks most about how to get the woman to 'do it.' But to a woman, sex is an act that leads to child rearing. And to make sure that the man is around to help take care of the kids, she's got to get some kind of commitment out of the guy, so that he doesn't run off after every skirt he sees. So she thinks about how to get a loving relationship going. But it's still sex she's thinking about and talking about."

"And you think that sort of psychological difference is *genetic*?"

"I don't know of any data on the subject, but it seems logical to me."

Clare considered the matter. "But what about the women's equality movement? Are we wrong to try to get men to do those things— like cooking and changing diapers—that have always been foisted off on women by the dominant males?"

Bill laughed. "Well, we can share the labor of taking care of the kids, but we can't share the labor pains, if you know what I mean."

"Ouch," said Clare, a hint of laughter in her voice.

"And I suspect that men are at least as good at taking care of kids as women are— maybe better."

"Better? What do you mean?" Clare said in surprise.

"Just last week my psych professor quoted a recent study showing that infants are more relaxed when held by their fathers than by their mothers. Maybe learning how to cradle a football in your arms teaches you how to cradle a baby, or something like that."

Clare sighed. "Okay, so you don't object to men and women sharing the burden of child rearing. That's progress, at least. But how do we get men to treat women like equals in *all* situations?"

"You can do that only if you give men something they want in return."

"Like . . . ?"

"Oh, like a lot of things. Like not demanding that we see the world from your viewpoint unless you're willing to look at things from the male point of view too. Like not demanding that a male 'commit' to a woman, and then telling him he's got a dirty mind when he wants sex in return. Maybe even admitting that you're as interested in the sexual *act* as men are."

"I'll have to think about that for awhile," Clare replied. Then she stood up, walked over to Bill, and put her arms around him. "What you're saying is that even if the equality movement succeeds, there will always be some differences in the way that men and women act and feel. Just because their genders are different."

"*Vive la différence*," Bill said.

Recommended Readings

Bell, A.P., Weinberg, M.W., & Hammersmith, S.K. (1981). *Sexual preference*. Bloomington: Indiana University Press.

Benbow, C.P. & Stanley, J.C. (1983). Sex differences in mathematical reasoning ability: More facts. *Science, 222,* 1029–1031.

Shepherd-Look, D.L. (1982). Sex differentiation and the development of sex roles. In Benjamin B. Wolman, ed., *Handbook of developmental psychology*. Englewood Cliffs, N.J.: Prentice-Hall.

Did You Know That...

- Sexual arousal and sexual climax are controlled by two different parts of the autonomic nervous system?

- William James believed that when you see a snake, you're afraid because you run away, not that you run away because you're afraid?

- Psychologists cannot agree whether emotions are subjective feelings, expressive behaviors, cognitive awareness of physical arousal—or a mix of these things?

- Women who believe they are "masters of their destinies" have shorter but more painful labor during pregnancy than do women who see themselves as "controlled by fate"?

- Some psychologists believe that "ventilating your feelings" does you little good and frequently harms the people you love?

- The "sink or swim" method of stress training is not particularly effective?

- There is "good stress" as well as "bad"?

12

Emotion, Stress, and Coping

"The Stress of Life"

Pilot David Milne pressed the button on his microphone and said, "Tower, this is Mid-Continental flight 474 heavy, turning onto downwind leg."

The radio squawked and bleeped in Dave Milne's ear for a second or two, and then the voice of the traffic controller in the tower came through loud and clear: "Mid-Continental 474 heavy, this is the tower. Descend to 3,000 feet and maintain speed 220 knots."

Dave Milne recognized the controller's voice as belonging to Bill Johnson, a good friend of his. Bill's wife, Chris, was a surgical resident at a hospital near the airport. Normally Dave would have said hello to Bill, but today was different, so Dave "went by the numbers" and kept the conversation impersonal. "Roger, Tower. Mid-Continental 474 heavy descending to 3,000, maintaining 220."

The huge airport complex was clearly visible to Dave through the cockpit windows as he banked the heavy, wide-bodied jet and headed "downwind" past the runway he would eventually be landing on. The landing pattern was U-shaped. Dave had just entered the upper left-hand corner of the U. He would pilot the plane down the left side of the U, then turn left and fly along the base of the U—the "base leg" of the pattern. Shortly thereafter, he would turn left again and enter the "final" or "upwind" leg of the pattern. Eventually, if all went well, he would land the plane on the runway—at the top of the right side of the U-shaped pattern.

The actual landing was a few minutes away, however, and Dave had a thousand things to do before he could bring his huge plane safely to ground. He glanced briefly at his copilot, who was going one-by-one through the long "checklist" of operations involved in the landing. The copilot also read the instruments and called out critical information on the plane's speed and altitude so that

Dave could keep his eyes on the runway as he brought the plane in for a landing. In fact, his copilot this trip was Mid-Continental's Senior Instructor, who was checking Dave out in the huge jet, and Dave certainly wanted to make a good impression on the man.

Dave grinned. This landing was going to be a piece of cake. He had flown for Mid-Continental Airlines for nearly 15 years, starting at the bottom and working his way up until he was captain of one of the smaller jets. Now he was switching over to the "heavies"—the huge, wide-bodied planes that most passengers preferred these days. The change-over to a much larger plane meant Dave had been required to learn many new skills, but he was confident that he had mastered them all. A piece of cake, he told himself.

The sound of Bill's voice from the control tower crackled through Dave's earphones again. "Mid-Continent 474 heavy, descend to 2,000, maintain 220 knots."

Dave acknowledged the controller's order, nodded to his copilot, and pointed the nose of the huge plane down a bit so that it would lose a thousand feet in altitude. There was no other traffic in the landing pattern, so Dave could keep his mind on flying the jet without having to keep an eye peeled for other planes that might get in his way.

Most pilots liked to say that flying a jet was a two-stage operation—you had hours of routine boredom while the plane was cruising at altitude, relieved by a few minutes of sheer terror when you took off or brought the jet in for a landing. Dave agreed, and he had had his share of hair-raising experiences during landings and take-offs. Particularly in bad weather. But the weather today was clear and the winds were light. Piece of cake, he told himself as he tried to relax a bit.

"Mid-Continent 474 heavy, turn left to 270, descend to 1,500, reduce speed to 200 knots," came Bill's voice from the tower.

Again Dave acknowledged the command. Technically speaking, he had complete responsibility for flying the craft. Thus, he could dispute or even ignore the orders the controller gave him. However, Dave almost always did precisely what the controller suggested. So, Dave banked the plane to the left until it had completed a 90 degree turn, and slowed the engines down a bit. Then he extended the flaps on the wings to give the huge ship the additional "lift" it needed when flying "low and slow."

They were on "base leg" now, flying along the bottom of the U-shaped pattern. Almost unconsciously he noted that the whining sound of the jet engines had decreased in intensity as he slowed the plane down for its landing. Piece of cake . . .

And then the terror started. Completely without warning, the copilot said in a loud voice, "Fire in number three engine!"

Instantly alert, Dave hit the emergency controls that would stop the flow of fuel and turn on the fire extinguishers in the number three engine. A fraction of a second later, he pushed forward the throttles on the other two engines to compensate for the loss of power. The wide-bodied jet had three engines— one on each wing, and one in the tail section. The plane could land safely on two engines—or even on just one, in a pinch. But all pilots were terrified by a fire anywhere in the plane. And they particularly feared a fire that started in an engine. Engines were simply too close to the plane's supply of fuel.

"Fire in number three engine extinguished!" the copilot cried.

Dave breathed a brief sigh of relief and began talking on the radio. "Tower, this is Mid-Continental 474 heavy. We've lost an engine! Request clearance for emergency landing!"

Moments later, Bill Johnson's voice came booming over the earphones. "Mid-Continental 474 heavy, you are cleared for a direct approach to the runway for an emergency landing. Fire trucks standing by. How can we help?"

Before Dave could respond, the copilot yelled at him, "Fire in number one engine!"

With one hand, Dave banked the plane and headed straight for the runway. With his other hand, he shut off the fuel and turned on the fire extinguishers in the number one engine. The stall warning alarm came on loudly, telling him that the plane was flying too slowly. Instantly Dave increased the power to the number two engine—the only one he had left—and prayed that he wouldn't run out of altitude before they reached the end of the runway.

"Fire still out of control," the copilot yelled.

Red warning lights flashed on several instruments. Dave tried to glance at each of them, to see what else had gone wrong with his ship. But he was too occupied with keeping the plane aloft and heading it toward the end of the runway to worry about them all. Safety was only a couple of miles away now—if he could get the plane there.

"Mayday, Tower, mayday. We've lost a second engine. I think we can make it, but . . ."

Suddenly the cockpit began to shake violently. The control panel lit up with so many flashing lights it looked like a Christmas tree gone wild. The stall warning screamed loudly for his attention, as did several other buzzing alarms. Dave felt an icy stab of terror in his heart as he tried desperately to take in and evaluate all the information that was assaulting his eyes and ears. And there, so close, just a couple of thousand feet away, lay the end of the runway.

"Stall speed! Stall speed!" the copilot cried.

Dave lowered the nose of the plane a couple of degrees in order to pick up speed, but the ship was flying so slowly now that it was difficult to handle. He fought with the controls, trying desperately to keep the wings level and aim the plane so it would touch ground just past the end of the runway. For a few brief seconds, despite the screaming alarms and the flashing lights, everything seemed to be under control, when . . .

"Fire in number two engine!" the copilot screamed.

Again Dave shut off the fuel and turned on the fire extinguishers. The jet's rate of descent increased rapidly, as if it had a burning desire to kiss the earth immediately. Dave pulled the nose up a little, scared green they didn't have enough momentum left to reach the runway. But suddenly, miraculously, the plane crossed over the end of the runway, flopping down like a wounded bird toward the narrow ribbon of concrete now less than fifty feet beneath them. They'd made it! Three engines gone, but they'd made it!

And then, without warning, the cockpit shuddered violently, and the world outside the cockpit windows went black. The control panel lights flicked off, the alarms stopped, and everything was still.

Dave sat there, stunned, wondering what had happened.

Then the copilot looked over at him and smiled. "Well, Dave, you just smashed up 60 million dollars worth of airplane and killed 300 passengers. How do you feel?"

Dave, still in shock, shook his head slowly. "What happened? We were headed straight in, and we had enough altitude. We should have greased right in . . ."

The copilot grinned. "Sure. But you forgot one thing."

"Forgot?" Dave said, a puzzled frown on his face.

"Yeah," the copilot said. "You handled the fires in the three engines pretty good, son. But you forgot to lower the landing gear."

Dave Milne shook his head groggily. "I guess I really bought the farm that time, didn't I?"

The copilot nodded and got up out of his seat. "You're not the first, Dave. We all do it." He patted Dave on the shoulder. "Come on, friend, I'll buy you a cup of coffee, and we'll talk it over. And then we'll try it again."

(Continued on page 335.)

Emotions

In Chapter 10, we said that the term "motivation" was derived from the Latin word meaning "to move." There is another common psychological term which also comes from the same Latin source: "emotion."

Motivated behaviors usually involve *trying to achieve a goal.* Emotional responses typically are associated with *achieving or not achieving a goal.* Thus, emotion and motivation are related, since they both are concerned with goal-oriented activities.

But emotions are more than just behaviors. If you experience great anger, your mouth goes dry, your stomach may churn, and your muscles may tense. You also *feel* this anger "inside you." You typically perceive what caused your anger, and can "categorize" the experience as being anger rather than hate or love. In addition, you probably are conscious of how being angry alters your own thoughts and actions, and how expressing your anger affects the people around you. Thus, you may choose to suppress your rage—or to express it—depending on what you think the consequences will be.

Five Elements of Emotionality

Now, how do we tie all these aspects of emotionality together to form a neatly packaged definition?

The answer is, not very easily. There is no single definition of "emotion" that all psychologists will agree upon. However, the five elements of emotionality mentioned most often by various theorists are the following:

1. Physical arousal or depression.
2. Feelings—usually those of pleasure or displeasure
3. Cognitive awareness and appraisal of the experience.
4. Emotionally expressive behaviors.
5. Environmental inputs and consequences.

Various theorists tend to emphasize one or more of these five elements. Generally speaking, though, we can divide the theories into the familiar three categories of "biological, intra-psychic, and social/behavioral."

Biological Theorists

To many biologically oriented scientists, emotion is primarily a *physical reaction* that involves rather special parts of your nervous sytem. To these scientists, your emotions have two major purposes: (1) to arouse your body for some kind of specific action (such as fighting or fleeing), or (2) to depress physical responses so your body can repair itself.

For the most part, biological theorists tend to see emotions as "instinctual survival mechanisms." For example, *pain* causes intensely unpleasant feelings that arouse you to move away from some inputs or, in the case of hunger, toward others. And *fear* is a drive that prevents you from approaching a dangerous situation before it can become painful. We will discuss the biological viewpoint more fully in a moment, when we describe the various "arousal mechanisms" in your body.

Intra-psychic Theorists

Some intra-psychic theorists emphasize the role of *subjective feelings*. Others focus on the *cognitive* aspects of emotionality.

Those psychologists interested in "feelings" often use terms such as *moods, passions,* and **affect** to describe the inner experiences associated with emotionality. Just as commonly, they will employ the terms *pleasant* and *unpleasant*. For the most part, "feeling" psychologists tend to believe emotions are unconscious and unlearned.

Those theorists interested in "cognitions" tend to focus on *conscious awareness* of subjective experiences. They often use such phrases as *cognitive appraisal of an experience* or *value judgments* in trying to explain emotionality. Most cognitive psychologists believe your *perception* of a situation creates both your physical arousal and your subjective feelings.

Social/Behavioral Theorists

Those theorists who take a behavioral viewpoint often think of emotions as *behavioral responses*. They do not speak of fear, but rather of fearful reactions to some external stimulus. They talk not of depression, but rather of massive inactivity or unresponsiveness.

However, many social psychologists hold that emotions do not exist just "in the mind" or just "in the body." Rather, these theorists say, your emotions are a product of your *interactions with your environment*. You learn to respond to situations in certain stereotyped ways. You also learn to "label" your feelings in a manner that will justify your feelings to yourself and to others. Furthermore, you *use* your emotional outbursts to achieve certain ends, and to communicate your inner experiences to others. According to these theorists, therefore, emotions are primarily determined by past and present *social inputs*.

Question: Which of the "five elements of emotionality" does each of these theoretical viewpoints seem to stress?

Emotions and Stress

There is one point almost all psychologists agree upon, however: Whatever emotions are, and wherever they come from, they can be quite *stressful* to the body and mind, which is to say that, for the most part, your feelings involve the expenditure of physical, mental, and behavioral *energy*. Learning to cope with your emotions, therefore, requires learning how to handle the stresses and strains of life.

In the first part of this chapter, we will look at your emotions from the biological, intra-psychic, and social/behavioral viewpoints. Then we will discuss various ways to cope with emotional stress. Finally, we will define emotions from a holistic point of view and show how they are related to cognitive (and other) activities.

The Biology of Emotions

Those psychologists who view emotionality as primarily a biological event tend to focus on *arousal* and *depression*. These scientists often perceive emotional reactions as being your body's way of preparing to respond to some kind of physical or psychological challenge. Perhaps you are in danger; then you must prepare yourself either to fight or to get out of the threatening situation. Or perhaps you are hungry and discover some food; then you must calm yourself down so that you can consume and digest your meal in comfort. In either case, your biological reactions are likely to be *reflexive*.

You don't have to "will" your sweat glands to secrete water or your teeth to start chattering when you are frightened or cold. Nor do you have to consciously direct your stomach to start digesting the food you've just eaten. These activities are handled for you *automatically* by the "lower centers" of your brain and nervous system.

Autonomic Nervous System

That part of your body which controls your emotional reactions is called your **autonomic nervous system**. It is connected to most of the glands and many of the muscles in your body.

Your autonomic nervous system has two major parts or divisions: (1) the **sympathetic**

"I THINK WE CAN RULE OUT STRESS."

Affect (AFF-fect). A psychological term meaning the conscious aspect of an emotion apart from any physical or behavioral reaction. Also means the visible display of an emotional experience. If you "lack affect," you don't respond emotionally—presumably because you don't experience any inner feelings.

Autonomic nervous system (aw-toh-NOM-ick). "Autonomic" means automatic or reflexive, without volition. The autonomic nervous system is a collection of neural centers that take care of most of your normal body functions (breathing, pumping of the blood, digestion, emotional reactions) that occur automatically—without your having to think about them.

Sympathetic nervous system. To have sympathy for someone is to experience common emotions or feelings with that person. The sympathetic nervous system is that half of the autonomic nervous system responsible for "turning on" your emotional reactions, or for arousing your emotions.

Parasympathetic nervous system (PAIR-ah-sim-pah-THET-tick). That half of your autonomic nervous system that is "beyond" or opposed to the sympathetic system. The parasympathetic system "turns off" or slows down most emotional activity.

nervous system and (2) the **parasympathetic nervous system**. In general, activity in your sympathetic system tends to excite or *arouse* you. Activity in your parasympathetic system tends to *depress* many of your bodily functions.

Your sympathetic and parasympathetic nervous systems work together in a *coordinated* fashion to control your bodily activities (see Fig. 12.1). When you need to be aroused, your sympathetic system speeds up and your parasympathetic system slows down. When you need to relax and "vegetate," your parasympathetic system increases its neural activities while your sympathetic system slows down. It is the *joint action* of the two systems that allows you to respond appropriately to most of the physical and psychological challenges you meet in life.

Sympathetic Nervous System

Your sympathetic nervous system consists of a group of 22 *neural centers* lying on or close to your spinal cord. From these 22 centers, axonic fibers run to all parts of your body—to the salivary glands in your mouth, to the irises in your eyes, to your heart, lungs, liver, and stomach, and to your intestines and your genitals. Your sympathetic nervous system also connects with your sweat glands, your hair cells, and with the tiny blood vessels near the surface of your skin.

Whenever you encounter an emergency—something that enrages you, makes you suddenly afraid, creates strong desire, or calls for heavy labor on your part—your sympathetic

In short, activity in your sympathetic nervous system prepares you for fighting, for fleeing, for feeding—and for sexual climax.

Question: Why do people often get red in the face when they get angry?

Parasympathetic Nervous System

Your parasympathetic nervous system connects to most (but not all) of the parts of your body that the sympathetic does. In general, parasympathetic stimulation produces physical effects that are the *opposite* of those induced by sympathetic stimulation. Activity in your parasympathetic system does the following things:

1. It closes down or constricts the pupils in your eyes.
2. It decreases the rate at which your heart beats.
3. It slows down your breathing.
4. It lowers your blood sugar level.
5. It increases salivation, stimulates the flow of digestive juices, and promotes the processes of excretion.
6. It retards sweating.
7. It controls penis erection in the male and nipple erection in the female during sexual activity.

Generally speaking, activity in your parasympathetic nervous system *conserves* or builds up your body's resources. For this reason, the parasympathetic is often referred to as the *vegetative* nervous system.

Question: Heroin causes the pupils to narrow to mere pinpoints, even when the person is sitting in relative darkness. Which part of the autonomic nervous nervous system does heroin affect most?

Homeostatic Balance

Increased neural excitement in the sympathetic system tends to *inhibit* activity in the parasympathetic, and vice versa. But the two systems are not really **antagonists** or competitors. Rather, they function together smoothly in a coordinated fashion to maintain an optimum balance between over-arousal and under-arousal.

For instance, parasympathetic stimulation is necessary for erection to occur in males and for vaginal lubrication in females. However, or-

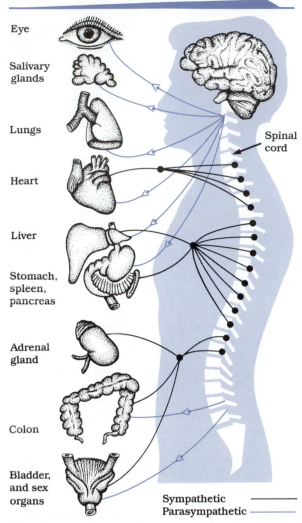

Eye

Salivary glands

Lungs

Heart

Liver

Stomach, spleen, pancreas

Adrenal gland

Colon

Bladder, and sex organs

Spinal cord

Sympathetic ──────
Parasympathetic ──────

Fig. 12.1 Schematic layout of the autonomic nervous system.

nervous system swings into action in several ways:

1. The pupils in your eyes open up to let in more light.
2. Your heart pumps more blood to your brain and muscles and to the surface of your skin.
3. You breathe harder and faster.
4. Your blood sugar level is elevated.
5. Your digestion is slowed down.
6. Your skin perspires to flush out the waste products created by the extra exertion and to keep you cool.
7. The sympathetic nervous system also controls orgasm and ejaculation during sexual excitement.

gasm and ejaculation are controlled by sympathetic excitation. Thus, sexual activity must begin with relaxation (parasympathetic stimulation) but typically goes on to arousal and climax (sympathetic stimulation). Too much sympathetic arousal or inhibition early in the sex act can lead to impotence in the male and disinterest or inhibition in the female. And too much parasympathetic stimulation will prevent orgasm in both sexes. Normal sexual activity thus requires you to maintain a *balance* between parasympathetic and sympathetic stimulation.

It is this *balanced coordination* of the two systems that, to a major extent, led biologists to theorize about *homeostasis* (see Chapter 10). And it was this same interplay between the two systems that drove early psychologists to create drive theory.

There is one major *difference* between the two systems, however: The sympathetic nervous system is connected to your adrenal glands, while the parasympathetic system is not.

The Adrenal Glands

You have two adrenal glands, one sitting atop each of your kidneys. As we mentioned in the last chapter, your adrenals produce hormones that influence sexual development and that control such bodily functions as urine production. But these glands also produce two chemicals that are referred to as the "arousal" hormones. The old names for these two hormones are **adrenalin** and **nor-adrenalin**. These days, the terms "epinephrin" and "nor-epinephrin" are more common.

When epinephrin and nor-epinephrin are released into your bloodstream by your adrenal glands, these hormones bring about all of the *physical changes* associated with strong emotions such as fear, anger, hostility, and sexual aggressiveness. That is, these two hormones act to *prepare* your body to meet an emergency by increasing your blood pressure and heart rate, speeding up your breathing, widening the pupils in your eyes, and increasing perspiration.

As you might guess from this description, the release of epinephrin and nor-epinephrin is under the control of your *sympathetic* nervous system, whose activities the hormones imitate or mimic. When you encounter an arousing situation, your sympathetic nervous system goes into action first, mobilizing your body's energy resources and also causing the secretion of the two "arousal" hormones. As you secrete epinephrin and nor-epinephrin, these hor-

Antagonists (ann-TAG-oh-nists). The Greek word *agonistes* means "competitor." An antagonist is someone who is opposed to, or competes with, a certain viewpoint or position. A protagonist is someone who is in favor of or who defends a certain position.

Adrenalin (ah-DREN-ah-lin). One of the two "arousal" hormones released by the adrenal glands. Also called epinephrine (EP-pee-NEFF-rin).

Nor-adrenalin (NORR-ah-DREN-ah-lin). The second of the two "arousal" hormones released by the adrenals. Injection of adrenalin or nor-adrenalin into the body causes a rise in blood pressure and pulse rate, an increase in the breathing rate, and a general speeding up of bodily functions. Also called nor-epinephrine (NOR-EP-pee-NEFF-rin).

mones continue the arousal process by chemically stimulating the *same neural centers* that the sympathetic nervous system has stimulated electrically.

But the hormones also increase the firing rate of the nerve cells in the sympathetic nervous system itself. This stimulation causes you to secrete more of the hormones, which increases activity in the sympathetic system, and so on until the emergency has passed or you collapse in exhaustion.

Why should you have two separate arousal systems? The answer seems to be this: Sympathetic arousal is quick—an "emergency alarm" that mobilizes your body almost instantly. But at times you need *sustained arousal*. It is more efficient for your body to maintain an aroused state by means of the adrenal hormones than by continuous activity in your sympathetic nervous system.

"Cold" Emotions

Until recently, there was little evidence that your autonomic system responds differently according to the *type* of emotion that you feel. Several studies have shown that your adrenal glands produce more epinephrin when you are afraid, but secrete more nor-epinephrin when you are angry. But both hormones are released to some degree in *all* arousal situations. Thus, we cannot tell *objectively* whether you are angry or afraid just by measuring the relative amounts of epinephrin and nor-epinephrin floating around in your bloodstream.

When human volunteers have been injected with large amounts of epinephrin or nor-epinephrin, they often report feeling as if they were "about to become emotional," but they can't say why. The arousal they experience does not seem "real" somehow, because it isn't fo-

Hans Selye

cused or directed toward any given object. Many of the volunteers described the experience as "cold rage."

Selye's General Adaptation Syndrome

More than 40 years ago, Canadian scientist Hans Selye first outlined the physical responses your body makes to stressful situations. Selye said that your reaction to stress almost always follows the same adaptive pattern. He called this pattern the **General Adaptation Syndrome**, or GAS. According to Selye, the GAS has three main stages or parts.

Stage 1: Alarm Reaction

Suppose that you suffer from a severe physical or emotional *trauma*. Your body will immediately respond with what Selye calls the *alarm reaction*, which is the *first stage* of the General Adaptation Syndrome. During this stage, your body and mind are in a state of *shock*. Your temperature and blood pressure drop, your tissues swell with fluid, and your muscles lose their tone. You don't think clearly, and as we will see in a later chapter, your ability to file things away in Long-term Memory may be disrupted.

Stage 2: Resistance

The second part of the GAS is the *stage of resistance*, or *countershock*. During this stage, your body begins to repair the damage it has suffered, and your mind begins to function more clearly. A small gland in your brain releases a complex hormone known as **ACTH**. The ACTH acts on your adrenal glands, causing them to release their own hormones. These adrenal hormones counteract the shock in several

ways, chiefly by raising your temperature and blood pressure.

However, you pay a price for resisting the shock, for your body uses up its available supply of ACTH and adrenal hormones at a rapid pace. If the stress continues, your adrenal glands will swell as they strive to produce enough hormones to neutralize the stress.

Stage 3: Exhaustion

During the first two GAS stages, your sympathetic nervous system is intensely aroused. However, if the emergency continues for too long, an overwhelming *counter-reaction* may occur in which your parasympathetic system takes over. You may fall into the third state—the *stage of exhaustion*. During this stage, you go into shock again because your body is depleted of ACTH and adrenal hormones. Further exposure to stress at this time can lead to depression, insanity, or even death.

Selye believed that many "diseases of adaptation"—high blood pressure, arthritis, and some types of ulcers—are caused by excessive stress.

Selye's GAS: An Evaluation

Hans Selye died in October, 1982. Almost everyone agrees that Selye made the concept of *stress* a respectable part of science. However, recent studies suggest that Selye's theory, while correct in many aspects, needs updating and revision.

In an interview in the August 6, 1983 issue of *Science News*, Nobel prize winner Julius Axelrod stated that recent research has led to two significant changes in Selye's theory. First, we now know that a great many hormones other than ACTH and the adrenal "arousal" chemicals are released during stress. The endorphins are one good example. Second, we now realize that the body *defends itself* against exhaustion. When you experience chronic stress, your body adjusts by using less of the stress hormones, ACTH, and the other chemicals involved in the GAS. Therefore, you are less likely to suffer from "death by stress" than Selye had imagined.

Despite these modifications in Selye's original views, Selye deserves credit for bringing stress-related problems to public attention.

The James-Lange Theory of Emotion

Selye's GAS deals with physical reactions to emotional stress, not with emotions themselves. In contrast, the theory proposed by William James in 1884 is much more complete.

But it gains this completeness by *reducing* the intra-psychic aspects of emotionality to mere "after-thoughts."

According to James, your body always takes the lead in emotional situations. Your feelings, James said, are mental responses to the changes that have *already occurred* in your nervous system, muscles, and glands.

To illustrate James's viewpoint, suppose you are walking through the woods one day and almost step on a huge rattlesnake. Chances are, you will momentarily go into shock. Then, almost immediately, your heart will start pounding, your hair will stand on end, and you will breathe more rapidly. And, if you are wise, you will slowly back away and then run for your life. Moments later—usually after you are out of danger—you will notice these physical reactions and *realize* that you are frightened.

You may think that you saw the snake, got scared, and then ran. But James said, this is not the case. Your bodily reactions precede and thus *cause* your feelings. As James put it, "We are afraid because we run; we do not run because we are afraid."

In 1885, the noted Danish scientist Karl G. Lange independently proposed much the same sort of explanation of emotional behavior. For that reason, this viewpoint is often called the *James-Lange theory of emotions.*

The Cannon-Bard Theory

The James-Lange approach led to a lot of highly emotional debate and, happily, a lot of useful research as well. For example, in 1937

"SEE, MY INTENSIVE-STRESS THERAPY REALLY WORKS. YOU ARE NO LONGER CONCERNED ABOUT YOUR MINOR ANXIETIES."

General Adaptation Syndrome (SIN-drome). A "syndrome" is a set of related symptoms that defines a particular disorder or behavior pattern. Selye's GAS is an attempt to describe the characteristic way in which the body responds to stress, particularly that caused by disease or physical trauma. As is true of most people trained in the medical sciences, Selye (SELL-ye) takes a biological view of emotionality.

ACTH. Adrenocorticotrophic (add-DREEN-oh-CORT-tih-coh-TROF-fick) hormone. For obvious reasons, almost always abbreviated as ACTH. A hormone released by cells in the pituitary (pit-TOO-ih-tarry) gland in the brain. ACTH stimulates cells in the "cortex" or head of the adrenal glands to release "arousal" hormones. "Trophic" comes from a Greek word meaning to nourish. Thus ACTH is a hormone that "nourishes" or stimulates cells in the adrenal cortex.

Walter B. Cannon pointed out three objections to the James-Lange theory: First, James-Lange assume your feelings are dependent upon activity in your sympathetic nervous system. However, people who (through accident or disease) have lost use of their sympathetic systems still feel emotions and show emotional behaviors. Second, the physical changes associated with emotion generally occur *after* the "feelings and behaviors" have started, not *before* they take place. And third, the *same* physical changes occur in very *different* emotional states—and in non-emotional states as well.

Cannon believed that emotional inputs were processed simultaneously by two different parts of the brain, the *thalamus* and the *hypothalamus* (see Chapter 10). According to Cannon, the thalamus controlled emotional *feelings*, while the hypothalamus controlled *bodily responses*. Thus, Cannon said, you would experience conscious "fear" of a snake even if your body were totally paralyzed because "fear" and "running" are mediated by different centers in your brain.

P. Bard advanced almost the same viewpoint in 1937. For that reason, this approach to the explanation of emotionality is often called the *Cannon-Bard theory.*

As it turned out, the same sorts of criticisms Cannon leveled against James and Lange were also raised against the Cannon-Bard theory. In 1960, Karl Lashley noted that people with a damaged thalamus still experience emotional feelings, and people with a damaged hypothalamus still show emotional responses. At about the same time, other scientists proved that both the *limbic system* (see Chapter 4) and the right hemisphere (see Chapter 5) were involved in mediating emotional feelings and behaviors.

Some aspects of both the James-Lange and the Cannon-Bard approaches appear in many modern theories of emotionality. Now that we've discussed the older viewpoints, let's see what a more recent theorist has to say about what emotions are—and where they come from.

Question: How do you know to run from a snake until you have *perceived* the snake and been aroused by this perception?

Evolutionary Theories of Emotion

Why do you have emotions? According to Charles Darwin, emotions help keep you alive. Over millions of years, Darwin theorized, species with "useful" emotions survived, while those with "inappropriate" emotions died out. Many biological theories of emotion are based on Darwin's evolutionary viewpoint.

Tomkins' Theory of Facial Expression
In his 1892 book *Expression of Emotion in Man and Animals*, Darwin suggested that facial expression of emotions was an animal's "innate method" of communicating its emotional state to other animals. In 1962 S.S. Tomkins modified Darwin's views by stating that your facial muscles respond *innately* to certain types of emotional situations. Tomkins notes that, worldwide, people have similar facial expressions when expressing joy, sadness, or anger. Therefore, Tomkins says, these facial responses must be coded for in the genes. But you don't use these facial reactions to communicate your "inner states" to others, as Darwin believed. Rather, Tomkins claims, you smile or frown innately as a reaction to a stimulus input. Feedback from your muscles then triggers off both the autonomic arousal and subjective "feelings" associated with the emotion. Following James-Lange, then, Tomkins says your body reacts *innately*, and your mind *interprets* these innate responses as "emotions."

Tomkins' approach to emotionality is an interesting one. And, as we will see, other scientists have incorporated some of Tomkins' views in their own intra-psychic theories. Generally speaking, however, the experimental data offer little support for Tomkins' position.

Question: If Tomkins is correct, could you experience emotions if your facial muscles were paralyzed?

Biological Theories: An Evaluation
By the 1970's, a number of theorists had made a very telling point against *all* the biological theories of emotion. The point is this: Bodily reactions do play an important role in *creating* and *sustaining* emotions. However, our feelings are so frightfully complex that we simply can't *reduce* them to mere hormonal and neural activity. To gain a more complete understanding of emotionality, we must look at intra-psychic variables as well.

Question: Some people report that they are most easily aroused sexually when they are hungry, or immediately after a frightening experience or a violent argument. Why might this often be the case?

Intra-Psychic Aspects of Emotionality

Roughly speaking, we can put intra-psychic theories into two major categories: those that emphasize "feelings," and those that focus on "cognitions." The scientists who believe inner passions are the crux of emotionality often emphasize the *unconscious*, *instinctual* aspects of feeling states. The researchers who take the cognitive view usually hold that you *appraise* a situation first, then react to it emotionally. A few theorists straddle the dividing line between these two positions.

Let's look at the "feeling" theories first.

Freud's Energy Theory
Sigmund Freud is undoubtedly the best known of the psychologists who view emotions as "inner passions." Like all other *drive theorists*, Freud related emotionality to basic needs. He also placed a strong emphasis on the importance of early experiences in determining later emotional problems.

Freud believed you were born with the capacity to feel two types of sensations—pleasure and unpleasure (or pain). These powerful sensory drives exist in the unconscious portions of your mind, Freud said. The "emotions" you are aware of as an adult—love and hate, anger and disgust—actually *differentiated* out of the primitive sensory drives through experience. That is, as you matured, you associated certain types of situations with pleasure, and other situations with unpleasure. For example, you learned to love your mother because she gave you pleasure by feeding you and caring for you. But your *love* for your mother exists in the *combination* of your conscious associations with your unconscious feelings.

Freud's view of the emotions has often been called an *energy theory*. He believed your body continually creates "psychic energy" much as a dynamo continually produces electrical power. Freud called this psychic energy **libido**. According to Freud, *libido* is the motivating force that "powers" all your thoughts, feelings, and behaviors. *Expending* libidinal energy is associated with sensory pleasure. *Repressing* libidinal energy almost always leads to unpleasant tension, anxiety, and other negative emotional states.

Whenever you suppress an unpleasant thought or emotion, Freud said, you *block the release of libidinal energy*. Psychic tension builds up in your unconscious mind in much the same way that physical pressure builds up in an overheated steam boiler. Some of the repressed energy will "leak out" in variety of ways—through unusual dreams, fantasies, "slips of the tongue," and feelings of anxiety. However, according to Freud, the best way to discharge the pent-up tension is through **catharsis**, which involves the open expression of your feelings.

Because Freudian theory is so rich and detailed, we will postpone a fuller discussion of his views until later. We should note, though, that one emotion frequently repressed is that of *anger*. From a Freudian point of view, releasing pent-up anger—particularly through *aggressive acts*—should always reduce stress through catharsis.

Type A Personalities

In 1973, Meyer Friedman and Ray Rosenman published a book entitled *Type A Behavior and Your Heart*. After years of studying heart patients, these two physicians concluded that many types of heart failure are due to "a particular complex of personality traits including excessive competitive drive, aggressiveness, impatience, and a harrying sense of time urgency." They named this behavioral syndrome "Type A Behavior." The opposite sort of behavior pattern—relaxed awareness, patience, and a lack of excessive aggression—they call "Type B Behavior."

According to Friedman and Rosenman, the hallmark of Type A Behavior is *aggressiveness*. Type A people are highly concerned with proving themselves to others. Therefore, they try to complete as many tasks as possible in the

Libido (lib-BEE-doh). The psychic energy created by your innate instincts. According to Freud, all behavior is "energized" by libido.

Catharsis (kah-THAR-sis). From the Greek word meaning "to purge, or to clean out." If you are constipated and take a laxative to "clean out" your digestive system, you have undergone a physical catharsis. Freud believed psychotherapy could act as a psychological catharsis to cleanse the mind of bottled-up libidinal energy.

shortest possible amount of time. Their pursuit of "measurable excellence" is so extreme, they leave themselves no time for leisure. They usually ignore or neglect their families. They have few close friends because most others interpret their aggressiveness as hostility or lack of trust. *Suppressing* aggressive instincts merely makes things worse, Friedman and Rosenman say, because "repression always leads to increased stress and tension."

Type A individuals also have many bad health habits. They skip meals, then "pig out" on rich, fatty foods. They often smoke too much and drink too much. They have no time for exercise, and their sleep habits are poor. All these behaviors put them "at risk" for a variety of stress-related illnesses.

Friedman and Rosenman believe that the major *physical* factors leading to heart failure are high blood sugar, high blood pressure, and high cholesterol intake. All these physical factors are, of course, made much worse by Type A Behavior. So it is the *personality pattern* that kills Type A people. Thus, therapy must be *psychological*, not *medical*. Friedman and Rosenman recommend that anyone who recognizes him- or herself as a Type A person should immediately change to a more healthy way of life or the person is likely to suffer a stress-related heart attack early in life. And, following the Freudian model, Friedman and Rosenman suggest that "cathartic discharge" of the emotions will be followed by a healthy decrease in blood pressure and other physical signs of tension.

Type A Behavior: An Evaluation

There are several problems with the Type A theory. First, Friedman and Rosenman see all people as being either Type A or Type B—there are no "in betweens" or "partials." Second, they talk at length about "aggressiveness," but never define the term. Third, they fail to consider either biological or environmental factors. Despite evidence to the contrary, they don't believe heredity plays much part in determining who will have a heart attack and who won't. Rather,

Magda Arnold Robert Plutchik Arnold Lazarus

they see Type A behaviors as being entirely determined by intra-psychic factors. Thus, they fail to see that individuals can be Type A's in some social settings, but Type B's in others.

Worst of all, Friedman and Rosenman offer little in the way of useful advice to Type A people on how to change themselves. Stern lectures and confrontation seem to be all they can offer their patients. Nor do Friedman and Rosenman offer experimental studies showing that Type A individuals can reduce their risk factors by "open expression of their emotions." Indeed, as we will see, there is good evidence that catharsis makes things worse for Type A's in many social settings.

There do seem to be individuals who fit the classic Type A behavior pattern. However, it seems likely these people are *over-reactors*. They apparently are easily aroused by almost any environmental input. Thus, their Type A activities are most likely the result of an *inherited* (or early-learned) hyper-sensitivity to stimulation. Changing the *behaviors*, of course, won't affect the underlying problem. Teaching them strategies to *cope with* their over-reactivity might help, however. We will return to this point momentarily.

Arnold's Theory of Emotions

As we mentioned, Freud viewed emotions as "feelings." Most American theorists have tended to place more emphasis on the role of cognitive activities in emotional experiences. Some have straddled the fence, however. For example, in 1960, Magda Arnold revised the James-Lange approach by putting *perception* into the picture. According to Arnold, you perceive a situation and then react to it in two ways. First, you *unconsciously* and *intuitively* "feel" that the situation is good or bad. You tend to approach

situations that make you feel good, while avoiding or fleeing from situations that make you feel bad. But according to Arnold, arousal and all other behavioral reactions *follow* your emotional evaluations rather than preceding them.

Once you have both "felt" and "responded behaviorally" to a situation, Arnold says, then you may well *appraise* the situation from a cognitive point of view. And, at that time, you may well make *conscious decisions* about the situation (and your own response to it). But according to Arnold, cognitions *follow* emotions rather than setting them off.

Question: In what ways are Freud's and Arnold's viewpoints similar? In what ways do they differ?

Cognitive Theories of Emotion

Those theorists who emphasize the "passionate" side of inner experiences (such as Freud and Arnold) tend to focus on the unconscious, intuitive aspects of emotionality. Those psychologists who prefer the cognitive approach are more impressed by the conscious, rational, explanatory side of emotional experiences. As we will see, though, these may simply be two sides to the same psychological coin.

Plutchik's Evolutionary Theory

One of the best-known cognitive theories is that proposed by Robert Plutchik, who teaches at Albert Einstein College of Medicine. Plutchik follows Darwin in believing that emotions have "evolutionary significance." And Plutchik is impressed by Tomkins' views on the role of facial expression in creating emotional experiences. However, Plutchik believes emotions are *conscious interpretations* of what happens to you when you become emotionally aroused.

In a 1980 book Plutchik edited, he states that emotion is not a subjective experience. Rather, he says, emotion is "a construct or inference based on various classes of evidence." The *classes of evidence* Plutchik refers to are your physical and behavioral responses to emotion-arousing environmental inputs. Some of these reactions are learned. However, the more important ones were built into your genes as evolutionary survival mechanisms.

When you go through an emotional upheaval, Plutchik says, you *evaluate* the experience. Then you *construct* a "cognitive appraisal" of what has happened to you. This appraisal includes your interpretation of your physical arousal, your unconscious feelings, your behavioral responses, and your conscious thoughts while the experience was occurring. It is the *sum total* of all these events that can rightfully be called an "emotion," Plutchik says.

Like many cognitive theorists (and some "feeling" theorists), Plutchik believes that emotions are **bipolar**. That is, he thinks emotions come in pairs of opposites. You are born with two innate emotional reflexes, he says: arousal/depression, and approach/avoidance. However, over time, these innate responses *evolve* into such conscious appraisals as anger/fear, acceptance/disgust, and anticipation/surprise.

Question: Most studies show that when you try to "appraise" an emotion, the intensity of your feelings decreases significantly. Does this fact support Plutchik's position or not?

Lazarus's Cognitive Theory

In an article in the February 1984 *American Psychologist*, Arnold Lazarus gives his cognitive approach to the study of emotions: "An emotion is not definable solely by behavior, subjective reports, *or* physiological changes; its identification requires all three components, since each one can be generated by conditions that do not necessarily **elicit** emotion." Thus, he says, emotions are actually composed of a *mix* of "action impulses and bodily expressions," various types of cognitive activities, inner feelings, and physical responses such as arousal or depression.

Lazarus was led to this point of view by the following facts: First, you can experience "arousal" just by exercising. So, emotion is *more* than just changes in your bodily processes.

Second, you can experience "feelings" that aren't really emotions. The "cold rage" you

Bipolar (buy-POLE-ar). "Bi" means two, thus anything that is bipolar has two poles or extremes to it. If you perceive love and hate as being opposites, then they can be put at the extremes of a bipolar scale.

Elicit (ee-LISS-it). To elicit is to pull out, to evoke, to stimulate into action.

might feel following an injection of epinephrin is one example. Another example would be sensory pleasure or pain, for Lazarus specifically states these are "sensations" and not "emotions." And, Lazarus says, you don't really *know* what you're feeling until you apply a *cognitive label* to your inner experience. Thus, the true value of the inner experience lies in the label, not the "feeling."

Third, you can learn to behave in a stereotyped manner that will make others presume you're experiencing an emotion when you're really just faking it. Actors (and other performers) do this all the time.

According to Lazarus, it is only when you *consciously participate* in an experience that has (a) physical arousal, (b) subjective feelings and evaluations, and (c) expressive behaviors, that you experience "emotion." And it is your *awareness* of the simultaneous occurrence of all three components that lets you evaluate the experience as "emotional."

Intra-psychic Theories: An Evaluation

In Magda Arnold's review of Plutchik's 1980 book, she criticizes the cognitive approach on several accounts. To begin with, she says, there is a great difference between "conscious appraisals" and "unconscious feelings." And you have only to inspect your own inner experiences to realize this is the case. Cognitive appraisals are *deliberate value judgments*, Arnold says. Emotions, however, are *intuitive* and *unconscious*. To confuse emotions with cognitions is to blur the distinction between "thoughts" and "feelings."

Furthermore, Arnold says, Plutchik's theory "suffers from inconsistencies. Plutchik says that emotions come in pairs of opposites: anger/fear, acceptance/disgust, anticipation/surprise. But the opposite of fear is courage; acceptance or affiliation is the opposite of enmity, not disgust; and anticipation is not the opposite of surprise." Arnold claims we have but to inspect our own emotions to know how wrong the cognitive approach is.

Even among theorists who agree that emotional experiences are really a mix of psychological and physical events, there is the problem of *which aspect comes first.* James and Lange said that behaviors and physical arousal precede emotional feelings and cognitive evaluations. Plutchik believes you evaluate a situation cognitively, and then you respond with arousal and expressive behaviors. Cannon and Bard held that you engage in *parallel processing.* That is, you "feel" and "behave" simultaneously. Lazarus seems to think you engage in a number of activities, then appraise what is going on cognitively. And it is your *appraisal* of the mix of activities that is the actual emotion.

How shall we resolve the issue? Since we are talking about definitions, and all definitions are in a sense *arbitrary,* there seems but one way out: You pays your money, and you takes your choice.

However, as complex as we have already painted emotional experiences as being, we have neglected one of the most important aspects of all: The effects of *environmental inputs* on the emotional process. Suppose we now look at the social/behavior approach to these problems.

Social/Behavioral Influences on Emotion

In fact, almost all theories of emotion make some mention of environmental inputs and behavioral outputs. It is the *relative emphasis* placed on biological, intra-psychic, and social/behavioral influences that allows us to put the theory in one of the three major categories.

Behavioral Theories of Emotions

Although most biological and intra-psychic theories include "expressive behaviors" in their definition of emotionality, the behaviorists don't always return the favor. The most radical view of all, perhaps, is that of B.F. Skinner. In discussing motivation, for example, Skinner said that hunger is *not* a drive, it is *not* an "internal state" of some kind, it is *not* a feeling or motive or urge-to-eat. Rather, Skinner said, "Hunger is the number of hours that the organism has been without food."

Skinner's view may seem radical, but there is an impressive logic to his position. Rather than dealing with biological mechanisms and intra-psychic feelings, he says, we should look at input/output correlations. We know perfectly well that the longer an animal has been without

food, the harder it generally will work to get food and the more it typically will eat when food is available. Given the strength of the correlation between deprivation and food consumption, do we really have to postulate internal "urges" and biochemical "itches" to explain why the animal eats as it does?

As you can guess, Skinner sees emotions as being *expressive behaviors* rather than "feelings," "cognitive appraisals," "passions," or "states of autonomic arousal." And he believes most expressive behaviors are learned. Thus, Skinner recommends that people with emotional disturbance should simply learn new ways of behaving. However, as the cognitive behavior modifiers showed more than 20 years ago, getting people to change their thoughts and feelings *in addition to their expressive behaviors* is a more effective type of therapy.

Skinner's major contribution to the study of emotions is probably this: He proved that most emotional reactions are determined by their *consequences.* The importance of "environmental consequences" to our understanding of emotions can be seen in several lines of research. Let's first look at a topic called "learned helplessness."

Learned Helplessness

Some 30 years ago, Richard L. Solomon and L.C. Wynne made several interesting discoveries while working with dogs. Solomon and Wynne used what is called a "shuttle box" to train their animals. At the start of a training trial, the experimenters put the dog in one side of the box. Then Solomon and Wynne turned off the light above the animal's head as a *warning signal.* Ten seconds later, they gave the dog mild shock through the metal grid floor of the shuttle box. The shock continued until the animal jumped over the barrier to safety on the other side.

On the first training trial, the dogs often became quite emotional. When the shock came on, they jumped about randomly, barked, and whined. Eventually they hopped over the barrier. But they did so only after receiving several seconds of shock. By the third trial, though, the dogs learned to *escape* (see Fig. 12.2). That is, they jumped over the barrier the moment the shock came on. By the 20th trial, the animals leaped the barrier the instant the light turned off. From this point on, they always *avoided* the shock.

Oddly enough, once the dogs had learned the "avoidance habit," they had great difficulty *unlearning* it. After the animals were uniformly jumping over the barrier whenever the light went out, Solomon and Wynne disconnected the shock apparatus. The dogs continued to jump for hundreds of trials each time the light went out, even though they would not have gotten shocked for "lingering behind."

Question: Solomon and Wynne eventually found ways to demonstrate to the dogs that they'd no longer be shocked if they didn't jump. What sorts of techniques do you think would work?

Unavoidable Shock

Many years later, Steven Maier, Martin Seligman, and Richard Solomon tried a variation on this classic experiment. They began by *first* putting the dogs in a chamber and giving them *unavoidable shock*. The dogs (as you might suspect) were fairly upset at first, and showed all of the emotional behaviors Solomon and Wynne's animals had displayed on their first trial. Eventually, however, the dogs settled down and

"coped" with the inescapable pain as best they could.

Then, Maier and his colleagues put the dogs in the shuttle box. Now the animals could learn to *avoid* the shock if they cared to do so. However, none of them did. Even though they could see safety on the other side of the barrier, *the animals refused to escape.* They simply sat there, apparently "depressed," and took the shock trial after trial.

Seligman tried a number of "tricks" to get these animals to jump. For instance, he put food on the other side of the barrier. The dogs ignored the food. He tried coaxing them over by calling to them. But the dogs sat passively, just accepting their "bad luck." Finally, Seligman tied ropes around their necks and pulled them over the barrier by brute force. He reports it sometimes took more than 30 "pulling sessions" before the dogs learned they could avoid the shock by voluntarily jumping the barrier.

Seligman believes the dogs had *learned to be helpless.* Since there was nothing they could do to escape the shock on the first trials, the ani-

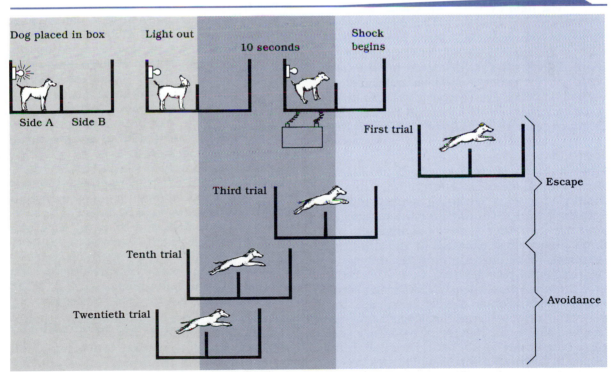

Fig. 12.2 Solomon and Wynne's avoidance experiment. First trial: Dog jumps over barrier long after shock begins. Third trial: Dog jumps immediately after shock begins. Tenth trial: Dog jumps between signal and shock. Twentieth trial: Dog jumps immediately after signal appears. (From Rachlin, *Behavior and Learning,* W. H. Freeman and Company. Copyright © 1976.)

Martin E.P. Seligman   Julian Rotter

mals simply "gave up" and "closed their minds" to thoughts of improving their lot.

Seligman's Theory of Learned Helplessness holds that when people (or other animals) experience outcomes that are independent of their responses, they come to expect their efforts to "gain control" will be futile. They become depressed and simply "suffer the stress" rather than trying to reduce it. And they frequently become prime candidates for stress-related diseases.

Learned Helplessness: An Evaluation

In an article published in *Contemporary Psychology* in January 1982, Melvin Snyder offers several criticisms of Seligman's Theory of Learned Helplessness. Seligman predicts that people who experience inescapable stress should (1) suffer decreased motivation, (2) experience emotional deficits, and (3) lose their ability to perceive significant changes in their environments. However, Snyder says, the research data don't support Seligman's position: First, humans often respond to inescapable stress with an *increased* effort rather than with *decreased* activity. Second, insoluble problems frequently lead to an *increase* in emotionality and anxiety rather than to *depression*. And third, individuals exposed to uncontrollable outcomes often *overestimate* the number of environmental changes that take place rather than *underestimate* them (as Seligman's theory would predict). Melvin Snyder concludes, however, that "despite [these] challenges to the theory, its place in the history of psychology is secure, even if only for its heuristic value. It has helped to focus attention on a vital set of issues concerning reactions to uncontrollable outcomes."

Since the notion of *personal control* is crucial to Seligman's position, perhaps we should look more closely at research on this topic.

Locus of Personal Control

One of your major motives is the need to predict and control your inputs. Evidence to support this belief comes from a variety of sources, including research on what is called the **locus of personal control**.

Almost 20 years ago, Julian Rotter noticed that some people believe they are **autonomous**. That is, they seem convinced they are masters of their own fates and take responsibility for what happens to them. They see their own *locus of personal control* as being *inside* themselves. And they believe that whatever rewarding inputs they get from their environments are due to their own actions. Julian Rotter calls these people *internalizers*.

On the other hand, many people believe they are helpless pawns of fate, controlled by *outside forces* over which they have little if any influence. These individuals feel their *locus of personal control* is external rather than internal, and that all rewards and punishments they receive are due to chance rather than to their own actions. Rotter calls these people *externalizers*.

According to Rotter, *externalizers* usually believe God or "fate" controls whatever happens to them. When faced with an external threat of some kind, externalizers either block off the stressful inputs, ignore them, or become depressed. *Internalizers*, on the other hand, don't believe in fate or "luck." They feel "getting ahead in the world" is primarily a matter of *what you do*, not what accidents befall you. When faced with a threat, internalizers tend to face the matter directly, or to remove themselves to temporary safety.

In fact, as many theorists have noted, both internalizers and externalizers have found a way to gain some *apparent* control over their inputs. Internalizers do so by noting the consequences of their acts, and changing their outputs accordingly. Externalizers gain "the illusion of control" by such acts as reading horoscopes, using magic, or appealing to such supernatural concepts as "ghosts" and "gremlins" to explain what happens to them.

Stress and Perceived Control

The concept of *personal control* is important for practical as well as theoretical reasons. For example, in a 1982 study, British scientists Jacqueline Scott-Palmer and Suzanne Skevington asked pregnant women to report their pain during childbirth. They also gave the women a questionnaire designed by Julian Rotter to determine where the women's locus of personal control was. Scott-Palmer and Skevington report that women who scored as externalizers had longer, less painful labors. Women who scored as internalizers had significantly shorter labors, but reported more intense pain. The British researchers believe the internalizers exerted "control" to get labor over with quickly, despite the pain. However, an equally valid conclusion might be that both groups of women had similar pain, but the externalizers simply repressed or denied it.

In a 1980 book on control, David S. Krantz and Richard Schulz suggest that middle-aged and elderly heart patients recover much better in an environment that encourages them to maintain personal control. Hospital environments in which the patient is treated as a child—or loses any measure of personal responsibility—seem to reduce the rate at which the patient recovers.

These reports are all quite interesting. However, there is one problem you must be aware of: As we will see in Chapter 21, there are no "pure" personality types. Concepts such as *locus of control* are useful, but we must not make the mistake of thinking everyone in the world must be either a "pure" externalizer or a "pure" internalizer. Indeed, many of us are "internalizers" in some situations and "externalizers" in others.

Locus of Organizational Control

Psychologists Patricia and Gerald Gurin have found that many individuals have an *internal* locus of control as far as their personal lives are concerned, but have an *external* locus of control on the job.

These people are quite effective in handling their own personal stresses—they know how to cope in many day-to-day activities, and how to face the strains of living with their relatives and close friends. But many of these individuals work for large organizations and lack the social or managerial skills to achieve their goals on the job. Thus—while at work—they see themselves as puppets pushed around by forces they don't really understand. Locus of *personal* control therefore includes a somewhat different set of attitudes and behaviors than does locus of *organizational* control.

Question: What kind of therapy could you give externalizers to convince them that—under certain conditions, at least—they could "control their destinies?"

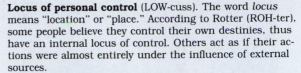

Locus of personal control (LOW-cuss). The word *locus* means "location" or "place." According to Rotter (ROH-ter), some people believe they control their own destinies, thus have an internal locus of control. Others act as if their actions were almost entirely under the influence of external sources.

Autonomous (aw-TON-oh-muss). From the Greek word meaning "independent," or "self-directed." If you make your own decisions, you are autonomous. If you obey other people's orders, you are not.

Reductionistic (re-duck-shun-ISS-tick). Biological theories try to "reduce" all aspects of human experience to neural excitation or chemical activity. A reductionistic theory, therefore, is one that attempts to explain highly complicated events in terms of very basic or simple processes.

Locus of Control: An Evaluation

Both "learned helplessness" and "locus of control" are attempts to explain why people react to stressful inputs as they do. However, these approaches place more emphasis on cognitive processes and behavioral outputs than on social inputs. Many psychologists hold that emotions are always the product of person-environment *interactions*. We can demonstrate the power of this viewpoint by discussing recent research on one of the most passionate of the emotions, *anger*.

Question: Is it better to express anger when you feel it, or to bottle it up inside you? What data can you give to support your answer?

Anger: A Social Process

"An emotion without social rules of containment and expression is like an egg without a shell: a gooey mess." This statement by psychologist Carol Tavris, is an excellent summary of her theory of *anger as a social process*.

Tavris explains her views in depth in her 1982 book *Anger: The Misunderstood Emotion*. "The social perspective on anger, I believe, explains the persistence and variety of this emotion far better than the **reductionistic** analyses of its biology or its inner psychological workings," Tavris said in a recent interview. "Anger is not a disease, with a single cause; it is a process, a transaction, a way of communicating. With the possible exception of anger caused by organic abnormalities, most angry episodes are social events: They assume meaning only in terms of the social contract between participants."

According to Tavris, our modern notions about anger "have been fed by the Anger Indus-

Carol Tavris

Expressing anger may make people feel better, but often causes more interpersonal problems than it solves.

try, psychotherapy, which too often is based on the belief that inside every tranquil soul a furious one is screaming to get out." This notion was made popular by Sigmund Freud, Tavris says. Freud referred to anger "as if it were a fixed amount of energy that bounces through the system: If you pinch it in here, it is bound to pop out there—in bad dreams, neurosis, hysterical paralysis, hostile jokes, or stomachaches." As a consequence, Tavris says, "therapists are continually 'uprooting' anger or 'unearthing' it, as if it were a turnip."

Because of Freud's popularity, Tavris claims, both psychiatry and the general public have come to believe that *suppressing anger* is medically dangerous. Thus, patients are often encouraged to "discharge their feelings," to relieve repressed energy, stress, and psychic tensions. You're told to "get it off your chest," or "blow off steam," or even to "let it all hang out." All these statements suggest there is some value in hitting, throwing, or even breaking things when you're frustrated.

The Consequences of Anger
But what do the *data* suggest? Just the opposite, Tavris believes. Expressing your anger can make you "feel good" temporarily. But what are the *long term* consequences, both for you and for the people you're angry at? "I notice that the people who are most prone to give vent to

their rage get angrier, not less angry," Tavris says. Why? In part because people give in to you when you're angry, in part because "ventilating" is self-rewarding. What about the objects of your anger, though? "I observe a lot of hurt feelings among the recipients of rage," Tavris says.

Expressing anger rather than learning to control it can have a devastating effect on social relationships, Tavris believes. For example, consider the stages of a typical "ventilating" marital argument: "Precipitating event, angry outburst, shouted recriminations, screaming or crying, the furious peak (sometimes accompanied by physical assault), exhaustion, sullen apology, or just sullenness." This cycle of rage is repeated again the next day, the next week, the next month, Tavris says, because "ventilating" *doesn't solve the personal problems that precipitated the rage.* And most of these problems come from an inability to observe the real *consequences* of our actions.

Controlling Anger
Tavris is not opposed to expressing anger. But she believes you should "ventilate" only when doing so will: (1) achieve rational goals, and (2) have positive consequences for all concerned.

How do you learn to master your emotions? Primarily by gaining *cognitive control* of what goes on inside you. First, you must learn how to relax, so that insults and bad experiences don't trigger an unconscious "arousal" in your sympathetic nervous system. Counting to 10 before retaliating against someone who angers you is an old but fairly effective first step. Another way is relaxation training, in which you learn voluntary control over your muscles.

Second, you should start measuring the actual consequences of your actions. Do you really "feel better" and "behave better" when you let it all hang out? How do other people respond? Are you helping matters, or making them worse? Only when you discover the *real* effects of your emotional outbursts are you likely to be motivated to change them, Tavris says.

Third, you must learn rational ways to solve life's problems—including those difficulties that occur in your relationships with others. In most instances, you will be able to find more effective techniques for communicating your desires and feelings to others than by merely "ventilating your emotions."

Social/Behavioral Theories: An Evaluation

Behaviors, thoughts, and feelings don't occur in a vacuum. Everything you think, feel, and do occurs within some social context. Therefore, we cannot describe emotions without taking environmental inputs and consequences into consideration.

All of which leads us back to the questions we raised at the beginning of the chapter: What are emotions? Are they physical arousals, subjective feelings, cognitive appraisals, social responses, or a mix of all these factors? We will try to answer this question in a systematic fashion momentarily. But we have one more topic to consider first. We noted earlier that almost all theorists agree that emotional experiences usually are fairly stressful. So, suppose we talk about stress management and then give a holistic definition of emotionality.

Coping With Stress

During your lifetime you have met many challenges, experienced many stressful situations, and worked your way through many emotional experiences. That is to say, you have *learned to adjust* to the problems that you face in life. Psychologists often speak of "learning to adjust" as *coping* with the world.

Your problems typically come to you as *inputs*, which you must *process* in some way and then *react* to. Thus, some methods of coping involve avoiding or even denying certain inputs.

Other coping strategies require you to change the way you "process" or think about problem-related inputs. Still other methods of coping involve altering your outputs—that is, changing the ways in which you respond or behave when the problem occurs.

But whether you attack the problem by working on your inputs, your internal processes, or your outputs, you will typically choose one of two major ways of adjusting—*defensive coping* or *direct coping*.

Defensive coping typically involves protecting yourself by getting away from the threatening inputs. Direct coping involves meeting the challenge head-on.

Defensive Coping

Most forms of defensive coping involve either mental or physical *escape* from the traumatic situation. You either flee from the problem and in the future avoid going near the stress-inducing situation—or you block out the threatening inputs and deny that the inputs are stressful.

Many of the *defense mechanisms* described by Sigmund Freud are types of defensive coping. The most common of these are *repression*, *denial*, *hysteria*, *displacement*, and *regression*. These defensive ways of coping involve shutting off the outside world, suppressing emotions, misperceiving situations, or reverting to childish behavior patterns. We will discuss Freudian theory more fully in Chapter 19. However, we should note that all the defense mechanisms are elaborate ways to escape the stresses of reality.

Unfortunately, running away from your difficulties usually offers only temporary relief from stress. In the long run, it may be better to confront your problems and find some way of solving them.

Question: Freud did not consider depression to be a defense mechanism. However, in what ways might depression be a defensive type of coping?

Direct Coping

Most forms of *direct coping* involve at least three steps:

1. An *objective analysis* of what your problem is, how it came into being, and how you are presently responding.
2. A clear statement of how things might be better—that is, a precise description of what your *ultimate goal* or adjustment would be.

The woman reporter under pressure to meet a deadline is probably experiencing "bad stress," while the collegiate crew could be experiencing "good stress."

Direct coping also requires that you set clear-cut goals, and then move toward these goals a step at a time. However, many people believe the best way to cope is to jump right into the middle of things. The experimental data, however, suggest otherwise.

Question: What kind of training does the military use to "make men out of boys?" How do sex role stereotypes affect the military's views on this subject? (Hint: Did you see the movie "An Officer and a Gentleman"?)

3. A *psychological road map*, or list of new approaches to life that you might use to help you reach your goal.

Direct coping is not always easy, and it is often very time consuming, for it requires that you "stand back" and look at things as unemotionally as you can. When you are caught up in the middle of a frightening or stressful situation, you may have neither the motivation nor the self-control to think things through rationally. Thus, you may need to seek professional help to learn how to deal with stressful inputs in a direct manner (see Chapter 22).

"Sink or Swim" Learning

In 1980, Lt. Col. William Datel reported an interesting set of experiments performed during the 1970's on Army recruits at Fort Ord, near Monterey in California. Each year, thousands of recruits are given their basic training at Fort Ord. Most of the recruits find the situation fairly stressful. They have little privacy, they are punished (often severely) for any mistakes, they are not allowed to talk back or argue with orders, and they are restricted to camp for the first several weeks of their stay at the camp.

Many recruits survive this stressful ordeal rather well, but a large number fall by the wayside. Some try to escape the situation by "going AWOL"—that is, by being absent without leave.

Others become ill or depressed. A few commit suicide.

When Colonel Datel was asked if he could find better methods of providing basic training, he first analyzed the situation psychologically. The philosophy in most army camps is that recruits must be "tempered in the fire of experience." Therefore, many trainers try to create the maximum amount of stress they can. One popular way of doing so is throwing recruits into dangerous situations to see who sinks and who swims.

Direct methods of coping—like all other habits—are usually learned best when you are rewarded for progress rather than being punished for failure. Knowing this, Colonel Datel set up an experimental unit at Fort Ord that trained a random selection of recruits using *positive reinforcement* rather than *punishment*. These men earned "points" for everything they did well, but were not severely penalized for their mistakes. The recruits in this experimental unit could trade in the points for various rewards—including the privilege of going into town the first night they were at the camp.

Colonel Datel followed his experimental recruits both while they were at Fort Ord and throughout their next several years in the Army. He compared their progress with that of a "control group"—namely, an equal number of recruits who went through the regular stress-oriented basic training at Fort Ord.

Datel's first discovery was that few of the men in the experimental program went "AWOL." This result alone saved the Army many thousands of dollars. Datel also found that his experimental subjects got better marks on such skills as rifle marksmanship and map reading than did recruits in the "control group." Furthermore, when the experimental subjects went into combat in Vietnam, they performed better under enemy fire than did the "control group" recruits. And more of the experimental group reenlisted at their end of their term of duty than did members of the "control group."

Despite Datel's data, the Army abandoned much of the experimental program a few years after Datel had set it up. Most military commanders apparently still believe that "sink or swim" techniques are the best way to help recruits learn to cope with stress.

Eustress

In an interview published a few years before his death, Hans Selye talked at length about **eustress**, or "good" stress. According to Selye,

Eustress (YOU-stress). From the Greek word *eu*, meaning "good." Euphoria is "good feelings." Eulogy means "to speak good" of someone, eugenics means "good genes," and the eucalyptus tree gets its name from "good shade." Eustress is the amount of stress you need in order to operate at an optimum level of performance.

we shouldn't try to avoid all stress. Rather, we should recognize what our typical response to stress is—and then try to adjust our lifestyles to take advantage of that response.

Selye believed that some of us are "turtles"—that is, we prefer peace, quiet, and a tranquil environment. Others of us are "racehorses," who thrive on a vigorous, fast-paced way of life. The optimum amount of stress we may require to function best is what Selye called *eustress*.

The problem with Selye's approach is this—he assumes you are born a "turtle" or a "racehorse." Thus, from Selye's point of view, there is little you can do about changing your response to stress other than trying to compensate for the genes that nature gave you. Few psychologists agree with Selye on this issue.

Society depends on eustress, for cultures are kept going by motivated people who are willing to learn how to cope with each other—and with their own individual needs and personalities. Thus, emotionality is necessary for life. The problem comes in discovering ways to make your emotions helpful to you rather than harmful. Needless to say, the more you know about your feelings, the better off you will be. And that means not only discovering what your emotions *are*, but learning effective ways of *handling them* as well.

Now that we have explored several theoretical approaches to emotionality, perhaps it's time to put them all together in a systematic manner.

Emotion: A Holistic Approach

In Chapter 5, we noted that you have two kinds of inputs, internal processes, and outputs: those associated with *information*, and those associated with *energy* and *matter*. In truth, though, it's difficult to imagine any stimulus that doesn't have *both* informational and energetic aspects. As we pointed out in Chapter 10, food is an energy input. But food also stimulates your pleasure centers, and it has symbolic values and "psychological meaningfulness" far beyond its ability to reduce hunger. In much the same fashion, getting an A on an examination, or learning something new about yourself in a psychology course, surely gives you "aroused pleasure" as well as cognitive information about yourself.

It seems likely that any input will be handled by two separate neural systems. The first, which includes the "straight-line sensory system" mentioned in Chapter 9, takes information directly through to the cortex. This is the *perceptual/cognitive* system, which includes several lower centers as well as the cortex. The second is the *motivational/emotive* system, which includes the limbic system (Chapter 4), the reticular system (Chapter 9), and the autonomic nervous system.

Both the perceptual/cognitive system and the motivational/emotive system probably "process" all inputs *simultaneously*, in parallel fashion. But the two systems surely feed back and forth to each other in a highly complex fashion. Under rather special circumstances, each system can operate independently. For example, you can feel aroused without knowing why, and you can "think" in abstract symbols (such as

equations) that may have little or no arousal value. Most of the time, though, your experiences are influenced by what is going on in both systems.

Why two systems? Perhaps the question should be, why not? You need your motivational/emotional system to stay alive. But having a well-developed perceptual/cognitive system surely adds to your ability to survive. For being able to reason gives you the power to *adapt* to changes in an ever-changing world in ways lower animals can't. And no small part of being able to adapt comes from learning "self-control," a term we often use to mean gaining voluntary control over your emotional outbursts, and acquiring the strength of will to resist motivational temptations. The perceptual/cognitive system thus can *guide* your emotions, while your motivational/emotive system can *energize* your thoughts and behaviors.

We now must turn our attention to adaptation, which is to say, to learning. As you will see, the motivational/emotive system apparently "learns" in quite a different fashion than does the perceptual/cognitive system.

Summary

1 Emotion has to do with **agitated movement**, most typically that associated with achieving or failing to achieve **goals**.

2 Biological theorists view emotions primarily in terms of **physical reactions**, such as arousal and depression. Intrapsychic theorists see emotions either as **subjective feelings** or as **cognitive appraisals** of complex experiences.

3 Behavioral theorists think of emotions entirely in terms of learned **expressive reactions**. Social theorists often view emotions as **social experiences** or **social contracts**.

4 Physical **arousal** and **depression** are controlled in large part by the **autonomic nervous system**.

5 The autonomic nervous system has two parts, the **sympathetic** and **parasympathetic nervous systems**.

6 Your sympathetic nervous system **arouses** you to handle such activities as fighting, fleeing, feeding—and sexual climax.

7 Your parasympathetic nervous system acts to **depress** those bodily functions that are aroused by sympathetic system

activity. The parasympathetic is sometimes called the **vegetative nervous system**.

8 The sympathetic and parasympathetic systems generally work together in a **coordinated manner** to achieve a **homeostatic** balance.

9 Physical arousal causes your sympathetic system to release **epinephrin** and **nor-epinephrin**.

10 The sympathetic system arouses the body almost immediately. Epinephrin and nor-epinephrin produce **sustained arousal**.

11 The **James-Lange theory of emotions** states that you are "afraid because you run, not that you run because you are afraid."

12 According to the **Cannon-Bard theory of emotions**, your **thalamus** controls "feelings," while your **hypothalamus** controls bodily responses.

13 In his **General Adaptation Syndrome** theory, Hans Selye says that your body goes through three rather distinct stages when stressed:

a The **alarm reaction**, in which your body's defenses are mobilized by activity in your **limbic system**, sympathetic system, and through secretion of epinephrin and nor-epinephrin.

b   The **stage of resistance**, during which your adrenal glands secrete **ACTH**.

c   The **stage of exhaustion**, during which your body may use up all of its ACTH and fall into **shock**.

14 Tomkins theorizes that **facial expressions** take the lead in emotions, and thus precede **subjective feelings** and **physical arousal**.

15 Freud believed the two innate emotions, **pleasure** and **unpleasure**, were correlated with discharging or suppressing **libidinal energy**. Releasing repressed libidinal energy leads to **catharsis**

16 Individuals "at risk" for heart disease often display such **Type A behaviors** as aggression, impatience, and excessive competition. **Cathartic expression** of emotions supposedly reduces **stress** in Type A individuals.

17 Magda Arnold believes emotions are **subjective feelings** that are **unconscious** and **intuitive** perceptions of the goodness or badness of a situation.

18 Plutchik believes emotions **evolved** from two innate **bipolar reflexes**, arousal/depression and approach/avoidance.

19 According to Lazarus, you have an emotion when you **consciously participate** in an experience that includes **physical arousal**, **subjective feelings**, **cognitive evaluations**, and **expressive behaviors**.

20 Skinner says that emotions are **learned behaviors** controlled by **environmental consequences**.

21 Seligman's **theory of learned help**-lessness holds that when you cannot control what happens to you, you suffer **motivational, emotional**, and **cognitive deficits**.

22 Julian Rotter believes that people respond to psychological pressures in different ways, depending in part on their own personal **locus of control**. **Internalizers** believe they are **autonomous**, while **externalizers** believe their reinforcers are controlled by fate.

23 Tavris claims emotions are **social contracts** controlled by personal and environmental **consequences**.

24 There are two main ways of adjusting to stress—**defensive coping** and **direct coping**.

25 Defensive coping strategies include such **Freudian defense mechanisms** as **repression**, **denial**, **hysteria**, **displacement**, and **regression**. Another method of coping with stress defensively is **depression**.

26 Direct coping methods involve **problem analysis**, **goal setting**, and moving toward the goal in **small steps**.

27 **Authoritarian** organizations foster an external locus of control by training their members to handle stress in a **sink or swim** fashion.

28 Selye calls the amount of stress you need to function properly **eustress**, or good stress.

29 From a **holistic** point of view, inputs undergo **parallel processing** by two neural systems, the **motivational/emotive** and the **perceptual/cognitive** systems. Emotions **energize** thoughts and behaviors, while cognitions **guide** them.

(Continued from page 315.)

"I can't believe I forgot to lower the landing gear," Dave Milne said to the Senior Instructor, who had been his copilot just moments before. "I've landed a jet a thousand times or more, and I've never once forgot the landing gear."

The Senior Instructor grinned. "Yeah, Dave, but you never had three engines catch on fire while you were trying to land, either."

"And I thought it was just a 'piece of cake,'" Dave said, mentally kicking himself for his stupidity. "Thank God it was just a simulator we were flying, instead of being the real thing."

"That's what simulators are for," the Senior Instructor said, and then opened the back door of the simulated cockpit and began climbing down the flight of metal steps that led to the ground of the hangar.

Dave followed the man slowly. At the bottom, he paused and gazed back at the machine. From the outside, it looked for all the world like a large wooden box supported on flexible legs. Inside, it was a perfect mock-up of the cockpit of the wide-bodied jet Dave was learning to fly—right down to the last button and knob.

As Dave had told his wife Susan earlier, the machine was controlled by a very large and expensive computer that *simulated* all of the sights and sounds of a real airplane. When you looked out of the cockpit windows, you saw exactly what a pilot would see trying to land or take off. When you banked the plane's controls to the left or the right, the visual world outside the windows tilted just as it would in real flight. When you pushed on the throttles to feed more fuel to the engines, the computer roared louder and louder. And the flexible legs supporting the cockpit allowed it to shake, shudder, and roll in a surprisingly realistic fashion.

But then, the simulators ought to be realistic, Dave told himself. They cost several million dollars each!

Dave and the Senior Instructor walked slowly toward the coffee shop, each man wrapped up in his own thoughts. Finally, to break the silence, Dave asked, "When did Mid-Continental start training pilots in simulators instead of in real planes?"

"Oh, the first really good simulators came on the market about 15 years ago," the older man replied. "Of course, the push to use them didn't come until the new wide-bodied jets appeared on the market. The new planes were so expensive that nobody could afford to lose one of them in a training acci-

dent. And fuel's so expensive now that we save all of it we can. So we use simulators instead of real planes, because simulators don't crash, and they don't use any fuel at all. I reckon they've saved hundreds of millions of bucks, not to mention countless numbers of lives."

They entered the little cafe, sat down in a booth, and ordered coffee.

"I can see they'd save money, perhaps," Dave said as he stirred his coffee. He started to lift the cup to his lips, but found he had difficulty in controlling it. "Good as they are, though, simulators aren't the real thing. You just aren't under the same stresses and strains that you are in a real plane."

The Senior Instructor laughed. "If you didn't feel any stress flying that thing, then why are your hands trembling?"

"Okay," Dave said. "So I'm still a little upset at doing poorly. But how do I know I wouldn't have performed better if my life had really depended on my remembering to put down the landing gear? Are you really as strongly motivated to learn when you know it doesn't matter if you make a mistake?"

"Good question," the Instructor said. "But the answer's just as good. Since we've been using the simulators, we've never had a fatal training accident. Before then, we cracked up several planes with trainees at the controls. And because the simulators let us test you in hundreds of situations you might encounter only once in your flying life, our pilots are much better trained than they used to be. Our flight safety statistics prove that

beyond a shadow of a doubt."

Dave nodded. "Sure. But every time I 'fly' the computer, I keep thinking to myself that there's something I'm *not* learning, namely, how to handle real-life stress. When you get through with me, I know I'll be able to land that simulator with all three engines gone. But how will I react if the same thing happens when I'm trying to land a real plane? How can you be certain that I won't go to pieces because I've never been tested in the fire of reality?"

The Instructor grunted. "Hope to hell you never are, Dave. And I know what you're talking about, because I was opposed to using simulators when we first bought them. I learned to fly in the military, and you know how those guys feel—you train a man to tolerate stress by pushing him over the breaking point again and again and again. Used to think that way myself, but then two things changed my mind."

"Two things?" Dave asked.

"Yep," the Senior Instructor said. "The first happened back in the 60's. A good friend of mine—a pilot for another airline—was taking a test ride in a DC-8 at an airport down south. He was just turning onto final approach when the man who was checking him out suddenly killed two engines to see how my friend could handle the stress associated with an unexpected emergency. Well, they weren't using simulators in those days, and my friend had never faced that particular problem before. I guess he panicked or something."

Dave shook his head sadly. "Bought the farm, eh?"

"Bought the motel, is what he did," the older man replied. "There was this fancy motor inn close to the airport, and the DC-8 plowed right into it and exploded. The motel was full of high school kids at a convention of some kind. Got pretty messy, I gather."

Dave Milne tried to picture the crash for a moment, but then blocked it out of consciousness. He let the Instructor sip his coffee for a few moments more before asking the man, "What was the other thing that convinced you simulators are a good thing?"

"Oh, yeah," the Instructor replied, pulling himself back to the present. "One of the first guys I trained in a simulator was this scrawny little runt of a guy, nervous as a balloon salesman at a convention of porcupines. He had done all right as a pilot in smaller planes, I guess, but he was downright scared that he wouldn't be able to handle a huge jet. If it had been up to me, I would have washed him out the first day. I just knew he'd come unglued if he ever faced a real emergency. But he'd been with the company a long time. So, I stuck him in the simulator and used the step-by-step method of training him how to handle stress. Started with tiny problems, and then built up to the big ones."

"How'd it go?" Dave asked.

The Instructor grunted. "Worked like a charm. The more he learned, the more sure of himself he became. By the time we finished his training, he could handle anything we threw at him. But that wasn't the thing that really convinced me, Dave. You see, this guy's *personality* changed right before my eyes. At first, he was as surprised at how well he was doing as I was. But the more he learned, the more sure of himself he became. Finally one day, after he had just licked the toughest emergency we could dream up on the simulator, he turned to me and laughed. 'I can do it!' he shouted. 'I never believed I could handle a big jet, but I bloody well can do it!'"

"And he could, huh?" Dave said.

The older man nodded, then grinned. "Yep, he learned real good. Too good in fact."

Dave looked puzzled. "Too good? You mean he cracked up a plane?"

"No," said the Instructor, "But he was so sharp and so sure of himself that another airline hired him away from us. He's now a senior pilot with United."

"Yeah," said Dave. "But maybe he was an exception. Teaching people how to handle stress step-by-step *sounds* like a good idea, but there are a lot of losers out there. Isn't that one good thing about the old 'sink or swim' method—it lets you weed out the losers?"

The Instructor grinned. "Maybe there aren't any losers, Dave. Maybe there are just people who don't get trained properly. Maybe they're losers because nobody ever taught them how to be anything else."

Dave frowned. "Yeah, okay, but how are you going to learn anything if you don't make mistakes? That's what training is all about, isn't it—learning from your mistakes?"

"Dave, we want you to learn how to *overcome* your mistakes, not die from them. So we don't let you pilot a real plane until *we* know—and *you* know—that you can do it well, really well."

Dave laughed. "If you remember to put the landing gear down," he said. "That really was a dumb mistake."

The Senior Instructor was silent for a moment. Then he sighed. "Yes, it *was* a dumb mistake, Dave. But the mistake was mine, not yours."

"Your mistake?" Dave said in surprise.

"Yep. You were only supposed to have two engines go out on you in the simulator today. But you handled the emergency procedures so well that I cut off the third engine on you too. Pushed you too far, too fast. If I'd done it the way the book says, you'd have learned how to handle the two-engine-out problem with no sweat. And then you could have gone on to three engines without ever making a real mistake. And without risking any loss of confidence on your part, either."

Dave grinned. "I don't think you have to worry about my losing any confidence."

The Senior Instructor nodded slowly. "Maybe not in your case, that's true. But with the next trainee, who knows? Anyhow, I'm still learning, just like you. And I hope you'll forgive my mistakes if I forgive yours."

"That's a deal!" Dave said happily.

"Okay, man, let's get back to work. We're going to keep at it until we both get it right."

Dave gave the Senior Instructor the "thumbs up" sign. "A piece of cake," he said with a smile.

Recommended Readings

Arnold, M. (1981) Reinventing the wheel. *Contemporary psychology, 26,* (7), 535–536.

Baum, A. & Singer, J.E. (eds.). (1980). *Advances in environmental psychology, Vol. 2: Applications of personal control.* Hillsdale, N.J.: Erlbaum.

Garber, J. & Seligman, M.E.P. (eds.). (1980). *Human helplessness: Theory and applications.* New York: Academic Press.

Glass, D.C. (1977). *Behavior patterns, stress, and coronary disease.* Hillsdale, N.J.: Erlbaum.

Plutchik, R. & Kellerman, H. (Eds.). (1980). *Emotion: Theory, research, and experience. Theories of emotion, Vol. 1.* New York: Academic Press.

Selye, H. (1978). *The stress of life* (rev. ed.). New York: McGraw-Hill.

PART IV

Learning and Memory

Did You Know That...

- Although a Russian named Ivan Pavlov is usually given credit, an American named E.B. Twitmyer was apparently the first to experiment with what we now call the "conditioned response"?

- Pavlov was able to train dogs willingly to withstand considerable pain to get food?

- Animals put in conflict-inducing situations often display behaviors that might lead us to assume the animals were "mentally ill"?

- The ancient Chinese presumed that accused criminals were guilty if they had trouble swallowing rice?

- The so-called "lie-detector" actually detects emotionality, not lies?

- A person with an abnormal fear (called a "phobia") can sometimes be helped by the same sort of conditioning techniques Pavlov used with his dogs?

- You can overcome "fear of exams" if you follow a technique called "desensitization"?

- Learning how to relax "on cue" is often a first step in learning how to overcome your fears?

13

Conditioning and Desensitization

"The Leningrad Connection"

"First of all, I'm only here because my wife wanted me to come," Kevin Lynn said to psychologist Dr. Nancy Wagner. "I have this little problem, I guess. Not really a problem exactly, just my own way of doing things. It doesn't hurt anybody but me, so what's the difference? Do you see what I mean?"

A spark of veiled amusement lit up Dr. Wagner's dark blue eyes. "No, Mr. Lynn, I don't see. But I'm sure I will if you tell me more about it."

Kevin Lynn ran a nervous hand through his thick black hair. "Well, it's a sort of very personal problem. Nothing really abnormal, or anything like that. But it cuts close to the skin, and I'm not exactly eager to talk about it. And when you stop to think about it, it's as much my wife's problem as my own."

The man had a bright, glib way of talking, but Dr. Wagner sensed he wanted to do something about his problem, whatever it was. So she nodded encouragingly and said, "Marital problems almost always involve both husband and wife. So why don't you tell me more about what's troubling the two of you?"

Kevin Lynn began to sweat a little. "Gee, you know, some things are very personal. Now, don't take this wrong, because I don't want to hurt your feelings. But . . . I mean, isn't there a *male* doctor I could talk to? I mean, there are some things . . ."

Dr. Wagner smiled reassuringly. "Mr. Lynn, I can't blame you for being reluctant to talk about sexual matters. But don't you think that women are often more understanding of a man's sexual problems than other men are? So just relax for a moment, lean back in your chair and get comfortable. And then see if you don't want to tell me what's troubling you."

Lynn stared at the woman

for a moment or two, then followed her suggestion. He sighed deeply as he let himself go limp. Then he began to talk.

"I don't satisfy her, Dr. Wagner. At least, I can't usually make it, well, *worthwhile* for her without a little something extra to turn me on." His voice dropped to a halting whisper. "I guess if I told you how screwed up I really am, you'd be pretty shocked."

Nancy Wagner smiled. "It depends on what it takes 'to turn you on.' The last man I worked with was impotent unless he took his teddy bear to bed along with his wife."

"You're kidding!"

"No, not at all."

Kevin Lynn giggled. "Well, maybe I'm not so bad off as I thought. And it's not that I *have* to have them, it's just that it's usually better that way . . ."

"Have what?"

The man sighed again. "The whips. I like the touch of a whip when it's bedtime. Gives me the power to get up and go, stirs my blood a bit. So when we got married, I bought my wife a couple of small whips—tiny ones, really—and asked her to use them on me. At first, she didn't want to. But when she gave in and tried them for a while, it was good, really good."

Kevin Lynn paused, remembering old times. "But now, she's read some stupid book, and she says I need help because I'm a masochist." He spat it out like a dirty word, MASS-oh-kist. "I guess that's pretty weird, isn't it? A guy who needs pain to get sexually excited?"

"It's a great deal more common than you probably realize. Pick up any of the underground newspapers and see how many 'personal' ads talk about whips and leather clothes and 'the need to be disciplined.'" Dr. Wagner smiled gently at the man. "And we may be able to give you more help than you suspect."

Lynn's voice quickened. "Gee, do you really think so? I mean, this book my wife read, it says I feel guilt and anxiety because I unconsciously think sex is dirty. So I've got to be punished first, to pay in advance for my sinful pleasures. Otherwise, I can't relax and do what comes naturally." He paused. "Is that what you think is wrong with me?"

The woman cleared her throat. "Mr. Lynn, there are many different views on what causes masochism. Some therapists believe that the real problem is *sadism*—or the desire to hurt other people. According to this view, some sadists can't tolerate the thought of hurting others. So, they hold their own hostile impulses in check by making other people hurt them instead."

Kevin Lynn shook his head firmly. "I don't like to hurt anybody. I just like to be hurt, you know?"

"I know," Dr. Wagner said. "Well, to continue, some psychologists believe that masochism is related to castration anxiety, that the man invites his wife to hurt him slightly as a way of warding off her attempts to castrate him."

"My wife doesn't think that way! Besides, I was into whips before I met her."

"Good point. Anyhow, still other psychologists think the problem is basically one of being *trained* to like or accept pain when you are very young."

Lynn frowned in confusion, not knowing quite what to think. "What do you believe, Doctor?"

The woman smiled. "There's a lot to be said for all those views, and just because one might be right doesn't mean that the others are wrong. Some types of therapy focus on understanding your past. Other therapies are oriented toward helping you change your future."

"Which would be best for me?"

Dr. Wagner frowned. "Ideally, we'd want to try both types of treatment at the same time. Masochism is sometimes a symptom of unconscious anxiety that needs to be uncovered if you're to learn to cope with your problem. In recent years, however, psychologists have found that many types of masochism are the result of improper learning when the person was young. In these cases, we 'condition' you to learn more appropriate ways of responding."

"How does this conditioning stuff of yours work? Do you have to whip me, or something?" Lynn's voice was eager and a bit mischievous.

The woman smiled. "No, we assume that sometime early in your life, you were rewarded for hurting yourself or being hurt by someone else. Perhaps one time you were terrified of something that involved sexuality or your own sex organs, and you got hurt, and somehow your anxiety was greatly reduced. Then pain would become associated in your mind with fear reduction. For example, did your parents have frequent fights?"

Lynn's face reddened in embarrassment. "Oh, I wouldn't say they were *frequent . . .*"

Dr. Wagner nodded. "I'm not trying to insult your parents, Mr. Lynn. But when a child's parents fight, the child may become terrified. If parents stop fighting in order to give love or affection to the child, then the child might unconsciously be conditioned to seek pain in order to reduce fear and anxiety."

"I don't seem to recall anything like that," Lynn said, still slightly embarrassed.

"This sort of conditioning could happen when you're so young that you don't remember it as an adult," Dr. Wagner said.

The man shrugged his shoulders, more at ease now. "Well, if you say so. But how do we start? Do I lie on a couch, or something? Or maybe a bed of nails?"

Dr. Wagner laughed warmly. "No, we'll talk about the origins of your masochism later on. But first, you will have to decide what you most urgently need help with right now."

Lynn thought for a moment, then said softly, "I guess my relationship with my wife comes first."

"All right, perhaps we can retrain you to enjoy sexual pleasure with your wife without having to suffer pain first."

An impish look crept over the man's face. "Couldn't we just train my wife to be a sadist? I mean, wouldn't that be just as quick?"

The woman laughed again. "I doubt she'd agree. Anyway, do you want your problem to control you, or do you want to control your problem?"

"Yeah, I guess you're right. What do we do first?"

"First, we teach you how to relax, and how to listen to your body. You see, pain has probably become a conditioned signal for sexual arousal in your case. If you skip the whips, you probably become nervous about whether or not you'll be able to perform sexually, am I correct?"

Lynn began to sweat a little. "Yeah, you got it right."

"Well," said Dr. Wagner, "Anxiety is controlled by your sympathetic nervous system. That's the part of your body that handles excitement. Unfortunately, erection is controlled by your parasympathetic nervous system, that part of your body which is involved in relaxation."

"So you're saying that I can't feel sexy unless I'm relaxed?"

Dr. Wagner nodded. "At the beginning of things, yes. And the more anxious you become about not being able to perform, the more your sympathetic nervous system turns on and the more difficult it is for your parasympathetic system to do its job."

The man nodded. "Yeah, that makes sense, in a strange kind of way."

"So we teach you how to handle your anxiety by learning how to relax. Then we'll make a list of all the situations that make you tense, beginning with things that aren't really all that disturbing and working up to things that make you break out in a cold sweat even just thinking about them."

"We'll make a little list, eh?"

The woman agreed.

"That's right. And then we'll start talking about the items on that list, starting with the simplest and working up to the most disturbing. If we can teach you to talk about these things while you're really relaxed, they won't make you very anxious any more. And if you're not anxious . . ."

". . . then I can make love to my wife without needing the whips, you mean."

Dr. Wagner smiled. "That's right."

Kevin Lynn pondered the matter for a long time. "Well, I guess it might work. How do we begin?"

"It's simple. First, stretch out your legs and make them as rigid and as tense as you can. Go ahead, do it now. Do you feel the tension?"

"Sure. It almost hurts."

"Good. Now, relax your legs completely. Relax your feet and your ankles and your thigh muscles. There. Now tense them up again. That's right, tense, tense, tense. Feel the tension? Okay, now relax again, just go completely limp. Now, can you tell the difference between tension and relaxation?"

"I sure can. There's a world of difference."

"Good," said the woman. "Next, we'll do the same thing with your arms, and then with your head and neck muscles. We want to get you to the point where you can discriminate tension from relaxation. Then you can command your body to relax any time you want to, and the muscles in your body will respond automatically."

Lynn grinned. "If I could do that . . ."

"Then your immediate problem would be solved, and you could go on to find out how the masochism got started."

"That sounds like a pain-fully slow process."

Dr. Wagner laughed lightly.

"I thought you liked pain, Mr. Lynn."

Kevin Lynn favored her with a broad smile. "Okay,

Dr. Wagner. You've got a deal."

(Continued on page 358.)

The Innate Reflex

In the early 1900's, a young man named E.B. Twitmyer began work on his doctoral dissertation in psychology at the University of Pennsylvania. Twitmyer was interested in *innate reflexes*—those automatic behavior patterns that are wired into your brain circuits by your genetic blueprint. And most particularly, he was interested in the **patellar reflex**, or knee-jerk.

You can evoke the patellar reflex in either of your legs rather simply (see Fig. 13.1). When you are sitting down, cross one leg on top of the other, leaving your uppermost leg hanging freely. Now, reach down with the edge of your hand and strike this leg smartly just below your kneecap. If you hit just the right place, you will strike your patellar tendon, which runs close to the surface of your skin at this point on your leg. Whenever you tap on this tendon, the lower half of your leg will swing forward involuntarily.

Why should your leg move reflexively when you stimulate your patellar tendon? The early biologists couldn't agree on an answer. Some

thought that when you hit the tendon, it pulled *directly* on the muscles and your leg twitched. Other scientists believed the sensory receptors in the tendon sent a message back to your spinal cord—and up to your brain—and the motor output center in your cortex responded by ordering the muscles in your leg to jump.

Thanks to research by Twitmyer and other scientists, we now know that the patellar reflex is mediated by nerve centers in the spinal cord. However, you can gain *voluntary control* over the reflex if properly trained. Thus, motor commands from the cortex can influence *expression* of the reflex.

E.B. Twitmyer

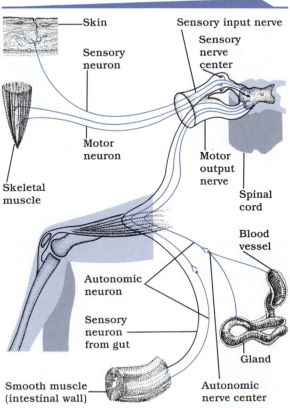

Fig. 13.1 The patellar reflex, or knee-jerk.

Twitmyer's Experiment

Twitmyer believed that the patellar reflex might be influenced by the *motivational state* a subject was in when the reflex was set off. So he asked fellow graduate students to be his subjects. Then he rigged up a small hammer that would strike the subject's patellar tendon when he let the hammer fall. Twitmyer didn't bother telling his subjects when he was about to stimulate their reflexes—he merely dropped the hammer and measured how far their legs jerked. But his subjects complained the hammer blow often caught them by surprise. Couldn't he ring a bell as a warning? Twitmyer

Patellar reflex (pat-TELL-are). The patella is the knee bone. If you strike your leg just below this bone, the lower part of your leg will jerk. This "knee-jerk," or patellar reflex, is an automatic response over which you have little volitional control.

Conditioned reflex (con-DISH-shunned). A learned response pattern in which a stimulus is bonded or connected to a response. The "conditions" for acquiring the reflex usually involve pairing a "neutral" stimulus (such as a bell) with a stimulus that innately sets off a reflexive response (such as striking the patellar tendon). Also called a "conditional reflex."

agreed, and began sounding a signal to announce the hammer drop.

One day when Twitmyer was working with a subject whose knee had been hit hundreds of times, he accidentally sounded the warning signal without dropping the hammer. As promptly as clockwork, the subject's knee jerked *despite the fact that his tendon hadn't been stimulated.* Although Twitmyer didn't realize it, he had just discovered the **conditioned reflex**, a response pattern upon which a dozen different psychological theories would later be built.

However, Twitmyer did appreciate the fact that he was on to something important, and he dropped his original research plans in order to investigate his discovery. He established some of the conditions under which this type of reflex occurred, and reported his findings at the 1904 meeting of the American Psychological Association.

Alas, the psychologists to whom Twitmyer spoke paid little attention to what he had to say. Discouraged by the frosty reception his ideas received, he dropped his laboratory research and became a clinical psychologist instead. And so credit for the discovery of the *conditioned reflex* passed by default to the famous Soviet physiologist, Ivan Pavlov.

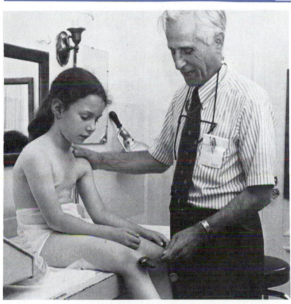
Tapping the patellar tendon with a hammer elicits the "knee-jerk reflex."

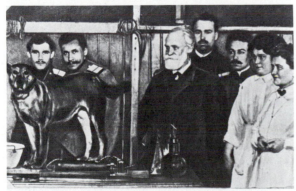
Ivan Pavlov (white beard) with his students and a dog in a training apparatus.

Pavlov's Conditioning Studies

Ivan Pavlov, who lived from 1849 to 1936, is perhaps Russia's most famous scientist. After taking his medical degree in 1883, Pavlov traveled in Europe, studying with various other scientists. In 1890, he founded the Institute of Experimental Medicine in Leningrad, which he directed the rest of his life.

Pavlov's early interests were in the biological processes of *digestion*, and he chose dogs for his experimental animals. He trained the dogs to lie quietly on operating tables or in leather harnesses while he studied what went on inside their stomachs before and after the dogs had eaten a meal. His experiments proved for the first time that the nervous system coordinates *all* digestive responses. Because of the pioneering nature of his work, Pavlov was awarded the Nobel Prize in 1904—the first Russian to be so honored.

Psychic Secretions

Digestion actually begins in the mouth, where *saliva* starts breaking up food particles chemically. So Pavlov began his work by studying the salivary glands. Pavlov soon found a way to measure the amount of saliva the glands produced. While the dog was in a harness, Pavlov would give food to the dog, then count the number of drops of saliva the glands secreted.

Dogs do not have to be trained to salivate when given food—they do so reflexively, or automatically. Salivation is therefore an innate *response* or reflex that is elicited by the *stimulus* of food in the mouth.

Pavlov wanted to determine the neural pathways that connected the stimulus receptors in the dog's mouth with its salivary glands. But his research was often interrupted by *peculiar responses* the animals would make. After an animal had gotten accustomed to being fed in the harness, its salivary glands would often "juice up" *before* it got the food. In fact, an experienced dog would usually start salivating if one of Pavlov's assistants merely rattled the food dishes in the sink or walked toward the dog carrying a plate.

Pavlov called these "unusual" reactions *psychic secretions*, which presumably were in response to some kind of *psychic stimulation*. These odd reactions infuriated him because they "got in the way" of his regular research. He did his best to ignore them because he wasn't interested in anything "psychological." However, the psychic secretions refused to go away. And so, in 1901, Pavlov began to study them systematically, hoping to get rid of these "annoyances." He told his friends this work surely wouldn't take more than a year or two to complete. In fact, Pavlov spent the last 34 years of his life determining the properties of these "psychic secretions."

Unconditional Stimulus-Response Connections

If you blow food powder into a dog's mouth, the animal will salivate reflexively. This response is determined by the dog's genetic blueprint. Pavlov called the food an **unconditional** or **unconditioned stimulus** (UCS), because the food's ability to evoke salivation is not *conditional* upon the dog's having learned the response.

The salivation *reaction* is also innately determined. Therefore, Pavlov named it the **unconditional** or **unconditioned response** (UCR), since it too is not *conditional* upon learning.

We might diagram this innate input-output connection as follows:

(innate stimulus-response
connection)

UCS ————————————————→ UCR
(food)   (salivation)

Conditional Stimulus-Response Connections

One of the first things Pavlov discovered in his research was this: If he sounded a musical tone just before he blew food into the animal's mouth, the dog eventually salivated almost as much to the *music alone* as it did to the tone *plus* the food powder. Apparently the animal learned to "associate" the *sound* of the tone with the *stimulus* of the food. And thus each time the tone sounded, the dog *anticipated* it would be fed. So it salivated to the tone just as it did to the food.

This sort of *conditioning* occurs in people as well as in dogs. The smell of bacon frying in the morning is enough to set your mouth to watering, but only because you have learned to associate the *smell* of the meat with how it *tastes*. In similar fashion, the clang of a dinner bell is often enough to set your stomach rumbling because your stomach muscles have been *conditioned* to expect food shortly after the bell sounds.

Technically speaking, this kind of learning involves an *association between stimulus inputs*. In the case of Pavlov's dog, the association is between a **neutral stimulus** (the tone) and an unconditioned stimulus (the food). We might diagram this associative learning as follows:

(learned stimulus-stimulus
connection)

Neutral S ————————————————→ UCS
(tone)   (food)

But the food powder "unconditionally" elicits the salivation *response* in the dog. So every time we pair the tone with the food, the dog salivates. Rather rapidly, then, the "neutral" tone takes on much the same ability to elicit salivation that the food has.

Pavlov called the tone a **conditional** or **conditioned stimulus** (CS), because its power to call forth the salivation response is *conditional* upon its being paired with the food powder. We can diagram the situation as follows:

(learned   (innate
stimulus-stimulus   stimulus-response
connection)   connection)

CS ——————→ UCS ——————→ UCR
(tone)   (food)   (salivation)

Once the dog has learned the connection between the tone and the food, you can present just the tone alone—without giving the dog food—and the dog will salivate. In similar fashion, once you have learned to associate the aroma of bacon with its taste, the mere *smell* of the meat will set off your salivary glands, even if you don't eat any of the bacon.

Question: Is the odor of bacon more likely to cause you to salivate when you're hungry or when you've just finished a large meal?

The "Conditioned Response"

But what can we call the salivary response when it is triggered off by the tone alone?

"HE SALIVATES."

Unconditional (unconditioned) stimulus. Abbreviated UCS. You are born with certain innate responses, such as the patellar reflex. These reflexes are set off (elicited) by innately determined (unconditioned or unlearned) stimuli. The blow to your patellar tendon is an unconditioned stimulus that elicits the unconditioned response we call the knee-jerk. The term "unconditional" is used to describe these stimuli, because their ability to elicit the response is not *conditional* on learning.

Unconditional (unconditioned) response. Abbreviated UCR. Any innately determined response pattern or reflex that is set off by a UCS. The knee-jerk is a UCR.

Neutral stimulus. Any input that does *not* set off a particular *unconditioned* reflex. A stimulus whose power to elicit a particular response is gained through learning. Since dogs don't normally salivate whenever a musical tone sounds, the tone is a "neutral stimulus" as far as the salivation response is concerned.

Conditional (conditioned) stimulus. Abbreviated CS. The CS is the "neutral" stimulus which, through frequent pairings with an unconditioned stimulus, acquires the ability to elicit an unconditioned response.

Conditional (conditioned) response. Abbreviated CR. Any reaction set off by a CS. A bright light (UCS) flashed in your eye causes your pupil to contract (UCS). If someone frequently rings a bell (CS) just before turning on the bright light (UCS), the sound of the bell (CS) would soon gain the power to make your pupil contract. Once this conditioning has taken place, the UCR (contraction) becomes a CR that can be elicited by the CS. Since pupil contraction can now be set off *either* by the CS or the UCS, the contractive response is *both* a CR and a UCR. In many cases, however, the CR looks slightly different from the UCR. In Pavlov's studies, for example, the CR usually consisted of fewer drops of saliva than did the UCR.

Surely it is no longer an *un*conditioned response because there is no innate connection between a "neutral" musical tone and salivation. Pavlov named this *learned* reaction to the neutral stimulus a **conditional** or **conditioned response** (CR).

Conditioning is the term Pavlov used to describe the process by which the previously neutral stimulus (CS) gains the power to elicit the conditioned response (CR).

Once the conditioning process has taken place, we can diagram the situation as follows:

(learned stimulus-response
connection)

CS   CR
(tone) ——————————————→ (partial
                                salivation)

The type of training developed by Pavlov is called by many names: Classical conditioning, reflex conditioning, Pavlovian conditioning, *respondent conditioning*, and stimulus-response (S-R) learning.

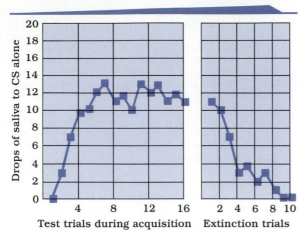

Fig. 13.2 The charts show first the acquisition of conditioned salivation in a trained dog, and then extinction.

Question: At the start of training, the animal may ignore the CS. After the CS-CR bond is established, however, the animal often gives a fairly strong *orienting response* to the CS. Why do you think this change occurs? (Hint: See Chapter 9.)

Conditioning: A Definition

Generally speaking, when psychologists use the term *conditioning*, they refer to some situation in which a *previously neutral stimulus* gains the power to elicit a *response* in a reflexive or mechanical fashion. So when we say that you have been "conditioned" to do something, we mean that you have learned to respond rather automatically to a particular stimulus.

Perhaps the most important point about conditioning is this: Because the learning is reflexive, you need not be *aware* that it has taken place.

Question: Can you figure out how you were *conditioned* to believe that, in our society, men shouldn't wear pantyhose?

Factors Affecting Conditioning

During the many years that Pavlov studied the conditioning process, he discovered several factors that affect this type of learning:

1. The more frequently the CS and the UCS are paired, the stronger the CR becomes (see Fig. 13.2). For example, up to a theoretical limit, the more often a tone is associated with food powder, the more drops of saliva

the tone will elicit. And the more frequently the CS and UCS are paired, the better the animal will remember the learning later on.

2. Conditioning is fastest when the CS is presented *immediately* before the UCS. For example, the optimum time interval for conditioned salivation in the dog is about half a second. If the tone is presented too long *before* the food—or is presented *after* the food—usually little or no learning occurs. However, the optimum time interval does vary from animal to animal, from species to species, and from situation to situation.

3. Conditioned responses are *unlearned* just as easily as they are learned. Suppose you train a dog to salivate. That is, you establish a CS-CR connection in the animal between a tone and salivation. Now you present the dog with the tone *without* giving it the food. You will find that the animal salivates less and less on each trial. Finally, the response will be **extinguished** completely (see Fig. 13.2).

4. An "extinguished response" is not completely *forgotten*. Suppose you condition a dog, then extinguish the response. Then you pair the CS with the UCS for a second round of training trials. The dog now will acquire the conditioned response much more quickly than it did the first time. Apparently the original conditioning has left a "trace" of some kind that makes relearning easier.

5. In similar fashion, suppose you *extinguish* a dog's conditioned salivation response and then let the animal sit in its cage for two weeks. Now you bring it back to the lab, hook it up in its harness, and again sound the tone. What will happen? As you might guess, the dog will have *forgotten the extinction* and it will again salivate. Psychologists call this *spontaneous recovery* of a previously extinguished response.

6. The mere passage of time can act as a conditioning stimulus. When Pavlov fed his animals regularly each half-hour, they began to salivate a minute or so before the next feeding was due, even though there were no *external stimuli* such as dish rattles to give them cues that it was almost time to eat.

Question: Pavlov believed the mere *pairing* of the CS and the UCS was sufficient for conditioning to occur—whether or not the subject wished to learn or found the experience rewarding. Look back over the past couple of pages. How many times have the terms "CS" and "conditioned stimulus" been paired? Are the two terms now associated in your mind? Were you conscious that you were learning? And the next time you watch television, look closely at the commercials. Do the advertisers seem to be using Pavlovian techniques to get you to like or remember their products?

Pavlov's Masochistic Dog

Pavlov believed "conditioning" could account for most types of human behavior. One way to prove his point, he reasoned, would be to produce in *animals* various abnormal behaviors some people thought could occur only in *humans.*

For instance, Pavlov wondered why a few individuals—called **masochists**—seemed to enjoy or seek out pain. Many psychologists believed *masochism* was the result of some "flaw" in the individual's personality. Pavlov suspected this "love of painful inputs" might be learned. To settle the matter—at least, in his own mind—Pavlov trained a dog to withstand extremely painful stimuli by using a "step-by-step" conditioning technique.

First, Pavlov marked off an area of skin on the dog's front leg. Then he stimulated this area with a weakly painful CS—and *immediately* gave the dog some food. The dog salivated to the food, but didn't flinch at the pain. Apparently the strong unconditioned salivation response *inhibited* the normal pain reflex.

Then, day after day, Pavlov slowly increased the intensity of the painful CS, each time pairing it with food. At no time did the animal respond as if it were being hurt. Indeed, the dog seemed more than willing to be put in the training harness and given the pain—since the pain *became a conditioned signal* that the dog would soon receive food.

Once the dog was fully trained, it would passively withstand incredible amounts of painful stimulation delivered to its front leg. However, if Pavlov applied the painful CS to any other part of the dog's body, the animal would instantly set up a great howl and attempt to escape from its training harness.

Pavlov concluded that when he touched the CS to the dog's front leg, the animal did not in fact *feel* any pain. Why not? Because the salivation response was so strong it *suppressed* all other responses *to the same stimulus*, Pavlov said. Apparently in dogs, as well as in humans, "You can't do more than one thing at a time." And whatever response is strongest tends to repress most other reactions that could be made to the same stimulus.

Extinguished (ex-TING-guished). To "extinguish" a response is to reduce the frequency (or intensity) of a learned response either by withdrawing the reward that was used during training, or by presenting the CS many times without the UCS. In fact, it is the "bond" or "connection" between the CS and the CR that is extinguished.

Masochists (MASS-oh-kists). Masochism (MASS-oh-kiss-em) is a sexual deviation in which pleasure is derived from pain. The pain may be psychological or physical, and may be self-inflicted or inflicted by others. The term comes from the name of the Austrian novelist Leopold V. Sacher-Masoch, whose stories frequently featured scenes in which sexual pleasure was associated with painful stimulus inputs.

Discrimination training. Teaching an animal to discriminate—that is, to react differently to fairly similar stimuli. If you can tell the difference between two things, you know how to discriminate between them.

Generalization (jen-er-al-eye-ZAY-shun). *Stimulus* generalization is the tendency to make the same response to two similar stimuli. If a monkey has been trained to lift its right paw when you turn on an orange light, it may also lift its paw when you turn on a yellow or a red light. *Response* generalization is the tendency to make a slightly different reaction to the same stimulus. If you hold down the monkey's right paw when you turn on the orange light, the response may generalize to the left paw instead.

The parallel between Pavlov's masochistic dogs and those humans who seek out pain or humiliation in order to gain pleasure (often sexual) is rather remarkable. But important as these experiments might have been to the discovery of a "cure" for masochism in humans, this research was regarded with considerable distaste by most other scientists, because it involved the deliberate use of painful stimuli.

Discrimination and Generalization

Perhaps the most interesting "mental health" experiment Pavlov conducted had to do with **discrimination training.** Pavlov began by showing a dog a drawing of a circle, then giving it food immediately. Very soon the dog became conditioned to salivate whenever it saw a circle.

Pavlov then tested the animal by showing it drawings of figures such as an ellipse, a pentagon, a square, a rectangle, a triangle, and a star. He found that the salivary response *generalized* to stimulus inputs other than the original CS (the circle). As you might suspect, this **generalization** followed a specific pattern—the more similar the other figure was to a circle, the more the animal salivated.

Pavlov then trained the dog to *discriminate* between the two stimuli by always giving food to the dog when the circle appeared, but never giv-

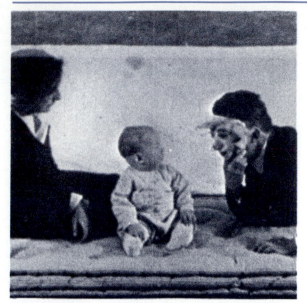

After conditioning Little Albert to fear white rats, Watson tested to see if the fear generalized to similar "furry" objects. Courtesy of Ben Harris.

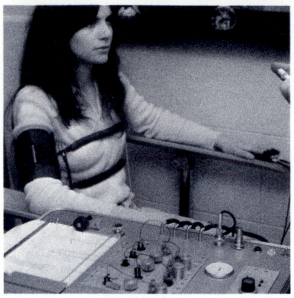

A polygraph (or so-called lie detector) records physical responses such as GSR, pulse rate, and breathing, while a subject is asked various questions.

ing it a reward when he showed it the ellipse. Soon the dog learned to salivate *only* when the circle was shown.

After Pavlov had established that the dog could discriminate between a circle and an ellipse, he tried to fool the animal. On subsequent trials, he presented the dog with ellipses that were closer and closer to being completely round. Eventually the animal's "cognitive system" was strained to the breaking point, for the animal could not perceive the difference between the positive CS (the circle) and the negative CS (the ellipse).

Overcome by stress, the animal broke down, snapped at Pavlov and his assistants, barked loudly, urinated and defecated, and tried very hard to get out of the restraining harness. If a human being had displayed the same behavior patterns, we probably would say the person was **neurotic** or "unable to cope."

How different Pavlov's two "mental health" experiments were! In the first case, an animal learned to give a *normal* response to a very abnormal stimulus input. In the second study—even though the dog received no painful stimulation at all—the animal gave an *abnormal* response to a very "normal" set of stimuli.

These two studies convinced Pavlov that "mental illness" was learned and was mostly a matter of mixed-up brain signals. (Pavlov took a purely biological view toward the causes of mental illness. As we will see in later chapters, there are intra-psychic and environmental influences that are at least as important.)

Question: Pavlov believed his dog became "masochistic" because it had learned that a food reward would always follow the pain. How could you use "extinction procedures" and "retraining" to bring about normal behavior patterns in the animal?

Conditioned Emotional Responses

Once Pavlov had shown the way, a number of other psychologists began experimenting with conditioning procedures, using humans rather than animals. John B. Watson, the father of behaviorism, was perhaps the first to study how emotional responses (such as fear) get established in children.

Watson and Little Albert

In one of Watson's most famous experiments, he and his second wife (Rosalie Rayner) conditioned a boy named Albert to fear a white rat. At the beginning of the study, Albert was unafraid of the animal and played with it freely. While Albert was doing so one day, Watson deliberately frightened the child by sounding a terrifying noise behind him. Albert was startled and began to cry. After several such experiences, he avoided the rat and cried if it was brought close to him. (This sort of experimentation is now forbidden by the American Psychological Association's Code of Ethics.)

In Pavlovian terms, Watson and Rayner had set up a *bond* between the sight of the rat (CS) and an arousal response in Albert's autonomic nervous system (CR). Once this S-R bond was fixed, the fear response could also be elicited by showing Albert almost any furry object. Put another way, fears often *generalize* to stimuli similar to the CS. The burnt child dreads not only the fire, but often comes to fear stoves, pots and pans, ovens, pictures of flames, and even stories about the great Chicago fire.

We will have more to say about conditioned fears (and how to treat them) in just a moment. First, let's look at how emotional responses such as fears are often measured in the laboratory.

Measuring Emotional Responses

Words are *stimuli*, just like bells and musical tones. If you were chased by a bull when you were a child, you probably experienced great fear. And you would still show some *conditioned autonomic arousal*, even now, if you read the word "bull," saw a picture of one, or were asked to think about one.

The Polygraph

We could *measure* your fear reaction to "bulls" by attaching you to a **polygraph**, a machine often (incorrectly) called a "lie detector." The polygraph would record your pulse, blood pressure, breathing rate, and the amount of sweat produced on the palms of your hands. The "palmar sweat," of course, would give a measure of your GSR, or *galvanic skin response*. These are all measures of autonomic arousal, as you know from reading Chapter 12.

Neurotic (new-ROT-tick). Abnormal or unusual behavior patterns are sometimes referred to as being "neurotic." A neurosis (new-ROW-sis) is a relatively mild form of mental disorder. As we will see in Chapter 22, however, psychologists do not agree on the causes and cures of neurotic behaviors.

Polygraph (PAHL-ee-graff). *Poly* means "many." A polygraph is a machine that makes a graph of many different responses simultaneously. Sometimes called a "lie detector," but it records emotional responses, not "lies."

Once you were hooked up to the polygraph, we could measure changes in your autonomic arousal. For example, if we showed you an emotionally "neutral" stimulus, your polygraph record presumably would remain calm and regular. If we then presented you with a picture of a large bull, or said the word aloud, the graph would note a sudden sharp *change* in your autonomic activity. We would then *assume* you had experienced some emotional arousal, such as that associated with fear, anxiety, or guilt. Notice, however, that the polygraph detects *emotions, not lies.*

Question: The ancient Chinese often gave criminal suspects rice to eat. If the suspect could swallow the rice easily, he or she was presumed to be innocent. What have you learned about the effects of autonomic arousal on salivation that might support the use of the "rice guilt detector"?

"Beating" the Lie Detector

University of Minnesota psychologist David Lykken has, for years, crusaded against the misuse of the polygraph. Lykken describes his views in his 1980 book *A Tremor in the Blood* and in an article published in *Discover* in 1981. According to Lykken, "there is no such thing as a lie detector. . . . There is no specific response that everyone emits when lying but never when telling the truth. When we lie about something serious, most of us experience some sort of inner turmoil, what Daniel Defoe described 250 years ago as 'a tremor in the blood'. . . . What we forget is that a false accusation can elicit an inner turmoil also—and the lie detector cannot tell the difference!"

To show what he means, Lykken describes the experience of a man named Floyd Fay, who, because he "flunked" a lie-detector test, was falsely accused of murdering a friend. Fay served two years in prison before the real killers

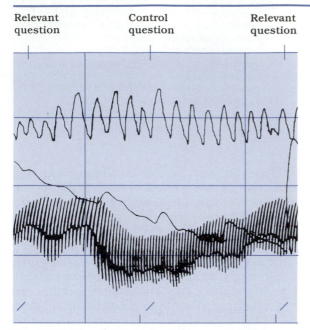

Relevant question Control question Relevant question

Fig. 13.3 A polygraph record.

David T. Lykken

The fear that children sometimes have of animals can be deconditioned, using desensitization techniques pioneered by Mary Cover Jones, a student of John B. Watson.

confessed. During that time, Fay read as much as he could about autonomic responses and polygraphs. In this particular prison, inmates were given polygraph tests if suspected of violating prison rules. Fay trained 27 inmates how to "beat" the polygraph by biting their tongues or secretly jabbing themselves with a sharp nail when the *control* questions were asked. Lykken states that "23 of the 27 managed to beat the lie test in this manner." Lykken also reports that in two large-scale studies published in 1976, half the suspects who were determined later to have been innocent actually failed the lie test.

Question: How would it affect your responses if you took a tranquilizer just before being given a polygraph examination?

Uses and Abuses of Polygraphs

David Lykken is not opposed to the proper use of polygraph tests. For example, he says, the polygraph is of considerable value in many scientific studies of autonomic responses. Second, the polygraph can help screen out innocent suspects in police investigations. The police can then spend their time investigating just the people who "flunk" the exams. And, as Lykken notes, many criminals who "believe" in the polygraph often *confess* when threatened with a test. (see Fig. 13.3).

But Lykken believes no person should ever be *convicted* just on the basis of a lie-detector test. The chances the test will be wrong are simply too great, which is one reason few courts admit polygraph records as evidence. Nor, Lykken says, should corporations or government organizations use lie-detector tests as "routine screening devices." Again, the odds are too large that people will be denied employment on the basis of some "expert's intuition."

Conditioned Emotional Responses: A Summary

Some of us are conditioned early in life to "feel guilty" when we lie. So we show autonomic arousal when we are untruthful. But we also may be trained—consciously or unconsciously— to respond to many other situations and stimuli with autonomic arousal.

If most emotional reactions are *learned*, then we might assume most of them can be *un-learned*, or extinguished. That particular insight has led to the development of a new type of psychotherapy called *counter-conditioning*.

Counter-Conditioning

In the July 1980 *American Psychologist*, Kansas State psychologist Franz Samelson describes the difficulties John B. Watson and Rosalie Rayner had trying to "condition fear" in Little Albert. At first they attempted to make him afraid of a flash of light (rather than a rat). They failed, in part because whenever they tried to frighten the child, Little Albert would pop his thumb into his mouth. Then he would sit peacefully thumb-sucking, instead of showing the normal "fear" response. According to Samelson, Watson and Rayner could get the fear reaction only when they kept Albert's thumb out of his mouth.

It seems likely the problems Watson and Rayner had in *conditioning* fear in Albert gave them the idea of how to *decondition* similar responses. If thumb-sucking "overwhelmed" Albert's fear response, perhaps they could "counter-condition" other children to recover from fear by teaching them a "relaxing" reaction like thumb-sucking. In 1924, a student of Watson's named Mary Cover Jones tried just that.

Phobia (FOE-bee-uh). From the Greek word for "fear." A phobia is a strong and often unusual fear of something.

To appreciate how counter-conditioning works, imagine that at some time in the future, your own 2-year-old son accidentally learned to fear small furry animals. You might try to cure the boy the way Mary Cover Jones did—by attempting to attach a *strongly positive* response to the fear-arousing stimulus.

The *sight* of a white rat would presumably upset your son—but the sight of food when he was hungry would surely make him happy and eager to eat. If you could somehow *bond* the "rat" stimulus to the "positive" eating response, you could "decondition" the child by making him like the rat rather than fear it.

You might begin the counter-conditioning procedure by bringing a white rat into the same room with your son while you were feeding him. At first, you would want to keep the animal so far away that your son could barely see it out of the corner of his eye. Since the animal wouldn't be close enough to bother him, he probably would keep right on eating. Then, step by step, you might bring the rat closer.

Since your son could not cry and eat *at the same time*, the CS-CR fear response would gradually *extinguish*. At the same time, the strength of the CS-CR "pleasure of eating" bond would increase. Eventually, your son would be conditioned to give a new response to the animal that was *counter* to his previous reaction. When Mary Cover Jones followed this procedure (actually using a white rabbit instead of a rat), she found that children soon learned to play with animals that had previously terrified them.

The important point about counter-conditioning is this—it almost always involves *breaking* an inappropriate S-R bond by attaching the *old* "S" to a *new* and more appropriate "R."

The Case of Anne M.

In a sense, Watson and Raynor created a **phobia** about rats in Little Albert. *Phobias* are intense, irrational fears about people, places, things, or situations. Usually these fears are so strong that the person with the phobia cannot control her or his reactions, even when the person clearly realizes that the terror is illogical and unreasonable.

Specific phobias—such as fear of snakes—are often created from a single emotion-charged encounter with the object dreaded. Just as likely, they can come about because of a series of highly unpleasant interactions. Some less specific phobias—such as being afraid of socializing with other people—are more difficult to explain in terms of emotional conditioning.

As an example of how *specific* phobias can be learned—and then unlearned—consider the case of Anne M., a middle-aged woman living near Cleveland. Anne M. shared a house with her mother, upon whom she was very dependent emotionally. One day the two women got into a quarrel at their home. At the end of the argument, the mother ran out into the street. Anne followed her mother to the door—just in time to see the older woman get hit and killed by a passing car.

As a consequence of witnessing the death of her beloved mother—and because she felt partially responsible—Anne developed a phobia about moving vehicles. She retreated to the security of the house and refused to come out. She closed the curtains on all the windows, for even the sight of an automobile or truck was enough to throw Anne into a violent panic reaction. Finally, her withdrawal from the rest of the world became so severe, she had to be hospitalized in a nearby mental institution.

Once in the hospital, Anne refused to leave. Her therapists tried to explore her guilt feelings and her anxieties about death. But even after years of treatment, Anne M. still panicked whenever she looked out of the hospital window and saw an automobile passing on the road.

Desensitization Therapy

At this point, two psychologists then at the University of Michigan—David Himle and Clayton Shorkey—attempted a form of counter-conditioning called **desensitization therapy**.

In their first talks with Anne M., Himle and Shorkey drew up a **hierarchy of fears**—that is, a list of disturbing *stimuli* arranged from least to most frightening. The act of actually riding in an automobile was the most frightening thing Anne could think of. Getting into a parked automobile was somewhat less disturbing. Thus, sitting in a car ranked *lower* on the hierarchy than did riding. Walking past a car was even less threatening, but was still more likely to induce panic than merely seeing a car or truck through a window. Merely imagining

what a car looked like evoked very little fear, so this item was at the bottom of the hierarchy.

When Himle and Shorkey began treating Anne M., they first got her to relax as much as possible. Once she was comfortable, they asked her to imagine seeing a car out of the window. Very rapidly she could tolerate seeing a car "in her mind's eye" without feeling any anxiety at all. Then they asked Anne M. to gaze out a window briefly, and got her to relax again. Soon Anne M. was able to look at cars out the window whenever she pleased.

At this point in her treatment, Anne M. had been conditioned to handle the lowest items on her fear hierarchy. For the stimulus of "seeing a car through the window" now elicited the conditioned response of *relaxation* rather than the conditioned response of *panic*.

Next, Himle and Shorkey asked her to imagine walking out the front door of the building and approaching a car. Once she could manage this imagery, they got her to leave the hospital building and actually touch a parked automobile outside. When she was relaxed enough to handle this real-life problem, they encouraged her to get inside the car and take a short ride.

To help Anne M. imagine what each step in her desensitization would be like, Himle and Shorkey built a scale model of the hospital and its grounds. The model included all the streets and highways in that area. Anne M. learned to move toy cars around the streets without becoming fearful. Once she had "thought out" a given journey using the toy cars, she was able to make the same brief trip in a real automobile.

At the end of just 10 training sessions, Anne M. was driven out of the hospital grounds on a short excursion—a trip that caused her little or no discomfort. Thereafter, with no further therapy, Anne M. began taking part in more of the social activities on the ward, including short visits to points of interest near the hospital. Once she could tolerate these brief trips, she spontaneously began visiting friends who lived in nearby towns.

The final test of Anne's desensitization came when she was invited to spend a few days with some relatives who lived several hundred miles away. Anne had to make the trip by bus. When she felt she was relaxed enough to handle this experience—which might well have rated right at the top of her original hierarchy of fears—she packed her bag and caught the bus.

Ironically, the vehicle broke down while on the expressway. Anne and the rest of the passengers had to sit by the side of the road for more than an hour while traffic buzzed furiously past them. However, Anne handled the situation without any panic and reached her destination safely. Thanks to desensitization training, Anne M. no longer had a phobic reaction to moving vehicles.

Question: Some college students become so frightened when forced to take an examination, they become violently ill. How might desensitization therapy be used to help them?

Desensitization: Pro and Con

Joseph Wolpe, a psychiatrist now working at Temple University in Philadelphia, is usually given credit for having popularized desensitization training. Wolpe believes that the secret of its success lies in never letting the phobic reaction get so strong that it cannot be *counteracted* by voluntary muscular relaxation (see Fig. 13.4). Wolpe and his colleagues achieve this goal by always starting with the least-feared item on the hierarchy and working up the scale. They also stop treatment momentarily whenever the client shows the slightest sign of distress.

Cognitive Desensitization

Attitudinal and other *cognitive* changes often occur during desensitization training. That is, the patient frequently reports *perceiving* the once-feared situation in a new and less frightening light. When Wolpe first began his work, he appeared to believe that these perceptual changes were the *result* of learning to handle disturbing stimuli in a relaxed fashion. That is, Wolpe thought that changes in *behavior* brought about the changes in *cognitive activities*.

Other behaviorally oriented therapists soon insisted Wolpe had put the cart before the horse. These psychologists noted that, during therapy, cognitive changes often occurred *first*. Once the patients had changed their "attitudes," they could relax more in the presence of the dreaded stimulus. As evidence, these therapists cited research suggesting you need not start at the bottom of the fear hierarchy and work up gradually to the most disturbing item. Rather, you can pick items at random and ex-

Fear of heights can be "desensitized" using counter-conditioning procedures.

Joseph Wolpe

Fig. 13.4 A patient and Dr. Joseph Wolpe during systematic desensitization. Note that the patient's index finger is raised to indicate that she is visualizing the scene required by the therapist.

pose the patient to them—as long as the patient doesn't become too disturbed by the procedure. Furthermore, many studies show that purely *mental* relaxation can be as powerful in helping cure phobias as is *muscular* relaxation. The use of mental rather than muscular relaxation is sometimes called **cognitive desensitization**.

In an article in the February 1981 *American Psychologist*, Wolpe comments on these subjects. He now differentiates between *cognitively based anxiety* and *conditioned anxiety*. According to Wolpe, cognitive anxiety is brought about by mental "errors or misinformation." Conditioned anxiety, though, is "based on autonomic conditioning" and is acquired in just the manner that Pavlov described. Conditioned anxiety occurs primarily in such simple situations as *specific phobias*. Wolpe believes that *both* cognitively based anxiety and conditioned anxiety are present in more complex cases, such as *non-specific phobias*.

Wolpe urges the use of desensitization therapy to treat conditioned anxiety. In his 1981 article, however, he does not make any specific recommendations about how to treat cognitively based anxiety.

Desensitization or "Natural Extinction"?

A survey of the literature suggests that *any* technique that keeps the patient in the "presence" of the feared object (or situation) for an extended period of time will help extinguish the fear. Desensitization may be effective, therefore, simply because it is an elegant way of getting patients to remain near the things they are afraid of until a sort of "natural extinction" takes place. And the more "cognitive" forms of counter-conditioning may work because they require the patient to *think* about the feared objects or situations until the same sort of natural extinction occurs. We will return to this point momentarily.

Psychoanalysis Versus Desensitization

In his 1981 article, Joseph Wolpe differentiates his approach to treating phobias from that favored by Freudian psychoanalysts. He believes phobias are "conditioned fears." However, Wolpe says, "According to psychoanalytic theory, mental activity is partly conscious and partly out of reach of consciousness in the 'unconscious mind.' Neurotic symptoms are regarded as the manifestations of emotional forces that have been 'repressed' in the unconscious."

Wolpe has little use for the psychoanalytic approach. He believes the success of psychoanalysis is due to the "brilliance with which Freud presented his theories. His writing weaves a magic web from which few can extricate themselves once enmeshed." However, Wolpe says, "Not a single one of [Freud's] propositions has ever been supported by scientifically acceptable evidence."

Few psychoanalysts would agree with Wolpe. Many analysts do admit that desensitization therapy can be effective with simple phobic reactions. But they cite case histories suggesting that complex phobias are better treated with techniques that *uncover the underlying cause of the patient's problems.*

Symptom Substitution

As an example of the psychoanalytic view of phobias, consider a young man who hates his parents and wants to kill them. Because this desire is unacceptable to him, the young man might develop a phobia about guns and knives. His fear then serves to keep him away from weapons he might use if his hatred ever got out of control. Merely "desensitizing" him to guns would make things worse, since it would keep him from facing the hatred that is at the root of his difficulties.

The psychoanalytic view is that phobias are almost always *symptoms* of an underlying personality problem. Thus, if you just remove the symptom without uncovering the underlying difficulty, other more devastating symptoms are bound to take its place.

Psychoanalysts offer many *case histories* in which symptom substitution has occurred. However, as we will see in Chapter 22, there is not much *scientific* evidence to support this fear of "symptom substitution."

Wolpe's Response

Wolpe's reply to the psychoanalysts is two-fold. To begin with, he believes that the symptom is usually what really bothers the patient. A man may continue to fear guns and knives long after his parents are dead and buried. Talking through his hatred for the long-gone parents may give the man considerable insight into his problems, but research suggests it usually does very little to help him overcome his gun phobia.

In the second place, Wolpe holds that what the analysts call "the underlying problem" is typically an attitude or perception that was *learned* by the same laws of conditioning as was the phobic reaction. Men aren't born with an instinctive hatred of their parents. It takes years of careful training—usually on the part of the parents themselves—to achieve that. If a therapist feels a patient's perceptions of her or his parents should be changed, conditioning techniques offer a fast and reliable methodology for doing so.

Which Position Is Correct?

In fact, there's little sense in fighting over which form of therapy is best, since all types of treatment have their uses. Indeed, it is likely that psychoanalysts unconsciously make use of counter-conditioning while treating their patients—although the psychoanalysts may not realize that they are doing so. For example, when they get their patients to "talk through" a fear time and time again, they actually are allowing a sort of natural extinction to occur. In similar fashion, many behaviorists don't stop at removing the symptomatic behaviors—they try to determine how and when the phobia was learned as well. And then they use desensitization techniques to "decondition" the emotionality connected with those early experiences.

Sometimes, in the heat of defending our theoretical positions, we all lose sight of the prime goal—namely, to get the patient back to normal as quickly and as surely as possible. And to do that, we probably should use any type of treatment that "works," no matter how revolutionary that therapy may seem when first introduced. We will raise this issue again at the end of the next chapter, after we have looked at a different form of learning called *operant conditioning*.

Cognitive desensitization. Pavlov and the early behavioral psychologists dealt entirely with *external* stimuli and *observable* responses. During the 1960's, psychologists discovered that Pavlovian techniques could be used to condition (or decondition) inner processes, such as thoughts and feelings. Desensitization seems to occur just as rapidly if the patient *thinks* relaxing thoughts (a cognitive process) as if the patient actually relaxes (an observable response).

Summary

1. The **conditioned reflex** was discovered by Twitmyer, but credit for its discovery is usually given to Ivan Pavlov.
2. Conditioning involves pairing a **neutral stimulus** (the CS) with an **unconditioned stimulus** (the UCS). The UCS already has the power to elicit the **unconditioned response** (the UCR). If the CS is paired with the UCS enough times, it *conditionally* takes on the power to evoke a reaction similar to the UCR. This "similar" reaction is called the **conditioned response** (the CR).
3. Pavlov paired a bell (CS) with food powder blown into a dog's mouth (the UCS). The food naturally evoked salivation (the UCR). Once the bell had been paired with the food for several trials, sounding the bell *without food* caused the dog to salivate (the CR).
4. All learning or conditioning is built on—or is an adaption of—**innately determined stimulus-response connections**, the UCS-UCR bond.
5. Conditioning is sometimes referred to as strengthening S-R bonds or **stimulus-response bonds**. The stronger the bond, the more likely it is the conditioned stimulus will elicit the desired conditioned response.

6   The more frequently the CS and the UCS are paired, the stronger the **S-R bond** becomes.

7   Conditioning proceeds fastest when the CS is presented immediately before the UCS.

8   An extinguished response is not totally forgotten. If the CS is again paired with the UCS, **relearning** usually takes fewer trials than did the original learning. Furthermore, extinguished responses often show **spontaneous recovery** after some time has passed.

9   Pavlov conditioned dogs to withstand pain by pairing a weak painful stimulus with a strong UCS, such as food. The food evoked salivation. Soon the **painful stimulus** also evoked salivation rather than escape.

10 If an animal is trained to respond to an orange light, this response may **generalize** to other similar stimuli, such as a red or yellow light. However, with the proper training, the animal can usually learn to **discriminate** among similar stimuli and give different responses to each.

11 If this discrimination becomes too difficult, the animal may show such **neurotic** responses as biting, barking, and defecation.

12 Watson and Rayner conditioned a boy called Little Albert to fear a rat by pairing the sight of the rat with a frightening noise. Mary Cover Jones **deconditioned** this sort of fear by pairing the sight of the animal with food.

13 The **polygraph** or "lie detector" measures **conditioned emotional responses**, not "lies" or "guilt."

14 Joseph Wolpe showed that conditioned fears can be **desensitized** or extinguished through **counter-conditioning procedures** that involve pairing the feared stimulus with relaxation. The patient makes a **hierarchy of fears** and learns to relax in the presence of stimuli low on the hierarchy of fears first, then **step-by-step** moves up the hierarchy.

15 Although **desensitization** (counter-conditioning) works well with **specific phobias**, it works less well with more complex fears.

16 There is some evidence that desensitization is effective because it keeps the patient in the presence of the feared stimulus long enough so **natural extinction** of the fear can occur.

17 **Psychoanalysts** believe desensitization merely removes the **symptom** and does not cure the **underlying cause** of fear. Wolpe believes the **symptom usually is the underlying cause**.

(Continued from page 344.)

"Well, what do you think about the desensitization program so far?" Dr. Nancy Wagner asked two months later.

Kevin Lynn grinned mischievously. "You really ought to ask my wife. After all, she's the one who whipped me into coming to see you."

Dr. Wagner clucked her tongue. "I thought the problem was that your wife *wouldn't* whip you."

"Just kidding," Kevin Lynn said. "Actually, it's going pretty well even without the whips." Then he paused, and a crimson blush spread over his pale face. "Except for the other night."

"Oh," replied the woman. "What happened the other night?"

"Nothing happened," Lynn said quietly. "That was the trouble."

Dr. Wagner nodded sympathetically. "Why don't you tell me about it, and then we'll pick up where we left off on the hierarchy."

Lynn sighed. "Let me relax a minute first." He tensed various parts of his body, then let them go limp. "Still feels good when I do that. But it just didn't work the other evening."

"What was the situation?" the woman asked. "Tell me what you were doing, what your wife was doing, and how you responded."

"She was lying in bed, watching television, eating some candy. Chocolates, I think." Lynn stopped abruptly. "Funny, suddenly I'm tense all over."

Dr. Wagner smiled reassuringly. "Relax for a moment. Completely relax. Okay?"

"Okay," said the man.

"Now, shut your eyes and listen to your body while I talk. The moment that you feel any tension, lift your right hand. Understand?"

"Okay," said the man, exhaling loudly.

"I want you to imagine your bedroom. Look at the chairs, and the dresser. Any tension?"

The man shook his head.

"Now look at the bed. Any tension yet?"

"Maybe a tiny bit. No big deal, really."

Dr. Wagner nodded. "That's progress. A month ago, you felt tense just thinking about the bed. Okay, now imagine your wife is lying in the bed. She's turned on the TV and is watching some program. Is that unusual?"

"Happens all the time, although I can usually give her a reason to turn the TV off—if I really want to."

Dr. Wagner grinned. "But that's a different kind of tension, so you just relax now. Keep your eyes closed, and imagine your wife watching the TV. Just as you walk into the bedroom and start to approach her, she reaches into a box of chocolates . . ."

"Stop," the man said. "That did it. I could feel it then."

"Chocolates," said the woman. "Why does that bother you?"

Lynn shook his head. "Haven't the foggiest." He sighed. "Oh, well, the tension seems to be gone now anyhow."

"Good," Dr. Wagner said. "Tell me if it returns. Now, what happened after you saw your wife eating the candy?"

"Hum," said the man, trying to remember. "We talked a bit, kidded around a bit. She was smoking a cigarette, but when I sat down on the bed, she went to put it out, and knocked the ashtray over. . . ."

Dr. Wagner leaned forward. "Suddenly you're sweating."

"The tension started just then," the man said.

"Relax. Just go limp, really limp."

Kevin Lynn sighed deeply, and then nodded when his muscles seemed relaxed.

"Stop me if the tension starts again," Dr. Wagner said. "Now, there seem to be four stimuli that, put together, cause the tension. You just stay as relaxed as you can while I name them. First, your wife in bed. Second, she's watching television. Third, she's eating chocolates. And fourth, she knocks over the ashtray."

"Stop," Lynn said. "There it is again."

"Well," the woman said. "It seemed to be the ashtray that you really reacted to. Now, I want you to relax deeply again. Go deep down inside your mind, and look for something about an ashtray. Did you ever knock one over?"

The man shook his head. "Not that I remember."

Dr. Wagner continued. "Well, did you ever see someone else knock one over? Your mother, perhaps, when you were a small child."

"Stop," Lynn said. "I feel tense again. Not much, but a bit."

"Just relax. Be calm," the woman said. And when the man sighed, she went on. "Okay, the ashtray is the clue. Did your mother smoke?"

Lynn shook his head. "No, but my father did." He stopped. "Oh, wow, I'm tense again."

"Relax, relax as deeply as you can," the woman said. "We're getting close now. I want you to think of a time when you and your mother and your father were together, and your mother was eating chocolates and watching television."

Kevin Lynn groaned loudly. "Oh, my God, it's all coming back to me now."

"Good, good," said Dr. Wagner. "Just go limp, and then tell me what you remember. If you get too tense, stop and relax, and don't worry about it."

"Incredible," said the man. "I completely forgot about it until now. I must have been nine or ten. Mom was watching television. She loved the tube. She used to say it was her only friend." He paused for a long time. "Funny, I wonder if she meant that she and my father didn't get along too well in bed."

"You're tensing up again," Dr. Wagner said. "Just relax."

Lynn sighed. "I guess I can finally think about things like that now. Anyhow, she made me stand in the corner in the bedroom, while she watched the tube. Seems like I was always standing in the corner for one reason or another. Anyway, this particular night, she was eating chocolates and watching the tube, and I really had to . . . to . . ."

"Urinate?" asked the woman.

"Yeah," the man said softly. "So I was squirming a bit, you know, and she got very upset because I was . . ." He shifted nervously in his chair.

"Touching your genitals?"

"That's right. I guess most kids do that, don't they, when they have to urinate?"

Dr. Wagner nodded her agreement. "They certainly do." She paused to think, then continued. "Now, I want to ask you a question, but I want you to relax deeply first. Okay?"

"Okay, I'm relaxed."

"Did your mother threaten to whip you when you touched your genitals?"

Lynn groaned again. "Oh, Lord, yes. All the time when I touched myself."

"Relax," commanded the woman. "It's all right. Now, tell me what happened next."

He paused. "You know something, this is getting pretty painful."

"I know. We can stop now if you like, and go on some other time."

Lynn shook his head. "No, we might as well get it all out in the open. Okay, I was standing in the corner, squirming around and touching myself, and my mother was watching the tube and eating chocolates and threatening to whip me if I didn't behave. Then my father came into the room, and . . ."

"You're tensing again."

"I can handle it," the man said gruffly. "Anyway, my father came into the room, and I guess they must have had another argument. Now that I think about it, they had lots of arguments. But this one was a lulu. Scared the hell out of me . . ."

"Very understandable," said the woman, soothingly.

"Yeah, well, I remember he called her a fat slob, and she said, uh, she said . . ."

"Relax," the woman said. "Take it easy."

Lynn nodded. "She said all he wanted to do was to, you know, mess around." Dr. Wagner nodded.

"Then they started shouting at each other, and my father got pretty mad, I guess. He probably had been drinking a little, you know?"

"I know," said Dr. Wagner.

The man sighed. "Anyhow, she said that he didn't deserve her, and . . ."

Dr. Wagner leaned forward. "Relax, Kevin. You're very close to the heart of the problem now."

"He screamed and rushed at her. I remember I got really scared." Lynn stopped. "There's something else, though, something I can't recall . . ."

"Are you fairly relaxed?" Dr. Wagner asked.

"Yeah," said Lynn. "I guess so. Why?"

Dr. Wagner smiled. "When your father rushed toward your mother, what did she do?"

"Oh, my God," the man said. "Of course! I remember now! She threw the ashtray at him, but she missed, and . . . and . . ."

The woman nodded. "I know, it hit you instead, didn't it?"

"That memory hurts," the man said softly. "It hurts like hell."

"Of course it hurts," Dr. Wagner said. "And it would have gone right on hurting all the rest of your life if you hadn't dredged it up and faced it squarely. I think you're doing beautifully."

Lynn frowned. "But I still don't see the connection completely. So my mother hit me with an ashtray. So what?"

Dr. Wagner sighed. "See if you can remember what happened after the ashtray hit you."

The man suddenly gasped for air. "Oh, my, that did it. That really did it. I had forgotten that part entirely."

"Relax as best you can, and tell me about it," she said.

"Okay. I remember I screamed, and they stopped arguing. My mother rushed over to me and grabbed me up. She hugged me to her breast and said she didn't mean it." Lynn stopped. "Oh, my," he said a moment later. "It all makes sense now."

Dr. Wagner nodded again. "Yes, it does, doesn't it? You got afraid and very tense, then you got hurt, and that stopped the argument and the fear. And then your mother hugged you and kissed you. One-trial conditioning, I'd say."

"Oh, my," the man said hoarsely.

The woman sighed deeply. "I think we've done enough for today. We can put the scene into the hierarchy the next time you're here. Shouldn't take too long to desensitize you to the whole thing. Okay?"

Kevin Lynn smiled. "Okay. But right now, I'm going home and break every ashtray in the house. And throw out all the chocolates."

"And the whips?"

"Yeah. Especially those. And then I'm going to kiss my wife, and . . ."

"And?"

Lynn grinned. "And then I'm going to show her I love her in the best way I know how."

"No sweat," said the woman.

"No pain," said the man.

Recommended Readings

Hergenhahn, B.R. (1982). *An introduction to theories of learning* (2nd ed.). Englewood Cliffs, N.J.: Prentice-Hall.

Kendall, P.C. & Hollon, S.D. (Eds.). (1981). *Assessment strategies for cognitive-behavioral interventions*. New York: Academic Press.

Lykken, D.T. (1980). *A tremor in the blood*. New York: McGraw-Hill.

Saxe, L., Dougherty, D., & Cross, T. (1985). The validity of polygraph testing: Scientific analysis and public controversy. *American Psychologist, 40,* 355–366.

Wolpe, J. (1981). *Our useless fears*. Boston: Houghton Mifflin.

Did You Know That...

- Most of the teaching techniques used in U.S. classrooms are derived from laboratory experiments with animals?
- Chimpanzees seem to have the same sort of insight (or "Ah ha!") experiences during learning as do humans?
- If you use an effective educational technology, you can teach a pigeon to bowl in a couple or hours or so?
- B.F. Skinner believes that rewards increase the probability that an organism will repeat the response it has just made?
- Most complex behaviors appear to be sequences of simple responses that have been "chained" together?
- The speed with which an organism responds is frequently dependent on the schedule of reinforcement the animal receives?
- Most of the animals you see perform on TV and in shows are trained by using techniques developed by Skinner and his associates?
- Some psychologists claim it is more effective to train alcoholics to become "social drinkers" than to try to get them to give up drinking entirely?

14

Operant Conditioning and Cognitive Skills

"That'll Learn You!"

I am writing this because I presume He wants me to. Otherwise He would not have left paper and pencil handy for me to use. And I put the word "He" in capitals because it seems the only thing to do. If I am dead and in hell, then this is only proper. However, if I am merely a captive somewhere, a little flattery won't hurt matters.

As I think about it, I am impressed most of all by the suddenness of the whole affair. At one moment I was out walking in the woods near my home. The next thing I knew, here I was in a small, bare room, naked as a jaybird, with only my good sense to stand between me and insan-ity. When the "change" oc-curred—whatever the change was—I was not aware of even a momentary flicker between walking in the woods and being here in this room. He must have a technology avail-able to Him that is very im-pressive indeed!

As I recall, I was worrying about how to teach my intro-ductory psychology class some of the more technical points of Learning Theory, when the "change" came. How far away life at the Uni-versity seems at the moment! I hope Dean Steiner will for-give me if I am now more con-cerned about where I am—and how to get out of here—than about cajoling un-dergraduates into under-standing Pavlov or Skinner.

Problem #1: Where am I? For an answer, I can only de-scribe this gray, windowless room. It is about 20 feet square and 12 feet high. The ceiling glows with a soft white light, and the spongy floor has a "tingly" feel to it, suggesting that it may be in constant vibration.

The only furniture in the room are "lumps" that re-semble a table and chair. On the table I found a rough sort of paper and a stick of graph-ite which I have sharpened into a pencil. My clothes are gone. The suit was an old one I won't miss, but I am worried about what happened to my watch. It was one of those fancy digital things, and quite expensive.

The #1 problem still remains, however. Where in the hell am I—if not Hell itself!

Problem #2 is a knottier one—*why* am I here? I have the usual quota of enemies, but even Dean Steiner isn't powerful enough to arrange for something like this. And I surely am not rich enough to kidnap. So, where am I, and why? And who is He?

There is no sense in trying to keep track of time. This room is little more than a sensory deprivation chamber, and I haven't the faintest notion of what hour or even what day it is. Well, if He wasn't bright enough to leave me my watch, He can't complain that I don't keep accurate records.

Or is that the problem I'm supposed to solve?

Nothing much has happened. I have slept, been fed and watered, and have emptied my bladder and bowels. The food was waiting on the table when I awoke last time. I must say that He has little of the gourmet in him. Protein balls are not my idea of a feast. However, they will serve to keep body and soul together (presuming, of course, they *are* together at the moment).

But I must object to my source of water. While I was asleep, a small nipple appeared on the wall. It produces a sweetish liquid when I suck on it. However, drinking this way is a *most* undignified behavior for a full professor to engage in. I'd complain to the Management if only I knew to whom I should complain!

Following my meal, the call to nature became a little too strong to ignore. Now, I was adequately toilet-trained, and the absence of indoor plumbing is most annoying. But there was nothing much to do other than choose a corner of the room and make the best of a bad situation. However, I have at least learned why the floor vibrates, for the excreted material sank out of sight moments later. Clever technology, but bothersome, since I have to sleep on the floor. I will probably have nightmares that the floor will gulp *me* up too, all in a piece.

You know, this place seems dreadfully quiet to me.

Suddenly I have solved two of my problems. I know both where I am and who He is. And I bless the day that I got interested in sensory psychology and the perception of motion.

The air in this room is filled with dust particles. This fact became important when I noticed the dust tended to pile up along the floor against one particular wall. At first I thought there might be an air vent there. However, when I put my hand to the floor, I could feel no breeze whatsoever. Yet even as I held my hand there, dust motes covered my hand. I tried this same experiment everywhere else in the room, but this was the only spot where the dust coated my hand.

But if ventilation was not responsible for the dust, what was? Suddenly there popped into my mind some calculations I had made when NASA first proposed building a wheel-shaped satellite and then setting it to spinning slowly in space. Centrifugal force would substitute for the force of gravity, and the outer shell of the wheel would appear to be "down" to anyone inside the wheel. It immediately occurred to me that dust would move in a direction *opposite* to the rotation of the wheel, and thus airborne particles would pile up against any wall that impeded their flight.

It also seemed that the NASA engineers had overlooked one important fact. Namely, that humans are at least as sensitive to angular rotation as they are to the pull of gravity. As I figured the problem then, if a man aboard the wheel moved his head a few feet toward or away from the center of the doughnut-shaped satellite, he would have sensed the angular rotation of the wheel. Rather annoying it would have been too, becoming dizzy every time you sat down or stood up.

With this thought in mind, I climbed atop the table and jumped off. Sure enough, I immediately felt dizzy. My hypothesis was confirmed.

I am aboard a wheel-shaped spaceship!

The thought is incredible, but in a strange way comforting. At least now I can postpone worry about heaven and hell and start considering other things. And, of course, I know who "He" is. Or rather, I know who He *isn't*, which is something else again. Since no country on earth has a space station like this one, He must be an alien!

I still have no notion of *why* I am here, however, nor why this alien picked me of all people to bring to His spaceship. One dreadful thought did occur to me, though. Maybe He's an alien scientist—a biologist of sorts—out gathering specimens. Is He going to cut me open to see what makes me tick? Will my innards be smeared over a glass slide for hundreds of youthful Hims to peer at under a microscope? Brrrr! I don't mind giving my life to Science, but I'd rather do it a day at a time.

Good God! I should have known it! Destiny will play her little tricks, and all jokes have their cosmic angles.

He is a *psychologist*!

Had I given the matter thought, I would have realized that whenever you come across a new species, you worry about behavior first, biology second. So I have received the ultimate insult— or the ultimate compliment, I don't know which. I have become a laboratory specimen for an alien psychologist!

This thought first occurred to me when I awoke after my latest sleep (which was filled with frightening dreams). Almost at once I noticed that one of the walls now had a lever of some kind protruding from it. Underneath the lever was a small hole with a container beneath the hole. When I accidentally depressed the lever, it made a loud clicking noise. Immediately, a protein ball popped out of the hole and fell into the container. For just a moment I was puzzled. This seemed so strangely familiar. Then, all at once, I burst into wild laughter.

This room is a gigantic Skinner Box!

For years I have been putting white rats in an operant chamber and making them press a lever to get a pellet of food. And now, after all those experiments, I find *myself* trapped like a rat in a Skinner Box! Perhaps this is hell after all, and He is just following the Mikado's advice to "let the punishment fit the crime."

Anyhow, it didn't take me long to discover that pressing the lever would give me food only at rather lengthy intervals. The rest of the time, all I get is a click for my efforts. Since I am never quite sure when the proper interval has passed, I stomp over to the lever and press it whenever I think it's getting close to dinner time. Just like my rats always did. And since the pellets are small and I never get enough of them, occasionally I find myself banging away on the lever with all the compulsion of a stupid animal. But I missed the feeding time once and almost starved to death (so it seemed) before the lever next delivered food. About the only consolation to my wounded pride is that I've already lost an inch or so around my waist.

At least He doesn't seem to be fattening me up for the kill!

I have been promoted. Apparently He has decided I'm intelligent enough to handle the Skinner Box. So I've been promoted to solving a maze.

Can you picture the irony of the situation? All of the classic laboratory apparatus is being thrown right in my face. If only I could communicate with Him! I don't mind being subjected to tests nearly as much as I mind being underestimated. Why, I can solve puzzles hundreds of times more complex than the ones He's giving me. But how can I tell Him?

As it turns out, the maze is much like the ones I have used. It's rather long, with 23 choice points along the way. I spent half an hour wandering through the thing the first time. Surprisingly enough, I didn't realize what I was in, so I made no conscious attempt to memorize the correct turns. It wasn't until I reached the final choice point and found food that I recognized what was expected of me. The next time I made fewer errors, and was able to turn in a perfect performance fairly rapidly. However, I'm embarrassed to state that my own white rats could have learned the maze somewhat sooner than I did.

Now that I am sure of what is happening to me, my thoughts have turned to getting out of this situation. Mazes I can solve easily, but how to escape apparently is beyond my intellectual capacity. Come to think of it, though, there was precious little my own experimental animals could do to get out of my clutches.

And assuming that I am unable to escape, what then? After He has finished putting me through as many paces as He wishes, where do we go from there? Will He treat me as I treated most of my rats? "Following the experiment, the animals were sacrificed," as we so politely put it in our journal articles. This thought doesn't appeal to me very much, as you can imagine. But perhaps if I seem particularly bright to Him, He may use me for breeding purposes, to establish a colony of His own. Now, that situation might have possibilities ...

Oh, damn Freud anyhow!

And damn Him too! I had just gotten the maze well learned when He changed it on me. I stumbled about like a bat in the sunlight for quite some time before I finally got to the goal box. I'm afraid my performance was pretty poor.

What He did was to reverse the whole maze so that it was a mirror image of what it used to be. Took me only two trials to discover the solution. Let Him figure that one out if He's so smart!

My performance on the maze reversal must have pleased Him, because He's added a new complication. He's trying me out on a "jump stand." I sit on a little platform facing three doors across an empty space. If I jump to the correct door, I get food. If I pick the wrong one, I fall into a pool of icy water. And if I don't jump at all, He shocks the devil out of me until I do!

I suppose I could have predicted what He would do next if I had been thinking in the right direction. The trouble is, I've been out of graduate school for too long. I took my first advanced course in learning theory from a strict Behavioral Scientist. "Dr. B-S," we called him. He was convinced that rats learned a maze mechanically, by relying entirely on stimulus-response bonds. The professor for my second course was a confirmed "mentalist," who insisted that rats learned a maze by creating a "cognitive map" of the apparatus in their minds. "Dr. Cog," we called him. And oh! the delicious battles he and "Dr. B-S" had when they debated in public.

The conflict between the two reached a peak when one of Dr. Cog's students started working with the Oddity Problem. Imagine yourself sitting meekly on a jump stand, staring at three doors across the water-filled gap. The two outer doors are white, the middle door is black. You try jumping at each of the white doors, and end up in the drink. So you leap toward the black door in the middle and find a nice meal of protein balls awaiting you. Thereafter—whether the black door is on the right, the left, or in the center—you jump toward it as quickly as you can. And you are always rewarded.

Now, the question is, *how* did you learn this trick? Dr. B-S insisted that you had "acquired the habit" of approaching the black stimulus and avoiding the white stimulus. But Dr. Cog contended that you learned to go to the "odd" color—in this case, black. This explanation infuriated Dr. B-S, who insisted that *oddness* is a "mental concept" rather than a true stimulus and that rats weren't capable of "conceptualizing."

Dr. Cog then proposed a Grand Theoretical Test: Namely, he would now show a rat *two* black doors and *one* white door and see what it did. If the rat had merely learned "to approach the black stimulus," it would leap wildly toward one of the black doors. But if it had learned to "approach the odd-colored door," it would jump to the white door *even though it had never before been rewarded for approaching white.* Dr. B-S scoffed, since rats obviously weren't bright enough to "think in concepts."

So, what do you think happened? Most of the rats Dr. Cog tested jumped to the white door the first time they saw it! Dr. B-S was furious, and Dr. Cog chortled smugly for weeks on end. Dr. Cog then rubbed salt in Dr. B-S's wounds by testing his rats on two doors with vertical stripes and one with horizontal stripes. And then on the reverse. Each time, most of the animals picked the "odd" stimulus. The results were so impressive that Dr. B-S threw up his hands in dismay and went to Hawaii on sabbatical. When he returned, he began studying biofeedback in humans, and never touched a rodent again.

What has all this got to do with me? Well, He must be a simple behaviorist, like old Dr. B-S. The last time He put me on the jump stand, I found myself facing two blue doors and a yellow one. I realized what was up instantly, and leapt toward the yellow. Success! Immediately He tested me with two yellow doors and a blue one. I jumped to the blue, and heard what I can only describe as a cosmic roar of frustration. I gather He wasn't very happy with what I had done.

Next up were two red doors and a green one. I "went for the green," and had no more than landed safely when the whole apparatus started to shake as if someone had kicked it in anger!

The next thing I knew, I was tossed rather roughly back in my cage. Since nothing has happened for an hour or so, I presume He's off sulking somewhere because my actions didn't confirm His expectations.

I suppose I should have realized it before now. Theories are typically born of the equipment one uses. If Skinner had never invented his blasted box, if the maze and the jump stand had not been developed, we probably would have entirely different theories of learning today than we now have. For if nothing else, the type of apparatus you use *reduces* the types of behavior your subjects can show. And your theories only have to account for the kinds of responses that show up in laboratory situations.

But if He has a problem, I have a worse one. What should I do next, now that I know what He expects of me?

Should I help Him confirm his narrow notions about behavior—and about the new species He's testing? Or should I prove to the monster that I'm more "cognitive" than He thinks I ought to be?

I'm sure He will shortly snatch me back for a final test. When I face those differ-

ent-colored doors, should I perform "stupidly" like the intelligent human being I really am? Or should I perform "intelligently" by acting like the dumb rat He wants me to be?

What am I anyhow? A man, or a mouse?

(Continued on page 387.)

Learning Theories

During the many years that you have gone to school, you must have had contact with dozens of different teachers. Some of them probably were strict **disciplinarians** whose "learning theory" was based on two beliefs: First, knowledge had to be pounded into your head through *constant repetition*. Second, it was better to *correct your mistakes* than to reward your progress. Holding a lesson book in one hand and a stick in the other, these teachers probably "drilled" you to spew back from memory whatever material they believed you should learn. These instructors apparently believed that learning is a matter of acquiring *behavioral responses*, and that these responses had to be forced on you by your external environment. If you survived their classes, you surely acquired a large number of facts. (Whether you remembered those facts for very long is another question.) But the constant threat of punishment may well have conditioned you to hate anything associated with school.

Other teachers may have been more concerned with creating an academic environment in which your inborn intellectual potential could grow like a seed planted in fertile soil. These instructors apparently believed that learning is a matter of acquiring *cognitive skills*, and that any attempt they made to "shape" your learning would bias you to perceive the world "their way" instead of "your way." Therefore, these teachers probably gave you a great deal of encouragement, but little or no academic guidance. Probably you enjoyed their classrooms. But the important question is this: Are such unstructured settings the most effective way to acquire the basic skills of life (including self-control)?

As you will soon see, the history of psychological learning theories—and the history of educational practice in the US—is little more than an account of the battle between theorists who believe teachers should condition their students to produce specific behavioral responses, and theorists who hold that teachers should merely encourage students to learn cognitive skills.

Thorndike's Theories

In a sense, the battle began with E.L. Thorndike, who influenced educational practices here almost as much as Pavlov did in Russia. Thorndike spent most of his academic career at Teachers College, a part of Columbia University in New York City. He helped create some of the very first intelligence and aptitude tests. And, with the help of C.L. Barnhart, Thorndike developed a series of dictionaries for school children that is still widely in use.

Thorndike believed that humans are descended from the lower animals and hence

E.L. Thorndike

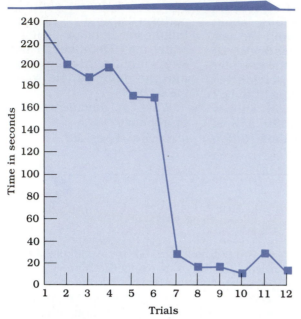

Fig. 14.1 The seventh trial shows a remarkable improvement in the time it took one of Thorndike's cats to open a puzzle box.

Fig. 14.2 Puzzle box used by Thorndike. In this version the cat can escape from the box and get food outside by pressing the treadle inside the box. A cord-and-pulley system unlocks the door.

learn the same way as do cats and rats. So, in 1890 he undertook some of the first laboratory studies ever performed on animal behavior, even though his main interest was human learning. His early work involved putting cats inside a "puzzle box." If the cat could figure out how to unlatch the door to the box, it escaped and was given a bit of food as a reward. At first the cat typically showed a great deal of what Thorndike called "random behavior." It sat and

scratched or licked itself, it mewed and cried, it paced the box, or it bit at the bars and tried to squeeze between them. Eventually, the cat would accidently press a pedal that was connected to the door. The door would fly open, and the animal would rush out and be fed.

In subsequent trials, the cat spent more and more time near the pedal and got out of the box sooner and sooner. Eventually the cat learned what was required of it. The moment it was placed in the box, it would press the pedal, escape, and claim its reward.

When Thorndike plotted on a graph the amount of time it took the cat to exit from the box on each trial, he came up with something that we now call a "learning curve" (see Fig. 14.1). Similar experiments on monkeys, chickens, and even humans yielded the same-shaped curves, a finding that confirmed Thorndike's original theory that animals and humans solve such simple tasks in much the same manner.

Trial-and-Error Learning

Thorndike believed that animals learn to escape from puzzle boxes by **trial and error** (see Fig. 14.2). That is, they perform various behaviors in a blindly mechanical way until some action is *effective* in getting them out of the box. Ineffectual actions—such as sitting and scratching—bring the animal little satisfaction. So these responses rapidly drop out of the animal's behavioral **repertory**. But those actions that gain the animal's release and lead to food are very *satisfying*, so these responses become strongly connected to the stimuli in the puzzle box. The "satisfying" responses thus are much more likely to occur whenever the animal is next put in the box.

Thorndike's Laws of Learning

The results of his puzzle-box experiments led Thorndike to formulate two basic laws of learning: (1) the **law of exercise**, and (2) the **law of effect**.

In part, the *law of exercise* states that the S-R connections you make are *strengthened by repetition*—in short, that practice makes perfect.

The *law of effect* holds that S-R bonds are also strengthened by the "effects" of what you do. These effects may either be "satisfying" or "punishing." Thorndike defined *satisfiers* as situations you willingly approach or do nothing to avoid. And he defined *punishers* as situations you typically avoid or do nothing to approach.

If the response you make to a stimulus somehow gives you pleasure or satisfaction, the connection between the S and the R will be appropriately *strengthened*. This is the first half of the "law of effect," and it holds today just as it did when Thorndike first announced it.

The second half of the law has to do with the effects of punishment on learning. Early in his career, Thorndike stated that "punishers" weakened or broke S-R bonds. But he changed his mind on this point later, when laboratory research proved that punishment *suppresses* responses temporarily, rather than breaking S-R connections. By then, however, many teachers had used Thorndike's laws of learning to justify the use of *aversive control* in the classroom. We will return to this point at the end of the chapter.

Cognitive Theories of Learning

As we noted in Chapter 8, you usually see what you expect to see. This perceptual principle holds in scientific investigations as well as in ordinary life. Thorndike surely *expected* his cats to learn by trial-and-error methods, before he began his work. Indeed, as **Gestalt** psychologist Wolfgang Koehler pointed out soon after Thorndike published his data, the puzzle box could hardly be solved in any way other than by trial and error.

Koehler was trained at the University of Berlin. He believed animals were capable of greater intellectual accomplishments than random solutions to puzzle boxes. He thought that—given the chance—they could discover *cognitive relationships* between objects and events. The animals could then use these "cognitive skills" to gain whatever ends they had in mind. Much of Koehler's research involved presenting various "intellectual" problems to chimpanzees, to see what kinds of solutions they might come up with.

Learning by Insight

Koehler's most famous subject was a particularly bright chimpanzee named Sultan. First, Koehler taught Sultan to reach through the bars of his cage with a stick and rake in a banana. After Sultan had mastered this trick, Koehler set the animal the much more difficult task of *putting two sticks together* to get the food. The banana was moved farther away from Sultan's cage, and the chimp was given two bamboo poles. When the two poles were fitted

Disciplinarians (diss-sip-plin-NAIR-ee-ans). From the Latin word meaning "teaching." We get our word "disciples" from the same Latin source. *Webster's New Collegiate Dictionary* defines *to discipline* as "to punish or penalize for the sake of discipline, to train or develop by instruction and exercise, especially in self-control."

Trial and error. To learn by making mistakes until you discover the correct solution to a problem. Usually involves learning without having someone to teach or guide you.

Repertory (REP-purr-torr-ee). A fancy term for "bag of tricks" or "stock in trade." Your own behavioral repertory is whatever skills, talents, or response patterns you possess.

Law of exercise. The first of Thorndike's two laws describing how stimulus-response (S-R) bonds are formed. The more frequently an S-R bond is "exercised," the stronger the bond becomes.

Law of effect. Thorndike's second law, which states that (1) satisfiers tend to strengthen S-R connections; (2) punishment tends to weaken S-R bonds. The first part of the law—describing the *effect* that reward has on learning—is generally accepted as being correct. However, we now know that punishment doesn't "extinguish" learning—it merely suppresses the learned response or causes the organism to avoid the learning situation.

Gestalt (guess-STAHLT). A German word that means "good form" or "good figure." Also means the tendency to see things as "wholes" rather than as jumbled bits and pieces. See Chapter 8.

together, they were just long enough to gather in the reward (see Fig. 14.3).

At first Sultan was confused. He tried to pull the fruit in with one stick and then with the other, but neither would reach. Despite the fact that this approach didn't get him the banana, Sultan repeated the behavior again and again. Then the chimp abandoned the banana and (perhaps in frustration) retreated into his cage to play with the sticks. So, Koehler decided the animal had failed the test. Koehler went home, leaving Sultan to be observed by an assistant.

Wolfgang Koehler

Fig. 14.3 Sultan in action.

E.C. Tolman

Not long after Koehler left, Sultan happened to hold one stick in each hand so that their ends were pointed toward each other. Gently, he pushed the tip of the smaller one into the hollow of the larger. *They fitted.* Even as he joined the two sticks together, Sultan was up and running toward the bars of his cage. Reaching through with the double stick, he touched the banana and started to draw it toward him.

At this point fate played Sultan a nasty trick for which Koehler was most grateful—the two sticks came apart! Annoyed at this turn of events, Sultan gathered the sticks back into the cage, pushed them *firmly* together, tested them briefly, and then "liberated" the banana.

These actions proved—at least to Koehler's satisfaction—that Sultan actually understood that *joining the poles together* was an effective way of lengthening his arm. Koehler used the term *insight* to refer to this very rapid "perception of relationships" that sometimes occurs in humans and animals. He believed that *insight* involved a sudden restructuring or reorganization of the organism's perceptual world into a new pattern or *Gestalt* (see Chapter 8).

As you might imagine, Ivan Pavlov did not take gladly to Koehler's experiments. As soon as the chimpanzee work appeared in print, Pavlov leapt to the attack. From his sanctuary in Leningrad, Pavlov issued one criticism after another. First, he accused Koehler of being a

"mentalist," which Koehler surely was. But Pavlov also unjustly criticized Koehler for performing "sloppy" experiments. (To Pavlov, a "sloppy" study was one in which the CS and the UCS could not readily be identified.) Since Koehler was much more interested in learning how animals solved real-life problems than in specifying CS's and UCS's, he ignored Pavlov's comments. But thanks to Koehler's work, Pavlov soon found himself assailed by a barrage of experiments from the US. Unfortunately for Pavlov, few of these studies yielded results that could easily be fitted into the Russian scientist's theory of conditioning.

Tolman's "Cognitive Maps"

One set of studies came from E.C. Tolman and his associates at the University of California, Berkeley. During the height of the Pavlov-Koehler controversy, Tolman and his group published a series of articles showing that rats apparently were much more "insightful" than either Thorndike or Pavlov thought they ought to be.

In most of Tolman's experiments, the rats were trained in very complicated **mazes**. Although the animals could reach the food reward at the end of the maze by a great many pathways, one path was typically much shorter than the rest and was preferred by the animals. When that pathway was blocked, however, almost all of the rats would instantly shift to the next most efficient way of getting to the food.

If at any time the experimenter moved the reward from one part of the maze to another, the rats responded immediately as if they had some kind of **cognitive map** of the maze. That is, the rats behaved as if they understood a great deal about the *spatial relationships* involved in getting quickly from one part of the maze to another.

The experiments by Tolman and other Gestalt psychologists clearly demonstrated that *some* rats, in *some* situations, acted as if they had acquired "cognitive skills" that helped them solve problems in real-life settings. Monkeys, chimps, and humans show a great deal more cognitive activity than do rats, however, so Gestalt theorists typically used primates as their preferred laboratory subjects. Because Pavlov, Thorndike, and the early behaviorists focused entirely on S-R bonds, they weren't interested in "mental processes." The rather mechanical behavior patterns of the lower animals appealed greatly to the behaviorists, and so they chiefly stuck to their rats, cats, and dogs. Finally, it took a bird-brained pigeon to show the narrowness of Pavlov's views, and to map out a kind of common ground between the Thorndikeans and the Tolmaniacs.

Operant Conditioning

The learning theories of Pavlov, Thorndike, and Tolman have all been applied in classroom situations. But the theoretical approach most frequently followed in schools today is surely that called **operant conditioning**, which was developed by by B.F. Skinner. We will compare operant conditioning with the other theories of learning later in this chapter. First, let's see why it is so powerful a method for teaching new behavior patterns to both pigeons and people.

Teaching a Pigeon to Bowl

Suppose that, as a final examination in one of your psychology classes, your instructor gives you a common, ordinary pigeon. The in-

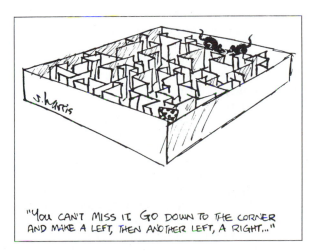

"You CAN'T MISS IT GO DOWN TO THE CORNER AND MAKE A LEFT, THEN ANOTHER LEFT, A RIGHT..."

Mazes (MAY-zizz). A network of pathways and blind alleys between a starting point and a goal, used chiefly to study problem solving in animals and humans. The first maze for laboratory animals was built by psychologist W.S. Small in 1900, and was similar to a famous maze made of hedges at Hampton Court Palace in England, which has delighted millions of visitors.

Cognitive map. Some psychologists (such as Thorndike and Pavlov) believe that animals learn each section of a maze by trial and error. Other psychologists believe animals acquire a "mental map" of the maze and can "think" their way through to the goal—rather than respond reflexively (and unconsciously) to the specific stimuli in each section. In fact, animals such as the rat seem to do a little of both.

Operant conditioning (OPP-per-rant). Skinner's technique for "shaping" responses by rewarding successive approximations to a goal.

structor then says that if you want to get an A in the course, you must teach the pigeon to bowl!

After you recover from your surprise, you take stock of the situation. The apparatus you can use is a large box with a wire screen over the top of it (see Fig. 14.4). Inside the box is a small bowling alley with a tiny ball at one end and pigeon-sized bowling pins at the other. In one corner of the box is a metal cup into which you can drop food pellets from the outside. Just above the food cup is a bell. Fortunately, the pigeon has already been trained to run to the food cup to get the pellets whenever you ring the bell.

Your instructor tells you that if you can teach the pigeon to bowl in a matter of two hours or less, you pass the exam and get your A reward. Keeping in mind all of the practical knowledge on learning theory you have acquired so far in this book, how would you go about educating your pigeon in order to satisfy your instructor, yourself, and, of course, the bird?

Pavlov's Approach

If you played the game according to Pavlovian rules, what would you do? Well, you might begin by ringing the bell and then pushing the pigeon toward the ball, hoping that an S-R connection of some kind would be established in the bird's nervous system. In fact, the pigeon would surely resent such an intrusion into its life space. Instead of learning to bowl when you rang the bell, it probably would learn to peck at your hand viciously. For Pavlovian conditioning is almost always built on *already-established unconditioned responses* (UCS's). If dogs did not salivate naturally when given food, how would you go about teaching them to salivate when you sounded a buzzer?

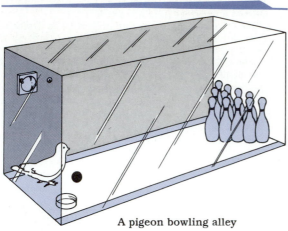

A pigeon bowling alley

Fig. 14.4 A pigeon bowling alley.

B.F. Skinner

If the pigeon already knew how to bowl, you could probably train it to give this response when you rang the bell. But you could read everything Pavlov wrote—in Russian or in English translation—without learning much about how to get a bird to bowl in the first place.

Cognitive Approach

If you turned to Tolman and the Gestalt theorists instead, you might decide to give the pigeon plenty of experience in the bowling box itself before you started the training. Once the animal had acquired a cognitive map of the apparatus, it would surely learn how to bowl much faster. But the relationship between striking the ball and knocking down the pins is an insight that comes hard to most pigeons—unless you facilitate matters a little along the way. And not even Koehler offered much practical advice about how this facilitation should be accomplished.

Trial-and-Error Approach

If you looked to Thorndike for help, you still might have troubles. You could utilize the law of effect by waiting until the pigeon *accidentally* knocked the ball down the alley. You could then ring the bell and give the bird some food, and this reward would increase the chances the bird would *repeat* its actions in the future. But how long would you have to wait until the pigeon *by accident* hit the ball straight down the alley the first time? The problem with Thorndike's approach, then, is that he doesn't give you a very efficient way of bringing about *the very first response.*

All of these components—*reward, repetition,* and *unlearned* or *innate responses*—are necessary if you are to train the pigeon and pass your exam. But putting them all together into a workable educational system took the genius of Harvard professor B.F. Skinner, who surely qualifies as being our most influential living psychologist.

B.F. Skinner's Techniques

According to Skinner, whenever you wish to change an organism's behavior, you always begin by defining *precisely* what it is you want to accomplish. For instance, to get your A, you must train the pigeon to bowl. But what do we mean by "bowling?" Do we have some objective, clear-cut, agreed-upon way of measuring the response pattern we call "bowling?" If so, then we know when to *terminate* the training, and we know when you've passed the exam.

Terminal Response or Goal

Bowling is obviously a complex *sequence of responses* that ends when the pigeon has whacked the ball down the alley toward the pins. Therefore, your goal must be that of getting the bird to hit the ball in the proper direction.

Skinner calls the *final* step in any chain of behaviors the *terminal response.* When the organism has performed this final act, the chain of responses is *terminated*—usually by a reward or punishment of some kind. Thus, when the pigeon finally "bowls," you will ring the bell and give the bird a pellet of food. And when the pigeon "bowls" regularly, you will terminate the training and receive your A.

The single most important thing about the terminal response, however, is that it must be *measurable.* As you will soon see, pigeons *can* be trained to bowl in two hours or less if you go about it the right way. However, how long do you think it would take to train a bird to be a "good sport"?

Question: College catalogues often state that the goal of a higher education is to turn students into "creative individuals" who are "good citizens" and "productive members of modern-day society." What might B.F. Skinner say about the *measurability* of such terminal responses?

Successive approximations to a goal. Rewarding any incremental (in-kree-MENT-tal) response that will lead the organism toward the terminal response. That is, reinforcing any slight behavioral change (increment) that represents a step in the right direction.

Reinforced. Concrete with steel rods inside it is called *reinforced* concrete, because the steel strengthens the concrete. Positive feedback reinforces an S-R bond by making it more likely the response will occur again the next time the stimulus input appears.

Taking a Baseline

Once you have a well-defined goal to work toward, you are ready to tackle the second stage in Skinner's analysis of behavioral change—that of determining what the organism is doing *before* you begin to train it. Skinner refers to these "prior responses" as the organism's *baseline behaviors*.

In order to determine the *baseline behavior*, you measure what the organism is already doing, and plot its responses on a graph or record of some kind. Skinner calls this "taking a baseline." Like the terminal response, the baseline behaviors must be stated in objective, measurable terms. Clever animal trainers (or people educators) always take advantage of the response patterns the organism brings to the training situation. You always build new learning on old, according to Skinner.

Successive Approximations

When you are sure of (1) the organism's baseline behaviors, and (2) the terminal behavior you hope to achieve, you are (3) ready to move from (1) to (2). Skinner suggests you do so in a *step-by-step* fashion called **successive approximations to a goal**.

Neither people nor pigeons typically change their behaviors in large, insightful jumps. We *can* do so occasionally, as the Gestalt theorists showed. But most of the time we change slowly, bit by bit, millimeter by millimeter. And we usually need to be coaxed and encouraged whenever we must acquire a new way of doing things. That is, we typically need to be rewarded or **reinforced** for each tiny step we make toward the goal. (We will have more to say about the importance of reward in a moment.)

The technique of *successive approximations to a goal* is one of the cornerstones of the Skinnerian system. But mastery of the step-by-step technique calls for rather a penetrating insight on your own part. Namely, you must realize that even the faintest, feeblest movement toward the goal is *a step in the right direction*, hence one

you must vigorously reward. Most people unfamiliar with Skinner's techniques seem unable or unwilling to analyze behavior in these terms. So, they give reinforcements grudgingly and infrequently. This fact may explain why most people would not be able to train a pigeon to bowl in two hours or less.

Behavioral Analysis

If we apply the Skinnerian *behavioral analysis* to the problem of getting your pigeon to perform, we can perhaps see how the technique works.

The terminal behavior your instructor has set is that of "bowling." But how shall we define it? Humans usually pick up the bowling ball in their hands and roll it down the alley. However, Mother Nature has given the pigeon wings instead of arms, and feathers are poor substitutes for fingers when it comes to lifting a heavy ball.

But could we teach an armless man to bowl? Couldn't the man kick the ball down the alley, or even butt it with his head? Do you really care how he manages it, so long as the ball zings down the alley and hits the pins?

One of the purposes of getting you to "take a baseline" of the pigeon's normal response patterns is this—it forces you to see what the bird *already* does that you can make use of during training. If you observe pigeons for a while, you will notice they use their beaks much as we use our hands. So if you can train the bird to hit the ball with its beak (so the ball rolls down the alley and hits the pins), you surely have taught the animal to "bowl" within the stated definition of the problem. And you surely should get an A on your exam.

Now that you know what your goal is, you can begin to take advantage of the baseline behaviors the pigeon already shows. At the start of training, the bird merely moves around nervously, inspecting its new environment. The final response you want from the animal is that of striking the ball with its beak. To make this terminal response, though, the animal must be standing *near the ball*. So your first task would seem to be that of getting the pigeon to move to where the ball is. But how to do it?

If you were training your child to bowl, you would probably explain to the child—in English—what you wanted the youngster to do. Or you could "model" the behaviors involved in bowling and tell the child to imitate you. Both verbal explanations and "modeling" are types of *feed-forward*. Then, when the child first approached the ball or picked it up, you would express your pleasure verbally. That's *feed-back*. But pigeons are non-verbal—they don't even speak "pidgin English." So, you can't use verbal explanations as "feed-forward." Instead, you use rewarding feedback until the bird achieves the behavioral output you have defined as the goal.

Question: How could you speed up learning, using a type of feed-forward as well as feedback? (Hint: One pigeon will often imitate the behaviors of another pigeon.)

Two Functions of Reward

Reward or positive reinforcement has at least two functions. First, it gives you *pleasure*, usually by satisfying some need or reducing some drive or deprivation state. But rewards also have an *informational* aspect to them, for they give you feedback as to how well you are doing, and how close you are coming to a goal. Both factors make it likely you will "do again" what you've been been rewarded for doing. Put more technically, positive reinforcement *increases the probability* that an organism will *repeat the response* that led to the appearance of the rewarding stimulus.

As we noted a few pages back, your pigeon has already been trained to go to the food cup when it hears the bell ring. Therefore, you can use the *sound of the bell* as a rewarding input whenever you want to let the pigeon know instantly it has made a step in the right direction toward the goal of bowling.

"Shaping" a Pigeon to Bowl

With these preliminaries out of the way, you would be ready to start passing your final examination. You know your goal; you know the bird's entering behavior; the animal is deprived of food; and you have an effective reinforcer available. What is your next step?

Actually, as Skinner points out, the next step is up to the bird. As it wanders around the box excitedly, at one time or another it will *accidentally* move toward the bowling ball. If you have the insight to recognize this simple movement as being "a step in the right direction"—and if you ring the bell *at once* and reward the animal with food—you will have no difficulty in training the bird to bowl. But if you insist the bird doesn't *deserve* a reward until it scores a strike, it may take you years to pass the exam—if you ever do.

Presuming you do sound the bell the first time the bird moves tentatively in the general direction of the ball, how does the pigeon respond? By running to the food cup to claim its reward. After eating the food, it will pause for a while near the food cup. But when pausing doesn't ring the bell, it will usually begin its random trial-and-error movements around the box again. Once more, as soon as it heads toward the ball, you sound the bell. And again the bird runs to the food cup and eats.

The fifth or sixth or tenth time the pigeon repeats this response, a very strange event often occurs. The bird behaves as if it has experienced a "flash of insight" into what is happening. That is, the pigeon acts as if it had discovered that it can actually control *your* behavior! All it has to do to *force* you to give it food is to move in a given direction.

Once your pigeon has learned the connection between *doing something* and *being rewarded*, you can go much faster with your training. Each time you sound the bell, the pigeon will dash to the food cup, then return at once to where it was the instant the bell rang. Now, on each successive trial, you merely wait until the animal accidentally moves one step nearer to the ball before you ring the bell. In a matter of minutes, the bird will be hovering over the bowling ball.

The Beak and the Ball

Once the bird is standing *over* the ball, you must find a way of getting the animal's beak *down to floor level*. Again, you go back to the natural responses the animal makes. As pigeons move, their heads bob up and down. Sometimes, then, the bird's beak is closer to the ball than at other times. An experienced animal trainer will soon perceive the bird's downward head movements as "good responses," and begin to reward them (see Fig. 14.5).

After several such reinforcements, the pigeon begins to return from the food cup holding its head a little lower than before. If you demand that the bird depress its head an additional inch or so on each subsequent trial, you can get it to touch the floor with its beak in a matter of minutes.

Question: Do you imagine that, at any time during training, the pigeon gains a cognitive awareness that it is "learning to bowl?" If you could somehow "explain" to the animal what you were doing, might this "cognitive understanding" speed up learning? Why?

On to the Goal

By now the pigeon's beak is close to the floor, and the bird is moving about near the ball. Within a few moments, its beak will touch the ball "accidentally." The skilled animal trainer now rings the bell joyously, knowing victory is near.

When the bird returns from claiming its reward, it typically takes a second swat at the ball. You reward it again. Soon, the pigeon is scooting back and forth from food cup to ball, whacking the ball each time it comes close to it.

Now it is up to you to shape the bird's "whacking responses" so the animal knocks the ball straight down the alley instead of merely hitting the ball at random. Such **shaping** should take only a few minutes, for at first you reinforce only those whacks that aim the ball in the general direction of the pins. Then you selectively reward those hits that are closer and closer *approximations* to your stated goal. The pigeon soon learns it will be fed only when it strikes the ball so it rolls straight down the alley and hits the pins.

An experienced pigeon handler can usually shape a hungry pigeon "to bowl" in less than an hour. (Training the animal to get a good score takes a little longer.)

Normal level

Fig. 14.5 Whenever the pigeon's head bobs below the normal level that it keeps its beak at, you ring the bell and reward the pigeon. Then, step by step, you reward it for moving its head lower and lower. Finally, the bird's beak will be on the floor, where the ball is.

Shaping. To "shape" a response is to bring it about using successive approximations to a goal. Thus *shaping* means "training an organism using operant conditioning techniques."

Negative reinforcement. Technically speaking, "positive" reinforcement is the *onset* or appearance of a stimulus input that "satisfies" an organism in some way. "Negative" reinforcement is the *termination* of a stimulus situation that the organism would ordinarily avoid. "Punishment" is the *onset* of a painful stimulus that the organism would ordinarily avoid, thus punishment is *not* (repeat *not*) the same thing as negative reinforcement. Punishment suppresses behaviors temporarily, or teaches an organism to avoid an unpleasant situation. Negative reinforcement strengthens behaviors by reducing a drive or terminating an unpleasant stimulus.

Question: Skinner has proved that almost any pigeon can learn to bowl, if trained in this step-by-step manner. Therefore, if *you* try to train a pigeon and it fails to learn, whose fault is it? Likewise, if you take a college course and don't do well, whom should we blame?

Analysis of Skinner's System

There are several fairly subtle points about the Skinnerian system that are sometimes overlooked:

1. Skinner differentiates between two "unpleasant" types of inputs, which have entirely different effects on behavior. The first is *punishment*, which is a painful input that the animal learns to avoid. The second is **negative reinforcement**, which occurs whenever you terminate a painful "drive state" such as extreme hunger. As we will see, *negative* reinforcement affects behavior in much the same way *positive* reinforcement does.

The difference between punishment and negative reinforcement is best seen in their *consequences*. Punishment *disrupts* behavioral sequences. It may occasionally *suppress* certain responses, but it does so only *temporarily*. And punishment seldom "wipes out" inappropriate behaviors. Thus, those teachers who threaten to punish you *unless* you perform correctly often teach you little more than to avoid them (and all academic settings).

Negative reinforcement, on the other hand, *strengthens* a behavioral sequence just as positive reinforcement does. Negative reinforcement is an input that *reduces* discom-

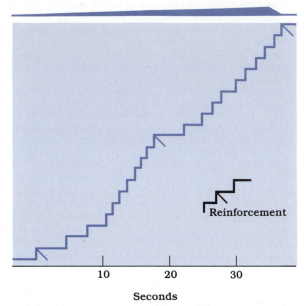

Fig. 14.6 A cumulative record of a pigeon trained to peck a button on a 10-to-1 fixed-ratio reinforcement schedule. Each vertical movement of the graph represents one press of the lever. Note that the pigeon responds more quickly just prior to a reinforcement than just afterward.

fort, while punishment is an input that *increases* pain or displeasure. Punishment leads to active avoidance and other types of emotional behaviors. Negative reinforcement, however, leads to approach behaviors and to learning.

The next time you visit a "marine world" of some kind, ask the animal trainers how they teach porpoises to perform in public. You'll find the trainers use reinforcement almost exclusively. If you punish a porpoise, it sulks in a corner for days. But if you give it food, you reinforce it both positively and negatively. First, the food tastes good. Second, it slightly reduces the animal's natural hunger. Animals don't hold trainers responsible for getting hungry. They do hold trainers responsible for the punishment they inflict, though. And if you punish a "killer whale," the consequences may be more disastrous for you than for the whale!

2. Notice that in teaching the pigeon to bowl, *no punishment* was necessary to get the animal to perform. The pigeon obviously *can* learn. If it fails to do so, the fault presumably lies with the teacher (or with the learning environment) and not with the student.

3. You control the *timing* of the reinforcement—but the pigeon determines whether it *wants* the reward you offered it. If the reinforcement is meaningful and satisfying to that particular bird, then the animal will work. But if you offer the animal something it doesn't want or need—or if you expect too much work for what you give the bird in return—it is free to rebel and ignore you. (Surprisingly, pigeons appear to enjoy this type of training and, once they have learned the task, will "bowl" again and again with but a minimal amount of encouragement.)

4. "Bowling" is obviously a very complicated set of responses that the animal has to learn in a *particular order or sequence*. You got the bird to learn one simple thing at a time, never demanding too much. You always encouraged the "right" things the pigeon did, and you ignored (or certainly didn't punish) its mistakes. And by doing so, you **chained** the sequence of responses together from its first approaching step to its last whack at the ball. However, the experienced pigeon will perform its bowling routine so smoothly and efficiently that it is not easy to see the various *individual responses* that have been chained together during training.

Question: If you can train a pigeon to bowl without using punishment, would it be possible to teach a child how to read and write without criticizing or spanking the child when she or he makes a mistake? Why aren't more children taught this way?

Schedules of Reinforcement

According to Skinner, at the beginning of training you should reward *each move* the bird makes toward the goal. However, once the pigeon has mastered a given response in the chain, you may begin slowly *fading out the reward* by reinforcing the response **intermittently**. You never fade out the reward completely. However, you can shift to a much less frequent *schedule* of reinforcement.

Continuous reinforcement is necessary at first, both to keep the animal eager to perform and to let it know it is doing something right. However, once the pigeon learns what that "something right" is, you may begin reinforcing the response every second time, then every third or fourth time, then perhaps every tenth time. If you fade out the reward very gradually, you can get a pigeon to repeat a simple response (such as pecking a button) several thousand times for each reinforcement.

During the fading process, the exact *scheduling* of the reward is crucial. If you reinforce *exactly* every tenth response, the bird will soon learn to anticipate which response will gain it food. As soon as it makes this tenth response and feeds, it will "take a break" because' it knows its next response never brings it any goodies. Skinner calls this **fixed-ratio reinforcement**, because the *ratio* between the number of responses required and the rewards given is fixed and never varies.

If we make a **cumulative record** of the time intervals between each response the animal makes, we would find it responds slowly just after a reinforcement, but more and more quickly as it approaches that response it knows will gain it the reward (see Fig. 14.6).

We can get the pigeon to respond at a more or less *constant* rate by tricking it a bit—that is, by rewarding it on a **variable-ratio schedule** rather than at a fixed ratio. Instead of reinforcing *exactly* the tenth response, we vary the schedule so that sometimes the third response yields food, sometimes the seventh, sometimes the eleventh, sometimes the twentieth—or any response in between. A hundred responses will yield *about* 10 rewards, but the bird will never know when the next reward is coming. When trained on variable-ratio schedules, pigeons respond vigorously and at a fairly constant pace.

We could also reward the pigeon using **interval reinforcement**. That is, we could reward the *first correct response* the bird made after (let's say) an interval of 2 minutes had passed. Generally speaking, however, *ratio* reinforcement is easier to use than is *interval* reinforcement.

Question: Do the slot machines in Las Vegas pay off on a fixed ratio or a variable ratio? Why?

"Shaping" Responses

"Shaping" any organism's responses is more of a psychological art than a science, and some people are much better behavioral artists than are others. Skinner says you should reward each successive step toward the behavioral goal you have in mind. But there are thousands of different response chains that might lead from the animal's baseline behaviors to the terminal goal. Unfortunately, Skinner doesn't tell you which one to pick, nor how to judge which pathway is best.

Lion tamers at the circus—as well as teachers at dog and cat "obedience schools"—often make use of Skinnerian principles in teaching

Chained. To write the word "cat" on a typewriter, you must first hit the "c" key, then the "a" key, then the "t." You will have made (at least) three different responses that are chained together to achieve the goal of typing the word "cat." Behaviorists believe complex human behavior patterns are mostly long chains of related responses that must be learned one at a time.

Intermittently (in-turr-MITT-tent-lee). If it rains on Monday, is clear on Tuesday, but rains again on Wednesday and Thursday, then it has rained intermittently during the week. If you reward a rat each third time it presses a bar, you are giving the animal intermittent reinforcement.

Fixed-ratio reinforcement. If you always reward a rat for each third bar-press it makes, the ratio between responses (bar-presses) and reward is fixed.

Cumulative record (CUE-mew-luh-tive). From the word *accumulate*, meaning "to acquire." As you grow older, your years are cumulative—that is, you never lose a year once you've lived through it. A cumulative record is an increasing graph or record of all the responses an animal makes in a certain time period. The record also shows the time between responses, and each reinforcement the animal receives.

Variable-ratio reinforcement. A schedule of reinforcement that involves rewarding the animal for *approximately* every 3rd (or 5th or 100th) correct response that it makes.

Interval reinforcement. Fixed-interval reinforcement involves rewarding the first response an organism makes after, say, 60 seconds. Variable-interval reinforcement involves rewarding the first response an organism makes, say, after *approximately* 60 seconds.

Instrumental conditioning. Also called "operant conditioning." A type of learning in which the organism must learn which of its responses will be instrumental in yielding a reward.

their beasts to perform dazzling tricks. But some lion trainers are much better at putting the "big cats" through their paces than are other animal handlers, just as some college instructors are more effective than others at rewarding successive approximations to educational goals. As you might guess, there is still considerable debate about what behavioral traits you should have in order to become an effective "shaper."

Question: Which parts of "shaping" seem to be left hemisphere traits? And which might be right hemisphere or "perceptual" traits?

Operant versus Respondent Conditioning

Skinner calls the type of learning he studies **instrumental conditioning**, or operant conditioning. Skinner chose the term "operant" because he believes the organism must learn to *operate*

Most animals used in movies and professional shows are trained using operant conditioning (reinforcement) techniques rather than punishment.

on its environment in order to get the reinforcers it desires. Stated in systems theory terms, the organism must somehow change its behavioral outputs until it finds one that is instrumental in bringing it the rewarding inputs it needs.

Skinner refers to Pavlovian training as **respondent conditioning**, because Pavlov taught his animals to *respond* in a specific way to a specific stimulus.

Elicited versus Emitted Responses

There are many differences between operant and respondent conditioning. Surely one of the most obvious ones is this—Pavlovian (respondent) learning is always tied to a unique and specific stimulus, while operant conditioning is not. Food powder blown into a dog's mouth **elicits** the salivary response. Pairing the bell with the food gives the bell the power to *elicit* the same sort of salivation—whether the dog likes it or not. The important point is that neither dogs nor humans go around salivating unless they are stimulated to do so by a highly specific sensory input. Respondent conditioning thus involves setting up involuntary, *elicited* responses to specific stimuli.

On the other hand, pigeons (and people) perform all kinds of actions that don't seem to be "elicited" or pulled out of the organism automatically. Rather, says Skinner we typically **emit** or produce a wide variety of behaviors rather freely. Those activities that are rein-

forced we tend to repeat. Those behaviors that aren't reinforced tend to drop out of our *behavioral repertory*.

Stimulus-Response Connections

Respondent conditioning involves attaching a *new stimulus* to an *already established response*. Thus, the important association in Pavlovian conditioning is that between the CS and the UCS. Once this connection is made, the connection between the CS and the CR follows rather automatically. Put another way, respondent conditioning is S-S-(R) learning.

Operant conditioning, however, involves attaching a *new response* to *already present stimulus inputs*. Thus, the important association is between the *response* itself and the *feedback* the response generates. This feedback, of course, is really a new sensory stimulus. So we can describe operant conditioning as (S)-R-S′ learning (where S′ is reinforcing feedback).

Pavlov didn't train his animals to respond in a new way. He merely taught them to give the same old salivation response to a new stimulus (the bell). Skinner, however, almost always teaches organisms to respond in ways they never have before. But the only new stimuli Skinner adds to the picture are those associated with reinforcement.

Voluntary versus Involuntary Muscles

Respondent conditioning typically involves those *involuntary muscle groups* controlled by the autonomic nervous system and the lower brain centers. Most emotional learning—such as acquiring a fear or a phobia—is a type of Pavlovian conditioning. The fear response is *already present* in the organism's repertory. All the respondent conditioning does is to attach the involuntary fear reaction to a *novel stimulus*.

Operant conditioning typically involves *voluntary muscle groups* controlled by the cortex and the higher brain centers. Motor skills—such as typing or playing football—are usually the result of operant conditioning. Put another way, acquiring a motor skill involves learning a new way of responding to stimuli that were already present in your environment.

The subtle differences between operant and respondent conditioning are probably of greater interest to learning theorists than to anyone else. For almost all real-life learning involves *both types of conditioning*. And both kinds of conditioning are built on the innate response tendencies that most organisms are born with.

Question: Suppose you trained a dog to press a bar to get food, using operant techniques. Do you think that, at some time during the training, the animal might learn involuntarily to salivate at the sight of the bar?

Biofeedback

For many years, psychologists believed it was nearly impossible to use Skinnerian techniques to help organisms gain voluntary control over their autonomic responses. Recently, however, a number of experiments using a technique called **biofeedback** have challenged this view.

Biofeedback in Medicine

Suppose you were a physician trying to treat a 40-year-old woman suffering from hypertension, or high blood pressure. And further suppose the woman was so sensitive to drugs that you couldn't use any kind of medication to help lower her blood pressure. What could you do to help?

You might begin by teaching her the "relaxation techniques" we discussed in the previous chapter. But surely it would help if the patient had some way of knowing when her blood pressure was rising, and when it was falling. You might then hook the woman up to a machine that gave her *visual feedback* about a specific

Respondent conditioning. Also called "classical conditioning" or "Pavlovian conditioning." So named because the organism always responds to presentation of the CS with the CR.

Elicits (ee-LISS-sits). To elicit is to pull out, to evoke, to stimulate into action. In Pavlovian conditioning, the stimulus that elicits the CR is always identifiable.

Emit (ee-MITT). The important association in operant conditioning is between the response itself and the reward that follows. If a rat is trained to press a lever only when a light is turned on, the rat is said to "emit" the response *in the presence of* the light stimulus—however, the light doesn't really elicit the bar-press response. It merely serves as a "discriminative" stimulus that lets the rat know that if it now emits a response, that response will be rewarded.

Biofeedback. Literally, biological feedback. Any mechanism that feeds back information on biological performance.

biological response (her blood pressure). If she *saw* the pressure was rising, she could "go limp" and try to think relaxing thoughts. And if she *saw* the pressure was falling, she could try to remember what she was thinking so she could repeat that calming thought in the future.

In their 1980 book *Biofeedback*, David Olton and Aaron Noonberg report considerable success in training hypertensive patients to gain voluntary (operant) control over heart rate and blood pressure. Olton and Noonberg have also found biofeedback useful in treating asthma, epilepsy, stomach disorders and migraine headaches. In all these cases, Olton and Noonberg state, the secret of success lies in finding some way of giving patients new types of feedback about their involuntary bodily processes. During a migraine attack, for instance, patients often experience great tension in their neck and facial muscles. When given visual or auditory feedback on how tense their muscles are, however, the patients often are able to reduce muscle tension voluntarily. According to Olton and Noonberg, this operant control of muscle tension frequently helps reduce the severity of the headache (see Fig. 14.7).

Biofeedback: An Evaluation

When biofeedback first appeared on the psychological scene, it seemed a "cure-all" for a variety of ills. However, recent findings have dampened the enthusiasm of all but the most ardent advocates of the technique.

Biofeedback does help *some* patients with certain types of problems. But the *cause* of the relief is now open to question. Take migraine headaches, for example. A recent study by Frank Andrasik and Kenneth Holroyd shows

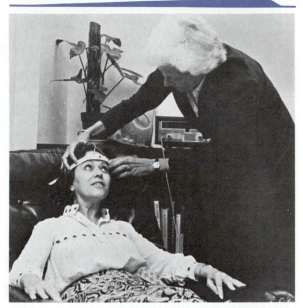

Fig. 14.7 This woman, using biofeedback, can reduce the pain of a migraine headache by learning to lower the temperature of her forehead.

that biofeedback can reduce the severity of the headache, but perhaps not for the reasons Olton and Noonberg suggested.

Andrasik and Holroyd tested four groups of students who suffered severe tension headaches. Subjects in the three experimental groups were individually connected to biofeedback devices that supposedly measured tension in (1) facial and neck muscles, and (2) in arm muscles. These subjects were informed they would hear a tone that would *decrease* in pitch as the tension in their muscles *dropped*. Andrasik and Holroyd suggested that, in order to "lower the tone," the students might try thinking peaceful thoughts, or just relaxing, or even try concentrating on the tone itself.

Subjects in the fourth group received no training or biofeedback at all, and thus served as controls.

The students in the first experimental group were given *accurate* biofeedback. That is, the tone *decreased in pitch* as tension in their face and neck muscles *decreased*, just as the experimenters had said it would. (However, the electrodes placed on their arms were fakes.) The subjects in the second and third groups were given *inaccurate* biofeedback. That is, the tone they heard *decreased in pitch* as tension in either face and neck muscles (group two) or arm muscles (group three) *increased*. So these stu-

dents were actually being trained to *raise* muscle tension rather than *decrease* it.

Andrasik and Holroyd state that all three experimental groups reported a significant reduction in the severity of their headaches, while control-group subjects did not. Thus, we can conclude that biofeedback training had some positive effect. The subjects in the first experimental group noted the fastest improvement. So, *relaxation* does have a quick and positive influence on reducing headaches. By the end of six weeks of training, however, the subjects in groups two and three reported the same level of headache reduction as did the students in the first experimental group.

How can an *increase* in muscle tension help reduce the severity of "tension headaches"? Andrasik and Holroyd believe that what we might call *cognitive skills* may be the answer. They report that all their experimental subjects developed "one or more mental exercises" to achieve success during biofeedback training. The students then used these mental exercises whenever they felt a headache coming on. According to Andrasik and Holroyd, "it may be less crucial that headache sufferers learn to directly modify [muscular tension] than it is that they learn to monitor the insidious onset of headache symptoms and engage in some sort of coping response incompatible with the further *exacerbation* of symptoms."

Put more simply, biofeedback may "work" for two reasons. First, because it actually helps you gain voluntary control over some of your bodily activities. But second, biofeedback may be useful clinically because it helps you learn "cognitive strategies" for disrupting or suppressing painful inputs. We will have more to say about this point in Chapter 16, when we discuss hypnosis.

There's an interesting point to be made here. Both biofeedback and Skinner's "shaping" technique started out as being purely *behavioral* types of training. However, both approaches appear to be more successful when they are used to teach people control of cognitive activities *as well as* control of behavioral outputs.

Skinner's Approach:
An Evaluation

B.F. Skinner has developed what is clearly the most advanced technology the world has ever known for helping people change their behaviors. It has probably done more *measurable* good for more people than any other type of psychological training technique. As powerful as the Skinnerian system is, however, it suffers from the same narrowness of view that afflicts most other psychological theories.

For one thing, Skinner views the organism as being a *passive receptor* of stimuli from the outside world. You have no "free will," because your actions are determined primarily by your past reinforcement history and your present environment. "People have assumed from the beginning of time that they initiate their own actions," Skinner said in an interview printed in the New York *Times* on September 15, 1981. "To suppose this is a great mistake." Instead of your *selecting* your own behaviors, he says, the environment does this for you. Skinner thus banishes all of motivational and cognitive psychology from what he calls "the scientific study of behavior."

Nor does he give much *credence* to biology. "I don't deny the importance of genetics," he said in the *Times* interview. However, Skinner believes that the only thing your genes do for you is to "program" you to respond to environmental inputs in an operant manner. Skinner thus dismisses most of biopsychology from his system.

And because he pays most attention to the effects that the environment has on *individual*

organisms, Skinner pays little attention to social psychology. Thus, the study of group processes and other social variables seems a waste of time. For from Skinner's viewpoint, "scientific psychology" consists entirely of the study of the effects the outside world has on the measurable behaviors of *individual* organisms.

Skinner and Self-Control

Skinner takes a very pessimistic view of the world these days, primarily because he views organisms as *passive* rather than *active living systems.* He looks at people from the outside in, and refuses even to guess at "what goes on inside the mind." He talks about feedback, but not about feed-forward. He measures biological rewards such as food, but ignores most intrapsychic reinforcers such as pride and self-esteem. And he refuses to deal with such concepts as perceptions, cognitions, and self-awareness. Thus he fails to understand the importance of such "systems properties" as *self-control.*

When Skinner trains a pigeon to bowl, *he* determines what the goal of the training will be, *he* measures the entering behaviors of the bird, and *he* selectively reinforces approximations to the goal. The bird *behaves*; Skinner *monitors* these behaviors and *gives the animal feedback* in order to shape its responses. Because Skinner can tell you what he is doing as he goes along, he can describe both the terminal response and the approximations in measurable terms. Thus, he doesn't need to talk about what goes on inside the pigeon's mind. And he can legitimately claim that such intra-psychic concepts as "thinking" and "self-control" aren't needed in order to explain behavior.

However, humans are more complex systems than are pigeons. Because of this complexity, you can use operant techniques to change your own outputs *voluntarily*—a technique now called "self-shaping." The problem for Skinner is that this sort of *self*-determined, *self*-monitored, and *self*-rewarded change is difficult to explain in purely operant terms.

Cognitive Behavior Modification
Skinner's demand that psychologists deal with measurable events was certainly a step in the right direction. And the techniques of *behavior modification* he developed in the 1940's and 1950's have obviously given us powerful tools for bringing about change. However, even Skinner's own students seem to have passed him by.

By the 1960's, several psychologists had shown that operant techniques could be used to shape thoughts and perceptions as well as overt actions. Intra-psychic events (such as attitudes and emotions) became "inner behaviors" that obeyed the same operant principles as did such "overt behaviors" as bowling. Simple operant technology thus evolved into *cognitive behavior modification*, and behavioral therapists started shaping their patients' thoughts and feelings as successfully as they shaped muscle movements.

As we noted, no one living has contributed more to psychology than has B.F. Skinner. But, in a sense, you demonstrate the narrowness of his viewpoint each time you have a creative insight, experience the joy of learning, think through a problem, or voluntarily control your thoughts, feelings, or behavioral outputs in order to achieve some personal goal.

Question: Do you consider alcoholism a disease (or perhaps a "mental disorder")? What do you think the *goal* of treating this problem should be, and what techniques do you think work best with alcoholic patients? What data do you have to support your beliefs? How would a *purely behavioral* view of the problem differ from yours, both in terms of *measurable goal* and *treatment plan*?

Behavior Modification *versus* Psychotherapy

Like Joseph Wolpe—whose desensitization therapy we described in Chapter 13—Fred Skinner believes that symptomatic behaviors associated with "mental disorders" are actually learned. Thus, therapy should consist of helping people learn new and healthier habits. Most psychotherapists, of course, take the opposite view. They see "mental illness" as being just that—a disorder of the mind, not a disorder of learned behavioral outputs.

The cognitive behaviorists stand somewhere in between these two extremes. They agree with Skinner that the ultimate focus in most types of therapy must be on learning new behavior patterns. But the cognitive behaviorists believe that teaching people how to control their own thoughts and feelings is often a very effective way of helping people learn to control their behavioral outputs.

We will discuss these issues at length in later chapters. But to give you a better understanding of both the strengths and the limitations of

the behavioral approach, let's look at recent research on therapy with alcoholic patients.

Question: If a symptomatic behavior has been heavily reinforced for many years, why might it not "disappear more or less automatically" once the underlying problem is solved? What type of *retraining technique* could you employ to reduce the strength of the symptomatic response?

Alcoholism: Disease or Learned Behavior?

Millions of Americans consume alcohol on a regular basis. But only about 5 percent of these people are "problem drinkers." What is wrong with this small group of individuals? Why can 95 percent of the population *voluntarily control* their alcohol intake, while the other 5 percent can't?

There are two main schools of thought today as to what alcoholism is and how to treat it. One school views alcoholism as a *disease*. The other school perceives problem drinking as a *failure to learn self-control techniques*.

Question: How would the term you used— "alcoholism" versus "problem drinking"—bias your beliefs both as to the causes and the cures of the disorder?

The Disease Model

The "disease model" of alcoholism was first put forward by E.M. Jellinek in 1960. According to Jellinek, alcoholism is a *medical disorder* that has a biological basis. Because of *defective genes* (or perhaps a combination of genetic and developmental problems), the alcoholic cannot control her or his drinking the way "normal" people can. The alcoholic becomes *dependent* on alcohol, and comes to *crave* it the way a heroin addict "craves a fix." Since this is a *chemical dependency*, Jellinek implies, the only solution to the dependency must be total withdrawal from drinking.

People who adopt the disease model generally believe alcoholism is a "progressive disorder." Therefore, there can be no "cure" for the problem. However, the course of the illness can be *arrested* if the alcoholic gives up drinking entirely. Thus, the goal of treatment must be **abstinence**, or complete *sobriety*. For, theoretically speaking, even one drink will reinstitute both the craving and the progressive physical deterioration. And, to help alcoholics achieve sobriety, disease-model therapists often use confrontation (and even punishment) to condition patients to avoid alcohol—much as Watson used a loud noise to condition Little Albert to avoid white rats.

Question: In Chapter 3, we reported data (the "think-drink" effect) showing that alcoholics who consumed alcohol but thought they were drinking tonic water showed no "craving" for alcohol. But alcoholics who drank tonic water believing it was alcohol did report "cravings." How are these data an attack on the disease model?

The Behavioral Model

In 1962, British physician D.L. Davies published a report that seemed to challenge Jellinek's disease model of alcoholism. Davies studied a group of 93 alcoholics for almost 10 years after they had received "abstinence training" in a hospital setting. Some of the patients had achieved and maintained sobriety. Most had fallen into alcoholic drinking patterns again. However, 7 of the 93 had become "normal, social drinkers." That is, while they did consume about the same amount of alcohol as the average non-problem drinker does, these ex-patients were no longer *alcoholics* in terms of their symptomatic behaviors.

Davies—and many other behaviorally oriented researchers—decided that the disease model was incorrect. These scientists further concluded that the major difficulty most alcoholics have is this: They never learned the type of "self-control" most people acquire early in life. The researchers then set out to find ways to *teach* alcoholics the cognitive and behavioral skills they lacked.

Sobriety versus Controlled Drinking

Rather than forcing alcoholics to achieve *total abstinence*, the cognitive-behavioral approach attempts to help them become "non-problem" drinkers. From this viewpoint, if the person no longer has any alcohol-related *difficulties*, then the alcoholism has been "cured" for all practical purposes.

In stark constrast, the disease-model position is that alcoholism *cannot be cured*. Disease-model researchers contend that patients who learn to moderate their intake are *still alcoholics*, despite the fact that most of them no longer have any significant alcohol-related problems.

Abstinence (AB-stin-nence). From the Latin word meaning "to hold (off)." If you abstain from drinking, you are engaging in abstinence from alcohol.

The question then becomes, how shall we decide which view is right?

The "Cure Rate" Controversy

You might think that scientific controversies such as this one would be settled on the basis of research findings rather than arguments. However, that's seldom the case in science or in any other human activity.

To begin with, alcoholism is a difficult problem to treat, no matter what view you take of its causes.

Second, research findings can often be interpreted in more than one way. For example, in the early 1970's, the National Institute on Alcohol Abuse and Alcoholism (NIAAA) commissioned the Rand Corporation to analyze data collected at three NIAAA treatment centers. The first Rand report was published in 1976. The data showed that *more than half* of the 597 patients treated from the disease-model perspective had returned to *uncontrolled* drinking 18 months after treatment. Only 24 percent "achieved and maintained sobriety for a substantial period of time."

Oddly enough, the first Rand report also showed that 22 percent of the patients had *voluntarily* achieved a normal level of "social drinking." They were not treated with this goal in mind. Rather, the patients apparently had learned to control their alcohol intake on their own.

Other Research Findings

The second Rand report involved a four-year follow-up of patients trained *either* from the "disease model" or the "learned behavior" perspective. The data showed that the "controlled drinking" approach achieved significantly better results than did abstinence training.

Given these data, you might ask why the controversy continues. In an article in the October 1983 *American Psychologist*, University of Washington psychologist G. Alan Marlatt offers this answer: "Scientific evaluations of treatment outcome such as the Rand reports have been branded as heresy by traditionalists in the field who claim that the publication of such results has itself precipitated relapse among otherwise abstinent alcoholics."

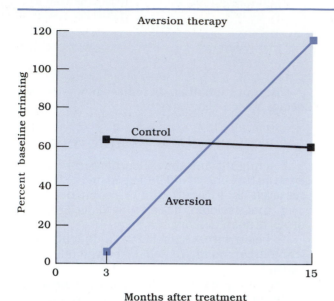

Aversion therapy

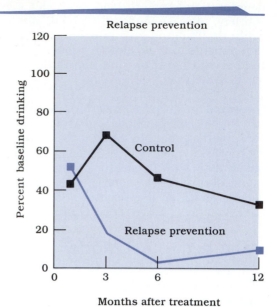

Relapse prevention

Fig. 14.8A and B Amount of alcohol consumed after treatment by two groups of experimental patients (and two groups of untreated controls) in study of controlled drinking by G. Alan Marlatt.

G. Alan Marlatt

Marlatt and most other cognitive behaviorists see the "alcoholism problem" as one of teaching people self-management skills. However, Marlatt says, most people who take the disease-model perspective refuse to accept "controlled drinking" as a worthy therapeutic goal. From their standpoint, turning an alcoholic into a social drinker is no more a "cure" than would be therapy designed to turn murderers into muggers.

Question: Which would you think is a *better* outcome, complete abstinence or controlled drinking? Why?

Psychotherapy *plus* Cognitive Behavior Modification

There are several purposes of this lengthy excursion into alcoholism, none of which has to do with proving one viewpoint wrong or the other right. For, as you will see, there is much to be said for both approaches.

First, the manner in which you *perceive* the human organism strongly influences how you will *diagnose* human ills, what types of *treatment* you will prefer, and what you will consider a *cure*. Thus, we often cannot decide matters "on the basis of empirical data," because scientists don't always agree on what the data actually are.

Second, the best form of treatment would seem to be a *mix* of techniques derived from the various perspectives. Perhaps a brief look at research from G. Alan Marlatt's laboratory may show why this is the case. The data also demonstrate how different the effects of using reward and punishment can be.

Aversion Training

More than a decade ago, Marlatt and his associates tried using *punishment* as a means of reducing alcohol consumption. Thirteen male chronic alcoholics were given **aversion training** in addition to abstinence training. That is, several times each day they were offered drinks they could consume or not consume, as they chose. But if they drank, they received a painful electric shock with each sip of alcohol. Marlatt and his colleagues hoped the *pairing* of pain with the sight, smell, and taste of alcohol would create a "conditioned emotional aversion" to drinking. Following this treatment, the subjects were studied for a period of 15 months to see how they fared "on their own." The results are shown in Fig. 14.8A.

Compared with an unshocked control group of chronic alcoholics given abstinence training but *no shock*, the subjects in the "aversion training" group showed an *immediate* reduction of alcohol consumption. However, when the two groups were tested 15 months later, the patients in the shocked group were now drinking much *more* than the control-group patients.

As Marlatt puts it in his 1983 article, "unless a new alternative response to drinking is established during the initial suppression stage . . . the old drinking patterns will gradually return as the impact of the aversion extinguishes over time."

Question: How do these results support Thorndike's law of effect, which states that "punishment *suppresses* responses temporarily rather than breaking S-R connections?"

Relapse Prevention Training

These results led Marlatt to give alcoholic patients cognitive-skills training instead of electric shock. He hoped this training would prevent relapse. According to Marlatt, "subjects in the relapse prevention group received a total of eight biweekly treatment sessions in which they practiced behavioral and cognitive coping skills to deal with a variety of high-risk situations for relapse (e.g., coping with anger, social pressure situations, etc.)." The data from this study are shown in Fig. 14.8B. As the graphs indicate, the skills training apparently was successful *in the long run*. However, note one important point: The *immediate* effect of "skills training" is an *increase* in alcohol consumption (as compared to the control-group subjects).

Marlatt believes *different skills* are needed at various stages in the therapeutic process. Early in treatment, as subjects struggle to achieve self-control, they have to learn how to *decrease* alcohol consumption. Later, they need to learn how to *maintain their gains*. As Marlatt puts it, "future treatment research may show that intervention procedures may be differentially ef-

Aversion training. Pairing punishment with an undesirable response with the hope that the pain associated with the punishment will generalize to the response and thus prevent its recurrence.

fective at each stage of the change process, from cessation (e.g., aversion therapy) to maintenance (e.g., relapse prevention)."

Question: How does the graph in Fig. 14.8B compare with the "trial-and-error" learning curve shown in Fig. 14.1? What does this comparison tell you about Thorndike's belief that "animals and humans learn the same way?"

A Holistic Approach

As we have said many times before, behavior is multi-determined. Thus, any attempt to change behavior must address all the factors that influence those response outputs.

Confronting an alcoholic with his or her problems may well lead to a suppression of drinking, just as Pavlov and Watson would have predicted. But the data suggest that this response suppression is often fairly temporary—just as Thorndike discovered was the case whenever threats and punishment are used. Rewarding alcoholics for learning new responses that compete with "the urge to drink" does help, just as Wolpe showed was frequently true with other types of "counter-conditioning." However, teaching alcoholics the cognitive skills involved in self-control is equally important. For you can't always have some external agency (such as Fred Skinner) standing over the alcoholic to administer positive reinforcement at just the right time.

Put another way, effective treatment of alcoholism may well need to begin with *external* control. However, the locus of control probably must be *internalized* if long-term success is your goal. And "internalized control" is the aim of most types of cognitive behavior modification.

Finally, *any type of therapy* probably goes better if you help the person solve a wide range of social and personal problems *in addition to* changing symptomatic behaviors.

To summarize, each of the various theories of learning tells us something important about how organisms acquire (and change) response outputs. But no one theory gives us the complete story.

We will discuss these matters again in several

later chapters. However, there is one important aspect of learning we've not yet touched upon—that of *memory*. So, it is to this topic that we now turn our attention.

Question: How could you use the various theories of learning to construct a holistic approach to education?

Summary

1   E.L. Thorndike assumed that humans learn in much the same way that animals do. His studies with cats in a **puzzle box** led him to believe most new behaviors come about by **trial and error learning**.

2   Thorndike stated learning is influenced by two laws:

   a   The **law of exercise** states that the more frequently an animal repeats an **S-R bond**, the stronger it becomes.

   b   The **law of effect** states that stimulus-response (S-R) bonds are strengthened if the effect of the response is **satisfying**. Early in his career, Thorndike believed punishment "broke" S-R bonds, but later he stated punishment only **suppresses** responses temporarily.

3   Thorndike, like Pavlov, believed all learning is mechanical or **reflexive**. **Gestalt psychologists**, such as Wolfgang Koehler, assume that animals are capable of solving problems mentally (through **insight**) rather than just through mechanical trial and error.

4   According to Tolman, animals do not learn a maze by acquiring hundreds of S-R connections. Rather, they make a **cognitive map** of the maze, which guides their behavior.

5   Skinner believes animals **emit** responses freely and that the environment **rewards** some of those responses but ignores or punishes others.

6   According to Skinner, **reinforcement** tends to increase the probability that an organism will emit the same response the next time it is free to do so.

7   Training an organism by operant (Skinnerian) techniques consists of several steps:

   a   The **terminal response** or goal of the training must be stated in measurable terms.

   b   The **baseline behaviors** (what the organism is doing before intervention begins) must be measured precisely.

   c   Those baseline behaviors that seem directed toward the terminal response are **rewarded**. All other responses are *ignored*.

   d   Each small step toward the goal is reinforced—a technique called **shaping**.

8   Generally speaking, **variable-ratio reinforcement schedules** yield smoother **cumulative records** (response curves) than do **fixed-ratio schedules**.

9   Punishment differs from **negative reinforcement**, which involves rewarding a response by terminating an unpleasant drive or stimulus.

10 Generally speaking, Pavlovian or respondent conditioning involves those **involuntary muscles** controlled by the **autonomic nervous system**.

11 Generally speaking, operant conditioning involves those **voluntary muscles** controlled by the **cortex** and **higher brain centers**.

12 The proper use of **biofeedback** can sometimes allow you to gain voluntary control over such involuntary responses as your heart rate, skin temperature, and so forth.

13 In the 1960's, many behavioral psychologists adapted Skinner's techniques to the shaping of thoughts and feelings, a technique called **cognitive behavior modification**.

14 The two major explanations of alcoholism are the **disease model** and the **learned behavior model**. Disease-model theorists believe the goal of treatment should be **abstinence**. Learning theorists believe that **controlled drinking**—which involves **skills training**—is a more achievable goal.

15 Alcoholism is probably best treated by a mix of **aversion training** (or social confrontation) during the early stages of therapy and **skills training** to maintain initial gains.

(Continued from page 367.)

FROM: Experimenter-in-Chief, Interstellar Labship PSYCH-192
TO: Director, Bureau of Science

Thlan, my friend, this will be an informal memo. I will send the official report along later, but I wanted to give you my impressions first.

The work with the newly discovered species is, unfortunately, at a standstill. Things went well at first. We picked what seemed to be a average but healthy animal and began testing it with our standard apparatus. I may have told you that this new species looks much like our usual laboratory subject, the White Rote. So we gave it a couple of the "toys" that the Rotes seem fond of—thin sheets of material made from woodpulp and a tiny stick of graphite. Imagine our delight when this new specimen made exactly the same use of the materials as have many of the Rotes. Could it be that there are certain innate behavior patterns to be found throughout the universe in the lower species?

The answer is of little importance, really. Your friend Verpk keeps insisting that the marks the Rotes make on the sheets are an attempt at communication, but that is, of course, utterly impossible. (Why did you saddle me with this idiot, anyway, when there are so many reasonable-thinking scientists available?) At any rate, this "scribbling" behavior did give us hope that the new species would behave according to accepted theory.

And at first this was the case. The animal solved the Bfian Box problem in short order, yielding as beautiful data as I have ever seen. We then shifted it to mazes and jump stand problems, and the results were equally pleasing. The animal clearly learns by bonding stimuli with responses in purely mechanical fashion.

Then, just to please Verpk, we tested it on the Oddity Problem. Now you and I both understand that lower organisms are not that bright, even if some cognitive theorists (whom I shall not name) disagree. For a few terrible trials, it seemed that those nameless theorists might be right! Which is to say that the animal *appeared* to react correctly even to stimuli it had never seen before! What an annoyance that would be, since we are committed to "protecting" species intelligent enough to form concepts.

Ah, well, not to worry. The Oddity Problem apparently overloaded its simple brain circuits, for the organism soon broke down and became quite ill. Probably just as well, since this species is obviously unsuited for further experimentation.

I am not sure what to do next, either with this specimen or the world from which we took it. One of the students has nursed the animal back to some sort of health, and wishes to keep it as a pet. Verpk, however, suggests we put it back where we found it, and that we begin a crash program to to see if these organisms really are concept-formers. Stupid suggestion, but I pass it along anyhow. My own belief is that we should sacrifice the animal and study its anatomy carefully to determine if it really is related to the White Rote.

But that is not why I write. Since this new species tends to break down readily under stress—much like Lavpov's Wogs—I see little sense in wasting our time in this part of the universe. We will not serve either our race or our glorious theories by studying what is clearly another stupid species.

The question is, then, should we stay here and continue our work as Verpk insists, or should we look for healthier and more normal animals elsewhere? And if we depart, should we first destroy the "home colony" so that these pests cannot be used in unscientific ways by those cognitive theorists whom I refuse to name?

Since all lower species are under your protection, we need your advice. My hope is that you will let us seek out new colonies and test our theories with *healthy* animals. For it is only in this fashion that science, as we know it, progresses.

Respectfully yours,
Iowyy

Recommended Readings

Hay, W.M. & Nathan, P.E. (Eds.). (1982). *Clinical case studies in the behavioral treatment of alcoholism.* New York: Plenum Press.

Hergenhahn, B.R. (1982). *An introduction to theories of learning* (2nd ed.). Englewood Cliffs, N.J.: Prentice-Hall.
Skinner, B.F. (1960). *Walden two.* New York: Macmillan.
Skinner, B.F. (1978). *Reflections on behaviorism and society.* Englewood Cliffs, N.J.: Prentice-Hall.

Did You Know That...

- You have not one memory system, but many different types?
- Your visual system momentarily stores an "exact photo" of what you see, but your brain "forgets" most of what your eyes see?
- Your Short-term Memory is limited to about seven items?
- Your Long-term Memory consists in part of "mental file cards" that allow you to reconstruct past events rather than remember them exactly?
- There are a number of mnemonics or "memory tricks" that can help you remember?
- Amnesia typically involves forgetting "what" but not "how to"?
- People suffering from aphasia sometimes can remember how to drive a car, but can't say the word "car" when they see one?
- Some scientists believe that, when you learn, your brain manufactures new "memory molecules"?
- Some experiments suggest these "memory molecules" can be transferred from one organism to another by injection?

15

Memory

"Where Is Yesterday?"

"Custard cups?" Bill Plautz said in a shocked tone of voice, as he unpacked the groceries. "You and Tom bought 32 glass custard cups?"

"Sure," Devin Eckhoff replied, a happy smile on his face. "They were only a dime apiece."

"You two paid 10 cents *each* for 32 glass custard cups?" Bill continued in an outraged tone of voice. "And you took the money out of our *grocery* budget?"

"Sure," Tom Laine said, sitting down at the kitchen table. "Better than taking it out of the beer budget."

Mike Keller looked up from his math book. "The four of us share and share alike in this apartment, Tom. So how could you and Devin spend $3.20 plus 16¢ sales tax for glass dishes, particularly when you know I don't even *like* custard!"

"The cups aren't for custard," Devin said. "They're for the worms."

"Oh," said Bill, his voice dropping a full octave on that single word. "Why didn't you say so?"

"You didn't ask," Tom responded.

Bill rummaged through the grocery bag a bit more. "And what is this tiny piece of beef liver for? Are we supposed to make a meal of this?"

"No, but the worms will love it," Devin said. "They don't eat very much, you know."

Mike sighed. "Neither will we, if you guys whoop off all our grocery money on worm dishes and beef liver."

"Well," Tom said. "You know we all agreed to work together on the research project that's required for our lab course in animal behavior."

"Yeah," Devin continued. "And we all agreed we'd try to condition planarian flatworms, to see if they could learn."

"Nobody's done it before, remember?" Tom said excitedly.

"I still don't see why we have to do this research project in our kitchen," Bill said, continuing to put away the food that Devin and Tom had bought.

"Because Professor Sauermann hates flatworms," Devin replied. "So he won't let us work in the animal labs."

Mike groaned. "That's no way to get an A on our project, you know. Doing research that Sauermann doesn't approve of."

"Our worm project is going to be so fantastic, he's bound to approve of it eventually," Tom said. "It might even make us famous!"

"Humph," Bill said, reaching the bottom of the grocery bag. "And what, may I ask, are these tiny camel's hair brushes for? Are we going to paint the worms different colors, or something?"

"We need the brushes to transfer the worms from the cups to the training trough," Devin replied. "You can't just pick 'em up with your fingers, you know. They're slippery little rascals, and they're only about an inch long."

"Speaking of worms, where are we going to get them?" Mike asked.

Tom laughed. "We're going to 'liberate' them from the pond in front of the biology building. I was over there yesterday. There are hundreds of the wee beasties crawling around in the muck at the bottom of the pond."

"And what about the training trough?" Mike asked.

"That's my department," Bill replied. "I'm working in Dr. Eastrum's chem lab this semester. He's got a dandy block of plastic he isn't using, and I can borrow his tools to gouge a tiny trough into it. And I've tucked away a

couple of thick brass pins I can insert at either end of the trough to use as electrodes to pass shock through the water in the trough."

Devin frowned. "We still need a shock source of some kind."

"Dr. Calvin was showing me through the Psych Department Museum the other day," Mike replied. "They've got boxes and boxes of junky old equipment stuck away in the back room. One entire box was filled with strange metal devices that Dr. Calvin called 'Harvard inductoriums.'"

"Called *what*?" Tom asked.

"Inductoriums," Mike replied. "They're an old-fashioned contraption invented at Harvard around the turn of the century. Psychologists used them to shock undergraduates in verbal learning studies, or something."

"Do you think it would work with worms in a water-filled trough?" Bill asked.

"Probably," Mike replied. "And think how impressed Dr. Sauermann would be if we told him we gave our planarians a 'Harvard education.'"

Devin laughed, then turned serious. "All right, you guys. It's time we got organized. Mike, you go over to the Psych Building and see if you can scrounge one of those inductoriums when nobody's looking. And Bill, you go over to Eastrum's lab and get that trough put together."

"What about you and Tom?" Mike asked.

Tom grinned. "We're off to the biology pond to free 32 flatworms from their muckish existence."

"What are you going to do if somebody catches you?" Bill asked.

"Oh, we'll worm our way out of it somehow," Devin replied.

"I found a couple of fat ones," Tom said, carefully brushing two flatworms off a leaf into the bucket of water that he and Devin had beside them.

"Great," Devin replied.

"Hey, what are you two guys doing?" a biology student asked, walking up to the pond.

Tom looked up at the young man. "Gathering specimens for an experiment."

"What kind of specimens?"

"Flatworms," Devin said casually.

"Oh, platyhelminthes," the biology student said knowingly. "What are you going to do with them?"

"We're going to train them in a conditioning trough," Devin replied.

The biology student shook his head in dismay. "Don't be silly. Worms can't learn."

"How do you know that?" Tom asked.

"Because I was reading Libbie Hyman's classic work on platyhelminthes just last week, and she says they can't learn. That's why," the student replied.

"Why can't they?" Devin responded. "They've got brains and a primitive nervous system. They've even got synapses?"

The biology student laughed. "Who cares about synapses? If worms could learn, a zoologist would have done the study already. And then it would be reported in Hyman."

"Well, did any zoologist you know of ever try to condition a planarian?" Tom asked.

"Of course not," the student replied. "It would be a

waste of time, because organisms that simple are incapable of forming associations."

Devin looked at Tom, and then grinned broadly. "Well, judging from the specimens I've seen today, I'm not sure that even biology students are capable of learning."

The biology student shifted uncomfortably on his feet. "Does the Chairman of the Biology Department know you're stealing our worms?"

"No," said Tom. "But we'll be sure to give the Biology Department credit when we publish our study proving planarians can learn."

"Yeah," Devin continued. "We'll mention you guys in a worm-sized footnote."

"Well, now, let's see," Bill said, laying out all of the equipment on the kitchen table. "We've got the worms . . ."

"Thirty-two fat and healthy specimens, housed in individual custard cups," Tom remarked in a happy tone of voice.

"We've got the trough gouged out of the plastic block that I swiped from Eastrum's laboratory. It's precisely 8 inches long, half an inch wide, and half an inch deep."

"And it's filled to the top with pond water," Mike added.

"Water, courtesy of your old buddies, Devin and Tom, who risked life and limb to steal it from the biology-building pond," Devin remarked.

"The electrodes at either end of the trough are connected to a 6-volt battery by means of a Harvard inductorium," Bill continued.

Mike interrupted him with a laugh. "Professor Calvin thought I was crazy, you know, borrowing such an *old-fashioned* piece of equipment."

"And we've got Tom's goose-neck study lamp to provide light to shine on the worms as the conditioning stimulus," Bill said.

"How many groups are we going to run?" Mike asked.

"Four," Bill said. "An experimental group that gets the light paired with the shock, and three control groups. With the experimental animals, we turn the light on for two seconds, then shock them. The light is the CS, the shock is the UCS."

"What's the UCR?" Tom asked.

"The 'scrunch' the worm makes when we shock it," Bill said.

Devin asked, "How are we going to prove to Professor Sauermann that the experimental animals have learned?"

Mike replied. "On each trial, we observe the worm to see what it does during the two seconds after the light comes on and before the shock starts. At the beginning of training, the animal shouldn't respond much to the light at all."

"Oh, I see," Devin said. "But as we train the animal, it should start 'scrunching' to the light more and more frequently."

"That's right," Tom said. "Because the light becomes a signal that the worm is about to get blasted. So it 'scrunches' in anticipation of the shock."

"But do we really need *three* control groups?" Mike asked plaintively, thinking of all the work involved.

Bill grinned. "Absolutely. We've got to prove it's the *pairing* of the light and shock that causes any change in the way the worms respond. So the first control group gets light, but no shock. The second group gets shock, but no light. And the third group gets both light and shock, but they're not paired. The response rate to the light should increase significantly in the experimental animals, and decrease in the three control groups."

"Okay, who does what when?" Devin asked.

"Mike and I will train two groups each day," Bill said, "And you and Tom can train the other two groups. We'll switch groups daily, to equalize the work."

"And when you and Mike are working, Tom and I can go play racquetball," Devin remarked.

"Yeah," Tom said, grinning. "And ever since Devin got hit in the eye with a ball, you should see him 'scrunch' whenever I serve him a zinger."

"Hey, man, you've got me conditioned!" Devin laughed.

They flipped a coin, and Bill and Mike won the honor of starting first. So while Devin and Tom went off to the racquetball courts, Mike and Bill settled down to work. Mike put a healthy planarian in the trough, and then told Bill to get ready. When the worm was crawling steadily in a straight line, he called out, "Now."

Immediately Bill switched on the light. Two seconds later, he turned on the shock for half a second. The Harvard inductorium buzzed noisily.

"Boy," Mike said. "You should have seen that baby scrunch."

"Before or after the shock?" Bill asked.

"After the shock," Mike

replied. "He sort of wiggled his nose for a fraction of a second when the light came on. But he didn't scrunch at all until you zapped him."

"Okay," Bill said. "We'll put down, 'Trial 1, W for Wiggle.'"

"Get ready for the next trial," Mike said moments later. And when the worm was again moving steadily in a straight line, he said, "Now!"

And again, Bill turned on the light for two seconds, and then the shock.

"Not even a wiggle that time," Mike announced. A few seconds later, he told Bill, "Ready. . . . Now!"

Bill applied the light and the shock.

"A scrunch!" Mike said excitedly. "A good, clean scrunch."

"Great," said Bill. "Let me observe the next worm while you run the light and shock."

"Sure," Mike replied. Then, as he waited for the animal to turn around at the end of the trough and start moving steadily again, he continued. "Do you *really* think these funny little critters are capable of learning?"

Bill thought a moment. "The worms will answer that for us, Mike. The important question is whether Devin will ever learn to wear goggles when he plays racquetball with Tom."

Mike sighed. "Oh, well. Maybe if worms can learn, humans can too." Then, noticing the planarian was again moving majestically down the trough, he said, "Ready. . . . Now!"

(Continued on page 414.)

Memory

What time is it?

When someone asks you for the time, how do you respond? Probably you look at your watch, or at a clock, and you give the answer almost automatically. As simple as this process may seem, however, we know very little about how your brain handles inputs such as this one. And we know even less about how your brain responds so appropriately—and so quickly. However, we are reasonably certain about certain aspects of this cognitive process.

To answer any question, you must make use of your **memory**. If someone asks you the time, you must first recognize that someone has spoken to you. Next you must check your memory banks to make sure you recognize the words and phrases the person has used. Then you must realize that you have been *asked a question* to which you might respond.

But while your brain is "checking all these things out," *it must have some way of remembering what the original question was*. If you had no way of holding the question in some kind of "temporary storage," you'd end up knowing you'd been asked a question without being able to recall what it was. However, you must remember several other things as well as what the question was. For example, you can't tell someone "what time it is" unless you can recall what a clock or watch is—and how to tell time. Nor can you respond to such questions correctly unless you can remember how to reproduce the words you must use in your answer. Memory, then, is a much more complicated process than it might seem at first glance.

As in the study of all other areas of psychology, there are certain *major problems* that memory researchers are trying to solve. Let's look briefly at what six of these problems are. For once you understand what some of the basic issues are, you will be in a better position to answer the question of how *you* answer such questions as, "What time is it?"

Six Important Issues

If we could solve the following six issues, we'd know a great deal more about your memory than we presently do:

1. How many types of memory—or memory systems—do you have?
2. What do you store in memory, exact copies of inputs or "processed" material of some kind?
3. Why do you store some things in memory, but not others?
4. How do you retrieve an item from your memory files?
5. What is forgetting, and what causes it?
6. What physical changes occur in your brain during memory storage?

As you will see, we can't answer any of these questions as fully as we might wish. However, discovering what we *do* know will surely give you greater respect for your own memory. And, who knows, this type of knowledge might even help you improve your own ability to remember things.

Memory Systems

In point of fact, you don't have just one "memory system," you have several different systems. Psychologists don't agree on how many systems there are, or how each functions. However, some 20 years ago, several psychologists advanced the theory that there were three major memory systems. These three systems are usually called *Sensory Information Storage, Short-term Memory,* and *Long-term Memory.*

The three-system "model" has guided most memory research since the 1960's. As you will see, however, recent studies cast some doubt on this issue. Since the three-system model is still dominant, though, let's look at it more closely.

Sensory Information Stage

What time is it?

When the image of those words first impinges on the retinas in your eyes, your rods and cones respond by sending a *characteristic pattern of nerve impulses* along your optic nerve to the visual centers of your brain.

Suppose that we flashed the words "What time is it?" on a screen for exactly one-tenth of a second. How long would your rods and cones continue to respond after the words had disappeared? The answer is—it depends. If you had been sitting in absolute darkness for several minutes, the words "*What time is it?*" would hang suspended in your visual field for quite some time. However, if you were sitting in a lighted room, the next thing you looked at would erase the phrase "What time is it?" from your visual system.

Your memory *begins,* then, in your receptors—in what psychologists call the **Sensory Information Storage** or SIS stage of information processing.

Under normal conditions—as you look from one object to another in your visual world—your visual system holds on to each stimulus pattern for but a fraction of a second before that pattern is replaced by yet another visual input. According to psychologists Peter Lindsay and Donald Norman, this storage time typically

Memory. From the Latin and Greek words meaning "to be mindful, or to remember." Your memory is your store of past experiences, thus the seat of your ability to recreate or reproduce past perceptions, emotions, thoughts, and actions.

Sensory Information Storage. The first stage of memory storage. Your sensory receptors hold a more or less exact copy of an input for a fraction of a second before that copy is "erased" by the next input. *up to 1/2 of 1 second*

Iconic memory (eye-KON-ick). The word "icon" (EYE-kon) comes from a Greek word meaning "a visual representation or image." Iconic memory is a visual form of Sensory Information Storage.

Echoic memory (eh-KOH-ick). An auditory form of Sensory Information Storage.

lasts from 0.1 to 0.5 seconds under normal viewing conditions. (As we noted, though, the storage lasts longer if no new stimulus "erases" the input.)

You can measure your own Sensory Information Storage time by using a technique Lindsay and Norman describe. Extend your index finger on one hand, and then wave your finger back and forth in front of your eyes while you stare straight ahead. You'll notice that a "shadowy image" trails behind your finger. Studies suggest this image lasts for about 0.25 second. (Swinging a flashlight around in a circle in the dark gives the same sort of "trailing visual image.")

Some psychologists refer to visual SIS as **iconic memory.** For the amount of information stored in visual SIS is much like that in an *icon,* which is a "detailed image" of a person or event. In similar fashion, auditory SIS is sometimes called **echoic memory,** because it seems to be an "exact echo" of an auditory input. However, by the time this sensory information reaches your cortex—and you become aware of what you are looking at—much of the rich detail is lost.

To put the matter another way, your *visual system* has a "photographic memory," but your *cortex* doesn't. We know this is the case because of studies begun at Harvard in the late 1950's by George Sperling.

Sperling's Research

Imagine that you are sitting in a dark room staring at a blank movie screen. Behind you, a slide projector clicks briefly, and the stimulus pattern shown in Fig. 15.1A flashes onto the screen. The pattern appears for a just 0.05 second (1/20th of a second, or 50 milliseconds), then disappears.

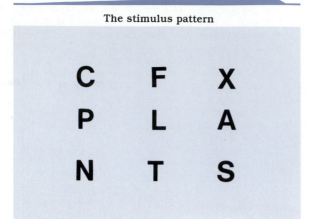

The stimulus pattern

C	F	X
P	L	A
N	T	S

Fig. 15.1A The stimulus pattern used in the Sperling experiment.

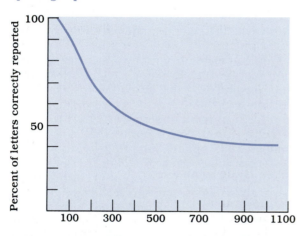

Fig. 15.1B When Sperling asked his subjects to report immediately, they could identify any of the nine stimulus letters. When the subjects' reports were delayed for half a second (500 milliseconds), they could identify but half the letters.

Your task in this experiment is to report all the letters you remember seeing during the 50 milliseconds exposure time. You do the best you can. But trial after trial, you can't recall more than 3 or 4 of the 9 letters. Does this result mean that your SIS system *recorded* only 3 or 4 of the letters? Not at all, as Sperling demonstrated almost 30 years ago.

Sperling suspected that his subjects actually *saw* all 9 letters, but forgot most of them during the time it took them to *report* what they had seen. So he changed the experimental procedure slightly. Immediately *after* presenting the stimulus pattern visually, he gave the subject an *auditory signal*. This signal told the subject *which letter to report*. For instance, one signal might ask the subject, "Which letter was in the upper right-hand corner?" Another signal would tell the subject to report which letter was in the center of the bottom row.

Suppose you were a subject in this type of study. Since the auditory signal occurred a fraction of a second *after* you had seen the 9 stimulus letters, you wouldn't know which of the 9 letters to pay attention to while the letters flashed on the screen. However, it wouldn't matter. For you would be able to remember *any* of the 9 letters you were signaled to report. So you obviously *saw* them all—and recorded them briefly in visual SIS. However, you would achieve this accuracy *only* if the auditory signal occurred within 100 milliseconds after the letters had disappeared from the screen. If the signal didn't come on until 500 milliseconds (1/2 second) afterwards, your performance would drop to the chance level (see Fig. 15.1B).

Sperling's research showed three important things: First, your SIS *records* inputs in much greater detail than previously had been suspected. Second, items stored in SIS are normally *forgotten* (or "erased") within half a second. Thus, the reason subjects in previous studies couldn't report more than 3 or 4 of the letters is this: During the time it took them to *report* the first 3 or 4 letters, they had actually *forgotten* the rest of the 9.

Last but not least, Sperling's studies suggested that the eye sends a *visual* copy of the input to the brain. When he delayed the auditory signal for more than one-half second, his subjects often made mistakes. But these were *visual* mistakes. That is, the subjects reported seeing a "P" rather than an "F." These letters are visually similar. However, the subjects seldom reported seeing an "X" when the letter actually was an "F." The importance of this point will become clearer in a moment.

Question: Many people believe your brain actually makes an "exact video tape recording" of everything you see, and that this "exact tape" is filed in your memory forever. What does Sperling's research suggest is the case?

Short-term Memory

Your eye obviously sends a very detailed representation of each visual input up to your brain. The lower centers in your brain then *extract the critical features* of the inputs and relay this information to your cortex. At this point, you become conscious of the input. Then you attempt to *categorize* the input and make certain cognitive decisions about it (see Chapter 9).

However, you must have some means of storing the input for a few seconds while you "think" about it. So your brain *codes* the input and tucks it away in "temporary hold" while the the input is being processed.

Question: How do the errors Sperling's subjects made support the belief that the lower centers *extract critical features* rather than sending the entire input to the cortex?

Defining Short-term Memory

Now, let's suppose you're a subject in yet another memory experiment. The experimenter shows you a card. Printed on the card are three large letters: C F M. You look at the letters for a few seconds, then the experimenter removes the stimulus card. Some 20 seconds later, the experimenter asks you what the letters were. You respond correctly. The fact that you can remember the letters for more than half a second shows that you aren't using SIS in this case. Could it be that you're using "permanent"

~ 30 seconds

storage instead? Let's continue the study and see.

Next, the experimenter asks you to repeat the task with different letters. But this time, you have to perform a difficult cognitive task during the 20-second delay: You must "count backwards by three's," starting at some arbitrary number such as 487. That means you must say, "487, 484, 481, 478 . . ." until told to do otherwise. After you have counted backwards for 20 seconds, the experimenter stops you and asks you what the three stimulus letters were. Now, how do you think you'd fare?

When George Murdock performed this study in 1961, he got the sort of results shown in Fig. 15.2. If you count backwards for just 3 seconds, you probably will recall but 2 of the 3 stimulus letters. If you count backwards for more than 6 seconds, you're lucky to remember 1 of the 3 letters. And, as Murdock showed, you'd perform at about the same level if you were given three words to remember instead of three letters.

Since you forgot so much so rapidly, it's obvious you're not using "permanent" storage to recall the letters. However, since you remember the letters for more than half a second, you can't be using SIS either. Psychologists use the term **Short-term Memory** (STM) to refer to this type of "temporary hold" during information processing.

A number of studies suggest that items filed in Short-term Memory remain available for recall no more than about 30 seconds before "vanishing forever."

Rehearsal

Why could you remember the 3 stimulus letters so well when you didn't have to "count backwards by three's"? If you've ever had to look up a phone number in a directory, you probably know the answer. What happens when you look the number up? Probably you silently repeat the number to yourself several times so you won't forget it during the length of time it takes you to close the directory, pick up the phone, and start dialing.

Psychologists use the term *rehearsal* to refer to the act of "silently saying things over and

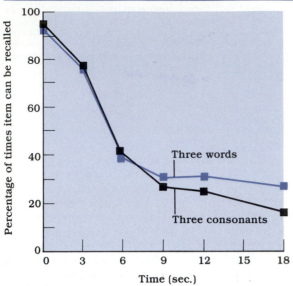

Fig. 15.2 When Murdock made his subjects "count backward" after exposing them to three consonants (or three words), the subjects couldn't "rehearse" and thus tended to forget. See text.

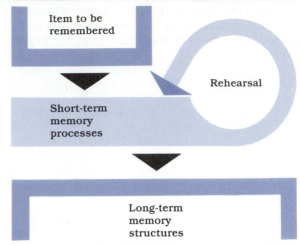

Fig. 15.3 Rehearsing an item keeps it current in Short-term Memory and helps move it to long-term storage.

over again." When you *rehearse* an item, you actually keep putting it back into temporary storage again and again. By *re-inserting* the item into Short-term Memory several times, you can keep it available for a period of several minutes (see Fig. 15.3).

Question: Most people must "rehearse" a telephone number continuously until they dial it. What does this fact tell you about the length of time an item typically remains in Short-term Memory?

Acoustical Coding

In describing George Sperling's research on visual SIS, we said the *type of mistakes* his subjects made was important. As it turns out, subjects in Short-term Memory experiments make quite different sorts of errors than the errors Sperling's subjects made. And this fact has given us a clue to how the lower centers of the brain actually *store* items in STM.

(Murdock)

When Sperling's subjects made mistakes, they often confused an "F" with a "P" or an "E." The fact that these letters all *look alike* suggests that *visual* SIS coding is *visual*. However, subjects asked to "count backwards by three's"

will typically confuse an "F" with an "X," but seldom with an "E" or a "P." What's going on here?

If you say "F" and "X" aloud, you'll hear the answer. For the initial sound you make when you say each letter is the same. But "F" doesn't *sound* at all like "E" or "P." Thus, you must be *translating* these visual inputs into *sounds* prior to tucking them away in Short-term Memory. We call this process **acoustical coding**. Technically speaking, *acoustical coding* refers to the tendency to "translate" certain visual inputs into something related to the sound or production of words when you put them in temporary memory storage.

Whenever a visual input involves *written or spoken language*, you tend to encode the input as sounds rather than sights. This fact shouldn't be too surprising. As you read this book, for instance, don't you "hear" yourself saying the words aloud? If you read a sentence, then close your eyes, it's the "sounds" made by your own "inner voice" you usually remember rather than the visual image on the printed page. Thus, with *language inputs*, what you actually file away in Short-term Memory is a sort of "auditory translation" rather than the visual input itself.

Not all Short-term Memory is made up of "auditory translations," however. Suppose we ask you to watch a young woman playing an accordion. Then we ask you to look away and describe what you saw. You might be able to do so in words alone, but the odds are you will recall *visual images* that you'd try to reproduce by *moving your own hands* the same way the woman had. *That* sort of Short-term Memory is obviously visual and muscular, not "acoustical coding."

Question: You encode the sight of a *word* acoustically, but not the sight of a beautiful *sunset*. Why does this fact suggest that many types of "thinking" are really a form of "inner speech"?

Familiar Items

Short-term Memory for familiar objects is generally much longer (and better) than for unfamiliar objects. For example, read the following sentence rapidly and then look away from the page and try to remember exactly what the stimulus sentence was:

Который час?

Chances are—unless you are familiar with the Russian language—you had a difficult time trying to remember what you actually saw. You surely sensed at once that the sentence was written in a language other than English. But could you "see" in your mind's eye each of the letters in that strange (to us) alphabet that the Russians use? Or was it more or less a jumbled blur?

Question: Would a camera have any more difficulty photographing the phrase in Russian than in English? What does this fact tell you about your STM and "acoustical coding"?

Memory "Interpretations"

Now glance quickly at the following stimulus sentence and then look away and try to visualize exactly what it says:

What time it is?

When this phrase appeared in Russian, your Short-term Memory couldn't "code" the words acoustically because (chances are) you couldn't say them aloud. But when the phrase appeared in English, you remembered it very well, because you knew the *sounds* of the words. Generally speaking, *familiar items* are much easier to "code into sounds" than are unfamiliar items. Your Short-term Memory can hold a familiar item for up to 30 seconds. Less-familiar items (such as the phrase in Russian) tend to drop out much more rapidly.

Question: Look again at the "stimulus phrase" one paragraph above. Does it *really* say what you

Acoustical coding (ah-KOO-stick-cal). Research suggests you "code" language inputs by converting them to sounds before you store them in Short-term Memory.

remembered it as saying? If you didn't perceive it correctly, what does this fact tell you about "interpreting" items before you store them in Short-term Memory?

Limited Capacity

Your Short-term Memory ordinarily cannot store more than 6 or 7 items simultaneously. At the moment that your brain inserts an item into Short-term Memory, that item is strong and clear and easy to recall, if you do so *immediately*. But shortly thereafter, your brain tucks away a second item, and then a third item, and a fourth. Although only a few seconds have passed, you will now have much more trouble trying to recall what the first item was.

By the time your brain has pressed 5 or 6 new items down on top of the first, that original item has lost most of its strength and has faded away. The new items appear to *interfere with* or erase the ones in front of them—just as each new visual pattern you look at wipes clean the stimulus you were looking at just a moment before (see Fig. 15.4).

While you are holding an item in Short-term Memory, you can recall it more or less at will. And you can keep the item around for several minutes by "rehearsing" it. However, once the item drops out of "temporary storage," it is likely to be gone forever—unless your brain decides to make a *permanent record* of the stimulus input.

Question: If you "rehearse" an item for a long enough period of time, you might well not forget it at all. What does that fact tell you about how items get shifted from Short- to Long-term Memory?

Long-Term Memory

If you stroll along a busy street, you may see a thousand different people in one short hour. Most of their faces will fade from your memory almost immediately. Yet some things (and faces) you remember vividly—or at least you think you do.

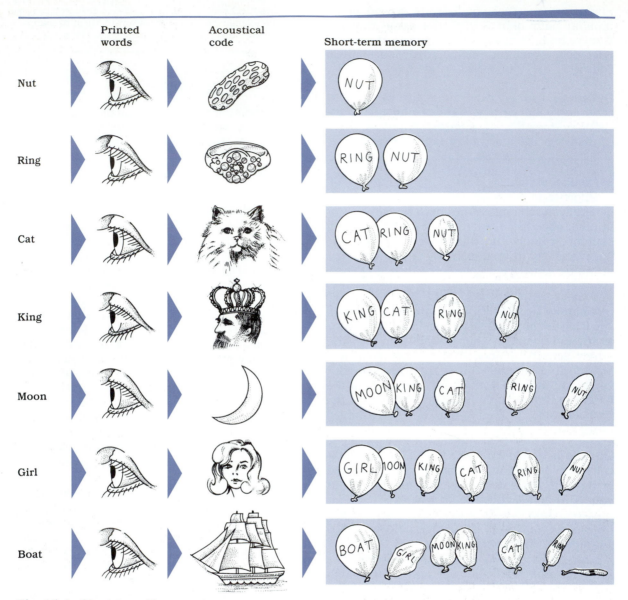

Printed words	Acoustical code	Short-term memory
Nut		
Ring		
Cat		
King		
Moon		
Girl		
Boat		

Fig. 15.4 Short-term Memory storage.

For example, try to remember the last long trip that you took. Can you recall *right at this instant* the exact date and hour that the trip began and ended? Chances are that you can't. But if you take the time to think about the details—and perhaps write them down as you go— you'll find you can *reproduce* a surprising amount of detail about that trip, even though it may have occurred months or years ago. However, if you inspect those memories carefully as they pop back into consciousness, you'll find they are *qualitatively* different from the imme-diate memory you have of a face you've just seen.

In fact, your recollection of things that happened long ago usually is hazy and incomplete at first. One reason for this haziness was offered more than 100 years ago by Hermann Ebbinghaus, one of the earliest and greatest investigators of human memory. Ebbinghaus suggested that you typically don't *remember* complex events. Rather, you recall a few "high points" and then *reconstruct* the experience piece by little piece.

Question: How might you use Thorndike's Law of Exercise and Law of Effect (see Chapter 14) to explain why people remember what they remember?

Reconstruction versus Exact Recall

Your SIS system briefly stores a more-or-less *exact copy* of the original sensory input. Your Short-term Memory is rather like an "instant replay" on television—a few seconds of highlight action that you can recall with considerable clarity for a brief period of time thereafter. But it is a "processed copy" of the input—rather than all the rich sensory detail—that you can replay at will until the input fades away into obscurity.

Your **Long-term Memory** seems to be much more complex, for it stores many different aspects of your experiences. First, it records certain *critical features* of your sensory inputs and files these according to various *memory categories*. These "memory categories" are much like the *cognitive categories* we discussed in Chapter 9. Second, your LTM creates an *acoustical representation* of the input. And third, Long-term Memory records information on how to *reproduce* the items you've filed away—that is, how to write and say things aloud.

When you draw on your Long-term Memory, it then *reconstructs* the event from the associa-

Long-term Memory. Your store of permanent memories. Inputs important enough to survive your Short-term Memory are transferred to long-term storage by some biological mechanism we don't yet understand. Salient (critical) features of an input are stored according to various categories. Long-term Memory also includes an acoustical coding of the input and information on how to reproduce the item in writing or speech.

tions and auditory representations it has in its files. However, Long-term Memory does not usually allow you to *relive* experiences in any great detail.

Item Storage and Retrieval

Your Long-Term Memory is practically limitless—rather like a huge library with billions of books stashed away on the shelves. You add thousands of new volumes to that library every day of your life, but you never seem to run out of shelf space for new arrivals. But how in the world do you *retrieve* the correct item when you're searching your memory files for it?

The answer seems to lie in how you *categorize* your experiences in the first place.

Hermann Ebbinghaus

Look at the people in this photo for a few seconds, then look away. How long do you think you can remember their faces?

Harold Goodglass

Memory Categories

In the November-December 1980 issue of *American Scientist*, Harold Goodglass notes that humans tend to tuck items away in permanent storage in terms of several rather specific categories. We can best illustrate these categories by asking you to consider how you might go about filing the word "chair" in Long-term Memory.

1. *Identity*. First you would try to remember the word itself, "chair." But, as you will see, you rapidly split up this category in a variety of ways.
2. *Class*. A chair is a piece of furniture. Thus, you would file this item not merely as a word unto itself, but as part of a **superordinate** class which would include such other items as "table," "couch," "bed," and "lamp."
3. *Attributes*. A chair is soft or hard, large or small, metal or wood, upholstered or plain. You may enjoy chairs, or hate them. Your memory of a chair, then, includes some notion of the various physical and psychological attributes that a chair has.
4. *Context*. You expect to see a chair in a living room, not inside a bathtub. But you may also remember a specific chair in an unusual context, such as an electric chair in a prison, or your mother's chair in her bedroom.
5. *Function*. You associate the word "chair" with certain verbs denoting its function, such as "sit," or "recline."
6. *Sensory Associations*. The word "chair" will be paired with the *sight* of typical chairs, with the *smell* of leather and wood, the *feeling* your skin has when you sit on a chair, and perhaps with a squeaking *sound* that old chairs make when you lean back too far in them.
7. *Clangs and Visual Patterns*. You not only file the *concept* of a chair away in your mem-

ory, but also certain salient features of the word itself, such as its *sight and sound*. Thus, "chair" will be stored according to its **clangs**, or "sound-alike" words (bear, pear). It will also be filed according to the visual pattern the letters c-h-a-i-r make, the initial letter of the word, the number of syllables in the word, and so forth.

8. *Reproductive Information*. Your Long-term Memory also includes information on the muscle movements needed to *say* the word "chair," to *write* it, to *draw* a picture of a chair, and so forth.

These eight "memory categories" are by no means the only ones having to do with *item storage* in Long-term Memory. But they are perhaps the most important ones, and those most studied by psychologists.

Question: How might "acoustical coding" of items in Short-term Memory make it easier to store the items in Long-term Memory according to "clangs" and "reproductive information"?

Mnemonics

If nothing else, the eight categories listed above may give you some notions about how to improve your memory. There are a variety of **mnemonics**, or "memory tricks," that psychologists have developed to help people remember things better. Some of these devices involve training you to *associate* whatever you want to recall with something already well established in your memory banks. Other mnemonics require you to use one or more of the eight categories in trying to memorize a specific item.

For example, if Mr. Bird looks like an owl, you can make an easy connection between his face and his name. Or you might pick a salient feature about his background and try to associate that with his name. Something like, "Mr. Bird flew into town three years ago," could do the trick.

If you have a list of terms you must memorize, you might write a poem that includes all the items in the proper order. Or you could take the initial letter of each term and memorize the letters themselves. For instance, music students often use the sentence, "Every good boy deserves favor" as a mnemonic to help them remember the notes of the music scale (EGBDF).

Psychologist Laird Cermak lists a great many helpful mnemonics in his 1978 book *Improving Your Memory*. Among other things, he urges you to (1) pay very close attention to the most important features of what you want to memorize; and (2) organize your thoughts in a logical way.

Question: "Sis" is an abbreviation for "sister." Can you make up a sentence using "Sis" that will help you remember "Sensory Information Storage"?

Forgetting

In an earlier chapter, we quoted Sigmund Freud's comment that you learn about the normal by studying the abnormal. In the field of memory research, that certainly is the case. For we have discovered a great deal about *memory* by studying *forgetting*. And we have learned an amazing amount about *item storage* in normal people by investigating the difficulties that brain-damaged people have in *retrieving* even the simplest of items from long-term storage.

Let's look at the most common types of "dis-remembering" in some detail.

Neural Decay

The SIS system in your receptors provides you with sharply etched neural impressions of the world around you. But this pattern of neural firing is quickly destroyed in one of two ways—either the receptor neurons adapt to the input (and hence the neural pattern *decays*), or the next visual input "erases" the first input.

Once an input reaches your brain, it may be put into Short-term Memory. But your Short-term Memory is very limited because, as new items are plugged into "temporary hold," older items decay and you thus forget them.

Neural decay is perhaps the simplest type of forgetting.

Interference

New memories interfere with old ones, and vice versa. There are two main types of "memory interference." The first has to do with *item storage and recall*. The second has to do with the fact that new inputs can actually distort or *transform* old memories.

Serial Position Effect

The *serial position effect* is an example of how learning one thing can interfere with storing and recalling other items. Let's again imagine that you are a subject in a memory study. The experimenter shows you a list of 20 words, one at a time, and asks that you remember as many of the words as you can. Since you see each word for only *one second*, you surely won't recall all 20 later on. But which ones will you remember?

When George Murdock ran a similar study in 1962, he got the results shown in Fig. 15.5. As you can see, Murdock's subjects tended to recall items at the beginning and end of the list much better than words in the middle. Apparently items at either end of the list *interfere* with your ability to recall the words in the middle. In short, the *position* of the item in the series affects how readily you can remember it later on.

Murdock also found that the *longer* you see the item in the first place, the better you tend to remember it. This unsurprising result might lead you to assume an item is "safe from interference" if you inspect it long enough and then

"WHEN YOU'RE YOUNG, IT COMES NATURALLY, BUT WHEN YOU GET A LITTLE OLDER, YOU HAVE TO RELY ON MNEMONICS."

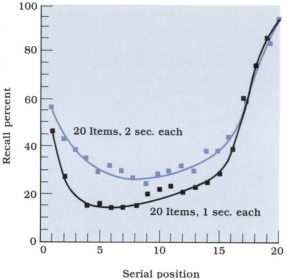

Fig. 15.5 Murdock's subjects tended to remember the first and last items in a 20-item list better than items in the middle, a result called the "serial position effect."

As in the Loftus study, here is the same vehicle approaching the corner where, at one time there was a stop sign, at another time a yield sign.

Elizabeth F. Loftus

file it away in long-term storage. However, that turns out not to be the case.

Memory Distortions

In an elegant series of studies, Elizabeth Loftus has shown that what you learn today may actually *distort* your memory of what happened to you yesterday. In one experiment, Loftus showed films of auto accidents to people, and then asked them questions about what they had seen. If she asked her subjects, "About how fast were the cars going when they *smashed* into each other?", her subjects gave much higher estimates of speed than did sub-

jects who were asked, "About how fast were the cars going when they *collided*?" Apparently, the use of the word "smashed" somehow *changed* the subjects' memories of what they had seen!

A week later, Loftus asked these same subjects if they had seen any broken glass in the films. In fact, there was no broken glass. But more of the subjects exposed to the word *smashed* "remembered" seeing broken glass than did those exposed to the word *collided*. Again, the question Loftus used to pull the memory out of long-term storage seemingly *changed the memory itself*.

In another experiment, Loftus showed half her subjects a series of photos involving a car. One photo showed the automobile approaching a yield sign. The other half of the subjects were exposed to the same series of photos, except that the car was shown approaching a stop sign. Loftus then asked the "yield sign" subjects what the car had done *at the stop sign*. Almost half of these subjects subsequently insisted that the sign had said "stop" instead of "yield."

According to Loftus, "No matter how well meaning or how well trained observers are, there are ways to make people see, hear, and even smell things that never were. . . . Every time we recall an event we must reconstruct the memory, and so each time it is changed."

In brief, items filed in your memory banks can be radically altered by new inputs—even though you are *unaware* that the change has taken place.

Question: How might the way that a lawyer *phrases a question* affect the answer a witness might give when testifying in court?

Rejection and Repression

In Chapter 9, we stated that the lower centers in your brain *reject* inputs (and parts of inputs) that are meaningless or unimportant to you. Although you are usually unaware of it, this "screening out" of trivial items goes on constantly and is a very necessary part of the forgetting process. (Can you recall *exactly* what the skin on your back felt like 20 minutes ago? How often do you need to recall such items?)

If a given stimulus input is threatening or disturbing, the emotional centers in your brain may *repress* the stimulus and hence make it very difficult for you to remember later on. The "perceptual defense" studies discussed in Chapter 9 are an example of this sort of repression.

Cataloging, Filing, and Retrieval Errors

You "hold" items in Short-term Memory temporarily while you decide how important they are. Meaningful items are usually transferred to Long-term Memory. This "transfer" usually involves cataloging the item in terms of the eight memory categories listed previously. Your brain also seems to make a "mental index card" for *each category* under which that experience will be filed. You use these index categories when

you try to *retrieve* an item from your memory storage banks. Mostly, this system works well. However, these "mental index cards" occasionally get catalogued in the wrong way, mis-filed, or even totally lost.

Cataloging errors seem to occur most frequently when you have to learn too many things at once. For example, if you are introduced to a dozen unfamiliar people at a party, you may well make some mistakes as you try to attach the right names to the proper faces. If you met one new person a day for a dozen days, you would have a better chance of getting the "file cards" filled out correctly.

Your memory also *mis-files* things occasionally, and thus you will have trouble locating it in your memory banks. The more similar two items are, the more likely it is that one of them will be filed in the place supposedly reserved for the other.

Old experiences are often hard to *retrieve*, because you have to scan the millions of similar index cards you've made since then to recover that one unique memory. Brand-new experiences are sometimes hard to remember, because you have such a limited number of cues as to their location in your long-term files.

According to a 1980 survey made by Elizabeth and Geoffrey Loftus, most people think Long-term Memory is much like a "video recorder"; thus you can *always* recover an item if you try hard enough. As the Loftuses note, though, the experimental data don't support this viewpoint. Indeed, a large number of scientific studies suggest that most of us *totally forget* much of what we've experienced in the past. And judging from the bulk of the laboratory studies on this subject, once an item is lost, it's probably gone forever.

As an example of the unreliability of memory, consider a series of studies performed by Russell Bernard and his associates at the University of Florida. Bernard and his colleagues got actual transcripts of conversations and social encounters. Then, a week or so later, they asked the people involved to recall their talks. In general, the subjects were correct in their recall *less than 50 percent of the time*. The subjects "remembered" talking to people whom they hadn't talked with, and they denied having conversations with individuals whom they had talked to at length. They made mistakes about "important" conversations just as often as they did about "trivial" conversations. Bernard believes that most people's memories of past events should not be entirely trusted—particularly in courts of law.

Memory Disorders

There are many types of memory disorders. Among the most common of these are the *amnesias* and the *aphasias*.

Amnesia

Memory is the process by which information is stored in your brain. *Amnesia* is the process by which this information is physically erased from your memory banks, blocked off from easy access, or prevented from being stored in the first place. Amnesia has both biological and psychological causes.

Forgetting "What" But Not "How To"

In an article published in the December 23 1983 *Science*, Larry Squire says there are two distinct Long-term Memory systems. The first, which Squire calls *procedural memory*, seems to store long-term habits and behavioral functions. These are "how to" functions—that is, motor skills, such as driving a car. The procedural ("how to") system seems to be mediated by "deep" brain structures, and usually isn't affected by strokes or disease. The second system, which Squire refers to as *declarative memory*, involves "stored representations of stimuli" and other cognitive functions. These are "what" functions, Squire says—such as what object the word "car" refers to. The declarative ("what") system seems to be mediated by cortical and other "higher" centers in the brain, and thus is more likely to be disrupted by accidents and illness. The same information may be stored in both systems, of course, although in slightly different form.

Retrograde Amnesia

Memory storage does not occur instantaneously. Rather, it takes up to 30 minutes for your Long-term Memory to file an item away. Any physical or psychological *trauma* that occurs to you during this half-hour-long **consolidation period** can prevent the item from being recorded in your memory banks. This type of forgetting is called **retrograde amnesia**, because a shock to your nervous system *now* can erase the memory of something that happened *several minutes earlier*. For example, people who survive a blow to the head in car accidents often can recall everything that happened immediately after the crash. However, they frequently can't remember anything that happened in the period *just prior* to the accident. Because these memories were still being "consolidated" at the

time of the crash, they got "erased" by the blow to the head.

Question: Why do the data on retrograde amnesia suggest that memory storage is basically a *physical* process?

Anterograde Amnesia

Memories already in long-term storage usually aren't affected by retrograde amnesia since they are already "consolidated." Severe brain damage and the diseases associated with old age, however, can cause a somewhat different type of forgetting, called **anterograde amnesia**. If you suffered from anterograde amnesia, you could retrieve *old* items with ease, but you no longer would be able to file *certain types* of new items in long-term storage.

In a 1983 report in the *Journal of Abnormal Psychology*, University of Toronto psychologist Daniel Schacter describes what it is like to play golf with a patient suffering from anterograde amnesia. This 58-year-old man had been a good golfer most of his life before suffering from **Alzheimer's disease**. Once the anterograde amnesia associated with Alzheimer's set in, however, his game become "horrendous."

There were some things the man could do perfectly. For example, he used golf jargon correctly, he teed up properly, he hit the ball well, and his selection of golf clubs was "virtually flawless." However, he couldn't keep score because a minute or two after playing a hole, he forgot how many strokes he had taken. Unless he could walk straight from the tee to his ball, he usually lost track of it. When asked what brand of golf ball he used, he simply couldn't recall. However, as Schacter notes, when the man had to pick out "his ball" from several examples, he was always correct.

According to Schacter, most of the patient's problems can be explained in terms of anterograde amnesia—that is, an inability to file new items away in Long-term Memory.

Psychological Amnesia

Psychological amnesia, caused by an emotional shock, is really a form of repression. Witnessing a terrible automobile accident can cause you to "block off" all your memories of that fateful day. The items are still in your long-term storage banks, however, and you could probably retrieve them if you tried hard enough to do so (or underwent psychotherapy).

True psychological amnesia is fairly rare, at least compared to memory loss caused by disease, accident, and old age. Indeed, some psychologists believe psychological amnesia occurs much more frequently on TV soap operas than it does in real life.

Aphasia

In his 1980 *American Scientist* article, Harold Goodglass defines **aphasia** as impairment in the ability to use or remember language. In right-handed individuals, aphasia typically results from damage to the left hemisphere of the brain. The exact type of language impairment the person suffers depends on what part of the left hemisphere is affected.

Goodglass notes that some aphasic patients can understand the spoken names of American cities and can locate them on a map, but may totally fail to understand names of common body parts. Other patients can understand nouns but not pronouns. For instance, one patient Goodglass describes could read the word "hymn" quite readily, but not the word "him." Still other patients can produce most verbs with ease, but can't produce nouns and adjectives.

Aphasic patients are better at naming things they can see than things they smell or words they hear. They are also better at remembering objects they can touch and feel (ball, spoon) than objects they experience at a distance (cloud, moon). They can occasionally write words they cannot say, or speak words they cannot write. There are many types of aphasia. All of them, however, seem related to one or more of the "eight memory categories" we described earlier.

Types of Aphasia

Those patients who cannot *name* objects readily are said to suffer from **anomic aphasia**. When shown a picture of a fork, an anomic aphasiac cannot say "fork." But the person may say something like, "You eat with it," or "I have one at home." And, of course, the person can *use* a fork properly when eating. One woman suffering from anomic aphasia described her daughter's marriage this way: "And then she, you know. . . .dum-dum-dedum" (humming the wedding march). According to Goodglass, most anomic aphasia results from damage to the border area between the temporal and the parietal lobes.

Damage to the rear portion of the temporal lobe can cause a type of problem called **Wernicke's aphasia**. If you showed a picture of a chair to someone with this disorder, the person

Consolidation period. The period of time (20 to 30 minutes) it takes your brain to file an input or experience away in Long-term Memory. Any trauma that disrupts your nervous system during the consolidation process will probably prevent that input from being put in permanent storage.

Retrograde amnesia (RETT-tro-grade am-KNEE-see-ah). "Amnesia" comes from the Greek word meaning forgetfulness. When you are hit on the head, you are likely to forget most of the things that had happened to you for 20 to 30 minutes prior to the blow—but you may very likely remember things that happened immediately after the trauma. The amnesia is "graded" because you will very likely forget *everything* that happened immediately before the trauma, *most* of what happened 5 minutes before, and *some* of what happened 20 minutes before. The term *retro* means "after the fact."

Anterograde amnesia (AN-terr-oh-grade). Memory disorder usually caused by trauma or brain damage involving inability to transfer items from Short-term to Long-term Memory. You can recall things prior to the trauma quite well, but not what happened to you an hour ago.

Alzheimer's Disease (ALTS-high-mer's). A disorder associated with old age, which usually involves an inability to file new items away in Long-term Memory. See Chapter 18.

Aphasia (ah-FAZE-ya). An impairment in the ability to use or remember language.

Anomic aphasia (a-NOM-ick). Memory disorder marked by the inability to recall the names of objects. Thought to involve a breakdown in stage one of memory retrieval.

Wernicke's aphasia (WERR-nick-ease). Memory disorder marked by the inability to locate an item precisely in long-term storage. Person often substitutes the class of the item for the item's correct name. Thought to involve a breakdown in stage one of memory retrieval.

Broca's aphasia (BROH-ka's). Memory disorder in which you cannot recall the "shape" or "sound" of an item, even though you may recognize the item as being familiar. Thought to involve a breakdown in stage two of memory retrieval.

couldn't say "chair" at all and might well use some made-up term like "chossi" instead. But the person also might substitute a name from the *class* of objects like chairs and say "stool" rather than "chair." A person with this problem obviously has difficulties *locating* an item in long-term storage.

Someone with damage to the "speech center" located between the temporal and frontal lobes is likely to suffer from **Broca's aphasia** (see Chapter 4). A person with this disorder has problems naming numbers and letters, but does reasonably well with colors. The individual often can recognize a word if shown it for a long time, but has difficulty pronouncing it. Thus, the person might say "tssair" rather than chair. These patients seem to have little memory of the "shape" of the word or the number of syllables it has.

According to Goodglass, damage to the upper portion of the temporal lobe may lead to con-

duction aphasia. If you showed the picture of the chair to someone with this disorder, the individual would typically make repeated efforts to get close to the word—but to no avail. The person might say, "Flair . . . no, swair . . . fair." Thus the person obviously knows both the *word* itself and the *sound* of that word. But the person simply cannot produce the sound correctly. Conduction aphasics also seem to know the first letter, the number of syllables, and the sound of the first syllable in the word. Thus, they can *locate* the word in their memory banks, and they know the sound and shape of the item. They simply cannot *reproduce* the word unless you say it aloud for them first.

Question: The initial letters of the four types of aphasia described are "A, W, B, C." What kind of mnemonic can you create to help you remember these four names?

Three Stages of Item Retrieval

According to Harold Goodglass, you probably go through three distinct stages when you are shown an item (such as a picture of a chair) and asked to retrieve the item's name from long-term storage:

1. First, you *recognize* the item and search through your memory banks for its "file card."
2. Second, you hunt for the *auditory representation* (or acoustical coding) of the item's name.
3. Third, you attempt to discover the set of *motor commands* that will permit you either to speak or write the name.

Patients suffering from anomic aphasia cannot recognize a word at all. They apparently suffer from a breakdown in stage one of the retrieval process. That is, they simply cannot *find* the right "file card" and often do not recognize the word when you say it aloud for them.

Patients with Wernicke's aphasia say "stool" for "chair." This fact suggests they can *get close to the right "file" card*, but must settle for the *class* of the item rather than for the item itself.

Patients with Broca's aphasia seem to *recognize* the word, but say "tssair" for "chair." This mistake suggests they suffer from a breakdown in the second stage of item retrieval. They can retrieve the item itself, and they can get close to the *sound* of the word. Indeed, they can often repeat the word when told what it is. But they cannot generally find the correct "acoustical coding" on their own.

Individuals with conduction aphasia recognize the stimulus word, can tell you what other words it sounds like, and indicate in a variety of ways they know the meaning of the word and most of its attributes. They simply cannot write the word or say it aloud. Goodglass believes that patients with conduction aphasia suffer from a breakdown in the third retrieval stage. They can find the "file card" and its "acoustical coding," but they have lost access to the "motor commands" that would allow them to reproduce the word as language.

Judging from evidence Goodglass presents, these three different stages of item retrieval are *mediated by different parts of the temporal lobe*. Just how your brain manages to work through all three stages so rapidly when you're asked to name an item, no one really knows. But, as we will see, scientists suspect that changes in your brain's *synapses* are intimately involved in storing items in Long-term Memory.

The Search for the Engram

Logic suggests there must be a *physical change* of some kind in your brain associated with storing that item away in your permanent memory banks. We call that physical representation of a memory an **engram**.

We *assume* there must be a different engram for each tiny bit of information you have ever learned. Your brain, therefore, should be jam-packed with billions of engrams. But we have no real proof for these assumptions, for no one has ever been able to put a finger on an engram or view one under a microscope. About all we can say is this—on the basis of the laboratory data gathered so far, different sorts of engrams appear to be stored in different parts of your brain.

The "search for the engram," as it is sometimes called, has occupied the attention of thousands of scientists for the past century or so. When scientists first discovered the amazing amount of electrical activity that occurs in the brain (see Chapter 4), they speculated that the engram might be an electrical loop or circuit of some kind. As long as the electricity flowed in its proper pathway through the brain, the engram was maintained. Early computers were built on this memory model. The problem was, if you shut off the electricity even for an instant, the computer lost its memories and had to be completely "reprogrammed" when it was turned on again.

Years ago, Ralph Gerard and his colleages tried to test this viewpoint using animal brains rather than computers. That is, Gerard and his colleagues tried to "turn off" all the electrical activity in an animal's brain to see if this act would erase the animal's memories. But how to accomplish this "turning off the juice"? As it happens, they found a way. When bears, hamsters, and other beasts go into the deep sleep associated with hibernation, their brain temperatures drop considerably and most electrical activity ceases. So Gerard and his group trained a hamster, then put it to sleep and cooled its brain down until they could no longer detect any electrical responses at all. Later they warmed the animal up again and checked to see what it would remember. The answer was, it could recall *almost everything*. The electrical-current hypothesis had failed, and scientists had to look elsewhere for the engram.

Question: Many types of digital clocks must be reset after a power failure. What kind of memory do these devices have?

Synaptic Switches

Computers store information in a variety of ways. One memory device used in computers is a simple *switch*, which can be left in either an open or closed position. When a message passes through the computer, the switches can route the information from one point to another—much the way the switches in a railroad yard can route a train from one track to another. If you ask a computer a simple question such as "what is $2 + 2$?", the computer routes your question through a series of switches until the final destination "4" is reached. Switches are not very complicated mechanisms. But given enough of them, the computer can store almost *any* information, no matter how complicated.

Most scientists believe that the *synapses* in your brain function in much the same way the switches in a computer do. When someone asks you a question such as "What is your name?", the message must cross over a number of synaptic switching points before you can answer it. If you could rearrange the functioning of these synaptic connections—opening some neural switches and closing others—you could send the message to any part of your brain that held the right answer.

It is generally agreed that the engram—the physical representation of whatever you remember—must involve some functional change

Conduction aphasia. Memory disorder in which you can find the item in memory, and can find its auditory representation, but cannot reproduce the item in speech without prompting. Thought to involve a breakdown in stage three of memory retrieval.

Engram (ENN-gram). A memory trace. The physical change that presumably occurs in the brain each time you store some item away in Long-term Memory.

RNA. Literally, ribonucleic acid (RYE-bo-new-CLAY-ick). Complex genetic molecule usually produced by DNA (the genes).

at the synapse. But there is not much agreement (or solid data) about how you go about shifting the switches in your brain. Recent research suggests that when you learn, one of two things must happen. Either your brain grows new nerve cells (which seems unlikely). Or the neurons already present in your brain *grow new dendrites* (or parts of dendrites). These dendrites then *make new synapses* with the axons of other neurons during some stage of learning (or memory storage).

The question then becomes, what *causes* dendritic growth at the synapse? No one knows for sure. However, many scientists believe some sort of *chemical change* has to occur at the synapse whenever you learn something.

The Biochemistry of Memory

Perhaps the first person to speculate in public that chemicals might be involved in memory storage was Ward Halstead. In 1948, Halstead advanced the theory that **RNA** and protein molecules might be the *engrams* that scientists had sought for so many years.

At about the same time, Swedish biologist Holger Hydén said much the same thing. However, Hydén believed that RNA, not protein, was the chief candidate. During the 1950's, Hydén and his colleagues taught various tricks to rats, then looked at the chemical composition of the animal's brains. Hydén and his group theorized that the brain of a trained rat should be *chemically different* from the brain of an untrained rat, and their research tended to support this belief. For they found noticeable changes in the amounts of RNA in the brains of trained animals (as compared with the brains of untrained rats).

Subsequent experiments in laboratories both here and abroad have generally confirmed the view that an organism's brain chemistry is *subtly altered* by whatever experiences the or-

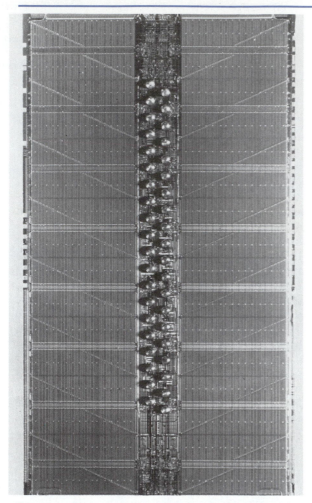

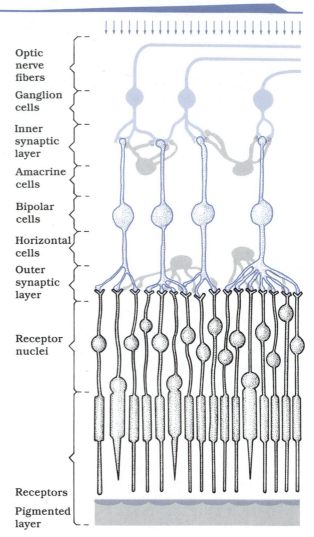

Optic
nerve
fibers

Ganglion
cells

Inner
synaptic
layer

Amacrine
cells

Bipolar
cells

Horizontal
cells

Outer
synaptic
layer

Receptor
nuclei

Receptors

Pigmented
layer

Compare the complexity of a computer chip with that of a much smaller area of the retina of the eye, which contains dozens of synapses. The retina can process more information, but at a slower speed, than do most chips.

Ward C. Halstead

ganism has. More important, it now appears that different types of psychological experiences can give rise to quite different sorts of chemical changes.

Whenever an *action potential* sweeps down the axon of a neuron, the cell responds by suddenly increasing its production of several chemical molecules, including RNA. The more vigorously a neuron fires, the more RNA it produces. And the more RNA a nerve cell produces, the more protein it typically manufactures as well. In short, nerve cells are not only generators of electrical activity, they are very efficient chemical factories too.

Chemical "Erasers"

You are not consciously aware of all the chemical changes taking place in your brain as they occur, of course. But if the changes didn't come about, you probably wouldn't be "aware" of anything at all! For example, what do you think might happen if, while you were studying for an exam, someone injected into your brain a chemical that destroyed RNA? How might that injection affect your ability to learn?

This question was first asked by E. Roy John. In the mid-1950's, John taught a cat a rather difficult task involving visual perception. Once the cat had learned the task, John injected **ribonuclease** into the animal's visual cortex. After the ribonuclease injection, the cat performed as if it had never been trained at all.

Memory Loss in Old People

One of the symptoms associated with senility is the type of *anterograde amnesia* we discussed earlier. That is to say, most senile patients are much better at recalling events that happened years ago than they are at learning new things. Psychiatrist D. Ewen Cameron spent many years trying to help older patients in several hospitals in Canada and the United States. His studies were, for a time, aimed at discovering whether or not the *body chemistry* of his patients was measurably different from that of other individuals who were just as old, but who were not senile.

In one of his experiments, Cameron found that senile patients had more *ribonuclease* in their bloodstreams than did non-senile oldsters. Cameron guessed this enzyme might be destroying brain RNA as fast as the senile person's neurons could manufacture it. And if RNA were involved in helping the brain store away long-term memories, then too much ribonuclease would *wipe out the engrams* before they could become permanent. If so, Cameron thought he might be able to help his patients by *lowering* the amount of ribonuclease in their bodies.

Cameron tried two different types of chemical therapy. First, he injected his patients with large amounts of yeast RNA, hoping the ribonuclease would attack this foreign RNA rather than the RNA produced by the patient's brains. While this approach seemed to help *some* senile patients recover *part* of their memory functions, the yeast RNA was often impure and caused many patients to come down with fevers. Hoping to avoid the fevers, Cameron gave

Ribonuclease (RYE-bo-NEW-klee-aze). A protein that breaks up or destroys RNA. Ribonuclease is found in most living cells.

his subjects a drug that was supposed to increase the *production of brain RNA*. Again, he was fairly successful—but only with people who had not slipped too far into senility. And once the patient was taken off the drug, the person's memory often began to deteriorate again.

Cameron died of a heart attack before he could complete his work. A group of scientists in Italy repeated his research and reported at least partial success, but no one in America seems to have picked up where Cameron left off. However, in the January 1982 issue of *Developmental Psychobiology*, Michael Warren reports that "elderly" mice who were good at problem solving had more RNA in their brains than did equally old mice who had difficulties with the same tasks. Warren notes that keeping the mice in "exciting environments" increased their brain RNA levels, while confining the mice to "sensory isolation chambers" decreased the amount of RNA in their brains. Warren believes that older humans who maintain an active life in stimulating circumstances need not fear a decline in their mental abilities.

Drugs and Memory

As we noted earlier, your long-term memories take time to form or *consolidate*. Anything that disrupts normal brain function during this consolidation period will interfere with your ability to remember. A number of chemicals, including some antibiotics, have been shown to disrupt memory consolidation in animals, if the drugs are given either before or immediately after training trials.

The other side of the memory coin is perhaps a bit more intriguing, however. For it is also true that anything that *facilitates* or speeds up your brain activity during the consolidation period will make it easier for you to form engrams.

We usually think of strychnine as a poison. In fact, it is a neural excitant. In large doses, it causes convulsions and eventual death. In very small doses, strychnine increases neural firing rates, much as does the caffeine found in coffee or cola drinks.

If you inject a rat with a tiny amount of

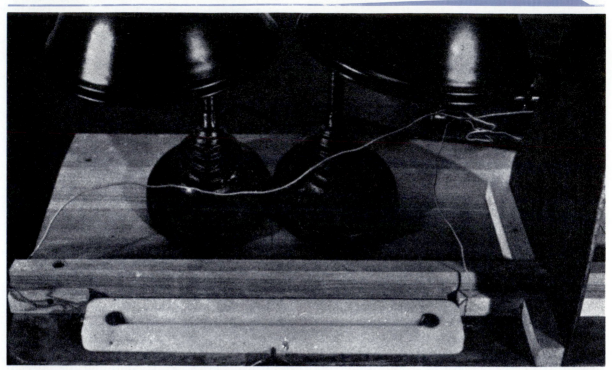
A water-filled training trough for planarians.

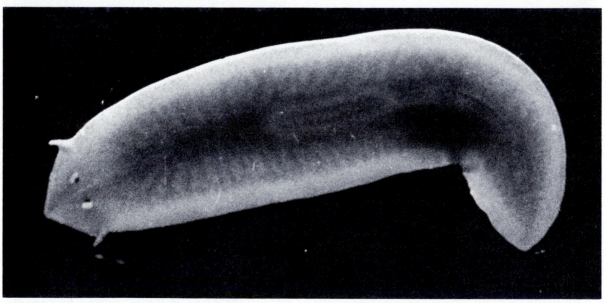
The fresh-water planarian has a true brain, a simple nervous system, a food tube in the middle of its body instead of a mouth, and can regenerate any missing part of its body.

strychnine just *before* you train it on a simple task, the rat typically will learn the problem faster. The explanation usually offered for this effect is that strychnine makes the animal more active and alert to its environment, hence it learns faster. However, you can cause a similar "memory facilitation" by giving the strychnine a few minutes *after* the animal has been trained. Now, when you retest the rat on the same problem a day or so later, the animal injected with strychnine will remember the task much better than does a rat injected with salt water.

How can a post-training injection speed up *learning*? It can't, for the rat given the strychnine takes just as long to *learn* the task as does the animal injected with salt water. What the drug apparently does is to make the animal's brain more active during the *consolidation period* following training. And the more active the animal's brain is *following the experience*, the more of the experience it remembers later on. However, the strychnine must be given within 30 minutes or so after the training, or the "facilitation effect" does not take place. A rat injected two hours after training remembers no better than does an uninjected animal.

Question: What do the strychnine studies suggest about the *length* of the "memory consolidation period"?

Memory Transfer

The most controversial evidence that the engram may be a chemical molecule comes from the so-called "memory transfer" experiments. Since I was personally involved in many of these studies, I hope you will forgive me for writing about them in the first person.

In 1953, when Robert Thompson and I were graduate students at the University of Texas, we attempted to train common flatworms, using Pavlovian conditioning techniques. We used light as the CS and shock as the UCS, and were able to show that the animals could make the same sorts of conditioned associations as did Pavlov's dogs.

The simple *planarian* flatworm we used in our studies reproduces both sexually and asexually. That is, a flatworm may mate with another planarian and subsequently lay eggs. Or its body may split in half, following which both head and tail sections will *regenerate* into complete worms.

The flatworm is the simplest animal to possess a true brain and a synaptic-type nervous system. It was this fact that got Thompson and me interested in working with these animals. In 1953, the synaptic theory of memory storage was just becoming popular. We reasoned that if synapses were important for learning, the flatworm should be capable of learning. Since our conditioning data convinced us this was the case, Thompson and I published our findings in 1955.

Regenerated Memories

When I came to the University of Michigan in 1956, my students and I continued where Thompson and I had left off. Daniel Kimble and Allan Jacobson helped with the first study, which involved training worms and then cutting them in half. We retested both heads and tails a month later, after they had completely regenerated all their missing parts. To our surprise, *both halves* of the worm remembered. We concluded there was not one engram, but several—scattered throughout the animal's body.

Shortly thereafter, E. Roy John and William Corning discovered they could "erase" a freshly-cut tail's memories by exposing it to ribonuclease while it regenerated. Subsequent experiments in Russia and in Turkey suggested that a strong solution of ribonuclease could erase memories even in uncut planarians.

Memory Transfer by Cannibalism and Injection

All of these experiments led me to believe that memory formation somehow involved the creation of new molecules, and that RNA played some part in the process. But how to prove it?

About 1960, it occurred to me that if two worms learned the same task, the chemical changes that took place inside their bodies might also be identical. If this were so, it might not matter how the chemicals got inside the worms. Provided the right molecules were present, the worm should "remember" whatever its chemical engrams told it to remember. Our attempts to test this odd notion took us not to the heart of the matter, but to the worm's digestive system.

In 1960 Reeva Kimble, Barbara Humphries, and I classically conditioned a bunch of "victim" planarians, then chopped them in bits and fed the "trained" pieces to untrained cannibalistic flatworms (our experimental group). We fed untrained victims to another group of cannibals (our control group). After we had given both groups of cannibals a couple of days to "consolidate" their meals, we trained both groups. To our delight, the planarians that had eaten educated victims learned much faster than did the worms that had consumed their untrained brethren. We seemed to have "transferred an engram" from one animal to another.

A year or so later, we extracted RNA from trained worms and injected it into untrained animals. These animals showed a "transfer effect," but worms injected with RNA from untrained planarians did not.

Robert Thompson   Jessie Shelby

RNA from a conditioned donor being injected into a recipient planarian.

In 1964 scientists working in the United States, Denmark, and Czechoslovakia reported similar success using rats rather than worms. And by 1984 several hundred successful memory-transfer experiments had been reported in the scientific literature. However, we are still far from proving conclusively that memories are coded in RNA, or that engrams can be transferred from one animal to another.

Are Memory-Transfer Studies Valid?

To begin with, there is the nagging question of *validity*. That is, when you inject an animal with chemicals taken from a trained donor, are you really transferring *specific memories* or are you merely giving the animal molecules that excite its brain activity as do caffeine and strychnine?

Jessie Shelby and I apparently answered that question for planarians some time ago. We first trained donor worms to go either to the light or the dark arm of a simple, water-filled T-maze. We then fed the donors to untrained cannibals. As we had expected, we got a highly specific "transfer effect." That is, the cannibals learned fastest when trained to go to the same-colored arm as had the donors they ate. However, the most interesting results came from a group of cannibals fed "conflicting instructions." These planarians ingested a "worm stew" made up of some donors trained to go to the light-colored arm and of some donors trained to go to the dark arm of the maze. The "conflicting engrams" these cannibals digested made learning more difficult than if they had ingested nothing at all.

Several other laboratories soon showed much the same sort of stimulus-specific transfer using rats and goldfish.

Are Memory-Transfer Studies Reliable?

An equally important question has to do with the *reliability* of the transfer effect. In 1970 James Dyal attempted to question everyone who had published articles on the transfer effect using rats and other higher animals. Dyal found that a number of well-known scientists had been *unable* to repeat the memory-transfer experiments successfully. However, *positive results* were reported by more than 100 scientists in a dozen different countries.

Still and all, many scientists remain highly skeptical of this research, perhaps with good reason. For despite the apparent validity and reliability of our studies, we never were able to prove that each memory you form is "coded" by an RNA molecule. Nor could we ever figure out a humane way of testing the transfer effect with humans.

Unraveling the "Memory Code"

But suppose your nerve cells *do* manufacture a unique new set of molecules for each of your memories. What a different world we could create if we could ever unravel this "memory code!" If we can ever devise *safe* drugs that would speed up learning, we might make college a more effective and less boring experience. And should we find ways to synthesize memories in test tubes, then students who "dropped chemicals" might be getting a higher education rather than merely "getting high."

Summary

1 The major problems that memory researchers study include **how many memory systems** there are, **what** you store, **why** you store some things but not others, **retrieval** processes, what **forgetting** is, and what the **physical basis** of memory storage is.

2 When sensory inputs arrive at your receptor organs, they are held for up to half a second in what is called **Sensory Information Storage**—an exact copy of the stimulus itself. Visual SIS is sometimes called **iconic** memory, while auditory SIS is sometimes called **echoic** memory.

3 **Short-term Memory** usually lasts for up to 30 seconds. You can increase the time an item is in STM by using **rehearsal**.

4 **Language inputs** are often translated into sounds while in STM, by a process called **acoustical coding**.

5 Usually you can store no more than **six or seven items** in STM.

6 Important inputs move from Short-term Memory into **Long-term Memory**, which is the permanent "memory bank" of your brain.

7 Your Long-term Memories seem to be filed by **categories**, so that you can **retrieve** items readily.

8 Your Long-term Memory also stores information on how to **reproduce** items—that is, how to say, write, or draw them.

9 Once you understand how your memory files items, you can use **mnemonics** or "memory tricks" to help you remember things.

10 There are many types of **forgetting**:
  a An input to Sensory Information Storage either **decays** rapidly, or is "wiped out" by the next input.
  b Items in your Short-term Memory **interfere** with each other, thus are continually forgotten.
  c Items in your Long-term Memory **interact** with each other, thus old items can be distorted or changed by new inputs.
  d Some inputs are **rejected** by the lower centers of your brain because they are meaningless or unimportant, while other inputs are deliberately (if unconsciously) **repressed**.
  e Your Long-term Memory also suffers from **cataloging, filing**, and **retrieval** errors.

11 **Amnesia** is a type of memory loss caused by brain damage or emotional trauma. Amnesia typically involves forgetting "what" you have experienced, but not "how to" do things.

12 It takes about 30 minutes for your brain to **consolidate** an item in Long-term Memory. Interruption of the consolidation process leads to a type of forgetting called **retrograde amnesia**.

13 Brain damage can also cause **anterograde amnesia**, in which new items are no longer translated from Short-term to Long-term Memory.

14 **Aphasia** is an impairment in the ability to use or remember language. There are several types of aphasia, but all seem to stem from damage to the **temporal lobe**.

15 According to Goodglass, retrieving the name of an item from long-term storage involves three steps:
  a You must **recognize** the item and search your memory banks for the item's "file" or identity card.
  b You hunt for the *auditory representation* of the item's name.
  c You try to discover the set of **motor commands** that will permit you to say or write the name.

16 The physical representation of a memory is called an **engram**. No one knows what the engram really is, but remembering does seem correlated with rearranging the **synaptic switches** in your brain.

17 Recent studies of the biochemistry of memory suggest that molecular changes may occur in your neurons whenever you learn something. The molecules involved in memory formation may be **RNA** and/or **protein**.

18 A series of controversial studies suggests that memories can be **transferred** from one animal to another under some circumstances. However, there is some question as to whether these experiments are **valid** and **reliable**.

(Continued from page 392.)

"Look at those learning curves!" Mike Keller said, as he finished plotting the data of their planarian experiment on graph paper.

"How'd they come out?" Devin Eckhoff asked. He was too engrossed in the latest issue of *Penthouse* to look for himself.

Bill Plautz picked up the curves that Mike had drawn. "Amazing. The experimental animals initially responded to the light about 20 percent of the time. But after 150 trials, their response rate went up to 92 percent."

"What about the control groups?" Tom Laine asked, momentarily putting down his copy of *People*.

"They all started off with an initial response rate of 20 percent, just like the experimental worms," Mike replied. "But all three control groups showed a marked decrease in responding over the 150 trials."

"So, what next?" Devin asked.

Bill cleared his throat. "We write the experiment up and turn it in to Dr. Sauermann."

"And pray for a good grade," Tom said, going back to his magazine.

"Yeah, I know that," Devin continued. "But what do we do next with the worms? I mean, we've got the equip-ment, and the animals, and the custard cups . . ."

"Yeah," said Mike. "We ought to be able to think of *something* outrageous to confound the scientific world with next."

For a few moments, the four of them sat in silence, each lost in thought. Then suddenly Tom glanced up from his magazine. "Hey, guys, look at this!"

"What is it?" Bill asked.

"It's an ad for a home permanent, that's what," Tom replied.

"Just what you need," Devin said slyly.

Tom threw the magazine on the kitchen table. "You're still angry with me because I beat you at racquetball this morning. But look at the ad and tell me what ideas it gives you."

Devin picked up the magazine. "The ad shows two absolutely gorgeous young ladies. That gives me lots of ideas."

"They're identical twins," Mike said, looking over Devin's shoulder to inspect the ad. "One has an expensive, beauty-parlor permanent, and the other has a $1.79 home permanent."

"Yes, but what does the headline on the ad say?" Tom asked.

Bill replied. "It says, 'Which twin has the home permanent?' But what's that got to do with worms?"

"Well," said Tom. "I've been doing a little reading on planarians."

"You mean you actually *read* that book by Hyman that you got out of the library?" Mike asked in an amused tone of voice.

"Sure," Tom answered. "And Hyman says that if you cut a planarian in half, the head will grow a new tail, and the tail will regenerate a new head. And the regenerated halves are *identical twins*, just like the two gorgeous twins in the ad. Doesn't that give you an idea for a new experiment?"

"What do you have in mind?" Mike asked.

Tom grinned. "Well, suppose we conditioned a worm, then cut it in half and let both pieces regenerate into whole planarians. Which half would retain the original training?"

"'Which twin has the memory, eh?'" Bill said.

"Right," said Tom.

"That's an easy question," Devin responded. "The head would remember. After all, it keeps the original brain. The tail has to regrow an entire new nervous system when it regenerates."

"Yeah," said Mike. "But wouldn't it be amazing if the

tail showed any retention at all of the conditioning, even though it had to grow a new head and brain?"

"That sure would upset those biology students," Devin said, a happy smile on his face. "I can just hear them now. 'If tails could remember, a zoologist would have done the study years ago.'"

"It's not mentioned in Hyman's book," Tom said. "I looked it up."

Bill shook his head. "It's really a nice idea, Tom. Very creative. But I don't think anybody would believe us if the tails remembered."

"Particularly not Dr. Sauermann," Mike added.

Tom thought the matter over for a moment. "I guess you guys are right. The scientific world just isn't ready for my brilliant insights yet."

Mike laughed. Bill snickered. Devin grinned, and picked up his copy of *Penthouse* again. But as he turned the pages, he asked, "Racquetball, anyone?"

"Sure," said Tom. "Go get your racquet. But if I cut you in half with my sizzling serve, I hope you don't regenerate into identical twins."

"Then you'd have twice as much trouble beating me," Devin replied.

Tom gathered up his equipment, then noticed that Devin was still reading his magazine. Tom crumpled a piece of paper into a ball and threw it at his roommate.

"Scrunch, scrunch," Devin said as he ducked. He put down the magazine and stood up. "I'll get my goggles too."

Recommended Readings

Cermak, L.S. (Ed.). (1982). *Human memory and amnesia.* Hillsdale, N.J.: Erlbaum.

Ellis, H.C. & Hunt, R.R. (1983). *Fundamentals of human memory and cognition* (3rd ed.). Dubuque, Iowa: Wm. C. Brown.

Fromkin, V.A., (Ed.). (1980). *Errors in linguistic performance.* New York: Academic Press.

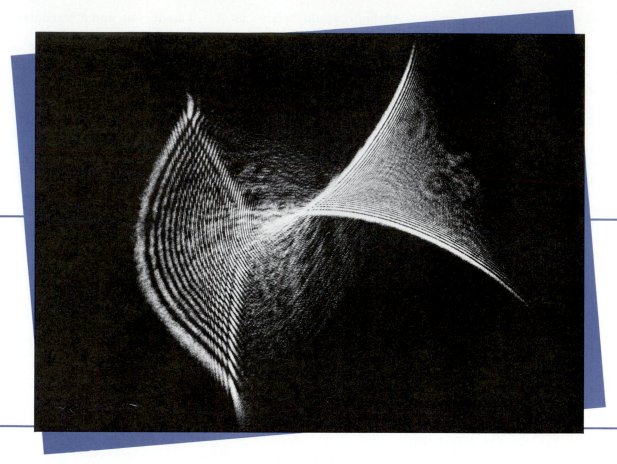

Did You Know That...

- Many of the "patent remedies" sold as medicine don't cure anything, but can make you mildly drunk?

- Perhaps half of the "cures" supposedly caused by pills or medicines are actually brought about by a psychological factor called the "placebo effect?"

- People who respond well to placebos tend to have had punitive parents?

- Hypnosis was discovered in the 1700's by a famous "quack" named Anton Mesmer?

- The French government once banned hypnosis because it supposedly made women too easy to seduce?

- Sigmund Freud rejected hypnosis because it didn't seem to help cure "mental illness"?

- People with rich fantasy lives often make good hypnotic subjects?

- Some psychologists believe that hypnosis is an altered state of consciousness, while others believe hypnosis is only a form of role playing?

- You appear to have two entirely different neural systems for controlling pain?

- You can learn how to reduce pain by using certain psychological techniques?

16

Hypnosis, Pain, and Placebos

"Mesmer's Magic Wand"

Are you sure you want to do it in class?" Brian Healy asked.

"Why certainly," Assistant Professor Don Powell replied, staring intently at his teaching fellow. "Hypnotic suggestion is a legitimate demonstration of mental functioning, a tool used extensively by respected members of the medical and dental professions. Isn't it time that hypnosis was taken out of the closet and brought into the open? It isn't a cure-all; it isn't a parlor trick; it isn't a mysterious force. It's merely mind over matter." Powell smiled. "Besides, the students will love it."

"I don't doubt that at all,

Professor Powell," the teaching fellow said. "But what if something goes wrong?"

"What could possibly go wrong?"

Brian Healy thought for a moment. "Well, what if the person you hypnotize doesn't come out of the trance? Who'd want to be hypnotized for life?"

"Nonsense!" Powell snorted. "I suppose at one time or another, some hypnotist must have experienced problems in bringing a subject back from a deep hypnotic trance. But I've never run across a fully authenticated case where that happened. What we do know is that if

you don't wake a person up deliberately, the person drops off into a restful, normal sleep and in a short time wakes up naturally. And with no physical ill effects, I might add emphatically," Powell added emphatically.

"Okay, you're the boss," Healy said. "But what if nobody in the class can be hypnotized? What would you do then?"

"Change the subject, probably," Powell said, perhaps a little too truthfully. "But it won't happen. In a class of 100, I'd expect roughly 15 students would not be hypnotizable at all, that about 65 would go into a light or medium trance, and that 20 would be capable of achieving a really deep hypnotic state. The subject's prior attitudes and experiences are the main controlling factor anyhow. If you think you can't talk when you're hypnotized, you won't talk no matter how much the hypnotist coaxes you. If you think you can't stop talking when you're in a trance, nothing will shut you up."

"Sounds like my mother-in-law. Nothing can shut her up either."

"Brian, no personal problems, please! We must approach this demonstration seriously. Hypnotism isn't a joke of some kind. It's a serious psychological tool. We are following in the great tradition of Braid, Charcot, and Freud. Just do as I tell you, and everything will turn out fine."

And, of course, it did. Professor Powell began the class with a lengthy discussion of the history of hypnotism, beginning with Anton Mesmer and his animal magnetism and concluding with recent experiments on the effectiveness of hypnotherapy. Much of the class was entranced. Next, he attempted to hypnotize all 100 students at once. Much of the class was tranced.

Then, as his final demonstration, Dr. Powell asked for a volunteer who might want to test out her or his mental powers. An alert, eager, wiry young man immediately stuck up his hand.

"What is your name, please?" Powell asked the volunteer.

"Elvis McNeil," the young man said, running one of his hands through his wavy hair.

"All right, Mr. McNeil. I'm going to put you into a trance, if I can. And then we're going to open up the pathways to your mind. We're going to unshackle all the latent mental powers you've always suspected you had. We're going to prove to you that your own mind—as untrained and untutored as it may be in its present state—can move mountains."

The young man began nodding in almost too-eager agreement, so Powell changed to rather a cautious tone of voice. "We won't do anything that could possibly harm you, of course. But there is always the possibility that you may feel a little foolish afterward. Is your ego big enough to withstand the laughter of your fellow students?"

"Gee, Professor Powell, I think my ego only has problems when people *don't* laugh at me," the intense young man said, carefully adjusting his glasses. "I'll go along with anything you want to try."

Powell smiled. "Excellent, my boy, excellent. Now just sit in this comfortable chair right here in the middle of the stage and start relaxing. Are you comfortable?"

Elvis McNeil nodded as he settled into the chair. Dr. Powell then pulled out a long, sharp hatpin and sterilized it over the flame of a match. "Would it hurt you if I jabbed this pin into one of your fingers?"

Elvis tensed a bit. "Of course it would. I thought you said it wouldn't hurt!"

"Since we won't try it until you're fully hypnotized, I guarantee you that you won't feel a thing. It's just a test to see if you're really in a trance. You won't mind, will you, as long as it's a scientific test of sorts?"

"Not if it unleashes the la-tent powers of my mind," McNeil said solemnly.

"Good," Powell replied, pulling a gold watch on a long chain out of his pocket with a flourish. "Now, Mr. McNeil, I want you to stare at this mystical timepiece that was given to me by my grandfather. See it swing back and forth before your eyes? Look at it closely, Mr. McNeil. Watch as it moves back and forth, back and forth, back and forth."

McNeil stared intently at the glittering gold watch.

Powell continued in a soft, crooning tone of voice, almost as if he were singing. "Your eyelids are getting heavier and heavier. Your eyelids are like lead, sinking slowly down over your eyes. You are getting sleepier and sleepier and sleepier. Soon you will be fast asleep, deep asleep. Soon you will see nothing but what I tell you to see. And you will hear nothing but the sound of my voice. Go to sleep, Mr. McNeil. Sleep. Deep, deep, deep sleep."

McNeil's eyes closed. He sat rigid, unmoving.

"Are you asleep?"

McNeil's head nodded slowly.

"Deeply, completely asleep?"

Again the young man's head nodded, almost mechanically.

"Hold your hand out, Elvis. That's right, straight out in front of you. Your hand is made of steel, isn't it? Impenetrable, painless steel. You can't feel a thing in your hand, Elvis. See, I can touch it, and you can't feel my touch, can you?"

"No."

"That's right, no pain at all. I can even stick this pin in your hand and it will cause you no pain at all. You can't feel a thing, remember. Now I will stick the pin in—like this!—and it didn't hurt at all, did it?"

The class gasped as Powell plunged the sterilized hatpin half-an-inch into the young man's hand. But McNeil didn't react. Instead, he shook his head slowly and whispered, "No, it didn't hurt at all."

Professor Powell removed the pin, inspected McNeil's hand, and put a small bandage over the tiny wound. Then he turned to the class and said, "So, you see, pain is ultimately controlled by the cortex. Your brain can turn pain off or turn it on, depending on the circumstances. Under hypnosis, you can be made to perceive things that aren't there, and you can be made *not* to perceive even very strong stimuli. Mr. McNeil here is obviously a very good hypnotic subject. So now let's put matters to a further test."

Powell motioned Brian Healy to come toward him. "Now, Mr. McNeil, you surely remember what my teaching fellow, Brian Healy, looks like. Right?"

McNeil nodded slowly.

"Well, in a moment, Mr. NcNeil, I'm going to ask you to open your eyes. But when you do so, Mr. Healy will be totally invisible to you. You simply won't be able to see Mr. Healy no matter where he is or what he does. Do you understand?"

Again the slow nod.

"Good. Now, please open your eyes."

Elvin McNeil blinked a couple of times and looked around cautiously.

"You can see me, right?" Powell asked, putting an arm around Brian Healy's shoulders. "But is there anyone else up here on the stage with me? Do you see anyone else here but me?"

McNeil said, "Only me. There's just you and me on the stage, Professor Powell."

"Right, absolutely right. You're a very perceptive person, McNeil. Now then, I want to help you open up the channels of your mind and tap the secret powers that lie dormant inside your skull. Would you like to learn those universal secrets, McNeil?"

Although he was still apparently in a deep trance, Elvis became excited. "Yes, yes," he cried loudly. "I want to learn the secrets of the universe! That's what I came to college for in the first place!"

"Then you should have taken this course sooner, right? Well, now, Mr. McNeil, let's begin by teaching you how to levitate objects—that is, how to make things fly through the air just by willing them to do so." Powell moved very close to the young man. "We'll begin with that empty straight chair on the other side of the stage. Do you think you can get it to float upward merely by giving it the mental command to rise?"

McNeil looked dubious. "If you say so . . ."

"Good. Good," Powell said, motioning Brian Healy to grab hold of the empty chair, which was some 15 feet away from McNeil. "Now, Elvis, all you have to do is to concentrate. Concentrate with all the hidden power in your cortex. Order the chair to rise. Do so now. Talk to the chair— give it commands out loud, and then watch what happens when your concentration becomes deep enough!"

McNeil took a deep breath. "All right, chair, you're going to rise. You're going to go sailing up into the blue like a toy balloon. Rise. Rise!"

As the young man spoke, Healy began to lift the chair slowly from the floor.

"Rise! Rise!" McNeil cried again.

The chair "rose" an inch or two each time McNeil urged it upward.

"Holy Moly, Professor Powell, it's working! What a trip!"

The chair suddenly dropped back onto the floor.

"You're not concentrating, McNeil. Keep your mind on the business at hand."

"Sorry, sir," McNeil said, and took another deep breath. "Okay, chair, let's float some more. Up, up and away!"

In Brian Healy's strong hands, the chair rose a foot off the stage.

"That's right, chair, keep going. Higher, higher, higher!"

The class began to giggle just a bit, not sure of what was going on. Healy lifted the chair until it was at the level of his waist.

"Don't stop now, get it on up there!"

Healy raised the chair above his head. Small beads of sweat began to pop out on his forehead. The chair was heavier than he had thought it would be.

"Higher! Higher!" McNeil screamed.

Quickly, Professor Powell interrupted. "That's high enough for the first time around, McNeil. We don't want to strain your cortex, after all. Why don't you tell it to dance instead?"

"Sure. I can do it. I know I can! Okay, chair, I want you to shake, rattle, and roll."

Healy twisted the chair over his head rhythmically,

following the beat of some distant drummer.

Suddenly McNeil burst out laughing. "It's a rocking chair! That's what it is. A crazy chair that dances because I've got rock in my head!"

"Be serious, McNeil, or you'll ruin everything," Powell warned him sternly.

As if in sympathy, the chair came crashing down onto the stage, and Brian Healy collapsed into it.

The class went wild with applause. McNeil beamed, confident the clapping was for him. Brian Healy stood up and took a bow, but Elvis appeared not to notice it and just smiled happily at his fellow students.

"And now, Mr. McNeil, I want you to wake up, to recover completely from the trance, as soon as I count to three," Professor Powell commanded. "Ready? One, two . . . THREE! You're awake!"

McNeil shook his head, then looked around slowly.

"Do you feel okay? Good," said Powell, not waiting for an answer. "And can you see Mr. Healy now?"

Elvis McNeil looked at the teaching fellow, then nodded. "Of course. He's right here on the stage with us."

"And how do you feel?"

"Fine, fine. But what happened? How did I get this bandage on my hand?"

"That's where I injected you with the secret powers. Don't you remember making the chair dance in the air?"

McNeil looked puzzled. "Oh, yes. I remember. How did I do that, Professor Powell?"

"Mind over matter, my boy. Concentration, that's what does the trick. Thank you very much for your assistance."

At that point, the bell rang, ending the class. Several students crowded around Professor Powell to ask questions. After he had answered as many as he could, he and Brian Healy headed back toward the office.

"What do you think the after-effects will be for poor Mr. McNeil?" Healy asked.

"After-effects?" Professor Powell said. "Why there won't be any. Elvis will find out what really happened, and he'll be embarrassed for a while. He's one of those students who takes psychology thinking that it's magic, or something. Now perhaps he'll see that the only way to unleash the powers of the mind is to study like crazy, learn all the facts about human nature, and then discover how to apply the facts wisely. Hypnosis is a marvelous tool, for some things. I think we proved that in class. But it's not a miracle cure for acquiring personal power or for gaining mystical control over the world. Besides, we proved another point that's even more important—you perceive what your mind wants you to perceive. Beautiful demonstration, didn't you think so?"

Brian Healy scratched his head. "Sure, Professor Powell. Sure."

(Continued on page 434.)

Mind Over Matter

The field of medicine has always attracted its share of quacks and **charlatans**—disreputable women and men with little or no medical knowledge who promise quick cures at cheap prices. The reasons why quackery thrives even in modern times are not hard to find.

To begin with, pain seems to be a chronic human condition. John Bonica is the founder of the International Association for the Study of Pain. In a 1984 article, he estimates that nearly one-third of the people in the US have persistent or recurrent chronic pain. According to Bonica, "chronic pain disables more people than cancer or heart disease, and it costs the American people more money than both." He estimates the price we pay for pain in the US is more than 70 billion dollars *each year.*

The second reason that charlatans still are with us is that many people lack the training necessary to evaluate medical claims. Given the choice between (1) a reputable physician who says a cure for cancer will be long, difficult, expensive, and may not work at all, and (2) a **patent remedy** salesman who says that five bottles of his "snake oil" will cure not only cancer, but tuberculosis, syphilis, warts, and bad breath as well, some individuals will opt for the bottles of snake oil.

Some patent medicines actually work. But the "snake oil" remedies sold by quacks are mostly bad-tasting concoctions that are highly laced with alcohol or narcotic drugs. People often drink them to drown their pains in the rising tide of pleasant intoxication. Little wonder that "snake oil" is a popular cure-all for minor aches and hurts!

The Correlation Illusion

Another reason that quack cures remain popular is what we might call the "correlation illusion." We all learn in school that if event B always *follows* event A, then B and A are *correlated*. That's true. But we then go on to presume that A somehow *causes* B to take place. That is, we infer a *causal connection* between two events merely because they are "co-related." Yet if there is one point you should learn about *statistics* from this text, it is this: "Correlations don't imply causality."

To make this point clearer, suppose that you overindulge at dinner and end up with a nasty stomach ache. A friend of yours offers you a sure-fire cure—dried frog eyes mixed with chicken blood! You hold your nose, swallow a spoonful of the dreadful medicine, and go to bed as quickly as you can. The next morning the stomach ache is gone. A miracle? No, for chances are you would have felt much better anyhow after a good night's sleep. And yet, the fact that you (1) took the medicine, and (2) that the pain later went away, might give you the *illusion* that A had caused B to happen. Merely because two events occur together frequently—

" I HATE TO BRING THIS UP, DOCTOR, BUT THERE'S A RUMOR GOING AROUND THAT YOU'RE A QUACK."

Charlatan (SHAR-lah-tan). From the Italian word meaning "to chatter" or "to talk noisily." A smooth-talking salesman of worthless medicines is a charlatan or quack.

Patent remedy (PAT-tent REMM-eh-dee). A packaged drug or medicine or "secret composition" whose name may be protected by a "patent" or "trademark." Many patent remedies are put out by reputable drug companies and are quite useful. Others, particularly those sold by a quack or charlatan, are worthless.

Placebo (plas-SEE-bo). From a Latin word meaning "to please." A harmless drug given for its psychological effect, especially to satisfy the patient or to act as a control in an experiment.

that is, merely because the two events are correlated—doesn't prove that one causes the other. (For more information on this point, see the Statistical Appendix to this book.)

Question: What connection do you see between Pavlovian conditioning techniques and how the "correlation illusion" occurs in the human mind?

The Placebo Effect

By far the most potent reason that quack medicines still are sold around the world has to do with what scientists call the **placebo** effect. A placebo is a pill made of sugar or ordinary flour. It does no harm at all, but when prescribed by a physician, the placebo may actually reduce pain and promote healing. How can a "sugar pill" help you recover more speedily from an illness? There are several reasons—some psychological, some biological, some social, and some a mixture of all three.

Expectancy

As we noted in Chapter 8, you see what you expect to see. You also *feel what you expect to feel.* If you are convinced that taking a pill will reduce your pain, chances are that you will *perceive* whatever pain you have as being less intense after you swallow that pill. Therefore, one reason why placebos "work" is that they alter the way you "process" pain signals coming from your body.

Locus of Control

Sugar pills are more effective with some people than with others. As we noted in Chapter 12, Julian Rotter has shown that people he calls externalizers believe their destiny is controlled by outside forces. Internalizers, on the other hand, see themselves as being responsible for what happens to them. Several studies suggest you are more likely to respond to a placebo if your "locus of personal control" is external than if it is internal. However, the reasons for this "responsiveness" in externalizers may be as much biological and social as intra-psychic.

Placebos and Endorphins

In 1978, Howard Fields and his associates at the University of California in San Francisco asked volunteers to rate how much pain they experienced after having a tooth pulled. Half the volunteers were given placebos. The other half were given a drug called **naloxone**. Naloxone *counteracts* the effects of the body's natural pain-killers, the *endorphins* (see Chapter 3).

Those subjects taking naloxone consistently reported a *worsening* of their pain after taking the drug. As Fields notes, the naloxone apparently "wiped out" the endorphins that the body usually releases when painful stress occurs. And it did so in almost every subject.

Those subjects taking the placebo fell into two sub-groups. About a third of the patients got almost immediate relief from the sugar pill. Fields calls these people "placebo reactors." The other two-thirds experienced little or no decrease in pain, and thus were "placebo non-reactors." Once Fields had identified the two sub-groups, he gave them both naloxone. The "reactors" reported an immediate *worsening* of their pain, but the "non-reactors" didn't.

Fields believes his study proves that one of the main effects placebos have is this—they cause the brain to release a sudden surge of endorphins. But the "placebo effect" is only likely to work in certain people—namely, those of us who have been *conditioned* to secrete endorphins, much as Pavlov's dogs were conditioned to secrete saliva when the bell rang.

We will have more to say about the endorphins and pain later in the chapter. First, let's look at how placebos are used (or misused) in medicine.

Question: Given the data so far, what percentage of the general population would you guess are "externalizers?"

Placebo Abuse in Hospitals

Several studies suggest that placebos are *just as effective as narcotics* in relieving the severe pain associated with abdominal surgery. But the sugar pills work with only one-third of surgery patients—presumably the same one-third of the general population who are "placebo reactors." Given the fact that narcotics are always dangerous, you might imagine that most hospital personnel would prefer to give sugar pills to "reactors" rather than morphine. However, as James Goodwin and his colleagues at the New Mexico School of Medicine discovered, this is seldom the case.

In 1979, Goodwin and his group reported that the medical staff gave placebos almost exclusively to those patients the staff thought were *faking pain*. As one physician put it, "Placebos are used with people you hate, not to make them suffer but to prove them wrong." Sadly enough, the fact that a third of the patients given placebos felt relief seemed to prove to the medical staff that many patients are "pain fakers."

Fortunately, as Goodwin notes, placebo *abuse* is a fairly rare event in most hospitals. Unfortunately, its *correct use* occurs just about as infrequently, presumably because most medical personnel haven't been taught what powerful pain-killers placebos can be with some patients.

Question: Placebos apparently are more effective if the *physician* incorrectly believes the pill is morphine rather than a placebo. What does this fact tell you about the importance of testing drugs using a "double-blind" procedure?

Placebos and "Cognitive Coping Strategies"

In a 1982 article in *American Health*, California psychologists Perry London and David Engstrom make an interesting point about placebos: Their effectiveness as pain-killers seems to reach a peak after three weeks of use, then slowly tapers off. By the end of 10 weeks of use, they often are of little use. (London and Engstrom note that morphine-like drugs show the same drop-off in effectiveness.)

In an attempt to extend the effectiveness of placebos beyond 10 weeks, London and Engstrom attempted to teach patients with lower back pain how to use "cognitive coping strategies." But London and Engstrom did so only *after* they had proved to the patients that *placebos work*.

London and Engstrom worked with a large number of lower-back pain patients. These individuals were told they would be receiving either placebos or "real" medication, but weren't told which they would get. The patients agreed to this test. London and Engstrom also gave the patients a "locus-of-pain-control" questionnaire based on Rotter's locus-of-personal-control test. The experimenters then selected 32 patients who seemed to be *externalizers* as far as their locus of pain control was concerned.

All 32 patients actually received placebos; none was given morphine. But all 32 reported considerable relief that "peaked" at the end of three weeks or so. At that point, London and Engstrom informed 16 of the patients they had been given sugar pills. London and Engstrom further told these 16 patients their *belief* in the treatment had actually been responsible for the pain reduction. But first, London and Engstrom offered to teach the patients *cognitive coping strategies* that would allow the patients to control their own pain voluntarily. All 16 patients in the experimental group agreed. The other 16 patients (the control group) continued to receive placebos without being told this was the case.

According to London and Engstrom, the experimental subjects reported *increased* pain relief after using these cognitive coping strategies for the next 10 weeks. However, the control group subjects reported *decreased* pain relief from just using the placebos. Indeed, by the end of the 10th week, the sugar pills were giving the control subjects no relief at all.

We will describe the cognitive strategies London and Engstrom used at the end of the chapter. First, however, let's look at another way of controlling pain, namely, *hypnosis*.

Question: What type of person do you think would be more easily hypnotized, a "placebo reactor" or a "placebo non-reactor"? Why?

Anton Mesmer and the Discovery of Hypnosis

One of the most famous quacks in all of medical history was a man named Anton Mesmer. Born in 1734 in a tiny Austrian village, Mesmer took degrees in theology and medicine at the University of Vienna (where Freud later taught). At the time that Mesmer began his medical practice, the prevailing view toward mental illness was that insanity was due to an imbalance of certain body chemicals called *humors* (see Chapter 20). Mesmer rejected the humoral theory in favor of the even more "humorous" notion that the mind was strongly affected by magnetic radiation from outer space.

Naloxone (nah-LOX-own). A drug that counteracts or antagonizes the effects of morphine and the endorphins.

"Cures" by Magnetism

Mesmer lived at a time when magnetism and electricity were new and exciting physical forces, and people still believed that the stars and planets radiated "magnetic fluids." Little wonder, then, that Mesmer thought that magnets could focus these "celestial fluids" on a sick person's body and thus restore the person to health.

One of Mesmer's first patients was a hysterical woman who complained of various pains, convulsions, and *agitations*. When Mesmer "magnetized" her stomach and legs, the woman's pains vanished for several hours. Mesmer became so successful at these "magnetic cures" that he took to wearing odd clothes and soon announced that, through his techniques, "the art of healing reaches its final perfection."

Mesmer never guessed that his "cures" might be due to the *the power of suggestion*. But this explanation did occur to Mesmer's colleagues at the University of Vienna. They investigated his techniques and decided his "cures" were a product of imagination rather than magnetism. Mesmer was thereafter expelled from the university, fled Vienna, and set up shop in Paris.

Mesmer's "Grand Crisis"

Paris in the 1780's was friendlier to Mesmer than Vienna had been, and he soon opened a healing salon that had in its center a huge tub containing "magnetized water." Twisted, oddly shaped rods stuck out from all sides of the tub. Mesmer made his patients sit holding hands in a closed circle around the tub so the rods could touch the injured parts of their bodies. The rods supposedly directed the "magnetic fluids" toward the wound and thus promoted healing.

To help things along, Mesmer dressed in a long purple robe and walked around the tub, touching his patients with a wand. He frequently urged them to yield themselves up to the magnetic fluids that surrounded them, saying they would be cured if only they could focus on the heavenly powers within their sick bodies. Some of the patients apparently went into trance-like states. They would sit or stand as if frozen in place, apparently unseeing and unhearing.

Mesmer had, in fact, discovered *hypnosis*, but made no real scientific study of what the

Anton Mesmer became the rage of Paris in the late 1700s when he convinced people that "magnetic fluids" could heal illnesses. Rich Parisians flocked to Mesmer's salons to touch injured parts of their bodies to metal rods that stuck out of tubs filled with "magnetic fluids."

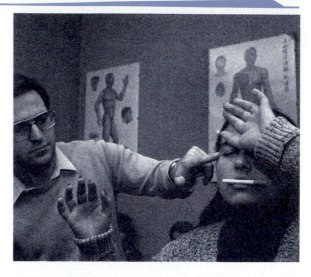

Under hypnosis, many subjects become insensitive to pain.

According to the famous French scientist Charcot, hysterical women made the best hypnotic subjects.

hypnotic state was like or what really induced it. Instead, he urged his clients "to reach farther into their minds." By continually pushing his patients psychologically, Mesmer drove many of them to reach what he called a "grand crisis," something we would call a *grand mal* convulsive seizure. Mesmer was convinced that

the "grand crisis" was responsible for the cures his clients reported. Other medical doctors were not quite so sure.

Mesmerism, the name soon given to the technique for inducing a trance state, became exceptionally popular in Paris. The French government offered Mesmer a reward of 20,000 francs to reveal the secret of his "cures." When he refused, the government appointed two committees to investigate his techniques. Benjamin Franklin, then the US ambassador to France, was a member of one. The committees were unanimous in their public reports—mesmerism was a hoax, and the cures were due to suggestion and imagination rather than to magnetism. The committees also sent a secret report to the French king, warning that the "grand crisis" was probably habit-forming and dangerous to your health. Furthermore, they told the king, women seemed to be particularly susceptible to the "grand crisis" and could easily be seduced while in this state.

So mesmerism was banned on moral as well as medical grounds. Mesmer retired to Versailles, a town near Paris, where he lived another 30 years—presumably basking in the magnetic radiations of the celestial bodies and, perhaps, occasionally trying to mesmerize a peasant or two.

Hypnosis

Until fairly recently, most scientists considered hypnotism more of a parlor trick than a legitimate psychological phenomenon. However, a few dauntless physicians and psychologists over the years did try to study hypnosis objectively.

James Braid, a Scottish physician, gave *hypnosis* its present name in 1842. He took the term from the Greek word for "sleep." After attending a session held by a wandering mesmerist, Braid became convinced that magnetic fluids had nothing to do with the effect. Rather, Braid felt, it was an abnormal or *intense form of sleep* that the hypnotist induced by somehow affecting certain centers in the subject's brain.

Shortly thereafter, Jean Charcot, a noted French professor of anatomy, began work in this field. Charcot soon reported he had found a close connection between hysteria and hypnosis. Other French scientists disputed Charcot's claims, believing that the hypnotic state was a result of **suggestibility**, not hysteria, although there seemed little doubt that hysterics often made good hypnotic subjects.

Freud and Hypnosis

It was into this sea of controversy that Sigmund Freud stepped in the winter of 1885. Freud had gone to Paris to study for a few months with Charcot. The experience marked a

Mesmerism (MEZZ-mur-ism). The first name given to hypnosis, or hypnotism (HIPP-no-tism, but often mispronounced HIPP-*mah*-tism).

Suggestibility. The state of following suggestions, of doing what you are told to do. If someone dares you to eat frog eyes, and you do, you are probably quite suggestible. The French anatomist Charcot (shar-KOH) believed hypnosis was merely a matter of some people's being highly suggestible.

turning point in his life. Prior to this visit, Freud had viewed mental illness as a *physical* problem. Thus, he had used massage, baths, rest, and electrical stimulation with his hysterical patients. When he returned to Vienna in 1886, he began thinking of insanity as having primarily *psychological* causes.

Following Charcot's lead, Freud used hypnosis to suggest to hysterics that their symptoms would vanish. But he soon ran into difficulties. For while the patients' symptoms did disappear, they usually came back again. Furthermore, Freud soon discovered that not all of his patients could be hypnotized. And those that could be hypnotized often became so dependent on his suggestions that they could not function in society unless they were under his hypnotic spell.

Renouncing hypnosis as a useless therapeutic tool, Freud instead developed *psychoanalysis*, which we will describe in a later chapter. But as Freud's influence grew, his negative opinions about hypnosis tended to discourage people from investigating the technique. It thus was not until the 1930's—when American behavioral psychologists took up the subject—that hypnosis again became a subject deemed fit for study in scientific laboratories.

Question: What similarities do you see between the return of hysterical symptoms "a few weeks after hypnosis" and the fact that placebos lose their power after a few weeks?

Suggestibility

What is hypnosis? Braid thought it a form of sleep. But the early behaviorists believed it was a state of narrowly focused attention in which the hypnotized person somehow becomes extremely *suggestible*. Clark L. Hull, the noted learning theorist, made a lengthy study of suggestibility and hypnosis. Hull was hunting for some simple test that would quickly tell who would be a good hypnotic subject. Perhaps because he looked at behavior rather than at a

Clark Hull

Theodore X. Barber

Martin Orne

person's "fantasy life," Hull was unable to find any one trait that was a sure-fire index of hypnotizability.

Suggestibility and Fantasy

Theodore X. Barber has recently developed a Suggestibility Scale that he uses in his research. The major questions on the Scale have to do with your ability to *imagine* yourself in a variety of unusual situations. One of the primary traits that the Scale seems to measure is the ease with which you can create mental fantasies.

In a 1981 report, Barber states that many women who are excellent hypnotic subjects—and who score high on his Scale—seem to have spent much of their adult lives lost in a world of fantasy. Most of these women began to fantasize early in life, as an escape from an unhappy childhood. As children they tended to have imaginary companions, and almost all of them believed their dolls and stuffed animals were actually alive. The majority of these women reported they sometimes had orgasms solely through sexual fantasy. But despite the fact that they spent "at least 90 percent of the time" lost in fantasy, these women were quite successful. All were either college students or graduates. One was a psychiatrist, another a psychologist, and all but one were married or had steady boyfriends.

Barber's research suggests there is a high correlation between the ability to "fantasize" and the ability to be hypnotized. As Barber notes, however, the fact that you are "suggestible" or are "addicted to fantasy" doesn't mean you can't live a happy and productive life.

Question: What is the relationship between being able to "fantasize" and being able to "dissociate yourself" from the aches and pains of reality?

Imagination and Parental Punishment

Data gathered by Ernest Hilgard and his associates at Stanford tend to support Barber's views on the close connection between suggestibility and fantasy. Hilgard's research suggests that the response you make to a hypnotist is partially determined by the type of upbringing you had. If your parents were inclined to punish you severely and frequently when you were young, chances are that you will be able to "go under" in a hypnotic trance rather easily. Hilgard gives three reasons why this may be the case. First, continual punishment can *condition* you to respond to authority automatically and without questioning what you are told to do. Second, you may learn to escape parental wrath by retreating into your own imagination. And third, you may find you can prevent punishment by learning to play various social roles. We will have more to say about this last point in a moment.

Question: Julian Rotter reports that most externalizers had punitive parents. Why isn't this fact particularly surprising?

Effects of Hypnosis

One of the fascinating aspects of hypnosis is that people often seem to do things while hypnotized that they couldn't (or wouldn't) do otherwise. Thus, individuals may perform *apparently* amazing feats of strength or withstand apparently large amounts of pain *if told to do so* while hypnotized.

However, as Theodore Barber notes, there is a strange quality of *role playing* to most of these feats. After studying the literature on the subject—and after testing many subjects in his laboratory—Barber comes to quite a different conclusion: Under hypnosis, you will perform only those acts that you *would perform normally* if the situation were right, and if your motivation were high enough. But even these factors are not usually enough. Barber states the major factor in hypnotic performance is the subject's *intense desire to please the hypnotist.*

According to Barber, hypnosis imparts no magic powers to the subject or to the hypnotist, nor does it enhance your physical or mental abilities. It merely *increases your motivation* to do things you might ordinarily not do—primarily because you don't want to disappoint the hypnotist.

Question: Who would be more likely to want to please an "authority figure" (such as a hypnotist), an externalizer or an internalizer? Why?

Hypnotic Age Regression

The early behaviorists were particularly impressed with the rapid access that hypnosis seemed to give to a person's early memories. They soon found that, while in a deep trance, subjects apparently could "relive" certain events of childhood. When told to "go back" to her 5th birthday, for instance, a young woman might begin to talk in a very childish voice. She would then recount in detail who was at her birthday party, what presents she got, what her parents said and did, and even what she dreamed later that night.

A few hypnotic subjects went much farther. When pressed to do so, some of them reported detailed conversations they thought had occurred between their mothers and fathers while they themselves were still being carried in their mother's womb. Other subjects recounted events that happened to them centuries before, when they were seemingly *living in a different body.* The "memory feats" these people performed under *hypnotic age regression* seemed fabulous indeed to those early psychologists who had not yet discovered the connection between hypnosis and fantasy.

Age Regression and Expectations

In a 1983 article in the *American Journal of Clinical Hypnosis*, University of Kentucky psychologist Robert Baker reports a study on hyp-

notic age regression. Baker used 60 students who he knew were good hypnotic subjects. He divided the 60 students into three groups. The first group heard a tape recording about a "new and exciting kind of therapy known as *past lives therapy.*" These students were also told, "You will be able to take a fascinating journey back in time." Under hypnosis, 85 percent of this group reported having had at least one other life.

A second group of 20 students heard a neutral description of "past lives therapy." These subjects were told, "You may or may not drift back in time to another lifetime." Under hypnosis, 60 percent of this group claimed they had lived another life.

A third group of 20 students were told that "past lives therapy" was a crazy sort of game developed "by a bunch of far-out therapists on the West Coast." The students were also warned that, under hypnosis, "You might accidentally drift back and imagine you're living in another lifetime." However, "Most normal people haven't been able to see anything." During their hypnosis sessions, only 10 percent of the students in this group reported having had another life.

According to Robert Baker, his research shows how readily people will "role play extreme [age] regressions on demand."

Hypnosis and Memory

Many police agencies now routinely make use of hypnosis in criminal investigations. In particular, the police hypnotize witnesses to help them recall details of events that seem lost to ordinary memory. In the April 1978 issue of *Human Behavior*, Martin Reiser of the LA Police Department claims that in 77 percent of the cases where hypnosis was used, "Important information was elicited from witnesses and victims that was not available by routine interrogation."

However, most psychologists now take rather a dim view of the use of hypnosis by the police. In a recent interview, Ernest Hilgard states, "It is well-known that hypnotists may implant memories, so that the hypnotized person accepts them as his [or her] own." And Martin Orne, past president of the International Society of Hypnosis, notes that what people remember under hypnosis is often *completely inaccurate.*

Question: As we noted in the last chapter, Elizabeth Loftus has shown that the questions you ask someone about an event can actually *transform* the person's memories. What problems does

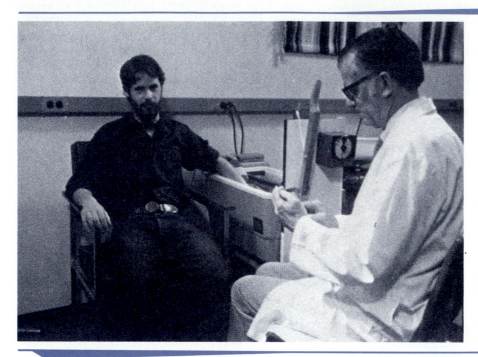

Fig. 16.1 Ernest Hilgard measuring the pain response of a subject whose arm is immersed in ice water.

Loftus's research raise about the use of hypnotism by various police agencies to "recover forgotten memories?"

Hypnosis and Pain

Theodore X. Barber believes that hypnosis is mostly a matter of "role playing." In particular, Barber uses this idea to explain the effects of hypnosis on pain. In doing so, Barber has mounted a direct attack on research by Hilgard.

Hilgard's Research

In a series of recent studies, Ernest Hilgard has shown that, while under hypnosis, a subject may both experience pain and simultaneously *not* feel it.

In one of his experiments, Hilgard asked 20 volunteers to hold their arms in ice water for 45 seconds (see Fig. 16.1). The water was painfully cold—as the subjects reported only too willingly if they were not hypnotized. Hilgard then "suggested" that they try consciously to control their experience of pain. Most of them were able to do so and now reported much less pain than before.

Next Hilgard hypnotized the subjects and suggested they would feel *no pain at all* from the ice water. While their arms were in the water, Hilgard asked them if they experienced pain. The subjects told him, "Some, but not much." Then Hilgard asked them to move a finger on the hand *not* in the water if the subjects *really* felt the pain at some "unconscious level." Most of the subjects immediately did so. Hilgard believes that *consciously* the subjects were suppressing the pain. But at some deeper level, Hilgard says, they apparently knew the pain was really there.

"Hidden Observers"

Hilgard believes hypnosis is an *altered state of consciousness* in which your consciousness can "split." One part of you acts in a hypnotized fashion and experiences no pain if the hypnotist tells you not to. But another part of your mind—which can communicate by gestures during the trance—remains unhypnotized and perceives the discomfort your conscious mind is repressing. Hilgard calls this part of the mind the subject's "hidden observer."

As we will see in Chapter 21, this "splitting of the mind" is very similar to the *dissociation*—popularly called "split personality"—that is occasionally found in mentally disordered individuals. Usually, when one personality "takes over," it temporarily *suppresses* any other personality patterns the person has. According to Hilgard, this same dissociation of personality may occur in normal individuals during hypnosis.

Question: Earlier in this chapter, we mentioned Hilgard's research showing that children escape parental wrath by retreating into their own imaginations. How do all these facts suggest that overly punitive parents may actually *train* their children to have a very simple type of "split personality?"

Is Hypnosis an "Altered State of Consciousness"?

Theodore X. Barber disagrees with Hilgard's definition of hypnosis as an "altered state of consciousness." He believes Hilgard's subjects may be unconsciously "faking" the presence of a *hidden observer*, just as people unconsciously "fake" any experience they think the hypnotist may want them to have.

In fact, Barber seriously doubts whether "hypnosis" actually exists! In a recent paper, Barber points out that Hilgard seems to define hypnosis in rather a circular way. "How do you know a man is in a hypnotic trance? Because he responds to suggestions. And why does he respond to suggestions? Because he is hypnotized!" According to Barber, hypnotism is actually made up of equal parts of "role playing" and learning how to control the way in which you *perceive* your sensory inputs.

"Conscious Strategies" for Controlling Pain

Over the past 20 years, Barber has conducted a series of studies in which he has taught people *conscious strategies* for reducing the intensity of pain. Some of these strategies are more effective than others, but the best of them seem to reduce pain at least as much as does a hypnotic trance.

For example, in one study, Barber asked subjects to immerse their hands in extremely cold water. Some of the subjects were told to try the sorts of "cognitive strategies for coping with pain" similar to those used by Perry London and David Engstrom with patients given placebos. Another group of subjects was given similar instructions while hypnotized. By all measures of "painfulness," the *cognitive strategies* for reducing pain were at least as effective as was hypnosis.

Barber concludes that, since hypnosis is no better as an **analgesic** than is "mental discipline," perhaps we should discard "hypnosis" entirely as a psychological concept. Not all psy-

Analgesic (an-al-GEE-sick). Any substance that reduces or "kills" pain. See Chapter 3.

Enigma (ee-NIGG-mah). From the Greek word meaning "to speak in riddles." Winston Churchill once said, "I cannot forecast to you the action of Russia. It is a riddle wrapped in a mystery inside an enigma."

chologists agree with Barber, and the matter is far from settled.

But it seems clear that, before we can make up our minds about what hypnosis is or isn't, we must face squarely a problem that we rather delicately ignored in Chapter 6—namely, what is *pain*?

Question: One "cognitive strategy" Barber teaches is that of "dissociating yourself from the pain." If you do so successfully, which part of you is experiencing the pain, and which part isn't? How does this question bear on the argument between Hilgard and Barber as to whether hypnosis is an "altered state"?

Pain

A century ago, most sensory psychologists believed there were four unique psychological experiences you could get from stimulating your skin—warmth, cold, pressure, and *pain*. Each of these four experiences was thought to be mediated by a specific type of receptor or nerve ending buried somewhere in your skin.

But further study turned up some troubling facts. There did seem to be receptors that were primarily concerned with temperature sensations, and other receptor cells that seemed to mediate the experience of pressure. But no one ever found a nerve ending that was *solely concerned* with the sensation of pain.

Investigations of the parietal lobe uncovered parts of the somatic cortex that, when stimulated electrically, gave rise to the experience of pressure or temperature (see Fig. 16.2). But no one ever found a part of the parietal lobe whose stimulation produced *pain*. Nor could a "pain center" be found anywhere on the surface of the cerebral hemispheres.

Every other type of sensation—vision, hearing, taste, smell, and "touch"—has both specific receptors and specific input areas in the cortex. What an **enigma** pain is, then, since it has *neither* special receptors nor cortical projection areas!

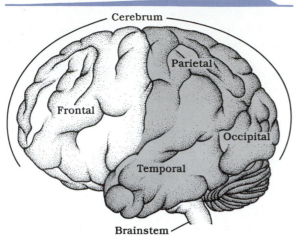

Fig. 16.2 The cerebrum, showing the parietal lobe.

David Mayer

But if no one could figure out how the pain signal got started in the skin—or where it ended up in the brain—there was no doubt at all about how it got from the "non-existent receptors" to the "invisible locus in the brain!" For it had long been known that pain sensitivity was quite well represented in the *spinal cord*.

Spinal Pathways

Your spinal cord contains *input* pathways that run from your body to your brain, and *output* pathways that run from your brain back to your body. Certain types of diseases that affect the spinal cord often give rise to continuous and vicious pain that can be relieved only by *cutting* some of the sensory pathways going up the spinal cord from the skin receptors. So pain obviously is an "input" message of some kind. But what kinds of stimulation set it off? And

why do drugs like the endorphins—which have their primary effects in the brain and not the spinal cord—reduce the experience of pain?

We will answer the drug-related question (as best we can) in just a moment. First, let's turn our attention to sensory stimulation as it moves from the skin up the spinal cord. For, if you are to understand why pain hurts as it does—and why placebos, hypnosis, and "cognitive strategies" can sometimes reduce or alleviate the pain—we must take another (very quick) look at how your skin receptors operate.

Fast and Slow Fibers

The basket cells and the encapsulated nerve endings in your skin send their messages to your brain primarily by way of special pathways in your spinal cord. The axons of these cells have an *insulating sheath* wrapped around them. As we noted in Chapter 2, this sheath is actually a special type of "support cell." Because this support cell insulates the electrical impulses that pass along the axon, the speed with which the neural messages flow is *faster* in these fibers than in nerves that lack this insulation. Insulated fibers are called **fast fibers**.

The free nerve endings, on the other hand, send their messages up your cord *slowly* by way of uninsulated axons. Since neural messages travel up to 30 times slower in your uninsulated nerve tracts than in the "fast fibers," the uninsulated neurons are called **slow fibers**.

If you implanted an electrode in the *fast fibers* of someone's spinal cord and stimulated these nerve cells directly, the person would report "pressure" feelings. If you stimulated the *slow fibers* instead, the person might report feeling pressure or temperature changes. But if the current was intense enough, the person might also report feeling *pain* from slow-fiber stimulation. However, if you stimulate both fast and slow fibers *simultaneously*, the person will not feel pain, no matter how intense the slow-fiber stimulation is. Apparently slow-fiber activity turns pain on, but fast-fiber activity somehow turns it off!

The best guess as to why this "stimulation analgesia" occurs has to do with *channel capacity* (see Chapter 9). The lower brain centers (at the top of the spinal cord) can process only so many inputs per second. Fast-fiber activity overwhelms these centers, so they "turn the switch" and screen out slow-fiber activity—and hence pain. You get the same sort of effect when you "scratch where it itches." The massive fast-fiber activity associated with scratching apparently overwhelms the mildly painful "itch input."

The Puzzle of Pain

Skin pain is obviously related to sensory inputs. Yet, the facts cited so far suggest that skin pain is *not a sensory modality* in the "sense" that vision, hearing, smell, and taste are modalities. But if pain isn't a sensory modality, what is it?

There is no one answer to that question that all scientists will accept. However, most psychologists do agree that pain is a *sensory warning signal* that is triggered off whenever tissue is damaged or stressed. Even if we accept this "warning signal" concept as a tentative definition, though, we still are left with many puzzles to solve about the *psychological experience* of pain.

The facts suggest that the body must have *two separate mechanisms for controlling pain*. One mechanism seems to involve a release of endorphins under stress. The other mechanism apparently involves a "blocking" of painful inputs at the level of the spinal cord. The first mechanism accounts for the pain-reducing effects of drugs such as morphine (and the endorphins). The second mechanism explains the analgesic effects of hypnosis, "cognitive strategies," and dissociation.

As you will see, the two pain-control mechanisms differ in a number of important ways.

Two Separate Pain-Control Systems

In a 1982 article in *Science*, Linda Watkins and David Mayer discuss much of the literature on pain, including their own research in this area. Watkins and Mayer were among the first scientists to conclude that, because the body "processes" painful inputs in two distinct ways, there must be two separate pain-control systems.

To help you understand the important differences between these two systems, let's see what happens when pain occurs. Suppose you accidentally step on a sharp tack. Immediately, the skin receptors in your foot will send a signal up your spinal cord—via the slow fibers—that some "damage" has occurred. As we mentioned in Chapter 9, this painful input message "splits" when it reaches the top of your spinal cord. The *sensory information* (about stepping on the tack) is passed on to your parietal cortex by way of the straight-line sensory system. How-

Fast fibers; slow fibers. Neural messages travel along axonic fibers at different speeds, depending on the thickness of the fibers and whether or not the axon is insulated by a Schwann cell (see Chapter 2). Uninsulated fibers are "thin and slow"; sensory inputs travel along slow fibers at a speed of about 10 feet per second. Some insulated fibers are so thick and fast that messages flow along the axons at about 300 feet per second or more.

ever, the *emotional significance* of the input is processed by your reticular system.

Since the painful input reaches your cortex by *two distinct neural pathways*, doesn't it make sense to theorize that there might be two separate systems for *controlling* the experience of pain? Let's call them the *emotion-suppressing system* and the *input-blocking system*.

Question: In Chapter 9, we noted that the reticular system controls the "orienting reflex," and that you orient toward inputs that have "emotional significance." Can you think of anything more "significant" than pain?

The Emotion-suppressing System

According to Watkins and Mayer, the emotion-suppressing system is a stress-related, "general alarm" mechanism for controlling pain.

When a painful input reaches your reticular system, it triggers off activity in your autonomic nervous system, much as Selye said occurred in all stressful situations (see Chapter 12). Your body releases epinephrin, nor-epinephrin, and a number of other chemicals that arouse you to action. But your body also *protects you against pain* by secreting endorphins (and other related substances).

This automatic release of endorphins during stress apparently reduces neural activity in the reticular system and other emotional centers in the brain. It also seems to slow down activity in the autonomic nervous system. You *experience* this reduced neural activity as a decrease in the "emotional significance" of the painful input. For example, surgery patients given morphine often report that, "The pain is still there; it just doesn't seem very important."

Watkins and Mayer believe that the emotion-suppressing system is "trained" primarily by means of Pavlovian conditioning. They point out, for example, that the sort of "learning" that occurs in the reticular system is of the "automatic" or unconscious variety (see Chapter 9).

TABLE 16.1 A Comparison of Two Hypothetical Pain-Control Systems

	Emotion-Suppressing System	Input-Blocking System
Neural Mechanisms	Reticular System, Autonomic Nervous System	Fast-Fiber Activity "Closes Spinal Gate"
Chemical Mechanisms	Endorphins and Related Substances	Unknown
Psychological Mechanisms	Stress-related Release of Endorphins May Become Conditioned via Pavlovian Conditioning	Cortical Control of Spinal Gate May Occur via Operant Conditioning
Psychological Effects	Decreases Emotional Arousal, hence Decreases Emotional Significance of Input	Blocks Input, hence Prevents Both Emotional Arousal and Consciousness of Input
Other Aspects	Explains Placebo Effect	Explains Analgesia Associated with Hypnosis, Dissociation, and "Cognitive Strategies"

To summarize: The emotion-suppressing pain-control system is mediated by the reticular system and the autonomic nervous system. Both these neural systems are easy to "condition" using Pavlovian techniques. The pain-reducing mechanism itself involves the release of endorphins (and other chemicals) under stress.

Question: As we mentioned in Chapter 13, Pavlov trained a dog to withstand physical discomfort by using pain as a signal the dog was about to be fed. Why might the dog not have experienced much conscious pain during this training?

The Input-blocking System

As we mentioned, painful inputs go up the spinal cord by way of the slow fibers. However, the inputs can be blocked at the top of the spinal cord by activity in the fast fibers. This fact suggests there is a "neural switch" of some kind at the top of the spinal cord that can turn pain "on" or "off." In 1965, Ronald Melzack of McGill University and Patrick Wall of University College in London named this switch the **spinal gate**.

According to Melzack and Wall, activity in the fast fibers "closes the spinal gate." And when the spinal gate is closed, painful inputs never reach *either* the cortex (via the straight-line system) *or* the autonomic nervous system (via the reticular system). Put more simply, when the spinal gate is closed, you neither become conscious of the painful input, nor do you respond to it emotionally.

Using data from both humans and animals, Melzack and Wall showed that the spinal gate can be closed by fast-fiber stimulation. This type of "input blocking" is an innate response to activity in the fast fibers. However, according to Linda Watkins and David Mayer, the *cortex* can also *learn* to "close the spinal gate." According to Watkins and Mayer, acquiring voluntary control over the spinal gate seems to involve operant (or Skinnerian) conditioning, not Pavlovian conditioning.

To summarize: The input-blocking system shuts out pain by "closing the spinal gate" so the painful stimulus reaches neither the reticular system nor the cortex. Fast-fiber activity is the "natural, unlearned" way to close the gate. However, by using a variety of "cognitive strategies" (including hypnosis), your cortex can gain operant control over the spinal gate (see Table 16.1).

Question: Hypnosis is sometimes described as "an abnormal narrowing of the focus of attention." What clues does this definition give as to the *mechanism* by which hypnosis reduces the experience of pain?

Conscious Control of Pain

Now that we have described the two pain-control systems in some detail, perhaps we can begin to make sense out of the various strategies scientists have developed to help people gain relief from the subjective experience of pain.

In their 1982 article, psychologists Perry London and David Engstrom list four techniques for pain control. The first technique seems aimed mostly at activating the emotion-suppressing system, while the other three appear to involve the input-blocking system.

Question: Which of the two pain-control systems would be more effective for reducing chronic pain? (Hint: The emotion-suppressing system influences the *significance* of the input. What does the input-blocking system do?)

Relaxation

London and Engstrom note that anything that reduces stress will usually give immediate reduction in pain. The first thing to do, therefore, is to learn how to relax. Reduce tension in all the muscles of your body that you can, by "going limp." Also, try to slow down your breathing, and breathe through your abdomen, not your chest.

Counter-conditioning through Imagery

London and Engstrom suggest that you learn to use pain as a stimulus that will automatically evoke a pleasurable mental image. Imagine yourself floating comfortably in a warm pool, listening to peaceful music. Then, whenever you feel pain, immediately try to call up your image of the peaceful pool. Since you can't experience "warm comfort" and "discomfort" at the same time, you will have counter-conditioned yourself against the pain.

Self-Instruction

London and Engstrom believe that "self-talk" is an important cognitive method for cutting off pain. Remind yourself that you can "switch pain off" whenever you wish. Try to make the pain "hurt less" bit by bit, and then give yourself a mental pat on the back for succeeding. Train yourself to be more positive in your approach to others, and encourage them to be more positive toward your attempts at self-control.

Monitoring Yourself (and Others)

Keep a log or chart that shows graphically how good you've gotten at controlling your pain. If you wish, you may arrange to have someone reward you for getting better at reducing your discomfort. Or, simply take pride in your own success.

Also, try to determine the response that the people around you make to your symptoms of pain. Your family and friends may unconsciously be rewarding you for expressing (and

Spinal gate. To gate something out means to keep something from entering. Melzack and Wall believe there is a nerve center in the spinal cord that "gates out" some sensations and lets others through to the brain. No one has yet located this "spinal gate" precisely or determined exactly how it works.

experiencing) pain. Or you may be using the pain as a way to control others—to get out of work or to avoid facing up to important interpersonal problems. Use direct coping strategies to work through these issues as best you can.

Question: Go back to the final pages of Chapter 10 and look over the plan for weight reduction offered there. What similarities do you see between learning to control caloric intake and learning to control pain? What do these similarities tell you about the general problem of "self-control"?

The Development of Pain-Control Strategies

As we noted earlier, externalizers tend to be much less sensitive to *acute* pain, or to the immediate consequences of the onset of pain. But externalizers have difficulties handling *long-term* discomfort, while internalizers usually develop fairly effective cognitive strategies for coping with chronic pain.

The approach you *presently* use in controlling painful inputs is very likely a mix of direct and indirect coping methods. You probably adopted this approach in part because of a genetic bias of some sort. But the most important influence surely is your past experience, particularly what happened to you during your early developmental years. As both Hilgard and Barber have shown, children whose parents were punitive tend to adopt indirect strategies involving conditioned release of endorphins and "conditioned dissociation" (such as fantasy). Children whose parents emphasized self-control skills are more likely to use direct strategies involving conscious monitoring of the consequences of their thoughts and behaviors.

Last, but surely not least, knowing the influence that parents have on children, you might well think carefully about the ways in which you plan to teach your own children to respond to (and control) pain.

Of course, it would help if you knew a bit more about how children usually grow up and mature. So, it is to the topic of *developmental psychology* that we now turn our attention.

Summary

1 Physicians have known for centuries that a **placebo** can be very effective in reducing pain—if the patient *believes* that the placebo is some powerful medicine.

2 Placebos work, in part, because they cause the release of **endorphins**. However, this **analgesic effect** occurs primarily in **externalizers**.

3 **Hypnotism** was first discovered by Anton Mesmer in the late 1700's, who thought he had "cured" his patients by putting them in a **trance state**.

4 Sigmund Freud used hypnosis to "remove symptoms" from **hysterical patients**, but abandoned the technique because it didn't always work.

5 Clark Hull and the early behaviorists believed that hypnosis was a state of narrowly focused attention in which the subject became extremely **suggestible**.

6 T.X. Barber has shown that people with rich **fantasy lives** often make good hypnotic subjects.

7 Ernest Hilgard believes that people with **punitive parents** often resort to fantasy as a way of **dissociating** themselves psychologically from parental wrath.

8 Under hypnosis, you may perform **unusual feats** of mind and body—but nothing that you couldn't do anyhow if **highly motivated**. The primary motivation for performing these feats seems to be a strong desire to **please the hypnotist**.

9 Subjects undergoing **hypnotic age regression** often act as if they had access to **past lives** or forgotten memories. Most of these experiences can be explained as a type of **role playing** engaged in to please the hypnotist.

10 Hilgard believes that, under hypnosis, the mind "dissociates" and that painful inputs not experienced by the conscious mind are felt by a **hidden observer**.

11 Barber believes that hypnosis is not an **altered state of consciousness**, and that Hilgard's data can better be explained in terms of role playing.

12 A century ago, pain was thought to be a sensory input similar to pressure, temperature, sights, and smells. Recent studies suggest that pain is a **sensory warning signal** rather than a sensory modality.

13 Pressure sensations are carried up your spinal cord by insulated **fast fibers**. Temperature sensations are carried by uninsulated **slow fibers**.

14 If stimulation from the slow fibers is greater than the stimulation from the fast fibers, the brain usually experiences pain. However, fast-fiber stimulation can **close the spinal gate** and thus prevent painful inputs from reaching the brain.

15 The body apparently has two separate **pain-control systems**.

16 The **emotion-suppressing system** involves the release of the **endorphins** as a natural reaction to stress. However, release of endorphins can become associated with neutral stimuli such as **placebos** by Pavlovian conditioning.

17 The **input-blocking system** involves shutting inputs out before they reach the brain by closing the **spinal gate**. Voluntary control over the spinal gate is acquired by **operant conditioning**, and apparently explains the analgesic effect of **hypnosis**, **dissociation** and **cognitive strategies** for reducing chronic pain.

(Continued from page 420.)

Assistant Professor Don Powell and his teaching fellow, Brian Healy, were correcting exam papers in Powell's office when a loud knock at the door interrupted their work.

"Come in!" Powell cried.

When Elvis McNeil walked through the door, the psychologist paled momentarily. Recovering quickly from his shock, Powell forced a broad smile. "Come in, come in, Mr. McNeil. Sit down! Make yourself comfortable! Why, we haven't seen you for several days! Wherever have you been?"

McNeil sat confidently in the chair that Powell had indicated. "Reading, sir. Reading every thing I could find about the powers of the mind."

Powell seemed a little flustered. "Er, well, yes. Interesting. Very interesting. We were afraid that you were angry with us—with Mr. Healy and me—about the little hypnosis demonstration we put on in class. I do hope you haven't stayed away from class because of some juvenile embarrassment . . ."

"Embarrassment? Of course not, sir! The very opposite."

"Then you aren't angry with us?"

"Certainly not, Professor. I came to thank you—and to ask for your help. You see, I've always been convinced I had a strong mind, that I had hidden talents which I simply couldn't bring out into the open and gain control of."

Powell and Healy looked at each other uneasily.

"Yes, Professor Powell," McNeil said, leaning toward the psychologist. "Even before I took your class, I had searched through all the occult literature. I answered ads in the magazines that offered to make me a mental giant if I would purchase a set of their long-suppressed secrets. I read the life histories of the mystics and tried to tap the power of the stars through astrology. But none of it worked very well. And then . . . and then, you opened the doors to my perception! You transported me to the pinnacles of power!"

Powell glanced sternly at Brian Healy, who was struggling valiantly to suppress a grin.

"Yes, well, I'm sure that's one way to look at it," Powell said hurriedly. "No harm done, then . . ."

"Oh, no. No harm at all. You see, I was sure I could really make the chair float around and dance without any help from you, if only I could find the key that would unlock my latent mental energies. Hypnosis did it, as you saw for yourself. So I've been reading all the books I could find on using hypnotism to unleash cortical forces. You really set my synapses to tingling!"

Brian Healy made a noise suspiciously like a muffled giggle.

"The trouble is," Elvis McNeil continued, not perceiving the reactions his words were evoking, "The trouble is, I can't seem to regain the powers I had while hypnotized that day in class. I mean, I've tried and tried. I've talked to one chair after another, and none of them will float—not even an inch. I feel I'm getting extremely close to the mental breakthrough I've always searched for. But I can't seem to make that final step. That's why I'm here."

"Yes?" said Professor Powell suspiciously.

"Sir, how much would you charge to hypnotize me again, and bring back the power?"

The psychologist was stunned. "Well," he said a few moments later. "Well, well. We'll have to think about that one for a while."

Elvis McNeil said hurriedly, "I can't afford much, but I'll pay whatever I can. Anything, anything to get that mystical magic back under my voluntary control!"

Powell gave the young man a wide-eyed look. Then he shook his head, almost sadly. "Yes, well, I do think we'd better have a long talk about mysticism and magic, McNeil. In private." Powell reached for his desk calendar. "Could you come see me tomorrow afternoon, say about 4 o'clock?"

"Certainly, sir. Any time you name."

"And let's keep our mouths shut about all this, shall we? I mean, we wouldn't want to let everybody in on the secret, now would we?"

"Certainly, sir. Anything you say."

"And in the meantime, I want you to go to the library and check out a book called *LSD, Marihuana, Yoga and Hypnosis* by Theodore X. Barber. Read it through carefully, particularly the section on hypnosis. Read it very, very carefully indeed. And if you're behind in any of your studies, use those latent mental powers of yours to catch up quickly. Okay?"

"Okay."

"And see me tomorrow at 4 p.m. sharp."

"Yes, sir. I can hardly wait!"

After Elvis McNeil had left the office, Professor Powell sat staring at the wall and tapping a pencil nervously on his desk. Then he turned to his assistant and said, "You know, Brian, when we teach this course next semester, instead of having a class demonstration on hypnotism, what would you think about showing a movie on the subject? I mean, maybe that's a fine way to demonstrate that while hypnosis can be useful, if improperly used it can cause, er, unexpected problems."

Brian Healy scratched his head. "Sure, Professor Powell. Sure."

Recommended Readings

Gibson, H.B. (1982). *Pain and its conquest*. London: Peter Owen.

London, P. & Engstrom, D. (1982). Mind over pain. *American Health*, *1*(4), 62–67.

Turk, D.C., Meichenbaum, D., & Genest, M. (1983). *Pain and behavioral medicine: A cognitive-behavioral perspective*. New York: Guilford.

Watkins, L.R. & Mayer, J.D. (1982). Organization of endogenous opiate and nonopiate pain control systems. *Science*, *216*, 1185–1192.

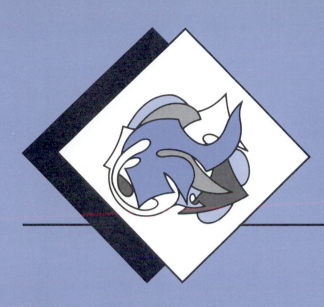

PART V

Maturation and Development

Did You Know That...

- The old expressions, "The child is father to the man," and "Man makes himself," while contradictory, are both partly correct?

- Baby geese who see a human (rather than their mother) immediately after hatching may grow up "thinking they're humans"?

- Women who are heavy drinkers are much more likely to have children with birth defects than are women who don't drink at all?

- Fetuses may learn simple associations while still in the womb?

- Most infants are mature enough to imitate facial expressions just an hour after birth?

- Infants may train their mothers almost as much as the mothers train the infants?

- The anxiety-filled dreams a pregnant woman has may be part of a "natural plan" to prepare the woman for motherhood?

- Down's syndrome children often show near-normal intellectual development if given special stimulation during their early years?

17

Infancy and Early Childhood: Physical and Emotional Development

"Where Sex Leaves Off"

Dr. Martin Mayer stared at the classroom, terrified. Through his thick-lensed glasses, the bright young faces seemed distorted, larger than life. The students swarmed around the room in constant motion, like bees defending their hive. High-school students, Mayer said to himself, have more energy than they know what to do with. How in the world could he have let himself in for something like this?

The man standing at the front of the classroom beside Dr. Mayer smiled mechanically. "All right, young people. Let's settle down now and listen. We have a special guest today, someone fa-

mous in the field of genetic psychology, or the study of inherited behavior patterns. He's come all the way from Mid-American University to give the annual Science Lecture this afternoon. And since he arrived earlier than we had expected, we've prevailed upon Dr. Mayer to address all the biology classes today. Isn't that kind of Dr. Mayer?"

Kind? They hadn't really given him the chance to refuse. He had written out the lecture he was going to give to the whole school. In very simple terms, he was going to explain his research program on genetic psychology. But what could he tell these

youngsters in addition to that? His graduate students at the U would listen to anything, of course—and listen politely. These bubbling, excited high-school students were too fresh and young to be polite, however. What did he know that could possibly interest them? A sinking feeling in the pit of his stomach began working its way up his digestive system.

The biology teacher droned on. "Dr. Mayer has published more than a hundred articles in various scientific journals, and he is co-author of the famous *Handbook of Behavior Genetics*. I'm sure you'll want to give him your closest attention.

And now let's welcome Dr. Mayer with a nice round of applause."

The students clapped loudly, and one or two even whistled. Dr. Mayer blinked twice. The co-author of the famous *Handbook of Behavior Genetics* was frankly petrified. Every face in the class was focused on him now, waiting expectantly. His wife, Elizabeth, would have called it a "pregnant pause." What had she told him, just before he got on the plane? "If you get stuck for something to say, just talk about sex. They'll listen."

Dr. Mayer adjusted his glasses on his nose. "With your permission, students, I'd like to talk about sex."

Their immediate rapt attention gave him all the permission he needed.

"As a scientist, I'm interested in sex—in all its aspects. Among lower animals, sex is primarily a matter of hormones and instincts. Among humans, it can also be an act of love. But among both humans and lower animals, sex is the beginning of life, not just the living end of things. For life starts where sex leaves off. And scientists who study the beginnings of life, as I do, must consider the biological as well as the social and moral consequences of the sexual act."

Mayer smiled at the students wanly. "A few months ago, I read Aldous Huxley's novel, *Brave New World*, for the third time. Huxley was a renegade, an artist born into a family of famous scientists. Late in his life, he studied the effects of hallucinogens like mescaline on human perception. But before he got interested in drugs, Huxley studied genetics. He was particularly interested in the social consequences of sexual behavior.

"Huxley came to the study of genetics naturally, for his grandfather had defended Charles Darwin's theory of evolution against attack by religious leaders in the 1860's. Darwin believed that animals mated rather freely, and their genes mixed rather randomly. When a male lion had sex with a female lion, neither of them was trying to create a super-lion. They were just following their blind instincts. Some of their lion cubs were, by chance, bigger and stronger than others, and these cubs survived. The weak cubs died because the environment in which they lived favored big, strong lions."

Mayer glanced at the students. They were still listening raptly, so he continued. "Humans are different, of course. We have the ability to select quite deliberately which of our offspring will survive simply by controlling the environment our children live in. And that ability puts us in a moral bind that lions don't have to face."

Mayer paused to take off his glasses and clean them. "Sometimes I think it would be great just to be a lion, so I wouldn't have to worry about the consequences of having sex."

Several of the students laughed.

"Control of the environment is perhaps the most difficult problem facing us at the moment," Mayer said, once his glasses were adjusted. "But Huxley saw that an equally difficult social issue would pop up in the near future. What would happen, he asked in *Brave New World*, if we could control the genetic process itself?"

Mayer frowned gently. "When two human beings—or two lions—mate, the sperm from the male unites with the egg borne by the female. One of the primary functions of the genetic message inside each sperm and egg cell is that of telling the cell how to grow and develop into an adult organism. The genes, then, are a kind of 'computer program' that instructs the cell in what its future behavior should be like."

Now the scientist smiled. "Ever ask yourself why you turned out to be a human instead of a lion? The answer lies in the genes you inherited from your mother and father. Human genes have different instructions in them than do lion genes. And you developed blue eyes—or brown ones—because your parents and grandparents' genes passed along 'biological instructions' that programmed your cells to turn out as they did. You had no choice in the matter—just as you will pass on your genes for eye color or skin color to your children, whether you or they like it or not.

"But what if we could *change* your genes before you started creating the next generation? That is, what if we could *reprogram* your genetic computer? Aldous Huxley was bright enough to see that, when scientists learned enough about genes, we could probably do just that."

Mayer shook his head. "See what I mean about the consequences of sex? Well, someday soon, we can go to a young married couple and say, 'Hey, what kinds of kids would you like to have? Do you want a big, blond football player for a son? Would you prefer a small, dark-skinned daughter as beautiful as the Queen of Sheba? Or would you rather your daughter became a physicist, a sort of Alberta Einstein? And is there any reason why she couldn't be both beautiful and exceptionally bright? And would you like for your son to have big hands—not so he could catch a football, but so he could play the piano like Van Cliburn?'"

Some of the students frowned, a fact that pleased Mayer immensely, so he kept on talking. "That's part of what *Brave New World* is all about. What I'd like to ask you today is the same question—when that great day comes and we know how to reprogram the genes of our children, what kind of kids would you like to have?"

The class sat silent, as if this was an idea they didn't really care to give much thought to.

"You," Dr. Mayer said, pointing to a young girl sitting in the second row. "How are you doing in biology?"

The girl blushed and the class giggled. Obviously biology wasn't one of the girl's better subjects.

"Are you getting an A+ in biology?"

The girl shook her head.

"Do you have to study more than you'd like in order to get grades that aren't as good as you wish?"

The girl nodded her agreement.

"Wouldn't it have been nice if your parents had 'spliced up your genes' to make you a 'brain,' so you could breeze through the biology book and learn it all very quickly? Wouldn't that help?" Mayer asked in a joking tone of voice.

"But then I wouldn't be

me," the girl wailed. "I'd be somebody else!"

Mayer turned quickly to a small but handsome young man sitting toward the back of the class. He had a guitar case lying beside his chair. "You, there, you're pretty good on the guitar, aren't you?"

"I'm just learning," the young man said shyly.

"But you'd like to be able to play as good as Segovia, or some of the popular rock stars, right? Did you know that the best guitar players seem to have much better finger coordination than average players have? The ability seems to be inherited, and all the practice in the world won't make you a performing genius if you don't have the right genes to start with. Don't you wish now that your parents had fixed up your finger genes before you were conceived?"

"Sure," the boy said quietly.

"You're smaller than average, too," Dr. Mayer continued. "Does that ever bother you, maybe just a little?"

The boy nodded slowly.

"Well, wouldn't you like your kids to be taller than the average? Wouldn't you want to see a genetic engineer to splice up your genes before you start having a family?"

One of the boys in the middle of the room interrupted. "But if everybody wanted their kids to be bigger than average, what would happen to the average?"

The class laughed.

"That's pretty unnatural, isn't it?" one of the girls asked.

"Of course it's unnatural," Mayer shot back. "Lions can't do it and neither can elephants. But we can already do these sorts of things

with bacteria. And it won't be long before we can do gene splicing at the human level. So maybe it's time we started to plan the consequences of what we'll be able to do. For instance, before you marry, you'll probably spend a lot of time deciding what your first house or apartment is going to look like. Don't you think you ought to spend just as much time planning what kind of children you'll have?"

"But you can't change human nature," the guitar-playing boy said.

"Ah, but you can," Mayer said. "Education is always an attempt to change human nature. But education starts too late in many cases, because you can't teach a child anything until after it's born. With genetic control, though, we can start 'educating' the child even before it's conceived."

One of the girls started to interrupt, but Mayer continued. "Nowadays, if you have ugly children, your friends and neighbors don't blame you for it because you couldn't do anything to change how they looked. But if your kids are badly dressed, or if you don't send them to school, that's a *conscious choice* and people hold you responsible. In the future, when we can reprogram genes at will, the world will hold you responsible for how pretty your children are—and for what native abilities they have. The lion can have sex without worrying about it. You can't. You'll have to decide whether you want your kids to be geniuses or just average types."

"But if everybody wanted their kids to be Einsteins, who'd collect the garbage?" complained a young man sitting in the front row.

"Beautiful question," Dr. Mayer said. "If there's a shortage of strong-bodied people who like to collect garbage, will the government require you to have kids who have an instinctive love for gathering up other people's trash?"

"I don't want anybody telling me what kinds of kids I've got to have," a young male student said. "Probably they'd try to make them all into robots."

"Hey, man, you're making *assumptions*," said another. "I mean, is garbage loving an inherited tendency?"

"Magnificent!" Dr. Mayer cried. "As far as we know, it's not. But maybe it could be. What kinds of *behaviors* do you think we can engineer into your children's genes?"

After a moment's pause, the guitar-playing boy responded. "You already said that finger coordination was inherited."

"Right. But someone born with the ability to move her or his fingers quickly probably could become a great violinist as well as a great guitarist. Or would be great at sewing or repairing computers. How would you feel if you had your future son's genes arranged so that he had superb finger coordination and he wanted to become a football player instead of a musician?"

"I'd send him to Notre Dame," said a large young man with an apparent interest in sports.

"Good idea," said Mayer. "But what other innate skills would you want to program into your future son to push him toward music? An inborn sense of rhythm? Is that something you inherit, or do you learn it from your parents? You, young lady," he said, pointing again to the girl in the second row. "What musical talents do you think are inherited, and which ones are learned?"

"I think you're trying to make us think too much," the young woman replied. "Why can't we just have kids and let them grow up the natural way, like our parents did?"

Mayer smiled. "For the same reason that we can't pretend that nuclear bombs don't exist. Genetic engineering is going to happen whether you like it or not, so you might as well start thinking about how it might affect you. As for me, I can't do anything about changing my children's genes because they're already born. But I can study behavior genetics in my lab so that your kids, or your grandchildren, can make decisions I couldn't make. But meanwhile, I've got a great big problem and it has to do with sex."

The class, which had become rather noisy during the discussion, suddenly quieted down again. Mayer smiled at how well things were going. His wife, Elizabeth, had given him very sound advice.

"Someday in the future, as Huxley pointed out, we'll have genetic engineering and we can order our kids from a catalog. But we already know that some diseases and maybe even some types of insanity have a genetic component. The facts are that some people carry the *wrong kind of genes*. If we were lions, nature would take care of things—lions with the wrong genes just don't survive in lion environments."

Mayer frowned. "The problem is, we're humans, and we tend to keep people alive no matter what's wrong with them, and no matter how much it costs. If we were 'natural' about things, the way lions are, we'd just let these people die when they were young. Until we have genetic engineering, and we can change these bad genes into good ones, what can we possibly do to protect ourselves from bad genes?"

The guitar-playing boy stuck up his hand. "Well," he said quietly, "why don't we just pass a law saying that people with bad genes can't have kids?"

The class exploded in anger.

(Continued on page 471.)

Human Growth and Development

In the previous 16 chapters, we have discussed the biological and psychological *sub-systems* that make up your body and mind. These sub-systems included your neurons and the various parts of your brain, your sensory inputs and perceptions, and your motives and memories. In the next five chapters, we will put these bits and pieces together to form a bigger picture of what you are like and how you got to be that way.

There are two traditional ways of covering human growth and development. The first approach—typically called *developmental psychology* or *child psychology*—involves discussing how various *aspects* (or sub-systems) of your personality grow and mature over time, particularly during your younger years.

The second method—often called the *life-span approach*—usually traces the maturation of a "typical" individual from birth through middle age to old age and death. The life-span approach tends to look primarily at the "whole person" as she or he passes through various stages or "life crises."

Since we will be interested in looking at your *whole personality* in several later chapters, we will adopt the life-span approach in studying human growth and development. However, we will not slight your various "sub-systems" while doing so. Chapter 17 will focus primarily on infancy and childhood. But these are also the years when physical growth and emotional development are of paramount importance. So we will cover these topics too in this chapter. In Chapter 18, we will talk primarily about the years from adolescence through adulthood to old age. With certain obvious exceptions, this span of life is a time of great mental and social maturation. So we will cover such topics as language learning and cognitive development in Chapter 18.

Finally, in Chapters 19, 20, and 21, we will put all this material together in quite a different manner as we look at *personality*—what it is, how it develops, and how psychologists try to measure it.

Before we can cover any of these topics, however, we must first discuss four important theoretical issues. As we will see, developmental psychologists often organize their research efforts (and their theories) around these four issues.

Developmental Issues

The four theoretical issues that run through all the literature on developmental psychology are as follows:

1. The matter of *continuity* versus *discontinuity*
2. The problem of *individual differences* and *human similarities*
3. The infamous *mind-body problem*
4. The *nature-nurture* controversy

Let's begin by looking at each of these four major issues briefly.

Continuity versus Discontinuity

Development implies *change*. But is that change constant and predictable, or not? Suppose we had studied you 10 years ago, and then gave you the same tests today. Could we have predicted a decade ago what you are like today? If so, then your development has "continuity" to it. If not, then your development has been relatively "discontinuous." Which do you think is the case?

In his 1980 book *Constancy and Change in Human Development* (edited with O.G. Brim, Jr.), Harvard psychologist Jerome Kagan notes that the term "continuity" has several meanings. First, it refers to a psychological quality that changes but little over a person's developmental years. "Once a fool, always a fool" is an example. Second, continuity can also mean that two traits will maintain the same *relative positions* during development. For instance, if you're better at math than English in first grade, then you should have higher grades in calculus than in literature as a college senior. And third, there is continuity across people. If you're at the top of your class in kindergarten, you should be valedictorian in high school.

"THERE'S ANOTHER HEREDITARY DISEASE THAT RUNS IN THE ROYAL FAMILY. YOUR GRANDFATHER WAS A STUBBORN FOOL, YOUR FATHER WAS A STUBBORN FOOL, AND YOU ARE A STUBBORN FOOL."

Kagan states there is some evidence that *physical* traits such as height and weight are "partially continuous." That is, if you're taller than average at four, you're likely to be taller than average when you're 14. But (as we will soon see) these physical traits are markedly affected by the environment you grow up in. As for *psychological* traits, Kagan notes they are so hard to measure that research often yields contradictory results. There does seem to be a tendency for such things as IQs and "personality test scores" to remain fairly constant over periods of time. However, this "continuity" tends to hold only when the individual's environment remains constant.

Writing in the October 1981 issue of *Contemporary Psychology*, Leon J. Yarrow observes that "Constancy and change have been poles of controversy before the advent of psychology as a science." Yarrow believes that the "continuity versus discontinuity" argument continues because we have over-simplified the issues involved. All traits are continuous—at least for brief periods of time. And, under some circumstances, all traits are discontinuous. When we define our terms properly, Yarrow says, the controversy disappears.

In this chapter, we will present some findings that seem to support the continuity position—and some data that seem to contradict that position. We then will discuss the matter more fully in Chapter 18.

Question: Two famous "old sayings" relating to development are as follows: "The child is father to the man," and "Man makes himself." Which saying takes the continuity position? Which the discontinuity position? What does the fact that these two sayings contradict each other tell you about this controversy?

Similarities versus Differences

You are YOU—a unique living system. You have your own psychological needs and personality traits that differ in many ways from anyone else's. But like most other humans, you probably have two arms and legs, a nose and mouth, two eyes and ears, hair, and skin. Even your values and opinions are probably similar to those of your family and friends.

So, what is more important about you—the fact that you are unique, or the fact that you share most of your thoughts, feelings, and behaviors with all other humans?

As we will see, some psychologists who study the human personality tend to emphasize the ways in which people are similar. These scientists assume you go through the same developmental **stages** that everyone must pass through, and that you will experience *life crises* similar to those all humans presumably experience. Other psychologists are more impressed by the fact that there are striking differences across individuals. These scientists note that even if you passed through the same stages as did most other people, you did so at your own speed and in your own way. And even if you encountered the same crises as did the person living next door, you surely solved your difficulties in your own unique fashion.

Actually, as you might guess, by far the *most important aspect* of your own development is the fact that you are like others in some ways, but different from everyone else in the world in other ways.

Mind-Body Problem

Does the mind control the body, or do bodily processes entirely determine what goes on in your "mind"? We have discussed the mind-body problem in several previous chapters. And we decided the best solution to this long-standing controversy was a holistic approach to understanding human beings.

In discussing physical development in the first part of this chapter, of course, we will tend to focus primarily on the "body" side of the mind-body equation. The "mind" part of the equation will surface when we begin talking about emotions. So, let's delay additional comments on this topic until then.

Nature-Nurture Controversy

There probably is no issue more violently debated in developmental psychology than the question of what is learned and what is innately determined. In truth, as we have noted so many times before, *everything* you do or think or feel is influenced by your genes, by what you have experienced in the past, and by your present environmental inputs. Thus, the issue really boils down to determining how nature and nurture *interact*.

The Four Issues

We will encounter these four issues constantly as we look at the material on human growth and development. Indeed, part of the delight in studying this area of psychology is that of learning how various theorists and researchers have tried to resolve the problems posed by these four issues. Let's keep that thought in mind as we now take a look at *infancy and childhood*, with a special emphasis on *physical and emotional development*. In Chapter 18, we will discuss adolescence, adulthood, and old age, while focusing in particular on social and cognitive development.

Genetic Development

As we noted in Chapter 11, you began life as a single cell. This egg cell—produced in your mother's reproductive organs—looked much like many other human cells. That is, the egg cell was a tiny round blob of material with a dark **nucleus** in its center. The nucleus contains what we might call the "managers" of the cell—its **chromosomes** (see Fig. 17.1).

Most of the cells in your body contain 23 *pairs* of chromosomes (see Fig. 17.2). If you looked at them through a microscope, each of these 46 chromosomes would seem to be a long strand of colored beads. These 46 chromosomes are composed chiefly of a substance called **DNA**. DNA is an *acid* because of its chemical composition. It is a *nucleic* acid because it is found chiefly in the nucleus of the cell. Your genes are composed chiefly of DNA molecules.

Stages. Some psychologists believe that development proceeds through a series of discrete steps or stages. Data reported in Chapter 18 suggest this may not be the case.

Nucleus (NEW-klee-us). From the Latin word meaning "kernel," as in the phrase, "This statement has a kernel of truth to it." The nucleus is the heart or center of any system.

Chromosomes (KROH-moh-sohms). From the Greek words *chromo*, meaning "colored," and *soma*, meaning "body." The genes of a cell are strung together like strands of colored beads. These "strands" are the chromosomes.

DNA. An abbreviation for deoxyribonucleic acid. The genes are composed chiefly of DNA molecules.

Cellular Division

Cells reproduce by dividing (see Fig. 17.3). When a cell divides, its nucleus splits in two. Half the DNA in the original nucleus goes into one of the daughter cells, while the other half of the DNA goes into the other daughter cell. (The term "daughter" is used even if the child will develop into a son rather than a daughter.) But before cell division takes place, the nucleus

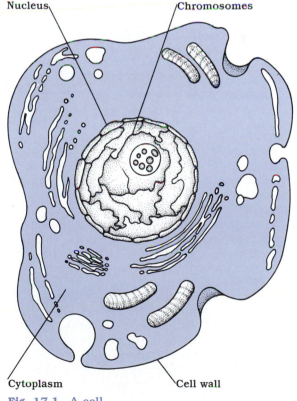

Nucleus

Chromosomes

Cytoplasm

Cell wall

Fig. 17.1 A cell.

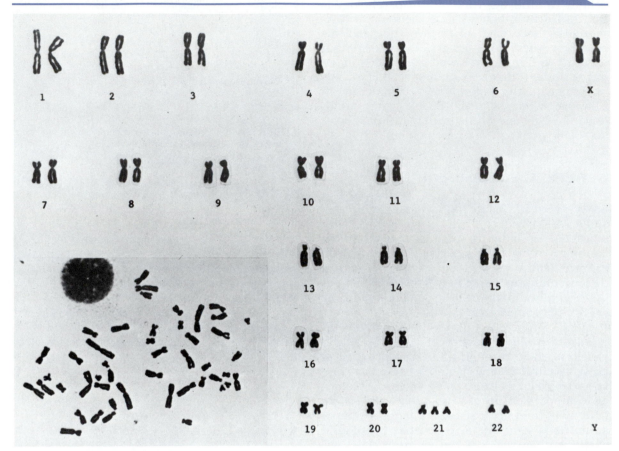

Fig. 17.2 Humans have 23 pairs of chromosomes, shown on the left as they might appear in a living cell. The 23rd pair is either XX or XY and determines the person's sex. If the 21st pair has an extra member, the person will suffer from trisomy-21, or Down's syndrome. (See Fig. 17.12.)

must *double* the amount of DNA present so each daughter cell will have its full complement of 46 chromosomes the moment the split occurs. Since the daughter cells have exactly the same DNA, the two cells are "identical twins."

The only exception to this rule is the case of the sperm and unfertilized egg cells. When an egg cell is produced through division, the original 23 chromosome pairs split in half *without doubling*, so that the egg cell contains exactly half the chromosomes it needs to survive and multiply. Thus, unless the egg cell is fertilized by a sperm cell—and receives the other 23 chromosomes it needs to survive—the egg cell will soon die. But since the sperm and egg have *different* DNA, they unite to form a cell that is *unlike* any cell in either the mother's or father's body.

X and Y Chromosomes

As we said in Chapter 11, the sperm cell differs from the egg cell in one very important respect: The 23rd chromosome of the sperm cell can be either the large X type or the smaller Y type. The 23rd chromosome of the egg cell is *always* a large X type.

If an X-type sperm is the first to enter the egg cell, the fertilized egg will of course have an XX 23rd chromosome pair—and the child will be female. If a Y-type sperm fertilizes the egg, the 23rd chromosome pair will be of the XY variety and the child will be a male.

Chromosomal Abnormalities

Because the human reproductive process is so complicated, it occasionally breaks down.

1.
The nucleus of a cell just beginning to divide.

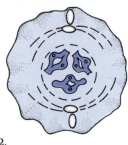

2.
The chromosome pairs begin to separate from each other.

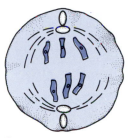

3.
The chromosomes of each pair pull far apart.

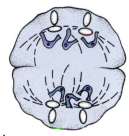

4.
The nucleus begins to divide.

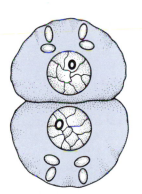

5.
Just before final division the cell has two functioning nuclei. The whole process takes approximately 3 hours. During the next several hours, each chromosome will replace its missing pair.

Fig. 17.3   Cell reproduction.

Sometimes the 23rd chromosome pair does not divide properly and the child ends up with but a *single* 23rd chromosome—always an X-type—or with one or more *additional* X or Y chromosomes. In what is called the **Turner syndrome**, the child's cells contain but a single X chromosome. Individuals who experience this chromosomal problem have female genitalia but lack ovaries. If given injections of female hormones at puberty, they develop the normal behavioral and physical characteristics of an adult female.

A child with an XXY 23rd chromosome will be physically a male—with penis and testicles—but with strong feminine characteristics. This condition—known as **Klinefelter's syndrome**—occurs in about one child out of every 900.

About 1 boy in 1,000 has two Y chromosomes and one X. The XYY male is typically taller than average, and most XYY males reach sexual puberty a year or more before the normal XY male does. About half of the XYY males suffer from moderate to severe acne—a much higher percentage than is found among normal men. Homosexual and many other abnormal patterns of sexual behavior are much more frequent in XYY males than in XY's. And, for reasons we still don't understand, the XYY condition appears primarily in white males.

Research reported in the 1960's and 1970's suggested that an abnormally large number of XYY males turn up in hospital wards reserved for the criminally insane. Some scientists at first believed the extra Y chromosome *caused* the criminal behavior to occur. However, current thinking takes a different view. The extra *male* chromosome causes the boy's adrenal glands to secrete abnormal amounts of testosterone during his development. This excess testosterone seems responsible both for the early onset of puberty and for the acne.

However, as we learned in Chapter 11, testosterone is also the "major motivator" of human behavior, and excess amounts of testosterone typically lead to an increase in *impulsive behaviors*. Most XYY males who get into trouble with the law appear to come from lower-class families in which the parents apparently lack the social skills needed to teach such an impulsive child how to control himself. XYY males born to middle- or upper-class families seldom show this lack of self-discipline, and thus seldom end up in prisons or mental hospitals.

In summary, then, the XYY male is at risk only if he is born to parents who fail to give the boy adequate training in self-control during his early years. It is thus the *interaction* between genes and social environment that causes the problem, not the genes alone.

Genetic Development   **447**

Identical twins, but not fraternal twins, have identical genes.

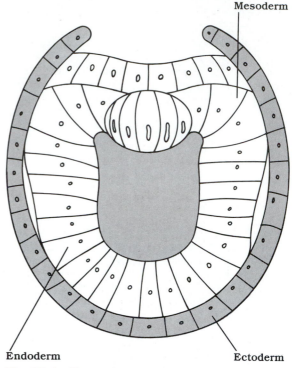

Mesoderm

Endoderm

Ectoderm

Fig. 17.4   The embryo at about two weeks, showing the three kinds of "derm."

Question: Some XYY males accused of crimes have asked to be pardoned, claiming their genetic disability "made them do it." If you were on the jury, what would your thinking be?

Trisomy-21

Occasionally the 21st chromosome pair does not divide properly, and the child is born with *three* 21st chromosomes rather than the normal pair. This **trisomy-21** condition leads to a type of mental, physical, and behavioral deficiency called *Down's syndrome*. In the past, the *mental retardation* often associated with trisomy-21 was blamed on the genetic abnormality. However, recent research suggests that Down's-syndrome children need not experience severe psychological problems *provided the child is given special treatment starting at birth*. Since this issue leads us into the area of cognitive development, we will delay further discussion of Down's syndrome until the end of the chapter.

The Beginnings of Life

At the moment you were conceived, you were no more than a single egg cell locked away in your mother's body. But within 24 hours after your conception, that original egg cell had grown large enough to divide into two daughter cells. At this point in your life, you might have become *identical twins*. Usually the first daughter cells remain close together and develop into a single individual. However, for reasons not clearly understood, these first cells sometimes separate and *each daughter cell* eventually creates a complete human **embryo**. Since the daughter cells were identical, the twins will be identical too.

Fraternal twins are much more common. Occasionally a woman will produce two (or more) eggs during her fertile period. If both egg cells are fertilized, they will both begin independent growth at the same time, and the woman will produce fraternal twins nine months later.

Since these two egg cells were fertilized by *different sperms*, they are no more identical than are brothers and sisters born to the same parents at different times.

If the two daughter cells remain linked after the first division, each of them will divide once more within a second 24-hour period. Within a third 24-hour period, all four of these cells will divide again. While this cell division goes on, the group of cells travels slowly down a tiny tube to the mother's womb. About nine days after fertilization, the rapidly forming human being attaches itself to the wall of the womb. At this point in your own life, you were about 0.5 millimeters (0.02 inches) in size.

Cellular Differentiation

Some two weeks after your life started, a remarkable change occurred in the tiny cluster of cells that made up your rapidly forming body. Up until this point, all of your cells were pretty much identical—because the "feed-forward" commands from the chromosomes were identical. But as we noted in Chapter 5, living systems are made up of sub-units that perform *different roles* in keeping the system alive. Thus, 13 to 14 days after fertilization, some of the chromosomes began giving out slightly different sets of "command" instructions. As a result, these cells began to produce slightly different proteins (and other materials).

As these new proteins and other molecules appeared, they forced the cells to *differentiate*— that is, to change shape, size, and function.

Fetal Development

By the 14th or 15th day of your life, you were made up of three clearly different groups of cells. One of these groups developed into what we call the **ectoderm**, a technical term that means "outer skin." Eventually these cells became your skin, your sense organs, and your nervous system.

Another group of cells, on instructions from their chromosomes, developed into what we term the **mesoderm**, or "middle skin." These cells eventually became your muscles, bone, and blood.

A third group of cells received instructions to become **endoderm**, or "inner skin." These cells turned into your digestive system.

At the moment that this differentiation into the three "derms" occurred, you were a hollow ball about 2.5 millimeters (0.1 inch) in size, and technically you were then an *embryo* (see Fig. 17.4). It was not until six weeks later—some

Trisomy-21 (TRY-so-me). From the Greek words *tri*, meaning "three," and *soma*, meaning "body." The modern term for mongolism, or Down's syndrome. A relatively common form of birth defect in which the facial features of the person somewhat resemble oriental or Mongolian characteristics. See end of chapter for more details, and the story that begins Chapter 18 for information on how Down's syndrome got its name.

Embryo (EM-bree-oh). An unborn child from the time of conception to the second or third month of development, when the child takes on vaguely human form and is thereafter called a fetus. From the Greek word meaning "to swell within."

Fraternal twins (fra-TURN-al). Twins born from two fertilized eggs. From the Latin word meaning "brothers," from which we get the word "fraternity."

Ectoderm (ECK-toh-durm). *Ekto* is the Greek word meaning "outer." *Derma* is the Greek word for "skin." A dermatologist (durr-mah-TOLL-oh-jist) is a medical doctor who specializes in treating skin diseases. A hypodermic is a needle that injects fluids under (hypo) the skin (derma).

Mesoderm (ME-so-derm). The "middle skin." The Greek word *mesos* means "in the center."

Endoderm (EN-doh-durm). The "inner skin." The Greek word *endon* means "inside" or "within."

Fetus (FEE-tuss). An unborn child after its second or third month in the womb, when it begins to take on vaguely human characteristics. Prior to this time, the child is referred to as an embryo.

Placenta (plah-SENT-ah). The organ inside a woman's womb that links the child's blood system with the mother's. A few drugs, such as thalidomide (thah-LID-oh-myde), can cross the placental (plah-SENT-al) barrier and affect the fetus. Most harmful chemicals, however, are screened out by the placenta before they can affect the fetus or embryo directly.

two months after your biological life began— that the three types of cells arranged themselves into vaguely human form, and the embryo thus became a **fetus**.

The Placenta

Developing cells—like developing children— are *unusually sensitive* to the environments they find themselves in. Fortunately, as you grew within your mother's womb, you were protected from most of the chemicals in her body by an organ called the **placenta**. This placenta acted as a barrier that blocked out most of the substances in your mother's blood that might have harmed your cells.

Illness can cause the pregnant woman's body to secrete somewhat different chemicals than is usual. If these chemicals (or the germs that cause them) infiltrate the placenta, they can upset the normal development of the fetus. If a woman has German measles during the third month of her pregnancy, for instance, the child is often born badly retarded.

Children can learn new motor skills—such as walking—only when neural pathways between their muscles and their brains mature and become functional.

Using twins, Gesell showed that early training on motor skills such as climbing stairs appears not to speed up physical maturation.

Various drugs also pass through the placenta and affect the fetus. For example, if the mother is addicted to morphine during pregnancy, the infant will be born with an addiction to morphine. Alcohol can also affect the fetus. Government researchers showed in 1982 that if a pregnant woman consumes three to five drinks, all blood is temporarily shut off to the fetus. The oxygen deprivation that results presumably can lead to birth defects.

About one child in a thousand is born with a set of physical defects called **fetal alcohol syndrome**, or FAS. In 1981, the Surgeon General issued a warning advising pregnant women to avoid alcohol entirely.

Effects of Physical Deprivation

Your genetic blueprint specified in rather general terms what you would be like and how you would grow. But this blueprint is always brought to life by orders from the chromosomes in each cell. And depending on circumstances, your growth and development can either be speeded up or retarded.

If a pregnant woman experiences starvation, her body protects the fetus by giving the unborn child almost all the resources the woman's body has available to it. Still, the child may be born much smaller than usual. If food-deprived children receive enough to eat immediately after birth, however, they usually catch up to

the size their genetic blueprints had set for their normal development. For example, consider a study on Korean children reported late in 1975 by Myron Winick, Knarig Meyer, and Ruth Harris. During the Korean conflict in the 1950's, many very young children in that Asian country were separated from their parents and were placed in orphanages. Most of these youngsters suffered from severe malnutrition before they entered the institutions. After the hostilities ended, some of these children were returned to their war-shattered homes. But many others were placed in foster homes in the United States. After several years of good care in the United States, however, *all* of these children were taller and stronger than the average child who remained in Korea.

It would seem that your genes *set limits* for your physical development. But it is the environment you were reared in that determines *where within these limits* your actual growth will fall.

Neonatal Growth and Development

In general, as soon as the newborn child's muscles, sense organs, and nerves are fully formed, the child begins to use them. But much of the human nervous system is not fully developed until the child is a year or two old—and some parts, such as the corpus callosum, continue to mature for many years.

As the noted child psychologist Arnold Gesell pointed out long ago, there are two general patterns of bodily development: (1) **cephalo-caudal**, which means development from *head to foot*; and (2) **proximal-distal**, which means development from *near to far*. The underlying principle explaining both patterns has to do with maturation of the connections between the central nervous system and the muscles.

The motor centers in the brain (see Chapter 4) send long nerve fibers out through the spinal cord to connect with the muscles in various parts of the body. Since the head muscles are closer to the brain than are the foot muscles, the head comes under the control of the motor centers long before the feet do. This is an example of *cephalo-caudal* development.

And since the muscles in the trunk of the body are closer to the spinal cord and brain than are those in the hands and feet, the shoulder and hip muscles come under control sooner than do those in the fingers or toes. This is an example of *proximal-distal* development.

The appearance of a new motor skill (such as crawling or grasping) always suggests that the brain centers have just become connected to the muscles involved in the new motor skill.

Effects of Early Training

Children develop at different speeds, in part because of their environments, but also because they follow different genetic schedules. Most children begin to walk between 12 and 18 months of age. No matter how much coaxing and practice the parents may give their 6-month-old child, the youngster will not walk much sooner than if the parents had simply let the child alone.

Many years ago, in his research on identical twins, Arnold Gesell showed that practice is not necessary for early motor development. In most of these studies, Gesell encouraged one twin to practice a skill (such as climbing stairs), while confining the other twin to a playpen. Training usually began well before either twin could be expected to display the skill and proceeded until the "experimental" twin had clearly mastered the desired behavior pattern. At that point, Gesell removed the "control" twin from the playpen and tested the child. The usual finding was that, right from the first trial, the "control" twin could perform the task almost as well as the "experimental" twin.

Fetal Alcohol Syndrome, or FAS. A developmental disorder associated with heavy consumption of alcohol by the mother during pregnancy. Child is born smaller than normal, often has malformations of the eyes, ears, and mouth, and may suffer from mental retardation and other physical and psychological abnormalities.

Cephalo-caudal (SEFF-ah-low CAWD-al). From the Greek and Latin words meaning "head" and "tail." Muscular development usually occurs first in the head region, then spreads downward toward the feet.

Proximal-distal (PROCKS-ih-mal DISS-tahl). Proximal means "close," while distal means "far." Muscular development usually occurs first in the center regions of the body and spreads outward to the hands and feet.

There are two exceptions to Gesell's findings. The first has to do with *special skills* such as swimming, skating, or playing a musical instrument. These behaviors need practice and guidance, and a child left to develop on his or her own usually does not do well without training. The second exception has to do with the *attitude* the child takes toward physical activities. A youngster who is encouraged to explore and engage in physical play is more likely to become active and outgoing than a child who is confined to a playpen. Thus, learning and physical development *always go hand in hand*.

Critical Periods

There is some evidence that the best time for a child to learn a given skill is at the time the child's body is just mature enough to allow mastery of the behavior in question. This belief is often called the *critical-period hypothesis*, the belief that an organism must have certain experiences at a *particular time* in its developmental sequence if it is to reach its most mature state.

Imprinting in Animals

There are many studies from the animal literature supporting the critical-period hypothesis. For instance, Nobel Prize winner Konrad Lorenz discovered many years ago that birds, such as ducks and geese, will follow the first moving object they see after they are hatched. Usually the first thing they see is their mother, of course, who was sitting on the eggs. However, Lorenz hatched goose eggs in an incubator, and then let the goslings see him instead of another goose. The freshly hatched geese followed him just the way they ordinarily would have followed their real mother.

After the goslings had waddled along behind Lorenz for a few hours, they acted as if they

Fig. 17.5 Konrad Lorenz followed by his grayleg goslings.

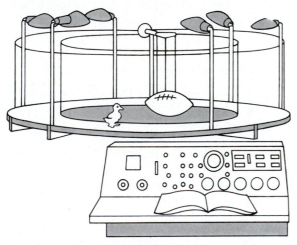

Fig. 17.6 Hess's apparatus for imprinting ducklings. The duckling follows the decoy around the circular runway.

thought they were humans, not geese. When Lorenz returned the goslings to their real mother, they ignored her. Whenever Lorenz appeared, however, they became very excited and flocked to him for protection and affection. It was as if the *visual image* of the first moving object they saw had become so strongly "imprinted" on their minds that, forever after, this object was "mother" (see Fig. 17.5).

Once the goose has been imprinted, this very special form of learning has long-lasting consequences. For example, when the birds Lorenz imprinted on himself were grown and sexually mature, they showed no romantic interest in other geese. Instead, they attempted to court and mate with humans.

Imprinting takes place in many (but not all) types of birds, and it also seems to occur in mammals such as sheep and seals. As we will see in a moment, however, there is still considerable argument as to whether anything like imprinting occurs in humans.

What Newborn Infants Can and Can't Do

Are there "critical periods" in human development? As it turns out, we cannot answer this question satisfactorily without knowing what things newborn infants can and can't do. A century ago, many scientists believed that a neonate had few if any innate abilities. For example, almost 100 years ago, William James stated that the newborn's sensory world was a "blooming, buzzing confusion." Taking a very strong "nurturist" position, James saw the neonate's mind as a "blank piece of paper." It was only when *experience* wrote on this piece of paper that the young child's mind began to form and develop, James said.

In recent years, however, the pendulum of scientific opinion has begun to swing back toward a "naturist" position. For example, we now know that almost from birth, an infant can sort out stimuli, remember, and predict future inputs. Neonates apparently can recognize their own names by two weeks of age, and they can distinguish among colors by the time they are three months old. They seem to develop depth perception by the fourth month of life. There is even some evidence that fetuses can acquire simple associations while still in the womb.

Prenatal Learning?

In the July 20, 1984 issue of *Science*, Gina Kolata describes a number of experimental studies that suggest that both animal and human fetuses can be *conditioned* to respond to specific stimuli before birth. For example, Anthony DeCasper, a psychologist at the University of North Carolina in Greensboro, notes that newborn infants have excellent hearing, a fact that suggests fetuses should be able to hear sounds while still in the womb. DeCasper performed several experiments showing that neonates preferred the sound of their mother's voice shortly after birth to the sound of women's voices they had not previously heard. They also preferred the sound of their mother's heart beat to the sound of male voices (including the sound of their father's voice).

In his most recent experiment, performed with Melanie Spence, DeCasper asked pregnant women to "talk" to their fetuses daily. During the last six weeks of their pregnancy, the women read aloud from *The Cat in the Hat* (a children's book) twice a day. Then, shortly after the infants were born, DeCasper and Spence tested them. The infants preferred hearing their mothers read aloud from *The Cat in the Hat* than from another children's book. DeCasper concludes that "prenatal auditory experience is sufficient to influence postnatal auditory preferences."

How much information fetuses can acquire before birth, we don't yet know. However, the fact that they can learn *anything* while still in the womb may help explain many of the early behaviors infants typically show.

Neonatal Learning

According to Richard M. Restak, "Only moments out of the womb, infants are capable of a wide variety of behaviors." Their eyes are alert, and they turn their heads in the direction of any voice they hear. They prefer female voices to male, but apparently search their visual world to locate the source of *any* human voice. They move their arms and legs in **synchrony** to human speech—but not to random noise, or many other sounds (such as tapping). Furthermore, they respond to any *human language*, but not to *artificial sounds* and broken-up speech patterns. They recognize their mother by the time they are two weeks old, but are more playful and alert in the presence of their father than of the mother.

Restak notes as well that a two-week-old infant apparently can integrate sights, sounds, and touch into a meaningful perceptual pattern or *schema* (see Chapter 9). The "mother" schema is particularly powerful. British researcher Genevieve Carpenter tested two-week-old babies in four different situations:

1. The mother speaking to the child in her own voice
2. A strange woman speaking to the infant
3. The mother speaking in the strange woman's voice
4. The strange woman speaking in the mother's voice

Imprinting (IM-prin-ting). To imprint is to make a permanent impression on something. In psychological terms, imprinting refers to the very rapid and long-lasting learning that occurs during the first day or so of a young animal's life, when it attaches itself emotionally to the first moving object that it sees or hears.

Synchrony (SIN-crow-knee). When a group of people "synchronize" their watches, they make sure the devices all show precisely the same time. To do something in synchrony with someone else is to respond in the same way and with the same rhythm.

The babies responded most positively to the first situation, thus demonstrating they can recognize their own mothers very early in life. However, the infants cried or became frightened by the third and fourth situations. Carpenter believes that the sound of the mother's voice coming from another woman's face "disrupted the infant's expectations," because this situation didn't fit the infant's schema of what the mother should sound like.

Expressive Imitation

According to Andrew Meltzoff of the University of Washington, an infant can imitate some facial expressions *one hour after birth*. But because such newborn children are difficult to work with, Meltzoff and his colleagues have performed most of their research on two-week-old babies. In an elegant series of studies begun in 1977, Meltzoff has shown that two-week-old infants will stick out their tongues or open their mouths fully the first time they see these expressive facial expressions in the adults around them (see Fig. 17.7).

Meltzoff's experiments seem particularly well controlled. The adults whose expressions the babies imitated were all strangers to the infants. The infants' responses were filmed and then judged by scientists who did not know what expression the baby was supposed to be imitating. Furthermore, Meltzoff did not tell the children's parents what he was up to. (In one early study when the parents were told, the mothers trained the infants to stick out their tongues before bringing them to the lab. As one mother put it, "I didn't want my baby to fail his first test.")

Meltzoff has also shown that two-week-old infants can *remember* facial expressions for brief periods of time. In one study, he stuck pacifiers in the babies' mouths and then exposed them to adults who either opened their mouths or stuck out their tongues. A few min-

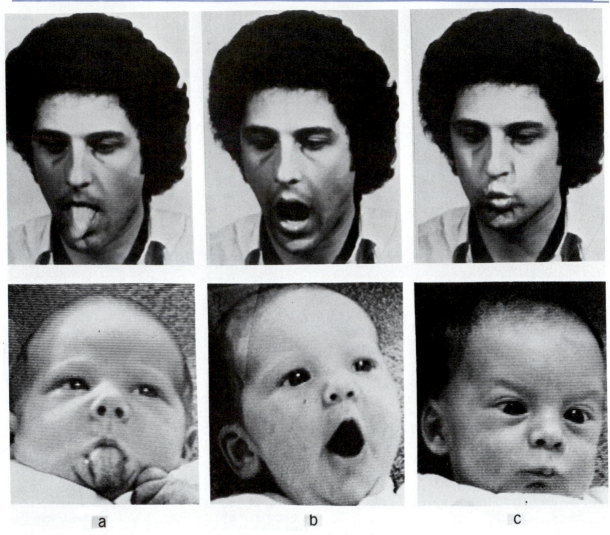

Fig. 17.7 Sample photographs from videotape recordings of two- to three-week-old infants imitating (A) tongue protrusion, (B) mouth opening, and (C) lip protrusion demonstrated by an adult experimenter.

utes later, when the pacifier was removed, the infants still gave the proper imitative response.

Nature or Nurture?

If newborns can do so much immediately after birth, doesn't that prove that most *mental development* is determined almost entirely by *physical growth*? And if that is the case, isn't most of what we call "personality" shaped by the genes, and not the environment?

Probably the *interactionist* position taken by Princeton researchers J.L. and Carol G. Gould is the one best supported by present data. Writing in the May issue of *Science 81*, the Goulds state that the genes *sensitize* newly born organisms to certain aspects of their environments. But both the environment and the training techniques actually used determine what infants learn (see Fig. 17.8).

Given the past history of the nature-nurture controversy, it's likely this issue will never be entirely settled. But as long as scientists continue to argue about what is innate and what is learned, the more we will learn about the factors that influence human growth and development. We can make this point rather dramatically by looking now at emotional development.

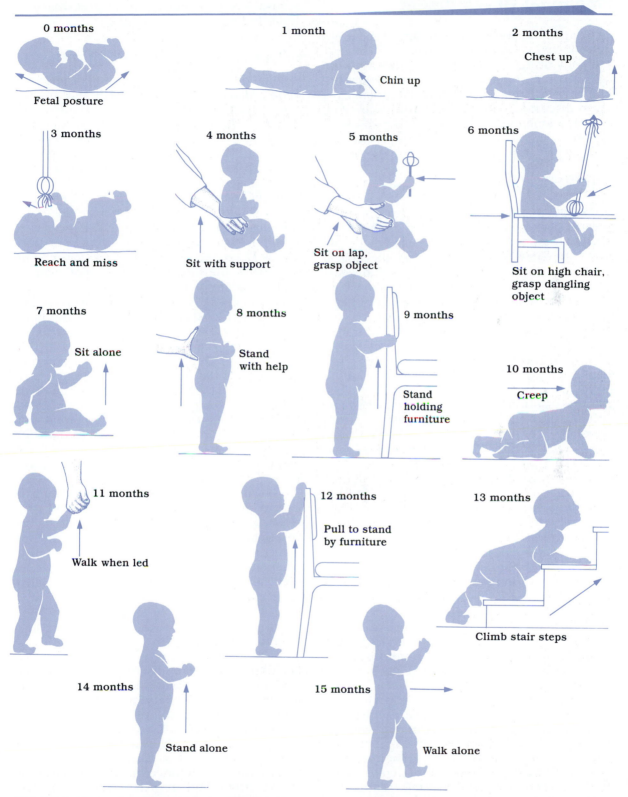

Fig. 17.8 Motor development in an infant.

Emotional Development

In Chapter 12, we discussed some of the problems of trying to study the emotions. The first difficulty brings the mind-body problem to the fore, since we must decide whether to emphasize physical reactions or mental experiences when discussing emotionality. But in covering the *development* of emotional responses in children, we cannot avoid the nature-nurture controversy either.

The Body/Nature Position

As you might expect, those developmental theorists who emphasize the physical side of emotions tend to believe that emotional reactions are chiefly inherited. In this, they follow the lead of Charles Darwin. As we mentioned in Chapter 12, Darwin believed that almost all human emotions are the result of inherited "animal instincts." These instincts have high survival value, for they allow organisms to *signal* their needs and desires to other organisms.

Modern theorists have refined Darwin's notions somewhat. They believe you inherited all of your emotional responses, true. But what you were born with were actually rather unspecific and undifferentiated physical reactions. The world you grew up in then "shaped" the specific manner in which you *express* your feelings.

For instance, in the 1982 book *Emotion and Early Interaction*, C. Malatesta states that infants learn to "display appropriate emotions" primarily through interactions with their mothers and other adults. Malatesta's research indicates that mothers influence their infants by "modeling" the appropriate reactions they want the youngsters to show. The mothers also selectively reward "appropriate" responses in the infants and punish emotional expressions the mothers believe to be "inappropriate." Malatesta says that early social contact with adults therefore serves to teach children cultural rules, gender-related rules, and personal rules involving emotional reactions.

In brief, then, the body/nature position is this: You were born with a set of undifferentiated emotional responses. Through contact with others, you learn to enhance and enlarge on some of these reactions, and to suppress and minimize others. But you *do not create new emotional expressions*. You merely *reshape* the responses you inherited. And you use these emotional expressions to signal your needs and arousal level to others, not to suggest what your inner feelings are like.

The Mind/Nurture Position

What do you try to convey to others when you smile? Merely that you are pleasurably aroused but unlikely to attack them (as Darwin suggested)? Or does your smile have *symbolic meaning*? That is, are you trying to tell people that your inner thoughts and feelings are highly positive, and that you want to share your warm glow with them?

Social-learning theorists, such as Michigan's Nancy Cantor, lean toward what we might call the "mind/nurture" perspective. When you were newborn, your emotions were determined primarily by neural activity in such lower brain centers as the limbic system, hypothalamus, and the brain stem (see Chapter 12). But in later childhood, social-learning theorists say, your cortex took over control from the lower brain centers. And as your cortex developed, your "mind" emerged. Your mind was at first "shaped" by your social environment and your genetic potential. You learned things in a fairly passive, reflexive manner. But as you grew, you gained the ability to think in symbolic terms. You discovered methods of changing your own thoughts and emotional responses *voluntarily*, and ways to alter your environment as well. Or, as we put it in Chapter 10, as you matured, you gained the ability to *choose*.

Body/nature theorists tend to view you as a passive recipient of what your genes and environment give you. Mind/nurture theorists see you as an active participant in your own development. You should keep both these theoretical positions in mind as we discuss the development of a very important emotion in infancy and childhood—that of *love*.

Love

Let us continue our discussion of emotional development by asking an apparently simple-minded question: What is love? The usual belief (in our society) is that love is an *internal state or emotional process*. Love certainly is an emotion, and it obviously has its *subjective* (or intra-psychic) aspects. This side of love has been written about for centuries by some of the wisest poets and novelists the world has known. When Elizabeth Barrett Browning wrote, "How do I love thee? Let me count the ways . . ." she told us as much about the subjective experience of love as any psychologist could.

However, love can also be approached *objectively*. For example, we may look at maternal love and say that it is an instinctual, biological response strongly influenced by the female's hormones. Or we may look at an individual's behavior and *assume* that only someone in love would act in that fashion. We can then study "loving behaviors" quite objectively, and draw conclusions about what internal processes might *mediate* these behaviors. These scientific investigations of love will never *replace* our subjective, poetic examination of this glorious condition—nor is there any reason why they should. But once we realize that love is, *in part*, a response to some living or inanimate object, we can make certain statements about love that we could not make otherwise.

Taking this viewpoint, we can see that, like all behavior, loving responses must be affected by a person's genetic blueprint, past experience, and present environment. We can also state that loving behaviors will *tend to increase* if they are followed by satisfaction and reward, and that they will *tend to decrease* if followed by pain, punishment, or lack of reinforcement. We do not usually think about love in these terms. But it is only by taking an objective view toward love that we can hope to identify the factors that influence the *development* of love and other emotions.

Question: How would your solution to the mind-body problem influence which aspects of "love" you decided could be studied scientifically?

Parental Love

Society demands that parents love—or at least care for—their children. So social factors surely influence both paternal and maternal love. But these social influences always *interact* with biological and intra-psychic factors.

In his book *The First Relationship: Infant and Mother*, Daniel Stern describes how mother and child form a **social dyad** almost immediately after the infant's birth. Stern has a laboratory at New York Hospital's Payne Whitney Clinic. For many years, he has filmed the reactions of mothers to their newborn children. He then slows the movies down and analyzes the pictures one frame at a time. By making this sort of "slow-motion analysis," Stern is able

to spot subtle mother-infant interactions that otherwise might be missed.

Stern reports that both the mother and her infant appear to have an "inborn mutual readiness" to respond to each other. This "readiness" apparently is a genetically determined *social behavior* in both the mother and the child. But it is also a pattern of interactions that society strongly reinforces once the behaviors occur.

Perhaps it is not as glamorous to study interactive patterns as it is to study "love." But as Robert Emde notes, we are more likely to understand these natural parental-child patterns if we look at them objectively. Emde is a psychiatrist at the University of Colorado Medical School. His studies suggest that the infant triggers off maternal and paternal behaviors in the parents as much as parents set off innate responses in the child. He sums up the matter thusly, "For years, theories described how mothers shaped babies, but we are now beginning to appreciate how much babies shape mothers." And how they shape their fathers, too, as Emde also points out.

The question then becomes, what are the crucial variables that determine parental/child patterns of interactions? Some of these variables are biochemical, and are determined by the genes. Other factors are psychological, and are influenced by past experience and the laws of learning. And some of the variables are social, for not all societies value infants as much as ours does.

We will look at the various influences on parent-child interactions in just a moment. But first, a reminder about a scientific "fact of life." There are some aspects of behavior we simply cannot study using human subjects. Therefore, in many studies, we use animal subjects instead. For instance, much of our knowledge of how hormones influence maternal care comes from experiments on rats, birds, sheep, and monkeys. As useful as the lower species are in this sort of work, however, we must always be careful in generalizing from animal subjects to the human level. And, just as important from an ethical standpoint, we must make sure the animals we use in our research are treated with as much concern for their welfare as if we were using human subjects.

T. Berry Brazelton   Jay Rosenblatt

These points made, suppose we begin by looking at some *biological* variables that affect parent-child relationships.

Hormonal Influences on Maternal Behavior

Harvard psychologist T. Berry Brazelton has for many years studied the ways that parents and infants react to each other. Brazelton states that a mother's emotional attachment to her infant does not appear "instantaneously, by magic" in the hospital delivery room. Rather, he says, this emotionality begins early in pregnancy and develops fairly slowly. It shows itself primarily in the *feelings and dreams* that many women experience during pregnancy.

Brazelton notes that most women experience considerable anxiety about themselves and their yet-to-be-born child during pregnancy. These fears are part of the normal attachment process, Brazelton says, and probably reach their peak a few days before labor begins. The anxiety and nervousness are needed in order to break old habit patterns and prepare the woman to take on the new role of mothering. These fears also provide the woman with the heightened arousal and energy she will need in order to care for her infant.

Brazelton believes that the attachment process has two aspects to it. The first is an *increased interest in infants*. Research suggests this part of the process develops rapidly, is controlled primarily by hormones, and is usually found only in pregnant females. The second part of parental attachment involves a need for *continued contact with infants*. This need seems to be psychological rather than biological in origin, develops rather slowly, is strongly influenced by reinforcement, and can be seen in males as well as females.

Hormonal "Triggers"

According to Jay Rosenblatt of Rutgers University, the hormone levels of pregnant females change dramatically just before labor starts. The amount of progesterone decreases sharply, while the level of estrogen increases (see Chapter 11). Rosenblatt states that "the onset of maternal behavior before delivery is based on this rise in estrogen." Rosenblatt calls this effect a "hormonal trigger" that significantly changes both *motives* and *behaviors*. "If, before a rat gives birth, we offer her a baby and a piece of food, she chooses the food. Right after birth, she chooses the baby. That is a motivational shift."

Rosenblatt notes that, prior to the change, a pregnant rat will avoid newborn rat pups taken from another mother. Immediately after the hormonal change—but before the female gives birth—she develops an intense interest in pups taken from other mothers, however.

Put more simply, progesterone merely makes it easy for the mother to *learn* to become attached to her offspring. This is the biological aspect of maternal attachment. However, it is the sight, sound, and smell of the pups that *reinforces* and thus maintains close contact with newborn infants. This is the intra-psychic aspect of the attachment process. And it is to this aspect that we must now turn our attention.

Intra-Psychic Aspects of Attachment

Jay Rosenblatt believes that most animals (and perhaps some humans) are frightened by contact with newborn infants. "It appears to be part of a basic fearfulness of anything new," he says. How, then, to get adults (other than pregnant females) to overcome this fear of novelty?

Desensitization may be one answer (see Chapter 13). In one set of studies, Rosenblatt confined virgin female rats to small cages. He then introduced newborn pups from other females. At first, the virgin rats kept as far away from the pups as they could. After four to seven days' exposure, however, the virgins began to accept the pups and started showing maternal behaviors toward them. Male rats exposed to the same desensitization process also displayed "maternal behaviors" toward the pups after a week or so. Generally speaking, the smaller the cage, the faster this behavioral change occurred.

It would seem, therefore, that *intra-psychic variables* take over in the attachment process where *biological variables* leave off. Desensitization is one such intra-psychic variable. Imprinting and something called "contact comfort" might well be two others. Let's look at both imprinting and "contact comfort" in some detail.

Question: Why might it help a human father accept (and eventually assist in the care of) his child if the man is present during the birthing process?

Does "Imprinting" Exist in Humans?

Once Konrad Lorenz had demonstrated imprinting with birds, scientists began hunting for similar effects in humans. Among the first researchers to report success were Marshall Klaus and John Kennell, professors of pediatrics at Case Western Reserve University in Cleveland.

In their 1976 book *Maternal-Infant Bonding*, Klaus and Kennell state there is a *critical period* in the first hour or so of life during which an infant can *bond* with its mother. This bonding takes place only if the mother and child are in close physical contact during the

"sensitive period," according to Klaus and Kennell. Supposedly, the "bonding" increases the mother's love for her child and makes her more attentive to the infant's need. Indeed, Klaus and Kennell believe the mother is likely to neglect or abuse the child if the "bonding" fails to occur.

Klaus and Kennell have presented such a large amount of evidence supporting their beliefs that most medical societies now recommend that mothers be given their infants to cradle immediately after birth—a practice that few doctors approved of prior to the Klaus-Kennell research. A survey of recent evidence supporting their position appears in the November 1981 issue of *Smithsonian* magazine.

Despite the data suggesting that "bonding" occurs in humans, however, some scientists remain skeptical. In his 1982 book *The Role of the Father in Child Development*, Michael Lamb reviews all of the experiments purporting to show that "bonding" occurs. Lamb is professor of psychology, psychiatry, and pediatrics at the University of Utah. He believes most of the "bonding" studies have such serious flaws that they offer little support for the position taken by Klaus and Kennell. "Taken together," Lamb says, "the studies . . . show no clear evidence for any lasting effect of early physical contact between mother and infant on subsequent maternal behavior. The most that can be said is that it may sometimes have modest short-term

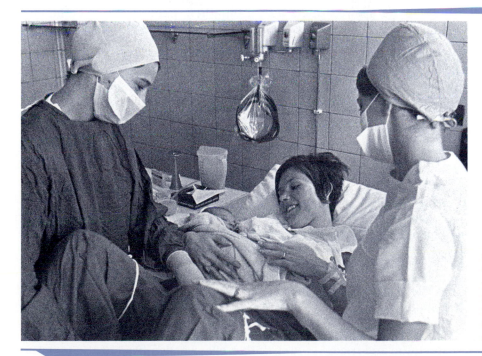

Some scientists believe that if mother and infant "bond" during first day of life, the infant's later development is enhanced.

Michael Lamb

Margaret and Harry Harlow in a laboratory with monkeys.

effects on some mothers in some circumstances."

Lamb notes that there are no known *ill effects* from early mother-infant contacts. But he fears that those mothers who were not allowed to hold their children immediately after birth may feel they are somehow "inadequate parents." That simply isn't so, Lamb says, and offers as proof the fact that most *adoptive mothers* are at least as loving as are "bonded" mothers. Thus, the question of whether any form of imprinting occurs in human infants has not as yet been completely decided.

Surrogate Mothers

Even if maternal "bonding" doesn't exist (or is relatively unimportant) in humans, it is a powerful force in many lower species, including the *primates*. The scientist who conducted the best long-term laboratory experiments on mother-child relationships in primates was Harry Harlow, who did most of his work at the University of Wisconsin. Since Harlow needed a place to house and raise the monkeys he used as subjects, he built the Primate Laboratory at Wisconsin. He and his wife Margaret (also a psychologist) devised a breeding program and tried various ways of raising monkeys in the laboratory.

The Harlows soon discovered that monkey infants raised by their mothers often caught diseases from their parents. So the Harlows began taking the infants away from their mothers at birth and raising the infants by hand. The baby monkeys were given cheesecloth diapers to serve as baby blankets (see Fig. 17.9). Almost from the start, it became obvious to the Harlows that their little animals developed such strong attachments to the blankets that, in the Harlows' terms, it was often hard to tell "where the diaper ended and the baby began." And if the Harlows removed the "security" blanket in order to clean it, the infant monkey often became greatly disturbed—just as if its own mother had deserted it.

What the baby monkeys obviously needed was an artificial or **surrogate** mother—something they could cling to as tightly as they typically clung to their own mother's chest. In 1957, while enjoying a champagne flight high over the city of Detroit, Harry Harlow glanced out of the airplane window and "saw" an image of an artificial monkey mother. It was a hollow wire cylinder, wrapped with a terrycloth bath towel, with a silly wooden head at the top. The tiny monkey could cling to this model mother as closely as to its real mother's body hair (see Fig. 17.10).

The Harlows gave the surrogate mother a functional breast by placing a milk bottle so that the nipple stuck through the cloth at an appropriate place on the surrogate's anatomy. The Harlows also developed ways to heat the cloth mother—or to cool it. They installed a mechanism that would rock the surrogate gently. Then they took infant monkeys away from their natural mothers and put them in with surrogates, to see how the infants would fare.

Question: What kinds of information about the emotional development of humans (and other species) can best be obtained from "real-life observations," and what kinds can best be obtained in a laboratory?

Contact Comfort

During the first two weeks of its life, warmth is perhaps the most important thing that a monkey mother has to give to its baby. The Harlows discovered this fact by offering infant monkeys a choice of two types of mother substitutes—one wrapped in terrycloth and one that was made of bare wire. If the two artificial

mothers were both the same temperature, the little monkeys always preferred the cloth mother. However, if the wire model was heated, while the cloth model was cool, the baby primates picked the wire substitute as their favorite for the first two weeks after birth. Thereafter they switched and spent most of their time on the more comfortable cloth mother.

Why is cold cloth preferable to warm wire? Something that the Harlows call *contact comfort* seems to be the answer. Infant monkeys spend much of their time rubbing against their mothers' skins, putting themselves in as close contact with the parent as they can. Prolonged "contact comfort" with a surrogate cloth mother appears to instill confidence in baby monkeys and is much more rewarding to them than is either warmth or milk.

According to the Harlows, contact comfort creates *emotional trust* in infant monkeys. If the infant is put into an unfamiliar playroom without its mother, the infant ignores the toys,

Fig. 17.9 Baby monkey in a cheese-cloth blanket.

Fig. 17.10 Baby monkey with surrogate cloth mother.

no matter how interesting they may be. It screeches in terror and curls up into a furry little ball. If its cloth mother is now introduced into the playroom, the infant rushes to the surrogate and clings to it for dear life.

After a few minutes of contact comfort, the infant apparently begins to feel more secure. It then climbs down from the mother substitute and begins tentatively to explore the toys, but often rushes back for a deep embrace as if to reassure itself that its mother is still there and that all is well. Bit by bit its fears of the novel environment are *desensitized*, and it spends more and more time playing with the toys and less and less time clinging to its "mother."

Question: How might you explain "trust" in terms of the infant's need to predict and control its environmental inputs?

John Bowlby

Nurturance in Human Infants

Why is "contact comfort" so important? Some scientists believe that sensory stimulation of the infant's receptor organs is necessary for the child's brain to develop properly. Whether a lack of **nurturance** causes a child's *brain* to develop in an abnormal fashion is still a matter of dispute. But several studies do support the notion that poor nurturance can affect a child's social and emotional development.

For example, psychiatrist Henry Massie showed home movies of mother-infant interactions to a group of impartial judges. The judges tried to guess which of the children experienced emotional problems later in life, and which children had grown up to become normal individuals. The movies, of course, had been taken years earlier, before anyone knew how the children would turn out.

At first the judges concentrated on observing the responses of the children themselves. But they soon found that all the infants behaved the same way. That is, the infants in both groups touched, gazed at, and responded to their mothers in similar fashion.

However, the judges could tell at once which children would become psychotic by watching *how each mother treated her child*. The mothers whose infants grew up to be normal touched their infants often, held them close, gazed at them frequently, and seemed very strongly attached to the children. The mothers of the children who later had emotional problems, however, gave "low-quality" nurturance. Since there was no observable difference in the way the infants reacted to the mothers, Massie concludes

it was the quality of sensory stimulation the mother gave to her infant that *predisposed* the child to become normal or emotionally disturbed at a later stage in the youngster's development.

Good Mothers and Bad

According to the Harlows, once a baby monkey has become *emotionally attached* to its mother (real or surrogate), the mother can do almost no wrong. In one of the Harlows' studies, they tried to create "monster mothers" whose behavior would be so abnormal that the infants would desert the mothers. Some of these surrogates shook so violently the infants couldn't cling to the surrogates. Other "monster mothers" would mechanically toss the infants aside from time to time. However, none of these surrogates apparently was "evil" enough to impart fear or loathing to the infant monkeys. The baby monkeys did show a brief period of emotional disturbance when the surrogates first rejected the infants. But as soon as the surrogates returned to normal, the infant would return to the "monster mother" and continue clinging, as if all were forgiven. As the Harlows tell the story, the only prolonged distress created by the experiment seemed to be that felt by the experimenters!

There was, however, one type of surrogate that uniformly "turned off" the infant monkeys. S.J. Suomi, working with the Harlows, built a terrycloth mother with ice water in its veins. Newborn monkeys attached themselves to this "cold momma" for a brief period of time, but then retreated to a corner of the cage and rejected her forever.

Anaclitic Depression

A human infant cared for by a mother with consistent behavior patterns rapidly builds up an emotional *attachment* to its mother, for the child learns that much of what is pleasant and satisfying comes through the actions of the mother. Psychologists call this an **anaclitic relationship**, the phrase coming from the Greek word meaning "to lean on."

J.A. Bowlby studied infant-mother attachments for a great many years. According to Bowlby, disturbing the anaclitic relationship can be dangerous. If it is the mother who *always* feeds the child, the infant soon builds up a *perceptual schema* that incorporates both "food" and "mother." When food appears, the child expects the mother to be there too, because the youngster is not yet mature enough to discriminate food from mother. If the infant is suddenly separated from the mother during the first few months of life, Bowlby says, the child may have considerable difficulty adjusting to changes in the environment.

Evidence supporting Bowlby's beliefs comes from research by psychiatrist R.A. Spitz. He studied the reactions of infants 6 to 12 months old who, for various reasons, had been separated from their mothers and put into institutions or foster homes. In their new environments, these infants received at best impersonal care. Almost as soon as the infants were institutionalized, they began showing signs of disturbance. They became quite upset when anyone approached them. They lost weight, became passive and inactive, and had trouble sleeping as well. Spitz calls this condition *anaclitic depression*.

The first sign of anaclitic depression is a behavior Spitz describes as "a search for the mother." Some babies quietly weep big tears; others cry violently. None of them can be quieted down by any type of intervention, although at the initial stage of the depression they still cling tightly to any adult who picks them up. If the mother does not return in 3 to 4 weeks, the infant's behavior changes. The child withdraws, lies quietly in the crib, will not play if offered a toy, and does not even look up if someone enters the room. The baby becomes dejected and passive, refuses food, and becomes more susceptible than usual to colds and other ailments.

Spitz believes that anaclitic depression might well account for some types of mental retardation, since the children he studied seemed to show considerable physical and intellectual impairment during and immediately after their periods of depression.

Psychologist Myron Hofer disagrees with Spitz, however. Writing in the 1981 book *Parental Care in Mammals*, Hofer claims the re-

Nurturance (NURR-tur-ants). To give nurturance means to take care of.

Anaclitic relationship (ann-ah-KLITT-ick). A strong, non-sexual love; the loving dependency and trust of a young child for its mother. The emotional attachment that builds up between a child and its mother.

actions of human infants to separation may be no more than responses to withdrawal of the sensory stimulation or "nurturance" provided by the mother. Thus, Hofer says, it is not a disturbance of the "mother schema," but simply a decrease in sensory inputs that causes the infant distress.

Question: Can you design an experimental study that might indicate whether Spitz's or Hofer's explanation was correct? Why would it be difficult to conduct this sort of research with *human* infants?

Parent-Infant Love: Learned or Innate?

As we noted earlier, most infants are born with a readiness to respond to the adults around them. If they are "nurtured" in a loving and stimulating way, they soon grow strongly attached to whoever takes care of them. However, the *strength* of the attachment process is influenced by the *consequences* of the adult-child relationship to both infant and parent.

According to Stanford psychologist Semour Levine, mother-infant contact *protects both of them from stress*. As evidence for this viewpoint, Levine cites several studies with monkeys showing that infant-mother contact lowers the levels of "stress hormones" in the bodies of both child and parent. Levine concludes that the mother-infant attachment "permits a mother to focus on her infant and the baby to focus on his mother. Through the mother-infant relationship, [the infant] develops a coping response. He finds he can do something about his environment."

Why do infants and parents form intense attachments? First, because their genes predispose them to do so. And second, because strong attachments reward both parent and child by making their environments more predictable and controllable. Thus, your genes make you want to *start* the attachment process going, while good experiences encourage you to *maintain* them. Like everything else, then, parent-child interactions are multi-determined.

Question: What responses *on the infant's part* would help reduce the mother's or father's stress levels?

Social/Behavioral Aspects of Emotional Development

Most early research on parent-child attachments focused on how the child's emotional development was affected by "good mothering." Slowly, over the years, psychologists came to realize two important things: First, mothers and infants constitute *social systems.* That is, the infant influences the mother as much as the mother affects her child. Second, at the human level, the father often plays as crucial a role in helping the child develop as does the mother. As we will see, the father's behavior affects the infant in two ways—through father-child interactions, and by the support the father gives the mother. Given these facts, it seems appropriate to turn now to a discussion of social/behavioral influences on emotional development.

We will begin by looking at how monkeys respond to being raised in *social deprivation.* Then we will turn our attention to father-child patterns of interaction.

Question: If you had been reared in complete isolation from all other humans until you were four, how would you have reacted if suddenly introduced to other children your age?

Peer Relationships

Monkeys raised on cloth surrogates appear to be fairly normal in their behavior patterns—at least while they are isolated from their **peers**. However, when the Harlows put *groups* of surrogate-trained monkeys together, the Harlows soon found they had a problem. Although these animals had never seen other monkeys during their entire lives, they responded to one another with excessive amounts of aggressive behavior. Eventually this hostility waned and then disappeared, but the animals' social behavior remained unusual, to say the least.

Many of these monkeys showed the kinds of *stereotyped* activities found in certain types of patients in mental hospitals. That is, some of the monkeys made oddly repetitive movements that seemed to have no function. Others froze into bizarre postures, or stared into space for hours on end. Sometimes, while a monkey was looking blankly out of its cage, one of its arms would rise slowly as if not really attached to the monkey's body. The Harlows refer to this as a *floating limb response,* and note that it is also seen in human patients who suffer from **catatonic schizophrenia**. If the monkey noticed its limb while it was "floating," the animal often jumped away in fear or even attacked its oddly-behaving limb.

As the Harlows point out, these infant monkeys had been raised in *partial* social deprivation. They had their surrogate mothers, and they often interacted with their human keepers. But the animals had never experienced the pleasures of socializing with other growing monkeys. Little wonder they didn't get along well with each other.

Peer Deprivation in Monkeys

In one of their best-known experiments, the Harlows tried to reproduce a human type of *anaclitic depression* in normal infant monkeys. These young animals were from birth raised in a large group with their mothers present. Then, for a period of several weeks, the mothers were taken away, leaving the infants to get along together as best they could.

As you might expect, the tiny monkeys went through much the same sort of anaclitic depression as do human infants. At the time of their separation, the baby monkeys searched actively for their mothers and cried loudly. Soon, however, they began to withdraw. Even though they had their peers to romp about with, they stopped playing and socializing. Instead, the babies huddled in corners alone, each clinging tightly to its own body.

Once the mothers were reintroduced, the infants went through a momentary period of frantic activity, most of which was aimed at clinging so tightly to the mother that she could never leave them again. Peer play soon became reestablished and the infants recovered normally.

In a further set of studies, the Harlows showed that it is not merely the loss of maternal "magic" that leads to severe depression. Rather, it is the deprivation of whatever form of social stimulation the organism is *accustomed to* at the time of separation that throws it into a state of hopelessness. Monkeys raised from birth in the presence of other infants their age (but without any mothers present) appear to grow up fairly normally. When these infants are isolated from their peers, however, they too fall into an anaclitic depression, just as if they had been separated from their mothers. When reunited with these peers, they engage in the same intense clinging as would an infant given back to its mother.

Question: The anaclitic depression occurs not merely because the infant is separated from its mother, but because its *expectancies* are grossly violated. How might this fact help explain adult depressions caused by loss of job, friends, or loved ones?

Isolation and Later Maternal Behavior

According to Harry Harlow, heterosexual love—the "urge to mate"—grows out of peer love. In one study, the Harlows put the partially deprived monkeys together so they might breed and hence provide more baby monkeys for experiments. But the animals refused to cooperate. Even when the Harlows introduced an experienced, normally raised male into the colony, he was a complete failure as far as impregnating any of the females was concerned.

The Harlows were finally able to get female isolates pregnant by confining them in a small cage for long periods of time with a patient and highly experienced male. But when these isolated females gave birth to their first monkey baby, they turned out to be the "monster mothers" the Harlows had tried to create with mechanical surrogates. Having had no contact with other animals as they grew up, these motherless mothers simply did not know what to do with the furry little strangers that suddenly appeared on the scene.

At first, the motherless mothers totally ignored their children. However, if the infant persisted, the mothers occasionally gave in and provided the baby with some of the contact comfort it demanded. Surprisingly enough, once these mothers learned how to handle a baby, they did reasonably well. Then, when they were again impregnated and gave birth to a second infant, they took care of it fairly adequately.

Maternal affection was totally lacking in a few of the motherless monkeys, however. To them, the newborn monkey was little more than an object to be abused the way a human child might abuse a doll or a toy train. These motherless mothers stepped on their babies, crushed the infant's face to the floor of the cage, and once or twice chewed off their baby's feet and fingers before they could be stopped. The most terrible mother of all popped her infant's head into her mouth and crunched it like a potato chip.

Peers. From a Latin word meaning "equals." Your peers are the people of your own age and social station whom you grew up with.

Catatonic schizophrenia (CAT-ah-TONN-ick SKITS-oh-FREE-knee-ah). *Schizophrenia* comes from the Greek words meaning "split mind." Someone whose mind is "split away from reality" is said to suffer from a severe form of mental illness, or schizophrenia. *Catatonia* means "under tension" or "contracted." A mentally disturbed person who "freezes" the body into strange positions has contracted her or his muscles abnormally.

We tend to think of most mothers—no matter what their species—as having some kind of almost-divine "maternal instinct" that makes them love and take care of their children, no matter what the cost or circumstance. And while it is true that most females have built into their genetic blueprint the *tendency* to be interested in (and to nurture) their offspring, this inborn tendency is always *expressed in a given environment*. The "maternal instinct" thus is strongly influenced by the mother's own early emotional development.

Question: What does the Harlows' research tell us about possible causes of child abuse in humans? (Hint: What kind of "maternal model" did the motherless monkeys have when they were young?)

Paternal Love

The noted anthropologist Margaret Mead once said that "fathers are a biological necessity but a social accident." However, data gathered by developmental psychologists tend not to support Dr. Mead's viewpoint. As Michael Lamb notes in his 1981 book, *The Role of the Father in Child Development*, fathers contribute significantly to an infant's emotional growth, although the father's contributions are often quite different from the mother's. While the father is just as capable of taking care of an infant as is the mother, one of the father's chief roles (at least in our society) seems to be that of *playmate* to the child.

Several studies reported in Lamb's book show that men are just as likely to nurture and stimulate their children as are the mothers. In fact, there is some evidence that fathers are more likely to hold their infants and to look at them than are the mothers. Furthermore, fathers are just as likely to interpret correctly the cues the infants give as are mothers. However,

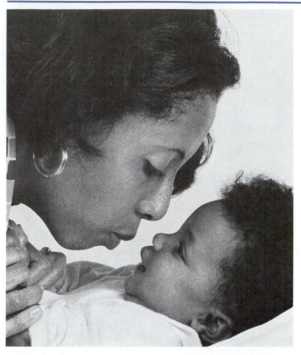

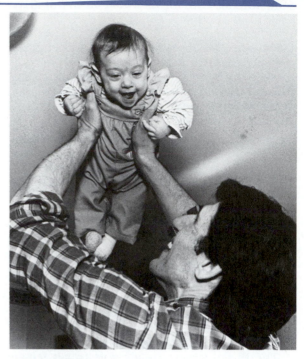

Mothers tend to talk to and gaze at their infants more than fathers, but fathers tend to touch their children and engage them in physical play more than do mothers.

in most real-life settings, men are less likely to feed infants and change their diapers than are women. This difference in parental behaviors seems due to cultural roles, however, and not to innate differences in male-female "instincts."

T. Berry Brazelton and his colleagues at Harvard found that fathers talked to their infants less than did the mothers. However, the men were much more likely to touch or hug the child than were the women. The fathers primarily engaged in rough-and-tumble play with their children, while the mothers were more likely to play conventional games, such as peek-a-boo. Brazelton notes that "when several weeks old, an infant displays an entirely different attitude— more wide-eyed, playful, and bright-faced— toward its father than toward its mother." One explanation for this, Brazelton says, is that the fathers apparently *expect* more playful responses from their children. And the children then respond to the father's expectations.

Paternal Deprivation

Given the fact that a father's influence on his child is more strongly emotional than intellectual, what would be the result of the father's

Mavis Hetherington

absence during the child's early years? Would boys react differently to paternal deprivation than would girls?

Several studies reported in the 1950's suggested that boys reared without fathers become less aggressive, more dependent, and have more "feminine" interests and behavior patterns than do boys who are brought up in normal families. Psychologist Joseph Pleck reviews these studies in the September 1981 issue of *Psychology Today*. Pleck states that most of these experiments are of questionable value. He concludes that boys who grow up without a "male identity figure" present are neither more nor less "masculine" than boys reared in intact families.

Father-Daughter Relationships

Research by E. Mavis Hetherington suggests that young girls may need their fathers if they are to grow up in a fashion our culture views as normal. Hetherington began by observing the activities of three types of girls: (1) those whose mothers had gotten divorces when the girls were very young; (2) those whose fathers had died when the girls were very young; and (3) those who had grown up in normal family situations. None of the girls had brothers. Although few of these young women had noticeable behavior problems, and all were doing reasonably well in school, there were marked differences in the way these adolescent girls *reacted to the males* in their environments.

According to Hetherington, girls reared by divorced mothers sought more attention and praise from males than did girls in the other two groups. They were also more likely to hang around places where young males could be found—gymnasiums, carpentry and machine shops, and the stag lines at school dances.

All three groups of girls appeared to have similar and quite normal relationships with other women. However, girls reared by divorced mothers dated earlier and more frequently than did the others, and were more likely to have engaged in sexual intercourse. By contrast, girls with widowed mothers tended to start dating much later than normal and seemed to be sexually inhibited.

Hetherington concludes that girls apparently need the presence of an adult male during their formative years in order to learn appropriate responses to men when they reach puberty.

Question: Would you expect father-deprived girls to be as active in sports as girls reared in intact homes?

Love and Psychotherapy

Given the great influence the people around a child have on the child's social and emotional development, it is understandable that infants who grow up in abnormal environments are likely to end up with abnormal emotions and behavior patterns. If parents and peers are absent—or if the child's father and mother are punitive, inconsistent, or unresponsive—the child will very likely need psychological help later in life.

But what kind of help? How do you teach someone to love?

We will attempt to answer some of these questions *at the human level* in later chapters. But we might mention how the Harlows attempted to solve similar problems with *monkeys* who were raised in social isolation (on terrycloth surrogates).

When the Harlows introduced these animals into normal monkey groups, the isolates responded with fear and withdrawal. When their terror of others had habituated, the isolates reacted with hostility and aggression. The Harlows figured that even these isolates could be trained to recover, but who could best act as a therapist for a socially withdrawn animal?

The Harlows reasoned that *contact comfort* was the key to turning an isolated monkey into a normal one. Therefore, they selected as their "therapists" socially normal female infants who were only three to four months old. The isolates were all males. The "therapists" remained with their natural mothers except during "therapy hours." Since these young female monkeys were all much smaller than the male isolates, the Harlows believed the babies would not threaten the isolates as much as would an adult animal—or a human. Then, too, persistence in therapy often yields rich rewards, and there are few things in life as persistent as a baby monkey in search of contact comfort.

So the Harlows built a "mental hospital" in which they could control the interactions between the isolates and the baby-therapists. At the beginning, the babies were allowed contact with their "patients" for two hours a day. At their first meeting, the typical male isolate (who had not learned to be aggressive) retreated to a corner of the "hospital" cage, hugged himself, and rocked back and forth, doing his best to ignore the infant. The infant's response was to approach the isolate and try to cling to him. Although the isolate rejected the "therapist's" overtures again and again during the first day or so, gradually his fear of the tiny stranger extinguished. The isolate stopped retreating from the infant and soon let her satisfy her need for contact comfort by clinging to his body (see Fig. 17.11).

Within a few days, the isolate was clinging to the infant with the same apparent pleasure that the infant derived. Within a few weeks, the isolates and "therapists" were playing together enthusiastically. Gradually, over time, most of the isolates' abnormal behaviors disappeared.

Fig. 17.11 A baby "therapist" comforts a monkey reared in isolation.

Fig. 17.13 A child suffering from Down's syndrome, or trisomy-21.

Female or male

Fig. 17.12 Trisomy-21. Note the three chromosomes instead of the usual 21st pair. (See also Fig. 17.2.)

By the time therapy had continued for 6 months, the isolates appeared to have recovered completely from their initial period of social deprivation. At this point the isolates could be introduced into normal monkey groups and could make a successful adjustment.

Question: How might we use the Harlows' research to design new types of psychotherapy for disturbed human children?

Learning about Love

We are just beginning to learn the *scientific facts* of emotional development. We still do not know which aspects of maturation are primarily controlled by the genes, and which are more strongly influenced by experience. Nor do we yet understand as much as we should about helping children overcome the sometimes crippling effects of early emotional trauma. But the data do suggest that the best way to make sure a child grows up to be emotionally healthy is for both parents to give it wise and attentive love.

But what do we mean by "wise and attentive love"? Recent research suggests that our loving behaviors must be judged by their *consequences*, not merely by our *intentions*. We can demonstrate that point rather dramatically by returning to the subject of chromosomal abnormalities, and by discussing more fully the developmental disorder called *Down's syndrome*.

Down's Syndrome

In their 1981 book *Human Development*, Diane Papalia and Sally Olds call Down's syndrome "the most common chromosomal defect" affecting a child's development. This disorder was once called "mongolism," because the child has an oriental-looking skin fold at the inner corners of the eyes. The young person also typically has a small head, a flat nose, a protruding and thick tongue, a defective heart, eyes, and ears, and a defective **thyroid** gland. The cause of the disorder is well known—an extra 21st chromosome (see Fig. 17.12).

According to Papalia and Olds, "the mortality rate for Down's syndrome children is very high early in life—especially for females—with 40 to 55 percent of them dying in their first year." These children seem to have defective immune systems, since they are particularly sensitive to viral diseases such as the flu. If their medical problems are handled properly, however, individuals with Down's syndrome often live until middle age.

Mental(?) Retardation

At the beginning of this chapter, we discussed both the mind-body problem and the nature-nurture controversy. The importance of these issues can be seen particularly well in a discussion of the "mental retardation" that usually accompanies Down's syndrome.

Until fairly recently, most developmental psychologists assumed all Down's syndrome children were doomed to be mentally handicapped because of their defective chromosomes. And it is true, as Papalia and Olds note, that when given "ordinary" training as infants, these children "have a limited intellectual potential, with most ranging from moderately retarded to dull normal." However, the *cause* of the retardation may be as much environmental as biological. As neurologist Mary Coleman notes in an article by Maya Pines in the June 1982 issue of *Psychology Today*, "Some of the retardation that is as-

Thyroid (THIGH-roid). A large endocrine gland lying at the base of the neck that produces growth hormones.

Plateau. In psychology, "to plateau" means to reach the limit of some developmental or growth curve.

sociated with Down's syndrome can actually be traced to a thyroid deficiency, which is easily corrected." Most of the children also suffer from middle- and inner-ear problems, which can be solved by minor surgery. "In the past," Coleman says, "People assumed that these children couldn't speak because they were dumb. But in fact, one major reason they were slow to speak was that they couldn't hear properly."

However, once the medical problems have been taken care of, the key to development is how much verbal stimulation and encouragement the children receive. Coleman recommends a program called *infant-stim*, which requires the parents of Down's syndrome children to spend several hours daily talking to and teaching the children. The parents are told to avoid punishment and give the children as much positive reinforcement as possible. Children treated with infant-stim usually show a remarkable jump in IQ within a few months. "The older literature on these children says that they **plateau** at 5," Mary Coleman says. "More recently, after the first infant-stim programs, people began to say that they plateau at 7. Then they said these children plateau at 12. I'm still waiting for them to plateau!"

In the past, because we presumed that Down's syndrome was "caused" entirely by a chromosomal defect, we often considered these children to be hopelessly retarded. Now that we see both the problem and the youngsters in a different perspective, we can be more optimistic. As we noted earlier, your position on both the mind-body and the nature-nurture controversies determines not only *how you perceive people*, but *how you treat them* as well.

Question: In the early 1980's, physicians began using "cosmetic surgery" to make Down's syndrome children appear more normal. The surgery involves removing the extra skin from the corners of the eyes, reshaping the nose, and trimming excess tissue from the child's tongue. Immediately after the surgery, the child often shows a dramatic rise in *cognitive development*. How could *cosmetic* surgery influence *cognitive* growth?

Physical and Emotional Development: A Summary

Children do not develop in bits and pieces—a smidgin of physical growth this week, a tad of emotional maturation next week. Rather, children grow in all ways at all times. Thus, separating physical development from emotional, social, and intellectual growth may be a handy pedagogical device. But, in truth, all these aspects of the maturing infant *interact*.

It should be obvious at this point that we cannot fully understand physical and emotional development without looking at how the mind matures. So, it is to the topic of cognitive development that we now turn our attention.

Summary

1 There are four main themes in developmental psychology—the **mind/body problem**, the **nature-nurture controversy**, **change versus constancy**, and **similarities versus differences**.

2 You began life as a single **egg cell** that contained 23 **chromosomes**. At the moment of **fertilization**, one of your father's sperms penetrated the egg and added 23 chromosomes of its own.

3 If an **X sperm** unites with the egg, the 23rd chromosome will be **XX**, and the child will be born a female. If a **Y sperm** unites with the egg, the 23rd chromosome will be **XY**, and the child will be born a male.

4 Sometimes the chromosomes of the mother and father contain **genetic defects**. If the child's cells contain but a single X chromosome, the child will suffer from **Turner's syndrome**. A child with an **XXY 23rd chromosome** becomes an infertile male and is said to suffer from **Klinefelter's syndrome**. A child with an **XYY 23rd chromosome** becomes a normal-appearing male but may have difficulty learning **impulse control**.

5 If the child's cells have three **21st chromosomes** rather than two, the child will suffer from **Down's syndrome**, or **trisomy-21**.

6 Two weeks after fertilization, the cells begin to **differentiate** or take on different roles. The three main types of cells are **ectoderm**, **mesoderm**, and **endoderm**.

7 During pregnancy, the fetus is protected from the mother's body by an organ called the **placenta**.

8 If the mother is starved during pregnancy, the child may be born smaller than usual. If the infant is given ample food, however, it will usually "catch up" to the size its **genetic blueprint** originally specified.

9 Physical development in the infant typically proceeds in a **cephalo-caudal, proximal-distal** direction.

10 Baby geese (and the young of other animals) often **imprint** on the first moving object they see or can follow. Whether imprinting or **affectionate bonding** actually occurs in humans is not yet decided.

11 The **critical-period hypothesis** states that the "best time" for learning to occur is when the organism is first ready to make a response.

12 There is some evidence that **fetuses** can learn **simple associations** while still in the womb. And only moments after birth, infants can **imitate** facial gestures, **search** visually for the source of human voices, and **move their limbs in synchrony** with the human voice. By two weeks, babies **recognize** their mother and form perceptual **schemata**.

13 Theorists who take the **body/nature** position on emotional development believe you are born with **undifferentiated emotional responses** that are selectively reinforced by your environment.

14 Theorists who take the **mind/nurture** position believe your **environment** shapes your emotions when you are very young, but you soon learn how to exercise **choice** in expressing your **inner feelings**.

15 Mother and newborn child form a **social dyad**. Evidence suggests that both mother and child have an **inborn mutual readiness** to respond to each other. Infants also **shape** parental responses as much as parents shape the child's reactions.

16 The increase in **estrogen** that occurs

just prior to birth may **desensitize** the mother and thus help overcome her innate fear of "little strangers."

17 A newborn monkey clings to its mother because she gives it warmth, food, and **contact comfort**. Contact with the mother (or her **surrogate**) appears to give the infant the **trust** that it needs in order to mature socially and emotionally.

18 Children who are treated inconsistently or who are given minimal stimulation by their mothers seem **predisposed** to suffer later psychological problems.

19 Maternal contact also allows the infant to build up **perceptual expectations** about its world. When its expectancies are grossly violated, the infant falls into an **anaclitic depression** and may die if not returned to its mother.

20 Female monkeys raised on surrogate mothers often treat their first infants cruelly.

21 When given the opportunity, human fathers seem as interested in and as responsive to their infants as are mothers.

22 Mothers tend to talk to their children more than do fathers, but **touch** and play with the children less.

23 Girls who grow up without fathers may either be strongly attracted to adult males or tend to avoid them, depending in part on whether the girls' mothers were divorced or widowed.

24 Monkeys raised on surrogate mothers can learn to get along with other monkeys if given **contact-comfort therapy** by normal monkey infants.

25 **Down's-syndrome** children suffer from a variety of physical problems. However, the **mental retardation** often associated with this developmental disorder can be overcome to a great extent if the child is given **intensive stimulation** during its early years.

(Continued from page 442.)

When the class calmed down a bit, Dr. Martin Mayer continued. "That's a very interesting approach," he said, nodding at the guitar-playing young man. "I presume you mean we could identify men and women who are carriers of the wrong kinds of genes, and prohibit them from having kids. Not from getting married or from having sex—but from raising a family."

"You're asking us to play God with human souls!" said one of the girls. "That involves religion, not genetics."

"We certainly must take religious views into account," Dr. Mayer said, polishing his glasses again. "But sex is also a matter of economics. Any of you students grow up on a farm?"

Several of the young people held up their hands.

Mayer put his spectacles back on his nose. "Well, I guess your daddies have a few cows around to give milk and to supply meat, right? And probably they buy the best breeding stock they can afford, because good cows give more milk and more butter fat than poor cows. And good bulls produce stronger offspring with better meat on them than do puny bulls. One good bull can service a whole lot of cows through artificial insemination. Even a scrawny little cow will have better offspring if her eggs are fertilized with genes from a first-rate bull. Perhaps we should do the same with humans. Maybe only the President should be allowed to have children."

"If only the President of the United States can have kids, he's going to be one busy daddy," one of the girls said laughing.

"Doesn't seem fair somehow," the boy sitting next to her said. "You've gotten rid of half the bad genes by using just one prime bull, but what about the scrawny cows? They're still passing along their scrawny genes to their kids. Why not have just one big mother cow that's as good as the bull?"

"Good idea," Mayer continued. "Just because a first-rate cow has good genes in her egg cells doesn't mean that she has to be burdened with carrying the calf until it's ready to be born. It's a waste of her time. So we've worked out a deal. After we inseminate the prime cow artificially, we let the fertilized egg grow for a few days, and then we remove the embryo and transplant it into the body of a scrawny cow and let her do all the work of carrying the little calf until it's ready to be born. A few months later, the scrawny cow gives birth to a super-calf with superior genes."

"Why bother?" a student asked.

"Financial reasons," Mayer responded. "Once we remove the embryo from the super-prime cow mother, she starts producing new eggs right away, which also can be fertilized artifically and then transplanted to the body of another inferior cow. That way, one super-momma can produce lots of superior calves each year instead of just one or two. It's still too complicated a technique for general use, but when the cost comes down, it's sure going to make a lot more money for the farmers."

"I know what you're going to say next," said the guitar-playing boy. "If it works with cows, why not try it with humans?"

"You've got to be kidding," one of the girls said. "I wouldn't want to carry somebody else's baby."

"Not even for a million dollars?" Mayer asked. "We're already doing embryo transplants at the human level— for women who can't conceive in the natural way. But why put limits on the technique? Suppose a rich lady offered you a million dollars if you'd let her doctor transplant her embryo into your body. That way you could carry the child for her while she went off on a fancy vacation somewhere. Then, when the child was born, she could pick the child up at the hospital and give you the million

dollars. How would you like that?"

"If I carried the baby, it would be mine, and no rich lady could take it away from me," the girl replied.

"Yeah, but what if the government decided you couldn't have kids," one of the boys said.

"Why couldn't I have kids, I'd like to know?"

"Because the government would say you didn't have the right kind of genes, stupid. Just like my daddy decides which of his cows can have calves and which can't," the boy added rather smugly.

"But I've got great genes!" the girl said. "And no government is going to tell me I don't! And even if they did, I'd just get Dr. Mayer to engineer my genes so they were the right kind. So there," she concluded, making a face at the boy who was tormenting her with his comments.

"What's the right kind of genes?" asked another girl.

"Yes, it all boils down to that decision, doesn't it?" Mayer said. "As Aldous Huxley pointed out in *Brave New World*, the day will surely come when we can engineer genes—if we know what kinds of kids we want to have. We can judge what kinds of cow we want because we value meat and milk production. But what do we value most in humans? Size? Strength? Intelligence?"

"That old Einstein wouldn't have done so well as a fullback for the Dallas Cowboys," an athletic young man said.

"I don't even want to talk about this, it scares me so," another girl said. "It's abnormal and immoral. It could never happen in the United States."

"That's probably what the cows thought a few years ago," said one of the boys.

"Well," said Mayer, "maybe it won't happen here, but the possibility of genetic engineering won't disappear just because we refuse to talk about it. In fact, just the opposite. But let's get back to that point about who should carry the baby. Is there any reason why a woman should have to go through a lengthy pregnancy? In *Brave New World* the embryos are grown in bottles rather than in their mothers' bodies. When they are ready to be born, the babies are uncorked like a bottle of fine wine. Maybe the day will come when each home has a mechanical incubator in it. You would watch your child's development before birth just the way you watch a plant grow and flower."

"That's outrageous," said the girl in the second row. "I don't want my baby born in a machine."

"You'd destroy the warm, maternal feeling every woman has when she's carrying her own baby," said another.

"I wouldn't love my baby if I didn't carry it myself," said another girl.

"And how would my baby feel if it learned that it had developed in a machine instead of inside me?" said another. "It just wouldn't love me as much."

"Do you really think that maternal love is dependent on carrying the baby yourself?" Mayer asked.

"Of course," said the girl in the second row. "You just wouldn't take care of the baby as well if it weren't for that special feeling of closeness you get when you're carrying the child. It just wouldn't be *yours*, and you wouldn't love it as much."

A girl in the middle of the room suddenly stood up, tears filling her eyes. "I'd like to say something. A woman doesn't have to carry a child, or give birth to it, in order to love the baby and see that it gets the best care and attention. And whether a child is born in a bottle or from its mother's body doesn't affect the love it has for the woman who brings it up. Maybe you ought to remember that I'm adopted. My adopted mother can't have children, so she and my foster father adopted me when I was just two weeks old. And they love me very, very much, both of them."

The class was absolutely silent for several moments. Then the bell rang.

"Thank you very, very much," Dr. Mayer said, a smile on his face.

Recommended Readings

Ambron, S.R. (1981). *Child development* (3rd ed.) New York: Holt, Rinehart and Winston.

Brim, O.G., Jr. & Kagan, J. (Eds.). (1980). *Constancy and change in human development*. Cambridge, Mass.: Harvard University Press.

Gould, J.L. & Gould, C.G. (1981). The instinct to learn. *Science 81*, May 1981, pp. 44–50.

Did You Know That...

- Children between one and six years of age may learn nine new words a day?
- Deaf children don't "babble" in quite the same way as normal children do?
- During the time you were learning to speak, your mother probably taught you the use of "social contracts" as well?
- Chimpanzees have been taught 100 or more words of an artificial language called "Yerkish"?
- Jean Piaget, perhaps the most respected child psychologist of this century, believed there were three kinds of knowledge, knowing "how," "what," and "why"?
- Many early theorists believed that a child would "explode" from surplus energy if it didn't release this energy in play?
- Piaget believed that play is "a child's work"?

18

Cognitive Development: Early Childhood and Adolescence

"Think about It"

"Cynthia, my pet," Horace Smythe called out loudly. "Come here at once."

Mr. Smythe hummed a nervous, off-key tune for a few moments, a Civil War melody that most of the US was humming in 1867. He picked up a small Ming vase from his desk, dusted it carefully, and put it down again. It was far too valuable a possession, as he frequently told his wife, to allow it to be cleaned by their Negro servant woman, Melissa. He had bought the vase from a local Chinese laundryman who, Mr. Smythe observed, "lacks the innate appreciation for culture that God in His infinite wisdom has given to members of the white race."

Then, since his wife hadn't yet appeared, Mr. Smythe stamped his foot impatiently on the old wooden floor. "Cynthia!" he cried. "Come here at once! I have marvelous news for you."

Cynthia Smythe walked briskly through the door, wiping her hands on a large towel as she did so. "Yes, Horace, what do you wish now? I was just helping Melissa prepare supper . . ."

"Bother supper," Mr. Smythe said. "I have just discovered why your nephew, Tommy, is an idiot, and I knew you'd want to know."

The woman sighed deeply. "Thomas is not an 'idiot' by any stretch of the imagination, Horace. And he's *your* nephew, too."

"Only by marriage, my pet. And he is most certainly an idiot, a *Mongolian* idiot. Dr. Down has just proven it."

"Mongolian?" the woman said in a puzzled tone of voice.

"Of course," Mr. Smythe said. "Has an oriental look about him, doesn't he? Especially the eyes."

"He doesn't look like any Chinese I've ever seen, Horace." Cynthia Smythe closed her eyes, as if to call her nephew's face to mind. "No, Tommy *is* a little different, naturally, but I wouldn't say he looked at all oriental."

Horace Smythe snorted in amusement. "Ha! You wouldn't say that if you had read Dr. Down's article."

The woman folded the towel in resignation and sat down. "Who is this Dr. Down, Horace?"

"Dr. John Langdon Haydon Down, to be precise, and he's the medical superintendant of Earlswood Asylum for Idiots in Surrey." The man peered over his spectacles at his wife. "That's just outside London, England, you know."

"Yes, Horace. I know."

The man smiled wanly at his wife, then turned his gaze back to the papers in front of him. "Well, I was just reading about Dr. Down's paper, 'Observations on an ethnic classification of idiots,' published in the *London Hospital Reports* for 1866. The good doctor has come up with an explanation for idiocy that is positively brilliant. Tommy is a 'throwback,' you see."

"A 'throwback' to what?"

"To a more primitive form of human development, of course," Mr. Smythe said in a superior tone of voice. "Modern biological theory tells us that the human fetus repeats all the stages of human evolution as it grows within the womb. It starts out as a single cell, and then it becomes fishlike. Next it turns into one of the lower mammals, such as a pig, and then grows into a little monkey."

The woman shook her head in amazement. "Tommy doesn't look any more like a monkey than you do, Horace."

"No, of course not. He's gone beyond that stage. But even when the fetus takes on a human appearance, it still must climb the evolutionary scale—from the black Ethiopian, up to the savage Malays or Indians who have dark brown skin. And from thence to the yellow-skinned peoples, the Mongolians. Finally, if all goes well, the fetus reaches the top rung of the developmental ladder."

Cynthia Smythe smiled. "The 'top rung' being a white American, I presume?"

"Or northern European," her husband replied. "I think our superiority to the dark-skinned human races is well established by now."

"The Bible says that we are all God's children, Horace."

"Cynthia, my pet, this is 1867, not the Dark Ages, and we must deal with the scientific facts. It is true, as Dr. Down points out, that all the races are descended from a single stock. But some of us—the whites, of course—have traveled farther down the evolutionary road than have the others. The inferior races may eventually catch up with us, of course, and it is our Christian duty to help them all we can. But in the meantime . . ." The man shrugged his shoulders eloquently.

The woman contemplated her husband's words for a moment. "What 'facts' does this Dr. Down present to prove his case?"

"Ah ha!" Horace Smythe said eagerly. "That's the real issue, isn't it? Well, remember that Dr. Down is a world-famous expert on idiocy. And among the patients at his hospital, he has found a very close connection between skin color and feeble-mindedness. The darker the color of the patient's skin, the more hopelessly stupid the patient appears to be. For example, the most terrible idiots of all have Ethiopian features—prominent eyes, puffy lips, dark skins, and woolly hair, just like Melissa's. 'White Negroes,' Dr. Down calls these poor, hopeless cases."

"Melissa's eyes are less prominent than yours are, Horace."

The man dismissed the woman's comments with a wave of his hand. "Pay attention, my pet. Slightly superior in intelligence to the 'white Negroes' are those idiots with Indian features—'shortened foreheads, prominent cheeks, deep-set eyes, and slightly apish noses,' according to Dr. Down."

"And I suppose Dr. Down believes that the Indian race is intellectually superior to the Negro?" the woman asked, a bemused look on her face.

"Naturally," Horace Smythe replied. "Even an idiot knows that to be the truth. But to continue, the least retarded inmates of all have slanted eyes and skins that have a 'slight, dirty yellowish tinge' to them. Just like the Mongols who inhabit China and the rest of the Orient."

Cynthia Smythe sighed. "And the Mongolian race is superior to the Indian, I presume?"

"Of course!" the man responded in a delighted tone of voice. "Black, brown, yellow, white—that's the natural order of the races on Earth, and that's the natural order of the idiots in Dr. Down's asylum, he says. Doesn't that prove the case, once and for all?"

The woman frowned. "Tommy's skin is about the same color as yours is, Horace. A bit more yellowish, perhaps, but . . ."

"But there you are, my

dear. Tommy's a throwback to the yellow-skinned Mongol stage, which is immediately below the white or Caucasian stage. He simply stopped developing when he reached the Mongoloid level, his yellow skin proves it. And that's why he's mentally retarded, and always will be. No sense in trying to work with the lad, of course, as your sister is foolishly trying to do. No, she should send Tommy away to an asylum."

"Or give him to the Chinese laundryman you bought the vase from, perhaps?" the woman said, in mock seriousness.

"Excellent idea!" Horace Smythe responded. "Like calls to like, you know. The laundryman is so uncultured he probably wouldn't even notice Tommy's feeble-mindedness."

"The laundryman . . ." the woman said slowly, as puzzling over the meaning of what her husband had said.

Horace Smythe gave a deep sign of satisfaction and leaned back in his chair. "Well, don't you agree? Hasn't Dr. Down come up with a brilliant insight into the biological causes of idiocy?"

The woman laughed. "I think the man's an imbecile, Horace."

"What!"

A look of gentle contentment spread across Cynthia Smythe's face. "I know little or nothing about science, but I do recognize utter nonsense when I hear it. And so should you, since the evidence is right before your very eyes."

"Evidence?" Horace Smythe wailed. He stared briefly at the Ming vase on his desk, then glanced at the paper he had been reading. "But I don't see . . ."

The woman rose from her chair. "Melissa needs help with the cooking, Horace. You think about it, and we'll discuss the matter further at supper. After all," she said slyly, "You're hardly an idiot like Tommy, now are you?"

(Continued on page 502.)

Cognitive Development

At the beginning of Chapter 17, we listed four major "issues" that cut across developmental psychology. Let's review those four topics as a way of introducing the field of cognitive development.

One of the issues was the mind-body problem. At first blush, it might seem that cognitive psychologists would uniformly resolve this issue in favor of the "mind." After all, we can hardly speak of "cognitive" development unless we are willing to admit that there *is* a mind—or at least that children have "internal processes" we can somehow follow over time. As you will see, however, there are many scientists working in this area who equate "cognitive development" with the growth of speech and problem-solving *behaviors*. From a behavioral point of view, *talking* is a physical rather than a mental response. So the mind-body problem remains important even in the field of cognitive psychology.

The second issue—the nature-nurture controversy—is probably of far greater importance, however. Are human infants born with an innate ability to think and process language, or are these skills almost entirely learned? Are there basic "structures of the mind" that are part of a child's genetic blueprint? Or are thinking and reasoning "programmed" into a child by the youngster's social environment? As you will soon discover, there are almost as many answers to these questions as there are psychologists working in the area.

The third issue has to do with developmental *continuity* and *discontinuity*. In the field of cognitive development, these topics show up primarily in the *stage theories* of mental growth. Stage theorists typically take the "continuity" viewpoint towards development. That is, they believe all children must pass through specific "stages" of mental maturation. These stages presumably are determined by the genes and therefore are primarily governed by the physical maturation of the body. That is, the mind is said to "unfold" just as a flower unfolds when it blossoms. The environment can speed up or slow down the *rate* at which the child's mind develops, just as it can affect the speed at which a flower opens. But (according to the "continuity" viewpoint) the environment cannot change the *direction* and *shape* of cognitive development any more than it can turn a rose into an orchid.

On the other hand, "discontinuity" theorists typically hold that cognitive growth is strongly influenced by the environment. They believe the

Neil Salkind

infant is born with potential to grow in many different ways and at a variety of speeds. The environment then encourages the development of a limited set of these cognitive skills, usually by providing the child with models and by rewarding the youngster for imitating these models. The environment may also ignore or even punish the child if he or she attempts to grow in directions not "approved" by the adults who care for the child. To these theorists, any continuity found in cognitive development is due to consistencies in the social and physical environment, not to the "natural unfolding" of the child's genetic potential.

The fourth issue is that of individual differences versus human similarities. "Continuity theorists" typically assume that the growth pattern for all children should be *similar across developmental stages*. Each child is unique, true, because each human has a different set of genes. But it is the "big picture" of intellectual development that stage theorists are most interested in. And this picture presumably differs little from one child to another. On the other hand, "discontinuity theorists" usually believe the consistencies we see in children are features of the cultures the children grow up in, not in the children themselves. Therefore, these psychologists tend to be more concerned with an individual child's pattern of development than in the fact that the child matures in ways similar to other children in the same environment.

These issues may seem highly theoretical to you, and hence of little practical importance. However, as we noted in Chapter 5, *theory determines practice*. Stage theorists believe a child cannot learn a given concept until the youngster's mind is "developmentally ready." Thus, if you try to teach something to a child, and the child does not learn, the problem lies

with the child's undeveloped mind, not with your teaching methods. Furthermore, stage theorists often insist that you *shouldn't try to influence a child*, since the pattern of mental growth is entirely determined by the genes.

We will touch on these matters again in the next chapter, when we discuss *personality*, and in Chapter 22 when we talk about psychotherapy. But you should keep all four issues "in mind" as we now look at the cognitive development of the child.

What Is "Cognitive" Development?

Before we can sensibly discuss what cognitive *development* is, we first should make clear that we have some notion of what *cognition* is. Actually, psychologists use the term "cognition" in many different ways. However, as Margaret Matlin notes in her 1983 book *Cognition*, the word usually refers to *mental activities*. Matlin lists eight types of mental activities that psychologists have paid particular attention to: perception, memory, imagery, language, concept formation, problem solving, reasoning, and decision making. We have already discussed many aspects of cognition in Chapters 8 and 9. In this chapter, we will focus primarily on the development of *language* and *reasoning* in children and young adults.

Language Development

According to Margaret Matlin, "Language acquisition is often said to be the most spectacular of human accomplishments." She cites research by S. Carey, suggesting that the 6-year-old child may have a mastery of about 14,000 words. And to acquire this large a vocabulary, Matlin notes, children must learn about *nine new words each day* from the time they start speaking until their sixth birthday.

In their 1984 book *Child Development*, Sueann Ambron and Neil Salkind remind us that learning a *first* language during the early years of your life is both simpler and more complex than learning a *second* language in high school or college. On the one hand, initial language learning was simpler than learning a second tongue because you were relating each new word directly to an experienced object, action, or quality—and not to a word in another language *about* that object, action, or quality. On the other hand, acquiring a first language is more complex because, when you were an infant, you were not merely learning a *new* language—you were learning "language" itself.

Learning to use language—and to use it properly—when you were a youngster changed your world profoundly, according to Ambron and Salkind. They note that having a *verbal label* to attach to an experience makes that experience easier to remember and deal with. "In fact," they say, "one reason most of us fail to remember much of what happened to us in our earliest years may be that we had not learned to use such verbal labels. We had nothing to file away in our memories as a coded symbol of the experience." (For a discussion of "memory categories," see Chapter 15.)

Question: Can you think of other reasons why you might have difficulties recalling early experiences? (Hint: How mature was your brain at the time?)

Language Acquisition

Ambron and Salkind say that the stages children go through while progressing from baby talk to adult communication are roughly identical—regardless of native tongue, socioeconomic class, and ethnic background. Children everywhere talk about the same things while going through these developmental stages. "They all speak of objects and situations, make demands, use mostly nouns and verbs, and talk *to* themselves a great deal but never *about* themselves or their relationship with others."

According to Ambron and Salkind, language acquisition has four aspects to it:

1. A knowledge of how to produce **phonemes**, which are the basic sounds of speech.
2. Learning **semantics**, or the meaning of words.
3. A mastery of **syntax**, or the rules by which words can be combined into sentences.
4. Discovering the **pragmatics** of language, or the appropriate social use of speech.

Let's look at each of these four aspects of language acquisition in more detail.

Phonemes

Obviously, an infant can't talk if it doesn't make sounds, and phonemes are the basic sounds that make up human speech. The developmental problem then becomes, how does an infant acquire the ability to produce phonemes? Do infants naturally (and spontane-

Phonemes (FO-neems). The smallest units of speech, such as "da" or "ba."

Semantics (see-MAN-ticks). From the Greek word meaning "to signify." Semantics is the study of meanings, particularly the meanings of words.

Syntax (SIN-tax). From the Greek word meaning "to arrange together." Syntax refers to the orderly structure of language.

Pragmatics (prag-MAT-ticks). From the Latin word meaning "skilled in law or business." Pragmatics is the study of the "practical rules" of some aspect of life or science.

ously) produce all the phonemes they will need in order to speak any human language? Or are they born with a readiness to imitate the sounds their parents (and others) say to them?

If you have been around infants very much, you probably have observed them happily chattering to themselves in a language made up of repetitive syllables, such as "da da da" and "ba ba ba." This type of early speech is called *babbling*, and occurs in all normal children between three and seven months of age.

Babbling frequently occurs early in the morning, when children first wake up and before they begin their daily "social life" with their parents and other adults. Normal patterns of babbling do *not* occur in deaf children. Deaf children may babble briefly, but then stop. This fact suggests that infants need to *hear* the sounds they are producing in order to continue producing them. Therefore, the *absence of babbling* may be a sign that the child needs special attention.

According to a 1983 report by Rachel Stark and Jennifer Bond of the J.F. Kennedy Institute in Baltimore, children everywhere make the same sounds when babbling. Until recently, scientists believed that children produced the entire range of human sounds when babbling. However, recent studies show that many speech sounds are almost never heard in babbling.

In summary, current thinking holds that the early acquisition of phoneme production has three distinct aspects to it. First, most children babble innately, but do not produce *all* the sounds of speech in their babbles. Second, parents selectively reinforce some sounds which then come to predominate. Third, children innately imitate phonemes not produced in their babbles, and parents reward the children for doing so. Eventually, the child can produce all the sounds found in its "native language."

Question: Is speech in humans innately determined, or acquired through learning?

Semantics

Words represent objects and actions. Thus, words have *meanings* that infants must learn as they progress from babbling to true communicative speech. The problem children face as they learn *semantics* is that most words have more than one meaning. "Drink," for instance, is both a noun and a verb. "I drink the milk," and "Give me a drink," are examples of how the same word can mean either an action or an object. Furthermore, words such as "sea" and "see," and "dear" and "deer," sound alike but have quite different meanings.

At about a year of age, infants begin uttering **holophrastic** or one-word sentences. The child may actually *say* single words earlier, but doesn't appear to grasp the *meaning* of words (and to use them to communicate) until the child is about one year old. At this stage, a single-word sentence may have several meanings. For example, "Cup" may mean "I see the cup," or "Get me my cup," or even "This cup is just like the one I use at home."

Most infants begin using two-word sentences about the 18th month. At first, these sentences are of the *agent + action* ("Mama drink") or *action + object* type ("Drink milk"). At this age, children also use negative statements, such as "No milk." They also use the so-called *Wh-questions*, such as "*Wh*ere milk?" or "*Wh*en drink?"

Some two-word sentences are called *telegraphic speech* because the youngster includes important words (such as nouns and verbs) but omits other parts of speech. Thus, rather than saying, "The cat is up the tree," the child may say, "Cat tree."

By the time children are two, most of them can speak in complete and fairly complex sentences, such as "Where is my milk?" and "I drank my milk." At this age, too, youngsters typically learn to change the meaning of words or sentences by changing the inflection they use. For example, "I drink *milk*?" might be a question asking if it's all right to drink milk rather than water. But "I *drink* milk!" might be the child's way of telling the mother the child has already consumed the milk.

Generally speaking, the meaning children assign to words tends to move from the overly general to the specific. Thus, at an early age, a little girl might use the word "Daddy" to refer to any adult male. Later, "Daddy" might refer just to males who look like her father. Finally, she learns to use "Daddy" only when referring to her father, and "Man" when referring to other adult males.

Noam Chomsky

At any point in a child's development, the *meaning* the child assigns to words tells a lot about how far the youngster's cognitive development has progressed. These "meanings" also give some clues as to the child's notions about the *rules* by which words can be combined into sentences.

Syntax

Where do children learn about *syntax*—the "grammar" or "rules" that govern language? These rules are often frightfully complex—so much so that even people who never make a mistake in English can't always tell you what "laws" they are following. And most parents don't *teach* syntax to their children—they just provide models and then correct the youngster's mistakes.

Put more informally, if you isolated two infants at birth (as Harlow did with his monkeys), would the children learn to speak spontaneously? If they did speak spontaneously, what language would they "invent?" Would different pairs of children dream up different languages? If so, would these invented languages have similar grammars? In short, is there an innately determined "universal language" underlying all types of human speech? Or is syntax entirely learned?

The nature-nurture debate in language acquisition probably reaches its peak in the area of syntax learning. Behaviorists—such as B.F. Skinner—have long insisted that children don't directly learn syntax at all (unless specifically taught it). Rather, they learn proper speech from imitation and "selective reinforcement." Thus, Skinner comes down strongly on the side of "nurture."

On the other hand, **linguists** such as M.I.T.'s Noam Chomsky have long taken the "naturist" position in this argument. Some 20 years ago, Chomsky stated that there is a universal *deep structure* or grammar underlying all human languages. Chomsky believes that languages are far too complex for children to learn in the short times it takes them to do so—unless the children are born with some innate knowledge of the "rules" or syntax that govern speech in all human societies.

By the *deep structure of language*, Chomsky means "the innate tendency to process information in linguistic form." To understand what Chomsky is talking about, consider the behaviors involved in walking. You had to *learn* to walk, didn't you? And you probably learned very quickly. But could you have acquired those motor skills so readily if the "deep structure" of walking weren't somehow inbedded in your genes? In similar fashion, could you have learned to talk if the neurons in your brain weren't genetically biased to produce spoken language as readily as they produce running and walking?

Who is correct, Skinner or Chomsky? The answer seems to be, "both of them." Skinner looks at how *verbal behaviors are acquired through learning*. Chomsky prefers to deal with the *innate aspects of linguistic development*. Thus, Skinner explains quite well how parents use selective reinforcement to "shape" the sounds children produce when babbling. But

Skinner doesn't explain *why* all children babble in similar fashion. Nor does he tell us how *words* become "mental symbols" for objects and actions in the physical world. Chomsky's strength lies in his attempts to explain those issues in cognitive development that Skinner simply ignores.

Pragmatics

Languages came about because people living together needed to *communicate* with each other. Communication involves more than phonemes, semantics, and syntax, however. It involves practical or pragmatic rules about when to speak and when not to speak, what is acceptable talk and what isn't. Put another way, children must learn not only how to communicate their needs, but also to predict what the *social consequences* of saying something will be.

Newborns cry to express their needs. As they acquire language, they find more complex ways to communicate. As Margaret Matlin notes, a seven-month-old child who wants a ball will reach out for the ball and make a fuss. By about nine months of age, the youngster will attempt to use adults to help gain what the child wants. That is, the child will alternately look at the adult and at the ball while fussing. By now, the child has learned there is a connection between making the right kind of sounds and getting the ball. Linguists often call this *intentional communication*, since the child announces his or her intentions in order to get assistance from someone else.

Society, however, puts constraints on *what* the child can say—and on *how* the child must say things, as well. Children soon learn there are some topics not to be discussed with adults (such as sex) and some words not to use in public (such as curses). According to Margaret Matlin, youngsters also learn to adapt the *complexity* of their speech to the person they're speaking to. For example, a four-year-old often will use simple words and sentences when speaking to a younger brother, but will employ much more complex speech when talking to adults.

"WHEN I SAY 'RUNNED', YOU KNOW I MEAN 'RAN'. LET'S NOT QUIBBLE."

Jerome S. Bruner

According to Jerome Bruner, parents often teach their infants social skills while teaching them language.

Social Aspects of Language Learning

According to Harvard psychologist Jerome Bruner, a child who is acquiring the "pragmatic rules" of language also may be learning something about "proper social behavior." In one recent study, Bruner made videotape recordings of mothers as they taught their children to communicate both verbally and nonverbally. According to Bruner, during the first few months of the child's life, a mother spends much of her time simply trying to find out what the infant is looking at. Then she begins trying to get the infant to look where she is looking. Once the mother discovers how to attract the child's attention, she begins to point out objects and give them names. She then rewards the child for learning these names.

Bruner also notes that, during language learning, the mother begins making *social contracts* with the child that serve as the pattern for adult behaviors. If the child grows restless, for instance, the mother may say, "Let's learn two more words, and then we'll go play." When the child fulfills a social contract, the mother often praises the youngster by saying something like, "See how well you did? Aren't you pleased with yourself?" According to Bruner, while the mother is "shaping language," she is also encouraging the child to monitor the consequences of the child's own actions and thus to become less dependent on the mother.

The Father's Role in Language Learning

Traditionally, in most societies, it is the mother who spends the most time with an infant. And it is the mother who is most responsible for nurturing the child. However, the father's role in teaching an infant to speak is also important, although his contributions are likely to be more indirect than direct.

Although fathers tend to talk to their infants less than do mothers, fathers apparently give the child *confidence*. Studies from several different cultures suggest that infants cope better with the appearance of strangers when their fathers have spent considerable time with the children. A child whose father is an involved parent is thus more likely to *perform verbally in public* than one whose father is uninvolved in caring for the child.

The Source of Language Learning

As we mentioned in Chapter 2, the "speech center" in the left hemisphere is physically a little larger than the same area of the right hemisphere in most right-handed humans. This size difference between the hemispheres exists to a much lesser extent in the higher primates, but is not found at all in lower animals. Furthermore, the vocalizations made by monkeys and chimpanzees seem to be primarily under the control of centers in the *limbic system* (see

Chapter 4) rather than under the control of the cortex (as is the case in humans). Electrical stimulation of the limbic system can call forth *all* of the vocal responses that monkeys are capable of making. Destruction of the "cortical speech center" in humans typically leaves them speechless. Destruction of similar areas of the monkey cortex does not affect the animal's vocalizations at all.

It would appear, then, that human brains are uniquely suited for language learning. However, many scientists have recently been successful in teaching chimpanzees to communicate ei-

ther in "sign language" or by pressing keys on a computer console.

For example, psychologists Sue Savage-Rumbaugh and Duane Rumbaugh have been able to train chimps to use an artificial language called **Yerkish**. To help the animals learn, the Rumbaughs present word-symbols on an overhead projector. The chimps respond by pressing illuminated buttons on a computer console. If the chimps use the word-symbols correctly, they are rewarded. Several chimpanzees have been able to learn 100 or more symbols, and use them as correctly as might a two-year-old child.

The Rumbaughs also have trained two apes to place items correctly into proper "cognitive categories." The Rumbaughs first taught the animals the general meaning of categories such as "tool" and "food." The animals were then shown specific items (such as a banana or a mechanical lever) and asked which category the item belonged to. In a 1980 report in *Science*, the Rumbaughs state the apes did an excellent job of sorting the items into the correct categories.

Other psychologists have taught apes to use **American Sign Language**, and have claimed that their animals could "create sentences" and "use language in a symbolic way," much as can very young children. However, there is a continuing controversy in the scientific literature about this research. For a detailed analysis of "ape language" often suggests that the trainers are *cueing* the animal's responses in various subtle ways, much as did the man who owned the famous "talking horse," Clever Hans (see Chapter 1).

Can apes speak? The answer depends on how you define "speak." Some apes can surely communicate their needs by way of "signing," or by pressing buttons on a computer console. But as Adrian Desmond points out in his 1979 book *The Ape's Reflexion*, no one has yet proven that ape language has "grammar." Nor is there concrete evidence that apes can manipulate symbols with, say, the sophistication of even a fairly young child.

One point seems very clear, however, as J.L. and Carol Gould note in the May issue of *Science 81*. Humans talk *spontaneously*, and do

At the Yerkes Regional Primate Center, a computer is used to teach another chimp, Lana, to communicate. Lana learns the name of an object she is shown by pressing keys that signify "What is?" (the object you are holding). The experimenter shows her the key that represents the object so that in the future she can ask for it by name.

In the Yerkes language, dubbed Yerkish, questions begin with a ? and name-of is a single word. A Yerkish conversation is carried out using an electric keyboard in which each key represents a word.

When keys are pressed, the words are projected in sequence on a display panel above Lana's keyboard. Lana and her teacher must read the projected images to get the message.

Set 1

Set 2

Fig. 18.1 Pictures similar to those used by Rosch et al. (1976).

so worldwide in their *natural environment*. Other animals do not. As the Goulds put it, "You cannot keep a normal, healthy child from learning to talk. . . . Chimpanzees, by contrast, can be [coaxed] into mastering some sort of linguistic communications skills, but they really could not care less about language: The drive just is not there."

Put more simply, humans are *programmed by their genes* to learn to talk, and they have a nervous system complex enough to support speech production. No other animal can make that statement.

Why Language?

In Chapter 5, we noted that a living system is an "organization of related sub-systems," and that the sub-systems "must be in communication with each other." You acquired language in part because your genes made it easy for you to do so, and because your parents reinforced you for talking. You could hardly become a "sub-system" within a family or a society without being able to communicate with other people or groups.

But you also learned to speak because speech serves your own personal needs. As we pointed out in Chapter 15, your memory banks are built around the sounds and structures of language.

And you not only *talk* and *remember* in words, you *think* and *reason* using language as well. Thus, speech is more than a means of communicating between social sub-systems—that is, among people and groups. Talking is also the method most of us employ when we form mental concepts and process information inside our minds.

Now that we have briefly described how language acquisition occurs, let's look at the development of those cognitive processes called "concept formation" and "problem solving." As we will see, these processes are heavily dependent on language.

Concept Formation and Problem Solving

According to Boyd McCandless and Robert Trotter, when a one-year-old girl uses the word "ball," she typically refers to her own relationship to the toy. *She* is always the one who plays with the ball, and she always does so in her *bedroom*. "Ball" refers to *her red ball*, not to anything else. If you gave her a round blue toy and insisted it too was a ball, she might become confused. Balls are (to her) red objects, not blue ones.

At about 18 months, however, the word is likely to take on an enlarged meaning. Now the girl uses "ball" to refer to round objects that she bounces on the floor, not just in the bedroom, but in the kitchen and outdoors as well. Other people may use the ball too, and balls can be red or blue or even striped. As McCandless and Trotter note, the girl's *concept* (or schema) for "ball" has obviously enlarged. But how does this miracle occur?

Question: What are the major differences between a "cup" and a "glass"? What does your answer tell you about your *concepts* of these two objects?

Concept Development

As we noted in Chapter 9, a "concept" is a category that *includes* some objects or ideas and *excludes* others. The rules of inclusion and exclusion *define* the concept or schema.

Very young children tend to be quite good at handling *basic-level categories*, but have problems dealing with superordinate categories. For example, look at Fig. 18.1. When Eleanor Rosch and her colleagues asked three-year-olds to select the two items that were alike, they had no difficulty at all with Set 1. A cat is a cat is a basic-level category. But the three-year-olds missed the correct answer in Set 2 about half the time. By the time they were five, however, the children almost always got perfect scores when given tests such as this one. Thus, as Rosch notes, concept development usually begins at the level of basic categories and moves outward to both superordinate and subordinate categories.

In a 1975 study, E.S. Andersen asked children of various ages to differentiate between a cup and a glass. Three-year-old children tended to call anything you can drink from a cup, even such odd "cups" as wine glasses and crystal goblets. Slightly older children tended to call anything made of glass or china a "glass," and every other type of container a "cup." By the time the children were 12, they usually called any object *with a handle* a "cup," and anything *without a handle* (particularly if made of glass or china) a glass. Andersen notes that the three-year-olds *overgeneralized* basic concepts. Slightly older children put objects in categories according to *how they look*. But 12-year-olds (and adults) tend to categorize primarily *according to use.*

Concept formation is often difficult for a child because not all concepts have well-defined boundaries. Andersen notes that 12-year-olds seemed to have gained an appreciation of the fuzziness of most concepts. Younger children, however, were often quite rigid in insisting that a given object *had to* fit within a given category because it possessed one or two specific attributes.

Question: If a "cup" always has a handle, what do you call those paper containers put out by the Dixie Company?

Problem Solving

Solving life's problems often boils down to finding the right concepts to describe a given situation or difficulty. Problem solving also involves discovering which "search strategy" is most likely to help you fit things into their proper categories.

Margaret Matlin notes that psychologists haven't studied the development of problem solving in children very extensively. There is, however, one classic study on the subject. In 1966, F.A. Mosher and J.R. Hornsby asked children aged six to eleven to play a game much like Twenty Questions. Mosher and Hornsby showed youngsters of different ages a set of objects much like those in Fig. 18.2. They asked the children to *name* each object first, to make sure the youngsters knew what each was. Then Mosher and Hornsby told the children to guess which *one* of the objects the experimenters had in mind. The children were told to use as *few questions* as possible. Mosher and Hornsby then recorded each child's guess.

According to Mosher and Hornsby, the children's guesses seemed to reflect two different *search strategies*:

1. Constraint-seeking questions. These were questions general enough to refer to more than one picture. "Is it alive?" is an example of a constraint-seeking question.
2. Hypothesis-scanning questions. These were very specific, and usually referred to just one picture. "Is it a doll?" is an example of a hypothesis-scanning question.

Mosher and Hornsby report the six-year-olds primarily asked hypothesis-scanning questions. The 11-year-olds, however, mostly asked constraint-seeking questions. Mosher and Hornsby conclude that, as children develop cognitively, they seem to acquire more efficient

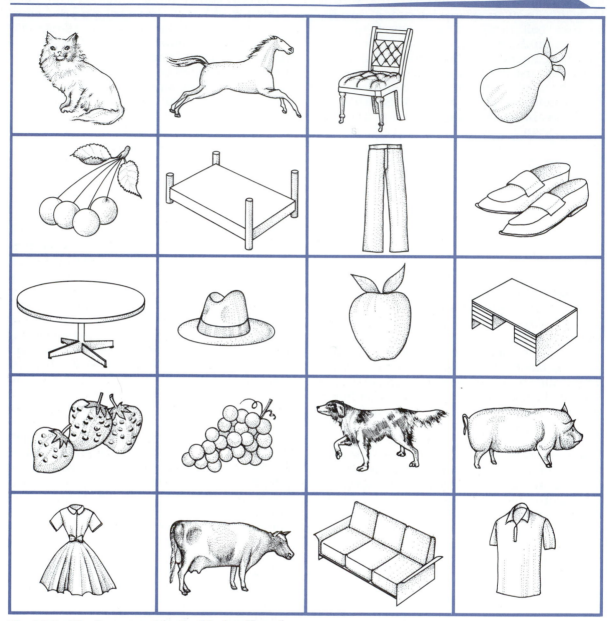

Fig. 18.2 The items used in the Mosher-Hornsby "20 questions" experiment. See text for detail.

search strategies. They cannot use these strategies effectively, however, until they are mature enough to know how objects can be linked together in superordinate concept categories. Children also gain the ability to handle **ambiguity** as they grow older.

Research suggests that younger children tend to be fairly rigid when fitting objects and ideas into cognitive categories, while older children tend to be more flexible. However, older children also have more *facts* about the objects they are asked to classify. Surprisingly enough, recent research suggests that facts may be just as important in "learning how to think" as are problem-solving strategies.

Question: Look back at page 9 in Chapter 1. What kind of search strategy does the scientific method seem to be? How would you go about teaching a 12-year-old child to use the scientific method in solving a real-life problem?

"Learning How to Think"

In the February 1984 *American Psychologist*, University of Pittsburgh psychologist Robert Glaser talks about how children "learn to think." Glaser notes that many educators believe there are general "cognitive rules" that can be taught to children, which presumably will help them solve academic and real-life problems. These rules are often said to be *content-free*, because they supposedly are strategies that can be applied to a wide variety of situations.

However, as we noted in Chapter 9, there simply aren't very many content-free strategies that are useful in the real world. Rather, as Glaser points out, most real-life problem solving involves the application of *knowledge*. Glaser defines "knowledge" as a combination of rules *plus* facts. The "facts" describe how to apply the rules in fairly specific situations. Glaser believes we cannot study the development of "thinking" and "reasoning" in children unless we first find out how much the children know about the world.

This point is made clear in a series of experiments by Robert Siegler, a psychologist at Carnegie-Mellon University. Much of Siegler's work involves the "balance beam" shown in Fig. 18.3. The beam is a sort of "teeter-totter" that can be locked into place.

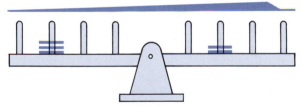

Fig. 18.3 A balance beam is used to identify children's rules for solving problems. On each side of the fulcrum are four pegs on which metal weights are placed. Depending on the arrangement of the weights, the beam ordinarily would tip to the left or right, or remain level. However, a lever (not shown) holds the beam motionless, regardless of how the weights are arranged. Children are asked to predict whether the beam would tip, and in which direction, if the lever were released.

As you know, there are two factors that determine which way the balance beam will tilt when released—weight and distance. The more weights there are on a given arm of the beam— and the farther the weights are from the center— the more likely it is that the beam will tilt in that direction.

In a 1983 article in the November-December *American Scientist*, Siegler states there are four "rules" that people use when trying to predict which way the teeter-totter will tilt. Rule 1 ignores distance entirely—it predicts that the arm with the most weights on it will tilt downward *no matter how far the weights on each arm are from the center*. Rule 2 does take distance into account, but over-emphasizes the importance of weight. According to Rule 2, the side with the most weights on it will *always* tip downward. Only if the two sides weigh the same does Rule 2 consider the distance factor. Rule 3 over-emphasizes the importance of distance. According to Rule 3, the side with the weights farthest from the center will almost always dip. Only Rule 4 multiplies "weight x distance," and only Rule 4 *always* yields a correct answer. A diagram of the four rules appears in Fig. 18.4.

Siegler put weights at different distances from the center of the beam, then asked children aged 5, 9, 13, and 17 to guess which way the beam would tilt when he released it. Siegler then asked the children to explain their guesses. More important, he also analyzed the *errors* the children made. By analyzing these errors, Siegler determined which of the four rules each child was using.

Siegler predicted the younger children would use Rule 1, while older children would use Rules 2 or 3. In fact, most of Siegler's predictions were correct. Five-year-olds tended to use Rule 1, 9-year-olds used Rule 2, 13-year-olds used Rules 2 or 3, and 17-year-olds used Rule 3 almost exclusively. Almost none of the children used Rule 4 during the first test. Oddly enough, some 20 percent of the children cited Rule 3 (weight and distance are both important, but distance is more important) *even though their errors showed they were actually using Rule 2*. Thus, Siegler says, merely *asking* children to explain their guesses isn't a particularly good

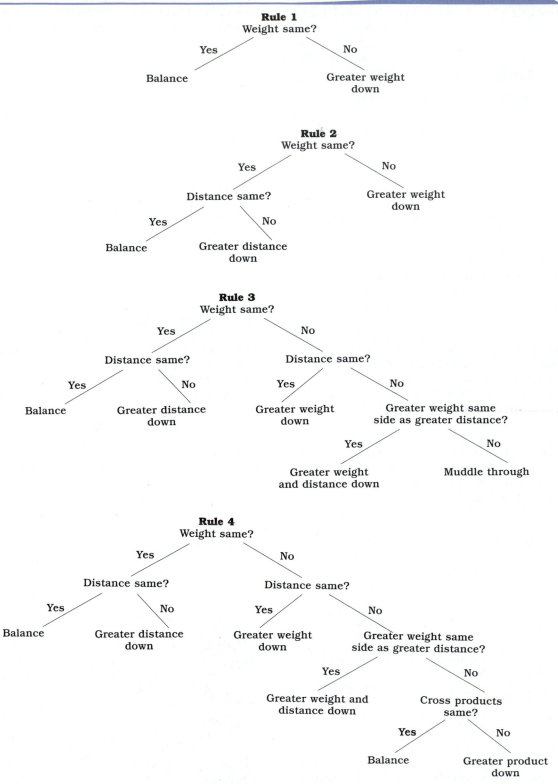

Fig. 18.4 Expected pattern of responses on the balance-beam problem.

way to discover how they actually think through a problem.

Teaching Children to "Encode"

Siegler says that the way a child perceives a problem depends on whether the child actually "encodes" the two important variables (weight and distance). By "encoding," he actually means "pays attention to." Siegler believes that children must *learn* to encode the crucial factors in any problem-solving situation.

To test his belief, Siegler asked a group of 5-year-olds and a group of 8-year-olds to guess which way the teeter-totter would tilt in one test situation. Then he released the balance and let both groups discover which way the teeter-totter actually tipped. Before this "feedback" session, both groups gave primarily Rule 1 answers. When Siegler tested the 8-year-olds again (after the feedback session), they tended to use Rule 2 rather than Rule 1. However, the 5-year-olds doggedly kept giving Rule 1 answers.

Why did the older children move on to Rule 2, while the younger ones didn't? Videotapes of the pre-feedback session showed the eight-year-olds had looked back and forth from one end of the balance to the other. Thus, says Siegler, these children were *aware* of distance as a possible factor even though they didn't use it at first. And because they "encoded" the distance factor, they could profit from feedback showing Rule 1 didn't work. However, the tapes showed that the five-year-olds ignored distance entirely. Because they didn't "encode" this variable when considering the situation, Siegler says, the younger children couldn't benefit from the feedback. Therefore, they continued to make mistake after mistake because they didn't *perceive* the situation properly.

Next, Siegler gave "training sessions" to a new group of five- and eight-year-olds. During these sessions, he taught the children to consider both weight and distance. Once the youngsters had learned how to "encode" both variables, almost all of them began giving Rule 3 answers.

Siegler believes that, developmentally speaking, there is no substitute for experience. But he advocates first training children how to encode their environments, then teaching them problem-solving strategies.

Like many other psychologists, Siegler is interested in how children acquire *knowledge*, which (as we noted) is facts plus rules. The person who made such studies popular was Jean Piaget. Indeed, Piaget's theory of cognitive development is really a theory of knowledge. Suppose we look at the theory first, then evaluate Piaget's contributions in light of recent studies by Siegler and other scientists.

Jean Piaget

Jean Piaget was one of the most respected figures in child psychology. He lived for 84 years. When Piaget died in September 1980, Harvard psychologist Jerome Kagan called him "the most influential developmental theorist of this century, if not of all time."

For some 50 years, Piaget was a professor at the University of Geneva and director of the Rousseau Institute. Trained as a zoologist, Piaget began his search for a "theory of knowledge" while still in college. This search soon led him to study the intellectual development of children.

Piaget was a gentle, wise man who loved children. But he also loved science, art, and religion. When he was 20, Piaget wrote a novel, *Quest*, about a young man named Sebastien who is concerned with such questions as, "Who am I?" and "What is the meaning of life?" The answers Sebastien discovers in the novel eventually became the basis for much of Piaget's theorizing about cognitive development. Indeed, most of Piaget's research on children appears to be little more than a life-long attempt to confirm the insights he had while still a very young man.

Jean Piaget was noted for his studies of cognitive development in children.

Mental Development

The basic psychological problem Piaget tried to solve can be stated fairly simply. When you were born, you were little more than a bundle of biological reflexes. You took in food, you excreted wastes, and you responded in a reflexive way to a variety of stimuli. But you did not "think" or solve problems. Nor did you have any real understanding of who you were or what the world is really like. Now, many years later, you are a conscious, self-directed, mature human being. You speak a complex language, you are capable of understanding the strange symbols of mathematics and nuclear physics, and you can create new things (such as poetry and music) if you wish to. You engage in **altruistic** behaviors that often benefit others more than they benefit you. And you probably have a firm sense of what is right and wrong, and how to make many things in the world (including yourself) better than they presently are.

Now, how did this miraculous change occur? That is, how did you develop from a passive "bundle of biological reflexes" into the infinitely complicated, self-directed human being you are today? Piaget attempted to answer these questions by developing a complex theory of cognitive development. His theory will make more sense, however, if we first look at where Piaget stood on the four developmental issues mentioned earlier in this chapter.

Piaget and the Four Issues

As far as the nature-nurture problem goes, Piaget was, in his own way, an interactionist. Indeed, he often called himself "the man in the middle" of this controversy. True, he believed you were born with certain *innate mental structures* that determined the shape of your cognitive development. These structures provided both your *motivation* to interact with your environment and guided the growth of your knowledge about the world. But Piaget thought the "shape of your mind" was affected by the environment you grew up in, too. Thus, he rejected Chomsky's notion that children are born with an "innate grammar" that helps them learn language. Children *construct* grammar in their own minds as they learn to talk, Piaget said, because their genes allow them to.

As far as the mind-body problem is concerned, Piaget came down clearly on the side of the mind. He paid little attention to behavior itself. Rather, it was the "mental functioning" that controlled behavior that interested him.

Unlike the behaviorists—whom he battled with constantly—Piaget did not believe you were "shaped" by your parents and professors. Rather, he said, "The child is the teacher." By this, he meant you were actively involved in your own cognitive development. Your social environment merely provided the inputs—your mind *interpreted* and *reshaped* these inputs to create the knowledge you presently have.

Piaget was also "somewhere in the middle" of the continuity-discontinuity controversy. According to Piaget, intellectual development *in all children* procedes through four clearly-defined stages. We will describe these stages in a moment. Since he believed that the later stages developed out of the earlier ones, Piaget was a "continuity" theorist. However, he also said that development occurred in "giant steps" (or stages), rather than being merely the slow and steady accumulation of knowledge and information.

And while Piaget studied children individually, he was more impressed by how similar cognitive development is in all children than by individual differences among children.

Now that we have briefly outlined Piaget's position on the four major issues in developmental psychology, let's examine his theory in some detail.

Equilibrium

At heart, Piaget was really an "information processing theorist" long before such a label existed. That is, he saw the mind as a kind of computer that used sensory inputs to construct an internal representation of the outside world. However, ordinary computers are *passive* instruments that must be "programmed" by external sources. To Piaget, the child's mind is an *active* computer that continually changes or reprograms itself. The mind accomplishes this miracle by *abstracting* reality. By "abstracting reality," Piaget meant the search for general laws that will allow your mind to understand why people and objects behave as they do.

Computers process data because they are built to do so. Thus, their motivation is supplied by external sources. Children, however, are motivated by an inner biological drive that Piaget calls the process of **equilibrium**. In Chapter 10 we discussed *homeostasis*, which is the body's innate tendency to move toward a need-free state. In a sense, the cognitive process of "equilibrium" is little more than the concept of homeostasis applied to mental rather than biological needs.

According to Piaget, you are born with the ability to construct an abstract representation of the world in your mind. But your attempts to do so are necessarily inaccurate, particularly when you are young and inexperienced. Sometimes, therefore, the things you experience may *contradict* your expectations. Whenever your *actual inputs* "contradict" your *expectancies*, you experience what Piaget called *dis-equilibrium*. And you are prompted to explain the contradiction.

In his 1980 book *Experiments in Contradiction*, Piaget described some of his studies in this area. For example, suppose you show two small wheels to a child. The wheels appear to be identical. However, only one wheel is "normal." The other wheel has a hidden weight on its rim. Then you ask the child to guess what will happen when you roll the wheels down a slight incline. The child predicts the wheels will move downhill. You then release the normal wheel which does, indeed, roll downhill just as predicted. But when you release the weighted wheel, it sometimes stands still or even rolls uphill. The fact that the weighted wheel did not behave as the child predicted is a *contradiction* that causes *dis-equilibrium* in the child's mind. This dis-equilibrium motivates the child to search for an answer that will resolve the contradiction and restore mental equilibrium.

Generally speaking, children resolve contradictions by changing the way they perceive or "symbolize" real-world objects or events. And when they do so, they usually will have achieved a greater understanding of themselves and the world around them. Piaget referred to this type of cognitive growth as "achieving a higher state of equilibrium."

Question: What similarities do you see between Piaget's "contradiction" study and Siegler's "feedback" experiments with the teeter-totter?

Dis-equilibrium

Dis-equilibrium is important in Piaget's theory for two reasons. First, dis-equilibrium *motivates* the child to resolve contradictions in order to re-establish equilibrium. Indeed, Piaget saw "the drive to maintain mental equilibrium" as being the major motive that fuels a child's cognitive development. Second, the *new equilibrium* the child achieves upon resolving the contradiction *is always higher* (more mature) than was the previous level of equilibrium. This new level is higher, Piaget said, because it

Altruistic (al-true-ISS-tick). From the Latin word *alter*, meaning "other." To be altruistic is to have a genuine concern for the welfare of others, to place the well-being of someone else above your own happiness or prosperity.

Equilibrium (ee-kwill-LIB-bree-um). Piaget believed people are motivated by an innate desire to match actual sensory inputs with their own abstract representations of reality. Any mismatch results in dis-equilibrium, which "drives" the person to change her or his mental structures to bring them into accord with reality.

is a *more accurate representation* of the real world.

Drive theorists believe that children eat to reduce their hunger pangs and thus restore homeostasis—not because they have an innate urge to grow and survive. Piaget took much the same approach in describing cognitive motives. He stated that children construct better abstractions about the world because they are driven to reduce dis-equilibrium and restore equilibrium—not because they have an innate urge "to learn about the world." Therefore, the best way to teach children, Piaget often said, was to present them with contradictions that they must resolve.

According to Piaget, all forms of psychological and social motivation flow from the innate need to establish equilibrium. In taking this view, Piaget resembles those drive theorists who say that personal and social needs are "secondary"—that is, acquired through association with primary needs. The important difference between Piaget and the drive theorists is this— your "optimum homeostatic level" remains much the same over long periods of time. For instance, each time you eat to reduce your hunger drive, you don't establish a "more mature" type of hunger. However, in Piaget's theory, each time you resolve a contradiction (in order to reduce dis-equilibrium), you create a more highly developed level of equilibrium.

Question: Given Piaget's early scientific training, why is it fairly understandable that he and the drive theorists define motivation in similar ways?

Structures of the Mind

Piaget said that you construct reality in your mind by trying to resolve contradictions. But you couldn't start doing that at birth unless you were born with some innately determined notion of what to expect from the world around you. Piaget called these "innately determined notions" the *structures of the mind*.

As we noted in Chapter 13, you were born with certain *innate reflexes*, which allowed you to respond automatically to inputs from the outer world during your first days of life. The sucking reflex is a good example, since infants suck and swallow without having to be taught how to do so. At birth, however, you began modifying these inborn reflexes because of your experiences with the outside world. Thus, new learning is always built on old, and *conditioned* reflexes are but adaptations of *innate* reflexes.

In much the same fashion, said Piaget, you were born with certain "mental reflexes." These innate cognitive structures allow you to process sensory inputs (and therefore represent reality) in a crude sort of way. At birth, however, you began to adapt these inborn mental structures as you constructed your own "mental action programs" for processing and responding to reality.

In Piaget's terms, each "mental action program" you have for thinking about and responding to the world is a *schema* (see Chapter 8). The history of a child's cognitive development is that of creating ever-more-complex **schemata**, or "action programs." Guiding the development of these mental structures, however, are the *functions of the mind*.

Functions of the Mind

You do not perceive yourself now in the same way that you did 10 or 20 years ago. Thus, your "self-schema" has changed over time, and will continue to change in your future years. But the growth of your "self-schema" was guided throughout your life by the same two mental *functions*. These "functions" are *organization* and *adaptation*.

By the term *organization*, Piaget referred to the mind's innate ability to put simple schemata together so they form a more complex cognitive structure. For example, a six-month-old infant knows how to push an object such as a ball aside. "Pushing" thus is one of the infant's cognitive schemata or "action programs." The infant also knows how to reach out and grasp a toy, such as a doll. "Reaching" is therefore a second but quite independent action program. At six months, the child is not mature enough to push a ball aside in order to grasp a doll that is behind the ball. At about nine months, however, the child can *integrate* these two schemata into a more complex mental structure. That is, the youngster can now intentionally push the ball out of the way and grasp the doll. Much of the process of cognitive development involves *organizing* simple schemata into more complex action programs.

Adaptation is the infant's innate tendency to adjust to the world by processing information in one of two ways. The child may try to incorporate inputs into already existing schemata, a process Piaget calls **assimilation**. Or, if the inputs simply will not fit the child's present view of reality, the child may be forced to change, add to, or reorganize its present schemata. Piaget refers to this process as **accommodation**.

Assimilation

Piaget was first and foremost a biologist. Thus, many of his notions of cognitive development are analogies to biological processes. For example, consider the process of digestion. You eat food, and your stomach breaks the food down into small particles. Your blood distributes these particles to the cells, which *assimilate* these particles by incorporating them into the structure of the cell. Biological assimilation therefore involves *changing* energy inputs to make them part of your body.

The process of *cognitive assimilation* works in much the same way. According to Piaget, when you "encode" an input in order to store it in your mind, you *break the input up* just as your stomach breaks food down into tiny particles. You then incorporate the "encoded" input into already existing mental structures, just as the cells assimilate food particles into already existing cellular structures. Cognitive assimilation thus involves *changing* sensory inputs to make them part of your mind.

For instance, a newborn girl tends to suck any small object that is put in her mouth. She soon builds up a mental schema related to "suckability" and assimilates all small objects into this category, whether they really fit there or not. Therefore, when she encounters any new small object, she often pops the object in her mouth at once.

Question: What similarities do you see between Piaget's views on how assimilation occurs, and Goodglass's theory (discussed in Chapter 15) of how inputs are encoded in *categories* while being stored in Long-term Memory?

Accommodation

Sometimes a given input simply will not fit within the schemata a child already has available. For instance, suppose an infant named

Mary finds a small red pepper and pops that into her mouth. Very rapidly, Mary will discover she must create a new schema, that of "not suckable." Any new experience that contradicts her already existing mental structures will cause Mary to resort to the process of *accommodation*—that is, to altering her schemata to make them fit reality.

Adaptation and Equilibrium

The adaptive functions of assimilation and accommodation are closely related to the equilibrium process. Earlier, we mentioned a study of Piaget's in which he showed a child two identical-looking wheels. At first, the child's cognitive structures regarding wheels were in a state of simple equilibrium, because all wheels the child had seen before had rolled downhill. So the child *assimilated* the two new wheels to the old structures. But when the wheel with the weight on its rim stood still (or rolled uphill), the child was faced with a contradiction between the child's prior mental structures and present sensory inputs. This contradiction brought about cognitive dis-equilibrium. The child *accommodated* by changing those schemata dealing with wheels. The act of accommodation resolved the contradiction and created a more mature level of understanding—that is, now the child understood that sometimes wheels can roll uphill too.

Schemata (ski-MAHT-tah). Plural of "schema." Schemata are mental structures that represent reality in some abstract manner. Similar to "perceptual schemata" that allow you to recognize and respond to sensory inputs (see Chapter 9).

Assimilation (ass-sim-il-LAY-shun). The process of adaptation by which inputs are altered in order to fit into present schemata or mental structures. "Coding" an input into memory categories for long-term storage is a form of assimilation.

Accommodation (ack-komm-oh-DAY-shun). The process of adaptation by which mental schemata are changed or added to in order to match them to reality. If a given input won't fit into any present schema, you accommodate by creating a new one.

Epistemology (ee-pis-tee-MOLL-oh-gee). The scientific study of how people acquire knowledge. According to Piaget, all children have an innate desire to learn about themselves and the outer world. Thus the study of child development, to Piaget, was epistemological (ee-pis-tee-moh-LODGE-ih-cal) in that it was the study of how the child's perception of reality changes over time.

Epistemology

One word Piaget used constantly was **epistemology**, which the dictionary defines as "the study or a theory of the nature and grounds of knowledge, especially with reference to its limits and validity." And much of Piaget's research was epistemological, in that it was aimed at discovering how *children come to know themselves and the world around them.*

As we noted earlier in this chapter, knowledge is a combination of accumulated facts *plus* a set of strategies for using those facts. Piaget's theory is actually an attempt to describe how the infant acquires both facts about the world and a set of "rules" for using those facts. And that is precisely what the study of epistemology is all about.

Piaget's Four Developmental Stages

According to Piaget, there are four major stages of cognitive development:

1. The sensory-motor period.
2. The pre-operational stage.
3. The stage of concrete operations.
4. The stage of formal operations.

Each of us goes from one stage upward to the next at slightly different ages. But the *average age* at which children attain each maturational level is said to be about the same in all cultures.

In the sensory-motor stage, the infant builds up simple schemata of the world. For instance, it may respond to all objects as if they were "suckable" until experience teaches it otherwise.

In the preoperational stage, children begin to acquire language. They begin to give names to objects, and thus can manipulate some aspects of the world "in their minds" once they have encountered the object in real life.

In the stage of concrete operations, children learn to conserve quantity when they discover that transformations are reversible. That is, the quantity of water doesn't change when you pour it from one container into another.

In the stage of formal operations, young people can reason and think in abstract terms. Thus, they "test the world" by planning and executing various types of experiments.

Sensory-Motor Period

The first of Piaget's four stages is called the *sensory-motor period*, which begins at birth and usually ends when the infant is about 24 months old. It is during this time infants build up their initial schemata, most of which involve the objects and people in its world.

As Sueann Ambron and Neil Salkind note in their 1984 book *Child Development*, the sensory-motor period actually has six parts:

Stage 1: Reflex activity (1st month of life)

Infants are born with innate reflexes that sustain them during their first days of life. By the end of the first month, however, infants begin to *use* these reflexes deliberately. For example, when really hungry, they will turn their heads in order to suck on a nipple.

Stage 2: Primary circular reactions (1–4 months)

At this age, infants (1) repeat chance behaviors that have brought them pleasure, and (2) start to anticipate future responses. Piaget calls these reactions "circular" because they are maintained by a *repeating pattern of reinforcement*. For instance, infants accidentally suck their thumbs, find this rewarding, and thus thumb-suck more frequently in the future. When put into a posture frequently associated with feeding, they may begin to make sucking motions in *anticipation* of being fed.

Stage 3: Secondary circular reactions (4–10 months)

In this stage, children turn their attention away from bodily movements toward objects and events in the external environment. Now they are mature enough to perceive some connection between *what they do* and what *happens to them*.

Stage 4: Coordinating secondary schemas (10–12 months)

At this age, infants begin to grasp what Piaget calls "means-ends relationships." For example, the child puts together two previously learned action schemas—pushing and reaching—in order to push a ball out of the way to grasp a doll.

Stage 5: Tertiary circular reactions (12–18 months)

In this stage, children become interested in objects themselves. For instance, the infant may repeatedly drop a ball from different heights and observe the ball's behavior. At this age, too, the child begins to test out various methods of *obtaining information* about the behavior of objects. Thus, the youngster not only drops the ball, but hits it and rolls it as well.

Stage 6: Symbolic representation (18–24 months)

It is at this stage of the child's cognitive development, Piaget says, that the infant truly begins to "think." By thinking, Piaget means *building an internal representation of the external world*. Children at this age can manipulate objects "in their minds"—by thinking about them—rather than having to move the objects with their hands. Prior to this stage, if the object wasn't *physically present*, it simply didn't exist for the child. "Out of sight, out of mind" is a good description of the child's previous level of development. By 18 months of age, though, the child can *symbolize* objects internally. Thus, the child begins to realize that objects exist even when the child cannot see or touch them. Piaget describes this as the concept of **object permanence**.

When youngsters gain the ability to represent objects symbolically, Piaget said, they pass from the sensory-motor period into the pre-operational period of development.

Question: What else does the child acquire during the first two years of life that allows the child to represent objects internally, using *easy-to-manipulate* cognitive symbols?

Pre-Operational Stage

During the sensory-motor period, the infant responds to its environment directly and rather automatically. But as the child acquires *sophisticated language*, the youngster passes to the second, or *pre-operational stage* of development, which runs from about age two to seven. Language gives the child the ability to deal with many aspects of the world in symbols, by talking and thinking about objects rather than hav-

> **Object permanence.** According to Piaget, a very young infant does not realize that an object has an existence independent of its own perceptions of the object. Once the infant is capable of symbolic thought, it builds up complex schemata involving the object and then realizes the permanence of the object.

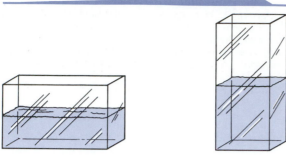

18.5 Conservation of quantity according to Piaget.

ing to manipulate them directly. Piaget believed that language also allows the child to *remember past events* and hence to *anticipate* their happening again.

During all the early developmental periods—and sometimes even much later in life—the child makes use of **egocentric reasoning**. But this type of thinking is particularly noticeable during the pre-operational period. By "egocentric," Piaget doesn't mean "selfish." Rather, he means that children cannot readily *differentiate themselves from their environments.*

The pre-operational stage is also marked by *perception-bound thinking.* That is, the child realizes that objects have permanence, but struggles with the fact that objects can undergo *transformations* without being destroyed or physically changed. By "transformations," Piaget means the fact that some aspects of an object may change, but the object itself remains intact. For instance, if you turn a sock inside out, then back again, the child is surprised to see that the sock remains the same. For when the youngster's *perception* of the sock changed, the child assumed the sock had been altered too.

Because the child doesn't realize that *transformations are reversible,* the youngster cannot **conserve** physical properties such as quantity and length. For instance, if you fill two identical, tall thin glasses with water, the child will agree both glasses have the same amount of water in them. But suppose you empty the water in one glass into a wide container (see Fig. 18.5). The water level is, of course, lower in the wide container than in the tall, thin glass. You "know" the fat glass holds the same *quantity* of water as does the thin glass because you can "conserve quantity" in your mind. But to a four-year-old, the tall glass now seems to have more liquid in it because the water level is

higher. The child doesn't realize that the process of pouring didn't *alter* the quantity of liquid in any way. So, if you now pour the water back into the tall, thin glass, the child is surprised that the water level rises because the youngster can't yet grasp the fact that transformations are reversible.

Not until children are four or five years of age do they seem capable of dealing with abstractions—such as love and hate, up and down, large and small. In Piaget's terms, children this age can think—that is, they can use language to generate expectancies—but they cannot *reason.* Reasoning, to Piaget, is the mental manipulation of abstract symbols, the process of "knowing why." Thus, when asked why a balloon flies, pre-operational children may respond, "Because it is red and has a string hanging from it." This is a "what" answer, not a "why" answer.

The pre-operational stage is a transition period. As the child acquires more complex language and mental structures, the young person moves into the stage of concrete operations.

Question: Piaget seems never to have used the shaping techniques (described in Chapter 14) to teach a child to conserve quantity. How might you go about pouring just a little bit of water back and forth from tall to wide glasses to see if children could be taught conservation of quantity at a young age?

Stage of Concrete Operations

By the time children reach the age of 6 or 7, they typically enter into what Piaget called the *stage of concrete operations.* Now young persons can conserve quantity, because they can perform this transformation mentally. But children this age usually cannot conserve weight until the 9th or 10th year. If you place two identical rubber balls in front of a young boy, he will assure you they weigh the same. But if you now cut one ball in pieces, he may say the cut-up pieces don't weigh the same as does the intact ball. According to Piaget, the boy's answer suggests he actually *perceives* weight in quite a different way than do older children. However, once the boy learns to conserve weight, he finally realizes that the whole is equal to the sum of its parts.

The concept of *number* is another acquisition the child usually makes during the stage of concrete operations. Suppose you lay out 10 pennies in two rows on a table, and show them to a girl still at the pre-operational stage:

The girl will see at once that the two rows are identical and that they both contain the same number of pennies. But suppose you widen the spaces between the pennies in the bottom row:

O O O O O
O O O O O

A pre-operational girl may say the second row has more pennies, despite the fact that she can count the coins in each row with no difficulty. Piaget emphasizes that *counting* is not the same thing as the *concept of number*, a schema the child usually attains only during the stage of concrete operations.

Question: If you ask a pre-operational girl, "Which row has the more pennies?", how do you know she understands you mean "more pennies" and not "more space"?

Stage of Formal Operations

The last of Piaget's four periods of intellectual development is called the *stage of formal operations*, which begins about age 12 and continues through the rest of the person's life. Some people may never really reach this stage, Piaget said. Or, if they do develop this far, they may not go very far into it. Whatever the case, children usually don't reach the last stage until at least age 12.

Prior to the 12th year of life, Piaget said, the child is limited to thinking in concrete terms. Only in the final stage can the young person think in completely abstract terms. At this level of development, people can solve problems in their minds by isolating the important variables and manipulating them mentally or perceptually. Now at last the individual is able to draw meaningful conclusions from purely abstract or hypothetical data.

It is during the stage of formal operations that the structures of the mind become complex enough to allow the individual to create a personal "theory of knowledge." This epistemological theory involves all types of knowledge— "how," "what," and most important, "why."

In a sense, Piaget's *stage theory* is an attempt to explain "why" children develop as they do. Now that we have briefly described it, let's see how others have reacted to his theory.

Egocentric reasoning (EE-go-SEN-trick). According to Piaget, young children cannot differentiate themselves from the external world. Thus, they see the world from a self-centered viewpoint.

Conserve. In Piaget's terms, to "conserve" something is to realize that an object is not necessarily transformed when it changes in some way. To Piaget, the mental process involved in transforming inputs was always reversible. But a child must be fairly mature to realize that this is the case.

Piaget and His Critics

One of the major criticisms leveled at Piaget is that many of his ideas were mere adaptations of early work by US psychologist James Mark Baldwin. As Robert Cairns pointed out in *Contemporary Psychology* in 1980, there is some truth to this accusation. For in 1897 Baldwin described the various stages of a child's cognitive development as part of his theory of "genetic epistemology." And he used terms such as "sensory-motor," "prelogical," "logical," and "hyper-logical stages." Cairns notes that Baldwin said the child must "*accommodate* to the stimulating environment, as well as *assimilate* events and ideas to which he is exposed."

It is difficult to take this criticism seriously, however. To begin with, Piaget acknowledged Baldwin's influence. Second, Baldwin was a theorist, not someone who engaged in research, and his theory was both incomplete and untested. Piaget spent almost 60 years testing, refining, and adding extensively to the ideas that Baldwin published at the turn of the century. Furthermore, Piaget's fame rests primarily on his astute observations of children's behavior, not on his stage theory of cognitive development.

Observations versus Experiments

There is also the problem of Piaget's methodology. Piaget performed "observations and demonstrations," not rigorously controlled experiments. Scientists who have conducted actual experimental studies have often gotten results Piaget wouldn't have predicted.

For example, University of Pennsylvania psychologist Rochel Gelman tested Piaget's notion of "conservation of quantity" with three- and four-year-old children. She showed them two rows of toy mice. One row had three mice in it, the other had five mice. The row with five mice, of course, took up more space than the row with three mice. She told the children that the three-mice row was the "winner," and then asked the youngsters to "find the winner" in a slightly different situation. This time she again showed the children rows of three and five mice. But now the distance between the three mice was increased so that they took up just as much space as did the row with five mice. All the youngsters immediately identified the three mice as the "winner." As one child put it, "It's still three—they just spreaded out." Obviously these "pre-operational" four-year-olds could conserve quantity, although Piaget said this cognitive ability did not appear until age seven or eight, during the stage of concrete operations.

Are There "Stages" of Development?

Susanna Millar points out that Piaget's "stage theory" includes three assumptions that may not be true. The first assumption is that intellectual development absolutely must proceed in 1-2-3-4 sequence. The *speed* at which a child matures may be sped up or retarded, but the *sequence of stages* must always be the same. The second assumption is that there are no halfway points between two stages. Piaget's third assumption is that all mental development can be described in terms of the logical operations a child employs while thinking. After reviewing the literature, Susanna Millar concludes that there is little *experimental* evidence to support these three assumptions.

Piaget's Subjects

The children Piaget spent a lifetime observing were for the most part white, middle-class youngsters reared in normal European homes. His four-stage theory appears to hold to some extent for such children. There is little good evidence to prove whether it holds in other cultures, however.

Are There "General Structures of the Mind?"

Piaget assumed there were "general structures of the mind" that the child could apply to all situations. In David Feldman's 1980 book, *Beyond Universals in Cognitive Development*, Feldman disagrees. He believes the child builds up *specific* mental processes for handling *specific* types of situations. And the child may do much better in some situations than in others, Feldman says. For instance, a seven-year-old genius may play chess at an adult level, but still may not be able to see the world from other people's point of view. What developmental stage shall we say this child is at?

In a recent book, John Flavell summarizes the present situation thusly: "I think it is fair to conclude that developmental psychologists are currently becoming increasingly skeptical of the theoretical use of the construct of 'cognitive-developmental stage' (many, indeed, never thought much of it). . . . My own hunch is that the concept of stage will not, in fact, figure importantly in future scientific work on cognitive growth." Flavell goes on to say that this "does not imply that there is no unity or consistency in cognitive functioning across situations. But it does imply that there may be less unity, consistency, and developmental interdependence than theories like Piaget's would have us believe."

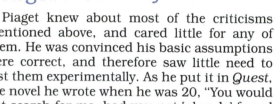

Piaget: A Summary

Piaget knew about most of the criticisms mentioned above, and cared little for any of them. He was convinced his basic assumptions were correct, and therefore saw little need to test them experimentally. As he put it in *Quest*, the novel he wrote when he was 20, "You would not search for me, had you not [already] found me." Thus, Piaget didn't seek the truth empirically, he merely tried to demonstrate to others the wisdom he had already found as a young man.

Right or wrong, Piaget has had a profound influence on educational practice. University of Pittsburgh psychologist Robert Glaser describes this influence in the February 1984 issue of *American Psychologist*. Prior to Piaget, Glaser says, teaching techniques in the US stemmed mostly from the work of E.L. Thorndike and other behaviorists. Many teachers believed that cognitive development was merely a matter of establishing thousands of specific stimulus-response connections. But Piaget insisted that *knowledge* was more important than reflexes, and that teachers should help children develop better schemata rather than merely "conditioning" the children by rewarding rote learning. Without Piaget, Glaser says, there might not be the focus on cognitive skills in psychology that there presently is. We will have more to say about this point in the next chapter, when we discuss *social learning theory*.

How shall we summarize Piaget's importance? Perhaps the old saying, "The king is dead. Long live the king!" says it best. We can underscore that point by looking briefly at one of the most fascinating aspects of cognitive development, that of *play*.

Play

The infant is born little more than an animal. If society does not condition the child, the youngster will remain non-verbal, non-social, and "retarded" (at least the child will seem retarded from our biased point of view). We typically call this conditioning process *education*, and believe that "study" is more important than "play." Recent studies suggest, however, that children may learn as much from seemingly random "play" as they do in the schoolroom.

Types of Play

There are several types of play, and children seem to pass through them in much the same "developmental stages" as Piaget described. Suppose we describe the types first, and then look at theoretical explanations of what causes playful behavior, and why it is so important.

Pre-Social Play

The first type of play that infants engage in is rightly called **pre-social**. That is, six-month-old infants play with dolls dangling from their cribs, with bells and rattles and balls and teddy bears, and they play with their own hands and feet. Only later do children learn the marvelous possibilities for play that other people offer.

Harry Harlow believed there were three types of pre-social play: (1) exploration play, (2) parallel play, and (3) instigative play. All three types of play first appear in what Piaget called the pre-operational stage.

Infants *explore* their environments by crawling around, inspecting, and playing with anything that drops into their narrow life spaces. A little later, children make the first step toward social contact with their peers by engaging in *parallel play*. Even before an infant is ready to interact with other children, the youngster may choose to play beside them—but not with them. A little later yet, the infant may engage in activities that are directly instigated by other people—follow-the-leader, mimicking, peek-a-boo. Yet in these behaviors the child does not really interact socially with the "leader." Harlow calls this *instigative play* and believes it is the final step toward true social interaction.

Social Play

As children pass from the pre-operational to the operational stage of intellectual development, their play becomes more complex and other people begin to become animate partners rather than mere objects to be manipulated. So-

cial play seems to be of three major types: (1) free play, (2) formal play, and (3) creative play.

Of the three, physical free play with other children is perhaps the easiest for the child, and hence often the first to appear. As Harlow points out, this sort of "rough-housing" is also the most disturbing to the middle-class parent who is often afraid the child will either hurt others or be hurt by them. Yet this type of activity may help children learn to tolerate minor frustrations and how to control their tempers.

As the child becomes more verbal, rough-and-tumble play drops off sharply, and formalized play begins. The mock fights of four-year-old boys develop rapidly into games of tag and "cops and robbers" in which the youngsters must follow *formal rules*. These rules, of course, constitute what Piaget would call "schemata."

In Piaget's terms, creative play is primarily a matter of *assimilation*—of "pretending" that things might happen that haven't yet happened. Piaget believes that creative play is the child's way of learning to manipulate symbols rather than objects. He calls it the "high point" of all types of play. He also calls it "a child's work."

But even if "play is work" in some sense, the question becomes *why* children engage in this activity at all. As we will see, there are many explanations.

Theories of Play

Most of us might assume that play is an activity that children fall into spontaneously, and that its major purpose might be that of making children more pleasant—or of keeping them occupied for a while. However, to some scientists, play has a deeper and more profound importance.

Both Plato and Aristotle urged parents to give their children toy tools to play with, to "shape their minds" for future activities as adults. This "educational" approach to play held until the 1800's, when philosophers suggested that play was the "unfolding" of innate talents and desires. These scholars told parents to leave their children alone, so the youngsters could freely determine what they wanted to do or become.

Research suggests that fathers help their children learn right-hemisphere skills such as emotional control and pattern perception when engaging the child in rough-and-tumble play.

According to many psychologists, "play is a child's business."

Piaget says an infant must first learn "how" before it learns "what." That is, the child builds up perceptual schemata of what the world is like by observing the consequences of its own movements.

Then, a little more than 100 years ago, British philosopher Herbert Spencer suggested what is now called the *surplus energy hypothesis* of play. Spencer thought each child was born with an energy-producing machine of some kind inside it. This energy had to be re-

leased regularly or the child would simply "explode." Spencer thought that all art came from play, as did Sigmund Freud. As we will see in the next chapter, Freud incorporated many of Spencer's ideas about psychic energy into his theory of psychoanalysis.

Although Spencer's ideas on the purpose of play were influenced by Charles Darwin's books on evolution, it was G.S. Hall who pushed evolutionary theory to what now seem absurd lengths. Hall believed that each child must **recapitulate** (relive) the behavioral history of the human race through play. Children couldn't become adults, Hall said, until they had worked their way through all the ancient behaviors built into their genetic blueprints over millions of years of evolution.

Question: Why would Hall have difficulty explaining children's fascination with airplanes and computers in terms of "reliving ancient behaviors?"

The Purpose of Play

What then is play, if it isn't blowing off steam or a way of stepping rapidly up the developmental ladder? The truth is, play serves so many different functions that no one theory can explain its many functions.

Play serves to stimulate the physical, emotional, social, and intellectual development of the child. And its hallmark is *pleasure*. Children who laugh while they are fighting seldom hurt one another. Adults who smile as they read textbooks seldom murder authors. Play is therefore a useful, necessary, vital part of life—but primarily because it *rewards* children (and adults) for learning the cognitive and behavioral skills they have to learn.

Cognitive Development: A Summary

As we trace your cognitive development from birth to early adulthood, several things become clear: First is the importance of your *genetic endowment*. You needed innate reflexes to survive your first days of independent life. Most of your subsequent mental and behavioral development stemmed from—and was based on—these inborn reflexes. However, your genes also gave you both the *motivation* and the *capability* to mature intellectually.

The second conclusion we can draw has to do with the importance of the environment you grew up in. Intellectual development results from the continual interplay between innate potential and environmental stimulation. Thus, while there are genetic limits to how far even the best of environments can take you, there are also environmental limits to how much of your genetic potential can be expressed.

The third conclusion has to do with the complex interplay between behaviors and cognitions. As Piaget pointed out, thoughts develop out of motor reflexes. You learn not merely by thinking and reasoning, but by doing—by testing your cognitive expectations against real-world feedback. But you can also test reality by using language. Which is to say, language lets you *behave without moving a muscle*. You can then anticipate the consequences of your actions before you act.

Finally, the data on cognitive development surely show the importance of your own personality in determining what and who you become. During infancy and early childhood, your cognitive development was determined primarily by the interaction between your genes and your environment. Then, as you matured, you gained the ability to alter both your environment and the way that you expressed your genetic potential. However, what you make of yourself—and what changes you attempt to make in the world around you—are strongly influenced by your own personality.

It is thus to the study of personality that we now must turn our attention.

Summary

1 **Cognitive development** refers to development in children of such **mental activities** as perception, memory, imagery, language, concept formation, problem solving, reasoning, and decision making.

2 Many **stage theorists** believe children would develop to a cognitive peak if merely left alone. Other psychologists hold that cognitive development is primarily **shaped** by environmental inputs.

3 **Language acquisition** refers to learning both **words** and the **rules** for using language correctly. Included in language acquisition are the learning of **phonemes**, **semantics**, **syntax**, and **pragmatics**.

4 Children **worldwide** between three and seven months of age **babble** by uttering repetitive **phonemes** such "da da da" but do not reproduce all the sounds in most languages. Parents **selectively reinforce** some babbled sounds, and urge infants to imitate those phonemes not produced during babbling.

5 At about one year of age, children produce **holophrastic** or one-word sentences, and produce two-word sentences about the 18th month. Many of these sentences are **telegraphic speech** that contains just the important words. Most children produce **complex sentences** by age two.

6 Some **linguists** believe humans have an innate tendency to process information in linguistic form, which they call the **deep structure of language**. Behaviorists, however, believe language production is entirely **learned**.

7 While acquiring language, the child also learns the **social rules** for proper use of speech.

8 Fathers appear to be more involved in **physical stimulation** of the child than in teaching it to talk.

9 Chimpanzees have been taught to "speak" 100 or more words and phrases, but whether their language has **grammar** and whether they can communicate in **symbols** is still a matter of debate.

10 **Jean Piaget** was one of the most respected figures in child psychology. For more than 50 years, he studied the child's **search for knowledge**, by which he meant the child's attempt to construct an **abstract mental representation** of the world.

11 According to Piaget, a child's motivation to develop comes from an innate drive to maintain **equilibrium**, a sort of **cognitive homeostasis**. When children's abstractions of the world don't match reality, they experience **dis-equilibrium**, which motivates them to change their inner representations of the world to bring them into accord with reality.

12 The two **mental functions** that guide development are **organization** and **adaptation**.

13 Organization is the tendency to create complicated mental structures out of simple ones. Adaptation is made up of two opposing processes, **assimilation** and **accommodation**.

14 Assimilation involves **changing inputs** to fit the child's present mental structures. Accommodation involves **changing mental structures** (or making new ones) to make them match present inputs.

15 According to Piaget, all children pass through four **developmental stages**, each of which grows out of (but is more complex than) the one preceding it.

16 During the **sensory-motor period** (birth to 2 years), the infant child learns to integrate its various sense impressions into complex **schemata**. In this stage, the child knows "how" and begins to learn "what," but doesn't know "why."

17 During the **pre-operational stage**, the child learns to speak and to deal with its world in **symbolic terms**. But its reasoning is **egocentric**, and it does not realize that objects can be **transformed** without being changed.

18 During the **stage of concrete operations**, the child learns to visualize a whole series of operations in its mind and to differentiate itself from the outer world. And it learns that the process of transformation is **reversible**.

19 During the **stage of abstract operations**, the young person gains the ability to think in purely **abstract terms**. That is, the child now knows "why" as well as "how" and "what."

20 Many psychologists have criticized Piaget's theory, but his fame rests primarily on his **observations of children's behavior**, not on his stage theory.

21 Harlow has listed several types of play:
a **Pre-social play**, which includes **exploration**, **parallel**, and **instigative play**.
b **Social play**, including **formal**, **creative**, and **free play**. Piaget considered creative play to be **pure assimilation**.

22 Play serves to stimulate the **physical**, **emotional**, **social**, and **intellectual development** of the child. Its hallmark is **pleasure**.

23 Early in life, **cognitive development** is determined primarily by the interaction of biological and social variables. Adults, however, gain the ability to **shape** both their own cognitions and the world around them.

(Continued from page 476.)

Horace Smythe speared a piece of meat with his fork, then held it up in front of his face. "Marvelous invention, the fork," he said. "Much more efficient than those peculiar chopsticks used by the Mongols, you know. Just goes to prove how superior the white race is, now doesn't it, my pet?"

"According to Godey's *Lady's Book*," Cynthia Smythe responded, "The fork was invented in the Middle East by one of those oriental races you and Dr. Down feel so superior to."

"What!" said the man with considerable surprise.

The woman nodded. "The

fork wasn't used in Europe until the Renaissance, and it didn't reach England until the 17th century. We've only had it in America since 1800 or so. But they've used it in the Middle East for hundreds of years."

"Humph," Horace Smythe replied. "I suppose you think that's evidence that Dr. Down's racial classification of the feeble-minded is incorrect."

"Well, that's one thing, of course."

Horace Smythe took some potatoes from the platter that the servant, Melissa, offered him. "And what else? What else?"

"As I understand it, Horace, Dr. Down believes that the human fetus must pass through several stages as it develops in the womb."

"Correct," the man replied in a pedagogical tone of voice. "The lowest is the Negroid, or black-skinned stage. Still primitives, most of the blacks." He glanced nervously at the servant woman. "Melissa excepted, of course. And then comes the brown-skinned, or Malay level, such as the Indians. Did you ever see an Indian who wasn't little more than a savage? Of course not."

"And then the fetus takes on Mongol or oriental features, correct?"

The man nodded eagerly. "Correct. The heathen Chinee, and all those other funny-looking people from the Middle and Far East."

"From which we get forks, Christianity, and a few other things we superior whites find so useful, eh, Horace?"

Mr. Smythe choked momentarily on a piece of food. "The oriental mind is devious, my pet, very devious. Imitative, true. But not really inventive. Mostly they just copy from us."

Cynthia Smythe smiled. "Like that exquisite Ming vase you bought from the Chinese laundryman, Horace? Nothing like it in the western world, you said. Whom did the Chinese copy that from, then?"

"A trivial point, my dear."

"And you still think that Tommy is a 'throwback' to the Mongolian stage of development?"

Horace Smythe nodded vigorously. "Makes complete sense to me. As a fetus, he stopped short of his final development into a Caucasian like us. He has the typical yellowish skin—you said so yourself. And he has Mongol eyes and dark hair, while his parents are blondes. So that proves that Dr. Down is correct in calling Tommy a Mongoloid, or Mongolian idiot."

"Balderdash," his wife said.

"Now, Cynthia, my pet. You shouldn't use such language. You are a mere woman, and thus you can't deal with facts as logically and as scientifically as Dr. Down and I can."

"Balderdash," his wife said again. "I can think of three very important facts that completely disprove your case."

"And what, pray tell, might those three facts be?" the man said in a very annoyed tone of voice.

"First, Tommy *does* look different from his parents, but he certainly *doesn't* resemble the Chinese laundryman."

Mr. Smythe snorted. "The exception that proves the rule."

"Second, why did the laundryman sell that exquisite vase to you?"

The man thought a mo-

ment. "He needed the money, of course."

"For what, Horace?"

Mr. Smythe squirmed in his chair. "Well, he had this feeble-minded child who needed medical attention. . ."

"A child who happens to look much like Tommy," the woman replied in a factual tone of voice. "What would Dr. Down call that child, Horace? A Mongol Mongolian idiot?"

"You're being entirely unreasonable, Cynthia."

The woman smiled. "And last, but surely not least, there's Melissa. Why did she come to work for us, Horace?"

"Money, of course. She is of an inferior race, and must work to support herself as best she can."

"And to support her niece, who is a feeble-minded young girl with many of the physical characteristics that Tommy and the laundryman's child have."

"So?" the man said coldly.

"So, how would you classify Melissa's niece? She can't be a 'throwback,' since you say that her race hasn't yet developed to the 'Mongol' level. What is she, then? A 'throw-forward' of some kind? And if she is, shouldn't she be brighter than Melissa?"

Horace Smythe sat quietly for a moment, poking at the food on his plate. "A 'throw-forward,' eh? Never thought of it that way."

Cynthia Smythe ate in silence while her husband pondered the matter.

After a while, the man sighed. "You know, my pet, I do believe that Dr. Down's ethnic scheme for classifying the feeble-minded isn't yet as perfect as it first seemed. Of course, he has described

Mongolian idiocy rather well, and given it a scientific label . . ."

"Horace, those children need loving care a great deal more than they need a fancy label."

"Well, my dear, you women always do look at the practical side of things. Which leaves it up to us men to look at the world from a more abstract, intellectual viewpoint, and to puzzle out the logic of the universe."

Cynthia Smythe nodded in amusement.

"And having given the matter my due consideration, I now perceive that the good doctor's logic *is* somewhat shoddy. 'Throwbacks,' indeed! Balderdash, that's what it is."

"If you say so, dear."

The man carefully dissected the meat on his plate. "Shocking that a man in his position would fail to see the facts, now isn't it?"

"I suspect you're right, dear."

Horace Smythe impaled a piece of meat with his fork, then put it in his mouth. He chewed the meat slowly, deliberately, then finally swallowed it. "You know, my pet, I wonder if I shouldn't write Dr. Down and share my insights with him . . ."

Recommended Reading

Ambron, S.R. & Salkind, N.J. (1984). *Child development*, (4th ed.). New York: Holt, Rinehart and Winston.

Matlin, M. (1983). *Cognition*. New York: Holt, Rinehart and Winston.

McCandless, B. & and Trotter, R.J. (1977). *Children: Behavior and development* (3rd ed.). New York: Holt, Rinehart and Winston.

Piaget, J. (1980). *Adaptation and intelligence: Organic selection and phenocopy*. Chicago: University of Chicago Press.

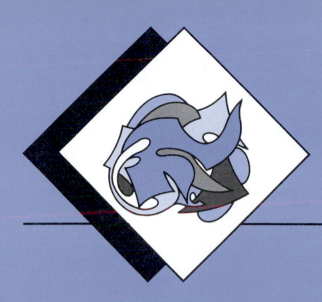

PART VI

Personality

Did You Know That...

- The study of personality involves identifying the distinctive patterns of thought, behavior, and experience that characterize your unique adjustment to life?
- Freud described your basic instincts as a "cauldron of seething excitement"?
- According to Freud, all children go through a "natural homosexual period"?
- Carl Jung believed people inherit "racial memories" he called archetypes?
- Alfred Adler believed you are motivated by a conscious desire to become superior to what you've been in the past?
- Erik Erikson states you must pass through eight developmental stages on your way to complete maturity?
- The old belief that you "lose 100,000 brain cells each day" is false?
- One theorist has suggested there are three types of older individuals—the "no-go" group, the "slow-go" group, and the "go-go" group?
- There is no *biological* reason why the majority of older people shouldn't be in the "go-go" group?
- We still don't have a personality theory that tells us all we want to know about the human condition?

19

Personality Theories: Psychoanalysis, Humanism, and Social Learning Theory

"The Span of Life"

The radio was playing a Golden Oldie, "As Time Goes By." Melanie Stein reached over and turned the radio off. "Where's Abe?" she asked.

"Late, as always," Fred Tanner said.

"I think his mother carried Abe for at least 10 months," Norma Gray said, laughing.

"And didn't toilet train him until he was five," Melanie added. "I swear, Abe is the sloppiest man I've ever met. A true anal expulsive personality, if I ever saw one."

"How can you *see* a personality?" Fred replied. "Sloppiness is a behavior, so you can see and measure sloppiness. But 'anal ex-

pulsiveness?' It doesn't exist, it's all in your mind."

"No," said Melanie, "It exists as a character trait in Abe's mind."

"I agree with Fred," Norma said. "Sloppiness is just your way of *explaining* Abe's unusual behavior. To make sense out of Abe's actions, you *attribute* the trait of sloppiness to his personality. But you do so in order to assimilate his actions to your own cognitive structures dealing with the development of the human personality."

Fred grinned. "And you maintain his sloppiness by verbally reinforcing him every time he's late."

"I don't 'verbally reinforce'

him, as you so pungently put it," Melanie replied. "I merely point out to him the underlying psychodynamic causes of his compulsive tardiness. Given insight into the problem, perhaps he'll change."

"The only way you'll change him is by rewarding him when he's on time, and ignoring him when he's late," Fred said.

"The 'shape' of things to come, eh?" Norma said, giggling just a bit.

Melanie shook her head in dismay. "Cut it out, you two. I can't take Skinner and Piaget this early in the morning."

"That's all right," Fred responded. "I can't take Freud except at dinner time—and then only with a grain or two of salt."

"Why, how perceptive of you," Melanie said in an overly affectionate tone of voice. "I'm delighted you find Freud such a rich intellectual feast."

"More of a famine, actually," Fred said. "Speaking of which, Norma, are there any more doughnuts? I'm starved."

As Norma got up to fetch more food, the door burst open. "Hi, gang!" Abraham Phelps cried loudly as he swept into the room. "I overslept again. Did you miss me?"

"I was just getting another round of doughnuts and coffee," Norma said. "Would you like some?"

"I do hope you have Jasmine tea as well as doughnuts," Abe said plaintively.

"Speaking of nuts . . ." Melanie said softly.

"Lipton's is the best I can do on a teaching assistant's budget," Norma replied, ignoring Melanie's comment. "Will that do?"

Abe sighed. "I suppose so." Then he brightened. "After all, it's the sharing that counts, not the substance being shared."

"Speaking of substance abuse . . ." Fred said softly.

"I heard that, Fred," Abe said. "You are suggesting that I overslept because I over-indulged last night. Not so. I was up late, true, but I was attending the monthly meeting of the Human Potential group. We locked consciousnesses and experienced new heights of awareness. And we didn't have anything stronger than Jasmine tea to drink."

"Speaking of tea groups," Norma said, returning from the kitchen with a tray,

"Here's your Lipton's." She gave Fred a couple of doughnuts and refilled Melanie's coffee cup. Then she sat down and opened a notebook. "Okay, gang, enough of this joshing around. We have serious work to do. We have all of 48 hours to prepare a joint lecture on personality theory for the 100 students enrolled in Dr. Damrosch's introductory psychology class."

"Our big chance as teaching assistants," Fred said.

"Yeah," Abe continued. "I like listening to Damrosch myself, of course. But he doesn't always cover the topics the students ought to be familiar with. Like humanistic psychology, for example. So this is our golden opportunity to get our own point of view across."

"*Points* of view, you mean," Melanie said.

"Yes, that is the problem, isn't it?" Norma said. "You, Melanie, are a Freudian."

"An ego psychologist, really," Melanie replied. "Freud focused more on the id, the libido, and the unconscious processes that shape the infant's personality. But his daughter, Anna, added to psychoanalytic theory by concentrating on the development of the ego and the conscious processes of the mind."

"You're out of your mind, just like Freud was," Fred said.

"If you would spend more time working with *people* and less time training *pigeons*, you might learn something useful about personality. But what can you discover about the human mind from studying bird brains?" Melanie said haughtily.

"Skinner learned more about human behavior from

working with animals than Freud did from all his patients," Fred replied.

"But birds don't have *personalities*, they have *pigeonalities*! So we shouldn't let you lecture at all," Melanie said in a triumphant tone of voice.

"Moving right along," Norma said, "We have Fred, here, who is a Skinnerian."

"A behavioral scientist, really," Fred interjected.

"Which can be abbreviated 'B.S.,'" Melanie said with a laugh.

"No, 'B.F.S.,' as in B.F. Skinner," Fred replied. "And we're scientific because we don't deal with unobservables, such as cognitive processes. We don't try to peer deep inside the cesspools of the mind, like you Freudians do."

"I've always said that behaviorism was only Skinnerdeep," Abe put in.

Fred got a little angry. "The fact that behavior modification *works* is the best evidence I know of that Skinner takes the right approach. You've got to agree with that."

Norma sighed. "I agree only partially. I tell my students that behaviorism predicts everything and explains nothing, while psychoanalytic theory explains everything and predicts nothing."

"But neither approach deals with the most important aspect of personality, the *will to good health*," Abe said in a healthy tone of voice. "Only the humanistic psychologists discuss the instinct to pull all of life's experiences together into a meaningful whole."

"Ah, yes," Fred replied. "You humanistic psychologists deal with consciousness and the itch to integrate, while the Freudians concentrate on unconscious repression and the urge to submerge."

"Enough already," Norma said. "Integrate is just what we've got to do today. We've got to pull all the different theories of personality together into one unified cognitive mass or Dr. Damrosch will repress our paychecks. Anybody got any ideas about how we might accomplish this miracle?"

"You're in charge, Norma," Abe said. "Any bright ideas?"

Norma considered the matter. "Well, we could point out that social learning theory—which happens to be my specialty—is a sort of combination of the best features of Piaget and Skinner . . ."

"No dice," Melanie said. "How you hope to explain epistemology and disequilibrium to undergraduates is beyond me. They want nitty-gritty stuff, like sex and aggressive instincts."

"No, they want *experience*," Abe said. "We could have them all hold hands and show them how the energy flows when you focus your attention on the transcendental levels of consciousness."

"Speaking of the transcen-

dental," Fred said. "Are there any more doughnuts?"

"How are doughnuts transcendental?" Norma asked.

Fred grinned. "Like most things mystical, doughnuts are soft, gooey, overly sweet, and very holely."

Norma groaned. "I will not reward your outrageous puns by getting you more doughnuts, Fred. But listen, all of you. We're getting nowhere. *Think*."

"That's the trouble with you cognitive types, Norma," Melanie said. "Your motto is, 'I think, therefore I am what I think I am.' But you neglect the emotions, and the unconscious determinants of thoughts and behaviors."

"Melanie is an expert on unconsciousness," Abe said. "She puts the students in her discussion section to sleep every time she lectures."

"Freud said that wit is aggression in disguise," Melanie replied. "In your case, he was half right."

"Hush!" Norma said. "We still haven't decided how to demonstrate the diversity of views on personality theory to the students."

Fred smiled. "We could let them listen to us hack away at each other. That ought to tell them something about

the state of the art."

"Yeah!" Abe said, enthusiastically. "We could stage a big debate among the four of us. And the students could vote for the winner!"

"They'd love it, that's for sure," Melanie put in. "They could displace all of their hostility toward Damrosch onto us."

Norma shook her head. "No, it wouldn't work. Oh, the students would probably enjoy seeing us hack away at each other. But we're supposed to add to their *knowledge*, not merely exercise their emotions."

"And asking them to vote for the 'best theory' would be like the kindergarten kids who didn't know the sex of a pet rabbit. So they took a vote. Skinner says such matters should be determined empirically, not by an appeal to the emotions," said Fred.

"But a debate surely would raise the level of their consciousnesses," Abe said defensively.

"Hold it!" Norma said loudly. "I've got the solution."

"What is it?" Melanie asked.

"Piaget to the rescue!" Norma replied.

(Continued on page 540.)

Personality Theory

Now that we know something about physical and emotional development in the early years, we are faced with a number of difficult problems. The first is the fact that psychological growth doesn't end at 12, or even at 30. You *continue to change*, develop, and mature in a great many ways throughout your span of life. And yet, some parts of your adult personality

are the same as they were when you were young. What aspects of your present-day functioning, then, are outgrowths of your early experiences, and which are not? This is the "continuity-discontinuity" issue we discussed in the last chapter, of course.

The second problem is this: If we are to study you scientifically, we must have some way of describing what we find. If you were completely unique, we could do little more than paint as

TABLE 19.1 Description of Personality Theorists

Theorist	Type	Emphasis	Viewpoint	Goal	Methods	Therapy
Freud	Traditional (Psychoanalytic)	Emotions, Biological Instincts, Unconscious Processes	(Biological) Intra-psychic	Explaining/ Helping	Case Histories	Psychoanalysis
Erikson	Traditional (Psychoanalytic)	Emotions, Biological Instincts, Unconscious Processes, (Conscious Processes)	(Biological) Intra-psychic Social	Explaining/ Helping	Case Histories	Psychoanalysis
Jung	Traditional (Jungian Psychoanalytic)	Emotions, (Biological Instincts), Unconscious Processes	(Biological) Intra-psychic Religious	Explaining/ Helping	Case Histories	Jungian Psychoanalysis
Adler	Traditional (Psychoanalytic/ Humanistic)	Emotions, (Biological Instincts), Conscious Processes	(Biological) Intra-psychic Social	Explaining/ Helping	Case Histories (Experiments)	Adlerian Psychoanalysis/ Humanistic
Trait Theorists	Traditional	Underlying Traits or Dispositions	(Biological) Intra-psychic	Describing/ Predicting	Tests	Psychoanalysis/ Humanistic
Rogers	Personologist (Humanistic)	Cognitions, Conscious Processes, Self-Actualization	Intra-psychic	Explaining/ Helping	Case Histories (Experiments)	Humanistic
Maslow	Personologist (Humanistic)	Cognitions, Conscious Processes, Self-Actualization	Intra-psychic	Explaining/ Helping	Case Histories	Humanistic
Murray	Personologist	Cognitions, Conscious Processes, Themas	Intra-psychic Social/Behavioral	Helping/ Predicting	Case Histories, Personality Tests	Humanistic
Skinner	Personologist (Behaviorist)	Learned Responses, (Denies Conscious & Unconscious Processes)	Social/Behavioral	Helping/ Predicting	Experiments	Behavior Modification
Social Learning Theorists (Bandura)	Personologists	Perceptions, Cognitions, Conscious Processes	Intra-psychic Social/Behavioral	Helping/ Predicting	Experiments	Cognitive Behavior Modification

accurate a picture of you as possible. But you are similar to other human beings in a great many ways. Therefore, we must find a basis for *comparing* your thoughts, feelings, and actions with those of the people around you.

The third difficulty we will encounter stems from the first two. Some people are more or less "normal." That is, they seem to adjust well to the world. These people are more or less content with their lives, they stay out of trouble, and make their own contribution to society. But other individuals are unhappy, seem not to adjust well to their circumstances, and appear to take more from the world than they give. What are we to do to help people *whose thought patterns are disordered*, whose emotions are unusual, and whose behaviors are often harmful to themselves and others?

The first two problems should sound familiar to you—they are two of the "four issues of developmental psychology" we listed earlier. In Chapters 17 and 18, we paid more attention to the other two issues—the mind-body problem, and the nature-nurture controversy. In the next two chapters, we will look more closely at "continuity versus discontinuity" and "individual differences versus human similarities."

The third problem—that of abnormal behavior, and what to do about it—we have touched on several times in this book. But, as we pointed out in Chapter 5, how you describe "psychological abnormalities," and what you try to do about them, depends to a great extent on your *theory of personality*. So, suppose we begin this chapter by defining **personality**. Then we can look at several theories that attempt to explain how you ended up with the personality that you presently have. We will save our discussion of abnormal psychology for Chapter 21, and our coverage of psychotherapy for Chapter 22.

What Is Personality?

Writing in the 1981 *Handbook of Behavior Therapy*, Nancy Cantor and John Kihlstrom state that "the field of personality may be defined as that subdiscipline of psychology which is concerned with the distinctive patterns of thought, behavior, and experience which characterize the individual's unique adjustment to his or her life situation." Your own pattern of personality, then, shows up in the way that you attempt to understand, respond to, and change the physical and social world in which you live.

Different theorists have, of course, emphasized different aspects of personality (see Table

Personality. From the Greek word *persona*, which means "mask." Those distinctive ways of thinking, feeling, and behaving that set you off from all other people. Your own unique way of adjusting to whatever situations you find yourself in.

Personology (purr-son-OLL-oh-gee). One of the two major approaches to the study of personality. Personology (a term coined by Henry Murray) takes a social/behavioral view, focuses on cognitive and perceptual processes, and emphasizes that personality development results from an interaction between the self and the environment.

19.1). However, there are two dominant approaches to the study of personality. Let's begin by discussing these two viewpoints.

Personality versus Personology

Writing in the November 1982 issue of *Contemporary Psychology*, University of Tulsa psychologist Robert Hogan notes that there are two main schools of thought in the study of personality.

The first school—which Hogan calls *traditional personality psychology*—"takes as its subject matter *human nature* and analyzes its forms of excellence and depravity." The "traditional" school stresses individual differences, practical problems, and psychological measurement.

The second school—which Hogan refers to as **personology**—takes as its subject matter certain *processes*, such as memory, perception, and information processing. The personology approach is "rooted in contemporary cognitive psychology . . . [and] stresses general laws, pure research, and an experimental methodology."

According to Hogan, *traditional* personality psychologists are primarily interested in unconscious processes, personality traits, and creativity. Generally speaking, they take an intra-psychic view of human nature—with a strong emphasis on emotions and motivation. *Personologists*, however, have a social/behavioral viewpoint. They typically focus on perceptual and cognitive processes. Personologists usually believe that behavior is the result of a continuing *interaction* between the conscious self and environmental inputs (see Table 19.1).

Freud (and the many people he influenced) and the trait psychologists described in the next chapter are examples of "traditional personality psychologists." Piaget, the behaviorists and social learning theorists, and (to some extent) the humanistic psychologists fall more within the "personologist" camp. Since you

Sigmund Freud

may be more familiar with the traditional approach, suppose we discuss *personology* for a moment, then turn to Freud as an example of the traditional way of viewing personality.

Personology

Nancy Cantor defines *personology* as the scientific study of what personality actually is, and how it grows and develops over an individual's life span. According to Nancy Cantor, personologists have four major goals:

1. To describe consistent patterns of individual differences.
2. To explain why a person thinks, feels, and behaves as she or he does.
3. To predict how a person will act in a new situation.
4. To help people change their **dysfunctional** thoughts, feelings, and behaviors.

As Cantor points out, some theorists place more weight on one or two of these goals than on others (see Table 19.1). And because traditional personality theorists and personologists have different goals, each group has developed its own methods of studying the human personality. The Freudians tend to look primarily at data gathered from *case histories*, trait psychologists utilize various *tests and observations*, while the social learning theorists often *perform experiments* to determine which environmental inputs affect thoughts and actions. But these differences are chiefly a matter of *relative emphasis* on goals and study methods. For the Freudians, humanistic psychologists,

and behaviorists do occasionally make use of psychological tests. And all personality theorists realize the importance of data gathered from scientific experiments.

Now that we have outlined some of the similarities and differences among the major personality theorists, let's look at each of them in more detail. We will start with the man who is surely the most famous theorist of all, Sigmund Freud.

Sigmund Freud

Freud was born in 1856 in what is now Czechoslovakia, but he lived for almost 80 years in Vienna. After taking his degree in medicine in 1881, Freud spent many years in the laboratory studying the human nervous system. Thus, Freud was *first and foremost* a biologist who came to the study of psychology in the middle of his life.

Freud was almost 40 when he married. Soon afterward, he left the laboratory and went into private practice. Much of his theory of psychoanalysis grew out of the observations he made of these patients.

Around 1885, Freud spent several months in Paris, studying hypnosis with Charcot. Freud's interest in personality theory seems to have begun about this time. As we noted in Chapter 16, he returned from Paris believing that hypnosis might be useful in curing some types of mental disorders. This view was strengthened by the success another Viennese psychiatrist, Josef Breuer, had achieved using hypnosis with a hysterical patient. Under hypnosis, Breuer had gotten this patient to relive some early, unhappy experiences. After the patient had "acted out" these childhood miseries, the hysterical symptoms seemed to disappear. (For more information on hysteria, see Chapters 16 and 21.)

Together with Breuer, Freud developed a technique called *catharsis*, which involves the re-enactment of emotional situations while under hypnosis. As we noted in Chapter 12, Freud assumed that some type of "psychic dynamo" inside the body produces "energy" that motivates thoughts and behaviors. Breuer and Freud believed traumatic experiences could *suppress this energy*. But like steam seeping out of the cracks of a boiler, some of this energy does escape—in the form of abnormal thoughts, emotions, and behaviors. Catharsis presumably helped because it *released* the dynamic forces that had been bottled up inside the patient. And once the "psychic pressure" had been reduced, the energy remaining would again be channeled into normal thoughts and actions.

As we stated in Chapter 16, Freud ultimately rejected hypnosis because it didn't work very well. Instead, he turned to *free association.* That is, he encouraged his patients to talk about all aspects of their past and present lives. "Talking through" their problems often brought repressed conflicts to light. Additionally, if Freud could get the patient to analyze a traumatic experience in unemotional terms, the patient often gained *insight* into what aspects of that trauma still bothered the patient. Freud called this technique *psychoanalysis.*

The Unconscious, Preconscious, and Conscious

Why did Freud's patients need his help? Like everyone else, these people had very strong physical needs, particularly a need for sexual expression. Their cathartic ("re-living") experiences suggested to Freud that sexual needs occurred even in newborn infants—if you interpret the word "sexual" in its broadest sense. But most of his patients had been punished for expressing their childhood sexual desires. This punishment appeared to drive their needs "underground," out of the patients' "streams of consciousness." Since the needs had not been satisfied, the energy associated with these needs was still present, lurking unconsciously "in the bottom of the patient's mind." Catharsis and psychoanalysis brought these hidden needs forward into consciousness. (For a discussion of *consciousness* as a "primitive term," see Chapter 5.)

But where were these lusty, unexpressed desires *hiding* in the mind? Charcot, in his at-

tempt to explain hypnosis, had suggested that there must be different *levels of consciousness.* Freud took Charcot's idea and made it very much his own. In 1913, Freud divided the human psyche into three levels or regions: The *conscious,* the *preconscious,* and the *unconscious* (see Fig. 19.1). (Freud did not use the term "subconscious" at all.)

The Conscious Mind

As we noted in Chapter 3, *consciousness* is a primitive term that cannot be defined precisely. Whatever you are aware of at any given instant is what you are "conscious of" at that instant. And in biological terms, conscious awareness seems to be a primary property of your left (dominant) hemisphere.

The Preconscious Mind

Long before Freud divided the psyche into three levels, German psychologists had likened consciousness to a cluttered stage in a darkened theater. A narrowly focused spotlight sweeps across the stage, illuminating now this, now that. As you sit in the theater, you see a continual flow of images flash into focus, then disappear into darkness. The narrow beam of the spotlight is your momentary consciousness. The rest of the stage is *potentially* visible to you—if and when the spotlight shines on it. But *at the moment* all you can perceive is what's within the tiny circle of light.

Following other German philosophers, Freud believed that your conscious mind includes *whatever you are aware of or paying attention*

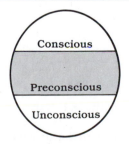

Fig. 19.1 Freud's "levels of consciousness."

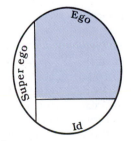

Fig. 19.2 Freud's "structures of the mind."

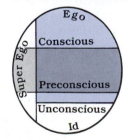

Fig. 19.3 "Levels of consciousness" occupied by the id, ego, and superego.

to at the moment. Your preconscious mind includes any sensory input or mental process that *you could become aware of*—if and when the spotlight of awareness shone on it.

Question: Which is larger, the conscious or the preconscious mind?

The Unconscious Mind

Freud's concept of the unconscious mind is exceptionally difficult to explain in simple terms. Briefly put, the unconscious contains all of those memories, experiences, images, feelings, and motives that you cannot voluntarily bring to consciousness or examine under the light of immediate attention. We can define it better by example.

In Chapter 9 we stated that you tend to *repress* unpleasant experiences. That is, you tend to put *blocks* on the spotlight so that it can't shine on some of the messier areas of your "mental stage" that you'd rather not look at. Repressed memories, then, are locked away in the "unconscious" portions of your mind.

As we noted in Chapter 12, you have innately determined reflexes and instincts that affect your behaviors and thoughts *whether you are conscious of them or not*. Your heart beats, your lungs breathe, and your adrenal glands secrete hormones, whether or not you're aware of what they're doing. Nor do you have *direct* consciousness of neural activity in the emotional or motivational centers of your brain. "Body language," then, and emotional "feelings" are typically a part of your unconscious mind.

As you discovered in Chapter 15, you tend to file items in long-term memory storage according to certain categories. You cannot recall many of your infantile experiences because you didn't file them in the same "memory categories" you use as an adult. These early memories are "unconscious" because you simply don't know how to retrieve them.

Then there are dreams and flashes of creative insight. You are, by definition, not conscious while you dream, and dreams are often very hard to bring to conscious awareness after they've occurred. Freud thought that the dream was an almost perfect example of an unconscious experience. As for insight, it often consists of perceiving a pattern of some kind. Where in your mind did this pattern form if not in your unconsciousness?

By now you may have perceived a pattern yourself. What Freud referred to as the unconscious portions of your mind seem to consist of

two things: processes that are mediated by the "lower" centers of your brain, and those that are mediated by your right (nonverbal) hemisphere.

We must raise an important issue about Freudian theory at this point. Freud died long before the split-brain research helped place most "unconscious processes" in the right hemisphere and lower centers of the brain. Indeed, Freud was vague about the relationship between "mind" and "brain." However, in 1895, he published a little-known work called the *Project*. In this book, Freud stated that he hoped all his concepts—such as "the unconscious" and "libido"—could eventually be tied to biological processes. In his later works, however, he often used these terms as *analogies*. That is, he used them as **theoretical constructs** (or explanations) rather than pretending they had any kind of concrete reality. Most experts on Freud still prefer to view concepts such as "id" and "ego" as theoretical explanations rather than as examples of actual structures in the brain.

Why did Freud make use of "fancy names" and "theoretical constructs"? Writing in the February 1982 issue of *Contemporary Psychology*, Rutgers psychiatrist Donald Spence offers an interesting speculation. In public, Spence says, Freud often liked to appear as a dominating "conquistador." In private life, however, he had a much softer side, which he liked to hide from most others. As Spence puts it, "Freud may have found it easier to refer to his tender feelings by giving them theoretical names (e.g., Oedipus complex, infantile sexuality) rather than labeling them directly, and we may wonder whether the importance of these other constructs stemmed in part from their function as indirect references to very private and deeply felt experiences."

Whatever the case, the "fancy names" that Freud used are now a deeply ingrained part of psychology. And anyone who wishes to understand Freud's personality theory must learn what he meant by the terms he used.

Libido

While Freud was mapping out the *regions* of the mind, he tried as well to determine the psychological processes that energized, focused, moved, and even blocked the spotlight of consciousness.

As we noted, Freud accepted the view that the body continually creates *psychic energy*, much as a dynamo continually produces electrical power. Freud called this psychic energy **libido** and believed that it is the motive force that "powers" *all of your thoughts, feelings, and behaviors.* A build-up of libidinal energy creates a painful drive state that forces you to become aware of some unsatisfied need. You then tend to focus on activities that will allow you to release the pent-up energy and hence reduce the drive. Therefore, *expending* libidinal energy is associated with sensory pleasure, while *repressing* libidinal energy almost always leads to painful tension and anxiety.

Question: How does Freud's view of human motivation compare with that of the drive theorists described in Chapter 10?

Id, Ego, and Superego

An infant is *conscious*, but it doesn't "know" enough to keep itself alive. How then does it survive its first years on earth?

The Id

According to Freud, you were born with a collection of basic instincts or biological drives that are the *source* of your libidinal energy. Freud called this set of instinctual drives the **id**, from the Latin word for "it." Your id is buried at the deepest level of your unconscious mind, far

removed from conscious reality. Freud described the id as a "cauldron of seething excitement" which has no inner structure or organization, which operates in illogical ways, and which seeks only the pleasures that come from discharging its pent-up energies.

Your id kept you alive when you were an infant because the id obeys the **pleasure principle**. That is, the id demands the *immediate* gratification of all its needs. Since most of these needs are related to bodily functions—such as hunger, elimination, aggression, and sensual stimulation—you survived because you were *biologically programmed* to release libidinal energy in life-sustaining ways.

Question: How does Freud's concept of the id compare to MacLean's concept of the reptilian brain (see Chapter 4)?

The Ego

Because the id is selfish and impulsive, your id helped you survive the first period of life. But as you grew, the "real world" began to make demands on you—and punished you if you didn't respond in socially appropriate ways.

As you were forced to delay gratification of some of your instinctual needs, Freud said, you gradually became aware there was a difference between your own desires and those of other people. And once you began to distinguish between yourself and the outer world, your **ego** or *conscious self* came into being.

Writing in the *Encyclopedia of Human Behavior*, R.M. Goldenson defines the ego this way: The ego is a group of mental functions or processes that enable you to perceive, reason,

"YOU MEAN YOUR BIG SMILE IS BOTTLED-UP AGGRESSION? MINE IS BOTTLED-UP HOSTILITY."

According to Freud, the ego emerges during toilet training in the anal stage, when the child's parents begin demanding that the child control its instinctual self-gratifying urges.

make judgments, store memories, and solve various problems. Your id was present at birth. Your ego developed slowly as you learned to master your impulses, delay immediate gratification of your needs, and get along with others.

Your ego is the part of your personality that is in communication with the external world. For the most part, then, your ego operates at a concious (or preconscious) level, but it includes some unconscious processes as well. Thus, like your id, your ego is subject to the demands of the pleasure principle. But as you mature, your conscious self is also influenced by what Freud called the **reality principle**—the practical demands of daily living. On occasion, however, your ego may be torn between the opposing forces of pleasure seeking and reality. It often resolves this conflict by trying to satisfy your instinctual desires (id) in socially approved ways.

The Superego

There is more to your personality, however, than id and ego, than pleasure principle and reality principle. For as you grow, the people around you demand that you adopt society's "rules and regulations." To do so, you must build up a *conscience* that keeps you from violating the rules, and an *ego-ideal* that you must strive to attain. Freud called this part of your personality structure the **superego** and regarded it as a part of your ego that splits off and begins to act on its own.

Freud stated that during the latency period, girls develop an intense love of their fathers (the Electra complex). They resolve this problem by identifying with their mothers.

According to Freud, your superego develops slowly (and unconsciously) during the first five years of your life, as you increasingly imitate the thoughts and actions of others—primarily those of your parents. But it develops rapidly as a defense against sexual desires during the "latency period," which we will describe in a moment. During adolescence and young adulthood, your superego matures even more, as you come into contact with adults (other than your parents) whom you admire and whose values you take on in part or in whole. For the most part, this socialization process occurs at an *unconscious* level, as your superego gains the power to criticize and supervise both your id and your ego. Your superego is, therefore, the "unconscious voice" that helps you discriminate social rights from wrongs without your being aware of why you do so.

Question: From Freud's point of view, why might some people be unable to give a logical reason for their hostility toward long-haired men or assertive women?

Psychosexual Development

Freud's notions about personality development came from many sources—from his knowledge of medicine, from his work with Charcot and Breuer, and from Darwin's theory of evolution. But mostly his theory sprang from his observations of his own patients. Freud was fascinated by the fact that most of his clients seemed to have gone through very similar developmental *crises* as children. Eventually he decided that you pass through various *psychosexual stages of development* that correspond to the maturational stage of your body at various times in your life. Each stage is associated with a unique crisis of some kind.

Oral Stage

The first crisis obviously was that of *birth*, when you were thrust out into the world and became dependent on others to meet your needs. True, you had innate reflexes that helped you survive by creating *libidinal energy* that had to be discharged. But the *manner* in which you release this energy changes as your body matures. When you were newborn, the brain centers that control your mouth movements were physically the most developed, so you released libidinal energy most easily through such oral activities as sucking and swallowing. Freud called this period—which lasts from

birth to about one year of age—the *oral stage* of development.

Freud believed that the oral stage was marked by a strong need for "nurturance." He noticed that many of his patients still expressed nurturance needs in disguised form. That is, the patients showed oral behavior patterns such as talking too much, overeating, excessive smoking, and a strong dependence on "mother figures." He presumed this "residue of their infantile experiences" had remained locked away in their unconscious minds because of traumatic experiences they had while in the oral stage. Freud decided that these patients had problems because, when they were stressed, they *regressed* to the oral stage. Thus, as adults, they tried to release libidinal energy through *adult oral activities*. Therapy for these patients obviously would involve some form of *catharsis* to allow the patients to discharge the libidinal energy that had been repressed while they were still in the oral stage. Treatment would also involve giving the patients *insight* into what their problems really were, and where their difficulties came from.

Anal Stage

The first developmental crisis you went through was that of birth. The second crisis came when you were just old enough to gain voluntary control over your bladder and bowels. Now, you could discharge libidinal energy by withholding or releasing urine and feces. At this time, however, your parents began making demands on you. These demands conflicted with your instinctual need to obtain immediate libidinal gratification.

Freud said this second crisis in your life reached a peak during toilet training, when your parents began insisting that you learn to *delay gratification*. He assumed you resolved this crisis by creating an *ego* or conscious self that could gain voluntary control over the release of libidinal energy through anal activities.

Some of Freud's patients were excessively neat, obstinate, and miserly. These three traits make up what Freud called the *anal character*, and he saw all three as attempts to punish the mother for the trauma of toilet training. The mother demanded that the child "be clean," so the patient became *unreasonably* tidy. The mother sat the child on a potty and demanded that the child "produce." The child rebelled by *withholding* its feces. As an adult, the patient still rebels by obstinately refusing to part with a single penny. Again, catharsis—and giving the patient insight into the roots of the problem—seemed to Freud to be the best therapy.

Phallic Stage

At age three or so, your sex organs began to mature, and so did the centers in your brain associated with sexual activity. Thus, you acquired a new avenue for discharging your instinctual energies. During this *phallic period*, boys build up a warm and loving relationship with their mothers, which Freud called the **Oedipus complex**. At the same age, girls experience an intense emotional attachment for their fathers. (Although Freud did not use the term, many psychoanalysts refer to this as the **Electra complex**.) Freud stated that, during the phallic stage, boys experience incestual desires to possess their mothers and compete with (or even kill) their fathers, while girls come to desire their fathers and fear or hate their mothers.

Freud believed that the phallic stage is marked by frequent masturbation. During the fantasies that accompany this self-stimulation, desires to "possess" the opposite-sex parent and destroy the same-sex parent break through to consciousness. These fantasies make the child fearful, for several reasons. First, they violate the *incest taboo* found in all societies. Second, the child becomes afraid the same-sex parent will discover what the child is thinking and harm the child.

Freud was probably much better at describing the psychosexual development of the male than of the female. For example, he tended to use masculine terms in describing both the "phallic" stage and the "Oedipus" complex. And he saw the crisis during this stage as being that of *castration anxiety*, a term that obviously fits males better than females. What Freud apparently meant, however, was this—the child fears that the same-sex parent will severely punish or even *mutilate* the child for desiring the opposite-sex parent. The child temporarily resolves these fears and anxieties by *repressing* all sexual desires and entering into the latency period. As we will see, however, these desires surface later in the child's development and, according to Freud, profoundly shape the child's personality.

In 1930, Freud wrote that the Oedipus complex "represents the essential part of the content of the neuroses. It is the culminating point of infantile sexuality which, through its aftereffects, decisively influences the sexuality of the adult." Men who fail to resolve their yearnings for the mother may delay marriage, or become attached to an older woman as a "mother substitute." Women who postpone marriage may well suffer from a "father fixation." Freudian therapy usually consists of giving the patient sufficient insight so that he or she can find ways to discharge the libidinal energy that was guiltily repressed during the phallic stage.

Latency Period

According to Freud, you entered the latency period at about age five or six, when you began *repressing* your infantile sexuality in order to deal with your "castration anxieties." (Repressing your sexual desires also gave you "rest time" to prepare for the stresses you would experience at adolescence.) During the latency period, you started to move out of the home more frequently, and your friendships with your peers took on greater importance in your emotional and intellectual development. Freud believed this was a *natural homosexual period*, during which boys found "heroes" among older male friends and teachers, and girls developed "crushes" on other girls and older women.

Genital Stage

The latency period ends at the onset of puberty. The Oedipus and Electra complexes come to the fore again briefly, but are normally resolved during adolescence. Boys overcome their hatred for (and fears of) their fathers by taking on the fathers' goals and standards. Thus, the young men "possess" their mothers symbolically by acting like their fathers. Girls find gratification and fulfillment in the feminine role, Freud said, as a result both of their mother's encouragement and of their father's admiration.

During this genital stage, Freud's patients consciously began to hunt for an idealized sort of "lifestyle" in which their main means of discharging libido came through heterosexual activities. Had all gone well during their psychosexual development, the patients would have become psychologically healthy adults. But all did not go well with many of them. Rather, the problems they faced during their early years were not resolved. These developmental difficulties kept surfacing during their adult years, causing the patients mental and sometimes physical pain. It was this fact that led Freud to state that *most adult personality traits* are determined during the early years of life. To Freud, then, your personalty ceased to develop (for the most part) after adolescence.

Defense Mechanisms

Freud's theory of psychosexual development is really the story of how the ego learns to resolve the conflicting demands made by the id, the superego, and the reality of the external environment. The ego has several *defense mechanisms* at its disposal to protect itself from being *traumatized* by the stress arising from these conflicts. These defense mechanisms allow the ego to deal with trauma *unconsciously*. If the ego did not make use of these defenses, it would have to use up psychic energy by facing the conflicts *consciously*. The defense mechanisms, Freud said, allow the ego to spend energy on growth rather than resolving conflicts.

The ego is not always aware of what the needs of the id and superego are, because many of these needs are unconscious. The occurrence of **signal anxiety** warns the ego that libidinal tensions have become so strong that it must either handle them or be disabled by stress.

Almost all of the defense mechanisms available to the ego have four characteristics in common:

1. They are ways of trying to reduce stress and anxiety.
2. They involve the denying or distortion of reality.
3. They operate at an unconscious level.
4. They operate mechanically and involuntarily (which is why Freud called them *mechanisms*).

Repression

One of the most important—and most frequently employed—of the defense mechanisms is *repression*. By repression, Freud meant the process by which the ego blocks off threatening

Oedipus complex (ED-ih-pus). A "complex" is a part of the mind that breaks free and begins to function on its own. Freud took many of his analogies from Greek mythology. Oedipus was a young man who inadvertently killed his father and married his mother. Freud believed that, during the phallic (FAL-ick) stage, all young boys develop an intense incestuous desire for their mothers and a strong hatred for their fathers.

Electra complex (ee-LECK-trah). Electra was a Greek woman whose mother killed her father. Electra then talked her brother into murdering their mother. Freud believed that all young girls (during the phallic stage) develop an intense incestuous desire for their fathers and a strong hatred for their mothers.

Signal anxiety. The internal or intra-psychic feeling that something bad is about to happen—"butterflies in the stomach." A warning to the ego that it is in danger of being overwhelmed by *traumatic anxiety* or stress if it does not find some way of releasing pent-up libidinal energy.

thoughts or desires and thus keeps them from sweeping into the spotlight of consciousness. Most of these experiences have undischarged libidinal energy attached to them in some way. In repressing these experiences, the ego has to use up some of its own energy sources. And the more painful the memory, or the stronger the unacceptable urge, the more energy the ego must expend in order to keep the material repressed. Eventually the ego may run out of steam, and bits and pieces of the repressed material may leak through to consciousness as slips of the tongue, or as symbols in dreams.

Regression

When some of Freud's patients experienced great stress, they fell back into childish behavior patterns. Some of them responded to stress by overeating or by drinking too much. Freud saw this as a *regression* to an earlier (oral) mode of pleasure. Or when a young male patient encountered heterosexual difficulties, he sometimes would resort to such immature forms of gratification as masturbation or homosexuality. This regression allowed the man to discharge libidinal energy in a "safe" way. But it also prevented him from trying to solve his present interpersonal problems.

Identification

As we noted earlier, people resolve their Oedipus or Electra crises by taking on the characteristics of their same-sex parent. Freud saw this process of *identification* as the ego's way of defending against incestual feelings. The young girl identifies with her mother out of fear of her mother's wrath—and thereby helps builds up the *unconscious* portion of her superego, the "conscience." In adolescence, the girl identifies with other women and thus strengthens the *conscious* portion of her superego, the "ego-ideal." Freud thus saw the superego itself as a kind of "super" defense mechanism that helped reduce anxiety by allowing the person to release libidinal energy in socially approved ways.

Denial

Many of Freud's patients seemed to be "deliberately" unconscious of certain painful facts. Freud decided that they were practicing *denial*, a defense mechanism by which the ego shuts itself off from certain realities.

Reaction Formation

A step beyond denial is *reaction formation*, in which the ego changes unacceptable love into acceptable hate (or vice versa). If a mother hates her child—a feeling she must deny conscious awareness of—the mother may smother the child with affection.

Projection

Another way a mother may deny her hatred for the child is through *projection*. That is, the mother's ego may pretend that the child actually hates *her*. The mother thus "projects" her unacceptable emotions onto the child.

Rationalization

Freud found that many of his patients offered him elaborate justifications for what were obviously illogical or immature actions. When he pointed out what they were doing, these patients usually would still refuse to confront reality. Rather, they would give him yet another *rationalization* or questionable excuse for acting as they did. This self-justification seemed to allow the patients to reduce any anxiety they had, and yet go right on behaving as they had.

Displacement

At birth, the objects of all our instincts are specified by our genetic inheritance. You don't have to teach an infant that food satisfies its hunger, because the child's body already knows this. But as the infant grows up, the *objects* of the child's instincts can change through learning and experience. That is, the child's ego gains the ability to *displace* the flow of of libidinal energy from one object to another. But the ego may use this ability inappropriately, as a defense mechanism. If a boy gets angry at his mother, he dare not hit her because he will be punished. Therefore, he displaces his anger toward a safe object—such as a doll—that cannot retaliate if the boy strikes it.

Sublimination

Over the years Freud and his followers identified a great many defense mechanisms, of which we have space to mention only the best known. The last one we will discuss is *sublimination*, which is at once a form of displacement and the most mature of the defense mechanisms. Freud thought that the energy an artist devoted to painting—or a scientist to the laboratory, or a politician to governing—was really energy that had been channeled away from sex or aggression or eating. Although this displacement was socially acceptable and sometimes highly creative, it seldom seemed to satisfy all the id's needs.

As we noted in Chapter 12, the defense mechanisms are really indirect or "defensive" ways of coping with stress and anxiety. By encouraging his patients to bring their unconscious problems to the fore—and thus deal with them at a conscious level—Freud was attempting to get his patients to use a more direct method of coping with their developmental difficulties.

Freud's Influence

Writing in the March 1982 issue of *American Psychologist*, Gary Leak and Steven Christoper give this evaluation of Sigmund Freud: "There can be little doubt that Freudian psychoanalysis is the 'first force' in 20th-century psychology. Psychoanalysis as a personality theory is the most comprehensive one available, detailing the structure, dynamics, and development of personality to a degree unsurpassed by its competitors." One reason for this influence is that Freud paid attention to the *unconscious* aspects of human behavior. Prior to Freud's time psychologists either studied overt behavior patterns or used introspection to study *conscious* activities. But neither introspection nor the study of conditioned reflexes yielded the insights into personality development that Freud gave the world.

Freud was one of the first "drive theorists." He believed that arousal was painful and that pleasure came primarily from the satisfaction of biological drives. Like most other early drive theorists, Freud grew up in a repressive and moralistic culture. Little wonder he saw the effects of punishment more clearly than those of using rewards. By making parents conscious of how they affected their childrens' development, however, he helped *change* the culture itself into a less punitive one.

But no theory is perfect. For example, Freud's position was altered considerably by his own daughter, Anna Freud. She placed much more emphasis on the ego than did her father, who saw behavior as determined more by the id and unconscious processes. In Volume 8 of her writings—published in 1981—Anna Freud also admits that her father's *theory* is much more completely developed than is psychoanalytic *treatment*. As Anna Freud puts it, "analytic understanding reaches further than analytic therapy."

Any theory as potent as Freud's is bound to have its critics. So suppose we look at two recent evaluations of Freud's position before we discuss other personality theorists.

Freud: Two Evaluations

In his 1981 book *Fact and Fantasy In Freudian Theory*, British psychologist Paul Kline discusses the extent to which modern scientific evidence supports Freud's position. Overall, Kline says, the results are fairly positive. For example, according to Kline, recent research by Raymond Cattell suggests that Freud's division of the personality into ego, superego, and id may be correct. It also seems true that adult patients do show combinations of traits that match Freud's "oral" and "anal" character types. However, Kline finds little or no support for the belief that these character types are the result of traumas that occurred during the oral and anal stages of development.

As for the Oedipus complex, Kline notes that "boys and girls do have sexual feelings toward the opposite sex parent of which they are largely unaware." However, the data do "not establish the Oedipus complex as the central conflict of mental life or show it to be the kernel of neurosis." Evidence for *castration anxiety* (in males) has been found in many different cultures, though.

Kline states that Freud's notion that repression is one of the "most important . . . defense mechanisms" seems to be supported by ample research data. Dreams do contain sexual symbols, Kline says, but Freud's belief that dreaming was often a type of "wish fulfillment" appears not to be correct in most cases.

And according to Kline, "psychoanalytic therapy has not yet been adequately evaluated and its efficacy remains in doubt." (We will have more to say about this point in Chapter 22.)

In their 1977 book *The Scientific Credibility of Freud's Theories and Therapy*," Seymour Fisher and Roger Greenberg draw similar conclusions. However, they do note that recent research has not supported Freud's views on homosexuality. And work by Wolpe and other behavioral psychologists has surely cast doubt on Freud's approach to treating many phobias and obsessions (see Chapters 13 and 22). After reviewing more than 1,900 scientific articles, Fisher and Greenberg conclude that much of Freudian theory is "scientifically alive and well."

In summary, then, Freud is still the dominant figure in traditional personality theory. When he was alive, people flocked to study with him, and his disciples restructured the fields of psychiatry and personality theory. However, not all of Freud's followers agreed with his emphasis on unconscious biological instincts, on infant sexuality, and on the unchangeable influence of a child's early upbringing. Among the most important of those theorists strongly influenced by Freud were Jung, Adler, and Erikson. Let's now look at each of these men in turn.

Carl Jung

Born in Switzerland in 1875, Carl Gustav Jung came from a family of theologians and medical doctors. As a medical student at the University of Zurich, he dabbled in biology, philosophy, archeology, mythology, and mysticism. Jung discovered Freud in 1907 and became something of a disciple until 1912, when Jung developed his own psychoanalytic theory.

Jung could not accept Freud's notion that the goal of "growing up" was to bring the infantile sexual instincts under control. Rather, Jung said, we are *religious* animals whose unconscious roots go back to the very beginnings of the human race. To Jung, the purpose of our existence is the integration of our conscious perceptions of the outside world with our unconscious, mystical experiences.

Jung believed in the ego, but he said it is made up of your feelings of identity and continuity. To Jung, therefore, the ego is the part of your mind that knows you are the same person today you were yesterday. But Jung didn't view the ego as striving to mediate between the childish id and the stern superego. Rather, it is a slowly-developing *structure* that pulls together

Carl Jung

Alfred Adler

Erik Erikson

all types of conscious and unconscious activity to form a new "whole." Jung called this integrative process **individuation**, which in many ways resembles what Piaget describes as the "building up of the self-schema." Jung, however, placed a great deal more emphasis on the ego's need to integrate unconscious with conscious processes than Piaget did.

To Freud, the unconscious was primarily the source of our psychic energies. But to Jung, there was not one unconscious but two—the *personal unconscious* and the *collective unconscious*.

The Personal Unconscious

By personal unconscious, Jung meant those half-forgotten ideas, wishes, and past experiences that are now so weak they are difficult to bring into consciousness. According to Jung, some of these thoughts and memories may be so closely related that they grow together into a *complex* or schema all of their own. This complex of associated experiences might then split off from the person's psyche. This split-off complex could then function independently, with a psychological life of its own. The purpose of psychotherapy, from a Jungian point of view, is often that of identifying these complexes and bringing them back into conscious control.

The Collective Unconscious

To Jung, the collective unconscious houses all of the "racial memories" that each person is born with. In his study of anthropology, Jung noticed that some myths—such as a "great flood," or the creation of the world—seem to appear in *all cultures*. Jung called these myths **archetypes**. He said that, through evolutionary processes, the *mental images* associated with these archetypes had become engraved on our genes. Thus, Jung said, each human being is

born with some unconscious "mental fragments" of the past history of the human race.

The most important archetype of all is that of the *self-concept*, for it encourages you to integrate all of your conscious and unconscious psychological processes into one meaningful whole.

Extroversion and Introversion

Jung's most widely accepted ideas have to do with *extroversion* and *introversion*. Jung said we are born with two innate *attitudes*, one of which leads us to look inward, the other of which leads us to look outward.

Some people seem to be born *introverts*—that is, they spend most of their time looking toward their inner or personal world. Other individuals focus more on the outside environment. Outgoing, highly social individuals are examples of what Jung meant by *extroverts*. Jung believed you are born with both tendencies, but that one usually comes to predominate. You are usually conscious of which attitude is dominant but, according to Jung, you may not realize that the other attitude often expresses itself unconsciously through your dreams and fantasies.

Jung versus Freud

Freud emphasized the role of biology in personality development. Jung preferred to think humans could rise above their animal natures. Freud believed that happiness often came from escaping pain or reducing anxiety, and he tended to attract patients who were highly anxious or pain-ridden. Many of Jung's clients were artists, mystics, or wealthy individuals who felt the need for spiritual guidance "outside the church." Freud focused on the early, developmental years, which he saw as determining the entire structure of an individual's personality. Jung worked to a great degree with older patients, and never did offer a complete account of how the personality is formed.

Perhaps the most telling difference of all between the two men, though, lay in their use of language. Freud was a superb writer who was a serious contender for the Nobel Prize in literature. Jung's books and articles were filled with obscure images and symbols. His greatest influence was perhaps not on psychology, but on art and mysticism. We will have more to say about this point in a moment.

Alfred Adler

Alfred Adler was born and educated in Vienna. He joined Freud's group a few years after taking his medical degree. Adler's first work was on the living conditions of Austrian tailors, a study that helped confirm his early bias toward the importance of environmental factors in determining personality. But fascinated as Adler was by Freud's ideas, he was the first to break away from "the master" and form his own group, the Society for Individual Psychology. Adler, then, was neither a Freudian nor a psychoanalyst.

Adler disputed Freud's notion that human behavior is dominated by the unconscious workings of the sexual instincts. Instead, said Adler, people govern themselves by a conscious need to express and fulfill themselves as unique individuals. Rejecting both Freud's theory of sexual drives, and Jung's emphasis on intrapsychic mysticism, Adler emphasized the importance of the social environment. He thought that people could shape their own destinies, and that they could build a superior society by satisfying their basic need to transcend their personal problems.

The Creative Power

To Adler, life is a conscious struggle to move from what he called a "felt minus" to a "felt plus." By this, Adler meant you have a innate urge to rise above your own inferiorities and to become superior to what you were in the past. It is not that you want to become superior to others. Instead, you want to perfect yourself.

Freud emphasized the sexual side of human nature. Adler denied the importance of sexual instincts and substituted "self-improvement" in their place. Freud and Jung emphasized the unconscious, unknowable inner influences on behavior. Adler believed that most of us are quite aware of our motives. We see our own *in-*

Individuation (in-dih-vid-you-A-shun). The process, according to Jung, by which the ego slowly builds up a self-concept or self-schema by pulling together all types of conscious and unconscious activity to form a unified whole.

Archetypes (ARK-ee-types). From the Greek words meaning "the original model, form, or pattern from which something is made or from which something develops." The archetypes that Jung referred to are the original models of myths, legends, and stories—instinctual thought patterns passed on genetically from generation to generation.

feriorities, and we strive to overcome them. We have an instinct for *self-realization*, for completion and perfection, which Adler thought was the driving force of life itself. Adler called this force the *creative power* and thought it was the "first cause" of all behavior.

The Inferiority Complex

As children, we learn very early that adults can do things that we cannot. This knowledge creates in all of us an *inferiority complex* that adds to our motivation to succeed. It also creates a drive for *compensation*, the urge to overcome our failures in one part of life by excelling in another. The small, weak boy may try to succeed in his school studies or become a great musician in order to *compensate* for his physical weakness.

Style of Life

Adler was an optimist. He believed that you have buried in your genes a basic need to cooperate with others and to work toward building a better society. But you need guidance from the adults around you in order to express this need. For it is only through training and experience that you develop your *style of life*—your own unique way of expressing yourself.

Adler believed that the "style of life" is the self-consistent, goal-oriented core of personality. In a sense, therefore, Adler's "style of life" is similar to Freud's concept of the ego. At first, Adler thought this style was fixed early in life. Later, he decided that you continue to mature even as an adult. Thus, Adler was one of the first theorists to emphasize *life-span development*.

Adler's emphasis on the importance of *social factors* in determining personality was, for a time, unique in psychoanalytic circles and helped give rise to what we now call "social psychology." And by assuring people that they were basically humane, open-minded, and in control of their own destinies, Adler encouraged the development of "humanistic psychology."

Indeed, as humanist Abraham Maslow stated shortly before his death, "Alfred Adler becomes more and more correct year by year. As the facts come in, they give stronger and stronger support to his image of man."

Freud versus Adler and Jung

Before his death in 1980, Walter Kaufmann was a professor of philosophy at Princeton. In his book *Discovering the Mind, Vol. 3: Freud Versus Adler and Jung*, Kaufmann compares the contributions of these three men. And, surely to the dismay of Jungians and Adlerians, Kaufmann comes down squarely on the side of Freud. "Nobody has contributed more to the discovery of the mind than Freud, but we must go beyond him. Adler and Jung tried to go beyond Freud while he was still living . . . but slowly and reluctantly, I have arrived at the conclusion that they obstructed rather than advanced our understanding of ourselves and others. Adler and Jung were singularly lacking in self-understanding, and their images of Freud were caricatures."

Why was this the case? Perhaps *language* is the key issue here. Writing in the February 1982 issue of *Contemporary Psychology*, Cal Tech psychoanalyst Louis Breger says, "Freud is a master of language and style; he writes clearly, considers alternatives and objections . . . is intellectually honest, and has a sense of humor. . . . [However], both Adler and Jung wrote badly, and they read even worse in the original German." Breger continues by saying that Freud can be read again and again, but "rereading Adler and Jung produces a different effect; there is less there than initially meets the eye. . . . Adler and Jung strike one . . . as forerunners of our contemporary psychological gurus."

Breger concludes that "Adler and Jung, each in their own way, are muddled writers because their theories are muddled; they could never be clear because they had a stake in not understanding themselves."

Kaufmann and Breger, of course, are fairly devout Freudians. So perhaps it is only natural that they should support "the Master" and criticize Freud's critics. What Kaufmann and Breger *fail to note* is that both Jung and Adler have many proponents today, and that both Jung and Adler made signal contributions to the understanding of the human psyche.

In a sense, however, Kaufmann and Breger are merely saying the sorts of things that Freud himself said of his ex-disciples. Freud called Adler "paranoid," "unintelligible," and "loathsome." And Freud referred to Jung as being "mentally deranged," "brutal," and "sanctimonious." Jung and Adler, of course, had equally terrible comments to make about Freud.

The reason for mentioning this controversy is not to open old wounds or to create new ones. Rather, it is to make it clear that science is a *very human occupation*. Personality theorists, like everyone else, have passions and prejudices as well as insights and inspirations. And people who hold opposing theories do not just debate their differences at polite academic tea parties. Rather, they often "slug it out" in public shouting matches that often resemble championship boxing matches. And to the winner go the spoils. For, as psychologist David Bakan noted in 1966, the *acceptability* of a scientific theory is determined only in part by the theory itself. Social factors—such as how loudly people argue for or against the theory, and the various "needs" of the listening public—are also influential.

Perhaps the most important point of all in this controversy is the bald fact that it *is* a controversy. Psychoanalytic theory has not "stood still." It is continually being altered and updated. Arguments about the "correctness" of Freud's position are thus of value, because they constantly force us to re-evaluate what we know (and don't know) about personality theory. It should be clear by now that we are still learning from Freud, Jung, and Adler.

These three important personality theorists are all dead now. The greatest living contributor to psychoanalytic theory is surely Erik Erikson. Suppose we continue our discussion by looking at how he has added to the Freudian position.

Erik H. Erikson

Freud was trained in the biological sciences. He emphasized the *psychosexual* side of your personality development, which he saw as being primarily under the control of your genes. Therefore, once you had resolved the heterosexual crisis that occurs during adolescence, you had reached the peak of your personal growth—at least as far as Freud was concerned.

However, other psychoanalysts soon came to believe there was much more to personality development than the biologically determined psychosexual stages. These theorists saw humans as being *social* as well as *biological* organisms. And following Adler's lead, they believed that development continued *throughout the entire span of life*.

Chief among these theorists was Erik H. Erikson, whose *psychosocial theory of development* has had a strong influence on traditional personality theory. Elizabeth Hall interviewed Erik Erikson in the June 1983 issue of *Psychology Today*. In her article, Hall says, "Erik Homburger Erikson is the only thinker to have put forth a coherent theory of personality development that covers the entire life span. Trained in Vienna as an orthodox psychoanalyst, he shifted his emphasis from the disturbed individual to the healthy personality, and enlarged his focus from the influence of the family to the influence of society." And because of this change in emphasis, Hall notes, Erikson's influence "extends far beyond the boundaries of psychoanalysis."

Erikson accepted most of Freud's notions on the importance of instinctual drives in young children. But Erikson insisted that it is the *conflict* between instincts and cultural demands that shapes the child's personality. Instincts are presumably pretty much the same from one child to another, but cultures differ remarkably. And cultures grow and develop, just as do human beings.

Freud and Jung emphasized the importance of past history on the maturation of the individual. Erikson, like Adler, emphasized the future. At any given moment in time, Erikson said, your *anticipation of future events* determines how you will behave in the "here and now."

Eight Developmental Stages

According to Erikson, you must pass through eight developmental stages on your way to complete maturity (see Table 19.2). Each of these stages is characterized by its own type of *crisis*, or conflict. Erikson saw these crises as being eight great tests of your character. Typically there are two *opposing tendencies* operating at the time of each crisis. One tendency is negative, in that it tends to retard development. The other tendency is positive, and promotes healthy growth. The crisis at each stage is resolved when the *relative balance* between the two tendencies swings either to the positive or the negative. And out of these crises grow the "strengths" that people need in order to mature and survive in a healthy fashion. These strengths include such things as hope, will, faith, and purpose.

TABLE 19.2 Erikson's Stages of Development

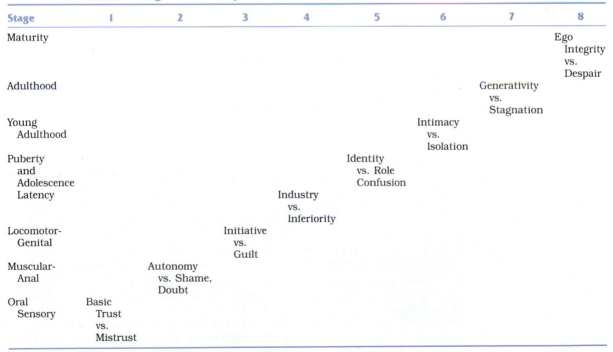

Stage	1	2	3	4	5	6	7	8
Maturity								Ego Integrity vs. Despair
Adulthood						Generativity vs. Stagnation		
Young Adulthood					Intimacy vs. Isolation			
Puberty and Adolescence				Identity vs. Role Confusion				
Latency			Industry vs. Inferiority					
Locomotor-Genital		Initiative vs. Guilt						
Muscular-Anal	Autonomy vs. Shame, Doubt							
Oral Sensory	Basic Trust vs. Mistrust							

Source: *Reprinted from* Childhood and Society, *Rev. by Erik H. Erikson, by permission of W.W. Norton & Company, Inc. Copyright 1960 ©1963 by W.W. Norton & Company, Inc.*

The second of Erikson's developmental stages is "muscular development." The child either succeeds at self-control and hence learns autonomy, or it fails and develops shame and guilt about its own abilities.

During the latency period, the child either succeeds and thus becomes industrious, or fails and develops a feeling of inferiority.

During young adulthood, Erikson said, people face the crisis of "intimacy versus isolation."

In maturity, the last of Erikson's developmental stages, the older person "returns to childhood" by working with children or perhaps by becoming childlike in some ways.

1. Erikson called the first developmental stage the "sensory stage," which corresponds to Freud's oral stage. To Erikson, the crisis at the sensory stage is that of learning a basic *trust or mistrust* of other people. As Erikson puts it, "a basic sense of trust means both that the child has learned to rely on his (or her) caregivers to be there when they are needed, and to consider himself trustworthy." If the mother (or someone else) meets the infant's needs, the child learns to depend on others in later life.

   In Erikson's words, "out of the conflict between trust and mistrust, the infant develops hope, which is the earliest form of what gradually becomes faith in adults." The infant gains the "strength" of hope, however, only if the mother is consistent in satisfying the infant's needs. If she is inconsistent, the tendency to mistrust becomes dominant. But the infant cannot be trusting in all cases. "Just imagine," Erikson says, "what somebody would be like who had no mistrust at all." Thus, it is the balance between the opposing tendencies that actually determines personality.

2. The second of Erikson's stages, similar to the anal stage, is that of *muscular development*. During toilet training the child learns to control her or his own muscles and begins to assert his or her individuality. The two opposing tendencies are **autonomy** and *shame and doubt*. If the child learns to control those bodily functions, the child becomes self-directed and autonomous. If the opposing tendency prevails, the young person may develop "a **precocious** conscience," and with it a sense of shame, or what Erikson calls "rage turned against the self." If this happens, the child may fear losing self-control and may suffer a loss of self-esteem.

   At this age, Erikson says, children often have to test the newly discovered notion that they are self-directing individuals. Therefore, they may occasionally "test the limits" with their parents by throwing temper tantrums and by generally acting in a negative way. Wise parents are neither too controlling and punitive, nor are they too permissive. Rather, they encourage children to learn the consequences of their actions, and to control themselves.

3. The third stage, that of *locomotor control*, is similar to Freud's phallic stage. The opposing tendencies at this age are *initiative* versus *guilt*. Children now turn from total dependency on the parents to *identification* with one or both parents. Urged by their instincts to possess the opposite-sex parent (at least in fantasy), children face the crisis of inner desires versus society's demands. If their superegos become too strict and strong, the children may experience excessive guilt and resort to repression as a means of handling their fears. However, if they resolve their Oedipal difficulties, the youngsters gain initiative and a sense of responsibility for controlling their own lives.

4. Both Freud and Erikson called the fourth developmental stage that of *latency*. During these (typically) school years, the opposing tendencies are *competence* versus *failure*. Children who do well in school and other activities learn they can succeed. Therefore, they become industrious. If the children do poorly, they experience failure and may develop a sense of inferiority.

5. At *puberty*, Freud thought, sexual interest returns and the individual must make the final adjustment, that of heterosexuality. Erikson saw the puberty crisis as that of either finding your *identity*, or of developing what he called *role confusion*. Erikson coined the term "identity crisis." At this age, you must decide what the future will hold and who you will become. By discovering who and what you want to be, you are able to plan your life and strive to achieve your personal goals.

6. Erikson postulated three final stages of maturation beyond the five Freud spoke of. The first of these stages, which occurs in young adulthood, presents you with the crisis of *intimacy* versus *isolation*. According to Erikson, "real Intimacy includes the capacity to commit yourself to relationships that may demand sacrifice and compromise. The basic strength of young adulthood is Love— a mutual, mature devotion." Erikson sees a great difference between "Intimacy" with a capital I and "intimacy," by which he means sexual activity. In his 1983 interview, he says, "Some people today may fool themselves in their so-called recreational sexual-

Autonomy (aw-TAWN-oh-me). Freedom; self-direction. The autonomic nervous system is usually "free" of conscious direction or control.

Precocious (pre-COH-shus). From the Greek words meaning "early ripening." To be precocious to be exceptionally early in your development.

ity and actually feel quite isolated because they lack mutuality—real Intimacy. In extreme cases, you could have a highly active sex life and yet feel a terrible sense of isolation because you're never there as a person; you're never perceiving your partner as a person."

7. One of Erikson's greatest contributions to personality theory has been his descriptions of what happens to people during their middle years. He sees the opposing tendencies here as being **generativity** and *stagnation*. Generativity is composed of three related activities—procreativity, productivity, and creativity.

As for procreativity, Erikson says, "I believe there is a procreative drive. There is an instinctual wish to have children, and it's important that we realize that." This urge, however, can be *sublimated* into productivity and creativity.

As for productivity, Erikson states that we have an innate drive to "take care of things. The Hindus call it the maintenance of the world." In part, this drive is a desire to make society better for one's children.

And as for creativity, it involves learning to accept the new rather than rigidly trying to maintain things as they were in the past. But creativity is also linked to procreativity, because it often involves child-like (id-like) activities. Erikson says, "Einstein used the word 'wonder' to describe his experience as a child, and he was considered childlike by many people. And I think he claimed that he was able to formulate the theory of relativity because he kept asking the questions that children ask."

Individuals who reject generativity typically become self-absorbed and stagnate.

8. Erikson's final stage is that of *maturity*. The opposing tendencies at this age are *integrity* and *despair*. Erikson defines integrity as "a sense of coherence and wholeness." He says further that integrity is at "supreme risk under such terminal conditions as [those that involve] a loss of linkages in **somatic**, psychic and social organization. What is demanded here could be simply called Integrality, a readiness to keep things together. The strength that grows out of resolving this final conflict is that of 'wisdom.'"

In a sense, Erikson has extended the tendency for generativity to this age as well. However, as he notes, "Old people can no longer procreate, but they can be productive, and they can be creative." Even if they no longer must take care of their own children, they can "care for" other children. "I'm convinced that old people and children need one another and that there's an affinity between old age and childhood that, in fact, rounds out the life cycle. You know, old people often seem childlike, and it's important that we be permitted to revive some qualities that we had as children."

If older people remain active—and if they still relate directly to society—they can *integrate* all of life's experiences and thus bring integrity to their egos or selfs. However, if they fail to solve most of their earlier crises, they may succumb to feelings of despair at the futility of existence.

Erikson: An Evaluation

Erikson's ideas—like those of Freud—are not always easy to test experimentally. And, like Freud, Erikson is a "traditionalist" in most senses of that word. For example, in the February 1984 issue of *Contemporary Psychology*, David R. Matteson notes that Erikson's choice of *identity* as the central theme of adolescence has a "male bias" to it, shared by most other Western personality theorists. "From my reading of the life span literature," Matteson says, "I believe our society has encouraged men to develop identity at the expense of intimacy and women the reverse. In mid-life, many women resume the task of developing mature identity, and many men reassess their priorities and finally develop interpersonal sensitivities." Matteson criticizes Erikson, therefore, because he (like Freud) pays little attention to the developmental pattern most women show.

Despite Matteson's criticisms, the fact that most psychoanalysts are impressed by Erikson's theory weighs in his favor. Surely, his emphasis on growth during the middle and later years is a signal addition to Freudian theory. And, if nothing else, Erikson deserves a vote of praise for two things: first, for insisting that the *society you grow up in* plays a strong role in determining how you resolve your inner crises. Second, for focusing attention on the personality changes that occur during the last half of the life span.

We will mention Erikson again later in this chapter, when we finish our discussion of life-span development. First, let's turn our attention to the other major approach to personality theory, *personology*. We will first discuss the humanistic psychologists. Then we will look at Henry Murray, who first gave "personology" its name half a century ago. Finally, we will cover the various behavioral approaches, including social learning theory. As you will see, all of these theorists take quite a different view of personality development than do the traditionalists such as Freud and Erikson.

Humanistic Theories of Personality

Freud believed that our destinies lie in our genetic blueprints, and that we more or less become what nature intended us to be. This predominantly biological view of human nature is rejected by a group of theorists who call themselves *humanistic psychologists*. They see us as being unique, set apart, and above all other life forms. We are not mechanisms wound up and abandoned to tick out our lives as our gene-clocks dictate. Rather, we are masters of our destinies, creative individuals capable of rising above our animal heritage.

According to the humanistic psychologists, we are motivated not merely to survive, but to become *better and better*. This process of continual psychological growth and improvement is what the humanistic psychologists call *self-actualization* (see Chapter 10).

There are many psychologists whose theories fall within the humanistic tradition. Of these, the best known are probably Carl Rogers and Abraham Maslow.

Carl Rogers

Carl Rogers taught for many years at the University of Chicago and at the University of Wisconsin. Rogers believes you were born with no

Carl Rogers

self-concept, and no self—but you do have an innate urge to *become* a fully fuctioning and actualized person.

At birth, all you had was a confusing set of sensory impressions, biological processes, and motor activities. Rogers calls this sum total of your experience the **phenomenal field**. As you matured, however, the outside world imposed a kind of order or logic on this field. And as you became aware of this logic, your *self* emerged and differentiated itself from the phenomenal field. The self is thus the *conscious* portion of your experience.

For Rogers, maturation is a matter of distinguishing your own body and thoughts from the objective, outside world. As you matured, your "self" began to build up expectations about its own functioning—that is, you took on values and made judgments about your own behavior. Some of these values came from your own desires (and from your genetic endowment). Other values were imposed on you by the society in which you live. Rogers believes you are mostly likely to run into developmental problems when society wants you to become something that conflicts with your own internal values or standards. If you yield to the demands of society too much, your psychological experience is distorted and your self-concept suffers accordingly.

According to Rogers, most of your experiences are *unconscious*—that is, below the threshold of awareness. But you can bring almost any experience above threshold if you merely give the experience a name or a label. That is, you make an unconscious experience conscious by developing *word-symbols* that allow you to describe (and hence think about) the experience. If a particular event threatens your self-concept, then you may refuse to symbolize this event in words or thoughts. But if you cannot tolerate some of your own behaviors, you will have problems achieving full actualization, because you are continually hiding

TABLE 19.3   Abraham Maslow's Whole Characteristics of Self-Actualizing People

They have more efficient perceptions of reality and are more comfortable with it.

They accept themselves and their own natures almost without thinking about it.

Their behavior is marked by simplicity and naturalness and by lack of artificiality or straining for effect.

They focus on problems outside themselves; they are concerned with basic issues and eternal questions.

They like privacy and tend to be detached.

They have relative independence of their physical and social environments; they rely on their own development and continued growth.

They do not take blessings for granted, but appreciate again and again the basic pleasures of life.

They experience limitless horizons and the intensification of any unself-conscious experience often of a mystical type.

They have a deep feeling of kinship with others.

They develop deep ties with a few other self-actualizing individuals.

They are democratic in a deep sense; although not indiscriminate, they are not really aware of differences.

They are strongly ethical, with definite moral standards, though their attitudes are conventional; they relate to ends rather than means.

Their humor is real and related to philosophy, not hostility; they are spontaneous less often than others, and tend to be more serious and thoughtful.

They are original and inventive, less constricted and fresher than others.

While they tend toward the conventional and exist well within the culture, they live by the laws of their own characters rather than those of society.

They experience imperfections and have ordinary feelings, like others.

Source: *Condensed from "Self-Actualizing People: A Study of Psychological Health," in* Motivation and Personality, *2nd ed., by Abraham H. Maslow, Copyright 1954 by Harper & Row, Publishers, Inc.; Copyright © 1970 by Abraham H. Maslow. By permission of the publishers.*

some of your own values or motivations from conscious expression. We will return to this point again in Chapter 21, when we discuss Rogers's views on psychotherapy.

When you can accept yourself completely, you become what Rogers calls a *fully functioning individual.* You are open to all experience, and you defend against nothing. You are aware of both your faults and your virtues, but you have a high positive regard for yourself. And most of all, you maintain happy and humane relationships with others.

Abraham Maslow

Carl Rogers's theory grew out of his long-time work as a psychotherapist. Thus, his theory is built in part on the study of abnormal and maladjusted individuals. To a great extent, this statement is also true of Freud's theory, and of Jung's, Adler's, and Erikson's.

Abraham Maslow, on the other hand, took his ideas about human behavior from studying highly creative and psychologically *healthy* people. Some of these individuals were his personal friends. Others—such as Lincoln, Einstein, Eleanor Roosevelt, and Beethoven—he studied through books, papers, and letters. Maslow assumed these individuals had achieved a high degree of self-fulfillment, or they wouldn't have

been so prominent and have demonstrated so much leadership. By determining the similarities among the members of this noted group, he arrived at the characteristics of a truly "self-actualized" person. A list of these characteristics appears in Table 19.3.

Most psychoanalytical theories focus on what can go wrong during the developmental years. That is, they emphasize the possibility of sickness, not the probability of success. Maslow's approach is different, for he looks primarily at the *healthy side of human nature.* As we noted in Chapter 10, Maslow has created a *hierarchy of needs,* of which self-actualization is the highest. Maslow acknowledges the strength of our biological instincts, but sees them as being "basic needs" easily satisfied in most civilized societies. But even our drives for food and sex are part of a more impelling intra-psychic urge— an active "will toward health"—that drives us up the developmental ladder toward self-actualization.

Humanistic Psychology: An Evaluation

Neither Rogers nor Maslow offered a full-fledged "theory of personality development," as did both Freud and Erikson. We discussed the pros and cons of Maslow's hierarchy of needs in

Chapter 10. His explanation of motivational development appeals to many people because of its simplicity. However, there is little in the way of experimental data to support his views, and his hierarchy is subject to all the criticisms raised against Piaget's and Freud's theories.

The major strengths of the humanistic approach appear to be (1) its emphasis on health rather than on sickness; and (2) its belief that people actively participate in shaping their personalities. The major weaknesses seem to be a de-emphasis on behavior and objective measurement, and a failure to explain in *precise terms* how personality is formed.

Maslow and Rogers did not consider themselves "personologists"—at least as we use the term today. However, as the following discussion of Henry Murray will show, the humanists surely fit within an earlier meaning of "personology."

Henry A. Murray

The term *personology* was probably first used by Harvard psychologist Henry A. Murray more than 50 years ago. Like Freud and Erikson, Murray was trained as a medical doctor. He also took a Ph.D. in biochemistry. In 1923 he purchased a copy of Jung's book *Psychological Types* the day it was published in the US. Shortly thereafter, he went to Switzerland to study psychoanalysis with Jung.

Murray's contact with Jung changed his career plans. When Murray was offered a job at the newly formed Harvard Psychological Clinic in 1927, he abandoned biochemistry and moved into the behavioral sciences. A few years later, he became director of the Clinic. For many years thereafter, he played a leading role in shaping the course of personality research in the US and abroad.

Murray frequently called himself a humanistic psychologist. He was that, and more. He was also a trait theorist (of sorts), a behaviorist (of a kind), a social learning theorist before the term came into being, and he was strongly influenced by psychoanalysis. Most of all, however, he was a *personologist*.

Murray's "Personology"

Because Murray didn't like the term "personality theory," he used "personology" instead. By *personology*, Murray meant the long-term study of personality development from what was really a holistic point of view. In a 1927

Behavioral trends. The combination of acts, plus the perception of the acts, plus the conscious awareness of the outcome or consequences of the acts. Put more simply, a behavioral trend is your conscious explanation of why you do what you do (plus an objective measurement of what you actually do).

Need integrates (IN-tee-greats). Your needs, plus your perceptions and cognitions related to those needs.

paper, he called for "a comprehensive investigation of the same organism simultaneously undertaken from a number of distinct standpoints over the entire [developmental] period or at least over a certain specified portion of the life span." Thus, personology was to deal with *observations* of people as they developed.

But what should the personologist observe? Bodily movements, of course. But movements have consequences or *effects* (as Murray put it), and the person doing the behaving can perceive the effects of his or her actions. Murray used the term **behavioral trends** to refer to an individual's *perception* of the relationship between actions and consequences. According to Murray, "behavioral trends" are the basic observational units of personology. In order to understand "what makes you tick," therefore, the personologist must study both your *actual behaviors* and your *perception* of your activities (behavioral trends).

Needs and Presses

Like most of the personality theorists discussed in this chapter, Murray was strongly influenced by Charles Darwin. For example, he believes you are primarily motivated to adapt to your environment and thus increase your chances for surviving. Murray uses the term *needs* to mean "internal motivational processes." By "needs," he means "processes in the brain" that account for the fact that you tend to *persist* in certain types of behaviors until your desires are satisfied.

But you behave in much the same way each time you satisfy a given need. Thus, over time, you tend to associate certain *images* of your own goal-oriented movements (and *images* of the goal itself) with the need you're trying to satisfy. Murray used the term **need integrates** to refer to a need *plus* the mental images you associate with reducing that need.

Whether you satisfy a need or not often depends on the environment. For the world you live in can either assist you in reaching your goals or it can thwart you. Murray used the term *positive press* to refer to an environment that accepts you (or facilitates your reaching your goals). By *negative press*, he meant an environment that rejects you (or that frustrates your goal-seeking behaviors).

Themas

Certain needs and certain environmental presses tend to "go together" with great frequency. Murray uses the term **thema** to refer to a "press-need combination." He believes that personology is, to a large extent, the study of "themas." That is, Murray says that personologists should study and attempt to explain "person-environment interactions."

Both Darwin and Freud believed that aggression was an "instinct" that aided survival. Murray would say that people often experience a need to be aggressive, which he calls "n Aggression." But you could satisfy this need in a variety of ways—perhaps by hitting people, perhaps by calling them dirty names, or even by engaging in fantasies about being a soldier or winning fights.

Suppose someone calls you a bad name. This insult activates your "n Aggression." You *perceive* your environment as (for the moment) being hostile and rejecting—which is to say that you experience "negative press." But you have learned not to hit people who insult you, because the consequences are often unpleasant. Instead, you typically back off from the insult and just daydream about getting even. Your "aggressive need integrate" would include your perception of the person who insulted you, your usual way of backing off, and your feelings when you daydream. And the fact that you *typically* engage in fantasy when faced with hostile environmental presses is a description of your "thematic disposition" for handling this need-press combination.

Murray: An Evaluation

Because of his creative approach—and because of his position at the Harvard Clinic—Murray has had a strong influence on the scientific study of personality in the US. However, as Berkeley psychologist Kenneth H. Craik notes in the November 1982 *Contemporary Psychologist*, Murray was at his best in the field of *personality assessment*. And many of his ideas were turned into personality tests. However, Murray did make two major contributions that go beyond standard trait theory:

1. First, Murray realized that needs are not merely "unconscious instincts." Rather, needs are mostly conscious. Furthermore, it is the way you *perceive* your need, not the need itself, that determines how you respond.

2. Second, he understood that your environment has a strong influence on the characteristic way in which you strive to satisfy your needs. Thus, he saw personality as an *integration* of personal and environmental facts.

As we will see, Murray's emphasis on *conscious perceptions* and *person-environment interactions* helped give rise to **social learning theory**.

Social Learning Theory

Henry A. Murray added something new to personality theory by emphasizing the importance of *organism-environment interactions*. True, *all* the other theorists recognized that the world you grew up in affected the structure of your personality, and that some behaviors are acquired. But Murray goes a step farther. He insists that it is not just the environment that helps shape your mind. Rather, it is your *perception* of the outside world—and your *perception* of your interactions with that world—that are important.

Although both Murray and Skinner are at Harvard and are the same age, the two men are natural antagonists. Skinner sees you as reacting passively to inputs from your environment. Murray insists that you actively interpret what you perceive. Skinner believes you respond automatically and blindly to the consequences of your actions—that is, to rewards and punishments. Murray says you consciously plan your activities based on a cognitive appreciation of the consequences of what you've already accomplished.

The problem is that Skinner tells you *how* you learn things, while Murray doesn't. And Skinner developed a highly effective way of teaching people new behaviors, while Murray didn't. If we could just *combine* the best aspects of Skinner, Murray, Freud, Adler, Piaget, Rogers, and Maslow into one grand theory, perhaps we could come up with a more adequate description of how people like you got to be the way you are. And that, indeed, is just what the *social learning theorists* appear to be trying to do.

Behaviorism and Social Learning Theory

As we noted in Chapter 14, by the 1960's the "pure" behaviorism of B.F. Skinner began to give way to "cognitive" behaviorism. For at that time behavioral therapists made three important discoveries. First, they found they could use Skinner's techniques to "shape" a patient's *thoughts* (cognitions) as well as the person's *actions*. Second, the therapists noted that patients frequently learned how to "self-shape." That is, the person could learn to use Skinnerian techniques to alter her/his own thinking and behaving "at will," without further guidance from the therapist (or anyone else). And third, many patients found ways to "shape" their external environments into helping the patients reach their own goals. All three discoveries, though, suggested that the behaviorists could not hope to explain human development unless they looked at intra-psychic processes as well as at environmental inputs and behavioral outputs. It was this addition of cognitive psychology to behaviorism that, in part, led to the creation of *social learning theory*.

According to Skinner, your actions are *directly* controlled by external stimuli. According to social learning theorists such as Albert Ban-

Thema (THEE-mah). You have certain stereotyped ways of responding to familiar situations—that is, to familiar "need-press combinations." Suppose we show you a drawing of two people talking, while a third person is eavesdropping in the background. You might interpret this familiar situation by saying, "The two people are telling horrible stories about the person who is listening, but the person will get even with them eventually." You would be interpreting the *thema* of this social interaction in one way. But another person might say, "The listener is trying to find out ways to make the two people talking like him, so he can become friends with them." This is quite a different thematic (the-MATT-tick) interpretation of the same situation. We will discuss themas (and how to measure them) more fully in the next chapter.

Social learning theory. A marriage of Skinner's behaviorism and cognitive psychology. Social learning theorists believe that learned cognitive processes mediate behavior. These processes are acquired through reinforcement, but also through such vicarious (vy-KAR-ee-us) processes as imitation and modeling. These cognitive processes are similar to Piaget's schemata.

dura, the social environment "shapes" your *cognitive processes*. These intra-psychic processes, in turn, determine how you will behave. Put more simply, Skinner says you react directly to your environment *as it really is*. Bandura says that you react to your *perceptions* of what the real world is like.

In a sense, social learning theory is an interesting mixture of Piaget, Murray, and Skinner. Social learning theorists often refer to themselves as "personologists," thus acknowledging their indebtedness to Murray's interactional approach. And the social learning theorists tend to emphasize cognitions, as did Piaget.

However, social learning theorists differ from earlier theorists in many ways. For example, Piaget believed that "mental structures" were determined primarily by the genes, but the social learning theorists see cognitive processes as being "shaped" the same way that Skinner says behavior is "shaped." Skinner says you learn because your actions are *directly* rewarded or punished. The social learning theorists agree with this point of view, but add something unique—the concept of *modeling*. That is, they say you can also learn by *observing the consequences of other people's actions*. You can then imitate those behaviors that yield rewards, and avoid those actions that bring unpleasant results. *Modeling*, therefore, is a form of "learning by observation" rather than "learning by doing."

In a nutshell, the social learning theorists believe that when you were young, your parents and the rest of your social environment shaped your behaviors the way that Skinner says pigeons are shaped to perform behavioral tricks. But as you *behaved*, you were also creating *cognitive structures* in your mind, much as Piaget and Murray claim is the case. These cognitions do at least two things for you. First, they allow you to observe and evaluate the actions of others, and to change your own behaviors consciously. Second, your cognitions allow you to *reshape your own environment*. As your external world changes, you respond to it differently. Thus, to the social learning theorist, the person-environment interaction is a continual process of *complementary shaping*.

Social Learning Theory versus Freud

Freud said that the social environment *brings out* the ego, but *doesn't change it*. For the basic structures of the ego are determined by the genes, not by conditioning. To social learning theorists, the "self-concept" is *entirely learned* and thus varies both from person to person and from culture to culture. But once your self-concept emerges, it *mediates* your social inputs. By doing so, your self-concept allows you to change not only your behaviors, but your environment as well.

Freud believed that abnormal behavior patterns were mere "symptoms" of some underlying abnormal thought process. Therefore, to cure the symptomatic behaviors, you had to resolve the underlying psychological conflict by giving the patient "insight" into what had caused the problem. Skinner disagreed. He said abnormal behaviors are entirely learned. Thus, they can be "cured" by shaping the person to act in a normal fashion. The social learning theorists take a middle position. They see abnormal behaviors as stemming from abnormal thoughts, but these thought patterns were learned. Therefore, you "cure" people by helping them reshape (1) their *cognitions* (including "self-cognitions"), (2) their *behaviors*, and (3) their environments. Which of these three you choose to work on first in therapy depends, of course, on you (and your therapist).

Social Learning Theory versus Humanistic Psychology

Carl Rogers thinks it is inhumane and immoral to "shape" a child in any way. Rather, he says, you provide a "permissive but encouraging environment" for the child, who then is free to develop in whatever manner he or she desires.

Social learning theorists believe you must be taught self-control and the techniques of self-change, because you have no "innate knowledge" about such matters. Therefore, refusing to give you guidance is both inhumane and counterproductive. Furthermore, you must learn to adopt a "give and take" attitude in your relations with society. For you can best meet your own needs if you help others around you achieve their own goals too.

Maslow believed the "will toward health" was built into your genes, so he saw no need to teach you *how* to achieve "self-actualization." The social learning theorists believe the "will toward health" must be learned—and they provide many effective techniques for helping you achieve "self-actualization" or any other goal you may wish to reach.

Social Learning Theory versus Skinner

As must be obvious, social learning theory is, in many ways, an extension of Skinner's work. But there are differences between the two approaches as well. As we mentioned, Skinner emphasizes behaviors, while social learning theorists deal with both behaviors and cognitions. And social learning theorists accept "observational learning," while Skinner doesn't.

In their 1981 article mentioned earlier, Nancy Cantor and John Kihlstrom note yet another difference, which has to do with *language*. Skinner sees language solely as an *external behavior* that is taught by the environment. Social learning theorists agree that speech is learned. But once learned, it can be internalized. Therefore, you can deal with the world by manipulating verbal symbols "in your mind" as well as by speaking them out loud. Social learning theory thus involves studying how you learn to *process informational inputs*—that is, how you think and reason—as well as discovering how you learn to behave.

The growing emphasis on the importance of learning is but one of several recent trends in personality theory. Now that we have discussed the theorists and their approaches, let's see what these trends are.

Recent Trends in Personality Theory

If you look back over this chapter, certain "developmental trends" in personality theory become apparent.

1. A shift from the "naturist" position of Freud and Piaget to the "nurturist" position of Skinner to the "interactionist" view of Murray and the social learning theorists.
2. A movement away from Freud's and Skinner's view of the organism as a "passive reactor" toward the social learning position that you are an "active participant" in the shaping of your own personality.
3. A trend away from Freud's emphasis on emotions, and an increasing emphasis on cognitive processes.
4. A shift from Freud's emphasis on unconscious processes toward a belief that conscious processes are the important elements in personality.
5. A movement away from Freud's belief that the personality structure was fixed at age 15 toward the belief that you continue to grow and mature all your life.
6. A decreased interest in "developmental stages," and a growing belief that the pattern of personality development is shaped by a *continuous interplay* between you and your social environment.

These "developmental trends" are nowhere more visible than in our viewpoint toward the adult years. Among traditional personality theorists, Erikson and Adler were the first to insist that personality continued to develop during adulthood and old age. But even Erikson places more emphasis on the early years. For example, he speaks of "the life *cycle*," and claims that "older people are naturally child-like." Therefore, he says, we can learn about the last years of life by studying the first years. However, most modern research suggests that older people who act in immature ways often do so in response to *cultural demands and expectations.*

In his 1982 book, *Life-Span Development and Behavior*, German psychologist Paul Baltes criticizes Erikson's "biological age-directed model." Human development is not "mapped out by the genes," Baltes says. Nor does development proceed in clearly defined stages. Rather, it is characterized by "reversibility, **reciprocal causality**, and pluralism." You can always change, you are always affected by

(and have an effect on) your enviroment, and there is no *one developmental pattern* that is best for all people.

Unfortunately, despite all the recent research by Baltes and others who share his viewpoint, we still don't have a personality theory that accounts for all the changes that occur over the full span of life. We can make that point most dramatically by briefly looking at what little we know of personality development during the adult years.

Maturity and Old Age

There is a cultural myth in Western society that, like a machine that has worn down from constant use, the older person should become slow-moving, mentally inflexible and rigid, and above all, asexual. Let us look at each of these points in turn.

Physical Changes in Maturity

There is no doubt that younger people typically expend more physical energy than do most people in their 40's and 50's. But this change in "body tempo" is probably due more to psychological and social causes than to something like "tired blood."

There are physical changes associated with aging, of course. Testosterone levels tend to drop in both males and females, and the hormonal alterations associated with **menopause** are well known. Older individuals often experience poor health. But long-term studies of hundreds of subjects in California suggest that many of the physical problems of mature individuals can be seen as poor responses to *psychological stress.* In their 1981 book *Present and Past in Middle Life*, Dorothy Eichorn and her colleagues report a significant relationship between mental health early in life and physical health during maturity. Those subjects who showed emotional stability and controlled re-

Current research suggests that maintaining an active interest in sex and other aspects of life helps prevent the onset of senility and other problems in older individuals.

sponses to stress as adolescents had far better health at age 50 than did those subjects who had poor stress reactions when young.

The Aging Brain

The human body tends to shrink slightly as it ages, and so apparently does the brain. In a 1982 report, M.J. de Leon and A.E. George of the NYU Medical Center report that the brain of a healthy 70-year-old is slightly smaller than that of a healthy 25-year-old. However, *sugar metabolism*—which is a measure of *activity* in the brain—is the same in the 70-year-old as in the 25-year-old. Thus, there is no medical support for the belief that older individuals *must* become "infantile" or *senile* because their brains either "shrivel up" or "stop functioning properly."

The belief that "you lose brain cells every day of your life" apparently got its start in 1958, when a noted scientist estimated that "humans lose 100,000 neurons a day after age 30." This belief is nonsense, according to Marian C. Diamond. She has studied the brains of both animals and humans for many years in her laboratory at the University of California, Berkeley. Diamond concludes that "in the absence of disease, our studies provide no reason to believe that normal aging in humans produces brain-cell loss until, perhaps, extreme old age."

Nor is there anatomical evidence that the nerve cells in older brains are not as *plastic* or responsive as are the neurons in younger individuals. Writing in the November 16, 1983 issue of *Science*, anatomists S.J. Buell and P.D. Coleman report the findings of their studies of different-aged human brains. Buell and Coleman state that the neurons of a healthy 80-year-old brain have just as many *dendrites*—and show similar growth patterns—as do neurons in much younger brains. As we pointed out in Chapter 15, most scientists believe that learning is accompanied by changes at the *synapse* that involve dendritic growth. Therefore, as Buell and Coleman state, their findings suggest that healthy 80-year-olds should be as *physically* capable of learning new things as are much younger individuals.

Senility and Alzheimer's Disease

In a 1981 book, Minnesota scientists J.A. Mortimer and L.M. Schuman note that only one elderly person in five will become senile. One common cause of senility is a disorder called *Alzheimer's disease*, which affects about a third of the patients who become senile. Only a small fraction of the population will fall prey to Alzheimer's disease. But caring for these patients is exceptionally expensive. Mortimer and Schuman estimate that *at least half of all Medicare costs* are spent on treatment of patients with Alzheimer's disease.

Medical researchers disagree both on what causes Alzheimer's disease and how best to treat it. At first it was thought to be the result of "hardening of the arteries," but recent studies show this isn't the case. Rather, current research suggests Alzheimer's may be caused by one or more viruses. Just which virus or viruses may be responsible isn't yet clear. We do know, however, that patients with this disorder have *abnormal brains*. Alzheimer's patients have lower sugar-metabolism levels than do normal individuals, and their brains contain reduced amounts of certain *neurotransmitters*. Their neurons also seem to have fewer dendrites and show less active growth than those of normal individuals. These findings have led scientists to say Alzheimer's patients have "slow-functioning brains."

Most medical treatment of Alzheimer's patients has proved to be of minor value. Marion Diamond believes the reason for this failure lies in our conception of Alzheimer's disease as a *medical disorder*. Diamond's research suggests that giving both animals and people stimulating environments actually *prevents* the types of brain changes found in Alzheimer's patients. Rather than hoping pills and surgery will "cure" the problems associated with senility, Diamond says, we should find new ways to keep older individuals active and in control of their lives. "The worst thing we can do is to consign elderly people to sedentary confinement in an unstimulating nursing home." To do so, Diamond says, is to perpetuate the false belief that brain-cell loss and mental deterioration always accompany old age.

Learning and Memory in Mature Individuals

As Leonard W. Poon and his colleagues point out in their 1980 book, *New Directions in Memory and Aging*, young people are perhaps more likely to "latch on to new ideas" than are older people. However, older individuals are generally able to learn more quickly those facts or skills that do not directly *contradict* their previous learning. Young people may be capable of taking in information more rapidly, and may have larger Short-term Memories, but older individuals are just as good at making decisions. *Processing speed* thus seems to be the major deficit that uniformly shows up in studies of learning in older people.

In a study of several thousand subjects, Oxford psychologist Patrick Rabbitt reports that most people over 70 prefer talking to one individual at a time. When older individuals are part of a conversation group, they apparently cannot *process information rapidly enough*. Thus, they tend to remember what was said, but not who said it. Or they recall who spoke, but not what was said. But Rabbitt also points out that some of the "memory problems" old people seem to have may be due to poor hearing or other physical defects rather than to mental deterioration. He notes as well that 5 to 10 percent of people past 70 have memories just as good as individuals in their 20's.

Perhaps the major "memory" problem that old people have is the *expectations* younger individuals have about memory loss in old age. As Samuel Johnson wrote more than 200 years ago, "if a young or middle-aged man, when leaving a company, does not recollect where he laid his hat, it is nothing. But if the same inattention is discovered in an old man, people will shrug their shoulders and say, 'His memory is going.'"

Sexuality in Older Individuals

There is not all that much agreement among the experts on how aging affects sexuality, much less *why* these changes occur. The generally accepted view of "sexual arousability" is shown in Fig. 19.4. From this point of view, males tend to reach their peak about age 18, then show a sharp drop that continues the rest of their lives. "Arousability" in women, however, tends to peak about age 35 or so and stays relatively high thereafter.

The truth of the matter is that there simply aren't enough studies—made in enough situations—to tell us all we need to know about sexuality in the later years. It is true that hormone levels reach a peak in the male at about age 18, and fall thereafter. But it is just as true that a 90-year-old male typically has a high enough hormone level to perform the sex act several times a week.

Almost all researchers in this area have come to the same conclusion: People who, in their

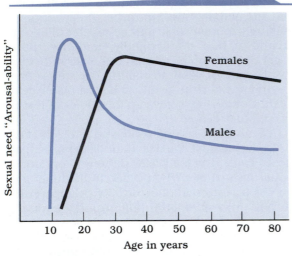

Fig. 19.4 Most psychologists believe that "sexual arousability" reaches a peak in males at about age 18 and thereafter declines, while "arousability" peaks in females at about age 35 and remains fairly constant thereafter.

later years, continue to have an active sex life typically look younger, have more energy, and show a greater zest for living than do people who shun sexuality. The older person's *psychological age* thus depends more on the individual's *self-concept* than on the person's *biological age.*

A Model for Aging

In an article in the February 1983 *American Psychologist*, Carl Eisdorfer proposes a "conceptual model for aging." He notes that, in all societies, older individuals tend to behave in ways that society believe are "acceptable." Thus, each culture has its own "model for aging."

Eisdorfer believes it is time our society rethought what its model should be. "The aged are now captives, the victims of a belief system that has most people over 65 identified with the small proportion of needy, dependent, and helpless individuals. Herb Shore once proposed that older people could be conceptualized in three different ways: The no-go group, the slow-go group, and of course, the go-go group. Are we so attached to the no-go and slow-go image that those who can and do go lose their options?"

What Eisdorfer is saying, of course, is that our *theories of personality development* are still too narrow. We simply have not integrated all of our scientific knowledge about the entire span of life into one complete theory or model. "If we must have a model," Eisdorfer says, "should we not accept the broadest model? In this case, a biopsychosocial model appears to best recognize the complexity of the situation." Eisdorfer concludes, however, that we are not likely to build this new model until we recognize how much the best-known theories of personality limit our conception of what life-span development is all about.

Someday, perhaps, we will have a master theory that tells us everything about the human personality that we want to know—one that is *holistic* enough to give us "deep understanding" of ourselves as well as the power to shape our personal development. But both understanding and shaping imply that we can somehow measure what it is we are trying to comprehend and change. So it is to the *measurement* of human personality (and personality traits) that we must now turn our attention.

Summary

1 The study of **personality** is concerned with identifying the distinctive patterns of thought, behavior, and experience that characterize the individual's unique **adjustment** to his or her life situation.

2 There are two major approaches to the study of personality theory. **Traditional personality psychology** focuses on unconscious processes, personality traits, and creativity, and takes an intra-psychic view of the human being. The second approach, **personology**, takes the social/behavioral view and focuses on cognitive processes and the interaction between the conscious self and environmental inputs.

3 Personologists attempt to **describe** consistent patterns of individual differences, **explain** why people think, feel, and behave as they do, **predict** how a person will act in the future, and **help** people change.

4 Psychoanalytic theory began when Freud and Breuer developed **catharsis**, a

means of releasing repressed **psychic energy**.

5 Freud described three "levels of consciousness," the **conscious**, the **preconscious**, and the **unconscious**.

6 An infant is born with a set of **instincts** or **biological drives** that motivate the child to live. Freud called these unconscious instincts the **id**. The energy supplied by these instincts is called the **libido**, or **life force**.

7 The id obeys the **pleasure principle**.

8 As the infant is forced to learn to delay gratification, the child's **ego** or conscious self comes into being. The ego obeys the **reality principle** when it takes into account the demands of the external environment.

9 The **superego** has two parts, the stern **conscience** that reflects the demands of society, and the **ego-ideal** that contains the individual's life goals.

10 Each stage in an infant's **psychosexual development** involves a crisis. The crisis during the **oral stage** is that of birth. The infant discharges libidinal energy through such oral activities as **sucking and swallowing**.

11 During the **anal stage**, the crisis is that of learning to **delay gratification**.

12 During the **phallic stage**, boys experience an **Oedipus complex**, or desire for the mother, while girls experience an **Electra complex**, or desire for the father.

13 The **incest taboo** crises associated with the phallic stage are resolved by **repression** of sexuality as the child moves into the **latency stage**, a natural **homosexual period**.

14 The **genital stage** begins at puberty. The child resolves its incestual feelings by taking on the characteristics of the same-sex parent. The child also begins to hunt for his or her **lifestyle**, or ego-ideal, which involves discharging libido through **heterosexual activities**.

15 The ego protects itself from **trauma** by using **defense mechanisms**.

16 According to Jung, we have two different types of unconscious: the **personal unconscious**, which contains our own individual memories, and the **collective unconscious**, which houses our **archetypes**, or racial memories.

17 Jung believed we have two **innate attitudes**, which he called **introversion** and **extroversion**.

18 Alfred Adler saw life as a struggle to achieve personal **superiority**, which is a movement from a **felt minus** or **inferiority complex** to a **felt plus**. We may **compensate** for an inferiority complex by trying to become **superior** in other ways.

19 According to Erikson, every human must pass through eight **developmental stages**, each of which is characterized by its own type of **crisis** or test of a person's character.

20 Each developmental crisis is marked by two **opposing tendencies**, one positive, one negative. The **relative balance** of the two tendencies determines whether the crisis will be solved in a healthy or unhealthy fashion.

21 The **humanistic psychologists** reject most psychoanalytic concepts, emphasizing instead the drive for **self-actualization**.

22 Carl Rogers believes that a **fully-adjusted person** can symbolize any experience in conscious verbalizations.

23 Abraham Maslow sees humans as having an innately determined **will toward health**.

24 The term **personology** was coined by Henry Murray, who believed **behavioral trends** are determined by an individual's **perception** of the consequences of his or her actions, by **needs** and by **environmental presses**.

25 **Behaviorists** such as B.F. Skinner believe that personality is entirely **learned** by direct experience with the **external environment**.

26 **Social learning theorists** such as Albert Bandura believe behavior is learned but is mediated by **cognitive processes**.

27 The changes that occur during the **later years of life** are multi-determined—that is, affected by genetic tendencies, past experience, and social expectations.

28 Except for those individuals suffering from disease, the brains of older individuals tend to be as **healthy and active** as are the brains of younger people.

29 Although hormone levels drop as people age, even elderly individuals can maintain an active sex life if they desire to do so.

30 Older individuals can readily learn **new behaviors** (and help prevent the onset of

senility) if they remain **psychologically alert** and open to new experiences during their later years.

31 No present **personality theory** adequately describes the final years of life.

(Continued from page 509.)

"Piaget to the rescue?" Fred asked in a tone of amazement. "Since when did he have anything practical to offer?"

"Piaget had lots of practical ideas about education," Norma replied. "The trouble is, you behaviorists are so eager to manipulate students into behaving 'properly' you never pay much attention to the real issues in education."

"Such as . . ."

"Such as the fact that we can't decide *for the students* which personality theory is best," Norma replied.

Melanie laughed. "Dr. Damrosch can decide, though. He makes up the final exam!"

Norma shook her head in disagreement. "No, Damrosch only decides which is the correct answer on the final—not which theory or theories the students will believe in after the semester is over. Piaget said again and again, 'The student is the teacher.' All we can do, really, is present the students with information. It's up to them to decide what to make of the information."

"Yeah," Abe said. "Students learn early in the game to give profs the 'right' answer on an exam, not the answer the students actually think is right."

"So, what do we do?" Fred asked.

Norma smiled. "Each of us will lecture for 10 minutes about our favorite theory."

"Who goes first?" Melanie asked.

"We'll draw straws," Norma responded. "And after we talk, we'll give the students a pop quiz."

"A quiz?" Marty said, surprised. "I thought we weren't going to ask them which theory was best?"

"We aren't," Norma said. "We'll ask them just two questions. The first will be, 'List the strengths of each theory.'"

"And the weaknesses," Melanie said.

Fred shook his head. "No, just the strengths. When we start hacking away at each other's weaknesses, we become emotional and get into trouble."

"Right," Norma said. "But the real clincher will be the second question."

"Which is?" Abe asked.

"Which is, 'What theory or theories would you like to learn more about?'" Norma replied.

Fred nodded. "Good idea. And we can pass out reading lists with additional references."

"Why do you call that a 'clincher?'" said Melanie.

Norma smiled. "Well, we've only got 10 minutes each. So all we can do is give very brief descriptions of very complex subjects."

"Yeah," Abe said. "Sort of, 'Previews of Coming Attractions.'"

"*If* the students go do the additional reading," Melanie said. "But how will we know?"

"Yes," Fred said. "But how will we score the quiz? Judging from what you've said, Norma, there isn't any one correct answer to your clincher question."

"Oh, but there is—if each of us does a good job of presenting his or her pet theory," Norma replied.

"What do you mean?" Abe asked.

"Well, Abe, wouldn't you be disappointed if most of the students didn't want to find out more about humanistic psychology?"

Abe nodded. "Sure I would. The students would be missing a rich and fulfilling experience if they didn't want to learn more about it."

"And you, Fred, wouldn't you be upset if the students weren't turned on by what you said about Skinner and behaviorism?"

Fred nodded. "Of course. Operant technology offers solutions to so many human problems, I'd feel the students were denying themselves a lot if they didn't want to read more about it."

"And you, Melanie. Don't you think the students should find out more about Freud and psychoanalysis than you can tell them in 10 minutes?"

"Freud still dominates personality theory," Melanie responded. "So they'd be silly if they didn't want to learn more about his insights."

Norma smiled. "I feel the same way about social learning theory. So, you see, there's just one correct answer when we ask the students which theory they'd like to learn more about."

"Which is?"

"All of them," Norma said. "Every single one of them."

Recommended Readings

Cantor, N. & Kihlstrom, J.F. (1981). Cognitive and social processes in personality: Implications for behavior therapy. In C.M. Franks and G.T. Wilson (Eds.). *Handbook of behavior therapy*. New York: Guilford Press.

Erikson, E.H. (1982). *The life cycle completed: A review*. New York: Norton.

Poon, L.W., Fozard, J.L., Cermak, L.S., Arenberg, D., and Thompson, L.W. (Eds.). (1980). *New directions in memory and aging: Proceedings of the George A. Talland Memorial Conference*. Hillsdale, N.J.: Erlbaum.

Shneidman, E.S. (1981). *Endeavors in psychology: Selections from the personology of Henry A. Murray*. New York: Harper & Row.

Did You Know That...

- According to an ancient Greek scholar named Galen, people with nasty tempers are strongly influenced by their livers?

- Harvard psychologist W.H. Sheldon said your personality was determined primarily by the shape of your body?

- British scientist Sir Francis Galton argued that "dumb" people shouldn't be allowed to have children?

- The first real intelligence test measured "mental age," and was developed by two French scientists?

- Intelligence tests predict academic performance reasonably well, but don't do a very good job of predicting success in later life?

- Raymond Cattell believes you have both "fluid" intelligence and "crystallized" intelligence?

- Several psychologists have shown that you can sometimes raise your own IQ score by taking special training?

- Studies show that racial differences on intelligence tests are due primarily to cultural backgrounds and test bias rather than to genes?

- Hermann Rorschach believed you would "project your personality" onto vague stimuli such as inkblots?

20

Individual Differences: Measurement and Meaning

"Measure for Measure"

"What is this 'Late Bloomer' test of yours, Mr. Flagg? I don't think I've ever heard of it," Jessie Williams said quietly. Tom Flagg had an athlete's physique, a handsome dark-brown face, and a ready smile. But Jessie had learned the hard way that she couldn't always tell the shape of a man's intentions from the shape of his physique. So she was wary of this young graduate student who had just walked into her fourth-grade school room. But she was also quite taken by his appearance.

"The 'Late Bloomer' test was devised by Professor Rosenthal at Harvard," Tom Flagg replied, hoping (for several reasons) to overcome the good-looking young black woman's obvious distrust. "You've been teaching fourth grade for several years, haven't you, Miss Williams?"

"Three years, Mr. Flagg. Exactly three years."

Tom grinned at the woman's precise way of expressing herself. "Well, maybe you've had a kid who seemed real dumb the first few months or so of school. Then, all of a sudden, the kid just took off and bloomed. Like a flower you'd forgotten to water until just then."

"I water all my flowers regularly, Mr. Flagg," Jessie replied. "I don't neglect any of them. Black or white, red or yellow—I hope they all bloom for me as much as they can."

Tom nodded appreciatively. If it wouldn't have prejudiced the results of his experiment, he would have tried to date her. He pulled himself together and resumed the conversation. "Mr. Washington, your principal, told me you were one of the best teachers he's ever seen. So I'm sure all your kids do learn a lot. But aren't you occasionally surprised when one of them does a lot better than you had expected?"

Jessie Williams shook her head. "I expect great things of them all. Maybe that's why I'm not surprised when they do well."

"Okay," said Tom, "I guess my test won't help you any. But maybe you can help *me* by letting me give it to your class anyhow. If I don't get to try out the test in enough classrooms, I won't get a good grade on my project back at the university. Even if you don't need the information, I do."

To his surprise, Jessie smiled broadly. "Well, why didn't you say so, friend? I'm always happy to help one of us get ahead. Tell me about these 'Late Bloomers' of Professor Rosenthal's."

"Well, it's really your bloomers I'm interested in," Tom said, and then blushed furiously as he realized what he had said. "I mean, it's a test devised by Professor Rosenthal and his associates at Harvard. They think they've found a way of telling in advance when a school kid is going to show a sudden spurt in intellectual achievement. Rosenthal says the test can also tell when a kid is going to backslide or tread water for a while. The change usually shows up in the kid's grades, although sometimes the IQ blossoms or backslides too."

"Some of our education books say that a child's intelligence is fixed at birth. Don't you believe that's so, Tom?" Jessie asked, a malicious twinkle in her eye.

Tom looked startled. "Well, I suppose that the limits to a person's mind are determined by the genes. But the rate at which people develop intellectually sure varies a lot. And the IQ you get depends as much on which test you take, who gives it, and how you feel when you take it as it does on how bright you really are. Have

you ever given any of your kids intelligence tests?"

"No, Tom. I'm not qualified to do that. I give achievement tests, but the school counselor tests their intelligence."

"But aren't you sometimes surprised at the scores the counselor reports on your kids?"

Jessie Williams smiled slyly. "I just don't pay them any mind."

"What do you do when the parents want to know what the kid's IQ is?"

"I tell them the story of my life, Tom," she said. "I was born in Mississippi, where my father was a tenant farmer. We moved North when I was 6. My first year in school they gave me a test and said my IQ was 87. As you know, that's what you might call 'dull normal.' You just don't learn very much about the world on a tenant farm in the back woods of Mississippi. But I loved school, and I had good teachers, and when I was in the seventh grade, I took another test. This time I got a score of 98. The counselor couldn't understand the change. So he gave me a different test, and I scored 104. He asked me what I wanted to do, and I said go to college and learn how to teach. He told me to forget it, that I'd never make it."

"But you did," Tom said, smiling to reassure her.

"Yes, I did," she said, a strong tone of confidence in her voice. "In high school they gave me another test. This time I tried very hard to impress the woman giving me the test, and I got a score of 111."

"The 'halo effect,' probably," Tom responded. "Good-

looking, eager children always score a little higher than uglies do because the tester gives them the benefit of the doubt. And I suspect you were very good looking indeed."

"You needn't flatter me, friend. I've already agreed to help you with your study. Anyway, the counselor said I might just get through college if I worked very hard, although you're supposed to have an IQ of 120 to graduate."

"So you went to the university and got your degree anyhow?"

"No, Tom, it wasn't that easy. My high-school grades were excellent but I didn't score too well on the college entrance examination. The university didn't want me. So I went to a community college for two years. I got all A's, and the university finally let me in. My last year there, I took another IQ test. This time I got a score of 122." She paused for a moment, then laughed. "But, of course, by then I knew the kinds of answers they wanted on the test."

Tom shook his head in amazement. His route to the university had been quite different. "And that's why you don't tell the parents what their kids' IQ scores are?"

"Right on. Now suppose you tell me what your study is all about."

"Okay," he said. "I'll give the Rosenthal 'Late Bloomer' test to all the kids in your room. When I've scored the results, I'll tell you which kids are supposed to 'bloom,' and which kids are supposed to backslide. Then, six months from now, I'll come back and see if that's what really happened."

A suspicious look crept into Jessie's eyes. "Why are you doing this, Tom? Doesn't sound much like an experiment to me."

"Rosenthal validated the test mostly in white classrooms. I want to see if it predicts for integrated classes as well."

"And you'll come back in six months to see what happened?"

Tom Flagg squared his shoulders a bit. "Well, your class is so important to me, I might just drop around a little more often than that—just to see how things are going."

She favored him with a broad grin. "You do that, Thomas. You do that very thing."

(Continued on page 566.)

Static Personality Theory

At the beginning of the last chapter, we noted that there are two major approaches to the study of personality—*traditional personality theory* and *personology*. As we noted, there are two main types of "traditionalists": (1) dynamic theorists (such as Freud), and (2) "static" theorists, who tend to be interested in human traits.

Dynamic theorists are primarily interested in the *process* by which your personality "grew and developed." That is, they tend to see your personality as a "functioning whole" that started out simple and matured over time into a complex system. In this regard, dynamic theorists are much like those biologists who study the development of a single egg cell as it grows into a much more complicated adult organism.

Static theorists typically are more interested in the *structure* of your personality. That is, they often focus on the basic elements of personality—the *traits* or *dispositions*—that are common to all people. In this regard, static theorists are much like those biologists who study the anatomy of adult organisms. For instance, your body has a limited number of organs—one heart, one liver, two kidneys, and so forth. If we know something about each of these organs—and how they interact with each other—we can explain a great deal about how and why your body functions as it does. In similar fashion, if we knew the basic *structures* that make up your personality—and how these structures interact with each other—couldn't we explain most of what you think and feel and do?

We discussed dynamic theories in the last chapter. Now it's time to see what static theorists have to offer in the way of understanding human behavior.

Temperaments, Types, and Traits

What are the basic structures of your personality? As you might guess from having read the previous chapter, there is little agreement among "static" theorists as to what the important elements of personality actually are. The three major approaches, however, seem to be *temperaments*, *types*, and *traits*.

In the *Encyclopedia of Human Behavior*, R.M. Goldenson defines *temperament* as "A general term for emotional make-up, including characteristic energy level, moods and mood changes, intensity and tempo of reactions to people and situations." If you believe that "moods" and "emotions" and "reactivity" are the basic structures of human personality, then probably you lean toward the "temperament" position.

On the other hand, you may prefer to "type" people rather than discuss their moods and tempers. For instance, aren't fat people usually "jolly types"? And don't tall, skinny people tend to be shy and intellectual? And aren't most of the muscular "jocks" rather aggressive and outgoing? If you see a connection between *body type* and *personality type*, then you are a "typologist."

More likely, you may perceive the human personality as a "collection of traits." That is, you might tend to describe people in terms of their characteristic ways of responding to situations. Aren't some people bright, while others are less intelligent? Don't some individuals strike you as being warm, enthusiastic, and accepting—while others seem cold, aloof, and critical? If you talk about people in these terms, you probably qualify as a "trait theorist."

Of these three "structural" approaches to describing personality, the study of tempera-

Galen

ments is probably the oldest. However, typologies and trait descriptions have been around for almost as long a time. Suppose we begin our study of static theories, then, by looking briefly at some of the older approaches. Then we will discuss trait theory in some detail. For of the three, the identification and measure of human traits is surely the dominant structural approach today.

Galen's "Four Temperaments"

Galen was one of the greatest medical doctors the world has known. Although he was born and educated in Greece a century or so after the death of Christ, Galen spent much of his adult life practicing medicine in Rome. His studies of the functioning of human and animal bodies were so excellent that he is often considered the father of modern physiology.

One of Galen's main interests was the various glands in the human body, and the chemicals these glands secreted. Like most other physicians 2,000 years ago, Galen called these glandular secretions the **humors** of the body. Galen stated that four of these humors were mainly responsible for creating four different types of *temperaments*. Galen believed that these "four temperaments" were the basic structures of the human personality.

As far as Galen was concerned, blood was a "humor." If a woman was most influenced by her blood, Galen called her a **sanguine** or "bloody" person. People with sanguine temperaments were supposed to be cheerful, hearty, outgoing, sturdy, fearless, optimistic, and interested in physical pleasures.

The second humor was *phlegm*, the thick, white material that you sometimes cough up when you have a cold. From Galen's point of view, phlegm was cold, moist, and unmoving. If

your bodily processes were dominated by too much production of phlegm, you had a **phlegmatic** temperament. That is, you were cold, aloof, calm, detached, unemotional, uninvolved, quiet, withdrawn, dependable, and perhaps just a trifle dull.

Galen believed that the human liver produced two different "humors"—yellow bile and black bile. He called the yellow bile *choler*, because it supposedly caused the disease we now refer to as "cholera." The **choleric** temperament was one easily given to anger, hate, and fits of temper—someone who gave in to most of his or her bad impulses.

Black bile was even worse, for it symbolized death in Galen's mind. If your personality was dominated by black bile, you had a **melancholic** temperament. That is, you were always depressed, unhappy, suicidal.

To Galen, *your biochemistry determined your temperament*, and your temperament determined your personality. It is unclear from Galen's writings whether he thought you had to be entirely one type or the other, or whether you could be a mixture of the four.

As "humorous" as Galen's theory may seem to you, it still lives on today. One of the dominant psychiatric beliefs about mental illness is that abnormal *behavior* is almost always caused by some abnormal *chemical imbalance*. Thus, a great many psychiatrists today treat mental illness just as Galen tried to—by giving patients pills that will change their inner chemicals and hence presumably will "cure" their unusual thoughts and behaviors.

Sheldon's Theory of Body Types

The belief that people with certain types of *body structure* are predisposed to have specific *personality structures* has been around a long time. For instance, in one of his most famous plays, William Shakespeare has Julius Caesar say, "Let me have men about that are fat; sleek-headed men and such as sleep o'nights. Yon Cassius has a lean and hungry look; he thinks too much; such men are dangerous." But while the common-sense belief that "body type determines personality" goes back many centuries, only in recent days have scientists offered *experimental* proof this might be the case.

One of the best known of the "typologists" was William H. Sheldon, a psychiatrist who worked at Harvard, Columbia, and the University of Chicago. Sheldon thought that the type of "constitution" (or physical makeup) you were born with *determined* the type of personality you ended up with.

In his book *The Varieties of Temperament*, Sheldon writes, "How shall we observe men, classify them, and measure them? . . . In this book we present a system for treating the problem of individual differences in terms of what appear to be basic components of temperament. These components in turn are tied back to and interpreted in terms of basic components of **morphology**."

By *morphology*, Sheldom meant "body type." And according to his theory, there are three major "morphologies":

1. The **endomorphs**, who have soft, rounded bodies and big stomachs.
2. The **mesomorphs**, who have hard, square, bony bodies with over-developed muscles.
3. The **ectomorphs**, who have tall, thin bodies with over-developed heads.

Sheldon took these terms from reproductive biology. As you may recall from Chapter 17, shortly after a child is conceived, the growing mass of cells develops three distinct layers. The central layer, called the *endoderm* or "inner skin," develops into the digestive system and internal organs. The middle layer—the *mesoderm* or "middle skin"—turns into bone and muscles. The outer layer, or *ectoderm*, becomes the central nervous system. According to Sheldon, your genetic blueprint usually causes one of these three layers to predominate—that is, to develop more rapidly and fully than the other two:

1. If your endoderm becomes dominant, your "gut" determines both your body type and your personality. You develop a roly-poly body and fixate on food. And, like other *endomorphs*, you become very social, enjoy relaxing and lazing about, you talk a lot, and you prefer the "sweet life" of physical comfort.
2. If your mesoderm gains the upper hand during your fetal development, your muscles dominate. You will have a square, heavy, *mesomorphic* body. And you will like sports, power, be energetic and assertive, courageous and sanguine.
3. If your ectoderm comes out on top, your brain will predominate and your body will develop long, thin legs and arms—and a big head. Like other *ectomorphs*, you will be introverted, inhibited, intellectual, and prefer being alone to being in a crowd.

Humors (HYOU-mors). The Latin word *humor* means "moist, wet, liquid." Galen (GAY-lun) believed your temperament was determined by the fluids secreted by your body. When you were in "good humor," you had good fluids bubbling around inside you.

Sanguine (SAN-gwin). From the Latin word *sanguis*, meaning "blood." Someone who hopes for the best, or is confidently optimistic, is a sanguine person.

Phlegmatic (fleg-MATT-tick). A watery, slow, unemotional person.

Choleric (KAHL-urr-ick, or koh-LAIR-ick). From the Greek word meaning "bile." Someone readily given to anger, or to losing her or his "good humor."

Melancholic (mell-ann-KOLL-ic). The Greek word *melan* means "black." Melanin (MELL-ann-inn) is the pigment in your skin that darkens when you get a suntan. Melan-choler is black bile. A melancholic individual is someone who is perpetually sad, unhappy, depressed.

Morphology (more-FOLL-oh-gee). The Greek word *morph* means "shape" or "form." Morphology is the study of biological forms, shapes, or body types. The word also means the structure or form of something, such as the human body.

Endomorphs, mesomorphs, ectomorphs (EN-doh, MEE-zoh, ECK-toh-morffs). Sheldon's three morphologies, or body types, that presumably determine personality traits.

Criticisms of Sheldon's Theory

In several experimental studies, Sheldon found a high *correlation* between various personality traits and body types. For instance, most of the mesomorphs he looked at seemed to be "extroverts," while most of the brainy ectomorphs tended to be "introverts."

Although Sheldon's findings were confirmed to some extent by other scientists, many questions have been raised about his research. First, because Sheldon believed that heredity played the major role in determining body type, he never looked at the effects of the environment or past experience on either morphology or personality.

Second, Sheldon never could offer any reasonable explanation of *why* or *how* your body type influences your thoughts, feelings, and behaviors.

Whether or not the *structure* of your body determines your personality remains an open question. However, the scientific evidence gathered so far gives little support to the notion that the type of body you have *determines* the structure of your personality.

Question: Can you think of any ways in which your body type *could* influence your personality? (Hint: What sorts of things do fat people typically find rewarding? Are these "rewards" learned, or inherited?)

Francis Galton

Trait Theory

According to *Webster's Third New International Dictionary*, the English word *trait* comes from a Latin term meaning "a brush stroke." The dictionary gives the current meaning of *trait* as "a distinguishing quality or feature, as of personal character."

Trait theory is much more popular these days than are typologies and theories of human temperament. The major reason for this popularity is perhaps obvious. Think of all the different people in the world. How can you hope to describe all of the complexities of 4 billion personalities in terms of just three body types or four temperaments? Trait theory has supplanted typologies because you can dream up as many different traits as your imagination can conceive of. Indeed, some theorists believe there may be as many as 20,000 traits.

Writing in the February 1983 *American Psychologist*, Fordham psychologist Anne Anastasi states that "trait theories . . . arose out of inquiries into the nature of intelligence." By this statement, Anastasi means that *modern* trait theory got its start about a century ago, when Sir Francis Galton tried to create the first intelligence test. So, we will begin with a discussion of Galton's work, then look briefly at more recent examples of trait theory.

Sir Francis Galton

Modern-day trait theory is a direct descendant of Charles Darwin's theory of evolution. Given that fact, perhaps it's not surprising that one of the first people to interest himself in measuring human traits was Francis Galton, who was Darwin's cousin. Darwin had said that evolution was a matter of "the survival of the fittest." In Galton's view, "fittest" meant "intel-

lectually gifted." He assumed that intellectual differences were due primarily to inheritance, not to training. Thus, the best way for the human race to survive, Galton said, was to encourage "gifted people" to have more children, and to discourage (or even prevent) "people of inferior intelligence" from reproducing. He called his approach **eugenics**, or "the science of improving the human race."

Galton's first problem was that of identifying those psychological traits that were somehow *correlated* with "superiority." His second problem was that of finding ways to *measure* these traits. By the time he had solved both of these difficulties to his satisfaction, he had

1. devised the first intelligence test
2. made the first scientific study of individual differences
3. proven that childhood experiences have an effect on adult thinking
4. developed the first psychological questionnaire
5. undertaken the first behavioral study of human twins
6. helped establish the use of fingerprints to identify people
7. made the first use of statistical correlations in a psychological study
8. written the first book on eugenics
9. measured the sensory and motor capabilities of almost 10,000 people.

Rather an impressive set of accomplishments, even for a man whose IQ was probably about 200. However, Galton's major contribution to trait theory surely came from his detailed studies of individual differences.

Individual Differences and Similarities

Galton published his first book on trait theory in 1869. Called *Hereditary Genius*, it was an attempt to prove that intelligence and creativity tend to "run in families." What Galton actually did, of course, was to show that children are more similar to their parents than they are to a random sample of unrelated individuals. And twins are more like each other than they are to distant cousins. Thus, trait theory—as defined by Galton and most other psychologists—is partially the study of human *similarities*.

But even twins will differ in many ways. If they are both musicians, one twin may have a finer sense of rhythm than does the other. So trait theory also concerns itself with the study of individual *differences*—what they are, and where they come from.

Galton defined traits as *measurable* and *consistent* patterns of human performance and character. And he assumed that traits were inherited and thus couldn't be altered to any significant degree. Earlier personality theorists tended to agree that traits were inherited, but defined them in quite different ways. Thus, even trait theorists have their similarities and differences.

Galton believed that once you have acquired a trait, it should last all your life. Galton also believed in the importance of *unconscious processes*. In one of his studies, he tried to give "free associations" to various words, and timed how long it took him to do so. He discovered that many of his associations came from his younger years. This finding suggested to him that childhood experiences—experiences he was normally unconscious of—had a large influence on his thinking as an adult. To Galton, then, your past is the major determinant of your present and future.

We will have more to say about Galton's studies of intelligence in a moment. First, let's look at how later theorists reacted to his position.

Question: What similarities and differences do you see between Galton's "free associations" and Freud's "technique of free association"?

Allport's Theory of Traits

Harvard psychologist Gordon Allport disagreed with Galton's position. Allport believed

Eugenics (you-JEN-icks). From the Greek words meaning "good genes." Literally, the scientific study of the hereditary characteristics of various races.

that the most important traits might be those that look to the future rather than to the past. Like many other humanistic psychologists, Allport saw people as being motivated primarily by the desire to *become*—that is, to change and grow. Allport believed that *conscious* desires control behavior more than do unconscious wishes or instincts. He also said that your values, hopes, goals, and aspirations were more reliable predictors of future experiences than were "mental associations" and the sorts of motor skills that Galton measured in his subjects. For Allport, the important traits were those that *motivated* you. For these tendencies not only provided the structure of your present personality, they guided your future as well.

Individual and Common Traits

Allport identified several classes of traits. To begin with, he pointed out the difference between *individual* and *common* traits. No two people are exactly alike. Therefore, all traits are individual and unique. But because all humans have similar genetic heritages, and because our cultures are all fairly similar, our behavior patterns are roughly comparable. All blonds are different, for example, because they are unique individuals. But they do all have light-colored hair. Thus we can talk about "blondness" as long as we remember that the differences among blonds are as important as their similarities.

Cardinal, Central, and Secondary Traits

Within a given individual, Allport said, there are *cardinal*, *central*, and *secondary* traits. If you had just one goal in life—perhaps to become president, or to help sick people get well—that would be a "cardinal" trait. According to Allport, however, few people are motivated just by a single cardinal trait.

More common are "central" traits—those few, important values or interest patterns that seem to color almost everything you do. Allport believed that most people have between two and ten central traits. For instance, the noted science fiction writer, H.G. Wells, once said that there were but two themes (central traits) to his life—his interest in promoting world government, and his preoccupation with sex.

Gordon Allport   **Raymond Cattell**

According to Allport, cardinal and central traits determine your major motives in life, and thus indicate the sort of person you will *become*. "Secondary" traits are those incidental, learned responses that differ markedly from one person to another—such as a preference for Chinese food, or a strong dislike of crowds.

Criticisms of Allport's Approach

Although Allport has had a great influence on modern trait theory, his approach has often been criticized. The first—and perhaps most important—problem with his theory is that of *consistency*. Presumably, if you have a trait, it should express itself most of the time. That is to say, the trait should be relatively *independent* of the environment in which the trait is ex-

pressed. Allport handles this criticism by noting that traits predict "typical" behavior patterns, not what you will do in extreme conditions or unusual situations. The fact remains, however, that Allport (like Galton) *neglected the importance of the environment* in determining thoughts and behaviors.

A second criticism of Allport's approach has to do with the *number* of traits that are needed to explain human behavior. Allport believed there were as many as 5,000 traits. Current estimates run as high as 20,000. If the goal of personality theory is to describe people in fairly simple terms, how can we possibly deal with a list of 20,000 traits? One solution to this problem has been offered by Raymond Cattell.

Cattell's Factor Analytic Approach

Raymond Cattell reduced the thousands of traits that Allport had listed to a mere 16. He did this by using a complex statistical technique called **factor analysis**—and by making certain assumptions about human behavior.

Surface Traits and Source Traits

Cattell's first assumption was that there are just a few "common factors" underlying all the traits other scientists had described. And his research soon suggested that many of the traits *clustered together*. From observing people, and from looking at the results of tests he gave his subjects, Cattell identified about 35 of these

---

TABLE 20.1.   The Sixteen Factors of Personality

1. Schizothymia (aloof, cold) vs. Cyclothymia (warm, sociable)
2. Dull (low intellectual capacity) vs. Bright (intelligent)
3. Low Ego Strength (emotional, unstable) vs. High Ego Strength (mature, calm)
4. Submissiveness (mild) vs. Dominance (aggressive)
5. Desurgency (glum, silent) vs. Surgency (enthusiastic, talkative)
6. Low Superego Strength (casual, undependable) vs. High Superego Strength (conscientious, persistent)
7. Threctia (timid, shy) vs. Parmia (adventurous, thick-skinned)
8. Harria (tough, realistic) vs. Premsia (sensitive, effeminate)
9. Inner Relaxation (trustful, adaptable) vs. Protension (suspecting, jealous)
10. Praxernia (conventional, practical) vs. Autia (Bohemian, unconcerned)
11. Naivete (simple, awkward) vs. Shrewdness (sophisticated, polished)
12. Confidence (unshakable) vs. Timidity (insecure, anxious)
13. Conservatism (accepting) vs. Radicalism (experimenting, critical)
14. Group Dependence (imitative) vs. Self-Sufficiency (resourceful)
15. Low Integration (lax, unsure) vs. Self-Sentiment Control (controlled, exact)
16. Low Ergic Tension (phlegmatic, composed) vs. High Ergic Tension (tense, excitable)

Source: *Reprinted from Personality Theories: A Comparative Analysis* by S. R. Maddi, by permission of Dorsey Press. Copyright © 1973 by Dorsey Press.

"trait clusters." To Cattell, though, these were mere "surface" expressions of more fundamental personality patterns. Cattell thus called these 35 clusters of related behaviors *surface traits*.

Once he had identified this limited number of "trait clusters," Cattell tried to *factor out* the basic relationships among the surface traits. He ended up with a list of 16 factors that he called *source traits*. To Cattell, these 16 source traits are the dimensions by which everyone's personality structure can be measured.

All 16 of Cattell's source traits are *bi-polar*. Which is to say that each trait has two extremes, such as "warm-cold," "bright-dull," and "relaxed-tense" (see Table 20.1). Cattell then devised a test that he believed would measure each person's location on all 16 of the source-trait scales. Cattell believed that your scores on this test described your "source traits" in objective, measurable terms. But to paint a complete picture of your personality, he needed additional information.

Cattell took his data about human behavior from three sources: (1) from records of people's lives, and from reports by friends and relatives; (2) from asking people what they thought they were like; and (3) from scores on objective tests such as his "16 Personality Factors Test." Only by analyzing all three types of data, Cattell said, could you give a complete description of an individual's personality and hence *predict* what the person would do in the future.

Criticisms of Cattell's Theory

Cattell's is surely the most comprehensive approach to the study of human traits. But his theory suffers from the same difficulties that all trait or type theories suffer from. First, he assumed your thoughts and behaviors are determined almost entirely by the structure of your personality. However, as we noted earlier, people tend to be more responsive to present environmental inputs than some trait theorists assume is the case.

Second, Cattell relied rather heavily on self-reports. But as we will see in future chapters, there is often a great difference between what you *say* your response will be in a given situation and how you *actually behave* when you face that situation in real life. Thus, test scores and interviews often do a very poor job of predicting future responses.

Third, although Cattell said traits are partially learned and partially hereditary, he gave no indication of how traits develop during the early years of life.

Factor analysis. A statistical device that presumably lets you discover the "underlying factors" that account for correlations or other relationships between variables. Your grade point average is highly correlated with the score that you get on an intelligence test. But a high GPA doesn't *cause* a high IQ, or vice versa. Rather, the underlying factor of *intelligence* presumably accounts for both your grades and your IQ. Factor analysis is one way of trying to determine what basic traits account for a variety of related behaviors.

Last, but surely not least, Cattell's list of 16 traits is quite different from lists prepared by other factor analysts. How are we to know which list is best? In truth, there is no way to know.

Given the problems associated with trait theory, why do we bother with it? The answer is simple: We can hardly hope to discuss individual differences meaningfully without having instruments available that *measure* these differences. And most present-day attempts to *measure human performance or personality* are based on some form of trait theory. Thus, almost all psychological tests—including intelligence and aptitude tests—stem from Galton's early efforts. Suppose we look at intelligence tests first, then go on to describing how psychologists measure other aspects of performance and personality.

Measuring Individual Differences

Technically speaking, a trait is a tendency or predisposition to respond to many different stimuli or situations in the same way. If you are kind to almost all the people you meet, then you possess the trait of kindness. If you are good at solving all types of problems, and if you adapt rapidly to all kinds of environmental challenges, then you possess what Cattell called the "source trait" of intelligence.

If we wanted to get an exact *measure* of your kindness, we might dream up a test for this trait—a "kindness scale"—that had 20 questions on it. We could ask things like, "If you saw an injured puppy lying by the side of the road, would you pick it up and take it to the doctor's or just ignore it?" Or, "Do you prefer to pat a person on the back, or kick the person in the seat of the pants?" If the test were a good one, then people who were kind *in real life* would get high scores, while people who were unkind *in real life* would get low test scores. Thus, just by knowing a person's score on the "kindness

Alfred Binet   Lewis Terman

test," you could *predict* the person's behavior in many situations.

Question: What numerical score should the average person get on a 20-point "kindness scale"?

Intelligence Tests

Traits such as kindness can be fairly easily measured—provided we can define the trait, and as long as we recognize that kindness might mean one thing in our culture, but something radically different elsewhere in the world.

But what about *intelligence*? How could we go about defining—and measuring—such a complex variable as this? Indeed, is intelligence really a *trait*? Cattell lists it as one of his 16 "source traits," as do other theorists. But not all psychologists would agree, believing that "intelligence" is a *combination* of a great many innate predispositions and learned behaviors.

Whatever the case, as we noted, trait theory got its start when Galton began searching for a way to measure "intellectual superiority." And the crude "intelligence test" he developed helped get the *mental measurement movement* going. So suppose we now look at length at intelligence tests.

The Binet-Simon Intelligence Test

One of the people most influenced by Galton's work was a Frenchman named **Alfred Binet**. In about 1890, he became interested in the differences between bright and dull children and tried to devise a simple scale that would allow him to distinguish the smart children from those who would have problems in school.

As we noted in Chapter 5, another French scientist named Paul Broca had theorized that *brain size* was related to intelligence, and (at first) Binet believed Broca was right. So Binet initially relied on physical measures—such as the size of the child's head or the pattern of lines on the palm of the child's hand. However, none of these scales correlated very highly with the child's performance in school, so Binet abandoned them. As Binet himself put it, "The idea of measuring intelligence by measuring heads [now seems] ridiculous."

In 1904 the French government asked Binet and a physician named **Théophile Simon** to devise a test that would allow teachers to identify "retarded" children so they could be given special attention in school. Since "measuring heads" hadn't worked, Binet and Simon decided that seeing how well the students performed ordinary tasks might give some indica-

Bead stringing is part of the Stanford-Binet intelligence test.

Fig. 20.1 Drawing of a diamond by a 5-year-old (left) and a 7-year-old (right).

tion of how bright the students were. So Binet and Simon pulled together a large number of rather simple problems that seemed to require different mental skills. Then they tried the test problems out on a large number of French school children of different ages. This technique allowed Binet and Simon to select appropriate test items for each age group. They found, for example, that the average seven-year-old could correctly make a pencil copy of the figure of a diamond, but most five-year-olds could not (see Fig. 20.1).

If a boy of nine got the same score on the test as did the *average* seven-year-old, Binet and Simon presumed that the boy's mental development was retarded by two years. The boy would thus have a "physical age" of nine but a "mental age" of seven. If an eight-year-old girl did as well on the test as the average eleven-year-old, then she had a mental age of eleven, although her physical age was but eight.

Later, psychologists in Germany and in the United States put the relationship between **chronological** (physical) age and mental age into an equation:

$$\frac{\text{Mental age}}{\text{Chronological age}} \times 100 = \text{Intelligence Quotient, or IQ}$$

A girl with a mental age of 6 and a chronological age of 6 would have an IQ of

$$\frac{6}{6} \times 100 = 1 \times 100 = 100 = \text{IQ}$$

By definition, she would be of average intelligence. A boy with a mental age of 7 and a chronological age of 9 would have an IQ of

$$\frac{7}{9} \times 100 = .777 \times 100 = 78 = \text{IQ}$$

A girl with a mental age of 11 and a chronological age of 8 would have an IQ of

$$\frac{11}{8} \times 100 = 1.375 \times 100 = 138 = \text{IQ}$$

The Binet-Simon test did so well at predicting the *academic performance* of school children that intelligence testing became a standard part of educational psychology. However, from the start, Binet was worried about the *misuse* of his test. As Jay Gould points out in his 1981 book *The Mismeasure of Man*, Binet didn't believe that intelligence could be captured by any single number, nor did he think intelligence was primarily inherited. He was afraid that teachers would "rank" their stu-

Alfred Binet (bee-NAY). Binet (1857–1911) was a French psychologist who, with Théophile Simon, developed the first well-known intelligence test.

Théophile Simon (TEY-oh-feel see-MOAN). Simon (1873) was a French physician who became more interested in psychological research than in the practice of medicine. Simon and Binet published their first intelligence test in 1905.

Chronological (kron-oh-LODGE-uh-cull). Chronos (KROH-nos) was the Greek god of time. Your chronological age is the actual number of months and years that you have lived.

dents according to some simple (and incorrect) scheme, and then respond to the rankings, not the students. So Binet refused to rank all the students he tested. He merely wanted to identify "slow students" in order to give them special help.

According to Jay Gould, American psychologists tended to ignore Binet's warnings. For example, the noted Stanford psychologist, L.M. Terman, made up his own version of the French scale early in this century. He called his device the Stanford-Binet intelligence test. It yielded a single number which Terman called the IQ. Other psychologists soon followed Terman's lead, and now there are hundreds of intelligence tests available. When used properly—by people who understand both the strengths and weaknesses of intelligence tests—these measures of individual differences can be of considerable value. As we will see momentarily, however, these tests have been abused almost as often as they have been properly used.

Before we can discuss the pros and cons of psychological testing, however, there is one point we should raise. Most modern intelligence tests don't actually measure "mental age." Instead, they make use of what are called *standard scores*. To understand what a standard score is, though, you first have to know something about what are called *normal distributions* of test scores.

Normal Distributions

Like most other trait psychologists, Binet and Simon were greatly influenced by Darwin's theory of evolution. Darwin had suggested that intelligence is *inherited* in much the same way as are skin color, height, and other physical characteristics. If a man and woman of average height (for their culture) could have 100 male children—so Darwin assumed—most of them would also be of average height. A few would be very tall, a few very short. But most of the boys would be about as tall as their father. If the cou-

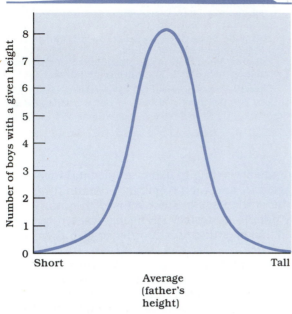

Fig. 20.2 Bell curve showing the height of 100 boys from one family.

Sandra Scarr

ple had 100 girls instead of boys, the girls would show the same *distribution of heights* and would average out much like their mother. If we made a graph of the height of the boys, it presumably would look something like what is shown in Fig. 20.2.

In technical terms, this is called a *normal distribution* of test scores—or a "bell-shaped curve." Many school teachers believe that the scores students make on a history or mathematics examination should "fit the curve," or be "normally distributed." A few students should get A's, a few should get F's, while most should get C's. The teachers then *write examinations that will give them the results they expect.*

Most intelligence tests are based on this same assumption of normal distribution of scores. Binet and Simon juggled their items around until their test yielded a bell-shaped distribution of "mental ages" for each age level. Modern test makers do much the same thing, but they work with "standard scores" instead of mental ages. That is, they *standardize* (or "weight") the actual scores on their test so these numbers will "fit the bell-shaped curve." They then assign IQ's "from the curve" rather than from the raw test scores.

If intelligence were in fact a single trait (like height), and if IQ were *entirely determined by your genetic blueprint*, then such a procedure might be justified. But are these assumptions really valid?

Is Intelligence a Single Trait?

The results of many psychological studies suggest that intelligence is not a single trait. Rather, it is made up of a great many related talents or abilities. Psychologists don't entirely agree what these "related" talents are, but they often mention such things as the ability to memorize words and numbers, to learn motor tasks, to solve verbal and numerical problems, to evaluate complex situations, to be creative, and to perceive spatial relationships. Indeed, in 1967, J.P. Guilford listed 120 "factors of intelligence," each one representing a different intellectual ability!

If intelligence is really a mixture of many different traits, then there is no reason to expect that IQ's should fit a bell-shaped curve. However, most trait theorists continue to believe that intelligence test scores should be normally distributed. The reason for this belief is simple—there seem to be more people of "normal" intelligence in the world than there are "geniuses" and "mentally retarded" individuals. These facts caused Charles Spearman and Raymond Cattell to rethink the concept of intelligence entirely.

Types of Intelligence

To Charles Spearman, the noted British psychologist, there were but two types of intelligence. He noted that, if you took 10 different intelligence tests, you would usually wind up with 10 different scores. True, the scores probably would be *related* to each other. But which one gave your *real* IQ? And why so many different scores?

Spearman decided each test item actually measured two factors. One he called *general* intelligence, or the "g factor." But each item also measured one or more *specific* types of mental ability, which he called the "s factors." Thus different tests yield different scores because each test tends to emphasize "s" or "g" to a different degree. However, the *mix* of "s" and "g" factors for each test could still fit a bell-shaped curve.

Raymond Cattell agrees that there were two "intellectual factors," but disagrees with Spearman on what they were. Cattell says you have *fluid* intelligence and *crystallized* intelligence. Your "fluid" intelligence is inherited, and involves such talents as the ability to think and reason. "Crystallized" intelligence involves learned skills such as being able to add and subtract, and the size of your vocabulary.

According to Cattell, your "fluid" intelligence sets limits on your "crystallized" abilities. If you aren't innately bright, all the training in the world won't help you get through school. However, if you have a high "fluid" intelligence, and you grow up in a deprived and unstimulating environment, you won't acquire many skills. And you won't get a high score on most intelligence tests, either. From Cattell's point of view, if everyone grew up in the best of all possible environments, "fluid" intelligence would be the major determinant of IQ—and test scores then would "fit the curve" almost exactly.

But what constitutes "the best of all possible environments"? Might not it vary from individual to individual? Whatever the case, since we know that many children are reared in unstimulating circumstances, is it ethical to make decisions about their schooling and career opportunities on the basis of IQ? The answer to that question might be "yes" if we believe that intelligence tests primarily measure *innate abilities*. But studies of the effects of early environment on IQ suggest this belief is false.

IQ and Early Deprivation

As we noted earlier, children who are reared in deprived environments often show remarkable improvements in their IQ scores if they are later given the proper intellectual stimulation. One of the first psychologists to make this point was H.M. Skeels. In the 1930's, Skeels shocked many of his colleagues by reporting he had been able to *increase* the IQ's of apparently retarded children by putting them in an unusual environment. Skeels took the children out of a

dreary orphanage and gave them to a group of retarded women to rear. The first children he studied were two little girls, whose IQ's rose from below 50 to near normal. Skeels believed the girls got higher scores because the retarded women gave them *massive stimulation and attention*, which children at the orphanage didn't receive. Skeels was thus one of the first psychologists to suggest that an enriched environment can have a dramatic effect on IQ.

The Minnesota Study

Several recent studies tend to confirm Skeel's findings. Sandra Scarr and Richard Weinberg studied several hundred children in Minnesota who were placed in foster homes. All the children were either black or of mixed racial background. Some of the foster parents were black, but many were white. Most were college graduates with professional jobs or responsibilities.

Scarr and Weinberg estimate that, judging from the adopted children's genetic backgrounds, they might have been expected to end up with IQ's well *below* the national average. Instead, they scored well above average and very close to youngsters brought up in natural homes similar to the ones the orphans were adopted into.

Scarr and Weinberg also report that the younger the child was when adopted, the higher the child's IQ tended to be. Generally speaking, black children adopted into middle-class white homes had higher IQ's than did black children reared in middle-class black homes.

There are at least two important conclusions we can draw from the Scarr and Weinberg study: First, intelligence test scores are strongly influenced by environmental factors. Second, orphans from disadvantaged homes who are reared by well-educated foster parents *of either race* have higher IQ's than they probably would have had if reared by their own parents.

Question: The obvious "control group" for this study would be white orphans reared in black foster homes. Why do you think Scarr and Weinberg were not able to find enough such children to make a meaningful comparison?

Does "Coercive Discipline" Affect IQ?

Sociologist Zena Blau of the University of Houston recently conducted a study of more than a thousand children in Chicago. Half of

Leona Tyler

the youngsters were black, the other half were white. In 1981 Blau reported that IQ's were lowest among children whose mothers have overly strict religious beliefs. Children whose mothers were from a non-denominational or non-religious background had the highest average IQ's—110 for whites, 109 for blacks. Children whose mothers belonged to "fundamentalist" religious groups tended to have IQ's that were 7 to 10 points lower. According to Blau, these religion-IQ differences hold even when you take into account the mother's social class, current occupational status, and education.

Zena Blau believes that environmental factors account for most (if not all) of the IQ differences between black and white children in the US. One of the most important environmental influences on cognitive functioning, she says, is the emphasis the mother places on teaching children "to think for themselves." Mothers with strong religious beliefs tend to use punitive and *coercive* measures to discipline their children. Mothers with non-religious backgrounds, however, are more likely to reward their children for learning self-management skills. Blau concludes, "In a society that is changing so rapidly, where self-control and self-direction are important to an individual's performance, the impact of the high-control religious institutions is adversive to a child's intellectual development."

As you might surmise, not all psychologists agree with Blau's position. Nor are they likely to do so until her work is confirmed by several other investigators. One psychologist who praises Blau, though, is Diana Teresa Slaughter, who is associate professor of education and of African American studies at Northwestern. Writing in the November 1982 issue of *Contemporary Psychology*, Slaughter says of Blau's

research, "This is a fine comprehensive study of the relationship between home environment and school achievement. . . . What is especially important, the study clearly indicates that the home environments of both black and white children are significantly implicated in [the children's] early intellectual development and their school achievements."

Can You Raise Your Own IQ?

Most intelligence tests place rather heavy emphasis on *reasoning*—the ability to work your way through a complicated mental task step by step. Cattell, Galton, and most other trait psychologists assume that "reasoning" is an inherited ability. Few psychologists doubt that *some* aspects of intelligence are determined by the genes. But are people poor reasoners because of their genes? Or is some aspect of that trait learned?

Several years ago, Benjamin Bloom and Lois Broder studied how college students with either low or high IQ's react to mental challenges. Bloom and Broder gave these subjects various problems to work on and asked the students to "talk out loud" as they proceeded. High-IQ subjects tended to read the instructions carefully, then diligently eliminated all the incorrect answers. The low-IQ students often skipped over the instructions, and lacked the patience to isolate the correct answers when faced with questions that required formal reasoning. The low scorers didn't seem to carry on an "internal conversation" with themselves, nor did they proceed through a step-by-step sequence of deductions. If the low-IQ students couldn't see the answer immediately, they felt lost and usually guessed.

Bloom and Broder were convinced that the low-scoring students had never acquired the proper cognitive skills. So they developed a training program aimed at helping these young people "learn how to think." First, they made the low scorers *read the instructions aloud.* Many of the students showed immediate improvement, because they were forced to pay attention to what was required of them. Next the students were asked to solve various problems *aloud.* After Bloom and Broder had discussed the student's solution with the student, the experimenters read the correct solution aloud. Then they asked the student to explain what had gone wrong, if the student had been incorrect. The students had many difficulties at first, and the instructors had to show tremendous patience. But once the students began to recognize that they actually could learn how to reason, they did so with increasing frequency. Although Bloom and Broder did not retest the students' IQ's after this training, the psychologists report most of their subjects got much higher grades in college thereafter.

California psychologist Arthur Whimbey has spent considerable time attempting to help people raise their IQ's. He points out that learning how to reason requires immediate positive feedback and much practice. If you wish to improve your own test performance, Whimbey says, you should work with a trained tutor, and you should use old tests and puzzle books as practice tools. You should think "out loud" as you work, listen to what you say, and try to figure out how you got the incorrect answer if you are wrong. Whimbey notes that following these techniques won't turn you into a genius. But he reports that many of the people he has worked with have increased their test scores by 20 or 30 points.

Reliability and Validity of Intelligence Tests

A psychologist who makes up a "measurement scale" of any kind has to prove two things to other scientists before they will accept the scale and use it themselves. First, the creator of the test must show that it is *reliable*. Second, the psychologist must provide evidence that the test is also *valid*.

At its simplest, the term "reliability" merely means that a test will yield the same results no matter how frequently you give it. However, Leona Tyler states that—when applied to instruments such as intelligence tests—reliability really means "accuracy." That is, a test is "reliable" if the results it yields are free from *chance effects*.

At its simplest, the term "validity" means that the test measures what it says it does. However, Leona Tyler also notes that modern psychologists take a more complex view of the term. To Tyler, you cannot judge the validity of a test unless you know all of the current research showing just what a test does and does not measure. Determining the validity of a psychological scale, therefore, is both a complicated and continuing undertaking.

With these definitions in mind, let's examine both the reliability and the validity of intelligence tests.

Construct validity (KON-struct). A test has construct validity if it yields the same sorts of scores or predictions that another test yields.

Are Intelligence Tests Reliable?

If intelligence were *absolutely fixed* at birth, psychologists would probably have little trouble making up tests that were highly reliable. However, intelligence tests measure *your present level of functioning*, not the underlying factor that Cattell calls "fluid intelligence." Thus, your IQ is always affected by your genes, your past experience, *and* your present situation. If you are unmotivated when you take a test, or if you are worried about something or have a toothache, you probably will do more poorly than if you were "up" for the exam. In similar fashion, if you grew up in a deprived environment, or if you never learned to reason, your test scores won't be as high as they otherwise might have been.

Intelligence tests are much more reliable than are many other psychological scales. And when given under the best of circumstances, they are fairly "accurate" in the sense that Leona Tyler uses that term. However, as we noted, no two intelligence tests will yield identical scores. And even if you take the same test several times, your IQ may vary considerably, depending on how you feel and what you have learned since the last time you took the test. Thus, your IQ *is not a fixed quantity*.

Are Intelligence Tests Valid?

Suppose you dream up a new intelligence test. Once it's created, how could you prove it really was a *valid* measure of intelligence? Well, one thing you might do is to give both *your test* and another *well-known test* to 1,000 or so people chosen at random. If the subjects who got high scores on your test also got high scores on the other instrument—and if the people who got low scores on your test also got low scores on the other test—then your test would have high **construct validity**. Put another way, if the scores on the two scales were highly correlated, that would suggest you had *constructed* your test in a *valid* manner.

But is "construct validity" enough? The mere fact that two psychological scales called "intelligence tests" yield similar scores surely doesn't prove that either test is *actually measuring intelligence*. Thus, you might wish to compare

Robert V. Guthrie

physicians were evaluated by colleagues, patients, nurses, hospital administrators—and gave self-evaluations as well. Taylor reports there was *no correlation* between "goodness" as a practicing physician and either medical school grades or IQ.

A second indication that intelligence tests can be valid *in certain circumstances*, Leona Tyler notes, is this fact: IQ's often predict how well people will do in various occupational *levels*. That is, if you have an IQ of 85, you probably will do better in an unskilled or semi-skilled job than you would trying to become a nuclear physicist. However, IQ's don't predict the success that people *within* a given occupation will have.

These data suggest that IQ can be a fairly reliable indicator of what sorts of special training people will need in school and on the job. Thus, we would be foolish not to employ test scores in those situations where they are known to be useful. The problem comes, however, when we use IQ's to make judgments in situations where they are known *not* to yield valid predictions. And, as we will see, we also can get into trouble when we use IQ's without realizing the various *biases* that are built into the tests.

Question: How high an IQ do you think you'd get on a test given entirely in Chinese?

Cultural and Racial Biases

Built into most intelligence tests is a *cultural bias* that we are not always aware of. Binet and Simon, for instance, took many of their basic ideas on intelligence from Paul Broca, who believed that the size of your brain determined the amount of your intelligence. As we noted in Chapter 5, Broca performed some very inexact measurements on brain size and incorrectly concluded that men were brighter than women and that whites were smarter than blacks.

Most modern psychologists reject Broca's notions about the superior mental abilities of males and whites. However, a few scientists do still cling to the belief in racial differences. In 1969, Arthur Jensen published an article in the *Harvard Educational Review* entitled "How much can we boost IQ and scholastic achievement?" In this paper—and in many books and articles he has published subsequently—Jensen claims that blacks are genetically inferior to whites as far as intelligence goes. Jensen's writings have, to say the least, created a

scores on your test with several real-world variables. For instance, we presume you need intelligence to succeed both in school and afterwards. Suppose that the subjects who got high scores on your test also got the best grades in school and showed the most achievement after graduating. This *correlation* between test scores and real-life performance would suggest your instrument had **empirical validity**.

Test builders usually offer their own *carefully limited* definition of what they think intelligence is, and then show that their particular test is valid within those limits. For instance, Binet and Simon assumed that "intelligence" was whatever mental properties were needed to succeed in French schools. Children who scored high on their tests generally got good grades—and were rated as being intelligent by their teachers. Students who scored lower on the Binet-Simon test got lower school grades—and were rated as being less intelligent by their teachers. Binet and Simon then used the correlations between test scores, teacher ratings, and grades to *validate* their intelligence test. And within the limits of their definition, Binet and Simon were correct.

Under certain circumstances, then, intelligence tests do yield "valid" results. First of all, there is a very high correlation between IQ and school grades. Thus, we can use intelligence test scores to predict which children will do well in school, and which children will probably get low grades. However, the tests do *not* predict academic performance very well when low scorers are given the kind of "special training" developed by Bloom and Bruder or by Whimbey. Nor are the tests accurate predictors of success in later life. In 1982, Utah psychologist Calvin W. Taylor and his colleagues studied more than 150 medical doctors presently in practice. The

storm of controversy. Let's look at the evidence that Jensen cites, then at the counter-claims.

Jensen begins by quoting a national survey of 81 different studies of black-white IQ's. According to this survey, blacks tend to average about 15 IQ points lower than do whites on standardized intelligence tests. Blacks also score somewhat below other disadvantaged minority groups. Jensen also claims that blacks from "upper-status" homes tend to obtain significantly lower test scores than do whites reared in similar circumstances. And in an attempt to prove these differences are not merely due to "cultural factors," Jensen makes two further points. First, blacks tend to do even worse on so-called "culture free" intelligence tests than do whites. Second, blacks tends to average 7–8 IQ points below American Indians. And, according to Jensen, American Indians who live on reservations have cultural environments that are typically rated as being far below the environments most blacks are reared in.

Had we not already pointed out that intelligence tests have a built-in bias toward certain cultural values, Jensen's points might deserve serious consideration. However, as Robert V. Guthrie points out in his book *Even the Rat Was White*, the psychologists who constructed most of the widely used intelligence tests were almost all middle-class white males. And most of them shared Jensen's view that intelligence is *primarily an inherited trait*. Thus, if blacks did poorly on standard intelligence tests, the test makers *presumed* this difference was due to "bad genes" and not to "bad environments." Guthrie also notes that, until recently, psychologists studying blacks tended to focus on *differences* between the races, not *similarities*. Little wonder, then, that Jensen's views received support from certain scientists (and from certain politicians).

As we have noted many times, *all aspects* of your personality (including your IQ) are determined by the interactions among your genes, your past experiences, and your present environment. Comparing blacks with whites (or any other group of people) is valid *only when the groups have similar past experiences and present social environments*. Many studies indicate that blacks who move from culturally deprived to more stimulating circumstances show a marked increase in IQ. So do whites, Indians, Koreans, and people of all other nationalities and races. Blacks reared in culturally advantaged environments have higher IQ's than do whites brought up in poor circum-

stances. Thus, intelligence tests, as presently written, probably tend to *underestimate* the innate potential of blacks—and of all other socially deprived groups, including many whites.

The Boston Study

In 1979, Regina Yando, Victoria Seitz, and Edward Zigler reported a study they had made of 304 children in the Boston area. All the subjects were eight years old when the study was made. Half the children came from upper-class homes, half from lower-class homes. Half the children from each class of home were black, and half from each class were white. The children in each of these four groups were carefully matched for IQ. The psychologists gave each child tests that measured such traits as creativity, self-confidence, autonomy, curiosity, frustration threshold, and dependency.

The results of the Boston study were, in many ways, fairly surprising. To begin with, Yando and her colleagues note that almost all of the differences between black and white children could be accounted for in terms of *social class*. Upper-class children—black or white—were very similar. So were lower-class children. However, disadvantaged children (of either race) were more creative in solving problems, and they were more likely to take risks and persevere at tasks despite frustration. Advantaged children had larger vocabularies and were better at step-by-step reasoning, but were anxious and overly concerned about failure. Disadvantaged black children attending predominantly white schools tended to suffer a loss in self-confidence, but did better academically than their peers in predominantly black schools.

Yando, Seitz, and Zigler also asked the children's teachers to rate each of the subjects. Teacher ratings did, in fact, predict academic skills. However, the psychologists note that these ratings might well have been due to "halo" effects. Thus, the fact that disadvantaged children failed to learn some cognitive skills in school might be due to the bias that the teachers showed against youngsters from lower-class homes.

Empirical validity (em-PEER-ih-kal). Two tests may yield the same sorts of scores or predictions, and thus have high construct validity because they agree. But to have high empirical validity, the tests must also predict real-world behaviors or accomplishments.

Early stimulation helps a child develop its intellectual potential.

Uses and Misuses of Intelligence Tests

As the Boston study suggests, early experience has a strong effect on functional intelligence. Thus, the *performance differences* that Jensen notes between blacks and whites on these tests probably reflect class differences rather than racial differences. Therefore, any time we make decisions about people based solely on their IQ's, we are likely to misuse the data the test gives us. For example, from about 1930 to 1980, the state of Virginia used IQ's to identify "feebleminded" individuals in state institutions. The 7,500 people so identified were then forcibly sterilized, "to prevent them from breeding."

Fortunately, most of the more blatant misuses of intelligence tests have now been halted, both by acts of law and by action of the American Psychological Association. For instance, in October 1979, Federal Judge Robert Peckham prohibited the State of California from using intelligence tests to place children with low IQ's in "classes for the mentally-retarded." Reviewing all the evidence to that date, Judge Peckham concluded that intelligence tests were culturally biased against minority children. Thus, said Peckham, these tests cannot be used to estimate some **hypothetical** "innate ability," such as "general intelligence."

Most psychologists agree with Judge Peckham's decision to ban the use of IQ's in "segregating" children in schools. Writing in the October 1981 issue of *American Psychologist*, Robert Glaser and Lloyd Bond note that "long-standing practices that were generated in the context of older social institutions have been justly criticized. . . . This criticism has stimulated changes that were both necessary and long overdue." But Glaser and Bond go on to state that "unfortunately, [the criticism] has also inevitably discouraged the use of tests in situations where they could be beneficial."

When can the use of test scores be beneficial? The entire October 1981 issue of *American Psychologist* is devoted to answering this and other questions related to mental measurement. D.J. Reschly points out that schools still need some method of identifying those children who need special help, and that subjective impressions are even more biased than are mental tests. Lynn H. Fox notes that tests are the best way known to identify gifted students from disadvantaged backgrounds. And Frank Schmidt and John Hunter report that IQ's are valid predictors of on-the-job performance. Schmidt and Hunter state that the best of these tests "are equally valid for minority and majority applicants and are fair to minority applicants in that they do not underestimate the expected job performance of minority groups."

Thus, intelligence tests do have a place in our society, and it would be foolish not to use them when they are valid, reliable, and do not discriminate against any group of people. However, we must be careful in what conclusions we draw from intelligence test data. In a 1977 paper, Leona Tyler notes that we cannot presently determine what aspects of intelligence are affected by our genetic blueprints, and which aspects are affected primarily by factors such as the environment. Therefore, comparisons of the IQ's of different races tell us nothing at all about such matters as racial superiority or inferiority. She also states that scientists who study such sensitive problems as racial differences have a special responsibility—to take into consideration the social consequences of their research.

Intelligence: A Holistic Viewpoint

In her 1983 article mentioned earlier, Anne Anastasi takes a holistic view toward what intelligence really is, and how we might measure it better. She says that such factors as cognitive skills, knowledge, motivation, and attitudes are all an integral part of what we call *intelligence*. A valid intelligence test would measure all these factors. To date, Anastasi notes, no such test exists. But as we free ourselves from our earlier, rigid beliefs that intelligence is made up of "g" factors and other traits determined primarily by the genes, Anastasi says, we will come closer to creating an adequate measure of intellectual performance.

Objective versus Subjective Tests

Although intelligence tests have received most of the publicity in recent years, there are many other types of psychological scales that attempt to measure traits or some other aspect of human performance or personality. Some of these tests are *objective,* in that they yield numbers that describe how much of a given trait you possess. Others tests are *subjective,* in that an expert must "analyze" your responses and then give a subjective evaluation of what the responses mean. (In the academic world, a multiple-choice test is usually "objective," while an essay exam is usually "subjective.")

Both types of test have been used for years in the study of human personality. Let's look at both kinds, then discuss the problems and benefits associated with using them.

Subjective Tests

Suppose that, because you were impressed with Freud's psychoanalytic theory of personality, you wanted to devise a means of getting at the *unconscious* aspects of a person's mind. You could hardly ask the person about such matters directly—using a pen-and-paper test—because (by definition) the person isn't aware of unconscious processes. But what would happen if you presented the subject with a variety of unstructured or *ambiguous* situations? Wouldn't you expect people to *project* themselves into the task given them? That is, shouldn't people perceive ambiguous stimuli according to their unconscious needs and desires? If they did, then you could easily interpret their responses to these *projective tests* according to psychoanalytic (or any other) principles.

Projective tests are among the most widely used subjective scales. So let's look briefly at several of them.

Word Association Test

The first of these "projective" instruments was a *word association test* devised by Galton

Hypothetical (high-poh-THET-ih-kal). Something is "hypothetical" if you *presume* that it exists. When you "make a hypothesis," you are offering a hypothetical explanation for something.

Thematic Apperception Test (the-MATT-tick app-purr-SEP-shun). A "thema" is a "need-press" combination, or the way that you tend to perceive (or explain) certain environmental/personal interactions. *Apperception* is defined as "the process of perceiving something in terms of your prior experience." The TAT is a set of vague stimulus pictures that you are asked to "tell stories about," presumably because you will perceive or structure the pictures in terms of your own personality. Hence the "themes" of the stories you tell will give the psychologist some clue as to your own "themas," or how you perceive various "need-press" combinations. See Chapter 19.

more than 100 years ago. It was subsequently revised by Carl Jung for psychoanalytic use in the early 1900's. The test consists of a list of highly emotional stimulus words that are presented to you one at a time. You are asked to respond to each word with the first thing that comes to mind.

Both Galton and Jung assumed that if you reacted to a word like "sex" by blocking (refusing to answer)—or if you started sweating, or fainted, or gave a wildly inappropriate reaction such as "firecrackers" or "death"—then you might have sexual problems that a therapist ought to look into. Sometimes the tester will use a polygraph, or lie detector, to check your physical reactions as you respond to the words (see Chapter 12).

The TAT

The **thematic apperception text**, or TAT, was developed by Henry Murray, whose "personology" we discussed in the last chapter. The TAT consists of a set of 20 stimulus pictures that depict rather vague but potentially emotional situations. You respond by making up a story telling (1) what led up to the situation shown in the picture, (2) what the people are thinking and feeling and doing right then, and (3) what will happen to them in the future. Each story you produce is scored and interpreted individually. The psychologist giving the test usually assumes you will express your deep-seated needs (such as "n Aggression") and personality problems by *projecting* them onto the hero or the heroine in the story. The way you describe the situation, of course, is an indication of what your own *themas* (or need-press combinations) actually are.

Inkblot Tests

By far the most famous of the projective instruments is the inkblot test, first devised in the 1920's by Swiss psychiatrist **Hermann Rorschach**. The Rorschach test is a series of 10 inkblots that are given to you one at a time. You look at each inkblot and report what you see—much as you might look at clouds passing overhead and tell someone what "faces" and other things you saw in the clouds. The psychologist then scores and interprets your responses according to one of several scoring methods.

Usefulness of Projective Tests

When used by a sensitive and perceptive psychologist, any one of the projective tests can yield a great deal of information about your personality. However, the bulk of scientific research suggests that most projective tests are neither very reliable nor particularly valid as presently used. In the 1982 edition of their book *Personality Assessment*, Richard Lanyon and Leonard Goodstein review nearly 10,000 studies on projective instruments. As for the Rorschach, they state that "the empirical basis for interpreting this test remains thin." Lanyon and Goodstein go on to say, "Although the volume of literature on the TAT is large . . . its status as a proven, clinical useful instrument is still in doubt."

Although many psychologists still report that projective tests are of considerable value in clinical practice, other scientists reject the notion that you can learn anything important about people by trying to interpret their responses to vague stimuli.

Question: It is sometimes said that Rorschach interpretations tell us more about the person doing the "interpreting" than they do about the person who took the test. Why might this sometimes be the case?

Objective Tests

Objective tests have several purposes. One is to *measure present traits, skills, and knowledge*. Another is to *predict future performance*. A few objective tests attempt to serve both purposes simultaneously.

Achievement Tests

An achievement test is a psychological scale that measures how much you have learned about a given topic. The test does *not* indicate either *why* you learned as much as you did, nor how much you *could have learned* under different circumstances. People with high IQ's will do poorly on achievement tests if they haven't learned much about the topic, or if they once knew the material but now have forgotten it. People with lower IQ's will do well if they have studied the subject thoroughly. Therefore, achievement tests presumably tell us little or nothing about your motivation or your IQ. *At their best*, they simply measure present level of performance.

Academic achievement tests are useful within school systems, but they don't necessarily give us much information about how well people will do after they have left the academic world. For instance, early in 1981 many city officials in Sacramento, California took a 6th grade math achievement test. The mayor missed 20 out of 25 questions, and the best score made by any of the officials was 80 percent correct. However, dozens of 6th grade students in Sacramento got perfect scores. Presumably the city officials once knew the material, but had simply forgotten it over the years.

Aptitude Tests

In its purest form, an aptitude test attempts to determine whether you possess enough of a certain trait—or certain personality factors—in order to succeed in some job or other situation. Some aptitude tests are fairly simple measures of such skills as mechanical or clerical aptitude. Other tests, such as those given to prospective airline pilots, measure a broader range of abilities. Scores on these *simple scales* tend to predict future performance fairly well.

Unfortunately, many devices that are called *aptitude* tests are really combinations of *achievement* and *intelligence* tests. The Scholastic Aptitude Test is one such, for it tends to measure how much you have already learned about a given academic subject and thus is an achievement test. The SAT also measures—to some extent—how "test wise" you are, and how good you are at solving the types of problems you are likely to face on examinations while in college. Since the SAT correlates rather well with intelligence test scores, it provides a rough measure of your IQ. And since SAT scores are reasonably good at predicting future grades in college, the SAT would seem to be a *valid* academic screening device.

However, according to Christopher Jencks and James Crouse, the use of aptitude tests may cause more problems than they cure. Writing in the 1982 book *New Directions for Testing and Measurement*, Jencks and Crouse note that aptitude tests are no better than achievement tests in helping universities find "'diamonds in the rough' who could be expected to overcome poor preparation and learn a lot if admitted." In addition, both kinds of tests are biased against students with disadvantaged backgrounds. Worst of all, however, selecting students on the basis of "aptitude" rather than accomplishment gives them the notion that "success depends on factors like 'smarts' over which you have no control." Thus, say Jencks and Crouse, aptitude tests actually encourage students to be lazy, since hard work can't improve their "aptitudes." Jencks and Crouse urge educators to abandon aptitude tests entirely and base college admissions solely on achievement.

Personality Tests: The MMPI

Not all objective tests attempt to measure achievement or aptitudes. Many personality tests are "objective," in the sense that they are made up of multiple-choice items and yield numerical scores. One such is the **Minnesota Multiphasic Personality Inventory**. The MMPI, as it usually is called, is widely used today as a device for detecting individuals who might have

Hermann Rorschach (HAIR-man ROAR-shock). A Swiss psychiatrist (1884–1922) who devised the famous inkblot test.
Minnesota Multiphasic Personality Inventory (mull-tee-FAZE-ick). An objective personality test that yields scores on many different scales. By looking at the *profile* of your test scores, a trained interpreter can often determine those areas in which you are "normal" (that is, like most other people) and those areas in which you might be somewhat abnormal, or might experience problems.

personality problems (or mental disorders). The MMPI was created to be as reliable as possible—and research suggests that its reliability is indeed fairly high.

In its original form, the MMPI consisted of some 560 short statements that were given to large numbers of people, some of them mental patients, some of them presumably normal. The statements mostly concern psychiatric problems or unusual thought patterns, such as: (1) Someone is trying to control my mind using radio waves; (2) I never think of unusual sexual situations; and (3) I never have been sick a day of my life. When you take the MMPI, you respond to each statement either by agreeing or disagreeing, or by saying that it is impossible for you to respond at all.

As you might expect, the mental patients used in the original sample reacted to many of the statements in quite different ways than did the "normal" subjects. Depressed or suicidal patients gave different responses than did patients diagnosed as being schizophrenic or paranoid. The authors of the test were able to pick out different groups of test items that appeared to form "depression" scales, "paranoia" scales, "schizophrenia" scales, and so forth. If an otherwise normal individual takes the test and receives an abnormally high score on the "paranoia" scale, the psychologist interpreting the test might well worry that the person could become paranoid if put under great psychological stress or pressure. By looking at the pattern or *profile* of a subject's scores on the different MMPI scales, a psychologist might also be able to predict what areas of the subject's personality needed strengthening.

This approach to the study of personality—judging people almost entirely in terms of their *objective* responses—gives the MMPI a very high reliability. Whether the MMPI is a *valid* index of personality structure is another matter altogether. For example, there is the nagging

"RORSCHACH! WHAT'S TO BECOME OF YOU?"

question of whether data gathered from the "normal" group used when the MMPI was first created is still accurate. The normal group was made up of visitors to the University of Minnesota hospital, of government workers in Minnesota, and of high-school graduates seeking job counseling. In his 1983 book, *The MMPI: A Contemporary Normative Study*, Mayo Clinic psychologist Robert Colligan states that "whoever takes the MMPI today is being compared with the way a man or woman from Minnesota endorsed those items in the late 1930s and early 1940s." Colligan notes that by 1980 a similar "normal" group gave quite different answers than did the "normal" group more than 40 years ago. Thus, modern-day MMPI scores based on the original sample may not be valid.

In their 1982 book mentioned earlier, Richard Lanyon and Leonard Goodstein state there are currently more than 5,000 published studies on the MMPI. Despite this "mountain of literature," though, Lanyon and Goodstein believe there is little scientific evidence that the MMPI is a valid measure of personality. Many personality theorists agree with Lanyon and Goodstein. However, other psychologists disagree and continue to use the instrument. Writing in the October 1981 issue of *American Psychologist*, Sheldon Korchin and David Schuldberg state that the MMPI "has gained and maintained a respected place in clinical practice. . . . There is no question that the test can yield, in the hands of a skilled interpreter, a differentiated picture of important personality characteristics of value to clinical decision-making."

Question: The MMPI correlates quite highly with diagnoses made by trained psychiatrists. As we will see in Chapter 21, however, there is growing evidence that psychiatrists often make mistakes about what is wrong with a patient. If these diagnoses are questionable, how valid can the MMPI be?

The Future of Trait Theory

In the 1860's, Francis Galton set out to describe and measure all human traits. Now, a century or more later, how is trait theory faring, and what does the future hold for it and the thousands of mental tests that the trait approach has spawned?

In a 1980 article in *Contemporary Psychol-*ogy, Wisconsin psychologist John Kihlstrom discusses the current state of trait theory. He writes, "After almost 50 years of factor analysis, the structural relationships among personality traits remain as obscure as ever. Even the most carefully constructed questionnaires purporting to measure some dispositional dimension fail to predict nontest behavior better than the person's own self-assessment given in ordinary language." Furthermore, Kihlstrom says, the *variability* of test scores for a given individual are so great he doubts that "'personality traits'" as such actually exist."

Kihlstrom's position is more extreme than that taken by most psychologists. However, there still is little agreement as to what a trait is, and even less consensus on how traits can best be measured. Because of this disagreement, as Korchin and Schuldberg note in their 1981 article, "there has been a decided decline and growing criticism of psychodiagnostic testing" in recent years. One criticism that Korchin and Schuldberg cite is that, like trait theory in general, test scores typically ignore the influence the environment has on human thoughts and behaviors. A second objection stems from the social consequences of testing and trait theory—consequences that we are still just beginning to learn about. A third problem is that raised by humanistic psychologists, who are more interested in the meanings people give to their lives than to their test scores. For example, Carl Rogers stated in 1942 that nothing a test score tells you about a patient matters much until the patient discovers the same thing for her- or himself during therapy.

Still and all, Korchin and Schuldberg believe that tests (and newer types of trait theories) will have growing usefulness in the future. They note that the *need* for diagnostic and predictive information about people is even greater now than in the past. What we have to do, they say, is to develop scales that are reliable and valid, but which satisfy ethical, social, and scientific standards better than those tests we have used in the past. They predict we will develop techniques that measure how traits and environments *interact*. They also believe that, in the future, psychologists will give greater weight to people's *own* assessments of their strengths and problems, rather than just relying on a battery of test scores.

Like all psychological theories, the trait approach has its strengths and weaknesses. At its best, it reminds us that humans have both similarities and differences. And it gives us ways of measuring both. At its weakest, it tends to put labels on people that they don't always deserve. The problem becomes, as we will see in the next chapter, that we then might respond to the *label* rather than to the *person*.

With that thought in mind, suppose we continue our study of personality by turning our attention to abnormal traits, thought patterns, emotions, and behaviors.

Summary

1 There are three main types of personality theorists: those interested in **temperaments**, **types**, and **traits**.

2 **Temperament** theorists (such as Galen) believe that body chemistry determines personality type. Galen assumed assumed the four main fluids or **humors** of the body were the major determinants of personality.

3 **Type** theorists (such as Sheldon) believe that body type determines traits. Sheldon believed people were mixtures of three body types, the **endomorph**, the **ectomorph**, and the **mesomorph**. Whichever type you became was determined during your fetal period.

4 The scientific study of **individual differences** probably begins with Francis Galton, who also devised the first **intelligence test**. Modern **trait theory** has been strongly influenced by Galton.

5 Modern theorists have rejected typologies, focusing instead on traits. Allport believed each person has one or two cardinal traits, up to ten central traits and up to 5,000 secondary or learned traits.

6 Raymond Cattell believes there are but two types of traits, **surface** and **source** traits. Using **factor analysis**, Cattell determined there are but 16 source traits, which determine some 35 surface traits.

7 Some psychologists define **intelligence** as a trait, but others do not. Galton devised a crude test, but the first true intelligence scale was the **Binet-Simon** test, which measured **mental age**.

8 **Intelligence Quotient**, or IQ, is often defined as mental age divided by **chronological age** times 100. Most modern intelligence tests measure IQ using **standard scores** rather than mental age.

9 Charles Spearman listed two types of intelligence, a **general** or "g" factor, and several **special** or "s" factors.

10 Raymond Cattell claims there are two intellectual factors, **fluid intelligence**, which is inherited, and **crystallized intelligence**, which involves learned skills.

11 Children brought up in deprived or **disadvantaged circumstances** generally have lower IQ scores than do children brought up in **stimulating environments**. Making the child's environment more stimulating can often help increase the child's **IQ**.

12 Disadvantaged persons in particular can raise their test scores by learning **cognitive skills**, such as step-by-step reasoning and how to take intelligence tests.

13 Intelligence tests are fairly **reliable**, but there is considerable question about their **validity**, since there is no agreement on what intelligence actually is.

14 A test has **construct validity** if it correlates well with other tests purporting to measure the same thing. A test has **empirical validity** if it predicts real-world behaviors. Intelligence tests do predict **academic achievement**, and thus have a type of empirical validity. But most tests **discriminate** against disadvantaged individuals.

15 Most studies suggest that blacks and whites from the same **social class** score about the same on intelligence tests. Thus, most racial differences on trait tests are caused by **environmental variables**, not genes.

16 **Projective tests**, such as the **Rorschach**, the **word association test**, and the **TAT**, contain ambiguous stimuli that you are supposed to "structure" in terms of your own personality. Both the **validity** and the **reliability** of these tests is questionable in most circumstances.

17 **Achievement tests** measure knowledge of a certain subject, while **aptitude tests** attempt to predict future performance. Many aptitude tests actually measure achievement and IQ, however, and thus may be **biased** against disadvantaged individuals.

18 The **MMPI** is a very reliable set of scales

standardized on a fairly large population. The MMPI also has **construct validity**, since it correlates well with **psychiatric diagnoses**, among other things.

19 The future holds promise that we will develop more accurate and reliable measures of personality traits. But these tests must satisfy **ethical, social**, and **scientific standards** better than those tests used in the past.

(Continued from page 545.)

"Well, Jessie, if I don't get my Ph.D., I can always blame it on you," Tom Flagg said, his smile belying the seriousness of his words.

"Did I mess up your experiment?" Jessie Williams asked in a concerned tone of voice."

"Royally. But luckily, you were practically the only teacher who did."

"None of my bloomers bloomed?"

Tom shook his head. "That wasn't the problem. Just the opposite. *All* of your kids bloomed, black or white, whether the test said they should or not."

"And that's bad?"

"Good for the kids. Bad for my experiment."

Jessie frowned. "Will it really hold you back from getting your doctorate in psychology?"

"No, not at all. As I said, the Rosenthal test predicted rather well for several other teachers." Tom stretched his muscular legs out in front of him. "I just wish that it hadn't."

Jessie looked puzzled. "But I thought you wanted the test to work? I thought you wouldn't get credit for your experiment if it didn't?"

"I couldn't tell you everything about the test, Jessie," Tom said sheepishly. "You see, Professor Rosenthal didn't really make up a test for 'Late Bloomers.' He was interested in people's expectancies instead. He figured if you told a teacher one of her children was going to 'bloom,' the teacher would pay a lot more attention to that child. And the kid would respond to the teacher's expectancies, and would really improve. But if the teacher expected the kid to backslide, she'd pick on the kid's faults and mistakes. Then the kid would become discouraged and wouldn't do well."

"Is that what this Professor Rosenthal found?"

Tom shrugged his shoulders. "In a lot of cases, yes. But it's an iffy sort of thing. Not everybody has been able to replicate Rosenthal's original results, and a lot of psychologists don't believe in it. Rosenthal still insists his results were valid, though, and I tend to believe him."

"But it didn't work with me, did it?" Jessie said, grinning.

"No, it didn't. Not that I'm complaining, you understand. It shouldn't work with really good teachers, because they wouldn't be prejudiced for or against kids just because of their test scores."

"Shower them with love and affection, and you help them all bloom as much as they can."

"Right," said Tom.

"Then why are you concerned if I didn't pay any attention to your test scores, Tom? I'm not suggestible enough for you?"

Tom laughed. "How did you guess?"

"Keep your mind on your experiment. What's troubling you, friend?"

Tom shrugged. "The fact that some teachers were influenced by the faked test scores that I gave them. I can maybe understand why some of the white teachers might be prejudiced in favor of white kids and against blacks—that's part of our culture, though it's changing some now. And maybe I can understand why some of the black teachers would be prejudiced against white kids and biased toward the blacks. Somehow you expect that. But why would white teachers be prejudiced against white kids, and black teachers prejudiced against black kids—just because some silly test said the kids were going to backslide, or do poorly?"

"Brother Thomas, we are all human beings," Jessie Williams said. "Our blood is the same color, our brains are the same size, our bodies are the same shapes, and we all learn our prejudices at our mothers' knees. I'm just lucky that I was taught to be prejudiced *toward*, instead of prejudiced *against*. But it's prejudice, just the same."

"You think love is prejudice?"

"Of course. Love is prejudice in favor of life."

Tom swallowed hard. "Well, do you think you might be prejudiced just a little in my direction?"

"It might happen to be so."

"Then maybe I ought to ask you out to the movies tomorrow night."

Jessie grinned. "You do that, Baby. You do that very thing."

Recommended Readings

Blau, Z.S. (1981). *Black children/ white children: Competence, socialization, and social structure*. New York: Free Press.

Guthrie, R.V. (1976). *Even the rat was white: A historical view of psychology*. New York: Harper & Row.

Jones, R.L. (Ed.). (1980). *Black psychology* (2nd ed.). New York: Harper & Row.

Scarr, S. (1981). *Race, social class, and individual differences in I.Q.* Hillsdale, N.J.: Erlbaum.

Tyler, L.A. & Walsh, W.B. (1979). *Tests and measurements* (3rd ed.). Englewood Cliffs, N.J.: Prentice-Hall.

Yando, R, Seitz, V., & Zigler, E. (1979). *Intellectual and personality characteristics of children: Social-class and ethnic-group differences*. Hillsdale, N.J.: Erlbaum.

Did You Know That...

- According to Kinsey, the average white married man aged 21–25 has about four sexual climaxes a week?

- Almost all definitions of "abnormality" have an element of subjectivity to them?

- Psychologists sometimes use the statistical term "two standard deviations from the mean" to describe most forms of unusual or abnormal behavior?

- A new diagnostic manual put out by the American Psychiatric Association describes hundreds of different "mental disorders"?

- Some scientists believe schizophrenia is caused by "bad genes"?

- Other scientists hold that schizophrenia is brought on by a "smothering mother"?

- A number of normal people who pretended to have severe mental problems were admitted to mental hospitals, diagnosed as being "psychotic," but had real difficulties getting out?

- There often is little agreement among psychiatrists as to which type of "mental disorder" a given patient actually suffers from?

- When a person develops abnormal behavior patterns, everyone the person has close contact with probably has helped bring about the abnormality?

21

Abnormal Psychology

"I'm Crazy—You're Crazy"

Steve May got out of the car, closed the door, then stuck his head back in through the window. "You really think it will work?" he said for perhaps the tenth time that day.

Dr. Mary Ellen Mann smiled reassuringly at the handsome young man. "Well, it worked for all of Professor Rosenhan's subjects. They all got admitted to the mental hospital without any trouble at all. Getting out seems to be the problem, not getting in. But I'm sure you'll be able to cope beautifully with any difficulties that may arise. Just get yourself in gear and go convince those people that you're crazier than a bedbug."

Steve thought about the matter for a moment or two. He had willingly committed himself to helping Dr. Mann with her research on the reliability of psychiatric diagnoses. But committing himself to a state mental hospital was a very frightening thought. He supposed that he couldn't really chicken out at the last moment, but still . . . "If they do admit me," the blond young man said, "you're sure that I can prove to them that I'm okay so they'll let me out?"

Dr. Mann snorted as she laughed. "As I told you, Steve, if you get stuck in there, you've got to get out on your own. Oh, I'll come rescue you

eventually, have no fears about that." She leaned toward him a trifle. "Or maybe you're afraid that you really are a bit nuts. Is that the problem?"

A rosy flush spread over Steve's face. "Of course not! I'm as sane as you are!"

Dr. Mann snorted even more loudly. "Just don't tell the psychiatrist that, or you may never get out!" Then she smiled warmly. "Good luck, Steve. I really appreciate your helping out my research this way."

Steve nodded slowly, then pulled his head out of the car window. Dr. Mann waved at him, then put the car into gear and slowly drove off.

Steve turned to look at the hospital. It was a huge, towering, forbidding structure. The thought of spending the next few days—or weeks, or months—in that place frankly scared him. But he had promised . . .

He walked slowly up the path and through the heavy, wooden door. The lobby inside was cool and almost empty. A nice-looking young woman sat behind a reception desk, filling in a form of some kind on a typewriter. Steve put on his best smile and walked over to her.

"Hello," Steve said.

The woman stopped typing and looked up at him. Her face brightened as she took in his handsome features and his muscular body. "Oh, hello," she said warmly. "What can I do for you? Would you like to see a patient?"

Steve returned her smile. "No, I want to be a patient, if you don't mind."

The woman's smile faded a bit. "Oh," she said briskly. "There's something wrong?"

Steve nodded. "Yeah. I need help. I hear voices."

The woman's smile faded away entirely, as if she had suddenly tucked him into a much less desirable category in her mind. "What do the voices seem to be saying?" she asked.

"They're kind of indistinct," he replied. "Mostly words like 'dull,' 'thud,' 'empty.' You know, things like that."

The woman nodded slowly, mechanically. "And what sex are the voices, male or female?"

Steve smiled wanly. "I can't always tell."

The woman frowned. "Are you in any pain right now?"

"No, not really," Steve said. "But I do think I need your help—for a while, that is, until the voices go away."

Again the woman frowned. "Well, we're pretty full these days. You'll have to see the admitting psychiatrist, of course. But he's very busy. And we'll have to fill out a lot of papers, and . . . "

Two hours later, Steve's fingers were almost numb from writer's cramp. He finished all the forms, and then sat patiently in the lobby for another hour or so until the psychiatrist could see him.

The psychiatrist was a pleasant man of about 40 who spoke with such a thick foreign accent that Steve couldn't always understand the questions the man asked him. Steve told the man about his voices—that they were indistinct and that they seemed to be saying 'dull,' 'thud,' and 'hollow.' The doctor nodded sagely, and muttered under his breath. Steve thought the man had said something like, "Existential crisis." Steve smiled inwardly. It was going just like Rosenhan's paper had suggested it would. Almost all of Rosenhan's subjects got the same sort of diagnosis.

Then the psychiatrist started asking questions about Steve's early life. When Steve admitted that he occasionally argued with his father, and that he really got along better with his mother, the doctor nodded sagely again. Steve thought he mumbled something like, "Very significant." And when Steve said that he wasn't always sure what his goals in life were, and that he now and again lost his temper, the psychiatrist muttered something under his breath that

sounded suspiciously like, "Poor impulse control."

Aside from the bit about the "voices," Steve answered the man's questions as honestly as possible, just as Dr. Mann had told him to do. At first Steve had been sure the psychiatrist would see through the game, and would announce loudly that Steve was "just faking it." But the doctor apparently took him only too seriously. To Steve's surprise, the psychiatrist never once asked him about his abilities and strengths, or what made him happy. The man obviously couldn't tell that Steve was really normal and healthy, and that thought frightened Steve more than he could admit.

Finally the psychiatrist leaned back in his chair, tapped a pencil on his desk, and stared silently at Steve for a few moments. "Look, Steven, I don't want to alarm you, but I do think I ought to be honest with you. You seem to be suffering from very real psychological problems. You were right to come to us. I'm sure that we can be of help. We'll keep you under observation for a while, and then we'll talk about getting you legally certified . . ."

"Legally certified?" Steve said in a horrified tone of voice.

"Of course. If you are to stay here more than 60 days, which will likely be the case, there are certain legal formalities we have to go through . . ."

"Sixty days! But what if I get better right away—like tomorrow?" Steve protested.

The psychiatrist allowed himself a brief, thin-lipped smile. "As you Americans say, we'll cross that bridge when we come to it." The doctor pressed a button on his desk and, almost immediately, a burly young attendant entered the office.

"Charles, this is Steven," the psychiatrist said. "He will be staying with us for a while. Please check him in and then put him on Ward A-5."

The attendant nodded, then said to Steve, "This way, please."

Steve got up and started to extend his hand to the psychiatrist. But the man was already busy working on the papers that would admit Steve to the mental hospital. So Steve picked up his small bag and followed the attendant out of the office.

"First, we'll check you in and get all your valuables stowed away," the burly attendant said.

"Oh," said Steve, "I'd rather keep them with me."

"Can't. It's the rule," the attendant said. "Got to stow it all away—your money and credit cards and all that stuff. Your watch and rings, too. We can't be responsible, you know. And we'll have to inspect your shaving kit and all your personal gear. No razors, you know, and you can't keep all your clothes either."

"Clothes?" Steve said in an unbelieving tone of voice.

"Belts, stuff like that. Might hurt yourself."

Steve had to hurry a bit to keep up with the attendant. "But surely I can keep my pictures, and my books, and things like that . . ."

"Nope. It's against the rules."

For a moment, Steve pan-

icked. The folly of what he was doing finally struck home. They were taking away all his "cards of identity," all his symbols of power, all his memories and mementoes. They were stripping him of his personality and turning him into a number, a card in a file, a statistic.

"We'll give you a shower and then get you some hospital clothes," the attendant said, opening a huge metal door and then locking it securely after they had passed through.

"But I just had a shower, about an hour ago," Steve protested as they walked down a long, bare corridor. "Do you think what I've got is catching?"

"Don't give me any trouble, man. I don't make the rules." The attendant unlocked another huge metal door at the end of the corridor and banged it shut behind them. They walked down a flight of metal stairs and then the attendant unlocked yet another door that had a small window in it. The window was covered with thick steel bars. The burly attendant told Steve to strip, took his things, and pointed to a shower room. When Steve returned, water still dripping from his hair, the attendant gave him a set of hospital clothes.

"You look fine," the attendant said. "Now, let's get on with it."

They walked down another long, bare corridor to a metal door that bore a small sign, "Ward A-5." Steve shook his

head in dismay. They had passed through four locked, steel doors already. If getting into the ward was this difficult, what would getting out be like?

"This is it," the attendant said, unlocking the door and walking into the ward. "Wait here until I find the nurse," the man said, shutting the metal door behind them.

Steve stood staring at the inmates. Several of them were watching a television set, but they didn't seem to respond to the program in any way. One middle-aged man rushed feverishly about the ward, as if looking for something he had lost. A younger man was rocking back and forth in a straight-backed chair. A third man was standing in a corner, quietly urinating.

My God, Steve thought. *You've got to be crazy to stay in a place like this.*

The attendant came back with a nurse, who gave Steve an efficient smile and then showed him where his bed would be. The man in the next bed was curled up in a fetal position, laughing quietly to himself, a serene smile on his face.

Steve stretched out on the narrow bed and stared at the ceiling. "Well, I made it in okay," he said aloud. "But how in the world am I ever going to get out of this place?"

The man in the next bed giggled softly.

(Continued on page 596.)

Warning: Controversial Material!

Like all other sciences, psychology has its agreed-upon facts and its controversies. Agreement tends to be highest in those areas of the behavioral sciences that touch on biology and physics—the brain and the nervous system, sensory psychology, and (to some extent) perception. Consensus is somewhat lower in the fields of motivation and learning, and lower still in developmental and social psychology. But *disagreement* among psychologists is surely at its greatest in the areas of personality theory, abnormal psychology, and psychotherapy.

Since we have already covered personality theory, you are aware of what some of these controversies are all about. As you read this chapter (on abnormal psychology), and the next chapter (on therapy), you will discover even more ways in which professional scientists and therapists disagree. Perhaps it will help, therefore, if you keep several points in mind as you go through this material:

1. The study of human abnormalities is one of the richest and most fascinating areas in all of psychology.
2. No one disagrees that these abnormalities exist. Rather, the controversy concerns how best to describe these conditions, where they come from, and what to do about them.
3. There is no way to be completely objective about abnormal psychology. Why is this so? Because the very word "abnormal" is based (for the most part) on subjective value judgments or interpretations.

What follows, therefore, is a *necessarily biased* presentation of the necessarily controversial material on abnormal thoughts, feelings, and behaviors. Before reading this chapter, you might wish to look over pages 20 to 21 again, to remind yourself of what the author's biases are. You might also wish to keep a list of those issues raised in this chapter that puzzle you, or that you disagree with. For surely that is the best way to discover what your own biases about abnormal psychology actually are.

Let's begin by trying to define some terms.

What Is a "Mental Disorder"?

Many of the great personality theorists—Freud, Jung, Adler, Erikson, Rogers, and the rest—based their ideas on the study of mentally disturbed patients. Most of these patients had problems that were *exaggerations* of the mental and behavioral traits that we all have. Therefore, the theorists presumed, the mental patient differs from the average citizen in the *quantity* (amount) of madness, not in the *quality* (type) of psychological problem. In short, the view of most theorists has been that we are all mildly abnormal, but some of us are more abnormal than others.

But does that view make sense? If everyone **deviates** from the norm one way or another, doesn't the word "normal" lose most of its meaning? And if we can't define the word "normal," what shall we make of the word "abnormal," which literally means "away from the normal"?

There is also the question of *what* about the person is abnormal, and how we should refer to the abnormality. The legal profession uses the word *insanity* to refer to many types of behavioral abnormalities, but psychologists typically avoid that term. Instead, we employ phrases such as "mental illness," "mental disorder," "behavioral disorder," or "problems of adjustment." These labels imply different *causes* and *therapeutic approaches*, of course. "Mental illness" suggests the abnormality is medical or biological in origin, and perhaps medication might help. "Mental disorder" implies the problem is primarily intra-psychic, thus psychotherapy might be called for. "Behavioral disorder" suggests the abnormality is learned and thus treatable with re-learning techniques. "Problems of adjustment" (or sometimes "problems of living") imply something unusual about person-environmental interactions, and thus a "systems" approach could be the therapy of choice.

As you will soon see, there is as little agreement over which of the four *labels* to use as there is over what *therapy* to employ.

No matter what term we use to describe psychological difficulties, though, all our concepts of the "abnormal" spring from a theory of what's "normal." So before we can discuss such topics as "mental illness," "behavior disorders," and "adjustment problems," we must first take a good, hard, objective look at the word "normal."

What Is Normal?

Writing in the *Journal of Abnormal and Social Psychology* in 1935, J.P. Foley defined *abnormal* as "a deviation from the statistical norms of a particular cultural group." There are good points and bad points about this definition. On the positive side, it notes (1) that abnormalities are *unusual* occurrences (at least in some *statistical* sense); and (2) that these abnormalities are always defined in terms of some specific culture or group. On the negative side, Foley's definition does not differentiate between "good" deviations and "not-so-good" ones.

Can there be "good" abnormalities? Of course there can be. If someone said you were "much brighter than average," would you be insulted? No, you probably would be pleased (or even flattered). Yet the person has said, really, that you are *abnormally* intelligent. Physical beauty, creative talent, great wealth, and even excellent health are other examples of what most people would consider to be "good" abnormalities.

In a statistical sense, the word "abnormal" is neutral. That is, it covers both positive and negative deviations from the average. *As most people use the term*, however, "abnormal" usually refers to deviations that are inappropriate, disabling, unhealthy, or even "undesirable" and "immoral." Thus, for the most part, when we use the word "abnormal," we're not only noting a departure from some statistical norm, but making a *value judgment* about the situation as well.

Some psychologists attempt to get around this difficulty by restricting their use of the term to certain specific situations. For example, E.J. Shoben states that normality consists of fulfilling your own potentialities as a human being. Any failure to live up to your own standards or ideals should be considered "abnormal," according to Shoben. However, as Melvin Zax and Emory Cowen point out in their book *Abnormal Psychology*, Shoben's approach raises as many problems as it solves. For instance, who sets standards, and where do ideals come from, if not the cultural group into which you're born? And statistically speaking, how close must you come to "fulfilling your own potential" to be considered normal?

Zax and Cowen believe that all definitions of "abnormal" must be based on some concept of what is "healthy" or "normal" for a given person in a given culture. If you decide to seek psychological help, you might well tell the therapist, "I have trouble sleeping," or "I have no appetite," or "I don't have any friends." As Zax and Cowen note, these *statements of your problem* imply a comparison to some standard (or norm) of how long you should sleep, how much you should eat, or how many friends you should have. And the therapist, in evaluating your difficulties, must always realize that some people sleep longer than others do, eat more than others do, and have more friends than perhaps you have (or want to have). So the therapist must not only deal with your own "norms", but also with the "norms" of the culture you live in. And the therapist must also have some way of *measuring* how far you depart both from your own and from societal definitions of normality.

Like it or not, then, you can't make much sense out of abnormal psychology until you learn a bit about statistical concepts of "the norm." So, let's look at how we might apply statistics to help understand and resolve the abnormalities of Mr. and Mrs. Smith.

"I CAN REMEMBER WHEN PARANOIA WAS UNUSUAL."

Psychological Deviants

Suppose a young married couple named Mary and John Smith are on the verge of divorce. They go to see a psychologist and ask for help. Even before the psychologist learns their names, this counselor knows several things about the Smiths. First, one or both of them is going to be suffering considerable psychological pain, distress, or anxiety. Second, things are probably worse for the couple now than at some time in the past. That is, their way of life has changed from its usual (normal) pattern. Third, they are bright enough to sense this departure from normal and to seek help.

Any deviation from a person's usual way of thinking, feeling, or behaving can be considered a symptom of psychological abnormality—provided that the person was reasonably "normal" (as defined by the person's culture) to start with. Generally speaking, if this deviation is slight, the psychologist is likely to believe the person suffers from what has generally been classified as a **neurosis**. (The fact that the deviation is "slight" doesn't mean that the person doesn't suffer from a great deal of pain, however.) If the deviation is large, the psychologist may worry that the person suffers from a more severe problem called a **psychosis**.

Not all psychologists use terms such as "neurosis" and "psychosis." And there is less than complete agreement on how to define these terms among those psychologists who do make use of these diagnostic labels. Indeed, the *terminology* in the field of clinical psychology is undergoing rapid change right now, a point we will discuss later in this chapter. For the moment, all you need to remember is that some people have relatively minor problems, while others have such major difficulties that they may need to be hospitalized at some point in their lives. It is the psychologist's job, in either case, to help the person solve the problem and return to "normal"—as defined by the society in which the person must live and function.

Sexual Dysfunctions

Mary and John Smith could have many quite different *kinds* of psychological difficulties. Later in this chapter we will describe what some of the more common types are like. But to help us understand what the word "normal" means, let us assume that either or both of them has what a psychologist might call a *sexual dysfunction*.

Suppose that, in their first interview with the psychologist, John complains that Mary is sexually inhibited, and that she consistently refuses him the pleasures of the marriage bed. Mary replies that John is a **satyr**—that is, he has an unusually strong sex drive. She claims

that he thinks of nothing but sex, talks of nothing else, and that he is interested only in her body and not in her mind or personality. (Of course, the problem might be the other way around—the wife might desire sex more frequently than the husband. But we will delay discussion of that situation for a moment.)

The psychologist might well assume that the woman was *normal*, but that the man's libido had gotten out of control and was ruining the marriage. Or the counselor might assume that the man had a *normal*, healthy appetite for sex, but that the woman was so *repressed* that she could not enjoy one of the finer aspects of marriage. Or the therapist might assume that *both* Mary and John showed symptoms of abnormality. How could the psychologist tell for sure?

Question: Psychologists always make *assumptions* about what is normal and abnormal for a particular patient. Do you think that male counselors might tend to make different assumptions about John and Mary Smith than would female counselors?

Cultural Norms

Normality is always defined *within a given context or culture*. No psychologist can come to any meaningful conclusions about the Smiths' problems if the counselor ignores the *social environment* in which the couple lives. That is, before the psychologist can concentrate on the unique aspects of the Smiths' difficulties, the therapist must ask how other people with similar backgrounds think, feel, and behave.

One question the psychologist would ask is, therefore, "What *values* about sexuality do the Smiths (and their culture) hold?" Another question would be, "What *past experiences*—pleasant or unpleasant—have the Smiths (and people like them) typically had?" Without knowing the answers to these questions, the psychologist could hardly hope to put the Smiths' problems in proper perspective.

However, the counselor would also need to know something about *actual sexual practices* in the world the Smiths live in. How many times do most young husbands expect sex each week? How frequently do most wives desire it? Do husbands typically *wish* to make love more frequently than their wives, or the other way around? How frequently do young married men achieve sexual climax? And is it always with their wives? How frequently do young married women reach orgasm, and is it always with their husbands? And, most important, how do the Smiths compare to other people in their segment of society?

Questions about sexual values and past experiences are often difficult to find answers to. But, as we saw in Chapter 11, the real controversy started when scientists started asking people *what they actually did* in the privacy of their bedrooms. Yet, logically speaking, how can we know what is "normal" sexual behavior until we know what's *statistically* "the norm" for most married people like the Smiths?

Sex and the Bell-Shaped Curve

Until Alfred Kinsey performed his pioneering research on human sexuality, no one really knew much about the "statistics of sexual behavior." But judging from a rough analysis of the Kinsey data, the average white married man aged 21–25 reaches sexual climax about three to four times a week. Using rather stilted language, Kinsey reported the young, married, middle-class, white male in the US achieved an average of about four *sexual outlets* per week. (Kinsey included all forms of sexual activity in his figures—including masturbation, homosexuality, bestiality, "wet dreams," and extramarital heterosexual contacts.)

Although Kinsey gathered his data more than 30 years ago, recent surveys tend to confirm his findings. Thus, we can use Kinsey's results to give us a "social context" in which to consider the Smiths' marital problems—but only assuming that the Smiths are white, middle-class people living in the US.

Even making these assumptions, there is still a lot more we need to know. If Mr. Smith desired 7 outlets a week, would you consider him abnormal? What if he demanded 17? And would John Smith be "far above normal" if he wanted 77?

Range

As you can see, knowing what the average is doesn't always help. The average score on most intelligence tests is 100. If you get a score of 101, are you "way above average"? Before we could answer, we would have to know the *range* of scores, as well as how those scores were *distributed* over the range. And the best way to find out would be to resort to that favorite psychological tool, the bell-shaped curve.

The range of IQ's on some tests goes from 0 to about 200. The tests are so constructed that most people's scores are bunched up in the middle of the distribution. Although some 50 percent of the scores lie above the mid-point of

Neurosis (new-ROW-sis). Also called "psychoneurosis." A mild form of mental disorder that usually does not keep the individual from living a reasonably successful life. Freud thought that the seeds for a neurosis were planted in early childhood.

Psychosis (sigh-KOH-sis). A severe and usually incapacitating form of mental disorder that often requires hospitalization.

Satyr (SAY-teer). An ancient Greek country god supposedly fond of wine, women, and song—but mostly fond of women. Represented in art as a horse or goat.

Mode. From the Latin word *modus*, meaning "to measure." The highest point or most frequent score on a bell-shaped distribution of scores.

Mean. That which is "middling" or intermediate in rank or order. The arithmatical average.

Median (ME-dee-an). From the Latin word *medius*, meaning "middle." The median on a superhighway is the paved or planted strip down the middle dividing the road in half. The median in a distribution is the score that cuts the distribution exactly in half.

Standard deviation. (dee-vee-A-shun). The standard deviation is a mathematical way of figuring out how much a test score deviates from the mean, median, or mode (usually the mean). The standard deviation thus gives you a precise way of measuring how significantly your own score on a test varies or departs from the norm.

the curve—and some 50 percent lie below it— most of the IQ's do not *deviate* very far from this mid-point (see Figure 21.1). Depending on how the mid-point is calculated, it is called the **mode**, the **mean**, or the **median**. If you are interested in how these terms are calculated, see the Statistical Appendix at the back of this book. However, "mode," "mean," and "median" are merely words that mean the *norm*, or the middle of the range of scores.

In the case of Kinsey's data on the sexual behavior of the (young, white, middle-class) male in the US, the mean, median, and mode are probably close together. Thus, for our present purposes, we can consider any of them the norm. The actual distribution of outlets per week probably looks something like the graph shown in Figure 21.2.

Now we can see that if Mr. Smith desired 7 outlets a week, he would be fairly close to the norm. But what if he wished 17? Would this fact make him ab-norm-al, or away from the norm? How far away is "away?"

Standard Deviation

Psychologists have a method of measuring deviations from the norm, which they call the **standard deviation**. If you are interested in learning more about this matter, you might wish to look at the Statistical Appendix. However, when all is said and done, the standard

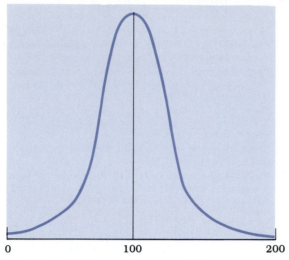

Fig. 21.1   A bell-shaped curve of IQ's.

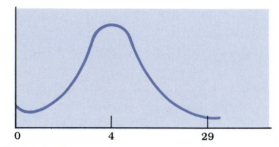

Fig. 21.2   Range of weekly outlets in young married men.

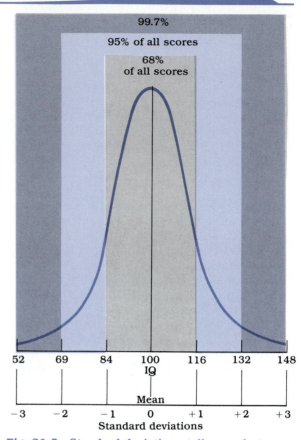

Fig. 21.3   Standard deviations tell you what percentage of scores fall within a certain distance from the mean.

deviation is little more than a fairly accurate way of measuring *percentages*.

Psychologists assume that, on any given test (or on the measurement of any given behavior), whatever *two-thirds of the people do* is probably pretty normal. On an intelligence test, for example, the norm (or mean) is arbitrarily set at a score of 100. On many such tests, about two-thirds of the people get scores between 84 and 116. As you can see from Figure 21.3, this fact means that about one-third of the people score within 16 points *below* the mean, and about one-third of the people score within 16 points *above* the mean. By definition, then, the *standard deviation* for such a test would be 16 points. If you score within one standard deviation of the norm, your performance is almost always considered "within the normal range."

If you got an IQ of 132 on the test, you would be 2 standard deviations above the mean, and you would be well above average. If you got a

score of 148 on the test, you would be 3 standard deviations above the norm. This exceptional score would put you in the upper two-tenths of a percent of the test population.

To summarize (so that we can get back to talking about *psychological deviations* from the norm):

1. If your performance on any measure is within 1 standard deviation of the norm, you are like two-thirds of the population and hence quite normal.
2. If your performance on any measure is between 1 and 2 standard deviations from the norm, you have departed somewhat from the average.
3. If your performance on any measure is more than 2 standard deviations from the norm, you are behaving differently than about 98 percent of the population. Thus, your performance should be considered *significantly* abnormal. You may score higher than the

rest of the people, or lower—but surely you are measurably *different* from the majority of the others.

Question: How many behaviors can you think of that are *statistically normal* (in that most people engage in them) but that aren't necessarily "good" or "healthy" or "moral"?

"Normal" Sexuality and the Standard Deviation

Now we're ready to put the Smiths' problem into context. Dr. Kinsey's surveys of sexual behavior suggest that young married men like John Smith have, on the average, 4 sexual outlets per week. The range is from 0 to more than 29. The standard deviation is about 2.

These facts mean that if John Smith desires sexual contact with his wife from 2 to 6 times a week, he is probably like two-thirds of all similar men that Kinsey talked to. In short, *within the society* in which the Smiths live, John's sexual demands would seem average, or nor-

mal. If he expected sex more than 8 times per week, John would be more than 2 standard deviations from the norm (for his culture), and thus his requests would be at least *statistically* abnormal (see Fig. 21.4).

Of course, in the long run, the problem that exists between Mary and John Smith is a personal one that cannot be solved by reference to bell-shaped curves. And any valid discussion of the Smiths' problems would have to include values and past experiences as well as actual behaviors. Yet the beauty of Kinsey's work was that he brought sexual behavior out in the open, so that it could be examined statistically as well as personally or theoretically. *Lacking* this important reference information, the psychologist might well make some very wrong decisions about how to help the Smiths. For we all tend to judge normality *in terms of our own behaviors and expectations.*

Question: How might the "personality theory" you believe in affect your judgment about who is "mentally ill" and who isn't? How would it affect your opinion of *what* is wrong with the person?

Classifying Abnormal Behavior Patterns

As you can gather, it is difficult to define psychological abnormality without a theory of some kind—or some set of data such as Kinsey's—to tell you both what is *statistically* normal and how any abnormality might have come about.

There is, unfortunately, no one master theory of human behavior that everyone agrees on. Psychologists and psychiatrists have worked out a variety of diagnostic schemes that are supposed to classify people according to their problems. Of these, the best known is surely the *Diagnostic and Statistical Manual of Mental Disorders*, first published by the American Psychiatric Association in 1952. The third edition (DSM-III) appeared in 1980.

DSM-III is quite different from DSM-I. In 1952, almost all the diagnostic categories were listed as *psychological reactions*. The experts who compiled DSM-I tended to believe in a theory of psychology put forth by the noted psychiatrist, Adolph Meyer. It was Meyer's view that "mental disorders" were best understood as awkward attempts to adjust to external demands. Thus, the people who created DSM-I perceived "mental disorders" as resulting from *imperfect person-environment interactions.*

DSM-II appeared in 1968. By that time, Freudian theory had become dominant in many

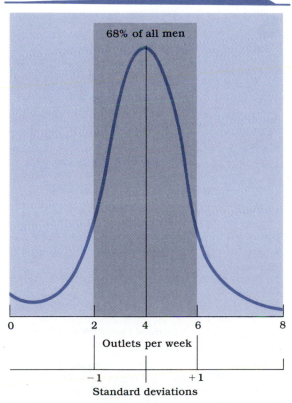

Fig. 21.4 According to Kinsey, two-thirds of all young, white, married, middle-class American males experience 2–6 sexual outlets per week.

TABLE 21.1   A Brief Outline of the Diagnostic Categories Included on Axis 1 and Axis 2 of DSM-III.

Axis 1: Severe Mental Disorders (Including Psychoses and Neurotic Disorders)

Disorders Usually First Evident in Infancy, Childhood, or Adolescence
Mental Retardation
Attention Deficit Disorders
  Hyperactivity
Conduct Disorders
  Undersocialized, Aggressive
  Undersocialized, Nonaggressive
  Socialized, Aggressive,
  Socialized, Nonaggressive
Anxiety Disorders of Childhood or Adolescence
  Separation Anxiety Disorder
  Avoidant Disorder
  Overanxious Disorder
Other Disorders of Childhood or Adolescence
  Reactive Attachment Disorder
  Schizoid Disorder
  Elective Mutism
  Oppositional Disorder
  Identity Disorder
Eating Disorders
  Anorexia Nervosa
  Bulimia
  Pica
  Rumination Disorder
  Atypical Eating Disorder
Stereotyped Movement Disorders
  Transient Tic Disorder
  Chronic Motor Tic Disorder
  Tourette's Disorder
Other Disorders with Physical Manifestations
  Stuttering
  Functional Enuresis
  Functional Encopresis
  Sleepwalking Disorder
  Sleep Terror Disorder
Pervasive Developmental Disorders
  Infantile Autism

Organic Mental Disorders
Dementias Arising in the Senium and Presenium
  Primary Degenerative Dementia
  Multi-infarct Dementia
Substance-Induced
  Alcohol
    Intoxication
    Withdrawal Delirium
    Hallucinosis
    Amnestic Disorder
  Barbiturates
  Opioid
  Cocaine
  Amphetamine
  Phencyclidine (PCP)
  Hallucinogen
  Cannabis
  Tobacco
  Caffeine

Substance Use Disorders
(Substance Abuse)

Schizophrenic Disorders
Schizophrenia,
  Disorganized
  Catatonic
  Paranoid
  Undifferentiated
  Residual

Paranoid Disorders
Paranoia
Shared Paranoid Disorder
Acute Paranoid Disorder
Atypical Paranoid Disorder

Psychotic Disorders Not Elsewhere Classified
Schizophreniform Disorder
Brief Reactive Psychosis
Schizoaffective Disorder

Neurotic Disorders
(Included in Categories Below)

Affective Disorders
Bipolar Disorder
  Mixed
  Manic
  Depressed
Major Depression
Other Specific Affective Disorders
  Cyclothymic Disorder
  Dysthymic Disorder (or Depressive Neurosis)

Anxiety Disorders
Phobic Disorders (or Phobic Neuroses)
  Agoraphobia
  Social Phobia
  Simple Phobia
Panic Disorder (or Anxiety Neurosis)
Obsessive Compulsive Disorder (or Obsessive Compulsive Neurosis)
Post-traumatic Stress Disorder

Somatoform Disorders
Somatization Disorder
Conversion Disorder (or Hysterical Neurosis, Conversion Type)
Psychogenic Pain Disorder
Hypochondriasis (or Hypochondriacal Neurosis)

Dissociative Disorders (or Hysterical Neuroses)
Psychogenic Amnesia
Psychogenic Fugue
Multiple Personality
Depersonalization Disorder (or Depersonalization Neurosis)

Psychosexual Disorders
Gender Identity Disorders
  Transsexualism

Paraphilias
  Fetishism
  Transvestism
  Zoophilia
  Pedophilia
  Exhibitionism
  Voyeurism
  Sexual Masochism
  Sexual Sadism
Psychosexual Dysfunctions
  Inhibited Sexual Desire
  Inhibited Sexual Excitement
  Inhibited Female Orgasm
  Inhibited Male Orgasm
  Premature Ejaculation
  Functional Dyspareunia
  Functional Vaginismus
Other Psychosexual Disorders
  Ego-dystonic Homosexuality

Factitious Disorders
Factitious Illness with Psychological Symptoms
Chronic Factitious Illness with Physical Symptoms

Disorders of Impulse Control Not Elsewhere Classified
Pathological Gambling
Kleptomania
Pyromania
Intermittent Explosive Disorder
Isolated Explosive Disorder

Adjustment Disorders
With Depressed Mood
With Anxious Mood
With Disturbance of Conduct
With Work (or Academic) Inhibition
With Withdrawal

Psychological Factors Affecting Physical Condition
Conditions Not Attributable to a Mental Disorder That Are a Focus of Attention or Treatment
Malingering
Borderline Intellectual Functioning
Adult Antisocial Behavior
Childhood or Adolescent Antisocial Problem
Academic Problem
Occupational Problem
Uncomplicated Bereavement
Noncompliance with Medical Treatment
Phase of Life Problem or Other Life Circumstance Problem
Marital Problem
Parent-Child Problem
Other Interpersonal Problem

Axis 2: Personality Disorders

Paranoid	Schizotypal	Narcissistic
Borderline	Dependent	Passive-Aggressive
Schizoid	Histrionic	Antisocial
Avoidant	Compulsive	Atypical, Mixed, or Other

psychiatric circles. And Freud, as you know, viewed "mental disorders" as having intra-psychic causes (and cures). What had been described in DSM-I as a schizophrenic *reaction*, therefore, became *schizophrenia* in DSM-II. Thus, DSM-II put the "locus" of psychological abnormalites *inside the mind*.

By 1980, when DSM-III was published, the pendulum had swung in yet another direction. Currently, professional psychiatry is (to a great extent) dominated by individuals who believe there is usually a *biological* cause underlying most psychological problems. Thus, in DSM-III, "schizophrenia" has become "schizophrenic *disorder*." And the "locus" of abnormality has been moved from "the mind" to "mind-body interactions."

As we will see, a great many psychologists object to DSM-III. One major complaint raised is that the people who created the *Manual* seem to believe in what is called the **medical model** of "mental illness." That is, DSM-III appears to be based on the notion that all abnormal thoughts and behaviors are but *symptoms* of some underlying "illness." (As we noted earlier, many psychologists prefer to view human abnormalities as being "problems of adjustment," "psychological difficulties," or "learned behaviors," rather than "symptoms of illness.")

We will discuss the good and perhaps not-so-good points of DSM-III a bit later. First, though, it will pay us to take a look at the 1980 *Manual* before we go any farther in our study of abnormal behavior patterns, sexual or otherwise.

DSM-III

DSM-III was designed to give specific diagnoses for *every* patient who might be referred to a psychiatrist (or perhaps to a psychologist)—no matter what the patient's problems might be. After interviewing the patient—and perhaps giving the individual various tests—the therapist rates the patient on each of five different **axes** or categories:

Axis 1. Clinical Syndromes and Other Conditions
Axis 2. Personality Disorders; Specific Developmental Disorders
Axis 3. Physical Disorders and Conditions
Axis 4. Severity of Psychosocial Stressors
Axis 5. Highest Level of Adaptive Functioning (during) Past Year

Let's look at each axis (or category of abnormality) in some detail.

Medical model. The belief—in psychiatry and psychology—that mental disorders are caused by some "underlying" or "deep-seated" psychological problem, just as influenza is caused by an infectious virus. In fact, what we call the "medical model" should really be termed "the infectious disease model," since there are many other "models" in the field of medicine.

Axes (AX-ease). The plural of "axis." An axis is a line about which something rotates. In the DSM-III, the five axes are really "categories" or types of information that the psychiatrist should use in making a diagnosis about what could be troubling a given patient. Whether it is the patient or the psychiatrist who "rotates" around these five axes is an open question.

Axis 1

Included on Axis 1 are most of the psychological disorders that the American Psychiatric Association officially recognizes as being "mental illnesses." Generally speaking, Axis 1 is made up of all those severe psychological or behavioral problems that would send you to see a therapist in the first place (see Table 21.1).

Axis 2

Technically speaking, Axis 2 is limited to what are called the *personality disorders*. In fact, Axis 2 is designed to let the therapist describe the patient's psychological traits or "enduring behavior patterns," rather than any problems that have occurred recently. Many patients will have disorders listed on both Axis 1 and Axis 2.

Axis 3

Axis 3 is a reminder that patients who seek psychological assistance may have physical ailments (such as cancer) that may be related to their mental disorders (such as depression). Included on Axis 3 are all the *physical symptoms* of any type of disease, damage to the brain or any other part of the body, and disabilities caused by accidents or drugs. The *psychological reactions* to these biological problems, however, are generally considered to be mental disorders that would be listed under Axis 1.

Axis 4

Axis 4 is a "social stress scale" that lists such traumas as the death of a loved one, changing (or losing) your job, and getting married (or divorced). Again, the patient's *psychological reaction* to these social traumas will probably be a mental disorder listed on Axis 1. Generally speaking, only those stressful events that occurred in the past 12 months are given serious consideration.

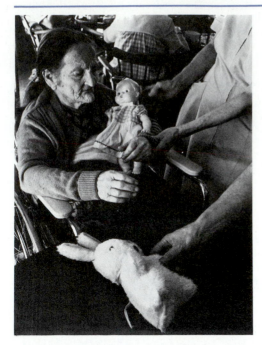

A patient suffering from Alzheimer's disease becomes senile and may revert to childish behavior patterns.

About 6 million US citizens are alcoholic.

Axis 5

Axis 5 is a scale running from "superior" to "grossly impaired" that describes your highest level of psychological adjustment for the past year.

Mental Disorders

As we noted earlier, DSM-III marks a radical shift in the psychiatric approach to classifying mental disorders. DSM-II was based in large part on psychoanalytic theory. Freud believed that almost all types of mental illness were due either to biological or to psychological causes. Some disorders were very severe, and were called the *psychoses*. Other forms were not as severe, and were called the *neuroses*. There were exceptions to this rule, however. A very severe neurosis of long duration might well have a greater negative effect on a patient than a very mild psychosis. Generally speaking, though, the psychoses are thought to be more debilitating to an individual than are the neuroses.

According to Freud—and DSM-II—the psychoses are characterized by a loss of contact with reality, a disorganized personality, and by extreme deviation from normal patterns of acting, thinking, and feeling. Some of these severe disorders had clear-cut biological causes and were referred to as **organic psychoses**. Other severe disorders had emotional causes and were referred to as **functional psychoses**. But the authors of DSM-II held that the neuroses *always* had emotional rather than organic causes.

DSM-III reflects a strong movement within the field of psychiatry away from Freudian theorizing. Instead of employing such diagnostic categories as "psychosis" and "neurosis," DSM-III uses the medical term "disorder." As we discuss the various *disorders*, however, we will also give their older names.

Disorders Evidenced during Infancy, Childhood, Adolescence

Axis 1 of DMS-III begins by listing a variety of mental disorders that "usually first manifest themselves in infancy, childhood, or adolescence." Some of them have clear-cut biological causes; others don't. We will talk about some of these disorders again in the next chapter.

Organic Mental Disorders

At the other end of the age scale from the childhood disorders are those problems associated with growing old. DSM-III refers to these as "**dementias** arising in the **senium** and presenium."

Senile Dementia (Senile Psychosis)

Many physical problems associated with old age can cause you to lapse into a child-like state commonly called a *senile dementia*, or *senile psychosis*. You may suffer from a series of slight strokes, or from *Alzheimer's disease* (see Chapter 18). In 1974 this type of mental illness accounted for almost 5 percent of the admissions to public mental hospitals. By 1984, this figure had risen considerably, in part because older people now make up a larger percentage of the population. (The actual percentage of older mental patients is hard to determine, since some half of them are put in nursing homes rather than mental hospitals.) The average age of hospital admission for patients diagnosed as senile is 75 for both men and women, although the problem may occur as early as age 60 or so.

Substance-Induced Organic Mental Disorders

Drug abuse can lead not only to behavioral changes, but to organic mental disorders as well. However, as the *Manual* notes, "in most cases, the diagnosis of these Organic Mental Disorders will be made in individuals who also have a Substance Use Disorder."

Substance Use Disorders

Addiction to, or overdose from, many types of drugs can lead to abnormal behavior and thought patterns. A person suffering from such abnormalities is said to have a *drug-induced psychosis*, or a "substance use disorder." We discussed many of the causes for drug-related problems in Chapter 3, and most of the types of drugs that people "abuse" are listed in Table 21.1. By far the most commonly abused substance, however, is alcohol.

Schizophrenic Disorders

In 1984, the National Institute of Mental Health reported on the "state of America's mental health." NIMH experts interviewed more

Organic psychoses (sigh-KOH-sees). Severe mental disorders that supposedly have a clear-cut physiological basis, such as brain damage, stroke, old age, drug abuse, and so forth. In fact, since people react quite differently to brain damage, strokes, old age, and drugs, there is no psychosis that is *entirely* "organic."

Functional psychoses. Severe mental disorders that have no measurable physiological cause. That is, mental disorders that appear to stem from malfunctions of the mind, not the body. In fact, since the body always reacts physiologically to psychological stress, there is no psychosis that is *entirely* "functional."

Dementias (dee-MENT-chee-ahs). From the Latin word meaning "mad," or "insane." A dementia is a severe mental disorder.

Senium (SEE-knee-um). From the Latin word meaning "old." Senium means "senile period," or "old age."

Volition (voh-LISH-shun). Voluntary control of your behaviors. See Chapters 9 and 10.

Dementia praecox (dee-MENT-chee-ah PREE-cox). The original name for schizophrenia. Means "insanity of the young."

than 20,000 people in five communities around the nation. According to the NIMH report, nearly 20 percent of American adults currently suffer psychiatric disorders of one kind or another. However, less than a million of these people are hospitalized at any one point in time. Some 50 percent of the hospital beds in the US are occupied by mental patients, the vast majority being people suffering from psychotic problems. Fortunately, many of these individuals recover completely after treatment and never need hospitalization again.

According to the NIMH report, about 1.5 million Americans suffer from *schizophrenia*. The term comes from the Latin words that mean "splitting of the mind." The use of this term is unfortunate, for the "multiple" or "split personality" we will discuss later as a type of dissociative disorder has nothing to do with schizophrenia.

General mental disorganization is usually the major hallmark of schizophrenia. The authors of DSM-III state that, "Invariably there are characteristic disturbances in several of the following areas: content and form of thought, perception, [emotion], sense of self, **volition**, relationship to the external world, and psychomotor behavior." Thus, if you badly distorted reality, or if you withdrew into a psychological shell and wouldn't come out, you would probably be diagnosed as suffering from schizophrenia.

An older name for schizophrenia is **dementia praecox**, from the Latin words meaning "youthful insanity." And schizophrenia *is* primarily a disorder of the young. In his 1978 study of thousands of people admitted to VA hospitals, Jeffrey Blum found that 45.7 percent of patients aged 17–24 were diagnosed as being schizophrenic. However, only 8.9 percent of patients over 65 years of age were classified as being schizophrenic.

About 27 percent of all the patients in Blum's study were classified as suffering from schizophrenia. Furthermore, this disorder is becoming increasingly more common. Only 21.2 percent of the VA patients in 1954 were classed as schizophrenic, while in 1974 the figure had risen to almost 31 percent. Schizophrenia affects men and women in equal numbers, but single males are particularly susceptible.

Causes of Schizophrenia

There is considerable argument in psychological circles as to whether schizophrenia really exists as a "single" mental illness, or whether we simply call people "schizophrenics" because we don't know what else to call them. The fact that so many people are diagnosed as schizophrenic suggests that this category may be too loose and too large to be meaningfully applied to the complex living systems we call human beings.

This controversy over what schizophrenia actually "is" can be seen in the variety of explanations offered for what causes this disorder. As you might surmise, there are three main types of theories—biological, intra-psychic, and social/behavioral.

Biological Correlates of Schizophrenia

In a 1981 article in *Psychiatry Research*, University of Nebraska researcher Charles Golden reports a study of patients suffering from chronic schizophrenia. Golden used a device that actually "scans" the brains of individuals from outside the body. Golden states that patients with schizophrenia have "less dense brains" than do normal individuals. Both hemispheres are equally affected. Golden says he cannot yet tell whether the decrease in brain density is caused by the schizophrenic disorder, or whether these patients simply have brains that did not develop fully.

Writing in the February 18, 1983 issue of *Science*, Jacinthe Baribeau-Braun and her colleagues report a series of studies on neural activity in the brains of schizophrenic patients. Baribeau-Braun and her group report that the schizophrenic patient "is unable to organize and maintain an effective strategy for process-ing information. The slowness and inefficiency of schizophrenic information processing could result from an inability to organize the processes in an optimal manner."

Why does the schizophrenic patient have difficulty attending to and processing inputs? Rochester University psychiatrist Rue Cromwell believes these individuals have some genetic flaw that prevents them from "blocking out" sensory stimulation. Thus, their brains may be "overwhelmed" by incoming stimuli and, rather than paying attention to "relevant" cues, they attend to "irrelevant" inputs instead. We will have more to say about this issue momentarily. However, the question remains, how is this genetic flaw expressed? Some researchers believe it shows itself in some type of altered brain chemistry.

Williams College psychologist Andrew Crider discusses this issue in his 1979 book, *Schizophrenia: A Biopsychological Perspective*. Crider concludes that no single neurochemical deficit can account for all the symptoms associated with schizophrenia. Crider believes that genes *predispose* an individual to schizophrenia, but the disorder becomes **manifest** only under certain environmental conditions. So it is to the psychosocial correlates of schizophrenia that we must next turn our attention.

Bateson's "Double-Bind" Hypothesis

One of the earliest psychosocial theories of schizophrenia came from anthropologist Gregory Bateson. In his studies of the families of schizophrenia patients, Bateson noted that the patients' mothers often communicated with their children using "contradictory messages." For example, the mother might *say* she loved the child, but say it in a manner (and with body language) suggesting just the opposite. The child was then caught in what Bateson called a "double-bind." That is, the child desperately wanted to understand and respond to what the mother was saying, but could neither decipher the "real" message the mother was giving nor tell the mother about the confusion she was causing. The child then supposedly withdraws from reality in an attempt to avoid further emotional turmoil.

Bateson's "double-bind theory of schizophrenia" has many attractive features to it. However, most research studies have failed to support Bateson's hypothesis.

The "Controlling-Mother" Hypothesis

In their 1981 book *The Family Shadow*, California researchers David Reynolds and Norman

Farberow suggest that a "controlling mother" may be the major cause of schizophrenia. Their book contains a detailed study of a short period in the life of a mental patient named "Chuck Smith." In order to discover what the world of the schizophrenic was like, Reynolds actually lived with Chuck and his family for a period of several weeks just after Chuck was released from a mental hospital. Reynolds's first observation was that "the pervasive boredom and meaninglessness of Chuck's way of life" made him "mentally and physically sluggish." This dullness also produced "a sort of personal numbness along with an unreal quality to the world [which] helped to cushion the steady undermining of optimism and hope experienced in the Smith household."

Reynolds sees Chuck's mother as being the main cause of the young man's problems. Jewel Smith was a depressive. And "like most depressives," Reynolds says, "she believed that love is a matter of controlling the loved ones and sought to control her family." Chuck's reaction to this was to escape into unreality. "Schizophrenia . . . provided Chuck with some protective distance from Jewel's smothering control." When Chuck was living at home, his "madness" allowed him to keep his mother at arm's length. And when that failed, Reynolds says, Chuck's mental disorder allowed him to enter the safe haven of the mental hospital.

Schizophrenia: An Interactive Model

In their 1981 book, John Strauss and William Carpenter propose what they call an "interactive-developmental-systems model" of schizophrenia. Strauss and Carpenter believe there is a genetic "predisposition" toward schizophrenia. However, this innate tendency is expressed only in certain stressful environments, particularly in "demanding" family situations. Thus, Strauss and Carpenter say, there is *no one, single cause* for this mental disorder. Rather, schizophrenia is a developmental problem determined by biological, intra-psychic, and social/behavioral factors. *All of these factors* must be present, Strauss and Carpenter believe, for the disorder to surface.

Types of Schizophrenia

DSM-III lists four main types of schizophrenia: disorganized, **catatonic**, paranoid, and undifferentiated. A fifth category, called *residual*, is reserved for patients who have made some sort of recovery or who are not presently showing all the symptoms of the disorder. How-

Manifest (MANN-eye-fest). Something that is "out in the open," or measurable, as opposed to something that is hidden.

Catatonic (kat-tah-TAHN-ick). There are two main types of catatonic schizophrenia. The first (called "catatonic stupor") often comes on rapidly. The patient becomes mute, stares blankly at the floor, and may assume a fixed, stereotyped posture which may be maintained for days or weeks. The second (called "catatonic excitement") is characterized by frenzied motor activity. The patient may talk incoherently at the top of the voice, rush frantically back and forth, tear off clothing, and without warning may attack someone or break up furniture. The two states may alternate—that is, a patient may be "stuporous" for a while, then lapse into excitement, then become calm and "freeze" into a strange posture for several days.

Paranoia (pair-uh-NOY-ya). A diagnosis given to those patients who show delusions of persecution or grandeur, or intense and irrational jealousy, but who do not seem to be schizophrenic. From the Greek word meaning "madness."

ever, most schizophrenic patients are not expected to recover fully, and they cannot be considered "cured" until they have been free of all symptoms for a period of "many years."

Paranoid Disorders

Some patients have well-organized delusions, severe types of jealousy, and feelings of being persecuted—but show no other evidence of mental illness (such as distorted thought patterns or inappropriate emotions). These patients are often diagnosed as suffering from **paranoia**. But as the authors of DSM-III note, "the boundaries of this group of disorders and their differentiation from other disorders, particularly severe Paranoid Personality Disorder and Schizophrenia, Paranoid Type, are unclear." The authors of DSM-III also state that deafness, moving to a new country, and other stresses may predispose a patient to the development of a paranoid disorder. The delusions caused by drug abuse are also considered to be a form of paranoid psychosis.

Other Psychotic Disorders

DSM-III lists several minor disorders here that resemble other psychoses but are of very brief duration. Since there is little agreement among psychiatrists on these disorders, we will not discuss them further.

Affective Disorders

People suffering from what we call the *affective disorders* (or affective psychoses) often

A 1984 NIMH report suggests that almost 10 million Americans may suffer from affective disorders, primarily depression.

seem stuck at one end of the emotionality scale or the other. That is, they usually are very "up" or very "down," although sometimes they "flip-flop" from one extreme to the other.

According to the NIMH report, almost 10 million people in the US currently suffer from one of the affective disorders.

Causes of Affective Disorders

There is little agreement among experts as to the cause of mania, depression, or the manic-depressive (bipolar) condition. As usual, there are the expected "narrow" theories that stress biological *or* psychological *or* social factors. But the trend appears to be toward "interactive" or "systems" models.

As John Wittrig points out in the February 1982 issue of *Contemporary Psychology*, "there is little doubt that having biological parents with either chronic schizophrenia or bipolar affective behaviors increases the probability of developing those [and related] conditions." Thus, there may well be a *genetic predisposition* toward mania or depression.

However, it may take a specific social situation to bring this predisposition to the fore. Writing in the December 1979 issue of the *American Journal of Psychiatry*, Julia Mayo and her colleagues blame the "family system" for most affective problems. According to Mayo, the *spouses* of manic-depressive patients often

perceived the mental disorder as a sign of "weakness of character and self-indulgence that had to be met with a firm display of power and control." The "normal" spouse then communicates to the children that daddy (or mommy) is "sick" through some fault of his or her own. To be loved—and to stay safely in the family system—you must remain "well." As a result, Mayo says, "each [member of the family] appeared to have developed his or her own idiosyncratic style of defensive coping to ward off the threat of expulsion from the family system."

Other researchers presume that both mania and depression are *acquired behaviors*. In Chapter 12, we described Martin Seligmann's research on "learned helplessness," which is very similar to depression. Leonard Ullman and Leonard Krasner take a similar stance in their book, *A Psychological Approach to Abnormal Behavior*. Ullman and Krasner describe several situations in which parents have unconsciously *trained* their children to be manic or depressive by paying attention to (and otherwise rewarding) the youngsters *only* when the children display manic or depressive behaviors.

As you can see, there is considerable controversy over both the cause of and cure for the affective disorders. However, in his 1982 article mentioned earlier, John Wittrig concludes that the affective disorders are multi-determined, and that only when we accept "the scientific principle of multiple causation" can we hope to understand mania and depression. Unfortunately, as Wittrig notes, to date we don't have an adequate model that includes all we know about these very human problems.

Types of Affective Disorders

DSM-III lists two major types of affective disorders—the *bipolar* disorder, and the *major depression*. There is considerable controversy among experts about *mania*. Some writers believe it is possible for individuals to suffer from a "manic psychosis" that never develops into a depressive condition. Other theorists contend that *all* patients who experience "manic episodes" will eventually become depressive. DSM-III takes the latter viewpoint, and therefore uses the term "bipolar disorder" to describe anyone who shows manic behavior.

There is a curious but not well understood relationship between manic and depressive episodes. Some patients swing wildly from one emotional extreme to the other, while some patients show only the depressive reaction. According to the authors of DSM-III, if the patient shows *both* schizophrenic thought patterns *and* severe mania or depression, the patient probably should be diagnosed as having both types of disorder simultaneously.

Question: What might Harlow's research on "depressed monkeys" tell us about the causes of some types of human depressions?

Neurotic Disorders

In a preliminary draft of DSM-III circulated in the late 1970's, the term "neurosis" was discarded completely. Probably no other aspect of the preliminary draft caused so much criticism. In the final version, the authors of DSM-III have again listed the neuroses—but in parentheses after their "new names." On page 9 of the *Manual*, the authors write, "When Freud first used the term 'psychoneurosis,' he was referring to only four subtypes: anxiety neurosis, anxiety hysteria (phobia), obsessive compulsive neurosis, and hysteria." Over the years, however, the term was broadened to include many disorders that didn't fit Freud's original four categories. And thus, according to the authors of DSM-III, "there [now] is no consensus in our field as to how to define 'neurosis.'"

In fact, most of what DSM-III calls "Anxiety Disorders," "Somatoform Disorders," "Dissociative Disorders," and "Factitious Disorders" are what once were called *neuroses*. The same might be said for some sexual disorders, "disorders of impulse control," and most of the other abnormalities that fill out Axis 1 and all of Axis 2 of DSM-III. We will list some of the more common types of neuroses below, following the DSM-III classifications.

Anxiety Disorders

Generally speaking, *anxiety* is the hallmark of these disorders. The authors of DSM-III estimate that from 2 to 4 percent of the general population have at some time had disorders that would be classified as anxiety disorders. However, the 1984 report from NIMH estimates that about 13.1 million people in the US (almost 6 percent of the population) *currently* suffer from anxiety disorders. Most of these individuals have phobic disorders, or "phobias."

Phobic Disorder (Phobic Neurosis)

As we mentioned in Chapter 13, phobias are abnormal or unusual fears that have no real basis in fact. If John Smith is unconsciously afraid of sexual activity, he may transfer this unacceptable anxiety to a fear of small or tight places. If the Smiths' bedroom is cramped for space, John may avoid the anxiety associated with entering his wife by refusing to enter the bedroom.

Panic Disorder (Anxiety Neurosis)

Fear begets fear, and panic leads to more panic. If John Smith is unconsciously worried about his masculinity, he may suffer from such acute anxiety that he is unable to perform sexually. The more he tries to satisfy his wife, the more anxiety he experiences, and the worse he performs. Eventually he may break out in a cold sweat if Mary so much as puts her arm around him in the kitchen, fearing that this show of affection is the prelude to another bedroom disaster.

According to the NIMH report, about 1.2 million Americans currently suffer from a panic disorder.

Obsessive Compulsive Disorder (Obsessive Compulsive Neurosis)

Suppose that Mary Smith had, during her childhood, picked up the attitude that sexual desires are evil and ought to be resisted even in marriage. And so she attempts to repress her natural instincts and urges, much to John Smith's dismay. But her sexual impulses become so strong that the only way she can keep

Multiple personality, though a rare type of dissociative disorder in real life, often appears in novels and movies, such as *The Three Faces of Eve.*

them safely repressed is to *think* continually about something utterly irrational—and keep *thinking* about it again and again and again.

Or perhaps she performs compulsive, repetitive *actions*—over and over and over. Usually these compulsive actions are symbolically related to her problem. For example, her mind may be filled with images of germs—she may see them everywhere. So she may wash her hands (or the bedroom floor) dozens of times each day in an attempt to prevent or get rid of the "dirty sexual thoughts" that flood her mind.

Obsessions typically deal with thoughts. *Compulsions* typically have to do with behaviors. In either case, the patient is diagnosed as suffering from an "obsessive compulsive disorder."

According to the NIMH report, about 2.4 million Americans currently suffer from an obsessive compulsive disorder.

Somatoform Disorders

Freud used the term *hysteria* to refer to this condition. The essential features are recurrent and multiple complaints about "illnesses" or "body dysfunctions" that apparently are not due to any physical disorder. The patient may experience pain that has no relation to medical problems. Or the individual may so fear having a particular disease that the patient goes to one doctor after another in an attempt to get someone to confirm the patient's fears. This latter type of disorder is called **hypochondriacal neurosis**.

Conversion Disorder (Hysterical Neurosis, Conversion Type)

If Mary Smith suffered from this disorder, she would tend to *convert* hidden or unacceptable wishes or impulses into organic symptoms. This "symptom conversion" presumably would be an attempt to divert her feelings of anxiety and perhaps to arouse sympathy and attract attention. If she insisted that her sex organs had no "feelings" at all, that they were "anesthetized," she might be converting her fears about sexuality into a bodily symptom.

Dissociative Disorders

These problems are also closely related to hysteria. The essential feature of most of these disorders is a sudden change in memory, consciousness, identity, or motor behavior.

Psychogenic Amnesia

A type of memory loss brought on by stress or psychological trauma, and not due to any organic problem. As we noted in Chapter 15, the person tends to forget "what" but not "how."

Psychogenic Fugue

If John Smith became badly traumatized by his relationship with Mary, he might assume a totally new identity. Usually this new personality would be more outgoing and uninhibited than his previous personality had been. John might also run away physically as well as psychologically—by moving to a new place. If he later returns to his old identity—and his old home—he probably won't remember what he did while in the **fugue state**.

Multiple Personality

If Mary Smith's desire for sex bothered her, she might repress all thoughts of sex. But these repressed sexual urges might be so strong that they split off into a *separate sub-personality* in order to find expression. Mary Smith might refer to this part of herself as "Miss Black," who periodically (usually in bed) seized possession of her body and "did wicked things" with John. In this form of "multiple personality," the dominant personality often forgets the behaviors that the minor personality engages in.

In his 1979 book, *Mindsplit*, New Zealand psychologist Peter McKellar describes in detail many of the most famous multiple personalities in psychiatric history. These cases include the patients described in the 1954 book *Eve*, and the 1975 book *Sybil*. Since the term *schizophrenia* means "split mind," many people wrongly presume that patients who suffer from multiple personality disorders must be schizophrenic. According to McKellar, this is seldom the case. In schizophrenia, "the personality . . . is not 'split' into a finite number of subsystems, it is 'shattered' into innumerable fragments." In cases of multiple personality, however, each "minor personality" is usually an *organized* and reasonably well-developed sub-system.

"...AND FLAIR SOAP HAS A SPECIAL OFFER FOR ALL YOU OBSESSIVE-COMPULSIVES WHO WASH YOUR HANDS BETWEEN 30 AND 50 TIMES A DAY."

Hypochondriacal neurosis (high-poh-kon-DRY-ick-cal). From the Latin word meaning "under the breastbone," which was assumed in olden days to be the "seat" of this disorder. A hypochondriac (high-poh-KON-dree-ack) is someone with a morbid concern about his/her health, or someone with delusions that she/he is sick.

Fugue state (FEWG). Our word "fugitive" comes from the same Latin source. A fugue state is one in which a patient "flees" from his/her old personality, often by getting on a bus or plane and moving to a new place.

Paraphilias (pair-ah-FILL-ee-ahs). From Greek words meaning "love of things above and beyond the normal." These sexual disorders involve a need for abnormal or unusual objects or stimulation in order to achieve climax.

Transvestism (trans-VEST-ism). From the Latin words *trans*, meaning "across," and *vestire*, meaning "to dress." A transvestite is a female who "cross-dresses," that is, who wears masculine clothes, or a male who wears dresses and feminine underwear.

Ego-dystonic homosexuality (EE-go diss-TON-ick). A type of homosexuality in which the person's ego becomes threatened or "torn apart" by the person's sexual thoughts or behaviors. A homosexual who is greatly disturbed by her or his own sexuality.

Depersonalization Disorder

If John Smith suffered from this disorder, he might occasionally feel that he had "lost touch with reality." He might believe he was "living a waking dream," and that his thoughts and movements were under someone else's control. He might even perceive the people around him as being "robots," or even see them as being "dead."

Psychosexual Disorders

There are four major types of psychosexual disorders:

1. *Gender identity disorders* have to do with a desire to be or dress like the opposite sex.
2. The **paraphilias** involve the need for unusual or bizarre imagery or acts in order to achieve sexual excitement. For instance, John Smith might be more excited by the sight of Mary's clothing than by Mary herself, which DSM-III describes as a "clothing fetish." But if John preferred to *wear* women's clothes, this would be a paraphilia called **transvestism**.
3. *Psychosexual dysfunctions* have to do with inhibited desire or performance, or with reaching orgasm too rapidly or too slowly.
4. The last category of psychosexual disorder is **ego-dystonic homosexuality**.

We covered many of these topics in Chapter 11. As we noted there, the prevailing view

Transvestism means "crossdressing," or wearing clothes typically worn only by the opposite sex.

Many psychiatrists believe that compulsive gambling is a mental disorder.

among psychologists and psychiatrists is that most of these behaviors are "abnormal" only in the statistical sense of the word. That is, they are unusual, but not pathological. While not all experts agree on this point, we might note again that both the American Psychiatric Association and the American Psychological Association now consider homosexuality an "alternative lifestyle," and not a "condition that requires punishment or therapy."

The only "mental disorder" that DSM-III recognizes as being associated with homosexuality is that which is *ego-dystonic*. By this term, the authors of the *Manual* refer to someone who experiences great guilt about her or his homosexuality. But the "guilt and anxiety" are what need treating, not the homosexuality itself.

Factitious Disorders

The term "factitious" means not real, genuine, or natural. Factitious disorders are, as DSM-III notes, characterized by physical or psychological symptoms that are produced by the individual and are under voluntary control. This tendency to "invent" illness is apparently more common among males than among fe-

males. The person with this sort of problem may often spend all of his/her life trying to get admitted to hospitals—perhaps in an attempt to escape from various problems, perhaps because the individual failed in an attempt to become a nurse or doctor. These disorders are not particularly common, and seem to be rather difficult to treat when they do occur.

Disorders of Impulse Control

These disorders include pathological gambling, **kleptomania**, **pyromania**, and the sorts of "explosive emotional outbursts" we will discuss in the next chapter (see "running amok"). These disorders are more common among males than females.

Adjustment Disorders

According to DSM-III, the essential feature of these disorders is the inability to cope with psychological or social stress (see Chapter 12). Depression, anxiety, and "acting out" are the main symptoms. DSM-III has, in fact, little else to say about this class of disorders.

Conditions Not Mental Disorders but Requiring Treatment

DSM-III lists a number of conditions that may cause a patient to seek treatment but that aren't really "mental disorders" and thus require a special diagnostic code. Most of these conditions are fairly minor problems that may require little more than "talking things over with an expert." Interpersonal difficulties, mild cases of antisocial behavior, simple grief, and various occupational problems make up the bulk of those on this list.

Personality Disorders

The authors of DSM-III state that "personality *traits* are enduring patterns of perceiving, relating to, and thinking about the environment and oneself, and are exhibited in a wide range of important social and personal contexts. It is only when *personality traits* are inflexible and maladaptive and cause either significant impairment in social or occupational functioning or subjective distress that they constitute *Personality Disorders*."

The personality disorders are coded on Axis 2 of DSM-III, not on Axis 1. Although many of the these problems are similar in type to the mental disorders described on Axis 1, they are thought to be "traits," not "mental illnesses." Thus, according to the authors of DSM-III, "the diagnosis of a Personality Disorder should be made only when the characteristic features are typical of the individual's long-term functioning and are not limited to discrete episodes of illness."

The major type of personality disorder not described elsewhere is that of the "antisocial personality."

Antisocial Personality Disorder

Whatever their causes or cures, most mental disorders typically give the most pain and unhappiness to the individual concerned. Someone with an *antisocial personality disorder*, however, is likely to cause more problems for others than for the person with the deviant behaviors. Many criminals fall into this category, as do "manipulators," "con artists," and some types of political rebels.

In previous diagnostic schemes, the terms "psychopath" or "sociopath" were often used to describe individuals with an antisocial personality disorder. Most of these people lack a superego or "conscience," and experience little or no guilt or anxiety about breaking social laws. They often appear to be greedy, impulsive, egocentric men and women who cannot comprehend the social consequences of their actions.

There is no agreement among experts as to what causes a person to experience this problem. However, according to the 1984 NIMH report, about 1.4 million Americans currently could be diagnosed as having antisocial personalities.

Kleptomania (KLEPP-toh-main-ee-ah). An irresistable urge to steal, usually without any need to do so.

Pyromania (PIE-roh-main-ee-ah). An irresistable urge to set things on fire, often for the perverse sexual excitement associated with "burning."

DSM-III: An Evaluation

Like all diagnostic schemes, DSM-III has both strengths and weaknesses. Let's look at the good points first.

Strengths of DSM-III

DSM-III has many strengths. To begin with, by focusing on the biological underpinnings of many "mental" disorders, DSM-III offers a broader view of the behavioral disorders than did DSM-II. Because DSM-II (1968) was heavily influenced by psychoanalytic theory, its diagnostic categories strongly suggested the use of psychotherapy (or "talk therapy"). However, because DSM-III (1980) is oriented more toward the biological end of the spectrum, its diagnostic descriptions seem to suggest the use of chemotherapy ("pills") rather than psychotherapy. Since chemotherapy is the "treatment of choice" for many mental disorders these days, DSM-III would seem to be closer to present-day practice than was DSM-II.

Second, because DSM-III was put together by psychiatrists, psychologists, and social workers, it has a broader scope than did previous *Manuals*. And because of this input from several professional fields, DSM-III contains more diagnostic categories than did DSM-II or DSM-I.

Third, since DSM-III has been widely adopted both in the US and abroad, the *Manual* adds some measure of standardization to the fields of psychiatry and clinical psychology throughout the world.

Fourth, DSM-III was tested more extensively prior to adoption than was either previous *Manual*.

And last, but surely not least, DSM-III answers a real need. We obviously must have *some* type of classification scheme in order to deal with the very human problems we find around us. And DSM-III is, quite simply, the best such scheme we presently have available to us.

Weaknesses of DSM-III

There are at least two kinds of problems associated with the 1980 *Manual*. The first type of difficulty is professional, while the second is scientific.

Any new classification scheme demands that people re-orient both their perceptions and their behaviors. Some mental health professionals accustomed to using DSM-II have raised questions about DSM-III that may do little more than reflect their own reluctance to change. Writing in the October 1981 issue of the American Psychological Association *Monitor*, Robert Spitzer attempts to deal with this issue.

Spitzer is a psychiatrist—a medical doctor—who chaired the group that developed DSM-III. Thus, some of his arguments are doubtless biased in favor both of psychiatry (as opposed to psychology) and to the use of the *Manual*. However, he does make some good points.

To begin with, Spitzer notes that many psychologists fear DSM-III is yet another attempt by the medical doctors to "take complete charge" of the behavioral sciences. Spitzer disagrees. He states that psychologists as well as psychiatrists helped prepare the *Manual*. More psychologists have bought copies of DSM-III than anyone else, including psychiatrists. And most recent textbooks on abnormal psychology have adopted the DSM-III classification scheme. By implication, it would seem that psychology has been more "accepting" of the *Manual* than has psychiatry. We will have more to say about this point in a moment.

Spitzer notes that one major objection to the *Manual* is that it "adheres to the medical model." Spitzer denies this is the case. He points out that nowhere in the book do the authors state that "mental disorders are medical disorders." Nor does the *Manual* "assume an underlying biological dysfunction or abnormality for all the disorders." These points are technically true. However, preliminary drafts of DSM-III *did* state that medical doctors should be the primary care-givers for *all* types of behavioral problems. If psychologists, social workers, religious leaders, and many psychiatrists had not complained loudly about this issue, the final draft would surely have reflected even more of a medical bias than it presently does. And, as we will see, most clinical psychologists still *perceive* DSM-III as having a "medical bias."

Scientific Problems with DSM-III

Many psychologists object to DSM-III on scientific rather than professional grounds. To begin with, because the authors of the present *Manual* have rejected Freudian theory, they have made DSM-III more **eclectic** in its approach than were previous versions. Thus, the categories listed above are little more than a hodge-podge of "labels" that are to be pinned on individuals who don't behave as most of us presumably do. Next, there is the difficulty associated with getting the right label on the right person—that is to say, can we be sure the *Manual* is reliable when used in real-life situations? Last but not least, we must somehow make sure that the diagnostic categories used are "valid" enough to tell us how to *help* the people we have labeled as being "mentally disordered."

We will have more to say about the problem of how to categorize people correctly in a moment. First, let's look at studies on the validity and the reliability of DSM-III in some detail.

Is DSM-III Valid?

As you discovered in the last chapter, there are two types of validity. If a test (or diagnostic scheme) correlates well with other tests or measuring tools, we say it has *construct* validity. But to have *empirical* validity, the test must be able to predict real-world events. As you will see, there are many studies showing that DSM-III has "construct" validity. Whether the "empirical" validity of the *Manual* is as high as it should be, however, is still a hotly debated topic.

Several studies have suggested that DSM-III has a higher "construct" validity than did DSM-II. For example, John Werry and his colleagues at the University of Auckland School of Medicine (New Zealand) found a significant correlation between DSM-III ratings of child patients and diagnoses offered by trained clinicians. Marsha Schroeder and her colleagues at the University of British Columbia found that DSM-III agreed with other measures for diagnosing "antisocial personality disorders" in prison populations. Still further evidence comes from a 1983 paper in the *Journal of Nervous and Mental Disease* by Canadian psychiatrist Edward Helmes and his colleagues. These researchers compared the ability of 12 diagnostic systems to correctly identify schizophrenic patients. Helmes and his group concluded that DSM-III was "one of the three most reliable" classification systems.

There are certain limitations to the use of DSM-III, however. Writing in the July 1983 issue of the *American Journal of Psychotherapy*, Georgetown University psychiatrist William Goldstein states that the *Manual* does a poor job of defining "borderline personality disorders." And Duke University researcher James Carter reports in the August 1983 issue of the

Journal of the National Medical Association that DSM-III "does not allow for the psychosocial stressor of racism," and thus may be an inappropriate instrument to use with blacks.

There is also some question about the validity of the *Manual* when used with female patients. Several authors discuss this problem in the July 1983 issue of the *American Psychologist*. Rutgers psychologist Marcie Kaplan notes that women's treatment rates for mental illness are higher than men's. In particular, women are more likely to be diagnosed as suffering from a "dependent personality disorder" than men are. One reason for this difference, Kaplan argues, is that the authors of DSM-III were predominantly male. Thus, Kaplan says, masculine-biased assumptions about what behaviors are healthy and what behaviors are "crazy" are built into the diagnostic categories of DSM-III. In that same journal, however, Janet Williams and Robert Spitzer deny Kaplan's assertions. In a test of 3,250 patients, Williams and Spitzer report that "there was no overall tendency for a female patient to receive a personality disorder diagnosis more often a male patient."

In the same issue of *American Psychologist*, Texas A&M psychologists Darrell Smith and William Kraft report a survey of 546 psychologists, most of whom were in clinical practice. The vast majority of these clinicians rejected DSM-III as a "useful diagnostic instrument." They also rejected the idea that "mental disorders" are a subset of medical disorders. Smith and Kraft urge all mental-health professionals to work together to develop a better diagnostic tool than DSM-III appears to be.

Despite all the controversy, the bulk of the research so far published suggests that DSM-III is more reliable and valid than previous *Manuals* were. However, most of these studies show that the *Manual* merely has high "construct" validity. We could show that DSM-III had "empirical" validity, if research indicated that the *categories* described in the *Manual* were those that occurred in real life. That is to say, does "paranoid schizophrenic disorder" as described in DSM-III really exist as a "mental disease" the way that (say) measles exists? Or is "paranoid schizophrenic disorder" a category that DSM-III *imposes* on people who actually suffer from quite different mental-health problems? In brief, do the "labels" that DSM-III puts on mental patients represent reality, or is it a matter of our "seeing what we expect to see" in the patients we treat? We will have more to say about "empirical validity" in a moment.

Perhaps, however, we shouldn't worry too

Eclectic (ek-KLECK-tick). From the Greek word meaning "to gather." To be eclectic is to "gather" or select the best aspects of several different theories or methods.

Pseudo-patients (SUE-doh). *Pseudo* means "false." Rosenhan's "pseudo-patients" were normal individuals who pretended to suffer from mental disorders in order to get admitted to various mental hospitals.

much about the *Manual*'s validity. For one of the statistical facts of life is that *no test can be valid if it is not reliable*. And, as we are about to see, many scientists have serious concern about the reliability of DSM-III.

Is DSM-III Reliable?

There is considerable evidence that psychiatrists who use the *Manual* often disagree on what diagnosis to make about a particular patient. Worse yet, psychiatrists sometimes cannot tell (in a reliable fashion) who is a "geniune" mental patient and who is "just faking it."

Rosenhan's "Pseudo-patients"

In 1973, Stanford psychologist David L. Rosenhan shocked the psychological world with a report of research he had undertaken on the reliability of psychiatric diagnoses. Rosenhan asked several "normal" people to try to get into mental hospitals by pretending to be mentally ill. These **pseudo-patients**, as Rosenhan called them, asked for voluntary admission to several public and private mental hospitals. The pseudo-patients all stated that they "heard voices," and thus needed help. Other than on this one point, these quite normal people told the admitting psychiatrists the *absolute truth* about their lives and feelings.

To Rosenhan's surprise, *all* of the pseudo-patients were admitted without question. They were all classed as being *psychotic*. About 95 percent of the time, they were diagnosed as being "schizophrenic."

Once the pseudo-patients were admitted, it was up to all of them to get *out* of the mental hospital as best they could. They were told to ask to see the admitting psychiatrist the next day, to say that the "voices" had gone away, and that they wished to be released. But getting out proved to be much more difficult than getting in. No matter how "normal" the pseudo-patients acted, they found it hard to convince the hospital staff there was now nothing wrong with them. On the average, it took the pseudo-patients more than two weeks to get out. And

David L. Rosenhan

on their release, all of their records were marked, "psychosis *in remission*," meaning that only the symptoms were gone. The "disease" presumably was still present, but hidden. One man was detained (against his will) for almost two months. He finally escaped because, as he put it, the hospital was driving him crazy.

When Rosenhan's article was published, it caused a furor. Many psychiatrists attacked him violently for daring to say they couldn't tell normal people from people who were mentally ill. Rosenhan then agreed to a further study. He promised to send an unspecified number of pseudo-patients to several hospitals in the near future. The admitting psychiatrists at these hospitals were asked to "guess" whether each patient they admitted during this time period was a pseudo-patient or not. In fact, Rosenhan sent out no more pseudo-patients. He merely checked all the psychiatric admissions at the end of the time period. To his surprise, he found that some 25 percent of the *actual* patients admitted were thought to be "pseudo-patients" by the psychiatrists.

Rosenhan concludes that psychiatric judgments of what is normal and what isn't—and what is "mental illness" and what is "mentally healthy"—are much less reliable than we had previously suspected.

Other Studies of Diagnostic Reliability

There are several published studies suggesting that psychiatric diagnoses can be highly unreliable. For instance, in 1949 Philip Ash arranged to have psychiatrists interview incoming patients jointly at a clinic, then diagnose them independently. The psychiatrists were in total agreement on specific diagnoses less than 10 percent of the time. They were in total *disagreement* about one-third of the time.

In a 1981 article, psychologist Walli Leff and

two colleagues report they asked staff psychiatrists and clinical psychologists at a VA hospital to indicate how much they agreed with a number of case-history diagnoses. Leff and his associates found very little agreement among the "experts."

Psychologists Maurice Temerlin and William Trousdale had psychiatrists and psychologists listen to a tape-recorded "clinical interview" with what was supposed to be a "disturbed person." In fact, the individual was an actor who was just pretending to have psychological problems. But 60 percent of the psychiatrists diagnosed the actor as being "psychotic." Only about 30 percent of the psychologists did so, and nearly 16 percent of them said the person was normal. But not one psychiatrist diagnosed the actor as being normal.

Not all reliability studies have yielded such dismal data, however. In the late 1970's and early 1980's, Nancy Cantor and her associates performed a series of studies on diagnostic reliability using DSM-III. Cantor and her colleagues found very high reliability—and good validity—in most of their research. However, they used rather a different testing technique than have most other scientists. To understand why Cantor's results are so special, you will need to know more about what she did, and why she did it.

Psychodiagnostics as "Cognitive Discrimination"

In Chapter 9, we noted the problems people have in trying to classify *concepts*. In Chapter 18, we also reported data suggesting that, as children mature, they discover that most cognitive concepts have very "fuzzy" boundaries. ("If all cups have handles, what do you call those paper containers produced by the Dixie Company?")

Nancy Cantor and Nancy Genero believe that many of the diagnostic categories in DSM-III have indistinct boundaries. Writing in the 1984 book *Contemporary Issues in Psychopathology*, Cantor and Genero state that "a diagnostic manual should ideally give as much attention to . . . the process of operating with fuzzy categories, as it gives to the descriptive content of those categories." The problem with DSM-III, Cantor and Genero say, is that it "encourages clinicians to become exceedingly focused upon a narrow set of typical examples." Instead, DSM-III should warn the clinician that many patients are *atypical*. That is, they do not fit readily into any of the categories given in DSM-III.

To solve the difficulties with DSM-III, Cantor and Genero suggest approaching **psychodiagnostics** as an exercise in *cognitive discrimination*, rather than as an exercise in psychiatric "insight." That is, one good way to improve DSM-III would be to study the cognitive processes people use *naturally* when they try to diagnose what is wrong with mental patients.

"Natural" versus "Theoretical" Categories

Cantor and Genero note that there are two main types of cognitive categories—"natural" and what we might call "theoretical." Natural categories have real-world existence. An example of a natural set of categories would be "animal, vegetable, and mineral." Theoretical categories may or may not exist in the real world. An example of a set of theoretical categories would be "fluid" and "crystallized intelligence."

Generally speaking, it is easier to fit objects into natural than into theoretical categories. Put another way, theoretical classification schemes yield more "atypical cases" than do natural schemes. Thus, according to Cantor and Genero, the fact that so many patients diagnosed using DSM-III are "atypical" suggests that the *Manual* may employ some categories that are more "theoretical" than "natural."

How do you tell whether concepts such as "schizophrenia" and "manic psychosis" are natural or theoretical? One way to do so, Cantor and Genero suggest, is to test the amount of agreement among trained observers when they attempt to use these categories to diagnose real-life patients. The higher the agreement—particularly in regard to atypical cases—the more likely it is that the concepts are natural.

"Priming" the Experts

Cantor and Genero began by selecting the records of 8 patients whose mental disorders had been diagnosed during lengthy periods of hospitalization. All the patients fell into one of four diagnostic categories: Bipolar Disorder (Manic), Bipolar Disorder (Depressive), Paranoid Schizophrenic, and Chronic Undifferentiated Schizophrenic. One patient in each category was "highly typical," while the other patient in each category was "atypical."

Cantor and Genero then selected two groups of "observers." One group was made up of 18 highly experienced clinicians (the "expert observers"). The second group was composed of 46 undergraduates taking a course in abnormal psychology (the "student observers").

Psychodiagnostics (SIGH-koh-dye-ag-NOSS-ticks). That field of psychology which concerns itself with classifying mental or behavioral tendencies, traits, or disorders.

Prototype (PRO-toh-type). A generalized model that represents a cognitive category. In Chapter 9, we noted that the robin is a prototype of the basic category we call "birds."

Exemplar (x-EM-plar). An example. Both penguins and robins are examples of birds, but the robin is a better prototype.

Cantor and Genero "primed" both groups with information about the four diagnostic categories being tested. Cantor and Genero used two types of priming materials. Half of each group of observers read material that described the *critical features* of each diagnostic category in A-B-C terms. Cantor and Genero call this the **prototype** priming condition. The other half of each group of observers read material that gave two examples of "typical" patients for each category. This was the **exemplar** priming condition.

After being "primed," the observers in both groups read the case histories of the 8 hospitalized patients and tried to put each patient into one of the four diagnostic categories.

The "Prime" Success Rate

Both the expert observers and the student observers assigned the "typical" patients to the proper diagnostic category in about 80 percent of the cases. The experts did slightly better than the students did. This high success rate with *typical* cases suggests that the DSM categories are, to some extent, "natural."

When faced with *atypical* cases, however, the success rate for both groups of observers dropped to about 25 percent. The difficulty that the observers had in fitting atypical cases into their proper niches suggests that the DSM diagnostic categories have fuzzier boundaries than they probably should have.

The high success rate with typical patients gives support to psychiatrist Robert Spitzer's contention that DSM-III has *construct validity*. However, the success that the Cantor and Genero "observers" achieved with typical patients would seem to hinge in large part on *priming*. For "priming" reminds the diagnostician ahead of time what the categories to be used actually are. In most real-life studies of the validity of clinical judgments, the diagnosticians are not required to "restudy" the categories just prior to making judgments. If nothing else, the Cantor and Genero research suggests that clinicians may need frequent reminders of what the critical features are that define diagnostic categories.

The low success rate the observers had with atypical cases tells us that the DSM-III categories are more "theoretical" than they probably should be. An analysis of the errors the observers made shows where the problems may lie. The observers seldom put a "manic" patient into the "depressed" category, nor a "depressed" patient into the "manic" category. Thus, the conceptual boundaries between "mania" and "depression" seem fairly clear-cut. Nor was there much confusion with "depression" and "schizophrenia," so the boundaries between these concepts are fairly well marked too. However, the observers frequently had trouble differentiating between "Chronic Undifferentiated Schizophrenia" and "Paranoid Schizophrenia." So the boundaries between the various types of schizophrenia are poorly drawn. In addition, the observers often confused patients diagnosed as "schizophrenic" with patients diagnosed as "manic." So the lines between "mania" and "schizophrenia" are very fuzzy. These results suggest that many of the DSM-III categories need extensive reworking.

Question: Most theorists believe that "mania" and "depression" are two sides of the same coin. What does the Cantor and Genero study suggest?

Evaluating DSM-III: A Summary

The Cantor and Genero experiment is important for many reasons. First, past versions of the *Manual* have been put together by highly qualified experts who argued—sometimes for months on end—about what the critical features of a disorder like "schizophrenia" actually were. This is, of course, a *theoretical* way of constructing diagnostic categories. A more *natural* way of doing so, Cantor and Genero suggest, would be to study the decision-making processes of people who actually have to diagnose real-life patients. A survey of the errors expert diagnosticians make might well help us create more sharply defined (and hence more "natural") categories than presently exist in DSM-III.

Second, the Cantor and Genero study reminds us that even expert clinicians probably need frequent "priming" if they are to function effectively. In Chapter 15, we noted many of the changes and distortions that creep into our Long-term Memory storage banks. These memory "failures" affect skilled psychiatrists and psychologists as much as anyone else. An occa-

sional bit of "priming" might well help experts in *any* field do better in their jobs.

Last, but not least, we might note that DSM-III is still based on the assumption that "mental disorders" are almost entirely *within the individual*, and not a property of the human *systems* we all are parts of. In his 1981 article in the *Monitor*, Robert Spitzer discusses this issue. "Certainly there is a need to develop a classification of disturbed dyadic (or family) units since the DSM-III classification is of behavior syndromes of *individuals*," Spitzer says. He hopes that DSM-IV (whenever it appears) will adopt more of the "systems" approach.

A Holistic Approach to Abnormal Psychology

From a General Systems viewpoint, all behavior is multi-determined. Which is to say that everything you do has not one cause, but many. Human problems, like human successes, are almost always due to *interactions* of biological, psychological, and sociological forces. Thus, any diagnostic scheme that does not view people *holistically* is bound to be relatively unreliable and invalid.

We can demonstrate this point by returning once more to John and Mary Smith. The authors of the DSM-III consider sexual inhibition in females as being primarily the *woman's* problem—a mental disorder (or personality trait) that resides in the woman's mind. But all personality traits (and mental disorders) have a biological background, and they are always expressed in social, interpersonal situations. In a small percentage of cases, sexual inhibition in women may be related to physical causes. But biological difficulties don't really *cause* the inhibition. Rather, the inhibition is the woman's *response* to her physical condition. And this response is chiefly determined by her own unique developmental history and the social environment she presently lives in. Sexual inhibition in men—which is defined by DSM-III as being the *man's* problem—can be seen in much the same light.

Sexual difficulties are seldom the exclusive problem of just the male *or* the female. A man may have problems with inhibition at the start of his marriage, but it is his wife's (often unconscious) responses to his condition that help keep him that way. A woman may dislike sex when she marries, but if her attitude does not change after the wedding, it is surely as much her husband's responsibility as it is hers. As

Masters and Johnson discovered more than 20 years ago, it typically is useless to treat one of the marriage partners and not the other. For, generally speaking, when a person develops abnormal behavior patterns, everyone the person has close contact with must be considered part of the cause.

In the long run, a theory of mental illness—or a set of diagnostic categories—stands or falls on its ability to help people get better. Thus, we cannot make a final evaluation of DSM-III, or any other similar scheme, until we discover what kind of "cure rate" it gives us. As we will see in the next chapter, the holistic approach to treating mental illness apparently yields a higher percentage of cures than does the "medical model" on which DSM-III is based. And perhaps that is the strongest evidence we can offer in favor of viewing human beings as highly complex living systems.

Summary

1 Most **mental disorders** can be viewed as "deviations from a **norm**."

2 Generally speaking, if the deviation from the norm is slight, the person is said to suffer from a **neurosis**. If the deviation is large, the person is said to suffer from a **psychosis**, and probably will require hospitalization or extensive treatment.

3 Psychologists often use the terms **mean**, **median**, and **mode** to describe the center of a **normal distribution** of test scores or behavioral measures. This distribution is often a **bell-shaped curve**. An abnormal behavior or score is one that departs two or more **standard deviations** from the norm.

4 Psychiatrists and psychologists use many different **diagnostic systems** to describe and interpret thoughts or actions that are presumed to be abnormal. One such system is described in the **Diagnostic and Statistical Manual of Mental Disorders**, the third edition of which was published in 1980.

5 **DSM-III** is based on the belief that most mental disorders have a **biological basis**. In contrast, **DSM-II** was based on Freudian theory, and **DSM-I** was based on the belief mental disorders came from abnormal person-environment interactions.

6 According to DSM-III, patients should be rated on five different diagnostic **axes**:
   a Axis 1 covers the **clinical psychiatric syndrome(s)** or major mental disorder(s) the patient suffers from.
   b Axis 2 lists the **personality disorders** or **personality traits** the patient showed, if any.
   c Axis 3 covers any **physical problems** the patient had, such as brain damage or disease.
   d Axis 4 describes any **social stressors** the patient had experienced in the past year.
   e Axis 5 states the patient's highest level of **adaptive functioning** during the past year.

7 A 1984 report by the **National Institute of Mental Health** suggests that some **20 percent of American adults** suffer from mental disorders.

8 The strengths of DSM-III are that it offers a broader view of the behavioral disorders than did DSM-II, it offers a measure of standardization, it was tested extensively prior to publication, and answers a real psychiatric need.

9 The professional weaknesses of DSM-III are that it is based on the **medical model**, and that some psychologists see it as a **grab for power** by psychiatrists. The scientific weaknesses of DSM-III are that, while it apparently has good **construct validity**, it may lack **empirical validity**. It may also be less **reliable** than it should be.

10 Worries about the reliability of DSM-III are based on studies showing that psychiatrists cannot always differentiate between real patients and **pseudopatients**, and that experts do not always agree on the **diagnosis** for any given patient.

11 Recent research suggests the **diagnostic categories** used in DSM-III may be based more on **theoretical categories** than on **natural categories**. However, giving experts a **priming session** often increases their ability to fit patients into proper diagnostic categories.

12 The best possible **diagnostic scheme** would be a **holistic approach** that took into account the biological, intra-psychic, and social factors that influence the disturbed individual's level of functioning.

(*Continued from page 571.*)

Steve May looked at the hamburger and burst into tears. "It's the most beautiful thing I've ever seen," he said.

Dr. Mary Ellen Mann nodded her head sympathetically. "Would you like a milk shake to go with it?"

"I'm not sure I could stand that much pleasure all at once," Steve replied in a serious tone of voice. Then he smiled. "But let's order one and see."

Dr. Mann motioned to the waitress and gave her the order. She watched with amusement as Steve demolished the hamburger and sucked up the milk shake in one long gulp. Then the young man sat back in his chair, a contented smile on his face, and uttered a very loud belch. The people at the next table glared at him. "Sorry," Steve said loudly enough for them to hear. "I forgot where I was."

"It's not where you are, but where you've been the past two weeks that I'm interested in," Dr. Mann said. "You said you'd tell me all about your stay at the hospital if I would buy you dinner. So, for starters, why a hamburger instead of a steak?"

"You miss the things you can't have," Steve explained. "Sometimes the food was okay, but mostly it was terrible. The food at that place is as crazy as the inmates sometimes act." He groaned. "You have no idea what obscenities can be inflicted on innocent objects such as hamburgers and green peas."

"Oh, yes I have," Dr. Mann replied. "I eat at the Faculty Club all the time. But start at the beginning. I want to know what happened, from the moment you walked through the hospital door until the moment you exited in the garbage truck."

Steve stirred his coffee slowly, considering what to say. "Well, I got in, as you no doubt know. The admitting psychiatrist never batted an eye when I told him I heard voices. He just nodded his head and then asked me what the voices said. When I said, 'dull,' and 'thud,' he nodded more vigorously and asked if the voices were male or female. I said I couldn't tell. That seemed to impress him mightily. Then he muttered the words, 'existential crisis.'"

Dr. Mann smiled. "Just as we suspected he'd do, eh? 'Existential crisis'—a type of psychosis that is described in many books, but that nobody's ever seen in real life."

"And then he asked me about my relationship with my mother, and did I have arguments with my father," Steve continued.

"The Oedipus complex, of course."

Steve smiled. "Of course. Seems I've never worked it out. He thought it significant also that I lose my temper a couple of times a year."

"Poor impulse control," Dr. Mann said. "You tend to belch in public places, and terrible things like that."

"I guess you do get back to the elementals in the mental hospital. Nobody thought twice about belching, or even crapping on the floor. They didn't even make you clean it up afterwards."

Mary Ellen Mann nodded.

"If the people around us didn't complain, we'd all act a lot crazier than we presently do. But to return to the subject, the psychiatrist never guessed you were a 'pseudo-patient,' like the ones in Professor Rosenhan's study?"

"No, he just asked questions for a while, then wrote down on the admission form that I was a certified nut."

"Which you probably are for letting me talk you into the whole affair," Dr. Mann said with a sigh. "I'm really sorry if you suffered very much, Steve."

"Oh, it wasn't all that bad. I did feel terrified at first, but I got over it after a while."

"Terrified of what?" Dr. Mann asked gently.

Steve grinned. "First I was worried that the 'crazies' might attack me. But of course they didn't. In fact, getting to know them was the best part of the whole experience. But after I realized I was physically safe, I got to worrying about not having any control over what was happening to me. I didn't have any money or power or status, so I tried to act sane and sensible and be nice to people. And I smiled a lot."

"Did it work?"

"Not hardly," Steve replied. "One nurse finally told me that smiling was a symptom of my underlying problems. So I stopped. Maybe she was right. Anybody who'd smile in there has to be out of touch with reality."

Dr. Mann frowned. "But they did treat you decently, didn't they?"

"The patients did. The staff treated me more like I was retarded, or some species of vegetable. There was one rather good-looking young nurse's aide I tried to get to know, but she wasn't about to get serious with a 'mental patient,' if you know what I mean. The nurses were much better, but I didn't see much of them. That's one of the things that frightened me."

"Why?" the woman asked.

Steve laughed. "You can't get out of that place unless the nurses and the social workers *see* you and realize that you're 'doing better,' as they put it. And most of them aren't around too much."

"Where are they?" Dr. Mann asked.

"In their offices, filling out papers, I guess." Steve May shook his head. "You can't convince people you're sane if they aren't around to be convinced."

Mary Ellen Mann sighed. "Rosenhan says that if we just valued the patients as people, if we treated them as human assets rather than as liabilities, we might learn a lot from them and simultaneously help most of them get better."

"Some of them don't want to get better," Steve said quietly. "They're afraid they can't cope 'outside,' and it's easier to stay where someone will take care of them. I tried to help a couple of them, as best I could."

"Like how?" Dr. Mann asked.

"Well," said Steve, "There was Crampy Joe. Nice guy, really, but he walked around all stooped over like he had the cramps. I started giving him a cigarette every time he walked upright."

Dr. Mann laughed. "Behavior modification to the rescue, eh? Did it work?"

Steve nodded. "It worked until the nurses made me stop. They said it was against the rules for one patient to perform therapy on another."

"A sobering thought, that," Mary Ellen Mann said. "And they never caught on to your game, did they?"

"Oh, many of the patients did," Steve said. "But the staff members never guessed. That's what terrified me most, I guess. The crazy people thought I was sane, but the sane people insisted I was crazy. After a while, I didn't know which group to believe. And that *really* worried me."

"And that's when you decided to get the hell out of there, eh?"

Steve grinned. "You bet. I tried to see the psychiatrist for two weeks, but I couldn't get an appointment. They just increased the number of pills they gave me. And I just kept on flushing them down the toilet, when nobody was watching."

"You aren't as crazy as you look," the professor said.

"No, but I did get to worrying about it." He smiled shyly at the woman. "For a day or two, I even thought you had cooked the whole deal up, because you thought I was nuts and it was the only way you could think of to get me into the looney bin. That's when I knew it was time to leave."

Dr. Mann laughed. "But why make your grand exit in a garbage truck?"

"Only way out. I noticed that the garbage truck always arrived right at lunchtime. So today I waited until they weren't looking and hid under the garbage. Once the truck was outside the gates, I dropped off, cleaned myself up as best I could, and hitch-hiked home. Then I took a very long shower, and called you."

Mary Ellen Mann gave a deep sigh. "Well, I do appreciate what you did, and we'll talk more about it later on. Do you have any final words of wisdom for tonight, though?"

Steve nodded. "Yes, I do. I realize that we can't improve the hospital system until we know it from the inside out, as well as from the outside in. And so you've got to have volunteers like me go in and look for you. But I have a favor to ask. If you talk anybody else into volunteering, tell them one thing for me, will you?"

"What?" she asked.

He smiled. "Tell 'em they're nuts."

Recommended Readings

Bean, P. (Ed.). (1983). *Mental illness: Changes and trends.* Chichester, England: Wiley.

Blum, J.D. (1978). On changes in psychiatric diagnosis over time. *American Psychologist, 33*(11), 1017–1031.

Matarazzo, J.D. (1983). The reliability of psychiatric and psychological diagnosis. *Clinical Psychology Review, 3*(1), 103–145.

Millon, T. & Klerman, G. (Eds.). (1984). *Contemporary issues in psychopathology.* New York: Guilford Press.

Task Force on Nomenclature and Statistics, American Psychiatric Association. (1980). *Diagnostic and statistical manual of mental disorders* (3rd ed.). Washington, D.C.: American Psychiatric Association.

Did You Know That...

- The term "to beat the devil" out of someone refers to a primitive form of psychotherapy?
- Many Cree Eskimos believe that they can be "possessed" by a witch or *witigo* who will make them cannibalize their relatives and friends?
- A male Chinese may sometimes suffer from a dismal fear that his penis is about to be drawn up into his stomach and disappear?
- Psychiatrists, psychoanalysts, and psychologists often disagree on how to define a "cure" of mental illness?
- A large number of mental patients will recover spontaneously even if not given treatment?
- One form of psychotherapy grew out of the theater?
- Encounter groups are good opportunities for people to explore and express themselves, but are not very effective as psychotherapy?
- Behavior therapists sometimes pay mental patients for getting well?

22

Psychotherapy

"The Odds in Favor"

Mark Evans looked at the little old lady standing by the slot machine. She wore cheap gloves to keep her hands clean, and dirty tennis shoes to keep her feet comfortable. As Mark watched her, she grubbed about in her huge purse, then produced a dollar bill and handed it to a scantily clad young woman who made change for the machines in the casino. The attractive attendant smiled as she handed the older woman a roll of 20 nickels. "Good luck," she said.

"Good juju," the little old lady said in response. Then she tottered along a row of slot machines until she found one to her liking. Mark

Evans moved over to watch her as she dumped her purse beside the one-armed bandit, then ever so carefully unrolled the nickels. She counted them one by one. Exactly 20. Examining one of the coins closely, she decided it would do. She spat on it, then rubbed the nickel gently between her gloved fingers to remove the tarnish.

"You'll rub all the luck off it, honey," said a large, red-headed woman who was dropping dimes into the next machine.

"Luck?" cackled the little old woman, taking a grimy cloth bag from her purse and shaking it at the slot machine. "Luck is just a matter

of chance, and I don't leave anything to chance. I put a hex on the machines, and they always pay off. I brought my juju bag with me today, so I can't lose. My juju is strong today. I feel its strength in my bones. You just wait and see."

The old lady dropped the coin in the machine and pulled the handle. The three reels spun wildly, then clicked to a stop, one by one. A plum, an orange, and a lemon. She shook her head, and deposited another nickel. Again the reels whirred into action and jerked to a stop—two lemons and a bell.

"Your juju is all lemons

today, dearie," the red-headed woman said.

The little old lady gestured wildly at the machine with the bag. "Juju!" she cried. "Give me a jackpot."

The reels produced a cherry and two bells, and the machine grudgingly coughed up two nickels as a reward.

"See! That's a good start. It's going to be a good day. I feel it in my bones!"

Mark Evans shook his head in amazement, then checked his watch. Time to meet his relative-in-law, Lou Hudson, from Chattanooga, Tennessee. Lou, who had married Mark's cousin Betty, was in Las Vegas for a convention of life insurance agents. Betty had called Mark a few days ago, asking Mark to take time out from his graduate studies at the University of Nevada to "show Lou the sights." That was the trouble with studying psychology in Las Vegas—sooner or later everybody you knew showed up and expected you to entertain them.

Lou Hudson turned out to be a thin young man with blond hair and blue but bloodshot eyes. "Stayed up half the night playing blackjack," Lou said, after the introductions were completed. "You wouldn't believe my luck. I was 200 bucks ahead, and I just knew I had a streak going. But then the cards turned against me. I barely broke even."

Mark Evans smiled. He had heard the phrase "broke even" enough to know that it usually meant losing a lot.

"Hey, man, this Las Vegas place is too much!" Lou gestured at the activity in the casino. "Hotels with gambling halls instead of lobbies, people running around 24 hours a day, throwing their money away like there wasn't any tomorrow! Bands playing, and free drinks, and nobody to tell you when to get up or when to go to bed. Why, it's a gambler's paradise!"

"You're here for a convention?" Mark asked, a touch of sarcasm in his voice.

"Yeah. I suppose I really ought to get around to some of the meetings pretty soon now," Lou said with a frown. "But I've been having so much fun, there just hasn't been time." His face brightened suddenly. "Hey, man, they've got every kind of game here you can imagine, haven't they? I mean, I like to gamble a little, just now and then you know. Poker, blackjack, the horses—strictly for small stakes. But they got things here I've only read about, like roulette. You ever play roulette?"

Mark Evans shook his head. "No percentage in it. The odds against winning are too great."

"Whatta ya mean, too great?" Lou demanded almost hostilely, leading Mark toward one of the roulette tables nearby. "See—36 numbers, half of them red, half black. You put a dollar chip on any one of them, and they spin the ball around the wheel. If the little ball drops into your number, the house pays you back 35 to 1. That's pretty good odds, isn't it?"

Mark groaned. "Lou, you forget the two green zeros at the top of the board. There are really 38 numbers, not 36. If you put a dollar down on all the numbers, it would cost you $38 a game. And you'd win back only $35, no matter what number came up. You'd lose $3 each time the wheel spun, because the odds are against you."

"Yeah, but if you pick a lucky number, and put a dollar on it 10 times in a row, and it hits twice, then you've won $70 and it only cost you $10. You can quit a big winner," Lou said.

"*If* you quit, which most gamblers don't. If you keep betting, it doesn't matter whether you play all 38 numbers once, or one number 38 times—you're going to spend $38 to win $35. Because your number is going to win just once in 38 times—on the average."

Lou was plainly annoyed. "You don't understand, man. Look at that fat man over there with the big diamond ring on his pinkie. He's got a stack of chips in front of him that would choke a giraffe. He's bound to be making money on the roulette wheel."

"The only way to make money in Las Vegas is to open your own casino, Lou. That man may be winning now, but if he plays long enough, he'll lose. Because the odds are against him."

Lou shook his head. "You may be right in theory, Mark, but look at that man's stack of chips. Maybe he's got a secret system or something. Maybe he knows what number's going to come up next."

Mark was beginning to understand why the casinos made so much money. "Lou, old man, if that wheel is honest—and out here, they almost always are—there's no way in hell that you or anybody else can make money at roulette if you play long enough."

"Well, how the hell *can* you win at this game, anyway?"

Mark thought a moment. "The only way I know of is to sit for hours and keep a record of each number that comes up. Sometimes the wheel does get out of balance. It gets biased toward one number, let's say 25. Out of 38,000 spins, 25 ought to come up 1,000 times. But if it comes up 2,000 times, or even 3,000, then you know something's abnormal about the wheel."

"You're saying I ought to just sit and take records first instead of just going with my hunches?"

"Absolutely," Mark replied, happy that Lou seemed to be getting the message. "You may not know *why* 25 is better than the other numbers, but the graph tells you it's a winner. So you go with the odds."

"Sounds like a lot of work to me," Lou said, taking a free drink from a cocktail waitress as she passed by. His hands trembled slightly as he sipped the drink. "Oh, I know. You've studied statistics and all that. But Mark, you've neglected the most important thing—the human factor. Man, when I get hot, I get really hot. I mean, I win big. It's like I've got some power over the cards, or the horses, or maybe even the roulette wheel. That kind of power is a helluva lot more important than sitting and watching a wheel turn round 38,000 times."

Mark sighed. "Lou, if you gamble to have fun, then you can just charge your losses off as entertainment expenses. But if you gamble for money—if you absolutely have to win—then you hunt for situations in which the odds are in your favor."

It was obvious that Mark's answer didn't satisfy Lou

Hudson. His bloodshot eyes opened wide. "But man, I'm a special case! I mean, I get these streaks when I'm hot as hell. How do you explain the power I have over the cards when I've got a streak going?"

"Lou," Mark said gently, "How much money do you have?"

"Me? Well, to tell the truth, I'm pretty near broke right now."

"And you've been gambling all your life. If you have all that power, how come you aren't a big winner?"

Lou took a big gulp of his drink. "Well, I've been down on my luck lately. But just wait until tomorrow. I'm gonna bounce right back with a big killing. I got that special feeling, you see . . ."

Mark sighed heavily. "Lou, friend, listen. How does the insurance company you work for manage to make money?"

Lou frowned. "Why they sell policies, of course. You wouldn't happen to need some life insurance, would you?"

"No, but pretend I did," Mark replied. "Suppose I bought a million dollar policy from you."

"Nice commission on a policy that big," Lou said dreamily.

Mark nodded. "Yes, but how can the company make any money when I might die an hour after I bought the policy?"

"It's simple," Lou said. "The company knows how many people your age are likely to die in any one year, and they charge enough to cover their expected losses and to make a little dough on

the side too."

"They go with the percentages, you mean."

"Sure," Lou replied. "They don't know who's gonna live, or who's gonna die. And I reckon they don't really care. They just go with the odds. I tell you no lie, Mark, those people are pretty hard-nosed when it comes to money." Lou stopped for a moment. Then his head drooped a little, and he continued in a voice grown suddenly hoarse. "Speaking of money, Mark, you wouldn't happen to have a little extra cash on you, would you? Just a temporary loan, you know. Until my luck turns good again."

Mark shook his head. "Sorry, man. The way tuition's shot up recently, students just barely get by these days. But what's the matter? Aren't you selling very many policies?"

Lou's bloodshot eyes filled with tears. "Oh, I sell a few. But the money always seems to go out faster than it comes in. Betty's pretty disturbed about it, I suspect. She says that I'm a compulsive gambler. And she ought to know, her being a psychiatric social worker. You're a psychologist, Mark. Do you think I've gone looney or something?"

Mark sighed. "I'm just a grad student, Lou, and there's lots of things I don't know yet. What do you think?"

"I think I've got a problem, Mark. I mean, I *hurt.* Deep down inside. I hurt real bad." Lou grabbed Mark by the arm. "Man, you gotta help me. What can I do to get rid of the pain? What can I do?"
(Continued on page 626.)

Research suggests that, in primitive cultures, "witch-doctors" and "native practitioners" have as high a cure rate with mental illness as do trained psychiatrists.

Turning Knowledge into Power

There's an old saying that "knowledge is power." Sometimes you study the world to figure out what makes things go. But as soon as you discover some significant relationships about the things you've been studying, you're likely to want to put your knowledge to use to make things go *better*.

At other times, when you're faced with a practical problem, you may try out something new. If it works to your satisfaction, you may sit down and attempt to figure out *why* the new technique succeeded—so that you can use it again, perhaps more effectively. In either case, you're trying to convert knowledge into power.

In the last chapter, we dealt with *knowledge*. For diagnostic schemes are really attempts to discover what abnormal behaviors people engage in, and to determine *why* people act, think, and feel in unusual ways. In this chapter we ask a *power* question—"How do you change or 'cure' abnormal behavior once it occurs?" Generally speaking, the more restricted your viewpoint is about what *causes* these abnormalities to occur, the more limited your power to *change* them becomes.

In many primitive parts of the world, for instance, people still believe in the "devil theory" of mental illness. Crazy people are thought to be *possessed* (or at least affected) by devils—outside spirits that take over a person's mental functioning for one reason or another. Let's look at some examples of the "devil theory" in action before we discuss more modern approaches to the problem of curing mental illness.

Primitive Approaches to Mental Illness

The Cree Eskimos and Ojibwa Indians of Canada occasionally suffer from a psychosis known as **witigo**, or devil-caused cannibalism. The first symptoms are usually a loss of appetite, vomiting, and diarrhea—as well as the person's morbid fear that she or he has been possessed by a *witigo* or witch, who lives on human flesh. The affected individual becomes withdrawn, brooding, and cannot eat or sleep. The person's family—fearing for their very lives—immediately calls in a "witch doctor" to cast out the witigo by saying magic words or casting spells. However, if a witch doctor can't be found in time, the disturbed individual may be overwhelmed by the witigo's powers and kill and eat one or more of the members of the family.

In Malaysia, in Southeast Asia, young males occasionally suffer from a different type of possession by devils, called **running amok**. At first the man becomes more withdrawn, depressed, and brooding than usual. Then he will suddenly leap to his feet with a blood-curdling scream, pull out a dagger, and begin stabbing anyone or anything in his path.

Therapy for "running amok" usually consists of killing the amoker before he can kill you, or keeping everyone out of the amoker's way until he kills himself. The few men who have survived this type of psychotic "seizure" have often said the world suddenly "turned black," and they had to slash their way out of the darkness with a knife.

In Spain and Morocco, the name given to this form of mental disorder is *juramentado*, the Spanish word for "cursed person." In the United States, we sometimes call it *homicidal mania*. DSM-III calls it "an explosive disorder of impulse control."

Question: Why would the *therapy* you suggested for "running amok" vary according to the *label* you put on the problem?

Koro

Many Chinese believe that mental and physical disorders result from an imbalance of Yang and Yin, the masculine and feminine "powers" that control the entire spiritual universe. Chinese males occasionally suffer from an odd phobia called *koro*—a dismal fear that their penis is about to be sucked up into their stomachs and disappear, causing death and other disappointments. To prevent this disaster, the man will hold on to his penis for dear life. When he tires, he asks for help from friends and relatives. The man's wife may "cure" the attack if she practices oral sex on him immediately, but this treatment is not always successful.

Koro is thought to be caused by a sudden upsurge in the strength of the man's Yin, or femininity. Thus, it can be cured by giving the patient "masculine" medicine containing a strong Yang factor—such as powdered rhinoceros horn. If this therapy fails, the man may use a special clasp that holds his penis out from his body mechanically.

On the Pacific island of Borneo, a similar disease affects women—who fear that their breasts and genitalia are being pulled up into their bodies. Therapy in Borneo often consists of asking a witch doctor to remove the curse, which presumably was laid on the woman by a "witch" jealous of the woman's physical beauty.

Question: Under what diagnostic category would a psychiatrist using the DSM-III put *koro*?

Four Issues Concerning Psychotherapy

Even in the United States—where most of us no longer believe in witches, demons, and evil spirits—our therapies almost always stem from our theories of what causes human behavior. If we see an organic psychosis as being due *primarily* to physical causes, we tend to treat the patient with physical measures, such as drugs, electric shock, and surgery. If we see a neurosis as being due *primarily* to a conflict between ego and superego, we use psychoanalysis to help bring some rational resolution to the conflict. If we assume that deviant behavior is *primarily* the consequence of inappropriate rewards and punishments, we might prescribe behavior therapy or somehow attempt to alter the person's social environment.

In this chapter we will discuss all these special forms of treatment, and the theories that gave rise to them. But before we can evaluate the various forms of therapy, we must raise several pertinent (and very hard-nosed) issues:

Witigo (WITT-tee-go). A Cree Eskimo word meaning an "ice witch" who eats human flesh. Also means the condition of being possessed by such a witch. The Ojibwa (oh-JIB-wah) Indian word for the same condition is *windigo* (win-dee-go).

Running amok (ah-MOCK). The Malaysian word *amok* means "furious attack." To run amok is to undergo a murderous frenzy and attack people at random. Similar to the Scandinavian term "going berserk" (burr-SERK) and the Spanish term *juramentado* (hoor-ah-men-TAH-do).

1. How successful is the therapy? That is, what is its "cure rate"? Would the patient have recovered anyhow, even if we hadn't done anything? Would a "witch doctor," or someone using a different form of treatment, have done as well? In short, does the therapy make a *significant difference* in helping the patient? Is it a *valid* form of treatment?
2. Assuming the therapy does make a significant difference, how *reliable* is it? Does it work all the time, or just occasionally? Is it effective with all sorts of patients, or does it succeed better with some than with others?
3. What are the *side effects*? What else happens to the patient when we apply the treatment? Is the "cure" sometimes worse than the disease?
4. And cutting across all these issues is the basic question: What do we mean by *cure*? How shall we define "improvement"? Just as important, how shall we measure it?

We will have much more to say about these issues as we discuss the three main types of psychotherapy. We will also find it all too customary for therapists of opposing views to call each other "witch doctors," and to accuse each other of using "black magic" rather than "scientific magic."

Biological Therapies

Two centuries ago, when the "demon theory" was the accepted explanation of most mental disorders, the therapy of choice was *punishment*. The belief was that if you would just whip a patient vigorously enough, you could "beat the devil" out of the person. The fact that many patients did improve after whippings was evidence enough to support the validity of the theory. It was not until *scientific investigations* suggested that the "cure rate" for unbeaten patients was higher than for those who were beaten that we finally hung up the whip in our

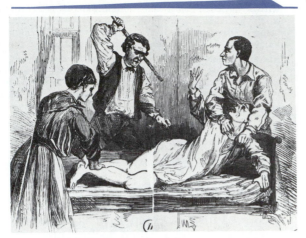

A century or so ago, many doctors believed mental patients were "possessed by devils." Treatment often consisted of "beating the devil out" of the person.

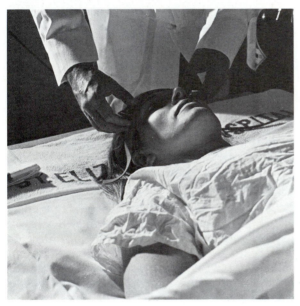

Although Electro-convulsive Shock Therapy continues to be used, particularly with severely depressed patients, recent research casts doubt on how effective it is in the long run.

lunatic asylums. Whether our present forms of psychotherapy are all that much more effective than "beating the devil" out of lunatics, however, is a point much debated today in psychology and psychiatry.

As we suggested in the last chapter, the organic psychoses do seem directly related to damage to the central nervous system or to genetic causes. Perhaps for that reason, many of the therapies used to treat organic psychoses are explicitly *biological*—the three main types being artificially induced seizures, psychosurgery, and drugs. (As we will see, these types of treatment are also occasionally used with patients who have functional psychoses.)

Convulsive Therapy

In 1935 a Hungarian psychiatrist named Ladislaus J. Meduna noted an odd fact—very few of the schizophrenic patients he worked with also suffered from epilepsy. Meduna concluded that seizures somehow *prevented* schizophrenia. If he could induce epileptic-type seizures in his schizophrenic patients, he reasoned, he might be able to cure them of their problems.

As a test, Meduna injected schizophrenic patients with drugs that caused seizures. Many patients did show some improvement, but an alarming number of them were severely injured or died from the treatment. Other patients showed intense apprehension about the unpleasantness of the experience. Meduna's treatment was abandoned as "barbaric," but the idea lived on.

Question: If therapy is extremely painful—be it whippings or convulsions—might some patients "get well" in order to avoid further treatment?

Electro-Convulsive Therapy

In 1938 two Italian psychiatrists—Ugo Cerletti and L. Bini—began using electrical current rather than drugs to induce seizures. If you were to be given electro-convulsive therapy (or ECT, as it is often called), the psychiatrist would probably apply it in the following way. First you would be given (1) a muscle relaxant, (2) a drug to prevent you from choking and perhaps a rubber device to put in your mouth to keep you from biting your tongue, and (3) a fast-acting anesthetic to put you to sleep. Then you'd be strapped to a padded bed in order to reduce the possibility of your breaking an arm or leg during the seizure.

When you were unconscious (from the drug), the psychiatrist would apply electrodes to your head, and pass a brief but fairly strong electrical current directly through your brain. Your muscles would become rigid for about 10 seconds, then you would go into convulsions much as if you'd had a *grand mal* seizure (see Chapter 2). The convulsions would last for a minute or two, but you would remain unconscious for up to 30 minutes and would be drowsy or confused for many hours thereafter. Because seizures induce *retrograde amnesia* (see Chapter 15), you probably would not remember the shock or the events immediately preceding it. Typically, you would be given ECT three times a week for a period of a few weeks—or until you showed some recovery.

There is considerable argument about the effectiveness of ECT. Many psychiatrists believe ECT can help with severely depressed patients. A few psychiatrists also believe ECT is effective with schizophrenic patients. But the data aren't all that clear. In his 1979 book, *Electroshock: Its Brain-Disabling Effects*, Maryland psychiatrist Peter Roger Breggin takes a different if somewhat extreme view. He admits some depressed patients do show improvement after ECT. However, he states that the effects of ECT on the brain are often "severe," "catastrophic," and "devastating."

Breggin believes that most of the "perceived benefits" of ECT are due to the *placebo effect*. He quotes extensively from the scientific literature to prove his point, and notes that the "cure rate" among psychiatrists who refuse to administer ECT is as high as or higher than that among psychiatrists who use shock extensively. Breggin urges that ECT be "prohibited by law."

In most psychiatric hospitals today, ECT is used primarily with deeply depressed patients for whom all other forms of treatment have failed. ECT does seem to be of some value with these types of patients. However, in the past it has been used routinely to help "cure" schizophrenia and many other types of disorders. There is no scientific evidence at all that ECT helps with these sorts of problems. Perhaps this is not surprising, for Meduna's original observations about schizophrenia and epilepsy were based on a mistaken idea. He apparently did not realize that all patients with epilepsy *and* schizophrenia were put in a different ward than the one he was working on.

Question: Some patients request ECT, particularly after they have been performing badly for a period of time. How might Freud's notions about the causes of *masochism* explain the patients' request for ECT?

Psychosurgery

As you will remember from reading the early chapters of this book, many types of emotional responses are controlled by the brain's *limbic*

Lunatic asylums (LOON-uh-tick as-SIGH-lums). In Europe during the Middle Ages, there was a common belief that insanity was caused by some influence the moon had on human behavior. *Luna* is the Latin word for "moon," thus mental illness came to be called "lunacy," and mentally ill individuals were called "lunatics."

Lobotomy (loh-BOTT-toe-mee). A surgical technique involving cutting the nerve pathways that run to any one of the four cerebral lobes. Usually means "prefrontal lobotomy," or cutting the connections between the thalamus (THALL-uh-muss) and the prefrontal lobes.

system (see Chapter 4). Portions of the thalamus and the frontal lobes are also involved in emotional reactions. In 1935, John F. Fulton and C.E. Jacobsen demonstrated that surgery on the prefrontal lobes had a *calming effect* on two chimpanzees they were working with. After learning of this research, a Portuguese psychiatrist named Egas Moniz decided that cutting the prefrontal lobes—an operation called a **lobotomy**—might help aggressive or hyperemotional patients. In 1936 Moniz and his associates reported that lobotomy did seem to be effective with some of these patients.

Lobotomies were introduced to the US in 1942 by Walter Freeman and his colleagues, and Moniz and Freeman later received the Nobel Prize for their work. Other psychiatrists soon reported that cutting the *connections* between the lower brain centers and the prefrontal lobes seemed to work just as well as *removing* the prefrontal lobes.

The question is, of course, "Work as well as what?" Many lobotomy patients do show an improvement after the operation, but many do not. And the fatality rate from the operation may run as high as 4 percent. Well-controlled comparisons of patients given lobotomies and those given other forms of treatment suggest that the operation is neither as effective nor as reliable as Moniz and Freeman had hoped. (We might note that the "fatality rate" must include Moniz himself, who died after being shot by one of his lobotomy patients).

Question: Why might many physicians be more interested in performing *operations* on patients with mental disorders than in giving the patients long-term *psycho*therapy?

Drug Therapy

There are a number of *psychoactive drugs*—that is, chemicals that have a psychological ef-

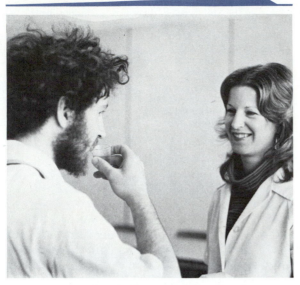

Many psychiatrists believe psychoactive drugs can help mental patients. However, the drugs often have bad side effects and probably do not by themselves "cure" the patient's mental and behavioral problems.

fect. We discussed many of them in Chapter 3. Among the most widely used psychoactive compounds are the major and minor tranquilizers and the antidepressants.

Major Tranquilizers

For many centuries medical practitioners in India have given tense or manic patients a drug made from the snake-root plant because it seemed to calm them down. We now call this drug **reserpine**. In 1953 the Indian physician R.A. Hakim reported that reserpine seemed to be effective with some schizophrenic patients. When Nathan S. Kline tried reserpine here in 1954, he stated that it brought about marked improvement in 86 percent of the schizophrenic patients he tried it with.

At about the same time, a French surgeon named Henri Laborit suggested that giving a powerful drug called **chlorpromazine** to schizophrenic patients might make them more manageable. The drug not only calmed these patients down, but seemed to relieve some of their symptomatic behaviors as well.

Reserpine and chlorpromazine were the first of the many tranquilizers now widely used with mental patients. One interesting point about these drugs is that patients often dislike and seldom "abuse" these chemicals. However, since the major tranquilizers make "disturbed"

patients easier to handle in hospitals, these drugs are now frequently prescribed by psychiatrists.

Beginning in the mid-1970's, a drug called *lithium carbonate* has been used with varying degrees of success with patients displaying bipolar affective disorders (manic-depressive psychoses). Lithium carbonate can have a calming effect during manic episodes. Whether it helps depressive patients, however, is a much-debated topic. Not all manic patients are helped by the drug, though, and it has dangerous (even deadly) side effects.

Minor Tranquilizers

Drugs such as Valium and Librium are called "minor" tranquilizers because they have less dramatic effects on behavior and mental functioning than do the major tranquilizers. However, Valium and Librium are among the most abused drugs in the US today, in part because many patients seem to enjoy their effects. These drugs are obviously addictive, and recent studies suggest they may cause birth defects if taken during pregnancy.

Antidepressants

As we noted in Chapter 3, these drugs are also called "psychic energizers." Except for the amphetamines, the antidepressants are seldom abused and have little effect on people not suffering from depressions. However, all these drugs have dangerous side effects, particularly when mixed with alcohol.

Drugs Alone Don't "Cure"

Scarcely a month goes by that the popular press doesn't serve up a juicy story about some new drug that seems to offer "miracle cures" for many types of psychological problems. Most of the reports need to be taken with a grain of salt, however.

First, as Nathan S. Kline and Jules Angst note in their 1979 book *Psychiatric Syndromes and Drug Treatment*, chemicals *by themselves* seldom solve mental, social, or behavioral problems. Even if the drug "cures" some underlying biological dysfunction, the patient will still need psychological and social help in adjusting to life. Thus, chemotherapy is at best no more than the *first step* in treating "mental disorders."

Second, there is the problem of side effects. Herbert E. Spohn is director of the Research Department at the Menninger Foundation. Writing in the March 1981 issue of *Contemporary Psychology*, Spohn notes that enthusiasm about drug treatment reached a high water-mark in the late 1960's, when some psychiatrists claimed that drugs were superior to psychotherapy. However, Spohn says, "In the 1970's enthusiasm gave way to a sober realism, as it came to be recognized that drug treatment of mental illness is a mixed blessing." Many types of chemotherapy have severe side effects that must, in turn, be treated with other medications. And long-term treatment with a number of medications—particularly with the antidepressants—often brings about an irreversible type of brain damage known as **tardive dyskinesia**. Spohn concludes that "it has come to be recognized, perhaps too late, that [psychoactive] drugs cannot rehabilitate discharged chronic patients, who by the thousands now lead marginal in-community lives, cheek by jowl with the normal population, who are disturbed and frightened by their residual psychopathology."

Third, not all of the drug research reported in the popular press has been as well planned and nicely controlled as we might wish. In particular, many drug studies have not been "double blind," and thus the results reported may well be due to placebo effects (see Chapter 16).

Perhaps a case history will demonstrate these points.

Mendel's Research

Werner Mendel is Professor of Psychiatry at the USC School of Medicine. He was also, for many years, the clinical director of the only public facility for treating acutely disturbed psychotic patients in Los Angeles County.

Like all psychiatrists, Mendel is a medical doctor. After receiving his MD degree at Stanford, he served a year as a psychiatric resident at St. Elizabeth's Hospital in Washington, D.C. Thereafter, Mendel spent several years as a resident at the Menninger Foundation in Topeka, Kansas—one of the best psychiatric training facilities in the world. Once his training at Menninger's was complete, Mendel was qualified to call himself a psychiatrist.

Next, he studied for several years at the Southern California Psychoanalytic Institute and completed his training as a psychoanalyst. He is an instructor at the Institute. After moving to Los Angeles, Mendel continued a series of experiments on the treatment of mental illness, which he had begun as a resident in Washington, D.C.

St. Elizabeth's Hospital was the largest of all the US government facilities dealing with psy-

Reserpine (ree-SIR-peen). From the word "serpent." So named because this tranquilizer was first discovered in the snake root plant in India.

Chlorpromazine (klor-PRO-muh-zeen). A tranquilizing drug whose usefulness with psychotic patients was first discovered in France.

Tardive dyskinesia (TAR-dive dis-kin-KNEE-see-ah). A "disfiguring disorder of motion control." Patients given psychoactive drugs often lose the ability to exercise normal voluntary control over their own actions. Recent studies suggest the incidence of tardive dyskinesia can be greatly reduced by *reducing* the amount (or dosage) of the psychoactive drugs prescribed. Oddly enough, the research also suggests that "cure rate" increases in many cases as dosage is *reduced*.

chiatric patients. When Mendel arrived at St. E's, he was put in charge of a ward of Spanish-speaking patients, most of whom came from Puerto Rico or the Virgin Islands. All of these patients were diagnosed as being hostile, aggressive individuals. And many were considered so dangerous to themselves and others that they were confined to "padded cells" or were kept in straight-jackets. Mendel says he usually took two attendants along with him whenever he visited the wards. And because the patients spoke little or no English, and Mendel spoke no Spanish, there was little he could do in the way of treatment.

Double-Blind Method

Fortunately, it was just at this time that news of the apparent effectiveness of reserpine spread to the US. The authorities at St. E's decided to test the drug. To make the test scientifically valid, they used the *double-blind method*. That is, they selected certain wards whose patients would be given reserpine. But they needed some *comparison groups* to make sure that the changes they noted in the patients

Werner Mendel

given reserpine (the "experimental groups") were due to the drug and not just to the fact that the patients had been given pills. So the researchers selected an equal number of wards whose patients were given "sugar pills" rather than reserpine. The pills looked the same no matter what was in them. The experiment was "double-blind" because neither the patients nor the doctors in charge of the wards knew which drug the patients on any particular ward were actually receiving.

The experiment ran for several months, during which any improvement in the patients was recorded as carefully as possible. Mendel's ward of Spanish-speaking patients was one of those chosen for the experiment.

Mendel reports that, almost as soon as the study began, he was sure his patients were receiving the reserpine—for they all calmed down dramatically. Within a short period of time they were so tranquil that many of them could be released from restraint. Mendel was convinced that a psychiatric revolution had begun.

Then the experiment ended and the results were announced. To Mendel's amazement, he learned his ward had been one of the "controls." All of his patients had received *placebos* instead of reserpine. Yet they had shown marked improvement! It occurred to Mendel that, when the experiment began, he unconsciously changed his attitude toward the patients. Convinced they were becoming more peaceful, he then treated them as if they were improving. And they did improve—not because of the drug but because of the way in which he responded to them.

The St. Elizabeth's experiment points up one dramatic difficulty in evaluating any psychiatric research: The good results that an experimenter obtains may be due to *chance factors*, or to factors the scientist *failed to control*. Drugs are always given in a social setting. The patient's attitude—and the doctor's—may be more influential than the chemical's effects on the patient's body. Likewise, if a surgeon communicates to the patient the belief that psychosurgery will surely solve the person's problems, the patient may very well get better after the operation—for all the "wrong" reasons.

Biological Therapies: An Evaluation

What goes on in your body surely affects what goes on in your mind—and vice versa. *Some* types of biological therapies will surely help *some* types of patients suffering from *some* kinds of mental disorders. Thus, we should *use* biotherapies when the data strongly suggest they are valid and reliable forms of treatment. And chemotherapy can often calm hospitalized patients down—and even allow their return to the community. However, the bulk of research in this area suggests we have not yet discovered any "magic pill" that will cure *most types* of psychosocial abnormalities.

With that sobering thought in mind, let's look at other types of treatment.

Intra-Psychic Therapy

Most personality theorists believe that abnormal thoughts and behaviors are mere symptoms of an underlying dysfunction in an individual's basic personality. To "cure" the symptom without handling the underlying problem would, therefore, be as senseless as giving aspirin to a yellow-fever patient. The drug might decrease the fever symptom, it is true. But aspirin won't kill the virus that is really responsible for the disease. Removing the fever with aspirin might delude patients into thinking they had been "cured" when, in fact, the patients might still be carrying the virus. A "deeper" form of therapy is necessary to kill the virus.

Intra-psychic therapy almost always focuses on making "deep changes" in the structure or the functioning of the individual's core personality. The belief behind this approach is that the symptomatic behaviors will disappear naturally as the cure progresses. As we noted in Chapter 21, this type of treatment is based on what is called the *medical model of mental illness*.

If you ever have need for intra-psychic therapy, you would seem to have your choice between two major types: (1) those methods that are primarily designed to help you understand your present self by giving you *insight* into what has gone wrong in your past; and (2) those techniques that focus on future goals in order to help you change your present mode of existence. (In fact, the difference between the two types may be more a matter of emphasis than anything else. Highly successful therapists appear to treat their patients in similar ways despite the fact that their theories may be quite different.)

Psychoanalysts usually follow the first method. That is, they concentrate on discovering traumas that occurred during psychosexual development in order to help patients set their "mental houses" in order. Psychoanalytic theory suggests that, if you complete your analysis and gain insight into your problems, you should experience a full recovery.

The humanistic psychologists, on the other hand, mostly follow the second method. They hope to make you aware both of your present condition and of your ultimate goals, so you can shorten the distance between the two and hence move toward self-actualization.

Psychoanalytic Therapy

There is no single accepted and approved method of psychoanalytic treatment—it varies widely according to the patient's needs and the analyst's skills and beliefs. Freud compared analysis to a chess game in which only the opening moves can be standardized. Thereafter, he said, endless variations may develop. Furthermore, in addition to "classic" Freudian analysis, there are a number of newer, briefer types of analytic treatment. Since most of the more modern approaches are extensions of Freud's original techniques, however, we will give primary attention to the "classic" analytic methods.

Freud viewed psychoanalysis as a way to bring about a basic reconstruction of the patient's personality. The analyst achieves this end in two ways. First, by encouraging the patient to build up an emotional relationship, or **transference**, with the analyst. And second, by getting the patient to freely associate about past thoughts and experiences. By *interpreting* these *free associations*, the analyst can often discover both the content and the dynamics of the patient's unconscious mental processes.

But the task is not an easy one. Psychoanalysis typically takes from two to five years to complete, and the 50-minute-long therapy sessions are usually held three to five times a week. Costs for a complete analysis typically run from 10 to 30 thousand dollars (or more). The most successful patients seem to be between 15 and 50 years of age. They must be bright, verbal, self-motivated, and be willing to cooperate with the therapist. Although psychoanalysis is occasionally used with individuals classed as "psychotic," the usual patient is a mildly disturbed or "neurotic" individual.

While Freud insisted that the medical degree was not necessary for the practice of psychoanalysis, more than 90 percent of American analysts are physicians who have gone through psychiatric residencies before becoming candidates at a psychoanalytic institute. During the several years of training required for graduation, the candidate undergoes a "training analysis" to make himself or herself aware of personal problems that might prejudice analytic interpretation of a patient's problems. As Freud noted in 1910, "Every analyst's achievement is limited by what his own complexes and resistances permit."

Transference

If you decided to undergo psychoanalysis, you would probably be treated by a male, since less than 10 percent of the analysts are women. You most likely would find your doctor in a private office completely cut off from the outside world. He might well ask you to lie down on his couch and then sit out of sight, just beyond your head, where he could take notes and observe your facial and bodily reactions.

Your analyst would ask you to free associate— that is, to say anything and everything that came to mind. But he would try to direct your attention to your inward world of feeling, emotion, and fantasy. In a variety of subtle ways, he would encourage you to "transfer" to him many of the intense emotional feelings you have for others. In a sense, he would become a "father figure" whom you could rely on and trust.

Free Association

Free association is the basic game plan of most forms of psychoanalysis. Freud believed that everything you do and say and think has a *cause*. Thus, even trivial and apparently meaningless statements may mask deep-seated emotional conflicts. The more you cut yourself off from conscious control—the more you let your unconscious mind come through to consciousness—the more easily you can bring the buried problems to the surface. If you cannot "free associate" very well, it may be that some part of your mind is blocking the expression of certain

Transference (trans-FURR-ents). In psychoanalysis, the patient is subtly encouraged to transfer to the analyst the emotions and attitudes the patient has concerning the "power figures" in the patient's life—chiefly her or his father and mother. That is, the patient is asked to act toward the analyst as the patient does toward the mother and father. Some of the transferred emotions may be warm and loving. Others may be cold, hateful, or angry. In either case, displacing the feelings onto the analyst may help release pent-up libidinal energy. At the end of treatment, the analyst must carefully remove the transference relationship so that the patient stands on his or her own.

There are currently more than 200 types of "talk therapy," in which patients discuss their problems with a therapist. There is considerable debate over the effectiveness of this type of treatment.

traumatic experiences. By noting the things you *avoid talking about*, the analyst can often get a feeling for what your problems are.

Interpretation

During the course of the treatment, your analyst would interpret your thoughts, feelings, and actions in terms of psychoanalytic theory. If inner blocks kept you from expressing important (repressed) material, the analyst might ask you to recall your dreams and talk about them.

Freud believed that many psychic conflicts express themselves in fantasy, particularly when the patient's defenses are down (as during dreaming). He felt it was not so much the actual content of the dream that was important. Rather, it was what the dream *symbolized* that must be discovered. For Freud, dream analysis was a "royal road" to the patient's unconscious and to the real significance of the patient's childhood experiences.

Psychoanalysis: An Evaluation

Psychoanalysis takes so long—and there are so few analysts available—that only a tiny frac-

tion of the people who need help ever undergo this process. Most patients settle for briefer, less intensive (and less expensive) types of treatment.

Psychoanalytic theory has influenced almost all other forms of intra-psychic therapy. Any form of treatment that concentrates on explaining the present in terms of past experience and unconscious motivations owes a large debt to Sigmund Freud.

Humanistic Therapy

Freud grew up in Austria, a land of kings and emperors who possessed "divine rights" their subjects dared not question. Austrian fathers typically claimed the same privileges—when the man of the family spoke, the children listened and obeyed. Perhaps it is understandable, then, that in psychoanalysis the fatherly analyst often sets the goals of therapy and urges the patient onward.

Modern humanistic psychologists reject the "divine right" of the therapist to determine what is mentally healthy for the patient. In humanistic therapy, the patient rather than the therapist is king. Humanistic psychologists—such as Carl Rogers and Abraham Maslow—emphasize the *conscious* determinants of behavior. All human beings are presumed to have a positive drive toward good mental health. As Adolph Di Loreto puts it in the April 1981 issue of *Contemporary Psychology*, Freud's patients may be depicted as fighting for their life, but Roger's and Maslow's clients are fighting for a better life.

The humanistic therapist does not look too deeply into your unconscious nor too far back into your past. For the present and future are considered much more important than events long since forgotten. Therapy, then, should consist primarily of making you aware of your present state of functioning. Therapy should also focus on how you see yourself now, how others perceive you, and what "ideal state" you would like to reach. Once you understand all these things clearly, the therapist need only provide you with feedback about whatever progress you are making toward becoming your "self-ideal."

Client-Centered Therapy

In Carl Roger's *client-centered therapy*, the client determines the goals of treatment and the speed at which these goals will be met. Like most humanistic psychologists, Rogers is loath to impose his own standards or values on his clients. Instead, Rogers tries to provide a "psychological mirror" in which the clients can see themselves. He believes the clients will use this reflected information to achieve whatever changes in themselves are necessary to meet their own standards.

If you went to see a "client-centered" therapist, you would most likely find a clinical psychologist who had taken the Ph.D. rather than a medical degree. You would sit in a chair rather than lie on a couch. And *you* would make most of the decisions about what the two of you would do together. The therapist would try to be warm, human, concerned, and supportive. But in theory, at least, the Rogerian therapist would seldom give advice or offer suggestions about what you ought to do or be.

Reflecting

As you talked about your problems, the therapist would frequently restate what you had said—*reflecting back* your own thoughts in slightly different form. In this way the therapist would provide you with an objective "mirror" of yourself and your own mental functioning.

Rogers believes therapists should give clients *unconditional positive regard.* By this, Rogers means the therapist should accept you and the things you did, rather than criticize you or make value judgments about your emotions and perceptions. Only by being non-judg-

mental, he says, can the therapist hope to build a relationship of trust and affection with you. And only when you experience such non-punitive conditions, Rogers believes, can you build sufficient courage to see yourself as you really are. This same supportive atmosphere helps you determine what your goals really are—and helps you decide what *you* want to become, not what you think the world wants you to become. But once you can see yourself objectively, and know where you want to go, your own internal motivation will push you toward a better state of mental health and acceptance of yourself.

Is Rogers a Rogerian?

Most of the people practicing intra-psychic therapy in the US today are neither "pure" Freudians nor "pure" humanistic psychologists. Rather, therapists tend to be *eclectic*—they make use of whatever psychological techniques seem to work best for them and their clients. And they may do so almost without realizing what they are doing. Carl Rogers is no exception. For example, in 1966 C. Truax studied movies of Carl Rogers as he performed therapy. Far from providing his patients with "unconditional positive regard," Truax says, Rogers was unconsciously "shaping" his patients by rewarding "healthy self-statements" with head nods and smiles. Rogers also tended to ignore any "unhealthy statements" the patient made. We will have more to say about unconscious "shaping" later in this chapter. For the moment, we need only note that even Carl Rogers is perhaps a bit more eclectic than he sometimes appears to be.

Transactional Analysis and Gestalt Therapy

Both Gestalt therapy and Transactional Analysis were developed by former psychoanalysts with strong humanistic leanings. Since both types of treatment are somewhat more likely to be used with groups than with individuals, we will postpone discussing them until later in this chapter.

The Effects of Intra-psychic Therapy

Many factors make it difficult to evaluate the effectiveness of psychotherapy scientifically. Science deals with objective events, things that can readily be measured. But by its very nature, intra-psychic therapy concerns itself with personality changes (and other variables) that seldom can be viewed in detail under a microscope. The success rates of various forms of

"MY ASTROLOGER SAYS ONE THING, MY GURU SAYS ANOTHER, MY PSYCHIATRIST SAYS SOMETHING ELSE — I DON'T KNOW WHO TO TURN TO ANYMORE."

H.J. Eysenck

treatment, then, must always be considered in terms of *what results both clients and therapists hope to achieve.*

"Art Form" versus "Applied Science"

Some psychiatrists see therapy as an "art form," thus something that cannot be measured objectively. One such person is Jerome Frank, a professor at the Johns Hopkins School of Medicine. Writing in a recent issue of the *American Journal of Orthopsychiatry*, Frank states that "psychotherapy is not primarily an applied science. In some ways it more resembles a religion . . . in others, the art of **rhetoric** or persuasion."

Frank goes on to compare therapy to music. "To try to determine by scientific analysis how much better or worse . . . Gestalt therapy is than Transactional Analysis, is in many ways equivalent to attempting to determine by the same means the relative merits of the music of Cole Porter and Richard Rodgers. To ask the question is to reveal its absurdity."

Jerome Frank believes that the effectiveness of therapy depends more on the therapist than the technique. Unfortunately, Frank does not give any standards by which to judge who is a "good" therapist, and who isn't.

Although Frank's viewpoint has its merits, other psychiatrists are willing to use less subjective measures of improvement—such as modifications in the patient's overt behavior and the gradual disappearance of neurotic or psychotic symptoms. At least these changes can be observed and agreed upon by people other than the therapist.

Writing in the February 1981 *American Psychologist*, Sol L. Garfield reviews 40 years of research on the effectiveness of psychotherapy. One of the most widely publicized studies on *psychoanalytic* treatment was performed at the Menninger Foundation and was published in 1972. The Menninger experiment involved 21 patients given psychoanalysis and 21 given analytically oriented "insight" therapy. Both sets of patients were followed for many years. In discussing the Menninger study, Garfield states that, "My understanding or interpetation of this material is that 6 patients were judged to be worse at the end of therapy, 11 were unchanged, 7 showed slight improvement, and 18 (or 43 percent) showed moderate or marked improvement. If one takes my interpretation as provisionally valid, the results cannot be viewed as a very convincing demonstration of the efficacy of psychotherapy—particularly when the therapy is so expensive and time-consuming."

In psychoanalysis, the *therapist* usually decides whether or not a "cure" has taken place. But in the humanistic therapies, the *patient* usually determines whether the therapy was successful or not. Rogers does have objective tests that measure changes in the client's *perceptions* of his or her progress, and the tests do seem to be reliable. Whether or not "perceptual changes" should be the major goal of therapy, however, is an open question. In any event, the "cure rate" claimed for humanistic therapy is usually in the neighborhood of 75 percent or so.

Eysenck's 1952 Report

In recent years, the behavioral psychologists and social learning theorists have leveled strong criticisms against the "unscientific ways" in which the effectiveness of psychotherapy is usually determined. Immediately after World War II, H.J. Eysenck investigated several thousand cases of mentally disturbed servicemen and women in British hospitals. Eysenck reported in 1952 that the overall improvement rate among those patients given psychoanalytic treatment was about 44 percent. The improvement rate for patients given any other form of psychotherapy (eclectic treatment) was about 64 percent. Several hundred other patients received no psychotherapy at all. Their physical ailments were treated as necessary, but they were given no psychological therapy. The improvement rate among these *untreated* patients was about 72 percent. These data led some scientists to compare psychoanalysis with "witch doctoring," and to suggest that psychoanalysis might actually *retard* the patient's progress.

As you might imagine, the psychoanalysts did not take such comments lightly. They pointed out that Eysenck's criteria for improvement were considerably different than their own, since Eysenck focused on easy-to-measure behavioral changes. For example, Eysenck ignored all of the basic alterations in the patient's personality that are the stated goal of most psychoanalytic treatment. The analysts also raised the important issue of patient selection. Some patients are better suited for analysis than others, and the usual feeling is that hospitalized psychotics make the worst clients of all.

Eysenck's *data* have stood up reasonably well, however. Edward Erwin discusses this issue in the May 1980 *American Psychologist*. Erwin notes that, some 30 years after Eysenck's original report, there still is little reliable scientific evidence showing that psychoanalytic therapy yields "cure rates" that are significantly higher than no treatment at all. However, this statement is true *only* if by the term "cure" we mean *measurable changes in behavior*. We will return to this important point later.

Spontaneous Recovery

Eysenck's criticisms of psychotherapy deserve more careful consideration than we have space for here, as do the replies of his critics. We should note, however, that people made **spontaneous recoveries** from their psychological problems long before we had any real form of therapy to offer them. In several recent studies, the spontaneous "cure rate" has turned out to be 40 to 50 percent. However the word "cure" is defined, it does seem as if the effectiveness of *any form of psychotherapy* must be measured against whatever changes would have occurred had the patient received no therapy at all.

Question: Why would it be more difficult to prove that therapy "works" using objective criteria than if you merely measured the subjective opinions of the clients and therapists?

Sloane's Temple Study

One of the best recent studies on the effectiveness of therapy was performed by psychiatrist R. Bruce Sloane and his associates at the Temple University School of Medicine in Philadelphia. These researchers selected 94 patients suffering from moderately severe neuroses and personality disorders, who had come to an outpatient clinic for help. Roughly one-third of the patients were treated with a brief form of psy-

Rhetoric (RETT-or-ick). The art of speaking or writing effectively.

Spontaneous recoveries. Any "cures" or improvements due to natural circumstances, and hence not due to therapeutic intervention. Research suggests that up to 50 percent of people who experience mental problems will recover "spontaneously" in a year or so, even if not given treatment.

choanalytic "insight" therapy. These patients, then, received intra-psychic *psychotherapy*. Another third received *behavior modification therapy*, a type of treatment we discussed in Chapters 10, 13, 14, and 15. The rest of the patients were told they would have to wait at least four months for help—and hence became an untreated *control group*.

Sloane or another psychiatrist interviewed each patient before treatment and gave an initial impression of how disturbed the patient was and what symptoms the person showed. These "assessing psychiatrists" did not perform therapy themselves—they merely *evaluated* the patients before (and after) treatment.

After the intake interview, the patient was randomly assigned to one of the three groups mentioned above. The patient was also given several personality tests, including the MMPI (see Chapter 20). At the same time, a research assistant interviewed a close friend or relative of the patient to get this person's evaluation of what might be troubling the patient.

Patients in the treated groups were given an average of one hour of therapy a week for four

R. Bruce Sloane

months. Patients in the untreated control group were called every few weeks to find out how they were doing—and were encouraged to "hang tight" until a therapist could see them. These calls, of course, were themselves a type of treatment. At the end of four months, all the untreated patients who still wished help were put into "insight" therapy.

After four months, all the patients were again interviewed by the assessing psychiatrist, who did not know (and was told not to ask) what kind of therapy (if any) the patients had been given. Each patient retook the personality tests, and the research assistant once more talked with the close friend or relative to determine what progress this person thought the patient had made. Psychiatric assessments of the patients were also made one year and two years after the experiment began.

Sloane and his associates measured as many different aspects of the therapeutic situation as they could. Some of the tests they employed were *objective*. That is, they were aimed at determining success in symptom removal, bettering job performance, improving relationships with others, and so forth. Other measures were *subjective*. For instance, the patients were asked how well they liked the therapists, and the therapists made subjective ratings of the patients. The patients also reported their own inner feelings as to how much they thought they had improved, and what anxiety they were experiencing. Both the assessing psychiatrist and the patient's friend or relative were asked what changes they saw in the patient's emotions and behaviors. In addition to these rather specific measures, the assessing psychiatrist, the patient, the friend or relative, and the patient's therapist (in two of the groups) made what Sloane calls "global evaluations" of the amount of improvement shown by the patient.

Results

The results of the Sloane study are both complex and fascinating:

1. Some 80 percent of the patients given *either* behavior therapy or "insight" psychotherapy showed significant *symptom removal*, but so did 48 percent of the patients in the no-therapy control group. Thus, either type of therapy is better than nothing, but spontaneous recovery did occur in about half the untreated patients.
2. Both of the treated groups showed a significant reduction in *anxiety*, but the no-therapy patients also improved so much that

Sloane and his colleagues conclude that the differences among the groups were not really significant.
3. The behavior therapy patients showed significantly greater improvement in their *work situations* than did the "insight" or no-therapy patients. The latter two groups of patients performed about the same.
4. Both the behavior therapy and the no-treatment patients were judged as significantly improved in *social adjustment*. Those individuals given "insight" therapy did not do as well.
5. The psychotherapists gave their patients significantly lower ratings of *sexual adjustment* than did anyone else. The behavior therapists gave their patients significantly higher ratings on the sexual adjustment scale than did anyone else. The patients gave themselves significantly higher ratings than did the insight therapists. Generally speaking, in most of the subjective ratings, the patients (no matter who treated them) and the behavior therapists were much more optimistic about recovery than were any of the other raters.
6. The *global evaluations* of patient improvement made by the assessing psychiatrists yielded the most marked differences among raters. As judged by the psychiatrists (all of whom had psychoanalytic training), 93 percent of the behavior therapy patients showed improvement, while only 77 percent of the "insight therapy" and 77 percent of the no-therapy patients showed improvement. As judged by the patients themselves, 74 percent of those in the behavior therapy group, 81 percent of those given psychotherapy, and but 44 percent of those in the no-therapy group felt they had improved. It would seem that those patients *denied* therapy believed they couldn't possibly have gotten much better without treatment, despite the objective evidence to the contrary seen by the assessing psychiatrists.

We might note that the patients in the two treatment groups probably had quite different perceptions of what improvement ought to be. The goal of psychotherapy is often that of giving the person better *understanding* of her or his mental processes. Behavior therapy is a broader-scale type of treatment, in which self-help and self-improvement in many areas are emphasized. It is possible that the "insight" patients did notice a marked improvement in their mental processes and, believing this to be the major goal of therapy, rated themselves highly. The assessing psychiatrists, knowing that things like good job performance and healthy social relations are also necessary to mental health, downgraded the "insight" patients because they had shown little improvement in these areas (while the behavior therapy patients had).

7. Additional findings by Sloane and his group were equally interesting. As we noted in several earlier chapters, one of the major objections raised against behavior therapy is that it merely removes symptoms without curing the underlying cause of the disorder. Hence other symptoms might crop up to replace those the therapy had banished. However, Sloane and his associates found no evidence for *symptom substitution* in any of the patients in any group. To the contrary, it seemed that when a patient's primary symptoms showed improvement, the patient often spontaneously reported improvement of other minor difficulties as well.

   Another objection brought against behavioral treatment is that it is a "cold and mechanistic way of pushing people around." In fact, the patients in behavioral treatment rated their therapists as being significantly "warmer, more involved, more genuine, and as having greater and more accurate **empathy**" than the insight patients rated their therapists as being.

8. Sloane and his colleagues found that their psychoanalytically oriented therapists did better with well-educated, middle- or upper-class, verbally fluent patients than with relatively uneducated or verbally passive patients. The behavior therapists did about as well with one type of person as with any other. Perhaps for this reason, none of the patients given behavior therapy got worse, while one or two people in the other two groups showed a *marked deterioration* over the four-month period.

Sloane's Conclusions

R. Bruce Sloane and his colleagues conclude that

behavior therapy is at least as effective as, and possibly more so than, psychotherapy with the sort of moderately severe neuroses and personality disorders that are typical of clinical populations. This [finding] should help to dispel the impression that behavior therapy is useful only with phobias and [simple] problems. In fact, only the behavior therapy group in this study had improved significantly on both the work

Empathy (EM-path-thee). From the Greek words meaning "to suffer with." Literally, the ability to understand fully another person's thoughts and feelings, or to experience the same emotions another individual is experiencing.

and the social measures of general adjustment at four months. Behavior therapy is clearly a *generally* useful treatment.

Question: Research such as Sloane's is sometimes criticized as being unethical because individuals in the control group are *denied therapy* for a period of time. Given the findings, what do you think?

"Sick Talk" and "Well Talk"

One of the most puzzling aspects of the Sloane study is that the psychotherapists saw *less* improvement in their patients than did the patients themselves, or the outside assessors. The behavior therapists were just the opposite—they saw more improvement than did the patients themselves. An explanation for this finding may come from research by a psychologist named Joel Greenspoon.

In the late 1950's, Greenspoon demonstrated how important the attitude of the therapist is in affecting the behavior of most clients. Greenspoon noticed that when a patient begins talking about sexual abnormalities, or about bizarre thought patterns, the therapist may unconsciously encourage the patient to continue talking. The therapist may lean forward, look very interested, and say to the patient, "Yes, yes, tell me more about that." But when the patient is speaking normally, or discussing solutions rather than problems, the therapist may believe the patient is making little or no progress. So the therapist may lean back and look disinterested. In Greenspoon's terms, there is always the danger that the therapist may unwittingly *reward* the patient for "sick talk" and *ignore* (or even punish) the patient for "well talk."

In more humanistic terms, getting the client to concentrate on achieving mental *health* may be more important than getting the client to understand the causes of his or her mental *illness*. It is possible that the insight therapists in the Sloane study *perceived* their patients as being a "collection of problems" rather than as a "collection of healthy possibilities."

Question: Given Greenspoon's findings, are you surprised that Rogers may have "unconsciously shaped" his patients toward better health?

Psychotherapy: An Evaluation

In 1980, the National Institute of Mental Health (NIMH) began a long-term study of the effects of psychotherapy. When the results of this research are finally reported, perhaps we will be in a position to speak more authoritatively about the "cure rate" for various types of psychological treatment. Preliminary findings from the NIMH study, however, suggest that most types of "talk therapy" can be of *some* value to *some* patients.

The major problem in evaluating psychotherapy obviously is that of defining what we mean by "cure" and "value." Almost every type of therapy—and almost every therapist—has a different way of measuring therapeutic success. Thus, no matter what the results of the NIMH study turn out to be, it is unlikely that the majority of psychologists will agree on what the effectiveness of treatment actually is.

Part of the problem may come from the use of the term "cure rate." For we have borrowed this term—almost unconsciously—from the medical profession. "Cures" almost always denote *measurable changes* of some kind. Yet such consequences of therapy as "feeling better" and "greater understanding" are internal processes that (by definition) cannot be measured objectively. Should we discard a type of treatment that uniformly helps clients "feel better" simply because the therapy yields no measurable *behavioral changes*?

"Values" are as subjective as "feelings" and "understanding." A century ago, if you had a problem, you talked it over with members of your family. (And if you were acting strangely, your family might have insisted on such a talk even if you didn't wish one.) These days, families are often widely scattered. And therapists often serve as sympathetic listeners for people who have no one else to talk to. Should we worry about "cure rates" in situations such as these?

We will have more to say about these issues at the end of the chapter. First, however, let's see what approach to psychotherapy social/behavioral theorists tend to take.

Social/Behavioral Therapy

Up until fairly recently, most of our laws, customs, and philosophies have been based on the assumption that psychological problems existed *within* an individual. When factors *outside* the individual contributed to "mental disorders," these factors were presumed to be primarily supernatural—gods, witches, and evil spirits. Most forms of biological and intra-psychic therapy can be seen as attempts to treat the patient by working from the inside out.

Within the last century rather a different point of view has emerged—a belief that "mental illness" is as much a disruption of relationships *between people* as it is a disruption of *one person's inner psychodynamics*. Abnormal behavior is almost always expressed in social situations. And unless "crazy people" disturb or upset others, they seldom are sent to mental hospitals or to see a therapist.

From a social/behavioral point of view, the goal of treatment is not merely altering the function of the patient's body or brain. Nor is the goal just to change the patient's personality. Rather, the purpose of treatment should be that of helping the patient *get along better with others*. Indeed, in many instances, the group of people around the patient may actually be contributing to the "craziness" without realizing it. In such cases the best form of therapy may be removing the person from that environment—or somehow getting other people to behave differently toward the patient. This type of treatment obviously works from the outside in.

The three major types of social-behavioral treatment are (1) group therapy, in which the patient learns better ways of responding to a group of people who often have similar problems; (2) behavioral therapy, including cognitive behavior modification, which we have discussed extensively in Chapters 10, 13, 14, and 16; and (3) **milieu therapy**, in which the patient's social environment or milieu becomes the focus for treatment.

Group Therapy

The history of group therapy probably stretches back to the dawn of recorded time. In a sense, the early Greek dramas offered a type of psychological release not much different from the psychodrama we will discuss in a moment. Bull sessions, prayer meetings, revivals—all these are the ancestral forms of today's encounter groups.

Group therapy did not gain any scientific notice, however, until 1905, when a Boston physician named J.H. Pratt made a fortunate mistake. Pratt found that patients suffering from tuberculosis were often discouraged and depressed. He first believed their despondency was due to ignorance on their part—they simply didn't know enough about the disease they suffered from. So he brought them together in groups to give them lectures about "healthy living." The lectures soon turned into very intense discussions among the patients about their problems. Pratt discovered his patients gained more strength from learning they were not alone in their suffering than they did from his lectures.

By 1910 group treatment was used by many European psychiatrists who gave "collective counseling" to people with similar psychological problems. Psychiatrist J.L. Moreno tried this method in Vienna with displaced persons, children, and prostitutes. In 1914 Alfred Adler suggested that group techniques might be a more effective way of helping large numbers of patients than the usual one patient/one therapist encounters.

In the *Encyclopedia of Human Behavior*, R.M. Goldenson notes that European psychoanalysts were for the most part hostile to group psychotherapy, but this form of treatment soon gained a firm foothold in the United States. Some of the major varieties are psychoanalytic

> **Milieu therapy** (mill-YOU). The French word for "social environment" is *milieu*. Milieu therapy involves changing the patient's environment in order to induce changes in the patient's mind and behavior.

group therapy, directed group therapy, inspirational group therapy, play group therapy, activity group therapy, family group therapy, encounter groups, and psychodrama.

Group Therapy Techniques

As you might guess, these various forms of group treatment differ considerably among themselves. But, as Jerome D. Frank puts it, they all seem to be based on the belief "that intimate sharing of feelings, ideas, [and] experiences in an atmosphere of mutual respect and understanding enhances self-respect, deepens self-understanding, and helps the person live with others."

Some types of groups are directed by a leader and have a rather formal treatment plan. One purpose of these "formal" groups is helping people *break through* their psychological resistances. In this sense, then, formal groups tend to be *confrontational* as well as highly directed. The group leader may give lectures or pass out written material that forms the basis of group discussion. This "structured" technique is used particularly with psychotic or withdrawn patients who would not, perhaps, be able to function effectively in a less structured social environment.

Other groups are more inspirational in character. They typically are led by someone with a strong personality who uses a variety of techniques (including strong criticism, or calling on higher spiritual powers) to inspire change in group members. Some groups concentrate mostly on encouraging the patients to form new behavior patterns and attitudes. Other groups concentrate on breaking down emotional resistances in their members. The 10,000 or more chapters of Alcoholics Anonymous, the Christian Science Church, est, the Seventh Step Foundation for ex-convicts, and even Weight Watchers, Inc., are examples of groups that rely heavily on inspirational or highly emotional devices.

Psychodrama

Moreno, who first used group therapy with socially displaced persons around 1910, later developed a type of treatment he called *psycho-*

"EVER HAVE ONE OF THOSE GREAT DAYS WHEN YOU'RE JUST BETWEEN MANIC AND DEPRESSIVE?"

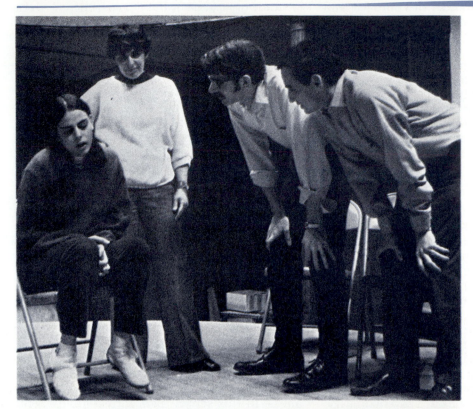

This psychodrama presents an example of "doubling"—two men on the right. The "director" is in the white sweater. The "auxiliary ego" is represented by the girl in the chair.

Dr. Jacob Moreno, creator of psychodrama, addressing a group at the New York Psychodrama Theater in the 1960's.

drama. The therapist usually serves as "director" for the psychodrama, which often takes place on a real stage. The patient stars as "heroine" or "hero" in a "play" that centers around some problem in the patient's life. Trained actor-therapists assist in the production. At times, a whole family or group may act out their difficulties. Moreno often invites audiences to watch the proceedings, for he believes that people in the audience can benefit from seeing problems similar to their own presented on stage.

Many types of group therapy that use "role-playing" techniques owe a debt to Moreno. For example, a group of teenagers in Philadelphia call themselves "The Connection." With the help of professionals, these young people prepare skits concerning such social issues as child abuse, rape, venereal disease, and pregnancy. The teenagers then present the skits to audiences made up of young people and their parents. The audience discusses the skits afterwards. According to Iris Stendig-Raskin, Coordinator of The Connection during the early 1980's, "At times it is very helpful for the audience to be able to discuss issues in terms of characters in the skits rather than say, 'This is my problem.'" Thus, says Stendig-Raskin, this type of psychodrama often helps increase communication between young people and their parents.

Transactional Analysis

A very different form of role playing is found in *transactional analysis*, or TA. In the 1950's, psychiatrist Eric Berne developed a personality theory that was, in part, an extension of Freudian psychoanalysis. Berne used the term "game" to refer to the stereotyped and often misleading interpersonal "transactions" that people frequently adopt in dealing with others. According to Berne, a game is a "recurring series of transactions, often repetitive and superficially rational, with a concealed motivation." He believed that each game is but a tiny part of a "script" that a person uses in "performing" various roles in his or her life. Briefly put, the goal of TA is that of consciously changing your behavior so that you no longer engage in unconscious role playing.

William and Martha Holloway describe TA as a therapy in which people learn they are responsible for their own feelings, but not for the feelings of others. The Holloways describe TA as "being for people who want to change and not those who want to be coddled." The Holloways further state that "change in TA groups is . . . contractual and decisional. . . . The duration and extent of the change process for any given individual is entirely dependent upon the goals which that person sets."

In previous chapters, we noted that infants require sensory stimulation in order to survive. The Holloways call this physical stimulation "giving strokes." Positive strokes result in "good feelings," while negative strokes result in "unpleasant feelings." As adults we often seek verbal or psychological "strokes" rather than physical ones. If we can't get positive "strokes," then negative ones are better than nothing. Much of the role playing we engage in, the Holloways say, is unconsciously aimed at "getting strokes."

Eric Berne believed we have three "ego states"—the Adult, the Parent, and the Child. Roughly speaking, the Adult, Parent, and Child ego states are similar to Freud's descriptions of ego, superego, and id.

According to the Holloways, the Parent ego state is a set of "memorized instructions we learned when young by observing how our parents acted toward us. When playing the role of a 'nurturing Parent,' we use terms such as 'I love you,' or 'You're beautiful.' When in a 'critical Parent' ego state, we use words such as 'always, never, must, should, ought to.'"

The Child ego state is one primarily made up of feelings. The "natural Child" ego state allows us to express our feelings as they actually are, the Holloways say. In the "adapted Child" ego state, we react as our parents told us we ought to when we were young.

The Holloways believe the Adult ego state is "like a computer." That is, "the Adult is the part of us that takes in and evaluates information,

Eric Berne

both from inside us and from the world around us. The Adult also estimates the probabilities and makes decisions." When in this ego state, we tend to "operate with little feeling," and our "Adult decisions are usually well-informed."

When two people speak, the Holloways say, the problem with communications is that one person may be speaking as an Adult, while the other may be in the Child or Parent ego state. The Holloways call this "crossed transactions." Thus, one goal of TA is to let you identify your states—and those of others—in order to understand how people communicate. Then you must learn to take responsibility for what you do, accept yourself ("I'm OK"), make a contract with yourself to live more successfully in the future, and realize that other people have the potential to do the same ("You're OK").

Gestalt Psychotherapy

Gestalt therapy has its roots in classical Gestalt psychology (see Chapter 8), psychoanalysis, and the analysis of nonverbal behavior. The main object of this type of treatment often seems to be that of *growth through exploration*. The explorations are sometimes emotional, sometimes perceptual, sometimes behavioral. The group leader (or individual therapist) helps clients experiment with new ways of acting and of viewing themselves, their problems, and the world outside them.

Gestalt therapy was begun by Fritz Perls. More than anything else, this type of treatment is based on Perls's belief that people should "take responsibility for themselves," and should "focus attention primarily on the here and now." In his 1978 book *Creative Process in Gestalt Therapy*, Joseph Zinker defines Gestalt therapy as an ongoing creative adjustment to the potential in the therapeutic situation.

One of the better descriptions of this type of treatment appears in a 1980 book *Beyond the Hot Seat: Gestalt Approaches to Group*, edited by Bud Feder and Ruth Ronall. Several characteristics of Gestalt therapy emerge from this book. First, members of Gestalt groups are expected to "be their own chairpersons." That is, they must accept responsibility for their actions. Second, group members are encouraged to focus not only on "here and now events," but also on their reactions to these events. For this reason, perhaps, *leaders* of Gestalt groups tend to explain their actions during therapy in terms such as, "It feels right," or "That's where I was at the time." Third, group members are urged to communicate openly with others. As one therapist puts it, "persons shall make contact with other persons."

Although Gestalt group leaders often speak in terms of "therapists and clients," the goal of Gestalt treatment is more **experiential** than that of achieving "measurable, objective cures."

Encounter Groups

Encounter groups vary so widely among themselves that no simple description of them is possible. In general, an encounter group is made up of people who have had little previous contact with one another. The group may meet one or more times a week for several weeks. Or the members may live together in close, intense contact for a day, a weekend, or even longer.

Encounter group participants are usually encouraged to bring their feelings out into the open and to learn more honest ways of communicating with each other. Often the focus is on some aspect of non-verbal experience—perhaps on developing better sensory awareness of bodily reactions, perhaps on learning how facial expressions communicate deep-seated emotions. As a means of helping group members strip away their defenses, a few encounter groups meet in the nude.

In his 1980 book, *Group Processes and Personal Change*, British psychologist Peter B. Smith lists two factors he believes are characteristic of successful encounter groups. First, the group gives "maximum support" to each member. Second, the group *confronts* each member with his or her faults, delusions, and excuses. Personal change occurs in encounter groups, Smith suggests, because the groups "accept" members as they actually are, while urging members to "face up" to their own inappropriate thoughts and feelings.

Evaluating Group Therapy

Perhaps the best evaluation of the effectiveness of different types of group therapy comes from a series of studies performed by psychologists Morton Lieberman, Matthew Miles, and psychiatrist Irvin Yalom. This research on group therapy began at Stanford in 1968 and is still going on. Over the years, Lieberman, Miles, and Yalom have studied almost every type of group treatment offered to the public. Typically, these researchers investigate the group leader's perceptions of what went on, and ask the participants to evaluate the experience immediately after treatment and at some later time. The scientists also ask close friends or relatives of the participants to rate the participants' progress.

In a recent book, Lieberman, Miles, and Yalom report that their studies offer little scientific evidence that group therapy is of much *therapeutic* value. Indeed, it may often do real harm. They state that about 8 percent of the participants are "casualties"—that is, people who show evidence of serious psychological damage that can be attributed to the group experience. Overall, however, about a third of the group members get better, about a third get worse, and the rest seem unchanged immediately after the experience.

According to Lieberman and his colleagues, there are *few differences* among the various types of group therapy as far as their *effectiveness* is concerned. Immediately after therapy has ended, almost 65 percent of the participants state that the experience was a positive one. However, six months later, less than a third of them are still enthusiastic about having undergone treatment.

Benefits of Group Therapy

Lieberman, Miles, and Yalom conclude that none of the groups they studied were particularly effective as *change agents*. However, the groups can excel at creating *instant, brief, and intense interpersonal experiences*. Lieberman and his colleagues believe this chance to learn something about yourself from the open reactions of others is important, and not often available in our society. But they believe that such experiences are not the crucial ones that alter people permanently for the better.

Environmental Therapy

One thing we have slowly come to realize in recent years is our sensitivity to our environments. The **ecologists** have demonstrated rather vividly the disasters that may occur when we pollute the physical world around us. But polluted psychological environments can kill or corrupt your spirit as readily as dirty air and water can kill or corrupt your body. Thus, the job of the *environmental psychotherapist* is similar to that of the ecologist—to identify sources of pollution and remove them. If the therapist cannot easily find ways of removing the "psycho-pollution" from your world, or of helping you live more happily despite the pollution, then more radical treatment is usually needed. Typically this treatment takes the form

Gestalt therapy (guess-SHTALT). The German word *Gestalt* means "good form." According to the Gestalt psychologists, we tend to perceive the world in "wholes," which are the "best possible forms." Gestalt therapy often consists of helping you "become a *whole* person again."

Experiential (ex-peer-rhe-EN-shall). Experiential psychology focuses on having (and sharing and understanding) experiences, rather than analyzing the experiences in some scientific fashion or setting measurable goals and striving to achieve them.

Ecologists (ee-KOLL-oh-jists). Ecologists are scientists who study the pattern of relationships between organisms and their environments.

of moving you to different surroundings—such as a mental hospital.

Mental Hospitals: Past and Present

Far from being *asylums* where people could flee when the storms of life became too threatening, early mental hospitals were little more than human garbage dumps, crammed with life's failures and misfits. As *ecological systems*, these institutions were often more abnormal and destructive to human egos than was the outside world the patients had sought relief from. Little wonder, therefore, that the "cure rate" in US mental hospitals remained very low from the 1700's until the mid-1900's.

Milieu Therapy

Social/behavioral therapists tend to see mental illness as being caused by *unhealthy living conditions*—not by character defects or mental weakness. It is the failure of society to *teach* people healthy behaviors—not the failure of people to *learn*—that causes insanity. The best form of treatment, therefore, would be putting the patient in a new milieu. Each aspect of this new milieu would be carefully designed to help the patient *learn better habits of adjustment*.

The term "therapeutic community" was coined by British psychiatrist Maxwell Jones in 1953 to refer to this type of *milieu therapy*.

In a way, the therapeutic community is rather like a non-stop, 24-hour-a-day encounter group. However, its primary function is *not* usually that of removing symptoms or merely changing behaviors. Rather, its aim is that of drawing the patient into normal relationships that will give the person confidence, self-esteem, and social competence.

The difficulty in evaluating milieu therapy is the same as with other forms of group therapy—terms like "confidence" and "self-esteem" refer to intra-psychic traits and hence are hard to define or measure objectively. Therapeutic communities certainly are far more humane forms of treatment than the old-style mental hospitals. But as we will see momentarily, there is a serious question as to whether milieu therapy is as effective in curing people as its proponents claim.

Token Economies

Rather a different type of environmental treatment is favored by behavior therapists, whose aim is that of changing habit patterns rather than altering inner psychological states.

Patients in mental hospitals often develop what is called an **institutional neurosis**. That is, the patients lose interest in the world and the people around them, develop hallucinations and fantasies, and become quarrelsome, resentful, and hostile. Institutional neurosis appears to be caused in part by the fact that, in most hospitals, patients often are "given" everything they might need by the staff. Under these conditions, many of the patients develop a rather child-like dependency on the staff.

Behavioral psychologists believe the best cure for institutional neurosis is making the patients take as much responsibility for their own improvement as possible. To help achieve this goal, the behaviorists have developed what they call the *token economy*.

In a token economy, each patient is encouraged to decide what rewards she or he wants to work for. The staff members then reinforce "socially approved" or "healthy" behaviors by giving the patients tokens. Staff members ignore "inappropriate" or "abnormal" behaviors. The patient is given the tokens as visible evidence that he or she is making progress. The patient then cashes in the tokens to "purchase" her or his rewards.

Perhaps the best study comparing the token economy to other forms of treatment was reported by Gordon Paul and Robert Lentz in 1977. Paul and Lentz contrasted the improvement rates in three groups of hospitalized patients—those given traditional "milieu" therapy, those put on a token economy, and those left on the usual ward without any special form of treatment. The patients in the token economy showed far greater improvement than did the patients in either of the other two groups.

The criticism most often raised against the token economy is that it is mechanistic and dehumanizing because it focuses on observable behaviors—on symptoms—rather than dealing with underlying, dynamic psychological problems. The behavioral changes that the token economies do bring about, however, seem to be very reliable (repeatable).

Evaluating Social/Behavioral Therapies

Behavioral therapies seem particularly effective at increasing "desirable" responses and at decreasing "symptomatic" or "undesirable" behavior patterns. And, as we noted in Chapter 14, cognitive behavior modification is useful in altering both perceptions and attitudes. These facts raise an interesting question: Since most types of "talk therapy" have failed to achieve the *measurable* results of behavioral treatment, why is psychotherapy still so popular?

There are several answers to that question. First, as we have frequently noted, the *goals* of psychotherapy and group treatment are often quite different than those of behavior modification. You do not go to a Chinese restaurant if you are hungry for Mexican food. Nor should you insist that, just because you prefer tacos and refried beans, everyone else should eat what you think is best.

Second, although several well-known studies of "cure rate" in psychotherapy have not yielded outstanding results, the *overall trend* may be more encouraging. In 1977, M.L. Smith and G.V. Glass reported on the use of a new "trend analysis" technique called **meta-analysis**. This technique involves analyzing hundreds of studies on the effects of therapy. Smith and Glass performed this "meta-analysis," and then added up the number of studies with positive results and the number of studies with negative outcomes. Smith and Glass report that their "meta-analysis box score" supports the belief that psychotherapy is effective. Several other authors have also reported favorable "box scores" using the meta-analysis technique. However, some researchers have gotten negative results when using meta-analysis. And behavioral psychologists (in particular) have been highly critical of the meta-analysis technique itself. So, the issue of the effectiveness of psychotherapy is still in some doubt.

Third, and most important, therapy is a *part of human experience*. As such, it can be best be understood in terms of such processes as perception, motivation, and learning. When you are faced with an ambiguous stimulus, you may well perceive it as you wish to perceive it. Thus, if you believe strongly in the usefulness of talk therapy, you will perceive a strongly positive trend in the research data. If you disbelieve in psychotherapy, you will pay more attention to the negative results than to the positive. And this statement is as true of *therapists* as it is of their *patients*.

Why would anyone believe strongly in the effectiveness of group therapy (for instance)? Because, as Lieberman and his colleagues discovered, it yields *immediate and significant changes in feelings and behaviors*. Most therapists—and many participants, as well—find such experiences extremely rewarding.

As we mentioned in Chapter 14, "behavior is determined by its consequences." The *immediate* result of most types of confrontational therapy is that both the therapist and the patient *feel immensely better*. So both patient and therapist are strongly reinforced. But suppose we look again at the research by Lieberman *et al.* on group therapy and at G. Alan Marlatt's studies on treatment of alcoholic patients (see Chapter 13). Both these lines of work suggest that the *long-term* effects of confrontation are typically negative. However, because the immediate outcome is so rewarding, many therapists and patients may be primed to see only the positive "short-term" effects achieved by psychotherapy.

As we mentioned in Chapter 13, however, it is possible that a *combination* of therapies may work better than any single type. Marlatt suggests that confrontation be used in the *early stages* of treatment for the immediate changes that it brings about. However, Marlatt says, the therapist should soon shift to teaching the patient those personal and social skills the patient needs in order to achieve and maintain *long-term improvement*.

Institutional neurosis. Hospital patients are often subtly encouraged to remain "sick" in order to stay in the hospital. The "sicker" the patient becomes, the more dependent the patient is on the hospital, and the more the institution justifies its own existence. When patients develop an abnormally strong dependency on a hospital or its staff, the patients are said to suffer from an institutional neurosis.

Meta-analysis (METT-ah). "Meta" means "beyond." Meta-analysis, developed by M.L. Smith and G.V. Glass, involves several steps. First, you survey *all* the published literature on a given topic, such as the effects of psychotherapy. Second, you judge whether each published study yielded positive or negative effects. Third, you add up the number of positive and negative studies. Fourth, you use statistical analysis to determine whether these results would have been expected by "chance alone." One problem with meta-analysis is that scientists tend to publish studies that yield positive results, but not to publish experiments that yielded negative or insignificant results. Thus, the published literature may have a "positive bias."

something extra to) what seems to be our inborn way of healing ourselves?

To answer this question, we might turn to Adolf Meyer, who is often called the "dean of American psychiatry."

Meyer's Holistic Approach

Adolf Meyer believed in the *holistic* approach to treating people, and recognized there were multiple causes for even the simplest of behaviors. Rather than passing verdicts on patients by labeling them as "schizophrenics" or "neurotics," Meyer preferred to discover both what was wrong and what was right with the patients at all levels of analysis—the biological, the psychological, and the sociological.

Meyer also attempted to determine those *normal* aspects of behavior that the patient might

Therapy and the Whole Individual

Despite all the controversy about the effectiveness of psychotherapy, one fact seems indisputable: Most "mentally disturbed" individuals get well whether or not they receive treatment. As the noted psychoanalyst Karen Horney said in her book *Our Inner Conflicts*, "fortunately, analysis is not the only way to resolve inner conflicts. Life itself still remains a very effective therapist." How then can we make sure that psychological treatment does speed up (or add

Karen Horney

still have available. He then tried to build on these psychological assets to bring about change. Meyer also believed that the patient should set both the goals and the pace of therapy, and that the therapist should work as hard at changing the patient's home (or hospital) environment as in changing the patient's psyche or behaviors. Meyer called his approach "critical common sense."

There are hundreds of different kinds of psychotherapy. The surprising thing is that almost all of them "work" with certain kinds of patients and with certain types of problems—and fail with others. If we apply Adolf Meyer's "critical common sense" to an analysis of the strengths and weaknesses of all the various types of therapy, we might discover that most successful forms of treatment have several things in common:

1. Psychological change almost always occurs in a supportive, warm, rewarding environment. People usually "open up" and talk about things—and try new approaches to life—when they trust, admire, or want to please the therapist. Criticism seldom changes thoughts or behaviors, and it often kills all chance of improvement. But sincere expressions of warmth and tolerance for "abnormalities" can provide the atmosphere in which change can occur.

2. Most successful forms of treatment can be seen as feedback mechanisms. That is, they provide you with information about your past, put you in touch with the functioning of your body, and make you aware of how your behavior actually affects other people. Feedback also helps you realize the distance between your desired goals and your present achievements, and offers information on how the social environment influences your thoughts, feelings, and behaviors. Ideally, a complete form of therapy would do all these things—and also help you learn how to seek out and make even better use of feedback in the future.

3. Magic can "cure" mental illness overnight; all other forms of psychotherapy take a little longer. If you believe that madness is a matter of possession by devils—or that it's due to a "poor attitude" on the part of the patient—then you might expect that beatings or sermons could cure the illness quickly. But if you believe it takes many years of stressful experiences (and perhaps a particular genetic predisposition) for a full-blown

psychosis to develop, then you might also expect the road to recovery to be a fairly lengthy one.

4. The attitudes of both the patient and the therapist are of critical importance. A Cree Eskimo woman suffering from *witigo* "knows" she needs a witch doctor. Will giving this woman a tranquilizer help her much? On the other hand, patients often see their therapists as being models of mentally healthy or socially approved behaviors. Effective therapists (witch doctors, psychoanalysts, humanists, or behaviorists) usually practice what they preach.

5. The best forms of therapy seem to build on strengths rather than merely attacking weaknesses. By helping the patient work toward positive improvement—toward problem solving, good social behaviors, and self-actualization—the therapist motivates the patient to continue to grow and change. Therapies that focus entirely on uncovering or discussing psychological problems may merely confirm the patient's attitude that sickness is inevitable.

The Future of Psychotherapy

It is likely that, in the coming years, we will take Adolf Meyer's ideas more seriously than we have in the past. That means we will treat the whole patient as a unique individual rather than treating just one aspect of the person's difficulties. Already in some hospitals there is a *team of therapists* available to work with each patient. One member of the team looks at the person's physical or biological problems. Another deals with the person's intra-psychic dynamics. A third helps the patient change behavior patterns. A fourth team member is an expert in altering social environments. The patient can then get as much—or as little—of each type of therapy as his or her own particular case demands.

Ideally, the goals of therapy should be spelled out in a written contract agreed to by the patient and all members of the therapeutic team. And the patient's progress should be recorded regularly on a graph of some kind, so all team members are aware of the patient's achievements. As this "team-contracting approach" increases in popularity, our success rate in curing mental illness is likely to show a significant increase.

All forms of therapy achieve some success. In 1975 the Research Task Force of the National Institute of Mental Health released a report covering 25 years of research on therapy and mental illness. According to the NIMH report, most types of psychotherapy yield a 70 percent "cure rate." The major exceptions are behavior therapy and drug therapy, both of which (when effectively utilized) have produced cure rates well above 80 percent. But, as the NIMH report suggests, perhaps the single most important thing we have learned about mental health in the past 25 years is that neither problems nor cures occur in a vacuum. No matter how well a patient may respond in a hospital setting—and no matter what insights a client achieves in a therapist's office—the ultimate test of therapy comes when the person returns to her or his usual environment. If the patient can function successfully and happily in the real world, we can then conclude that a "cure" has indeed taken place.

It is thus to the complexities of the social environment that we now must turn our attention.

Summary

1   In primitive times (and societies), insanity was said to be caused by **possession**. That is, a **devil** of some kind was thought to take over the sick person's mind.

2   Primitive forms of **psychotherapy** typically involve the use of magic to "cast out the witch," or painful whips to **beat the devil** out of the patient.

3   As our scientific explanations of the causes of human behavior have changed, so have our types of treatment. In evaluating any form of therapy, we must ask ourselves several questions:
    a   How successful or **valid** is the treatment?
    b   How **reliable** is the therapy?
    c   Are there unfortunate **side effects**?
    d   How shall we define "success" or **cure rate**?

4   Biological treatment typically involves the use of **electro-convulsive shock, psychosurgery**, and **chemotherapy** or drugs.

5   **ECT** is most often used for **depression**, while **lobotomies** are used with aggressive or highly emotional patients. Both types of treatment have bad side effects and have not been proven scientifically to be of great worth except in very special cases.

6   The **major** and **minor tranquilizers** and **antidepressants** have limited uses, but many can be **abused** and all may have dangerous side effects.

7   There are many forms of intra-psychic treatment, including **psychoanalysis, humanistic therapy**, and **eclectic therapy**.

8   In psychoanalysis, the client is encouraged to undergo a **transference relationship** in which the analyst becomes a kind of "father figure." The therapist often **interprets** the client's **free associations**, feelings, and dreams in psychoanalytic terms in order to determine the client's unconscious **psychodynamics** and motivations.

9   In humanistic therapy, the client sets his or her own **therapeutic goals** and determines the **pace** at which treatment proceeds.

10 In **Rogerian** or **client-centered therapy**, the therapist gives the client **unconditional positive regard** while **reflecting back** the client's thoughts or feelings.

11 All therapy must be judged in relationship to the rate of **spontaneous recovery** patients show without treatment. In most recent studies, this rate has been between 40 and 50 percent.

12 In the **Menninger** study of psychoanalytic treatment, the "cure rate" was about 43 percent. However, many patients showed little improvement or even were worse at the end of treatment.

13 The cure rate for humanistic therapy, for eclectic psychotherapy, and for most types of **insight therapy** is about 70 percent.

14 The **Sloane study** suggests that "insight" therapy is better at changing a patient's **self-awareness** than at removing symptoms or changing behaviors. **Behavior therapy** is at least as effective with most patients as is psychotherapy, and is better at helping people improve

job **performance** and **social ad-justment**.

15 Research by Greenspoon shows that therapists may **unconsciously shape** patient responses by rewarding them for **sick talk** or **well talk**.

16 Environmental therapies include many types of **group therapy**, as well as attempts to change the patient by altering the patient's **milieu** and **social behaviors**.

17 Group therapies seem better as ways of encouraging people to explore and express themselves than as **change agents**.

18 **Milieu therapy** involves changing the patient's environment so that the person may grow in psychologically healthy ways.

19 **Behavioral psychologists** often use a **token economy** to help patients overcome **institutional neuroses**.

20 Most effective therapy takes place in a **warm, supporting environment** in which patients are given appropriate **feedback**. The **attitudes** of both patient and therapist are important, as is **building on strengths** rather than merely correcting weaknesses.

21 It is likely that, in the future, a **team approach** to treatment will prove to be highly effective, particularly if **patient-therapist contracts** are employed.

(Continued from page 601.)

"I *hurt*, Mark," Lou Hudson repeated, ignoring all of the boisterous activity in the gambling casino as he poured out his heart to Mark Evans. "I've lost almost everything we own. The house, the car, everything—gambled it all away. I've borrowed from everybody in the family and lost it all on the horses. I'm even going to lose Betty and the kids if I can't shape up somehow. But I get those urges, you understand, those times when I just know that I've got a winning streak going, and I have to play my hunches. I've got to get help of some kind, Mark, but what should I do?"

"What does Betty think you should do?"

"She wants me to join the Chattanooga chapter of Gamblers Anonymous. They're a bunch of people just like me that get together regularly to talk over their problems and help each other out. Betty says they've helped lots of folks."

"So, why don't you join and see what they can do for you?"

"Cause it would make your uncle angry at me. I mean your Uncle John, the psychoanalyst. He says I have an unconscious desire to punish myself by losing all the time. He thinks I ought to lie on a couch for a few years and find out what's wrong deep down inside me. He says that group therapy just doesn't get at the roots of the problem."

Mark smiled at the thought of Lou lying on a couch. "Well, why don't you try psychoanalysis, then?"

"Because of your Cousin Sophie," Lou said.

"The Rogerian?"

"Yeah. She thinks I need nondirective theory to help me achieve self-actualization. Sophie's a wonderful woman, Mark, and she's awful easy to talk to. Every time I say something to her, she just says it back to me in different words. Trouble is, she isn't talking to your Uncle John, and I owe her almost as much money as I owe him."

Mark decided that he needed a drink too, and hoisted a glass off the tray of a passing cocktail waitress. "So, why don't you go in for a little self-actualization?"

Lou groaned. "Your Aunt Beverly would never approve."

"You mean the behavior therapist?"

Lou nodded. "Yeah." He swallowed half his drink in a single gulp. "Man, you've got more different kinds of shrinks in your family than I ever heard of!"

"Psychology runs in my family the way that insanity runs in others. But what does Aunt Beverly, the behaviorist, think?"

"She tells me that all the other forms of therapy are unscientific. According to her, I'd do better to find a witch doctor than to go to your Uncle John for psychoanalysis. She wants to set up a behavioral program that will reward me for not gambling. And I hate to tell you how much I owe that woman, Mark."

"The cure rates for some kinds of behavioral therapy are very impressive, Lou. So why don't you try it?"

Lou shook his head in dismay. "Because it would make everybody else in the family mad as hell at me, including my wife Betty. I wouldn't mind going to any of them if I was sure they could help me. But how can you be sure you're going to be cured, Mark?"

"You can't be, Lou. Any more than you could be sure that if you sold me a life insurance policy, I wouldn't die the next day. All you can do is play the odds."

"What do you mean?"

"Ask each of the shrinks in the family to tell you what the cure rate is for compulsive gambling with their type of therapy. Take a good, close look at what they consider successful treatment to be, and how they measure success, and what the cost to you is going to be. Then pick the one that gives you the best odds for your time and money."

Lou Hudson blinked his bloodshot eyes as he pondered the matter. "That's being pretty hard-nosed about a very human predicament, isn't it?"

"Being hard-nosed about human predicaments is what keeps insurance companies and gambling casinos in business, Lou. You can't be sure that the therapy with the best overall cure rate is going to work for you and your own unique set of problems, but the fact that the odds are in your favor gives you a bit of a head start."

"Yeah," said Lou reluctantly. "I see what you mean."

"But what do *you* want to do, Lou? That's the most important factor of all."

"I kind of like the advice your Cousin Oscar gave me, and I owe him more than anybody."

Mark laughed. "Ah, yes, Cousin Oscar. What does the black sheep of the family recommend?"

Lou grinned. "Well, he knows of this woman who's a fortune teller. She lives in the same trailer park that Oscar lives in. He says that if I slip her a few bucks, she might look into her magic crystal ball and give me a tip on the races. Oscar says she's almost always right. If I could just win a few big ones, Mark, I could pay back my debts, stop gambling, and then I wouldn't need any therapy at all. What do you think of that?"

Mark shook his head. "No dice. If she's so good with crystal balls, how come she lives in a trailer instead of a mansion?"

Lou frowned. "Yeah, I see what you mean. Bad odds, eh? But what can I do? No matter whose therapy I pick, I'm going to make everybody else in the family madder than a wet hen."

Mark scratched his nose. "I think I have an idea. Lou, *you* haven't got a problem. The *family* has a problem. So we ought to come up with a family group solution."

"What do you mean? Me get a divorce from Betty?"

"No, Lou, nothing that drastic. But I suspect everyone in the family would rather give you free therapy than continue to lend you money."

Lou Hudson rubbed his eyes with the back of his hands. "Maybe you've got something there, Mark. I'd better go call Betty on the phone and see what she thinks."

As the two men walked toward the door of the casino, the little old lady in tennis shoes stopped them. She held up a coin. "My juju's deserted me today, boys, but I feel a change coming over me. This is my very last nickel, and I've got to get a winner. Where do you think I ought to put it?"

"Back in your purse," Mark said.

"Naw, Mark, you don't understand us gamblers." Lou closed his eyes and turned around three times. Then he pointed to a small slot machine far down the row. "Try that one, lady. I gotta hunch."

The little old woman trotted obediently down the row of one-armed bandits and paused to look the machine over carefully. Then she spat on the coin gently, rubbed it lovingly between her gloved hands, dropped the nickel in the slot, and pulled the handle. The reels spun wildly. The first one stopped on a bar. The second one did likewise. When the third reel clicked into place, it too sported a bar.

Suddenly the machine exploded. A bell rang loudly, and lights flashed off like skyrockets.

"Jackpot!" the woman screamed. "I did it, I did it! I've got my juju back! The magic power is with me again!"

A small crowd of people gathered around to watch the

slot machine pay off.

Lou Hudson looked at the woman and smiled wanly. "She probably spent $50 in nickels just to win one $10 jackpot. And now she'll put all those nickels right back in the machine, won't she?"

Mark nodded in agreement. "If she's a compulsive gambler, she will."

"You think I can stop that kind of nonsense, Mark?"

"If you really want to, and you get good help," Mark said, "the odds are definitely in your favor."

The slight young man with bloodshot eyes grinned in response. "I'll bet on that!"

Recommended Readings

Breggin, P.R. (1979). *Electro-shock: Its brain-disabling effects.* New York: Springer.

Garfield, S.L. (1983). *Clinical psychology: The study of personality and behavior* (2nd ed.). New York: Aldine.

Feder, B. & Ronall, R. (Eds.). (1980). *Beyond the hot seat: Gestalt approaches to group.* New York: Brunner/Mazel.

Kline, N.S. & Angst, J. (1979). *Psychiatric syndromes and drug treatment.* New York: Aronson.

Yalom, I.D. (1970). *The theory and practice of group psychotherapy.* New York: Basic Books.

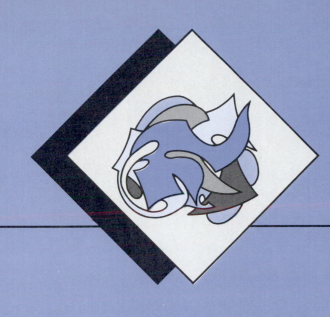

PART VII

Social Psychology

Did You Know That...

- You tend to perceive your actions as being responses to your environment, but tend to attribute the actions of others to personality traits or flaws of character?

- When you meet someone, you tend to judge them more by their looks and "body language" than by what they say or are like "deep down inside"?

- You have a "psychological bubble" around you that you defend whenever anyone intrudes on this "personal space"?

- Student juries give longer sentences to unattractive "rapists" than they do to handsome men accused of the same crime?

- How close people sit to each other when talking may depend on what language they are speaking?

- Women students with "low social competence" seem to perceive social distress in others accurately, but don't always respond appropriately?

- Married couples tend to establish "personal territories" in their homes, but unmarried couples living together don't generally do so?

- Guards who behave cruelly toward prisoners are often just normal people who are responding to what they perceive to be "society's rules"?

23

Person Perception, Attribution, and Social Roles

"The Best of Intentions"

Day 1

I was walking home from the meeting when I saw the police car sitting in front of our apartment house. They had come for Charlie, of course. Charlie is my best friend and bosom buddy.

Charlie and I have been rooming together for two years now ever since we came to college here two years ago. He is a top-notch person, and since we are both pre-legal, we have decided to open up an office together when we get out of Law School. Charlie is a super jock, the sort of guy you'd really want on your team. He is also a born leader, always coming up with great ideas about things

to do and giving me advice on what to wear and how to act. Which I guess I sometimes need. I suppose that when we do open that office, his name will be first on the door.

It was Charlie who read the ad in the student newspaper. The one offering to hire us at $25 a day to take part in this two-week-long "prison" experiment that this Dr. Mark Matossian is running. That struck us as a great way to earn some big bucks over the summer vacation. So we showed up, got interviewed, took all those psychological tests, and signed away our rights. I was sort of skeptical about that, you know. Agreeing to give up our basic rights

to privacy, and all those good things. But, as Charlie pointed out, it was only for two weeks. And besides, they promised they wouldn't use physical punishment of any kind on us. So when Charlie volunteered, I felt sort of obligated to go along with him. And now I am going to make almost 300 bucks, and help science besides.

Funny that they should have selected me to be a guard, and Charlie to play the prisoner's role. Well, maybe the tests showed he was more impulsive or something like that.

I arrived at the apartment house just as the cops were dragging Charlie out the door. He sure did look surprised! We learned at the Guards' meeting this afternoon that the local police were cooperating with Dr. Matossian. They had agreed to pull the prisoners in unexpectedly, charge them with suspicion of armed robbery, search them, fingerprint them, and take "mug shots" of their faces. Then the cops put blindfolds on the prisoners and we picked them up and drove them over to school where the "mock prison" is. Which we did, all in the spirit of good, clean fun, you understand. Tried to get them in the mood, so to say.

They needed some mood-setting because the prison is pretty "mock," I tell you no lie. Just some rooms in the basement of the Psych Building, with bars painted on the doors and the tiny windows. Dr. Matossian said he is repeating a study performed by some professor at Stanford named Philip Zimbardo, who found that isolating people from society was dehumanizing. Well, okay, what's new? But these prisoners are hardly going to be "isolated from society." There will be us guards, three to a shift, and Dr. Matossian and his students who will be the Prison Staff and actually live there. Plus the guys—the prisoners, I mean—will be allowed visitors twice a week. So I do not think this study is going to work very well.

But maybe it will be fun anyhow, plus the money.

Dr. Matossian asked us to keep diaries, which he will collect, and we are to write down everything we think and do, even if it seems critical of him and the staff. I don't like criticism or hassling people anyhow, so he

shouldn't worry.

Charlie put on a big smile and tried to look very nonchalant when the policemen escorted him out of the apartment. Several of the neighbors were standing outside, watching. I will have to explain to them later what it is all about. I admire Charlie for taking it so calmly. Of course, I did not let on I knew him, since that is one of the Rules.

At the meeting today we decided on the Rules and Regulations for the Uni-Prison. Mostly, they are just commonsense things to keep an institution running properly. There is to be no physical abuse, although we can lock a prisoner up in the isolation room if he breaks the Rules. Which, given the sensible nature of the Regulations, a prisoner would be stupid to do anyhow. Charlie being anything but stupid, I figure he will do OK as a prisoner. Unless his Irish impulses get out of hand, or something.

I am not so sure about me in the role of a Guard. Sorry. We are to refer to ourselves as Correctional Officers. Anyhow, I put on my uniform at the apartment after the Police Officers took Charlie away. The dumb-looking khaki pants and shirt are a size too big and I feel uncomfortable in them. But I have a whistle and a billy-club, just to make me look "official." And they gave me a neat pair of mirrored sun glasses. Before I left, I stood in front of the mirror for a few minutes. Funny thing. I look pretty tough in that outfit, maybe because you can't see that my eyes are laughing. Mostly at myself.

Then I went over to the Uni-Prison and checked in. They started bringing the

"Numbers" in about half an hour later. I call them "Numbers," because that is how I am to address them. Good old Charlie is now #853, which is written on both sides of the nightshirt he wears. He was one of the first Numbers brought in. We stripped him down, then sprayed him with a "de-louser" which, it turned out, was only deodorant. Well, they are going to need that deodorant, because they are not going to get a shower while they are in prison. That is one of the Regulations.

Charlie got a little bit teed-off when we put the steel chain around his ankle and then required him to stand naked in the exercise yard for 20 minutes before we gave him his nightshirt. Well, it was necessary to remind him that he is a Prisoner even when he's bare-assed. Of course, underneath, I felt just as foolish as he did, but I don't think he or the other guys noticed. A Correctional Officer should not be embarrassed, since he is just doing the job for which he is being paid.

When we checked the guys in—the Numbers—we gave them a nylon stocking to put on over their heads. Makes them harder to tell apart, but they are just Numbers, after all. They have got nothing on under the nightshirts, and that does lead to some comical situations. Charlie complained right off that he wasn't a woman and didn't like wearing a skirt, but I told him to shut up because that is one of the Rules.

Warden Matossian then assembled the Staff and the Numbers and gave them an Official Welcome. He did a pretty good job of role playing, I do say that. His talk was really pretty patriotic.

"Listen," he said to the Numbers, "you have shown that you are unable to function outside in the real world. You lack the responsibility of good citizens of this great country. We of this prison, your Correctional Staff, are going to help you learn what your responsibilities as citizens of this country are. Here are the Rules. We expect you to know them and to be able to recite them by number. If you follow the Rules, repent for your misdeeds, and show a proper attitude, you and I will get along just fine.

"Rule #1: Prisoners must remain silent during rest periods, after lights are out, during meals, and whenever they are outside the prison yard.

"Rule #2: Prisoners must eat at mealtimes and only at mealtimes.

"Rule #3: Prisoners must not move, tamper with, deface, or damage walls, ceilings, windows, doors, or other prison property.

"Rule #4: Prisoners must address each other only by their numbers.

"Rule #5: Prisoners must address the guards as 'Mr. Correctional Officer.'

"Rule #6: Prisoners must obey all lawful commands and orders issued to them by Correctional Officers.

"Rule #7: Failure to obey any of the above rules may result in punishment."

Now, that's what I call *sensible* rules for a place like this!

Well, after the Warden had welcomed them, we put the Numbers away in their cells for Rest Period, and then I was off for the evening. I went back to the apartment, which I admit was sort of empty, what with old #853 being in

Prison. Of course, he got himself into this, so I guess it serves him right. But I do not know yet whether I am going to enjoy this experience at all.

Day 2

This morning when I got to work the guys on the night shift told me that they didn't have much trouble handling things. Some of the Numbers broke the Rule about not conversing after Lights Out, but the guys said they stopped that nonsense in a hurry. Charlie likes to talk a lot, so I was not surprised to learn that my old buddy #853 got himself shouted at a few times. Sort of wish I'd been around to hear what they said to him.

We got the #'s through the morning ritual pretty well. Part of their job is to sweep up the place. Naturally #853 complained about having to clean the toilets. Back at the apartment, that's usually my chore. Old #853 got a taste of what's good for him, for a change. I would have given him a chit to see the movie that night if he had done a good job, but he bitched too much, and that's against Regulations. Then at lunch he acted up something awful. Broke the Rules all over the place. Lunch was sausage and potatoes, and being his roommate, I am well aware that he does not like sausage very much at all. So #853 refuses to eat them, although that's illegal, because Rule #2 says that #'s *must eat* at mealtimes, which means that they must eat *everything* we give them, right?

So I said, "Listen you dumb twerp. Just because you are bigger than me doesn't mean that you are going to get away with break-

ing the Rules. You don't scare me, 853. You eat that damn sausage or I'll stick it in your ear and let you digest it that way." Of course I didn't say "ear," but you know what I mean.

Well, that must have teed him off, or something, because he started arguing with me and abusing me, which is definitely against the Rules. So the other guys and I just grabbed #853 by his nightshirt and led him away to solitary confinement. Which is really just a closet he's got to stand in, but is just what he deserved.

Even then he didn't calm down much, and I had to go down two or three times to shut him up. He got a little nasty the last time, so I shook the billy-club at him, just to let him know who was boss. I wouldn't ever use it, of course, because that's against the Regulations. But it was a little frightening to have this guy I thought I knew threaten me with verbal abuse and physical gestures. Finally, I couldn't take it any more, so I went and got the other guys and we got a couple of sausages and took them down to the "hole" and stuck them in #853's hands.

"Listen 853," I told him in no uncertain tone of voice. "You are going to hold on to those sausages until you see fit to obey the Rules and Regulations and eat them."

To tell the truth, even with the other guys around to protect me, I was a little worried because 853 has got one helluva temper, him being Irish and red-headed and all that. Of course, I couldn't *see* the color of his hair because of the nylon stocking pulled over his head, and maybe that made the difference. Anyhow, 853 shook the sausages at me and stepped forward, like he might be going to hit me with them. So in self-defense I held up my billy-club. Funny thing. He stopped and stared at me, and then he sort of trembled or shivered, like he had a chill. Then he burst out crying, and turned around and hid his face in a corner. I just let the old sissy cry, since he brought it all on himself.

Jeez, I hate sissies. So before I left for the day, I deliberately got in a loud conversation outside the "hole" with one of the Correctional Officers. I had a date that night, and so did the other CO, and we spent a lot of time describing just what we were going to do with the ladies that evening. I figured that would teach 853 a lesson, because he certainly did like his nocturnal activities before he got sent to Prison.

Day 3

The first thing that the guys told me when I came on duty was that 853 still refused to eat the sausages, so they were starving him until he gave in. He had missed supper and breakfast both, which is only proper, under the Rules. I saw right away we had trouble on our hands, because he was setting the other Numbers a very bad example. What would happen if everybody behaved that way? So I called his two cellmates into the yard, and then I handcuffed 853, sausages and all, and brought him out too.

"Listen you Numbers. This stupid jackass is disobeying the Regulations, and we cannot let him get away with the gross violations of the Rules he is guilty of. Therefore, we are going to take away your eating privileges until your cellmate here gives in and eats the sausages we have provided to keep him alive."

Well, naturally, the other two #'s are not very happy. But we told them to shut up and to get back on the Routine. Which, I am happy to say, they did without too much complaint. Except for 853, the #'s are mostly a bunch of sheep. Then as I am taking 853 back to the "hole," Warden Matossian came up and asked me to remove the handcuffs. I am not sure why he did this, since I was just trying to keep 853 from escaping. Which is what I am paid to do.

At lunchtime, when we wouldn't let them eat, the other two #'s stood in front of the "hole" and tried to talk some sense into 853. Which, I am sad to say, they failed to do, so they went hungry. I would feel sorry for 853, except he is obviously just being stubborn to show off, and now he is hurting others besides himself. Which is a downright crime, if you ask me.

Naturally, this whole nasty business upset the Routine so much that nobody knew which way was up. Finally, things got so bad that I suggested we ought to take away the eating privileges of all the #'s until 853 showed he was sorry for his misdeeds and corrected his bad attitude and behaved like any decent human would. The other CO's agreed with me, but they were a little worried about keeping discipline if all the #'s went hungry.

When we told the #'s of our decision, they got pretty surly. In fact, one of them started wise-mouthing a bit and showing off, but I tapped him lightly with my billy-club, and he got back into line.

Day 4

I was barely asleep when the CO's on the evening shift phoned. They said the #'s had gone crazy and were rioting! The Evening Shift got the the #'s cornered by spraying them with a fire extinguisher, but they needed reinforcements.

As I rushed over to help, I really got angry thinking what a sissy jerk 853 turned out to be. Embarrassing us all with that stupid, childish behavior. Why didn't he just give in and obey the Rules, like everybody else?

Well, when I got there, I guess I taught him a lesson, didn't I?

(Continued on page 656.)

Social Psychology

In the first chapters of this book, we described *psychobiology* as the junction point between two academic disciplines—biology and psychol-ogy. Writing in the April 1984 issue of *Contemporary Psychology*, Canadian psychologist James Olson says, "Most professionals would agree that social psychology is the scientific study of human social behavior. . . . The field has evolved from two distinct disciplines, sociology and psychology."

When we described psychobiology, we noted that *biologists* who work within the field often take quite a different view than do *psychologists*. The same thing is true of social psychology. James Olson goes on to say, "It is striking how much social psychologists who were trained within sociology differ from those who were trained within psychology in their conceptualizations of the science and in their preferred research strategies." As you read through the next three chapters, you will find this is indeed the case.

But aside from being a marriage of psychology and sociology, what is *social psychology* all about? How does it differ from all the other areas of psychology we have already discussed? According to Michigan psychologist Theodore Newcomb, the major difference is that social psychology pays attention chiefly to *relations between people*, while most of the rest of the field focuses on *the individual*. Tufts psychologist Jeffrey Rubin prefers the following definition: "Social psychology is the study of the ways in which people influence, and are influenced by, each other." These two conceptions of the field are similar. But you should remember there is no one, agreed-upon definition of "social psychology," as you read about the ways in which you relate to and are influenced by others.

Newcomb believes there are several major issues social psychologists typically deal with. Five of the most important issues are as follows:

1. In describing social relationships, should we look at how the individual affects the group, or how the group influences the individual?
2. When we attempt to study social variables, should we look primarily at internal processes such as *attitudes*, or at objective events such as *behaviors*?
3. Are social responses mostly learned, or mostly determined by the genes?
4. Should we be more interested in relatively consistent features of individuals and social organizations (*structures*) or in those aspects that change fairly readily (*functions*)?
5. Is social psychology primarily a *theoretical* or an *applied* science?

Some of these questions may sound a bit familiar. But let's look at them briefly from a new perspective as we begin our discussion of social psychology.

Ken. Literally, "ken" means your range of vision. However, "ken" also refers to your range of perception, understanding, or knowledge.

The Individual or the Group?

In Chapter 5, we noted that individuals are *sub-systems* within groups, that groups are "sub-systems" within organizations, and that organizations are the sub-systems that make up societies and cultures. Generally speaking, social *psychologists* tend to focus on responses *within* a single organism. That is, they anchor themselves at the level of the individual and look up the "systems" ladder toward groups and (perhaps) organizations. However, societies and cultures are so far up the scale that they are beyond the **ken** of many social *psychologists*.

Social psychologists, on the other hand, come to this field from the perspective of sociology. They stand at the top of the "systems" ladder and look down toward the individual. To many *social* psychologists, the individual is about as interesting as a single neuron in your brain would be to most clinical psychologists.

If you take a course in social psychology in the Department of Sociology, you will mostly learn about such topics as "socialization," "organizational structures," "cultural symbols," and "social deviance." If you take a course in social psychology in the Department of Psychology, you will probably cover such issues as "attitude change," "person perception," "attribution theory," and "social roles." Since this is a book on *psychology*, we will start with the individual and work our way up to groups and some types of organizations. And we will mostly talk about such things as attitudes, attributions, and roles.

Attitudes or Behaviors?

Traditionally, social psychologists have focused more on measuring and describing *attitudes* than on *behaviors*. Since attitudes are "internal processes," this argument boils down to the mind-body problem revisited.

The traditional way of defining an attitude is as follows: It is a consistent way of thinking about, feeling toward, or responding to some environmental stimulus or input. Thus, attitudes are composed of cognitive, emotional, and behavioral components. Some social psychologists emphasize the cognitive aspects of attitudes, some focus more on emotions, while a few try to deal with both cognition and affect. Whatever the case, these scientists come down on the "mind" side of the question.

Other social psychologists prefer to deal with measurable behaviors. For example, writing in the July 6, 1981 issue of the *Wall Street Journal*, social scientist Peter Drucker discusses the problem of trying to predict actions from attitude surveys. Drucker says, "In a good many social matters, attitudes are secondary and attitude surveys are a snare and delusion. What matters is what people do, not what they say they will do."

Since we have discussed the mind-body problem many times already, we need not restate all the issues here. We might note, however, that social learning theory offers a compromise between the two extreme positions. As you probably will remember, social learning theorists believe that attitudes are "cognitive structures" that allow you to process environmental inputs in consistent ways. Thus, in many (but not all) situations, attitudes actually control behaviors. But the social learning theorists also believe that you "acquire new cognitive structures" as you learn new behavioral habits. So to explain social relationships completely, you must deal *both* with attitudes and behaviors.

Learned or Innate?

Most psychologists believe that *some* aspects of social responses are influenced by the genetic blueprint. Perhaps the need most people have to *explain* their own behaviors and the actions of others is one example of a genetic tendency. However, the *expression* of most social needs appears to be learned. Hence, the emphasis in social psychology is much more on the "nurture" side of the issue than on the side of genetic inheritance.

Consistency versus Change

Some social scientists emphasize the *consistent features* of individuals, groups, and organizations. British researcher Mower White discusses this matter in her 1982 book *Consistency in Cognitive Social Behavior.* White believes an individual's attitudes, behaviors, personality characteristics, and social relationships should be "mutually compatible." By this, White means there should be a *consistent pattern* to the way you act, think, and feel in social situations. Furthermore, White says, "like attracts like." You are attracted to other

Kurt Lewin   John M. Darley

people who are similar to you, because their attitudes and behaviors are compatible with yours. White sees this same sort of "compatibility" in groups and organizations.

Other theorists believe that change and flexibility are the hallmarks of social responses. Behavioral psychologists, for instance, think you are attracted to others because you find them *rewarding* in some way. And since rewards are learned—and vary from person to person and situation to situation—the "consistency" lies in the way rewards function, not in the personality structure of the individual.

As we noted earlier, some aspects of *all* behaviors are relatively consistent, and some are relatively changeable. To emphasize one more than the other would be like a heart surgeon's paying attention only to the structure of your heart, while ignoring the way your heart functioned.

Question: How could you explain "compatibility" in terms of an innate need to "predict and control environmental inputs"?

Theories or Applications?

As we mentioned in Chapter 1, the field of psychology is split down the middle. Some scientists spend most of their time generating knowledge—that is, in performing experiments and creating new theories. Other psychologists are more interested in putting knowledge to use—that is, they like to help people, groups, and organizations solve real-life problems.

Although there are a great many theories (and theorists) in social psychology, the field has always leaned ever so slightly toward applications. There are many reasons for this "emphasis on the applied." To begin with, social problems are often highly visible and of obvious importance. And many social psychologists were originally attracted to the field because they were strongly motivated to *change society* in some fashion. For example, Kurt Lewin was a pioneer in the field of social psychology. Writing in the *Handbook of Social Psychology*, Morton Deutsch describes Lewin's approach in these words: "Lewin devoted much of his scientific work to furthering the understanding of the practical day-by-day problems of modern society." Lewin did so by developing a technique he called *action research*. The goal of "action research" is to find ways to achieve social change in the real world. Deutsch notes that "Lewin's work on social psychology reflected two basic personal orientations which [can be] summed up in the term 'scientific citizen.'"

It is also true that a lot of social research *of necessity* takes place in real-life settings. Much of learning theory stems from laboratory studies of rat and pigeon behaviors. But there are both ethical and practical constraints on the study of human subjects. For instance, we can't bring two people who are friends into a laboratory and deliberately create hostility and conflict between them. We can, though, study hostility and conflict *as they already exist* in real life. We might try to find ways of reducing interracial tensions in an integrated school or housing project, for example. Discovering new methods of helping people "get along better" would not only solve a pressing social problem, but would create new knowledge as well. Little wonder, then, that many social psychologists have adopted Kurt Lewin's motto, "The world is my laboratory."

The "Social Interaction Sequence"

There is no one "best way" to discuss social psychology. However, one good method is to begin with the individual and "work upward." In this chapter, therefore, we will look at the *individual in social situations*. That is, while keeping in mind that you are a unique person, we will focus on how you relate to others (and how they relate to you). And a good way to start is to look at what John Darley and Russell Fazio call the "social interaction sequence."

Writing in the October 1980 *American Psychologist*, Darley and Fazio state that, "Perception is a constructive, interpretative process. Such interpretation is particularly critical in

the perception of other people. The actions of another person do not automatically convey meanings, but are given meanings by the perceiver." With this thought in mind, Darley and Fazio state that the "social interaction sequence" typically has five distinct steps:

1. When you meet someone, you develop a *set of expectancies* about the other person.
2. You then *act* toward the person in a way that is consistent with your expectancies.
3. The other person *interprets* the meaning of your actions.
4. Based on this interpretation, the other person *responds*.
5. You then *interpret* the meaning of the other person's response.

Generally speaking, if the other individual's actions *fit your expectancies*, you are likely to continue generating further interactive sequences without pause. If your expectancies are not confirmed, however, you may either break off the relationship, or try to find some explanation for the unusual behaviors. Under some conditions, you may even change the way you perceive the other person, if her or his actions aren't as you anticipated they would be.

As we go through the chapter, we will touch on each of these five points in the social interaction sequence. And we will begin by trying to find out how you *generate a set of expectancies* about others. That quest leads us immediately into the topic of "person perception."

Question: What do you think Darley and Fazio's position would be on the "mind-body problem"? What about the "nature-nurture" issue?

Person Perception

One common social sequence is this: You meet someone new, you decide you like this person, and thus you see the individual more frequently in the future. Eventually, you form a warm friendship with (or even get married to) the person. Social psychologists have spent a great amount of time studying—and theorizing about—this type of social interaction. You may perceive this sequence of events as "happening naturally." Social scientists, however, have discovered that your perceptions and actions throughout the sequence are strongly affected by factors you may be unaware of.

When you meet someone new, the first thing you do is to *perceive* the other person. But what

Harold Kelley

influences your perception of this other individual? And what affects the way the other person views you? The answers to these questions make up the fascinating field of *person perception*.

Defining "Person Perception"

What is "person perception"? In the May 1981 issue of *Contemporary Psychology*, Edith Greene and Elizabeth Loftus say the meaning of this term has changed in recent years. They state, "Traditionally, it has been thought to be the study of how people perceive their human environment. It concerns our ability to know another individual's intentions, attitudes, emotions, ideas, and possible behavior. It is how we know that one person is friendly, another a cheat, and a third is depressingly angry." According to Greene and Loftus, we must now add the term "person memory" to the older definition, because perceptions are primarily *learned*. Thus, the way you perceive someone will depend to a great extent on what kinds of "codes" you use to file your memories of people in long-term storage.

But your perceptions are also affected by your needs. So the area of *person perception* must take into account not only social *perceptions*, but social *memories* and *motives* as well. Let's attempt to illustrate these points by describing "person perception" in more detail.

First Impressions

Suppose some good friends of yours have talked you into taking a blind date to a party. They paint a glowing picture of your date as a kind of super-person in order to get you to agree to the date. When the fatal moment comes, and you meet the person, what sorts of things do you look for first? That is, what *immediate stimulus clues* influence your *judgment* of the individual?

Obviously, your answers to these questions may be somewhat different than other people's answers. But the social psychologists who study person perception have come up with some generalities that might interest you.

If you have read Chapter 8, you will remember the primary rule of perception: *You see what you expect to see.* Before you meet your date, your friends will have *biased* your perceptions by their descriptions of the individual. If they have told you the person is warm, affectionate, responsive, and outgoing, you will probably *look for* these attributes in your date as soon as the two of you meet. Certainly your *attitude* toward the person will be different than if you have been told your date is rather intellectual, cold, withdrawn, quiet, and self-possessed.

The question then becomes, how do attitudes affect perceptions?

Attitudes

As we noted earlier, an *attitude* is a consistent way of thinking about, feeling toward, or responding to some aspect of your environment (or toward yourself). Thus, an attitude is actually a sort of "cognitive structure" that allows you to process and respond to social inputs in an efficient manner. But an attitude is also a "mental program" for *coding* experiences in order to store them in Long-term Memory. Therefore, your attitudes affect not only your *present* perceptions and responses, they also help determine your *future* memories of what you saw and did in the present. We can prove that point by looking at how you form "first impressions" of the people you meet.

Reputations

When your friends describe your blind date to you, they are telling you something about that person's *reputation*. That is, your friends are describing how most people perceive your date, or the attitude most people have toward the person.

Social psychologist Harold Kelley tested the importance of "reputations" in a study performed at MIT in the late 1940's. Kelley told a large class of undergraduates they would have a visiting lecturer for the day, and that the students would be asked to evaluate this man at the end of the class. Kelley then passed out a brief biographical note about the teacher, presumably to help the students with their evaluation. Although the students did not realize it, the description half the class received referred to the lecturer as being "rather a warm individual," while the description given the rest of the class called the man "rather a cold intellectual."

After the class had read the printed comments, the man arrived and led the class in a 20-minute discussion. Kelley watched the students and recorded how often each of them asked a question or made a comment. Afterward, the students were asked to rate the man on a set of attitude scales and to write a brief description of him.

Although everyone in the class had witnessed *exactly* the same performance at *exactly* the same time, the manner in which each student responded was measurably affected by the descriptions each had read. Those students who had been told the instructor was "warm" tended to rate him as much more informal, sociable, popular, good-natured, humorous, and humane than the students who had been told the same man was "cold."

More than this, the subjects *reacted* to the man quite differently. The students who were told he was warm spoke to him in class much more frequently than did the students who were told he was cold.

Judging from Harold Kelley's research, once you believe you won't like a person, you tend to

Autistic hostility (aw-TISS-tic). Autism (see Chapter 1) is the act of withdrawing into oneself, of shutting off external stimulation. Autistic hostility is the act of cutting off or denying favorable inputs about people or things we don't like. "My mind is made up—don't confuse me with facts."

Stereotypes. A stereotype is a fixed or unconscious attitude or perception—a way of responding to some person or object solely in terms of the the person's (or object's) class membership. The failure to treat people as individuals, each different from the other, is the act of stereotyping.

avoid further contact with him or her. Theodore Newcomb has called this avoidance response **austistic hostility**, and suggests that it may apply to interactions among groups as well as among individuals.

Question: How might Kelley's research help explain the difficulty that Rosenhan's "pseudo-patients" had in convincing mental hospital staffs that they (the "pseudo-patients") were really normal or sane?

Stereotypes

When you don't know a given person's "reputation," your initial impressions are likely to be affected by the **stereotypes**, or biased perceptions, that you have about certain types or groups of people. If you assume that all blacks are lazy, dull, ignorant but musical, you will tend to "see" these attributes even in an energetic, bright, black doctor who perhaps couldn't carry a tune in a handbag. If your attitude toward Jews is that they are intelligent, emotional, and penny-pinching, you may respond to each Jew as if she or he had to fit your stereotype.

Any time you react to an individual *primarily* in terms of that person's membership in some group—or in terms of that person's physical characteristics, race, or religion—you are guilty of *stereotyping*. That is, you have let the reputation of the group influence your perception of the individual who belongs to that group.

Put in more cognitive terms, when you "stereotype" people, you are using what Piaget called the process of "assimilation" (see Chapter 18). That is, you are forcing your perception of the individual to fit your *schema* for remembering or classifying that type of person. When you change your perception to fit the facts, you are "accommodating" to the real world by altering your schema.

"WHO'S GOING TO BE AT THIS PARTY? I'D LIKE TO KNOW HOW ECCENTRIC I SHOULD LOOK."

Question: How would you explain Newcomb's concept of "autistic hostility" in terms of Piaget's "process of assimilation"?

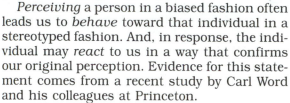

✓"Self-Fulfilling Prophecies"

Perceiving a person in a biased fashion often leads us to *behave* toward that individual in a stereotyped fashion. And, in response, the individual may *react* to us in a way that confirms our original perception. Evidence for this statement comes from a recent study by Carl Word and his colleagues at Princeton.

Word and his group asked *white* undergraduates to interview both *white* and *black* job applicants. In truth, the so-called applicants were confederates of the experimenters, who had been trained to act in a consistent manner no matter how the undergraduates behaved toward the applicants. The interviews were videotaped. An analysis of the tapes showed the white undergraduates tended to adopt what Word calls an *immediate* interview style when talking with white applicants. That is, the interviewers tended to use proper language and were quite friendly and outgoing. When talking with black applicants, however, the undergraduates tended to adopt what Word calls a *non-immediate* way of interviewing. That is, the interviewer's speech deteriorated into a sort of "white imitation of Black English" filled with grammatical errors and sloppy pronunciation. The interviewers also were less friendly, less outgoing, and much more reserved in the way they treated the blacks. The "immediate" and "non-immediate" styles presumably reflect the prejudiced *perceptions* the undergraduates had about whites and blacks.

In their second experiment, Word and his colleagues attempted to find out how people *respond* to obvious prejudice. In this study, Word trained white confederates to use either the "immediate" or "non-immediate" style in a consistent fashion. The confederates then interviewed *white* job applicants. Again, the interviews were videotaped. Analysis of the tapes showed that the white applicants subjected to the "non-immediate" style *performed less adequately* and were *more nervous* than were whites who experienced the "immediate" style.

Put in simple terms, when you perceive someone in a stereotyped fashion, you *predict how they will respond*. You then may act toward that individual in a manner that almost *forces* the person to respond in ways that con-firm your stereotyped expectations. Social psychologists call this sequence of behaviors *self-fulfilling prophecies*.

Question: How does the research by Word and his associates compare with Rosenthal's "Late Bloomer" study described in the story that begins Chapter 20?

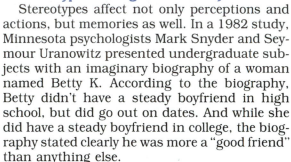

Stereotyped Changes in Memory

Stereotypes affect not only perceptions and actions, but memories as well. In a 1982 study, Minnesota psychologists Mark Snyder and Seymour Uranowitz presented undergraduate subjects with an imaginary biography of a woman named Betty K. According to the biography, Betty didn't have a steady boyfriend in high school, but did go out on dates. And while she did have a steady boyfriend in college, the biography stated clearly he was more a "good friend" than anything else.

A week after the students had read about Betty K., half of them were told she had just gotten married and was living with her husband. The other students were informed that Betty K. was now involved in a lesbian relationship. After giving the students this "additional information," Snyder and Uranowitz asked their subjects to answer a series of questions about the information they had read the *previous* week. According to Snyder, "when we examined their answers, we found that the students had reconstructed the events of Betty's past in ways that supported their own stereotyped beliefs about her sexual orientation." That is, those students who believed Betty was a lesbian remembered that Betty didn't have a steady boyfriend in high school. But they either forgot she had a steady boyfriend in college or over-emphasized the fact that he was "just a good friend." However, those students who believed Betty was now married tended to remember she dated a lot in high school, but forgot she didn't have a steady boyfriend at that time. And they recalled her "close relationship with a man in college," but forgot the two were "just good friends."

Your memory of things past obviously affects your present actions. But your present stereotypes just as obviously influence how and what you remember. Mark Snyder puts it this way: "As long as stereotypes make it easy to bring to mind evidence that supports them and difficult to bring to mind evidence that undermines them, people will cling to erroneous beliefs."

Primacy Effect

Stereotyping not only affects Long-term Memory, but Short-term Memory as well. For instance, suppose you meet someone with bright red hair, and you happen to stereotype red-heads as being "hot-tempered." If you are strongly impressed by this individual's "prime" physical characteristic, you may unconsciously *force* all other aspects of the person into this "prime" memory category. Later, then, you may recall the individual as *being* "hot-tempered," even if the person was calm and rational all the time you were with the person. Psychologists call this tendency to "label" people in terms of one first-observed characteristic the **primacy effect**.

Research on the "primacy effect" goes back to the 1940's, when psychologist Solomon Asch gave a group of subjects a list of adjectives describing someone they might meet. Half the subjects were told the person was "intelligent, industrious, impulsive, critical, stubborn, and envious." The other subjects were given the same list, but in opposite order: "Envious, stubborn, critical, impulsive, industrious, intelligent." The subjects were then asked to write a brief paragraph evaluating what they thought the person might be like.

A subject told the person was "intelligent . . . envious" wrote: "The person is intelligent and fortunately he puts his intelligence to work. That he is stubborn and impulsive may be due to the fact that he knows what he is saying and what he means and will not therefore give in easily to someone else's idea of what he disagrees with."

A subject told the person was "envious . . . intelligent" wrote: "This person's good qualities such as industry and intelligence are bound to be restricted by jealousy and stubbornness. The person is emotional. He is unsuccessful because he is weak and allows his bad points to cover up his good ones."

You can perceive any person you meet in dozens of different ways. Presumably, the first information you get about a person pulls one particular memory schema to the "top of the memory bin." Once that happens—according to the primacy effect—you are likely to "assimilate" any other data about the person into the schema you first used to categorize that individual.

Recency Effect

Psychologists often speak of a **recency effect**, which can either counteract or reinforce

Primacy effect (PRY-muh-see). *Primus* is the Latin word for "first." Whenever you remember your first impressions of a stimulus (or person) better than your second or third, you are demonstrating the power of the primacy effect.

Recency effect. The tendency to be more influenced by your last or most recent impressions than by your initial impression.

the primacy effect. If you have recently used a given schema to categorize people—and have found it useful—you are very likely to apply it to the next person you meet. Thus, if one of Asch's students had already encountered a lot of "envious" people that week, the student might well have perceived almost anyone that way, despite the fact that "intelligent" was first on the descriptive list the student received.

Question: What kind of first impression do you think you give the people you meet? *Why* do you think they perceive you this way? Are strangers more influenced by what you are really like "deep down inside," or by how you look?

Two Channels of Communication

The way you perceive someone you have just met is obviously affected by such *internal processes* as attitudes, reputations, stereotypes, the primacy effect, and the recency effect. But perceptions are also influenced by *present stimulus inputs*. Suppose you want to influence the way someone else *perceives you*. How do you communicate with that person to give him or her a good first impression of yourself?

Actually, you have but two main channels of communication—what you do with your body, and what you say with your tongue. The way you look and dress and move—these are part of your *body language*. What you say, the opinions you express, and the verbal responses you make—these are part of your verbal language. Surprisingly enough, when it comes to first impressions, people are often more influenced by your looks and physical movements than they are by what you actually say.

Question: Suppose you met two people, one with obvious good looks, the other with average looks. Which person do you think would be the happier? Why?

Research suggests that most social interactions are strongly influenced by "body language" and by eye contact.

Physical Appearance

According to Ellen Berscheid, the less chance you have to know the people around you well, the more likely you are to judge people in terms of their appearance. "My guess is that anything that increases the number of brief encounters with other people increases the importance of physical attractiveness," Berscheid said recently. "People don't have a record of behavior to judge by, and they have to go on superficial characteristics."

Berscheid's own research at the University of Minnesota supports her statements. In one recent study performed with colleagues at the University of Wisconsin, Berscheid found that "most people consider attractive people to be more sensitive, stronger, more modest, more sociable, more outgoing, kinder, more interesting, and sexually warmer and more responsive than their unattractive peers." Berscheid says most people believe good-looking individuals "have prestigious jobs and happy marriages and . . . enjoy life to the fullest." But this perception of good-looking people is based almost entirely on their looks, not on any *facts* about what they are really like.

Karen Dion, of the University of Toronto, has performed research that tends to support Berscheid's views. Dion asked subjects to make judgments about second-grade children who had committed minor misbehaviors. She reports the subjects usually judged the misbehavior as being "much more serious" if the child was unattractive. Furthermore, Dion says, her subjects believed the unattractive children were more likely to have a "chronic predisposition to commit bad acts" than were handsome children.

Similar evidence on the "power of good looks" comes from a study by Marsha Jacobson, a psychologist at the University of Dayton. Jacobson asked undergraduates to read a fictionalized account of a rape case. The students were then shown photographs of the supposed "victim" and of the accused "rapist." The students had to indicate whether they believed the "victim's" story, or the "rapist's" alibi. If the students found the "rapist" guilty, they were to indicate how many years in jail the man should serve.

Some of the students in the Jacobson study were shown pictures of a very attractive "victim," and of a rather unattractive "rapist." Other students saw photos of an unattractive "victim," and of a very handsome "rapist." (The physical attractiveness of the supposed "victim" and "rapist" had been judged by a panel of psychology graduate students.)

Marsha Jacobson reports both male and female undergraduates showed more sympathy for the "victim" when she was attractive than when she wasn't. Thus, they were more likely to "convict" the rapist (handsome or not) if the "victim" was good-looking. No matter which photo of the "victim" the students saw, however, 82 percent of them thought the unattractive "rapist" was guilty, while only 57 percent of the students who saw photos of a handsome "rapist" voted to convict the man of the crime. The students also passed out much longer sentences to the unattractive "rapist" than to the handsome one.

Beauty may be "in the eye of the beholder," but it obviously does shape our perceptions of others to a greater extent than many of us would like to believe is the case.

Question: Why do you think beautiful children tend to score higher on individually administered intelligence tests than when they take a written test administered to a whole group of children?

Non-Verbal Communication

You can't do all that much about changing your looks. But you can alter your physical movements—that is, the way you present yourself to others. Whether you know it or not, you have a characteristic way of dressing, of combing your hair, of moving your arms and legs, of looking toward or away from people as you speak or listen, of smiling, of frowning, and of giving feedback. This "body language" may not be an accurate indicator of what you are "really like." However, experiments suggest many people you meet will judge your *intentions toward them* primarily by the way in which you communicate non-verbally.

But what makes up your own unique brand of body language? What can a stranger tell about you just by watching you behave? To begin with, and perhaps most important, is the simple fact that you are either *male or female.* As we pointed out in Chapter 11, every culture has different *social expectations* about the ways that women and men should look and behave. Your *age* is also an important aspect of your "body image," as is (obviously) your skin color and how good-looking you are. The clothes you wear, the way that you move, even such seemingly trivial behaviors as how close you stand to the people you meet and the eye contact you give them—all these things "communicate" information to the people you meet.

Once people have *stereotyped* you according to your sex, size, age, skin color, dress, and physical beauty, they *expect you to behave in certain ways.* Generally speaking, if your behavior *confirms* these expectations, most people will gain a good "first impression" of you. However, if your actions *disconfirm* people's expectations, you are not likely to win very many popularity contests.

Question: Is there any objective truth to our culture's stereotypes about men and women? About young and old people? Why is this the case? (Hint: what about "self-fulfilling prophecies"?)

Behavioral Congruence

Person Memory, a 1980 book edited by Reid Hastie and several other social psychologists, contains several chapters on how your perception of others changes over time. One important process that influences *perceptual change* is what Hastie calls **behavioral congruence**. If the way people act later on tends to *confirm* your initial perception of them, then their behaviors are "congruent" with your first impression. If their later actions *disconfirm* your first impression, you experience "discongruence." According to Hastie and his colleagues, when

Behavioral congruence (kon-GRUE-ence). Congruent behaviors are those that fit your expectations or match a stereotype. When behaviors and expectations don't match, you are motivated to resolve the discrepancy. Usually you explain or "rationalize" the behaviors and maintain your prior expectations.

most people experience discongruence, they tend to "rationalize" (or explain away) any data that don't reinforce their original impressions.

Oddly enough, Hastie's research shows that most people remember *incongruent* behaviors better than *congruent* ones. Hastie believes that congruent behaviors are readily coded and filed away in Long-term Memory. But when someone acts in an unexpected way, you must try to "explain the behavior" before you can tuck it into long-term storage. Hastie believes you remember incongruent actions more readily because it takes more time to process them.

Question: What similarities do you see between "behavioral discongruence" and Piaget's concept of "cognitive disequilibrium"?

Personal Space

How close people stand to you when they first meet you can often influence your impression of them. California psychologist Robert Sommer has for many years studied what he calls *personal space.* Sommer believes you carry an "invisible bubble" around your body that encloses what you consider to be your own, personal psychological space. He notes that in a number of studies, subjects have shown a dramatic increase in nervousness when an experimenter moved to within a foot or so of them. Most of the subjects "defended their territories" by either moving away from the intruder, or by becoming increasingly hostile.

Sommer states that the size of your own personal space bubble is influenced by such factors as your personality, status, and the present social situation. For middle-class Americans, this private area extends outward about two feet from any part of the body. For people in the Middle East and South America, the space is usually much smaller. For Scandinavians and Japanese, the bubble is typically larger. However, the size of each person's "space bubble" may expand or contract, depending on the circumstances.

In a 1982 article in the *Journal of Personality and Social Psychology*, Nan Sussman re-

Robert Sommer

Research suggests that your concept of "personal space" varies not only according to your culture but also according to the language you speak.

ports that personal spaces varies with the language you're speaking. Sussman asked students from three different cultures to "sit and converse" in their *native tongues.* The students from South America sat closer together than did students from the US. But Japanese students sat several inches farther apart than did the Americans.

Sussman then asked other groups of students from South America and Japan to "sit and converse in English" rather than in their own languages. She reports the South American students sat eight inches *farther apart* when speaking English than when talking in Spanish. And the Japanese students sat significantly *closer* to each other when talking in English than when conversing in Japanese. Apparently these students were quite aware that the size of the "space bubble" in the US was different from their own—and they tried to imitate our space requirements while speaking in our tongue. Learning to speak a foreign language apparently involves not only memorizing verbs and nouns, but also discovering what kind of "body language" goes with the "spoken language."

Question: When you change roles—as from Correctional Officer to Prisoner—why does the size of your personal space often change?

Body Posture

Even when you stand at just the right distance from people "to make them comfortable," the way that you *hold your body* influences the impressions that you give others. In our culture, most people assume that if you lean toward them, you like them (and perhaps are inviting intimacy). But if you lean away from them, they may assume you dislike or reject them.

In a study on body posture, psychologist Albert Mehrabian asked men and women to act out the way they would sit when speaking to someone they liked or disliked. Mehrabian reports that both men and women leaned *forward* to express liking, but that men (more than women) leaned back or became more tense when addressing someone they disliked.

Once you have established a "proper distance" to stand from an individual, any further movement you make may signal a change in your feelings. Psychologist Donn Byrne and his associates set up an an experiment in which couples were selected by a computer for blind dates. After the young man and woman had gotten to know each other briefly, they were called into Byrne's office and stood before his desk for further instructions. The subjects were then separated and asked to fill out a questionnaire indicating how much they liked their dates. Byrne and his colleagues report that couples who liked each other moved closer together in front of the desk than did couples who didn't care much for each other.

Question: Why might strangers in a crowded elevator stare straight ahead and avoid conversation?

Eye Contact

Movements of your face and eyes are often as critical to the first impression you give as are how close you stand and whether you lean toward or away from someone. For the eye contact you make with people often controls both the flow of conversation and their initial opinion of your honesty and aggressiveness.

The "rules of eye contact" vary considerably from one society to another, and thus seem to be primarily learned behaviors. However, the *reason* there are "rules" is probably grounded in innate emotional responses. Among both primates and people, intense "mutual gazing" is a mark of intense emotionality. Primates usually respond hostilely to being stared at. (Next time you're at a zoo, try staring directly at a monkey's eyes and watch how the animal responds.) Among humans, "mutual gazing" of any duration occurs primarily among (1) lovers, (2) two people locked in some kind of emotional confrontation, and (3) a mother and her infant.

Humans avoid the emotionality of direct "mutual gazing" by developing rules that govern who looks at whom, and when. For example, if you happen to be a middle-class adult, you probably gaze *at* people when they are talking or lecturing. For staring directly at a speaker is your way of encouraging that person to continue conversing—particularly if you also nod or smile in apparent agreement. When you look *away* from whoever is talking, however, you signal that you are bored or that you want to take over the talking role yourself.

When *you* are telling a story or making a point, though, chances are you will gaze *away* from your audience—particularly if you are trying to think through what you are talking about. While you speak, you may glance back at your audience from time to time to make sure they are still with you (that is, still looking at you), then look away again as you continue talking.

These "rules of eye contact" vary dramatically from culture to culture, and from one segment of society to another within a particular culture. For example, individuals brought up in lower-class environments in the US have eye signals that are the direct opposite of those found in middle-class society. People reared in lower-class homes tend to stare directly at people when talking, but avert their eyes when listening to show respect (particularly if listening to someone of higher status).

You learn these "rules of eye contact" so early in life that you may not be aware of how strongly they influence your perceptions and behaviors. Unless you understand how these rules affect your first impressions, however, you are likely to *misinterpret* the eye signals that someone from another culture or socio-economic class gives to you.

Question: If a man stared at you intensely while talking to you, what motives would you *attribute* to him? If he averted his eyes while listening to you, would you think he was showing disinterest or respect?

Responding to "Body Language"

According to Connecticut researchers Dana Christensen and her colleagues, *recognizing* body-language cues is fairly easy for most people. But *responding appropriately* may be harder. Christensen and her group gave 130 undergraduate women a "social competence" questionnaire. The experimenters then selected 15 of the women with the highest scores, and 15 women who got low scores on "social competence."

Next, Christensen and her associates asked the students in both the "high" and "low" groups to interview a young woman. They were told to ask this woman 10 prepared questions about each of three topics: the woman's extracurricular activities, the courses she was taking, and her family life. The students were specifically instructed to *move on to the next topic* if the woman seemed uncomfortable.

The woman being interviewed was a confederate trained by the experimenters to act in a normal fashion when being asked about the first topic. However, when the students reached the second topic (academic courses), the woman always started showing visible signs of distress. She wrung her hands, avoided direct eye contact, stammered, and hesitated for long periods before responding.

Christensen *et al.* report that the students with high "social competence" scores moved on to the next topic (or stopped the interview) almost immediately. The students with low "social competence" scores, however, continued the questioning for much longer periods. When the experimenters asked the students in the "low" group about their actions, the "low" students all claimed they had *detected* the signs of stress at the same time that the "high" students did. So "perceiving" body language wasn't the issue. Rather, it was a matter of *interpreting* and *responding accurately* to the situation.

Students with "low" social competence scores offered many excuses for their actions. Some said they continued the questions because, from their point of view, "the woman had no reason to be upset about such trivial questions." Others responded that the woman was "so hopelessly tense about being interviewed that changing the subject wouldn't have helped."

Christensen and her colleagues conclude that most women students can "read" social cues rather well. The trouble the low-scoring students had, however, came from their "tendency to make judgments about how others should behave rather than being open to how they are actually behaving."

Question: How would *you* define "social competence"?

Territoriality

Wild animals often have clearly defined "territories" that they mark off and defend. Do humans have "territories" too? If so, what purpose do they serve?

One set of answers to these questions comes from a 1975 study by Paul Rosenblatt and Linda Budd. These experimenters asked married and unmarried couples the following questions:

1. Do you have your own separate bed or your own special side of a bed that's exclusively yours to sleep on?
2. Do you have a certain and separate area of the closet in which you store your own things?
3. Do you have a certain and separate portion of the bathroom in which to place items such as your toothbrush?

Rosenblatt and Budd report that, although the unmarried couples had lived together for the same amount of time as had the married couples, the two groups gave quite different responses to the questions. Generally speaking, the married couples had "staked out individual territories" and respected each other's rights. The unmarried couples, however, were significantly less territorial.

According to Rosenblatt and Budd, the married couples apparently had decided their relationship could not endure unless they settled "territorial rights" early in their marriage. However, the unmarried couples took a different view. Either they saw the relationship as being so temporary it wasn't worth the effort to argue about such things. Or, as Rosenblatt and Budd put it, "they sensed that staking territorial claims and setting boundaries would commit them to a long-term relationship that neither wanted."

Question: Would having clear-cut territories reduce or increase the stress most people feel when forced to live together in crowded conditions?

The Attribution Process

By now, you have learned some of the rules that influence the way you perceive people, particularly someone you've just met. But why do you do so? For instance, why do you often "stereotype" people? According to Fritz Heider, you do so to *avoid stress*. Heider notes that most of us become alarmed whenever we cannot guess fairly accurately what will happen to us next. By using what Heider calls the **attribution process**, we attribute to others motives that make their actions more predictable (and hence less stressful) to us.

As Heider pointed out in 1958, when you perceive a woman's actions as being an expression of her character, you are actually *attributing* certain personality traits to the woman. Most of these *attributed traits* are stereotypes, for she may not possess these traits at all. But once you stereotype her, you have a ready-made attitude or perception to fit her. Therefore, you not only can predict her actions (or so you think), but you have a way of *responding* to her as well.

Edward E. Jones noted in 1976 that we use the attribution process to *explain our own faults* as well. But we attribute these faults to the environment, not to our own personality. We see ourselves as merely reacting to whatever situation we find ourselves in. However, when we observe inconsistent behaviors in *others*, we tend to ignore the social background. Instead, we attribute their actions to some inner need, motive, or flaw of character. That is, we perceive ourselves as being *forced* to act in inappropriate ways from time to time. But when others misbehave, we perceive them as *wanting* to behave that way.

Psychologists Richard Lau and Dan Russell call this the "I win because of me; I lose because of you" effect. In a 1980 article in the *Journal of Personality and Social Psychology*, Lau and Russell report that many athletes tend to take credit for their wins, but blame their losses on others. Lau and Russell studied the explanations offered by professional players and coaches after important baseball and football games. More than 80 percent of the time, the athletes claimed that "wins" were due to their own superior performance. About half the time, however, they attributed "losses" to such factors as bad luck, bad officiating, or injuries to key players.

Question: Is the attribution process a "direct" or an "indirect" method of coping with stress (see Chapter 12)?

Kelley's Theory of Personal Relationships

The person who has advanced attribution theory the most in recent years is Harold H. Kelley, who is now at UCLA. His thinking about the attribution process is shown most clearly in his

1981 book *Personal Relationships: Their Structures and Processes*.

Kelley is interested more in long-term relationships between people than in "first impressions." He believes that three concepts are crucial to understanding enduring *dyads*, or two-person relationships. These three concepts are *interdependence*, *responsiveness*, and *attribution*.

Interdependence

By "interdependence," Kelley refers to the belief that the *outcomes* of a relationship depend in large part on both the individual and the joint actions that people in a dyad undertake. For instance, suppose you are married. Both the benefits and the costs of the marriage—to you and to your spouse—will depend not only on what each of you does individually, but also on the *joint actions* the two of you perform. Therefore, to get the most out of your marriage, you must not only pay attention to what you do, but you must be able to *anticipate* what your spouse will do as well. Much of your own behavior, then, is dependent on your predictions of how your spouse will behave in certain situations.

If your predictions about your spouse are accurate, you can often use this knowledge to maximize your own personal gains. But if you do, your spouse may suffer. Therefore, the relationship may break apart unless you are responsive to your spouse's needs as well as to your own.

Responsiveness

By "responsiveness," Kelley means that you take your spouse's needs into account when making decisions about your own behavior. If your partner does the same, Kelley says, both you and your spouse will probably assume this means you have a loving, interdependent relationship. That is, you will *attribute the trait of lovingness* to each other.

To Kelley, the essence of a good personal relationship is the fact that the partners care about one another. And this caring is most readily visible in situations where one partner gives up benefits or endures costs out of consideration for the other.

"This is... ROGER. HE SPEAKS ONLY... IN BODY LANGUAGE."

A uniform is often "part" of a social role.

Attribution

Even loving couples occasionally have problems. Kelley has shown that marriage partners are inclined to explain problems in their relationship in terms of *attributed traits* rather than in terms of *specific behaviors*. Thus, a wife who is upset with her husband typically won't speak of the actions that bother her—he leaves his dirty underwear on the floor for her to pick up, doesn't listen to her, or won't help her with the housework. Rather, she will describe the problem in terms of his personality and his presumed attitude toward her—he is sloppy, lazy, and doesn't love her. This attribution of the causes of his misbehaviors constitutes what Kelley refers to as a *sanction*. That is, the wife calls attention to what the husband is doing wrong and *challenges* him to prove that her attribution of the causes is incorrect.

The husband, on the other hand, will attribute his faults to environmental stress, such as problems he is experiencing at work. He perceives himself as still being deeply in love with her, and believes she ought to forgive him for his minor misbehaviors because his *intentions*

are good. When his wife fails to forgive him, he attributes her anger to such traits as "moodiness" and "bad temper."

If the husband changes his behaviors, the wife may not be satisfied, if she thinks he is merely trying to appease her. Because she *attributes* his actions to "underlying traits and attitudes," she wants an *attitudinal change* from him rather than a mere shift in the way he acts. At this point, Kelley notes, the husband is in something of a bind. Since his wife can never *see* his attitudes or intentions *directly*, the only thing he can do is to change his behaviors toward her. But she is always free to *interpret* these behavioral changes any way she wishes, and he cannot prove her wrong.

Question: How does the attribution process help explain the popularity of the "trait approach" to describing human personality?

When Attributional Conflicts Occur

In a book entitled *New Directions in Attribution Research*, Harold Kelley and his colleagues describe those situations in which attributional conflicts are most likely to occur between two people.

The first observation Kelley and his associates make is this one: People make use of the attribution process most frequently in situations of conflict of interest. Thus, you are much more likely to use the attribution process when interpreting "bad" behaviors than "good" behaviors, because "bad" actions are more likely to lead to conflict.

The second observation by Kelley *et al.* is that most attributional conflicts aren't about which factors were *present* in the conflict situation. Rather, the dispute usually concerns which factors were *crucial*. For instance, suppose a couple argues about why the husband no longer engages in sports. He says, "I'm very busy now, and sports are just a waste of time." She may respond, "Sure, you say they're a waste of time, and maybe they are. But the *real* reason you've given them up is because you're lazy." Since there are always many factors present in any social situation, the person using the attribution process can almost always find one to suit his or her fancy.

Kelley and his colleagues believe that attributional conflicts are usually irresolvable. Why? For three reasons. First, there are no objective (behavioral) standards by which one person can *prove* another's attributions are wrong or his or her own attributions are correct. Second, most people *genuinely believe* they have an accurate understanding of why they act as they do—and that their explanations of "why" are justified by "the facts." Third, most people perceive *explaining* their actions as a "good behavior" designed to reduce social stress. Thus, when you use the attribution process, you may actually see yourself as "playing the peace-maker's role." And most of us are extremely reluctant to give up what we perceive as being "socially approved roles."

Social Roles

Attributions are *highly personal* explanations for behaviors. But you may also excuse your actions in terms of *social expectations*. That is, you may describe what you did as "merely playing the role that society has put you in."

As we shift our attention from attributions to social roles, we move slightly up the ladder—away from the individual toward larger social systems. For "traits" are generally perceived as intra-psychic factors. Roles, however, are *systematic behavior patterns* that are embedded in the structure of groups, organizations, and societies rather than inside the individual's psyche. You *are* generous or stingy. But you *play the role* of doctor, lawyer, merchant, or thief.

Put another way, a *social role* is a more or less stereotyped set of responses that you make to related or similar situations. Some roles (such as socially approved "masculine" and "feminine" behaviors) are a basic part of your **repertory** all through your life and are influenced by your genetic blueprint (see Chapter 11). Other roles seem to be entirely learned, such as that of "leader" or "manager." Whatever the case, one *important purpose* of most roles seems to be that of making "social interactions" go more smoothly.

There are many types of roles. And, as Shakespeare put it centuries ago, "One man in his time plays many parts." This much everyone admits, just as most psychologists agree that much role learning occurs through imitation. However, there is little agreement on how and why you switch from one role to another in certain situations. And there also isn't much consensus on which social roles are the most important ones to study.

Social psychologists have researched the *leadership role* for many years, however. And

while theorists disagree on why certain individuals become leaders and others don't, some aspects of the leader's role are fairly well defined (at least for our culture). Given the amount of information we have on the subject of leadership, therefore, suppose we look at this topic first.

Question: Assume you have a "social interaction sequence" with a physician. How would your knowledge about *social roles* affect the way you perceived and responded to this individual? Would you have reacted differently had the other person been a "janitor" rather than a "doctor"? Why? And how does the presence of clearly understood roles help reduce stress in "social interaction sequences"?

Leadership Roles

Many years ago, Harvard sociologist Robert Bales and his colleagues performed a classic set of experiments on leadership. Their subjects were groups of male college students brought together in a laboratory and given certain intellectual problems to solve. Bales *et al.* measured the men's verbal behaviors as objectively as they could. And at the end of each problem-solving session, the experimenters asked the subjects to rate each member of the group in a number of ways, including how much the man liked the others and which men seemed to be leaders or have the best ideas.

Two Types of Specialists

Bales and his associates found that two types of people got high scores on the leadership rating scales: The "idea generator" (or *task specialist*) and the "social facilitator" (or *social-emotional specialist*).

During group sessions, the task specialist gave opinions and made suggestions more often than anyone else. He kept reminding the group of its goals and brought the group back to the task at hand whenever the members strayed from problem solving. These behaviors apparently caused other group members to rate the man as a good leader or idea generator.

The social-emotional specialist, on the other hand, was much more likely to *ask* for sugges-

5. Self-actualization needs

4. Esteem needs
(Social learning theory operates on this rung)

3. Belongingness or love needs
(Perceptual theory operates on this rung)

2. Safety needs
(Arousal theory operates on this rung)

1. Physiological needs
(Drive theory operates on this rung)

Fig. 23.1. Maslow's hierarchy of needs

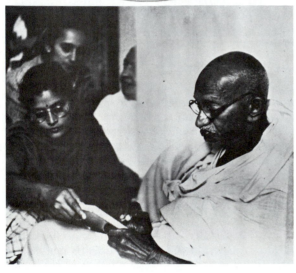
Mahatma Gandhi, Hindu nationalist teacher, surrounded by young followers.

Robert F. Bales

Jay Hall

Question: What similarities do you see between the two types of "specialists" in the Bales study and the functions associated with the two hemispheres of the brain?

tions than to give them. He was particularly sensitive to the needs of others. He made extensive use of praise and other forms of feedback, and he smoothed over arguments in order to create what Bales calls *group solidarity*.

According to Bales, the "task specialist" directed the cognitive or intellectual resources of the group, and was respected for his knowledge and expertise. The "social facilitator" directed the emotional resources of the group, and was warmly liked for his ability to keep the group functioning as a **cohesive** unit.

Successful Managers

Brandeis psychologist Zick Rubin believes it is a rare person who is a "natural-born" expert at controlling both the cognitive and emotional processes of groups of people. According to Rubin, such greatness is found only in a very few leaders—Gandhi of India, Mao of China, Winston Churchill of Great Britain, and Franklin Roosevelt of the United States.

A study reported in 1979 by Texas psychologist Jay Hall, however, suggests that leadership skills are more a matter of training than of innate ability. In the course of his survey, Hall measured the attitudes and behaviors of more than 17,000 managers in 50 different US business and government organizations.

Hall began by scoring his subjects on the Rhodes *Managerial Achievement Quotient*, which measures how rapidly and how far a man has risen "through the ranks" in the organizational structure. According to Hall, only some 10 percent of the men had "high MAQ's," which is to say that only 10 percent of the men had received frequent and rapid promotions. About 50 percent of the men received "average MAQ's," while some 40 percent of the men had progressed so slowly that they received "low MAQ's."

Next, Hall gave his subjects the *Work Motivation Inventory*, a test based on Maslow's *hierarchy of needs* (discussed in Chapter 10). (See Fig. 23.1.) Hall found clear-cut differences among the three groups of managers in terms of what seemed to motivate them. The "successful" managers were most interested in *self-actualization*—that is, in becoming better both as supervisors and as concerned human beings. The "average" managers were motivated by *ego and status needs*. The men with "low MAQ's" were partially motivated by status needs, but more by *security needs* (such as not being fired). Apparently, the most successful managers had risen to the top of Maslow's motivational ladder, while the least successful men were stuck on the bottom rungs.

Question: Do you think "successful managers" *perceive* subordinates differently than do "unsuccessful managers"? Why would the traits you *attribute* to your own subordinates affect the way in which you would attempt to manage them?

Participatory Management

Some organizational leaders *tell* people what to do. Other managers encourage their subordinates to *participate* in the decision-making process. According to Jay Hall, the greatest difference between successful and unsuccessful managers lies in how frequently the men make use of *participatory management*. The "unsuccessful" managers did not encourage much participation at all from their subordinates. The men with "average MAQ's" asked (and took) the advice of the workers relatively infrequently. The "successful" managers, however, almost always sought the opinions and consent of the people who worked for them.

Jay Hall believes that a manager's *goals* in large part determine how successful the man-

ager will be. Hall reports that men with "high MAQ's" show both a strong interest in achieving organizational goals *and* in helping their subordinates satisfy their personal needs. Managers with "average MAQ's," on the other hand, feel a strong urge to "get the task done," but they show considerably less concern about what happens to their employees in the process. The unsuccessful managers appear to be protecting themselves. They seem to have little commitment either to the goals of the organization or to satisfying the needs of those individuals whom they supervise.

Question: What similarity do you see between Hall's "unsuccessful managers" and the "women with low social competence" described earlier in this chapter?

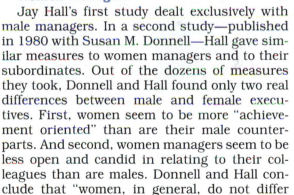

Women Managers

Jay Hall's first study dealt exclusively with male managers. In a second study—published in 1980 with Susan M. Donnell—Hall gave similar measures to women managers and to their subordinates. Out of the dozens of measures they took, Donnell and Hall found only two real differences between male and female executives. First, women seem to be more "achievement oriented" than are their male counterparts. And second, women managers seem to be less open and candid in relating to their colleagues than are males. Donnell and Hall conclude that "women, in general, do not differ from men, in general, in the ways in which they administer the management process."

According to Jay Hall, there is a certain irony in these results. For one of the main problems that women managers have is that males *perceive* the women as being skilled at handling social-emotive resources, but as being poor at task achievement. In fact, the truth is just the opposite—males (in general) are less oriented toward achievement than are women managers, and males may be more skilled at interpersonal relations than the present crop of female managers are. Yet, as long as males dominate the work scene, it is their *perceptions* of women that make the difference, not the actual behaviors of the women themselves.

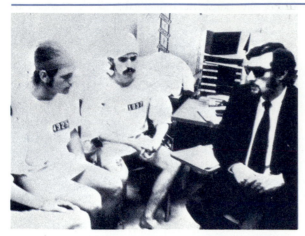

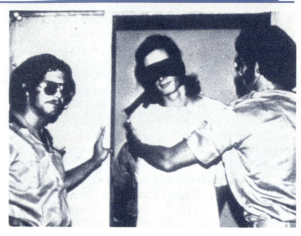

Philip Zimbardo and his students at Stanford University studied the dehumanizing effects of a mock prison environment.

Harry C. Triandis   Philip G. Zimbardo

Question: What similarities do you see between Jay Hall's findings and Werner Mendel's discovery (Chapter 22) that his patients at St. Elizabeth's suddenly showed improvement when he started to perceive them differently?

Roles as "Behavioral Intentions"

Illinois psychologist Harry C. Triandis believes your actions are determined primarily by two things: habits, and behavioral intentions. *Habits* are those stereotyped ways you have of responding to specific situations. Your *behavioral intentions* are, more or less, whatever set of goals you are trying to reach at any given moment. These momentary goals are affected by many things—the roles you have learned, your emotional reactions, and your cognitive expectancies. Thus, according to Triandis, you can predict an individual's behavior much better if you know a person's intentions than if you merely know the individual's habits.

Exchange Theory

Triandis views the process of human interaction from the perspective of *exchange theory*. That is, he believes social relations are governed by "exchanges of resources." You want things from me, and I want things from you. If you know my intentions, you can guess at what I want—and what I am willing to pay for satisfying this goal. But the intentions you *attribute* to me are strongly influenced by *your own social expectations*.

In his 1977 book *Interpersonal Behavior*, Triandis reports a series of studies on what happens when two people from different cultures meet and interact. He finds that most subjects assume that someone from a different country *must have the same intentions as they do*. Thus, most Greeks will explain the behavior of Americans in terms of Greek tradition and culture, while Americans find it difficult to believe that Greeks aren't motivated by precisely the same intentions as we have.

Triandis believes the first thing you must do when you learn a new role is this: You have to discover what *behavioral intentions* are associated with that role. Thus, when you meet someone new, learning the person's role expectations will tell you a great deal about that person's intentions. Therefore, you learn about other people's roles in order to find what "social exchanges" they are interested in.

Zimbardo's "Jail"

As we noted, roles are little more than a set of behavioral expectancies. For example, you could play the role of a police officer if you were called upon to do so. You would know you were "just acting a part." However, someone watching you perform might well *attribute* your actions to some deep-seated character trait. The fact that most people in our culture tend to perceive behaviors as being caused more by attributed traits than role playing may explain why the public reacted so negatively to research performed several years ago by Stanford psychologist Philip Zimbardo.

In the summer of 1971, Zimbardo and his students studied the "roles" that people play in prison situations. Zimbardo and his group took over a basement corridor in the psychology building at Stanford and converted it into cells, an exercise yard, observation rooms, and a closet that served as the "hole" for solitary confinement. They turned nearby rooms into space for the guards, the "warden" (Dr. Zimbardo) and his students, and for the videotape equipment.

Next, Zimbardo put an ad in two local papers offering to hire students to play the roles of prisoners and guards for a two-week period. Zimbardo interviewed all the volunteers, screened them for physical and mental health problems, and then selected the 21 men who seemed most healthy, mature, and "normal." On a random basis, 11 of them were chosen to be "guards," while the other 10 were to be "prisoners."

The subjects were told the details of the study and all voluntarily agreed to "play the game" for a period of up to 2 weeks. They were paid $15 a day for participating, and knew that if selected as prisoners they would lose all rights to privacy during the 14-day period the experiment was to run. The guards worked 8-hour shifts, but (unlike the prisoners) were allowed to leave when their shifts were over.

The guards were given special uniforms designed to look "official." They were issued police night-sticks, whistles, and reflecting sunglasses (to prevent eye contact with the prisoners).

The prisoners were required to wear muslin smocks with no underclothes, a light chain and lock around one ankle, rubber sandals, and a cap made from a nylon stocking. Each prisoner was given a toothbrush, towels, soap, and bed linen. No personal belongings were allowed in the cells.

Persons and "Non-persons"

Zimbardo and the guards developed a set of "rules" the prisoners were expected to memorize and follow while in jail. One of the most important rules was that the prisoners were to be addressed only by the "numbers" painted on their muslin smocks. The prisoners were expected to "work" in order to earn their $15 daily payment. Twice a week, the prisoners were allowed visitors. The guards could also give them a variety of "rewards" for good behavior, including the right to exercise in the "yard" and to attend movies.

The first clue as to how the study would turn out came during the "count" of the prisoners the guards took three times daily. The first day, the "count" took 10 minutes or less. But by the second day, the guards starting using "count time" to harass the prisoners, so the time increased. By the fifth day, some of the "counts" lasted for several hours as the guards berated the prisoners for minor infractions of the "rules."

Zimbardo designed his experiment in an attempt to study some of the conditions that lead to *depersonalization*. He quickly discovered that one primary factor was the behavior of the guards. True, the prisoners had given up their identities and become "numbers." But they were still human beings, despite the smocks they wore and the chains around their ankles. However, the guards rapidly began treating the prisoners as "non-persons" who weren't really humans at all.

As far as "depersonalization" went, however, the *reactions* of the prisoners were probably just as important as the *actions* of the guards. Instead of protesting their treatment, the prisoners began to act in depressed, institutionalized, dependent ways—exactly the role behaviors shown by real-life prisoners and mental patients. And, as you might guess, the more the prisoners acted like "non-persons," the more they were mistreated by the guards.

By the end of the sixth day, the situation had nearly gotten out of hand. The guards began modifying or changing the prison "rules" and routines to make them increasingly more punitive. And even some of Zimbardo's students got so caught up in the spirit of things, they neglected to give the prisoners some of the privileges they had earned.

At this point, wisely, Zimbardo called a halt to the proceedings.

Question: How do the actions of the guards and the reactions of the prisoners fit Darley and Fazio's "five-step social interaction process"?

The Results

After stopping the experiment, Zimbardo and his students interviewed all of the subjects and analyzed the videotapes they had made during the six days. Perhaps their most important finding is that the subjects simply "became" the roles that they played. *All* of the 11 guards behaved in abusive, dehumanizing ways toward the prisoners. Some of them did so only occasionally. But *more than a third* of the guards were so consistently hostile and degrading that Zimbardo refers to their behavior as *sadistic.*

The prisoners, on the other hand, showed a reaction which (in Chapter 12) we called *learned helplessness.* Day by day, the prisoners did less and less, initiated fewer conversations, became more surly and depressed. Five of the prisoners were unable to cope with their own reactions and asked to leave. But the other five seemed to accept their fates and (in a few cases) didn't even bother to "request parole" when given a chance to do so.

The second important finding Zimbardo made is obvious but, to most people, simply unbelievable: There was absolutely *no prior evidence* that the subjects would react as they did. Before their random selection as guard or prisoner, the two groups did not differ from each other in any way that Zimbardo could discover. All 21 were healthy, normal, mature young men—and not one of them predicted he would act as he did. Furthermore, there is no reason to believe that the study would have turned out any different *had the roles of the two groups been reversed.*

One of the personality tests Zimbardo used is the F-Scale, which measures **authoritarianism**. Surprisingly enough, the guards didn't differ from the prisoners on this scale, nor were the "sadistic" guards more authoritarian (as measured by the test) than were the more "humanitarian" guards. However, the prisoners who refused to leave were, generally speaking, the ones who scored as being the *most authoritarian.* Zimbardo believes these men were psychologically better prepared to cope with the highly structured and punitive environment of the prison.

The third finding is perhaps less surprising. At no time did any guard ever *reward* a prisoner for anything. The only "correctional" techniques the guards ever employed were criticism, punishment, and harassment.

Question: Given the data, can you be *really* sure that you wouldn't have played the guard or prisoner role exactly as Zimbardo's subjects did?

Public Reaction

The results of his experiment distressed Zimbardo so much that he made them available to the news media almost immediately. Public reaction was swift, and primarily punitive. Many critics found it inconceivable that a "noted Stanford professor" would undertake such a dehumanizing study. Most of these same critics also suggested that Zimbardo must have picked a very abnormal bunch of young men for his subjects, because ordinary citizens surely wouldn't behave in that fashion.

In fact, there is no better illustration of the *attribution process* at work than Zimbardo's study. At first the prisoners blamed their behaviors on the situation they were in. But eventually they became depressed and attributed their failure to cope to their own "innate trait of spinelessness." The guards justified their harassment in terms of "being paid to do the job," as well as the "criminal instincts" they perceived in the prisoners. The critics attributed both the brutality of the guards and the "helpless" behaviors of the prisoners to innate character flaws in *those* specific men. No one caught up in the experiment—including, at times, Zimbardo and his students—perceived that the *environment* was almost entirely responsible for the behaviors of both guards and prisoners. No one saw that the men were just "playing roles."

Question: One of the problems that psychologists often face is this—their research findings occasionally contradict rather cherished notions other people have about human behavior. If you had been Dr. Zimbardo, how would you have gone about trying to convince people your results were valid?

Social Roles versus "Attributed Motives"

Social roles are patterns of attitudes, emotions, perceptions, and behaviors that are "the norm" for a particular group, organization, or culture. They seem to be learned early in life, primarily through observation and imitation.

Although some aspects may be innately determined, *roles are primarily determined by the social situation*.

Most of the things you do, think, and feel are strongly influenced by the conditions you grew up in and by your present social milieu. But society still *attributes* the causes of human behavior to such internal processes as "personality" and "character." So if you find yourself attributing motives and intentions to other people, perhaps that is merely a role you have been taught to play.

Fortunately, however, there are ways to change both perceptions and roles.

Changing Perceptions, Changing Roles

At the beginning of this chapter, we listed five steps that John Darley and Russell Fazio believe "define" the social interaction sequence: First, you perceive someone else (usually in a stereotyped fashion) and generate expectancies about that individual. Next, you act in accord with your perception. Then the other person interprets the "meaning" of your action, and responds accordingly. Finally, you interpret the

Authoritarianism. An authoritarian is someone who believes that discipline and punishment make the world a better place. Someone who believes in "following the rules" set down by higher authority. Generally speaking, most authoritarian individuals also have an external locus of control. See Chapter 12.

other person's response and then either break off the interaction or move on to another five-step sequence. Darley and Fazio note, however, that occasionally there is a sixth step to the sequence. That is, at some point you may pause and wonder why *you* responded the way you did.

Most of the time, of course, you may interpret your own actions as appropriate and as being "caused" by the other person. But, occasionally, you might well learn something new about yourself. And as a result of this gain in self-knowledge, you could change your perception both of yourself and of others.

Now that you know something about person perception, stereotypes, attribution conflicts, and role theory, perhaps you might wish to add step six to more of your own social interaction sequences.

Summary

1 Five important issues **social psychologists** deal with are:
   a Should the focus be on the **individual** or the **group**?
   b Is social psychology the study of **attitudes**, or **behaviors**?
   c Are attitudes and behaviors **learned** or **innate**?
   d Should the focus be on **consistent features** (such as social structures) or on **changeable aspects** (functions) of groups and organizations?
   e Is social psychology primarily **theoretical** or **applied**?

2 Generally speaking, social **psychologists** focus on the individual, while **social** psychologists look at group and organizational structures and functions.

3 **Attitudes** are consistent ways of thinking about, feeling toward, or responding to some environmental stimulus or input.

4 The **social interaction sequence** has five steps: (a) You meet someone and **generate expectancies**; (b) you **act** in accordance with your expectancies; (c) the other person **interprets** the meaning of your actions; (d) the other person then responds; and (e) you then **interpret** the meaning of the other person's response.

5 **Person perception** is defined as the process by which you come to perceive, remember, and respond to people as you do.

6 **First impressions** of people are determined by such factors as **prior attitudes**, **reputations**, **stereotypes**, the **primacy** and **recency effects**, and by **autistic hostility**.

7 We tend to attribute **good traits** to good-looking people and **bad traits** to less attractive individuals.

8 Most people tend to think that your body language signals your **intentions**, or your **underlying traits and motives**. Research suggests people with **low social competence** may be better at detecting body language signals than in responding to them properly.

9 Each of us seems to have a **personal space** around us that we defend as our **psychological territory**.

10 Each culture has its own rules for **eye contact** that determine the ways in which people converse with each other.

11 In order to predict and influence the actions of others, we use the **attribution process**. That is, we attribute motives and intentions to them that make their behaviors understandable to us. However, we often see our own actions as responses to the **social environment**.

12 Harold Kelley believes that long-term relationships are determined by **interdependence**, **responsiveness**, and **attributions**.

13 Relationships are interdependent because the **costs and benefits** are a joint function of the behavior of both partners.

14 Marriage partners are inclined to explain problems in terms of **attributed traits** rather than **observed behaviors**.

15 People are more likely to use the **attribution process** in conflict than in non-conflict situations.

16 Research on problem solving in small groups suggests that there are two types of **leadership roles**, the **task specialist** and the **social-emotional specialist**.

17 Studies of 17,000 US managers suggest that successful supervisors are motivated by the need for **self-actualization**, while less successful managers are motivated by **security** and **status needs**.

18 Successful managers tend to use **participatory management** techniques, while average or below-average supervisors tend to manage in an **authoritarian** way.

19 Women managers tend to be slightly more **task oriented** than men, who seem to be somewhat better at **social relations**.

20 Triandis views the process of human interaction as little more than an **exchange of resources**. In order to get what we want from others, we must therefore guess their **behavioral intentions**.

21 Zimbardo's **jail study** suggests that abnormal behaviors such as **authoritarianism**, **social aggression** and **depersonalization** may be nothing more than **role behaviors** determined primarily by the **social milieu** in which they occur.

22 An occasional **sixth step** in the **social interaction sequence** is that of **changing** your attitudes, perceptions, and behaviors, based on what you have learned from the sequence.

(Continued from page 634.)

Day 5

I don't understand why Warden Matossian stopped the experiment. We had the riot under control, and we hadn't violated the Regulations. I mean, it isn't really physical punishment if you just *poke* the #'s a little. That sort of stuff goes on in jails all the time, doesn't it? And how else were we going to get 853 to obey the Rules?

I looked at some of the video tapes that Dr. Matossian took, particularly the last one showing how we settled 853's hash. And I had to grin. I don't think I will ever forget the sight of him standing there, with that sausage sticking out of his mouth.

I watched that final tape twice, and even if I do say it myself, I think I came out of the whole thing looking pretty darn good. Like, when I got there, all of the #'s were backed into a corner of the yard, and the CO's on the evening shift were pointing the nozzle of a fire extinguisher at them. Old 853 was shaking one of those stupid sausages at the CO's, and they were shaking their billy-clubs back at him. But nobody was getting anywhere. And I saw what I had to do, right off.

I told the CO with the nozzle to keep me covered, and motioned to the other two CO's to come with me. Then we marched right up to 853.

"Grab his arms, men," I said, and they did. He seemed shocked and started to struggle, but the CO's straightened him out right away. Then I grabbed the sausage and stuck it right in 853's face. "Listen, twerp," I said, "we are going to finish this business *right now*. Then you are going to *apologize*, and we are going to get back on the Routine, just like the Rules say."

853 gave me some smart-ass reply, so I jabbed his nose with the sausage and said, "I will give you 5 seconds to start eating, or I am going to cram this thing down your throat, and it will serve you right if you choke."

He gave me this peculiar look, like he didn't recognize who I was because of my mirror sunglasses, or something. Then I started to count, "One . . . Two . . . Three . . . Four . . . Five!"

Well, at that moment 853 opened up his mouth to say something, and I jammed the sausage right between his teeth. "Bite," I said, in a firm tone of voice. But all that animal did was grin at me defiantly. So, I jabbed him in the stomach with my billy-club. Just a firm little poke, but sudden like, if you know what I mean. Well, his teeth chomped shut automatically, and there was the first bite of the sausage inside his mouth.

"Now chew," I said. And to help things along, I jabbed him another good one. I guess the sausage must have had a lot of pepper in it, because his eyes started to water. He stared at me sort of funny, and then his eyes watered some more.

And then, ever so slowly, #853 started to chew.

And everybody breathed a sigh of relief. The Rules were Obeyed.

For some reason, that's when Dr. Matossian came out and stopped the game. I mean, why then? We had it all under control, and could have gone right back to the Routine. That way, we'd have earned the full 300 bucks.

Well, even if Charlie did cost me the money, he taught me something important. I was looking at the tape, see, and I had this sudden insight.

Old friend Charlie was *enjoying* himself, getting all that attention for flouting the Rules that way. The way I see it, Charlie has got some basic flaw in his moral character. He's just a little *bent*, if you know what I mean. Fortunately, I discovered the truth in time, before asking him to take on the role of my legal partner.

Not that I don't still like the kid, sort of. I'm not even mad that he won't converse with me, because I figure he's depressed about how he behaved. He did say we ought to go talk to Dr. Matossian and apologize for what happened, but I don't see much sense in that. He can go if he wants to, but I have nothing to apologize for.

I was just doing my job.

Recommended Readings

Kelley, H.H. (1979). *Personal relationships: Their structures and processes*. Hillsdale, N.J.: Erlbaum.

Mehrabian, A. (1981). *Silent messages: Implicit communication of emotions and attitudes* (2nd ed.). Belmont, Cal.: Wadsworth.

Miller, A.G. (1982). *In the eye of the beholder: Contemporary issues in stereotyping*. New York: Praeger.

Zimbardo, P.H. (1975). On transforming experimental research into advocacy for social change. In M. Deutsch & H. Hornstein (Eds.), *Applying social psychology*. Hillsdale, N.J.: Erlbaum.

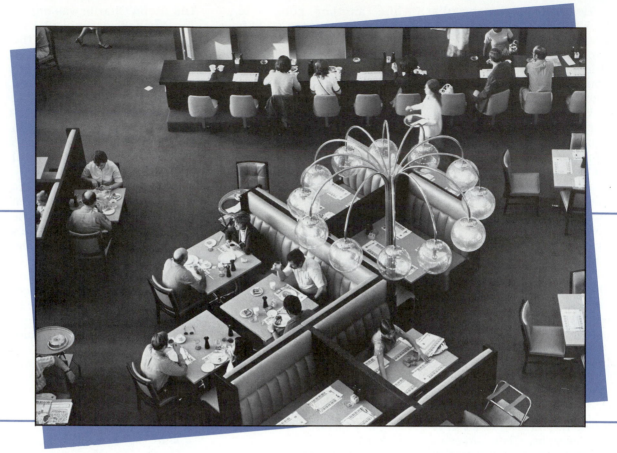

Did You Know That...

- Social psychologists are sometimes more interested in how you relate to other members of a group than in what you are like as an individual?

- One of the major characteristics of a group is the shared acceptance of group rules, norms, and goals by all the members?

- If everybody else in your group says that a red rose looks blue to them, you may actually perceive the rose as being bluish?

- Many people who claim they are not influenced by group pressures actually are strongly influenced in a negative way?

- Two-thirds of the subjects tested in an obedience study were willing to shock a person to (seeming) death if ordered to do so by the experimenter?

- You may be more likely to aid a wounded stranger if you are alone than if other people are present?

- When you do something that conflicts with your moral code, you may be more likely to change your perception of yourself than to change your behavior?

- Hostile groups may become friendly if rewarded for cooperating with each other?

24

Social Groups

"Two (or More) to Tango"

"Tell me, Mr. Kraus, what area of psychology are you most interested in?"

Norman Kraus squirmed around in the hard, wooden chair. It pained him that his adviser, Professor Ronald Ward, kept such uncomfortable chairs in his office. Professor Ward's seat, of course, was a soft armchair covered with English leather.

"Well, sir, I'm most turned on by social psychology, I guess."

"Good, good. Bloody important field," the Professor said. "Many excellent experiments that you could replicate as your training research."

Norm Kraus squinted at his adviser. Ward spoke with a slight Oxford accent that oddly annoyed Norm. He assumed the man took this means of reminding everyone that he had spent several years in England. Then it dawned on Norm what Ward had said.

"Replicate?"

"Yes, of course. We expect our first-year graduate students to replicate, or to repeat as exactly as possible, some piece of published research. Learn by doing what's already been well done, that's our motto."

"If you don't mind, sir, I'd really rather do something

new, something no one's tried before."

Professor Ward nodded sagely. "Yes, I'm sure you would. And did you have something particular in mind?"

Norman Kraus stopped to consider. "No, but I thought we could figure something out."

The Professor's lips pursed into a bitter-lemon smile. "There, you see what I mean. Our attitude is that students should learn to walk before they attempt to run. Try something we know will work first, before they exercise their presumed creativity." Ward coughed discreetly, then continued. "Now, what part of social psychology would you like to work on?"

Norm's anger might have boiled over had he not suddenly recalled his father's advice: "If you want to get along with people, you have to go along with people." Much as Norm hated compromising his own standards, he recognized that his father's comments certainly applied to the present situation. But a devilish urge still prompted him to say, "I'd like to find out why people knuckle under to other people."

Professor Ward glanced at the young man sharply, then frowned. "I presume you are referring to the conformity experiments. The early studies by Muzafer Sherif and Solomon Asch opened the field up, of course, but I've always liked the work that Bob Blake and his group did at Texas back in the '50's. Particularly their use of tape recorders to create synthetic social environments. Have you read Blake's experiments?"

The wooden seat was getting more uncomfortable by the moment. "No, sir."

Ward leaned back in his leather armchair, lit his pipe, and continued. "Asch had students guess the length of lines—a very easy task if no one were around to influence their decisions. But when the students had to judge immediately after several other subjects had spoken, matters got sticky. The other subjects were 'stooges,' paid by Asch to lie about which line was longest. If the stooges gave patently stupid judgments, the students often 'knuckled under' and gave incorrect reports themselves. The presence of the group of stooges was apparently so

intimidating that many of Asch's subjects conformed to the false group standard."

"And what did Blake do?" Norm asked, in a slightly desperate tone of voice. This stuff sounded even duller than the flatworm research another professor had tried to talk him into doing.

Ward tapped his pipe on an ashtray and continued. "Blake and one of his graduate students proved that the stooges didn't have to be physically present. Just hearing a tape recording of the stooges' voices was enough to pressure the subject into conforming. They reported this research at the 1953 meeting of the American Psychological Association in Cleveland, as I recall."

Inwardly, Norm Kraus groaned. Professor Ward's memory for trivial detail was legendary. He should have been a cop instead of a professor, Norm told himself. But aloud he said, "Gee, that's interesting. Do you remember exactly what they did?"

Professor Ward smiled, delighted at the chance to show off. "They used the auto-kinetic effect, as did Sherif. You may recall that if you look at a stationary pinpoint of light in a dark room, the light seems to dance around like a firefly. Because the apparent movement is created by the person's own eyes, everybody sees a rather different dance. Given a 10-second exposure to the light, some people will say that it moved a few millimeters, some will say it danced several meters, while others may insist that it hardly moved at all."

Fireflies? Norm thought. In an experiment on *social* psychology? Maybe he had

better go back to the worms after all.

The psychologist plowed right on, as if not noticing Norm's dismay. "Because the auto-kinetic effect is so subjective, it's rather easy to pressure people into conforming to group standards. But that's not what the experiment looked like to the subjects, who were undergraduate males at Texas. They were told it was a study on visual perception. The US Air Force, so the subjects were informed, wanted to find out how people judged the movement of tiny lights on the horizon. So the psychologists had devised a complicated and very expensive piece of apparatus that simulated the movement of airplanes in a night-time sky."

"What was the apparatus like?" Norm asked, beginning to be interested in spite of himself.

Ward snorted with amusement. "An empty tin can with a hole punched in one end. There was a flashlight bulb inside the can that could be turned on and off from the next room. Blake and his student hired four stooges to sit in the dark room and give false reports on how far the light moved. The real subjects were called into the room one at a time and sat directly in the middle of the stooges. During each trial, the light went on for 10 seconds, after which each person was asked to report how far it seemed to move. The four stooges always gave their reports first, before the real subject did.

Norm looked puzzled. "Didn't the real subject know the others were stooges?"

"Certainly not. They looked and acted just like real subjects would have acted—they asked questions and complained about the stupidity of the study. Of course, they asked exactly the same questions with each real subject. Anyhow, the stooges gave ridiculous reports. For example, on the first trial the four stooges reported that the light moved 1.6 centimeters, 1.7 centimeters, 1.9 centimeters, and 2.1 centimeters. Who can make measurements like that in the dark?"

"But it worked?" Norm asked.

Professor Ward lit his pipe again. "Only too well. About two-thirds of the subjects were greatly influenced by what the stooges said."

"And that was news?"

"No, but the second part of the study was. In this part, the subjects sat in the room alone and merely heard the tape-recorded voices of the stooges. Naturally, the subject didn't know a recording was being used. He had met the stooges in person before the start of the experiment and was told they were sitting in different rooms. The stooges asked the same questions and made the same comments on tape as they had in the real-life condition. And, as you might assume, the stooges gave the same ridiculous reports on how far the light moved."

Norm wiggled around on the hard chair. "So, what happened?"

Professor Ward smiled benevolently. "The subjects were just as influenced by the synthetic social background recorded on tape as they were when the stooges were physically present. We seem to conform to imaginary groups as much as to real ones." Ward paused to grind at his pipe with a metal tool. "Yes, I think you ought to replicate that experiment as your training research."

Norm could feel the crunch coming. "But couldn't I jazz it up a bit, just to make it more exciting?"

The Professor looked at the young man sternly. "You will learn a great deal more if you first do it exactly the way the Texas group did. Of course, if you have a streak of serendipity in your personality, you might turn up something unexpected anyhow. But be so kind as to try it our way first."

"But Professor Ward, I don't think . . ."

"Mr. Kraus," the Professor barked in a tone of absolute authority, "Our departmental rule is clear. We will expect you to replicate the Blake work *exactly*, as your training research. Report back to me after you've set things up and have run a few pilot subjects. Do you understand?"

Through gritted teeth, Norm Kraus muttered, "Yes, sir."

(Continued on page 681.)

What Is a Group?

In the last chapter, we looked at how your social environment affects you *as an individual*. In this chapter, we will discuss *groups* of people— how groups are formed, what keeps them together, and what the structures and functions of groups are. But the first question we must ask is, what *is* a group, and why would you want to belong to one?

Social Groups

Whenever you set up a continuing relationship of some kind with one or more other people, you have in fact either started a new **social group** or joined one already in existence. In the strictest of terms, a group is a *system*—that is, *a set of persons considered as a single entity*.

Actually, this definition is so narrow that it is of little practical use. For it implies that groups exist "in the mind of the beholder" rather than in real life. More broadly speaking, a group is a system of two or more individuals who are psychologically related, or who are in some way *dependent* on one another. This dependency usually involves *seeking a common goal*. Thus, groups, like all other living systems, are *goal oriented* (see Chapter 5).

You belong to dozens, if not hundreds of groups. Some are *formal membership groups*. For instance, you apply for membership in most colleges, religious groups, and tennis clubs. But you are born into *family groups* and *ethnic groups*. Some groups, such as "all the people attending a party," are fairly temporary or very informal systems. Other groups—such as friends and lovers—are informally structured but may exist for months or years.

Interaction groups are composed of people who relate to each other face-to-face.

The most important groups in your life are typically those that (1) last a long time, and (2) are made up of people with whom you have frequent, face-to-face encounters. For obvious reasons, these are called *interaction groups*.

Interaction Groups

Whenever you set up a new friendship, you have begun an interaction group. That is, you have given up some part of your own personal *independence* to create a *state of interdependence* between you and the other person. Whenever you join or create a group, you lose the privilege of "just being yourself" and of ignoring the other group members. But you may gain many things that compensate for this loss.

Some of the rewards for group membership are social. For example, you now have someone to talk to—someone to be with and to share things with. Other rewards are more practical or task oriented. For instance, pushing a car out of the mud, rearing a family, playing tennis, and having sex are activities that typically are more reinforcing if two or more individuals participate.

Most interaction groups, then, are made up of people who have affection and respect for each other, who have similar attitudes toward a number of things, or who have a common set of goals and interests.

Question: In the previous chapter, we reported that unmarried couples living together didn't establish "personal territories," while married couples did. How would you explain this result in terms of "group membership"?

Group Structure and Function

As Theodore Newcomb notes, groups typically form when two or more people sense that the pleasure of each other's company would be more *rewarding* than remaining socially isolated. Most such groups are informal. That is, an informal group does not have a *stated set of regulations* governing the behavior of its members (as does a formal group). But informal groups do have "informal rules," most of which are based on *cultural expectations* of how people should behave when they are together. If you misbehave at a party—if you are too noisy, if you spill drinks on people, or assault the host or hostess—you might well be asked to leave.

As Newcomb points out, one of the major characteristics of any group is the *shared acceptance of group rules by all the members*. This acceptance may be conscious or unconscious, but it is almost always present in one form or another.

Part of the fun of forming a friendship group (becoming friends or lovers) often is trying to understand what the other person or persons want. That is, the early pleasures of *dyadic relationships* often come from determining what *rules of the game* the two of you believe ought to be followed. If the person is very much like you, perhaps little or no discussion of the rules may be necessary. If the person is very different from you, the dyad may not last for long (although it can be an exciting relationship at the very beginning). In most cases where the members of a dyad are neither too similar nor too different, however, each person will compromise a little. For no group can maintain itself unless there is some minimal agreement or **consensus** as to what its members can and can't do.

Social group. A set of persons considered as a single unit. Two or more individuals who are psychologically related to one another. In certain rare instances, such as a child playing with an imaginary companion, or when one person hears tape-recorded voices of others, one or more members of the group may not be real (living) people, or may not be physically present.

Consensus (con-SENSE-sus). From the Latin word meaning "to feel together, to agree." A consensus is a harmony of viewpoints, opinions, or feelings. One common language mistake we often make is saying "consensus of opinion," for the word "consensus" all by itself means "agreement of opinion." Our word "consent" comes from the same Latin source.

Question: How do group rules (a type of group "feed-forward") make life less stressful for members of the group?

Group Norms

Newcomb notes that the ability to predict the behavior of people and objects in our world appears to be innately rewarding. One of the most reinforcing aspects of belonging to a group is that each member can to some extent predict what the other members are likely to think and do in most situations. Perhaps that is why group rules are almost always stated in terms of behavioral or attitudinal *norms*. That is, the rules specify what the average or *norm-al* behavior of each member should be, or what role(s) each member should play.

Newcomb states that no group member will fit all the norms *exactly*, just as no one is *exactly* average in all aspects of intelligence or sexual behavior. Most groups tolerate some deviation from the norm, so long as the member is not perceived by the group as playing "too abnormal" a role. The more similar the group's members are to each other, and the more em-

phasis the group places on "following the rules," the less deviation the group will usually tolerate. Perhaps we can demonstrate this point with an example.

Suppose we measure the attitudes toward premarital sex of two different groups—a class of students taking introductory psychology, and a group of young adults at a campus church or religious center. We will ask the members of both groups to record their agreement or disagreement with the following statement by placing a check mark on the 9-point attitude scale shown in Figure 24.1.

After both groups respond, we measure the position each person has marked on the 9-point scale. We can then use the number closest to each check mark as a *scale score* that fairly accurately represents each member's attitude toward the statement on premarital sex. And, since we have a number, or score, for each person, we can calculate the mean or *average attitude* for both groups. This average would, presumably, be the group norm. We can also calculate the *range* and the *standard deviation*

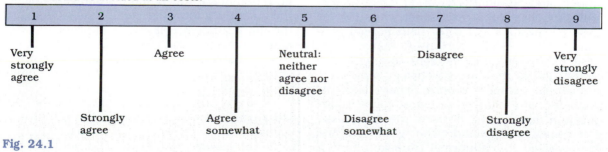

"Premarital sex is generally so damaging from both a psychological and moral point of view that it should be avoided at all costs."

1	2	3	4	5	6	7	8	9
Very strongly agree		Agree		Neutral: neither agree nor disagree		Disagree		Very strongly disagree
	Strongly agree		Agree somewhat		Disagree somewhat		Strongly disagree	

Fig. 24.1

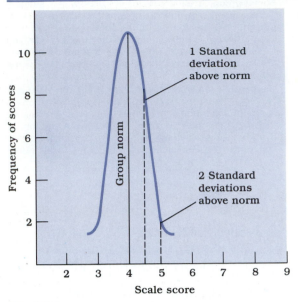

Fig. 24.2

People in an elevator don't usually form a group unless an emergency strikes, thus giving the people a common goal.

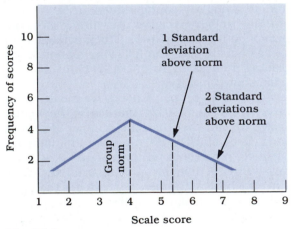

Fig. 24.3

of scores for both groups. (See Chapter 21 and the Statistical Appendix for a discussion of "range" and "standard deviation.")

For the sake of this discussion, let us assume that the mean or norm for both groups happened to be a scale score of 4: "Agree somewhat." This result might suggest to you that the church group and the psychology class were very similar, since the norm seems to be the same in both groups. But ask yourself this question: If your own position was a 6 ("Disagree somewhat"), would either group perceive you as being "too abnormal" to belong to that group?

The answer is—it depends on what each group's standard deviation is. Church groups, in general, are much more **homogeneous** in their attitudes toward sexual behavior than are the more random collections of students who make up classroom groupings.

The distribution of scores for the church group *might* look like those shown in Figure 24.2.

However, the distribution of scores for the classroom group *might* look like those shown in Figure 24.3.

As you can see, your score of 6 would be more than 2 standard deviations from the church-group norm, but well within the "normal" range for the psychology class. Presumably, the church group would consider your attitude "significantly deviant," while the classroom group probably would not.

Generally speaking, the more homogeneous the group, the smaller its standard deviation will be on most scales. And the more **heterogeneous** the group, the larger its standard deviation will be on most measures.

Question: What do you think would happen to the standard deviation of the church group's scores if you attacked the group for being narrow-minded on the subject of premarital sex?

Group Cohesion

According to Theodore Newcomb, *cohesiveness* is the psychological glue that keeps group members sticking together. The more cohesive a group, the longer it will typically last and the more resistant it will be to external pressures.

In ordinary situations, cohesion is often a function of the homogeneity of the group—the more homogeneous the attitudes or behaviors of the members, the more cohesive the structure of the group will be. However, even such heterogeneous groups as introductory psychology classes can be made momentarily cohesive if the group is threatened by some outside force.

People riding together in an elevator are not usually considered a group, for they have no real psychological interdependencies, and their attitudes are likely to be very dissimilar on most subjects. However, if the electric power fails and the people are trapped together in the elevator for several hours, this very heterogeneous bunch of people may quickly form into a group. They will give each other psychological support and comfort, and work together on the goal of escaping.

As soon as the people are released from the stalled elevator, however, the common threat to their survival is removed. At this point, the heterogeneity of the members' attitudes and behaviors will probably overcome the temporary cohesion and the group will disband. (Individual members of the group may be similar enough to strike up friendships as a result of the experience, however.)

Question: Why do groups that were close-knit in high school tend to become less cohesive if some of the members go on to college, while others don't?

Homogeneous (ho-moh-GEE-knee-us). From the Greek words meaning "same kind." The more alike members of a group are, the more homogeneous the group is. In more technical terms, the smaller the standard deviation of a distribution of test scores, the more homogeneous the scores are.
Heterogeneous (HETT-turr-oh-GEE-knee-us). From the Greek words meaning "different kinds." The more dissimilar the members of a group are, the more heterogeneous the group is, and hence the less cohesive the group is.

Group Commitment

The members of a group system often are free to abandon the group whenever they wish. But a group can survive only if it can hold its members together. One of the functions of any group, then, seems to be that of inducing the highest possible *commitment* among its members. For the more committed to the group's norms and goals the members become, the more cohesive the group typically will be and the more homogeneous its attitudes.

In an interesting study of 19th-century communes, psychologist R.M. Kanter found that these groups often demanded considerable sacrifice from their members. Some communes required their members to sign over all money and worldly goods to the group and thereafter to work on commune property "for free." Other communes prohibited their members from wearing jewelry or expensive clothes, from smoking tobacco, eating meat, or having sex. Kanter reports that communes demanding such sacrifices tended to last longer than communes that did not.

A similar finding comes from an experiment by social psychologists Elliot Aronson and Judson Mills. They offered college women a chance to participate in a discussion group—if they were willing to pay a price. Half of the women were required to suffer a very embarrassing initiation in order to "buy" entrance to their discussion group. The other half of the women were put through a much milder form of initiation. Those who suffered less embarrassment liked their discussion group significantly *less* than did the women who had committed themselves to paying the much higher psychological price.

Question: Which country club would seem more desirable to you, one that charged a $1,000 membership fee or one that charged but $100?

The Shakers lived in communes in the last century.

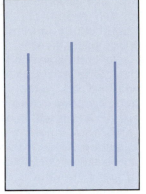

Standard line, 8″   8 3/4″   10″   Standard line,
                           line   line   8″

Fig. 24.4 The lines used in Solomon Asch's experiment.

Group Pressures to Conform

Most of us believe our attitudes toward such things as sexual behavior, politics, economics, and religion are primarily the result of our own decision making. In truth, as Harold Kelley points out, we use the groups we belong to as reference points, or guides, for much of what we think and do.

According to Kelley, **reference groups** influence your behavior in at least two ways: first, by providing comparison points which you use in evaluating yourself and others. Second, by setting standards and rewarding you when you conform and punishing you when you do not conform to these norms. As Kelley has shown, members who express opinions, attitudes, or judgments too far from the reference-group norm are typically pressured by other members to fall back into line.

Question: Your most important reference group is usually your family. How did members of your family *set and enforce* group norms when you were growing up?

The Sherif Experiment

The study of how groups induce their members to conform to group norms is one of the most fascinating areas of social psychology—and probably one of the most relevant. Scientific experiments on this topic date back to 1935, when social psychologist **Muzafer Sherif** first demonstrated the effects of group pressures on visual perception. Sherif asked students to observe a pinpoint of light in a dark room and tell him how much the light moved.

When the students made their judgments sitting alone in the room, each went his or her own way. But when the students were tested in groups, the first members to give their judgments created a perceptual "group norm" that the others had trouble resisting.

Attitudes expressed verbally in groups almost always tend to be more homogeneous than those the group members express if questioned in private.

Question: Can you explain the phrase "divide and conquer" in terms of destroying group cohesion and reducing group pressures toward conformity?

The Asch Experiment

Several years after Sherif reported his findings, social psychologist Solomon Asch carried the matter a step farther. Asch first tested the perceptual abilities of a group of students who served as "control subjects" for the latter part of his experiment. Asch showed these controls a white card that had a black line 8 inches long drawn on it, as shown in Figure 24.4. He referred to this as the "standard line" and asked the controls to remember it well.

Then Asch removed the first card and showed the subjects a second card that had three "comparison lines" drawn on it. The first of these lines was 8.75 inches long, the second was 10 inches, while the third was the same 8-inch length as the standard. Asch then asked the control subjects to report *privately* which comparison line matched the standard. To no one's surprise, the controls picked the correct answer some 99 percent of the time.

With his "experimental subjects," Asch played a much more subtle game. He asked these volunteers to appear at his laboratory at a certain time. But when each young man arrived, he found several other students waiting to participate in the experiment. What the experimental subject did not realize was that the others were stooges—that is, the others were "confederates" of Asch who were paid to give occasional false judgments. After the stooges and the experimental subject had chatted for a few moments, Asch ushered them into his laboratory and gave them several opportunities to judge line lengths for him. The judgments were given *out loud*, so that everyone could hear, and much of the time the stooges reported *first*—before the experimental subject did.

During the first two trials, the stooges picked the *correct* comparison line—as did the experimental subject. But on the third trial, each of the stooges calmly announced that the 10-inch line matched the 8-inch line! These false judgments created an *incorrect group perceptual norm*, and apparently put the experimental subjects under tremendous pressure to conform. In this first study, the experimental subjects "yielded" to group pressures almost one-third of the time by reporting that the two lines matched. In later studies, when the judgments were more difficult to make, the experimental subjects yielded to the group of stooges about two-thirds of the time.

Size of Group
In another experiment Asch varied the number of stooges who reported before the experi-

Solomon Asch

mental subject did. While the presence of one, two, or three stooges did induce some conformity, the maximum pressure to yield apparently was reached when there were four stooges giving false reports. Having 14 or even 40 stooges doesn't increase conformity much more than having four. However, if even one stooge out of 40 gives the "correct" answer, the homogeneity of the group is broken and much (but not all) of the "group pressure" is lifted. Under these conditions, the experimental subject "yields" only about one-fourth as often as when the stooges give a unanimous report.

Reasons for Conforming
The importance of the Asch study lies not merely in its dramatic demonstration that people tend to conform to temporary reference groups, but in the *reasons* they gave for doing so.

If you were to ask the subjects who "conformed" *why* they judged the 8-inch line as being as long as the 10-inch line, *most of them* would look at you sheepishly and confess that they couldn't stand the pressure. They might say they figured something was wrong, or they thought the stooges "saw through a trick" they hadn't recognized, or they simply didn't want to "rock the boat" by giving a judgment that went against the group norm.

The few remaining "conformers" are far more interesting, however. For they typically insist they *actually saw* the two lines as being identical. That is, they were not conscious of "yielding" at all.

Group norms not only influence your attitudes toward complex social issues, but your perceptions of even the simplest objects as well.

What Makes People Conform?

Shortly after Asch reported his initial results, a number of psychologists began to study how groups *induce conformity* in their members. Perhaps the most detailed of these studies was a series of experiments by Robert R. Blake,

Robert Blake

Harry Helson

Harry Helson, and their colleagues at the University of Texas.

In one of the first of these, which I performed under Professor Blake's direction, we demonstrated that the "stooges" did not have to be physically present in order to pressure the experimental subject into conforming. If the subjects merely heard tape-recorded voices of the "stooges," the subjects still conformed about two-thirds of the time.

In further studies, Blake and his students showed that subjects would volunteer for difficult tasks, donate large or small sums of money to a fake charity, violate social rules ("Don't Walk on the Grass!"), and change their reported attitudes toward war and violence in order to conform to the behavior of various groups of stooges.

Adaptation-level Theory

Robert Blake is a social psychologist with a long-standing interest in group behavior. Harry Helson, however, was an experimental psychologist who spent many years studying visual perception in individuals, not groups. Some of Helson's best-known research had to do with the effects of the *background* on the perception of a visual stimulus—for example, the fact that a white rose appears reddish when seen on a background of blue-green velvet (see Chapter 8).

Originally, Helson had little interest in social psychology. However, he soon perceived that the stooges in Blake's studies were really a "social background" that affected perceptual judgments much as the blue-green velvet "colored" the perception of the white rose. Thus, conformity behavior could be explained by reference to **Adaptation-level Theory**, which Helson had devised to account for the way that humans perceive the world. The discovery that their in-

terests were similar led Blake and Helson to form a research group—and to jointly direct a series of experiments that helped clarify the conditions that induce people to conform to group norms.

According to Adaptation-level Theory, all behavior (including conforming) is influenced by three factors:

1. *Stimulus factors.* These influences include the task or problem set before the subject—what the subject looks at or is told to do.
2. *Background factors.* These influences include the social situation or context in which the stimulus is presented.
3. *Personality factors.* These influences include such matters as innate response tendencies, traits, and past experience.

According to Adaptation-level Theory, if you want to understand why people do or do not yield to group pressures, you must look at all three factors in detail.

Stimulus or Task Variables

The physical properties of the stimulus you must judge in a conformity experiment have a lot to do with whether or not you will yield to group pressures. In general, the *vaguer* the stimulus, the more likely it is that you will conform.

Attitudes about almost anything are easier to shift than are *judgments of concrete facts*. However, strong *personal preferences* for things like food are harder to influence than are guesses about such vague facts as the distance from New York to London.

The more *difficult the stimulus task* appears to be, and the more *confusing the instructions* about the task, the more likely it is that the group will be able to influence your behavior. For this reason, perhaps, group pressures are most effective if you must judge the stimulus from *memory*.

Situational or Background Variables

If the group is to have an influence on you, you must know what the group's opinion or norm actually is. One of the most important situational factors, therefore, is how much information you have about what the group is like, and what you know about the beliefs of the other group members. In general, the more *knowledge* you have concerning the group, the more strongly you will feel pressured to yield.

Group pressures to conform develop when stimulus and background factors are in conflict—that is, when your perception of the stimulus *differs significantly* from that offered by some reference group you belong to. Up to a point, the larger the difference between your judgment and that of the group, the more likely it is you will be influenced by group standards. However, if the matter is carried to ridiculous extremes, the pressure on you may lift. It is all very well to ask you to report that an 8-inch line is the same length as one 10 inches long. It is something else to expect you to report that an 8-inch line is identical to a line several feet in length.

The way you perceive the other group members is also critical. The more *prestige* or status or competence members of the group seem to have—or the more *trustworthy* they appear to be—the more powerful agents they become in pressuring you to conform. You are more likely to conform to friends than to strangers, and more likely to yield to strangers who say they like you than to strangers who don't.

The more *out in the open* you are forced to be in making your judgments, the more likely it is that you will yield to group pressures. If you are told that the whole group must come to a *unanimous decision* on the matter at hand, you will be strongly pressured to yield. Also, the greater the *reward* for yielding, or the more *importance* the judgment is supposed to have, the more likely it is that you will be swayed by incorrect or inappropriate group norms.

Question: Why is it particularly important that juries, who often decide matters of life and death, should always take secret ballots?

Personality Factors and Past Experience

Some people seem to conform much of the time, some practically never. Most of us, however, yield in some situations and not in others. The *personality traits* of the individual who readily yields to group pressures have often been measured—but not all of these studies have come up with the same results. There are at least three reasons why this conflict might be expected.

First, as we noted in previous chapters, some of our personality tests are not as valid and reliable as we would like them to be.

Second, with the notable exception of the investigations by Asch, Sherif, and by Blake and Helson, many of these studies of the "conformist personality" have never been replicated. As a general rule, you probably should not trust any scientific finding until it has been successfully repeated several times.

Adaptation-level Theory. A theory proposed by Harry Helson that accounts for judgments, perceptions, and attitudes in terms of three factors—the physical and social dimensions of the stimulus input, the background in which the stimulus appears, and the personality structure (traits, attitudes, past experiences) of the perceiver. Often called A-L Theory.

Third, there is no reason why we should expect that all people who conform to group norms should have the same sort of personality. In fact, judging from Zimbardo's research on prisoners and guards (see Chapter 23), we might assume we would *all* yield if the situational factors were strong enough.

But there are literally dozens of studies in which personality traits have been correlated with yielding or conforming. Looking at the broad picture, we find that yielders are reported to have had harsh parents who gave their children very little "independence training." Yielders are also reported to be "followers" rather than "leaders," but are rather rigid and *authoritarian* in the way they respond to rules. Men who yield more than average are reported to score as being more "feminine" than average on masculinity tests.

Past experience also has its effects on conformity. If you are an expert on the task at hand, or if the experimenter somehow makes you *think* you are an expert, you are less likely to yield. If you are rewarded for going against the group, you tend to yield less often than if you are punished for refusing to conform.

Some *cultures* may be more "conformist" than others. For example, Stanley Milgram found in 1961 that Norwegian subjects conformed to group pressures more than did French subjects. Later research suggests as well that Soviet children are more likely to yield to group pressures than are Israeli youngsters. Thus, the *society* you grow up in may, in part, determine whether you tend to yield to or resist group pressures toward conformity.

Question: Would you expect "internalizers" or "externalizers" to be more likely to conform to group pressures?

Negative Conformity

In our society, we all make use of reference groups, and we all conform to group norms at one time or another. Indeed, as we will see, one of the *chief functions* of a group is to induce "normative behavior" in its members. And yet we often talk as if we placed a high premium on being independent of the people around us. People brag (and even write songs about) "doing things *my* way." But are we really as non-conformist as we often think we are?

In one study, Blake and Helson discovered a very amusing thing about many people who consider themselves to be "independent thinkers." In fact, they yield to group pressures just as much as do the rest of us, but they yield *negatively.* Let us return to our attitude scale on premarital sex to see what these *negative conformers* are like (see Fig. 24.1).

"Premarital sex is generally so damaging from both a psychological and moral point of view that it should be avoided at all costs." Suppose we ask a young man to respond to this statement while he is *alone,* and he marks #8, "Strongly disagree." Later, we present him with a similar statement that he must respond to *publicly,* after four stooges have given their opinions out loud. The stooges have been paid to say that they too "Strongly disagree" with the statement. What would you think of this young man if he now switches and gives his score as #2, "Strongly agree?" Is this man really acting *independently* of the stooge group? If you wanted to trick him into doing something, couldn't you figure out a way to do so?

Question: How might you use the information on stimulus, background, and personality factors to minimize the effects of group pressures on your own behavior?

Obedience

One interesting sidelight to the conformity studies is this—in most of the experiments, the subject was never told that he or she *had to yield* to the group norm. Indeed, many of the subjects were quite unaware they had given in to group pressures. Some people even *denied* they had done so. So let us next ask a very important question: What might the results have been had the subjects been *ordered* to yield by the experimenter?

The Milgram Experiments

The answer to this question may well come from a fascinating set of experiments performed by psychologist Stanley Milgram in the 1960's at Yale. His subjects were men who ranged in age from young to old, and who came

Stanley Milgram

from many different walks of life. These men were paid to participate in what they thought was a study on the effects of punishment on learning.

"Teachers" and "Learners"

In the first experiment, each man arrived at Milgram's laboratory to find another subject (a stooge) also present. The stooge was supposed to be the "learner" who would have to memorize a list of word pairs. The experimental subject was supposed to be the "teacher" who would punish the stooge if he made any mistakes. The stooge was sent into another room and was strapped into a chair so he couldn't escape when the punishment became severe. The stooge was then out of sight for the rest of the experiment.

Sitting in front of the experimental subject was a very impressive piece of electrical equipment that *supposedly* was a powerful shock generator. In fact, the machine was a fake. *No shock was ever delivered during the experiment.* This "fake" generator had 30 switches on it to control the (apparent) strength of the electrical current. Labels on these switches ranged from "Slight Shock" (15 volts) to "Danger: Severe Shock" (420 volts) to "XXX" (450 volts).

The first time the stooge made a mistake, the subject was to give him 15 volts of shock. For each subsequent mistake, the subject was to increase the shock intensity by flipping on the next-higher switch. The apparatus was so ingeniously designed that none of the subjects guessed the stooges actually weren't receiving shocks from the machine.

At the beginning of the session, things were easy for the experimental subject. The stooge got most of the word pairs correct, and the "shocks" delivered for making errors were presumably very mild. As time wore on, however, the stooge made more "mistakes" and the "shocks" became more and more severe. When the shock level reached what seemed to be a fairly high point, the stooge suddenly pounded on the wall in protest. Then the stooge *stopped responding entirely*, as if he had fainted or had suffered an attack of some kind.

At this point the experimenter told the "teacher" to continue anyway—no matter how dangerously high the shock might get. If at any time the subject wanted to stop, the experimenter told him in a very stern voice, "Whether the learner likes it or not, you *must go on* until he has learned all the word pairs correctly. So please go on." However, the experimenter never *forced* the "teacher" to continue.

What would you do in this situation? Would you refuse to cooperate, or would you "obey" the experimenter and go on shocking the stooge right up to what you believed were the limits of the electrical generator?

And how do you think most other people would react if they faced this challenge?

Some "Shocking" Facts

After Milgram had completed his first study, he asked a great many college students how they thought most people would react when told to shock the "learner." If you are like Milgram's

students, you will insist that you—and most other people—would refuse to continue the experiment when a dangerously high shock level was reached (and particularly when the "learner" apparently had fainted or died in the other room). But, in fact, your guess (at least about other people) would be wrong. For out of the first 40 subjects Milgram tried, *almost 65 percent* continued to "obey orders" right up to the bitter end. Most of these subjects were extremely distressed about doing so. They complained, they showed tension, and they said they wanted to stop again and again. But some 65 percent were *completely obedient* in spite of their inner conflict.

Question: What similarities do you see between the people who "obeyed" Milgram and the young men in Zimbardo's experiment who became "brutal" in their behaviors toward men who were playing the role of prisoners?

Factors Inducing Obedience

In Adaptation-level Theory terms, the verbal orders to Milgram's subjects were "stimulus factors," while the behavior of the stooge can be considered part of the "background or situational factors." By manipulating each of these factors in subsequent experiments, Milgram was able to determine a variety of ways in which obedience can be increased or decreased.

As you might expect, the weaker the stimulus, the fewer the number of people who obeyed. When the experimenter stood right over the experimental subjects, breathing down their necks and ordering them on, about 65 percent followed through to the end. But when the experimenter was out of the room and gave his orders by telephone, only some 22 percent of the subjects were completely obedient.

In the first experiment, the subjects could not see or hear the stooge in the other room. In subsequent studies, Milgram altered this "background factor." If the stooge began moaning, or complaining about his heart, fewer subjects obeyed orders. Having the stooge physically present in the same room so that the subject could see the supposed pain from each shock reduced obedience even more. And if the subject had to grab hold of the stooge's hand and force it down on a metal "shock plate" before each punishment, very few of the subjects followed instructions to the end. Put more simply, the subjects were more likely to deliver severe punishment if they couldn't see the *consequences* of their actions.

"IT'S ENDLESS. WE JOIN A COUNTER CULTURE — IT BECOMES THE CULTURE. WE JOIN ANOTHER COUNTER CULTURE — IT BECOMES THE CULTURE..."

Members of homogeneous groups (the priests) have more similar attitudes and greater group cohesion than do members of heterogeneous groups (the classroom).

Group Pressures and Obedience

In a later experiment, Milgram added the group-pressures technique to his own method of studying obedience. In this experiment, Milgram used three stooges with each experimental subject. One of the stooges, as usual, was the "learner" seated in the next room. The other two were supposed to be "teachers" working in a team with the subject.

The experiment proceeded as before, except that one of the stooge-teachers backed out as soon as the "shock" reached a medium-low intensity. Saying that he refused to continue, this stooge simply took a seat as far from the shock machine as he could. When the "shock" reached a medium-high level, the other stooge-teacher also refused to go on. The subject then was faced with *conflicting social norms*. The experimenter kept pressuring him to continue, while the "group" of stooge-teachers was exerting pressure to stop. Under these conditions, the "social background" factors won out over the "stimulus" of the experimenter's orders. More than 90 percent of the subjects refused to complete the experiment.

We are taught to obey, just as we are trained to conform. If you consider the great rewards and massive punishments that groups can administer to their members, perhaps it is not so surprising that many of us obey and conform rather readily.

Question: What do you think would have happened in Zimbardo's prison study had the "warden" *ordered* the guards to punish the prisoners severely for infractions of "the rules"?

Attribution Theory and Obedience

Before we go any farther with our discussion of obedience, let's ask a question. Suppose, in one of his studies, Milgram had allowed the "teacher" to *set the shock level himself*. That is, rather than insisting that the "teacher" blindly increase amount of shock given the "learner" after each trial, suppose Milgram had told the "teacher" to decide how much punishment would be "appropriate." The "teacher" could increase the shock to the maximum level, keep it in the "mildly painful" range, or decrease the shock to almost zero.

Under these circumstances, how much shock do *you* think the "average teacher" would eventually administer? And what percentage of the "teachers" do you think would give the maximum amount of electricity? Why not write your predictions down on a sheet of paper, and then see what actually happened.

In fact, Milgram actually performed this experiment and reported the results in 1974. He began by giving all the teachers themselves a mildly painful shock of 45 volts, so they would "understand how shock felt." Thereafter, the "teachers" were allowed to administer (false) shock to the "learner" that could vary from 15 up to 450 volts. Milgram found that almost all of the "teachers" maintained the shock in the "mildly painful" range (45 to 60 volts). Only one "teacher" out of 40 administered the maximum shock of 450 volts. That finding itself is very interesting. However, an extension of this research by Martin Safer of Catholic University of America yielded even more intriguing results.

Safer began by showing a film of Milgram's research to 132 students in an introductory psychology class. He then asked the students to *predict* what the "teachers" would do if allowed to set their own shock levels. Safer found that the students systematically *overestimated* the amount of shock they thought the "teachers" would administer. They guessed that about 12 percent of the "teachers" would give 450 volts, and that the average "teacher" would end up giving about 175 volts!

Safer believes that his students *attributed evilness to the "teachers."* That is, the students apparently assumed most people have a "cruel streak" in them, and that they will express this trait if given a chance. Safer points out the paradox of his findings. First, before learning about Milgram's research, most students presume that *almost nobody* would shock an innocent "learner." When they learn what actually happened in Milgram's laboratory, however, the students attributed the results to some character flaw inside the "teachers." For the students failed to perceive that the "teachers'" actions were due to the *social environment*, not to some personality trait. Thus, when asked how the "teachers" would react when allowed to set their own shock levels, the students predicted on the basis of *attributed traits*, not on the basis of the actual situation the "teachers" were in (and responding to).

Martin Safer concludes that *few people* "appear to have insight into the crucial situational factors affecting behavior in the obedience . . . experiments."

Question: What level of shock did *you* think the "teachers" would use? What have you learned about your own perceptions from these studies?

The Ethics of Deception

The Milgram studies, the Zimbardo prison research, and many other experiments raise a number of complex but important questions about the *ethics* of using humans as subjects in scientific experiments. One of these questions involves the morality of *deceiving* the subjects as to the real purpose of the study, even if the experimenter believes such deception is necessary because people seldom act naturally when they know they're being observed.

Milgram's Critics

When Milgram's research was published, a storm of protest was raised by sincerely concerned individuals who urged that studies such as Milgram's be banned or prohibited. This same barrage of criticism, as we noted in the last chapter, occurred when Zimbardo released the results of his prison experiment. In consequence, a number of codes of ethics were proposed, but workable guidelines for experimentation on humans are not easy to agree upon. For, given a little time and motivation, we could all think of certain types of studies in which deception might be morally justified, and other experiments in which misleading the subjects would be both a legal and an ethical outrage.

In his 1982 book *Ethical Problems in Psychological Research*, German psychologist Heinz Schuler notes one of the most disturbing aspects of experiments such as Milgram's. That is, the experimenter typically has *far greater power and social prestige* than does the subject. Thus, says Schuler, there always is an "unspoken contract" between the researcher and the subject. The experimenter implicitly promises not to abuse her or his power, and the subject promises to respond as accurately as possible. As far as Milgram's studies are concerned, Schuler has this to say:

> The experimenter failed to keep his word. The terms of an implicit contract were not observed, and the trust of the subjects was misused.

However, Schuler also states that "A good experiment—that is, a valid experiment—is one that subjects cannot see through, one in which they tacitly accept the investigator's definition of the situation." Since none of Milgram's subjects "saw through" the situation, apparently (from Schuler's point of view) Milgram's studies were *valid* but not ethical.

Question: Which do you think is more important—that a research study be a *valid* representation of how the world really is, or that it be conducted in an *ethical* manner?

When Is Deception Ethical?

Obviously we should always consider the *actual results* of experiments before drawing hasty conclusions about what is ethical, and what isn't. Viewed in this perspective, Milgram comes off fairly well, for he did discover some fascinating facts. More important, there is no evidence reported in the scientific literature that any of his subjects suffered ill effects. In truth, Milgram seems to have employed little more deception in his work than is used regularly on TV programs such as "Candid Camera." Yet the nagging question—"When is it ethical to use deception?"—remains for the most part unanswered.

Some of the emotional reaction to Milgram's experiments probably stemmed from the rather unflattering picture his results gave us of ourselves. Had most of Milgram's subjects *refused* to obey blindly, perhaps he would not have been so vigorously attacked. Milgram's research—as well as Zimbardo's, and the early research on conformity—suggests that we all have "psychological blind spots" about the true *causes* of human behavior.

However, despite the emotionality of some of Milgram's critics, the issue of experimenter responsibility remains a crucial one, and the American Psychological Association has recently taken a stand against the unwarranted use of deception in similar research. Similar codes are now in force in several other countries, including Poland, Germany, France, and the Netherlands.

We will have more to say about these complex ethical issues in the next chapter.

Question: Under what circumstances do you personally think that deceiving subjects in a scientific experiment might be ethically warranted or justified?

Bystander Apathy

Milgram created problems for his subjects because he told them what to do. In real-life conflicts, there often isn't anyone around to give you directions, and you must act (or fail to act) on your own. If there are other people around when a crisis occurs, however, you may look at them as "models" of what you ought to do. And you may assume that *they are as responsible as you are* for taking action (or not doing anything) in an emergency. Thus, if your "models" fail to react, you may feel strong group pressures to follow their lead. Keep that thought in mind as we describe a particularly gruesome murder.

Early one morning in 1964, a young New York woman named Kitty Genovese was returning home from work. As she neared her front door, a man jumped out of the shadows and attacked her. She screamed and attempted to defend herself. Because she screamed loudly, 38 of her neighbors came to their windows to see what was happening. And because she fought valiantly, it took the man almost 30 minutes to kill Kitty Genovese. During this period of time, not one of those 38 neighbors came to her aid—and not one of them even bothered to call the police.

Bibb Latané

woman. While the people were in an office filling out the forms, the woman went into the next room. Shortly thereafter, the subjects heard a loud crash from the next room, and the woman began moaning loudly that she had fallen and was badly hurt and needed help.

Now, how many of the subjects do you think came to her rescue?

The answer is—it depends. Some of the subjects were exposed to this little drama when they were all by themselves in the testing room. About 70 percent of the "alone" subjects offered help. Another 40 subjects faced this apparent emergency in pairs. Only 8 of these 40 people responded by going to the woman's aid. The other 32 subjects simply sat there listening to the moans and groans.

Were the subjects who failed to rush to the woman's assistance merely apathetic and uncaring? In this case, yes. Many of the "apathetic bystanders" informed the experimenters they hadn't really thought the woman was seriously hurt and were afraid of embarrassing her if they intervened. But we should note that the subject's *perception* of the emergency was strongly

The Darley-Latané Studies

Kitty Genovese's death so distressed scientists John Darley and Bibb Latané that they began a study of why people refuse to help others in similar situations.

In one experiment, Darley and Latané staged a disaster of sorts for their subjects. They paid people 2 dollars to fill out a survey form which was given to them by an attractive young

The Kitty Genovese murder scene. At location (1), she drove into the parking lot. She noticed a man in the lot and proceeded to location (2) toward a police telephone box. Here, the man caught and attacked her with a knife. She got away, but he attacked her again at location (3) and finally at location (4).

influenced by whether or not there was someone else present in the testing room.

In another experiment, subjects heard a young man (presumably in the next room) discuss the fact that he frequently had seizures similar to grand mal epilepsy. Shortly thereafter, the stooge began crying for help, saying he was about to have an attack and would die if no one came to help him. About 85 percent of the subjects who were "alone" rushed to the stooge's assistance. However, only 62 percent of the subjects who were in pairs offered aid, while but 31 percent of those in 5-person groups overcame their apathy.

Latané's "Theory of Social Impact"

In an article in the April 1981 *American Psychologist*, Bibb Latané proposed a "theory of social impact." Latané states, "As social animals, we are drawn by the attractiveness of others and aroused by their mere presence. . . . We are influenced by the actions of others, stimulated by their activity and embarrassed by their attention. . . . I call all these effects, and others like them, 'social impact.'"

Latané believes the impact of your social environment can be determined by three factors: the *strength*, *immediacy*, and the *number* of people around you. The more people involved in a given situation, the more *diluted* you will perceive your own responsibility as being. Thus, Latané says, each person who witnessed Kitty Genovese's murder felt but a fraction of the responsibility for helping the woman or reporting the crime. Therefore, while the murder itself had a strong and immediate impact on the neighbors, the *number of people* was so great that it diluted each person's sense of responsibility to the point where no one took action.

Question: Consider those 38 neighbors as an Asch-type "conformity group." Why would each person be under strong pressures *not* to intervene if none of the other 37 did?

Subways Are for Slipping

Darley and Latané note that most of Kitty Genovese's neighbors said after the murder that they didn't *perceive* anything really terrible as taking place. This inaccurate perception then excused the neighbors' failure to take action—at least in their own minds.

Research by I.M. Piliavin, J. Rodin, and J. Piliavin tends to confirm the accuracy of this explanation. In the late 1960's, Piliavin and his group turned the New York subway system into an experimental laboratory. Four people involved in the study would board one car of a subway train through different doors. Once the train was underway, one of the male experimenters would stumble down the aisle, slip, and collapse on the floor, face up. Two of the experimenters recorded how long it took the "innocent bystanders" in the subway car to come to the stooge's aid. If no one helped out, one of the other experimenters would then assist the stooge.

From a humanistic point of view, the results of the Piliavin research are fairly encouraging. When the "victim" was carrying a white cane, and acting as if he were blind, people came to his aid in 95 percent of the tests. Even when the stooge reeked of whiskey and pretended to be drunk, he received assistance in about half the tests.

Question: People tend to conform to groups less in situations in which they think they are experts. What would happen to "bystander apathy" if we began teaching children how to handle social emergencies as part of their normal training in school?

Who Intervenes, and Why

Writing in *Social Psychology Quarterly* in 1981, psychologist Ted Huston and his colleagues offer an interesting comparison between people who have helped crime victims and those who have not. The state of California has long compensated **Good Samaritans** who are injured when they intervene to give assistance in holdups, asaults, burglaries, or other serious crimes. Huston *et al.* interviewed 32 people who had received "Good Samaritan" awards and contrasted them with 32 "control subjects"—individuals from the same community who were identical in most other ways but hadn't intervened in a crime for at least the previous 10 years.

According to Huston and his group, the "interveners" and the "controls" had strikingly similar scores on standardized personality tests. The interveners were no more sympathetic or socially responsible, nor were they more likely to *state* they would be willing to help others. The one *personality test difference* was that the interveners *perceived* themselves to be stronger, more aggressive, and more emotional than did the controls.

In terms of *experience with crime*, however, there was a marked contrast between the two groups. The interveners had witnessed crimes at least nine times as often as had the control subjects (although the two groups lived in the same community). In addition, the "Good Samaritans" had themselves been crime *victims* more than twice as often as the controls. Just as important, the interveners had much higher levels of training in such skills as life saving, first aid, and self-defense.

Huston and his associates note that helping out in crisis situations may be habit forming. Some 34 percent of those individuals who received "Good Samaritan" compensation reported they had intervened in at least one crime other than the one they got the award for.

Question: Suppose you witnessed a crime and didn't intervene. How would you explain this failure to yourself afterward? Would you be more likely to change your *attitude* toward yourself, or would you strive to change your *behavior* in crisis situations?

Cognitive Dissonance

Not all the conflicts we face involve a choice between satisfying group expectancies or satisfying our consciences by living up to a moral code. Sometimes the problem has to do with trying to *explain to ourselves* why we do what we do.

Doomsday Prophecies

Over the years, Leon Festinger has conducted a series of intriguing studies on how human beings react to situations involving social conflicts. In one of his first studies, Festinger worked with H.W. Riecken and Stanley Schachter. These social scientists made an extensive study of a "doomsday group" whose leader had predicted the world would end on a certain day. As the fatal day approached, the members of the group became more and more excited and tried to convince others to repent and join their group in order to "save their souls." When "doomsday" arrived, the members of the group gathered together to await final judgment and to pray for deliverance. To their amazement, the day passed, and so did several other days, and the world continued to speed on its merry way.

And how did the leader of the "doomsday group" respond to the failure of her predictions? Apparently, by finding a "rational excuse" for what actually happened. Several days after the date the world was supposed to end,

she told the members of her clan that "God had spoken to her, and had spared the world in answer to the group's prayers." The group members then reacted with great joy. Rather than rejecting the leader, they accepted her more warmly and believed even more firmly in her prophecies.

Changing Perceptions to Reduce Conflict

The "failed prophecy" study led Festinger to hypothesize that people tend to reduce mental conflict by changing their *perceptions* of what really happened to them. In perhaps the best known of his experiments—reported in 1959 by Festinger and J.M. Carlsmith—college students were asked to do about 30 minutes of very tedious and boring work. The subjects performed these repetitive and uninteresting tasks while alone in a laboratory room.

After the students had completed the chores, Festinger and Carlsmith offered some of them a dollar as a reward to tell the next subject what an exciting and thrilling task it had been. Other subjects were paid 20 dollars for doing exactly the same thing. Afterward—no matter how good a "selling job" the person had done—each subject was asked to give her or his actual opinion of how pleasurable the work was.

Festinger and Carlsmith report that the students paid but one dollar thought the chores were really pretty interesting and enjoyable. However, the subjects paid 20 dollars rated the tasks as being dull, as did a group of subjects

Leon Festinger

Muzafer Sherif

emphasize the importance of intra-psychic processes in determining how individuals think and behave. These "inventions" include most of our theories about "traits," "attitudes," "personality factors," and "mental illness."

Question: What similarities do you see between Festinger's theory of cognitive dissonance and Piaget's description of how "disequilibrium" drives us to change our perceptions of the world?

who were not asked to "sell" the experiment to another student.

Why did the subjects paid but one dollar rate the work as being much more pleasant than one might have expected? Festinger believes they had a difficult job rationalizing their own actions. For they had *lied* to the other subject about how interesting the task was supposed to be. The subjects paid 20 dollars for lying apparently were willing to face the fact that they had "fudged" a bit for that much money. The students paid but a single dollar couldn't admit to themselves that they'd "sell out" for so little money. Therefore, Festinger says, they apparently changed their *perception* of the enjoyability of the task "after the fact."

Dissonance Theory

In the early 1960's, Festinger suggested that in conflict situations we experience **cognitive dissonance**. That is, whenever we do something we think we shouldn't, we face the problem of explaining our actions to ourselves and to others. Festinger stated that we are usually highly motivated to reduce cognitive dissonance when it occurs, and we do so chiefly by changing our *beliefs or attitudes* to make them accord with our *actual behaviors*—and then we go right on behaving the way we always had.

Perhaps you will have noticed a certain similarity between the group-pressures experiments, the obedience studies, the research on bystander apathy, and the cognitive-dissonance experiments. In all these cases, the conflict arose when people failed to recognize that we all are immensely sensitive to group pressures, and it is a *natural function of a group* to exert these pressures.

Given the fact that so few of us ever perceive what strong control our environments exercise over us, perhaps it is not surprising we invent all kinds of "rational explanations" that over-

Inter-Group Conflict

For the most part, the studies on conformity, obedience, and cognitive dissonance have dealt with individual subjects put under strong psychological pressure to avoid conflict with other members of a group, or with their own value systems. From the standpoint of General Systems Theory, however, we can consider the group itself as a kind of "super-organism" that should be subject to social pressures to conform to the standards set by other groups or organizations.

Groups should also show many of the same sorts of *internal processes* (structures and functions) as do individuals. Not unexpectedly, most of the factors that influence individual conformity and internal conflict have their direct parallels when we study the behavior of groups as groups.

Sherif's "Camp" Experiments

Muzafer Sherif was one of the first social psychologists to undertake scientific experiments on conflict between groups. Several years ago, Sherif and his colleagues helped run a camp for 11- and 12-year-old boys. These youngsters were all from settled, well-adjusted, white, middle-class, Protestant homes. The boys were carefully selected to be happy, healthy individuals who had no difficulty getting along with other young men their age. None of the boys knew each other before being admitted to the camp. Nor did any of them realize that they were to be subjects in Sherif's experiments.

Eagles and Rattlers

The camp itself had two rather separate housing units. The boys living in one unit were called the "Eagles," while the other group's name was the "Rattlers." Since there were no pre-existing friendships among the boys, group

commitment and cohesion in both units was very low on the first day of camp. Then Sherif gave both the Eagles and the Rattlers various real-life problems that could be solved only if the boys *in each separate unit* worked together effectively. As each unit overcame the difficulties Sherif put to it, the boys came to *like* the other boys in the same unit more and more. The Eagles and the Rattlers each became a "natural group," and commitment to the specific group (and to its particular emerging norms) increased significantly.

Competition versus Cooperation

After the Eagles and the Rattlers had shown considerable cohesion, Sherif introduced a series of contests designed to make the two groups hostile toward one another. As the groups competed for prizes, conflict developed, since one group could win only at the expense of the other. Very soon the Eagles were making nasty comments about the Rattlers, and vice versa. Most of this hostility consisted of one group's *attributing* selfish or hostile motives to the other group. Name calling, fights, and raids on the cabins belonging to the other group became commonplace. At the same time, Sherif reports, there was a marked *increase* in cooperativeness and cohesiveness *within* each of the groups.

Reducing Inter-group Hostilities

Once the groups were at each other's throats, Sherif tried to bring them back together again. In his first experiment, Sherif attempted to unite the two groups by giving them a common enemy—a group of threatening outsiders. This technique worked fairly well, in that it brought the Eagles and the Rattlers closer together. But they still held *hatred* for their common enemy.

The next year Sherif repeated the group-conflict experiment with a different set of boys. Once inter-group hatred had reached its peak, Sherif brought the two units into very pleasant, non-competitive contact with each other. They sat together in the same dining hall while eating excellent food, and they watched movies together. However, this approach didn't succeed, for the groups merely used these occasions for fighting and shouting at each other.

Sherif then confronted the hostile groups with problem situations that could be solved only if the two units *cooperated* with each other. First, a water shortage "suddenly developed," and all the boys had to ration themselves. Next, Sherif offered to show the whole camp an exciting movie—but to see it, both

units had to pool their resources. And one time when all the boys were particularly hungry, the transportation for their food "broke down." It could be fixed only if both groups worked together quickly and effectively.

Sherif reports that his technique succeeded beautifully. The two groups did indeed cooperate—reluctantly at first, but more and more willingly as their initial efforts were reinforced.

Before the crises occurred, almost none of the boys had friendships outside their units. Afterward, some 30 percent of the friendships were inter-group rather than in-group. During the hostile period, about one-third of the members of each group rated the members of the other group as being "stinkers," "smart-alecks," or "sneaky." Afterward, less than 5 percent of the boys gave the members of the other group such highly unfavorable ratings.

Effects of Group Membership on Perception

Group membership has a strong effect on perception. For instance, during the hostile period, several of the boys were asked to estimate how many jellybeans were in a jar. When the boys were told the jellybeans had been collected by a member of their own group, the boys tended to *overestimate*. When told the candies had been collected by a member of the other group, however, the boys tended to *underestimate*.

In a similar study reported in Henri Tajfel's 1982 book *Social Identity and Intergroup Relations*, British boys were given a simple perceptual task to perform. The task involved estimating the number of dots that flashed on a screen. Then each boy was taken aside individually. Half were told they were "overestimators" as far as guessing dots was concerned. The rest were informed they were "underestimators." Next, each subject was asked to divide a sum of money between two other boys—one supposedly an "overestimator," the other supposedly an "underestimator." As you might guess, the subjects tended to award more money to someone they thought *shared their own trait* than to someone they perceived as "being different."

Question: Do you join groups because they are made up of people like yourself? Or do you join groups and then *become* similar to the people who make up the group?

Social Identity Theory versus Social Learning Theory

Henri Tajfel had a strong influence on many social psychologists in England. Tajfel explained most group behaviors in terms of what he called "Social Identity Theory." According to Tajfel, you first define *who you are*. Then you join groups of other people whom you *perceive* as being similar to you in one way or another.

Tajfel believes that, at some point in your life, you "categorize" all the people around you into various groups. Then you deliberately affiliate with some of those groups—but not with others. The groups you join *define your social identity*. As Tajfel puts it, social identity is "the portion of an individual's self-concept that results from knowledge of his or her membership in some social groups together with the value and emotional significance attached to that membership."

Tajfel further presumes that you wish to "attain or maintain a positive social identity." Therefore, he says, you are strongly motivated to distinguish between *your* groups and *other* groups by assigning positive traits to your groups and negative traits to others. Tajfel suggests that one major reason people are prejudiced against others is because of this need to "maintain a positive social identity."

As you might surmise, many American social psychologists disagree strongly with Tajfel. For instance, according to social learning theory, you typically are pushed into groups by your environment. Then you *learn* the group's norms and adhere to them (rather than picking groups in terms of norms you already have.) Thus, if your group *happens* to take a preju-

diced view toward some other group, you are likely to *acquire* this prejudice as a consequence of group membership. But because the prejudice is *learned*, it can be *unlearned* through experience.

In fact, the truth seems to lie somewhere between these two extremes. As we noted earlier, you are "born into" family, religious, and other types of groups. You then take on the values of these groups through the *socialization* process during your early years. But, later on, you obviously pick some groups to join because the members share values you already have. And then you become even more like the members of the groups you've voluntarily joined.

Question: Suppose you voluntarily joined a group, and then discovered that other members of the group strongly rejected someone who was a good friend of yours. How would you resolve this conflict?

Conflicting Attitudes

When you feel conflict *within yourself*, as Festinger has shown, it is often because your hold two or more attitudes that are dissonant. And when hostility arises *between two groups*, as Sherif has demonstrated, it is often their norms or group attitudes that are in conflict. Turning enemies into friends thus is sometimes a matter of changing their attitudes and actions toward one another.

In the next chapter we will take a careful look at how attitudes are formed, how consistent they are, how they are changed, and how attitudes relate to behaviors.

Question: Suppose you wished to help a group of whites get along better with a group of blacks. What would you try to do, and what changes would you hope to make in the attitudes and attributions of *both* groups in order to promote cooperation?

Summary

1. A **group** is a set of persons considered as a **social system**—a collection of two or more individuals who are psychologically related to or dependent upon one another and share common goals.

2. **Interaction groups** are made up of individuals who have frequent face-to-face encounters and who share **common attitudes**.

3. One of the major characteristics of any group is the **shared acceptance of group rules** by all the members.

4 The more similar the members, the more **cohesive** the group and the more **homogeneous** it becomes.

5 The more cohesive a group, the more **commitment** the members are likely to have toward the group and its goals.

6 Our **reference groups** are those we look to as social **models** or **norms**.

7 Reference groups give us **feedback** on our behavior by rewarding movements toward and punishing movements away from the **group norm**.

8 Whenever we make a judgment or give an opinion that is different from one shared by other group members, we typically find ourselves under strong psychological **pressure to conform** more closely to the group standard or norm.

9 Conformity behavior can be explained in terms of Helson's **Adaptation-level Theory**. A-L Theory states that judgments, perceptions, and attitudes are influenced by three factors—the stimulus, the background in which the stimulus appears, and the personality and past experience of the individual under pressure.

10 Some people are **negative conformers** who tend to move away from the group norm, no matter what they perceive it as being.

11 Milgram's research suggests that, when given orders from a higher authority, most of us tend to show **obedience** even if we sometimes end up hurting ourselves or others. We are particularly likely to obey orders if the people around us are doing so.

12 Latané's **theory of social impact** states that the impact of the social environment is determined by the **strength, immediacy**, and the **number** of people around you. **Bystander apathy** occurs in part because groups tend to **dilute** feelings of responsibility.

13 **Cognitive dissonance** develops when you hold two conflicting attitudes. According to Festinger, all people act to **reduce dissonance**, usually by changing the way they **perceive** the situation rather than by changing their actual behaviors.

14 Sherif has shown that **inter-group conflicts** can be reduced if the groups are either **threatened** by an outside danger or **rewarded** for working toward a common goal.

(Continued from page 661.)

"All right, Mr. Kraus, please calm down and tell me what happened."

Norm Kraus leaned forward excitedly, hardly noticing the hardness of the chair in Professor Ward's office. "Well, the Blake experiment worked just like it was supposed to. I put a flashlight bulb inside an empty cocoa box to make the auto-kinetic light, and I got some friends to act as stooges. We made tape recordings of their voices, but I wanted to start with the situation where the subject was sitting right in the middle of my four friends."

Taking a quick breath, the young man hurried on before Ward could interrupt him.

"I got an undergraduate named Dan Gorenflo to volunteer for the experiment. I introduced Dan to the stooges, and then we all went into the lab. The cocoa box was hidden behind a black curtain that I didn't open until the lights were off when nobody could see what it was. Then I gave Dan and my friends the song and dance about airplanes moving on the horizon, turned off the overhead light, and left them to adapt to the dark."

"Sounds fine so far," Ward said.

Norm Kraus smiled. "The lab next door was my control room, where I ran the experiment. I could open the curtains, turn the flashlight bulb off and on, and talk to the subjects over a loudspeaker. I put a mike right in front of Dan so I could hear his voice. And, of course, I could also hear the stooges and make sure they said what they were supposed to say."

Professor Ward nodded in an absent-minded fashion. "Yes, yes, just like Blake and his student did it. But how did your stooges know what to say?"

"I gave them their responses written out on a card."

Ward's eyebrows rose a millimeter or so. "And they read these numbers in the dark?"

Norm smiled broadly. "I wrote the numbers in dark-glow paint. The stooges could just make out the numbers if they squinted at them."

"Didn't this Dan Gorenflo fellow get suspicious?"

"No, sir. You see, I gave him a card with a scale marked across it in centimeters, also in dark-glow paint. It looked just like the cards the stooges had. I told them to look at their cards frequently to make sure they could judge how far 1 centimeter was."

Professor Ward coughed politely. "Not half bad. But how did it go?"

Norm beamed. "Beautifully, at least at first. I was sitting in the control room recording Dan's reactions. The first trial, he seemed to ignore the group. But on the next 14 trials, he hit the midpoint of their judgments right on the nose. I couldn't believe it! I was so excited at the end of the test that I rushed over to the next room to congratulate everybody and turn on the lights. And that's when it happened."

"Dare I ask what?"

"Well, Dan came bolting out of the lab and went rushing down the hall toward the toilet. I had to chase after him to catch up. He was shouting at me over his shoulder, 'Don't believe a word I said. You can't use my results.'"

"Did he tell you why?"

Norm nodded. "Yes, sir, he did. He said, 'You put me in a bad seat. I couldn't see the damned light at all. I just said whatever the other subjects said. You shouldn't do things like that, it curdles the stomach.'" Norm frowned rather

theatrically. "And then Dan rushed into the john and was sick all over the place."

Ward picked up his pipe and stuffed it with tobacco. After a moment, he asked, "Why do you think Dan responded that way? Were the group pressures to conform that strong?"

Norm tried to hide the smirk that kept creeping over his face. "Serendipity, sir. After I left your office the last time, I looked the word up."

"Oh, yes, the Persian fairy tale about the three princes of Serendip, or Sri Lanka, as it is called today. They were always going out on expeditions to search for something like iron and discovering a mountain of gold instead. Serendipity is the gift for finding very valuable things you weren't really looking for. Invaluable in scientific research, serendipity is." The Professor smiled rather warmly. "And you think you have the gift?"

Norm attempted a modest grin. "Well, I did luck onto something strictly by accident. It isn't every day you can upset a subject that much without laying hands on him."

"All right, Mr. Kraus, tell me exactly what happened."

Norm Kraus leaned back in the hard chair and relaxed. "Well, at first I couldn't figure it out, and neither could the stooges. But then I checked out each piece of equipment, just to make sure. Guess what I found?"

"I'm veritably breathless with anticipation," Ward said, smiling with encouragement.

"The flashlight bulb had burned out! As far as I can tell, the light went on during the first trial, but then it got shorted or something. I kept saying the light would go on

. . . NOW. And the stooges kept giving their reports. But for the last 14 trials, the light simply didn't appear."

"Why didn't your friends, the stooges, notice it?"

"They were too busy trying to read the night-glow numbers on their little cards. Besides, it didn't matter to them if they couldn't see the light at all. Their job was just to read off their reports."

Professor Ward poked at the tobacco in his pipe with a match. "But why did the poor young man get sick?"

"How would you like it if you were sitting smack in the middle of four people who all acted as if they could see something that you saw once, but couldn't see thereafter? Dan told me later that he looked and looked, but the light just wasn't there. He thought maybe he was going crazy. But he didn't want to upset the experiment, so he just sat there and gave the same reports the stooges were giving. He couldn't disobey orders by leaving, and he couldn't violate the group standard by saying he didn't see what everybody else was seeing. The stress was so great that his stomach curled up into a tight little ball. He said he'd never felt so much pressure in his life."

A stern tone crept back into Professor Ward's voice. "I hope you explained things to him and tried to make amends."

"Oh, yes sir. I took him over to the clinic and had the doctors examine him. They gave him a tranquilizer and two aspirins and told him to call them in the morning if he didn't feel better. While we were walking back to Dan's place from the clinic, I told him about what we had done, and why. Now he wants to be a stooge if we continue the experiment."

"If?"

Norm sighed dramatically. "Well, sir, it does seem we've discovered an interesting way to measure psychosomatic responses to social stress. I was talking to some of the doctors at the clinic about it. They thought we might do some joint research. You know, trying to figure out how group pressures toward conformity can lead to ulcers and hypertension and things like that. I realize that's not a replication of the Blake experiment, and I wouldn't want to break the rule . . ."

Professor Ward interrupted. "Mr. Kraus, we have *two* departmental rules about graduate students. The first is that they should begin by repeating a piece of published research. The second rule is that, if students find something exciting on their own while performing the replication, we expect them to follow it up. You wouldn't want to violate our departmental standards, now would you?"

Norm Kraus smiled slyly. "Oh, no sir."

"Good work, Norm. I'm pleased with your progress. Let me know if I can help, and keep me posted on how you come along. And by the way, why don't you call me Ron instead of Professor Ward?"

Norm could hardly believe his ears. "Yes sir, Profes . . . I mean, bloody good of you, Ron!"

Recommended Readings

Corey, G. & Corey, M.S. (1982). *Groups: Process and practice* (2nd ed.). Monterey, Cal.: Brooks/Cole.

Festinger, L. (Ed.). (1980). *Retrospections on social psychology.* New York: Oxford Press.

Latané, B. (1981). The psychology of social impact. *American Psychologist, 36*(4), 343–355.

Tajfel, H. (Ed.). (1982). *Social identity and intergroup relations.* Cambridge, England: Cambridge University Press.

Did You Know That...

- You are probably exposed to 1,500 different ads each day of your life?

- Although you may reject propaganda if it comes from what you consider to be a biased source, later on you may forget the source and be influenced by the message?

- Many student activists of the 1960's have found ways to maintain their "radical attitudes" despite pressures to change?

- People involved in presenting propaganda are often more affected by it than is the intended audience?

- Propaganda messages that arouse a high degree of fear are usually not as effective as low-fear appeals that tell you how to cope with the threatening situation?

- Some youthful offenders who were exposed to a "scared straight" program actually became *worse* than did similar offenders not treated with scare tactics?

- You cannot make valid ethical judgments about persuasive attempts unless you understand how strongly influenced you are by the attitudes and behaviors of the people around you?

25

Persuasion, Communication, and Attitude Change

"The Mind Benders"

Hey, listen, I need your advice. Did I do a dumb thing, or didn't I? *I* think I won the contest. And that's the most important thing, isn't it? But there's this little voice, down in my gut, that's sort of laughing at me.

It all happened this way. I was walking through the Psych Building yesterday, and I saw this notice on the bulletin board:

SUBJECTS NEEDED FOR PSYCHOLOGICAL EXPERI-MENT!!!
EARN $2 AN HOUR (AND MAYBE MORE)
WE NEED SUBJECTS WHO ARE HIGHLY COMPETITIVE

FOR STUDY OF DECISION-MAKING PROCESSES
MEET TUESDAY AT 3 P.M. IN ROOM 108

Well, competition is my middle name. I mean, like, didn't I win the silver medal in the 100-meter dash my senior year in high school? (I would have won the gold if I hadn't stumbled on a pebble, you know.) And don't I try to set the curve on every exam I take? (And like I probably told you, I did that very thing on the first organic chemistry quiz last year.) I mean, I *like* winning, and that's no joke.

So, like yesterday was

Tuesday, and it was 2:45 when I saw the notice. I was supposed to meet my buddy Nick Suino at the dojo to practice karate. I want to be a black belt some day, and so does Nick. (Nick practices at the dojo more than I do, but I think I've got more natural talent, if you know what I mean.) Anyhow, I knew Nick would understand if I was a little late. And besides, I needed the money to pay for my karate lessons. So I cruised down the hall to room 108.

There were half a dozen people there already, and a couple more came in right afterwards. I didn't know any of them, but they looked like a bunch of turkeys to me. Not a real winner in the bunch, if you know what I mean. I sat and watched them for a few minutes, trying to psych them out. And then this nice looking lady walked in through the door.

"Hello," she said in a friendly tone of voice. "I'm Dr. Abbott, and I'd like to thank you all for showing up. I'm interested in how people make decisions, and I need your help in my research. If you want to stay and be a subject in today's experiment, it shouldn't take more than an hour of your time. I'll pay you two dollars for taking part, and there's a possibility that you can win a bit more than that."

Hey, man, that really turned me on! So I listened to this Dr. Abbott very carefully indeed. She smiled this nifty smile of hers, and then she said something kind of funny. "Before we go any farther," she said, "I have to give you a warning. We're going to play a game today. If you're lucky, you can win a little bit of money. However, if you're not careful, you might lose not only the two dollars I'll give you, but some of your own money as well."

Now, you know me. I'm the most careful guy who ever lived, particularly when it comes to those green notes with the dead presidents on them. So I knew her warning wasn't aimed at me. But it must have touched a sore point with some of the turkeys, because a couple of them got right up and left. Got rid of the losers, as far as I was concerned.

Then this Dr. Abbott passed out some forms. You know, the kind they always give subjects—name, ad-dress, student ID number, that sort of thing. I wrote my name, JIM SAMONS, in big block letters like I always do, and filled in the rest of the blanks. Then I took the form up to Dr. Abbott and handed it to her with a great, big smile. "When do we start?" I asked.

"As soon as everyone hands in their forms," she said, smiling back.

"Great," says I, and sat down again. Pretty soon the turkeys had all given Dr. Abbott their forms, and then things got rolling.

First, Dr. Abbott gave us all two crisp new one-dollar bills. Nice feel to them. "That money is yours, for partici-pating in the experiment," she said. "You can quit right now, and be two dollars ahead of the game. That's fine with me. But if you want to stick around, you might win a little more."

Nobody left, specially not me. Then she pulled another dollar out of her pocket and held it up for us to look at.

"See this dollar bill? I'm going to auction it off to the highest bidder. If you can get it for less than a dollar, of course, you'll make money on the deal."

Well, I mean, who in his right mind would pay more than a buck for a buck? says I to myself. Big deal.

Then this Dr. Abbott added a twist. She said, "However, there are a couple of rules you have to understand. First, we'll start the bidding at a nickle, and you have to make your bids in 5¢ incre-ments. So the next bid would be a dime, then 15¢, and so forth. If you make the *highest bid*, you pay me what you bid and I give you the dollar. Those are the easy rules. The hard rule is this: If you make the *second-highest bid*, you have to give me what you bid but you *don't* get the dollar in return."

What is this? I said to my-self. And then I saw the beauty of it. If she just gave the dollar to the highest bid-der, the first person to offer her 95¢ would take the buck. But if some turkey offered her 95¢, and I then offered her a full dollar, I'd win abso-lutely nothing because I'd have to give her back the money right away. But the *turkey would be stuck with losing 95¢!* Hey, what a great game this was going to be! Because you had to decide how much you were willing to risk losing as well as figuring out how much you wanted to win.

"Now," Dr. Abbott said, "How many of you want to participate in the auction?"

A few more turkeys exited at this point, but I stuck up my hand. This was going to be a great contest of wills. I just hoped I wouldn't chicken out too early in the game because, of course, I didn't want to be second-highest no matter what.

We all gathered round Dr. Abbott. "Okay," she said, "Let's start the bidding at a nickle. Who wants to offer me 5¢ for this dollar?"

"I do," says I.

"Ten cents," says a turkey. Another bids 15¢, another 20¢, and we soon got right up to half a buck. "Fifty-five cents," says I.

Funny thing. At this point, everybody stopped for a few moments. I figured I had the buck won right then. But after a few seconds, the guy who had bid 50¢ upped the ante to 60¢. I found out later his name was Tracey Winter-meyer. I guess he figured he didn't want to lose half a buck, and I couldn't blame him. As for me, I knew I couldn't lose. So I bid 65¢, and this Tracey cat immediately said 70¢. I bid 75¢. Eighty cents, he says, and I bid 85¢ right away. Ninety cents, the idiot says, and I offer 95¢ right away. I mean, I was determined to win, even if it was only a nickle.

Well, Tracey scratched his chin and mumbled to himself for a while. Then, can you believe it? The dumb jerk actually bid a dollar! I mean, bidding a dollar for a dollar!

Then it was my turn to cogitate. Because it suddenly occurred to me that I was going to lose, no matter what, thanks to this idiot's stupidity in trying to outbid me. If I quit now, I'd owe Dr. Abbott 95¢. Oh, I'd still make $1.05, since I had her two bucks to start with. So I was still playing with her money, so to speak. But if I bid $1.05, I'd only owe her a nickle and I'd make $1.95 since I would win the dollar.

Unfortunately, this Tracey dumbbell wouldn't leave well enough alone. "I bid $1.10," says he.

I thought about that for a while. Obviously this cat had an ego problem, and I had to keep that fact in mind. So I casually smiled at him, friendly like, and bid $1.15.

But the jerk immediately jumped to a buck twenty. A buck and a quarter, says I. A buck thirty says he.

Hum, says I, suddenly feeling trapped. This can go on all day, and it's only going to get worse. I've got to make a dramatic move, something that will force him to give in.

Two bucks! says I.

Tracey gave that bold move of mine considerable thought. Then he sort of whispered, two-oh-five.

I've got him on the ropes! He's weakening, and if I just make a large enough gesture, he can back out gracefully. So I smiled again and casually said, I bid FOUR BIG BUCKS.

A sickly look spread over the poor guy's face. "I guess I quit," says he.

The kid wins again! says I.

"Yes, you won the dollar," Dr. Abbott said. "But you've got to pay me four dollars for it." So I coughed up the two bucks she had given me, plus a dollar of my own cold cash and let her keep the dirty dollar she had put up to auction. Then she collected $2.05 from Tracey because he had the second highest bid. He looked a sick sort of green.

Dr. Abbott told the other turkeys they could leave, but she asked me and Tracey to stick around. Once we were

alone, she offered us our money back plus the two dollars we started with if we would answer some questions. Which we were glad to do, I kid you not.

The questions? Oh, things like what we were thinking about as we made each bid, and why we kept on going. What we hoped to gain, and when we realized that we were likely to lose a bundle if we kept on bidding.

Finally, she asked both of us why we didn't offer to split the difference with each other so that nobody would lose.

Well, I mean, I knew the answer to that. There's got to be a *winner*, doesn't there? And that means somebody's got to lose, and I knew it just wasn't going to be me. Like I told you, I'm a winner.

So, Dr. Abbott told us both to go to the library and look up a book by Allan Teger called *Too Much Invested to Quit*. I'm going to do that any day now.

I talked to my friend Nick about all this, and he thinks I'm the biggest turkey of them all. So, that's why I decided to ask you what you think.

I mean, I *was* the winner, wasn't I?

(*See related story on page 705.*)

Attitudes

At the start of Chapter 23, we listed five significant issues that concern social psychologists. One of these issues dealt with what the *content* of social psychology should be. Namely, should researchers and theorists pay attention to such internal processes as *attitudes*? Or should they focus almost entirely on measurable outputs, such as *behaviors*? More to the point, perhaps, can you predict what people will *do* if you know their attitudes, and vice versa? We will deal with the attitude-behavior issue (as best we can) in this chapter.

Another issue we raised in Chapter 23 was that of the "individual versus larger social systems." So far, we've looked mostly at social psychology from the individual's point of view. In

You are probably exposed to more than 1500 advertisements a day.

this chapter, we will try to discover how groups, organizations, and societies try to *influence* the behavior of their various sub-systems (including individuals).

And, as we noted, a third important problem in social psychology has to do with the *relative* emphasis put on theoretical or on practical issues. We will save most of our discussion of applications for the next (and concluding) chapter. But, as you will soon learn, this chapter touches more on the "real world" than on the laboratory. Take, for example, advertising . . .

Ads and Attitudes

What brand of toothpaste do you use? No matter what your answer, there's a much more interesting question to ask: How did you happen to pick that particular brand? Whatever reason you give, chances are that you probably won't list *advertising* as the factor behind your choice. And yet, if you think about it, how would you have known about this brand if it had never been advertised? Furthermore, if you were subjected to "blind" tests (where you couldn't tell which brand you were using), are you absolutely confident you could pick your favorite toothpaste or brand of beer, soup, or cigarette from others on the market?

Most of us like to think our decisions to buy a particular product, to vote for a certain politi-

cian, or our opinions about war and sex and minority groups are *rational* decisions. However, while we do sometimes think through such matters logically, our viewpoints are often created *unconsciously*, without our being aware of how various forces in our social environments shape our thoughts and preferences. One such force is advertising.

You probably encounter about 1,500 ads each day of your life. Americans spend more money each year on advertising than they do on education, or on pollution control, mental health, poverty relief, or scientific research. If the advertisers didn't believe they could influence your attitudes toward their products—whether or not you were aware of their efforts—would they spend so much?

Whenever a teacher critizes or praises a certain theory, whenever a religious leader preaches, whenever a parent "lectures" or a friend offers advice—aren't these people trying to affect your attitudes? And whenever you "dress up to make a good impression," or compliment someone in authority, aren't you "advertising" too?

In the past several chapters we have talked at length about how attitudes (or personality traits or types of behavior) are created. In this chapter, suppose we look at why attitudes are important, why some of them remain fairly stable throughout our lives, and why other attitudes appear to be so changeable. We will then discuss the relationship between attitudes and behaviors, and the ethics involved in trying to persuade people to change.

Question: How has the author of this book attempted to influence your attitudes toward psychology?

Attitude Stability

In an earlier chapter we defined an attitude as a relatively enduring way of thinking, feeling, and behaving toward an object, person, group, or idea. And, as we noted, attitudes almost always involve some bias or pre-judging on your part. When you *label* someone as "stingy" or "psychotic," you both state an attitude and reveal the way in which you perceive the person. In a sense, then, attitudes are *perceptions* (cognitive schemas) that involve emotional feelings, and that predispose you to act in a certain way.

You could not do without attitudes, for many reasons. To begin with, the attitude (or schema) you have of someone or of some object allows you to *predict the future behavior* of that person or thing. If you made no pre-judgments about things, you would have trouble walking across a street or carrying on even the simplest of social conversations. For example, when you tell a man wearing an ecology button that you "hate pollution," you not only can predict the man's response but also influence his attitude toward (or perception of) you.

Question: How do attitudes help reduce social stress?

Attitudes and Memories

A second important aspect of attitudes has to do with memory. As you learned in earlier chapters, you seem to file your experiences in Long-term Memory according to certain *categories*. That is, you attach "cognitive labels" to the important features of the experience, and then file the memory according to these "labels." When you try to remember something that happened in the past, you search your memory files using this same set of cognitions. Another word for "labels," of course, is *attitudes*.

Psychologists believe that the more you know about a person, thing, or idea, the more *stable* your attitude will usually be. Likewise, the more strongly you feel about something, the more difficult it will probably be to get you to change the "memory labels" attached to that thing. Furthermore, the better your attitude allows you to predict future events or inputs, and the more you are rewarded for holding a certain percept, the less susceptible that percept or attitude is to being changed.

Since the attitudes of individuals are affected by the groups to which they belong, *attitude consistency* is also a property of social groups and organizations. Generally speaking, the more important a given attitude is to the continued functioning of a group, the less likely it is that group members will give up or change this attitude.

Question: Studies show that most college students have attitudes very similar to those held by their parents. Can you think of at least five reasons why this might be the case?

Newcomb's Study of Bennington Women

As Theodore Newcomb notes, liberal arts colleges are populated by professors who often have very liberal political opinions. When a student from a politically conservative family arrives on such a campus, the student often comes under fairly intense social pressure to change her or his attitudes. If you were such a student, do you think you would change, or would you retain your old attitudes despite the pressure?

Bennington College

Newcomb answered this question many years ago. At the time he began his research, he was teaching at Bennington, a woman's college in Vermont noted for its fine programs in the liberal arts. Because the student body was limited to about 600, Newcomb was able to work with the entire college population in his study of political attitudes.

Most of the women attending Bennington in the mid-1930's came from wealthy and rather conservative homes. The faculty members, however, were quite liberal in their views. Indeed, they felt duty-bound to familiarize the students with the social and political implications of a Depression-torn America and a war-threatened world. Therefore, the faculty encouraged the students to become politically active and socially concerned.

The college itself, nestled between the Taconic and the Green mountains of Vermont, was physically isolated from much of the rest of the world. The nearest town, a village of less than 15,000 people, offered few excitements. The students visited the town infrequently, and went home for the weekend less than once a month. Hence, the students made up what advertising executives call "a captive audience."

Student Reference Groups

In the first part of his research, Newcomb found that the more prestige or *status* a woman

Theodore Newcomb

Studies of people who belonged to the "Free Speech" movement in 1964 show that they have maintained their radical beliefs by seeking out environments that shelter them from conflicting viewpoints.

had among her fellow students, the more likely it was that she was also very liberal in her views. Conservative students typically were looked down upon; liberal students were very much looked up to. Seniors were significantly less conservative than were freshmen.

Under these conditions, the entire college population acted rather like a *reference group* that rewarded liberal attitudes and punished political conservatism. Those women who *identified* with the college community tended to become much more liberal during their four years at Bennington. By their own admission, many of them were quite conscious of how they had changed. As one woman put it, "what I most wanted here was intellectual approval of teachers and the more advanced students. Then I found you can't be reactionary and be intellectually respectable."

Those women who *resisted* the liberal college tradition tended to identify more with their parents than with their classmates. As one woman said, "I'd like to think like the college leaders, but I'm not bold enough and I don't know enough. So the college trend means little to me. I guess my family influence has been strong enough to counterbalance the college influence." Newcomb notes, incidentally, that this woman was given to severe emotional upsets and told the college staff she felt "alone and helpless except when with her parents."

Question: How many Bennington women would have become politically liberal had they lived at home and commuted to their classes?

What if they had taken most of their courses by television and seldom met their teachers or other students?

25 Years Later

To find out how their attitudes would change over time, Newcomb followed 150 of the most liberal of these women for the next 25 years of their lives. Although he originally had suspected the students might revert to a more conservative position, this turned out not to be the case with many of them. In fact, during the entire 25 years, most of the women remained liberal in their outlooks *despite family pressures*. But why?

Newcomb reports that most of these women *deliberately* set out to remain liberal in spite of their social backgrounds. They tended to select liberal (or non-conservative) husbands who would reinforce their political views. They found little pockets of liberalism in their environments and tried to stay entirely within these pockets. And they kept in close touch with their Bennington classmates who were also liberal. These students also tended to ignore those "old classmates" who weren't as liberal as they.

Newcomb believes that if maintaining a given attitude is important enough, you will consciously or unconsciously select environments that will continue to support that attitude. You may also shut out incoming sensory messages that might tend to disrupt the attitudes you already hold (a form of *autistic hostility*).

1960's Student Activists

Writing in the July 1981 *American Psychologist*, Alberta J. Nassi reports data that confirm Newcomb's findings. In 1964, highly liberal students at the University of California at Berkeley formed a loosely knit organization called the "Free Speech Movement." As a protest against university policies, they tried to shut down the school by staging a variety of demonstrations. Many of the students were arrested. Nassi looked at how these "student activists" had fared 15 years afterwards. She reports they "do not appear to have grown out of the political philosophy that galvanized their activist youth." That is, they still hold relatively radical or liberal attitudes toward most things. Nassi notes they have maintained these attitudes much as the Bennington women did—by seeking environments that would protect them from change. Most of them had found jobs in "social service" and "creative" occupations, and tended to socialize with people who held similar views.

The Newcomb and Nassi studies are among a very few aimed at measuring *stability* of attitudes. Attitude *change* is much easier to investigate, in no small part because the subjects need not be studied over such a long time span. Indeed, it seems that much of what we know about attitude stability comes from experi-

"WHAT YOU WANT IS 'MACHO', THE MAGAZINE THAT TELLS YOU HOW TO WEAR YOUR SHIRT OPEN, PUT ON SOME GOLD CHAINS, AND HAVE YOUR HAIR STYLED SO THAT YOUR OWN MOTHER WOULDN'T RECOGNIZE YOU."

ments designed to change people's opinions. So now let us look at the factors that bring about shifts in attitudes. Perhaps this information will be useful not only if you wish to change someone's mind—but also if you wish to protect yourself against the influence of the millions of people who would like to persuade you to be different than you presently are.

Question: Ethnic and religious minority groups often tend to "flock together" even when they are economically free to do otherwise. How might this tendency be related to a desire to maintain attitude stability within the group?

Persuasion and Attitude Change

Suppose you are in the market for a new automobile. You shop around, looking at Fords, Plymouths, Chevrolets, AMC Eagles, and a number of other cars. As you can now see, you come to this situation with a number of biases, or attitudes, about cars in general and these automobiles in particular. If your prior attitude toward Plymouths is highly favorable, how might an AMC sales person try to change your viewpoint?

In 1940, Solomon Asch pointed out there are two basic ways to induce attitude change toward an object like an automobile. The first way is to change the *object* or product itself, so you are forced to change your attitude toward the car. The second way is to leave the car "as is" but somehow get you to change your *perception* of its good and bad points. In either case, the sales person must somehow get certain types of information across to you. For without new *sensory inputs* of some kind, your attitudes will presumably remain very stable. Thus, the most important aspect of **persuasion** is the *flow of communication* from the outside world into your nervous system.

Question: What sorts of television commentators are you most likely to watch or to place faith in?

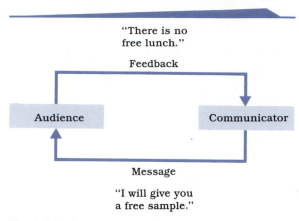

"There is no
free lunch."

Feedback

Audience   Communicator

Message

"I will give you
a free sample."

Fig. 25.1 Successful communication depends on feedback from the audience to the communicator.

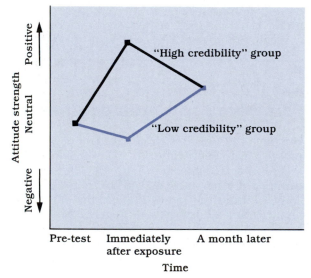

Fig. 25.2 The "sleeper effect." Effects of exposure to propaganda on "effectiveness of atomic submarines."

The Communication Process

Psychologists tend to look at persuasive communication as having four main factors—the communicator, the message, the audience, and the feedback loop between the audience and the communicator.

The *communicator* is the person (or group) trying to induce the attitude change. As we will see, the way that the audience *perceives* the communicator often affects the readiness with which the audience will change.

The *message* is the information the communicator transmits to the audience. The type of language or pictures used, and the channel through which the communicator chooses to transmit the message, can be of critical importance.

The *audience* is the person or group whose attitude is to be changed. Obviously a clever communicator will wish to know as much as possible about the personalities and attitudinal characteristics of the audience in order to make the message as persuasive as possible.

Until fairly recently, the *audience-communicator feedback loop* was perhaps the least-studied aspect of the communication process. Yet it is of crucial importance. For unless the communicator knows what type of response the audience *actually* makes to the message, the communicator is very likely to misjudge the success of the persuasive project (see Fig. 25.1).

Let us see, then, what kinds of experimental evidence social scientists have provided, so we can understand the effects of each of these four influences on persuasion.

Question: Why do you think the audience-communicator feedback loop was so little studied until recently?

The Communicator

If your best friend told you that a given product was incredibly good, would you be more likely to believe this communication than if you heard a TV announcer say the same thing on a television ad? Chances are you'd put more **credibility** in your friend's endorsement than in the TV announcer's. And credibility seems to be one of the most influential traits a communicator can possess.

The first reliable experiments on communicator credibility probably came from a group of Yale psychologists almost 30 years ago. This group of scientists, led by Carl I. Hovland and Irving L. Janis, were pioneers in the study of the communication process. Some of their early findings have stood the test of time. However, as we will see, many of their conclusions are of limited value because they were *laboratory* studies. And the real world is—for better or worse—much more complicated than scientific laboratories are. Suppose we first look at what Hovland, Janis, and their colleagues found. We will discuss the limitations of their findings a little later.

High-Credibility Sources

In one of the first of the Yale studies, Hovland and Walter Weiss tested the influence of "trustworthiness" (credibility) on attitude change. They began by making a list of "communicators" they figured were very trustworthy, and another list of communicators they figured few people would trust. The "high-credibility sources" included the *New England Journal of Biology and Medicine*, a Nobel-Prize-winning physicist, and *Fortune* magazine. The "low-credibility sources" included a noted gossip columnist, the Soviet newspaper *Pravda*, and a well-known American publication that specialized in scandals and sex-oriented stories. When Hovland and Weiss asked students to judge the credibility of these sources, about 90 percent of the subjects rated the first group as being very trustworthy and rated the second group as being exceptionally untrustworthy.

Next, Hovland and Weiss tested the "attitude toward the effectiveness of atomic submarines" in two similar groups of students. They found that most of the students were rather neutral about this highly complex topic. If we were plotting their attitudes on a graph, we would say the students were right in the middle—at the "neutral" point on the graph shown in Figure 25.2.

Hovland and Weiss then wrote a "message" in which they argued that atomic submarines would indeed be a very important weapon in any future war. They showed this message to the two groups of students. The first group was told the message came from one of the high-credibility sources (such as *Fortune*). The second group was informed the message came from one of the low-credibility sources. Immediately after exposing the students to the message, Hovland and Weiss retested their subjects' attitudes.

As you might guess, the subjects in the "high-credibility" group tended to accept the arguments. That is, their attitudes about the importance of atomic submarines became significantly more positive. The students in the "low-credibility" group tended to reject the arguments as being "biased and untrustworthy." If anything, their attitudes became slightly more negative.

Apparently you tend to move *toward* the position of someone you trust, and *away* from the position of someone you distrust—even if this movement involves giving up your original attitude.

Question: How does this study compare with the experiment on "negative conformity" mentioned in the last chapter?

Credibility (kred-ih-BILL-it-tee). From the Latin words meaning "worthy of lending money to." Literally, the power or ability to inspire belief.

Sleeper effect. As Hovland and Weiss showed, people tend to remember the facts of an argument rather well, but often forget the source of those facts. The credibility you place in a source may cause you to accept or reject a message as soon as you see or hear it. However, the facts are somehow "sleeping" in your Long-term Memory and will emerge on their own long after you have forgotten who told you those facts.

The "Sleeper Effect"

Had Hovland and Weiss stopped their work at this point, we might well have misunderstood the real importance of communicator credibility. However, they continued by retesting all their subjects a month later. To their surprise, they found significant attitude changes in both groups over this period of time. The attitudes of the "high-credibility" subjects became significantly *less* positive, while the attitudes of the "low-credibility" subjects became significantly *more* positive. As Fig. 25.2 suggests, the students had apparently forgotten the *source* of their information on submarines, but remembered the *arguments* rather well. Hovland and Weiss call this the **sleeper effect**.

The sleeper effect suggests that the credibility of a source has an immediate and often strong effect on whether you accept or reject incoming information. However, once the message has gotten through to you, chances are you will soon forget the source and recall only the information itself.

"Sleeper Effect" or "Delayed Treatment Effects"?

Writing in the December 1981 *Developmental Review*, Yale psychologist Victoria Seitz claims the sleeper effect is but one example of what she calls "delayed treatment effects." Seitz notes that children have many experiences during their developmental years that have no immediate effect on behavior. However, these experiences often have a strong influence at some future time. For example, children in "Head Start" programs often don't show much immediate progress. However, a year or two later, the children's cognitive development is often significantly better than that of similar youngsters not given the "Head Start" experience.

There are many other types of "delayed treatment effects" in the psychological literature. All of them tend to prove what we said at the start of Chapter 23: "An attitude is actually a sort of

The effects of early intervention, such as the Head Start Program, may be delayed until later in life.

Irving L. Janis

'cognitive structure' that allows you to process and respond to present inputs in an efficient manner. But an attitude is also a 'mental program' for *coding* experiences in order to store them in Long-term Memory." And as we learned in Chapter 15, memories are active, not passive. What you remember tomorrow depends not only on *what* you learned today, but also on your *attitude* toward what you learned today.

Credibility and "First Impressions"

A number of further experiments by Hovland, Janis, and their associates demonstrate that the factors that influence credibility are much the same as those that influence first impressions (see Chapter 23). People whom you like, or who are like you, or who seem to be act-

ing naturally rather than "playing roles," are people whom you typically trust. Persons with high social status—such as doctors, scientists, and church leaders—are somehow more believable than are people with low social status.

Writing in the *Polish Psychological Bulletin* in 1981, psychologist Stanislaw Mika states that credibility is higher if the communicator is a member of a positive reference group, and if the message is communicated in technical rather than "street" language. Particularly if the audience is made up of educated subjects, credibility is greater if you give the audience "both sides of the question" rather than just the side of things you're trying to promote. According to Mika, the perception of the communicator's credibility also depends on the level of anxiety of the recipient and the level of anxiety arousal of the message. Subjects with a high anxiety level tend to perceive the communicator who arouses strong anxiety as being less credible than someone who presents messages that do not evoke strong anxiety.

To summarize, it is your *perception* of the communicator—and the motives you *attribute* to this person—that determine how much you will be influenced.

Question: If you were trying to sell a cold remedy on television, what kinds of TV actors would you choose, and how would you have them dress?

The Message

In 1956, University of Michigan professor Sam Eldersveld decided to run for mayor in Ann Arbor as a "class project" to help his political science students learn about politics in the "real world." Eldersveld planned and carried out his campaign with the assistance of his students. The students not only performed several interesting experiments during the heat of the contest, they also managed to get their professor elected (he became a very effective mayor).

In one of the Ann Arbor studies, potential voters were approached in one of three ways. Either the voter received four mail appeals to vote, or the voter was contacted in person, or both. A fourth group of voters served as an "untreated control group." A much higher percentage of the voters contacted *in person* actually voted than did voters who received just mailings (or no messages at all). The combination of mail appeals and personal contact was no more effective than was just asking the voter in person.

In another study, Eldersveld compared the *content* of the appeals. Some voters were given highly *emotional* arguments—either by mail or by personal contact. Others were given very *rational* reasons for voting. As it turned out, the content of the message seemingly didn't much matter. But again, personal contact was much more effective in "bringing out the vote" than were mail appeals—no matter what the content of the appeals happened to be.

Question: How could you be sure that the voters sent messages by mail actually read them?

Fear-arousing Messages

Many of us seem to believe that people would behave in more socially acceptable ways if someone in authority just threatened them enough. In recent years, for instance, nation-wide campaigns against venereal disease, the use of hard drugs, cigarette smoking, and the dangers of not wearing seat belts have emphasized the "hellfire and damnation" approach. That is, the main thrust of the **propaganda** has been to describe in exquisite detail the terrible consequences of various types of misbehavior.

But are such threats really as effective as we sometimes think them to be? The experimental evidence suggests that the actual effects of "the punitive approach" are more subtle and complex than we might previously have guessed.

In 1953, Irving Janis and Seymour Feshback investigated the effects of fear-arousing communications on high school students. These scientists picked "dental hygiene" as their topic. They wrote three different 15-minute lectures on tooth decay. The first was a "high-fear" lecture that contained 71 references to pain, cancer, paralysis, blindness, mouth infections, inflamed gums, ugly or discolored teeth, and dental drills. The second or "moderate-fear" lecture was somewhat less threatening. But the third or "minimal-fear" lecture was quite different. It made no mention at all of pain and disease. Instead, the "minimal-fear" message suggested ways of *avoiding* cavities and decayed teeth through proper dental hygiene.

Janis and Feshback presented each of the three appeals to a different group of 50 high-school students (a fourth group of students heard no lecture at all and thus served as a con-

"AT LEAST WITH WASHINGTON AS PRESIDENT, WE WON'T HAVE A CREDIBILITY GAP TO WORRY ABOUT."

Persuasion and Attitude Change **695**

Although the prisoners who participated in the "Scared Straight" program enjoyed their attempts to "straighten out" juvenile offenders, there are conflicting reports on how effective the program actually was.

trol group). Janis and Feshback found that *immediately afterwards*, the subjects exposed to the "high-fear" lecture were highly impressed with what they heard. A week later, however, only 28 percent of the "high-fear" group had brushed their teeth more often, and 20 percent of them were actually *doing worse*. In marked contrast, the "low-fear" students were not particularly impressed with the lecture—but a week later 50 percent of them were "brushing better" and only 14 percent were doing a worse job.

The high-fear appeal apparently evoked strong emotional responses in the students, many of whom thought that being frightened was somehow "good for them." When it came to actually *changing behaviors*, though, the high-fear message simply didn't work as well as did the minimal-fear message. In fact, for reasons we will discuss in a moment, the high-fear propaganda seems to have had exactly the opposite long-term effect that you might have predicted.

Counter-propaganda

Propagandists often point out that it is not enough to change the attitudes an audience has. You must also make sure that the audience resists any further attempts that might push the audience back toward their original beliefs. Effective propaganda, then, not only causes attitude shifts but also protects against *counter-propaganda*.

A week after the high-school students in the Janis-Feshback experiment had listened to the dental hygiene lectures, the experimenters exposed the students to information that contradicted what they had originally been told. The students were then asked whether they believed this counter-propaganda or not.

Twice as many subjects in the high-fear group were affected by the counter-persuasion as were subjects in the minimal-fear group. Janis and Feshback conclude that "under conditions where people will be exposed to competing communications dealing with the same issues, the use of a strong fear appeal will tend to be less effective than a minimal appeal in producing stable and persistent attitude changes."

Question: Given the data on the long-term results of the "high-fear" approach, why do so many communicators still make use of this technique?

Fear and Failure

Why don't fear and threats work the way many people think they should? Janis and Feshback offer two reasons. First, there seems to be a tendency for people to *repress* frightening information. Second, our emotions can *arouse* us, but they don't always *direct* us in our thoughts and behaviors. Janis and Feshback believe that fear-inducing communications focus your attention on *problems* and not on *solutions*. You become excited by the terrifying message, but you don't know how to avoid or prevent the disaster the message warns you of. In fact, the fearful message may do little more than convince you that disaster is inevitable, and so you give up and do nothing at all.

In Chapter 14, we described G. Alan Marlatt's research on therapy with alcoholic patients. Marlatt discovered that when the treatment was primarily punishment oriented and "confrontational," many patients stopped drinking immediately. When tested a year later, however, most of these patients were actually *drinking more* than before they started therapy. When therapy consisted of teaching the patients "self-control skills," most patients showed an immediate but slight increase in alcohol consumption. A year or so later, though, these same patients were drinking significantly less than when therapy started. The parallels between the Janis-Feshbach studies and the Marlatt experiment are, in their own way, fairly striking.

Question: Given Marlatt's data, can you think of a third reason why fear and confrontation may fail in the long run?

Scared Straight

In the spring of 1979, a film called "Scared Straight" was shown on many American television stations. The movie shows how inmates at a prison in New Jersey used "scare tactics" to frighten troubled young people into avoiding further scrapes with the law. The youths spent several hours in the prison, mostly listening to the convicts describe the effects of homosexual rape, fights, and prison brutality. The film is highly dramatic, and implies strongly that the "Scared Straight" program has been a great success. The film won an Academy Award in 1979. After the movie was broadcast, many state legislatures debated whether or not to make such treatment compulsory for all juvenile offenders.

Unfortunately, the actual data did not support the effectiveness either of the first version of the program or of the film's fear-arousing message. A year after "Scared Straight" won its awards, Rutgers professor James O. Finckenauer reported a detailed study of the juvenile offenders involved in these jail visitations. Finckenauer discovered that only some 60 percent of the juveniles in the program avoided further arrest. By contrast, some 90 percent of highly similar offenders in Finckenauer's control group "went straight"

> **Deterrent** (dee-TURR-ent). From a Latin word meaning "to frighten, or to discourage from acting." Punishment is usually thought to be a highly effective deterrent that keeps "sane" people from committing crimes. In fact, many studies suggest that fear of punishment seldom keeps people from doing things that they really want to do, or that they find particularly rewarding.

without being scared. Worse than this, of 19 youngsters who had no criminal record before they visited the New Jersey prison, 6 later broke the law.

California psychologist Roy V. Lewis reports on a similar program in the June 1983 issue of *Criminal Justice and Behavior.* Several years ago, the inmates at San Quentin began a confrontational type of intervention they called the "Squires Program." Lewis reports that 53 delinquent young males who met with the San Quentin prisoners showed an immediate improvement in attitudes relative to 55 similar males in an untreated control group. However, a follow-up a year later showed no differences between the two groups in number or severity of subsequent criminal charges. In fact, those young men who were "high risk" delinquents actually did worse after being in the Squires Program than did similar "high risk" youths in the control group.

Question: Despite the negative data, the *prisoners* who actually confront the youthful offenders typically believe their programs are quite successful. How would their attitudes compare with the leaders of therapy groups (discussed in Chapter 22) who incorrectly believed that *all* members of their groups showed improvement?

Nothing Succeeds Like Success

According to *attribution theory*, you see your own actions as being a response to environmental circumstances. But you see the actions of others as being determined primarily by their personality or character traits. Therefore, you may believe that "punishment works" because others need a fear-evoking **deterrent** to keep their anti-social impulses under control. But the data show that many criminals—particularly youthful offenders—simply don't have the *social skills* to succeed in a complex environment. What would happen if juvenile delinquents were given skill training rather than being threatened?

Tim Walter

Carolyn Mills

In 1979, Carolyn Mills and Tim Walter gave an answer to this question. They reported achieving a marked reduction in anti-social behaviors among a group of youthful offenders who were given special training in how to get and hold a job. Mills and Walter began with a group of 76 young people aged 14–17 who had been arrested four times or more prior to the start of the experiment. Mills and Walter randomly selected 23 of the young people to be a "no-treatment control group." The other 53 were put into a behavioral training program.

In the first part of their program, Mills and Walter recruited a number of local business people who were willing to offer employment to youths "on probation." These business people signed contracts agreeing, among other things, to give the young people day-by-day feedback on their performance and to meet with the experimenters weekly to discuss the youths' progress.

Next, Mills and Walter asked the youths to make a list of the behaviors they thought would be *expected* of them while working. If the subjects could not guess, they were given a list of job-appropriate activities produced by the employers. The youths then "role played" the behaviors they thought would help them get and hold the job. They were rewarded for learning these skills and, once they were on the job, they got written feedback *daily* by the employer.

When the subjects had been successful "on the job" for a period of several weeks, Mills and Walter began helping the youths gain skills in handling personal and school-related problems (rather than focusing primarily on job-related tasks). All in all, the subjects were followed for a period of 18 months or more.

Mills and Walter report that more than 90 percent of the experimental subjects had no further arrests, while but 30 percent of the control subjects stayed out of trouble. Some 85 percent of the experimental subjects stayed in school, but only 14 percent of the control subjects did.

Mills and Walter note two further points of interest. At the beginning of their intervention program, their subjects got considerable verbal harassment from their peers for "giving in to the system." However, as the subjects began earning good paychecks, many of these peers voluntarily requested placement in the training program. Second, while the training program was fairly costly, the "re-arrest" rate among the trainees was so small that the juvenile court sponsoring the program ended up saving many thousands of dollars.

In summary, we might conclude that changing people's attitudes may be important—but teaching people the skills that will allow them to *maintain healthy attitudes* may be the best form of propaganda presently available to us.

Question: Does criticism or punishment for inappropriate behaviors *by itself* tell you what to do in order to succeed?

The Audience

In terms of Helson's Adaptation-level Theory, the "message" is a *stimulus* factor, while the social context in which the message appears is a *background* factor. The character traits and past experiences of the audience are, as you might expect, *personality* factors that affect how the audience will perceive and respond to the message.

Obviously, the most persuasive messages are those created with all three factors in mind. A good communicator thus attempts to discover as much as possible about the audience, and then *shapes* the message to suit both the occasion and the people receiving the message.

The Cincinnati Study

Knowing something about your audience doesn't always guarantee you will be able to get your message *through to them*, however. Several years ago, Shirley Star and Helen Hughes helped lead a monumental advertising campaign designed to inform the citizens of Cincinnati about the great value of the United Nations. Star and Hughes began by taking surveys to determine what people thought about the UN. The groups who knew the least about the UN (and who liked it the least) included the relatively uneducated, the elderly, and the poor.

Once Star and Hughes knew the characteristics of their target audience, they carried on a six-month "pro-United Nations" campaign. Unfortunately, the messages apparently reached or persuaded few of the target population. Instead, the propaganda was effective primarily with young people and with the better-educated and relatively well-to-do segment of the general public. These were, of course, the very people who were already favorably disposed toward the world organization.

In marked contrast to these results, studies by several investigators show that more than two-thirds of the American public learned about the assassination of President John F. Kennedy within 30 minutes after the news first broke. And more than 95 percent of the population knew about Kennedy's death within 90 minutes after the first radio bulletin hit the airwaves. The vast majority of the public, however, first learned about the assassination from *friends and relatives*, not from the news media.

Obviously mass communications *are* successful from time to time—but primarily when the "message" meets some need the audience has, or when the information imparted is so important or stimulating that people *talk to each other* about what has been printed or broadcast.

Question: How might you explain the response of the "target audience" in the Star and Hughes study in terms of *autistic hostility*?

Audience Responses

Why did the Cincinnati campaign fail? There probably are many different reasons. To begin with, we have no guarantee that Star and Hughes knew what kinds of messages would be most likely to reach their target audience (the poor, the uneducated, the elderly). Nor can we be sure that those involved in creating the propaganda knew what sorts of appeals would convince the targets to change their attitudes.

A more glaring mistake, however, was that Star and Hughes did nothing to establish feedback loops to monitor the *effects* of their propaganda campaign while it was going on. The Cincinnati communicators talked—the audience was merely supposed to listen and to respond appropriately. We will have more to say about this point in a moment.

The one "success story" in the Cincinnati study was that people *actually engaged* in the propaganda campaign showed significant attitude change in the desired direction. As they

Almost 95 percent of the US population knew about President John F. Kennedy's death within 90 minutes after the first news bulletin, but the vast majority learned about the assassination from friends and relatives, rather than from the news media.

worked on the project, this group of people apparently became more and more committed to making the study a success. Since the group was favorable toward the UN, anyone who joined the group was under strong pressure to conform to the group norm. These individuals also had the greatest exposure to the persuasive messages.

Question: How successful would the Mills and Walter study of juvenile offenders have been had the experimenters not monitored continuously the youths' actual "on the job" behaviors?

Mass Hysteria

Sometimes the audience receives a "message" not from a "communicator" but from other members of the audience itself. If the "message" is of the wrong kind, the result can be *mass hysteria*.

There are a surprisingly large number of mass hysteria cases in the psychological literature. Writing in the September 18, 1982 *Science News*, Wray Herbert states, "The earliest known occurrences of [mass] hysteria were in medieval Italy, where outbreaks of 'tarantism'—or dancing mania—were fairly common. Particularly in the summer, people would flock into the streets dancing maniacally until, exhausted, they collapsed." These days, according to Herbert, mass hysteria more likely leads to medical symptoms, such as nausea, vomiting, rashes of various kinds, headaches, and fainting.

Many cases of mass hysteria have appeared recently in schools. For example, in 1973 at a high school in Alabama, a couple of members of the marching band fainted while performing during a football game. Within a few minutes, 55 other members of the band became seriously ill. Six girls fainted, and 36 students had to be taken to the hospital. In a Louisiana high school, several girls got sick after hearing rumors that another student had fallen ill with typhoid fever. In a midwestern high school, a single case of gonorrhea was followed almost immediately by 84 cases of hysterical gonorrhea. And on May 21, 1979, a sixth-grade boy at an elementary school in Norwood, Massachusetts, fainted during assembly. Within a short time, one-third of the students became ill. By the end of the day, 34 severely ill children were hospitalized, and another 40 to 50 were treated at school.

Who Becomes Hysterical—and Why

According to Wray Herbert, outbreaks of hysteria typically follow a set pattern. First, a number of people in a group or organization happen to be anxious or aroused about something. Second, a new stimulus is introduced, such as a strange odor, or one person with legitimate medical problems becomes ill. At this point, the "contagious hysteria" occurs. Other people suddenly *interpret* their own arousal as a "sign of disease," and develop genuine **psychosomatic** symptoms.

Most victims of mass hysteria appear to be suffering from fairly severe stress. For example, in almost all the cases where high-school band members have become hysterically ill, the weather was hot, their clothing was uncomfortable, and (perhaps most important) their team was losing.

Question: How would you interpret "mass hysteria" in terms of the Hovland and Janis "communicator-message-audience-feedback" model? How might group pressures to conform add to the hysteria?

The Yale Studies: An Evaluation

As Richard Petty, Thomas Ostrom, and Timothy Brock point out in their 1981 book *Cognitive Responses in Persuasion*, the Yale studies by Hovland, Janis, and their associates dominated research in the field of social psychology in the 1950's. However, during the 1960's, many experimenters had difficulties in replicating some of this work. There seem to be three reasons for these difficulties.

First, Hovland and Janis assumed that what they found in the laboratory would readily translate to real-life situations. But that turned out not to be the case. The Star and Hughes study is a good example of why the Yale approach failed. In the *laboratory*—using college students as subjects—the Star and Hughes persuasive attempts would have succeeded. In *real life*—when the target audience was the poor and uneducated segment of the population—the message failed to get through. The Yale approach was tested on "willing student subjects," not "the unwilling general public." And the theory that Hovland and his group at Yale developed was far too simple to be applicable in most situations outside the laboratory.

Second, Hovland assumed that the "audience" was a passive receptacle into which the communicator poured a message. Indeed, Hovland once defined his research as the study of "who says what, how, and to whom." The Yale group almost completely ignored the *response* of the audience to the inputs that it received. However, as research in the 1960's soon showed, the audience was anything but passive. Indeed, the audience frequently would argue with the communicators, reject what was said to them, or refuse to listen further to a given message or communicator. By the 1970's, most scientists studying the persuasive process had begun to focus as much on active audience responses as on "communicator, message, and (passive) audience."

Third, the Yale group had assumed that *attitudes control behavior*. But by 1965, psychologists had discovered an unexpected difference between what people *said* their attitudes were, and what people actually *did* in real-life settings. Most of us conform at one time or another—but we seldom *perceive* ourselves as being "conformist." And few authoritarian people are likely to refer to themselves by that name on a pen-and-paper test. Furthermore, many of us apparently have very inconsistent or conflicting attitudes.

One great benefit of the Yale research, then, was that it led social psychologists to pay more attention to the differences between attitudes and behaviors.

Attitudes versus Behaviors

According to most social psychologists, whenever you state an attitude, you are making a prediction about your future thoughts, feelings, and behaviors. But what are we to think if your attitudinal statement doesn't predict what you actually do at some future time?

Chinese and Blacks Keep Out!

The research study that first opened up this problem was reported many years ago by R.T. LaPiere. Just after the Second World War, LaPiere spent considerable time driving through the US with a Chinese couple as his companions. Despite the very strong "anti-Chinese" prejudice to be found among many Americans at that time, LaPiere and his friends were refused service only once during 10,000 miles of travel.

Later, when they were safely home, LaPiere

Psychosomatic (SIGH-koh-so-MATT-tick). From the words meaning "mind" and "body." Many psychologically stressful situations cause physical symptoms (such as ulcers or high blood pressure). These symptoms are said to be "psychosomatic" in origin.

sent questionnaires to all the hotels and cafes where they had stopped. One item on the questionnaire asked, "Will you accept members of the Chinese race as guests in your establishment?" More than 90 percent of the places responded with a very firm "no," and yet all but one of these hundreds of establishments actually had accepted the Chinese couple without question or comment. Obviously there was a very marked difference between "attitude" and "behavior" on the part of these establishments.

In a similar study reported in 1952, B. Kutner, Carol Wilkins, and Penny Yarrow had three young women visit various restaurants in a fashionable suburban community in the northeastern part of the US. Two of the women were white; the third was black. The two white women always arrived at the restaurant first, asked for a table for three, and were seated. Shortly thereafter, the black woman entered, informed the head waiter or hostess that she was with friends who were already seated, found the table, sat down with the two white women, and was served without question.

Two weeks after each visit, Kutner, Wilkins, and Yarrow wrote a letter to each restaurant asking if they would serve blacks. Not one replied. The experimenters then called the manager of each establishment on the phone. The managers uniformly responded in a very cool and distant manner, suggesting that they held a highly prejudiced attitude toward serving blacks. Yet, as in the LaPiere study, this attitude was simply not translated into action when the restaurant personnel were faced with seating a black person.

Since 1965, there have been dozens of similar experiments, all of which suggest that attitudes (as measured by questionnaires) are often poor indicators of what people actually do, think, and feel in real-life situations. Furthermore, there is often little relationship between attitude *change* and a subsequent change in the way a person *behaves*. Just as important, as we noted in the previous chapters, people often change their behaviors without changing the attitudes related to the behaviors.

Question: How would you explain LaPiere's results in terms of Adaptation-level Theory?

Attitudes toward Attitudes

In their classic book *Opinions and Personality*, M. Brewster Smith, Jerome Bruner, and Robert W. White ask a most important question: Of what possible use to you are your opinions? The answer to that question is not an easy one to find. Smith, Bruner, and White believe that attitudes or opinions *serve needs*. That is, whenever you express an attitude, you are really describing some need or goal that you are "driven" to fulfill. When you state your attitudes to the people around you, therefore, you presumably are hunting for others with similar needs who might assist you in achieving mutual goals. Like most social psychologists, Smith, Bruner, and White believe that attitudes are *internal processes* that somehow guide or direct your behaviors.

A radically different approach to the subject, however, was stated in the late 1960's by Daryl Bem. According to Bem, attitudes are simply *verbal statements* about your own behaviors. Bem believes most of what you do is under the control of external stimulus inputs, and that you aren't consciously aware of most of these "controlling inputs." Bem points out that LaPiere really measured two quite different responses that occurred in two very different environments. LaPiere's questionnaire seemed designed to elicit negative responses from the hotel and innkeepers to whom it was sent. But when LaPiere presented himself and a well-dressed Chinese couple at the desk of the hotel, the stimulus situation was so different from that evoked by the questionnaire that the behavioral response of the innkeeper was bound to be different as well.

Bem believes that there really are no such things as "attitudes," unless you wish to consider them as verbal explanations of why you do what you do. Attitudinal statements then don't predict behaviors well at all—they merely give a *rationalization* of what you've already done. We might summarize Bem's position as follows: "How do I know my attitude until I see what I've done?"

Psychological Traps

Yet another explanation of the LaPiere study comes from a 1981 article by Jeffrey Z. Rubin. Once you "invest too much" in a situation, Rubin says, you may continue in a given line of behavior simply because you can't find an easy

way out. Rubin calls these situations "psychological traps." For example, you call someone on the phone and are put on hold. You wait a while and wonder if you shouldn't hang up. But if you do, you'll just have to call again. So you wait some more. Then you decide that, since you've waited so long already, you will "lose" the time you've already waited if you hang up. So you wait still longer . . .

Rubin gives another example of a psychological trap that seems unbelievable to many people—until they get caught up in it. Some years ago, Yale economist Martin Shubik auctioned off a dollar bill to friends at a cocktail party. The money went to the highest bidder. The "trap" came from the fact that the person who made the second-highest bid also had to pay whatever that person had bid, but didn't get the dollar. Rubin reports that "several researchers have had people play the Dollar Auction game under controlled laboratory conditions and have found that the participants typically end up bidding far in excess of the $1 prize at stake, sometimes paying as much as $5 or $6 for a dollar bill."

The interesting question is why people would engage in such a self-defeating course of action. According to Boston University psychologist Allan Teger, participants in the Dollar Auction typically offer two reasons for their behavior. The first reason has to do with economics—they genuinely want the money (at first). Then they are motivated by a desire to regain their losses or to avoid losing more money. The second reason is intra-psychic—a desire to "save face," a desire to prove yourself as the "best player," or an urge to "punish the other person." However, these are all *after-the-fact* attitudes expressed by people to explain why they behaved in a self-defeating manner.

Rubin's work suggests that when, for example, two white women are seated in a restaurant, the manager *has an investment* in these customers. Thus, when a black woman arrives to join the two whites, the manager may feel "trapped." For to refuse service to the newcomer means "a messy scene" in which the white women may get up and leave. Thus, the *social situation* may determine which of two attitudes ("not wanting to serve blacks" versus "not wanting to make a scene and lose customers") actually prevails.

Question: Do most attitude questionnaires specify the social situation in which the attitude is to be expressed?

Reciprocal Determinism

Are your thoughts and actions regulated by internal processes such as attitudes? Or by environmental inputs that directly influence your visible behaviors? Do you "change your mind," and let your actions follow suit? Or do you first change the way you act, and then alter your attitudes to fit your behaviors?

According to Albert Bandura, you do both at the same time. Writing in the April 1978 issue of *American Psychologist*, Bandura states that "explanations of human behavior have generally favored unidirectional causal models emphasizing either environmental or internal determinants of behavior. In social learning theory, causal processes are conceptualized in terms of **reciprocal determinism**." Bandura goes on to say that, from his point of view, psychological functioning involves a *continuous* interaction between behavioral, cognitive, and environmental influences.

Bandura believes that you first build up "behavioral standards" by observing others and by noticing the consequences of their actions. You may then test these standards yourself, to determine if you will be rewarded or punished for thinking and acting in a given way. Once your standards are set, though, you tend to *evaluate* future social inputs in terms of (1) the situational context in which the input appears, (2) your own internal standards, and (3) the possible consequences of acting or thinking in a given way. But these three factors are *reciprocal influences* on each other. Other people influence your internal standards, true. But, as Newcomb has shown, you tend to avoid people who don't share your standards and seek out those who do. And, as we noted in Chapter 10, when you're trying to lose weight, you use your internal standards to help you stay away from pastry shops, because you know you will respond to the sight of cookies by purchasing and eating some.

The notion of "self-regulating systems" lies at the heart of Bandura's position. He sees you not as the "passive audience" for persuasive messages from your environment, as Hovland does. Nor does he view your mind as a "behavior-producing machine," as do trait theorists. Nor does he assume that all of your responses are learned reactions triggered off by external inputs, as does Bem. Instead, Bandura believes that there is a reciprocal *interplay* between your social inputs, your perceptions, and your responses. You continually evaluate the consequences of perceiving a given stimulus in a particular way.

Reciprocal determinism (ree-SIP-pro-cal dee-TURR-min-ism). Bandura's belief that psychological functions are a joint function of behavioral, cognitive, and environmental influences.

And you change both your behaviors and your attitudes in order to achieve your own particular goals.

The Ethics of Attitude Change

Whatever solution you take to the attitude-behavior (mind-body) problem, there is a deeper issue involved. We *do* know ways of inducing attitude change, and we *do* have methods for creating new behaviors. Given this knowledge, we must then face the following issue: *Who has the right to use these powerful techniques?*

Is it right to talk someone into buying an expensive new car? Is it ethical to convince people that the United Nations is worthy of support? Is it a morally responsible act to persuade a mentally disordered person to seek professional help? Is it ethical to teach children religion or economic theories? Shouldn't all individuals be free to make up their own minds without interference from persuasive sources?

The ethical questions involved in persuasion and attitude formation are numerous and complex. And the questions become even more difficult to answer in cases of *unintentional* persuasion, such as the influence parents have on their children or the subtle and indirect propaganda found in many textbooks, movies, newspapers, and television programs.

Psychology, as an objective science, is not in a position to answer ethical questions. Psychology can, however, attempt to provide some of the information and facts that you will need in order to make your own ethical decisions. One important point that psychology makes about attitude formation is this: *No one is free of the influence of others or free of the responsibility of influencing others*. Every member of society is involved in attitude formation, both as communicator and as audience. Whenever two or more people get together, the outputs (messages) of one individual become the inputs of others. And this exchange of outputs can result in behavior or attitude change.

If everything you do in the presence of someone else affects that person, then the only way you can hope to judge the ethical value of your actions is to have an *objective* understanding of how your behavior influences others. And since you acquired many of your own attitudes from others, you will also need to learn as much *scientific* information as possible about how you were "shaped" to be what you presently are. For only when you know the full facts of how people communicate with and influence each other can you hope to make good ethical decisions about human attitudes and actions.

As Carl Rogers noted long ago, people need people, and no one ever achieved self-actualization without considerable assistance from hundreds of other individuals. The debt you owe these people, in return, is to help them achieve their own unique goals.

And perhaps that is what ethics is all about, at some deep psychological level—helping others so that they in turn can help you. Therefore, the more you learn about human behavior (and attitudes), the more likely it will be that you can achieve your own form of self-actualization, and the more likely it will be that you can be of *optimal* assistance in helping others.

Social Psychology: A Summary

In the past, we've tended to explain most of what people think and do in terms of "genes" and "inner desires." Only in the last century or so have we become aware of the tremendous influence the social environment has on our thoughts, feelings, and actions.

Social psychology grew out of personality theory (with a large dose of sociology thrown in for good measure). Thus, when the field was very new, some social psychologists paid more attention to what people *perceived* (and the *attitudes* people had) than to what people *actually did* in real-life situations. Then, the behaviorists came along and took the opposite stance—they ignored inner psychological processes and focused almost entirely on measurable behaviors.

Having swung to both extremes, social psychology seems to have returned to a middle ground of sorts. The social learning theorists—such as Bandura—have reminded us that you can influence your environment, just as it influences you. So we cannot throw the "mind" out of social psychology any more than we can throw the environment out of intra-psychic psychology and biological psychology.

As we pointed out in Chapter 5, you are a *system*. You are made up of sub-systems (your cells and organs), and you are a sub-system within such larger social systems as groups and organizations. You cannot understand yourself (or other people) unless you look at the "big picture." That is, you must learn as much as you can about inputs, inner processes, *and* behavioral outputs if you really want to *understand* human behavior.

Now that we've covered many of the theoretical aspects of social psychology, it's time we turned our attention to more practical subjects. We'll do just that in the next (and final) chapter.

Summary

1 Although some of our opinions, feelings, and preferences are the product of **rational decision making**, many of our attitudes are unconsciouly influenced by attempts of other people to **persuade** us to think and act as they do (or as they would like us to think and act).

2 Attitudes are important because they allow you to **predict** future events. They also aid you in **remembering** past experiences.

3 In general, the more you know about something, the more **stable** and **consistent** your attitude toward that thing will usually be.

4 The stronger you **feel** about something, the more difficult it probably will be to get you to change your perception of or attitude toward that thing.

5 The more you are **reinforced** for holding a certain **percept**, the less susceptible that percept or attitude is to being changed.

6 In Newcomb's study of Bennington women, he found that students felt **group pressures to conform** to the liberal environment at the college. The most liberal of the students tended to seek out or create post-college environments that would help them **maintain** their liberal attitudes.

7 The Bennington students often showed **autistic hostility** to non-liberal attitudes and opinions.

8 **Student activists** from the 1960's have tended to maintain their "radical" attitudes over the years, much as have the Bennington women.

9 The **communication process** is influenced by at least four different factors: the **communicator**, the **message**, the **audience**, and the **feedback** (if any) from

10 Immediately after hearing a message, we tend to accept the word of **high-credibility sources**, but reject the word of **low-credibility sources**. Several weeks later, we tend to be more influenced by the actual content of the message than by its source—a phenomenon called the **sleeper effect**.

11 Many studies suggest that **person-to-person communication** is by far more effective than **mass communication** involving the news media.

12 When we receive **fear-arousing messages**, our first impression may be that the stimulus is a very persuasive one. However, studies show that fear usually achieves little more than **repression** and does not protect the audience from **counter-propaganda**.

13 Youthful offenders exposed to the first **scared straight** program actually had a higher rate of subsequent arrests than did a control group not exposed to the fear-arousing experiences.

14 Youthful offenders given **job-skill training** and **positive feedback** about their attitudes and behaviors showed a much lower rate of subsequent arrests than did control-group subjects.

15 The more a **propagandist** constructs the message to fit the prior beliefs and attitudes of the audience, and the more the communicator pays attention to **audience feedback**, the more successful the persuasive attempt will usually be.

16 **Mass hysteria** can occur when groups of people are under **stress** and are exposed to a **novel stimulus**.

17 The Yale researchers had problems because (1) they ignored the **social context** in which persuasion occurs, (2) they assumed the audience was **passive** and thus ignored **feedback**, and (3) they presumed that **attitudes always determine behavior**.

18 Some studies suggest that attitudes are poor predictors of what people actually do. One reason may be that attitudes are **verbal statements about your own behaviors**. Or, you may invest so much in a situation you are **psychologically trapped** into behaving in ways counter to your attitudes.

19 Bandura believes psychological functions are determined by **reciprocal determinism**—a continuous interaction between behavioral, cognitive, and environmental influences. Thus, you change both your attitudes and behaviors **simultaneously** in order to achieve your goals.

20 The **ethical questions** raised by research on attitudes are highly complex and not easily answered. However, we probably should evaluate ourselves objectively in terms of what we really do, rather than evaluate ourselves subjectively in terms of our intentions and attitudes.

(*See related story beginning on page 685.*)

Her Imperial Majesty, Katherin III, Queen of Nacerima, banged her solid-gold gavel on the table. It had been given to her by her grateful subjects. The gold gavel made a satisfyingly loud noise as it bit into the tabletop. "The meeting will come to order," she said in a regal tone of voice.

The Queen's ministers, seated around the table, stopped their chattering and turned to give Her Imperial Majesty their undivided attention.

Once the group had quieted down the Queen continued. "I regret to inform you that we have just received a dismaying report from our intelligence services. The Aissurs are at it again!"

"Oh, no," murmured the Minister for Intermural Affairs.

"Oh, yes!" said the Queen firmly. "They are escalating the gold war, which is to say they are trying to outspend us again. They are raising international tensions to an unbelievable level, which is to say they are trying to top us again. We, the Queen, cannot believe the Aissurs would undertake such a foolhardy venture, merely to attract world attention." Her Majesty paused, sighed, and then said plaintively, "But then, what else could we expect from heathens like the Aissurs?"

"Harrumph," said the Minister for Indignant Responses. "Precisely what insult have our hereditary enemies the Aissurs heaped on us this time?"

The Queen sank into her plush velvet chair. A depressed look crept slowly over her face. "Well, it's this way. As you know, it was just a month ago that we personally attended the opening ceremonies for our crowning achievement, the Katherin III Home for Homeless Orphans."

"Hear, hear," said the Minister for Appropriate Comments.

"One hundred forty-four stories high, built of shining glass and steel, the Home for the Homeless points a victorious finger to the sky. It is concrete proof to the entire world that *we care!*" Her Majesty said proudly.

"Did they ever work out the problems with the elevators?" asked the Minister for Nagging Doubts.

"That isn't the point," the Queen replied testily. "The point is that the Aissurs have just signed a secret contract with Mammoth Construction Company to erect a new tower in their capital city. It is to be a Home for Abandoned Animals, and it is to be 166 stories high!"

An angry murmur swept through the group of ministers.

"Brinksmanship!" cried the Minister of Eternal Truths (formerly known as the Minister of Propaganda).

"Horribly expensive!" cried the Minister of Financial Possibilities (formerly known as the Tax Man).

"I'll bet they're reserving the top floors for abandoned birds, so they won't even *have* to put in elevators,"
opined the Minister for Nagging Doubts.

"We cannot tolerate this threat to our international image," Her Majesty said in a very majestic tone of voice. "For decades now, the world has looked to Nacerima for leadership in the field of *caring*. The Katherin III Home for Homeless Orphans was designed to be our ultimate statement on the subject. Our architects assured us that 144 stories was the tallest structure humans could possibly build. It was also 24 stories higher than the highest building in Aissur. But now, I regret to say, we are about to be topped."

"It will bankrupt the Aissurs," said the Minister of Financial Possibilities.

"No," replied the Queen, "They will simply raise taxes again. The peasants of Aissur never complain about such things."

"If they do, they're shot," said the Minister of Eternal Truths.

"What are we to do?" asked the Queen. "We cannot abandon our world leadership."

The Minister for Nagging Doubts pulled at his ear as if lost in thought. "Well," he said finally, "we could mount a propaganda campaign pointing out that Homeless Orphans are more important than Abandoned Animals . . ."

"Not to the British," replied the Minister of Intermural Affairs.

"Couldn't we just add a 1,000 foot TV antenna to the Katherin III Home?" asked the Minister for Insightful Solutions.

"We could even put a birdhouse at the top of the antenna," said the Minister of
Financial Possibilities. "That way we could kill two birds with one stone."

Her Majesty glowered. "No, we must take no half-way measures. Our response to this insult from the Aissurs must be bold and creative. Therefore, we have commanded our architects to design the ultimate in ultimate buildings." The Queen turned to the Minister for Creative Fantasies. "Show us your plans."

The Minister for Creative Fantasies smiled and pulled out a huge blueprint. When unrolled, the plan covered the entire length of the table. And as soon as the other ministers saw the design, they gasped. For the blueprint showed a structure at least 400 stories high with a 4,000 foot lightning rod atop it.

"Incredible!" said the Minister for Appropriate Comments.

"An unanswerable challenge!" cried the Minister for Intermural Affairs.

"Hideously expensive," said the Minister of Financial Possibilities.

"I'd hate to be in that thing during a windstorm," murmured the Minister of Nagging Doubts.

"We will call it the Katherin III Tower for Terrified Toddlers," the Queen said grandly. "It is such a bold leap upward that the Aissurs won't even dream of challenging our world supremacy in the field of international *caring* for decades to come!"

"But how will we pay for it?" asked the Minister of Financial Possibilities. "The populace nearly revolted when we raised taxes to pay for the Home for Homeless

Orphans."

"Contributions!" cried the Queen. "We will ask the people to give from the bottoms of their hearts so we can top the Aissurs.

"But who will be the first to give?" asked the Minister of Nagging Doubts.

"I will," the Queen contributed. She raised the solid-gold gavel given to her by her doting subjects. "This will be my gift to the Tower fund." She looked around the table. "Naturally, each of you will be eager to match my generosity."

There was some shuffling of feet and clearing of throats. Then the Minister of Financial Possibilities frowned, took off his Mickey Mouse watch, and put it beside the gold gavel. The Minister for Intermural Affairs added a rhinestone brooch, and the Minister for Creative Fantasies reluctantly removed a small diamond from his right earlobe. One by one, each of them put something of value on the table until only the Minister of Nagging Doubts was left. He squirmed in his seat, then said, "Couldn't we end this whole business by building the tower in neutral territory, and asking the Aissurs to come up with half the cost?"

"Nonsense!" thundered the Queen. "We will not share the glory with those heathens!"

The Minister of Nagging Doubts sighed, then pulled out his wallet. He took out a single dollar bill, put it on the table, and then showed everyone that his wallet was now completely empty.

"Victory is ours!" cried the Queen triumphantly.

They all cheered. Someone proposed a toast to the Queen. The Minister of Financial Possibilities gathered up the loot, and they all got up and trooped into the next room for drinks. Only the Minister for Appropriate Comments lingered behind. He recited aloud some lines from a poem by Robert Southey:

"And everybody praised the duke,
Who this great fight did win."
"But what good came of it at last?"
Quoth little Peterkin.
"Why, that I cannot tell," said he;
"But 'twas a famous victory."

And then he went to join the crowd.

Recommended Readings

Bandura, A. (1978). The self system in reciprocal determinism. *American Psychologist, 33*(4), 344–358.

Janis, I.L. (1982). *Stress, attitudes, and decisions: Selected papers.* New York: Praeger.

Petty, R.E., Ostrom, T.M., & Brock, T.C. (Eds.). (1981). *Cognitive responses in persuasion.* Hillsdale, N.J.: Erlbaum.

Sieber, J.E. (Ed.). (1982). *The ethics of social research: Surveys and experiments.* New York: Springer-Verlag.

Stumphauzer, J.S. (Ed.). (1979). *Progress in behavior therapy with delinquents.* Springfield, Ill.: Charles C. Thomas.

26

A Conclusion

Like most scientists, I believe in the future. I suppose I always have. I am much more interested in new things than in old. And I am more intrigued by what a person might become than by what a person has already been. Indeed, about the only time I think about yesterday is when I need information that might let me better understand what tomorrow could be like.

Humans seem to be the only animals that can look far into the future and plan accordingly. This ability to change some parts of the present world *deliberately* in order to shape the world of tomorrow is, in my opinion, one of the essential characteristics of being human.

Science is (among other things) the fine art of predicting the future in objective terms. It is therefore one of the most *human* of occupations. It took people a long time to learn how to make their predictions accurate, however, for at least two reasons:

1. Being emotional or subjective is probably more immediately rewarding for most of us than is being rational or objective. Perhaps this fact is not too surprising. As we noted in Chapter 4 when we discussed Paul MacLean's "Theory of the Triune Brain," the nervous systems of lower animals are dominated by emotional centers. The "thinking" or "processing" centers in the cortex reach their fullest development in humans. But these are *additions to* (rather than subtractions from) the basic blueprint of the highly reactive animal brain.

   The sheer size of the human cortex gives us the potentiality of bringing the lower centers—and hence our passions and desires—under *voluntary control*. As we mentioned in Chapters 9 and 12, we need training and experience in order to learn how to be rational. However, we need precious little training to be emotional.

2. Even when early men and women attempted to view the world in objective terms, they often lacked sufficient data to make good predictions. It probably wasn't until around the year 1600 A.D. that we had gathered enough hard, unemotional facts about the world—and had the proper mathematical

The Industrial Revolution gave us control over the physical environment, but gave us little knowledge about how to help people survive in that environment.

tools—for science to prove a worthwhile occupation.

The Industrial Revolution

Perhaps because it is easier for most of us to look at *things* objectively than for us to be "unemotional" about ourselves, the physical (or "thing") sciences were the first to develop. Modern physics and astronomy date from the 1600's. Chemistry came a little later. These scientific disciplines soon matured enough to let us understand and predict the behavior of a few objects under certain specified conditions—for that kind of prediction is science's job. But once we could *guess* how physical things would behave, we could also hunt for ways to *control* the future behavior of these objects. This ability to control "things" marked the rise of physical technology.

The first major applications of physical technology in Europe began in the mid-1700's, and led to what we call the "Industrial Revolution." Before this time, almost everyone in Europe lived on farms or in relatively small towns, and almost every "thing" was handmade. Life changed little from one generation to another. A man typically became what his father had been, and a woman married the sort of man her mother had married. As greater and greater application of the physical sciences gave hu-

mans the ability to shape their physical environments, however, the tempo of cultural change speeded up noticeably.

The Medical Revolution

By the 1800's, we had learned enough to begin viewing our bodily reactions in an objective manner. Biology became a true science, and medical technology became a reality. As the "Medical Revolution" gathered steam in the early 1900's, we discovered ways to predict and control some of our biological reactions. Because of this applied knowledge, we are now bigger, stronger, healthier, and we live longer than at any previous time in human history.

The Psychological Revolution

During the last part of the 1800's and the first part of the 1900's, we took the next step up the ladder—we discovered ways to look at our minds and behaviors objectively. Psychology and the social sciences came into being. We are just now starting to build a technology based on our new-found objective knowledge of ourselves. We call this technology *applied psychology*—that is, the application of psychological facts and theories to the solution of real-life problems. In short, we are now in the midst of what might be called the "Psychological Revolution." The cultural changes this third revolution has brought about are, in their way, as "mind-blowing" as those caused by the Industrial and Medical Revolutions.

What will scientific psychology be like in the future? That question is difficult to answer, since it depends in part on the often unpredictable outcomes of all the thousands of experiments that psychologists are conducting right at this moment.

The future of applied psychology is somewhat easier to predict, however, since tomorrow's technology will lean heavily on today's scientific knowledge. In these final pages, let me share with you my *guesses* about the changing world of human behavior, and what these changes might mean to you. Other psychologists will surely see things differently, and predictions are often little more than wild speculation.

Still, it might pay us to try to answer three interesting questions:

1. What will the world be like in the year 2000?
2. What kinds of job opportunities might be open to you then?
3. What types of psychological services will probably be available to you by the end of this century?

In defense of my answers to these questions about the year 2000, let me remind you of one fact. At least half of the *types* of jobs available to college graduates today simply didn't exist as "job classifications" 25 years ago.

The Future of Biological Psychology

There seems little doubt that we will shortly gain a great deal more control over our heredity (and hence our instinctual behaviors) than we would have dreamed possible a few years back. In 1973 scientists at the University of Wisconsin announced they had synthesized a gene in a test tube. That is, they took ordinary chemical molecules and combined them to "build" a very simple gene. By the late 1970's, other scientists had shown that "artificial genes" could function *normally* in very simple organisms. By the early 1980's, researchers had transferred "active genes" from one simple organism to another. And by 1985, dozens of corporations had been formed in the US alone to exploit the possibilities of "genetic engineering." Thus, is seems clear that in the very near future we will indeed be able to change a person's heredity

(genes) both before and after that person is born (see Chapter 17).

Once the biologists give us greater control over our inheritance, psychologists will be able to determine with much greater precision what the genetic contribution to behavior really is. We should also be able to learn much more about how to overcome genetic handicaps that people already have. By the year 2000, many psychologists should be employed as "genetic counselors," giving advice to prospective parents both before and after they get married. Other psychologists will be able to offer physically handicapped people much better training than now exists. These psychologists may also offer surgeons advice on what kinds of drugs and operations might be helpful to maximize the *psychological* potential of brain-damaged individuals.

The Two Hemispheres

There is no part of biological psychology presently more exciting than the study of the functions of the two hemispheres. As we noted earlier, there is a growing body of evidence that such "mental illnesses" as schizophrenia and autism are related to a *functional imbalance* between the two halves of the brain. Fifty years ago, autism was thought to be a type of schizophrenia. But in the last two or three years, brain scan research has clearly shown this isn't the case. Autistic children process information primarily with their right hemispheres, while patients diagnosed as schizophrenic process inputs primarily with their left hemispheres. I would guess that our whole approach to treating these two "mental disorders" will change markedly in the next decade. Instead of locking schizophrenic patients up in asylums, or using just chemotherapy, we surely will begin training them to process information with *both hemispheres*.

We are also likely to be able to help normal children who have language problems by measuring how they input information to their two hemispheres. In the June 29, 1979 issue of *Science*, Joseph Cioffi and Gillray L. Kandel report that young boys tend to process information in quite a different manner than do young girls. When Cioffi and Kandel gave "word-shapes" to more than 100 young subjects, the girls tended to respond to the "word value" of the stimulus, while boys tended to respond to the "visual shape" of the input. Boys also tend to have more language-development problems than do girls, while girls typically have more difficulty learn-

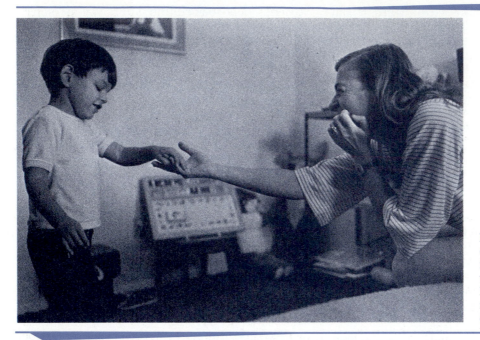

Because autistic children process information primarily with their right hemispheres, they must be taught communication skills.

ing spatial concepts and the correct use of mathematical symbolism than do boys.

There are also differences in the brains of men and women. According to University of Chicago psychologist Jerre Levy, the right ear and eye are more sensitive in women, while the left ear and eye are more sensitive in men. Levy believes the left hemisphere dominates in women, the right in men. The cause for this difference in hemispheric dominance may be the corpus callosum, which is thicker in women than in men. Because puberty occurs earlier in women than in men, the callosum doesn't "stretch out" as much in women as it does in men, Levy says. Because sexual maturity stops the "lateralization" of the brain, Levy says, women have *less-lateralized brains*. Thus, women are better at integrating processes that occur in both hemispheres. Men, Levy believes, are better at tasks that depend on the dominance of one hemisphere, such as spatial perception and mathematics.

Support for Levy's views comes from a 1982 report by Stanford psychologist J. Merrill Carlsmith. According to Carlsmith, girls who *matured late* "matched or outscored their male counterparts in mathematics." Like Jerre Levy, Carlsmith believes late maturity allows for a greater "lateralization of the brain." Therefore, Carlsmith says, late-maturing women should have the same range of cognitive abilities as do men. Carlsmith also notes that *early-maturing*

males (who have less-lateralized brains) tend to do better at verbal tasks than do *late-maturing* males.

If further experiments support Levy and Carlsmith, perhaps we eventually will "custom-tailor" the high school curriculum to the individual needs of both young men and women. For example, we could give girls (and early-maturing boys) special training in mathematics and perceptual skills. And we could give boys (and late-maturing girls) special training in language and "integration skills."

Behavioral Medicine

There are very few psychologists working in hospitals today. By the year 2000, however, hospitals may employ more psychologists and behavioral technologists than they do physicians and surgeons. This surprising situation will be a direct consequence of the three revolutions we mentioned earlier. For thanks to our increased knowledge of the physical and biological sciences, the major health hazards are no longer diseases that have a purely biological cause—such as pneumonia, influenza, and tuberculosis. Medical technology has "cured" us of these maladies, for the most part. But medical technology is presently ill equipped to help us with health problems that have an intra-psychic, behavioral, or social component. For few

J. Merrill Carlsmith   Marty Merrill

physicians are trained in psychological technology.

Writing in the August 1982 *American Psychologist*, University of Hawaii psychologist Jerrold Michael has the following to say about a new field usually called "behavioral medicine":

> Society, the federal government, and perspectives on health care are changing. New attention is being given to how individual behavior and our physical environment influence health. Half of the mortality in the United States is due to unhealthy behavior or life-style, and a further 20 percent is due to environmental factors. Disease prevention and health promotion represent developing trends in health policy.

There have been many attempts to define this new field. For instance, in an article entitled "What is Behavioral Medicine?" published in 1977 in *Psychosomatic Medicine*, G.E. Schwartz and S.M. Weiss offer the following definition:

> "Behavioral medicine" is the field concerned with the development of behavioral science knowledge and techniques relevant to the understanding of physical health and illness and the application of this knowledge and these techniques to diagnosis, prevention, treatment and rehabilitation.

The assumption underlying most approaches to behavioral medicine is this: Our biological systems *interact* with our intra-psychic and our social/behavioral systems. From this viewpoint, it would seem that the next breakthroughs in medicine will come from the wise and humane use of a psycho-technology that helps coordinate the inputs and outputs of all three systems.

Already many of my students are working with doctors and patients at several medical facilities in the Ann Arbor area. The students have been particularly successful with "problem patients" whose thoughts and behaviors interfere with improvement in their physical health. Helping patients stay on diets, give up smoking, and stay on medical treatment plans are three of the areas that the student-therapists have done well in. And sometimes the students can achieve near-miracles with patients the medical profession has difficulty handling.

Cortical Blindness

In 1984, Marty Merrill earned her doctorate in psychology at Michigan working with brain-damaged patients who suffer from "cortical blindness." There usually isn't anything wrong with these patients' eyes. So visual inputs from the eyes still do get through to the visual cortex in one fashion or another. However, because the patients have suffered extensive brain damage, the visual inputs simply aren't "processed" effectively after they reach the visual cortex. As a result, the patient cannot "see" at all.

(To understand what "cortical blindness" is like, imagine a camera hooked up to a videotape recorder. Like your eyes, the camera takes in a visual image and converts it to an electrical signal that is sent to the tape recorder. But if the recording head is damaged, the recorder can't store the incoming signal on magnetic tape. The tape, then, is "blank"—even though the camera keeps sending a clear signal to the recorder.)

One of the patients Marty Merrill worked with was a 14-year-old girl whom we will call Eliza. About five months after her 14th birthday, Eliza had a heart attack and went into a coma. She remained unconscious for some five weeks. Because her brain was deprived of oxygen during (and following) the heart attack, Eliza's cortex was badly damaged. Brain scans showed that the visual input areas in the occipital lobes were almost totally gone, as were certain parts of the cortex in the parietal lobe. (The parietal cortex is the "input area" for sensations from the skin, muscles, and tendons—including the muscles that control the eyes.) She also suffered damage to several "lower centers" in her brain. Electrical recordings suggested that visual inputs from the eyes reached her cortex more slowly than they should have, and Eliza's cortex simply didn't "process" the inputs properly. A few weeks after coming out of the coma, Eliza could detect the onset of a very bright light if you shone it directly into her eyes. Other than that, however, she wasn't conscious of "seeing" anything at all.

The medical doctors who worked with Eliza pronounced her "blind." She couldn't see, so she had to be pushed around in a wheel chair. Her "postural reflexes" were totally absent, so she couldn't maintain her body in an upright position. Thus, she had to be strapped into the wheelchair.

Psychological tests showed that Eliza had suffered gross impairment to her memory system. She did still understand language and could speak in a fairly normal fashion. She could remember her name—but she couldn't remember her birthday. She could repeat words and short sentences, but not long sentences. Nor could she execute *sequences of spatial movements* such as "Raise your right arm and then wiggle your hand." Worst of all, Eliza couldn't perform such "automatic" verbal habits as repeating the alphabet. (These deeply ingrained "automatic" habits tend to survive all but the most severe types of brain damage.) There was considerable doubt, too, as to whether Eliza could *learn* much of anything at all.

Because patients with this amount of neural damage almost never recover when given just medical treatment—surgery or drugs—the doctors believed Eliza would never be normal again.

"Shaping" Eliza To See

Four months after Eliza came out of the coma, Marty Merrill began working with the young woman. First, Marty gave Eliza a series of psychological tests. Psychological testing is part of medical practice in many rehabilitation settings. The tests showed that Eliza had not recovered at all.

For a number of reasons, Marty decided the next thing she would do was to train Eliza to "name colors." Marty and another medical psychologist, Donald Kewman, began by showing Eliza four 8″ x 11″ sheets of colored paper and asked Eliza to say what the four colors were. Surprisingly enough, Eliza did guess "blue" correctly, but she missed red, yellow, and green. Marty praised her for getting "blue" right and told Eliza the names of the colors she'd missed. Then Marty tried again—rewarding correct responses with verbal praise and correcting mistakes gently. Within two days, Eliza could consistently identify the colors she had been trained on—but she still couldn't recognize colors she hadn't been taught to identify.

Next, Marty and Donald Kewman worked on form recognition. She showed Eliza four different shapes—circle, square, triangle, and cross. Each form came in four colors—red, blue, green, and yellow. One by one, Marty showed Eliza each of the 16 form/color stimulus cards and asked the young girl to identify both the color and the shape. At the beginning, Eliza could give the colors but not the shape. Then Marty began "tracing the contours" of each shape by running her fingers around the edges of the form before asking Eliza to name it. Again, she rewarded correct responses and gently corrected mistakes. In less than a month, Eliza could consistently identify the four shapes and their colors. However, Eliza could not identify other shapes (such as a heart and a star) until she had been trained with those forms too.

Marty then decided to teach Eliza how to read. First came "letter recognition." Eliza did poorly at first, for she confused letters with similar shapes (B and D, A and H). After a week of training, though, Eliza could breeze through the entire alphabet. Then came "word recognition." Once more, the young woman had problems at the start. But within two weeks, she could read and comprehend simple words and phrases. Sentence recognition took an additional month.

Six months after the visual retraining started, Eliza could read even small print in textbooks. More surprising than this, when her visual acuity was tested using the Snellen charts (see Chapter 7), she could now "see" as clearly as before the coma. In fact, although she had used glasses previously, the eye doctor told her she didn't really need them now. At this point, she returned to school.

Teaching Eliza to Remember

About the time Eliza began to recognize letters, she began to report that she could "see things" again. Her posture improved dramatically, and she began to walk again without running into anything. Soon thereafter, she could get around entirely on her own.

Eliza still had many problems, however. She could read—but she couldn't write. She had no memory of how to form written letters. So Marty taught her. Eliza also had no memory for "written grammar." She couldn't spell, nor could she pronounce many words correctly. And she couldn't tell time. So Marty taught her these skills too. Eliza had been fairly good at mathematics before the coma, but afterwards she couldn't remember even such simple tasks as how to add and subtract. Again, Marty was able to retrain Eliza in a fairly short period of time.

Eliza continued to have problems with *verbal* memory and with *sequences* of skilled movements. Eliza could walk, but she was fairly clumsy. And she had forgotten how to dance. Marty "modeled" the appropriate movements, and rewarded Eliza for imitating the correct responses. Marty also had the girl *reverse* the direction of learned movements since Eliza had difficulty "reversing" any kind of motor sequence. Eliza recovered very rapidly. She could remember from one training session to another the exact *sequence* of learned movements. She learned to identify objects by touch less than three months after learning to read short phrases.

By the end of training, Eliza had normal verbal memory, normal motor memory, normal visual memory, and most of her cognitive functions had recovered as well. She was not entirely "normal," however. She still did slur her words when emotionally excited, and sometimes she had to be reminded to attend to *how* she walked.

The Importance of Eliza

Marty Merrill's work with Eliza is important for several reasons. First, it is an example of how effective "behavioral medicine" can be. Second, it tells us something important about the brain. Eliza's cortical visual input areas were almost totally destroyed—the brain scans proved that. With training, however, two things probably occurred: (1) Parts of her brain that previously hadn't been involved in "visual processing" took over these functions; (2) the damaged visual areas may have learned to "process" information in new ways.

Third, this "applied research" demonstrates how much the psychologist can tell the medical doctor. The brain scans indicated that damage to Eliza's visual cortex was more extensive than was damage to the parietal cortex. But the fact that Eliza regained the ability to see but still couldn't identify objects by touch suggests that the parietal lobe damage was *functionally* greater than that to the occipital lobe.

Last, but surely not least, the Case of Eliza reminds us that our *diagnostic categories* (such as "cortical blindness") are statements of how the patient *presently* is, not a description of what the patient *could become*. Since no other patient diagnosed as being cortically blind had ever recovered as Eliza did, the doctors thought her case was hopeless. But then, no other patient had ever been retrained using the "shaping" and "modeling" techniques Marty Merrill tried. An accurate diagnosis, therefore, doesn't always tell you how to treat the problem being diagnosed.

Since working with Eliza, Marty Merrill has been able to retrain a second cortically blind patient to "see." Given this *pattern* of success, we can expect that behavioral retraining techniques will eventually become a standard part of the medical regimen with cortically blind patients. Behavioral retraining takes much longer (and requires different skills) than does medical diagnosis and treatment. That's just one reason why I believe that, by the year 2000, there may be more psychologists working in hospitals than there are physicians.

Applied Psychology Involving Drugs

Drugs and surgery hold little hope for patients such as Eliza. But chemotherapy can be effective in helping make *behavioral* changes under certain circumstances. For example, we already know that chemicals such as caffeine speed up learning, and that "downers" typically retard it. By the year 2000, psychologists may use a wide variety of drugs that will help people achieve goals not presently within their reach. Chemicals to slow down or help reverse the process of senility are a possibility, as are drugs that will help prevent some types of mental illness. It is highly probable that all such compounds will be used *in conjunction with* psychological and social/behavioral treatment, but there is no reason not to use drugs if they can be helpful.

As we learn more about "consciousness," we will surely discover more effective means of inducing whatever "altered states of consciousness" anyone might desire to experience. Both drugs and biofeedback techniques seem likely candidates in this type of research.

Applied Psychology Involving Sensory Processing

Computers are crude models of our brains. As we gain more insight into how your cortex "processes" sensory inputs, we should be able to build dramatically better yet simpler computers than we presently have. It is already theoretically possible to use, for example, the brain of an ant or a worm as a "biological computer." That is, we should be able to "store " inputs in a tiny living brain and later retrieve these inputs in the form of motor outputs. The problem at the moment is in controlling the sensory inputs and the motor outputs. Biological computers should be able to handle complex decision making much better than present-generation electrical or mechanical computers—and brains are likely to be smaller and easier to handle than machines. Thus, it is possible that some "computer technologists" in the year 2000 will be, in effect, animal trainers rather than machine tenders.

Biological engineering will be a part of our future whether we like it or not. But it seems reasonably certain that it will always be used *along with* improved ways of "engineering" our thoughts and behaviors. So let us look next at what applied intra-psychic psychology may be like in 2000 A.D.

Applied Intra-psychic Psychology

Technology implies measurement. The more accurately you can describe or measure anything, the better chance you have of being able to exercise some kind of control over it. As you may have gathered from the earlier chapters in this book, one of the major problems with the intra-psychic or subjective approach to human existence is that internal events are most difficult to describe in quantitative or measurable terms. For this reason alone, we can probably expect greater immediate technological development in biological and behavioral psychology than in the intra-psychic area.

There are a number of highly promising developments, however, that we should take note of. Personality theory in the past has been based on the assumption that your character was fairly well fixed by the end of the first few years of your life. Freud, for instance, thought that only superficial or "surface" changes occurred in people once they had passed the years of early adolescence. Personality tests were usually designed to measure the intellectual and emotional traits a person already possessed, not the traits the person *might acquire* with training and encouragement.

My guess is that by 2000 A.D., we will have entirely new types of intelligence tests. Some will involve the use of EEG machines and computers to measure the *speed* with which the brain "processes" incoming information. Other more psychologically oriented tests will determine the *quality* of your decision-making skills and the rapidity with which you can acquire and utilize new information. These tests will probably be oriented more toward measuring performance in "real-life" situations than present intelligence scales, which tend to focus on certain academic skills.

The humanistic psychologists emphasize growth and perpetual change. One of the great-est challenges of the coming 20 years will be to develop new types of intra-psychic tests that will tell us more about the *potentialities* of people than present tests do. We will have to find new types of traits to measure (as best we can) that emphasize the process-of-becoming rather than "fixed" or supposedly unchangeable traits such as "intelligence" or "mental disorders." The humanistic psychologists are also likely to discover more about human (and humane) goals and values in the coming years than we presently know. In many ways, the humanists are in a unique position—that of functioning as a conscience or "superego" that can help keep the more applied technologies oriented toward *ethical* solutions of human problems.

Psychotherapy

Psychotherapy is one of the most important and exciting areas in psychology because it involves *people helping people*. As we noted earlier, however, the positive changes that sometimes occur during the early stages of psychotherapy aren't always sustained over the long haul. There are many reasons why this is so. To begin with, most psychotherapy stems from Freud, and Freud tended to emphasize emotions rather than cognitive and behavioral skills. As traditional types of therapy begin to incorporate some of the techniques used in cognitive behavior modification and social learning theory, the long-term success rate should rise.

Another problem with traditional types of psychotherapy has been the failure of some therapists to understand how the patient's behavior affects the *therapist*. Helping others change is a tremendously reinforcing experience. Most forms of talk therapy yield significant improvement in attitudes—and a lot of emotional release—during the first therapeutic sessions. These changes may so strongly reinforce the therapist that she or he might overemphasize the importance of immediate emotional expressivity and downplay the importance of long-term behavioral improvement. Then, when the initial improvement isn't sustained, both the therapist and the patient may *attribute* the failure to the patient's character without understanding they are making use of the attribution process. As psychologists learn more about the factors that determine human change—and as therapists use more of this knowledge in their practice—the "cure rate" for psychotherapy might well show a dramatic improvement.

It is also true that we may have expected too much from psychotherapy in the past. Many

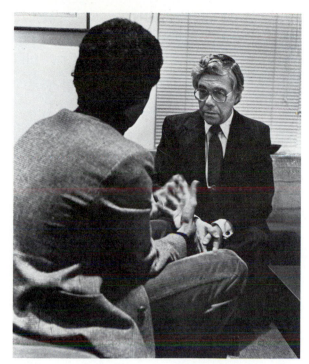

"Talk therapy" remains a popular form of treatment for emotional problems.

psychologists now believe that "talk treatment" is really a form of *psychological exploration* rather than a type of *treatment*. In a society as mobile as ours, it is not always easy to find someone to talk your troubles over with. More than this, not even your friends can always guide you through a full-fledged "investigation into the self." And yet, that is just what most forms of psychotherapy turn out to be.

We might suspect, therefore, that in the future people will seek out a therapist when they have minor problems and anxieties, or when they want to find out more about their own intra-psychic functioning. For more severe problems, however, a *combination* of therapies is more likely to yield good results. This combination will surely include biological therapy, behavioral therapy, family therapy, and work counseling as well as the more traditional types of psychotherapy.

Applied Developmental Psychology

One of the fastest-growing fields within the behavioral sciences is that of *developmental psychology*. Although this term once meant much the same thing as *child psychology*, we now realize that people continue to change throughout their lives. In the future, develop-

mental specialists will work with people of all ages, helping them solve whatever "growth" difficulties arise at any time in a person's life.

Life-long Learning

As our health gets better and our lives get longer, we will realize that there is no reason why we should commit ourselves to one occupation, or to one style of life, and stick with it forever. Indeed, studies of "job burn-out" and "career plateauing" suggest many people may *benefit* from changing occupations in mid-life. By the year 2000, therefore, some psychologists may specialize in helping middle-aged individuals acquire new job skills.

For that matter, we now realize that education should not stop when some college places a degree in a person's hands. Rather, learning should continue to the moment of the person's death. So even those middle-aged individuals who are content with their jobs may well decide to take additional college courses just to "freshen up their minds."

Later Life

Some of our greatest untapped resources are the skills and abilities of our senior citizens. As we learn how to maintain psychological youthfulness even when our bodies have started to creak and groan a bit, we will need specialists to help older people continue to be useful and contributing members of society.

Death is as much a part of the business of living as is life itself, yet we often avoid the topic, and it has seldom been studied scientifically. Developmental psychologists will probably be called upon as much to help people prepare psychologically for facing death as for facing life.

Applied Cognitive Psychology

The computer has revolutionized the way people think. But it has also dramatically altered the way that people "think about thinking." As we attempt to build machines that process information and make decisions the same way that humans do, we are forced to build ever-more-accurate models of the cognitive processes that allow us to survive in this complex world of ours. Little wonder, then, that cognitive psychology is one of the fastest-growing areas in the behavioral sciences.

Computers will also have a profound effect on education. As we discover more about how people learn, we surely will find new ways of helping people to learn *better*. We know from Skin-

Studying human-computer interactions may teach us important facts about human-human interactions.

ner's research on "programmed learning" that students acquire information faster when they are allowed to work at their own pace. Computers can be programmed to measure each student's knowledge and ability. Then the computer can "customize" the manner in which it presents data to each student. It will reward progress and gently correct mistakes. And, unlike most teachers, computers never get punitive when students don't learn at an "acceptable" speed. My suspicion is that, by the end of the century, most types of classroom learning will be handled by computers. The teachers will then be free to act as "models," as "resource persons," and as "mentors" for the students.

Computers are already changing the workplace. Many data-processing jobs now performed "at the office" could just as readily be done in the home. All you need is a computer terminal that is hooked into a central processing machine via the telephone line. Many corpo-

rations are using this approach already. Some workers seem to thrive on working at home, for they can work at their own pace and on their own schedules. Others miss the social excitement and challenge that comes from being around their fellow employees. But computers can even provide social stimulation. Already there are "networks" of people who use computer terminals to send and receive messages from each other—and to talk over work-related and personal problems. Perhaps by the next century, the computer will let us add to our "extended families" just as the telephone has in the past.

Applied Social/Behavioral Psychology

The engineering profession really got its start with the beginning of the Industrial Revolution.

Part of an engineer's job is to take known scientific data and use them to transform the physical environment. But in doing so, engineers often discover new scientific principles on their own. And, in putting well-known scientific theories to practical tests, the engineers may uncover flaws in the theory that laboratory scientists were unaware of.

One of the most important new professions is that of behavioral engineering—women and men who use psychological data to help create new and more satisfying social and work environments. My private opinion is that, by the year 2000, half the psychologists in the US will be employed in jobs demanding behavioral engineering skills. Let us look at some of the things they might be doing.

Community Mental Health

Writing in their 1980 book *Helping in the Community: Behavioral Applications*, Garry Martin and J. Grayson Osborne say:

> Behavioral community psychology projects may be more likely to examine behaviors that are collectively significant to society and that occur in locales other than the clinic, for which there should be societal consequences (as contrasted with individual consequences). But this approach does not rule out projects with individuals, in clinics, for which there are consequences dispensed by individuals.

As Yale psychologist Seymour Sarason noted in an article in *American Psychologist* in 1981, from a historical point of view, clinical psychology has emphasized work with individuals. But, according to Sarason, "the substance of psychology cannot be independent of the social order. It is not that it *should not* be independent but that it *cannot be*." People always live with—and are affected by—other people. As clinical psychologists move out of the "sheltered environment" of their private offices and into the "real world of people," they are likely to face many new challenges. Let's look at what some of these challenges might be.

"Parenting" Skills

Already we have a great many community mental health centers scattered across the US and Canada. We will need many more of them, for they tend to focus on changing "systems" rather than just working with individuals. The data suggest, for instance, that many parents who mistreat their children were mistreated by their own parents. If we are to stop this destructive behavior toward innocent children, we will have to find effective ways of teaching some parents to manage their children without resorting to violent physical punishment. Since most high schools and colleges fail to give training in "parenting skills," probably the community mental health centers will have to fill the educational gap.

In the future, psychologists may discover better ways of helping parents solve the problems associated with child abuse.

What we call "mental illness" tends to run in families partly because of genetic factors, in part because certain types of parental responses induce "insane" (that is, disordered) behavior in children. To break this self-perpetuating pattern of mental illness, we will need more effective forms of family counseling. Much of this counseling will be systems-oriented "family therapy." We will also have to make some rather difficult moral decisions concerning society's right to intervene in unhealthy family situations when the parents may resent or fight against outside intervention.

Sheltered Environments

Mental hospitals as we presently know them may well vanish during the first part of the next century. These "asylums" will be replaced by clinics, re-education centers, halfway houses, group homes, and other forms of "sheltered environments," where people with mental problems may go for relatively short periods of time. Behavioral engineers—working in teams with psychiatrists, clinical psychologists, and social workers—will help these disturbed people find solutions to their problems. The patients will then be eased back into society bit by bit, rather than being discharged abruptly with little in the way of after-care. Behavioral psychologists will also be involved in helping to change the social environment (such as a family situation) into which the patient will return.

The importance of the "step-by-step" method of bringing mental patients back into society is emphasized in recent work by Wayne State psychologist Jacobo A. Varela and his students. Varela noted that many ex-mental patients were housed in cheap hotels where violence was rampant. Terrified by their new environment, the patients often remained locked in their rooms and thus were even more cut off from other people than when they had been hospitalized. Varela and his students slipped notes under the doors of the patients' rooms inviting them to join "rap" groups in the hotel that would discuss problems they all had in common. Varela states that 19 out of 20 ex-patients responded enthusiastically and "came out from behind their locked doors." Unfortunately, this type of carefully engineered "after-care" is seldom offered by the present mental-health establishment.

The sprawling concrete prisons we presently send criminals to will also slowly fade from the scene. As we gain greater control over the social environment, fewer people will "want" to become law-breakers. Rehabilitation and re-education are much more effective ways of dealing with criminals than are merely punishing them and locking them away behind bars. Thus, prisons should develop into "schools for social and personal learning" and be staffed as much by psychologists as by wardens and guards. And prisoners—like ex-mental patients—should be given extensive assistance after leaving jail in order to help them learn the skills necessary for day-to-day survival. However, given the "urge for vengeance" that seems to afflict us all, and because of the strong belief that "punishment works," prison reform will probably come much more slowly than will changes in mental hospitals.

Industrial Psychology

Writing in *American Psychologist* in 1982, R. Fox, A. Barclay, and D. Rodgers define "professional psychology" as that "which is concerned with enhancing the effectiveness of human function. Therefore, a professional psychologist is one who has expertise in the development and application of quality services to the public in a controlled, organized manner . . ."

Enhancing the effectiveness of human function" is one of the main tasks of *industrial psychologists* and *organizational psychologists*.

Psychologists have long been employed by business firms and governmental agencies. One of the chief functions of these industrial psychologists has been that of personnel selection. A great many intelligence and aptitude tests have been developed that, under the right conditions, allow psychologists to evaluate the knowledge and skills of potential employees. Psychologists also have tried to develop "job descriptions" that would state what abilities were needed to handle a particular position. It was then up to the psychologist to match the person to the job. As we learn more about how to help people grow and develop, however, industrial psychologists will probably spend more time *training* personnel than in *selecting* them.

Improving Job Performance

A worker's performance is not dependent entirely on her or his own talents. It also depends on the type of encouragement and feedback the worker's supervisor gives, and on how rewarding and satisfying the job happens to be. In his 1978 book *How To Improve Human Performance*, Thomas K. Connellan points out that gaining some control over their own destinies—that is, being able to participate in deci-

Large corporations often call in psychological consultants for assistance, much as individuals seek help from psychotherapists.

Thomas K. Connellan

sion making—is a major reinforcer for most workers. And as we noted in Chapter 23, most successful supervisors do in fact use "participatory management" as one of their main managerial tools.

Giving employees appropriate feedback on job performance is a large part of "participatory management." Indeed, the so-called *quality control circles* used by many Japanese companies are little more than feedback devices in which both workers and managers can let each other know "how things are going" and suggest ways of improving matters.

The Hawthorne Effect

For almost half a century, industrial psychologists have spoken of the "Hawthorne Effect," meaning that one must be careful in real-life experiments because subjects will often produce the results they think the experimenters

want. The effect gets its name from a series of studies performed at the Hawthorne (Chicago) plant where the Western Electric Company manufactures equipment for AT&T. This research, done between 1926 and 1932, was designed to discover how much productivity and morale might be improved when the experimenters made various changes in the work environment.

According to the initial reports the experimenters issued, productivity increased *no matter what the experimenters did.* The usual interpretation of these data has been that the subjects knew they were being measured. Hence they worked harder whether the experimenters made conditions better or worse. Psychologist H.M. Parsons has recently re-examined all of the original data in this study. Parsons shows that productivity increased *only* in those situations in which the workers could have gotten some feedback as to how well they were performing. Parsons believes the so-called "Hawthorne Effect" offers strong support for the belief that productivity tends to increase *primarily* when employees are given appropriate feedback about their performance.

Management "By Exception"

Generally speaking, most American managers and supervisors "manage by exception." They typically *ignore* appropriate work behaviors and focus on *punishing* inappropriate or off-target behaviors. But as Thomas Connellan points out, "management by exception" actually tends to punish productive responses and reinforce (with attention) unproductive and disruptive responses.

As an example of how behavioral engineers might help managers overcome this tendency to "manage by exception," suppose we look briefly at industrial absenteeism. Connellan notes that employees who stay away from their jobs cost the US more than $40 billion a year. In some companies, 10 percent of the employees are likely to be absent on a given day. For many years the "cure" for absenteeism has been punishing those workers who had no excuse for their failure to show up at work. Most managers *attributed* the cause of "playing hookey" from work to some innate character flaw in the employees' personalities.

In fact, as recent studies show, high absence rates are primarily an index of poor employee morale and of job dissatisfaction. In general, the more a worker dislikes the supervisor and/or the work group, the more likely it is that the worker will have a high absentee rate. When jobs are extremely scarce, threatening to fire an employee may have some effect on absenteeism. When jobs are more plentiful, rather a different solution seems to be called for. Many corporations have found that offering workers "time off" for good attendance often cuts the absentee rate in half.

However, as E.E. Lawler and J.R. Hackman showed in 1969, by far the best way to reduce absenteeism is to ask employees what incentives or job changes they want, and then to reward the workers with what they asked for when they do show up for work. (Some employes may prefer other rewards than "time off.")

Industrial corporations often count their buildings, machines, and profits as "corporate assets." As psychologist Rensis Likert points out, however, the finest resources available to any company are the skills and talents of its employees. Two of the major jobs for future industrial psychologists will be (1) to help executives measure these human assets, and (2) to treasure these assets by developing work environments that are optimally satisfying to all employees.

Organizational Development

In the January 1982 issue of *Contemporary Psychology*, Clayton Alderfer defines organizational development as "a professional field that attempts to improve human organizations by using the theory and methods of behavioral science." The problem with this field is that we know much more about people working in organizations than we do about organizations themselves. There are at least two good reasons for this lack of knowledge about organizations:

First, psychology has always focused more on the individual than on larger social systems. As Edgar Schein points out in the third edition of his book *Organizational Psychology*, "Organizations begin as ideas in the minds of people." Thus, Schein's book carries the term "organization" in its title, but Schein writes more about people in organizations than about organizations themselves.

Second, there probably have been a thousand times as many studies of individuals as of groups, and a thousand times as many studies of groups as of organizations. So we simply *know more* about individuals than we do about larger social systems.

A Theory of Behavior in Organizations, published in 1980 by James Naylor, Robert Pritchard, and Daniel Ilgen, is essentially an application of social learning theory to the study of organizational development. Naylor and his colleagues assume that productivity is a function of the *collective perceptions* of the individuals within the organization. If employees perceive a given act as likely to yield a reward, they will perform that act. Therefore, managers shouldn't just offer reinforcers for good behavior. Rather, these authors say, management should also attempt to alter the "attitudes and perceptions" employees have about work-related actions. As an application of cognitive behavioral psychology to the workplace, the book is excellent. As a description of how organizations function, the book has certain obvious weaknesses.

Systems Theory for Organizational Development, a 1980 book edited by Thomas Cummings, is quite a different kettle of fish. Most of the authors of the various chapters attempt to apply an information-processing model or General Systems Theory model to the study of large organizations. Will McWhinney's chapter on "how to design an organization" is a particularly apt description of how to use systems technology in creating and maintaining new social systems.

In the future, I suspect, psychologists will probably adopt the strategies found in both these new books. That is, they will utilize *change strategies for individuals* (as Naylor *et al.* suggest), and they will apply various psychological theories to the *study and understanding* of social systems (as described in the Cummings book).

Applied Social Psychology

As we begin to use the behavioral sciences to bring about changes in groups and organizations, social psychologists will become involved in such tasks as helping groups, organizations, and even countries resolve conflicts. One way to increase conflict resolution would be to make people more aware of how much social havoc the *attribution process* can wreak. (If you want to see the attribution process at work in international affairs, read what commentators in the Soviet have to say about American *motives*, what the Arabs say about the Israelis, what the Israelis say about the Arabs, and so forth.) We will never have "one world" until all of us stop attributing cultural differences to personality flaws rather than to learned responses.

For more than two decades now, social scientists at the University of Chicago have been studying how juries make decisions. As you might guess, jurors are likely to attribute crimes to character defects, and thus to decide guilt and innocence on a biased basis. At some time in the future, surely, we will want to restrict jury membership to those individuals who have some knowledge of the social (as well as the intra-psychic) variables that influence human behavior.

Perhaps the most important thing that psychologists can bring to human affairs, however, is the knowledge that all social change has costs as well as benefits. "Cleaning up the environment," for instance, is a very expensive proposition. Social psychologists might well help us estimate precisely what the price of change will be—and then work out informational programs that will encourage people to make the sacrifices necessary to achieve worthy goals.

Psychology In Your Future

Fifty years ago most Americans were employed in producing "things"—farm products and manufactured goods. Today more than half of all Americans are employed in service occupations—that is, in processing information, helping other people, or taking care of people's possessions. As we learn more effective ways of assisting one another, the need for psychological services will grow tremendously. The behavioral sciences have rapidly become one of the most popular undergraduate majors in US colleges and universities. My own estimate is that by the year 2000 at least 10 percent of the US work force will be able to lay claim to the title "psychologist" or "behavioral engineer."

Whether you choose to become a psychologist yourself is a decision only you can make. But perhaps reading *Understanding Human Behavior* has given you some notion of what the future possibilities in psychology will be. At its best, psychology can offer you the tools to shape your body, your mind, and your social environment somewhat closer to your heart's desire. We do not know what the real limits of human potential are—we know only that people are capable of greater growth and development than we dreamed possible a mere 50 years ago.

Now that you have discovered what psychology is all about, perhaps you can use your new-found knowledge to help plot your own course into the future.

Let me close by thanking you for making me your guide through some of the frontiers of psychology, and by wishing you the happiest of life's journeys.

Statistical Appendix

The Red Lady

I was sitting in the student union not long ago, talking with a friend of mine named Gersh, when two young women came over to our table and challenged us to a game of bridge. The two women—Joan and Carol were their names—turned out to be undergraduates. They also turned out to be card sharks, and they beat the socks off Gersh and me. Joan was particularly clever at figuring out how the cards were distributed among the four bridge hands—and hence good at figuring out how to play her own cards to win the most tricks.

One hand I will never forget, not merely because Joan played it so well, but because of what she said afterwards. Joan had bid four spades, and making the contract depended on figuring out who had the Queen of Diamonds—Gersh or me. Joan thought about it for a while, then smiled sweetly at Gersh. "I think you've got the Red Lady," she said, and promptly captured Gersh's Queen of Diamonds with her King.

Gersh, who hates to lose, muttered something about "dumb luck."

"No luck to it, really," Joan replied. "I knew you had 5 diamonds, Gersh, while Doc here had only 2. One of you had the Queen, but I didn't know which. But since you had 5 of the 7 missing diamonds, Gersh, the odds were 5 to 2 that you had the Little Old Lady. Simple enough, when you stop to think about it."

While Gersh was dealing the next hand with noisy frustration, Joan turned to me. "I know you're a professor, but I don't know what you teach."

"Psychology," I said, picking up my cards for the next hand. The cards were rotten, as usual.

"Oh, you're a psych teacher! That's great," Joan said with a smile. "I really wanted to study psych, but they told me I had to take statistics. I hate math. I'm just no good at figuring out all those complicated equations. So I majored in history instead."

Statistics—A Way Of Thinking

I shook my head in amazement at what Joan said. I don't know how many times students have told me much the same thing—they're rotten at mathematics, or they just can't figure out what statistics is all about. But these same students manage to play bridge superbly, or figure out the stock market, or they can tell you the batting averages of every major league baseball player, or how many miles per gallon their car gets on unleaded gasoline.

Statistics is not just a weird bunch of mathematics—it's a way of thinking. If you can think well enough to figure out how to play cards, or who is likely to win the next election, or what "grading on the curve" is all about, then you're probably already pretty good at statistics. In fact, you surely use statistics intuitively every minute of your life. If you didn't, you'd be dead or in some institution by now.

Sure, a few of the equations that statisticians throw around get pretty fancy. But don't let that fact discourage you. I've been a psych prof for more than 20 years, I minored in mathematics, but even I don't understand all the equations I see in the statistical and psychological journals. However, those "fancy formulas"

Learning how to use statistical reasoning is no more difficult than learning how to play bridge.

are usually of interest only to specialists. Forget about them—unless you happen to be a nut about mathematics.

The truth is that you *already know* most of the principles involved in basic statistics—if, like Joan, you're willing to stop and think about them. Yet many psych students reject statistics with the same sort of emotionality that they show when somebody offers them fried worms and rattlesnake steak for dinner. Well, worms are rich in protein, and rattlesnake meat is delicious—and safe to eat—if you don't have to catch the snake first. But you may have to overcome some pretty strong emotional prejudices before you're willing to dig in and see what snake meat (or stat) is all about.

Odds and Ends

I've been a gambler all my life, and I really enjoy trying to "psych people out" at the bridge or poker table. So maybe I didn't get conditioned to fear numbers and "odds" the way a lot of people do. But whether you realize it or not, you're a gambler too. And you (like Joan) are pretty good at figuring out all kinds of odds and *probabilities*. Every time you cross the street, you gamble that the odds are "safely" in your favor. Each time you drive your car through a green light without slowing down, you gamble that some "odd" driver won't run the red light and hit you broadside. Every time you study for a true-false exam, you're gambling that you can learn enough to do better than somebody who

" I THINK YOU SHOULD BE MORE EXPLICIT HERE IN STEP TWO."

refuses to study and who just picks the answers randomly. And whenever you go out with somebody on a date, you're gambling that you can predict that person's future behavior (on the date) from observing the things that the person has done in the past.

So you're a gambler, too, even if you don't think of yourself as being one. But if you're going to gamble, wouldn't it be helpful to know something about odds and probabilities? Because if you know what the odds are, you can often do a much better job of achieving whatever goals you have in mind.

One way or another, almost everything in statistics is based on *probability theory*. And, as luck would have it, probability theory got its start some 300 years ago when some French gamblers got worried about what the pay-offs should be in a dice game. So the gamblers—who were no dummies—hired two brilliant French mathematicians to figure out the probabilities for them. From the work of these two French geniuses came the theory that allows the casinos in Las Vegas and Atlantic City to earn hundreds of millions of dollars every year, that lets the insurance companies earn even more by betting on how long people will live—and that lets psychologists and psychiatrists employ the mental tests that label some people as being "normal" and other people as being "abnormal."

The Odds in Favor

If you want to see why Joan was so good at playing bridge, get a deck of cards and pull out the 2, 3, 4, 5, 6, 7, and Queen of Diamonds. Turn them face down on a table and shuffle them around so you won't know which card is which. Now try to pick out the Queen just by looking at the back of the cards.

If the deck is "honest" (unmarked), what are the odds that you will pick the Red Lady instead of the 2, 3, 4, 5, 6, or 7? As you can see, the odds are exactly 1 in 7. If you want to be fancy about all this, you can write an equation (which is what Joan did in her mind) as follows:

The probability (p) of picking the Queen (Q) is 1 out of 7, therefore

$$pQ = 1/7$$

Next, shuffle the cards again, place them face down on the table, and then randomly select 2 of the cards and put them on one side of the table, and the remaining 5 on the other side of the table. Now, what are the odds that the Queen is in the stack of 5 cards (Gersh's bridge hand), and what are the odds that the Queen is in the stack of 2 cards (my bridge hand)?

Well, you already know that the probability that any 1 card will be the Queen is 1/7. I have 2 cards, therefore, I have two chances at getting the Queen, and the equation reads:

$$pQ \text{ (Me)} = 1/7 + 1/7 = 2/7$$

Gersh had 5 cards, so his probability equation is:

$$pQ \text{ (Gersh)} = 1/7 + 1/7 + 1/7 + 1/7 + 1/7 = 5/7$$

So if you dealt out the 7 cards randomly 70 times, Gersh would have the Queen about 50 times, and I would have the Queen about 20 times. No wonder Joan wins at bridge! When she assumed that Gersh had the Queen, she didn't have a sure thing—but the odds were surely in her favor.

Outcomes and Incomes

Now let's look at something familiar to everyone, the true-false examination. Suppose that you go to a history class one day, knowing there will be a test, but the teacher throws you a curve. For the exam you get is written in Chinese, or Greek, or some other language you simply can't read a word of. The test has 20 questions, and it's obviously of the true-false variety. But since you can't read it, all you can do is guess. What exam score do you think you'd most likely get—0, 10, or 20?

Maybe you'd deserve a 0, since you couldn't read the exam. But I'm sure you realize intuitively that you'd most likely get a score of about 10. Why?

Well, what are the *odds* of your guessing any single question right, if it's a true-false exam?

If you said, "Fifty percent chance of being right," you're thinking clearly. (See what I mean about statistics being a way of thinking?)

The probability (p) of your getting the first question right (R_1) is 50 percent, or 1/2. So we write an equation that says:

$$pR_1 = 1/2$$

The probability of your getting the first question wrong (W_1) is also 50 percent, or 1/2. So we write another equation:

$$pW_1 = 1/2$$

Furthermore, we can now say that, on the first or any other equation, the

$$pR + pW = 1/2 + 1/2 = 1$$

Which is a fancy way of saying that whenever you guess the answer on a true-false exam, you have to be either right or wrong—because those are the only two *outcomes* possible.

Now, suppose we look at the first two questions on the test. What is the probability that you will get *both* of them right, if you are just guessing at the answers?

Well, what outcomes are possible? You could miss both questions (W_1W_2), or you could get them both right (R_1R_2), or you could get the first answer right and the second answer wrong (R_1W_2), or you could get the first one wrong and the second right (W_1R_2).

Thus, there are 4 different outcomes, and since you would be guessing at the right answer on both questions, these 4 outcomes are *equally likely to occur*. Only 1 of the 4 outcomes (R_1R_2) is the one we're interested in, so the odds of your getting both questions right is 1/4.

$$pR_1R_2 = 1/4$$
$$pW_1W_2 = 1/4$$
$$pR_1W_2 = 1/4$$
$$pW_1R_2 = 1/4$$

and

$$pR_1R_2 + pW_1W_2 + pR_1W_2 + pW_1R_2 = 1/4 + 1/4 + 1/4 + 1/4 = 1$$

In a sense, getting both questions right is like selecting the Queen of Diamonds when it is 1 of 4 cards face down on the table in front of you. In both cases, you have 4 equally likely outcomes, so your chances of getting the Queen (or being right on both answers) is 1 out of 4, or 1/4.

As you can see, if you're taking an exam, playing bridge, or trying to add to your income by buying a lottery ticket, it will surely pay you to consider all the possible outcomes.

Actually, we can figure the odds of your answering the first 2 questions correctly in a much simpler way. We simply multiply the odds of your getting the first question right (pR_1) by the odds of your getting the second question right (pR_2):

$$pR_1R_2 = pR_1 \times pR_2 = 1/2 \times 1/2 = 1/4 = 25\%$$

Maybe you can see, too, that the odds of your getting both answers *wrong* would be exactly the same:

$$pW_1W_2 = pW_1 \times pW_2 = 1/2 \times 1/2 = 1/4 = 25\%$$

If the exam had just three questions to it, the odds of your getting all the answers right by chance alone (that is, by guessing) would be:

$$pR_1R_2R_3 = pR_1 \times pR_2 \times pR_3 = 1/2 \times 1/2 \times 1/2 = 1/8 = 12.5\%$$

To put the matter another way, on a 3-question exam, there are 8 different outcomes:

$$R_1R_2R_3$$
$$R_1R_2W_3$$
$$R_1W_2R_3$$
$$R_1W_2W_3$$
$$W_1R_2R_3$$
$$W_1R_2W_3$$
$$W_1W_2R_3$$
$$W_1W_2W_3$$

Since only 1 of these 8 possible outcomes is the one you want ($R_1R_2R_3$), the odds in your favor are only 1 in 8.

If the test had 4 true-false questions, there would be 16 different outcomes—twice as many as if the test had but three questions. These outcomes would range from $R_1R_2R_3R_4$, $R_1R_2R_3W_4$. . . .all the way to $W_1W_2W_3R_4$ and $W_1W_2W_3W_4$. If there are 16 different outcomes, only one of which is "all answers right" or $R_1R_2R_3R_4$, what would be the odds of your guessing all the answers right on a 4-question true-false test?

(If you said, "1 in 16," congratulations!)

Now, let's take a giant leap.

If the exam had 10 questions, the odds of your getting all 10 answers right by guessing would be:

$$pR_1R_2R_3R_4R_5R_6R_7R_8R_9R_{10} = 1/2 \times 1/2 \times 1/2 \times 1/2 \times 1/2 \times 1/2 \times 1/2 \times 1/2 \times 1/2 \times 1/2 = 1/1024$$

So if you took the exam 1024 times and guessed randomly at the answers each time, just *once* in 1024 times would you expect to get a score of 0, and just *once* in 1024 times would you expect to get a score of 10.

Now, at last, we can answer the question we asked you a few paragraphs back: If you took a 20-question exam on which you had to guess at each answer, what exam score do you think you'd most likely get—0, 10, or 20?

Well, what are the odds that you'd get a score of flat 0? In fact, the odds are astronomically against you, just as they are astronomically against your getting a score of 20 right. In either case, the probability would be:

$$pW_{1\text{-}20} = pR_{1\text{-}20} = 1/2 \times 1/2 \times 1/2 \ldots$$
$$(20 \text{ times!}) = 1{,}048{,}576 \text{ to } 1!$$

So the odds are more than a million to one that you won't get all the answers right or all the answers wrong on a 20 question true-false exam just by guessing. Which might give you good reason to study for the next exam you have to take!

Normal Curves

Next, let's throw in some pictures just to liven things up a bit. Statisticians have a way of plotting or graphing probabilities that may make more sense to you than equations do.

Let's make a diagram of the *distribution* of outcomes when you take an 10-question true-false exam (See Fig. A.1):

As we mentioned earlier, the number of possible outcomes in a 10-question exam is 1024. So the odds of getting all 10 questions right by just guessing ("by chance alone") would be 1 in 1024. Not very good odds. But the probability of your getting 4, 5, or 6 questions right would be well above 60 percent! That makes sense, because just looking at the curve you can see that better than 60 percent of the possible outcomes are bunched up right in the middle of the curve.

Descriptive Statistics

The curve we've just drawn is the world-famous, ever-popular "bell-shaped curve." In fact, the curve describes a *random distribution of scores* or outcomes. That is, the curve describes the outcomes you'd expect when students are forced to guess—more or less at random—which answers on a true-false exam are correct. Naturally, if the exam were written in clear English, and if the students knew most of the material they were being examined on, the curve or *distribution of scores* would look quite different.

There are many sorts of "outcomes" that fit the bell-shaped curve rather nicely. For example, if you randomly selected 1,000 adult US males and measured their heights, the results you'd get would come very close to matching the bell-shaped curve shown in Fig. A.2. Which is to say that there would be a few very short men, a few very tall men, but most would have heights around 5'10". The same bell-shaped curve would fit the distribution of heights of 1,000 adult women selected at random—except that the "middle" or peak of the bell-shaped curve would be about 5'5".

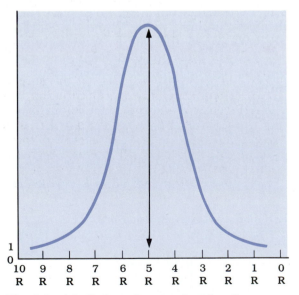

Fig. A.1 A bell-shaped curve showing the distribution of "right answers" expected by chance alone when taking a 10-item true-false exam.

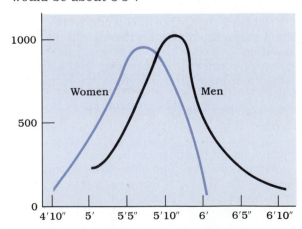

Fig. A.2 A bell-shaped curve showing the distribution of heights of a thousand men and a thousand women selected at random.

Measures of Central Tendency

As we noted in Chapter 21, intelligence tests are constructed so that the scores for any age group will approximate a bell-shaped curve. In this case, the peak or "middle" of the distribution of IQ's will be almost precisely at 100. A very few individuals would have IQ's below 50, a very few would have scores above 150. But some two-thirds of the scores would fall between 84 and 116 (see diagram page 576).

Why this bulge in the middle as far as IQ's are concerned? Well, think back for a moment to the true-false test we were discussing earlier that had 10 questions on it. There are 1024 possible outcomes. If you wanted to get all 10 questions right, there was only one way you could answer the 10 questions—all had to be correct. But there were 256 ways in which you could answer the questions to get a score of 5—right in the middle.

There is only one way you can earn a top score on an intelligence test—you've got to answer all the questions rapidly and precisely the way the people who constructed the test say is "right." But there are thousands of different ways you can answer the questions on the usual test to get a "middle score," namely, an IQ between 84 and 116.

In a similar vein, there are precious few ways in which you can earn a million dollars, but there are dozens and dozens of ways in which you can earn between $15,000 and $20,000 a year. So if we selected 1,000 adult US citizens at random, asked them what their incomes were, and then "took an average," what kind of curve (distribution of incomes) do you think we'd get?

Whenever we measure people psychologically, biologically, socially, intellectually, or economically, we often generate a distribution of outcomes that looks very much like a bell-shaped curve. Each person in the world is unique, it's true. But it is equally true that, on any given *single* measuring scale (height, weight, grade-point average, income), most people's scores will be somewhere in the *middle* of the range of possible outcomes.

Psychologists have a variety of tools for measuring the "middle" of any curve or distribution of outcomes. These techniques are often called *measures of central tendency*, which is a fancy way of saying that these techniques allow us to measure the center or midpoint of any distribution of scores or outcomes.

Mean, Median, Mode

1. *The Mean.* The *mean* is simply the statistical "average" of all the scores or outcomes involved. When you figure your grade-point average (GPA) for any semester, you usually multiply your grade in each course by the number of credit hours, add up the totals, and divide by the number of hours credit you are taking. Your GPA is actually the *mean* or mathematical average of all your grades (see Table A.1).

2. *The Median.* Since the mean is a mathematical average, it sometimes gives very funny results. For example, according to recent government figures, the "average" US family was made up of about 4.47 people. Have you ever known a family that had 4.47 people in it? For another example, if you got two As and two Cs one semester, your average or "mean" grade would be a B. Yet you didn't get a B in any of the courses you took.

There are times when it makes more sense to figure the exact *midpoint score* or outcome, rather than figuring out the *average* score. At such times, psychologists often use the *median*, which is the score that's in the precise middle of the distribution—just as the "median" of an expressway is the area right down the middle of the highway.

The median is often used as a "measure of central tendency" when a distribution has one or two extreme scores in it. For instance, if 9 people earn $1 a year, and a tenth earns $100,000, what is the *mean* income of these 10 people? About $10,001 a year, which is a misleading statistic, to say the least. However, the *median* income is $1, which de-

TABLE A.1   Table of Grade Point Averages

Course	Hours Credit	Grade	Hour × Grade
History	3	A	3 × 4 = 12
Psychology	4	A	4 × 4 = 16
Mathematics	4	C	4 × 2 = 8
Spanish	4	B	4 × 3 = 12
TOTALS	15		48

GPA = 48/15 = 3.2

scribes the actual income of the *majority* of the group somewhat better than does the mean of $10,001.

3. *The Mode.* The word *mode* is defined in the dictionary as "the prevailing fashion or most popular custom or style." When we are talking about distributions of scores or outcomes, *mode* means the most popular score. That is, the mode is the highest point (or points) on the curve. If the distribution has two points that are equally high, then there are two scores that are *modal*, and we can call the curve *bi-modal* (having two modes).

Skewedness

If the distribution of scores is more or less bell-shaped, then the mean, median, and mode usually come out to be the same. But not all curves do us the favor of being so regular in shape. For example, suppose you were interested in whether a particular teacher—Dr. Johnson—started and ended her classes on

time. To find out, you take a very accurate watch with you all semester long and make a scientific study of Dr. Johnson's behavior.

During the term, let's say, there are supposed to be 50 lectures by Dr. Johnson. So the number of possible start-time scores or outcomes will be 50. For the most part, Dr. Johnson begins on time, but occasionally she starts a minute or two early, and sometimes she's a minute or two late. Now and again, she is fairly tardy in getting to class, and once she didn't show up at all. But she *never* begins a class more than two minutes early. If you put all of her starting times on a graph, it would look something like the curve on the left side of Figure A.3. If you plotted all her closing time scores on a similar graph, it would look like the curve on the right in Figure A.3.

The term we use to describe these curves is *skewedness*, which means they are "slanted" or "pushed out of shape." In the starting-time example, the curve slants out far to the right-hand side, so we say that the curve is "skewed to the right." The other curve has a tail that slants out to the left, so the curve is "skewed to the left." As is the case in many distributions where the scores are measures of reaction times or beginning times, the mean, median, and mode are fairly different.

Range and Variation

There are two more important concepts we have to get out of the way before we can finish our discussion of *descriptive statistics*—which is to say, statistics that measure or describe something. The first concept is the *range* of possible scores or outcomes; the second is the *variability* of the scores. The first concept is easy to understand, but the second will take some careful thought on your part.

What is the *range* of possible scores on a 10-item "fill in the blanks" test? From 0 to 10, of course. And since you can't guess as easily on this type of test as on a true-false examination, you can't really tell ahead of time what the class average is likely to be. The range on a 100-item test would be from 0 to 100—and again, you have no way of knowing before you take the test what the "mean" or average score is likely to be.

Let's suppose that you took a 10-item "fill in the blanks" exam and got a score of 8 right, which also turned out to be the mean or average score for the whole class. Then you took a 100-item "fill in the blanks" test and again you got a score of 8, which again turned out to be the class average. What does knowing the *range* of

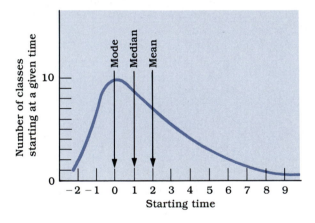

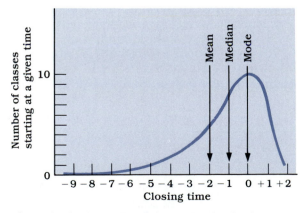

Fig. A.3 A plot of Dr. Johnson's "beginning times" and "closing times."

possible scores tell you about the level of difficulty of the two tests? Wouldn't you say that the 100-item test was considerably more difficult, even though the class average was the same on both tests?

Now, let's add one more dimension. Suppose that on the 10-item examination, *everybody in class* got a score of 8! There would be no *variation* at all in these scores, since none of the scores *deviated* (were different from) the mean. But suppose on the 100-item "fill in the blanks" exam, about 95 percent of the class got scores of flat zero, you got an 8, and a few "aces" got scores above 85. Your score of 8 would still be the *mean* (but not the median or mode). But the *deviation* of the rest of the scores would be tremendous. Even though you scored right at the mean on both tests, the fact that you were better than 95 percent of the class on the 100-item test might well be very pleasing to you.

The variation or variability of test scores is simply a measure of *how spread out across the range* the scores actually are. Thus, the variability of a distribution of scores is a very important item to know if you're going to evaluate how you perform in relation to anybody else who's taken the test.

The Standard Deviation

If you know the range of scores, plus the mean, median, and mode, you can usually get a fairly good notion of what shape the curve might take. Why? Because these two bits of information tell you something about how the scores are *distributed*. If the mean, median, and mode are almost the same, and they fall right at the center of the range, then the distribution curve must be "vaguely" bell-shaped, or regular in shape.

But why do we say "vaguely" bell-shaped? In Chapter 24, we discussed the distribution of scores on an attitude questionnaire in two different groups. In the homogeneous group, as Fig. A.4 shows, the range of scores was very small. But in the heterogeneous group, as Fig. A.5 shows, the range was much larger. The means for the two distributions were the same, and if the groups had been large enough, we might even have found that the ranges of the two distributions were the same. However, in the homogeneous group, the scores were all bunched up close to the mean, while in the heterogeneous group, the scores were broadly *dispersed*, or spread out.

In Chapter 21, we found that we needed a concept we called the *standard deviation* to describe the *dispersion of scores* across the range (or around the mean). The larger the standard deviation, the more widely the scores vary around the mean (and the more heterogeneous the group probably is). The smaller the standard deviation, the more bunched up the scores are around the mean (and the more homogeneous the group probably is).

We can now define the *standard deviation* as a statistical term meaning the variability of scores in a distribution.

There are a variety of mathematical formulas for figuring out such statistics as the standard deviation. Once upon a time, students were required to memorize these formulas and grind out statistical analyses using nothing more than their brains (and perhaps their fingers and toes to count on). Nowadays, however, even cheap pocket calculators will figure out the

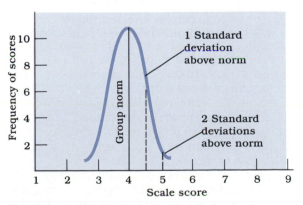
Fig. A.4 A distribution of attitude scores for a homogeneous group.

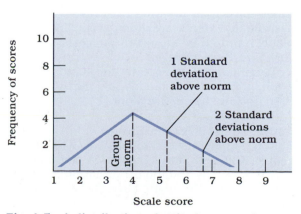
Fig. A.5 A distribution of attitude scores for a heterogeneous group.

standard deviation of a distribution of scores almost instanteously (if you input the right data in the first place). If you wish to learn one of the formulas for calculating the standard deviation—or if you are required to do so—you will find them in many places, including the *Student Manual* that accompanies this book.

However, as we said earlier, statistics is more a way of thinking than it is a bunch of fancy formulas. *Descriptive statistics* are short-hand ways of describing large bunches of data. They are "thought tools" that let you think about the world in convenient symbols.

Let's now see how you can use "descriptive" statistics to help you *make inferences* or draw conclusions about the data you're mulling over in your mind.

Inferential Statistics

Whenever you test a hunch or a scientific hypothesis, you often are hunting for *reliable* differences between two groups of subjects or between two sets of data. Again, there are *many* different formulas for figuring out how reliable (or important) the group differences really are. But one of the simplest—and most often used—is the standard deviation. By convention, scientists accept differences as being "real" if the means of the two groups depart by 2 or more standard deviations from each other.

We pick the figure 2 standard deviations for a very understandable reason. If on a bell-shaped curve we measure out from the mean a distance of 2 standard deviations, we will take into account about 95 percent of all the IQ scores described by the curve. Any score falling outside of this distance will be there *by chance alone* less than 5 percent of the time. So the odds of your getting an IQ of 132 are but 5 in 100, or 1 in 20. Since these odds are pretty impressive, we can assume that your score didn't occur "by chance alone," and thus the score suggests you are "brighter than average."

To summarize, the greater the standard deviation, the greater the odds are that the score didn't occur "by chance alone."

Differences Between Groups

Now, suppose we compare the IQ's of two people, Bill and Mary. Bill has a score of 84, which is exactly 1 standard deviation from the mean of 100. He might have "below average" intelligence, true. But he's so close to the mean that we might as well call him "average" since he might have been overly tired when he took

the test. (In fact, even if his *true* IQ was 100, Bill would get a *measured* score of between 84 and 100 about one-third of the time that he took the test. Can you guess why this would be the case?)

Mary has an IQ of 116, which is exactly 1 standard deviation above the mean. But again, her score isn't all that different from the mean, so we could (technically speaking) say that she too has "average intelligence." (She too would be expected to get a *measured* score between 100 and 116 one-third of the time if her *true* IQ was 100. And, like Bill, she would also get a *measured* score between 84 and 100 a third of the time.)

Since both Bill and Mary have IQ's that "vary" from the mean but 1 standard deviation, their scores of 84 and 116 don't differ reliably from each other, right?

Wrong! (As if you didn't know that intuitively anyhow.)

Bill's score differs from Mary's by *2* standard deviations, thus the odds are at least 20 to 1 that Mary's *true* IQ score is significantly higher than Bill's. (And wouldn't you have been willing to make a small wager that was the case the moment you knew what their scores were?)

Significant Differences

Whenever you hear scientists say that their "findings are significant at the 5 percent level," you can translate this to mean that their groups differed by about 2 standard deviations. In general, if the odds are not at least 20 to 1 in support of the hunch you're trying to prove, you probably shouldn't use the word "significant" in describing your results.

There are many different tests or formulas you could use for calculating whether the results of an experiment were significant or not. Among the best-known of such statistical devices are the *t-test* and the *critical ratio*. Should you ever need to employ one of these tests, you'd do well to read about them in a statistics text.

TABLE A.2   Relationship between IQ Score and GPA

	Entrance Test IQ Score	Grade Point Average (GPA)
Ann	152	3.91
Bill	145	3.46
Carol	133	2.77
Dick	128	2.35
Elmer	112	1.51
Σ (Sum of)	670	14.00
Mean	134	2.80
SD	15.54	0.94

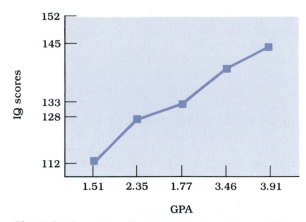

Fig. A.6 A scatter diagram showing the positive correlation between IQ's and grade-point averages.

Correlation Coefficients

In several chapters of this book, we have mentioned the term *correlation* to suggest that two events or traits were somehow connected or associated with each other. The mathematics underlying correlations are not too difficult to understand. However, the correlation concept itself has a "problem" buried deep within it that makes it one of the most misunderstood and misused ideas in all of human experience. We'll come back to this problem in just a moment. First, let's look at how one figures out if two sets of scores are correlated.

As we noted in Chapter 20, there is a strong relationship between IQ's and grades in school, and for a very good reason. Intelligence tests are usually devised so that they will predict academic success, and the items on most such tests are juggled around until the final score does in fact yield the expected predictions. Thus, if we give intelligence tests to all incoming freshmen, and we know their grades at the end of their first collegiate year, we should expect to find the sort of relationship between these measures shown in Table A.2.

Just looking at the rank orderings of these scores, you can tell that a strong correlation exists between the two distributions. As Fig. A.6 shows, if we plotted the data on what is called a *scatter diagram*, we'd get pretty much a straight line. (A scatter diagram shows how the scores for each subject are *scattered*, or distributed, across the graph or diagram.)

If we reversed the scores, so that Ann has an IQ of 152 but a GPA of 1.51, Bill got an IQ of 145 and a GPA of 2.35, and so forth, we'd get a scatter diagram that looked like the one in Fig. A.7.

Generally speaking, the closer the scatter diagram comes to being a straight line tilted to the right or left as these are, the higher the correlation between the two variables (scores).

There are several formulas for figuring out the *mathematical* correlation between two sets of scores that we needn't go into here. All of these formulas yield what is called a *correlation coefficient*, which is merely a "coefficient" or number between +1 and −1.

A correlation coefficient of +1 indicates that the two sets of scores are *perfectly correlated in a positive way*. Which is to say, the person who got the highest score on one test got the highest on the second test, the person who got the second highest score on one test got the second highest on the other test, and so forth.

A correlation coefficient of −1 indicates that the two sets of scores are *perfectly correlated in a negative way*. Which is to say that the person

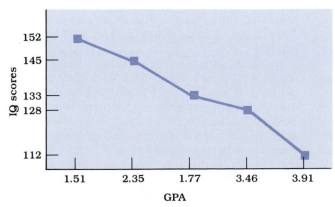

Fig. A.7 A scatter diagram showing a negative correlation between IQ's and grade-point averages.

who got the *highest* score on the first test got the *lowest* score on the second, the person who got the second *highest* score on the first test got the second *lowest* score on the other test, and so forth.

A correlation coefficient of +.75 suggests there is a strong (but not perfect) association between the two sets of scores. A coefficient of −.75 would indicate the same strength of association, but in a negative direction.

A correlation coefficient of 0 (or close to it) tells you that there is little or no significant relationship between the two sets of scores.

Uses and Abuses of Correlation Coefficients

The ability to make quick correlations is just about the most useful trait that your mind has available to it. Whether you realize it or not, your brain is so built that it automatically makes connections between incoming stimuli. Think back to the discussion of Pavlovian conditioning you read about in Chapter 13. When you ring a bell, and then give food to a dog, the animal's brain soon comes to associate the sound of the bell with the appearance of the food. When the dog eventually salivates to the sound of the bell *before* food arrives, its nervous system has calculated a crude sort of "correlation coefficient" between the onset of the bell and the presentation of the food. Since (in the experiment) the two events *always* occur together, the correlation coefficient of the two events would be close to +1. Thus, the dog can anticipate (predict) the stimulus input "food" as soon as the stimulus input "bell" has occurred.

If dogs could talk, how might they explain their conditioned responses? Don't you imagine that Pavlov's beasts might explain matters in *causal* terms? That is, might not a well-conditioned canine remark that the bell has "magic powers" that cause the food to appear?

As peculiar as this notion may sound to you, evidence in its favor comes from some real-life experiments. In several studies, bell-food conditioned animals have later been trained to turn on the bell themselves by pressing a bar in their cages. What do you think the animals do when they become hungry?

As we mentioned earlier, the concept of correlation has a problem buried in it. The problem is this: We too often assume that if event A is *correlated* with event B, then A must somehow *cause* the appearance of B. This "causal

assumption" gets us into a lot of trouble. For example, does the sound of the bell really *cause* the food to appear? Do high IQ's really *cause* students to get good grades? As you can see, the answer in both cases must be a resounding *no*.

Scores on an intelligence test don't cause much of anything (except, perhaps, favorable reactions from college admissions committees). The underlying trait of intelligence presumably causes both the high IQ and the good grades. Thus, *intelligence* is responsible for the correlation between the two events, just as the Pavlov's desires were responsible for the correlation between the bell and the food.

There are times when highly significant correlations may seriously mislead us. As we have mentioned several times, there is a high correlation between going to a psychotherapist and "getting better." But as many studies have shown, you are just about as likely to show improvement if you *don't* seek help as if you do. But the fact that you (1) went to a therapist and (2) solved some of your problems may incorrectly convince both you and your therapist that it was the *treatment* that primarily caused your improvement.

At their very best, correlations can help us predict future stimulus inputs and give us clues as to what the underlying causal connections among these inputs might be. However, in daily life, we too often misuse correlations. If you want to make your psychology teacher very happy indeed, say "Correlations don't determine causes" over and over again—until you're conditioned to believe it!

Stat and Everyday Life

Why statistics? Or, to phrase the question more precisely, is there any correlation between knowing something about stat and knowing something about yourself and the people around you?

As it happens, the difference between knowing stat and not knowing it is highly significant. All of your future life you will be performing "little experiments" in which you try to understand the people around you. It's likely (at the 5 percent level) that you will probe your environment better if you know how to interpret the results of your informal experimentation. If you are introspective, an understanding of correlations and conditioning could help tell you some very important facts about how you have acquired many of your values and attitudes. And, if nothing else, understanding what a bell-shaped curve is all about could save you a lot of money should you ever happen to visit Las Vegas.

The second reason for imposing statistics on you, willy-nilly, is that you may wish to take further courses in psychology. If you do, you may be encouraged (or even required) to perform one or more controlled experiments, either in a laboratory or in a real-life setting. Therefore, you might as well learn the first law of statistics right now:

Your statistical inferences are never better than your experimental design will allow.

The topic of how to design a good experiment has filled many a thick textbook, and there's little sense in subjecting you to more grief than we've done already. What we can say is this—the secret of good experimentation lies in *controlling variables*. If you want to pick a random sample of people for a political poll, make sure your sample is *really random*. Just asking a few of your friends what they think won't do, because your method of choice was highly biased—and hence not random at all.

Several times in this book we've mentioned the concept of a "control group" that some scientist(s) used in an experiment. There probably is no more powerful way of making sure your results are reliable than by incorporating as many groups as possible in your study—one group to *control* for each factor (variable) that might influence the results of your study.

But, most important of all, if you must run a scientific study, think it through carefully *before you start*. Then you can design your study

intelligently so that the data you gather will be easy to analyze, and so your expected results will be as truthful and as reliable as you can make them. Scientists are probably about as honest and as open in their work as any professional group can be. And yet all of us may unconsciously bias our results if we feel passionately about the subject we're studying. So we should use control group after control group—just to make sure that we screen out our unconscious biases before they can affect our results. Anything that you love, or that is important enough to you, is worth working hard for—and worth being entirely honest about.

Animals show a lot of intelligent behaviors. They "sing," and monkeys even draw pictures of a sort. But only human beings run experiments, control for bias, select their subjects randomly, and perform statistical analyses. Being a scientist is thus one of the most *humane* occupations you can have, because we all need reliable and valid data about how things are now so we can make things (including ourselves) better in the future.

As it happens, I love science. To me, it is a "fun game," a way of wisdom, and a means of achieving self-actualization. My parting hope is that you will someday come to appreciate this art form as much as I do. And if the scientific love bug does bite you, perhaps then and only then will you come to enjoy statistics and experimental design as much as most scientists do.

I wish you the best of luck!

(Meanwhile, Gersh and I are reading several books on probability theory as applied to bridge. Joan and Carol, you'd better watch out!)

For permission to use copyrighted materials the authors are indebted to the following:

Chapter 1: p. 2, © Ellen Pines Sheffield/Woodfin Camp & Associates; p. 6, from CLEVER HANS *(The Horse of Mr. von Osten),* by Oskar Pfungst, edited by Robert Rosenthal, A Henry Holt Edition in Psychology, Holt, Rinehart and Winston, Inc.; p. 18, (left) © Martine Frank/Magnum Photos, (right) © Sybil Shelton/Peter Arnold, Inc.

Chapter 2: p. 24, © Arthur Tress; p. 29, (top) courtesy of American Museum of Natural History, (bottom) Arthur Jacques, Rhode Island Hospital; p. 36, (left) © Joel Gordon 1979; p. 38, (top right) courtesy of Norman Geschwind, Beth Israel Hospital, Boston, (bottom) Arthur Jacques, Rhode Island Hospital; p. 40, (both) Russell Dian/HRW photo; p. 42, courtesy of Roger Sperry, California Institute of Technology; p. 44, By permission of Michael S. Gazzaniga, Cornell University Medical College, photos courtesy of Worth Publishers, Inc., New York.

Chapter 3: p. 52, © Peter Angelo Simon 1976/Photo Researchers; p. 58, courtesy of Wilse B. Webb, University of Florida Sleep Laboratories; p. 60, photos by Theodore Spagna, from *Dreamstage Exhibit Catalog,* copyright © 1977 by Allan Hobson and Hoffmann-LaRoche, Inc.; p. 61, By permission of Wilse B. Webb, University of Florida Sleep Laboratories; p. 62, from *Measurement and Characteristics of Nocturnal Sleep,* by Wilse B. Webb and Harman W. Agnew, Jr. In PROGRESS IN CLINICAL PSYCHOLOGY, VOLUME VIII, eds. L.E. Abt and B.P. Riess, 1969. Reprinted by permission of Grune & Stratton, Inc. and the author; p. 66, The Bettmann Archive; p. 74, courtesy of Solomon H. Synder, The Johns Hopkins University School of Medicine; p. 76, (left) © Joel Gordon 1981, (right) courtesy of Oakley Ray, VA Medical Center, Nashville; p. 80, (left) courtesy of Addictive Behaviors Research Center, University of Washington, (right) © Phyllis Graber Jensen/Stock, Boston.

Chapter 4: p. 86, UPI/The Bettmann Archive; p. 92, (left to right) The Bettmann Archive, National Library of Medicine, The Bettmann Archive; p. 94, (left) Culver Pictures; p. 100, (left) © George Roos/Peter Arnold, Inc., (right) courtesy of Leonard D. Eron, The University of Illinois at Chicago; p. 104, (top and bottom right) courtesy of Nathan Azrin, Nova University, (bottom left) German Information Center; p. 110, The University of Michigan News and Information Services, photo by Bob Kalmbach.

Chapter 5: p. 114, © Bill Ross 1985/Woodfin Camp & Associates; p. 122, © Shirley Zeiberg/Photo Researchers; p. 124, (right) © Joel Gordon 1983; p. 126, (left) Reproduced with permission of AT&T Corporate Archive, (right) courtesy of Karl H. Pribram, Stanford University; p. 130, (left, second from right, right) The Bettmann Archive, (second from left) Culver Pictures; p. 132, © Christopher S. Johnson/Stock, Boston.

Chapter 6: p. 138, © Dan Budnik 1985/Woodfin Camp & Associates; p. 144, (left) © Bruce Roberts/Rapho, Photo Researchers; p. 146, Museum of Modern Art/Film Still Archives; p. 148, (top) © Joel Gordon 1979; p. 150, © Tom McHugh/Photo Researchers; p. 152, (bottom left) © Robert Houser 1977/Photo Researchers, (bottom right) © Anestis Diakopoulos/Stock, Boston; p. 154, (bottom right) courtesy of Zwiren & Wagner.

Chapter 7: p. 162, © Arthur Tress 1976/Photo Researchers; p. 170, (bottom left) © Michael Philip Manheim 1973/Photo Researchers, (bottom right) © Hella Hammid/Photo Researchers; p. 171, © Eric Kroll/Taurus Photos; p. 180, © Michael Weisbrot; p. 182, © Peter Marlow/Magnum Photos; p. 186, University of Texas News and Information Service.

Chapter 8: p. 190, © Dave Burnett/Photo Researchers; p. 194, Russell Dian/HRW photos; p. 204, (top left) © Michael Mather/Peter Arnold, Inc.; p. 206, (top left) The Minneapolis Institute of Arts; p. 207, © Terraphotographics/BPS; p. 208, (bottom right) Russell Dian/HRW photo; p. 210, (top left) © William Vandivert, published in *Scientific American;* p. 212, (top) The Bettmann Archive, (bottom) © Kenneth Karp; p. 214, (right) courtesy of Marshall M. Haith, University of Denver.

Chapter 9: p. 224, © Sybil Shelton/Peter Arnold, Inc.; p. 228, © Thomas Ives; p. 230, courtesy of Irving Maltzman, University of California, Los Angeles; p. 232, (bottom) courtesy of University of California, Los Angeles; p. 234, © Joel Gordon 1984; p. 238, (left) courtesy of K.D. Broota, University of Delhi, (right) courtesy of Graham Wagstaff, The University of Liverpool; p. 240, courtesy of Norman F. Dixon, University College London; pp. 243 & 245, both from COGNITION by Margaret Matlin. Copyright © 1983 by CBS College Publishing. Reprinted by permission of Holt, Rinehart and Winston, CBS College Publishing; p. 248, (top right) © Paul Conklin/Monkmeyer Press Photo Service, (bottom right) courtesy of Robert Glaser, University of Pittsburgh; p. 252, (right) courtesy of Birth Defects Foundation, March of Dimes.

Chapter 10: p. 258, © Joel Gordon 1981; p. 263, Iowa State University of Science and Technology Information Service; p. 264, (bottom left) © Joel Gordon 1982, (right) courtesy of Brandeis University; p. 266, (top) © Ginger Chih/Peter Arnold, Inc., (middle left) © Erika Stone/Peter Arnold, Inc., (middle right) © Sybil

Name Index

Subject Index